D1491504

The Marshall Cavendish Illustrated Encyclopedia of

SCIENCE AND TECHNOLOGY

The Marshall Cavendish Illustrated Encyclopedia of

SCIENCE AND TECHNOLOGY

Marshall Cavendish London & New York

Academic Advisor:
Professor John Taylor, M.A., Ph.D.,
Professor of Mathematics,
King's College,
University of London.

Editors:
Michael Bisacre
Richard Carlisle
Deborah Robertson
John Ruck

Published by Marshall Cavendish Books Ltd.,
58 Old Compton Street, London W1V 5PA.

Some of this material was first published
by Marshall Cavendish Limited in the
encyclopedia *Tree of Knowledge*

First printing: 1979

Printed in Great Britain by Severn Valley Press Limited

ISBN 0 85685 744 0

Introduction

The quality of our lives, both at home and at work, is largely dependent on technology – the science of industry – which is itself dependent on scientific research for progress. *The Illustrated Encyclopedia of Science and Technology* explains this complex subject with clarity and detail.

The scientific part is sub-divided for ease of reference and deals with the basic principles which govern the universe, the laws of thermodyamics, the harnessing of power, the character of chemical elements, the phenomenon of electricity, the nature of sound and light, astrophysics and relativity.

The technological 'miracles' of today, which are directly attributable to these discoveries are then examined and discussed. The answers to the age old question 'how does it work?' are provided on every subject from the transistor radio to the nuclear missile. How can technology serve the needs of the consumer? How is it advancing transport and communications? The encyclopedia answers these questions and thousands more.

Photographs and diagrams drawn from government agencies, institutes, and industry expand and reinforce the text.

The articles are also complemented by illustrations of experiments, flow charts and models, which all serve to provide a lucid understanding of this vast area of knowledge.

Contents

Part I Science Today

Part II Technology Today

Part I

Science Today

Paul Brierley

Chapter 1

Matter and Energy

Oil molecules indicate the presence of *foraminefera*, a form of *protozoa*, found on the sea bed and evident in fossil fuels.

Atoms and Molecules

Everyone nowadays has at least a vague idea of the atomic theory of matter. The theory gives a picture of all matter as being composed of basic building blocks, the 92 different sorts of naturally-occurring atoms corresponding to the 92 different naturally-occurring chemical elements. In addition, there are over a dozen man-made elements.

At the centre of each atom is a tiny *nucleus*, very heavy and positively charged, which is made up of particles called *protons* and *neutrons*. The nucleus is surrounded by a cloud of much smaller particles, the negatively charged *electrons*.

The 92 natural elements have from one to 92 protons in the nucleus and these protons carry its positive electric charge. But while the number of electrons surrounding the nucleus corresponds to the number of protons, the number of neutrons can vary. These particles carry zero electric charge (although of approximately the same mass as a proton). The protons attract the electrons because they have opposite electric charges, as unlike charges attract each other whereas like charges repel each other. Overall, each atom is electrically neutral, as the positive charges in the nucleus are balanced by the negative charges of the electrons.

The difference between an atom of one element and an atom of another lies simply in the numbers of protons, neutrons and electrons they each contain. For example, an atom of helium has two protons, two neutrons and two electrons, while a carbon atom has six protons, six neutrons and six electrons. The particles are exactly the same in each case, it is only the numbers that are different.

Atoms can combine together to form *molecules*, such as the two-atom gas molecules of hydrogen (H_2) and oxygen (O_2) and the three-atom molecule of water (H_2O). Molecules may be much bigger than this however, and some which occur in living or organic substances contain thousands of atoms.

An atomic theory of matter had been conceived by early Greek philosophers, notably Democritus (about 420BC) and Epicurus (about 300BC). This atomic theory was not accepted by many other important philosophers, however, and Aristotle (384-322BC) rejected Democritus' theory in favour of the view that all matter was composed of different combinations of the 'four elements'—earth, water, air and fire.

This concept displaced the atomic theories and formed the basis of alchemy, the study of matter that dominated science up until the seventeenth century. Alchemy was widely practised in Arabia, China and Renaissance Europe, and two of its main objectives were to find a way of turning a base metal, such as lead, into gold and to find a 'elixir of life'.

Alchemy was supported by religious leaders of the time, whereas atomic theories with their implied atheism were suppressed by Jewish and Christian teachers. Many earlier texts survived, however, including the *De rerum natura*

Above: John Dalton, the English philosopher who devised the first scientific theory of the atomic structure of matter. He was born at Eaglesfield, Cumberland, in September 1766, and by the age of 12 he was teaching at his local school. He had a life-long interest in meteorology, and kept a daily record of the local weather from his early childhood to his death in July 1844. This interest in the weather led him to study the atmosphere and subsequently the nature of gases and their properties. Through his experiments with gases, he arrived at the conclusions which formed the basis of his atomic theory. When he died over 40,000 people filed past his coffin.

Below: A molecule of nucleic acid, a heavy, complex organic acid which combines with a protein to form a nucleoprotein, an important part of the nucleus of a living cell. The helical bands represent chains of a compound called a nucleotide, and carry four other compounds, adenine (A), thymine (T), cytosine (C) and guanine (G). Bonding between T and A and between C and G holds the chains together.

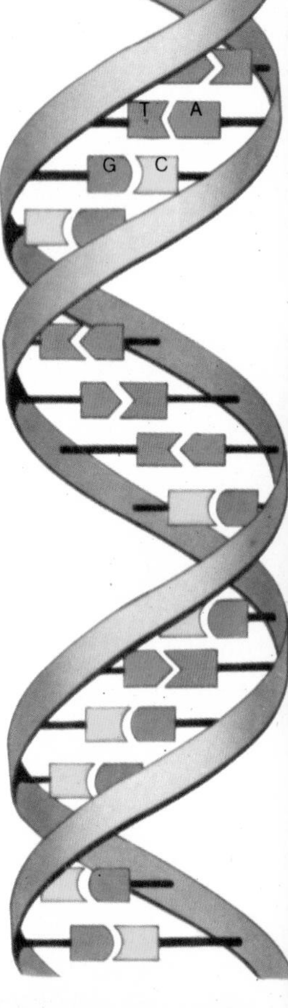

Above: An atomic model of a crystal of common salt, sodium chloride. The shape and the physical properties of a crystal are determined by the forces which bind the atoms together, forces which include ionic and covalent bonds, the metallic bond and the van der Waal's forces. The ionic bond is the electrical attraction between charged atoms and the covalent bond involves pairs of atoms sharing electrons. The metallic bond occurs in crystals of metals, where the positive metal ions are neutralized by a cloud of electrons which move freely throughout the lattice. This arrangement gives metals their characteristic physical properties, including their ability to conduct electricity. Van der Waal's forces are weak bonds caused by momentary disturbances in the electron clouds within the lattice.

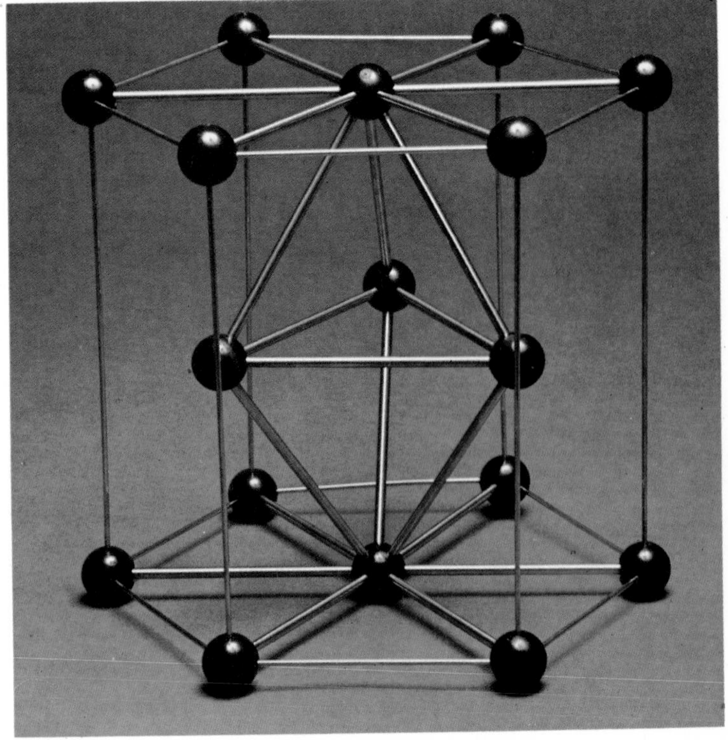

Right: There are a large number of crystal shapes, which arise from the way in which the atoms are grouped together. This hexagonal shape is a model of a zinc crystal.

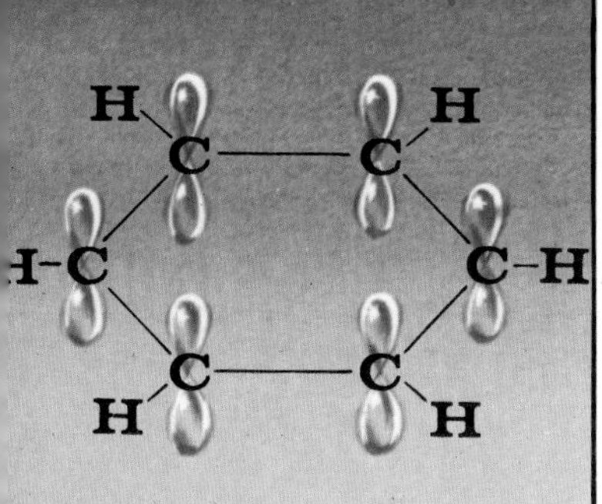

ar shaped electron orbits carbon atoms

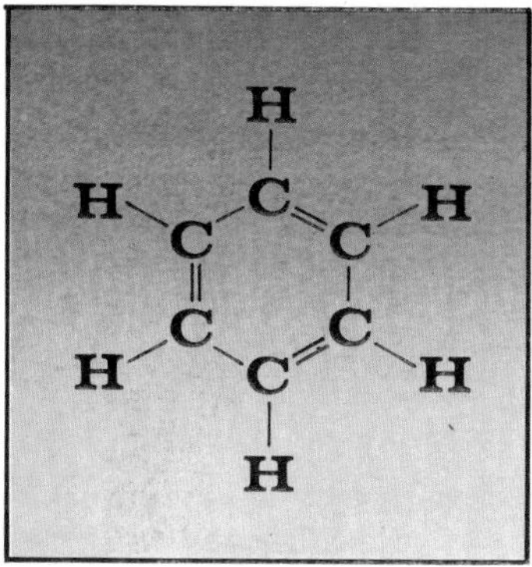

Alternate single and double bonds between carbon atoms

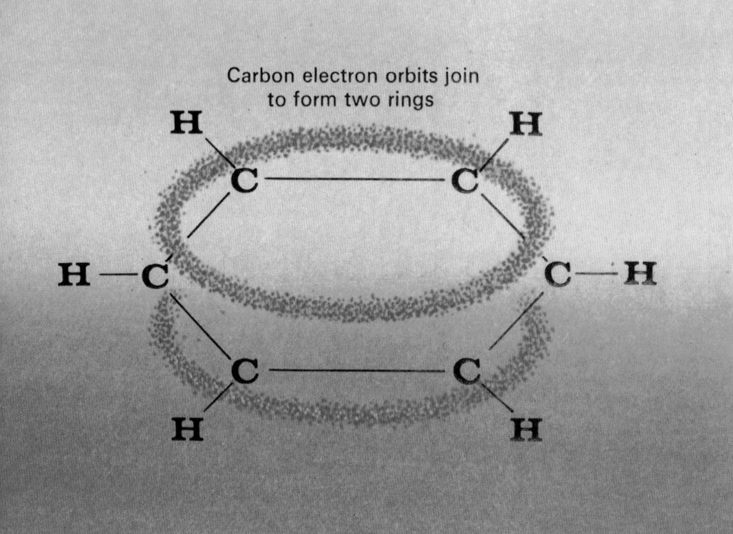

Left: The structure of benzene (C_6H_6) was a mystery for over a century, because its chemical properties were not consistent with its presumed structure pf single bonds linking the hydrogen atoms to the carbon atoms, and alternate single and double bonds linking the ring or carbon atoms. The explanation was that some of the shared electrons travel in tear-drop shaped orbitals at right angles to the carbon atoms and, because these atoms are so close together, these orbitals overlap to form ring-shaped orbitals above and below the carbon ring. Benzene is used in making aspirin, aniline dyes, and some types of plastic.

Above: This sheet of clear plastic was charged up by bombarding it with electrons. When it was discharged at one edge, the departing electrons created this pattern in it.

Below: This cutting torch uses a stream of plasma (ionized gas) carrying a current of about 250 Amps.

('On the Nature of Things') written in the first century BC by the Roman poet Lucretius. In the first half of this six-volume poem, Lucretius described and defended the theories of Epicurus, and it was used as a source of reference by several seventeenth and eighteenth century philosophers.

At the beginning of the nineteenth century, John Dalton (1766-1844) produced the first atomic theory to be backed up by experimental evidence. Following on from the work of A. L. Lavoisier and J. L. Proust, Dalton investigated the way that elements forming chemical compounds combine in definite proportions by weight. He was then able to work out the relative weights of the atoms of various elements, including hydrogen, oxygen, nitrogen and sulphur.

For example, he calculated that when hydrogen and oxygen combine to form water they do so in the ratio, by weight, of one part hydrogen to seven parts of oxygen (it is actually eight parts of oxygen, Dalton's analysis was slightly incorrect). From this he deduced that an oxygen atom was seven times heavier than a hydrogen atom, because he assumed that a water molecule contained only one atom of each. In fact, a water molecule contains two hydrogen atoms and one oxygen atom, and oxygen is about sixteen times heavier than hydrogen.

Despite these errors, however, the theory formed the basis for a serious scientific study of the atomic structure of elements, and during the nineteenth century scientists were able to identify about 90 (out of 92 naturally-occurring) different sorts of atom.

Inside the atom

Investigations of the structure of atoms themselves began in the late nineteenth century. The crucial experiments involved investigation of the nature of the 'matter' taking part in electrical discharges in sealed tubes not unlike fluorescent lighting tubes.

Before 1890, rays streaming from the negative electrode or *cathode* of such tubes had been observed and were named *cathode rays*. The physicist J. J. Thomson (1856-1940) showed that the rays, when subjected to magnetic or electrostatic fields behaved exactly as negatively charged particles would be expected to.

These electrons, as the cathode rays were renamed, were assumed to be constituents of atoms. However, because it was difficult to separately measure either their electric charge or their mass, no-one knew how they fitted into the atom or how important they were.

Thomson proposed a model of the atom, the 'plum pudding atom', consisting of a not very massive sphere of positive charge in which thousands of plum-like electrons rotated in rings. This model needed a very large number of electrons in the atom because it was thought that they accounted for most of the atom's mass.

New experiments soon made Thomson's model unrealistic. When positively charged *alpha particles* (each comprising two protons and two neutrons) were directed on to thin films of atoms, a significant number bounced backwards. This could not have happened if Thomson's model had been correct; the positively charged 'pudding' would not have been able to repel the particles because it

was too light. Additionally its positive charge would have been neutralized by the electrons and so would not have repelled the positively charged particles.

Ernest Rutherford (1871-1937) proposed a different model which explained the backward scattering, and this model has been the basis of our understanding ever since. If the positive charge in the atom is heavy and concentrated, not light and diffused as in the Thomson model, then the experimental results can be explained. Rutherford's atom consists of a small (10^{-13}cm) heavy nucleus with a positive charge, surrounded by a diffuse cloud (10^{-8}cm) of light electrons.

It is tempting to visualize Rutherford's atom as a miniature solar system, with the nucleus as the sun and the electrons as the planets. In place of gravity, the attraction between the oppositely charged nucleus and electrons would hold the atoms together. But, according to the old laws of electromagnetism, even this picture would have been impossible. If the electrons revolved around the nucleus they would radiate electromagnetic waves, lose energy and spiral into the centre, attracted to the nucleus by its positive charge. According to the old laws, the atom could not be stable.

An excellent, though temporary, solution to the problem was provided by Niels Bohr (1885-1962). Instead of radiating continuously and spiralling in to the centre the electron, according to Bohr, could travel only on certain discrete closed orbits. The electron would radiate but it would do so suddenly, and at the same time jump between one orbit and another of lower energy (as if the Earth suddenly jumped into Venus' orbit).

Cavendish Laboratories

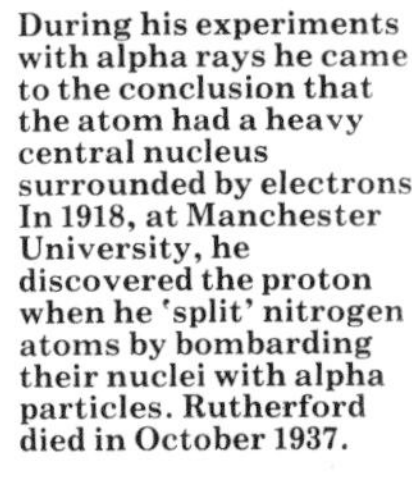
Above: Sir Ernest Rutherford, Lord Rutherford of Nelson (right), the founder of nuclear physics. He was born near Nelson, New Zealand, in 1871 and went to Cambridge University in 1895 to work with J. J. Thomson. He investigated radioactive decay, which led him to the discovery of alpha and beta radiation. During his experiments with alpha rays he came to the conclusion that the atom had a heavy central nucleus surrounded by electrons. In 1918, at Manchester University, he discovered the proton when he 'split' nitrogen atoms by bombarding their nuclei with alpha particles. Rutherford died in October 1937.

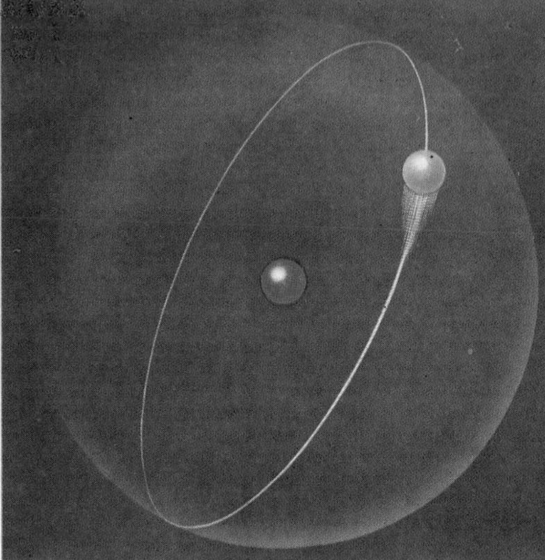

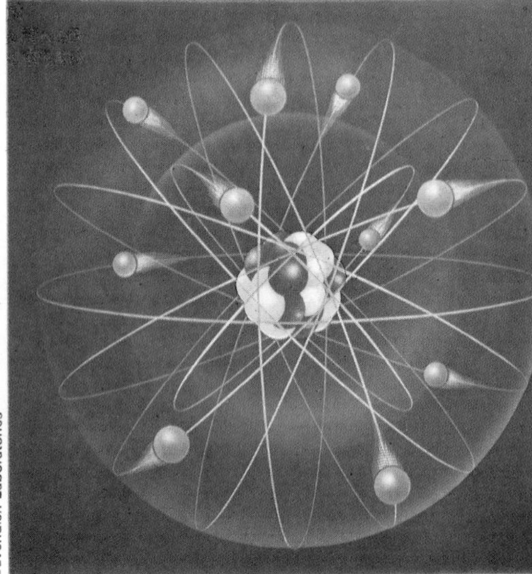

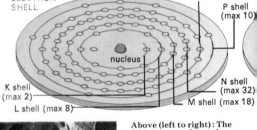

ELECTRON SHELL
O shell (max 23)
P shell (max 10)
nucleus
K shell (max 2)
L shell (max 8)
M shell (max 18)
N shell (max 32)

Above (left to right): The first diagram shows the maximum number of electrons which can occupy electron shells K to P. The second diagram shows hydrogen, which has a single electron which occupies one of the available energy states in the K shell, and the third shows helium, whose two electrons fill its K shell.

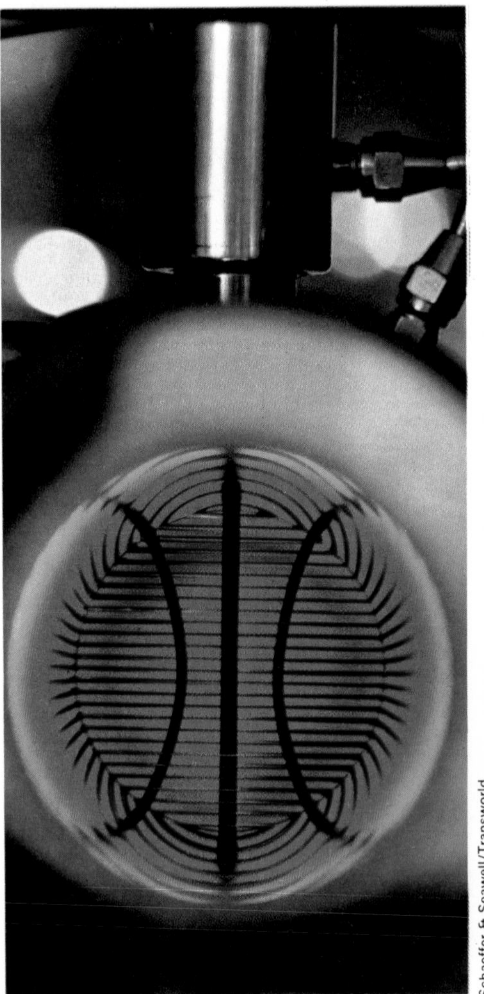
Schaeffer & Seawell/Transworld

UKAE

Left: Prospecting for uranium using an instrument called a spectrometer, which detects any radiation from the rock which would indicate the presence of uranium ore. Uranium atoms emit alpha particles and thus gradually decay into 'daughter' elements, which in turn decay until they eventually become lead.

Far left: The ripple patterns in the light given off by an electrical discharge depend on the atomic structure of the electrodes between which the discharge occurs. The study of these patterns has helped scientists understand more about the structure of atoms and molecules.

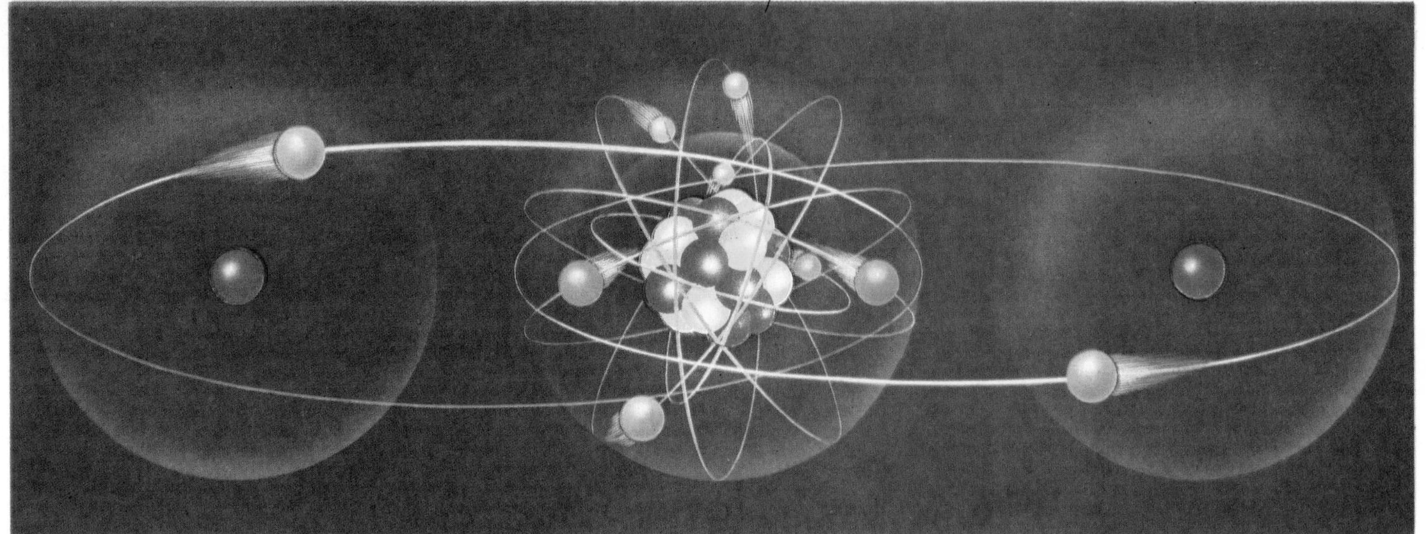

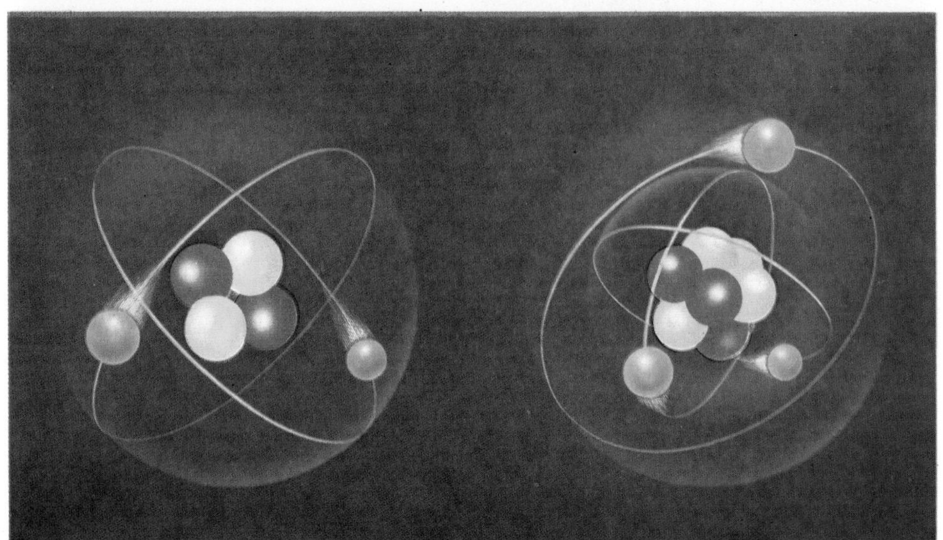

Top, far left: Hydrogen has a single proton in its nucleus, orbited by one electron.

Above: When two hydrogen atoms combine with an oxygen atom to form a molecule of water, the hydrogen atoms share their electrons with the oxygen atom which has two unfilled states in its outermost shell.

Far left: Neon, like helium, is inert because its outer electron shell is filled.

Left: An atom of helium, on the left, has two protons and two neutrons in its nucleus, and two electrons. Lithium-7 (right), an isotope of lithium, has three protons, four neutrons, and three electrons.

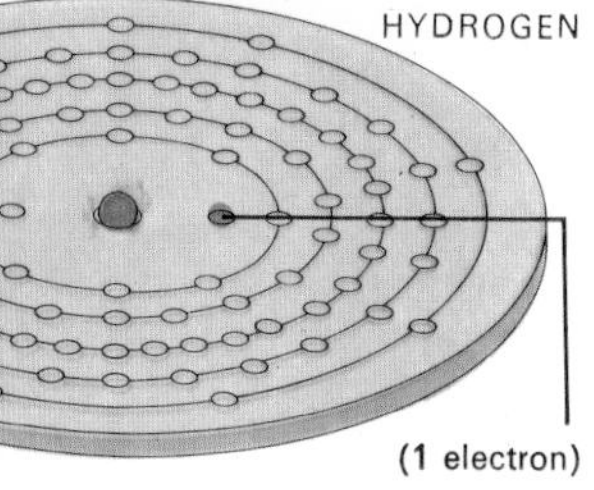

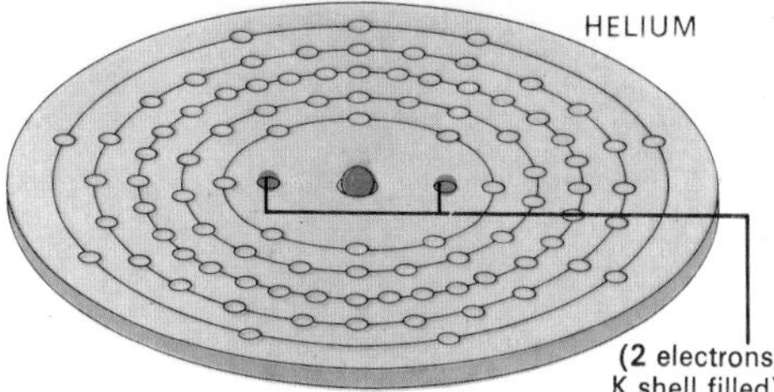

Left: The chemical properties of an atom depend on the number of electrons and unfilled energy states in its outermost shell. Helium has its outermost shell filled by its two electrons and so, having no spare electron or energy state which it can share with other atoms, it cannot react or combine with them.

Finally, there was an orbit of minimum energy (like Mercury's orbit), from which the electron would not radiate. Once the electron reached this *ground state* it was stable.

Within a dozen years, the physical results of Bohr's model had been refined and justified by a new physical theory, *quantum mechanics*. Through this, nature was viewed in quite a different way. In the new theory, a particle's position and velocity could not simultaneously be measured with absolute precision (*Heisenberg's uncertainty principle*) and the concept of force, as it had been known, disappeared.

Our present understanding of electron structure in atoms is based on the system of discrete energy levels (like Bohr's orbits) that quantum mechanics allows, together with a new principle discovered in 1924 by Wolfgang Pauli (1900-1958): the *exclusion principle*.

The exclusion principle forbids more than one electron being in any possible 'state' of an atom or molecule. The states are sub-divisions of the energy levels, which surround the nucleus like a series of concentric shells and are known as the K, L, M, N, O, P and Q shells respectively, the K shell being the innermost. In naturally-occurring elements, the maximum numbers of states, and thus electrons, which can exist in these shells are 2, 8, 18, 32, 23, 10 and 2 respectively.

If it were not for the exclusion principle all electrons would fall to the lowest state, the level of minimum energy. The chemical properties of atoms are determined by the electrons in the outermost (highest) energy levels.

Molecular bonds

The way in which chemical behaviour, that is, the formation and properties of molecules, is determined by the electrons in the atom's highest energy levels, can be described in terms of different sorts of molecular bond.

The *ionic bond* occurs when one atom in a two-atom molecule has only one or two electrons in its outermost level, and the other atom has room for one or two more in its outermost level or *electron shell*. The electrons pass from the first atom to the second, so the first atom becomes positively charged because it has lost electrons and the second atom becomes negatively charged because it has gained electrons. These *ions*, as the charged atoms are now called, attract each other with their opposite charges, forming a stable molecule. One example is salt where sodium atoms lose their highest electrons to chloride atoms.

The other simple sort of bond is the *covalent bond*. This occurs when similar atoms form molecules, such as the gas molecules hydrogen (H_2), oxygen (O_2) and nitrogen (N_2). The electrons are shared between the two atoms, being clustered between the two positively charged nuclei and attracting them both.

Isotopes

The amount of positive charge on a nucleus is determined by the number of protons within it. The number of protons in the nucleus is the *atomic number* of the atom, and this is also the number of electrons the atom possesses.

The mass of the nucleus is determined by the number of protons plus the number of neutrons. The mass of a proton is about the same as the mass of a neutron and over 1,800 times the mass of an electron.

The atomic weight of an element should be just the number of protons and neutrons together, but some elements were found to have atomic weights which are not whole numbers. This was an unsolved problem for more than a century until it was realized that although atoms of a given element had a fixed number of protons, the number of neutrons was variable. The different forms were called *isotopes*, and the elements found in nature are mixtures of different isotopes.

The discovery of isotopes ushered in the nuclear age, an age of the study and application of nuclear forces. It was found that nuclei heavier than uranium could be built up and that nuclei could be broken apart. Nuclear bombs have been made, but the question of why the nucleus does not fly apart on its own, as it might be expected to due to the positively-charged protons repelling each other, has not yet been really answered.

But the questions the Victorians asked, 'Are atoms real? Can they be seen?' have been answered. Photographs of atoms taken by electron microscopes and field emission microscopes, in which streams of electrons take the place of the visible light used in optical microscopes, are as real as the pictures on a television set.

Elementary Particles

All matter, living or dead, is composed of atoms, which were originally thought to be solid and indivisible. Towards the end of the nineteenth century, however, scientists began to realize that the atoms themselves were made up of even smaller particles. The physicist J. J. Thomson established that electrons were constituents of atoms, then in 1911 Ernest Rutherford proposed the theory that the atom had a central nucleus around which the electrons were grouped.

The idea of the nucleus led to the science of nuclear physics, the study of the nucleus and its components. Rutherford suggested the existence of the proton in 1914 and in 1932 the neutron was discovered by James Chadwick. Particle physics, the study of matter at its deepest, most fundamental level, is an extension of nuclear physics and developed from it almost by accident.

In 1934 the Japanese physicist Hideki Yukawa suggested that the force keeping the protons and neutrons together in the nucleus was due to a new particle, which came to be called a *meson*.

A systematic search for new particles began and about 30 were discovered during the next two decades, including one with the properties Yukawa had predicted. But the hope that the new particles would provide a detailed explanation of the structure of the nucleus was not completely realized. Emphasis shifted to the problem that seemed more basic, namely, the ways in which the new particles interacted with each other. Experiments designed to investigate this question revealed an embarrassing number of new particles and particle-like phenomena.

Gravity and electromagnetism

Following the discovery of the electron it was possible to think of atoms as being made up of electrically charged particles between which two types of force acted. One force was electromagnetism, due to the electric charges of the particles, and the other was gravity, although its effects were only slight.

The presence of gravitational forces on this scale was in accordance with Sir Isaac Newton's universal law of gravitation. This states that between any two objects in the universe, even such small objects as particles, there is an attractive force proportional to the masses of the objects and inversely proportional to the square of the distance between them.

In this idealization, the particles created smooth, continuous electromagnetic and gravitational *fields* or areas of influence around them. If a particle moved, the fields would change and the forces on other particles would consequently be altered.

Quantum theory

Einstein upset this simple picture of particles and fields. He found a circumstance in which it was more sensible to regard light, one of the forms of electromagnetic radiation, as being composed of a stream of particles rather than being a

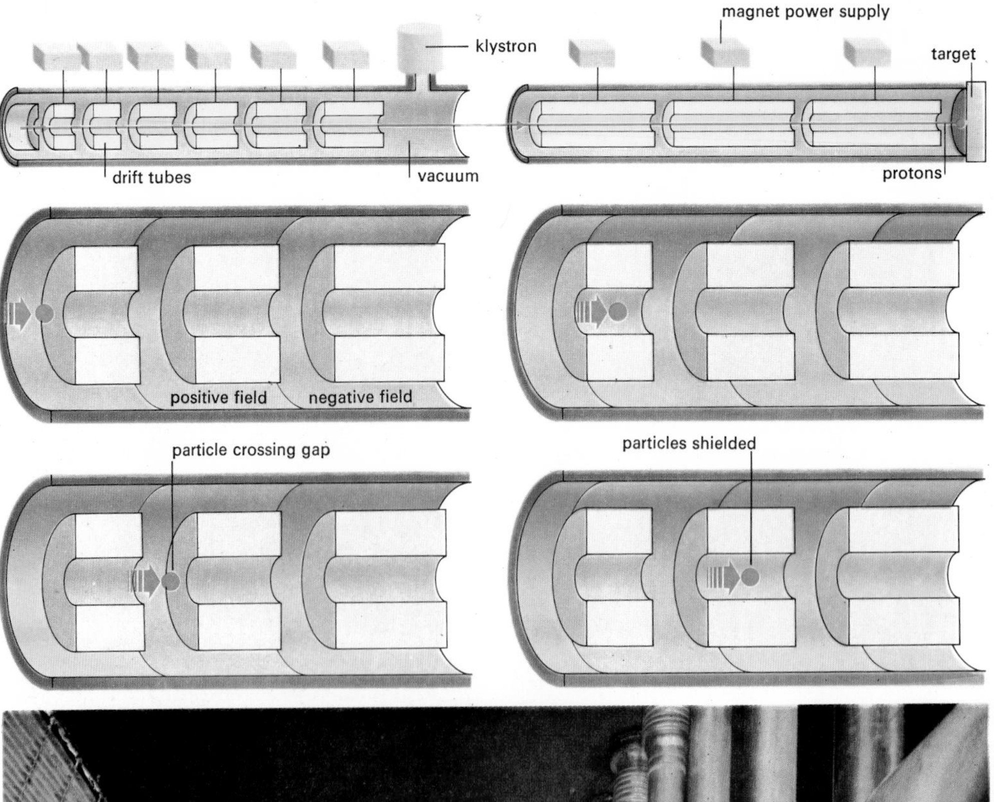

Picturepoint

Rutherford Laboratory

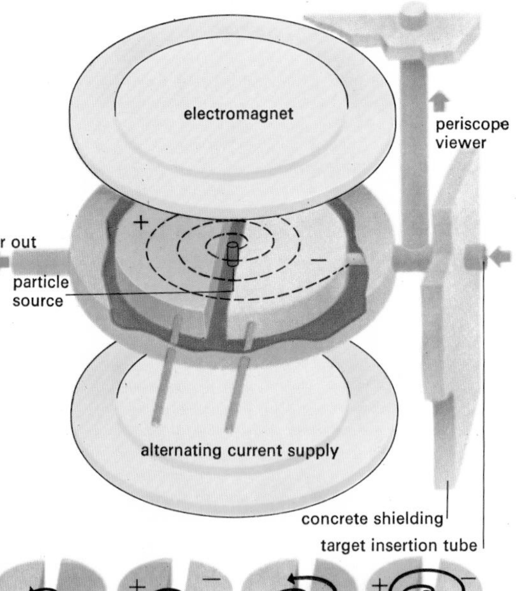

Above left: In a linear accelerator, particles such as protons are accelerated along a tube by high frequency alternating electric fields supplied by a device called a klystron. A proton is accelerated when there is a negative field ahead of it. As the field is alternating—constantly changing from negative to positive and back—the protons have to be shielded from the positive field so that they are not decelerated by it. They travel through a series of 'drift tubes' which provide this shielding. The timing of the field and the lengths of the tubes are arranged so that the field is negative when the protons cross the gaps between the tubes, and positive when they are within the tubes and shielded by them. When the protons hit the nuclei of the target atoms they break them up into particles.

Left: The interior of a linear accelerator.

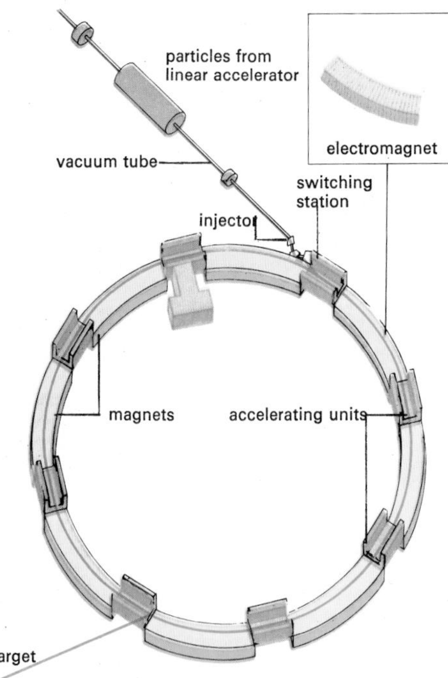

Left: A 7 GeV proton synchrotron.

Above: A synchrotron is fed with accelerated particles from a linear accelerator and as they travel round the machine they are further accelerated each time they pass one of the accelerating units. When they reach a high enough velocity they are diverted out of the synchrotron to the target. The energy a particle possesses depends on the accelerating voltage. Particle energies are thus expressed in terms of 'electron volts'. For example, the tube of a television is a simple form of accelerator, accelerating electrons with a voltage of about 10,000 V. Thus each electron hits the screen with an energy of 10,000 electron volts or 10keV. Accelerators commonly operate at MeV (mega, or million, electron volt) and GeV (giga, or 1,000 million, electron volt) energy levels.

Left: A cyclotron has a pair of hollow, D-shaped units mounted in a vacuum chamber between the poles of a powerful electromagnet. These units are alternately charged positive and negative, so a particle put into the centre will spiral outwards and accelerate until it reaches the outer edge and hits the target.

Below: The Van de Graaff generator produces a very high voltage by accumulating an enormous amount of electrostatic charge and this voltage can be used in a laboratory to accelerate particles. This picture shows the top of the six million volt generator at the nuclear laboratories at Aldermaston in England.

UKAEA

smooth, continuous field of energy.

The circumstance in question was known as the *photoelectric effect*. It had been discovered that, under certain conditions, light shining on a metal surface caused electrons to be emitted from it. The effect would occur only if the light was towards the blue end of the spectrum. A red light, even if it were intense or left on for a long time, would not cause the emission.

Einstein's explanation was that light was composed of particles called *photons*. The energy of a photon was proportional to the frequency of the light, and so was higher for blue light than for red light because blue light has a higher frequency. The emission of an electron from the metal surface was due to it being struck by a photon. A blue photon had sufficient energy to do this, but a red one did not.

The explanation of the photoelectric effect in terms of discrete bundles or *quanta* of energy carried by photons was in fact the second time such an idea had been used. Five years before, in 1900, Max Planck (1858-1947) had introduced the idea of discrete quanta of energy in his discussion of the spectrum of energy emitted by objects heated to incandescence.

Planck and Einstein forced physicists to accept that the electromagnetic field sometimes behaved like an assembly of particles (the photons) and sometimes like a continuous wave.

Quantum mechanics

In the 1920s, Prince Louis de Broglie suggested that the wave and particle aspects of light had to be considered together, not separately, since the energy of the particle depends on the frequency of the wave. In addition, he proposed that other particles besides the photon could also behave like waves. If this were so, electrons would be expected to exhibit characteristic interference patterns such as occur when two stones are dropped into a pond and the spreading ripples overlap. Three years later precisely such an effect was found.

The next step was taken by Werner Heisenberg, Wolfgang Pauli and Max Born, who developed a form of *quantum mechanics* which gave a complete understanding of the structure of stable atoms. Quantum mechanics predicted stable energy states for electrons in the presence of a positively charged nucleus. With the help of Pauli's exclusion principle, Bohr's theory of the atom was given a firm basis.

Paul Dirac applied the new quantum mechanics to the electromagnetic field and showed how it could be regarded as an assembly of photons. The resolution of the wave-particle paradox was that the intensity of the wave could be regarded as the density of particles in it. In certain situations the density would be so high that the grainy nature of the wave could be overlooked. In other situations, with low density, the fact that there was a wave at all might be neglected.

Almost all physics was explained by quantum mechanics. The structure of the atom and the formation of molecules could be understood, and electromagnetic radiation (such as light, radio waves and X-rays) was emitted and absorbed in accordance with Dirac's theory. All physics and chemistry, for example the formation of crystals and magnets and the action of solvents and adhesives, could be described in terms of particular effects of electromagnetic radiation.

In the stage of understanding reached by 1930, the original two long-range forces ruled all nature: gravity for very large masses on an astronomical scale (its effects being so weak at atomic levels that it could be ignored) and electromagnetism operating everywhere else. By analogy with the concept of the photon as the quantum (or particle) of electromagnetic radiation, many people suppose that the gravitational field is also composed of particles, which are called *gravitons*. As yet, however, there is no experimental evidence for them.

Strong and weak forces

After the discovery of the neutron, and the realization that the nucleus consisted of a collection of positively charged protons and uncharged neutrons, it became clear that a third basic force must exist in nature. This force was necessary to overcome the repulsive forces between the positively charged protons that would tend to push them apart. In addition, this *strong* or *hadronic force* would have to be very attractive and very short range to explain the small size of the nucleus (10^{-13} cm) as opposed to the overall size of the atom (about 10^{-8} cm), and to explain the fact that the nuclei, shielded by the electron clouds, seem to have no effect on one another.

Yukawa suggested that this strong force was transmitted by mesons, the mesons carrying the strong force in the way that photons carry electromagnetism.

There is one further force in nature, the so-called *weak force*. It is not thought responsible for creating any 'bound

Right and below: A storage ring collects bursts of particles from an accelerator and builds them up into two intense beams of particles travelling in opposite directions around the ring. The beams are then fired at each other so that very high energy collisions occur between the particles, and new particles are created by the break-up or combination of the original particles. This diagram and the picture on the right show the rings at the European Centre for Nuclear Research (CERN) near Geneva. Protons from a linear accelerator are further accelerated in a synchrotron then directed into the rings.

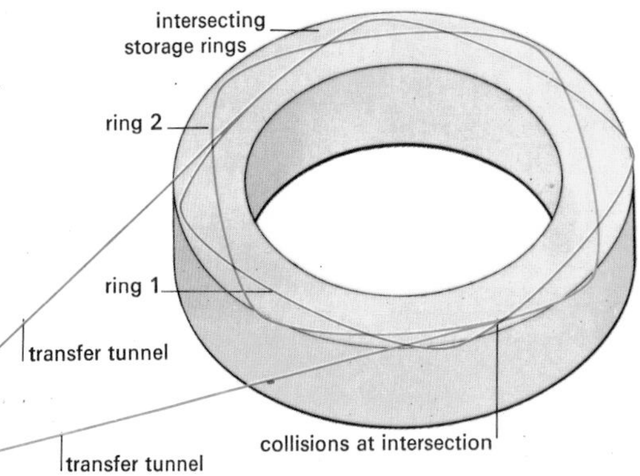

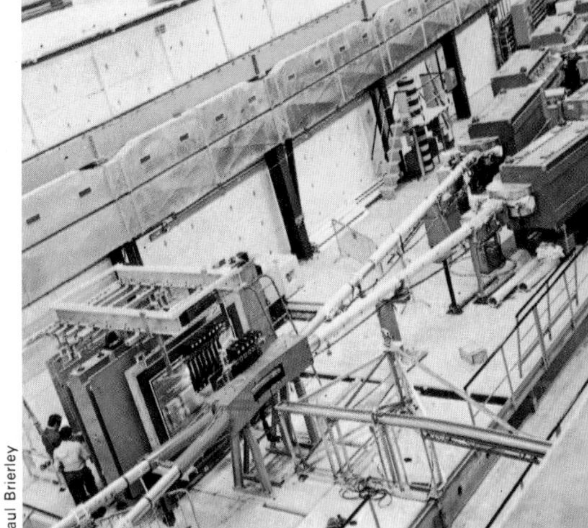
Paul Brierley

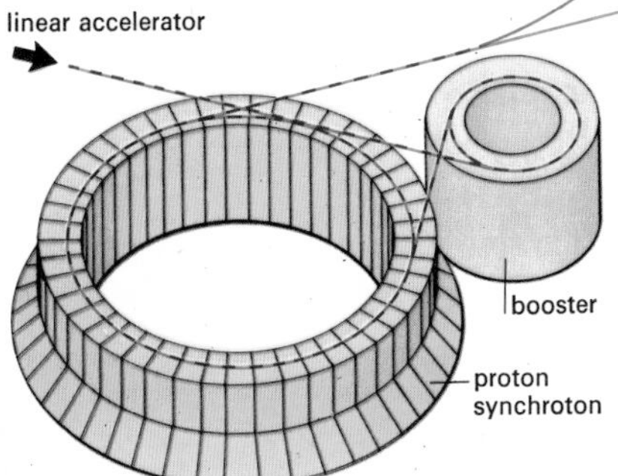

Below and right: One of the devices used to detect and identify particles produced by accelerators is the bubble chamber. The chamber contains liquid hydrogen which is kept under pressure by a piston. The particles are fired into the chamber, the pressure is momentarily released and the particles leave a trail of bubbles in the liquid as they pass. The chamber is surrounded by powerful electromagnets; the size and charge of a particle can be found from the curve and the direction of the path it takes under the influence of the magnetic field. The particles' tracks are recorded by cameras.

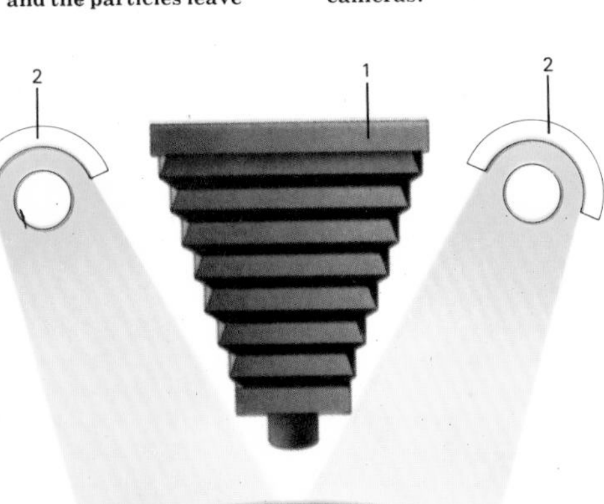

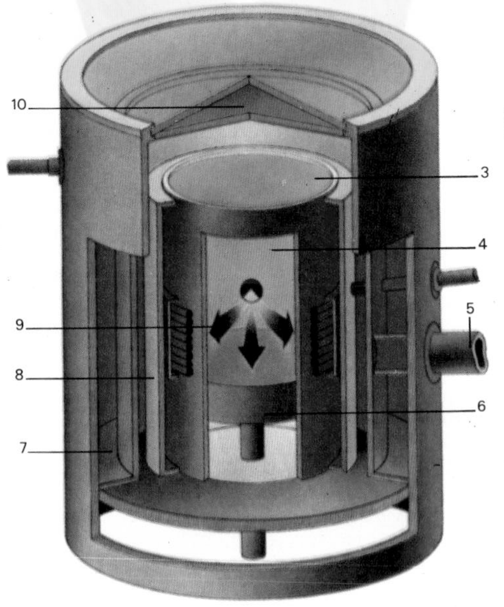

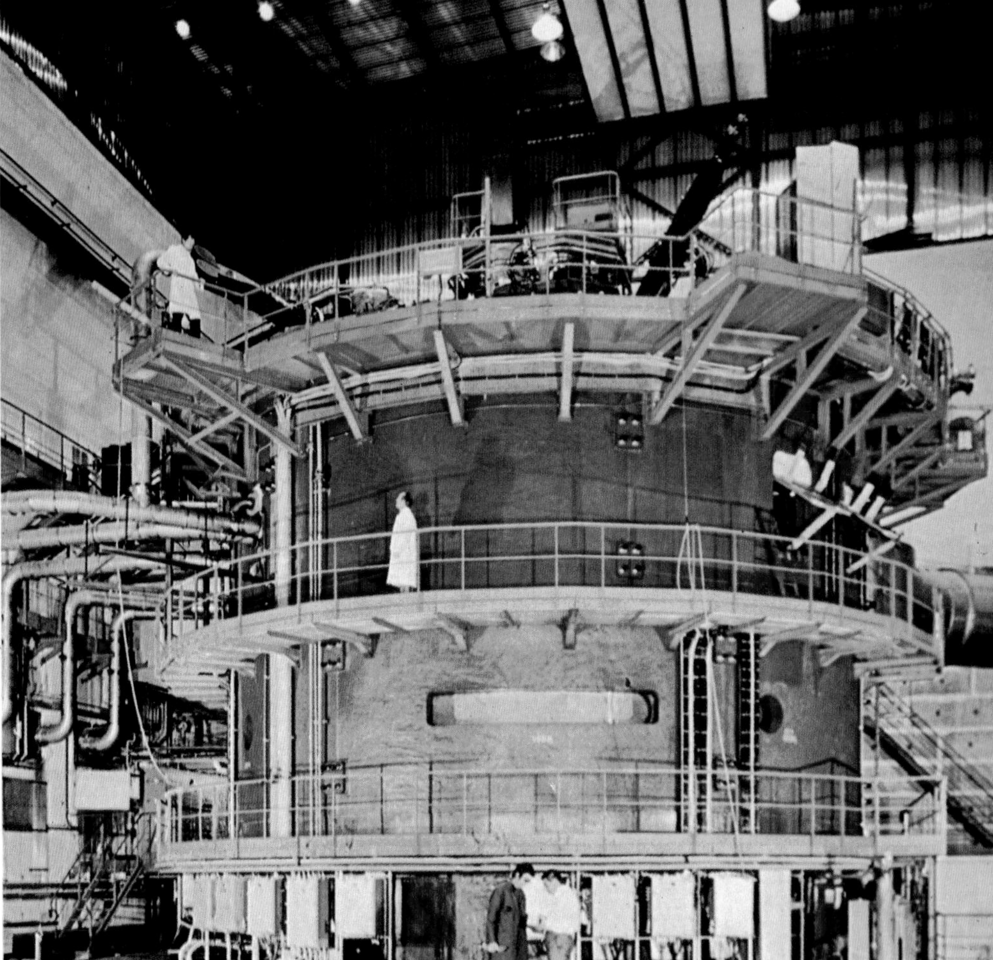
CERN

1 Camera
2 Lights
3 Bubble chamber window
4 Liquid hydrogen
5 Pipe to vacuum pump
6 Piston
7 Radiation shield
8 Liquid hydrogen chamber cooling tank
9 Beam of particles
10 Radiation shield window

CERN

Right: An aerial view of the CERN complex near Geneva. There are two laboratories, CERN I and CERN II, employing a total of about 3,650 staff. A super proton synchrotron, about 5 km (3 miles) in diameter, is being constructed for CERN II, capable of a peak energy of 400 GeV. CERN's 1975 budget was 247 million US dollars.

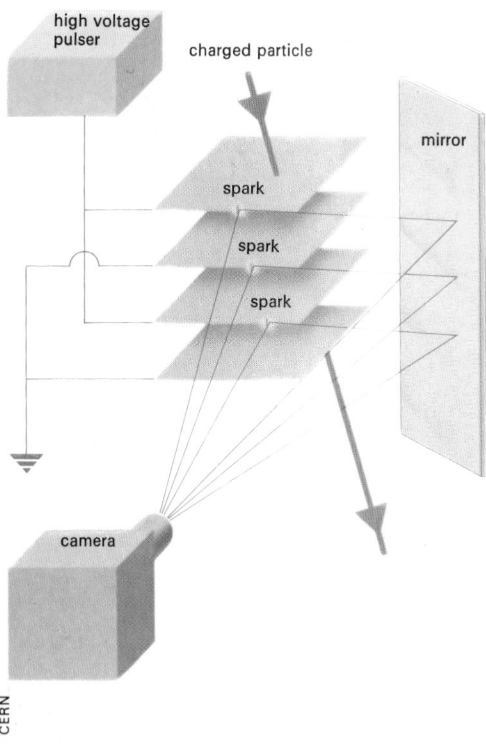

Above and above right: In the spark chamber particle detector, a stack of aluminium foil sheets, separated from each other by a gap of about a centimetre, is enclosed in a chamber containing an inert gas such as argon. A high voltage is applied to the plates and any charged particle passing through leaves a track of ionized gas in its wake. The ionized gas is electrically conductive and allows a spark to jump from one plate to the next along the route taken by the particle. The sparks are observed by a film or television camera. The photograph above shows the two mirrors of a spark chamber used at CERN in studying leptons—which include electrons, muons and neutrinos.

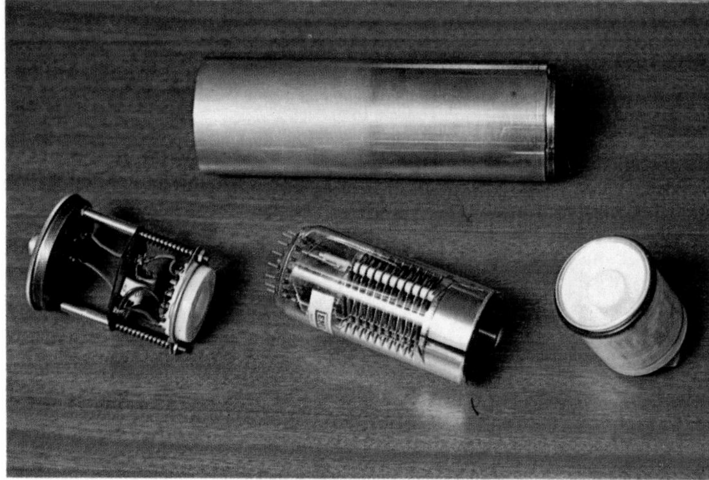

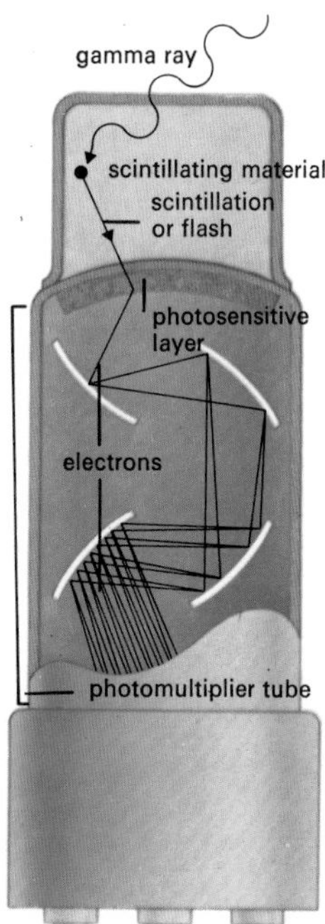

Above and left: The rate at which particles are being produced in an experiment can be measured by a scintillation counter. Some materials, such as certain types of plastic, give off a flash of light when a high-energy charged particle passes through them. The top of the counter, on the right in the photograph, contains a block of one of these scintillating materials. When a particle passes through it, the flash of light is picked up by the photomultiplier tube, a device which converts it into an electrical pulse. This pulse is relayed to a computer which counts and times the pulses. The accuracy is within a thousandth of a millionth of a second.

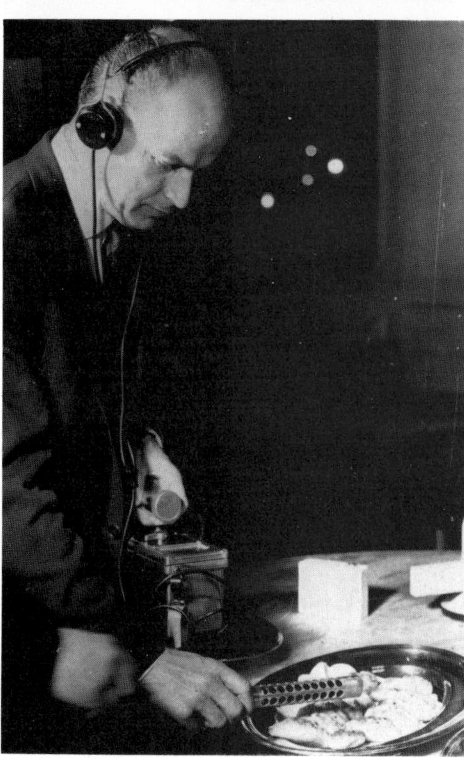

Right: At a banquet in Paris for the Soviet leader Nikita Kruschev in 1960, all the food was checked with a geiger counter in case it had been poisoned with a radioactive substance. Any charged particle passing through the detector causes an electrical discharge which is indicated by a click in the phones.

states' like the solar system, the atom or the nucleus, as gravity, electromagnetism and the strong force do. It is, however, thought to be responsible for the decay of many particles, in particular for the decay of a free neutron into a proton, an electron and a neutrino (a particle with no charge). The weak force is held responsible for all interactions involving neutrinos. A neutrino has so little mass, and such a weak interaction with matter, that only rarely will it disturb it as it passes through.

It is believed that the weak force may be transmitted by a particle called the *intermediate vector boson*, W, which was predicted by Yukawa in 1938.

Antiparticles

Conservation of energy is one of the principles of physics which, it is assumed, is never violated. Energy may change its form—it may reside in the mass of a particle at rest, and then become partly rest mass and partly the kinetic energy of the particle's decay products—but it is never created or destroyed. Energy is thus conserved absolutely.

Another quantity which is conserved absolutely is net electric charge, Q. This is slightly more subtle than energy conservation, because electric charge can in fact be created or destroyed, but only in pairs of opposite charges. For example, pairing a negative electron with a positive electron produces a zero electric charge, and it is the net charge which never changes.

The positive electron or *positron* is the *antiparticle* of the ordinary negatively charged electron. It has the same mass as an electron, only it is oppositely charged. The electron pairs gave rise to the idea of antiparticles generally and so, when sufficiently powerful particle accelerators became available in the 1950s, there was great interest in whether an antiproton could be created. This was much more difficult than creating the electron pairs because the rest mass energy required is nearly 2,000 times greater.

Particle accelerators are machines which accelerate particles to enormous velocities. These particles then bombard target atoms to break up their nuclei and create new particles. The antiproton was found and it then became possible to conceive of an 'antiworld' made up of antiatoms—antiprotons surrounded by positrons. Such a world meeting ours would annihilate both in a great flash of light.

The existence of the antiproton brought into the open another absolutely conserved quantity, *baryonic charge* B. Like the electric charge, it is conserved net. It allows creation or destruction of proton-antiproton or neutron-antineutron pairs, but forbids their creation in single particles. The baryonic charge of electrons and mesons is zero, and it can be said that protons do not decay into positrons because the baryonic charge would not be conserved. If it were not for the conservation of baryonic charge, atoms would disintegrate into light and a flux of neutrinos.

Isomultiplets and strangeness

The discovery of the mesons and higher mass particles with baryonic charge +1 disclosed two further patterns or symmetries. Every particle had a place in a group called a *charge multiplet* or *iso-*

UKAEA

Right: The blue glow of Cerenkov radiation in a pool of water containing used fuel rods from a nuclear reactor. This radiation is caused by particles travelling faster through the water than light can. As the particles travel through the water they make its atoms give off this characteristic blue glow.

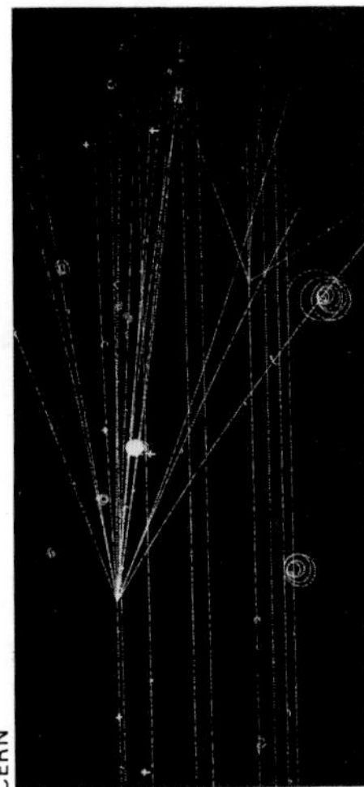

CERN

Above: A bubble chamber photograph showing the spray of mesons given off when a 20 GeV proton beam hit the stationary protons of the hydrogen atoms in the chamber.

Below: A beam of deuterons, each comprising one proton and one neutron, emerging from a cyclotron.

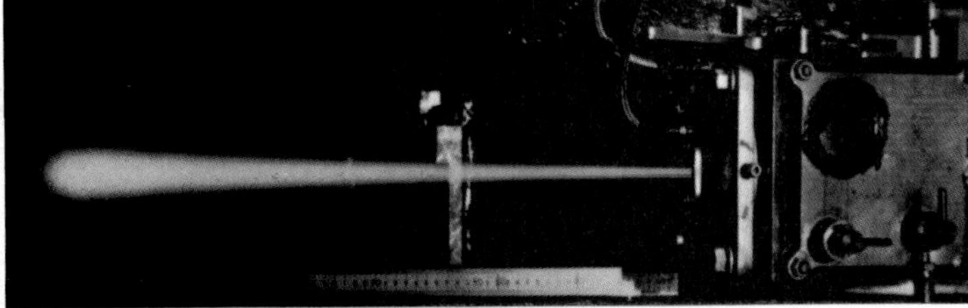

AERE

Below: Some of the known particles shown in an imaginary accelerator beam. The lightest particles are at the top; those on the left are positively charged, those in the centre neutral and those on the right are negatively charged. Also shown are a hydrogen atom and its corresponding anti-hydrogen atom.

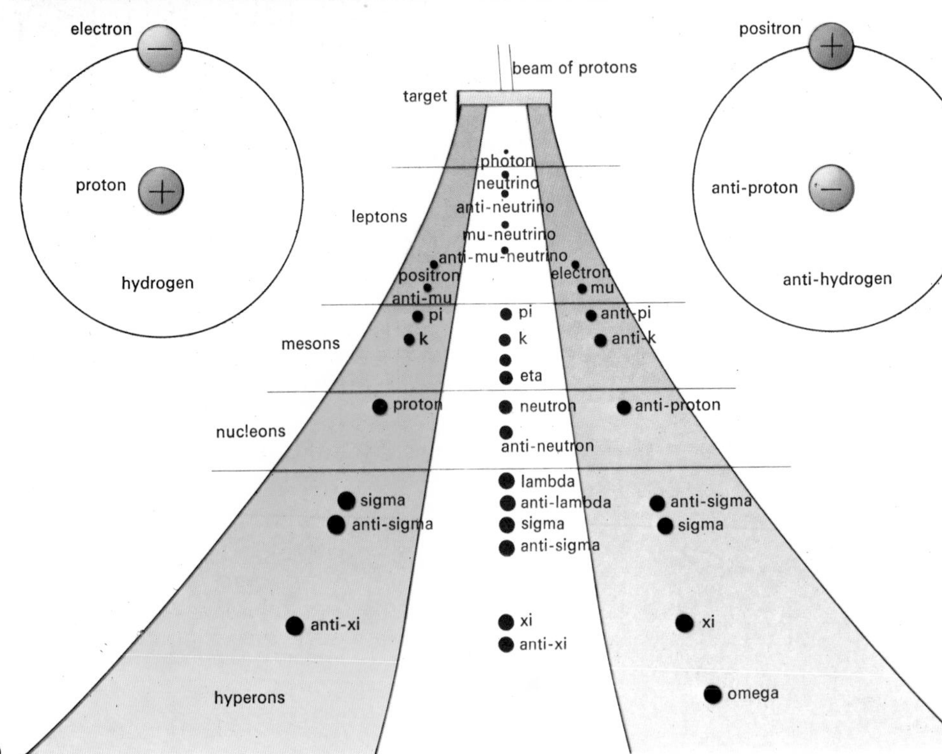

multiplet, each group consisting of particles having approximately the same mass but differing electric charges. For example, the proton and neutron form a multiplet. Their masses are nearly the same, but their electric charges are different, being one and zero respectively. Another example are the *pi mesons* or *pions*, the mesons predicted by Yukawa; their masses are the same but they can have either a positive, negative or zero charge.

The other pattern that was discovered was the operation of yet another kind of charge conservation, but this one was peculiar. The accelerators, by banging protons together, created many more particles. Some of these had a baryonic charge of +1 but were more massive than pions, and these higher mass particles were never produced singly. This suggested that a new sort of charge, which was termed *strangeness*, S, was being conserved. It would be zero for pions and nucleons (protons and neutrons), but possibly different for the heavier particles.

Quarks

The structure of the many particles that have now been detected is not yet fully understood. One theory is the *quark* model, which is able to account for the multiplets and for the strangeness of the observed particles in terms of just three basic particles and their antiparticles, the quarks and the antiquarks. The quarks have been allocated various values of electric and baryonic charge and strangeness, so that known particles can be explained in terms of combinations of quarks, or quarks and antiquarks.

The original quark model does not explain everything, however, and since it was originated in 1963 by Murray Gell-Mann and George Zweig it has been greatly modified. One modification requires 12 kinds of quark. In addition to the three 'flavours' of quark, *up*, *down* and *sideways*, there is a fourth flavour, the *charmed* quark. As well as the four flavours of quark they come in three 'colours', red, yellow and blue. The various flavours and colours of the quarks depend on their mass, electric charge, strangeness and whether or not they possess the additional property known as 'charm'.

The quarks are considered to be truly elementary particles, that is, they are basic and indivisible. They are thought to be the constituents of the *hadrons*, the particles such as protons and neutrons which interact by means of the strong force. The other elementary particles are the *leptons*, a group which are not affected by the strong force. These are the electron and the *muon*, which interact through the electromagnetic force, and the electron neutrino and the *muon neutrino* which interact through the weak force. In addition to the four leptons there are also four corresponding anti-leptons.

Despite the fact that hundreds of particles have now been discovered, the answers to the original questions about the nature of energy and forces, and just what exactly the smallest constituents of matter are, have not yet been fully answered. The new, immensely powerful accelerators now coming into use may provide some of the answers; but there is still a great deal that remains beyond our understanding.

Electricity and Magnetism

Electricity and magnetism are phenomena which arise from the nature and behaviour of the electrically charged particles—the *protons* and *electrons*—which together with the uncharged *neutrons* are the principal constituents of atoms. The exact nature of an electric charge is still unknown, but it can be measured, and its effects can be predicted and put to use, being the basis of all electrical and electronic equipment.

The charge carried by a proton is called a *positive* (or +ve) charge, and that carried by the electron is called a *negative* (or —ve) charge. A pair of similar charges, two positive ones for example, will repel each other, but two unlike charges, one positive and one negative, will attract each other.

The region around a charged particle in which these forces of attraction and repulsion operate is called an *electric field*. The strength of the force a particle can exert, and thus the intensity of its electric field, decreases as the inverse of the square of the distance from it. This means that if the distance from the particle is doubled, the strength of the force will be quartered, and if the distance is trebled the force will be reduced to one ninth.

Objects normally have no net electric charge as they contain as many electrons as they do protons, and so their positive and negative charges are balanced. If, however, electrons are taken from an object, it will have a net positive charge. Conversely, if it is given extra electrons it will have a net negative charge.

These effects can be created by rubbing a substance which has an affinity for electrons with one which is willing to give some up. For example, when dry hair is combed with a plastic comb the hair becomes positively charged and the comb

Below: Michael Faraday was born in September 1791, and after a very basic education he was apprenticed to a London bookbinder. While working there he read an article on electricity in a copy of the *Encyclopaedia Britannica* and this interested him so much that he decided to take up the study of science. In 1812 he went to work for Sir Humphry Davy at the Royal Institution, and this was the beginning of his scientific career. In 1823 he discovered methods of liquifying gases; in 1825 he discovered benzene. His most important work, however, was his study of the relationship between electricity and magnetism.

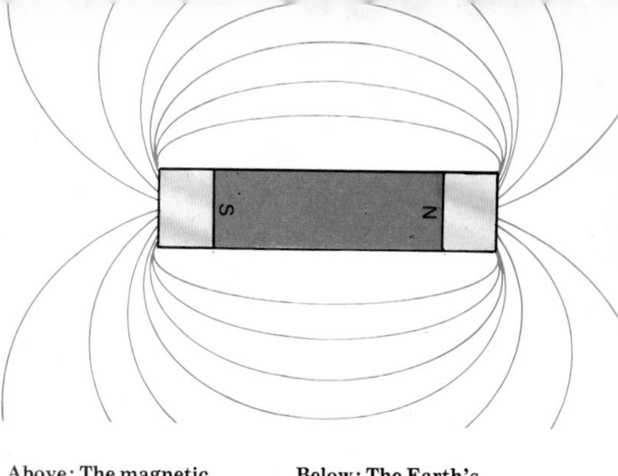

Ferrofluidio Corp.

Above: The magnetic field of a bar magnet can be represented by lines of force which form closed loops around it, leaving the magnet at one pole and joining it again at the other. If a magnet is placed under a piece of paper, and iron filings spread on top, the filings will group together along the lines of force.

Below: The Earth's magnetic field may be caused by electric currents, circulating horizontally, within the liquid rock between the core and the crust. These currents may be produced by friction within the planet due to its rotation and they produce a magnetic field at right angles to their plane of rotation.

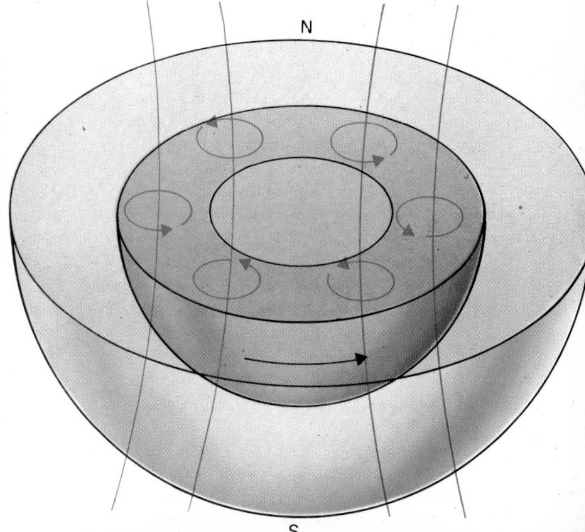

Below: The induction coil is a device for producing high voltage pulses. There is a soft iron core, around which is wound a primary coil and a secondary coil. Interrupting the electrical current in the primary coil creates a very high voltage in the secondary which has many more turns of wire wound on it.

Right: The disc dynamo built by Faraday in 1831. The copper disc is rotated with its edge between the poles of the magnet, so that it cuts through the lines of flux. This causes electric currents to be set up within the disc—and the electricity is collected by copper brushes which rub against the disc.

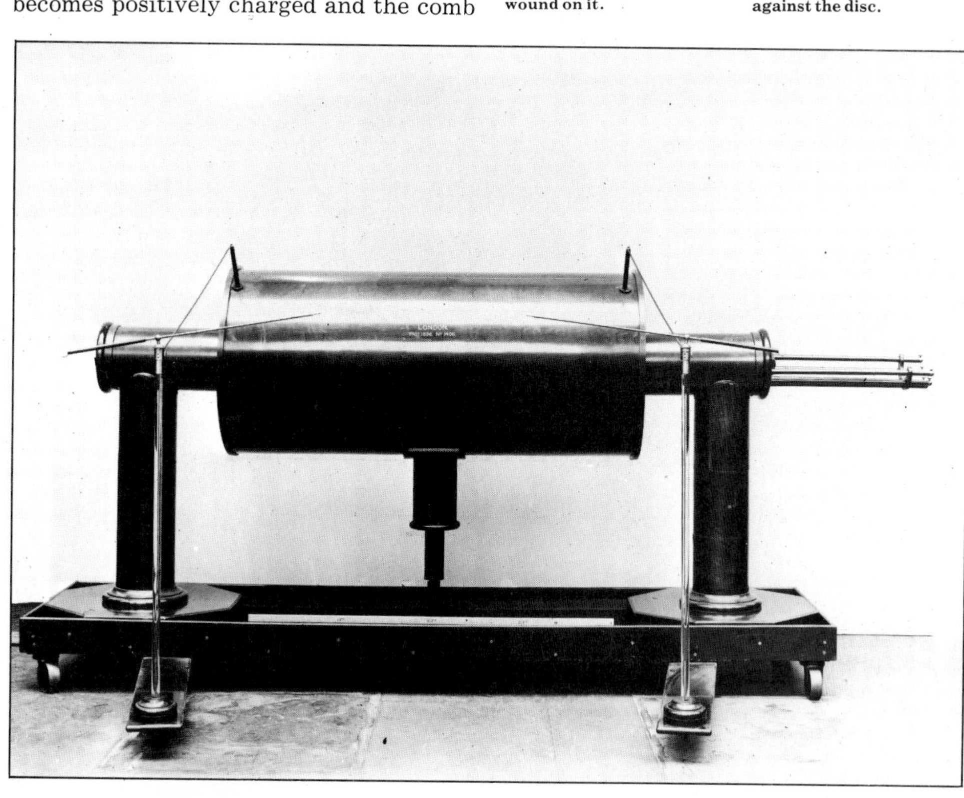

Michael Holford

negative. If the comb is then held near the hair, strands of hair will be attracted towards it because of their opposite electric charge.

This type of attraction is called *electrostatic* attraction because, apart from the initial transfer of electrons during the combing, it is due to stationary or *static* charges.

If the difference in charge between two objects is great enough a *static discharge*, in the form of a spark, may occur as the surplus electrons on the negatively charged object jump across to make up the deficiency on the positively charged object. A spectacular example of this is the lightning flash which occurs between highly charged thunderclouds and the ground.

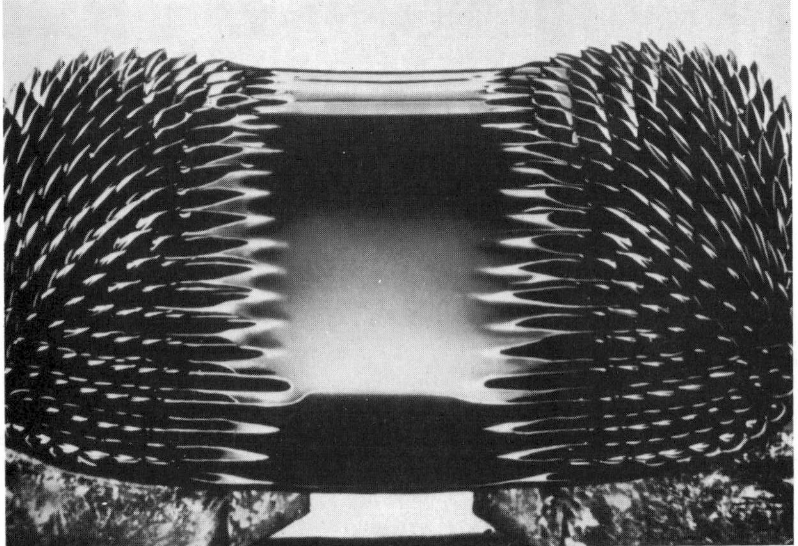

Above and left: These two pictures show the spikes formed on the surface of magnetic fluids (also called ferrofluids) when subjected to a vertical magnetic field. Ferrofluids contain particles of ferrite, a ceramic material made from an iron oxide and small quantities of other metal oxides. The particles are coated with a type of plastic so that they can slide over each other with virtually no friction, and the fluid is made by suspending the particles in water. Because the particles are so small, they do not settle at the bottom of the water and the resulting fluid still has almost the same consistency as water. Despite appearances the spikes are fluid.

Electric current

An ordinary electric current is the flow of electrons around a circuit, created when one end of the circuit is made more positive or negative than the other. A good example of a simple circuit is that of an electric torch.

Chemical reactions inside the battery continually create a surplus of electrons at one terminal and a deficiency at the other. When the circuit is completed by switching the torch on, the electrons in the circuit, that is in the connections to the lamp and in the lamp filament, move towards the terminal that is deficient in electrons, drawn to it by its net positive charge. As the electrons move towards the terminal, electrons from the other terminal move into the circuit to take their place.

The result is a steady flow of electrons around the circuit from one terminal to

Paul Brierley

Left: Iron filings spread on top of the windings of a linear electric motor show the nature of its magnetic field. The motor is constructed so that its magnetic field travels along it, and so any metallic object placed on top will be carried along by the moving field while also supported by it.

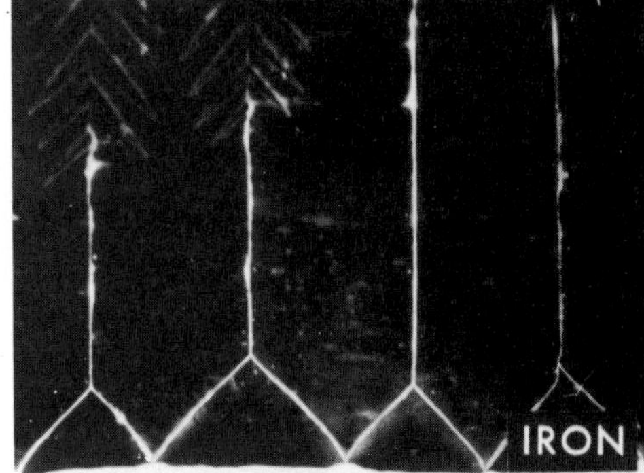

Top and above: These two pictures show how crystals of iron behave when they are magnetized. The upper picture shows a sample which is not very highly magnetized, and the lower one shows the internal strains created when the magnetization is increased. This causes the crystals to deform as the atoms re-align.

Left: A Leyden jar, one of the first devices built for storing electric charges. The glass jar has a metal lining and a metal covering. When a high voltage is applied across these two metal sections, one becomes positively charged and the other negative. This picture shows the stored charge being discharged.

Right: Some of the wide range of resistors used in electronic circuits. The resistance of these devices is utilized to reduce the current flowing in a particular part of a circuit, or to reduce the voltage level at a given point in a circuit. The commonest types are made of carbon powder mixed with clay and resin.

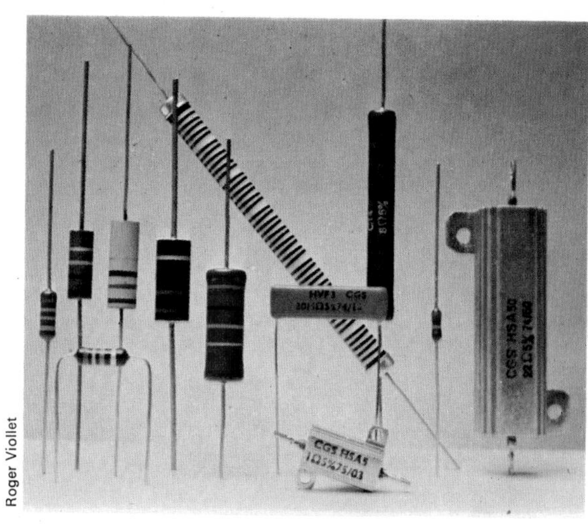

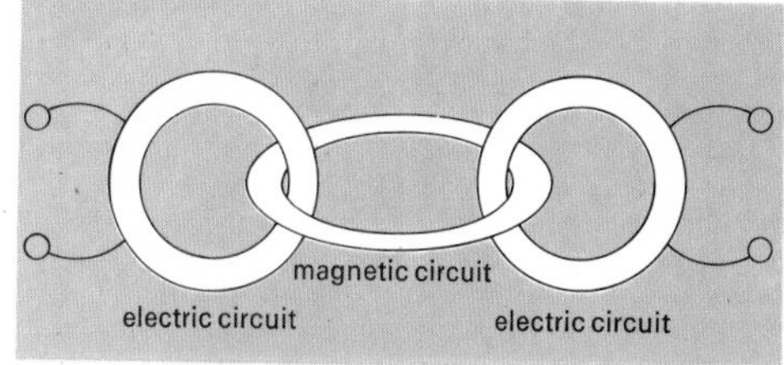

Left: This diagram illustrates the way in which the electric and magnetic circuits of a transformer are interlinked. The current in the primary electric circuit, on the left, sets up a magnetic circuit, centre, which then causes a current to flow in the secondary electric circuit on the right.

Right: In an electromagnetic machine, the forces involved act at right angles to each other. In a motor, for example, the current in the rotor will set up a magnetic field at right angles to its direction of flow, and the turning force on the rotor will be at right angles to both the current and the magnetic field.

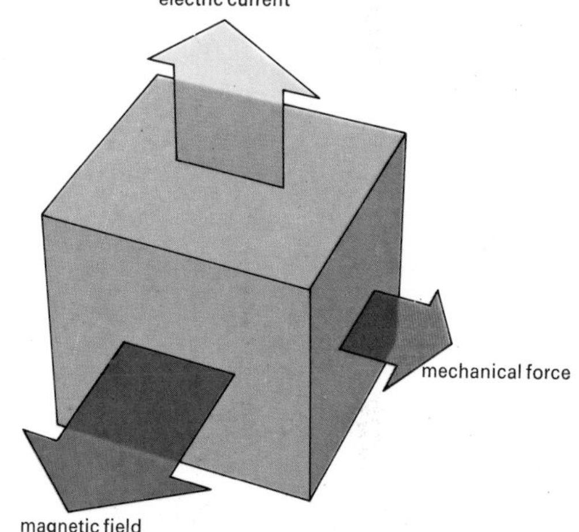

the other, kept going by the chemical reactions within the battery. Until it was realized that electric current was a flow of electrons from a negatively charged area to a positively (or less negatively) charged area, it was assumed that current flowed from positive to negative.

Ohm's law

The amount of current flowing through a circuit depends on two factors: the voltage applied to the circuit and the opposition to current flow within the circuit.

The voltage is a measure of the difference between the levels of charge at each end of the circuit. This difference, known as the *potential difference*, provides the *electromotive force* (emf) which drives the current around the circuit, just as pressure drives water through a system of pipes.

In a *direct current* (dc) circuit, where the current flows smoothly in one direction only, the opposition or *resistance* to current flow is caused by collisions between the electrons and the atoms of the material through which they are passing. These collisions interfere with the electron flow and so reduce the rate at which they can pass through the material.

Metals are good conductors of electricity because they have a low resistance. This is because their atoms are arranged in crystal structures, and the outer electrons of the atoms are free to move within the crystal lattices.

At the other end of the scale, insulating materials (which have a very high resistance) have their electrons tightly bound within their molecules, and so it takes a great deal of voltage to make them move through the material.

The relationship between voltage, current and resistance is expressed by *Ohm's Law*, formulated by the German physicist Georg Ohm (1789-1854). This states that the resistance (R) of a circuit is the ratio of the voltage (V) to the current (I), that is, $R = V/I$. It can also be expressed as voltage = current x resistance, or $V = IR$.

Magnetism

When a charged particle such as an electron is stationary it is surrounded by its own electric field. When it moves, however, an additional field, a *magnetic field*, is set up. This occurs whenever an electric current flows, but it also happens within an atom because the electrons *spin* while moving in their orbits. In the atoms of most substances the magnetic fields produced by the electrons cancel each other out, but in others there is a net magnetic field and the atom itself behaves like a tiny magnet.

In the materials known as *ferromagnetic materials*, of which iron is the best known example, the application of a magnetic field will pull the magnetic fields of the atoms into line. The fields are then acting in unison, and the material becomes a magnet. Pure or 'soft' iron will not retain its magnetism when the magnetizing force, produced for example by the electric current flowing in a coil of wire, is removed. The atoms will return to their random alignment, instead of remaining in the aligned state. Steel, however, is iron alloyed with carbon, and the resulting structure is such that the atoms remain aligned after the magnetizing force has been removed.

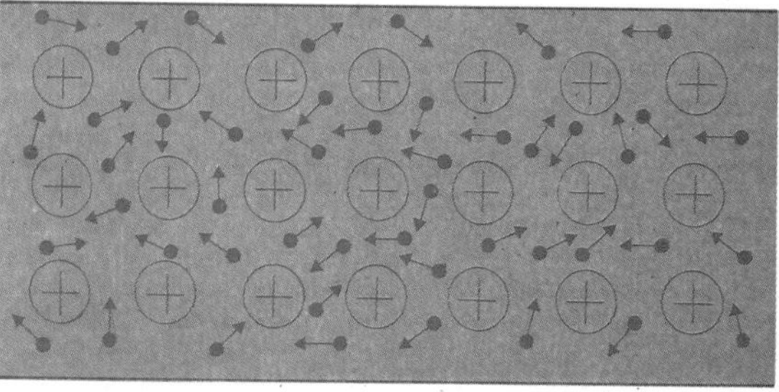

Above and below: Metals are good conductors of electricity because of the way in which electrons are free to move around within their crystalline structures. When no voltage is applied to them they move around at random, as shown above. However, applying voltage makes them drift towards the positively charged end, as in the diagram below. This electron drift is what constitutes an electric current in solid conducting materials.

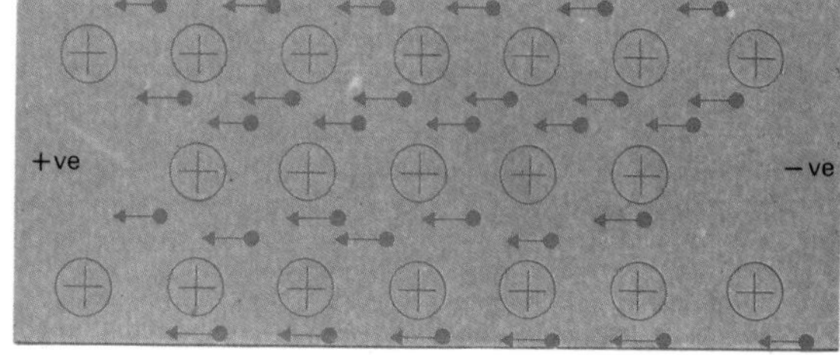

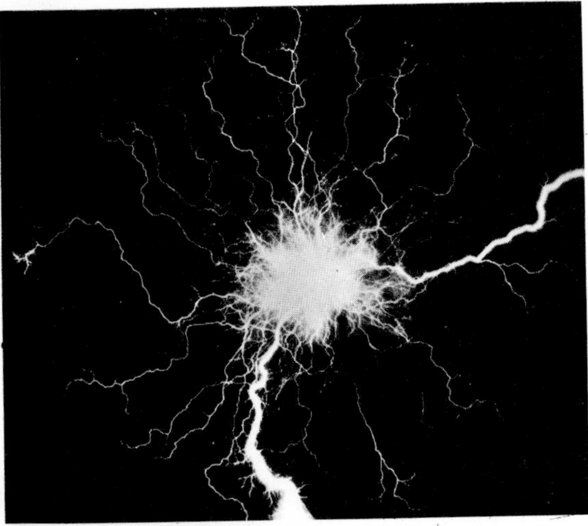

Roger Viollet

Above: A lightning flash is a very powerful discharge of static electricity. The thundercloud's charge is created by friction, caused by powerful air currents within it. This charge eventually becomes so great that a massive discharge occurs between the cloud and the ground or objects on it, such as trees.

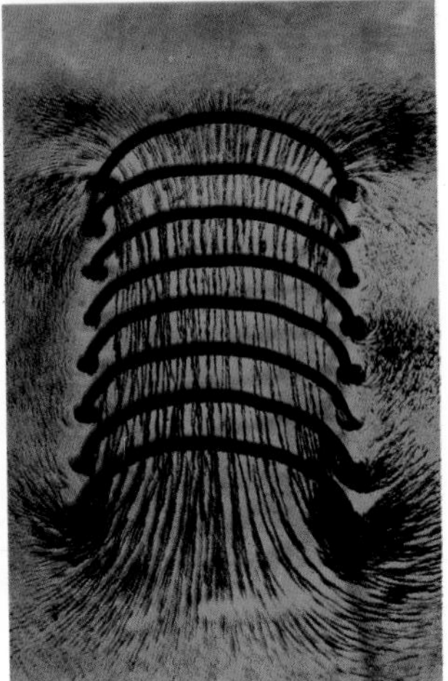

Snark

Left: Iron filings show the pattern of the lines of force around a coil carrying a current.

Below: An electromagnet consists of a soft iron bar with a coil wrapped round it. When current flows in the coil, the bar acts like a permanent magnet because of the magnetic field passing through it.

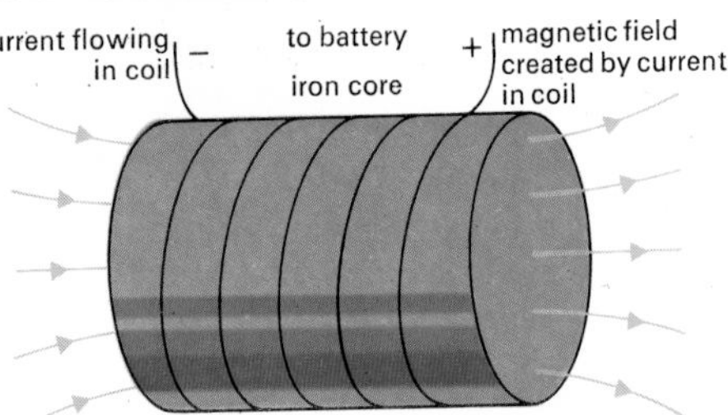

Reyrolle Parsons Ltd

Above: A 'flashover' discharge during the testing of an insulator of the type used in high voltage electricity supply systems. The voltage at the top of the insulator is steadily increased, until it becomes so high that it breaks down the resistance of the air around it and causes a discharge.

Below: The ribbed glass insulators on a 400 kV transmission line. The insulators hold the lines, which are uninsulated themselves, away from the steel tower which is carrying them. The sections of line on either side of the tower are connected by lengths of line which bypass the insulators and the tower arms.

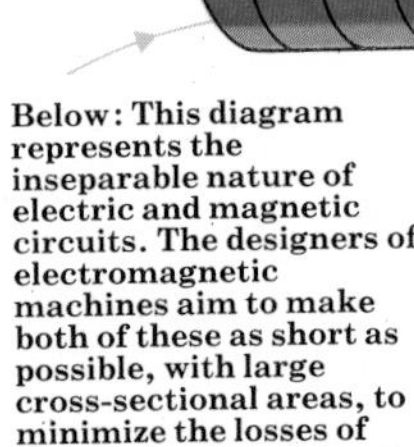

Below: This diagram represents the inseparable nature of electric and magnetic circuits. The designers of electromagnetic machines aim to make both of these as short as possible, with large cross-sectional areas, to minimize the losses of energy due to resistance and reluctance within the circuits.

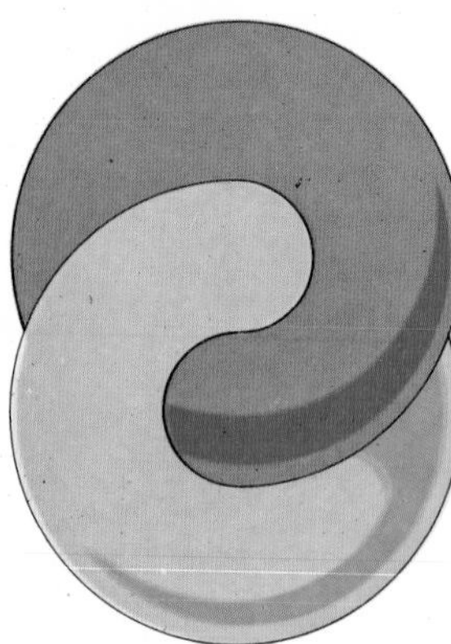

Paul Brierley

Just as there are two types of electric charge, positive and negative, a magnet has two *poles*, one at each end. These poles are called 'north' and 'south' respectively, and two similar poles will repel each other while two unlike poles will attract each other. However, an object cannot have just one pole, in the way that it can have either a positive or a negative charge. Poles always exist in pairs, one north and one south.

If a bar magnet, a small bar of magnetized steel, for example, is suspended by a piece of thread tied around its middle, it will turn so that its north pole points to the Earth's magnetic north. This is the way a compass needle works, and the reason why the magnetic poles are called 'north' and 'south'. The north or 'north seeking' pole always swings towards the north, and the south or 'south seeking' pole likewise always swings towards the south.

Electromagnetism

In 1831, Michael Faraday (1791-1867) made many important discoveries which demonstrated the relationship between electricity and magnetism. He found that a coil of wire carrying an electric current produced a magnetic field, and behaved like a bar magnet. Such an *electromagnet* could exert a force on a piece of unmagnetized ferromagnetic substance, on a permanent magnet, or even on a similar current-carrying coil. It would also exhibit polarity, having a north and a south pole, and it would obey the rules of attraction and repulsion between poles.

Light and Sound

Much of our awareness of the world around us comes from information received by our eyes and ears. Our eyes respond to visible light, which is one of the many forms of *electromagnetic radiation* (other forms include radio waves and X-rays), and our ears respond to sound or *acoustic radiation*. Electromagnetic and acoustic radiation can both be thought of as travelling in waves. The waves on the sea are the most familiar examples of waves, but light and sound also reveal a wave-like nature when studied closely in the laboratory.

Sound

When we hear a sound it is because the air is vibrating, alternately pushing and pulling our eardrums and forcing them to vibrate. So to make a sound that can be heard by others we must obviously make the air vibrate somehow. This is not difficult; any object that vibrates, such as a drumskin or a vocal cord, pushes and pulls at the air which surrounds it. Every time it moves forward it presses against the air in front and when it recedes again the air has to rush back to fill the partial vacuum thus created. In other words the air in front of the vibrating object (which can be called a *sound source*) is subjected to an alternating pressure.

The air of course is composed of separate molecules, many millions of them in every cubic centimetre, and the molecules next to the source are unhappy at having to suffer the alternations in pressure, so they pass the strain on to their neighbours, who pass it on to their neighbours in turn. In this way the pressure alternations at the source are passed through the air. Every time the source vibrates another cycle of alternating pressure is passed along and the succession of these pressure cycles moving through the air constitutes a sound wave.

Such a wave moves through the air at a fixed speed—the velocity of sound, which in dry air at sea level is about 344 metres/sec (770 mph). Sound waves can travel through almost any gas, liquid or solid but they cannot travel through a vacuum, because in a vacuum there are no molecules to transmit the pressure to their neighbours. In liquids and solids sound waves move faster than in gases like air—about 1,400 metres/sec (3,130 mph) in water and 5,000 metres/sec (11,180 mph) in steel.

The number of vibrations made by the source in a second (the number of *cycles per second*) is known as its *frequency*, and since all the molecules affected by

Picturepoint

Above: This device, in a Tokyo street, is indicating the sound level in the vicinity. The number it is displaying represents the local sound level in decibels. The formula for decibels is 10 x log EN/ER, where EN is the sound energy present and ER is the energy of the quietest sound the ear detects.

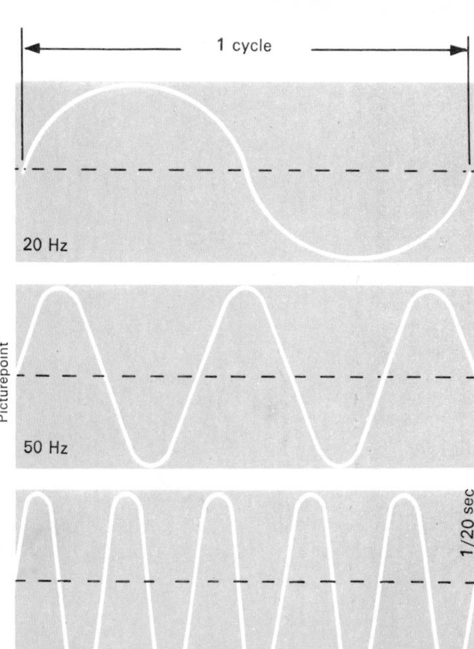

Right: Sound waves can be represented by graphs, with the vertical axis representing the intensity or amplitude of the sound, and the horizontal axis showing seconds. The frequency of the wave is the number of complete cycles per second. One cycle per second is known as 1 Hertz (1 Hz).

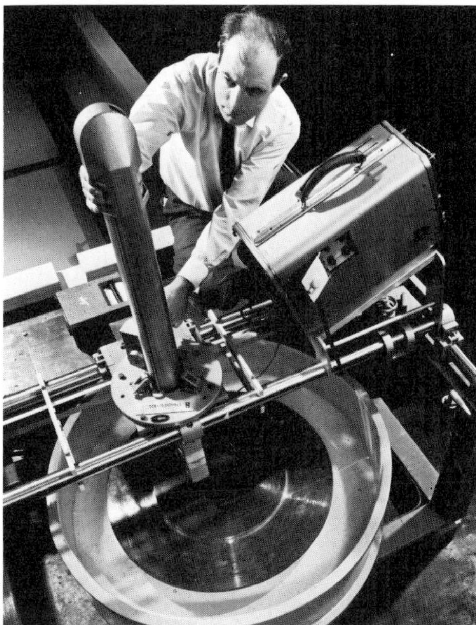

UKAEA

B & K Labs

Left: Ultrasonic waves are used to detect flaws in engineering materials. The test sample is scanned with pulses of very high frequency sound which normally travel right through it. If they meet a flaw in the material, however, they are reflected back again. The machine will detect these reflections and thus record the presence of the flaw.

Above: High levels of sound are dangerous to health, causing hearing defects and creating fatigue which can lead to accidents. This picture shows sound level monitoring apparatus analyzing the noise in a workshop.

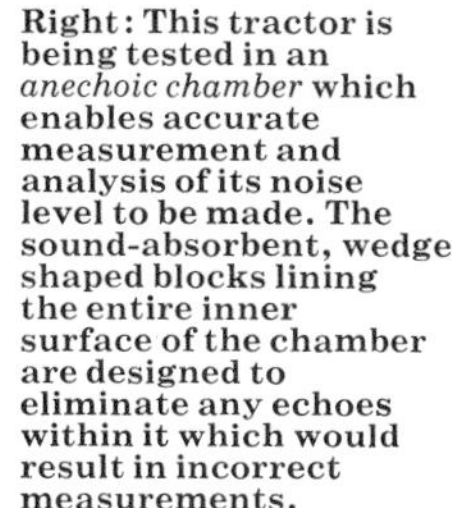

Right: This tractor is being tested in an *anechoic chamber* which enables accurate measurement and analysis of its noise level to be made. The sound-absorbent, wedge-shaped blocks lining the entire inner surface of the chamber are designed to eliminate any echoes within it which would result in incorrect measurements.

Below: Echoes occur when sounds strike a hard surface and are eventually reflected back to their source.

Picturepoint

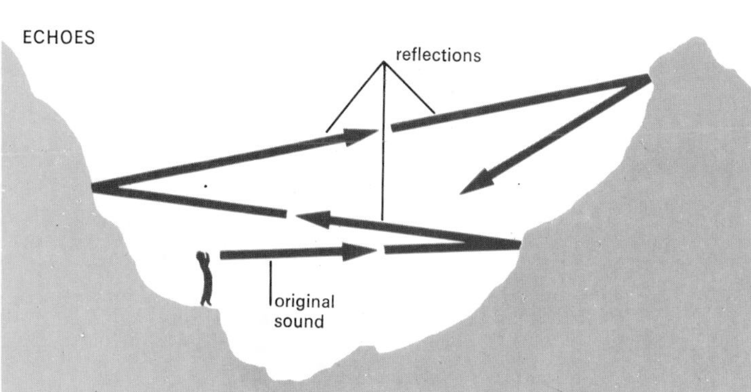

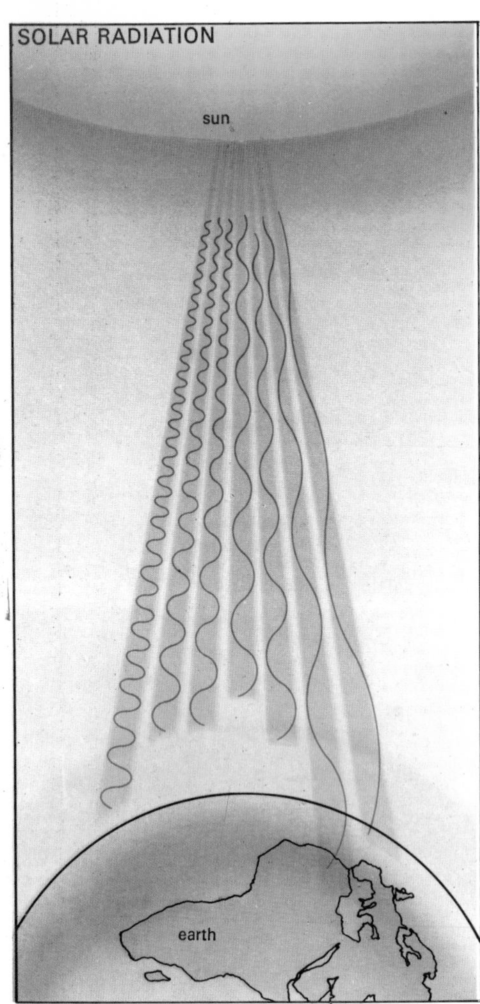

the wave it produces vibrate at the same frequency we can talk of the frequency of the wave. Frequencies are measured in *Hertz* (symbol *Hz*), one Hertz being one complete cycle of vibrations (from maximum to minimum and back to maximum) per second.

The speed at which sound travels is independent of its frequency, and so the peaks of high frequency sound waves are closer together than those of low frequency waves. The distance between successive wave peaks is known as the *wavelength*, and the wavelength of any type of wave can be calculated by dividing its velocity by its frequency.

Speech and music are a mixture of frequencies from about 20 Hz to 20,000 Hz (20 kHz). The higher frequencies are heard as treble notes and the lower as bass. Frequencies below 20 Hz are felt rather than heard; a large part of the vibration caused by earthquakes is in fact due to low frequency sound waves moving in the Earth's crust. Sounds above 20 kHz cannot be detected by human ears, although they are audible to other animals such as dogs and bats.

Electromagnetic waves

Electromagnetic radiation can be thought of in two ways, either as continuous waves of energy or as streams of 'particles' or pulses of energy known as *photons*. Whether it is considered as waves or as particles depends on which particular properties of it are under discussion; in some cases its behaviour is best explained by its wave-like properties, and in others it is better to think of it as streams of photons.

THE ELECTROMAGNETIC SPECTRUM

ultra violet
infra red
x-rays
microwaves
visible
gamma rays
EHF SHF UHF VHF HF MF LF VLF
radio waves
0.001 nm 0.01 nm 0.1 nm 10 nm 100 nm 1000 nm 0.01 mm 0.1 mm 1 cm 10 cm 1 m 10 m 100 m 1 km 10 km 100 k

Far left: The sun sends a wide spectrum of electromagnetic radiation to the earth, much of which is absorbed by the atmosphere. The sun's radiation includes low frequency radio waves (on the right) and high frequency X-rays and gamma rays (on the left). Microwaves, infra-red rays, visible light and ultraviolet rays are in between.

Snark

Left: This enormous structure is a radio telescope, used by astronomers to detect the radio waves emitted by stars. The energy of the waves reaching the earth is extremely low, and the dish-shaped part of the radio telescope acts as a reflector, focussing the waves on to the actual aerial so that a stronger signal is obtained.

Right: Rainbows are the result of a phenomenon called *refraction*. When light passes from one medium, such as air, to another, such as water, its angle is altered slightly. The size of this change depends on the light's wavelength, red (long wavelength) light being affected less than blue (short wavelength) light. Sunlight passing through raindrops will, if the angle is correct, be split into its component colours by the raindrops in such a way as to form a rainbow.

Below: Photons (blue) striking a photoelectric material, dislodge electrons (red), creating an electric current.

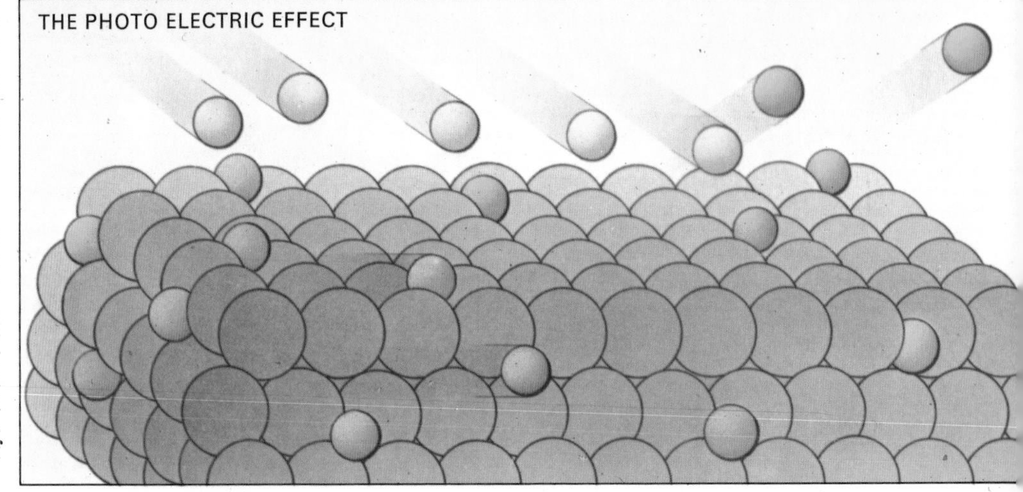

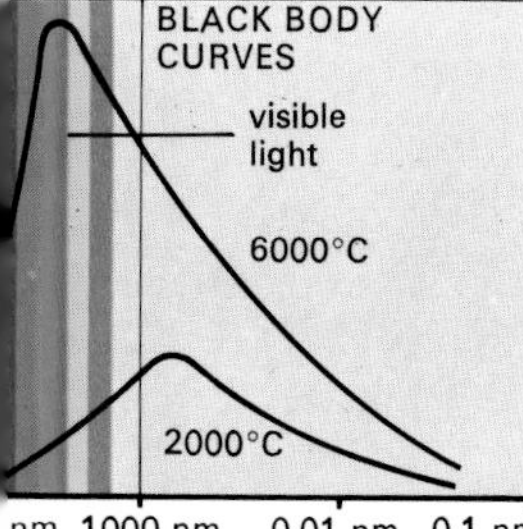

Above: 'Black body curves' show the distribution of energy radiated at various frequencies by heated objects. These curves show how an object at 6,000°C radiates more energy, at higher frequencies, than one at 2,000°C.

Right: A microwave antenna. Microwaves, because of their high frequencies, can be made to carry more information than lower frequency radio waves.

Left: The whole electromagnetic spectrum, from gamma rays, through the visible region, to the longest radio waves.

Cable & Wireless

Colour Library International

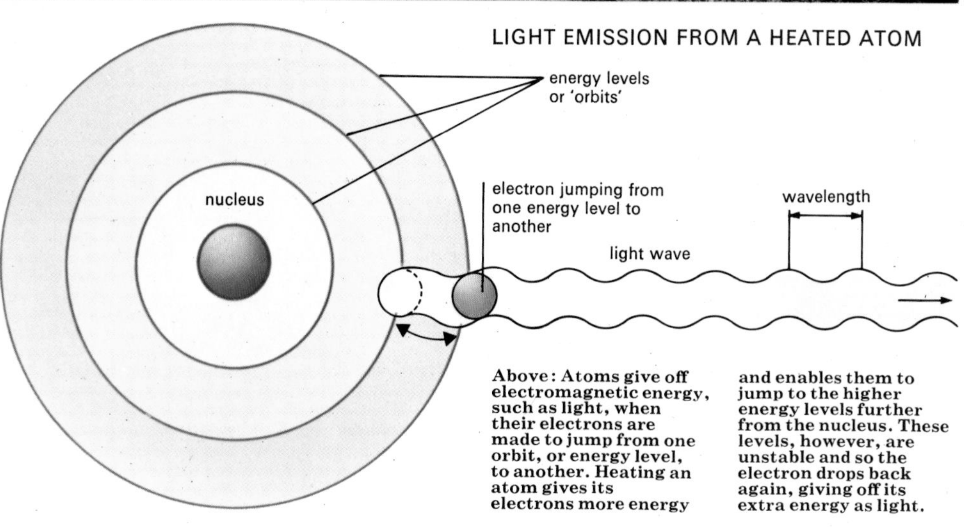

Above: Atoms give off electromagnetic energy, such as light, when their electrons are made to jump from one orbit, or energy level, to another. Heating an atom gives its electrons more energy and enables them to jump to the higher energy levels further from the nucleus. These levels, however, are unstable and so the electron drops back again, giving off its extra energy as light.

The optical properties of light, for example, such as reflection and refraction, are related to its wavelength and so in these aspects light is best thought of as waves. The photoelectric effect, on the other hand, where light falling on to certain materials causes an electric current to flow in them, is best explained in terms of high-energy photons striking electrons in the material, freeing them from their atoms so that they can travel through the material as an electric current.

Unlike sound, which is propagated by the mechanical vibrations of the molecules of substances, electromagnetic radiation originates at a sub-atomic level and travels most easily in a vacuum where there are no atoms or molecules to impede its progress. An electromagnetic wave has two components, an electric field and an associated magnetic field that travels along with it.

Anything which produces either an alternating electric field or an alternating magnetic field is also a source of electromagnetic radiation. An alternating electric current flowing in a wire, for example, creates both an alternating electric field and an alternating magnetic field around it, and these two fields spread out together from the wire as an alternating electromagnetic field. This alternating field travels as a wave-like series of alternations in the strengths of the electric and magnetic fields, the 'peaks' of the waves being at points where the field strengths are greatest. As with sound, the frequency of the wave equals the frequency of the source, and the wavelength, that is the distance between two successive points on the wave where the fields are equal, is found by dividing the velocity by the frequency. The higher the frequency, the shorter the wavelength.

The velocity of electromagnetic waves in a vacuum, as calculated by James Clerk Maxwell who first suggested their existence in 1864, is an incredible 299,792·458 km/second (186,282 miles/sec, or 670,615,200 mph). This is the same as the measured velocity of light, a coincidence which persuaded physicists to accept the existence of electromagnetic waves long before their transmission was first demonstrated by Heinrich Hertz in 1887. It was also obvious that one of their forms is visible light itself.

Visible light, however, is only the most obvious form of electro-magnetic radiation, which can be observed also as radio waves, microwaves, infra-red and ultraviolet light, X-rays and gamma rays. All these differ from each other only in wavelength and frequency, and there is a certain amount of overlap between these different groups, the highest frequencies of one group being the same as the lowest of the next.

The longest wavelengths are those of radio waves, which range from over 1000 km down to about 10 cm, and these are the simplest to generate artificially. An alternating current of the right frequency is passed through a straight wire aerial, creating an alternating magnetic field around the aerial which radiates the waves into the air. An equally simple aerial can be used to detect radio waves, which induce a tiny alternating electric current in any wire which points at the same angle and direction as the transmitting aerial.

Shorter electromagnetic wavelengths,

unlike radio waves and microwaves, cannot be produced electronically. Infra-red radiation, which covers the wavelengths from 1 mm down to 1 micrometre (a millionth of a metre), is produced by the natural vibrations of atoms, particularly those in solids. Atoms are composed of electrically charged particles, and when these vibrate they create alternating electric and magnetic fields which project themselves away as infra-red rays. The hotter an object gets, the faster its atoms vibrate and the higher the frequency (hence the shorter the wavelength) of their radiation.

Since it is generally true that any emitter of waves will also absorb them, infra-red waves readily give up their energy to the atoms of any solid they encounter. This raises the temperature of the absorbing solid, so that infra-red can also be considered as radiated heat.

If an object is heated above about 530°C (986°F), it begins to radiate appreciable amounts of radiation at wavelengths as short as 750 nanometres (1 nm is 1 thousand millionth of a metre), which human eyes can detect as red light. Visible light wavelengths range from this down to 390 nm for violet light. Anything heated above about 1,200°C (2,192°F) radiates a mixture of visible light wavelengths which appears white to our eyes. This is the physical meaning of the terms 'red hot' and 'white hot'.

Shorter still than visible light is ultraviolet light, a term used to describe electromagnetic radiation with wavelengths from 390 nm down to 1 nm. Ultraviolet waves can be produced, like infra-red, by atomic vibrations, but the temperature must be about 5,000°C (9,032°F) before a significant amount is produced. The sun and other stars are at higher temperatures than this and consequently radiate a good deal of ultraviolet, but the bulk of their output is still in the visible range. However, ultraviolet and some visible light can also be produced at much lower temperatures by changes in the energy of electrons in atoms and molecules.

According to the *quantum theory*, electrons orbiting atomic nuclei can only have certain definite energy levels, and each time an electron changes from one energy level to another it emits a short burst of electromagnetic radiation called a photon. The frequency of the photon is directly proportional to the change in the electron's energy, and the possible energies of electrons are such that the emitted photons are visible or ultraviolet light. The higher the frequency of the photon, the more energy it possesses.

Black Body Radiation

The relationship between frequency and energy was first explained by the German physicist Max Planck (1858-1947) in 1900. The explanation was contained in Planck's quantum theory, which he formulated when studying the spectrum of radiation emitted by heated objects. Physicists had been unable to explain why, when an object was heated, it gave off much less high-frequency energy than they expected it to.

Planck's explanation was that the energy was emitted in discrete bundles or *quanta* (photons), and that a quantum of high frequency contained more energy than a low frequency one. Consequently the energy needed to enable an object to

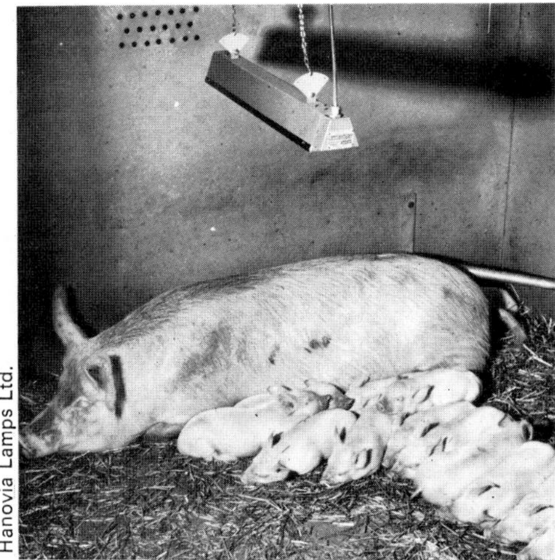
Hanovia Lamps Ltd.

Picturepoint

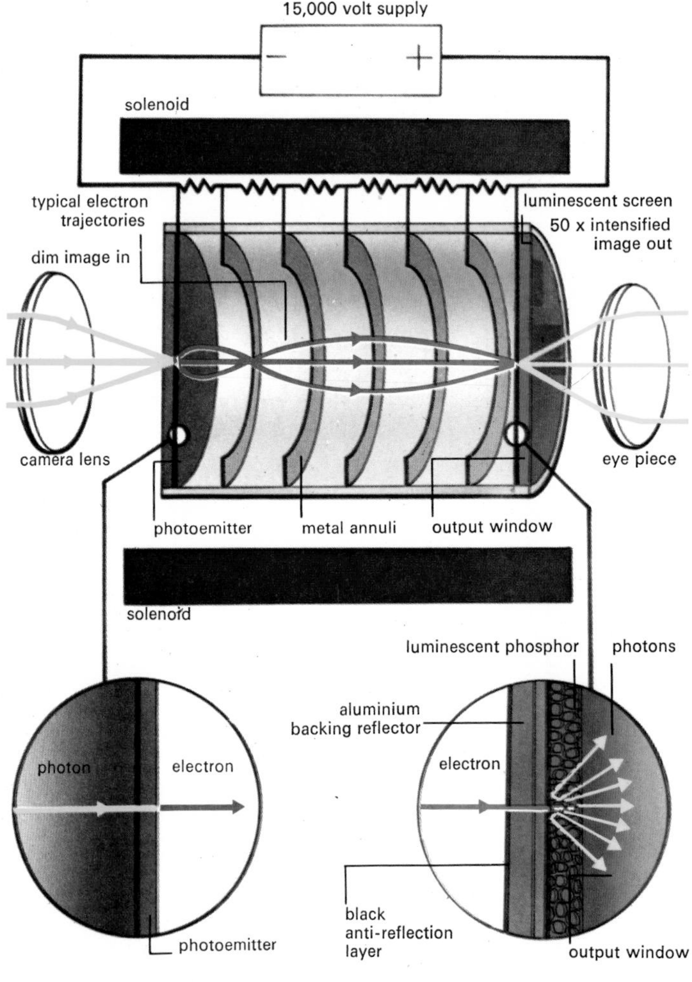

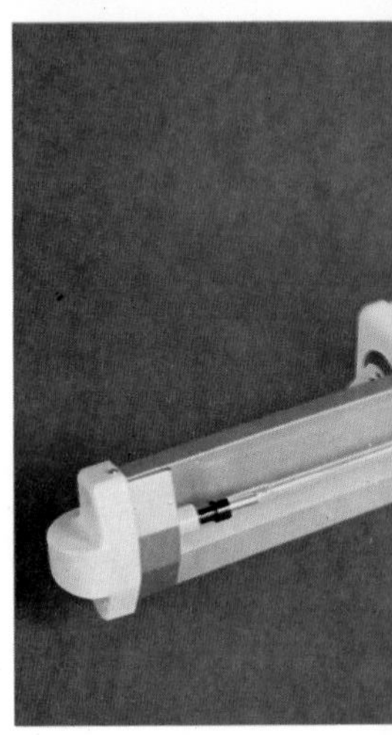

Above: Over 80% of the light emitted by an ultraviolet bactericidal lamp is 254 nm ultraviolet, which kills most kinds of germs.

Left: An image intensifier takes a dim image and focusses it onto a *photoemitter*. This emits electrons in proportion to the pattern of light of the image. These electrons are accelerated by the 15,000 volt supply, and focussed by the solenoid's magnetic field, and when they hit the luminescent screen they make it give off photons, creating a bright picture of the original scene.

Below left: An image intensifier gun sight and (below) Stonehenge viewed at night through an intensifier.

RCA

Pilkington P.E. Ltd

Far left: A litter of young pigs and their mother being kept warm by an infra-red heater. Infra-red radiation raises the temperature of any solid object on which it falls, but passes through air without heating it. Infra-red heaters such as this one provide ample warmth for the objects they are intended to heat, but do not waste energy by heating up the air around them.

Left: Banknotes can be 'marked' with Anthracene, which does not show up under ordinary light, but when lit with ultraviolet light it absorbs it and re-emits it as visible light. This effect is called *fluorescence.*

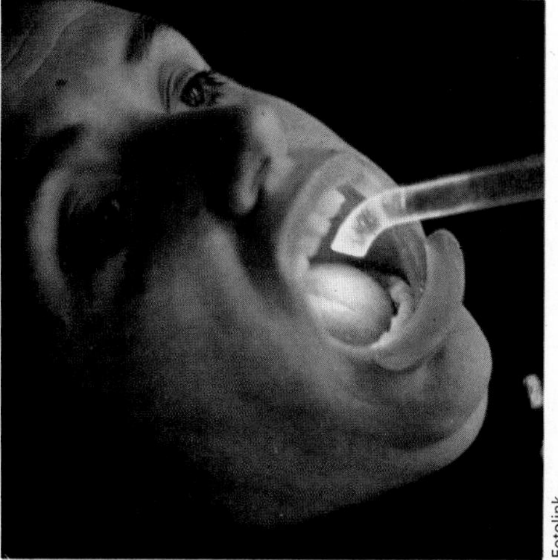

Fotolink

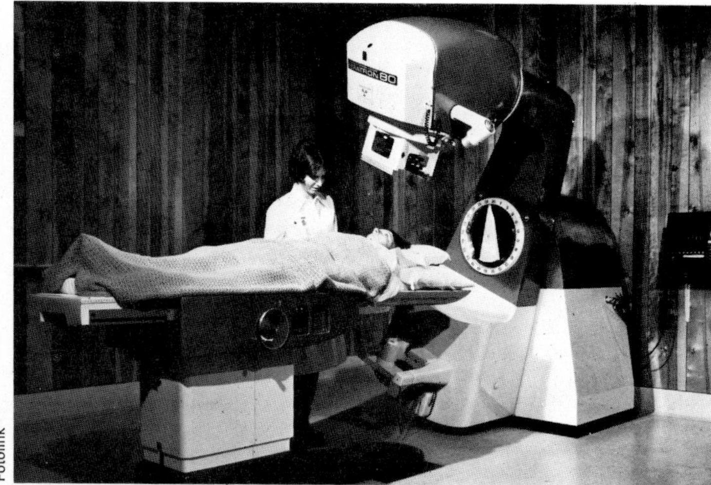

UKAEA

Hanovia Lamps Ltd.

Rolls Royce

Above left: Ultraviolet light is the component of sunlight which causes sunburn. Its effects on skin tissue can be used medically: this picture shows a powerful ultraviolet lamp being used to seal a patient's gum tissue after a tooth has been extracted. The light also kills any germs present.

Above: Gamma rays can be used to destroy the cells of tumor tissue. This machine uses radioactive cobalt as a gamma ray source.

Left: Gamma ray and X-ray photography are used to study the internal structure of machinery. Here, a jet engine is being studied with X-rays.

THE DOPPLER EFFECT

wave front

direction of plane

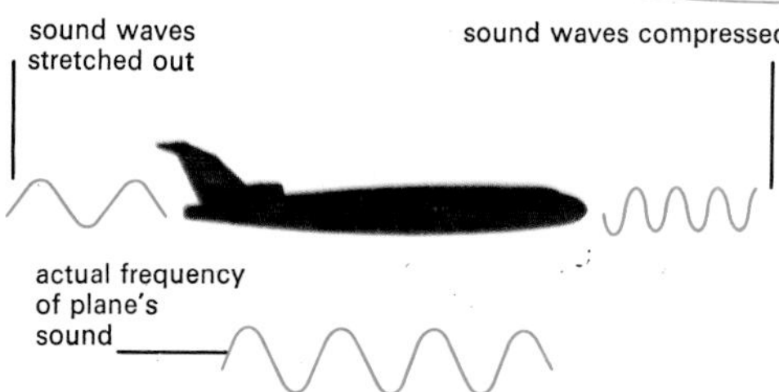

Left: The pitch of the sound of an object travelling towards an observer sounds higher than it really is because it 'compresses' the sound waves in front of it. The sound appears lower when the object is travelling away, because the sound waves are 'stretched out'. This is called the *Doppler effect*, and at extremely high speeds it has a similar effect on the frequency of light coming from an object. The light from an approaching object appears bluer than it is, as its frequency is higher, and conversely that from a receding object appears redder. The effect was discovered by C. Doppler in 1842.

form and emit high frequencies was greater than that needed for the formation of low frequencies. In the case of a heated object, the higher its temperature the more energy was available for the emission of radiation. Thus a relatively moderate amount of heat was required to make the object give off low frequencies (in other words to make it red hot), but a great deal more heat was needed to make it give off higher frequencies (to make it white hot). This is why a piece of metal can be made to glow red at about 530°C, but must be heated to around 1,200°C or more to make it glow white.

The energy levels at different frequencies, radiated by an object heated to a given temperature, can be predicted by using data based on the behaviour of the theoretical 'black body'. This theoretical body, being perfectly black, absorbs all the energy from all frequencies of radiation falling on it, but it radiates this energy at different frequencies. The amount of energy it emits at a given frequency depends on its temperature.

X-rays and gamma rays

X-rays have extremely short wavelengths, from 10 nm down to 0.001 nm. The longer X-rays are called 'soft' and the shorter 'hard'. Some soft X-rays are produced by electron energy changes in atoms, but they are usually generated by firing high speed electrons at a metal target. The sudden deceleration of a charged electron when it hits the target causes a very rapid change in the electric field surrounding it, which leads to the emission of radiation in the form of an X-ray photon.

Gamma rays, shortest of all electromagnetic radiation, are emitted as a result of energy changes in the elementary particles which comprise an atomic nucleus. They can be generated, somewhat haphazardly, in the core of a nuclear reactor, but are produced naturally in any radioactive process such as the disintegration of radium. Some gamma rays have wavelengths in the hard X-ray range—others are as short as 0.0001 nm (one billion billionth of a metre).

The Foundations of Chemistry

We take the world around us very much for granted. But do we know what the wallpaper, the paint, the furniture, the transistor radio and the man-made fibres in our clothes are made of? Even if we were given the basic ingredients we would still need to know how to change them into the final product.

Chemistry is largely concerned with finding out more about substances, including their components and structure, their properties and how they can be made. The chemist's job is to analyse and synthesize things. In the past 30 years this has led to a vast range of new products: plastics, man-made fibres, dye-stuffs, fertilizers, medicines, synthetic rubbers, refrigerants, detergents, fire-fighting chemicals and rocket fuels, the list is endless. Chemistry has also gone hand in hand with physics; for example, in the development of the semiconductors used in transistors and integrated circuits.

The building blocks

All these achievements depended on a knowledge of the basic chemical *elements* or building blocks of matter. For about 1,600 years it had been left to the alchemists to try to untangle these secrets. Misguided by Aristotle's philosophic theory that all matter was composed of 'four elements'—earth, air, fire and water—and dedicated to the pursuit of turning base metals into gold and finding the 'elixir of life', they actually halted the progress of science.

However, in 1661 Robert Boyle correctly defined an element as 'a substance which cannot be split into anything simpler by a chemical change'. The search for elements began and within 100 years Antoine Lavoisier, the brilliant French chemist, had listed 27 of them. Today all 92

Derby Museum

Above: White phosphorus was unwittingly discovered by a German alchemist, Hennig Brand, in 1669, while looking for the elixir of life. He filled a retort with urine and heated it. The glowing residue was the element phosphorus. It was not until 100 years later that the search for elements began seriously.

ELEMENTS SHOWN IN THE PERIODIC TABLE

Ar Argon
Ac Actinium
Ag Silver
Al Aluminium
Am Americium
As Arsenic
At Astatine
Au Gold
B Boron
Ba Barium
Be Beryllium
Bi Bismuth
Bk Berkelium
Br Bromine
C Carbon
Ca Calcium
Cd Cadmium
Ce Cerium
Cf Californium
Cl Chlorine
Cm Curium
Co Cobalt
Cr Chromium
Cs Caesium
Cu Copper
Dy Dysprosium
Er Erbium
Es Einsteinium
Eu Europium
F Fluorine
Fe Iron
Fm Fermium
Fr Francium
Ga Gallium
Gd Gadolinium
Ge Germanium
H Hydrogen
He Helium
Hf Hafnium
Hg Mercury
Ho Holmium
I Iodine
In Indium
Ir Iridium
K Potassium
Kr Krypton
La Lanthanum
Li Lithium
Lu Lutetium
Lr Lawrencium
Md Mendelevium
Mg Magnesium
Mn Manganese
Mo Molybdenum
N Nitrogen
Na Sodium
Nb Niobium
Nd Neodymium
Ne Neon
Ni Nickel
No Nobelium
Np Neptunium
O Oxygen
Os Osmium
P Phosphorus
Pa Protactinium
Pb Lead
Pd Palladium
Pm Promethium
Po Polonium
Pr Praseodymium
Pt Platinum
Pu Plutonium
Ra Radium
Rb Rubidium
Re Rhenium
Rh Rhodium
Rn Radon
Ru Ruthenium
S Sulphur
Sb Antimony
Sc Scandium
Se Selenium
Si Silicon
Sm Samarium
Sn Tin
Sr Strontium
Ta Tantalum
Tb Terbium
Tc Technetium
Te Tellurium
Th Thorium
Ti Titanium
Tl Thallium
Tm Thulium
U Uranium
V Vanadium
W Tungsten
Xe Xenon
Y Yttrium
Yb Ytterbium
Zn Zinc
Zr Zirconium

1st period
2nd period
3 Li 4 Be 5 B
3rd period
11 Na 12 Mg 13 Al
4th period
19 K 20 Ca 21 Sc 22 Ti 23 V 24 Cr 25 Mn 26 Fe
5th period
37 Rb 38 Sr 39 Y 40 Zr 41 Cb 42 Mo 43 Tc 44 Ru
6th period
55 Cs 56 Ba 57 La 58 Ce 59 Pr 60 Nd 61 Pm 62 Sm 63 Eu 64 Gd 65 Tb 66 Dy 67 Ho 68 Er 69 Tm
7th period
87 Fr 88 Ra 89 Ac 90 Th 91 Pa 92 U 93 Np 94 Pu 95 Am 96 Cm 97 Bk 98 Ct 99 Es 100 Fm 101 Md

Left: In 1940 scientists found they could make synthetic elements by bombarding uranium with atomic nuclei. Shown here is plutonium, atomic number 94. It is being handled by remotely-controlled tongs. A radioactive metal of the actinide group, it was used in some of the first atomic bombs instead of uranium.

UKAEA

Below: Many compounds in our world occur as mixtures which can be separated in various ways; by filtering, by gravity differences and by distillation. Air can be separated into its gases by liquefying and distilling it. Here salt is being extracted from sea water simply by letting the water evaporate off in the sun.

naturally-occurring elements, of which about 70 are metals, have been identified. In addition, about 14 artificial ones have been made during nuclear reactions, but being radioactive they are often short-lived.

If a massive chemical analysis of the Earth's crust was possible, the abundance of elements would be approximately 50 per cent oxygen, 26 per cent silicon, 7 per cent aluminium, 4 per cent iron, 3 per cent calcium, 2.5 per cent sodium, 2.5 per cent potassium, 2 per cent magnesium and all the other elements together 3 per cent.

Relatively few elements are found 'free' in nature; most occur chemically combined with one or more other elements, forming *compounds*. There are, however, rules governing which elements combine and the proportions in which they combine. A compound is a pure substance with its own properties, often widely different to its constituent elements. For example, when sodium, a soft, highly reactive metal, is burned in chlorine, a poisonous choking gas, a harmless compound is produced, sodium chloride or household salt.

There is a further complication; in the world around us most compounds and any 'free' elements exist as *mixtures*, which are held together by physical rather than chemical means. The air, sea water, soil, rocks and crude oil are all mixtures of this kind. The separation of mixtures is important to many industries, for example, in oil refining, in the desalination of sea water, in the extraction of metals from mixed ores, and in brewing.

ZEFA

Atoms and the Periodic Table

Each element is, in fact, made up of millions of tiny particles known as *atoms*. The structure of these atoms helps to explain the chemical and physical properties of the various elements and how they form compounds.

At the heart of the atom is a cluster of positively charged protons and uncharged neutrons, which together form the nucleus. Surrounding the nucleus is a cloud of negatively charged electrons. These electrons are so light in comparison to the nucleus that an atom of hydrogen could be compared to a pea orbited by a speck of dust. In reality electrons are very important as they alone are responsible for chemical changes, but only the outermost ones are involved in these changes.

The electrons have to go into particular energy levels or concentric 'shells' around the nucleus and there is a maximum number of electrons which can exist in each shell. There are never more than eight electrons in the outermost shell. Those with the full complement of eight are chemically very stable. They are the rare or 'inert' gases; neon, argon, krypton, xenon and radon.

In all atoms the number of protons in the nucleus equals the number of elec-

rare (inert) gases
electropositive metals
non metals
transition metals
hydrogen
rare earths and actinides
elements with both metallic and non-metallic properties

8 O	9 F	10 Ne												
16 S	17 Cl	18 Ar												
29 Cu	30 Zn	31 Ga	32 Ge	33 As	34 Se	35 Br	36 Kr							
47 Ag	48 Cd	49 In	50 Sn	51 Sb	52 Te	53 I	54 Xe							
72 Hf	73 Ta	74 W	75 Re	76 Os	77 Ir	78 Pt	79 Au	80 Hg	81 Tl	82 Pb	83 Bi	84 Po	85 At	86 Rn

Left: A modern Periodic Table. Above the symbol for each element is its atomic number, equal to protons in the nucleus. In each period all elements have the same number of electron shells. Broad classes exist, but sometimes they include smaller families having the same number of electrons in their outermost shell.

Courtesy, Director of the Institute of Geological Sciences

Above: In a solid the atoms stack in an orderly fashion, giving rise to beautiful crystalline forms. This applies equally to atoms of the same kind (as found in elements like iron, copper, sulphur and iodine), or different kinds, as in this compound, a natural mineral form of calcium carbonate, called calcite.

trons, making them electrically neutral. For example, the second lightest element is the gas helium which has two protons and two neutrons surrounded by two orbital electrons which fill the K shell. This makes helium as stable as the inert gases, which is why it is much safer to use helium in balloons than highly inflammable hydrogen. On the other hand, lithium, the lightest solid element, has three protons, four neutrons (the number of neutrons does not have to equal the number of protons) and three electrons. It is highly reactive because the third electron has to go into the second shell where it is loosely bound and easily lost to another atom.

Each element is assigned an *atomic number* based on the number of protons in the nucleus. It is also given an *atomic weight*, which is equal to the total number of protons and neutrons in the nucleus. (The electrons are so light they can be ignored.) Naturally this does not say how many grammes an atom weighs, but is useful for comparing the relative weights of elements.

Apart from the atomic numbers of elements, some system of classification other than metal or non-metal was sought. The first successful attempt to place the elements in some order was made by a Russian chemist, Dmitri Mendeleyev, in 1868. He noticed that when elements were listed in order of increasing atomic weight there was a definite periodic repetition of those with similar properties. He placed the elements in rows and columns and, as only about 60 elements were then known, left spaces and predicted the properties of the 'missing' elements. Today, this *Periodic Table* is complete and slightly more complex.

Elements may be grouped together on the basis of having the same number of electrons in their outermost shell. For example, all the halogens—fluorine, chlorine, bromine, iodine, and the unstable radioactive member, astatine—have seven electrons in their outermost shell. Elements can also be arranged in horizontal rows or periods. All the elements in a period have the same number of electron-shells, but they themselves may differ widely chemically because they have different numbers of electrons in the outermost shell. For example, in the third period we find the highly reactive soft alkali metal sodium, plus aluminium, sulphur, the reactive gas chlorine and the inert gas argon.

In broader terms elements may be classified as being rare gases, electropositive metals, non-metals, transition metals, the rare earth elements and the actinides or radioactive elements—uranium, thorium, plutonium and so on. The transition metals are interesting as they have two unfilled electron shells—normally elements only have the outermost shell unfilled—and this gives them the ability to form a wider range of compounds. Iron, chromium, and copper are transition metals.

Symbols are widely used in chemistry. The Swedish chemist Berzelius first suggested our short-hand way of writing down elements and their compounds. The symbol for an element is usually an abbreviation of its present or original name: P for phosphorus, Zn for zinc, but Fe for iron from the Latin *ferrum*, and Na for sodium from the Latin *natrium*. The subscript numbers in a molecule or compound represent the numbers of atoms of each element present.

A molecule of water, whose symbol is H_2O, has two hydrogen atoms and one oxygen atom. Sulphuric acid, H_2SO_4, has two hydrogen atoms, one sulphur atom and four oxygen atoms. This universal chemical shorthand comes in very useful when describing chemical reactions. For example, when dilute sulphuric acid is poured on to a small piece of zinc, hydrogen gas bubbles off and the zinc dissolves, forming zinc sulphate, or, as in this equation:

$Zn + H_2SO_4 = ZnSO_4 + H_2 \uparrow$

The arrow pointing up indicates a gas, while one pointing down would indicate a precipitate (or insoluble solid) forming in a solution, rather than the new compound remaining in solution.

Right: Chemical analysis is an important part of routine quality control testing of many products. Here a 'wax appearance test' is carried out on a fuel oil. This is necessary because, although a lot of wax is removed from the oil in refining, small amounts remain and may block filters by precipitating out when it gets cold.

Far right: A simple chemical reaction is used to reduce the carbon content of iron to make steel. When oxygen is blown on to molten iron, the carbon and oxygen unite as carbon monoxide gas which then passes out of the metal. This reaction is *exothermic*; no extra heat is needed as the reaction creates heat during bond formation between the atoms.

Below: This apparatus measures the absorption of light at a particular wavelength, which is unique for each element. The sample is injected into the flame and burned, which causes it to give off light. Here motor oils are tested to ensure the correct amount of additives is present in the oil blend.

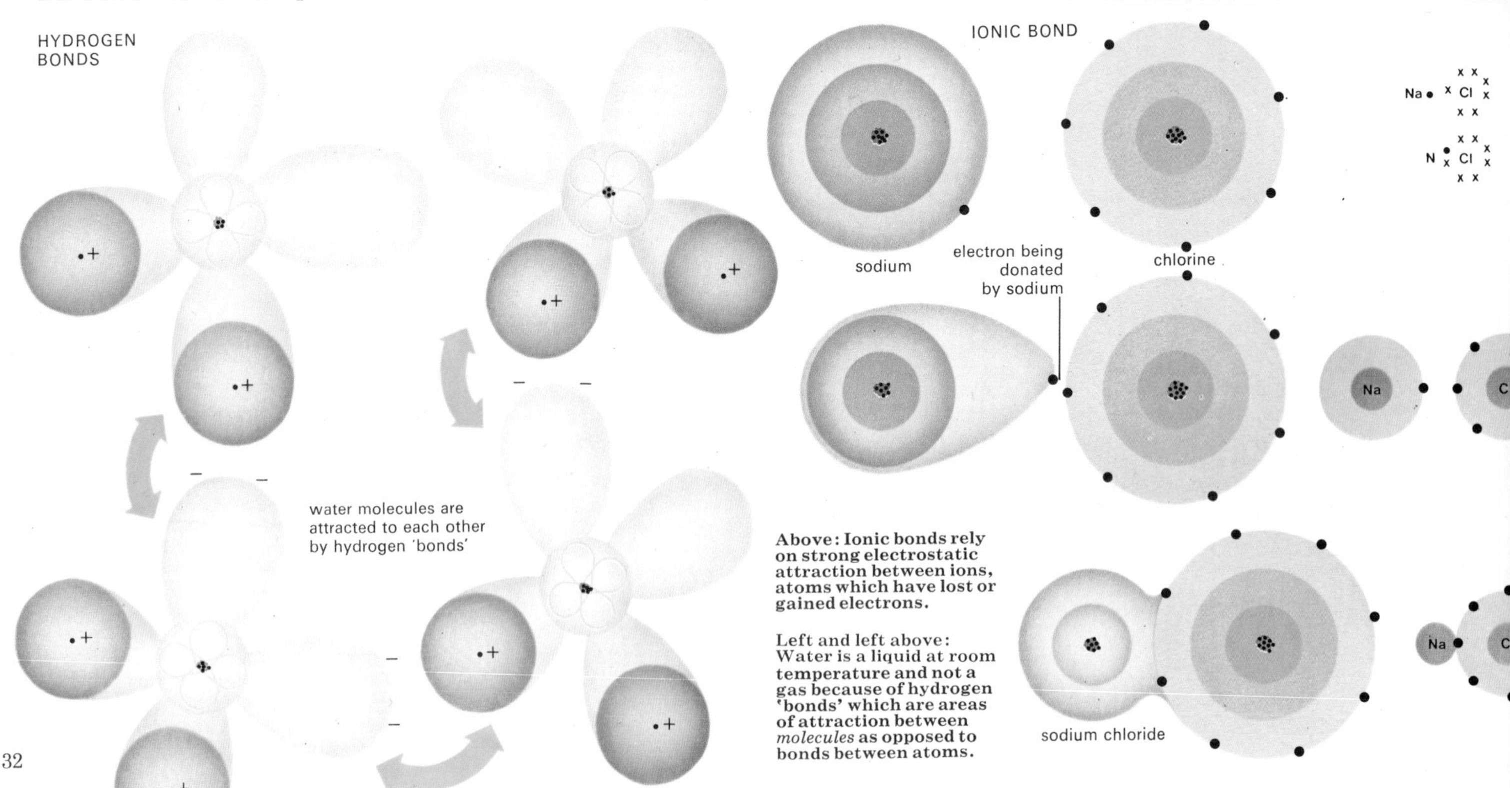

Above: Ionic bonds rely on strong electrostatic attraction between ions, atoms which have lost or gained electrons.

Left and left above: Water is a liquid at room temperature and not a gas because of hydrogen 'bonds' which are areas of attraction between *molecules* as opposed to bonds between atoms.

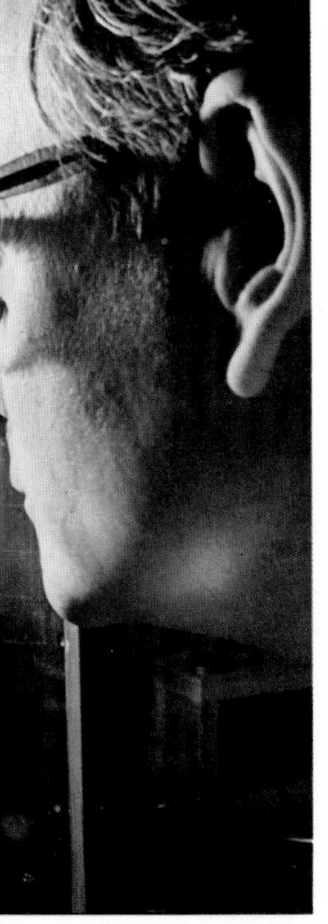

BSC

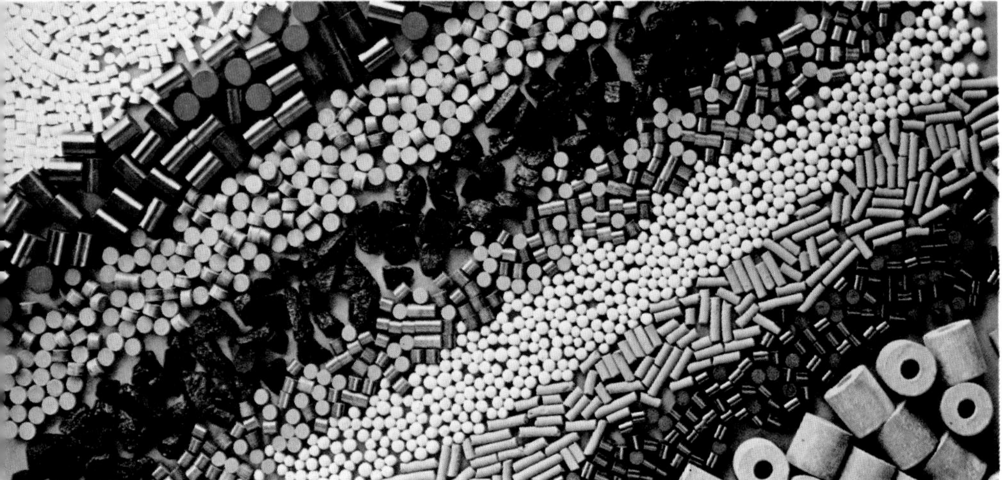

Left and below: Covalent bonds link atoms in molecules by sharing electrons, to give strange shapes where orbitals overlap. In water the two hydrogen nuclei are held at a 105° angle, keeping one side of the molecule positive and the other negative, which is useful for hydrogen bonding. Below, the gas methane.

Above: A selection of catalysts used in the oil and chemical industries. Chemical reactions are often difficult to get started or very slow, so to speed things up catalysts are used. They do not chemically change themselves. The black coal-like lumps are iron oxide, used for making ammonia from hydrogen and nitrogen.

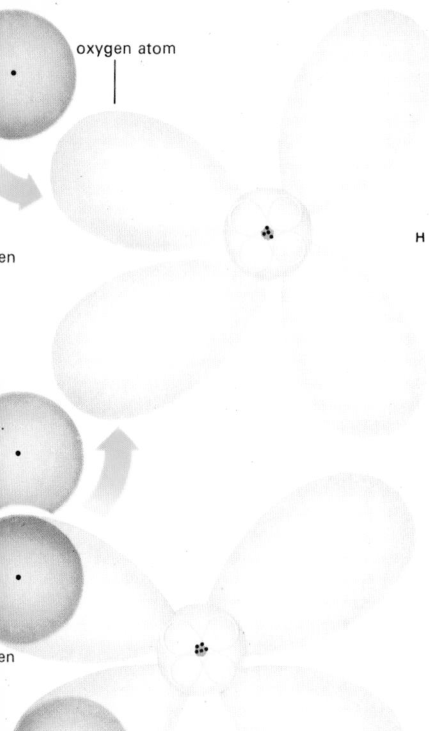

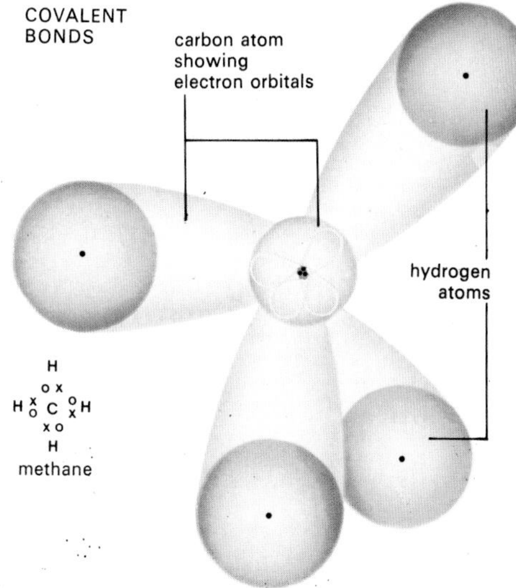

Valency and bonds

When elements form compounds the *valency* or combining power of one element with another is determined by the number of atoms of hydrogen that will combine with one atom of the element. For example, oxygen has a valency of two because two atoms of hydrogen combine with it to form water. But the full story of combining or bonding is more complex than this. Atoms tend to be able to combine by forming the stable inert gas configuration of eight electrons, and there are two ways of doing this.

In an *ionic* or electrovalent bond, such as that formed by sodium chloride, the sodium atom readily loses its single outer electron. This leaves it with a proton in the nucleus which is now unneutralized as it no longer has a negatively charged electron to balance its own positive charge, and the sodium atom then becomes a special type of atom—a positive *ion*, or *cation*. Chlorine, however, has seven outermost electrons and willingly accepts another to achieve the stable eight electron state, becoming a negative ion, or *anion*. The sodium ion, Na^+, and the chloride ion, Cl^-, are held together by a strong electrostatic attraction. Ionic compounds are usually solids, the ions being packed together in a stable pattern called a crystal lattice.

Apart from losing and gaining electrons, bonds may be formed by sharing electrons between atoms. These are known as *covalent* bonds. For example, in the gas methane, CH_4, the carbon atom has four electrons in its outermost shell and each hydrogen atom has one electron. By mutual sharing of electrons each hydrogen atom can have the stable two electron state, while the carbon ends up with a stable eight electron state. Sometimes more than one electron pair is shared between atoms, forming a 'double' bond or sometimes a 'triple' bond, as in acetylene. Both these bonds are less stable than a single bond. Covalent bonding is widespread in carbon compounds found in plants and animals. Some elements are also covalent bonded: oxygen, O_2; nitrogen, N_2; and chlorine, Cl_2. Only covalent compounds or elements form these discrete particles of two or more atoms known as *molecules*.

All chemical bonds have two things in common; they arise from a stable arrangement of electrons around the atoms involved, and they result in more stable 'low energy' compounds being formed. This means that energy is required to break the bonds, but when they are being formed it is released, often as heat. For example, a tiny piece of sodium dropped on to water vigorously reacts with it to give the compound sodium hydroxide, and much heat is produced in the process of forming bonds.

Chemical reactions often only occur at high temperatures; copper reacts with oxygen to give black copper oxide only if they are heated together. However, extra heat is produced as the result of bond formation between the copper and the oxygen. Thus, to recover pure copper from its oxide, that much energy would need to be absorbed before the bonds could be broken. It is this release of energy during chemical bonding that provides the heat when fossil fuels are burned. Indeed, knowledge of such chemical changes can provide chemists with the key to the search for new materials.

Elements of Nature

The usefulness of the various naturally-occurring chemical elements varies almost as much as their chemical and physical properties. Some, such as the gases oxygen and nitrogen, are essential to living creatures, while others, such as astatine, have little or no practical importance. This article deals with the nature and properties of some of the most important elements and the ways in which they are used.

Oxygen and nitrogen

Oxygen (O) and nitrogen (N) are the two main constituents of the earth's atmosphere. Pure dry air contains, by volume, approximately 21 per cent oxygen and 78 per cent nitrogen, the remainder being a mixture of other gases, including hydrogen and inert gases such as argon and helium.

In addition to the vast amount of oxygen within the atmosphere, it is also the most abundant element within the crust of the earth, where it occurs in combination with other elements such as iron, silicon and aluminium. Water, which covers over 70 per cent of the earth's surface, is made up of oxygen in combination with hydrogen.

Oxygen is an *electronegative* element, accepting electrons from other elements (which, in giving electrons away, are thus *electropositive*) when it combines with them to form compounds. Pure oxygen can be obtained in small amounts by heating certain of these compounds, such as potassium chlorate and manganese dioxide, but on a commercial scale it is extracted from air.

Oxygen and water are both essential to living creatures, but oxygen also has many industrial uses. One of the most important is in cutting and welding metals, where it is burned together with acetylene gas to produce a very hot flame which melts the metals. It is also used in making iron and steel, where it is used to help burn away impurities in the molten metal. Liquid oxygen is used in rocket engines, where it is burned with a second fuel, such as kerosene, to produce the powerful stream of exhaust gases which drive the rocket.

Nitrogen, the principal constituent of air, occurs in combined form as Chile saltpetre (sodium nitrate, $NaNO_3$) and, in addition, it is a constituent element of proteins and so is a part of all living organisms.

Nitrogen is a very stable, non-reactive gas at normal temperatures, but at high temperatures the bonds holding the atoms within the nitrogen molecules break up, and the freed nitrogen atoms become very reactive. In a pure form it can be obtained either by heating suitable nitrogen-containing compounds or by extracting it from air.

Nitrogen is prepared industrially by the fractional distillation of liquefied air. The boiling point of liquid oxygen is 90°K (—183°C) and that of liquid nitrogen is 78°K (—195°C), so the two gases can easily be separated by controlling the temperature of the liquid air so that the nitrogen 'boils off' leaving the oxygen behind. One of the most important uses of nitrogen compounds is in the manufacture of fertilizers, while others are used in making explosives. Liquid nitrogen is widely used as a coolant.

Silicon

After oxygen, silicon (Si) is the next most abundant element in the earth's crust. It occurs mainly as *silica* (SiO_2), which is the main constituent of sand, and as metallic silicates such as $K_2Al_2Si_6O_{16}$, a compound of potassium, aluminium, silicon and oxygen which is one of the group of rocks known as *feldspars*. Silicon is also found in *kaolinite* ($Al_2O_3.2SiO_2.2H_2O$), which is one of the main ingredients of china clay.

Silica occurs in either crystalline or *amorphous* (noncrystalline) forms. A good example of crystalline silica is quartz, while the precious stone opal is composed of amorphous silica.

Silica is the main ingredient of glass and silicon itself is used in many important synthetic materials such as synthetic rubbers. These *silicone rubbers* are more resistant to chemical attack than other rubbers. The enormous range of silicon-based products includes oils, greases, waxes and polishes, and solid resins such as those used for electrical insulating materials.

Sand, which is mostly silica, is used in large quantities for making concrete and mortar. *Kieselguhr* or *diatomaceous earth* is a type of silica formed in the earth from the skeletons of tiny organisms called diatoms. It is used in making fireproof cements and clays, as a filtering medium,

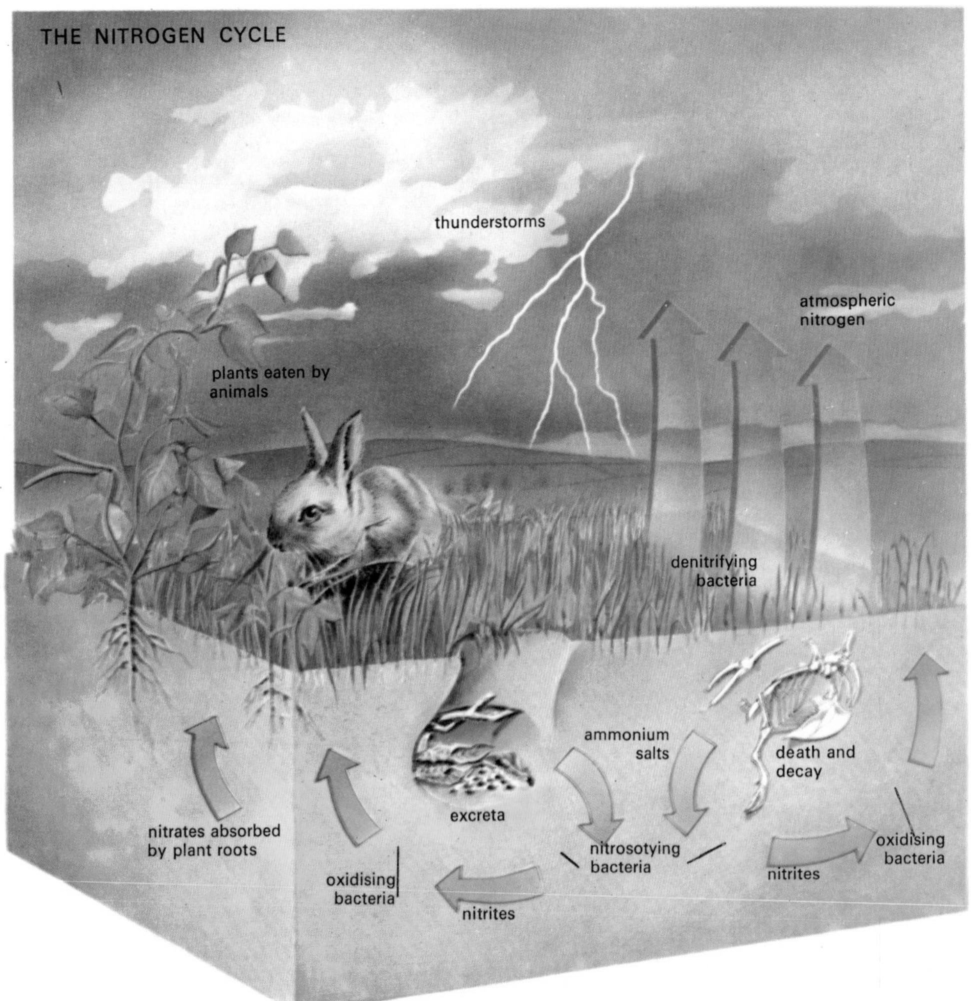

Left: The *nitrogen cycle*, the natural circulation of nitrogen compounds between plants, animals, the soil and the air. Nitrogen from the atmosphere is converted into various nitrogen compounds within the soil by the action of bacteria living in the roots of plants such as peas and beans. In addition, some nitrogen compounds are formed during thunderstorms. Nitrogen compounds in the soil are absorbed by plants, and then by animals which eat the plants, being returned to the soil in excreta or by the decay of dead animals and plants within the soil. Some nitrogen is returned to the atmosphere by the action of denitrifying bacteria.

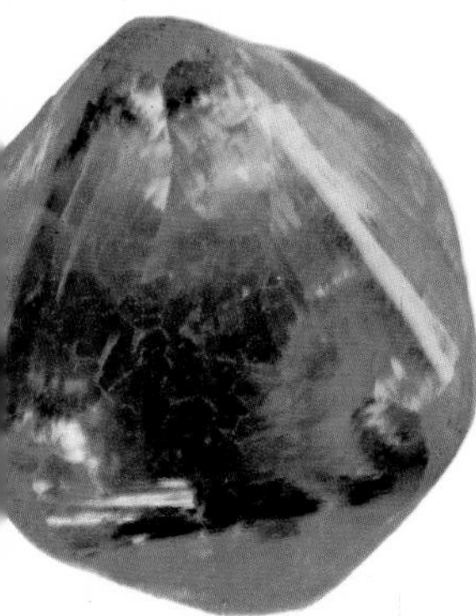

Left: Diamond, one of the allotropes of carbon, is the hardest substance found in nature. Carbon will only crystallize into diamond at very high temperatures and pressures. Synthetic diamonds are now produced in large numbers, using apparatus capable of producing over 90,000 times atmospheric pressure at over 2,000°C (3,630°F), developed in 1953.

Below: The hardness of a diamond is due to the way in which the atoms are arranged within the crystal structure.

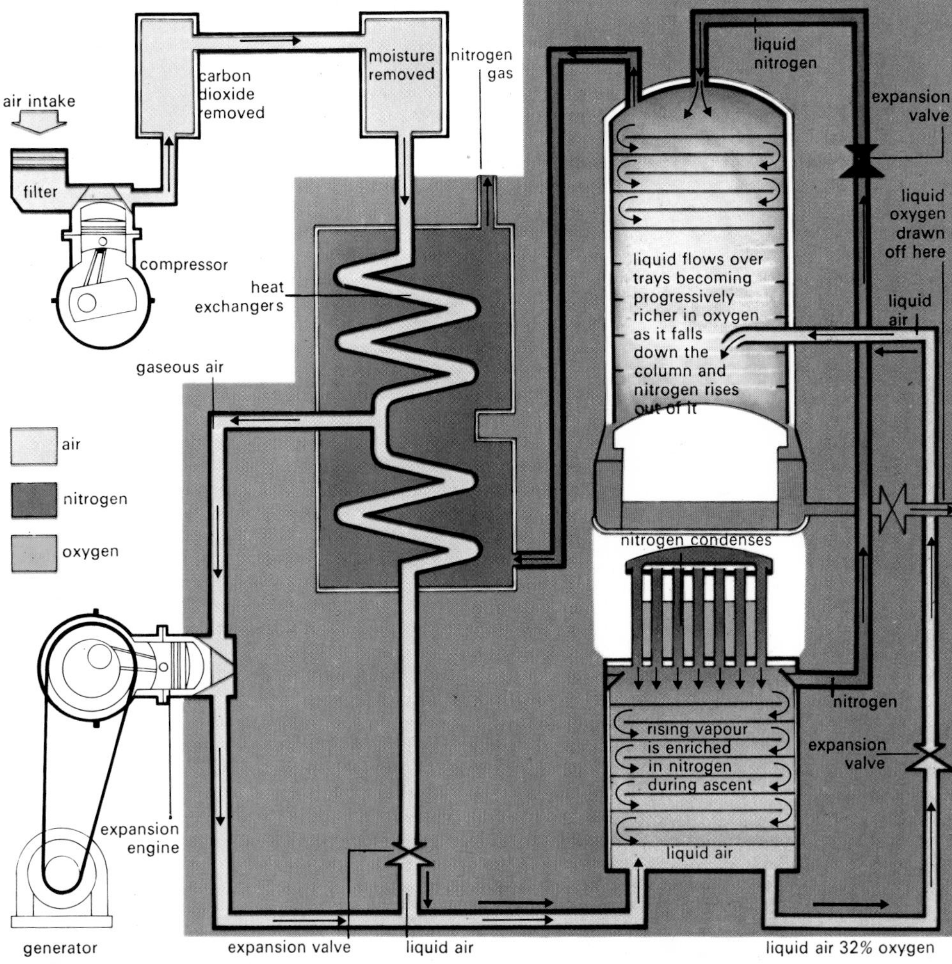

Right: Graphite, the second main form of carbon, has its atoms bonded together in layers. These layers can slide easily over each other, and this gives graphite its soft, slippery nature.

Left: A synthetic crystal of quartz, a form of silica (silicon dioxide, SiO_2). Silica occurs widely in nature, one of the commonest forms being sand.

Below: The rate of chemical decomposition of radio active compounds is reduced at low temperatures, and so they are stored in liquid nitrogen. This keeps them at below 78°K (—195°C), which is the boiling point of liquid nitrogen.

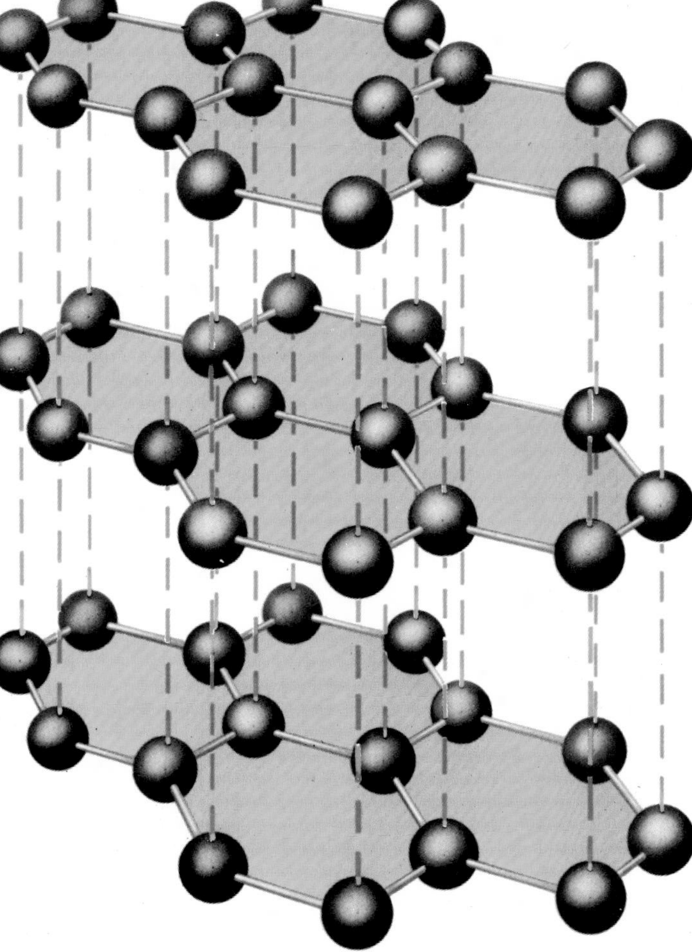

Above: Oxygen and nitrogen are obtained by the distillation of liquid air. Air is compressed and passed through absorbent materials which take away the carbon dioxide and moisture, then it is cooled in the heat exchangers. Next it is expanded so that its temperature drops further and it liquefies. Some of this expansion takes place in an expansion engine, which drives a generator to provide some electricity for the plant. In the distillation column the nitrogen boils out of the liquid first, as it has a lower boiling point than oxygen. The remaining liquid is almost pure oxygen.

and in the manufacture of explosives. Dynamite, for example, is made by absorbing nitroglycerine into a keiselguhr base.

Carbon

Compared with the great amounts of oxygen and silicon within the earth's crust, the amount of carbon (C) within it is very small—it comprises only about 0.3 per cent of the crust. This relatively small quantity, however, belies its extreme importance to living creatures. The molecules that form the basis of life, such as RNA and DNA, are based on carbon, and animals obtain their energy by the oxidation of the *carbohydrates* (compounds of carbon, hydrogen and oxygen) contained in the food they eat.

Carbon is also important to industry, being the basis of fossil fuels such as coal, and occurring in combination with hydrogen to form the *hydrocarbon* fuels such as oil and natural gas.

There are two naturally-occurring forms of crystalline carbon, both of which are pure carbon despite the great differences between them. These two forms or *allotropes* of carbon are diamond, a clear, very hard crystal, and graphite, a soft, smooth, black substance.

James Blake

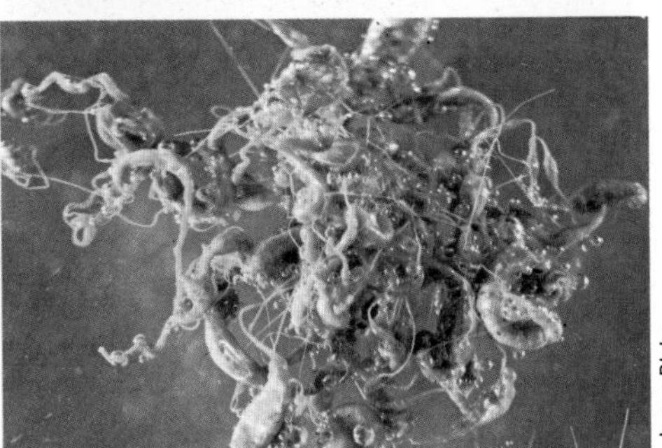

James Blake

James Blake

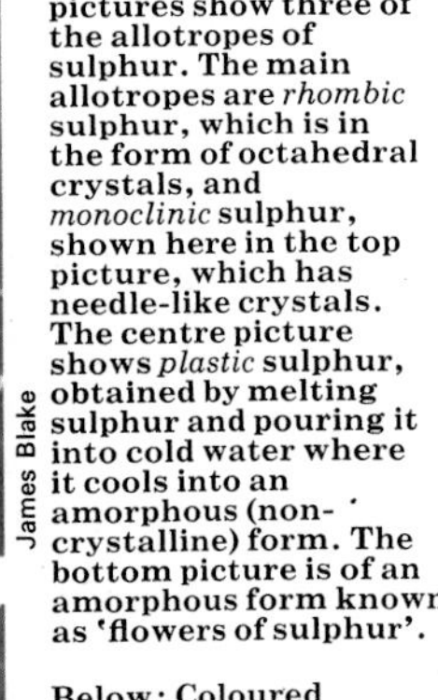

Left: These three pictures show three of the allotropes of sulphur. The main allotropes are *rhombic* sulphur, which is in the form of octahedral crystals, and *monoclinic* sulphur, shown here in the top picture, which has needle-like crystals. The centre picture shows *plastic* sulphur, obtained by melting sulphur and pouring it into cold water where it cools into an amorphous (non-crystalline) form. The bottom picture is of an amorphous form known as 'flowers of sulphur'.

Below: Coloured firework flames are produced by the addition of various compounds to the basic gunpowder mixture. Brilliant white flame is produced by potassium, sulphur, arsenic or antimony compounds or by magnesium powder. Red flames are produced by strontium and lithium salts, green by barium salts, yellow by sodium salts, and blue by copper salts. Lithium, sodium and potassium belong to a group of elements called the *alkali metals*.

J. F. Millies/ZEFA

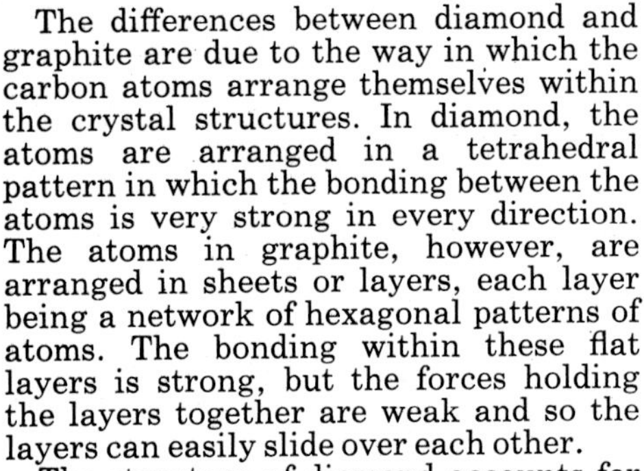

The differences between diamond and graphite are due to the way in which the carbon atoms arrange themselves within the crystal structures. In diamond, the atoms are arranged in a tetrahedral pattern in which the bonding between the atoms is very strong in every direction. The atoms in graphite, however, are arranged in sheets or layers, each layer being a network of hexagonal patterns of atoms. The bonding within these flat layers is strong, but the forces holding the layers together are weak and so the layers can easily slide over each other.

The structure of diamond accounts for its hardness and transparency, and also for the fact that it will not conduct electricity—its electrons are held tightly within it. On the other hand the ability of graphite layers to slide over each other gives this form of carbon its characteristic softness and also makes it a good lubricant. It is a good conductor of electricity and has many applications in the electrical industry. Another very common use of graphite is for the 'lead' of pencils.

Carbon and its compounds are so important that a whole branch of chemistry is devoted to the study and uses of these substances. This is known as *organic chemistry*, its name deriving from the role that carbon plays in the structure and life of plants and animals.

Sulphur

Sulphur (S), a hard, yellow substance, has been known for over 3,000 years. It was widely used by the Mediterranean civilizations in various medicines and the sulphur dioxide (SO_2) fumes given off by burning sulphur have been used for

Left: Incendiary bombs often use a material called *thermite*, which is a mixture of magnesium, iron oxide and aluminium powders that reaches a temperature of 2,500°C (4,500°F) when it ignites. Napalm, an incendiary oil, contains petrol, polystyrene and white phosphorus.

Imperial War Museum

Below: Sodium, one of the alkali metals, is so intensely reactive with air or water that it must be stored under paraffin oil. If it is exposed to air it rapidly oxidizes to sodium oxide, and if it comes into contact with water it reacts violently to produce sodium hydroxide and hydrogen gas.

James Blake

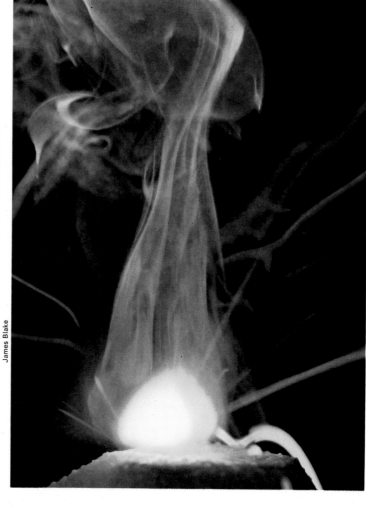

Right: The violent reaction created when a piece of sodium metal is placed on a wet surface. The hydrogen gas given off is ignited by the heat produced during the reaction. When this reactive metal is combined with the poisonous gas chlorine, the result is harmless common salt.

Dave Kelly

centuries for bleaching cloth.

Deposits of pure sulphur occur in many areas, including the southern USA and Sicily. It also occurs in combined states such as the sulphides of zinc (ZnS), lead (PbS) and iron (FeS_2), and sulphates such as *gypsum* ($CaSO_4.2H_2O$, hydrated calcium sulphate). Sulphur may also be present in crude oil.

The principal industrial use of sulphur is for making sulphuric acid (H_2SO_4), which is used in the manufacture of fertilizers, paints, detergents, plastics, synthetic fibres and dyes. Sulphur is also used in making rubber during the *vulcanization* process which makes the rubber stronger and more durable, and many drugs, such as the antibiotics penicillin and sulphonamides, contain sulphur compounds.

The halogens

The name 'halogen' comes from the Greek words meaning 'salt producer', as these elements will readily combine with other elements to form salts. The original members of this group were chlorine (Cl), bromine (Br) and iodine (I), which occur as salts in sea water, and later on the elements fluorine (F) and astatine (At) were added to the list. Fluorine and chlorine are gases at room temperature, bromine is a liquid and iodine and astatine are solids.

The chief characteristic of the halogens is the fact that they each have a valency of 1, their outer electron shells being one electron short of the number needed to give them the stable eight electron configuration.

Their compounds are known as the halides, and those formed with the more electropositive metals are held together by ionic bonding. Halides formed with non-metallic elements and the less electropositive metals have covalent bonding.

The halogens are highly electronegative, having a great affinity for electrons and readily forming negative ions. This is what makes the halogens so reactive. Their high electronegativity also makes them powerful oxidizing agents; it is this property which makes chlorine, for example, effective as a bleach and as a disinfectant.

The most common chlorine compound is ordinary salt, sodium chloride (NaCl), and other chlorine compounds are used in plastics (polyvinyl chloride, pvc), weedkillers, insecticides and drycleaning fluids. The bromine compound silver bromide is one of the light-sensitive compounds used in photographic film, and ethylene bromide is added to petrol to prevent lead (from the anti-knocking additive tetraethyl lead) from building up within the engine.

Iodine is widely used as an antiseptic and within the human body small quantities of iodine are essential for the proper functioning of the thyroid gland. Fluorine is the most active chemical element and one of its best-known uses is in the production of compounds used to make teeth more resistant to decay. Other fluorine compounds are used as refrigerants, aerosol propellants, firefighting chemicals and anaesthetics. Non-stick pan coatings are made of the fluorine-based plastic called *polytetrafluoroethylene* (PTFE). Astatine is the least important of the halogens and also in fact one of the least important of all elements, as its most stable isotope is very short-lived, having a half-life of only 8.3 hours.

Alkaline earth metals

The alkaline earth metals are a group of very reactive metals, namely beryllium (Be), magnesium (Mg), calcium (Ca), strontium (Sr), barium (Ba) and radium (Ra). The most important are calcium, which makes up about 4 per cent of the earth's crust, and magnesium, which accounts for about 2 per cent of the crust. Being so reactive, none of the alkaline metals occurs in an uncombined state.

The chief sources of calcium are calcium carbonate ($CaCO_3$), which occurs in many forms such as limestone, marble and calcite; gypsum and fluorspar (CaF_2). Natural chalk is a form of calcium carbonate, but the manufactured chalk used for writing on blackboards is calcium sulphate ($CaSO_4$). Calcium is an important constituent of bones and teeth, but the metal itself is not widely used in industry in its uncombined form. Calcium compounds, however, have many applications, a good example being limestone, which is used in cement making. Limestone is also used in steelmaking, where it acts as a flux which absorbs impurities from the molten metal.

Two important ores of magnesium are *dolomite* ($MgCO_3.CaCO_3$), a combination of magnesium and calcium carbonates, and *carnallite* ($KCl.MgCl_2.6H_2O$), potassium magnesium chloride, which is also an important source of potassium salts. *Chlorophyll*, the green colouring material in leaves, is a mixture of two substances known as chlorophyll-a and chlorophyll-b. These are complex compounds of carbon, hydrogen, oxygen, nitrogen and magnesium, their respective chemical formulae being $C_{55}H_{72}O_5N_4Mg$ and $C_{55}H_{70}O_6N_4Mg$. Magnesium also occurs in sea water, constituting about 0.5 per cent of it by weight.

Magnesium compounds are used in medicines, and the very light but strong magnesium alloys have many applications in the engineering industries.

Organic Chemistry

Organic chemistry is the branch of chemistry that deals with almost all the compounds that contain carbon. The exceptions, such as the carbon oxides and sulphides and the carbonates of metals, are considered to be chemically more similar to *inorganic* (non-carbon) compounds.

Organic chemicals are so named because those discovered first occurred in living organisms, and it was thought that they were the result of the action of some mysterious 'vital force' produced within living cells. This assumption gave rise to the belief that organic compounds could not be produced synthetically, as the necessary vital force would not be present.

The division of chemistry into organic and inorganic branches was the result of the work of the Swedish chemist Jons Jacob Berzelius (1779-1848). He believed in the vital force theory, which persisted throughout the first half of the nineteenth century. The first opposition to this theory had come in 1828 when Friedrich Wöhler (1800-1882) synthesized an organic compound known as urea ($H_2N.CO.NH_2$) from ammonium cyanate ($NH_4.CNO$), but the final blow to the theory did not come until 1860, when Pierre Berthelot (1827-1907) published a detailed treatise on the synthesis of organic compounds.

In the early days of organic chemistry the organic compounds were divided into two main groups, the *aliphatics* (from the Greek word *aleiphar*, meaning 'fat'), which were related to fatty substances, and the *aromatics*, which were related to the aromatic oils and spices (from the Greek word *aroma*, meaning 'spice'). These two main groups are today further divided into several smaller groups.

Aromatic compounds are derived from the benzene ring structure of six carbon atoms, whereas most aliphatics have straight or branched chains. *Alicyclic* compounds are aliphatics which are based on rings instead of chains.

Aliphatic compounds

The aliphatic group includes the aliphatic hydrocarbons called *alkanes*, *alkenes* and *alkynes*, which are made up of carbon and hydrogen, and the compounds of carbon, hydrogen and oxygen known as *alcohols*, *aldehydes*, *ketones*, *carboxylic acids* and *carbohydrates*. It also includes more complex substances containing additional elements such as nitrogen, sulphur and phosphorus, such as the amino acids and proteins which are fundamental constituents of living matter.

The alkanes, also known as the paraffin hydrocarbons, have the general formula C_nH_{2n+2}, where n represents a whole number. Thus the gases methane and ethane have the formulae CH_4 and C_2H_6 respectively. One of the most important sources of paraffin hydrocarbons is crude oil, which is a complex mixture of many different hydrocarbons.

Among the range of hydrocarbons yielded by fractional distillation of oil are the light gaseous ones such as methane and propane (C_3H_8); light liquids such as petrols (with from five to ten carbon

Ronan

Distillers

Above and above right: A fifteenth-century distillery and a modern whisky distillery. The first step in the production of spirits is the fermentation of a fruit or cereal base, during which yeasts convert sugars into alcohol. The weak alcohol solution thus obtained is then heated in a still so that the alcohol boils away, leaving the water behind. The alcohol condenses at the top of the still and runs down the outlet pipe.

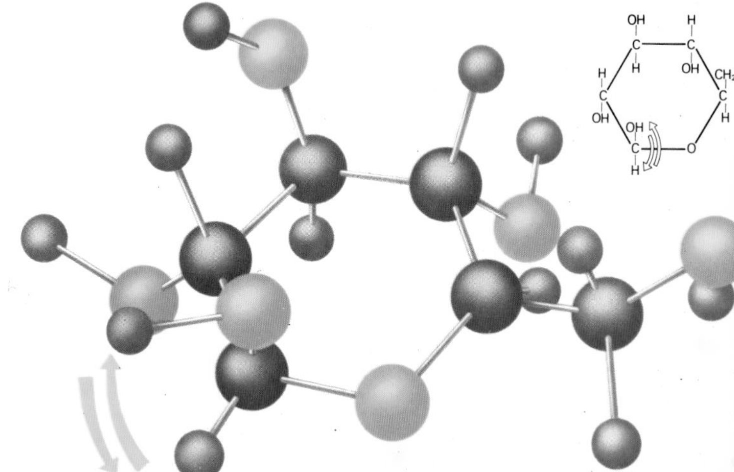

Right: A model of a molecule of the type of glucose called β-D-glucose. The carbon atoms are shown in black, the oxygen in red, and the hydrogen in blue. Glucose is a *monosaccharide*.

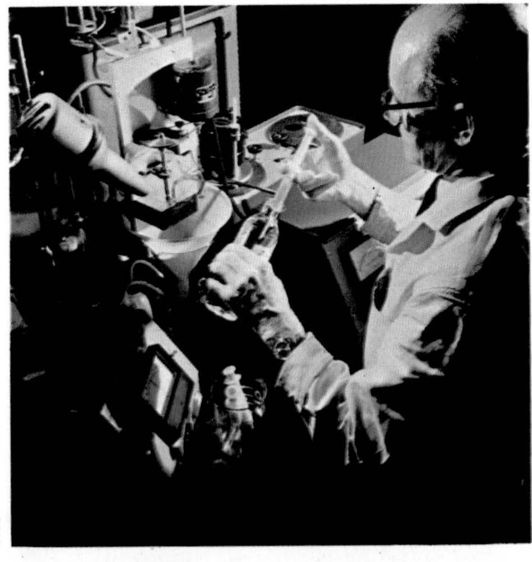

Esso

Above: A laboratory test to determine the viscosity or thickness of a motor oil. The most widely used lubricating oils are mineral oils, derived from crude oil, but in certain applications vegetable oils such as castor and palm oils are often used, either on their own or added to mineral oils.

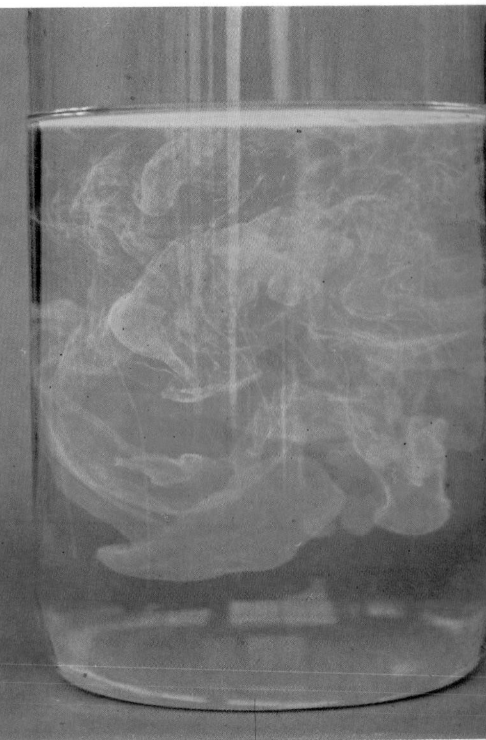

BASF

Right: The bright green dye uranin, first discovered in 1871, is an aromatic compound often used in cosmetics and for colouring bath salt tablets. A closely related dye called Eosin FA is used for making red ink, and it is also used to give a pink tint to the salt used for clearing ice from roads.

Above: The aromatic compound Rhodamine Base B Extra is a colourless powder, but when it comes into contact with the weak hydrochloric acid in perspiration it becomes Rhodamine FB, which is red. It can therefore be used as a thief detector, as it will dye the skin of anyone handling objects coated with it.

Below: Plastics are composed of heavy organic molecules known as *polymers*, networks or long chains of atoms built up by joining together smaller, simpler molecules known as *monomers*. The chemical process of forming a polymer from its component monomers is known as *polymerization*.

atoms per molecule); paraffin oils (kerosenes) with 10 to 16 carbon atoms; gas oils (C_{14} to C_{20}) and lubricating oils (C_{20} to C_{70}).

An important difference between the alkanes, alkenes and alkynes is the number of hydrogen atoms each contains in comparison with the number of carbon atoms in it. The alkanes are *saturated* hydrocarbons, that is, the carbon atoms are combined with the maximum possible numbers of hydrogen atoms (ie 'saturated' with them) and are joined to each other by single bonds. Alkenes, on the other hand, are *unsaturated;* the carbon atoms are not combined with the maximum number of hydrogen atoms and are joined by double bonds. The alkenes have a general formula C_nH_{2n} and include butylene (C_4H_8) ethylene (C_2H_4) and propylene (C_3H_6). The most important alkene is ethylene, which is used in the making of ethylene glycol (antifreeze) and the plastics polystyrene, pvc and polythene.

The alkynes are highly unsaturated, with relatively few hydrogen atoms per carbon atom and triple bonding between the carbon atoms. The alkynes have a general formula C_nH_{2n-2}, the most important alkyne being the gas acetylene (C_2H_2). Acetylene is highly reactive and one of its chief uses is in oxy-acetylene welding and cutting equipment.

Alcohols, another important group of aliphatic compounds, are formed by joining a *hydroxyl group* (consisting of one oxygen atom and one hydrogen atom) to an *alkyl radical*. Alkyl radicals are derived from the alkanes; they are essentially alkanes with one of the hydrogen atoms removed and thus have a general formula C_nH_{2n+1} (the alkanes being C_nH_{2n+2}). The names of the radicals are formed by changing the -ane of the alkane to -yl, for example methane's radical is methyl, and that of ethane is ethyl. The names of the alcohols are obtained by changing the final -e of the alkanes to -ol; thus we have methanol (methyl alcohol, CH_3OH), ethanol (ethyl alcohol, C_2H_5OH) and propanol (propyl alcohol, C_3H_7OH).

Ethanol is the alcohol found in alcoholic drinks and it is mixed with methanol, pryidine (C_5H_5N), petrol and a violet dye to make methylated spirits.

The oxidation of alcohols produces two further groups of compounds, the aldehydes and the ketones, which are both closely related. Further oxidation of aldehydes or ketones produces carboxylic acids. The general formula for aldehydes is $C_nH_{2n}O$, which is the same as for ketones. Despite this, however, the atoms of aldehydes are arranged differently within their respective molecules. Both contain a *carbonyl group*, comprising a carbon atom and an oxygen atom, but in aldehydes the carbonyl group is attached to a hydrogen atom and to an alkyl, while in the ketones it is attached to two similar alkyl groups or to two different alkyls.

The simplest aldehyde, and one of the most useful, is formaldehyde, H.CHO. When dissolved in water it forms formalin, which is used to preserve biological specimens. Formaldehyde is also an important germicide and an ingredient of several types of plastic. Other aldehydes are chloral, CCl_3CHO, used in making DDT, and benzaldehyde, C_6H_5CHO. which is used as a solvent and is the main constituent of oil of bitter almonds.

The best known ketone produced by the oxidation of alcohol is probably the solvent acetone, CH_3COCH_3. Methyl ethyl ketone, $CH_3COC_2H_5$, and methyl isobutyl ketone, $(CH_3)_2CHCH_2COCH_3$, are also used as solvents.

Carbohydrates

One of the most important groups of aliphatic organic compounds is that known as the *carbohydrates*, which includes such substances as sugars, starches and plant fibres. Their name is derived from the original idea that they were simply *hydrates* of carbon, that is, carbon atoms combined with water and having the general formula $C_x(H_2O)_y$. This idea was later found to be an oversimplification, as the molecules consist of chains of carbon atoms with the oxygen and hydrogen atoms arranged around them.

Carbohydrates, in common with most organic compounds, will form *isomers*. When compounds are composed of molecules containing large numbers of atoms, it is possible for these atoms to arrange themselves in many different ways within the molecules. This means that two or more compounds, with different properties, can have the same molecular formula; these compounds are known as isomers.

For example, the carbohydrate glucose, $C_6H_{12}O_6$, is one of 16 possible compounds with that formula, although only three occur naturally. Glucose is a *monosaccharide*, which is the simplest form of carbohydrate. *Disaccharides* are formed when two monosaccharides combine,

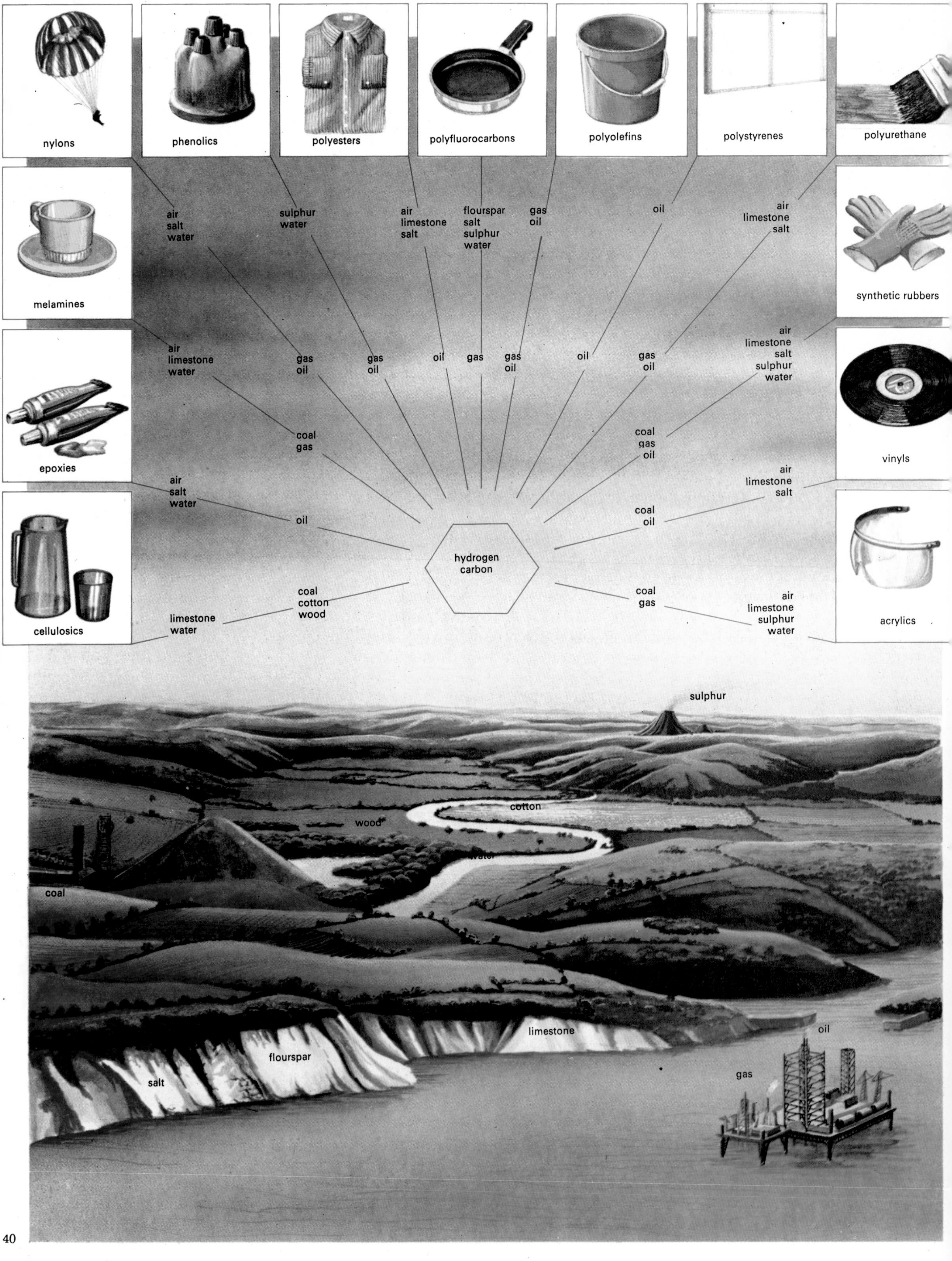

nylons

phenolics

polyesters

polyfluorocarbons

polyolefins

polystyrenes

polyurethane

melamines

synthetic rubbers

epoxies

vinyls

cellulosics

acrylics

air
salt
water

sulphur
water

air
limestone
salt

flourspar
salt
sulphur
water

gas
oil

oil

air
limestone
salt

air
limestone
water

gas
oil

gas
oil

oil

gas

gas
oil

oil

gas
oil

air
limestone
salt
sulphur
water

coal
gas

coal
gas
oil

air
salt
water

air
limestone
salt

oil

coal
oil

hydrogen
carbon

coal
cotton
wood

coal
gas

limestone
water

air
limestone
sulphur
water

sulphur

cotton

wood

water

coal

limestone

oil

flourspar

salt

gas

Left: The most common types of plastic, and some of the raw materials used during the polymerization process. The main starting materials are hydrocarbons, and the other substances involved are used as sources of their constituent elements; salt, for example, is a source of chlorine.

Above: Cosmetics are made up from a wide range of organic substances. Lipsticks are mixtures of several types of waxes, oils and fats shown here.

Above right: Soaps are made by reacting fatty acids, such as stearic acid, with caustic soda (sodium hydroxide, NaOH).

Below: This beaker contains two liquids (one dyed red) which do not mix with each other and so one floats on top of the other. Hexamethylene diamine is dissolved in one, and sebacoyl chloride in the other; when they meet at the interface between the two liquids they combine to form nylon.

losing one water molecule between them. *Polysaccharides* are compounds with very large molecules formed by the combination of several monosaccharides.

One common carbohydrate is cellulose, a polysaccharide, which is the main constituent of plant cell walls and thus of plant products such as cotton and wood. It is also used in making plastics such as celluloid and Cellophane.

Starches are also polysaccharides; they are important constituents of many foods, including potatoes, vegetables and cereals. Sugars include glucose and the disaccharides sucrose (cane, beet and maple sugars) and lactose (milk sugar). Glucose and another monosaccharide, fructose (fruit sugar) are constituents of invert syrup and honey.

Aromatic compounds

The second main group of organic compounds are the aromatics, substances which are very important to many industries such as the plastics, drugs, and dye industries. The aromatic compounds are based on the compound benzene, C_6H_6, which can be thought of as having its carbon atoms arranged in a hexagon with alternate single and double bonds between them. There is a hydrogen atom bonded to each of the carbon atoms of this *benzene ring*, and the aromatic compounds are formed by replacing one or more of these hydrogen atoms with atoms of other elements. The main sources of benzene and its derivatives are coal tar and petroleum.

Chemically benzene is not very reactive, nor does it easily form addition products in the way that ethylene does, but suitable industrial processes have been developed and benzene has become the starting compound for a great range of important organic substances.

One of these processes is *halogenation*, which involves substituting the hydrogen atoms of the benzene for atoms of a halogen, such as chlorine or bromine. When chlorine is used, the compound chlorobenzene, C_6H_5Cl, is formed. This is a useful industrial solvent, and it is also used in drug manufacture.

Alkylation of the benzene ring involves attaching an alkyl radical, for example $-CH_3$ or $-C_2H_5$, to the ring in place of a hydrogen atom. The radical is called the *side chain*, the attachment being formed by one of the carbon atoms of the side chain. The compounds obtained by alkylation are good starting points for the formation of more complex molecules.

Toluene, $C_6H_5CH_3$, is the simplest alkylation compound and it is used as a solvent for gums, resins and plastics. It is also used in the manufacture of the high explosive TNT, which is trinitrotoluene $C_6H_2.CH_3.(NO_2)_3$.

Xylene, $C_6H_4(CH_3)_2$, is synthesized from toluene. It is a solvent of rubber and plastics and it is also used in making synthetic fabrics such as Terylene.

Nitration involves substituting hydrogen atoms of the benzene ring by a corresponding number of *nitro-* ($-NO_2$) *groups*. One of the most important nitration products is nitrobenzene, $C_6H_5NO_2$, which can then be reacted with hydrogen to make aniline, $C_6H_5NH_2$. Aniline is an important chemical in the manufacture of such things as plastics, dyes and drugs.

Carboxylic acids

Carboxylic acids may be formed from either aliphatic or aromatic substances. Their chief characteristic is that they contain *carboxyl* (COOH) *groups*, which are made up from a carbonyl (CO) and a hydroxyl (OH) group. The simplest carboxylic acid is formic acid, HCOOH, which is found in ants and is also what gives stinging nettles their sting. Other aliphatic carboxylic acids are acetic acid, CH_3COOH, the main ingredient of vinegar, and the *fatty acids* such as palmitic acid, $C_{15}H_{31}COOH$, and stearic acid, $C_{17}H_{35}COOH$, which occur in natural oils such as tallow and palm oil.

Among the aromatic carboxylic acids, benzoic acid, C_6H_5COOH, is used in dyes, medicines and as a food preservative, and various derivatives of para-aminobenzoic acid are used as local anaesthetics, for example Novocaine.

John Topham Picture Library

Chapter 2

Harnessing Power

The sun radiates energy at a rate of 380 million million million megawatts. The energy output from this solar furnace at Alburquerque, New Mexico – one of the largest in the world – is 5 megawatts.

Hydraulics

One of the simplest methods of transmitting power is by using a liquid under pressure, and any device operated by this means is a form of hydraulic mechanism. The theory of hydraulics is based on two principles. The first is that liquids are virtually incompressible even when subjected to very high pressures and the second, which was discovered by the French scientist Blaise Pascal in the seventeenth century, is that pressure applied to an enclosed liquid is transmitted with undiminished force in every direction.

To calculate the pressure exerted by a force, the value of the force is divided by the area on which it is acting. (Force is measured in such units as *Newtons*. One Newton or 1 N is the force required to move a 1 kg mass with an acceleration of 1 m/sec^2. The *pound-force* is also used and is the force exerted by gravity on a 1 lb mass.) Pressure can thus be expressed as Newtons per square metre (N/m^2) or pounds-force per square inch (or psi). For example, if two cylinders, each containing a piston, are connected by a pipe filled with a liquid, a downward force on one piston will create pressure which will be transmitted through the liquid to the other piston, exerting an upward force on it. If the area of the first piston is 10 cm^2 and the force on it is 10 N, the pressure in the liquid will be 1 N/cm^2. This pressure will be transmitted to the other cylinder, so the pressure under the second piston will also be 1 N/cm^2.

The pressure on the second piston is the same regardless of its area, a fact which leads to the astonishing power potential of hydraulic mechanisms. By making the area of the second piston ten times that of the first one, any force acting on the first one produces ten times that force on the second one. Thus if the area of the second piston is 100cm^2, a pressure of 1 N/cm^2 acting on it will push it upwards with a force of 100 N (calculated by multiplying the pressure in the liquid by the area of the piston).

Some research into the principles of hydraulics was carried out by Archimedes as early as 250BC, but it was not until the late eighteenth century that the first hydraulic mechanism was made. This was a hydraulic press built by Joseph Bramah, which consisted of a large cylinder containing a piston to which a ramrod (or ram) was attached. A small hand-operated pump was used to pump water, under pressure, into the cylinder. The water drove the piston along the cylinder, pushing the ramrod against the material to be pressed.

Since that time the use of hydraulic machinery has expanded rapidly to every industry, chiefly because of the simplicity of the components required and because the liquid can be carried through small bore (narrow) piping to operate mechanisms at a distance from the source of pressure. This latter feature is a great advantage on aircraft and ships. Water was used in the early hydraulic mechanisms, which is why they are still called 'hydraulic', from the Greek words *hudor* (water) and *aulos* (a pipe). Light mineral oils or castor-based oils are now used as the liquid because of their low freezing point and their lubricating properties.

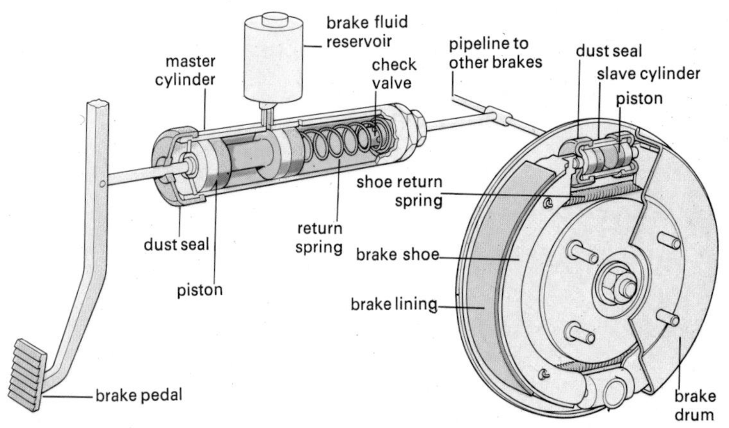

Left and below: One of the simplest hydraulic systems in everyday use is that used to operate the brakes of a car. A master cylinder, primed with hydraulic fluid from a small reservoir, is connected by tubing to a slave cylinder at each of the four wheel brakes. The master cylinder contains a piston which is operated by the footbrake pedal. When the pedal is depressed, pressure is created in the fluid, and this pressure is transmitted to the slave cylinders at the wheels, where it pushes on a pair of pistons. In drum brakes, the pistons force the brake shoes against the inside of the drum. In disc brakes, the pistons are forced inwards to make pads grip the brake disc.

John Goldblatt

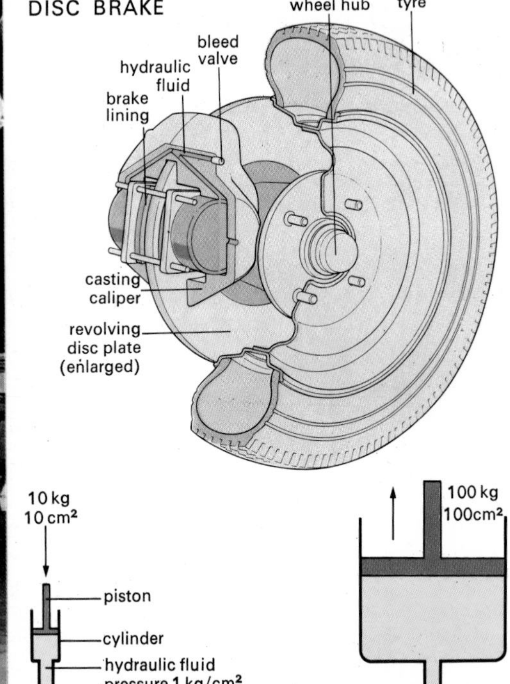

Above: This drawing shows how a hydraulic system can multiply a force. The large cylinder has 10 times the area of the smaller one, so a force exerted on the smaller piston will result in a force 10 times greater on the larger one. The smaller piston, however, must move 10 times as far as the larger one.

Above left: The nosewheel of the BAC TSR2 supersonic strike and reconnaissance aircraft was operated hydraulically, as are all modern retractable undercarriages. Early hydraulic undercarriages were operated by hand pumps, but these were soon replaced by high pressure pumps driven by the aircraft's engines.

Spectrum

Left: On this hydraulic car jack the pump is operated by pushing the handle up and down, which forces oil from the reservoir within the jack body through a non-return valve and against a piston. The piston is linked to the lifting arm, and as the pressure increases it pushes the arm upwards, tilting the car clear of the ground.

Zefa

Above left: Simple hand-operated hydraulic mechanisms have many applications in addition to the common hydraulic car jack. This picture shows a hydraulic roof support being positioned in a uranium mine. These roof supports work on a similar principle to the car jack, having a pump mechanism operated by a hand lever.

Above: Excavators make extensive use of hydraulic systems. The arms and buckets are operated by hydraulic rams, and hydraulic motors are used to drive the wheels or tracks. The pumps are driven by the machine's diesel engine; the selector valves are operated by levers and pedals in the driver's cab.

cks

›st hydraulic systems now use power-ven pumps to pressurize the liquid and sure an adequate supply, but hand mps are still used for servicing and ting components and in case of ergency if the main supply fails. They e also used in many simple mechanisms ch as the lifting jacks used to raise hicles when a wheel is being changed. The pump is incorporated in the jack dy, the lower part of which is used as a servoir for the liquid. The upper part of e body forms a cylinder containing a ston, and it is the upper end of the ston which is placed under the vehicle. eration of the hand pump transfers the uid from the reservoir to the cylinder ere it is applied to the piston, lifting it d the vehicle. The jack is lowered by ening a needle valve which allows the uid to by-pass the pump and return to reservoir.

essure control

hen power-driven pumps are used in draulic systems, additional components e required to safeguard the system ainst excessive rises in pressure when e mechanisms have reached the end of e operation they are performing, or en they are not being used. In these cumstances provision must be made for -loading (disconnecting) the pumps en the maximum pressure is reached, order to prevent overheating of the uid and undue wear on the pumps.

The section of a hydraulic system con-rned with the supply of liquid under essure is termed the power system. In rtain industrial applications it is sup-ed by the manufacturers as a separate it called a *power pack*. Present day draulic systems operate at pressures m about 68 to 340 bar (1000 to 5000 i) and power packs are made in rious sizes to suit the pressure and lume of liquid required to operate the chanisms. The function of the compo-nts is the same whether they are sup-ed as a power pack or incorporated in e hydraulic system as a whole.

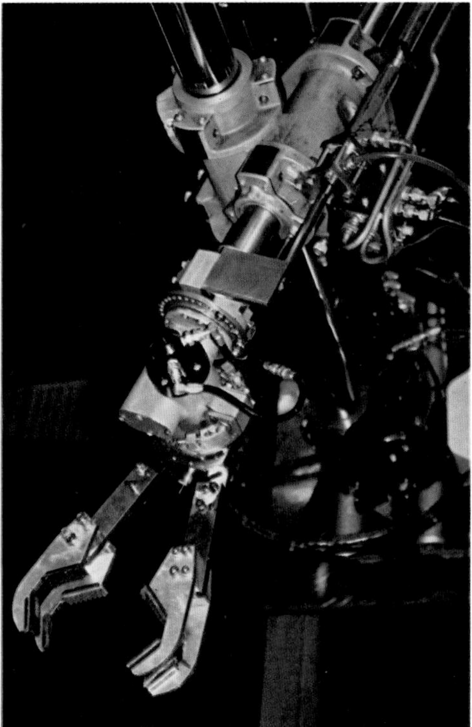
Paul Brierley

Left: Remotely controlled mechanical arms can be operated by means of hydraulic rams and motors. Devices of this type are used in automatic machine tools for transferring the workpiece from one operation to the next. They are also used for handling dangerous substances such as nuclear fuels.

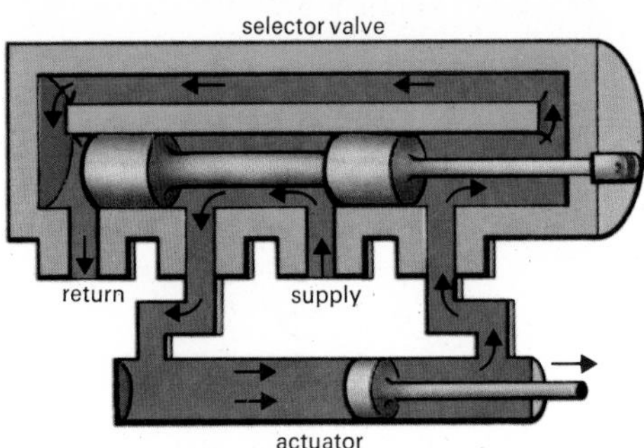

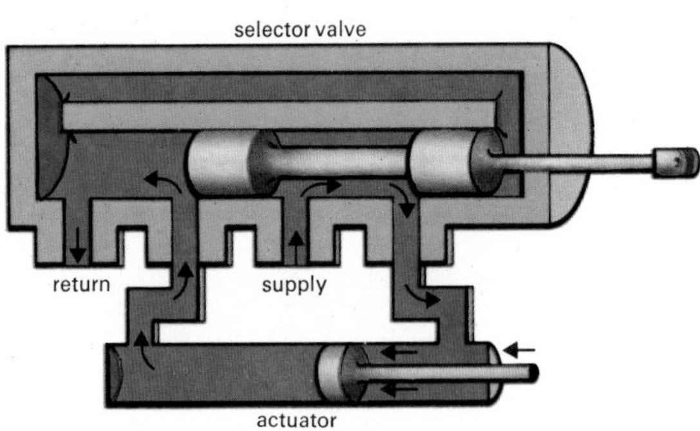

Above: These two diagrams show how a selector valve controls the movement of an actuator in a hydraulic system. The position of the selector valve determines whether the actuator will move to the right, as in the upper diagram, or to the left as in the lower diagram. The arrows indicate the fluid flow.

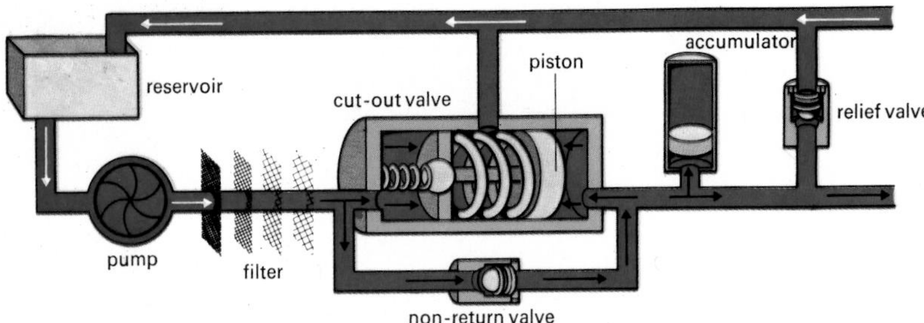

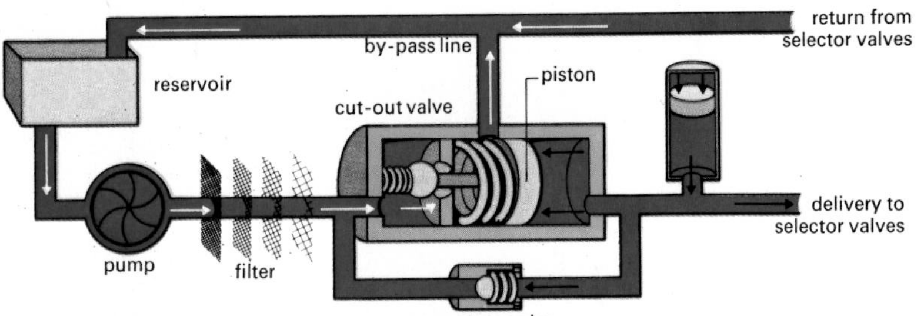

Above: In a hydraulic power pack, fluid from the reservoir is pumped into the delivery line through a non-return valve, as shown in the upper diagram. If the pressure exceeds a certain value the piston in the cut-out valve moves to the left, allowing the fluid to return to the reservoir, as in the lower diagram.

Above: Some of the complex hydraulic systems used to fold back the wings of a carrier-borne jet fighter so that it takes up less space on the ship. Aircraft use a great deal of hydraulic equipment for operating the flight control systems, such as the rudder, flaps and elevators.

Below: This 1889 photograph shows the hydraulic lift on the Eiffel Tower, Paris. During the late nineteenth century many cities installed systems of hydraulic mains, using water as the fluid, which customers used to drive machinery like lifts or cranes, in the same way as electric mains are used today.

Roger Viollet

Power systems

A typical power system or pack contains a reservoir, one or more power-driven pumps, a filter, a relief valve, an accumulator, a check valve (non-return valve) and either a cut-out valve (pressure regulator) or a pressure switch.

The reservoir contains a supply of liquid for the pumps and accommodates the returning liquid from the system. The pumps deliver liquid under pressure into the system, and the filter keeps the liquid clean. The accumulator smooths out any fluctuations in pressure. It stores a supply of liquid under pressure for emergency use or to supplement the main supply.

The cut-out valve off-loads the pumps by automatically re-routing the liquid from the pumps back to the reservoir when the maximum system pressure is reached. The non-return valve holds the pressurized liquid in the system when the pumps are off-loaded, and the relief valve is provided as an additional safeguard should the cut-out valve fail to operate.

The pressurized liquid is piped from the power system to a selector valve and then to the *actuator* or *hydraulic motor* which operates the mechanism that the system is powering. A pipe carries the returning liquid back to the reservoir.

Where pumps are driven by electric motors a pressure switch may be used to stop the motors when the maximum pressure is reached. This enables the cut-out valve to be dispensed with and saves electricity. The switch is designed to start the motors again when the pressure drops.

On aircraft and vehicles the pumps are usually driven by the engines, but on stationary equipment they are invariably driven by electric motors. The most common pumps are the *gear pump* and the *radial cylinder pump*. The gear type pump has two intermeshing gears within a close-fitting casing, which draw the liquid in through one port and force it out through another.

The radial cylinder type has an odd number of cylinders (usually from 5 to 11) arranged in a block around a drivi shaft. The shaft operates pistons insi the cylinders. Oil enters through a pc in the side of each cylinder and the pist forces it out through a valve in the to

Actuators and motors

If the mechanism being driven by t hydraulic system has a reciprocati action or requires lifting or lowering, is operated by an actuator or jack, whi consists of a cylinder having a piston a ramrod. The cylinder is fixed to the ma structure and the ramrod extends retracts to operate the mechanism. cases where continuous rotary motion required, however, it is usual to employ hydraulic motor. Some tracked vehicle for example, use hydraulic motors drive their tracks.

Hydraulic motors are similar in desi to rotary pumps, except that the operati is reversed. Pumps are rotated by mechanism to pressurize fluid, where motors are rotated by pressurized fluid operate a mechanism.

Two types of motor are in common u the *gear motor* and the *vane motor*. T gear motor has a pair of gears like th of the gear pump, and the fluid is forc between them to make them revolve a drive the mechanism, the fluid bei expelled into the return line.

The vane motor has a rotor fitted w a number of movable, radially extendi vanes which are spring loaded to pr against the motor housing. The rotor eccentrically mounted in the housing that when liquid under pressure is through an inlet on one side of the ro it passes between the rotor and t housing, turning the rotor as it goes. T outlet to the return pipe is on the oppos side of the rotor to the inlet.

Applications

The range of applications for hydrau power is enormous. Hydraulic systems used on ships, railway locomotives, a craft, computer disc drives, earthmovi machines, refuse trucks and fact equipment. On a modern 250,000 tonne tanker, for example, there may be so 35 km (22 miles) of piping connecti over 100 actuators which open and cl the various valves used for loading a unloading the oil. The selector valves mounted on a huge console and each c has an indicator to show whether valve is open or closed. This syst enables the tanker to be loaded or loaded using a minimum of personnel w the maximum of efficiency.

Energy, Work and Power

There is a considerable difference between the common usage of the words energy, work and power, and their strictly scientific definitions. The scientific meaning of the word 'energy' is founded on the idea of movement; anything that moves is said to have *kinetic* energy because of its motion. This idea is then extended to allow the definition of the word to include the capability of producing movement. An object which, because of its circumstances or position, can produce motion if required is said to have *potential* energy.

A fully-wound clockwork spring, for example, has potential energy. This is converted into kinetic energy when the spring unwinds and drives the gears of a clock mechanism or a clockwork toy.

Forms of energy

Defining energy as either potential or kinetic may at first glance appear quite straightforward. An object has kinetic energy if it is moving, and potential energy if it is capable of producing motion. In practice, however, this distinction is less clear, as in the case of a gas under pressure.

If this gas is free to push a piston it will expand and produce motion, but before it expands it can be said to have potential energy. After it expands, the piston that it moves then has kinetic energy, and the whole action could be said to represent an energy conversion from potential to kinetic.

In fact the 'potential' energy in the compressed gas existed because the molecules of the gas were in continuous motion, hammering against the piston to produce the effect we call pressure. Thus the gas actually possessed kinetic energy and all that happened during the 'conversion' was that the kinetic energy of the random movement of countless molecules of gas became the kinetic energy of the ordered movement of one solid object in one particular direction.

The definitions of the various forms in which energy can be found therefore depend largely upon the manner in which we wish to consider them. In the example above, the 'potential' energy of the compressed gas can be increased by raising its temperature—this causes the molecules to move faster, so that they each possess a higher kinetic energy. However, to be more specific, the energy of the gas can be said to consist of heat or *thermal* energy. Other forms of energy include *radiation* energy, such as light, radiant heat, radio waves and X-rays, *chemical* energy, and *nuclear* energy.

Chemical energy is energy given off by a chemical reaction, such as the heat given off when a fuel is burned. For example, when methane gas burns, the carbon and hydrogen atoms in the methane molecules combine with the oxygen molecules in the air to form carbon dioxide and water. A certain amount of the energy that was holding the original molecules together is not needed to hold the new ones together and is given off as heat. This kind of reaction is the basis of the power of all explosives.

Aspect

Above: An atom has a central nucleus, made of protons and neutrons, with electrons in orbit around it. In a fission reaction, a free neutron (shown here in black) penetrates the nucleus (shown here in red) of a suitable fuel, such as uranium-235, and splits it, releasing more neutrons which then split neighbouring atoms. This process spreads throughout the fuel, giving off vast amounts of energy.

Left: In the uncontrolled chain reaction in a nuclear bomb, all the energy is given off in a fraction of a second, with terrible results.

Picturepoint

Above: The chain reactions within a nuclear reactor are basically the same as those in an A-bomb, but they are controlled so that the energy is given off gradually in the form of heat. This heat is used to raise steam to drive electricity-generating turbines.

Du Pont

Left: Explosives such as gelignite or TNT work by rapidly releasing large amounts of chemical energy—the product of a chemical reaction during which the atoms which make up molecules recombine to form different ones. Nuclear energy, on the other hand, is a result of the re-arrangement of the particles which make up the atoms themselves.

This chart show energy conversions involved in the generation and use of electricity. The two pictures on the right show a water turbine under construction and the turbine hall of a coal-fired power station. In a hydroelectric power station, the potential energy of the water

M. T. Walters

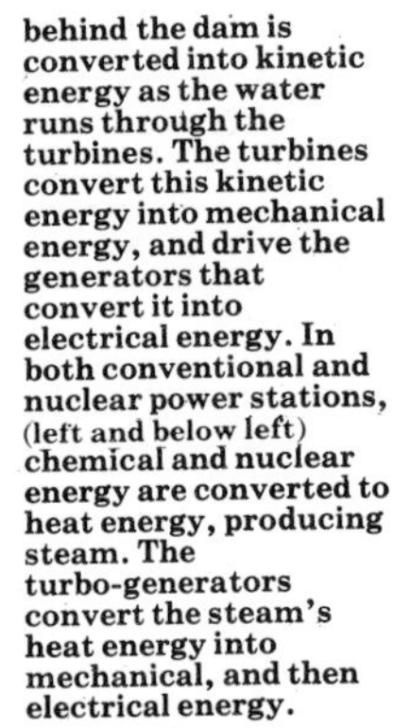

behind the dam is converted into kinetic energy as the water runs through the turbines. The turbines convert this kinetic energy into mechanical energy, and drive the generators that convert it into electrical energy. In both conventional and nuclear power stations, (left and below left) chemical and nuclear energy are converted to heat energy, producing steam. The turbo-generators convert the steam's heat energy into mechanical, and then electrical energy.

Electricity is a convenient form of energy which can easily be converted into many other forms, for example light, heat, mechanical and sound energy. Many devices employ more than one conversion, for example the bell converts electricity to mechanical energy and then to sound.

CEGB

Work

Work can be defined as movement against a force; for instance, lifting an object involves doing work against the force of gravity. The work done on an object by a force is calculated by multiplying the value of the force by the distance through which it moves the object.

Energy is the capacity to do work; it can be converted into work, and work can be converted into energy. A good example of this is the operation of a drop-hammer piledriver, where a crane lifts a heavy weight then drops it to drive a pile into the ground.

Energy is produced by burning fuel in the crane's engine, and this is converted into work to lift the weight. At the top of the weight's stroke, the work done on it has been converted into potential energy. When the weight is dropped, the potential energy is converted into kinetic energy, and when it hits the pile this kinetic energy is converted back into work to drive the pile into the ground.

Thermodynamics

The conversion of work to energy, or energy to work, leads to scientific facts that make nonsense in everyday language. For example, a sack of flour resting on the floor has zero potential energy. If a man lifts it, he will have done work on it and given it potential energy. If he then puts the sack gently back on to the floor, he takes its potential energy away from it again.

Since he has lifted the sack and given it potential energy, then put it down and taken the energy away again, scientifically speaking the net energy input to the sack, and thus the net work input, is zero. The man has done no 'work' in lifting the sack and putting it down again, even though he has actually used energy.

All energy changes (such as from chemical to mechanical or from electrical to mechanical) result in a certain amount of energy being 'lost' during the change, as though it had drained away into a universal lake of unusable energy. This is known as increasing *entropy*, since the energy 'lost' cannot be regained for further use.

For example, an electric motor which converts electrical energy into mechanical energy, actually delivers less energy that it receives. The 'missing' energy is used up in several ways; for example, in overcoming the electrical resistance of the wiring of the motor, and in counteracting the friction of the bearings. This energy is wasted in the form of heat and sound, and in wearing away the bearings. It is, in fact, dissipated in such a way that it can never be recovered.

A little of the energy in the Universe is lost every time an energy change occurs, as in the case of the electric motor. It has been predicted that eventually all the energy will have drained away and become unusable. This will be the 'end' of the Universe—still a long way off yet—sometimes called the 'heat death' of the Universe because then everything will be at the same temperature. As all energy derives ultimately from a flow of heat, without temperature differences there can be no such flow, and thus no more usable energy can be obtained.

The relationship between thermal (or heat) energy and kinetic (or dynamic) energy is explained by two laws, the *First and Second Laws of Thermodynamics*, which were formulated during the nineteenth century. The First Law, also known as the *Law of Conservation of Energy*, states that the total amount of energy is constant, and energy cannot be created or destroyed, only converted from one form to another.

The second law implies that energy will not flow 'uphill'; it must be pushed up,

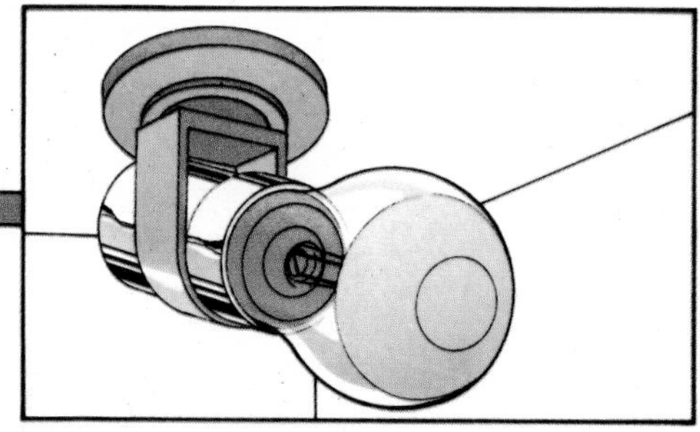

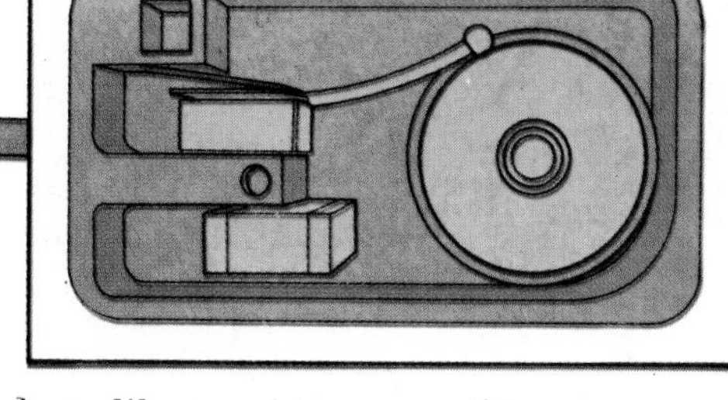

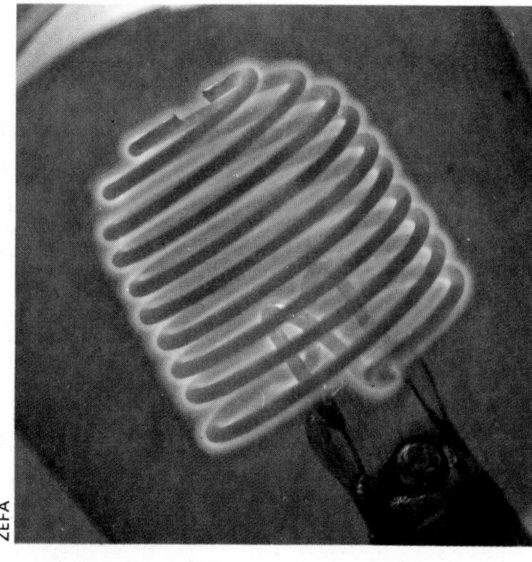

ZEFA

Above: Current passing through a light bulb filament raises its temperature so that it gives off light.

Above right: When a car battery is charged, electrical energy is converted into chemical energy and stored. When the battery is used, this energy is converted back into electricity.

Right: The term 'horsepower' was devised by James Watt in the eighteenth century. One horsepower is the power needed to raise 550 lb through a height of 1 foot in 1 second, that is, 550 ft.lb/sec. It is about 50% more than a horse can maintain over a period of time.

British Leyland

just like pushing something upwards against the force of gravity. One result which is relatively obvious is that heat cannot flow from a body of lower temperature to one of higher, unless work is done on it. But a more far-reaching example brings home the full impact of the Second Law and its relationship to entropy.

A warm object which is at rest may have the same energy as a cold object which is moving, the energy in both cases being the total kinetic energy of the molecules of the object. In the first case, the molecules are moving at random within the object, and in the second case they are all moving in an orderly manner in one direction.

However, there is an essential difference between, for example, a warm brick which is static and a cold one which is moving (and so possessing the same amount of energy). Eventually the cold brick will hit the ground and come to rest, becoming warm as the kinetic energy of the orderly motion of its molecules is converted (when the molecules are 'shaken up' by the impact) into the kinetic energy of random molecular motion within the brick. The entropy of the brick, which is a measure of the randomness or disorder within it, has inevitably increased.

On the other hand, the reverse cannot happen; the random motion of the molecules of a warm brick cannot by chance become an orderly motion, so that the brick suddenly becomes cold and throws itself into the air. An input of energy is necessary to change the random motion into an orderly motion, in other words to decrease the entropy of the brick.

It is clear from these examples that the natural tendency is for entropy to increase; and work must be done in order to decrease it.

The Second Law of Thermodynamics dictates that a block of ice (in which there is little molecular motion, and low entropy) may not spontaneously form itself from water vapour in the air in the Sahara Desert at noon. Similarly, a refrigerator must be supplied with energy in order to withdraw heat from within it, in other words to decrease its entropy.

Power

Power is the rate at which work or energy is supplied, transferred or consumed. The relationship between energy and power is a simple one—power is energy divided by time. For example, if a machine has a power output of one horsepower, it can deliver 550 ft.lb. of energy per second.

Above: Measuring engine power on a hydraulic dynamometer. The engine drives a rotor which forces fluid against a casing. The force on the casing is measured and multiplied by the speed of the engine to calculate the power.

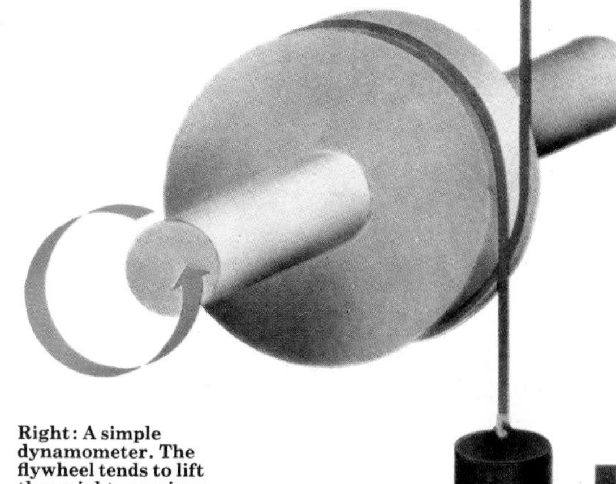

Right: A simple dynamometer. The flywheel tends to lift the weight, causing a reduction in the spring balance reading from which the torque can be calculated.

Electrical Machines

The basic principles behind such electrical machines as motors, generators and transformers were discovered by Michael Faraday (1791-1867) during the first half of the nineteenth century. Faraday discovered that if a piece of a conducting material, such as copper wire, was moved in a magnetic field, an electric current would flow in it. In addition, if current was passed through a piece of copper wire which was within a magnetic field, forces would be set up which made the wire move. These two discoveries led to the development of dynamos and motors.

Faraday also found that if a varying electric current was passed through a coil of wire, a similarly varying current would be induced to flow in a second coil placed next to it. This was the basis of the transformer.

Dc machines

The simplest type of direct current (dc) machine consists of three main components, the *stator*, the *rotor*, and the *commutator*. The stator is a horseshoe-shaped permanent magnet, and the rotor is mounted on a shaft, free to rotate, between the two poles of the magnet.

The rotor has a coil of copper wire, through which the current flows, wrapped around a soft iron core. The ends of the coil are connected to the commutator, which acts as a sort of rotating switch to reverse the direction of the current within the coil twice per revolution of the rotor.

When direct current is passed through the coil, a magnetic field is produced. The coil in effect becomes a magnet, suspended within the field of the horseshoe magnet. It is then forced to turn so that its lines of magnetic flux line up with those of the horseshoe magnet, with its north and south poles next to the south and north

ASEA

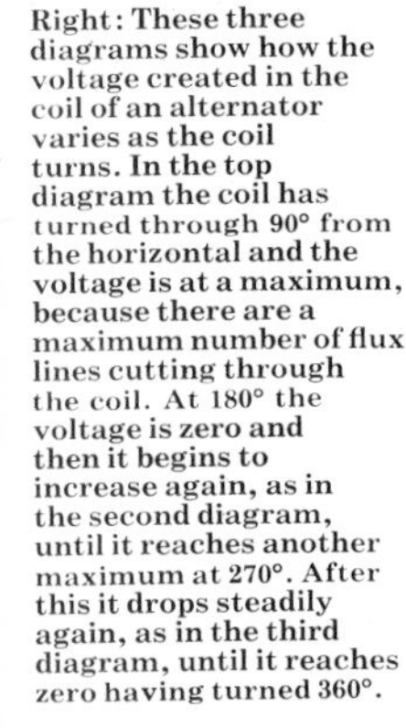

Right: These three diagrams show how the voltage created in the coil of an alternator varies as the coil turns. In the top diagram the coil has turned through 90° from the horizontal and the voltage is at a maximum, because there are a maximum number of flux lines cutting through the coil. At 180° the voltage is zero and then it begins to increase again, as in the second diagram, until it reaches another maximum at 270°. After this it drops steadily again, as in the third diagram, until it reaches zero having turned 360°.

Left and below: In a hydroelectric power station, the alternators are driven by water turbines which are turned by the force of water passing down through them. The picture on the left shows the tops of the turbine units at a modern hydro station in Scotland, while the picture below shows the water pipelines supplying a small hydroelectric power station in the Pyrenees mountains in south-west France.

Below right: Most power stations use steam turbines to drive the alternators. This is a turbogenerator at a nuclear power station, where the steam is produced by the heat from a nuclear reactor. This alternator generates 22 kV at 50 Hz. The power is developed in the stator, and the dc supply which creates the magnetic field of the rotor is generated by the small machine at the near end of the unit.

Below left: One of the earliest electrical machines was the Wimshurst machine. It generated static electricity by means of the friction between a rotating glass disc and a stationary metal one.

Roger Viollet

Science Museum

UKAEA

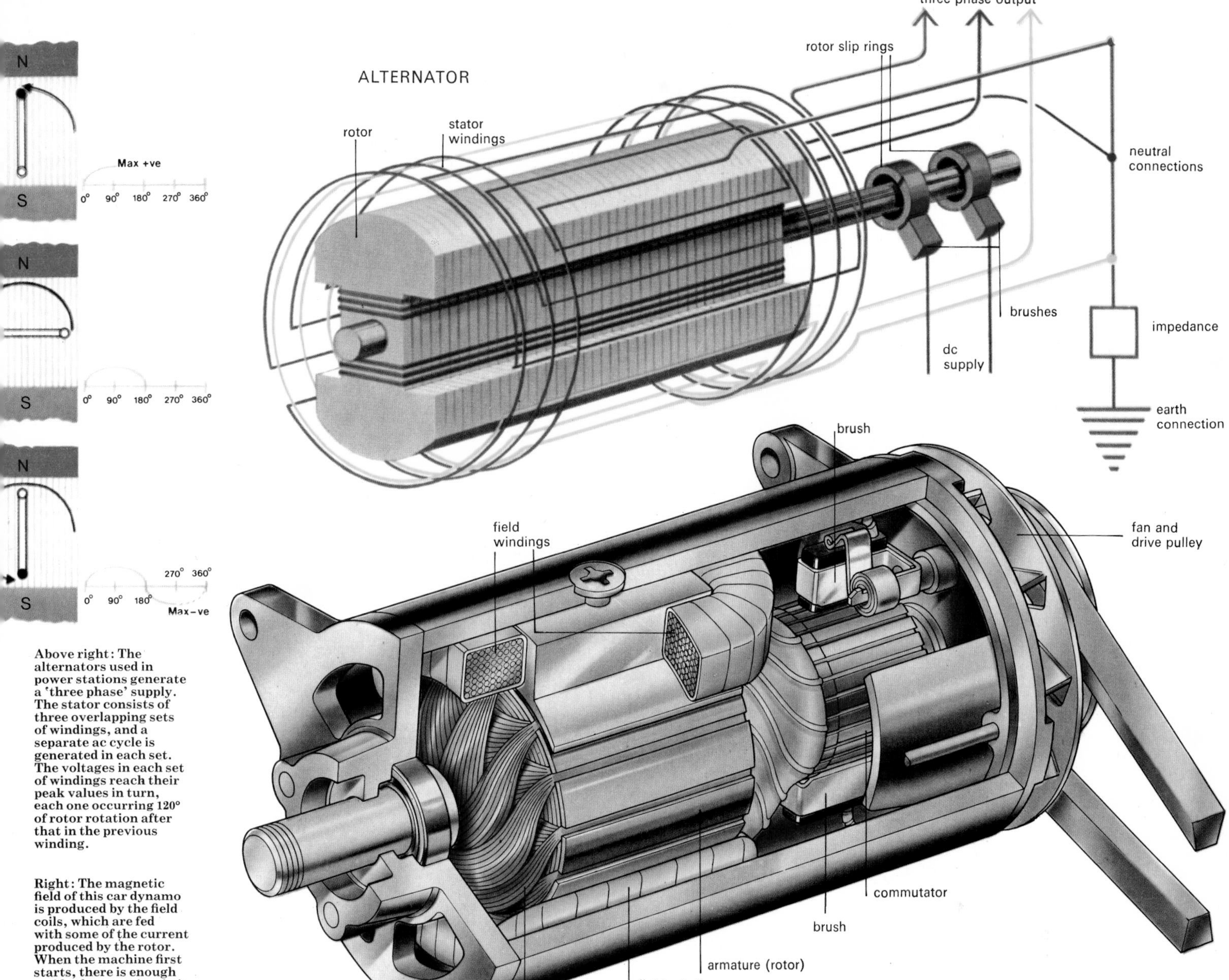

Above right: The alternators used in power stations generate a 'three phase' supply. The stator consists of three overlapping sets of windings, and a separate ac cycle is generated in each set. The voltages in each set of windings reach their peak values in turn, each one occurring 120° of rotor rotation after that in the previous winding.

Right: The magnetic field of this car dynamo is produced by the field coils, which are fed with some of the current produced by the rotor. When the machine first starts, there is enough residual magnetism in it to provide a field until the rotor begins producing current.

poles respectively of the magnet.

Just as the coil reaches the position where its field aligns with that of the magnet, however, the direction of the current flow within it is reversed by the action of the commutator. Its magnetic field is thus also reversed, and the coil then has to move around another 180° to keep its field in line with that of the magnet. Already moving when its field was reversed, the coil continues moving in the same direction. By reversing the current flow each time the coil is about to line up its field with the magnet's, the coil can be made to rotate continuously.

In practice, dc motors have a number of separate coils, wound round the core in sequence, and the commutator is a series of copper strips to which the ends of the coils are connected.

A simple dc machine like this can also be used as a dynamo to produce dc electricity. The rotor is turned mechanically, and as the coils turn they cut through the magnetic flux lines of the stator magnet so creating a current within them. This current is collected from the commutator by carbon brushes and taken away by wires to supply an electric circuit. A common example of this is the dynamo driven by a car engine, which supplies the electrical system and charges the battery. Large dc machines often use electromagnets in place of permanent magnets to provide the main magnetic field.

Alternators

To produce an alternating current (ac), another principle of electromagnetism is employed. This is the fact that the current induced in a coil rotating within a magnetic field is proportional to the rate at which the coil cuts through the lines of flux of the magnetic field.

These lines of flux pass from one pole of the magnet to the other and as the coil passes near the poles it is almost in line with the flux lines. At this point it cuts them at a maximum rate. On the other hand when the coil is at right angles to the poles it is also at right angles to the flux lines and cuts through a minimum number of them.

The result of these different rates is that the voltage induced in the coil at any one time depends on its position in relation to the magnetic field. The voltage is at a maximum when the coil is in line with the poles, it falls to a minimum when the coil is at 90° to the poles, and then it rises to a maximum again as the coil once more lines up with the poles. After a further 90° of rotation the coil is again producing a minimum voltage.

At the second maximum, however, the coil is the opposite way round in relation to its position at the first maximum. As the direction of the magnetic field remains unchanged, this reversal of the coil means that the current induced in it will flow round it in the opposite direction and the voltage will have the opposite polarity, that is, negative instead of positive or vice versa.

In effect the voltage and current produced by such a coil build up smoothly to a maximum in one direction, fall to zero, and then build up to a maximum in the other direction, with each 180° of its rotation. In 360° of rotation this alternating voltage (and current) goes through one whole *cycle*, from one maximum to the other and back again.

The *frequency* of an ac supply is the number of complete cycles per second, one cycle per second being known as 1 *hertz* (1 Hz), named after the German physicist Heinrich Hertz (1857-1894). For example, if the coil rotates at 50 revolutions per second (3,000 rpm), the frequency will be 50 Hz.

In Europe, the frequency of the mains

supply is 50 Hz, produced by *alternators* (mostly driven by steam turbines) running at 3,000 rpm. In North America the mains frequency is 60 Hz and the alternators run at 3,600 rpm.

On most small alternators the current produced by the rotor is collected by brushes from a pair of copper rings, called *slip rings*, mounted on the rotor shaft, each ring being connected to one end of the coil. Other alternators, including the large ones used in power stations, avoid having to collect large amounts of power through brushes and slip rings by keeping the coil stationary and rotating the magnetic field within it. The power developed in the coil (or stator, as the stationary part of any motor or generator is known) can then be collected by fixed connections. In this case the rotor may be a permanent magnet or an electromagnet fed with a relatively small amount of dc power through brushes and slip rings.

Ac motors

There are several types of ac electric motor, of which the *induction motor* is the most widely used in industry, largely because of its simplicity of design. This type uses a rotating magnetic field produced in the stator to induce *eddy currents* in the rotor which in turn produce their own magnetic field. These currents are produced whenever a magnetic field is moved relative to a conductor. And as long as there is a difference in speed of rotation—that is, as long as the rotor is moving more slowly than the stator field —eddy currents are created and the attraction between the two magnetic fields effectively pulls the rotor round.

The stator consists of a series of electromagnets, and these are connected in such a way that an alternating current passing through them creates a pattern of north and south poles which move around the stator in sequence. The rotor is made of a slotted steel core, with bars of low-resistance copper or aluminium in the slots making a kind of 'cage'. The bars are connected together at the ends of the core and provide paths for the induced eddy currents.

The *synchronous motor* uses the same kind of rotating field as the induction motor, but the rotor is made of permanent magnets or dc electromagnets. The field of the magnetic rotor is synchronized with the rotating field. It follows it at exactly the same speed, since no relative motion is needed to produce its magnetism.

If the stator is arranged so that a single pair of poles appears to rotate around it, the motor will run at the same speed as the supply frequency—50 revolutions per second for a 50 Hz supply, or 60 rps for a 60 Hz supply. Doubling the apparent number of poles will give a third of the speed. Electrical machines of the synchronous type are more often used as alternators than as motors, as the simpler, more robust induction motor is usually preferable for most applications.

Two other forms of synchronous motor are the *reluctance motor* and the *hysteresis motor*. In the reluctance motor the rotor

DC MOTOR

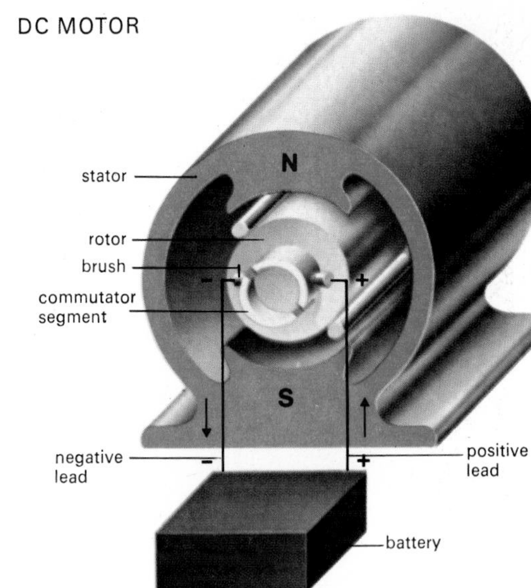

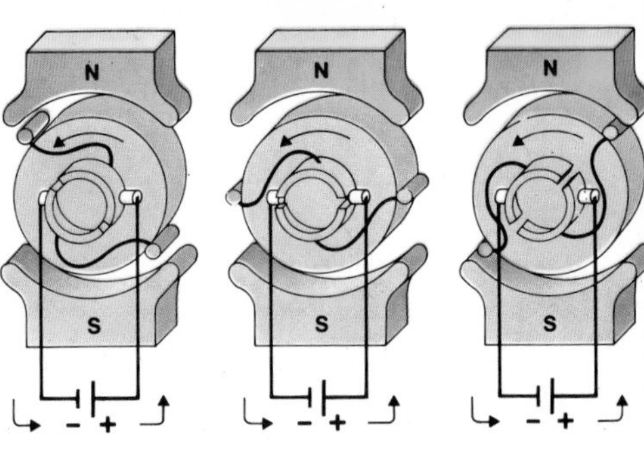

SYNCHRONOUS MOTOR

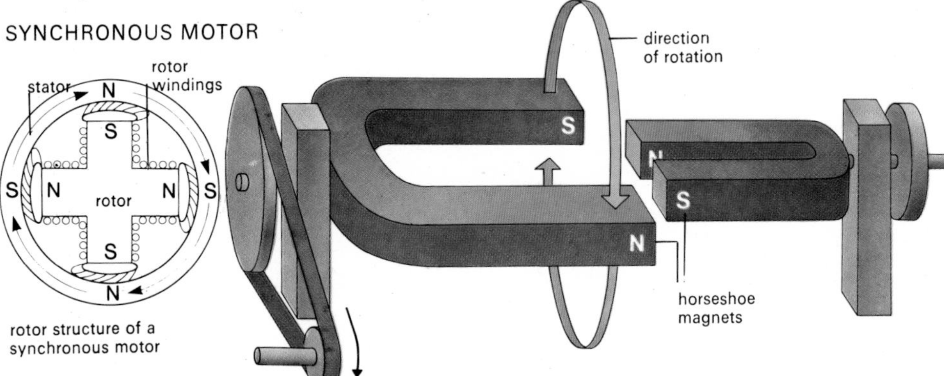

SQUIRREL CAGE MOTOR

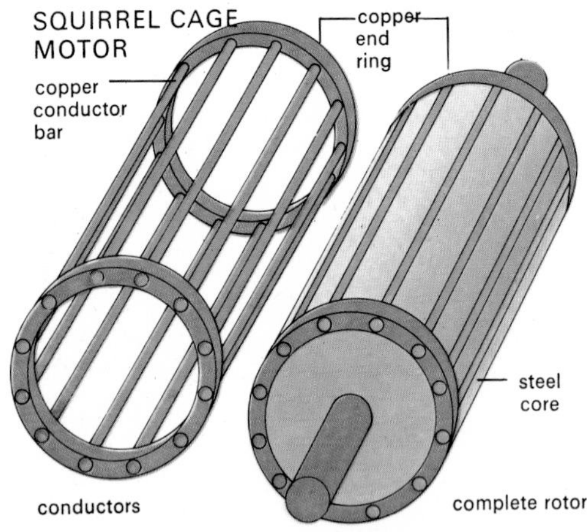

Above: The synchronous motor has a rotating magnetic field in its stator which attracts the field in the rotor and pulls it round with it, just as the magnet on the right will turn if that on the left is rotated. The diagram on the far left shows the way this happens in an actual motor. The rotor is fed with dc.

Right: A great deal of heat can be generated within big transformers, and so a cooling system is necessary. This transformer, at a 400 kV substation in England, has a special insulating oil circulating through its windings to carry away the heat, which is then dissipated by the banks of cooling radiators on its right.

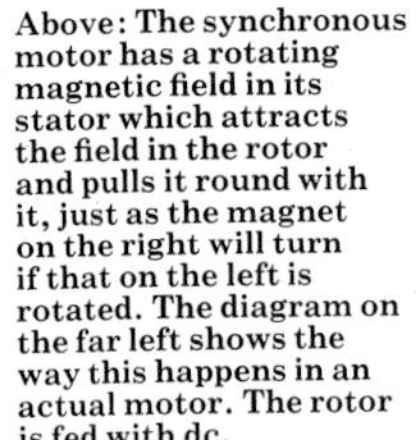

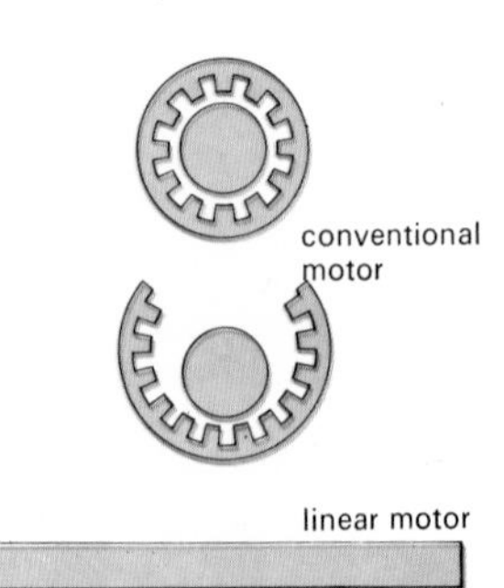

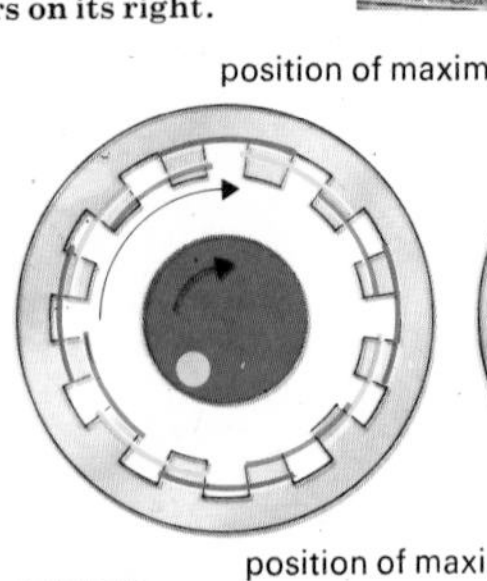

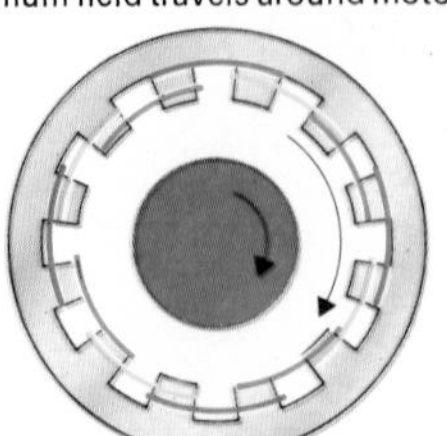

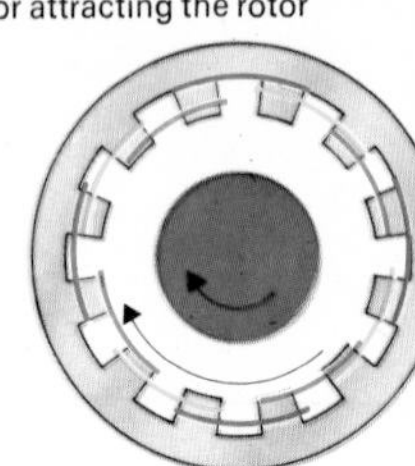

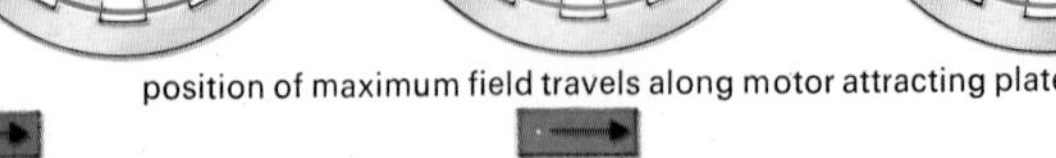

Above: Many induction motors are called 'squirrel cage' motors because of the way the rotor conductors are arranged. Eddy currents induced in the rotor by the rotating magnetic field of the stator produce forces which drag the rotor around, trying to make it catch up with the rotating field.

Right: In a normal induction motor the field travels in a circular path around the stator windings, pulling the rotor with it. A linear motor is like a normal one which has been unrolled. The field travels along the windings, carrying a suitable conductor, such as an aluminium plate, with it.

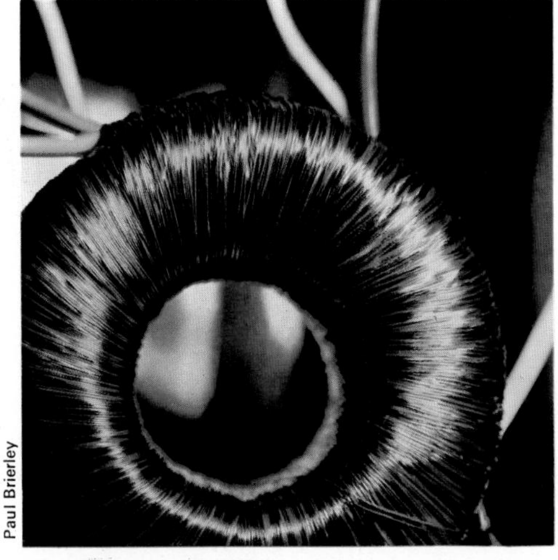

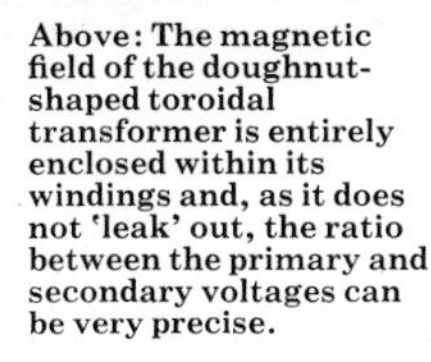

Above: The magnetic field of the doughnut-shaped toroidal transformer is entirely enclosed within its windings and, as it does not 'leak' out, the ratio between the primary and secondary voltages can be very precise.

Far left: The commutator of a simple dc motor changes the direction of current flow in the coil every 180° of rotation.

Left: Many dc motors have electromagnets instead of a permanent magnet stator to provide the stationary magnetic field.

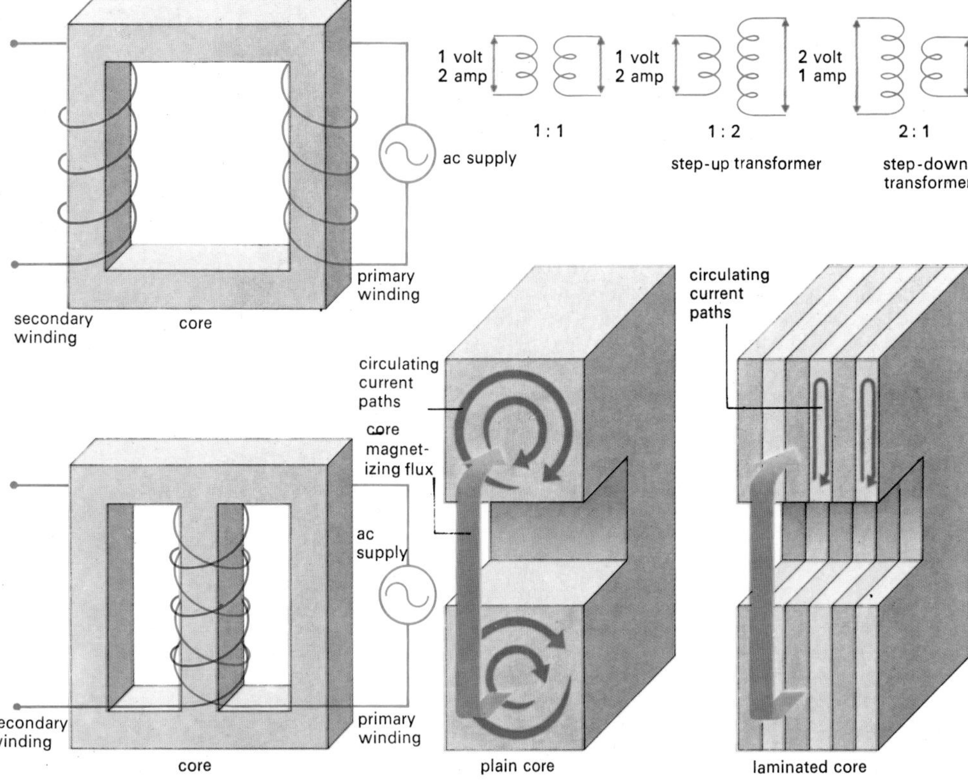

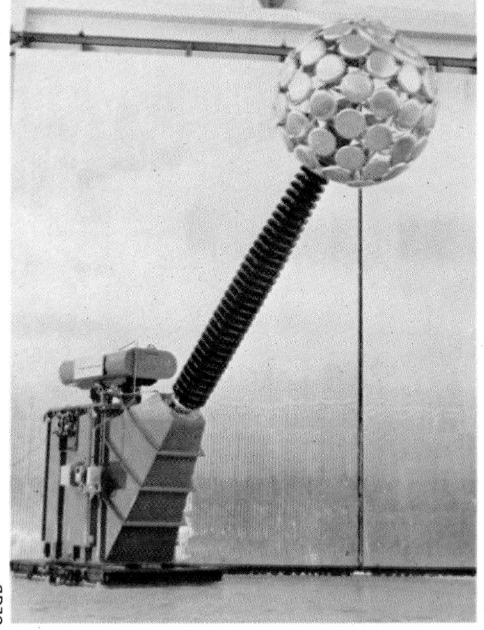

Above: In a transformer, the ratio between the primary and secondary voltages is the same as the ratio between the numbers of turns of wire in the primary and secondary windings. The ratio between the primary and secondary currents, however, is the inverse of this winding ratio. The diagrams also show the two main winding layouts for power transformers, and the way a laminated core reduces the induced circulating currents which cause power losses. Two main kinds of power loss occur: the 'iron loss' is power used in magnetizing and demagnetizing the core; the 'copper loss' is power used in overcoming the electrical impedance of the windings.

Left: This transformer produces 600 kV output for testing heavy electrical equipment. Voltage is discharged from the plates making up the sphere at the end of the long, ribbed insulator.

is an unmagnetized piece of steel with a toothed circumference, and the stator has a correspondingly toothed inner surface. The rotor moves so as to line its teeth up with those of the stator, as this provides the path of minimum *reluctance*, or resistance to the passage of magnetic flux, between the stator and the rotor.

The rotor must be given a spin to start it, but once it is moving it will keep going at a synchronous speed because the magnetic polarity of the teeth of the stator changes every half cycle of the ac supply. Each rotor tooth is pulled round from one stator tooth to the next by this constantly reversing magnetic field. Because they run at the precisely controlled speed of the ac mains, these cheap and reliable motors are widely used to drive electric clocks.

The hysteresis motor has a smooth steel rotor which is capable of being permanently magnetized. As the moving magnetic field of the stator passes a point on the rotor, that point becomes a small permanent magnet which follows it round. It eventually catches up with the moving field and locks on to it, so that the rotor behaves like the rotor of a synchronous motor.

All types of ac electric motor can be made in linear form, that is, with the stator windings arranged in a line rather than in a circle. This arrangement produces a magnetic field which moves along the line of windings and will carry any suitable piece of conducting material along with it. *Linear motors* thus produce straight-line motion instead of rotary motion and so are becoming popular for driving travelling cranes, sliding doors and baggage handling systems. They may also be used in the future for driving high speed transport systems such as railways.

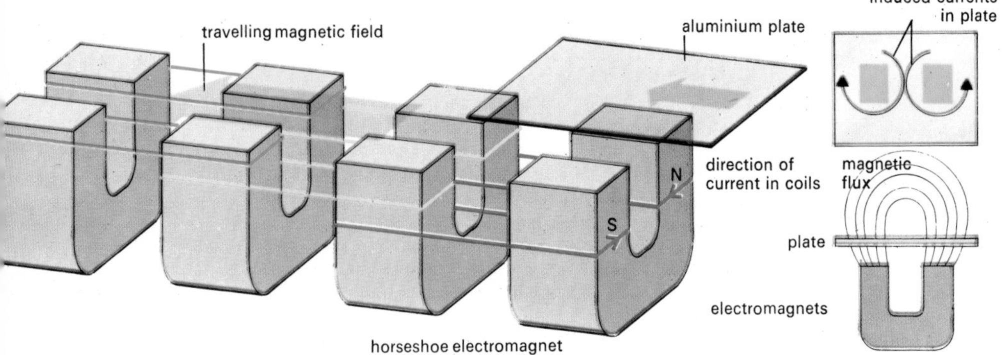

The Internal Combustion Engine

The internal combustion engine was one of the most important inventions of the nineteenth century. Its development and its applications have had far-reaching effects throughout the world—its use has revolutionized transport, its manufacture has spawned vast new industries and its technology has inspired developments in many other fields of engineering.

The internal combustion engine is so called because the heat energy that it converts into mechanical energy is produced within it by the repeated explosion of a mixture of fuel and air. For instance, if petrol gasoline vapour is mixed with the right proportion of air, the resulting mixture can be ignited by means of a spark. As it explodes it expands rapidly, and this expansion is what drives the pistons.

Early designs of these engines used coal gas as the fuel and were based on steam engine technology. The first reasonably successful engine was built by the Frenchman J. J. E. Lenoir in 1859. The Lenoir engine, however, suffered from a low power output and high fuel consumption, so many attempts were made to produce a more efficient design. This was eventually achieved in 1876 by Nikolaus Otto in Germany and his company, Otto and Langen, produced about 50,000 engines during the following 17 years.

E. P. Barrus

Above: A two-stroke outboard motor engine. It is a V-6 engine, having two banks of three cylinders set at an angle to each other to form a V-shape. The total cylinder capacity is 2448 cc (149.9 in^3), and the power output is 149 kW (200 hp).

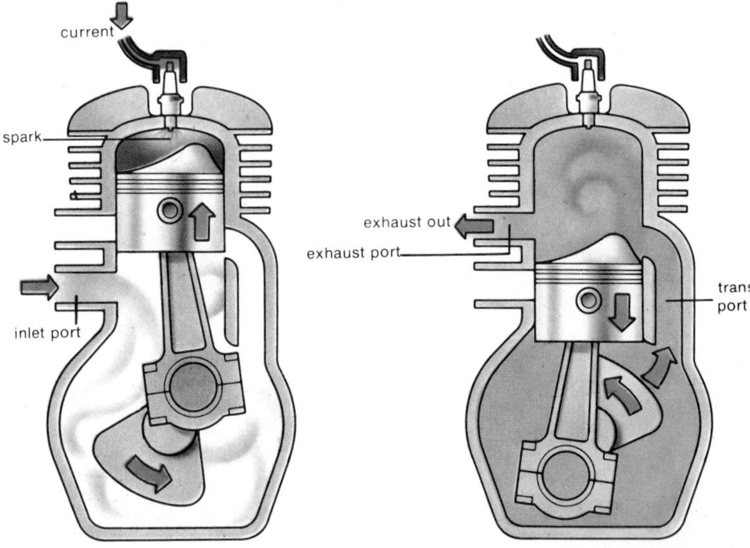

Right: The two-stroke cycle. As the piston moves up to compress the fuel/air mixture in the cylinder, the next charge of mixture is drawn into the crankcase via the inlet port. After the compressed mixture in the cylinder has been ignited by the spark plug, the expanding gases drive the piston down the cylinder. As the piston descends it pushes the mixture in the crankcase up the transfer port and into the cylinder. The mixture entering the cylinder pushes the exhaust gases out through the exhaust port, then the piston starts to rise and the cycle begins again.

Petrol engines

The basic components of an internal combustion engine are the cylinder, closed at the top by the cylinder head, and the piston which moves up and down within it. The piston is connected to a crankshaft by a connecting rod, so as the piston moves up and down the crankshaft is turned.

The fuel and air are mixed by the carburettor and this mixture is then drawn into the cylinder by the suction created during a downward stroke of the piston. When the piston rises again, the mixture is compressed as the space between the top of the piston and the cylinder head decreases. This compression raises the temperature of the mixture, making it more explosive.

Just before the piston reaches the top of its travel, the mixture is ignited by an electric spark created by current jumping across the gap between the two electrodes of a spark plug, screwed into the cylinder head.

By the time the piston has reached the top of its travel, the explosion which began in the mixture around the spark plug has spread rapidly throughout the rest of the mixture in the cylinder. The resulting expansion of hot gases created by the burning mixture drives the piston down again.

The power of the explosion is thus converted into a downward movement of the piston, and this motion rotates the crankshaft. The rotation of the crankshaft is then used to drive, for example, a car or a motorcycle.

The simplest form of petrol engine is the two-stroke engine, in which there are two strokes of the piston, one up and one down, for each ignition of fuel. On a two-stroke engine the mixture is drawn into the cylinder via the crankcase, the casing below the cylinder which encloses the crankshaft.

As the piston rises to compress the mixture in the cylinder, the low pressure created in the crankcase below it sucks in fresh mixture through an opening, the inlet port, in the side of the bottom of the cylinder where it meets the crankcase.

Meanwhile, the mixture already in the cylinder has been compressed and ignited, and the piston is on its way down again. As it descends it uncovers two other openings in the cylinder wall, which were closed off by the sides of the piston during its upward compression stroke.

One of these ports is the exhaust port, through which the burned exhaust gases escape, and the other one, on the opposite side of the cylinder, is the transfer port. The transfer port is the top opening of a passage leading down to the crankcase, and as the piston moves down it pushes the mixture in the crankcase up the transfer port and into the cylinder. As the mixture enters the cylinder it pushes the remaining exhaust gases out through the exhaust port.

The piston now rises again, covering the exhaust and transfer ports and so sealing the cylinder, compressing the mixture ready for ignition. The impetus required to push the piston back up the cylinder is provided by a relatively heavy flywheel, fitted to the end of the crankshaft, whose inertia keeps it turning after it has been set moving by the down-

Right: The four-stroke cycle. On the first stroke, the induction stroke, the piston moves down and the inlet valve opens, allowing mixture to enter the cylinder. On the second stroke, the compression stroke, both valves are closed and the piston moves up to compress the mixture. After the mixture has been ignited the piston is driven back down on its power stroke. As it rises again on its exhaust stroke the exhaust valve opens and the exhaust gases are driven out of the cylinder. The exhaust valve then closes, the inlet valve opens, and the next induction stroke begins.

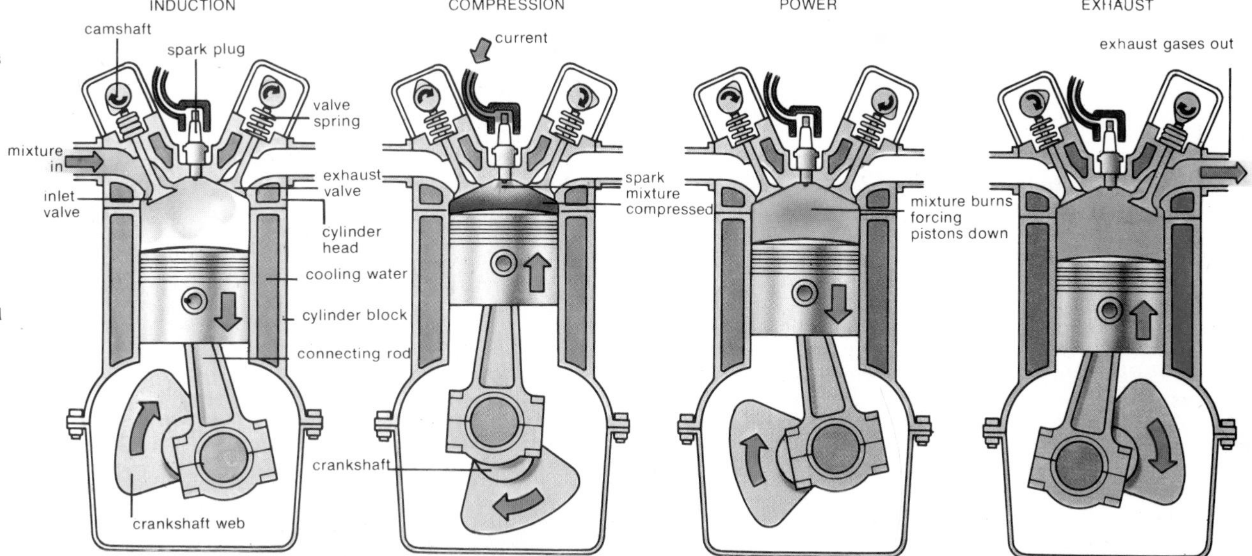

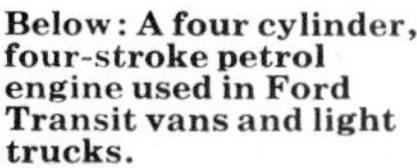

Below: A four cylinder, four-stroke petrol engine used in Ford Transit vans and light trucks.

Ford

ward power stroke of the piston.

The four-stroke engine is more complicated than the two stroke because there is a separate stroke of the piston for each of the four stages of the combustion cycle. In addition, cam-operated valves are used to control the entry of the mixture and the exit of the exhaust gases, the mixture entering the cylinder directly and not via the crankcase.

The first stroke of the cycle is a downward stroke of the piston, during which the inlet valve is open to allow mixture to be drawn into the cylinder. The inlet valve then closes and the piston moves up on the second stroke, the compression stroke, to compress the mixture which is then ignited by the spark plug. The expansion of the burning mixture drives the piston back down on its power stroke.

The cycle is completed by the next upstroke of the piston. As the piston rises, the exhaust valve opens and the exhaust gases are forced out of the cylinder. Then the exhaust valve closes and the cycle begins again.

Carburation

As the air is drawn through the carburettor by suction from the engine, it passes through a narrow passage called a *venturi* or *choke* (barrel). This narrowing of the air's path causes an increase in its velocity, and this increase in velocity causes a decrease in the air's pressure.

A small nozzle or *jet*, connected to the fuel supply, is positioned at the venturi, and the low pressure air flow sucks a fine spray of fuel out of the jet. This fine spray vaporizes and mixes with the air, in a ratio (by weight) of approximately 15 parts air to 1 part fuel. The amount of mixture drawn into the engine, which determines its speed, is controlled by a flap-like *butterfly valve* or *throttle* connected to the accelerator control.

On engines with more than one cylinder, the carburettor feeds the mixture into a *manifold*, a set of pipes connecting it with each of the cylinder inlets. Each cylinder draws mixture from the carburretor in turn. Many large engines have more than one carburettor, or a carburettor with more than one choke, to improve the flow of mixture to the cylinders.

A high voltage of up to 30,000 volts is needed to create the spark across the spark plug gap, and this voltage is supplied by the *ignition coil*. Current from a low voltage supply (such as the 12V supply from a car's battery) is fed into the low tension (lt) winding of the coil, which consists of a few hundred turns of copper wire wound on a soft iron core.

The flow of current sets up a magnetic field in the coil. When the current flow is switched off by a set of contact breaker points, operated by a cam driven by the engine, this magnetic field dies away or 'collapses'. The collapsing magnetic field creates or *induces* flow of current in the high tension (ht) winding of the coil. In comparison to the few hundred turns of relatively heavy wire which make up the lt winding, the ht winding consists of many thousands of turns of fine copper wire. This also is wound around the soft iron core.

When one coil induces a current in another, as in an ignition coil, the ratio of the initial voltage to the induced voltage is the same as the ratio of the number of turns of wire on the first coil to the number of turns on the second coil. This means that if the second coil has a thousand times more turns than the first, the induced voltage will be a thousand times greater than the initial voltage.

The high voltage pulse created by the coil is fed to the spark plug, where it travels down the centre electrode to its tip, which is inside the cylinder, and then sparks across to the other electrode. On multi-cylinder engines the pulses from the coil are fed to the *distributor*, which then distributes them to each cylinder in turn.

On many modern engines the current in the low tension circuit is controlled by an electronic circuit instead of by a mechani-

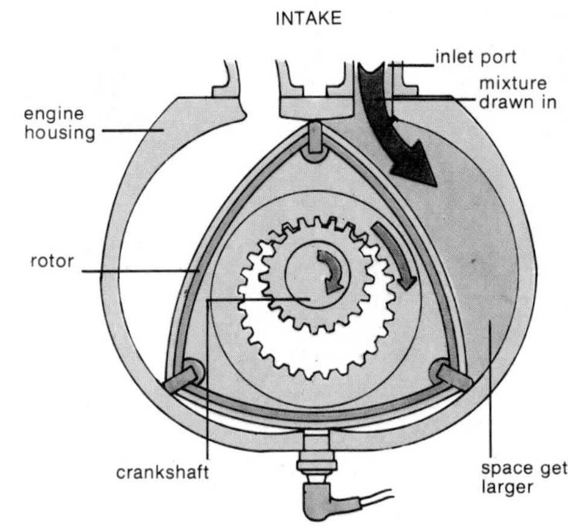

Picturepoint

ROTARY MOTOR CYCLE ENGINE

1. Air intake for carburettor
2. Carburettor
3. Cooling passages in rotor housing
4. Thermostatic switch for radiator fan
5. Inlet port (exhaust port below)
6. Wax thermostat
7. Rotor set trochoid pump for metering oil
8. Coolant pump rotor
9. Coolant pump volute
10. Ignition contact breaker (3 sets of points)
11. Oil filter
12. Oil sump inlet strainer
13. Chain tensioner
14. Multi-plate clutch
15. Twin drive chains from engine to clutch
16. Kick starter shaft
17. Kick starter freewheel mechanism
18. 5 speed gearbox
19. Chain lubricator
20. Drive chain to rear wheel
21. Electric starter
22. Spark plug
23. Tip seal
24. Rotor
25. 3 phase alternator
26. Combustion chamber

Above: A four-stroke diesel engine for use in particularly heavy commercial vehicles.

Below: A diesel draws in air, compresses it to raise its temperature to over 550°C (1022°F), then sprays in the fuel which ignites spontaneously in the hot air and drives the piston down on its power stroke.

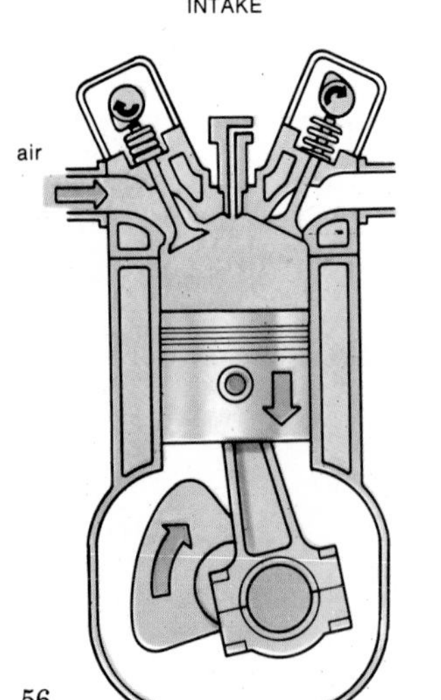

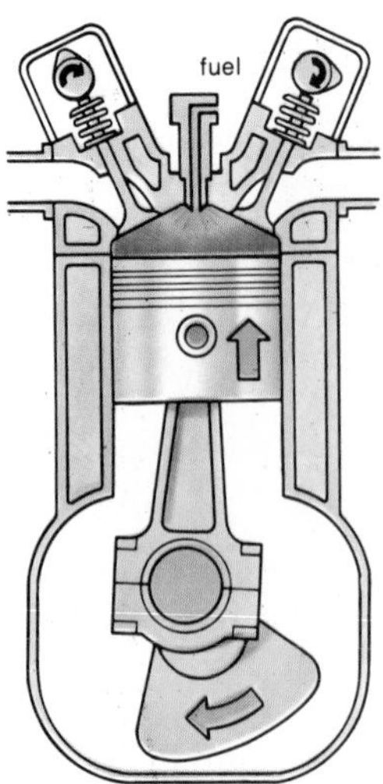

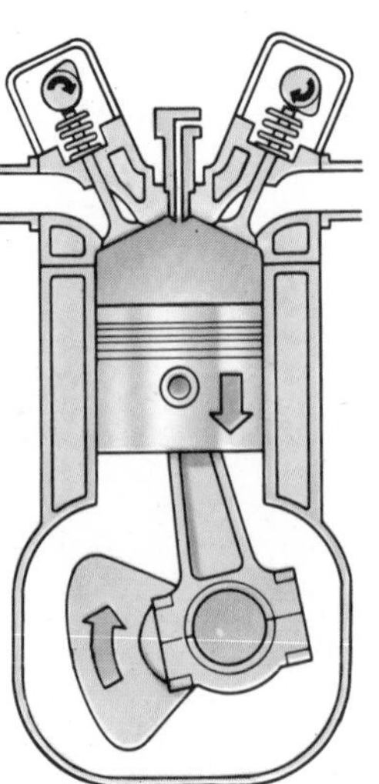

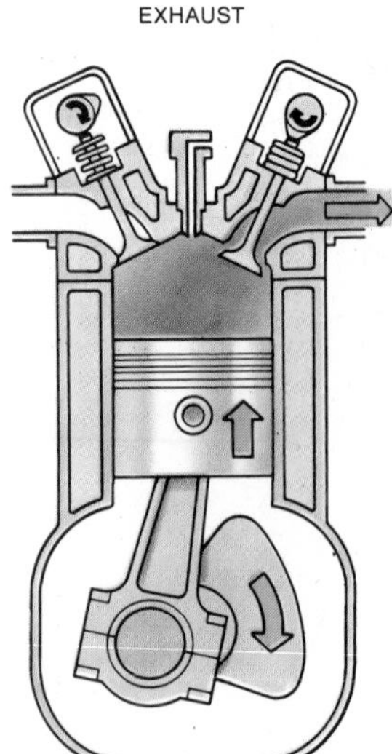

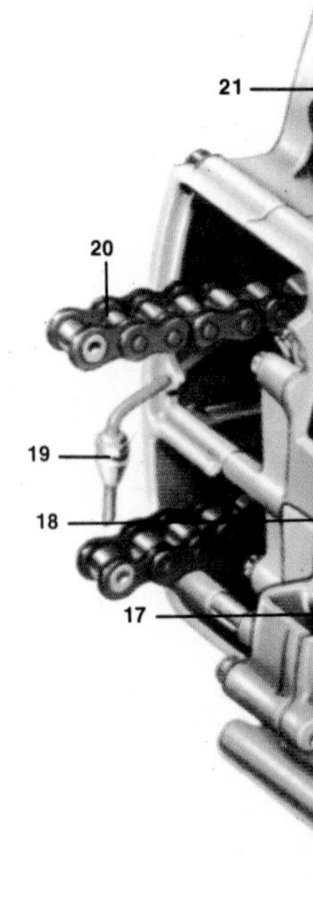

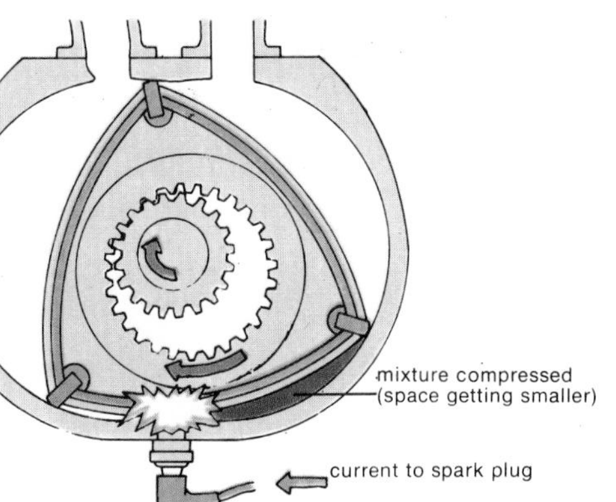

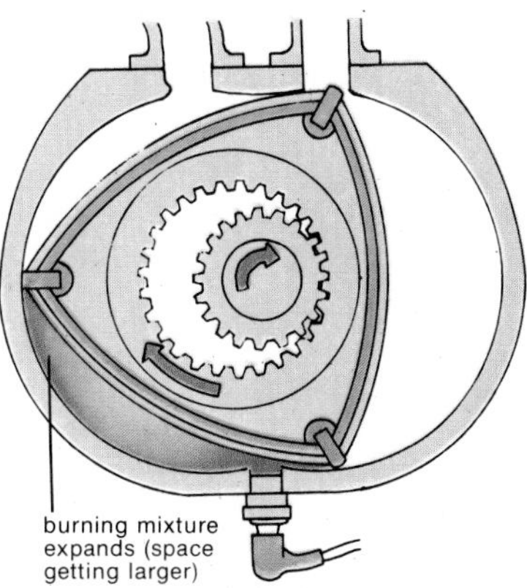

EXHAUST

Above: A Wankel rotary engine has a three-lobed rotor which rotates eccentrically around a fixed gear. This turns a crankshaft (not shown) which passes through the centre of the fixed gear and fits into the central recess of the rotor. As each face of the rotor passes the inlet port it draws in fuel mixture. The rotor then compresses the mixture and the spark plug ignites it. The exploding gases expand and push the rotor on round. The rotor tip seals may be lubricated by oil mixed with the fuel, or by oil sprayed directly into the rotor housing.

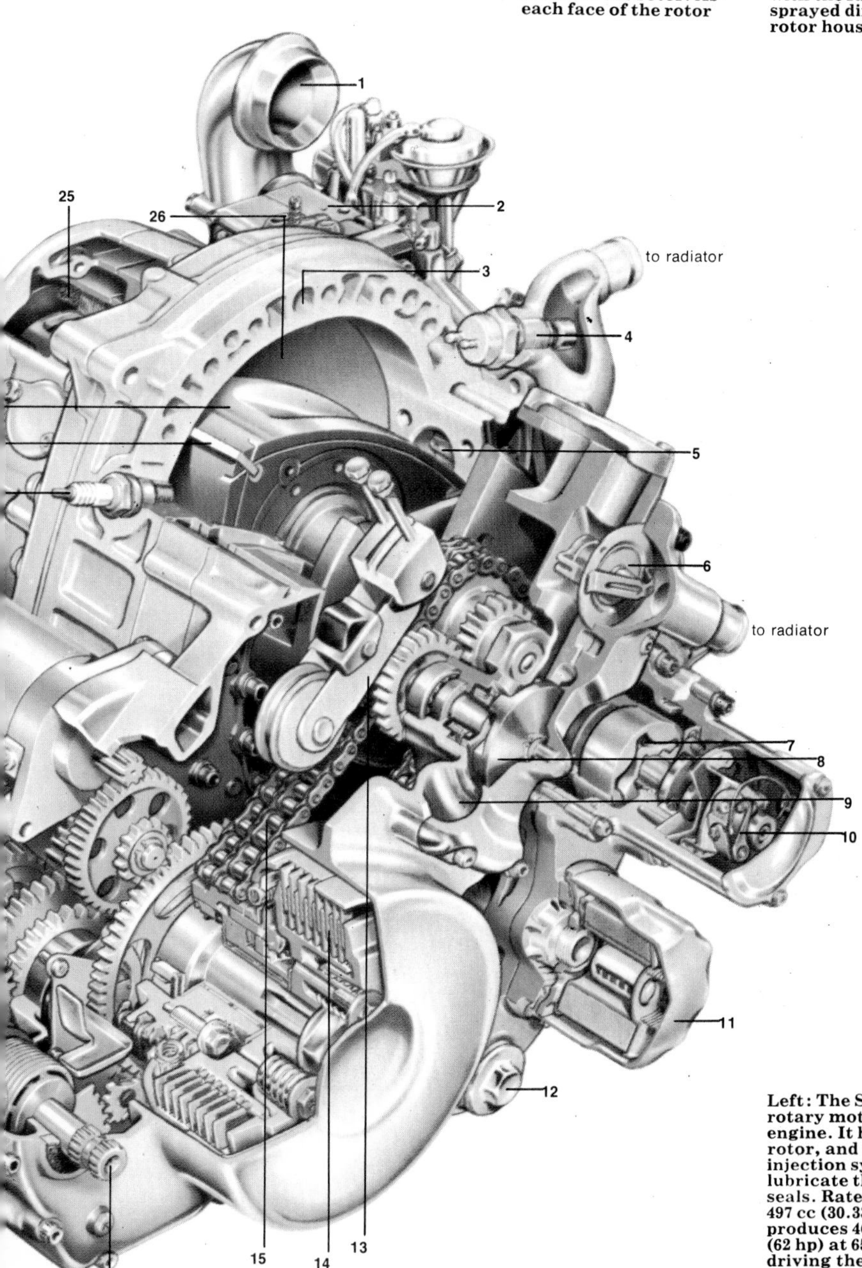

Left: The Suzuki RE5 rotary motorcycle engine. It has a single rotor, and an oil injection system to lubricate the rotor tip seals. Rated capacity is 497 cc (30.33 in^3), and it produces 46.2 kW (62 hp) at 6500 rpm, driving the bike through an integral five-speed gearbox.

cal contact breaker unit. Some also use fuel injection systems instead of carburettors, the petrol being sprayed directly into the cylinder instead of being mixed in a carburettor.

Diesel engines

The first diesel engine was built by Rudolf Diesel at Augsburg in Germany in 1897. Diesel engines, which may be either two-stroke or four-stroke, differ from petrol engines in several important respects. Only pure air is drawn into the cylinder on the induction stroke of the piston, and it is compressed to a much greater degree than is the fuel/air mixture of a petrol engine.

This high compression of the air raises its temperature to well over 550°C (1022°F). As the piston nears the top of its travel a measured amount of fuel is sprayed into this hot air by an injector nozzle fed by a pump unit.

The air is so hot that the fuel ignites spontaneously as it mixes with it, without needing a spark to set it off. As there is no carburettor, the speed of a diesel engine is controlled by altering the amount of fuel delivered to the injector by the pump. There is an injector in each cylinder of a multi-cylinder diesel engine, and the pump delivers a shot of fuel to each injector. Diesel engines can be modified to run on almost any kind of inflammable fuel, but most of them run on diesel oil.

Cooling and lubrication

The combustion process inside the cylinders of an engine creates a large amount of heat, so without some form of cooling the temperature of the engine would rise rapidly. This would lead to a loss of performance and possibly internal damage due to the expansion of engine components; for instance the pistons could jam or 'seize up' within the cylinders.

Air-cooled engines have cooling fins on the outside of the cylinders, which increase their surface area so that the heat is carried away quicker by the surrounding air. Greater cooling is achieved by using a fan, driven by the engine, to blow air through the fins.

Water-cooled engines have water circulating in passageways around and between the cylinders to carry the heat away, and the water itself is cooled by passing it through a radiator. Most water-cooled engines have fans to draw air through the radiator and so increase the rate of cooling of the water.

Steam Engines and Turbines

Despite a tendency to regard steam power as a symbol of obsolescence, it continues to provide much of the energy used in modern society and there is, as yet, no practical alternative. Indeed, even the most advanced nuclear power station reactor is merely a source of heat to produce the steam which drives the generator turbines. Steam engines and turbines are good examples of energy conversion systems, in this case converting heat into mechanical energy.

The heat energy in steam is in a very convenient state for conversion into mechanical energy. Steam engines and turbines do this by expanding a supply of steam from a small volume at high pressure to a large volume at low pressure, with a corresponding fall in temperature. In steam engines this expansion moves a piston to-and-fro in a cylinder; turbines use it to give velocity to a flow of steam which then turns a rotor. Both machines are *external combustion heat engines*, that is, their fuel is burnt outside the working section. This permits better control of the combustion, and so the fuel can be burned under optimum conditions for avoiding atmospheric pollution.

Steam is generated in boilers heated either by furnaces fired by any convenient fuel such as oil or coal, or by some flow of hot fluid like the coolant from a nuclear reactor or the waste gases from a metal-smelting furnace.

The main types of boiler are the *shell* boiler, the *fire-tube* boiler and the *water-tube* boiler. The shell type boiler is cylindrical with internal flues, and is often set in brickwork containing *return flues* which carry the heat round to heat the outside of the boiler shell. The 'Lancashire' boiler, with two furnaces, is typical of this class.

In fire-tube boilers, as used on locomotives, the hot gases from the furnace pass through an array of small tubes immersed in water. In the water-tube boiler, on the other hand, arrays of small tubes carry the water through the combustion chamber. Although this type is more expensive to build, it is the most suitable for high pressure work, and is commonly used to supply turbines.

Steam engines

Most steam engines are *double acting*, that is, both sides of the piston are used to produce power, one side of the piston making a power stroke during the exhaust stroke of the other. The sequence of events during one revolution begins when steam is admitted to the cylinder just before the end of the previous stroke.

Next, the inlet port closes (known as *cut-off*) and the steam expands, driving the piston back down the cylinder. Just before the end of the power stroke the exhaust port opens, (known as *release*), and on the return stroke most of the steam is driven out of the cylinder. Finally the exhaust port closes and the remaining steam is compressed until admission begins again.

In most engines the whole sequence of events for both sides of the piston is

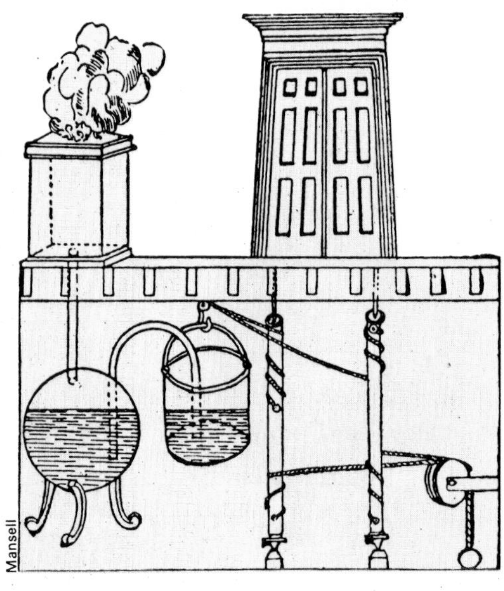

Above: The fact that heat could be converted into mechanical energy was known almost 2,000 years ago. This system, devised before 100AD by Hero of Alexandria, used the expansion of hot air beneath the fire on the the hollow altar to drive water from the container into the bucket—which then descended and opened the temple doors.

Right: Newcomen's 'atmospheric' engine of 1710. Steam from the boiler 'a' was admitted to the cylinder 'c' and this pushed the piston up. A jet of cold water was then sprayed into the cylinder, condensing the steam, and the piston was driven back down by atmospheric pressure acting on its top surface.

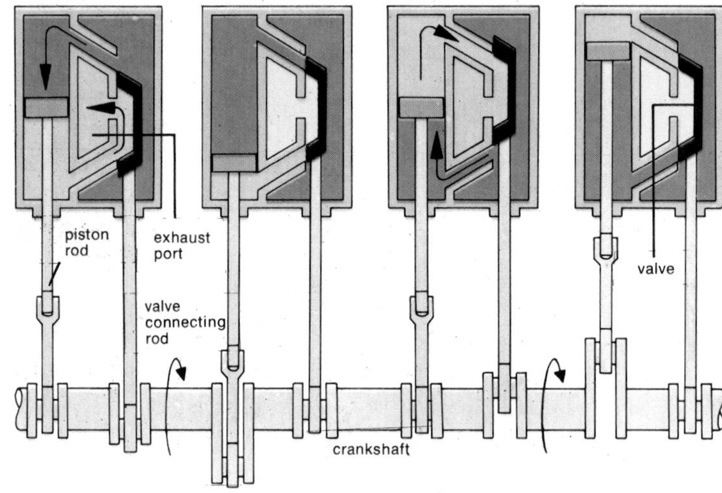

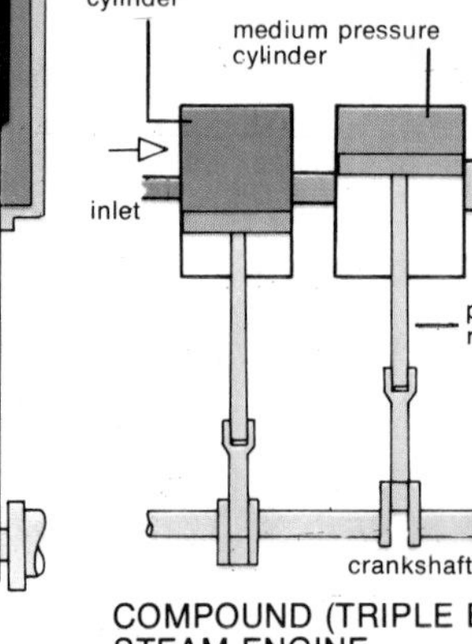

Above left: The operating principles of a double-acting steam engine, showing the action of the slide valve which controls the supply of steam to the cylinder.

Above: In a triple expansion engine the steam is passed from one cylinder to the next as its pressure drops.

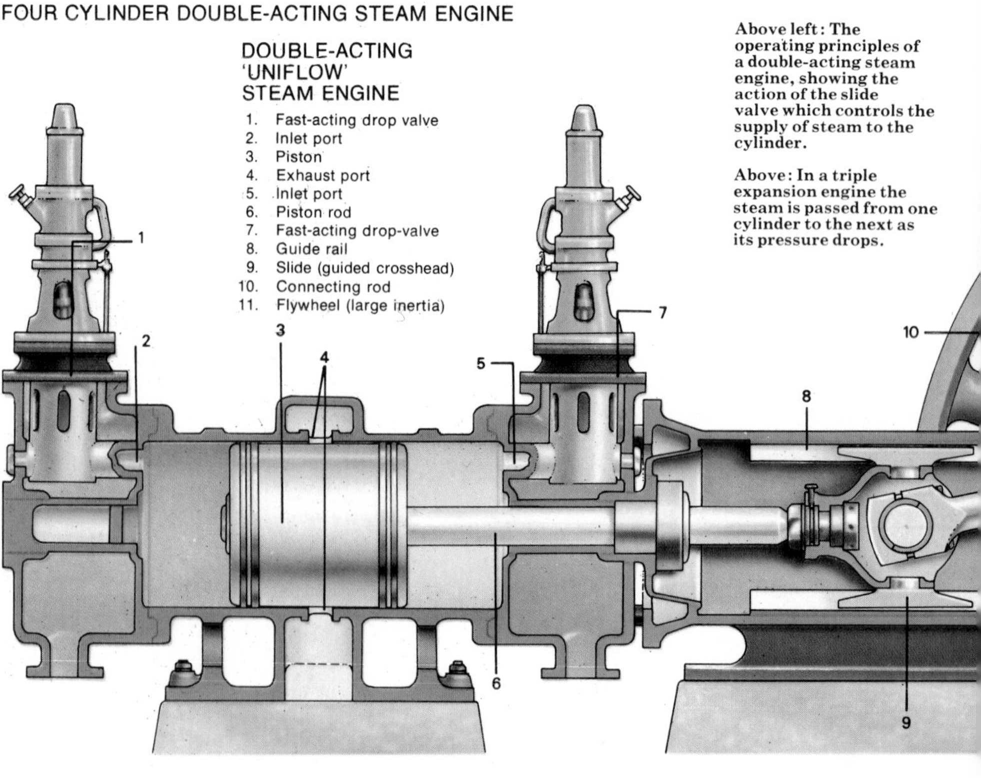

Mansell

Left: James Watt was working as an instrument repairer in Glasgow University in 1763 when he was given a model Newcomen engine to repair. It occurred to him that the alternate heating and cooling of the cylinder was very inefficient, and so he designed an engine with a 'separate condenser'. This was a separate chamber into which the steam was led for condensation, so that the cylinder could be kept hot, and this greatly improved the engine's performance. He went on to design engines which drove rotating shafts instead of rocking beams, and he also invented the double-acting engine. The *watt*, the metric unit of power, is named after him.

John Watney

Radio Times Hulton Picture Library

Above: A two-cylinder high pressure steam engine which was installed in a small cargo boat.

Left: An early pioneer of the French motor industry, the Marquis de Dion, driving a steam tricycle which he built in 1897. The engine is at the front and drives the rear wheel.

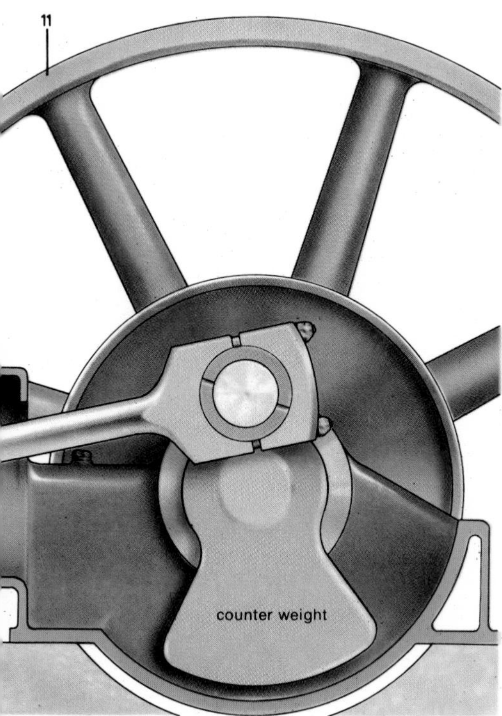

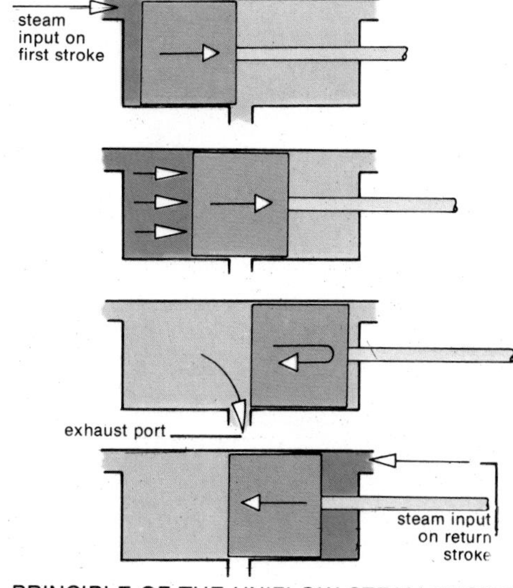

Left: A diagram of a uniflow steam engine, which has an inlet valve at each end of the cylinder and a ring of exhaust ports half way along it.

Above: In the uniflow engine, steam is admitted at each end in turn, driving the piston up and down the cylinder and escaping through the exhaust ports.

controlled by a single D-shaped valve, which slides along the cylinder to open and close the ports in sequence. Some large stationary engines have separate inlet and exhaust valves for each side of the piston.

The to-and-fro motion of the piston is converted into rotary motion by a crank linked to the piston rod by a connecting rod. The inertia of a flywheel carries the crank on round past the places where the rod is in line with the crank arm and has no turning effect on it.

As the crank turns, the angle between the connecting rod and the piston rod is constantly changing. To allow for this, the connecting rod must be pivoted where it meets the piston rod. The most common arrangement uses a metal block which slides along guide rails at the end of the cylinder and connects the piston rod to the connecting rod. This sytem, the *guided crosshead*, is the one used on steam locomotives and in marine engines.

Some *single-acting* engines, where one side of the piston is used to produce power, have the connecting rod attached directly to the piston by a metal pin, the *gudgeon pin*, as in a petrol engine or diesel engine.

Compound engines

In a single cylinder, if the difference between the volume of the steam at cut-off and its volume at release is very large, the temperature variations of the cylinder wall which result will cause heat losses. These are unacceptable because the lost heat has to be replaced by burning more fuel, or else the temperature variations must be reduced by limiting the pressure of steam admitted to the cylinder to such an extent that the power of the engine is greatly reduced.

A solution to this was found by using a small, high pressure cylinder whose exhaust steam was passed into a larger, low pressure one. Such combinations are called *compound engines* and were made in several forms, some of which are still found in industrial engine-houses.

Triple expansion engines, with high pressure (HP), intermediate (IP), and one or two low pressure (LP) cylinders were used extensively in ships. The Atlantic liner *Olympic* (1911-36) had two such engines, each with a 1372 mm (54 in) HP cylinder, a 2134 mm (84 in) IP cylinder, and two 2464 mm (97 in) LP cylinders. Each engine developed 11,185 kW (15,000 hp) at 75 rpm.

Quadruple expansion engines were also used at sea, particularly in German ships around the turn of the century. One example, the *Kaiser Wilhelm II* built in 1902, had a total of eight cylinders and produced 16,033 kW (21,500 hp).

Uniflow engines

Uniflow engines are double-acting engines which release most of the expanded steam through a ring of exhaust ports in the cylinder wall. The ports are about half way along the cylinder, so that during most of the power stroke of either side of the piston, the piston is either between the inlet valve and the exhaust ports or closing off the exhaust ports.

A total expansion greater than in most compound engines is achieved in one cylinder at an almost constant wall temperature. Many large engines were built on this principle between 1908 and

Below: The upper drawing shows the steam path through a compound turbine which has six high pressure and four low pressure stages. The lower drawing shows the steam flow in a radial flow turbine. A rotating disc carries rings of blades which move within the fixed blades, and the steam flows outwards through them.

COMPOUNDED TURBINE

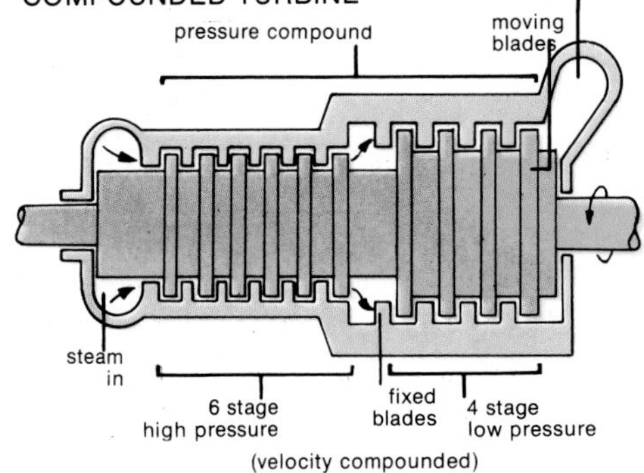

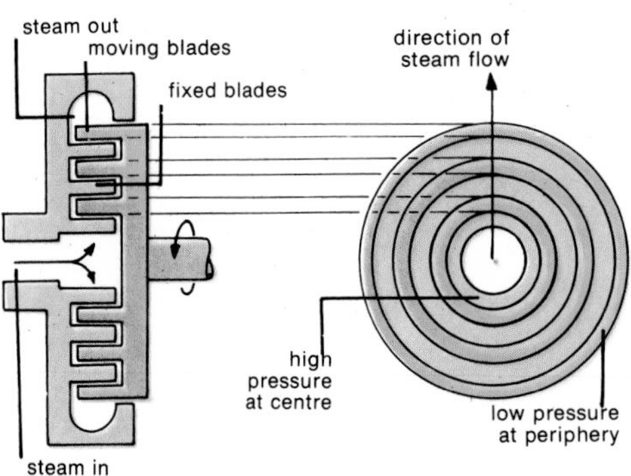

PRINCIPLE OF RADIAL-FLOW TURBINE

Right: Another of Hero's inventions, the 'Aeolipile', a kind of steam turbine. The tubes fixed to the hollow sphere had their ends bent over in opposite directions. The sphere was mounted over a boiler. Steam passed into it through the hollow bearings, to escape through the tubes and rotate the sphere.

Radio Times Hulton Picture Library

Below right: A single stage velocity-compounded turbine. The steam enters through the admission valve, and passes into the nozzle passages where it expands as its pressure drops. This expansion increases its velocity and it then passes rapidly through the blades, turning the rotor as it goes.

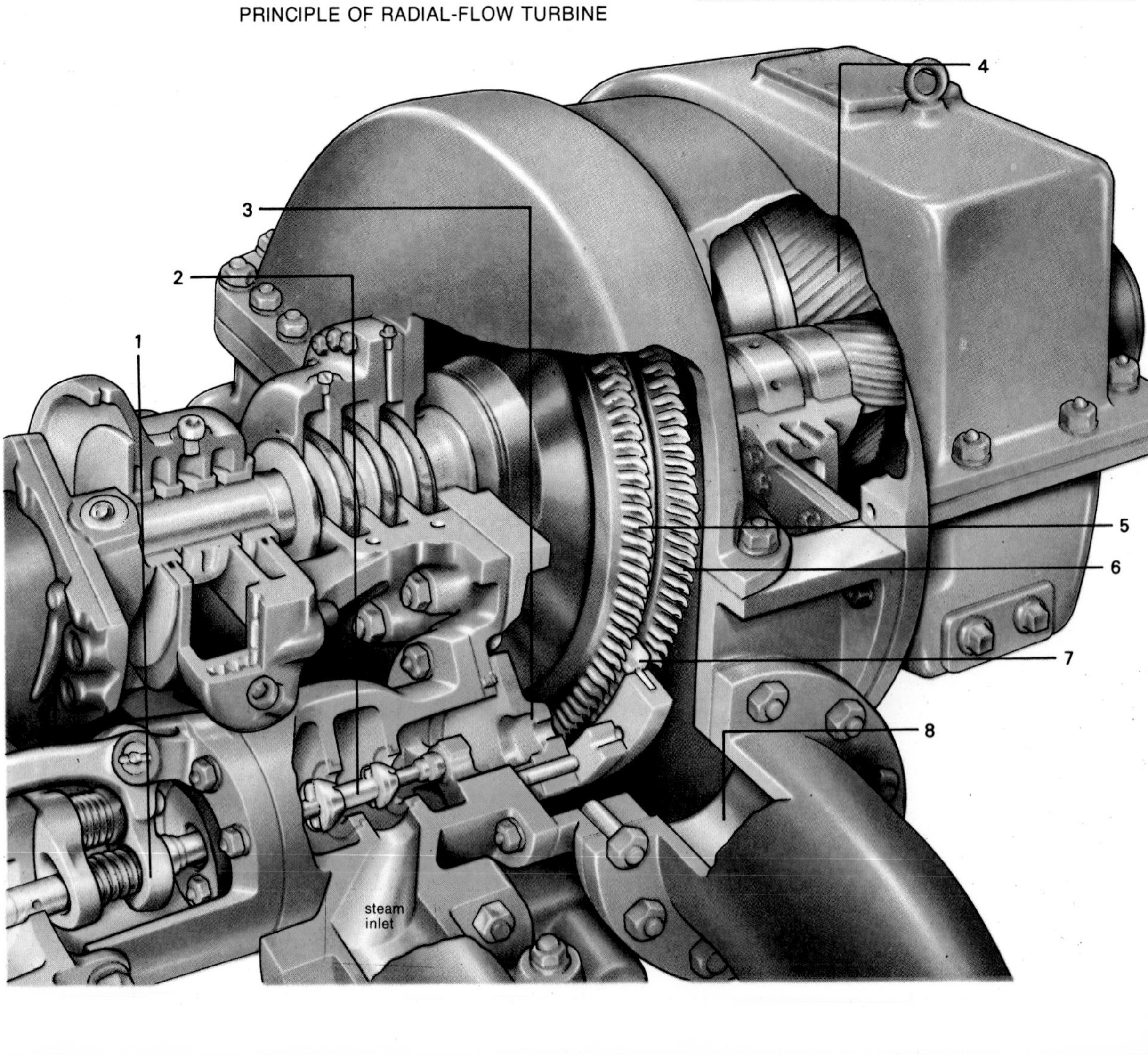

SINGLE-STAGE VELOCITY-COMPOUNDED TURBINE

1. Inlet valve governing mechanism
2. Inlet valve
3. Steam nozzle
4. Speed reduction gears
5. Moving blades (first set)
6. Moving blades (second set)
7. Intermediary fixed blades
8. Steam outlet

steam inlet

Photri

Above: The rotor and blades of the first turbine built by Sir Charles Parsons in 1884. The steam entered at the centre and flowed outwards towards the ends, turning the rotor at 18,000 rpm. The turbine was used to drive an electricity generator on board a ship and it remained in use for 16 years.

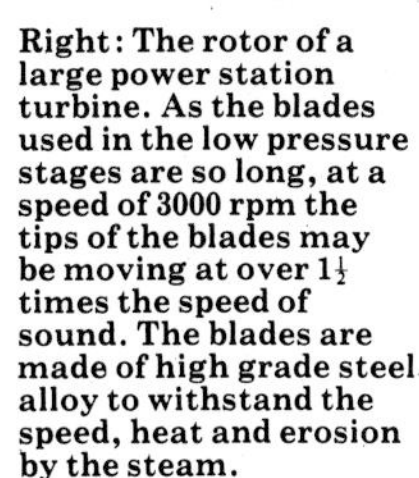

Below: This miniature turbine set was used in the Second World War to provide electricity for paratroops' radio and signals equipment. A fire was lit beneath the boiler to the left, and the steam was passed through the hoses to the generator turbine on the right. Power output was about 48 watts (8 amps at 6 volts).

ASEA

Right: The rotor of a large power station turbine. As the blades used in the low pressure stages are so long, at a speed of 3000 rpm the tips of the blades may be moving at over 1½ times the speed of sound. The blades are made of high grade steel alloy to withstand the speed, heat and erosion by the steam.

John Watney

1958, several uniflow cylinders being used in parallel for the largest. A five-cylinder German engine of the 1930s produced 22,371 kW (30,000 hp) to drive a rolling mill in a steelworks, and was the most powerful steam engine ever built.

Steam engine applications

Almost every type of machine that moves has at some time been driven by steam, either directly or through shafts and belts. In Victorian times the steam engine provided the power to print newspapers, spin and weave textiles, pump water, and power washing machines in 'steam laundries'. Portable steam engines ploughed and drained the land, threshed corn, drove fairground machines and even vacuum cleaners for cleaning-contractors. There were even steam driven scalp massage brushes in some barbers' shops.

Most of these applications will never return, but one which may be revived is the steam car. Several types were built in considerable numbers before the First World War, but went out of favour as the petrol engined car grew more efficient.

Steam turbines

The first practical steam turbines were built in the late nineteenth century by Carl De Laval in Sweden and Sir Charles Parsons in England. The main working part of a turbine is a rotor, which carries a set of blades, and is contained inside a casing which has a set of fixed blades to direct the flow of steam. A rotor can be regarded as a sort of windmill, each blade being a sail and the flow of steam acting like an enormously strong wind.

Expanding steam moves very fast: for example, expansion from a pressure of about twelve times atmospheric pressure down to about half atmospheric pressure produces a velocity of about 1100 m/sec (3600 ft/sec). The optimum speed of the moving blades for the transfer of kinetic energy from the steam to the rotor is half that of the steam. For instance, in the above example the ideal rotor speed would be 550 m/sec (1800 ft/sec). This is not always possible to achieve, however, and so the turbine may not be able to extract all the available energy from the steam.

Excessive steam speeds which can lead to this kind of energy loss are often avoided by using several sets of fixed and moving blades, and allowing only a fraction of the total pressure drop to occur in each set. Such turbines are said to be *pressure-compounded*. The blades are made progressively longer from the inlet to the exhaust end to allow room for the greater volume of steam at the lower pressures. This is comparable to the progressive increase in the size of the cylinders of a compound steam engine, where the high pressure cylinder is smaller than the intermediate and low pressure cylinders.

When a large pressure drop cannot be avoided, the steam leaving a row of moving blades is often re-directed on to a second, and sometimes a third, row of moving blades without further expansion. This sytem is called *velocity-compounding*.

There are two basic classes of turbine blading: *impulse*, in which the steam expands only in the fixed blades, and *reaction*, in which the steam expands in both the fixed and the moving blades. Steam has to be admitted to the whole circumference of the rotor when reaction blading is used, but impulse blading can be worked with some of the inlet nozzles shut off if required. Large turbines often have both types of blading, carried by several rotors in separate casings.

Power station turbines

The very large turbines used in power stations run at constant speeds, the speed being determined by the mains frequency of the system for which they are generating electricity. In most European countries, for instance, the frequency is 50 Hz (50 cycles per second) and the speed of the turbines is 3000 rpm. In North America, the frequency is 60 Hz and so the turbine speed is 3600 rpm.

A single line of rotors driving one alternator (ac generator) is used for powers up to 300 MW (300,000 kW). Two lines, interconnected on the steam side but with separate alternators, are used for greater power, sometimes as much as 600 MW. Such turbines are called *cross-compounded*.

Double-flow rotors, in which steam is admitted half-way along the cylinder and expands outwards towards both ends, are often used. These avoid excessive blade lengths for handling the large volumes of steam at the low pressure end and balance the pressure thrusts of reaction blading. The low pressure ends of the largest turbines comprise several double-flow rotors working in parallel.

Marine turbines

Smaller turbines are used in ships than in power stations because their size and speed must suit propeller requirements. The turbine may drive the propeller shaft through a set of reduction gears, or it may drive a generator which powers an electric motor that in turn drives the propeller shaft.

Large marine turbines are cross-compounded to save length. For example, the *Queen Elizabeth II* has two turbines, each developing 41,013 kW (55,000 hp) from two cross-compound rotors, one impulse and one double-flow reaction.

Jets and Gas Turbines

The invention of the jet engine had a tremendous impact on aviation. The world's first military jet was the German Messerschmitt Me 262, which went into service as a light bomber in 1944, and the first jet airliner was the de Havilland Comet, which made its first commercial flight on 2 May 1952. The jet engine is now extremely important in the field of aviation, but the gas turbine engine from which it was derived is also important in many others areas, including marine propulsion and electricity generation.

In both the gas turbine and the jet engine, air is drawn in at the front and compressed. Then fuel is burned in the compressed air, and the resulting gases expand rapidly through a turbine section.

One of the earliest patents for a gas turbine engine operating on similar principles to modern ones was that issued to John Barber in England in 1791, but the first successful engines were not built until the early twentieth century.

Dave Hoskings

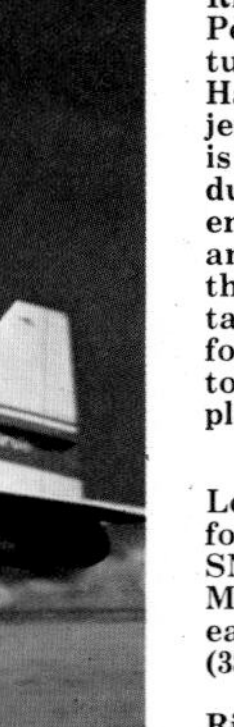

Right: The Rolls-Royce Pegasus vectored-thrust turbofan used by the Harrier vertical take-off jet. The jet exhaust is emitted through the ducts at the sides of the engine, which can be angled to direct the thrust downwards for take-off, to the rear for forward flight, or to the front to make the plane fly backwards.

Left: The Concorde uses four Rolls-Royce/SNECMA Olympus 593 Mk 602 turbojet engines, each developing 17,260 kg (38,050 lb) thrust.

Right: An Olympus 593 engine. The original Olympus engines were developed in the early 1950s, and turboshaft versions are used in ships and generators.

Picturepoint

ZEFA

Right: The Vickers Viscount airliner uses four Rolls-Royce Dart RDa 7/1 Mk 525 turboprop engines, each developing 1484 kW (1990 hp).

Far right: A Pratt and Whitney JT9D turbofan on a Boeing 747 airliner. The JT9D-7W version of this engine produces 21,320 kg (47,000 lb) of thrust.

Rolls Royce

Left: A Lynx helicopter is driven by a pair of Rolls-Royce BS 360 Gem turboshaft engines mounted side-by-side behind the main rotor shaft. The engines, capable of producing 670 kW (900 hp) each, drive the rotor via a reduction gearbox, and a transmission shaft takes the drive to the tail rotor.

ZEFA

Right: The McDonnell Douglas DC-10 airliner is powered by three General Electric CF6-50A turbofans, two of which are mounted under the wings with the third, shown here, in the tail.

Below: Checking a Rolls-Royce RB211 turbofan with an X-ray camera mounted on a fork lift truck.

The Swiss firm of Brown-Boveri ran a successful gas turbine in 1906 which was identical in principle to modern engines. This engine had an *axial* compressor, so named because the air enters and flows through it parallel to the axis of rotation of the compressor. The compressor consists of a series of discs or rings, each carrying blades projecting radially like spokes, which are assembled into a strong, light drum capable of rotating at high speed.

This compressor *rotor* revolves inside a closely fitting casing which has sets of stationary blades (*stator* blades) which just fit between the revolving blades of the rotor. When the rotor is spinning at high speed, air is drawn in and compressed as it passes through the sets or *stages* of fixed and moving blades, before being discharged at the rear of the compressor.

In early engines as many as 20 stages of blading were needed for a pressure ratio of 3:1, that is, for the outlet air to be at three times the pressure of the inlet air. Today it is possible to build compressors of much higher efficiency, which can achieve a pressure ratio of 30:1 with twelve stages.

With such high compression the air

John Ross/Robert Harding

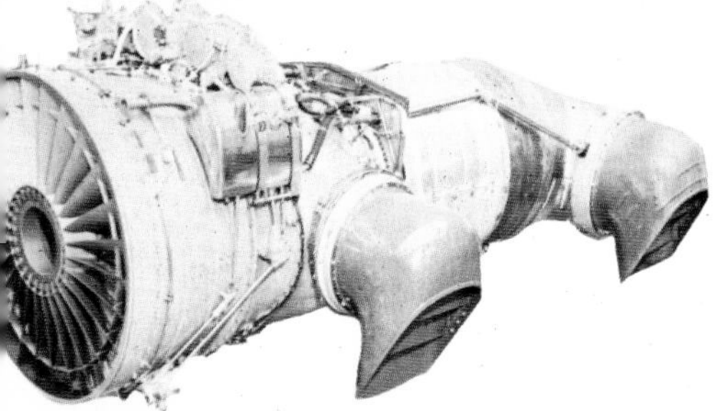

Rolls Royce

becomes so hot that the downstream stages have to be made of *refractory* (heat resistant) alloys.

From the compressor, the hot, high pressure air is fed through the combustion chamber where the fuel is added to it. A few gas turbines have run on pulverized coal or peat, but almost all use liquid fuels. An advantage of these engines is their ability to run on a wide range of fuels and, although most run on kerosene it is possible to run gas turbines on heavy oils, high-octane petrol or natural gas.

An enormous amount of heat energy can be generated within the combustion chamber of a modern engine. As much as 37,350 kW (50,000 hp) can be produced in a combustion chamber whose volume is less than that of a briefcase.

From the combustion chamber the gas, now at perhaps 1300°C (2372°F), flows at high speed through the turbine section of the engine. Like the compressor, this consists of several axial stages, each separated by a row of stator blades which direct the flow on to the row of rotor blades immediately downstream, causing the rotor to revolve at high speed.

The rotor drives the compressor, usually by means of a simple drive shaft. It may also drive the machinery that the turbine is powering, or additional turbines may be used for this purpose.

Turboprops and turboshafts

The *turboprop* engine is a gas turbine engine which drives an aircraft propeller. The drive is taken from the turbine to the propeller via a gearbox because of the great difference in the rotational speeds of the rotor and the propellor.

For example, the Canadian Pratt and Whitney PT6 engine, used on many light transport planes such as those built by de Havilland of Canada, has a drive ratio of 15:1, linking a 33,000 rpm turbine with a 2,200 rpm propeller. The latest version has a 22.74:1 gearbox ratio, the 30,017 rpm turbine driving a larger propeller at only 1,320 rpm for lower noise.

In some engines, instead of having one turbine to drive both the compressor and the propeller, there are two turbines. The gas from the combustion chamber passes first through the compressor drive turbine, and then through the *free turbine*, which is mounted on a separate shaft to the compressor and its turbine. The propeller gearbox drive is taken from this shaft.

Sometimes a free-turbine type of turboprop is installed 'back to front', with the compressor at the rear and an arrange-

Right: The Rolls-Royce RB211 turbofan has three shafts or 'spools', carrying the low, intermediate and high pressure turbines and compressors (the low pressure compressor being the fan). The Lockheed L-1011-200 TriStar is powered by three RB211-524 engines, which deliver 21,775 kg (48,000 lb) thrust each.

Rolls-Royce RB-211
1 ip turbine
2 lp turbine
3 hp turbine
4 annular combustors
5 bleed air cooling
6 hp compressor discs
7 hp compressor blades
8 ip compressor discs
9 ip compressor blades
10 fan casing
11 guide vanes
12 33-blade titanium fan
13 inlet guide vanes
14 lp (fan) shaft
15 shaft coupling
16 engine core
17 ip shaft
18 hp shaft
19 rear shaft bearings
20 turbine discs
21 tail cone

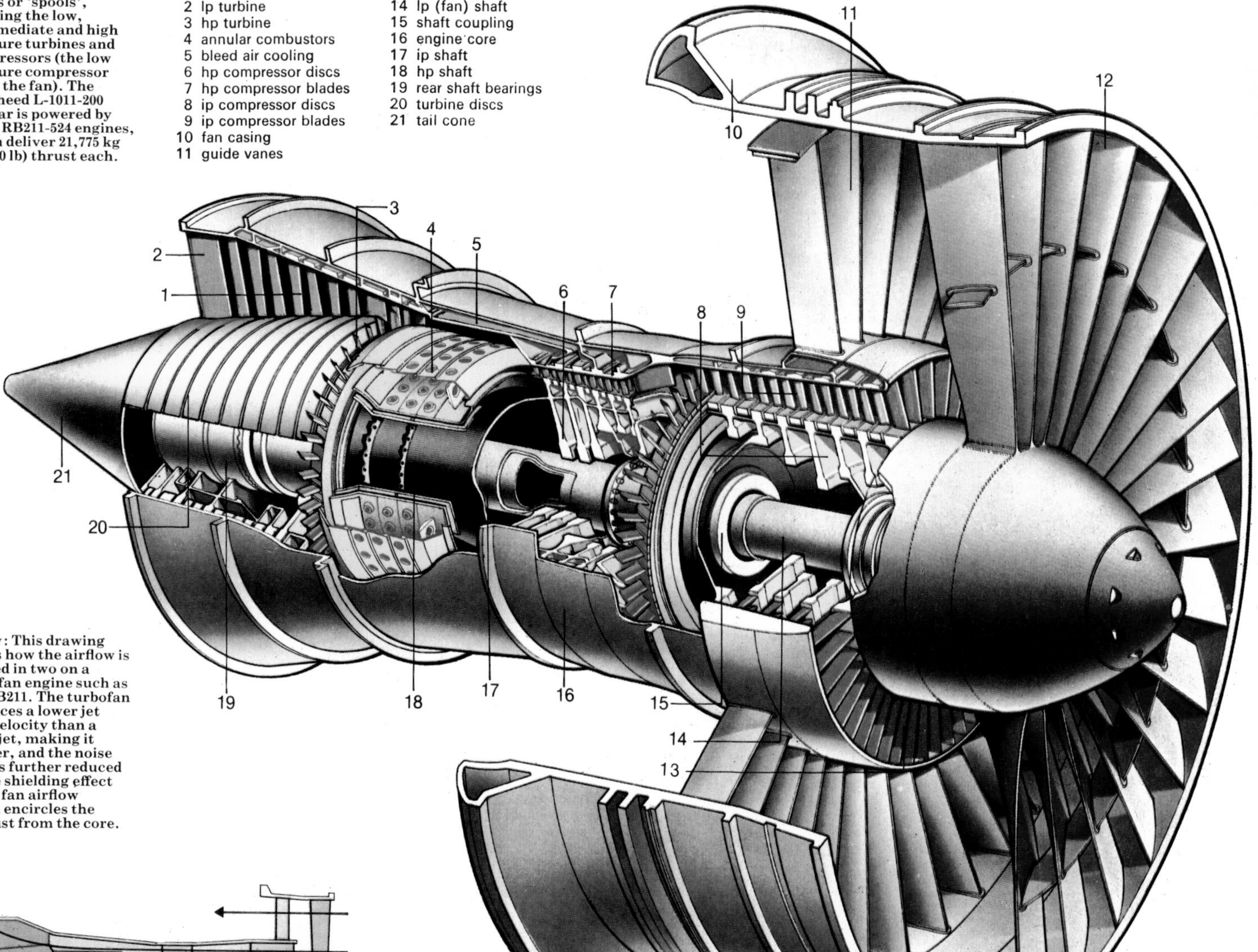

Below: This drawing shows how the airflow is divided in two on a turbofan engine such as the RB211. The turbofan produces a lower jet flow velocity than a turbojet, making it quieter, and the noise level is further reduced by the shielding effect of the fan airflow which encircles the exhaust from the core.

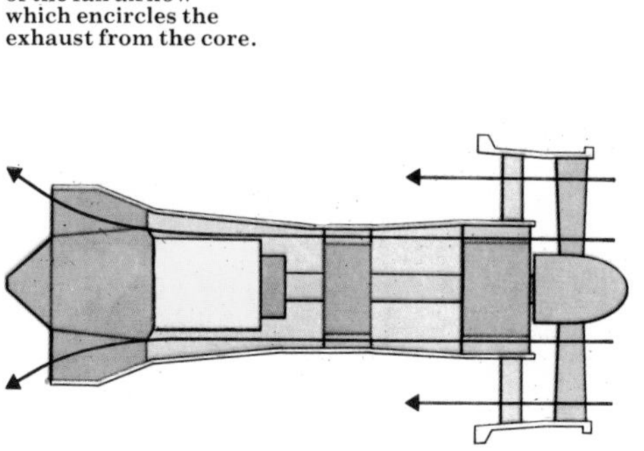

ment of ducts and vents to guide the inlet air into the compressor and deflect the exhaust gases away from the inlet. This simplifies the drive shaft arrangements which would be necessary to drive a front propeller if the engine were installed in the normal way.

Turboprops have not been produced for large aircraft since 1955, except for a small number of specialized military aircraft. Smaller turboprops, however, are being produced in increasing numbers for private and business aircraft and short-range transport aircraft. The small turboprop is gradually eating into the last remaining market for the aircraft piston engine.

Turboshafts are gas turbines used as a source of shaft power. They are used to drive naval craft of all kinds, fast container ships, hydrofoils, hovercraft, trains, electricity generators, and large-scale oil and gas pumping units. They are also being developed for use in heavy road trucks and other vehicles.

Turbojets and turbofans

The first jet engines were developed independently in the 1930s by Frank Whittle in England and Dr. Hans von Ohain in Germany. The jet is basically a gas turbine engine; the essential difference is that the turbine section extracts only a part of the energy of the gas flow. This extracted energy is just sufficient to drive the compressor in a *turbojet* or the compressor and a fan in a *turbofan*. The rest is used to accelerate the gas out through a nozzle at the rear of the engine —so driving the aircraft forward.

Newton's third law of motion states that for every action there is an equal but opposite reaction. In the case of the jet engine, pushing large amounts of gas rearwards at high velocity is the action, and the reaction to this is the forward thrust on the engine.

Whittle's first engine ran in April 1937, and the first British jet plane the Gloster E28/39 flew in May 1941. By the end of the Second World War, refined forms of this engine had been built in Britain and the USA for use in fighter aircraft.

Whittle's engine used a *centrifugal* compressor, because despite being fatter and less efficient than an axial compressor it was already well developed and easier to make. This type of compressor is essentially a spinning disc on which curved walls fling the airflow outwards at high velocity. Around the disc, often called the *impeller*, is a fixed deflector or *diffuser* in which the airflow is turned rearwards and slowed down. Its pressure rises as it is slowed.

Centrifugal compressor technology has since developed greatly, and almost all gas turbines designed for light planes, road vehicles, and small stationary power units use these cheap and robust compressors. At speeds higher than 30,000 rpm they can develop a pressure ratio exceeding 7:1.

Whittle's engines used an array of separate combustion chambers or 'cans' and expelled the gas discharged from the turbine through a simple short nozzle. Such an engine is called a *turbojet*. It is the simplest of all gas turbines, but tends to be noisy and is less efficient in aircraft propulsion until supersonic speeds are reached.

Since 1950 the gap between the noisy, high-speed turbojet and the quieter low-speed turboprop has been filled by a broad range of engines at first called *ducted fans*, but today called *turbofans*. Some early types were aft-fan engines, in which an additional turbine was added to the rear of the jet and provided with very long blades, which acted on the air flowing past the outside of the engine, rather like a multi-bladed propeller.

Nowadays the fan is mounted at the front of the engine, and it is essentially an oversized axial compressor, usually having one (but often as many as four) stages. The air it compresses is divided into two parts. That compressed by the inner part of the fan enters the main compressor and passes through what is known as the 'core' of the engine.

The core consists of the compressors, combustion chamber and turbines. In the Pratt and Whitney TFE 731 engine, for example, there is a four-stage low pressure axial compressor, a single stage high pressure radial compressor, an annular combustion chamber, then a single stage high pressure and a three stage low pressure turbine.

The rest of the fan airflow, which is usually from two to six times greater than that passing into the core, is discharged through a separate outer fan duct and used to provide forward thrust, rather like the rearward airflow from a propeller. If the fan is designed to run at a lower speed than the turbine, it is driven from a reduction gearbox mounted in front of the compressor.

The turbofan creates a greater rearward flow than the turbojet, but at a lower velocity. This reduction in the jet flow velocity makes it very much quieter. The turbofan is today by far the most important aero engine (except for light aircraft). The latest designs have three separate shafts, each rotating at its own best speed. One carries the fan, one an intermediate pressure (ip) compressor, and the third the high pressure (hp) compressor. Each shaft has its own turbine and the shafts are concentric (mounted one within the other), with the hp shaft outermost.

Afterburners

Engines for supersonic aircraft need to be slim but powerful. Most modern military aircraft compromise by using a turbofan with a low *by-pass ratio*—the ratio of the fan or secondary airstream to the core or primary airstream. In these military engines the fan airflow is not much greater than the core airflow.

Virtually all supersonic aircraft have an afterburner which adds fuel to the gas flow downstream of the turbine. The fuel burns in the gas, giving a much higher jet velocity and temperature. This gives extra thrust, but at the expense of greatly increased fuel consumption, and so it is used mainly for take-off and, in the case of military aircraft, to give more engine power during combat manoeuvres.

An engine which has an afterburning or *reheat* system has to have a propelling nozzle whose diameter can be reduced when afterburning is not in use. As the nozzle is a large item, subject to severe stresses at about 1200°C (2200°F), it is not easy to make it open and close. The most common method is to use rings of inner and outer 'petal' flaps which are accurately positioned by hydraulic or pneumatic actuators located in cooler areas away from the nozzle.

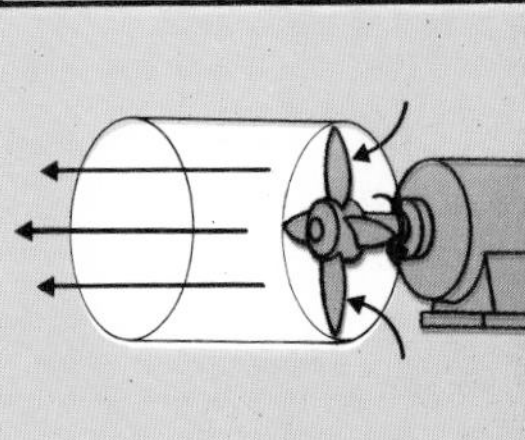

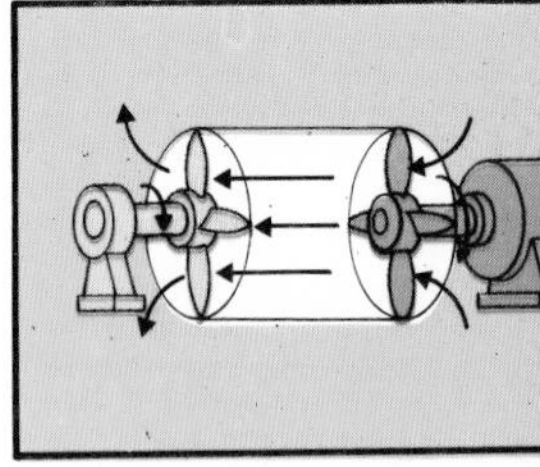

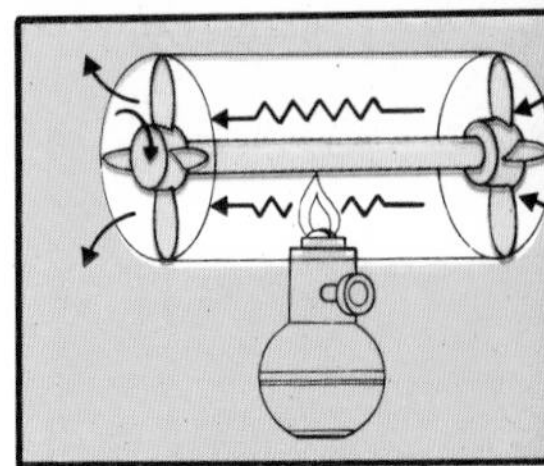

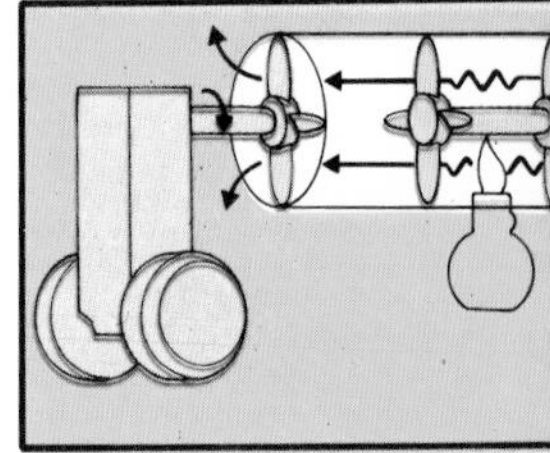

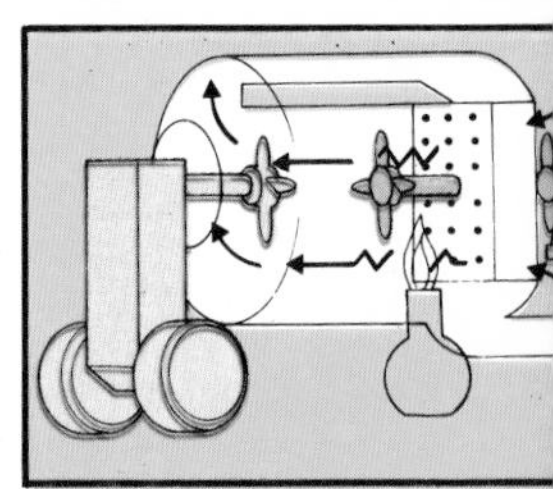

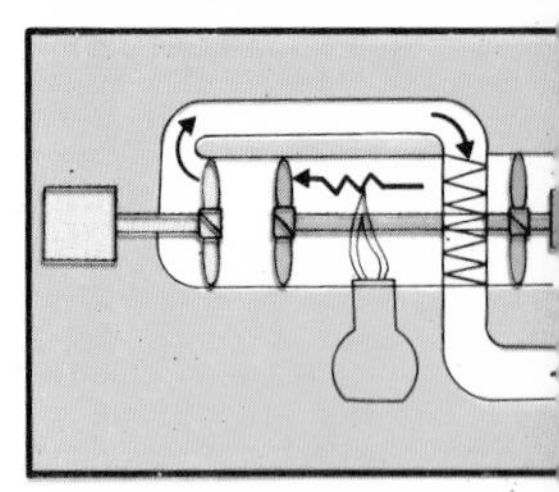

The series of six diagrams on the right show the underlying principles of the gas turbine engine, and the way it can be used to drive a car or a truck.

In the first diagram, an electric fan is drawing in air and blowing it through a hollow cylinder, rather like a turbine compressor blowing air through the engine core. If a freely mounted fan is placed at the end of the cylinder, as in the second drawing, the airflow from the electric fan will make it rotate, like a turbine rotor. If heat energy is added to the airflow between the two fans, the air will expand and accelerate, creating enough energy to enable the second fan to drive the first, as in the third diagram, and the electric motor can be dispensed with.

In a turbine, this heat energy is supplied by burning fuel in a combustion chamber between the compressor and the rotor, and the engine is started by an electric starter motor or by blowing compressed air through it. If sufficient energy is produced by heating the air between the fans, only part of it will be needed to drive them.

The remaining energy can be used to drive a third fan, shown in the fourth diagram, and a load. In a gas turbine, this third fan is the free or power turbine and it is used to drive, for example, an aircraft or ship propeller, the wheels of a car or a truck, or an electricity generator. Any heat energy remaining in the gas after it has driven the third fan can be used to help heat the air from the first fan before fuel is burnt in it, and thus less fuel has to be burned to raise the turbine gas to its working temperature.

The heat from the exhaust gas is transferred to the air from the first fan in a device called a heat exchanger, as in the fifth drawing. The final drawing shows how the simple fans and other components shown in the other drawings relate to the components of an actual gas turbine engine. The advantage of having the power turbine on a separate shaft is that the speed of the compressor is unaffected by the load on the power turbine.

British Leyland

British Leyland

Left: The experimental Rover-BRM gas turbine engined sports car taking part in the Le Mans 24-hour race in 1965. It finished the race with an average speed of 160.6 kph (99.8 mph).

Right: A gas turbine powered frigate. Gas turbines are used in many types of ship, and are usually adapted from aero engines.

Below: A mobile gas turbine powered generating unit used to provide emergency electricity supplies.

Centrax

Vosper Thorneycroft

Right: The British Leyland 2S 350R gas turbine truck engine. It is started by a 24 V electric starter motor, which accelerates the compressor while fuel is sprayed into the combustion chamber and ignited by an electric ignitor plug. Once the engine has reached a quarter of its top speed the starter and ignitor are switched off, and the engine accelerates up to its idling speed, which is half its top speed.

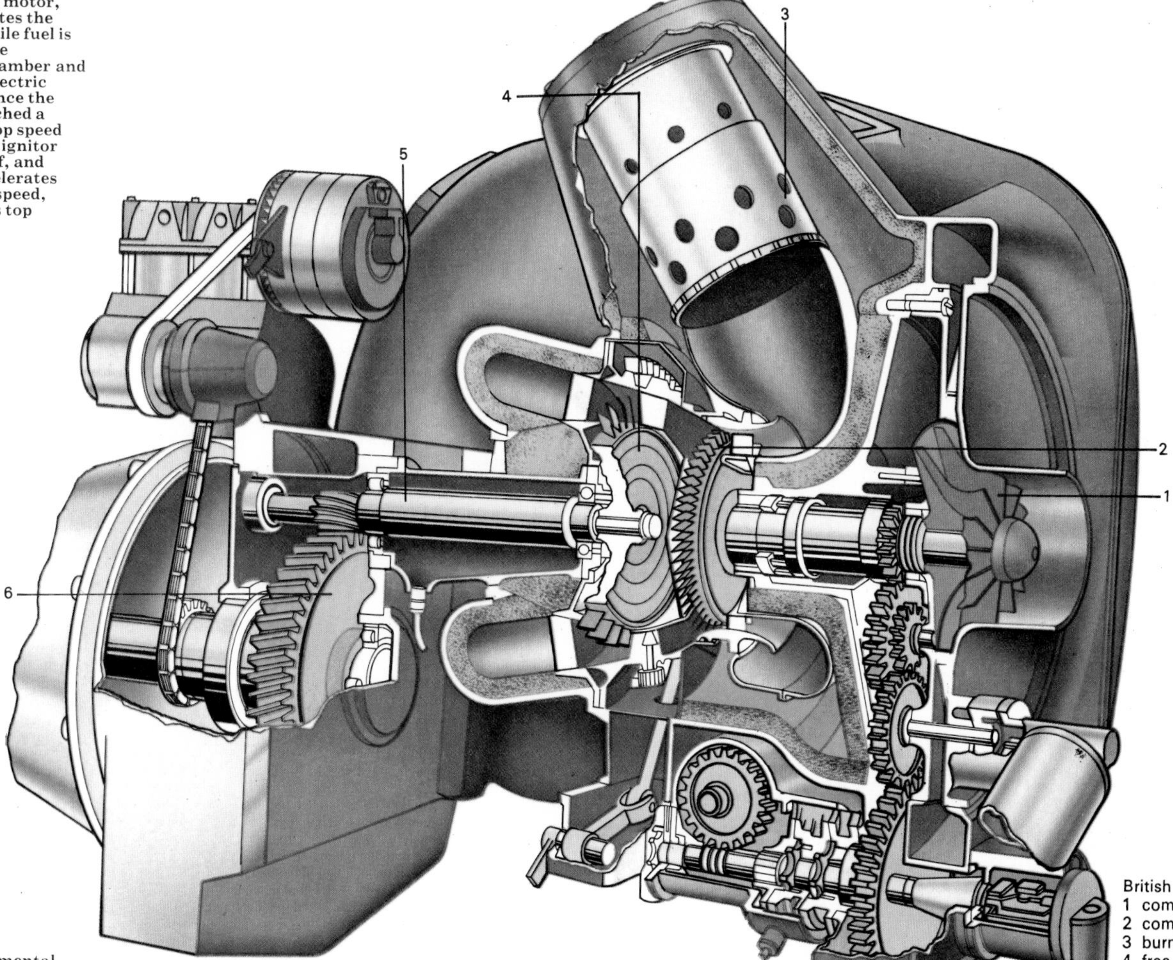

British Leyland 2S 350R
1 compressor
2 compressor turbine
3 burner
4 free (power) turbine
5 drive shaft
6 reduction gears

Left: An experimental articulated truck powered by the British Leyland 2S 350R gas turbine engine, a cutaway drawing of which is shown above right. The engine produces 260-300 kW (350-400 hp), can run on either petrol or diesel oil, and is designed for a life of 12,000 hours without major breakdowns.

Nuclear Power

The nucleus of an atom, the tiny central core around which the electrons are grouped, consists of positively charged particles called protons and uncharged particles called neutrons. The essential difference between an atom of one element and an atom of another lies in the numbers of protons and neutrons each possesses.

If the nucleus of an atom is split up, a process known as nuclear *fission* takes place, and a vast amount of energy is released as the protons and neutrons are scattered. Some of these will recombine to form fresh nuclei, creating atoms of lighter elements than the original one. For example, splitting a uranium atom may result in the formation of barium and krypton atoms and the liberation of three free neutrons. If one of these neutrons strikes the nucleus of a neighbouring uranium atom it will split it, and the process will begin again.

This sequence of a neutron striking a nucleus and splitting it, releasing more neutrons which then go on to split more nuclei, is called a *chain reaction*. In an atomic bomb, this chain reaction is allowed to proceed unchecked, resulting in a very rapid build-up of an enormous amount of energy which is released in a violent explosion. In a nuclear reactor, on the other hand, the speed at which the reaction spreads, and thus the rate at which the energy is released, is carefully controlled. The energy is given off in the form of heat, which is then used to raise steam to drive, for example, electricity generator turbines.

Only a few elements are capable of undergoing a fission chain reaction since this requires large, relatively unstable nuclei. These elements are known as *fissile* materials, and one of the most widely used is the isotope of uranium called uranium-235 (^{235}U) which has 92 protons and 143 neutrons in its nucleus.

Even with a suitably fissile material, a chain reaction will only be self-sustaining if there is a sufficient mass of the material (and thus enough fissile nuclei present) to ensure that as many neutrons as possible are able to collide with nuclei and split them, freeing more neutrons to keep the reaction going. If the mass of a piece of fissile material exceeds this mass, which is known as the *critical mass*, a self-sustaining chain reaction will begin spontaneously.

In the case of uranium-235, for example, the critical mass is about 50 kg (110 lb). Below the critical mass a reaction can only be sustained if neutrons are constantly supplied from an external source.

Fermi's pile

The first controlled nuclear reaction was created by Enrico Fermi (1901-1954) in Chicago on 2 December 1942. Fermi had already shown that neutrons could be slowed down by releasing them in a *moderator* such as water or graphite. The neutrons bounce off the atoms of the moderator, losing energy and slowing down as they do so. These neutrons are called 'thermal' neutrons because when slowed they possess about the same level of energy as the heat energy possessed by the atoms or molecules of the substance through which they are passing. The slow neutrons are more efficient at causing fission than fast ones.

Fermi's reactor or 'pile' consisted of a pile of graphite blocks, throughout which lumps of uranium were dispersed. Strips of neutron-absorbing cadmium were provided as control rods, regulating the speed at which the chain reaction could proceed by absorbing some of the free neutrons, while counters and foils were used to measure the rate at which neutrons were being produced.

At *criticality*, when enough fuel had been assembled for a chain reaction to take place, the pile was about 7.8 m (24 ft) across and 6.2 m (19 ft) high. Criticality was approached by adding successive layers of graphite and uranium to the pile, and it finally contained about 6 tonnes of uranium, of which 0.7% was the lighter isotope ^{235}U, and 99.3% was ^{238}U (92 protons and 146 neutrons).

At this time it was understood that when ^{238}U captures a thermal neutron the resulting compound nucleus ^{239}U does not undergo fission, but disposes of the energy it gained during the capture (known as its *energy of excitation*) by emitting high energy photons of the form of electromagnetic radiation known as *gamma radiation*. Later, it emits two electrons (*beta particles*) in succession as two of its neutrons decay into photons.

The resulting nucleus, with 94 protons and 145 neutrons, is ^{239}Pu, an isotope of a previously unknown element, plutonium. Like ^{235}U, plutonium-239 is a fissile material suitable for making atomic bombs, and is to be used in the new Fast Breeder reactors now being developed.

AERE Harewell

Above: The world's first nuclear reactor, built by Enrico Fermi in 1942.

Keystone

Right: Enrico Fermi was born in Rome on 29 September 1901. He studied in Pisa, and later went to work with Max Born at Gottingen, returning to Italy in 1924. He became Professor of Theoretical Physics at Rome University in 1927, and investigated quantum statistics, beta decay and neutrinos, but his most important work was the study of radioactivity and neutron bombardment for which he received a Nobel Prize in 1938. In that year, he left Italy to work in the USA, joining the University of Chicago in 1941. He died in Chicago in 1954.

Below: A diagram showing how the fuel, moderator and control rods are arranged in a nuclear reactor. The moderator slows the fast neutrons so that they react more readily with the fuel, and the neutron-absorbing control rods control the speed of the reaction. The diagrams at the bottom show six types of nuclear power station.

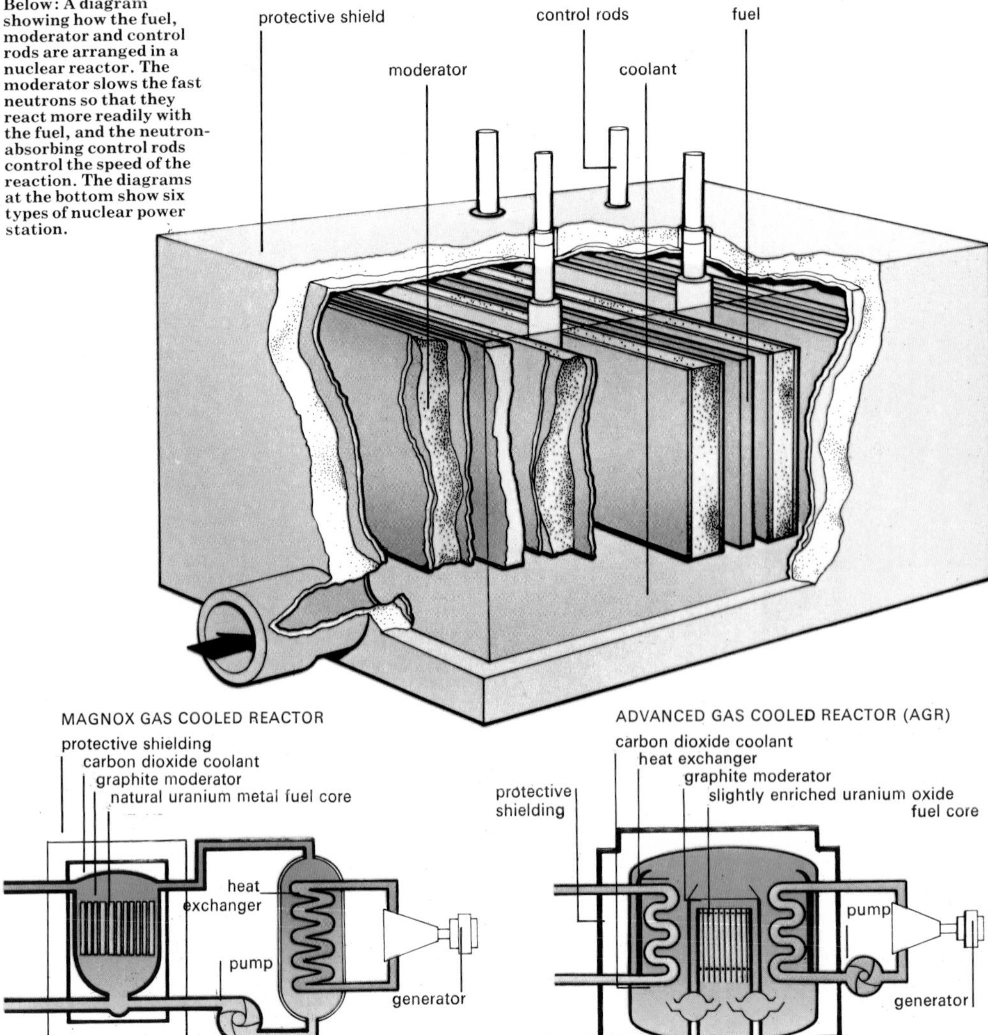

Left: Loading fuel elements into an Advanced Gas Cooled reactor at Hinckley 'B' power station in Somerset, England. Each fuel element consists of 36 stainless steel fuel pins, filled with uranium oxide pellets inside a graphite sleeve. When fully loaded the reactor contains 2,464 fuel elements.

Below: The top of the experimental High Temperature Reactor at Winfrith, Dorset. This reactor, known as the 'Dragon' reactor, is a helium-cooled, graphite-moderated reactor, and is one of the projects set up by the European Nuclear Energy Agency. Supported by 12 countries, this project was started in 1959.

UKAEA

UKAEA

The bomb dropped on Hiroshima used ^{235}U as its fissile material, but the Nagasaki bomb used ^{239}Pu. In both cases, the explosion was achieved by using conventional high explosives to force pieces of the fissile material together to form a *supercritical* mass, which then exploded almost instantly as the chain reaction spread through it.

Modern reactors

Modern *thermal reactors*, so named because they use thermal neutrons, use one of three moderators to slow the fast neutrons given off by fission and make them thermal neutrons. These are graphite, which consists of pure carbon; 'heavy' water, which is *deuterium* (symbol D, an isotope of hydrogen which has one proton and one neutron in its nucleus) combined with oxygen; and 'light' water, which is just ordinary water. As they collide with the moderator nuclei, the neutrons lose energy, rather as the cue ball is slowed down by collisions on a snooker table.

Of the three moderators, graphite was originally favoured, especially in the United Kingdom, where it is used in the Magnox and Advanced Gas-cooled Reactor (AGR) power stations. Looking to the future, graphite is the moderator used in the helium-cooled High Temperature Reactor (HTR), pioneered by the international Dragon Project at Winfrith in England.

The use of heavy water has been developed mainly in Canada, its particular attraction being that it is the least wasteful of neutrons. In Britain, it is to be used in the Steam Generating Heavy Water Reactor (SGHWR), which has been chosen for the next generation of nuclear power stations.

Light water is the most compact moderator, an important consideration in nuclear power plant for submarines and surface ships. Light water reactors have been highly developed in the USA and USSR, not only for ship propulsion, but also as power station reactors.

Magnox reactors are fuelled with uranium metal clad in a magnesium alloy, but most present-day nuclear reactors have fuel in the form of pellets of uranium oxide sealed in long metal tubes or 'pins'. These pins are grouped together in fuel 'elements', several hundred of which are required to charge the reactor. Typically, the fuel stays in the reactor for 3 to 5 years before it must be removed.

The heat which fission generates in the fuel pins is carried away by a stream of liquid or gas coolant, which is passed through heat exchangers, where steam is raised in secondary circuits for feeding the turbo-generators. In the Boiling Water Reactor (BWR) and in SGHWR, the primary coolant is water, but its pressure is adjusted so that boiling occurs in the fuel channels. The steam so generated may be fed direct to the turbine.

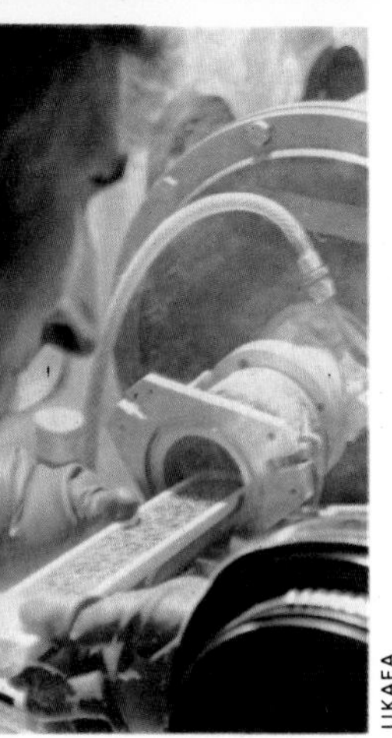

Left: Unloading pellets of uranium-plutonium oxide fuel from a furnace which forms the pellets from a powder mixture. There is a radiation-proof glass shield between the operator and the fuel, and he handles it by means of special gloves fitted into the shield. This type of fuel may be used in future Fast Breeder reactors.

Right: The coolant pipes at the bottom of the prototype Steam Generating Heavy Water Reactor at Winfrith. This prototype produces 300,000 kW of heat, which raises the steam to drive generator turbines that generate 100,000 kW of electricity for supply to the National Grid.

UKAEA

UKAEA

URIZED WATER REACTOR (PWR)

tive shielding
urised water coolant and moderator
iched uranium oxide fuel core
heat exchanger

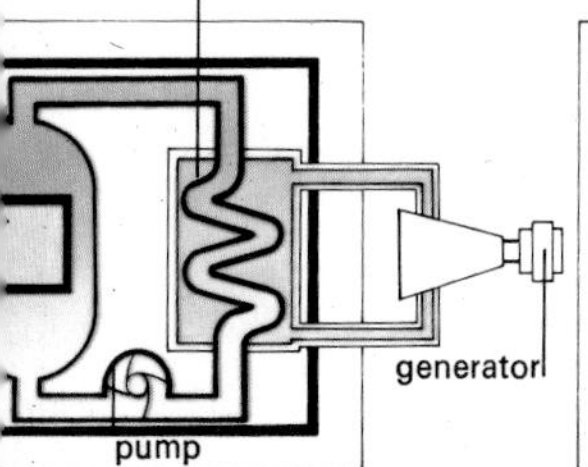

BOILING WATER REACTOR (BWR)

protective shielding
water coolant and moderator
enriched uranium oxide fuel
generator

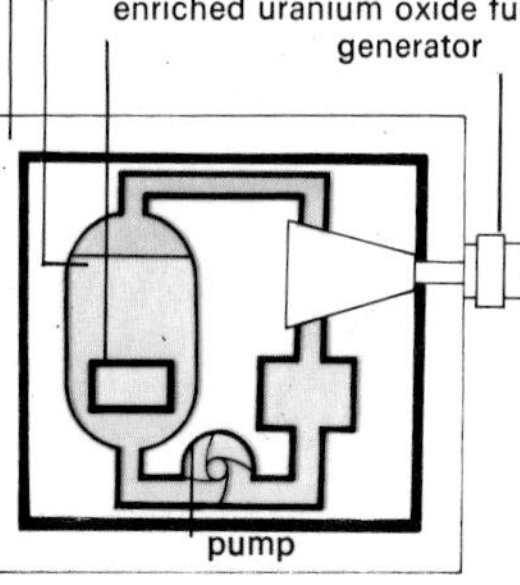

HEAVY WATER REACTOR

protective shielding
slightly enriched uranium oxide fuel core
heavy water moderator
steam and water coolant

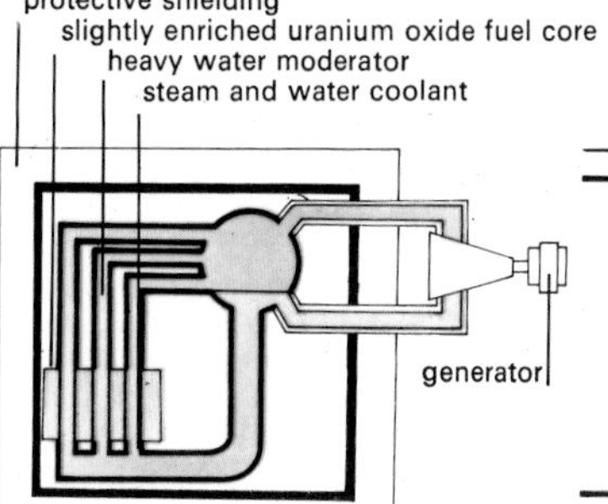

FAST BREEDER REACTOR

protective shielding
fuel core of plutonium and uranium oxides
liquid sodium coolant
heat exchanger

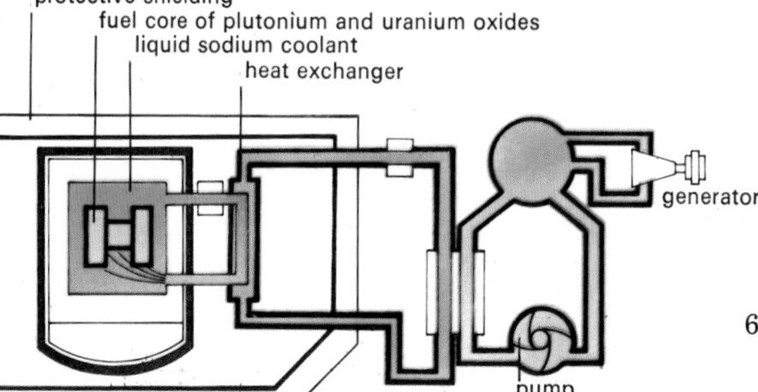

Right: The energy of the Sun and other stars is believed to be produced by a nuclear fusion reaction which fuses hydrogen into helium. These diagrams show three possible ways that this could happen. The first step (1) is either the fusion of two protons (which are hydrogen nuclei) into deuterium plus a positron and a neutrino, or the fusion of two protons plus an electron into deuterium and a neutrino. (2) The deuterium then combines with another proton to form helium-3 and a photon. (3) About 86% of the helium-3 fuses with itself to form ordinary helium-4, liberating two protons. (4) Alternatively, the helium-3 combines with a nucleus of helium-4 to

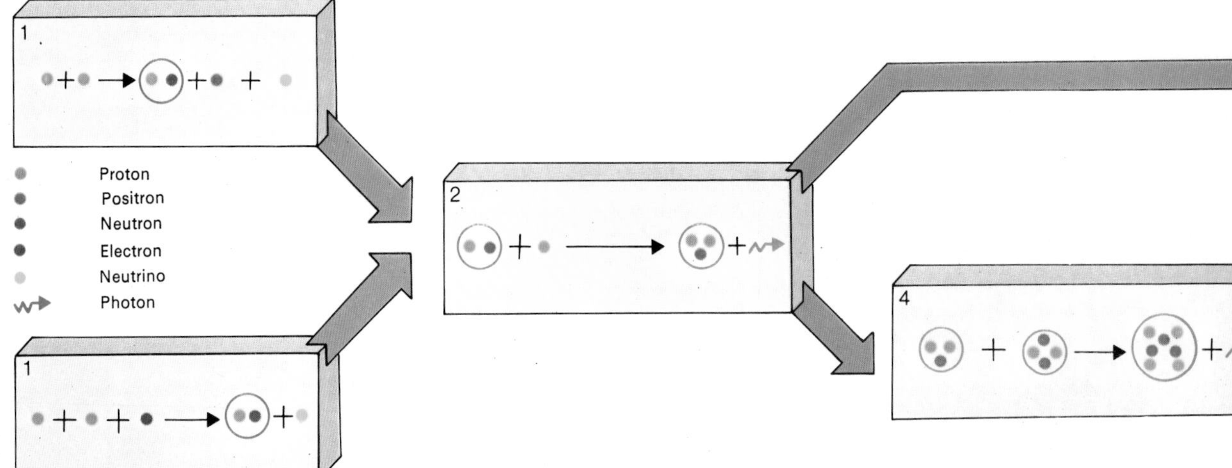

Although in general gas-cooling offers prospects of higher temperatures, and thus higher efficiencies when generating power, it tends to be less compact than water-cooling.

Whichever coolant is used it must be maintained at high pressure, either by enclosing the fuel, moderator and coolant in a pressure vessel, or by placing the fuel elements in pressure tubes through which the coolant is forced. The reactor is surrounded by a concrete case called a 'biological shield', several feet thick, to protect the operators from radiation.

Radiation

There are three types of radiation which may be given off during atomic reactions, or when a *radioactive* element decays. The unstable nucleus of such an element achieves stability by giving off particles, gradually transmuting itself through a series of lighter elements.

Uranium, for example, decays through a series of 'daughter' elements until it eventually becomes lead. The rate of decay of a radioactive element is measured in terms of its *half life*, which is the time taken for half the atoms initially present to decay into the next daughter element in the particular series. Half life times range from fractions of a second to millions of years. For example, ^{238}U has a half-life of 4.5 x 10^9 years, whereas astatine has a half life of only 8.3 hours.

The three types of radiation are known as *alpha*, *beta* and *gamma* radiation. Alpha radiation is the emission of alpha particles, each of which consists of two protons and two neutrons. Beta radiation is a stream of beta particles, either negatively charged electrons or their positively charged counterparts, positrons. Gamma radiation is similar to, but stronger than, X-rays and is given off by atoms which have surplus energy following the emission of an alpha or beta particle or after the capture of a neutron. All three forms of radiation are dangerous to living things, and can cause burns, cancers, infertility and genetic damage.

Waste disposal

When fuel elements have come to the end of their useful lives, they are withdrawn from the reactor by remote control and placed in deep 'cooling ponds' nearby. There they remain for about six months, to allow much of the radioactivity of the fission products to die away. They are then transported in heavily shielded casks, which may weigh up to 100 tons, to a re-processing plant, such as that at the Windscale Works of British Nuclear Fuels Limited.

Here, the fuel is dissolved in acids and the residual uranium and plutonium are recovered. Of the fission products, the inert gases, krypton and xenon, and some tritium, are released to the atmosphere. The rest of the tritium and small proportions of other fission products are discharged into the sea or pumped into suitable underground strata.

Much the greatest part of the fission products is stored in jacketted stainless-steel tanks, behind concrete shielding, with arrangements to dissipate the heat released by radioactive decay. Ultimate disposal of these wastes, which will remain radioactive for many centuries, is likely to be their incorporation into insoluble glassy substances that can be stored in water-filled ponds.

Fast Breeder Reactors

Present types of thermal reactor suffer from a serious limitation; they can, at best, consume only about 1 or 2% of the uranium available, most of the ^{238}U having to be rejected as useless because there is not enough ^{235}U available to create the chain reactions necessary to consume it. World resources are uncertain, but it seems likely that uranium could be in short supply early in the next century, if the installation of these types of power plant continues at an increasing rate. Two ways around this difficulty are being explored. One is to substitute thorium for ^{238}U in a thermal reactor, in which case a new fissile material, uranium 233, would be generated. By feeding this back into thermal reactors, it should be possible to consume much of the available thorium.

The other line of development is that of the controversial *fast breeder reactor*, which should be able to consume a high proportion of the uranium reserves, through the recycling of plutonium back to the reactors. As its name implies, the fast reactor employs no moderator, so that the neutrons retain their high velocities as they move through the core of the reactor. This avoids the difficulty which restricts the usefulness of plutonium as a fuel for thermal reactors, in which it tends to form higher isotopes, such as ^{240}Pu, instead of undergoing fission, when it absorbs neutrons. Because such wasteful losses of neutrons are minimised in the gas reactor, their absorption in ^{238}U can be used to breed at least one new ^{239}Pu nucleus for each that is destroyed.

Right: Assembling a cluster of fuel pins for use in a Fast Breeder reactor.

Below: This enormous machine at Hinckley 'B' nuclear power station is used for refuelling the reactor. When fully operational, Hinckley will generate a total of 1250 MW of electricity. During the operating year from April 1 1974 to March 31 1975, the Central Electricity Generating Board in England and Wales generated 210,948 million kW hours of electricity, of which 23,137 million were generated by nuclear power stations. The percentage of the heat energy produced by the nuclear stations that was converted into electricity was 25.49%.

UKAEA

UKAEA

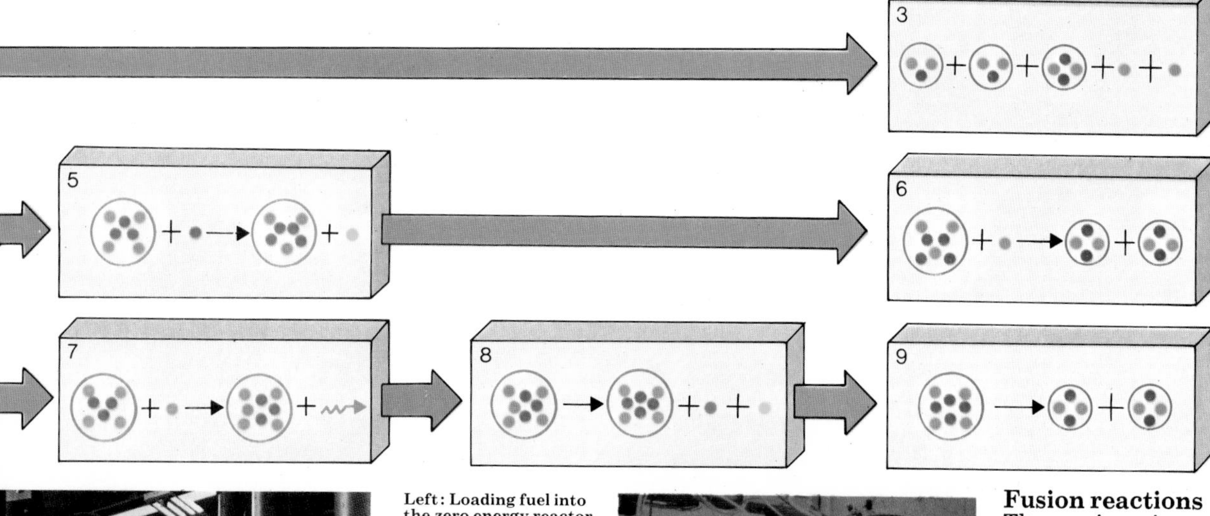

form beryllium-7 and a photon. (5) This beryllium-7 nucleus nearly always absorbs an electron and becomes the nucleus of lithium-7, emitting a neutrino in the process. (6) The lithium-7 nucleus then combines with a proton, and this makes it split up into two nuclei of helium-4. (7) Less commonly, the nucleus of beryllium-7 formed in stage (4) absorbs a proton, thus becoming a nucleus of boron-8 and emitting a photon. (8) This boron-8 then decays into beryllium-8 and gives off a positron and a neutrino. (9) In turn the beryllium-8 nucleus then splits in half to make two helium-4 nuclei Fusion reactors may be able to fuse deuterium to make helium and produce enormous energy.

UKAEA

Left: Loading fuel into the zero energy reactor Zenith II at Winfrith. A zero energy reactor is an experimental unit which does not produce any useful energy, but is designed to give information which can be used by nuclear power engineers in the design of full-scale reactors. This reactor uses 5 tonnes of fuel.

UKAEA

Right: The design and construction of fuel elements is continually being improved to ensure the most efficient, safe and reliable operation of nuclear reactors. In this test, an SGHWR fuel pin is being heated in an atmosphere of steam to simulate the conditions that would arise following the loss of coolant from a reactor core.

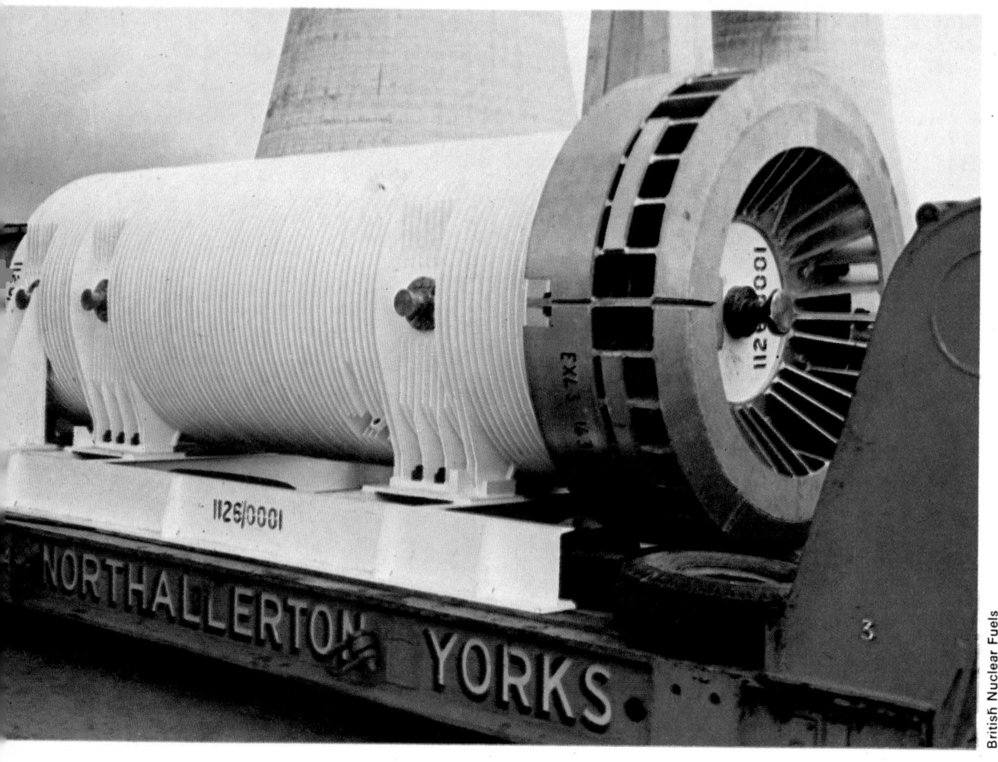

British Nuclear Fuels

Below: This container, known as an Excellox 3 flask, is used for transporting used nuclear fuel by road to the British Nuclear Fuels reprocessing plant at Windscale, Cumbria. During reprocessing any unused ^{235}U is recovered from the fuel for future use. The Windscale plant is the biggest in the world, processing over 2,000 tonnes a year.

Fusion reactions

The engineering and safety problems of the fast breeder reactor are formidable, so it is perhaps as well that an entirely different approach to the problem of utilising nuclear energy is being attempted. Its availability from uranium and thorium depends on the fact that these heavy elements can be split into lighter ones with an accompanying release of energy. Energy can also be obtained, however, by a sort of reverse of this process, the fusing together or *fusion* of two light nuclei to make a heavier one, a process which is accompanied by a release of nuclear energy.

The easiest fusion reaction to use a source of power is the D-T reaction. In this, the nuclei of two isotopes of hydrogen, the *deuteron* (the nucleus of deuterium) mass two, and the *triton* (the nucleus of tritium), mass three, fuse together. They form a helium nucleus, mass four, with the emission of an energetic neutron, mass one, and the liberation of energy. This is the basic reaction of the H-bomb.

Deuterium is available in almost unlimited quantities in the ocean, but tritium must be produced artificially from lithium by bombarding it with neutrons so that it absorbs them. In the H-bomb, lithium deuteride is detonated by neutrons and compression from an A-bomb trigger. In a controlled thermonuclear reactor, as at present envisaged, the reactant hydrogen isotopes would form an ionised plasma, periodically raised to temperatures at which the nuclei have kinetic energies of motion sufficient to enable them to react, despite the electrostatic repulsion of their positive charges.

The main reaction space would be surrounded by a lithium-containing blanket, in which the escaping neutrons are absorbed to maintain the supply of tritium. The technology of such reactors has yet to be successfully demonstrated, but world reserves of lithium are sufficient to provide an energy source comparable to that of uranium as it would be used in fast breeder reactors. Over the next few decades, the choice between uranium-based fission and lithium-based fusion may be dictated by environmental and economic considerations.

One great advantage of fusion is that it produces helium, a safe, inert gas, and less highly dangerous wastes than fission reactions. In the longer term, the more difficult fusion technology affords the prospect of almost unlimited energy supplies.

Fossil Fuels

The fossil fuels are so called because they are formed from the remains of plants and other living organisms that existed on earth millions of years ago. Peat, lignite and coal, for example, were formed from the remains of the trees and plants in ancient forests which sank into swamps and were subsequently covered by layers of mud which later became rock.

Petroleum (crude oil), on the other hand, probably originated from the remains of plants and animals living in seas and lakes. These remains settled on the sea or lake beds where they were gradually buried under layers of sediment. Slowly the organic remains were converted into petroleum and natural gas.

Picturepoint

Above: The Pitch Lake on the West Indian island of Trinidad. Pitch is a very heavy, semi-solid form of oil, and one of its main uses is as road tar.

Camera Press

Left: This power station in county Offaly, Eire, burns milled peat to raise the steam that drives its generator turbines. It produces 40 MW of electricity, and burns 280,000 tonnes of peat per annum.

Below: A crude oil distillation column. Crude oil, heated in a furnace, enters the column near the bottom. The constituent 'fractions' of the oil rise to various heights in the column; those with the lowest boiling points rise to the top.

Peat

Peat is the initial stage in the formation of coal and was probably the first of the fossil fuels to be used by man. It is found in bogs, where it has formed from decayed rushes, reeds, mosses and sedges by the action of water and bacteria.

The formation of peat requires certain climatic and topographic conditions. There must be soil capable of retaining water at or near the surface, and the average temperature must be low enough to prevent rapid evaporation and decay, but not so low as to prevent the abundant growth of vegetation. The temperature best suited to the formation of peat is between 5° and 9°C (42° to 48°F), and so peat bogs are found in the temperate zones of the earth. For example, they cover large areas of swamp and fen land in northern Europe, varying in depth from 6 to 12 metres (20 to 40 ft).

Freshly cut peat contains up to 80 per cent of water, and so before it can be used as fuel it has to be dried out, either mechanically or by leaving it in the open air so that the water evaporates. When burnt in domestic fires, peat gives out a good heat and leaves a clean ash, but it produces a lot of smoke.

Properly dried peat yields almost as many by-products as coal does. Peat gas, for example, has been used successfully as a fuel for internal combustion engines and for various types of furnace. It does, however, require a longer and more complicated purification process than that needed for coal gas.

The process of extracting gas from peat also yields many valuable organic compounds, including alcohols and phenols, which are used as raw materials in a great number of industrial processes such as the manufacture of plastics, drugs, dyes and waxes.

Finely-shredded peat can be made into an exceptionally strong wrapping paper, while chemical treatment under pressure converts peat into a hard fibre suitable for making furniture and flooring.

In agriculture, peat makes a good absorbent litter for cattle, while cleaned peat is an excellent fodder. Ammonium sulphate, which can be obtained from peat, is a very good fertilizer.

Coal

Although outcroppings of coal have existed since prehistoric times, the use of coal as a source of heat is comparatively recent. To the ancient world, coal was merely a kind of black stone, and even the early metalworkers had no use for it as they did all their smelting with wood or charcoal.

There is some evidence that the ancient Britons used a certain amount of coal, and that the Romans learned of its value from them. The first definite written reference to coal, however, occurs in the Anglo-Saxon Chronicle, which was compiled in about 990AD. Among the first official references is one in a charter provided by King Henry III, in 1259, authorizing the inhabitants of Newcastle to dig coal from their fields.

During the following five centuries, the use of coal for domestic fires grew rapidly, and the soft, easily obtained coal which was used gave rise to serious pollution in the form of smoke and soot. It was heavily taxed, and in many places its burning was prohibited because of the danger to public health.

The consumption of coal increased rapidly during the eighteenth century, following the advent of the Industrial Revolution. In addition to its use as a fuel for steam engines, it became valuable as the source of coke, a hard, porous form of carbon used in steelmaking and also a fuel itself.

Shell

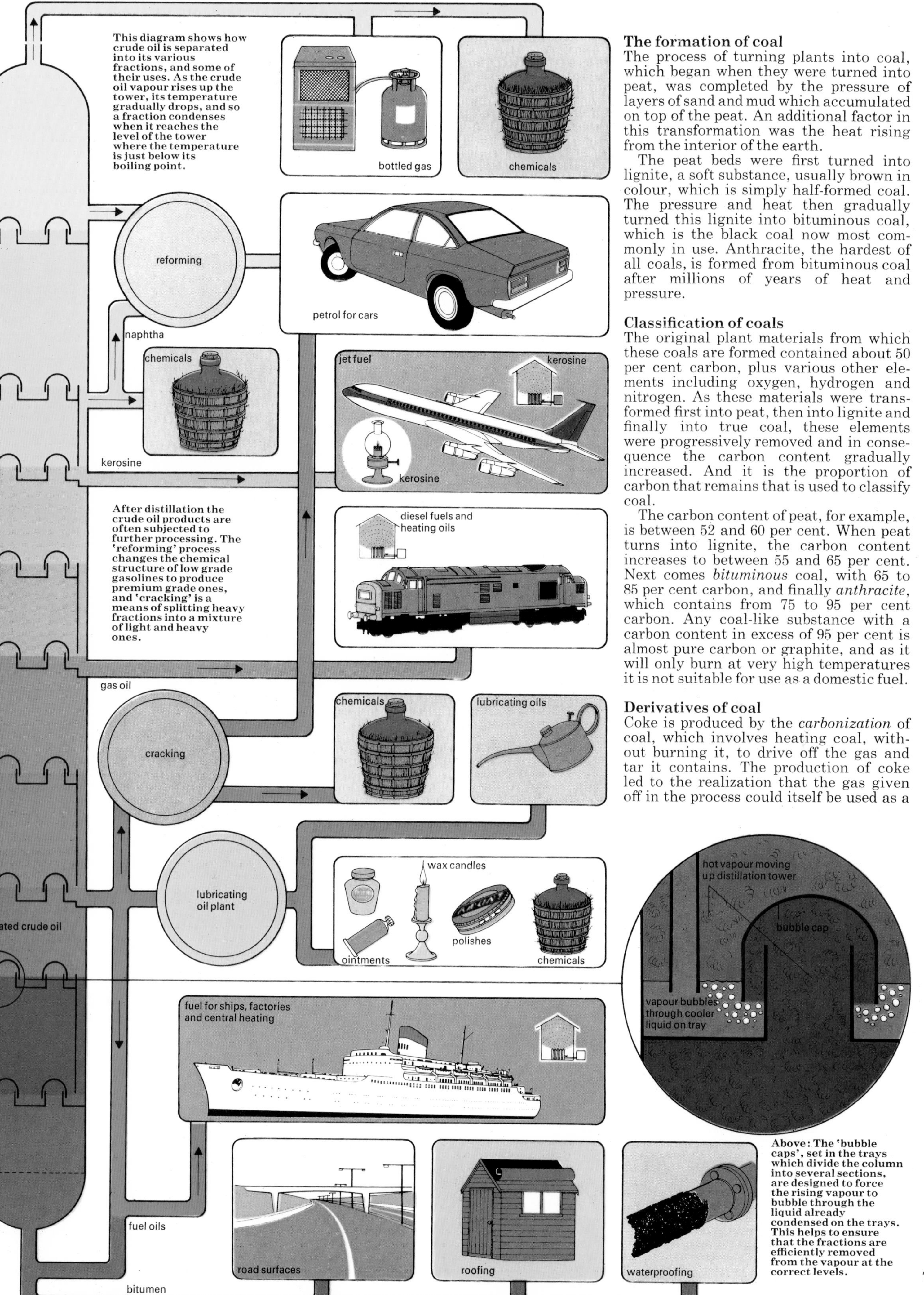

This diagram shows how crude oil is separated into its various fractions, and some of their uses. As the crude oil vapour rises up the tower, its temperature gradually drops, and so a fraction condenses when it reaches the level of the tower where the temperature is just below its boiling point.

After distillation the crude oil products are often subjected to further processing. The 'reforming' process changes the chemical structure of low grade gasolines to produce premium grade ones, and 'cracking' is a means of splitting heavy fractions into a mixture of light and heavy ones.

Above: The 'bubble caps', set in the trays which divide the column into several sections, are designed to force the rising vapour to bubble through the liquid already condensed on the trays. This helps to ensure that the fractions are efficiently removed from the vapour at the correct levels.

The formation of coal

The process of turning plants into coal, which began when they were turned into peat, was completed by the pressure of layers of sand and mud which accumulated on top of the peat. An additional factor in this transformation was the heat rising from the interior of the earth.

The peat beds were first turned into lignite, a soft substance, usually brown in colour, which is simply half-formed coal. The pressure and heat then gradually turned this lignite into bituminous coal, which is the black coal now most commonly in use. Anthracite, the hardest of all coals, is formed from bituminous coal after millions of years of heat and pressure.

Classification of coals

The original plant materials from which these coals are formed contained about 50 per cent carbon, plus various other elements including oxygen, hydrogen and nitrogen. As these materials were transformed first into peat, then into lignite and finally into true coal, these elements were progressively removed and in consequence the carbon content gradually increased. And it is the proportion of carbon that remains that is used to classify coal.

The carbon content of peat, for example, is between 52 and 60 per cent. When peat turns into lignite, the carbon content increases to between 55 and 65 per cent. Next comes *bituminous* coal, with 65 to 85 per cent carbon, and finally *anthracite*, which contains from 75 to 95 per cent carbon. Any coal-like substance with a carbon content in excess of 95 per cent is almost pure carbon or graphite, and as it will only burn at very high temperatures it is not suitable for use as a domestic fuel.

Derivatives of coal

Coke is produced by the *carbonization* of coal, which involves heating coal, without burning it, to drive off the gas and tar it contains. The production of coke led to the realization that the gas given off in the process could itself be used as a fuel, and that the coal tar was a valuable source of many useful organic compounds such as benzene, toluene and phenol.

Coal gas is a mixture of several gases, typically 50 per cent hydrogen (H_2), 25 per cent methane (CH_4), and 10 per cent nitrogen (N_2), plus small amounts of carbon monoxide (CO), carbon dioxide (CO_2), ethylene (C_2H_4), benzene (C_6H_6) and oxygen (O_2).

Coal tar contains over 200 compounds, many of which are important raw materials for a wide range of industrial processes. These include the production of fats, soaps, dyes, drugs, flavouring essences, solvents, tars, plastics, explosives and insecticides.

Another means of obtaining useful by-products from coal is the *hydrogenation* process. Powdered coal is processed with hydrogen gas at high temperatures and pressures, and this produces a form of oil which is then further processed with hydrogen to make petrol and diesel oil. The hydrogenation process also yields ammonia (NH_3) and a wide range of light hydrocarbons.

Petroleum

The name 'petroleum' is derived from the latin words *petra*, meaning 'rock', and *oleum*, meaning 'oil'. It thus means 'rock oil', so distinguishing it from animal or vegetable oils. Petroleum deposits are trapped beneath layers of impervious rock, but in some places they have seeped to the surface and collected in pools. The lighter constituents have evaporated out of these pools, leaving behind surface deposits of pitch or bitumen, very heavy, semi-solid forms of oil.

Only a small amount of the petroleum formed beneath the earth's crust rose through fissures in the rock to collect in pools, and most remained trapped beneath domes of impervious rock. Normally there is a layer of natural gas above the petroleum, and frequently a layer of salt water beneath it. In many cases the richest deposits of petroleum lie beneath a great depth of rock and can be reached only by massive and costly drilling operations.

Although the Chinese had been drilling for oil as long ago as 320BC, their wells were never very deep. The first serious modern attempt to drill for oil was by Edwin L. Drake, who drilled a successful well about 30 metres (100 ft) deep in Pennsylvania in 1859, and this marked the beginning of today's petroleum industry.

Petroleum from the early oilfields was primarily used for domestic lighting and heating oils, but towards the end of the nineteenth century it became very important as the source of fuel for the new internal combustion engines. Today, however, petroleum is much more than just a source of fuel, and even the natural gas associated with it, which was once considered a waste product and burnt away, is carefully collected and distributed for domestic and industrial use. Natural gas is a mixture of several gases, the principal ones being methane (CH_4) and ethane (C_2H_6).

Petroleum, often called 'crude oil' or simply 'crude', is a complex mixture of an enormous number of hydrocarbon compounds, together with small amounts of compounds of other elements. The exact composition of a crude oil depends on many factors, such as its age and the types of organism from which it was formed. Every deposit of crude oil is a unique mixture, whose exact composition differs even from deposits separated from it vertically or horizontally by only a few metres of rock.

The chief hydrocarbons present belong to the *paraffin*, *naphthene* and *aromatic* groups of organic compounds. The paraffins are compounds with a general formula C_nH_{n+2}, and the carbon atoms within them are arranged in straight or branched chains. The naphthenes, also called *cycloparaffins*, are formed by the removal of two hydrogen atoms from each end carbon atom of a paraffin chain, and then joining the chain together to form a ring. The simplest naphthenes have only one carbon ring per molecule, and can be sub-divided into the *cyclopentanes*, with five carbon atoms in the ring, and the *cyclohexanes*, which have six carbon atoms in the ring.

The aromatics are compounds based on the benzene (C_6H_6) ring. They are extremely useful to the chemical industry, but they must be removed from fuel oils because they adversely affect their burning properties.

The non-hydrocarbon compounds present in crude oil are mainly compounds

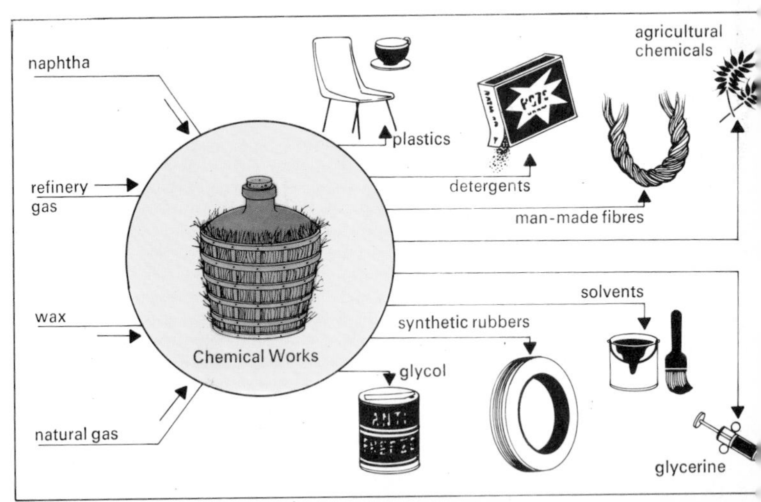

Right: The starting materials for many useful chemicals can be derived from naphtha, refinery gas, waxes or natural gas. Naphtha is one of the lighter fractions obtained from crude oil, and like the other substances it can be broken down into a number of simpler but highly reactive compounds. The high reactivity of these compounds means that they can be combined with each other and with other compounds to form hundreds of useful substances, such as plastics, synthetic fibres, detergents, fertilizers and insecticides. Glycol is the basis of antifreeze, and glycerine is used in drugs, cosmetics, explosives and food processing.

Esso

Above: Measuring the sulphur content of petroleum products. The samples are burned, and the combustion gases given off are collected and analyzed so that the sulphur content can be calculated. Sulphur compounds are a source of air pollution, so they must be kept to a minimum in motor fuels.

Below: A general view of a modern oil refinery. The world's refineries produce over 3,000 million tonnes of products annually, including fuels, oils, gases, waxes, bitumen, and the chemical *feedstocks* which are the basis of the vast range of oil-based products such as plastics and detergents.

Shell

Picturepoint

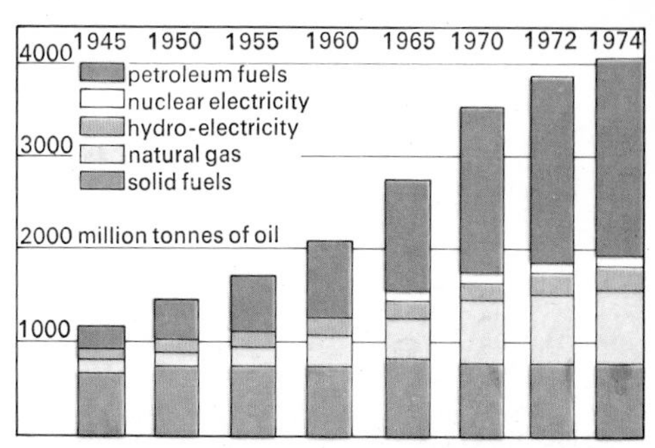

Right: The growth in world energy demand (excluding China, the USSR and Eastern Europe) from 1945 to 1974. The contribution of non-oil fuels is expressed in terms of the amount of oil which would provide the same amount of energy. In 1974, petroleum fuels provided 51% of the total energy supplied.

BAC

John Goldblatt

Above left: Oil derivatives are the raw materials for some of the most important plastics now in use. Ethylene, for example, is used in the manufacture of polyethylene (better known as polythene), and benzene is one of the chief raw materials used in the production of nylon.

Above: The world's airlines are some of the biggest consumers of petroleum fuels. Jet aircraft fuels are based on a type of paraffin known as aviation kerosine, often blended with a low-octane gasoline. This picture shows a British Airways *Concorde* refuelling at Singapore.

Above: Most candles are now made from paraffin wax obtained from crude oil. They are made by pouring molten wax into a mould containing the wick, or by forcing small particles of solid wax into a mould at high pressure and compressing them around the wick, which is usually made of plaited cotton.

Shell

Right: Cattle can be protected from parasitic insects and infective organisms by passing them through a bath or 'dip' of water containing chemicals which kill off the insects and germs. Many agricultural chemicals, including such pesticides, are made from the by-products of oil refining.

of sulphur, nitrogen and oxygen. Crude oil may contain as much as 7 per cent sulphur, up to 2 per cent nitrogen, and up to 1.5 per cent oxygen. Other elements present in very small amounts include vanadium, nickel, chlorine, arsenic and lead, as well as particles of material from the rock containing the crude.

The petroleum is refined by *fractional distillation*, which involves heating it in a tall tower so that the various compounds are distilled out of it and rise to various levels in the tower. The lightest compounds such as the gases, which have low boiling points, rise to the top, and the heavier oils with higher boiling points are collected lower down.

The distillates may then be further processed by *cracking* or by *reforming*, both of which involve the use of *catalysts*. These are substances which assist in creating a chemical reaction, but which themselves remain unchanged by the reaction. Catalytic cracking, often called 'cat cracking', is a means of breaking down the heavier distillates to form lighter compounds. Reforming is used to change low-grade distillates into higher grade ones, for example a low grade motor fuel can be reformed into a higher grade one.

Petroleum derivatives have an enormous range of uses—making plastics, artificial rubber, detergents, anaesthetics, insecticides, explosives, chewing gum, wax polishes, dyes, cosmetics, food preservatives, artificial silk, adhesives, medicines, paints and a large number of chemicals. It was this enormous and important range of petroleum derivatives that prompted the Shah of Iran to comment that 'oil is too good for burning'.

Gas Production

The earliest users of gas were the ancient Chinese. They used natural gas, piped through bamboo tubes, for lighting; and even obtained salt from sea water by evaporating it in iron tanks heated by burning natural gas escaping through fissures in the ground. The modern use of gas, however, did not begin until the late eighteenth century, when engineers in France and Britain succeeded in building practical coal-gas lighting systems.

Experiments in producing gas from coal had been carried out by many people during the seventeenth and eighteenth centuries. But although many individual gases were discovered and analyzed, none of the experiments resulted in a practical application of gas. For example, Jean Tardier, a French chemist, published a treatise in 1618 which described how he had produced gas by heating coal in an iron pot. He had intended to use the gas for lighting, but the lamp he built was far too clumsy and dangerous for practical use.

One of the first major developments came in 1765 when a man called Spedding, the manager of Lord Lonsdale's coal mine near Whitehaven, Cumberland, tapped gas from a burning bed of coal to light the mine's offices. Despite the success of this project, however, it was almost 30 years before the next major advance in gas production.

In 1792 an engineer named William Murdock built a small iron retort in the back garden of his house in Redruth, Cornwall. Coal gas from the retort was stored in a small gasholder, and then ducted through piping to provide illumination for his combined home and offices. Some years later he built a gas lighting system for the Birmingham works of his employers, Boulton and Watt, who made steam engines and mill machinery.

Boulton and Watt subsequently began building and selling gas-making and lighting equipment, which was designed by Murdock in association with another member of the firm, Samuel Clegg. At this time each customer had an individual gas-making plant to supply the gas for the lighting, and Murdock rejected the idea of a single gas works supplying gas by pipeline to local consumers.

The founder of the modern system of gas distribution was F. A. Winsor, an international financier. He had no technical or scientific qualifications, and knew nothing of gas-making, but he was convinced that selling gas rather than gas-making equipment was financially viable. Despite bitter opposition, Winsor formed the Gas Light and Coke Company in London in 1812. Samuel Clegg, who had left Boulton and Watt and set himself up as a designer and builder of gas equipment in 1806, was appointed chief engineer.

Thanks to Winsor's energy and enthusiasm and Clegg's engineering genius, the company's first plant was built and in production within a year. Then the necessary pipelines were laid, and by the end of 1813 gas street lighting had been installed in Westminster. The success of the Gas Light and Coke Company led to the installation of gas systems in cities

Gas Council

Above: One of the last British plants for making gas from oil-based feedstocks. In 1968 oil gas plant accounted for 73.1% of the total British gas-making capacity, and coal gas plant for only 11.2%. By the middle of the 1970s, however, natural gas had almost completely replaced other forms of gas.

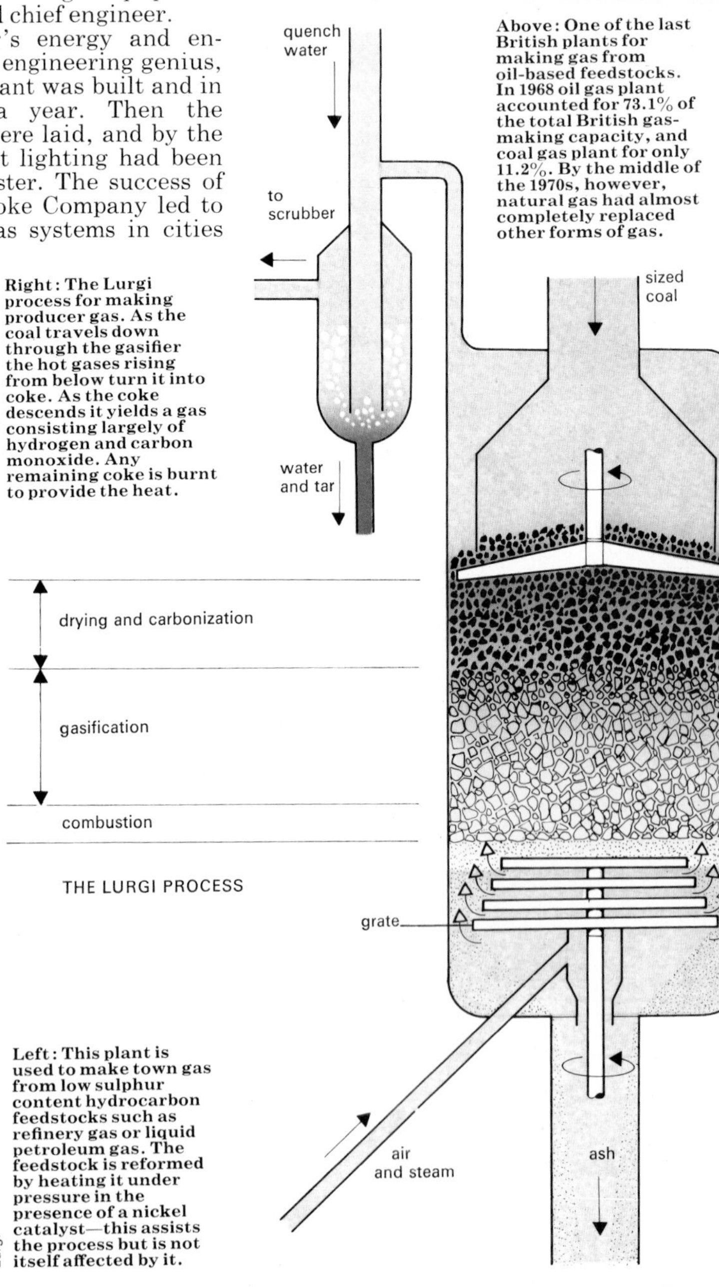

Right: The Lurgi process for making producer gas. As the coal travels down through the gasifier the hot gases rising from below turn it into coke. As the coke descends it yields a gas consisting largely of hydrogen and carbon monoxide. Any remaining coke is burnt to provide the heat.

quench water
to scrubber
water and tar
sized coal
drying and carbonization
gasification
combustion
grate
air and steam
ash
THE LURGI PROCESS

Lurgi

Left: This plant is used to make town gas from low sulphur content hydrocarbon feedstocks such as refinery gas or liquid petroleum gas. The feedstock is reformed by heating it under pressure in the presence of a nickel catalyst—this assists the process but is not itself affected by it.

Left: When a system is converted from town gas to natural gas, the pipes must be cleared of the town gas they contain before the natural gas is put into them. This picture shows town gas being burned off from a pipe in the street during North Sea gas conversion work in London.

Spectrum

Above: The first commercial gas installations had their own gas-making equipment as there was no piped distribution system. An alternative to having an individual gas plant was to have a gasholder to which gas was delivered when needed; this picture shows a French gas delivery cart.

Mary Evans

North Thames Gas Board

Above: A rail truck for collecting hot coke discharged from the retorts of a gas works. Coke was invented in the 17th century by Derbyshire brewers, who found that when they burned coal to heat the liquor from the mashed barley, the result was an undrinkable beer. This was due to the sulphur in the coal. They solved the problem by 'charring' the coal to make coke. Only later was it realized that useful gases and tars were given off during the charring.

Left: A coal gas works. In many countries coal gas production at such plants has ceased because of the availability of natural gas which also has a higher calorific value.

London News Agency

throughout Britain and abroad, and the company itself continued in operation until the British gas industry was nationalized in 1948.

The use of gas for cooking and heating began in the middle of the nineteenth century, with the introduction of gas stoves in 1840 and gas fires in 1855. The modern use of natural gas also began during this period, with the formation of the Fredonia Gas Light and Water Works Company in the US in 1858.

In addition to coal gas and natural gas, a certain amount of gas is made from oil, and processes are being developed for the manufacture of substitute or 'synthetic' natural gas from coal.

Coal gas

Coal gas is made by the *carbonization* of bituminous coal, a process involving heating coal in the absence of air. The coal is heated in retorts or ovens to a temperature of approximately 1,350°C (2,462°F), so that it softens and releases its gas.

This gas is thick and brown in colour because of the presence of coal tar vapour, and it also contains ammonia (NH_3) and hydrogen sulphide (H_2S) gases. These gases and the tar are removed by passing the gases through a series of purification processes. The purified coal gas is itself a mixture of gases, and its exact composition depends upon the type of coal used and the kind of oven or retort in which it was made.

The main constituent, however, is hydrogen which makes up approximately half the volume. It also contains 25 to 35 per cent methane (CH_4), up to 10 per cent nitrogen (N_2) and as much as 6 per cent carbon monoxide (CO). It also contains small amounts of gaseous hydrocarbons, carbon dioxide (CO_2) and oxygen. Completion of the carbonization process leaves a residue of coke, which is cooled and graded to be used again as fuel.

There are four main types of carbonization plant for the production of gas: *continuous vertical retorts*, *horizontal retorts*, *coke ovens* and *intermittent vertical retorts*. The most widely used type, however, is the first.

A continuous vertical retort system consists of a number of ovens grouped in units of four. The coal is fed in through gas-tight valves at the top of the retorts, which are heated by *producer gas* burnt in ducts around the outside. This gas is made in what are called *producers*, in which coke is heated with air and steam to yield a gas consisting mainly of nitrogen, carbon monoxide and hydrogen.

The coke formed in the retorts is extracted from them by a discharge mechanism, and fed into a sealed chamber from which it is removed at regular intervals. The coke is so hot when it leaves the retort that it would ignite spontaneously on contact with the air if it were discharged without first being cooled. This cooling is done by constantly spraying water into the coke chamber.

The gas yield from any given quantity of coal is increased by passing steam into the base of the retort. The steam provides preliminary cooling of the coke, and reacts with the carbon it contains to form *blue water gas*, a mixture of carbon monoxide and hydrogen. This gas passes up through the retort and mixes with the crude coal gas.

The mixture of gases and steam produced in the retorts is collected and passed to a water-cooled condensing system. Here its temperature is reduced to between 15° and 20°C (59° to 68°F). This causes most of the tar vapour to condense out, together with the steam. Most of the ammonia and other impurities are removed simultaneously as they dissolve in the condensed steam, forming what is known as *ammoniacal liquor*.

The remaining ammonia and tar are removed from the gas by passing it through washers, where it is bubbled through weak ammoniacal liquor. Residual tar can also be removed by an electrostatic system, operating at up to 50,000 volts, which separates the tar from the gas by electrostatic attraction. The hydrogen sulphide is removed from the gas by passing it over grids covered in hydrated iron oxide, which absorbs the hydrogen sulphide and is converted into iron sulphide.

To prevent corrosion of the distribution mains or user's equipment and appliances, the final purification stage removes any water. Finally the gas is dried by contact with either glycerine or calcium chloride, then piped to storage holders ready for distribution.

Most gas works also produce what is known as *carburetted water gas*. This is the result of enriching blue water gas with vaporized gas oil, a form of diesel oil. The carburetted water gas is mixed with the coal gas at the inlet to the gasholder, and the mixture is known as *town gas*.

One of the more recent developments in coal gas production is the *Lurgi process*, which can produce gas from grades of

ZEFA

Gerolf Kalt/ZEFA

Left: A natural gas flare at a German gas processing plant. Natural gas is composed primarily of methane and ethane, and is found beneath the earth either alone or with crude oil. There are extensive natural gas deposits in north Africa, the USSR, the USA and beneath the North Sea.

Above: Storage tanks for liquefied natural gas. Liquefication of the gas greatly reduces its volume, making it easier to store and transport in large quantities. One of the major exporters of liquid natural gas is Algeria, and this gas is carried in the pressurized holds of specially built tankers.

Lurgi

coal formerly thought unsuitable. The coal is gasified by high-pressure streams of steam and oxygen, and as all the carbon is converted into gas there is no coke residue. The gas produced contains less impurities than ordinary coal gas, but its burning quality is lower and so it has to be enriched by the addition of butane (C_4H_{10}) or methane (CH_4).

Oil gas

Gas can also be made from mineral oils. This was originally done by 'cracking' crude oil, which meant reacting it with steam at temperatures of over 1,000°C (1,832°F) to split it into various liquid and gaseous hydrocarbon compounds. It was later found that most liquid hydrocarbons could be used as 'feedstocks' (raw materials) and a large number of processes were developed for making gas from them.

Oil gas is of high quality, and is low in impurities. It contains a mixture of hydrocarbons, including methane, acetylene and benzene, and it can be mixed with town gas and distributed in the normal way through a system of pipelines.

Natural gas

In many parts of the world there are valuable deposits of natural gas, either in association with oil or on their own. This gas was once considered as little more than a nuisance when discovered during drilling for oil, and was merely disposed of by burning it at the oilfields. This is still done in many areas, particularly at oilfields in remote desert areas far from any potential consumers of gas.

Today, however, oil-producing countries are beginning to collect and process this gas, either for export in liquefied form or to provide fuel and feedstocks for their own developing industries and cities. Saudi Arabia, for example, was burning off over 110 million cubic metres (4,000 million cubic feet) of gas per day in 1975, but is now planning to build a system to collect and distribute this gas.

Natural gas has been the major source of gas in the United States since the 1930s, and gas from beneath the bed of the North Sea is now the primary source of gas for Britain and other northern European countries.

Natural gas is composed primarily of methane, together with ethane and small amounts of propane (C_3H_8), butane and nitrogen. Its *calorific value*, that is, the amount of heat that can be obtained by burning a given volume of it, is over twice that of town gas. This poses a problem when a gas network is to be changed from using coal gas to natural gas; either the natural gas must be processed to make it into a gas similar to town gas, with the same calorific value, or else all the appliances and equipment in use on the network must be converted to make them able to use the natural gas efficiently and safely.

When Britain began using gas from the North Sea it was decided to convert the system to handle natural gas, because although the cost of conversion was enormous it was estimated that the cost of *reforming* natural gas into town gas, over a period of 30 years, would be over four times the cost of a ten-year conversion programme. In addition, as the natural gas had over twice the calorific value of the town gas, the existing gas network would, in effect, be able to provide twice the amount of energy.

Deleu/ZEFA

Above: Gasholders are built in concentric sections which fit inside each other like the sections of a telescope. This allows the holders to expand or contract vertically, depending on the amount of gas within them, thus maintaining the gas pressure and helping to prevent any air entering the gas.

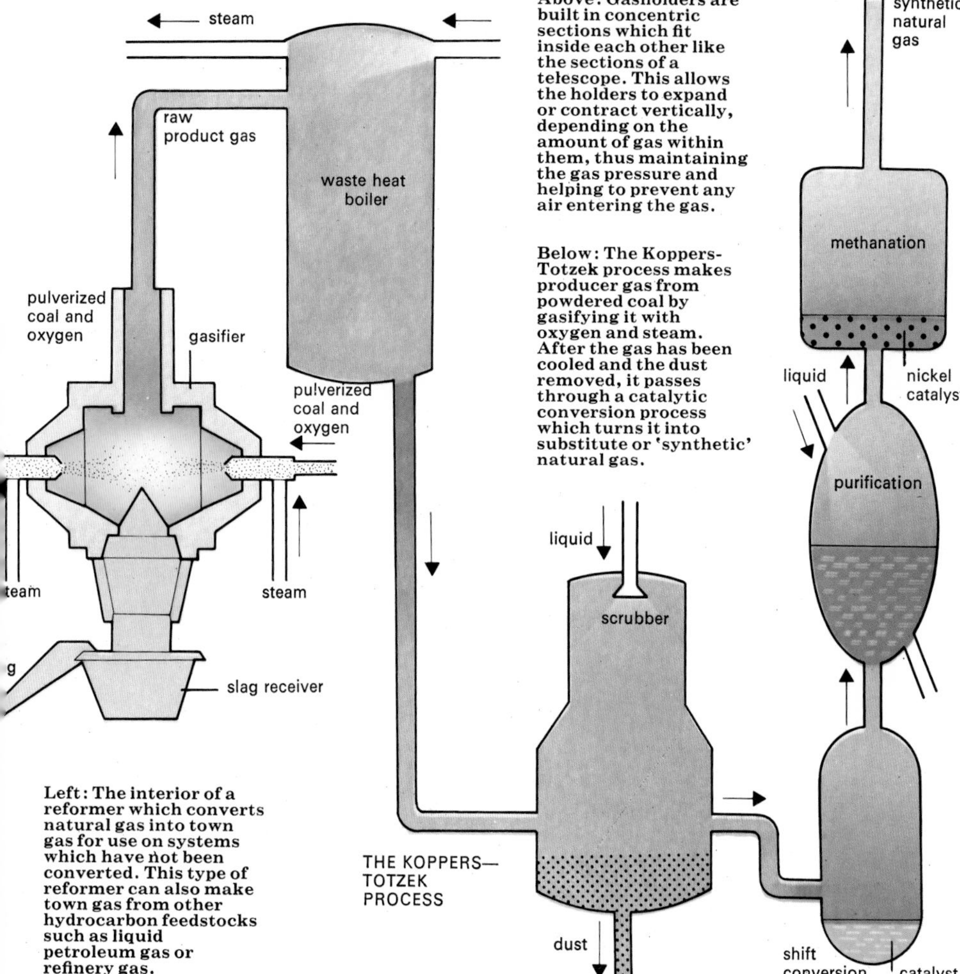

Below: The Koppers-Totzek process makes producer gas from powdered coal by gasifying it with oxygen and steam. After the gas has been cooled and the dust removed, it passes through a catalytic conversion process which turns it into substitute or 'synthetic' natural gas.

Left: The interior of a reformer which converts natural gas into town gas for use on systems which have not been converted. This type of reformer can also make town gas from other hydrocarbon feedstocks such as liquid petroleum gas or refinery gas.

Batteries and Fuel Cells

An electricity battery consists of one or more electric *cells*, which are devices for producing electric currents directly from chemical reactions. Electricity made in this way is much more expensive than that made by mechanical generators, but batteries, being compact and portable, are a better choice for many applications. The chemical generation of electricity is possible because many chemical reactions involve simply an exchange of electrons between atoms of different kinds.

The electrical nature of such reactions can easily be shown by passing a direct current through distilled water to which a little acid has been added to improve its ability to conduct electricity. The result is that the water splits up into bubbles of hydrogen and oxygen gases which can be collected separately.

This process of breaking down liquids by electricity is known as *electrolysis* and is widely used in industrial chemistry for separating many different compounds into their simple constituents. An electric cell performs electrolysis in reverse, forming compounds from simpler constituents in such a way that electricity is produced by the chemical reactions taking place.

In principle the action of an electric cell is simple. A current is created in a wire by feeding in electrons at one end and sucking them out at the other, causing the electrons to flow through the wire as an electric current. This is accomplished by attaching each end of the wire to a metal plate which is immersed in an *electrolyte*, a chemical solution of some *ionic* compound. When such a compound is dissolved, its molecules split into two or more parts which are kept apart by the molecules of the liquid it is dissolved in. Some parts of the dissolved molecule have a positive electric charge and are known as *positive ions;* other parts have a negative charge and are called *negative ions*.

For example, when sulphuric acid (H_2SO_4) is dissolved in water, the two hydrogen atoms are separated from each other and from the rest of the molecule. Because each loses an electron in this process, they become hydrogen ions and are denoted by the symbol H^+ to indicate that they have a positive charge. The rest of the molecule stays together as a sulphate ion, which is negative because it has gained two extra electrons (from the hydrogen atoms), and it is denoted by the symbol SO_4^{--}.

Sulphuric acid in water was used as the electrolyte in the first modern battery, invented by the Italian physicist Count Alessandro Volta (1745-1827) in 1800. The basic electric cell of this battery is perhaps the simplest of all. One end of the wire in which the current is to flow is connected to a plate made of zinc and the other to a copper plate. Both the plates, which are known as *electrodes*, are immersed in the electrolyte but do not touch each other.

The electrolyte reacts with the plates, feeding electrons to the zinc and extracting them from the copper in the following manner. The hydrogen ions from the sulphuric acid capture electrons from the

Left: This battery, comprising 200 cells, was built by Sir Humphry Davy in the basement of the Royal Institution, London, to provide electricity for experiments and demonstrations. The picture is from a French book of 1870.

Below: A battery of silver-zinc cells built for use in a satellite. Silver-zinc cells have an alkaline electrolyte and their electrodes are made of silver oxide and zinc. They give high power in relation to their size and weight when compared with other types of battery, and their high cost is considered worthwhile for such items as satellites. These batteries provide power for the satellite when it is in the earth's shadow and there is no light to drive its solar cells—or they take over if the solar cells break down.

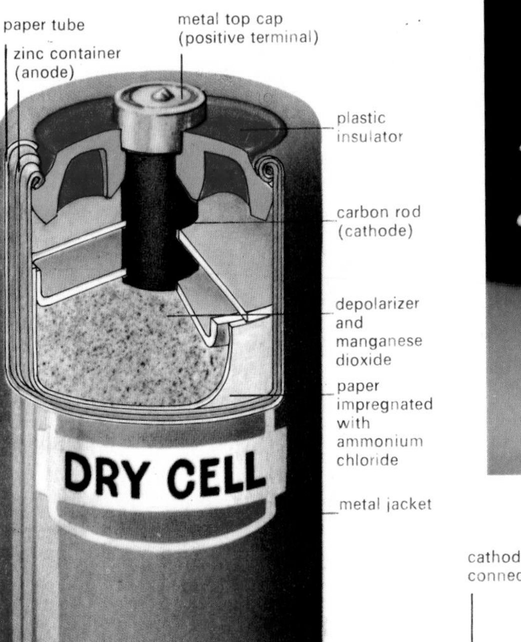

Above: A dry cell of the kind used in radios and flashlights. This particular design has a carbon rod surrounded by a depolarizer and the manganese dioxide which forms the cathode (positive electrode). The rod and cathode are surrounded by paper impregnated with ammonium chloride electrolyte, and are contained within the zinc cup which is the anode (negative electrode). During operation, electrons travel from the anode, through the external circuit and into the cathode via the carbon rod.

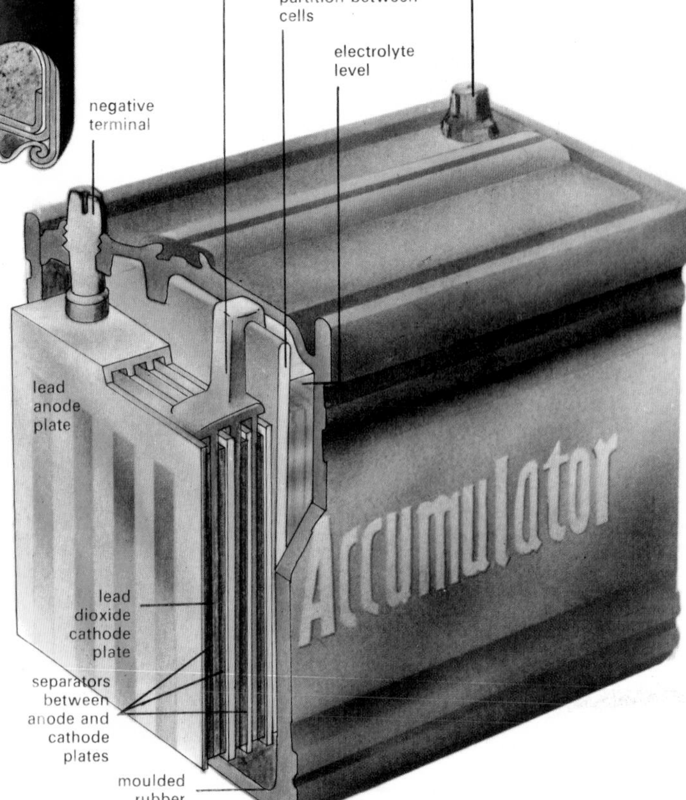

Right: This car battery has a lead anode, a lead dioxide cathode, and a dilute sulphuric acid electrolyte.

Paul Brierley

Above: Francis Bacon, who designed the first efficient fuel cell. The idea of combining hydrogen and oxygen in an electrolytic cell, producing water and electricity, was first demonstrated by Sir William Grove in 1838. Bacon began working on this idea in the 1930s, and in 1959 he introduced a hydrogen-oxygen cell capable of producing 6 kW of power. Bacon's work was taken up by Pratt and Whitney in the USA, who built the fuel cells used in the Apollo moon missions. Fuel cells are now being built for large-scale power production.

Below: Bacon's 6 kW fuel cell, built in 1959.

Francis Bacon

atoms of the copper plate and change into hydrogen atoms, which are insoluble and escape from the solution as gas. Sulphate ions capture zinc atoms to make molecules of zinc sulphate. The zinc atoms each abandon two electrons in favour of the two spare electrons on the sulphate ion. These two abandoned electrons move through the wire, as an electric current, to replace those lost at the copper plate.

If the external wire connection between the plates is broken (which is in effect what happens when, for example, a radio or a flashlight is switched off), so that electrons cannot travel from plate to plate via the wire, the reactions will soon come to a halt. This is because a layer of electric charge, caused by an excess or deficiency of electrons, builds up on each plate and prevents the ions of the electrolyte from approaching the plates closely enough to capture electrons or atoms. Thus the available chemical energy is held in check until the circuit is completed again and electrons can again flow through the wire.

Primary cells

The arrangement just described can only produce current as long as there is zinc available to be converted into zinc sulphate. Once the zinc plate has completely disintegrated, the reactions which drive the current can no longer proceed as there is no 'fuel' left to feed them. Such a cell, which can be used only once, is known as a *primary cell*. The commonest primary cell is the familiar 'dry' cell, which is almost universally used to power flashlights, transistor radios and other devices which need only a small amount of power.

This cell, also known as a *Leclanché* cell after its inventor, Georges Leclanché (1839-1882), is not really 'dry' at all. The active ingredient is still a solution of an ionic compound (ammonium chloride, NH_4Cl) in water, but there is so little water present that the solution is a thick paste. Into this paste is inserted a rod of carbon, which is a good conductor of electricity, and the whole is enclosed in a casing of zinc. As long as the carbon and zinc are unconnected no reactions take place in the cell, but as soon as they are connected by an external circuit a current begins to flow as electrons are extracted from the paste via the carbon rod and fed through the circuit into the zinc casing.

One product of the reactions in the Leclanché cell is hydrogen gas and, as this accumulates at the carbon rod, it begins to interfere with the operation of the cell if current is allowed to flow for very long. This phenomenon is known as *polarization* and is partly offset by including some manganese dioxide (MnO_2) in the paste. This *depolarizer* reacts with the hydrogen to remove it from the carbon surface.

Secondary cells

The principal disadvantage of a primary cell is its short life. Obviously it would be more useful to have a cell which could be restored to its original condition once it had discharged all the available chemical energy stored in it. Fortunately it is possible to do this with some types of cell. Other electric cells, however, rely on reactions which are reversible. In these, the chemical compounds whose formation gives rise to the current can be changed back to their original components simply by passing a current through the cell in the opposite direction. They are then free to recombine as before to make current.

Such cells are called *secondary cells* and a set of them is called a *storage battery* because it enables charge produced by other means (usually generators) to be 'stored' for later use.

Storage batteries may be divided into two types, acid and alkaline, according to the nature of the electrolyte. The principal acid battery is the familiar lead-acid *accumulator*, almost universally used in motor vehicles. Each cell of this battery consists of a plate of lead (Pb) and a plate of lead dioxide (PbO_2) both immersed in an electrolyte of dilute sulphuric acid.

At the positive plate, the lead dioxide reacts with the hydrogen and sulphate ions of the acid to make lead sulphate ($PbSO_4$) and water, extracting two electrons from the external wiring to balance the reaction electrically. At the negative plate, the lead metal reacts with the sulphate ions to make lead sulphate and feeds two electrons to the external wiring to maintain the electrical balance. The net effect of this is to produce a current of electrons from the negative to the positive plate.

When no more lead or lead dioxide remains the cell is exhausted. It can be regenerated (recharged) by passing a direct current through the cell from the negative to the positive plate. This induces the lead sulphate to break down again to lead on the negative plate and to lead dioxide on the positive.

During the recharging, the electrical energy put into the cell creates the chemical energy that breaks the lead sulphate into lead and lead dioxide, and combines the sulphate ions (freed from it) with the water to form dilute sulphuric acid. When the cell is subsequently used, these chemical reactions are reversed and the chemical energy is turned back into electrical energy. The electricity used in recharging the cell can thus be thought to have been 'stored' by the cell.

Alkaline batteries, as the name implies, have an alkaline electrolyte, usually

Right: Hydrogen gas, which can be used to run fuel cells producing electricity for domestic and industrial premises, could be produced by the electrolysis of water. The electricity required for the electrolysis could be generated by using natural energy sources such as the wind, waves or sunlight. The energy available from these sources is variable and unpredictable—there may be plenty at times when demand for electricity is low, and little when demand is high. Electricity itself cannot be stored, so it cannot be generated during periods of low demand and kept until it is needed. If it is used to make hydrogen, however, the gas, and in effect the energy used to make it, can be stored almost indefinitely, and distributed by pipeline in the same way as natural gas and town gas are conveyed.

Below: When dc electricity is passed through water, hydrogen gas collects at the cathode and oxygen gas at the anode.

Right: In a hydrogen-oxygen fuel cell the two gases react with the electrolyte, producing water and electricity.

Below: These two diagrams show how fuel cells, running on hydrogen produced by the system shown on the left, could replace the existing electricity supply system. The cycle of events would be as follows: natural energy sources produce electricity, which is used to obtain hydrogen from water. The hydrogen is then distributed to fuel cell units, on the consumers' premises, which produce electricity by combining the hydrogen with oxygen from the air to make water.

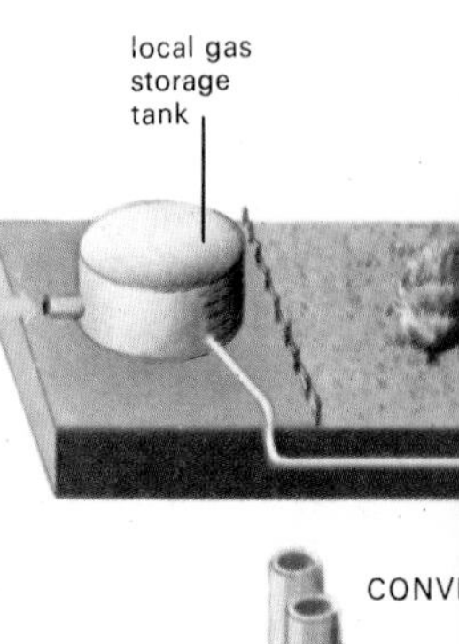

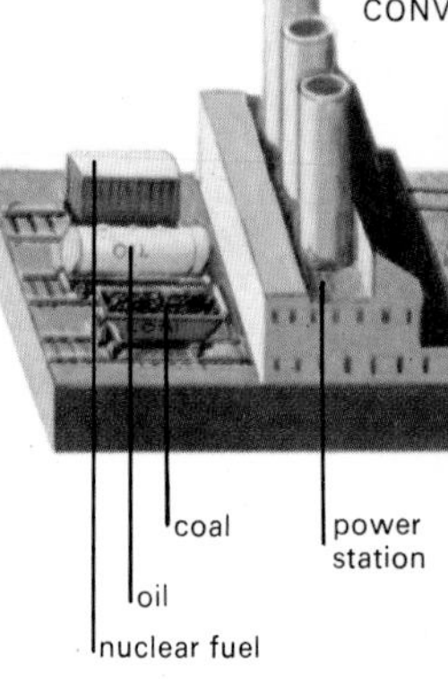

potassium hydroxide (KOH). A common type of alkaline cell has one plate made of an oxide of nickel (Ni) and one of iron (Fe), and for this reason it is often known as the *NiFe* battery. Each cell weighs less than a lead cell but gives out only 1.2 volts. So for a 12 volt battery ten cells are needed as against six lead cells, which means that a NiFe battery ends up no lighter than a lead accumulator. Another type of alkaline cell, which has plates of silver oxide (AgO) and zinc (Zn), can give from two to ten times as much electrical energy for the same weight, but it is not widely used because of the high cost of silver.

Fuel cells

Even a secondary cell, however, cannot be used continuously. Its ability to be recharged is certainly a considerable advantage, but recharging takes several hours during which the cell cannot be used to provide current. So to obtain an uninterrupted current at least two batteries are needed and some means of recharging. All these problems are overcome in the *fuel cell*. In this, unlike any of the cells described above, the substances whose reactions drive the current are not contained within the cell but are fed into it as required to sustain the reaction.

The first efficient fuel cell was produced, after many years of development work, by the English engineer Francis Bacon in 1959. Fuelled by hydrogen and oxygen gas, it is still the most reliable and widely used type and was chosen for the Apollo space missions.

The Bacon cell is filled with an alkaline electrolyte, potassium hydroxide in water, which is bounded by two very special electrode plates. They are made out of porous metal into which the electrolyte can penetrate, although it cannot pass right through. On the other side of one electrode is hydrogen gas, at a pressure which is carefully controlled so that the gas also can only penetrate part way into the plate. The other electrode is fed with oxygen gas in the same way.

The chemical and physical properties of the electrodes are crucial to the operation of the fuel cell, for it is only in the pores of these that the gases come into contact with the electrolyte. At the positive plate hydrogen molecules combine with *hydroxyl* ions (OH) from the electrolyte and release electrons into the electrode. At the negative plate oxygen atoms capture electrons from the electrode metal and combine with water molecules to make hydroxyl ions which dissolve in the electrolyte.

If the electrodes are connected outside the cell, the reactions will continue and current will flow from the positive to the negative plate as long as hydrogen and oxygen are supplied. To encourage the reactions to proceed at a reasonably rapid rate, the electrodes are made of a metal which acts as a catalyst. The best for this purpose is platinum, but since this is expensive Bacon cells use nickel which works very well at a temperature of about 200°C (392°F).

Another very promising type of fuel cell uses a metal carbonate as electrolyte. At the operating temperature of 700°C (1,292°F) the electrolyte separates into metal and carbonate (CO_3^{-}) ions. The fuel is carbon monoxide (CO) at the positive plate, which reacts with carbonate ions to make carbon dioxide gas (CO_2) and supplies electrons as a result.

At the negative plate, oxygen combines with the carbon dioxide, extracting electrons from the plate as it does so, to make more carbonate ions. Fuel for this cell is cheap because the higher temperature allows air to be used at the negative electrode to supply oxygen, so a supply of

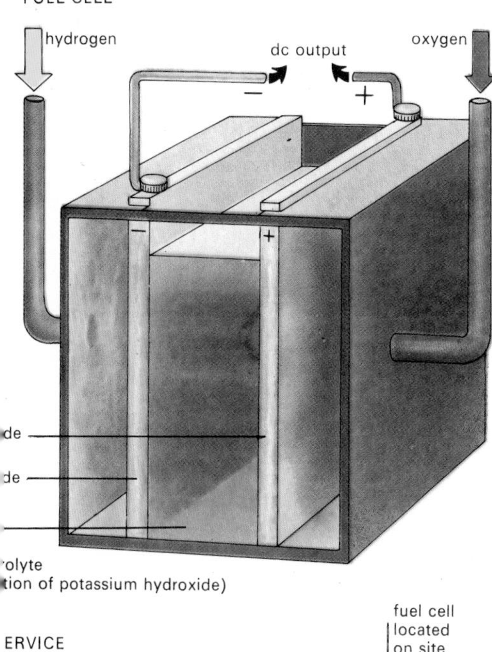

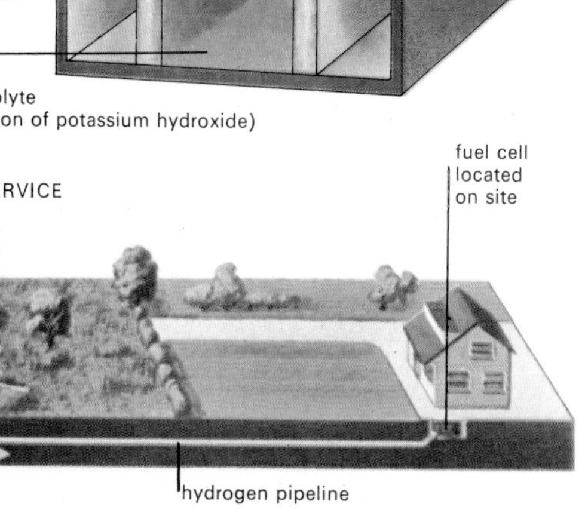

Above: One of the fuel cell elements used in a 25 MW power unit capable of supplying the electricity for a town of 20,000 people. The power unit consists of a fuel conditioner, which produces hydrogen from natural gas, hydrogen-oxygen fuel cells, and an inverter which turns the dc output into alternating current.

Left and below left: A great deal of work is going into the development of electric cars. At present these are powered by batteries, but future designs may use fuel cells running on fuels such as liquid hydrogen, hydrazine (N_2H_4), or powdered metal-hydrogen compounds (hydrides).

Electricity Council

pure oxygen is not required, and carbon monoxide is obtained as an inexpensive by-product in the distillation of coal tar.

Fuel cells are beginning to find more and more applications in industry and transportation. They are not at present particularly suitable for small vehicles, because the ancillary equipment needed to heat up the cell initially and remove surplus water (from the Bacon cell) or carbon dioxide (from the carbonate cell) produced by the reactions adds significantly to the weight of a small installation. However they are ideal for long-term supply of electricity in environments such as space stations and underwater habitats, where it is impractical to install conventional generating equipment.

Fuel cells are also beginning to look more attractive for some applications which have previously been the exclusive province of thermo-mechanical generators, because a fuel cell (unlike a conventional primary or secondary cell) is more efficient at converting chemical energy to electricity. Unfortunately the initial cost of a fuel cell installation on a large scale is at present far too high for it to be widely used, about ten times that of a conventional plant, even though running costs are lower.

Chapter 3
Scientific Method

One of the many uses of the laser beam-gas velocities and turbulence being measured within the manifold of a car by laser anenometry.

Logic and Games

Logic and the theory of games are two fields of mathematics concerned with the study of decision-making. In logic, the object is to determine the truth or falsity of the arguments used in arriving at a decision, but game-theory deals with situations in which a decision has to be made between two conflicting requirements, both of which may be true. Logic and game-theory are closely related, and in some circumstances a combination of both may be required.

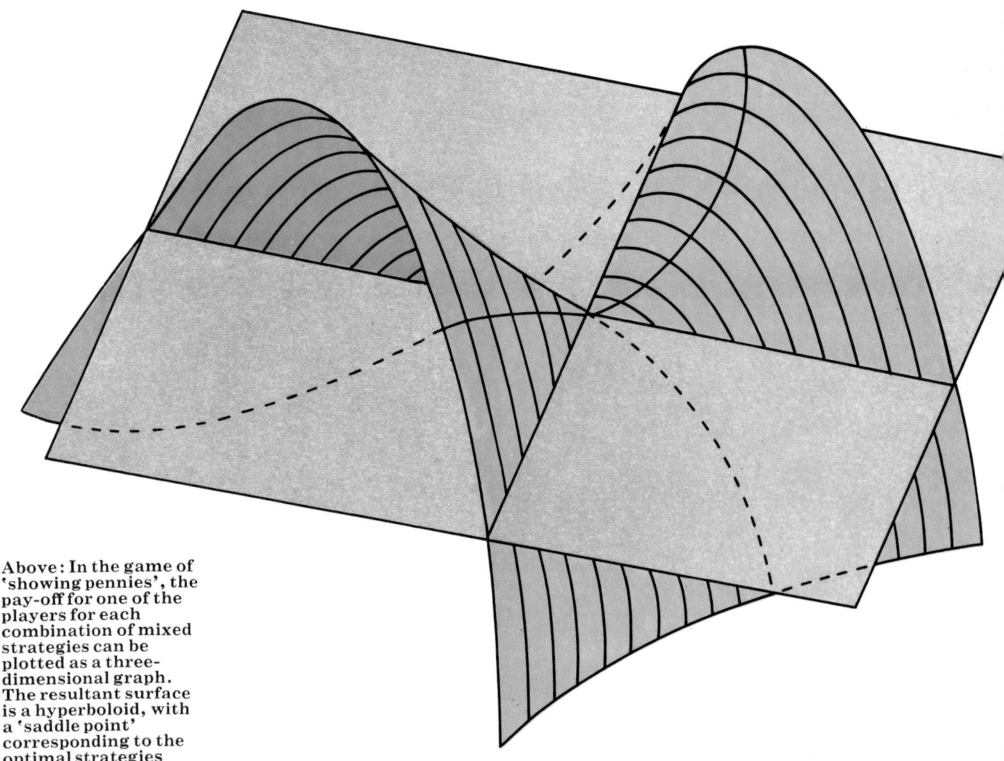

Above: In the game of 'showing pennies', the pay-off for one of the players for each combination of mixed strategies can be plotted as a three-dimensional graph. The resultant surface is a hyperboloid, with a 'saddle point' corresponding to the optimal strategies which can be used.

Game Theory

The theory of games was first suggested by Borel in 1921, but the basic result of the theory was proven by John von Neumann in 1928. The games in question are those of strategy, such as parlour games, chess and poker, but a complete analysis of real games such as these tends to be extremely complicated and so it is best to study the ideas of the theory in terms of very simple games.

Even simple games, however, show features which are important not only in game theory but also in its application, as suggested by von Neumann, to economics. Von Neumann argued that the social sciences had made little progress in applying mathematics to their theories because the type of mathematics available was devised with physics in mind, and thus a new kind of mathematics was needed.

The simplest form of game theory deals with two-person games such as 'showing pennies'. In this game the two players, call them 'P' and 'Q', each show a coin simultaneously. With the pay-off rules that if both have displayed heads or both tails, P pockets both, but if they have displayed different faces then Q pockets both, it is obvious that the best strategy each player can adopt is to show heads or tails at random and hope for the best.

If, however, the pay-off rule to Q is changed slightly, so that in the case of a mixed showing the player showing heads has to pay, in addition to what was to have been paid under the previous rules, an extra half the value of the coin to the player showing tails, the situation is quite different. Thus if P shows heads and Q shows tails, then P pays Q $1\frac{1}{2}$, and if P shows tails and Q shows heads, then Q receives only $\frac{1}{2}$ instead of the 1 that would have been paid under the previous rules.

The game under the new rules has, on first examination, the appearance of being just as fair as the earlier version, for Q's greater gain on one occasion is counterbalanced by a lesser gain on another. This appearance, however, is deceptive.

Suppose that P chooses to show heads on average 3 times out of 8, in a long run of games. Then, on average, by showing heads Q can expect to pay P 1 in $\frac{3}{8}$ of the games and to receive $\frac{1}{2}$ from P in the remaining $\frac{5}{8}$ of the games. This would give Q an average loss of 1/16 per game.

But if Q shows tails instead of heads, a similar calculation shows yet again an average loss for Q of 1/16 per game. From P's point of view, this strategy provides an expected average gain of 1/16 per game, whatever Q may do.

A similar argument for Q shows that the best strategy is to show heads for $\frac{5}{8}$ of the games in order to ensure that the loss is no worse than 1/16 whatever P may do. The game is said to have a *value* of 1/16 to P, and the strategies described are called *optimal strategies* for P and Q. Since the specification of the optimal strategies is in terms of average numbers of different moves over a large number of plays of the game, they are called *mixed strategies*. If the optimal strategy for Q had been, say, to show only heads, it would have been a *pure strategy*.

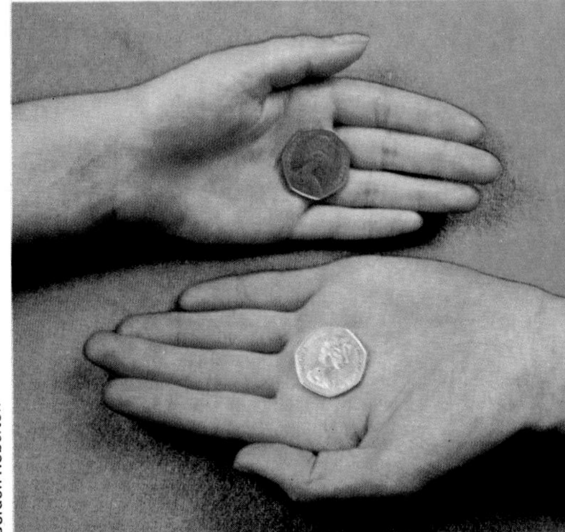

Gordon Roberton

Above and below: The game of 'showing pennies' is a simple form of two-person game. The simplest pay-off rules are that when both players ('P' and 'Q') show heads, as above, or tails, as below, P wins both coins, but if one shows heads and the other shows tails, then Q wins both coins. When playing to these rules, the optimal strategy for each player is simply to show heads or tails at random and hope for a maximum number of wins. Over a large enough number of plays each player will have won the same number, and so these rules offer no unfair advantage to either of the players.

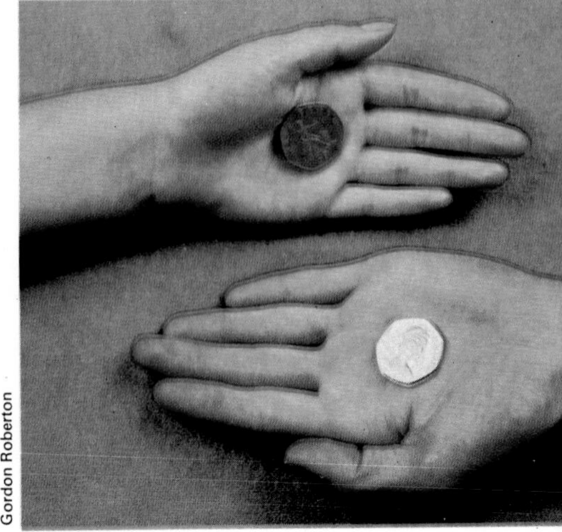

Gordon Roberton

Games for more than two players

A simple analysis such as the one above would not be possible if the game were one, like chess, in which there are a large number of strategies open to each player. However, von Neumann was able to show that, in any such two-person game, there are always optimal mixed strategies and the game has a unique value.

The economic application concerns *duopolies*, situations in which two firms are competing for the same market, and the different strategies are their different promotional options. As soon as the number of players (or firms) increases to three, the situation is quite different, for now the deciding factor is which, if any, of the players agree to co-operate with each other. Moreover, von Neumann's version of the theory of three-person games is now widely regarded as being incomplete, since it excludes any discussion of what factors determine such co-operation.

Little is known of the theory of four-person games. Attempts have been made to augment von Neumann's theory of three-person games, notably by Kemeny in 1959, but the determination of the complete theory is still in the future. It is known, however, that not all games (with any number of players) will have solutions in von Neumann's sense, although

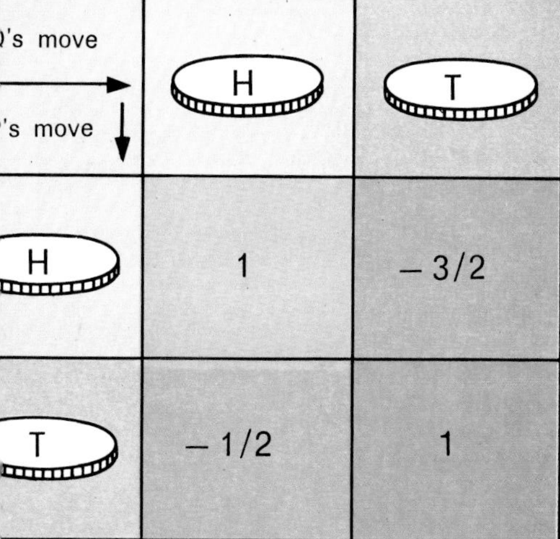

)'s move → / 's move ↓	H	T
H	1	– 3/2
T	– 1/2	1

Above: The pay-off chart for the 'showing pennies' game, when in the case of a mixed showing the player showing heads has to pay an extra ½. This chart shows the pay-offs for player 'P', the minus figures indicating payments by P to player 'Q', and the other figures payments by Q to P.

AP

Right: John von Neumann (1903-1957), author of the *Theory of Games and Economic Behaviour*, with his wife Klara and his dog Inverse. In addition to his work on the theory of games, von Neumann was the leader of a team which built one of the first computers to use a stored program of operating instructions.

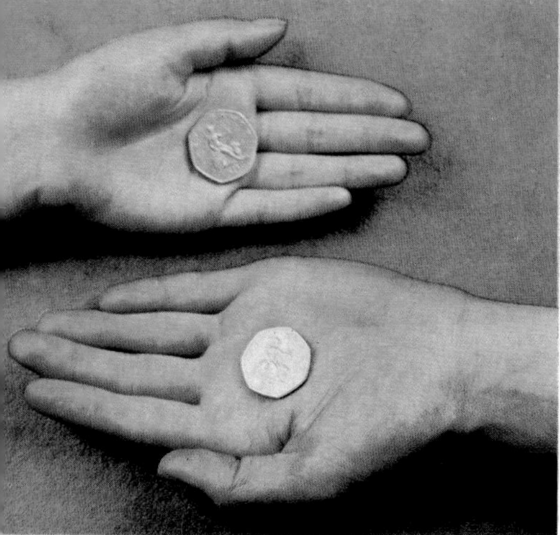

Gordon Roberton

Above and below: A small variation in the pay-off rules of the game of 'showing pennies' can result in an automatic advantage to one of the players. If the rules are modified so that, in the case of a mixed showing, the player who shows heads has to pay an additional ½ to the other player, then if P shows heads and Q shows tails, above, P pays Q 1½. If Q shows heads and P tails, below, then P only pays Q ½. Under these rules, P can adopt a strategy which will provide an average gain of 1/16 per game, regardless of any attempt by Q to adopt a strategy to prevent it. The game has a *value* to P of 1/16.

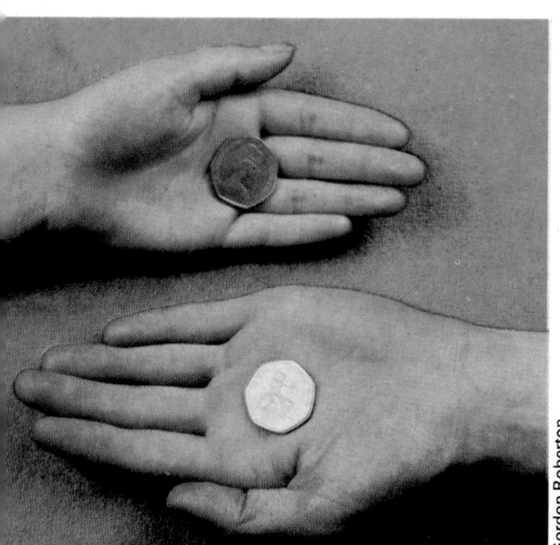

Gordon Roberton

the greatest number of players for which a theory, like his 1928 one for two-person games can be determined, is still not known.

Logic

Modern mathematical logic has evolved, over the last 100 years, from the form of logic established by Aristotle in the fourth century BC. The Aristotelian logic was based on the use of *propositions*, sentences, used in arguments, which are either true or false. It made the assumption that all propositions could be put into one of four forms.

Each of these forms contained two terms, known respectively as the *subject* and the *predicate*, these terms being linked by words such as 'is', 'are', 'is not' or 'are not', with the subject being qualified by words such as 'all', 'no' or 'some'. Examples of propositions containing such terms are 'All men are mammals' (subject 'men', predicate 'mammals'), and 'No mammals are cold-blooded' (subject 'mammals', predicate 'cold-blooded').

This form of logic then went on to make the further incorrect assumption that most valid arguments could be analyzed into the form of three such propositions, namely two *premisses* and a *conclusion*. Using the two propositions mentioned above as the premisses, the conclusion would be derived by getting rid of the *middle term*, 'mammals', which occurs in both premisses, to give the conclusion 'No men are cold-blooded'.

Aristotle and his successors through the Middle Ages codified all the valid forms of this kind of argument, known as *syllogisms*, and found 19 of them.

Venn diagrams

Arguments of the Aristotelian type can be represented graphically by means of *Venn diagrams*, which were invented by the British mathematician John Venn in the nineteenth century. The argument mentioned above can thus be represented by three overlapping circles, representing men, mammals and cold-blooded animals respectively.

The areas where the 'men' and 'mammals' circles overlap the 'cold-blooded animals' circle are shaded to indicate 'emptiness', because no members of either of these groups are cold-blooded. Similarly, since no men are not mammals, the area of the 'men' circle which does not fall within the 'mammals' circle is also empty.

The diagram thus shows that all men are mammals, some mammals are men, but no men or mammals are cold-blooded.

Boolean algebra

Some attempt at making this form of logic more mathematical was made by Lully (1234-1315), a monk of Aragon, and later by Leibniz (1646-1716) in Germany, but no real progress was made until the middle of the nineteenth century. In 1847 and 1854, the English mathematician George Boole (1815-1864) published details of his work on mathematical logic. Boole was still working with syllogisms, but he invented a way of setting them out in algebraic form which later evolved into *Boolean Algebra*.

His system of notation is as follows. Each *set* of objects under discussion is assigned a letter from the alphabet, such as x, y and z. The entire range of objects under discussion, called the *universe of*

Photri

Left: The German philosopher Gottfried Leibniz (1646-1716) was one of the first to attempt the formulation of a mathematical notation for logic. He also suggested that, once logic could be adequately expressed mathematically, it should be possible to build a machine capable of using these mathematical equations to resolve arguments and solve problems—which, in a way, is what modern computers are doing.

Right and below: Computers can be programmed to play games, but in view of the enormous range of strategies possible in games such as chess, their success has been rather limited.

Photri

Aberdeen University/Alphabet & Image

Below: Simple arguments can be represented by Venn diagrams like this one, in which the relationships between sets are shown by intersecting circles which represent them.

Below: This Venn diagram represents the premisses 'All men are mammals' and 'No mammals are cold-blooded', and the conclusion 'No men are cold-blooded'.

discourse, is represented by the figure 1, and in addition there is a set which contains no members, called the *empty set*, which is represented by an 0.

The product of two sets, for example xy, represents the *common part*, that is, objects which are both x and y. Where $xy = 0$, the set 'xy' is an empty set and so x and y have no common part. In this case, $x + y$ will be the set of objects which are either x or y. Subtraction of terms is also possible, for instance $x - y$ is the set of objects which are x but not y, and $1 - x$ is the set of objects which are not x.

Using his algebraic logic, Boole was able to show that two of the nineteen forms of Aristotelian syllogism were, in fact, invalid. One of the two invalid forms is exemplified by 'All men are cowards, All men are mammals, therefore, Some mammals are cowards'. Using x, y and z for mammals, cowards and men respectively, Boole would write the premisses as $z(1 - y) = 0$ and $z(1 - x) = 0$, and the conclusion as xy 0, meaning xy does not equal 0. This conclusion certainly cannot follow, since the two algebraic premisses would also be true if $z = 0$, that is, if there were no men at all. Since we are concerned with the form of the argument and not with the particular terms involved, this possibility cannot be ruled out, and so this form of syllogism is actually invalid.

Modern logic, which deals simply with propositions, arose obscurely in the work of both Frege (1848-1925) in Germany and Peano (1858-1932) in Italy, and was brilliantly codified by Whitehead and Russell in *Principia Mathematica* (1910-1913).

..aws of Chance

..ematical probability provides a ..s of determining the likelihood of ..occurrence of a particular event, .. that a series of other events have ..dy occurred. The theory can be ..ssfully applied to an enormous .. of situations, from simple ones— .. as whether a tossed coin will come .. showing heads or tails—to the ..lex and subtle probabilities involved ..antum mechanics.

.. tossing

..ose that a coin is tossed a very large ..er of times, and that after each toss ..esult is written down, writing 'H' if ..oin lands heads uppermost and a 'T' ..ands tails uppermost. Assuming that ..oin is evenly balanced, and that it .. lands on its edge, we can expect a ..ly equal number of H's and T's. In .. tosses, a 'fair' coin will produce ..t 500 H's and 500 T's; if we had ..ded 700 H's and only 300 T's it ..d look very much as though the coin .. biased, so that on a single toss it ..d be much more likely to land head-..ıp than tail-side-up. Intuitively, ..ability is a measure of the *likelihood* .. event.

..ppose that, over a long sequence of .. tossings, the proportion of H's in ..rst 'n' tosses is p_n (H), that is, the .. number of H's in the first n tossings, ..ed by n itself. Then, as n gets very .. we find (by practical experience) .. the sequence of numbers p_n(H) ..s down and gets closer and closer ..ome fixed number, called p(H), .. is the *probability* that on a single ..he coin will land head-up.

..ce p_n(H) is a proportion, it, and ..fore p(H), must lie between zero ..ne. If the coin is fair, then p_n(H) ..get nearer and nearer to $\frac{1}{2}$ as n in-..es, so that for a fair coin the proba-.. of a 'head', p(H), is $\frac{1}{2}$. If p(H) is ..ent from $\frac{1}{2}$, then the coin is biased ..as a definite tendency to land with a ..ular face uppermost.

..ce we have excluded the possibility ..the coin lands on its edge, the pro-..on of tosses in which the result is .. H or T must be 1 for all values of ..d so the probability p(H or T) must ..e 1. After n tosses the number of H's ..the number of T's must be n, and ..fore $p_n(H) + p_n(T) = 1$, so that .. + p(T) = 1. But since p(H or T) = 1 ..neans that p(H) + p(T) = p(H or T), ..s, the probability of an H plus the ..bility of a T is equal to the proba-.. of getting an H or a T.

..inty

..roperties that we have found for ..bility in the case of coin-tossing ..eneral ones. Suppose we have any ..iment, the result of which is one of ..ossible outcomes which we label ..E_2, . . . E_k and call *events*. We ..e that only one of these events can .. at a time. Then, if the experiment is ..ted *independently* (so that the out-.. of one does not affect the outcome .. next) a large number of times under ..cal conditions, the proportion of .. the event E_i occurs will get close .. probability $p(E_i)$ for each value of

Bruce Coleman

Above: Random sampling is a quality control method used by manufacturers which involves testing a small, random sample of goods from each batch produced. If the goods in the random sample are up to standard, then there is a high probability that the entire batch is satisfactory.

PASCAL'S TRIANGLE

1 1
1 2 1
1 3 3 1
1 4 6 4 1
1 5 10 10 5 1
1 6 15 20 15 6 1

Right: The figures in this triangle are arranged so that they can be used to calculate the probabilities of combinations. For example, the third horizontal row shows the odds governing the likely numbers of boys or girls in a three-child family. Adding the figures gives a total of 8; the least likely combinations, of boys only or girls only are indicated by the end figures—giving odds of 1 in 8. The chances of there being two girls and one boy, or vice-versa, are shown by the middle figures—3 in 8.

Below: The chances of a family of seven children being all the same sex are 1 in 128.

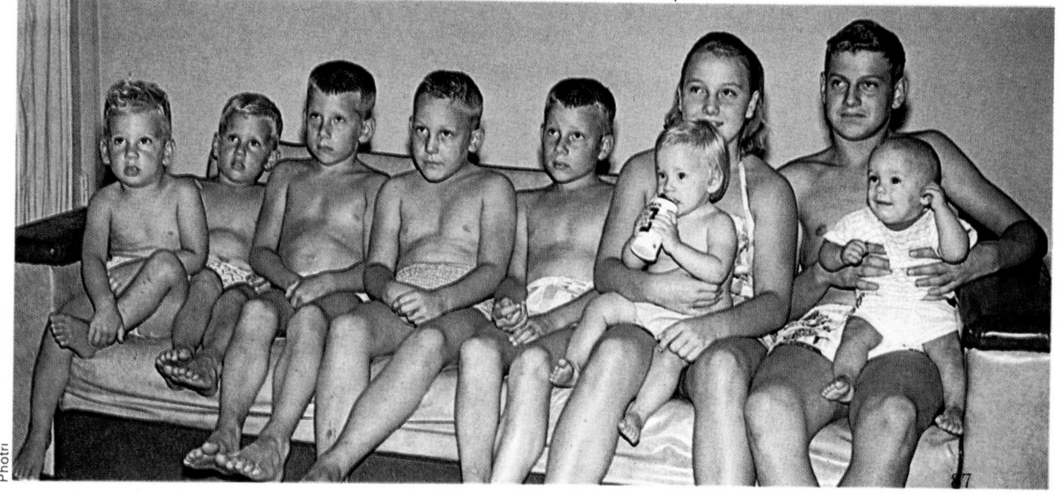
Photri

The zero on a roulette wheel ensures a balance in favour of the casino. Since it is neither red nor black, nor between 1 and 36 it is rarely bet upon, and when it does come up all other stakes are forfeit to the bank.

ZEFA (UK) Ltd.

Keystone

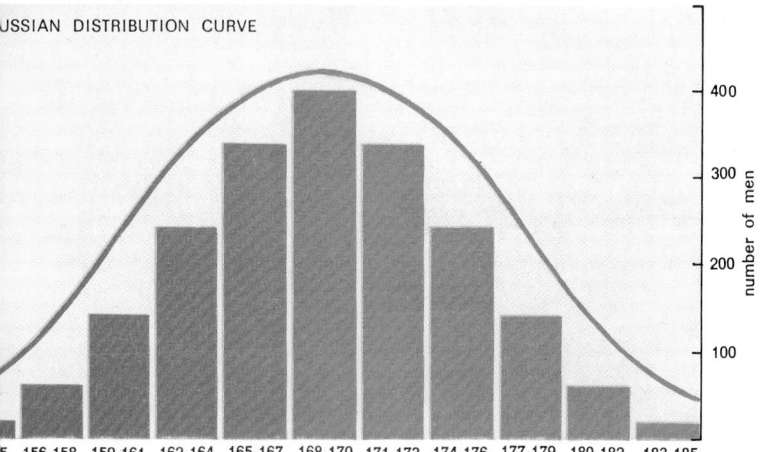

Above and left: If the heights of a large number of men are measured, and plotted on a graph, the result is a diagram which shows how the number of individuals in each height category falls away smoothly to either side of the middle range of heights. The curved line is a *Gaussian curve*, and this shape of curve is obtained whenever large numbers of variations about an average point are plotted on a graph like this. For any such set of variables, once the average values and the upper and lower limits are known, the Gaussian curve can be used to find the probable distribution of individual variables within a sample group of them.

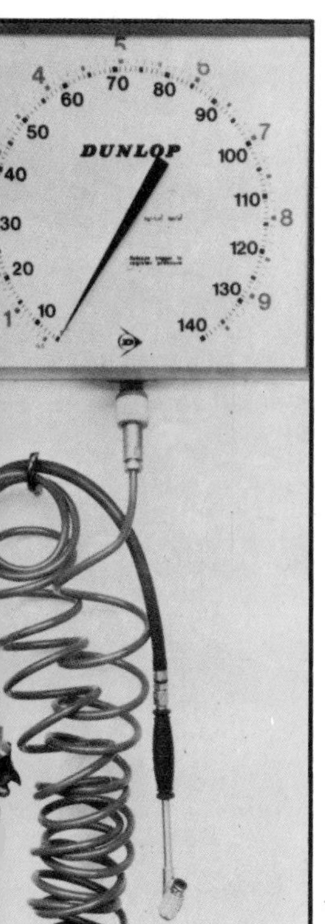

Dunlop

Left and below: Probability theory is widely used in statistics, but statistics involve measurements and are thus affected by the principle of *uncertainty*. This principle can be expressed as the fact that it is impossible to measure something without altering it in some way. Thus the tyre pressure gauge, on the left, has to let some air out of the tyre in order to measure the pressure, and this loss of air reduces the pressure. If the current in an electric circuit is to be measured, inserting an ammeter, below, into the circuit makes it a different circuit to that whose current was to have been measured.

Eagle Int.

1, that is for $i = 1, i = 2, \ldots i = k$.

These probabilities will always lie between zero and one; they will add up to one, that is, $p(E_1) + p(E_2) + \ldots p(E_k) = 1$; and they will satisfy the expression $p(E_i) + p(E_j) = p(E_i \text{ or } E_j)$, where '$E_i$ or E_j' denotes the outcome that 'either E_i or E_j' occurs, where E_i and E_j are any two of the possible outcomes of the experiment. The demonstration of these properties is exactly the same as in the coin-tossing, and an event which has a probability of 1 is said to be *certain*.

Some simple examples of an experiment with 'k' outcomes are:

(i) throwing a die, with event E_i defined as 'the die shows the number i' for $i = 1, 2, \ldots 6$. Here, $k = 6$ and $p(E_i) = 1/6$ for $i = 1, 2, \ldots 6$ if the die is fair.

(ii) throwing a die with E_1 defined as 'the die shows the number 1 or 2' and E_2 defined as 'the die shows the number 3, 4, 5 or 6'. Here, $k = 2$ and if the die is fair $p(E_1) = 1/3$ and $p(E_2) = 2/3$.

(iii) drawing a single card from a pack of 52 playing cards, with the event E_1 being 'the card is a club', E_2 being 'the card is a diamond', E_3 being 'the card is a spade' and E_4 being 'the card is a heart'. Here, $k = 4$ and $p(E_1) = p(E_2) = p(E_3) = p(E_4) = \frac{1}{4}$.

Conditional probability

Consider drawing a single card from a pack of playing cards (without a joker). The probability that the card is the four of diamonds is 1/52. This is because there are 52 cards in the pack, all of which are equally likely to be drawn, and so all have the same probability, p. Since some card must be drawn, the sum of these probabilities is 1, that is, $52p = 1$, or $p = 1/52$.

But suppose we are told that the card drawn is a diamond, what is the probability of it being the four of diamonds? In this case the card is one of thirteen possible cards (the number of diamond cards in the pack), and again all are equally likely to have been drawn, and so the probability is 1/13.

This is an example of *conditional probability*, and it is the probability that the card is the four of diamonds conditional on the fact that it is known to be a diamond.

Independence

When we mentioned earlier the repeating of experiments *independently* under identical conditions, we meant that the outcome of one experiment had no effect upon the outcome of the next. For example, when tossing a coin it is usually reasonable to assume that the result of one toss will not depend upon the result of the previous toss, nor will it affect the result of the next.

A well-known example of the concept of independence is as follows. If a coin is tossed twice, then, it was argued by the French mathematician D'Alembert (1717-1783), there are three possible results, namely (i) two heads, (ii) one head, one tail, and (iii) two tails, and so the probability of each of these results must be 1/3.

If you perform the experiment a large number of times, and calculate the proportions of occasions on which each of these results was obtained you will find that result (ii) occurs roughly half the time while results (i) and (iii) each occur about a quarter of the time, and this contradicts the argument that the probabilities are each 1/3. What is the explanation?

The essential part is that event (ii) splits into two parts, (iia) that the first toss gives a head and the second toss gives a tail, and (iib) that the first toss gives a tail and the second a head. Then events (i), (iia), (iib) and (iii) are really equally likely and so each have a probability of $\frac{1}{4}$. Event (ii) in fact has a probability of $\frac{1}{2}$, compared with the $\frac{1}{4}$ of events (i) and (iii).

As another example, consider families with three children. If, as is approximately biologically correct, we assume that the sexes of the different children are independent of each other and that each child is equally likely to be a boy or a girl, then the probability that a family of three children consists only of boys is $\frac{1}{8}$.

The possible families can be written as BBG, BBB, BGG, BGB, GBG, GBB, GGG and GGB, where 'G' denotes a girl and 'B' denotes a boy, and the order of the letters gives the order in which the children are born. There are thus eight different but equally likely possibilities, only one of which gives a family of boys only, and so the probability is $\frac{1}{8}$.

Alternatively, since the series of different children are independent, p(BBB) =

$[p(B)]^3$, and since each child is equally likely to be a boy or a girl, $p(B) = \frac{1}{2}$, so that $p(BBB) = 1/2^3 = \frac{1}{8}$.

Simple calculations of the sort described above occur in a very wide range of 'real-life' situations. An important example of this is in the field of genetics, where probabilistic models are used in attempts to determine, for example, the chances of a child inheriting a particular disease or defect when it has occurred previously in the family.

Probability theory often produces some surprising results. A good example of this is to suppose that we have a room with 23 people in it. Since there are 365 days in an ordinary year, it would seem surprising if two of these people had the same birthday. Yet the probability of this happening is more than $\frac{1}{2}$, and if we were to look at a large enough number of rooms all containing 23 people, randomly selected from the population as a whole, then we would find that in more than half of these rooms two of the people would share the same birthday.

Determinism

We have talked above of experiments, such as coin-tossing, being repeated

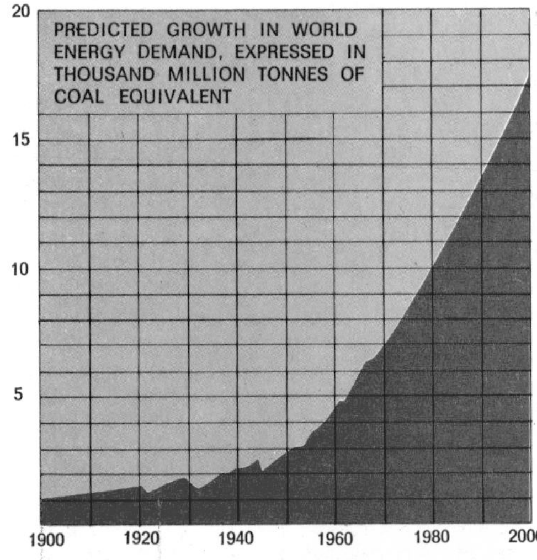

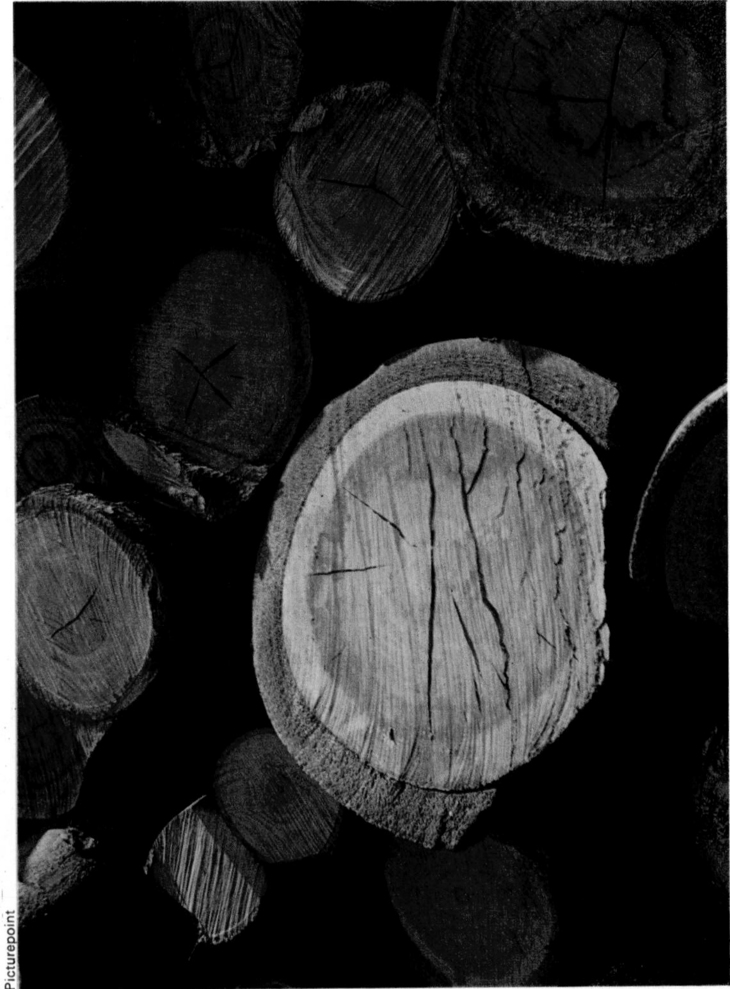

Picturepoint

Above, right and left: Past climatic variations can be detected by studying the thicknesses of the layers of sediment deposited annually by the meltwaters from glaciers, or by measuring the thicknesses of tree rings. This form of *inductive reasoning*, the derivation of general conclusions from the study of particular items or facts, is also used by statisticians when they use a known set of facts to predict future trends, such as the growth in the world's demand for energy up to the year 2000.

Syndication International

Left: Harold Wilson's surprise defeat in the 1970 General Election in Britain was regarded by many observers as an example of the effect of public opinion poll forecasts upon the attitudes of voters. According to the uncertainty principle, asking someone for their opinion on something may, by making them think about it, cause them to subsequently alter it. However, in view of the relatively small sample of voters questioned by the opinion poll interviewers, this could not have accounted for the fact that the actual election result was practically the opposite of that predicted by the polls. It is more likely that many Labour Party supporters did not bother to vote because the polls predicted such an easy victory for Labour.

Inigo Everson/Bruce Coleman

Bruce Coleman

Above: Long before the mechanism of the solar system had been realized, people 'knew' that the sun would always rise in the east and set again in the west; this conclusion had been arrived at by a crude form of inductive reasoning—it always had, and therefore it always would.

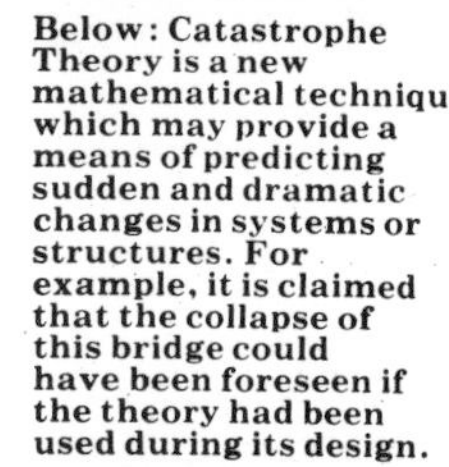

Below: Catastrophe Theory is a new mathematical technique which may provide a means of predicting sudden and dramatic changes in systems or structures. For example, it is claimed that the collapse of this bridge could have been foreseen if the theory had been used during its design.

Keystone

under identical conditions. If a card is drawn from a pack, and 'under identical conditions' means that the cards are in the same order within the pack and the chosen card is in the same position, then this experiment will always have the same result.

Similarly, any student of classical mechanics knows that if, when coins are tossed, all positions, velocities and external forces are kept the same, then it follows from Newton's laws that the final result will be the same. So when discussing repeating experiments under identical conditions, and finding the probabilities of different outcomes from the proportions of occurrences of these outcomes, it certainly does not mean that the conditions will be quite so identical. If they were, then the experiments would be completely deterministic—that is, the results would be pre-determined and there would be no need of probability.

In fact, the observed sequence of results has its origin in the *uncontrollable* variations in the initial conditions which occur when the experiments are actually performed. In the physical world, uncertainties of this sort lead to results of the type discussed. At a more fundamental level, in atomic and nuclear physics (quantum mechanics), probabilities arise which are of a totally different nature—the probabilities are *intrinsic* to the systems, and no amount of knowledge of the initial conditions can ever remove them. This possibility that the physical world contains intrinsic probabilistic aspects poses problems for philosophers who have traditionally inclined towards a deterministic, cause-and-effect view of the world.

The Nature of Mathematics

To ask the nature of mathematics is to pose a question to which the answer is by no means clear. The reason for this strange state of affairs is to be found in the historical development of the subject.

The origins of counting and number systems are lost in antiquity, but as long as 4,000 years ago the Akkadian arithmetic was a high point of Babylonian culture. Unlike most modern counting systems, including our own, where the number 10 plays a basic role, this Babylonian system was based on the number 60. Irrespective of the actual symbols used, or the numbers upon which they are based, all developed counting systems are precise formulations of the concept of the *natural number*.

To the obvious natural numbers, such as 1, 2, 3, 4 and so on, we now usually add the *zero*, 0, which did not in fact appear as a genuine number (as distinct from a sign to indicate a space) until the Hindu arithmetic of the ninth century AD.

In due course the ideas of space and length, that is of *geometry*, were added to those of counting. Geometry arose as a practical subject, out of such problems as those involved in the surveying of the land around the Nile delta which was subject to annual flooding, but from about 500 BC onwards it was developed as a theoretical subject by the Greeks.

Pre-eminent in early Greek geometry was the proof of the theorem of Pythagoras, which stated that the square of the longest side of a right-angled triangle was equal to the sum of the squares of the other two sides. Thus for a triangle whose sides are 3, 4, and 5 units long, the square of the longest side is 25, which equals $3^2 + 4^2$, or $9 + 16$, the sum of the squares of the other two sides.

Calculus

To the Greek mathematicians such as Pythagoras, the concept of 'number' meant natural number. Fractions were only used in commerce; in geometry a ratio was not a fraction, but a separate entity. Later mathematicians, however, adopted a more general idea of number, considering first the *rational numbers* or fractions, and then the *real numbers*, those involving decimals instead of fractions.

Whereas the natural numbers increase in definite steps of one at a time (1, 2, 3 etc), any two rational or real numbers always have a range of other numbers in between. For example, between 1 and 2 lie other real numbers such as 1.3, 1.5 or 1.875. It is thus possible to think of a *continuously varying* real number.

This opens the way for the development of *calculus* and *mechanics*, two branches of mathematics which developed together during the seventeenth century. In mechanics, the basic idea is not the *point*, as in geometry, but the *particle* or *moving point*, whose position changes with time. The new mathematics of the seventeenth and eighteenth centuries expressed this in terms of the idea of a *variable*, such as the time or the distance of a particle from a fixed reference point.

	EGYPTIAN	BABYLONIAN	GREEK	ROMAN	MAVAN	II WEST ARABIC	HINDU
1	I	▼	A	I	•	I	१
2	II	▼▼	B	II	••	2	२
3	III	▼▼▼	Γ	III	•••	३	३
4	IIII	▼▼▼▼	Δ	IIII	••••	۴	४
5	III II	▼▼▼ ▼▼	E	V	—	٩	५
6	III III	▼▼▼ ▼▼▼	F	VI	• —	6	६
7	IIII III	▼▼▼▼ ▼▼▼	Z	VII	•• —	7	७
8	IIII IIII	▼▼▼▼ ▼▼▼▼	H	VIII	••• —	8	८
9	III III III	▼▼▼▼▼ ▼▼▼▼	Θ	IX	•••• —	9	९
10	∩	◀	I	X	=	I•	१०

Above: The modern numerals for 1 to 10, used by western cultures, compared with their counterparts from older civilizations.

Below: Three counting systems—decimal (based on the number 10), binary (based on 2) and hexadecimal (based on 16).

DECIMAL	BINARY	HEXADECIMAL
1	1	1
2	10	2
3	11	3
4	100	4
5	101	5
6	110	6
7	111	7
8	1000	8
9	1001	9
10	1010	A
11	1011	B
12	1100	C
13	1101	D
14	1110	E
15	1111	F
16	10000	10
8 +4 12	1000 +100 1100	8 +4 C

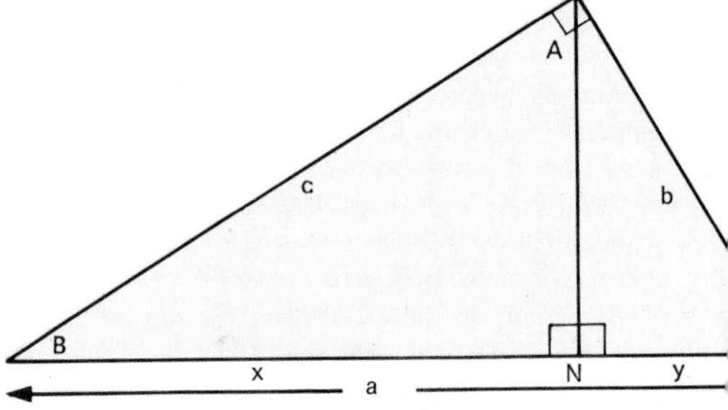

Above: Triangles ABN and ABC are *similar* triangles. Although they are different sizes, they each contain the same angles between their sides—ABC is simply a larger version of ABN.

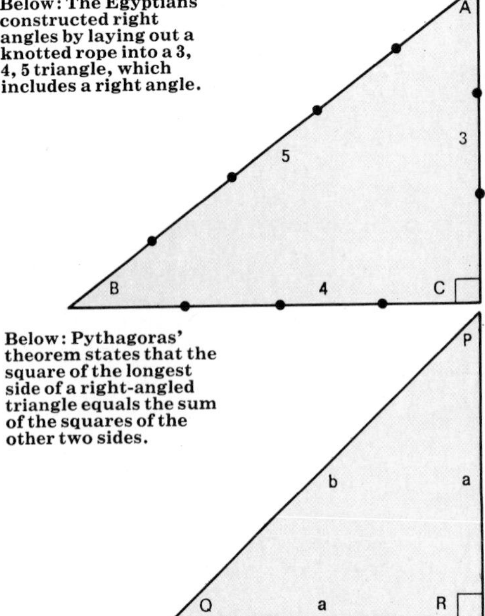

Below: The Egyptians constructed right angles by laying out a knotted rope into a 3, 4, 5 triangle, which includes a right angle.

Below: Pythagoras' theorem states that the square of the longest side of a right-angled triangle equals the sum of the squares of the other two sides.

Below: Pythagoras, one of the most famous Greek mathematicians, was born on the island of Samos in about 572 BC. He is best known for his theorem concerning right-angled triangles.

Radio Times Hulton Picture Library

Roland Michaud/John Hillelson Agency

Above: The work of the Greek mathematicians was known to the Arabs. This is part of a 15th century commentary on Euclid by Al-Tusi.

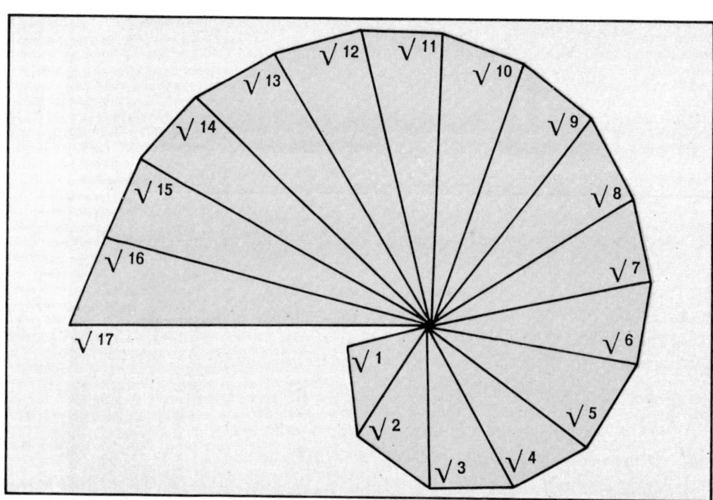

Right: A Greek geometrical construction based upon lines, radiating from a common point, whose lengths represent the square roots of the numbers 1 to 17. The lines joining the ends of these lines are all the same length, which gives the construction its shell-like shape.

Below: The shell of the pearly nautilus has a similar form of construction to the type of figure shown on the right. These creatures, which grow up to 20 cm (7.8 in) long, are found in the Indian and Pacific oceans, and as they grow they add new chambers to their shells. The animal's head is at the wide end of the shell.

Kodak/Alphabet & Image

Below: An example of a natural geometrical construction—the cell wall structure of a micro-organism called a diatom.

Picturepoint

The dependence of one variable upon another, say of variable 'x' upon variable 't', was expressed in the form 'x is a *function* of t', which was written '$x = f(t)$'.

The idea of *velocity* (the speed of an object *in a given direction*), which had given great difficulty to mathematicians during the thirteenth century, was now much easier to handle, for a function can be represented by means of graph. It was then possible to understand the velocity, at any instant, of a particle moving in a curved path, as that which it would have were it to continue in a straight line moving just as it was at the instant under consideration.

The velocity would be a function of the time, and if a graph showing the particle's position at various times were drawn, the velocity at any instant could be found by drawing a tangent to the curve of the graph at the time under consideration.

Infinite series

Many of the problems of calculus thrown up by mechanics would have proved too difficult without the use of the mathematical device of an *infinite series*. Some such series had been known for some time: the series '$1 + \frac{1}{2} + \frac{1}{4} + \frac{1}{8} + \ldots$', where each term is half the preceding one, is one example. This series may be said to have a 'sum' of 2 in the sense that, however many terms are added together they will never reach 2, but on the other hand they will get as near to 2 as desired.

But the original idea that it was sufficient for the terms to decrease in order to be able to associate a sum with a series was shattered by the series '$1 + \frac{1}{2} + \frac{1}{3} + \frac{1}{4} + \ldots$'. In this series, the third and fourth terms together add up to more than $\frac{1}{2}$, as do the fifth, sixth, seventh and eighth. Therefore if a sum were to be associated with such a series it would be more than '$1 + \frac{1}{2} + \frac{1}{2} + \ldots$', and so it would, in effect, have no upper limit.

Despite the difficulties involved in determining the sums of infinite series, such series were often found to be useful in solving practical problems. During the eighteenth century it was suggested that the value of an infinite series should be defined in terms of the value of the function which gives it, the term 'function' in this case meaning an algebraic expression.

The general idea of a function did not evolve until the nineteenth century, when the intuitive but clumsy idea of a 'variable' having values expressed, by an algebraic formula, in terms of the values of another variable, was finally displaced by that of a *mapping* between two *sets*.

In mechanics, for example, the relationship between time and the position of a moving particle could be expressed in this manner. The time would be represented by the set of all real numbers, and the distance at any one time between the particle and its starting point by the set of distances that it was possible for the particle to have. The mapping would then associate a unique member '$f(t)$' of the second set with each member 't' of the first.

Reductionism

The concept of set was first clearly formulated by Georg Cantor in 1872, and it influenced the discussions about the philosophy of mathematics which arose in a gradual way as part of a general *reductionist* programme in the nineteenth century.

One instance of this programme is the clarification of the status of *non-Euclidian geometry*, a form of geometry not based upon the traditional form of geometry established by the Greek mathematician Euclid around 300 BC. Such geometries had been produced in earlier times, and the question arose whether it was consistent to suppose, for example, a plane geometry in which from a point outside a line, no parallel to the line could be drawn.

This can be seen to be consistent (if ordinary geometry is consistent) by exemplifying it as the geometry of *great circles* on the surface of a sphere. A great circle is one whose diameter is the same as that of the sphere itself, and it is impossible to draw two great circles on the surface of a sphere without them intersecting. For the reductionist programme, the consistency problem in non Euclidian geometry was *reduced* to that of ordinary, Euclidian geometry.

There were other fields in which a reductionist programme was carried out. For example, ordinary geometry can be reduced to algebra by the use of a *co-ordinate system*. In this system, which was largely due to the French philosopher René Descartes (and is thus known as *Cartesian*), the position of any point can be fully described by means of its distances from two lines or *axes*, one vertical and one horizontal. Using Cartesian co-ordinates, any geometrical relationship between two points can be expressed in terms of algebra.

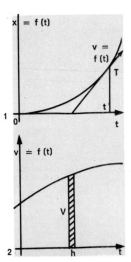

Left: 1. A graph of the position, x, at any time, t, of a moving particle which was originally at rest at x = 0, and then gradually accelerated. The velocity at point T can be thought of as that which the particle would have if its position graph were a straight line at a tangent to the curve at point T.
2. In a velocity/time graph of a moving particle, the shaded area is of size hv, and represents the approximate distance the particle travelled during time h.

Right: 3. The reduction of geometry to algebra employs a pair of fixed co-ordinate lines to describe the position of any point 'P'.

G. F. Allen/Bruce Coleman

Right: The curved path of a jet of water from a fountain forms a type of curve known as a *parabola*, and the outline of each group of jets is itself a parabola.

Below: 1. Instead of the older, graphical representation of a function, the modern picture is of two *sets*, T, called the *domain*, and X, the *range*, with a *mapping* 'f = T — X' between them.
2. Three possible geometries of parallels. Top: Euclidian—only one possible parallel to a line can pass through point 'P'. Centre: hyperbolic geometry—two parallels can pass through 'P'. Bottom: elliptic geometry—no parallel can be drawn.

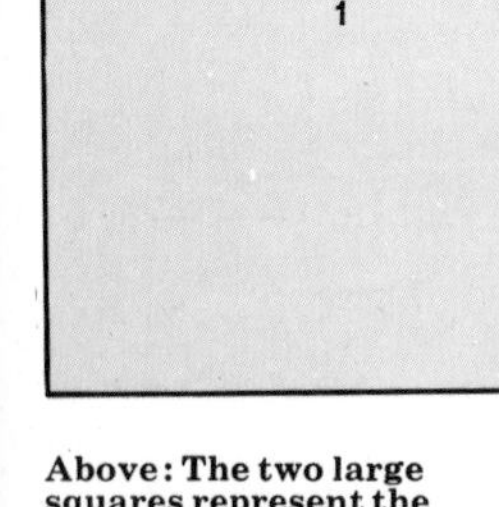

Above: The two large squares represent the infinite series '$1 + \frac{1}{2} + \frac{1}{4} + \ldots$', which never quite adds up to exactly 2.

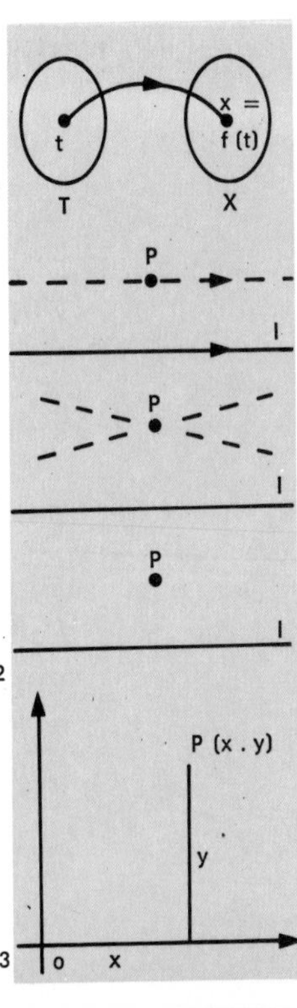

Bruce Coleman

ZEFA

Syndication International

Left: The woman's body and its distorted mirror image are *topologically* identical because the 'surface' of the image, although

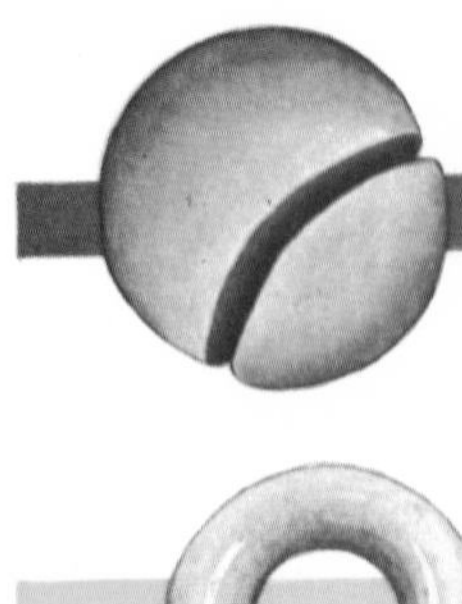

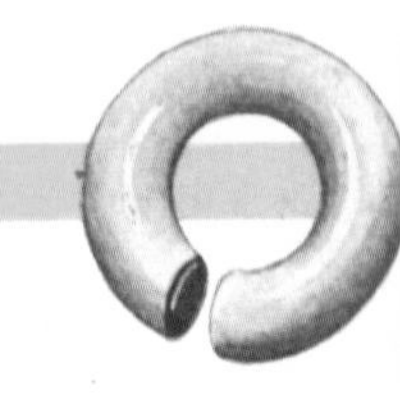

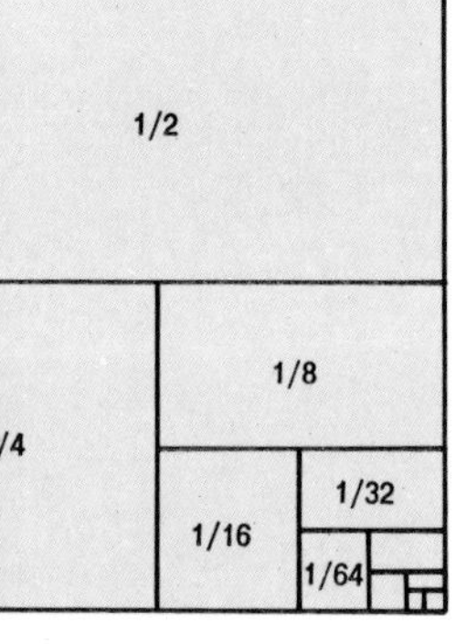

Left: Albert Einstein (1879-1955), whose mathematical theories of relativity were proven only later by practical experimental results. The concept of relativity is an example of the way in which mathematics is used to discover more about the physical universe.

Radio Times Hulton Picture Library

Right: Academician Andrei Kolmogorov of the Soviet Union, a prominent modern mathematician who devised an abstract calculus for use in probability theory.

Novosti

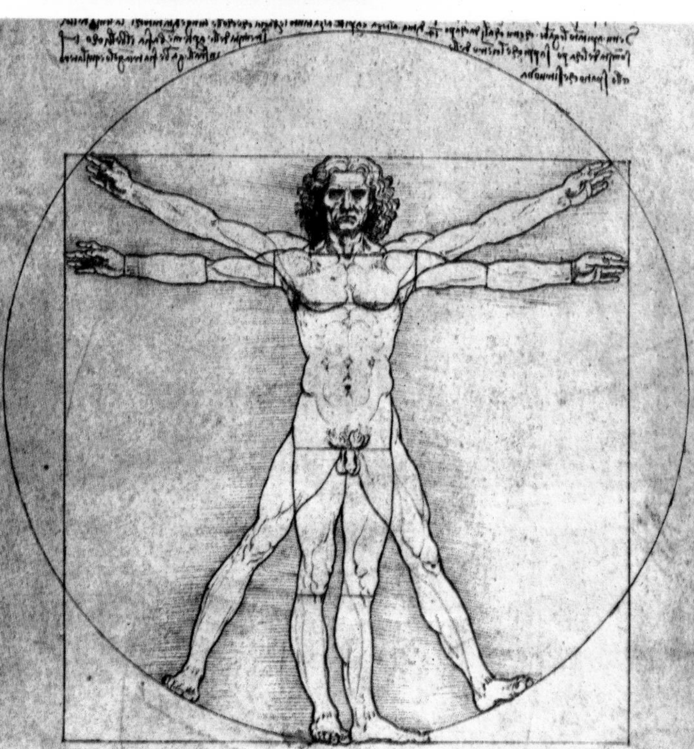

Below: A drawing by Leonardo da Vinci (1452-1519) which illustrates the geometrical nature of the proportions of the human body.

Mansell

Below: Parallel lines often appear to converge, but, like an infinite series and its 'sum', they never actually do.

distorted, has the same mathematical properties as the body's surface.

Below: the topological *genus* of an object is the number of times it can be cut without dividing it into two parts—none for genus 0, one for genus 1, and two for genus 2.

Set theory

Every attempt at a thorough reductionist programme since the work of Gottlob Frege in 1879 has depended upon the idea of a set. A set is simply a collection of all its members, and its members themselves may be sets. For example, the set of all people includes the set of all men, the set of all women, and the set of all children—and these in turn can be sub-divided into other sets.

Cantor had concluded that every well-defined decidable property defines a set, that is, the members of a set are just those possessing that property. In 1899, however, Cantor discovered to his surprise that his theory was plagued with contradictions. Russell attempted to resolve these contradictions in 1903, but with no real success.

The foundations of mathematics had suddenly been shown to be quite unsure. Russell and Whitehead, in 1919, suggested that a sure foundation was to be found in logic, but when they looked for it there they found that the logic which was taught at the time was a tissue of trivialities and nonsense that had been handed down almost unchanged from the Middle Ages, and so they had to begin again.

Their greatest triumph was the precise formulation of arithmetic, including a formula for the definition of the number 1. Another approach to the problems of the foundations of mathematics was begun by Hilbert in 1899. He was able to formulate geometry in better terms than those used by Euclid, and he turned his attention to the concept of truth, which is essential to both mathematics and logic.

The difficulties encountered in discussions about truth are exemplified by: (The sentence in these brackets is false). If we suppose this sentence to be true, then it asserts its own falsehood, which contradicts our supposition; but if we assume it to be false, this assumption is exactly what the sentence is saying, so that the sentence is therefore true and our assumption is again contradicted.

During the first 30 years of this century it became apparent that the consistency of much of classical mathematics depended upon the corresponding result for the arithmetic of natural numbers. As a result of this, Gödel, in 1929, devised a way of expressing the letters of the alphabet, and combinations of them such as words and sentences, by a numerical code. By this means, the truth or falsity of sentences could be determined arithmetically.

Gödel was able to prove that any system that was rich enough to describe elementary arithmetic, the arithmetic of natural numbers, would inevitably be either inconsistent or incomplete. Using his numerical code, he could construct an arithmetic statement which was essentially equivalent to: (The statement in these brackets is unprovable.)

There is no paradox as there was in the previous example. But if the sentence is true, it is an example of a true but inprovable sentence, so the system is uncomplete. If, on the other hand, it is false, it is an example of a false but provable sentence, and so the system is inconsistent. So, although the technical achievements of mathematics are not in question, its real nature still remains in doubt.

Time Measurement

Throughout the ages, concepts of the nature of time have been governed by spiritual and physical requirements. Until comparatively recently, natural rhythmic patterns such as life and death, day and night, winter and summer, led to the conception of time as a *cyclic* quantity, one that repeated itself at regular intervals.

The first methods of keeping track of the passage of time were based on observations of the movements of the sun, moon and stars. As the cyclic nature of these movements became apparent, it was realized that they could be used to indicate such things as, for example, the right times to plant crops. The Egyptians also used the rising of the star Sirius to predict the beginning of the annual flooding of the Nile, which occurred (coincidentally) a few days later.

From their astronomical observations, the Egyptians produced a calendar based on a 365 day year. Their studies of Sirius, however, indicated that the length of the *solar year* (the time taken for the Earth to orbit the Sun) was, in fact, 365¼ days. The Romans, who had been using a calendar based on the *lunar month* (the number of days between full moons), adopted a 365¼ day calendar in 45 BC. This was the *Julian Calendar*, introduced by Julius Caesar and calculated by Sosigenes of Alexandria.

The Julian Calendar, to avoid the problem of having to fit a quarter of a day into each year, ran for three years of 365 days then one of 366, a *leap year*, to give an average year length of 365¼ days. The solar year, however, is only 365.242199 days long, not 365.25, and so the Roman year was, in fact, 11 minutes too long. This gave a cumulative error to the Julian Calendar, which was eventually rectified by Pope Gregory XIII in 1582.

By this time the Julian Calendar was ten days out, and Gregory decreed that 5 October 1582 should become 15 October. In addition, he ordered that century years would only be leap years if they were divisible by 400, a ruling which reduced the number of leap years sufficiently to keep the calendar in step with the solar year. Gregory's calendar, known as the *Gregorian Calendar*, is the one used in Western countries today, and it is only out by 26 seconds per year.

The Egyptians astronomers noticed that the time taken for one revolution of the Earth about its axis was constant if measured against a star, but varied throughout the year if measured against the Sun. They therefore used the stars as the basis for their time measurement. Time based on star observations is known as *sidereal* time, whereas time measured against the Sun is known as *solar time*.

There are two reasons for the irregular length of the solar day. Firstly, the Earth is in an elliptical orbit about the Sun, and as a result is moves faster when near the Sun, in January, than it does when it is farther away, in July. Secondly, the Earth's axis is inclined at an angle of 23½°, causing a variation in the angular velocity of the equator relative to the Sun.

Above: The sundial is one of the oldest devices for measuring time. As the Sun travels across the sky, the shadow of the sundial's *gnomon* moves around the face of the dial to indicate the time.

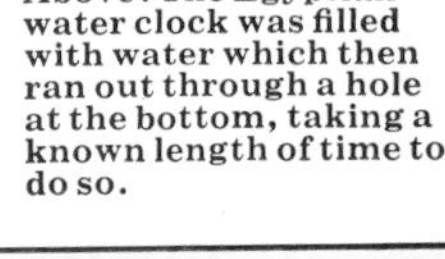

Above: The Egyptian water clock was filled with water which then ran out through a hole at the bottom, taking a known length of time to do so.

Right: A model of a pendulum escapement mechanism designed by Galileo Galilei (1564-1642). The fact that the time of one swing of a pendulum was dependent on its length, and not on the angle through which it swung, was first discovered by Galileo in 1581. It was not until 1656, however, that the first really satisfactory pendulum escapement was designed, by the Dutch astronomer Christiaan Huygens (1629-95).

Below: Sand glasses were simple timing devices designed so that it took a certain time for all the sand to fall from one half into the other.

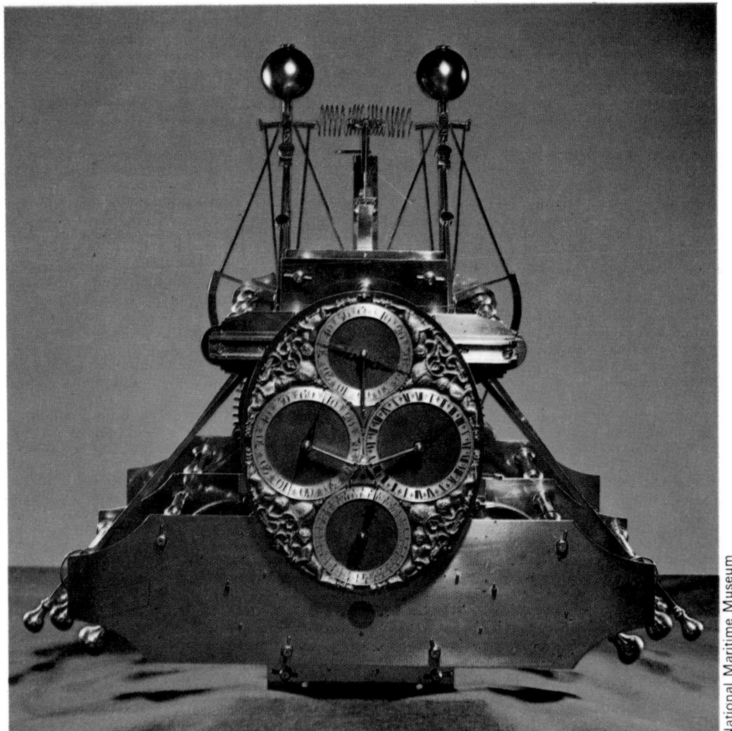

Right: The first of four chronometers built by John Harrison between 1728 and 1759 to provide accurate timekeeping for ship navigation.

Michael Holford

National Maritime Museum

The average or *mean* solar day was devised to accommodate this irregularity. Mean time varies from actual solar time by anything up to about 16 minutes. The difference between solar time and mean time is called the *equation of time*, the word 'equation' in this context being used to mean 'that which is needed to make things equal'.

Early clocks

The linear concept of time, in which time is considered as an independent, continuous function in its own right, was made possible by the invention of mechanical clocks. The first mechanical clocks were probably invented in the late thirteenth century, but it was not until the seventeenth century that reasonably accurate models were produced.

The earliest devices for measuring the passage of time were sundials, the first known forms of which were made by the Egyptians. In its simplest form, the sundial consists of a stick or *gnomon* which casts a shadow onto a scale marked off in hours. As the Sun moves across the sky during the day, the shadow cast by the gnomon moves around the scale, indicating the solar time.

The determination of time at night or

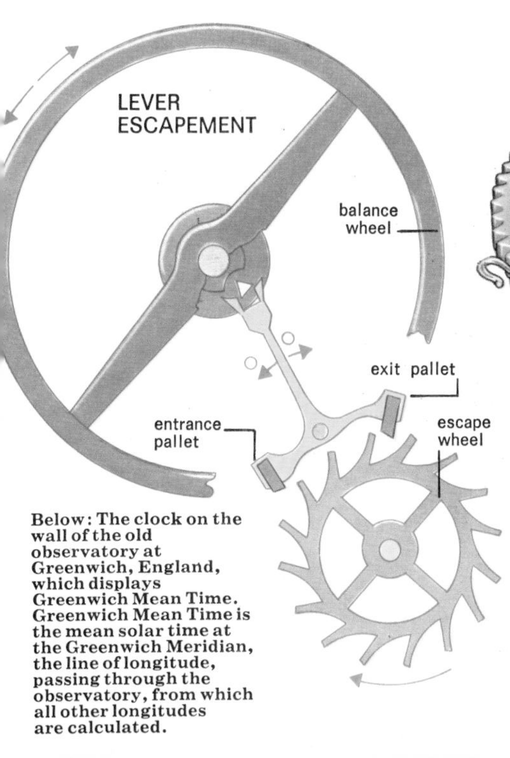

WATCH MOVEMENT
ratchet wheel
centre wheel
balance spring
mainspring
balance wheel
escape wheel

Below: The clock on the wall of the old observatory at Greenwich, England, which displays Greenwich Mean Time. Greenwich Mean Time is the mean solar time at the Greenwich Meridian, the line of longitude, passing through the observatory, from which all other longitudes are calculated.

Above left: A lever escapement mechanism. The two pallets engage with the escape wheel one at a time, permitting it to turn one tooth at a time. The oscillation of the pallets is produced by the coiling and uncoiling of a hairspring mounted within the balance wheel, and the escape wheel gives each pallet a small push as it disengages from it so as to keep the oscillations going.

Above right: A watch mechanism incorporating a lever escapement mechanism. The speed of the watch is adjusted by increasing or decreasing the tension of the hairspring, which alters the rate at which the balance wheel oscillates. The escapement controls the speed at which the mainspring unwinds to drive the hands of the clock, and the ratchet wheel stops the mainspring from unwinding without driving the mechanism.

Right: The mechanism of an alarm clock, which has an additional spring for driving the alarm hammer.

Keystone

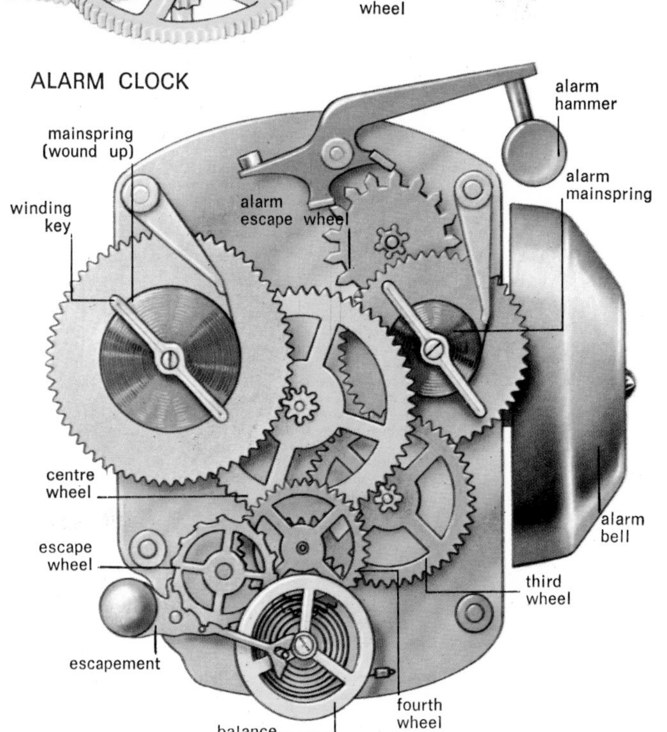

in cloudy weather was not possible with a sundial, and so a variety of devices were developed which used forms of observable regular motion or changing circumstances. These devices included the *clepsydra* or water clock, in which time is indicated by the gradual flow of water from a bucket-shaped container with a small hole in its base.

The basic components of a mechanical clock mechanism are a source of rotational force, a means of regulating the speed of the rotation produced by this force, and a system of gears to transmit this regulated motion to the hands of the clock. The first clocks were driven by weights. A falling weight was attached to a rope wound around a horizontal drum, so that as the weight fell the drum was turned.

The speed at which the drum turned was regulated by a *foliot* and *verge escape ment*. The foliot was a horizontal rod with a weight attached to each end, and fixed at its centre to a vertical rod, the verge, which was pivoted so that it, together with the foliot, could oscillate about its long axis.

As the foliot and verge oscillated, two short projections or *pallets* engaged, one at a time, with the teeth of a crown wheel. The crown wheel was driven by the weight drum, and the motion of the pallets allowed it to turn a distance of one tooth at a time. The crown wheel gave a small push to each pallet as it left its teeth, and this maintained the oscillation. The speed at which the crown wheel, and the associated gearing which drove the clock hands, could turn was determined by the rate of oscillation of the foliot and verge.

Clocks driven by springs instead of weights first appeared in the late fifteenth century, but speed regulation by means of a pendulum was not introduced until the middle of the seventeenth century. The period of swing of a pendulum depends upon its length, and so the speed of rotation of a toothed wheel can be regulated by the action of a pair of pallets connected to a swinging pendulum. The pendulum, whose length is carefully

Omega

Above: The photofinish camera records the finish of a race on a moving strip of film, on to which the finishing times are projected. The timing begins at the start of the race, and is initiated by a signal from the starting mechanism, for example from a contact linked to the trigger mechanism of a starting pistol.

Above right: An example of a photofinish picture. The timing is accurate to 1/1,000th of a second.

Omega

Above: The type of watch used by American astronauts, which was also used by the Russians during the Apollo-Soyuz mission.

Blick

Right: An attendance recorder is a clock, used in many factories and offices, which records the times at which the employees arrive and leave. Upon arriving or leaving, an employee inserts a card into the machine, which stamps it with the time and the day of the week. The cards provide a record of the hours worked, and can be used in calculating wages.

Below: The world is divided into time zones, shown here as either ahead (—) or behind (+) Greenwich Mean Time.

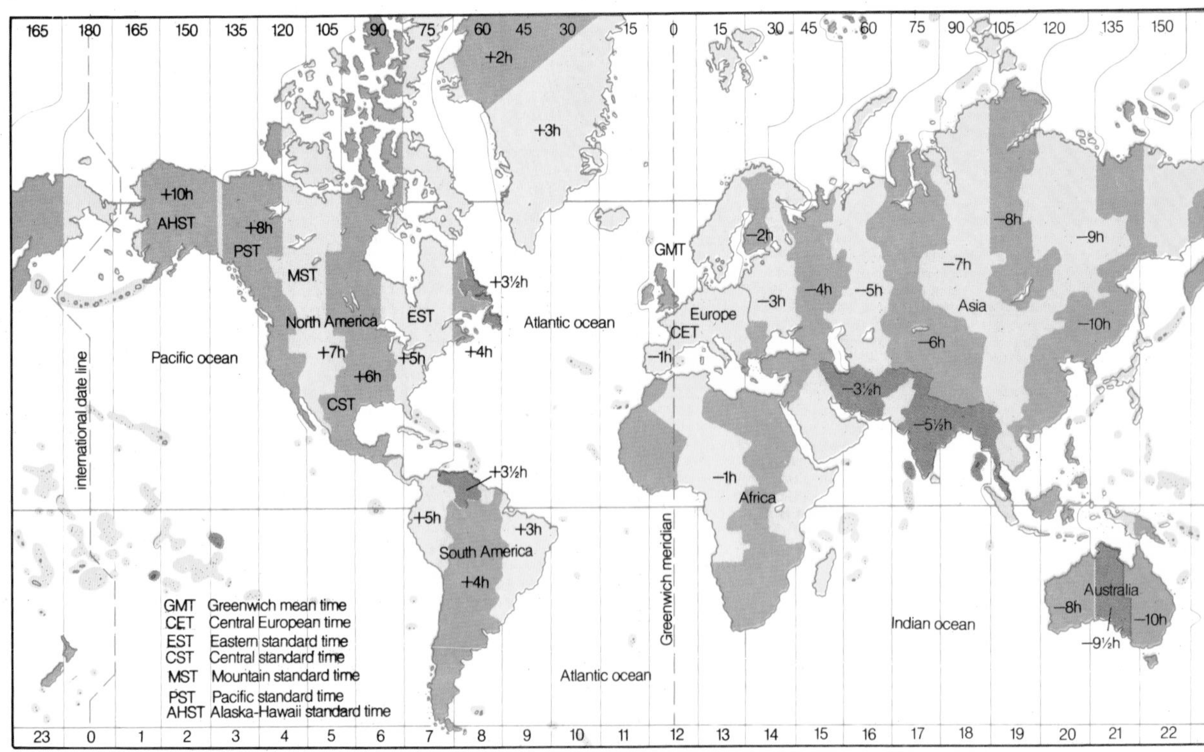

Below: An experimental hydrogen maser atomic clock. These devices use the natural vibrations within hydrogen atoms to control the frequency of a quartz crystal clock and maintain its accuracy. Hydrogen maser clocks have an accuracy of within one ten thousand millionth of a second per day.

NPL

calculated to give the required rate of operation of the pallets, is kept swinging by impulses given to the pallets by the weight or spring driven wheel.

Another form of escapement control, now widely used in clocks and watches, was invented by Robert Hooke in the middle of the seventeenth century. This is the *spiral balance spring* or *hairspring*, a fine coiled spring mounted within a wheel, which when set in motion coils and uncoils to create continuous oscillations analogous to those of a pendulum. These oscillations are used to operate a pair of pallets, usually via a lever arrangement, which control the speed of the main mechanism.

Chronometers

The expansion of trade and the increase in the numbers of long sea voyages during the sixteenth and seventeenth centuries encouraged the production of more accurate clocks, which were essential to accurate navigation. The main problem was the determination of longitude, which could only be achieved with a clock that would keep accurate time aboard ship.

By the eighteenth century, the pendulum clock had become accurate to about one second per day, but it was useless at sea because the regular swing was upset by the motion of the ship. Large inaccuracies were also likely with spring balance clocks due to the considerable temperature variations often encountered.

In 1714, the British Government set up a Board of Longitude, which offered a prize of £20,000 to anyone who could devise an accurate means of determining a ship's longitude. If this was to be done by means of a clock, it would have to be accurate to within three seconds per day, anywhere in the world.

The prize was won by John Harrison, who between 1728 and 1759 constructed four *chronometers*, accurate clocks for use in navigation. His fourth model won the Board's prize; on a voyage of 156 days it showed an error of only 54 seconds.

Below: The upper drawing is a simplified view of the atomic beam chamber of a caesium atomic clock. The lower drawing shows the paths of the atoms through the beam chamber, and the way their energy states are changed if the resonator frequency is correct.

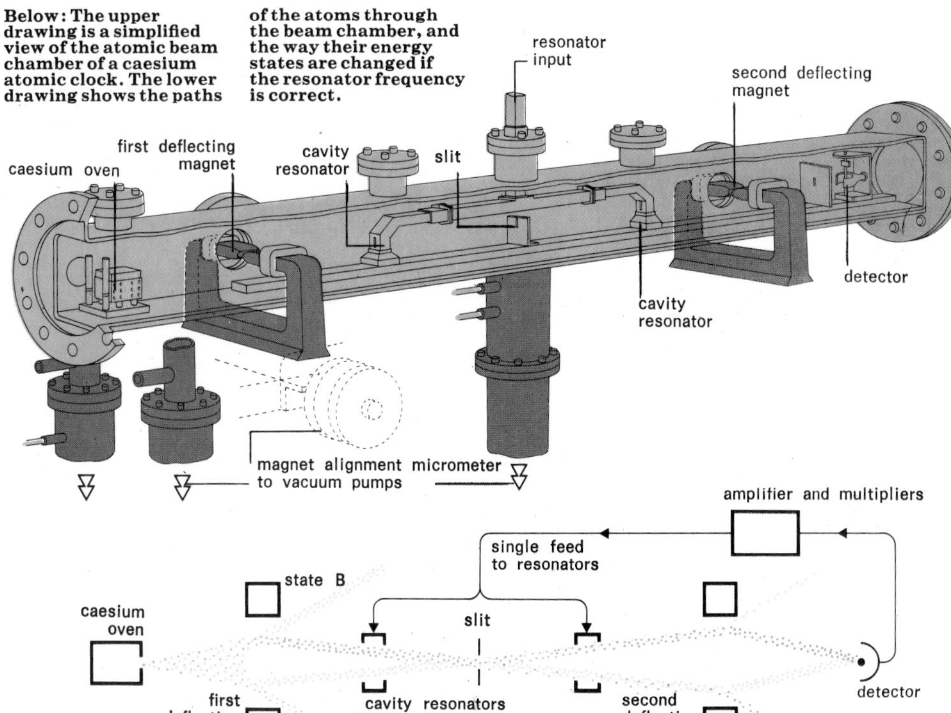

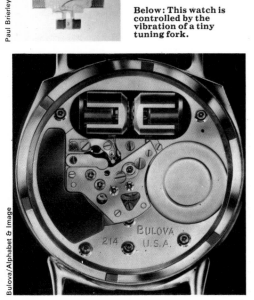

Paul Brierley

Left: The components of an all-electronic digital watch.

Right: This chart shows how the accuracy of time-keeping has improved since the fourteenth century.

Below: This watch is controlled by the vibration of a tiny tuning fork.

Bulova/Alphabet & Image

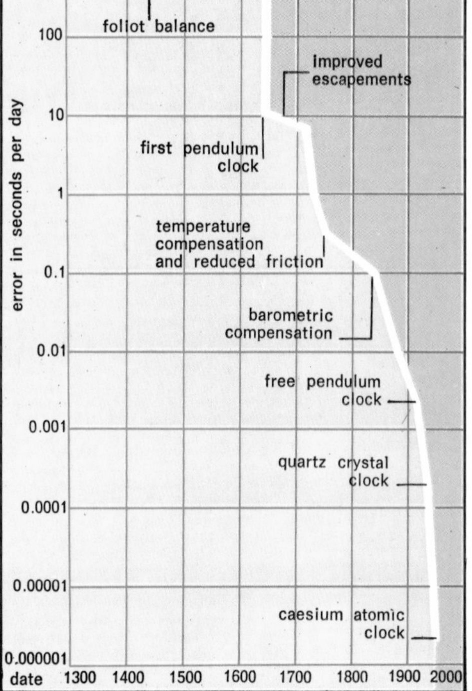

Modern clocks

Although most clocks and watches are still mechanically-driven, electric clocks and electronic watches are becoming increasingly popular. Electric clocks may be battery-powered, having a small motor controlled by a balance spring, or driven by a mains-powered motor. The speed of these mains motors is precisely controlled by the frequency of the mains supply, and a simple gear mechanism takes the drive directly from the motor to the hands of the clock.

Just as the mechanical clock uses regularly oscillating functions, such as those of a balance spring or a pendulum, to control its movement, the *quartz crystal* clock uses the electrically-induced vibrations of a piece of quartz crystal. Quartz crystal is *piezo-electric*; that is, when a voltage is applied to it it will distort slightly, and conversely if it is distorted it will produce a small voltage.

In a clock, the crystal is stimulated electrically to make it vibrate at its *resonant frequency*, the frequency at which it will vibrate the most easily. This frequency, which can be maintained very accurately, is determined by the size and shape of the crystal. When the crystal has been made to vibrate at its resonant frequency, it produces voltages at that frequency, and these can be used either to drive a small motor geared to the indicating mechanism of a clock, or to drive circuits controlling a liquid crystal or light-emitting diode display. A small amount of the crystal output is fed back to it to keep it vibrating. Quartz crystal clocks can be built to have an accuracy of less than 1/30 second per day.

Another form of natural resonance which is used for time measurement is that of atoms such as those of caesium. The caesium atom can be at one of two energy states, depending upon the direction of spin of its outer electron. If the atom is passed through an electromagnetic field whose frequency is 9,192 MHz, it will change its energy state.

In the caesium clock, a beam of caesium atoms given off by caesium heated in a small oven is directed through an electromagnetic field. The 5 MHz output from a quartz clock is multiplied to give the 9,192 MHz that controls the electromagnetic field. If the quartz clock is producing exactly the right frequency, a maximum number of atoms will change their states, and this is registered by a detector. The frequency of the clock is automatically adjusted to produce the maximum number of changes, which means that it is kept as close as possible to 5 MHz.

Part of this 5 MHz output is used to drive a clock display unit, which indicates the time to within one second in 1,000 years. A newer type of atomic clock, the hydrogen maser clock, is even more accurate.

Weighing and Measuring

An organized system of weights and measures is fundamental to many human activities, particularly those associated with science, industry and commerce. Any comprehensive system must include the three basic quantities of mass, length and time, and should also cater for the measurement of temperature, electricity and magnetism, and light.

Two measuring systems have been of major importance during the last few hundred years. These are the *metric* system, used by most European countries, and the *imperial system*, used by Britain and those countries which were once part of the old British Empire. In most countries, however, the old metric and imperial weights and measures are being phased out, and the *SI system* of units (Système International d'Unités), a more accurately-defined version of the old metric system, is being adopted.

The SI system has six basic units. These are the *metre* (m), the unit of length; the *kilogram* (kg), the unit of mass; the *second* (s), the unit of time; the *kelvin* (K), the unit of temperature; the *ampere* (A), the unit of electrical current; and the *candela* (cd), the unit of luminous intensity.

Units and standards

Measurement involves the comparison of an unknown quantity with a similar known quantity. For example, the measurement of length with a ruler is a visual comparison of the unknown length with a scale of known lengths marked on the ruler. The basis for any measurement is the direct or indirect reference to some definitive standard. It is important to distinguish between 'units' and 'standards', a unit being in itself an abstract conception which is meaningless unless it is referred to the primary standard for the quantity to be measured. This primary standard may be an arbitrary material standard such as the international prototype kilogram, or a naturally-occurring invariable phenomenon such as the wavelength of the radiation from a krypton-86 lamp.

Length

Early units of length were based on the dimensions of the human body, and many of the imperial units of length were derived from such units. For example, the yard was the distance from the spine to the fingertips (with the arm outstretched), and the foot was the length of one foot. A yard was also taken to be the length of one stride, and the world 'mile' came from the Latin for 'a thousand paces'. A cubit was half a yard, the distance from the elbow to the fingertips.

The first official standard yard, established by King Edward I of England in 1305, was an iron bar subdivided into three feet of twelve inches each. Fortunately for his subjects who were unable to obtain access to this standard, the inch was also defined as the length of three grains of barley laid end to end.

Subsequent standard yards were also made of metal, Britain and the US

Michael Holford

Above: Part of the 'Nilometer' on the southern tip of Roda, an island in the Nile near Cairo. The Nilometer, which is a form of depth gauge, was used to measure the rise of the Nile during its annual flooding, which begins in late June and reaches its maximum rate of flow in September.

Bruce Coleman

Right: Stonehenge, which stands on Salisbury Plain in southern England, is one of the best known of the many neolithic structures found in north west Europe. It has been suggested that the builders of these structures used a standard length unit, the 'megalithic yard' 82.9 cm (2.72 ft) long.

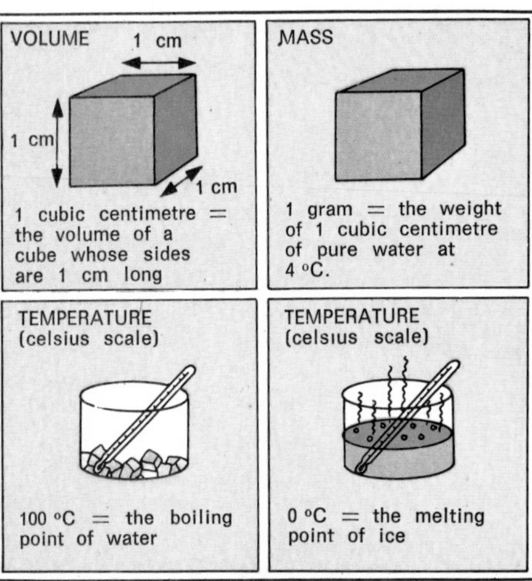

VOLUME
1 cm
1 cm
1 cm
1 cubic centimetre = the volume of a cube whose sides are 1 cm long
MASS
1 gram = the weight of 1 cubic centimetre of pure water at 4 °C.
TEMPERATURE (celsius scale)
100 °C = the boiling point of water
TEMPERATURE (celsius scale)
0 °C = the melting point of ice

Left: The cubic centimetre is the volume of a cube whose sides are 1 cm long, and one gram is the mass of 1 cubic centimetre of pure water at a temperature of 4°C. The Celsius temperature scale uses the melting point of ice as its zero and the boiling point of water as its 100° point.

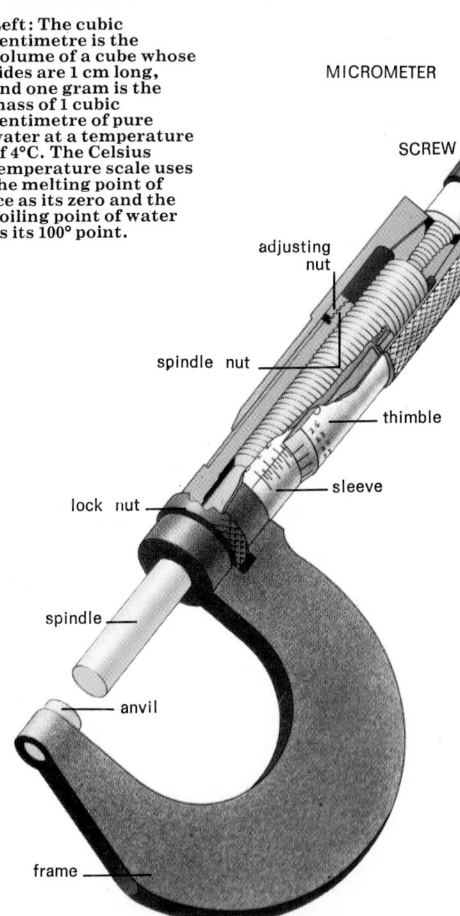

Above: The micrometer, a precision measuring device used in engineering. When the thimble is turned, the spindle is moved towards or away from the anvil, and the distance between them is indicated by the scales engraved on the thimble and the sleeve.

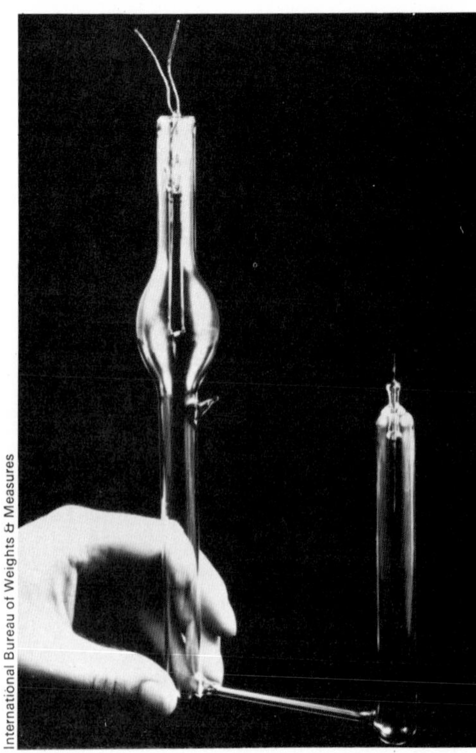

International Bureau of Weights & Measures

Left: A krypton-86 lamp of the type used to produce the light whose wavelengths are used to define the metre. The lamps used can produce the specified wavelength to an accuracy of 1 part in 100 million (1 part in 10^8), but the standard may eventually be re-defined in terms of the wavelengths of a stabilized helium-neon gas laser, which can be reproduced to an accuracy of 1 part in 10^{10} (10,000 million).

Right: The international prototype kilogram, and the platinum-iridium bar which was formerly the standard metre.

Keystone

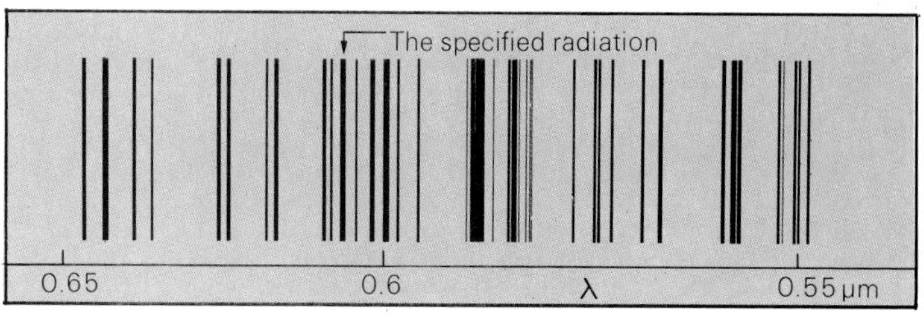

Crown Copyright/NPL

Above: Part of the spectrum of the light obtained from a krypton-86 lamp. The metre is now defined as that length which is equal to 1,650,763.73 of the wavelengths of the specified radiation, which has a wavelength of approximately 0.60578 microns (millionths of a metre).

Above: Three views of the tower of the Deutches Museum in Munich. The tower carries three large weather instrument displays: a hygrometer, which measures humidity; a wind speed and direction indicator; and a thermometer and barometer which measure air temperature and pressure.

Below: The bimetallic strip thermometer is operated by a coiled strip of two metals, one of which expands or contracts more with changes in temperature than the other one, bending the strip as shown. The clinical thermometer contains mercury which expands along the tube when heated.

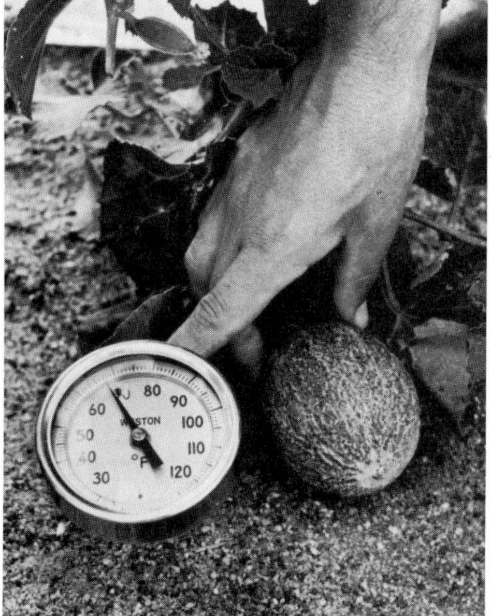

Transworld

Above: A rotary thermometer, calibrated in degrees Fahrenheit, being used to measure soil temperature. The Fahrenheit scale was invented in Holland in 1724 by Gabriel Fahrenheit, but most countries adopted the Celsius scale devised in 1742.

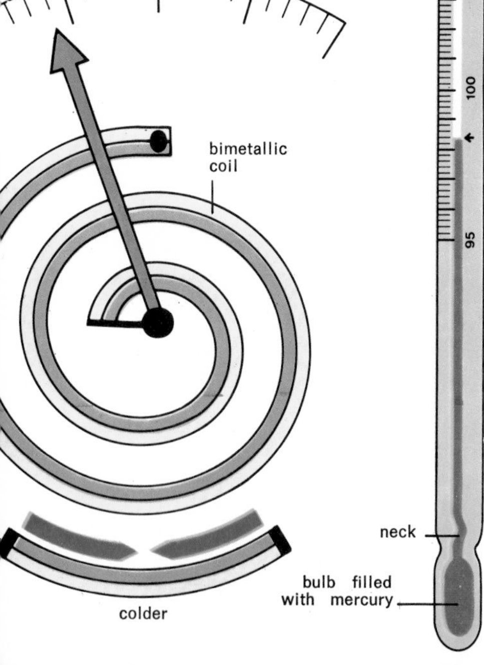

International Bureau of Weights & Measures

adopting bronze and brass standard yards respectively in the first half of the nineteenth century. In 1893, however, the US decided to define the yard as 0.9144 of a metre, and this definition was adopted in 1959 by Britain, Canada, Australia, New Zealand and South Africa.

The metre, the basic unit of the metric system—which was devised in France at the end of the eighteenth century—was originally defined as one ten millionth of the distance from the North Pole to the equator, along a line passing through Paris. When the length of the metre had been calculated, a standard metre in the form of a bar of platinum was made, one metre being the distance between the end faces of the bar.

This standard was replaced by a bar of platinum-iridium alloy in 1889, but the metre is now defined in an altogether different manner. Since 1960, the metre has been defined as the length equivalent to 1,650,763.73 wavelengths of the orange radiation corresponding to the transition of a krypton-86 atom from energy level $2p_{10}$ to energy level $5d_5$. This radiation is produced by a krypton-86 lamp, an electric lamp filled with krypton-86 gas, enclosed in a vacuum chamber at a temperature of 63 K (—210°C).

Mass and volume

The metric system was first formulated on the basis of natural quantities. The metre was based on the size of the Earth, and the gram, the unit of mass, was based on the weight of pure water. The original definition of the gram was that it was the mass of one cubic centimetre (1 cm = 1/100 m) of pure water at a temperature of 4°C. A platinum cylinder, weighing the same as 1,000 cubic centimetres of water, was adopted as the standard kilogram.

There was now a neat relationship between length, mass and volume. A litre was defined as the volume of a cube whose sides were 0.1 m long, a volume of 1,000 cubic centimetres. However, due to the difficulty, at that time, of obtaining a really precise measurement of volume, the standard kilogram did not in fact weigh precisely the same as 1,000 cubic centimetres of water.

It was therefore decided to define one litre as the volume of one kilogram of water (at 4°C), and so the litre became, in fact, 1,000.028 cubic centimetres. In 1964, however, the litre was redefined to be the exact equivalent of the cubic decimetre (precisely 1,000 cubic centimetres).

The current standard kilogram, known as the international prototype kilogram, is a cylinder made of 90 per cent platinum and 10 per cent iridium, and it is kept at the International Bureau of Weights and Measures (the BIPM) at Sèvres, near Paris. Duplicate standards are kept at national standards offices throughout the world, the British national copy, for example, is copy number 18 and it is kept at the National Physical Laboratory near London.

Temperature

The primary unit of temperature is neither material nor reproducible, being a measure of heat intensity. Its nature dictates that the unit should be defined in terms of a scale relative to the difference between two standard temperatures. As it is not possible to compare directly two temperatures in the same manner as two lengths or masses can be compared, some indirect effect of heat must be used to provide a measurable quantity.

The earliest method of doing this was to employ the expansion of a liquid, contained in a glass tube, when it was heated. In this method, two fixed standard points, an upper one and a lower one, are marked on the tube. The range between these fixed points is called the *fundamental interval*, and it is divided into a scale of units or *degrees*.

A number of these *thermometer* scales have been devised, using a variety of easily-obtained natural temperatures to provide the upper and lower fixed points. Gabriel Fahrenheit (1686-1736) used a mixture of ice and salt to provide his zero or lower fixed point, and human body temperature to provide his upper fixed point. He originally divided this range

Alphabet & Image

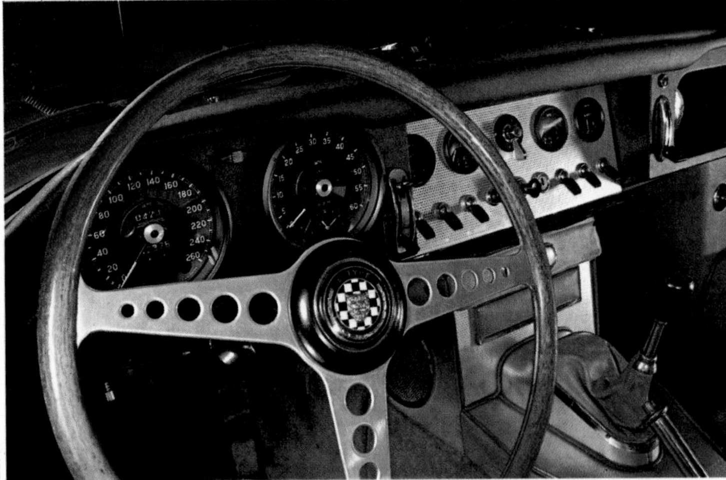

ZEFA

Left: Oil prospectors using a gravimeter to detect local changes in the force of gravity due to changes in the density of the underlying rock. The gravimeter contains a weight suspended from a delicate balance mechanism which indicates changes in the pull of gravity on the weight.

Above: The speedometer and rev counter are tachometers, which measure rotational velocity. The rev counter is calibrated in revolutions per minute, but the speedometer indicates the car's speed although in fact it is responding to the rotational velocity of a gearbox shaft.

Below: A speedometer mechanism. A flexible drive cable, connected to a gearbox shaft, turns a permanent magnet. The magnet drags the stator and pointer assembly round against the force of a spring; the distance the pointer moves depends on the speed at which the magnet is turning.

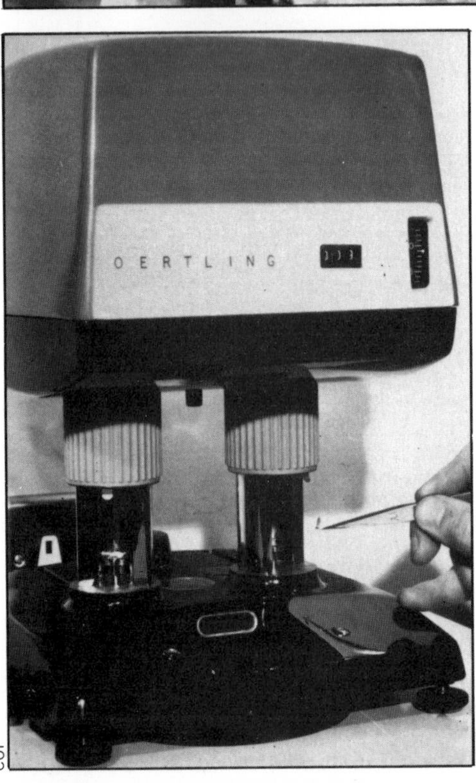

COI

Left and below left: Two precision weighing instruments. The one on the left, a deci-microbalance, is accurate to one tenth of a microgram (one microgram is one millionth of a gram). The machine below has an electronic digitali display, and a printer to record its measurements.

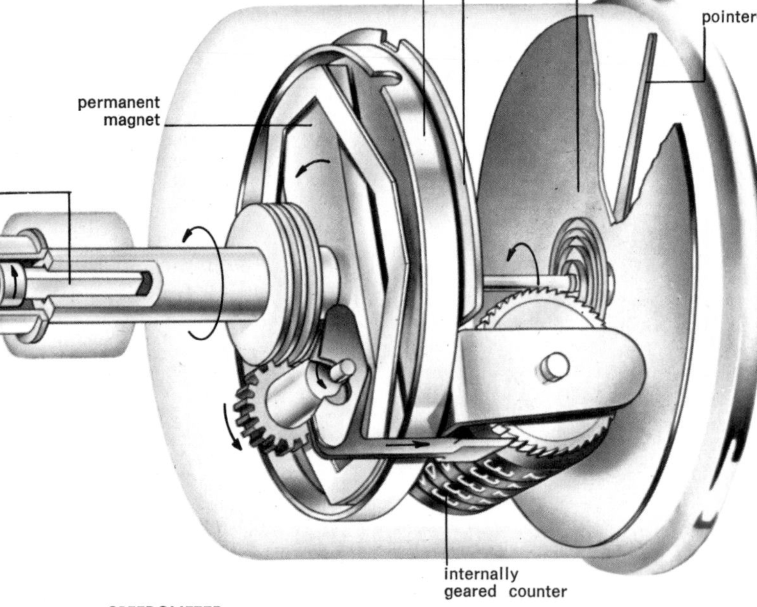

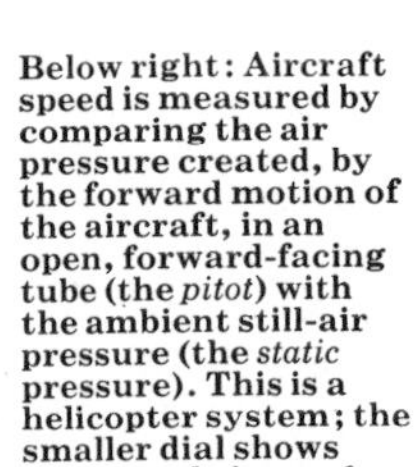

Below right: Aircraft speed is measured by comparing the air pressure created, by the forward motion of the aircraft, in an open, forward-facing tube (the *pitot*) with the ambient still-air pressure (the *static* pressure). This is a helicopter system; the smaller dial shows the lateral airspeed.

Oertling Ltd

GEC-Marconi

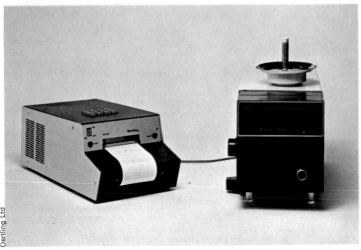

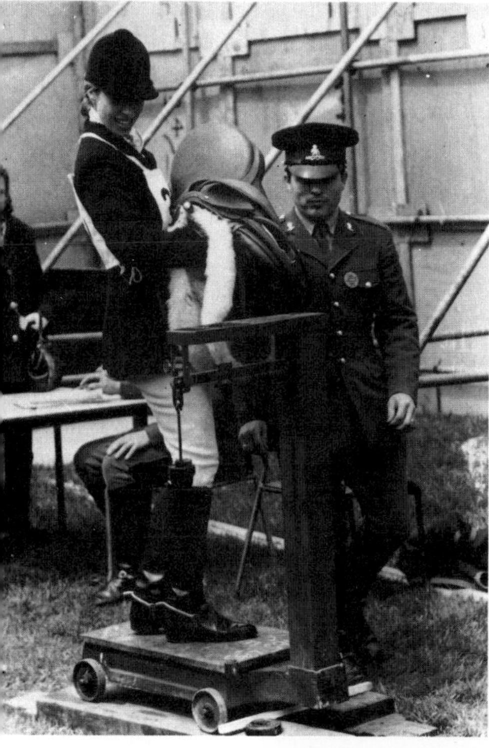

Keystone

into 96 degrees, but later adjusted it so that he obtained an exact 180° between the freezing and boiling points of pure water. On his revised scale, which was adopted by many countries in 1724, the freezing and boiling points of water are 32° and 212° respectively, and body temperature is 98.6°

The Swedish astronomer Anders Celsius (1701-44) proposed a scale of temperature with 100° representing the freezing point and 0° the boiling point of water His scale was quickly adopted as the *centigrade* scale, but the values 100 and 0 for freezing and boiling were reversed. In 1948 the centigrade scale was officially named the Celsius scale.

The SI unit of temperature is the kelvin, which is named after the physicist Lord Kelvin (1824-1907). A Kelvin is the same size as a degree Celsius, but the zero point on the Kelvin scale is a much lower temperature than that on the Celsius scale. In 1787 Jacques Charles discovered that when the temperature of a gas was altered by 1°C, its volume changed by 1/273 of its volume at 0°C. Kelvin proposed that this change in volume was due to a change in the energy of motion of the molecules of the gas. Continuing this line of thought, he went on to suggest that this change in energy of motion applied to all molecules, whether in solids, liquids or gases.

The heat energy possessed by an object or substance, of which its temperature is a measure, is retained in it as the kinetic energy possessed by its molecules due to their motion. Kelvin predicted that, since 1/273 of the energy at 0°C was lost for every 1°C drop in temperature, then at —273°C there would be no heat energy left in a substance. Therefore, —273°C was the lowest possible temperature, and should be considered as *absolute zero* and used as the zero point for an absolute scale of temperature. Absolute zero has been found to be slightly less than —273°C, and as a result degrees Celsius are converted to kelvins by adding 273.15.

Above: HRH Princess Anne weighing in during a three-day equestrian event. This type of weighing machine is a form of beam balance. The weighing platform is connected to one side of the beam, very close to the pivot, so that it can be counterbalanced by the comparatively small weights hung at the other end, a long way from the pivot. Exact balance is obtained by moving the sliding weight along the calibrated beam.

Michael Holford

Right: These Roman bronze scales also have a movable weight on one side of the beam. The object to be weighed was placed in the left hand pan, and a weight was placed in the other. The movable weight was then positioned to give an exact balance.

Photri

Below: The pitot tube on the nose of an experimental jet. Pitot tubes are either mounted on the nose, the wing, or fuselage of aircraft, and the static vents are usually fitted on the fuselage.

Electricity and light

Electrical units are based nowadays on the definition of the ampere, which is the unit of electrical current. The ampere is defined as that current which produces a force of 2 x 10^{-7} newtons per metre of length between two parallel, infinitely long conductors of negligible cross-sectional area, when the conductors are placed 1 m apart in a vacuum and the current is passed through them. The newton is the SI unit of force, being the force required to give a mass of 1 kg an acceleration of 1 m/sec^2.

Luminous intensity is measured in candelas, which have replaced the older units such as the *international candle.* The candela is the luminous intensity of 1/600,000 square metre of the surface of a black body which is at the temperature of freezing platinum (2042 K), under a pressure of 101,325 newtons per square metre.

Time

The basic unit of time is the second. This was originally defined simply as 1/86,400 of a mean solar day, but it was re-defined in 1955 as 1/31,556,925.9747 of the year 1900. With the development of atomic clocks, however, it became possible to provide an even more precise definition of the second.

Between 1955 and 1958, the National Physical Laboratory in England, in collaboration with the US Naval Observatory, obtained a definition of the second based upon the natural resonances within caesium atoms. This definition, adopted as the SI unit of time in 1967, is that one second is the duration of 9,192, 631,770 periods of the radiation given off during transitions between two energy levels of the caesium-133 atom.

Derived units

From the basic SI units, the metre, kilogram, second, kelvin, ampere and candela, all other units of measurement may be derived. Examples of derived units are the square metre (m^2), a unit of area, the metre per second (m/sec), a unit of linear velocity and speed, and the newton (N), a unit of force.

A seventh basic SI unit, which is rarely encountered in everyday life, is the *mole.* The mole is used as a measure of the amount of substance present in a given sample or system. One mole of a substance is the amount present when it contains the same number of *entities*, which may be atoms, molecules, electrons, or other specified particles, as there are atoms in 0.012 kg of carbon-12.

Scientific Analysis

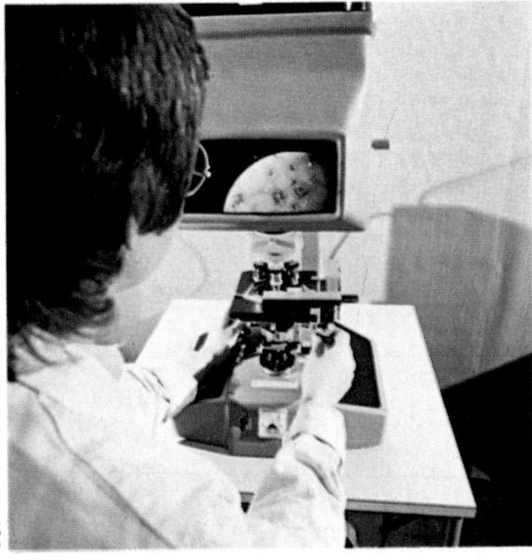

Above: The microscope is one of the basic tools of scientific analysis. This one is fitted with an optical projection system which projects the image of the specimen on to a screen, instead of the user having to peer into the eyepiece. This makes it easier to use and produces a clearer image.

Right: Crystalline tartaric acid (dihydroxy-succinic acid) viewed through a microscope at x 30 magnification in polarized light. The polarized light creates these coloured effects in the crystal which enable its structure to be seen more clearly than in ordinary non-polarized light.

Scientific analysis represents a composition of procedures and techniques associated with man's enquiry into the physical substance of his environment. Early practical demands probably originated from metallurgists needing some method of determining the percentage purity of gold and silver. Since then a wide variety of analytic instruments of observation and measurement have been developed to satisfy the demands of all branches of science. These may be of direct application such as the chemical balance and the microscope, or they may use some property of matter to provide results indirectly—for example, the spectrometer.

Analyses fall broadly within two categories: *qualitative* analysis which encompasses the detection of what a material is made of; and *quantitative* analysis which determines how much of the material is present.

Microscopy

Microscopy is an analytic process which had its origins among biologists, although its potential in the fields of crystallography and metallurgy was soon realized. In 1683, Anton van Leeuwenhoek (1632-1723) was the first to set eyes on bacteria, using a *simple microscope*, one fitted with a single lens.

There is a limit to the magnification obtainable with a simple microscope, however, and for further resolution of detail a *compound microscope* is necessary. The compound microscope, which is the type generally used, consists of two powerful converging lenses of short focal length.

Microscope use is very diverse; from its origins as a tool of direct observation it is now essential in many fields of qualitative and quantitative analysis. Physical observations are generally of colour, optical density, size, shape and surface characteristic. Chemical observations are mainly the study of precipitation reactions where a material is brought into solution and the colour and form of the precipitate crystals are noted when a test reagent is added.

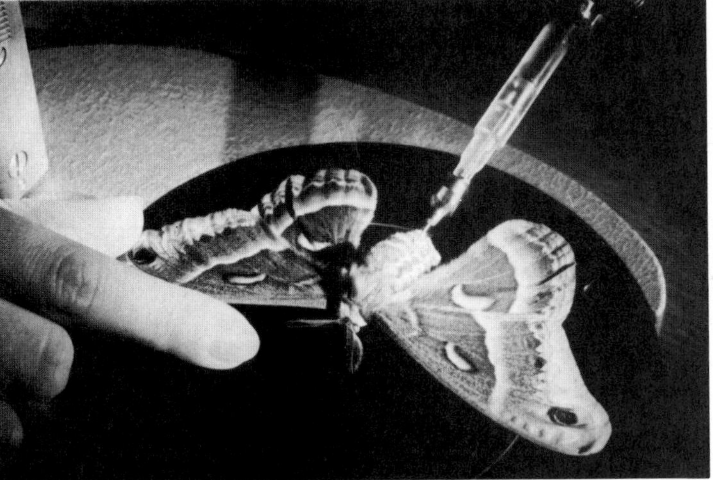

Left: A male silkmoth being injected with a radioactive substance as part of a biochemical analysis of its metabolism. The way in which the substance is broken down or metabolized, and distributed through the insect's tissues, can subsequently be analyzed by tracing the radioactivity.

Right: This apparatus is used for the microdistillation of weighable amounts of substances. This involves heating them to separate off their constituents, which vaporize at different temperatures and so can be collected separately for subsequent analysis. This enables the composition of the substances to be found.

Electron microscopes

No matter how well an optical microscope is made, there is a limit to the amount of detail it can resolve, and this limit cannot be overcome optically because it is due to the nature of light itself. In order to be able to distinguish between two closely-positioned particles, the light source used must have a wavelength of not more than twice the distance between them.

Visible light is restricted to a small band of wavelengths of the electromagnetic spectrum, its wavelength being of the order of about 0.5 microns (1 micron = 1 millionth of a metre). This means that an optical microscope cannot resolve details of less than about 0.25 microns. During the 1920s it was discovered that when electrons are accelerated, they travel with a wave-like motion similar to that of light, but with a wavelength over 100,000 times shorter.

This led to the invention of the electron microscope during the 1930s. The electron microscope uses a beam of electrons in place of light, and the beam is either directed right through the specimen, or reflected off its surface.

In the *transmission electron microscope*, an ultra-thin specimen is placed in the path of an electron beam, which passes through it and produces an image of it on a phosphorescent screen. The *scanning* electronic microscope, on the other hand, scans a fine beam of electrons across the surface of a specimen. As the beam hits the surface of the specimen it drives off 'secondary' electrons from it, which are drawn towards a detector. The detector produces a signal which is amplified, and used to drive a cathode ray tube that produces an image of the specimen.

A third type of electron microscope, the *scanning transmission electron microscope*, uses a similar scanning and detection principle to the scanning instrument, but the electrons are beamed right through the sample as in the transmission instrument. Modern electron microscopes can resolve details as small as 0.0002 microns.

Chromatography

Chromatography was initially developed as a means of separation of complex mixtures in the fields of organic chemistry and pharmacology, where chemical differences are so slight as to be insufficient to afford a means of separation, whereas molecular physical differences exist which are used as a means of resolution. Although several investigators applied chromatography more or less accidentally during the nineteenth century the Russian Mikhail Tswett (1872-1920) was the first to appreciate the underlying principles.

Chromatographic techniques involve manipulation of a few of the general properties of molecules. These are: first, solubility, the tendency of the molecule to dissolve in a liquid solvent; secondly, adsorption, the tendency for a molecule to attach itself to a finely divided solid; and thirdly, volatility, the tendency for a molecule to evaporate.

Tswett was interested in separating the pigments contained in the leaves of plants which he dissolved in ether. He then poured this solution into a vertical glass column filled with calcium carbonate and, as he continued to wash the solution through the column with more solvent, he found that it separated into a series of coloured bands which travelled slowly down the column to the bottom, where

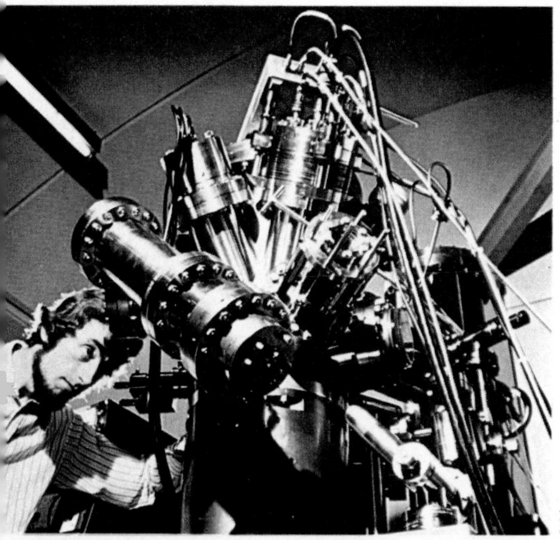

COI

Left: Optical microscopes are limited to a useful maximum magnification of about x 2,000 because the wavelength of visible light prevents the resolution of details below 0.25 microns apart. Electron microscopes, on the other hand, can produce magnifications as high as x 1,000,000.

Right: A small transmission electron microscope like this one is usually mounted on a desk-type console. The electron beam, generated by a 60 kV electron gun, passes through the specimen and creates an image of it on the screen. The largest transmission microscopes, nearly three storeys high, operate at 3 MV.

BASF

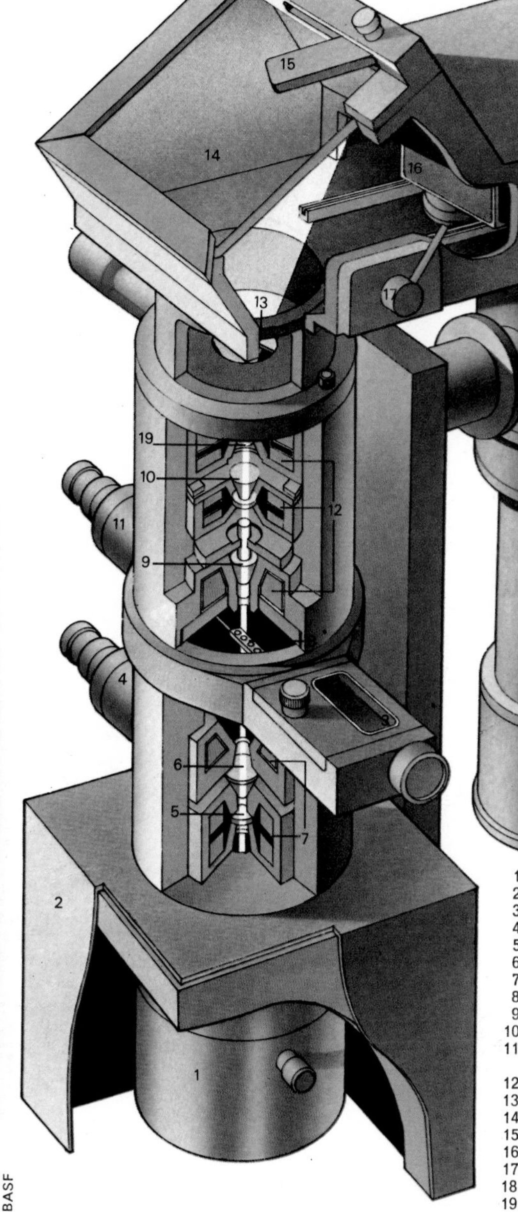

1. 60 KV Electron gun
2. Steel frame
3. Specimen stage
4. Condenser control
5. First condenser lens
6. Second condenser lens
7. Cooling jackets
8. Specimen holder
9. Objective lens
10. First projector lens
11. Specimen rotation control
12. Cooling jackets
13. Camera shutter
14. Phosphor coated screen
15. Exposure meter
16. 70 mm camera
17. Camera retraction lever
18. Vacuum chassis
19. Second projector lens

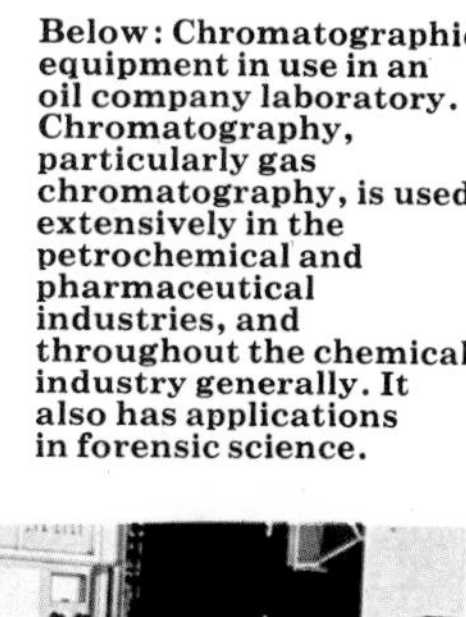

Left: A basic gas chromatograph. The gas is dried by the dessicant, and its flow rate and pressure are monitored by the flow meter and manometer. The constituents of the sample are identified by the different times at which they emerge from the column. Gases used include argon, nitrogen and hydrogen.

Below: Chromatographic equipment in use in an oil company laboratory. Chromatography, particularly gas chromatography, is used extensively in the petrochemical and pharmaceutical industries, and throughout the chemical industry generally. It also has applications in forensic science.

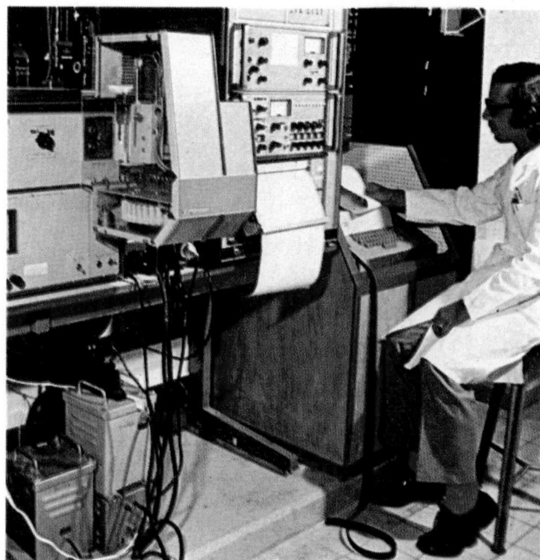

Shell

they could be individually collected.

As the dissolved chemical compounds constituting the pigments were washed through the column, the ones that had an affinity for the large surface area of the finely divided calcium carbonate, the *adsorbent*, had their progress delayed. The ones completely inert to the surface passed through the column at the same rate as the solvent.

Not only do different substances have widely varying adsorption characteristics but differing solubility tendencies as well. As it is highly unlikely that two different substances will exhibit quantitatively the same pair of physical properties, an interaction of these features will lead to the band separation of the compound, which will have their own characteristic rate of downward migration. These bands can be detected as they emerge from the column, isolated, and identified. Modern column chromatography, as it is called, is little different from the method used by Tswett, but alumina and silicia gel are the most commonly used adsorbents.

Since its inception chromatography has been continuously modified but the basis remains the same, that of two *phases* with a substance distributed between them, separation requiring one of the

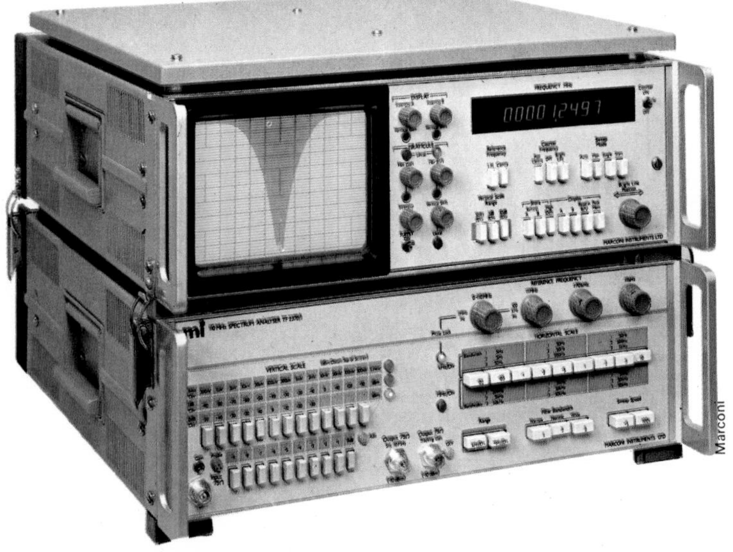

Right: This electronic spectrum analyzer is used to examine the component frequencies and waveforms of electronic signals.

Below: The *nuclear magnetic resonance* (NMR) spectrometer is used to analyze the structure of molecules. The sample to be analyzed is placed in a strong magnetic field and exposed to radio-frequency radiation. It will absorb radiation energy at frequencies corresponding to the magnetic resonance frequencies of its atomic nuclei, those at which they change their direction of orientation within the magnetic field. The frequencies at which energy is absorbed indicate the types of atoms present.

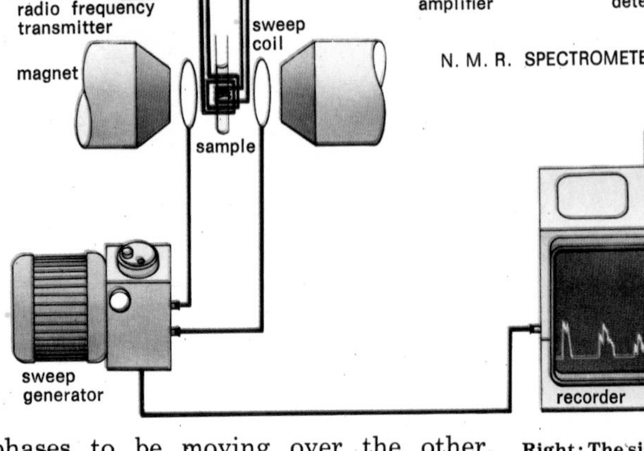

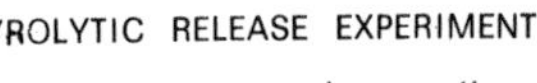
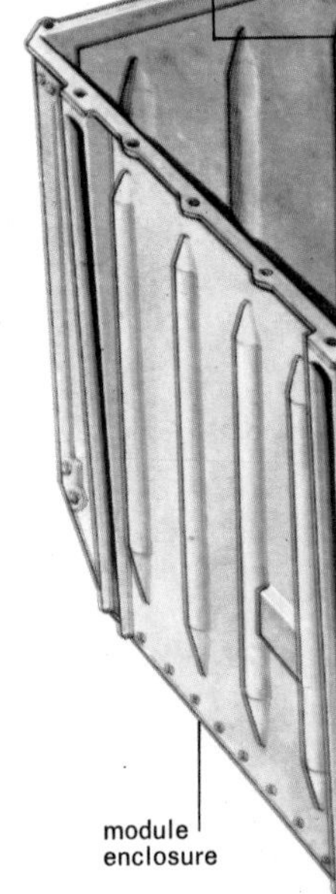

Right: The equipment used in the life detection experiments carried out by the Viking 1 and Viking 2 spacecraft on soil taken from the surface of Mars. There were three sections to these experiments: the *pyrolytic release* experiment, which looked for evidence of photosynthesis; the *labelled release* experiment, which looked for signs of metabolic activity; and the *gas exchange* experiment, which looked for changes in the composition of the gases surrounding a soil sample that would indicate that some form of respiratory activity was taking place within the soil.

phases to be moving over the other, stationary phase. The moving phase may be a liquid or a gas; the stationary phase may be a solid adsorbent or a liquid film, the former being called *adsorption chromatography* and the latter *partition chromatography*.

Partition chromatography depends on the difference in solubility a compound may have in two different liquids. One of the liquids is kept stationary as a liquid film by impregnating it in an inert support, such as kieselguhr, cellulose or some other finely divided solid. The substance to be separated is dissolved in the moving phase, its progress being delayed according to its relative solubility in each of the liquids. Substances with different solubilities may be separated, the solutes more soluble in the moving phase progressing faster.

Gas-liquid chromatography (a form of partition chromatography) apparatus consists of a liquid film support packed in a small diameter tubular column, usually several metres long. The moving phase, an inert gas such as argon, is allowed to flow through the column, which is generally placed in an oven so that it can be heated to facilitate separation of high boiling point materials. The sample mixture is injected into the head of the column and passes down the tube under the influence of the carrier gas.

The individual compounds proceed at a rate dependent upon their affinities for the stationary phase, those with a strong affinity being retained longer than those with a weak affinity. A detector at the column exit produces a signal as the compounds emerge, which is amplified and displayed on a chart recorder.

Right: The size of the equipment used by the Viking landers in their search for life on Mars can be seen from this picture of the assembly of one of the complex miniature laboratories. Each one contained three automated units which performed the life detection experiments, plus associated equipment for handling the soil samples and a computer. The soil samples were dug from the Martian surface by a telescopic digging device and transferred automatically to the three experiments. The control analysis was carried out by repeating the experiments with soil samples that were sterilized to kill off any organisms present.

TRW Inc

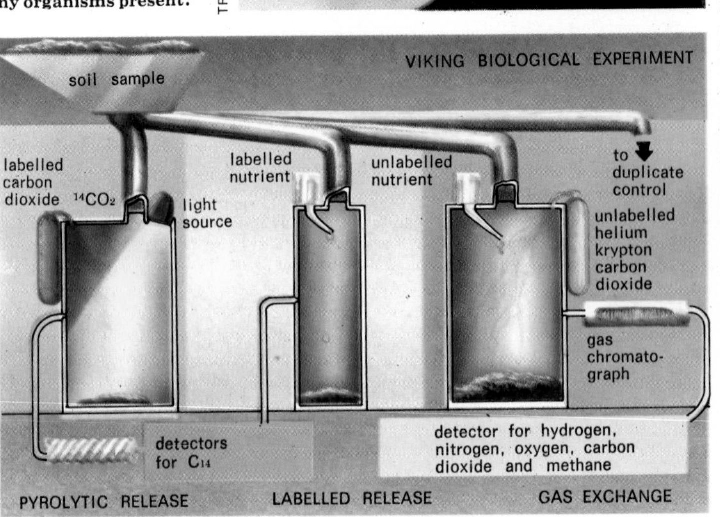

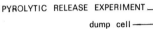

Below left: The biological experiments performed by the Viking spacecraft. In the pyrolytic release experiment, a soil sample was kept in a container in which the Martian atmosphere was supplemented with carbon dioxide containing ('labelled with') radioactive carbon-14. The sample was bathed in light similar to Martian sunlight then the gases surrounding the sample were removed. It was then heated to see if it gave off any carbon-14, which would indicate that carbon had been removed from the gases by a photosynthetic organism. In the labelled release experiment, the sample was treated with a nutrient containing carbon-14, so that any living organism present to absorb the nutrient would give off carbon to the surrounding air, including carbon-14 which could be detected. In the gas exchange experiment, a gas chromatograph was used to detect any changes, caused by the respiration of a living organism, in the gases around the sample.

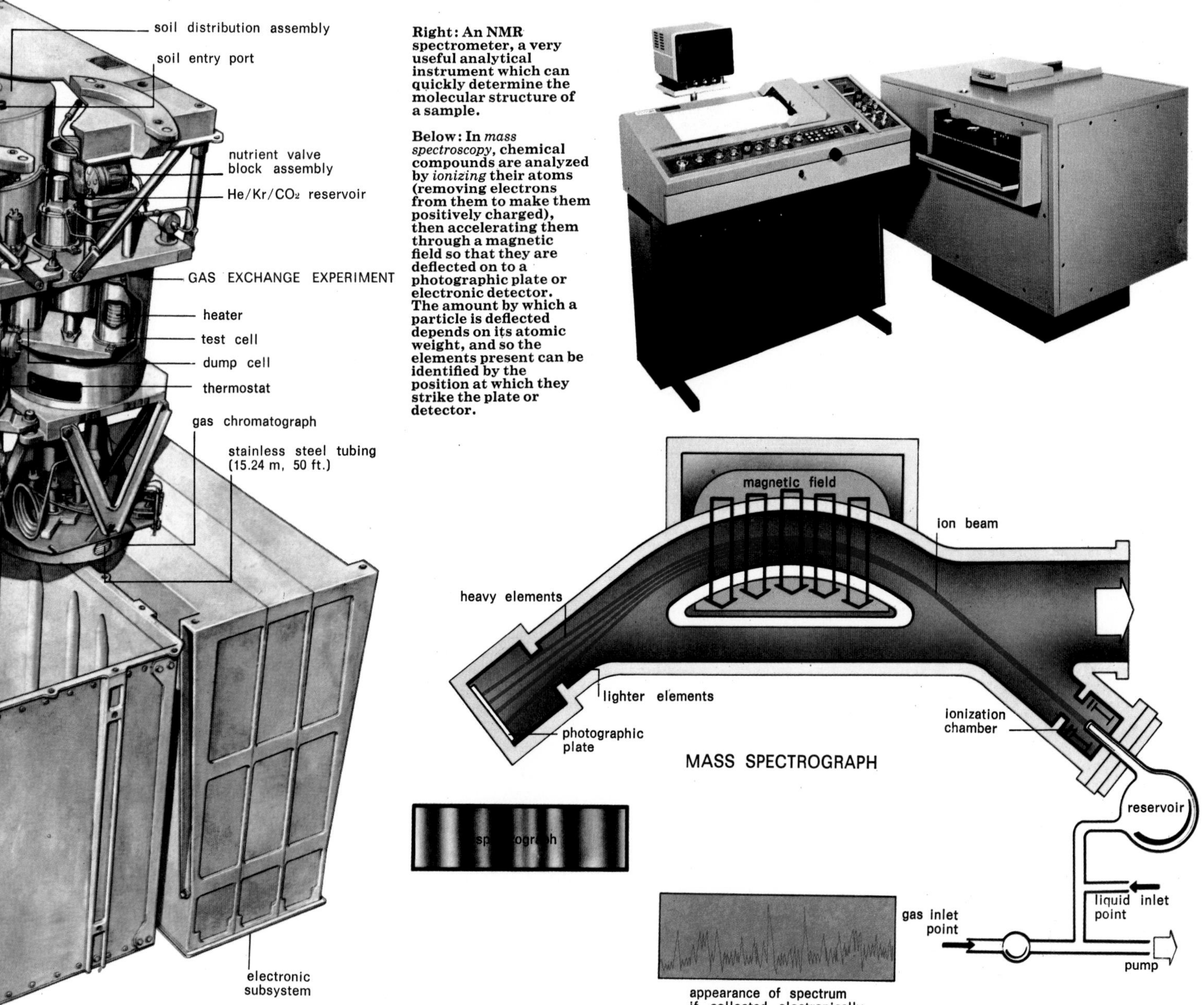

Right: An NMR spectrometer, a very useful analytical instrument which can quickly determine the molecular structure of a sample.

Below: In *mass spectroscopy*, chemical compounds are analyzed by *ionizing* their atoms (removing electrons from them to make them positively charged), then accelerating them through a magnetic field so that they are deflected on to a photographic plate or electronic detector. The amount by which a particle is deflected depends on its atomic weight, and so the elements present can be identified by the position at which they strike the plate or detector.

This display is called a *chromatogram* and ideally takes the form of peaks, each indicating the presence of a particular component. The retention time in the column is characteristic for each compound, allowing qualitative analysis to be made upon comparison with a standard sample chromatogram.

Spectroscopy

Newton was the first to discover that when a beam of white light strikes one of the faces of a triangular glass prism, the beam is bent or deviated from its straight path and resolved into a series of rainbow-coloured bands called a spectrum. Newton's spectrum, however, was impure, as the colours overlapped. An instrument for producing and measuring a pure spectrum is called a *spectrometer*, which by focusing the light admitted via a narrow slit or *collimator* on to the prism produces a series of distinct or *monochromatic* colours.

The spectrum produced by the white light of the Sun is a series of closely-adjacent radiations called a *continuous spectrum*. By contrast elements, when incandescent, produce light of distinct colours of particular wavelengths called a *line spectrum*.

The study and analysis of spectra is called *spectroscopy*, which involves observing and measuring the radiations emitted by atoms and molecules when they are excited by means of energy which is normally thermal or electro-magnetic in nature. Atoms consist of a nucleus surrounded by electrons moving in certain orbits corresponding to levels of energy. If supplied with an amount of energy at an appropriate frequency the electron will jump to another orbit, where it will have a higher energy level.

The difference between the energy states is equal to the energy supplied. Conversely, under favourable circumstances an electron may jump from a high to a low energy orbit, emitting energy in the form of electromagnetic radiation. The frequency of this radiation is proportional to the amount of energy it contains.

In a hot body, thermally excited atoms emit and absorb visible and invisible radiation of discrete and characteristic wavelengths due to energy changes between electron orbits, normally producing a radiation spectrum of more than one wavelength.

The first known spectroscopic observations to distinguish individual atomic transmissions were those of Josef von Fraunhofer (1787-1826) in 1814. Fraunhofer developed a spectrometer capable of resolving the spectral lines named after him, which arise from the absorption of solar radiation by the atoms in the cooler gas surrounding the Sun and by atoms in the Earth's atmosphere. The same spectroscopic techniques were soon applied to the analysis of other atomic emissions, for every element has a unique electronic structure, capable of producing a specific and identifying spectrum. Furthermore, the intensities of the lines of emission indicate the concentrations of the atoms present in the sample, so that a quantitative analysis is possible.

Any substance will absorb radiation of the particular wavelength that it emits at a high temperature. Thus, if radiation from a hot source emitting a continuous spectrum is passed through a transparent sample or vapour, the *absorption spectrum* is deficient in the wavelengths that the sample would emit if it were raised to the same high temperature. Absorption spectroscopy is a valuable analytic tool as it is easy to control and does not destroy the sample. By measuring the proportion of incident light absorbed the molecular concentrations may also be determined.

Navigation

Navigation probably originated on the waterways, such as the Nile and the Euphrates, around which the first major civilizations developed. From these simple beginnings, navigation became steadily more complex as the distances travelled and the speeds and numbers of craft increased with the spread of civilization and trade. Although the basic principles remain the same, the intervening centuries have provided a host of navigational aids and techniques to match the development of transport technology.

Navigation is a composite problem requiring the establishment of position, speed and direction. It is characterized by four main aspects: the determination of the destination; the choice of a suitable route; the estimation of course and speed; and a regular or continuous monitoring of the progress of the craft.

Early navigation

Early navigation in rivers, or in coastal waters in sight of land, was a relatively simple process, using landmarks and coastal features as visual references. Out at sea, however, the early mariners used the Sun and the stars to determine the direction in which they were heading.

The mapping of the heavens was started by the Babylonians, who regarded the heavenly bodies as being mounted on a celestial sphere, a hollow globe of great size which surrounded the Earth and rotated around it from east to west. In the north of the celestial sphere, around its upper pivot as it were, the stars did not change position as much as stars at other parts of the sphere, so a bright star near the centre of this pivotal area could act as an almost-stationary visual reference. In the northern hemisphere, the star occupying this position at present is the Pole Star (Polaris), which is part of the constellation of the Little Bear (Ursa Minor).

Gradually, the positions of celestial bodies were tabulated, and in conjunction with a calendar men could make observations with simple instruments to ascertain their latitude. One of the earliest instruments was the Greek astronomers' *astrolabe*, simplified for use by mariners and developed by the Portuguese in the 15th century for their oceanic voyages. Latitude could be found by observation of the angles between the horizon and the sun or certain stars, the simplest being the angular altitude of the Pole Star, as this angle approximately equals the latitude of the place of observation.

Solar observations were also useful in determining the time, the sun reaching its highest altitude at noon. This altitude also provided latitude, if combined with data (listed in simplified astronomical tables) concerning the angles and position of the Sun throughout the year. By comparing the local latitude with that of an already tabulated latitude of their destination, they were able to deduce their distance north or south of the destination. This furnished them with the rudiments of setting and maintaining course by sailing to the appropriate latitude and then running east or west to their destination, but without a knowledge of longitude a 'fix' of position was impossible.

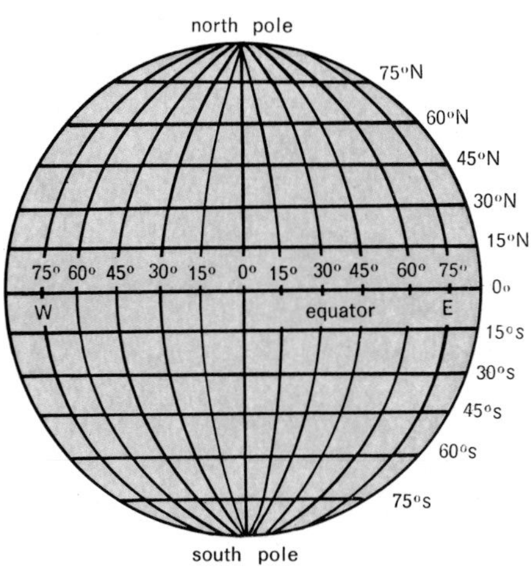

Above: Any point on the Earth's surface can be identified by its latitude and longitude. Lines of latitude are imaginary circles drawn round the Earth, the *Equator* being the line of zero latitude (0°). Lines of longitude are circles drawn through the poles, zero longitude (0°) being the *Greenwich Meridian*.

Radio Times Hulton Picture Library

Right: A pair of seventeenth century Arabian *astrolabes*. The astrolabe had many uses including finding the time of day, and the rising and setting times of the Sun and stars. The Portuguese version, the *mariner's astrolabe*, measured the angle of the Sun or stars to indicate latitude.

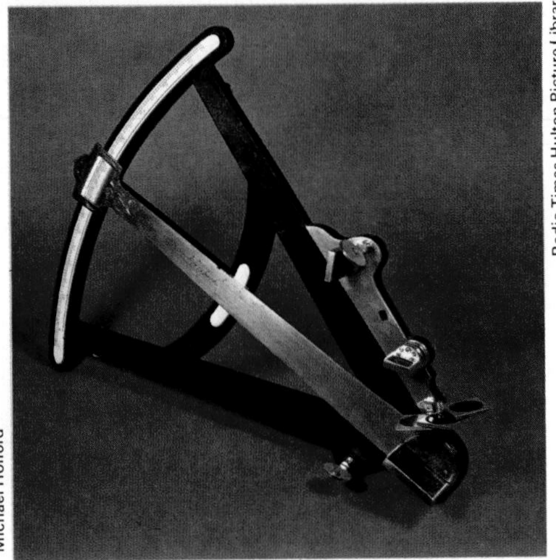

Michael Holford

Above: James Hadley's *octant* enabled navigators to make accurate measurements of the altitude of the Sun or stars, so that they could find their latitude. The observer viewed the horizon through a sight, and adjusted the movable central arm of the instrument until the reflected image of the Sun or star appeared in a mirror placed in line with the horizon. The altitude was indicated on the curved scale.

Below: A *sextant* made by Hadley in 1785. The sextant, a more accurate version of the octant and capable of measuring a greater angle, was invented in 1757 by John Campbell.

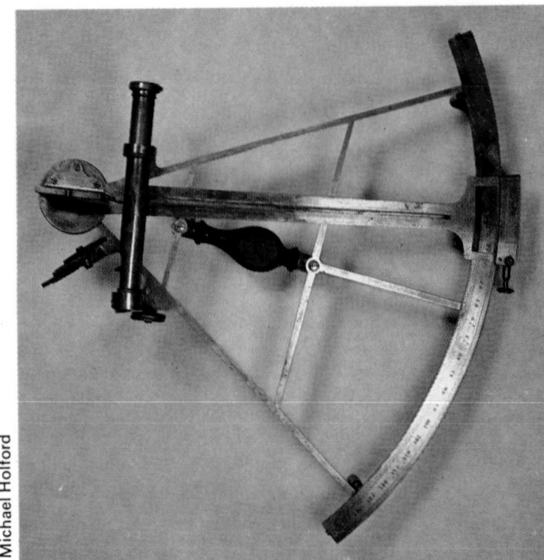

Michael Holford

SHIP'S COMPASS

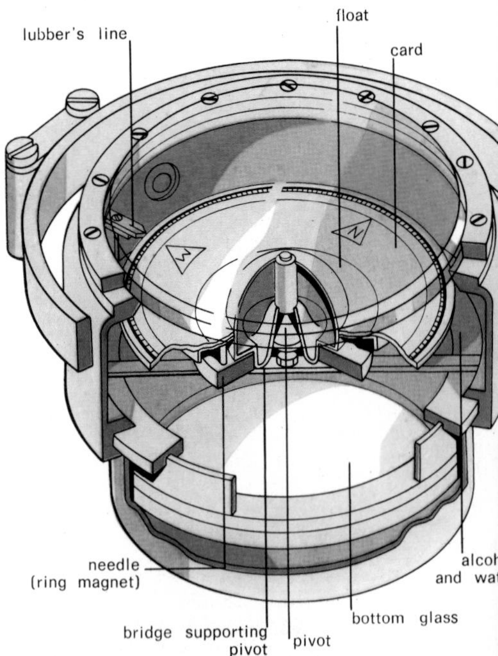

Above: A mariner's compass. A magnet is attached to the bottom of the compass card, which is mounted on a float in water and alcohol so it stays horizontal as the ship moves. The 'north' on the card points to magnetic north, and the ship's direction is indicated by the *lubber's line*.

Right: The type of gyroscope used in many gyrocompasses. The gyroscope is a rapidly-spinning wheel which is controlled in such a way that it keeps itself pointing towards true north (the geographic north pole, as opposed to the magnetic one). It is unaffected by movement or by magnetism.

Picturepoint

Left: The D-shaped scanner of a ship's radar system. Radar is a valuable navigation aid, providing information on the range and bearing of the coastline and other vessels. It is particularly useful at night and in bad weather when visual observations are not possible.

Syndication International

Right: Checking the accuracy of the *precision approach radar* at an RAF airfield in England. Precision approach radar is one of the many navigational aids used to guide aircraft safely down to the runway; the most advanced *instrument landing systems* can land an aircraft fully automatically.

Port of London Authority

Right: The operations room of the Thames Navigation Service in Gravesend, which is run by the Port of London Authority to ensure the safe navigation of vessels using the River Thames. The operations room is equipped with seven radar sets and several vhf radio consoles. Tide gauge readings obtained automatically from five separate points are displayed on tv monitor screens. The service broadcasts half-hourly bulletins on the state of the tides, the weather, ship movements and other navigational information. Over 1,000 ship movements per week are monitored and assisted by this service.

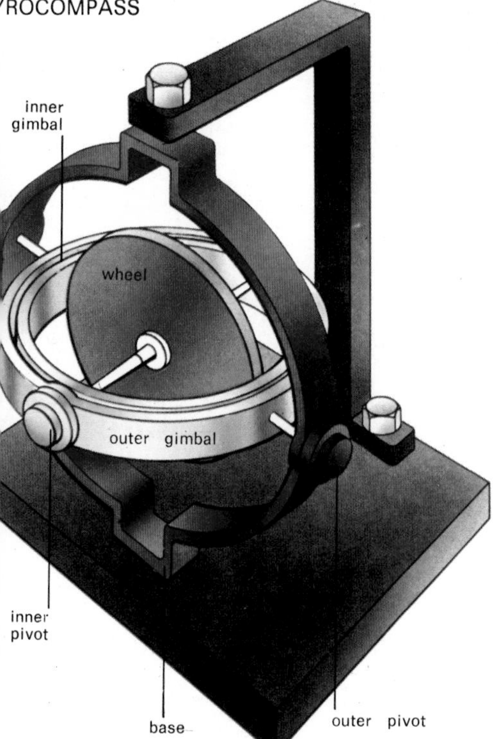

Dead reckoning

The mariner's compass, first known in Europe in the 13th century, introduced navigation as a science. The discovery of the directional properties of the lodestone, or of a magnetized needle, which if freely suspended appeared miraculously to point towards the Pole Star, even when she was invisible, made all-weather voyages possible. The compass depends upon the horizontal component of the attraction of the earth's magnetism for its directive force and thus by being free to rotate in a horizontal or *azimuth* plane determines bearing relative to the magnetic pole.

As the magnetic poles are moving slowly about the geographic poles, the compass does not show true North but aligns itself at an angle to it. This difference is called the *magnetic variation* and alters daily, but it is predictable and is listed in almanacs.

The discovery of the compass facilitated steering a course but ignored the vagaries of the wind, the tide and the current. It was therefore impossible to reckon accurately how far and on what bearing the ship lay from its destination.

The process of estimating position based on a record of known progress is known as *dead reckoning*, from the practice of throwing a log overboard (from the bow of the ship) which was assumed to be 'dead' in the water. By noting the time for the log to pass the length of the ship an estimate of speed could be made.

The English adapted this to the *log and line*. A log thrown overboard into the water was attached to a line knotted at regular intervals, and the line was paid out for about half a minute, timed on a sandglass. The length between each successive knot was chosen so that during the timed interval the number of knots paid out represented the number of nautical miles per hour (Knots) at which the ship was travelling. The speed was regularly recorded so that the distance travelled could be calculated. A record of the ship's direction of travel was also kept, and so by drawing a line on a chart which corresponded to the direction and distance travelled, the ship's position could be ascertained.

The ambitious voyages resulting from the expansion of trade created a demand for accurate maps, so that bearings from port to port could be known with some precision. Sailor's charts at this time mapped the world as plane and flat, and

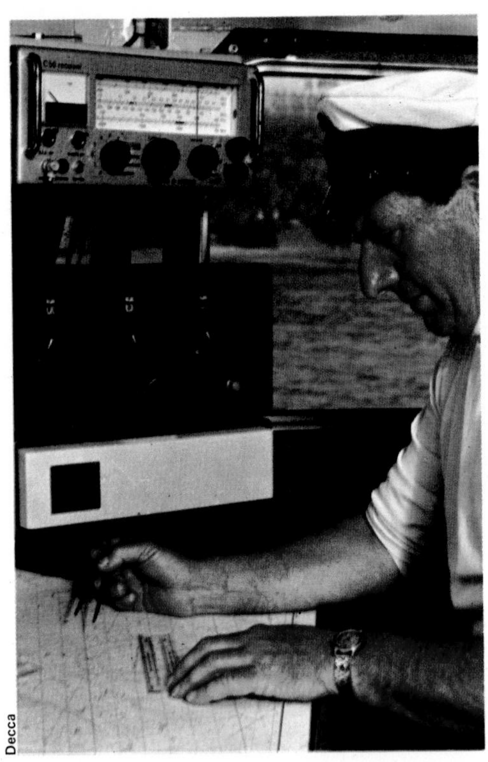

Decca

Above left: A Decca Navigator Mk21 receiver in use on a lifeboat. The Decca system uses groups of 'master' and 'slave' transmitters, operating in the 70-130 kHz band, which are positioned so that phase differences are created between the signals from the master and those from the slaves.

Above: The signals from a Decca master/slave combination produce hyperbolic lines along which the signal phase differences are zero. The receiver detects these phase differences and also responds to signals which are transmitted at one minute intervals to identify the individual Decca 'lanes', the areas between the hyperbolic lines. The receiver displays the Decca co-ordinates and lane numbers, which are then used in conjunction with a lattice overlaid on a standard navigational chart to establish the ship's exact position. The Decca system has a range of about 480 km (300 miles).

Below: A map display of an aircraft *inertial navigation* (IN) system. An IN system computes an aircraft's speed and position by data obtained from *accelerometers*, which register its horizontal and vertical accelerations, and gyroscopes, which register changes in direction and attitude.

marked with *rhumb lines*. A rhumb line, also known as a loxodrome, is a line which crosses every line of longitude at the same angle. Lines of latitude are rhumb lines, as they cross every line of longitude at an angle of 90°. By using the rhumb lines, routes could be planned along lines of constant direction.

The inaccuracies caused by ignoring the convergence of the meridians at the poles was acceptable in the low latitudes of the Mediterranean, but introduced large errors when sailing further North or South.

The great Flemish mathematician Gerardus Mercator (Gerhard Kremer, 1512-94) devised a projection in which straight line rhumbs were true. In this projection, while the meridians remained parallel and equidistant the lines of latitude, although parallel, were spaced in inverse ratio to the convergence of the meridians. Rhumb lines drawn between points with a ruler were correct, crossing every meridian at an equal angle. Such routes could be simply maintained using a compass on a constant course.

The position of a craft is known when both its latitude and longitude have been defined. Latitude and longitude are both measured in *degrees*, and for greater accuracy one degree can be divided into 60 *minutes*, and each minute into 60 *seconds*. The determination of longitude is inseparably associated with the measurement of time. As the earth rotates on its axis, successive meridians pass beneath the sun at an interval of four minutes for every degree of longitude. By comparing local time with a standard time at a reference meridian, say Greenwich at 0° (Greenwich Mean Time), the time divergence gives the difference in longitude, one hour forward or backward equalling 15° East or West.

Astronomical observations give local time but to deduce standard time some predictable phenomenon was required, which was independent of, and could be seen from, the observer's position on earth. The obvious answer was a clock, although it was not until the eighteenth century, when John Harrison succeeded in designing a marine timekeeper (or chronometer) that was sufficiently accurate, that one could be carried on ship.

In addition to the chronometer, a method involving lunar distances relative to celestial bodies was proposed, for in principle any fast-moving object can be used for timekeeping provided its motion is predictable and it can be accurately observed. However, the existing instruments lacked the precision required and the method only became practicable with the invention of James Hadley's *octant* in 1731. The octant was the fore-runner of the modern sextant, and was designed for measuring the angle between a celestial body and the horizon to determine latitude.

It could also measure the angle between the Moon and a given star, and once this angle was known the exact time, and the longitude, could be calculated from astronomical tables.

Radio navigational aids

As radio waves, under perfect conditions, travel as a wave about a straight line axis their reception with a suitable receiver, or *Direction Finder* (DF), may be considered analogous to a line of sight bearing. By noting the bearings of two or more shore based stations a position fix may be obtained.

If a loop aerial of a receiver is placed at right angles to the direction of radio waves, the wavefront will strike each side of the loop simultaneously and there will be no signal. If the loop is aligned parallel to the path of the wave it will strike the two sides at slightly different instants of time and a difference signal

Ferranti

Right: The Transit satellite navigation system is based on eight satellites travelling in polar orbits around the Earth (orbits which pass over the north and south poles). As a satellite passes overhead, a ship using the system receives three separate transmissions from it. As the satellite's position changes during the intervals between the signals, the receiver can compute the ship's position in a similar way to taking a fix from three separate ground-based transmitters. The ground system computes the details of the satellite's orbit and transmits this data to it every 12 hours.

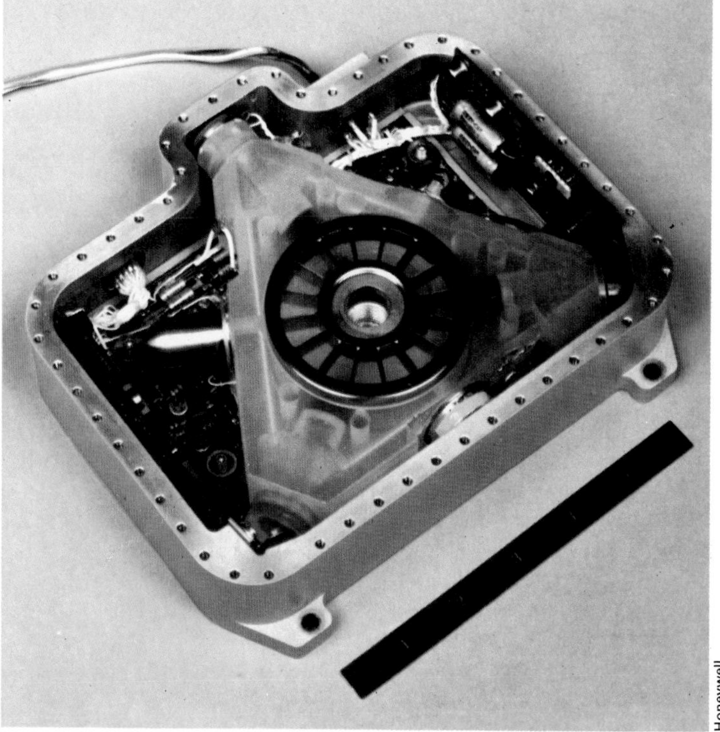

Above: A laser gyro developed for use in navigation systems. Instead of using a rapidly-spinning wheel, the laser gyro has two laser beams, one moving around clockwise and the other one anti-clockwise. If the gyro is rotated about its axis, the frequencies of the beams alter, and these changes in frequency are used to compute rotation rate.

Left: The sensing element of the inertial guidance system built by Ferranti for the European Launcher Development Organization satellite launch vehicles. The element contains three gyros and three accelerometers which sense the vehicle's motion.

Ferranti

Honeywell

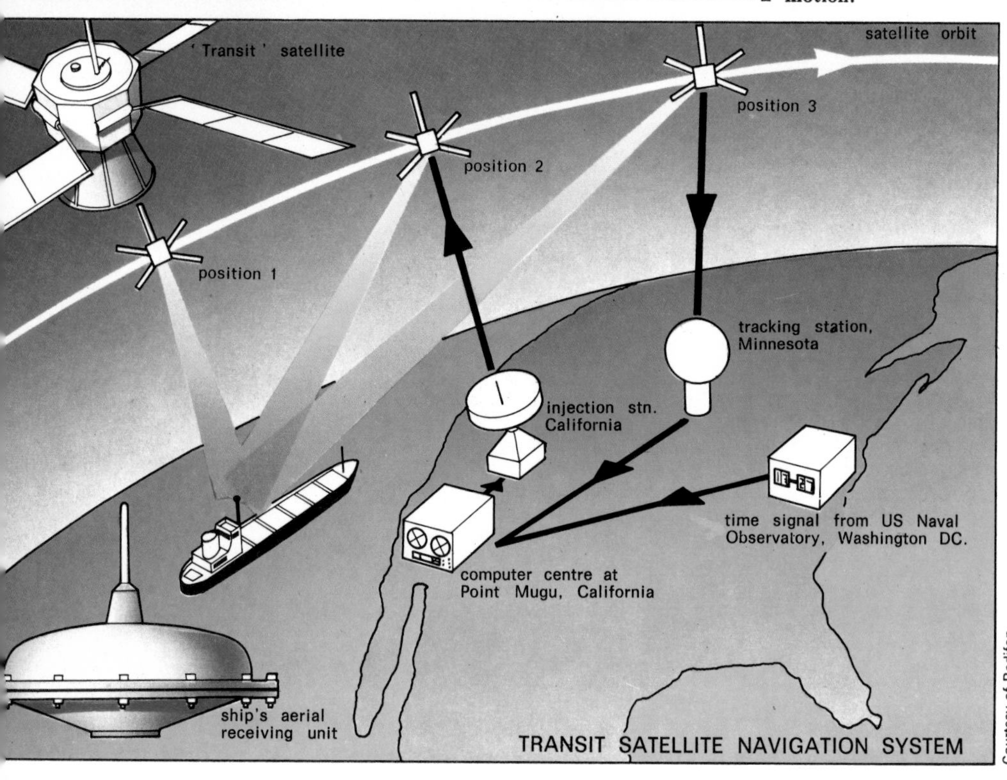

Courtesy of Redifon

will appear. Thus the signal intensity in the receiver alters from a maximum to a minimum as the aerial is rotated relative to the bearing of the transmitting station. Marine radio beacons along the coast or in lightvessels transmit a steady signal on which the bearing is taken, and a morse signal for identification.

A sophisticated omnidirectional version of marine DF is *vhf omnirange* (VOR). A beacon transmits two signals, one omnidirectional and one rotating, and the bearing of the beacon relative to the receiver is indicated by phase differences between the two received signals.

Most civil air traffic is routed along busy airways in controlled airspace. These airways are separated into height bands as well as different headings. The position of the aircraft in space is prescribed by ground authorities by means of radio and radar contact. At present the most widely used navigation aid is VORTAC, a radio system in which numerous ground beacons along airways send out signals that enable aircrews to check their bearing and distance to the next station. The bearing is checked against a VOR transmitter while distance is estimated using *Distance Measuring Equipment* (DME), which transmits a pulse from the aircraft to interrogate a responsive ground beacon called a *transponder*, which in turn transmits a signal back to the 'plane. The total time (measured from the aircraft) for the sequence to occur defines the distance from the plane to the beacon.

More flexible use of the total airspace is obtained with a phased group of ground stations that send out interlocked signals to create a hyperbolic pattern of position lines. There are a variety of systems available, which are in wide use by both shipping and aircraft. *Decca*, highly accurate to within a few yards up to 480 km (300 miles), from a Decca transmitting station, covers busy coastal shipping areas but is not suitable for ocean position finding and *Loran C*, although primarily designed for aircraft, can be used by ships.

Relativity

The publication of Albert Einstein's Theory of Relativity in the early years of this century marked a great advance in man's understanding of the physical world. Unfortunately, the theory has a reputation for incomprehensibility, partly because of the complexity of some of the mathematics, but also because its conclusions seem to contradict common sense.

Relativity is primarily a theory about the motions of moving bodies. It was formulated in two stages: the *Special Theory* (1905) considers only bodies moving at a constant velocity relative to each other, while the *General Theory* (1915) also deals with acceleration and gravity.

The Special Theory

Einstein was led to the Special Theory by a crisis which faced physicists at the beginning of this century. Some forty years earlier the great British physicist James Clerk Maxwell (1831-1879) had shown that light consists of waves of electric and magnetic fields. These spread out at a velocity which can be calculated from the electrical properties of a vacuum, and this velocity agrees well with the experimentally measured speed of light (300,000 km per second). Nineteenth century physicists assumed that these waves must travel in some 'medium', the *ether*, just as sound waves require air in order to propagate. The ether, however, must fill the entire Universe, both matter and vacuum, because light traverses both transparent bodies (like glass or water), and the vacuum of space.

The ether was thus thought to be a universal background, and all movement could be measured *absolutely* with respect to it. Since the Earth orbits the Sun at a speed of over 29 km per second, its motion through the ether should have been detectable by optical methods. A precision instrument to achieve this was built by Albert Michelson (1852-1931) and Edward Morley (1838-1923) in 1887 at the Case School of Applied Science in Cleveland, Ohio. In their *interferometer*, a light beam was split into two beams at right angles to one another by a half-silvered mirror. Each beam was reflected back by a mirror at the end of a ten-metre arm, and recombined in an eyepiece.

The light beam which moved out and back *across* the Earth's direction of motion should have taken slightly less time, according to the ether theory, than that which moved with the motion, and then been reflected back against it. This small difference should have shown as a change in the pattern of bright and dark stripes (interference pattern) seen when the beams recombined. Michelson and Morley rotated their apparatus back and forth through 90°, so that the two interferometer arms would reverse roles, and expected to see a corresponding change in the interference pattern. Not the slightest change was observed. The simple ether theory was incorrect, and modifications to explain the negative result of the Michelson-Morley experiment were not very satisfactory.

Einstein, however, realized that the problem lay in a misunderstanding of Maxwell's results—even by Maxwell himself. As a simple example, imagine two laboratories, one fixed on the Earth, and another in a moving train. As long as the train moves at a *constant speed* (relative to the Earth), the occupants cannot tell that they are moving, unless they look out of the windows. Indeed, they could claim that they are stationary and that the Earth is moving backwards.

Einstein generalized this idea in his *Principle of Relativity*. It states that the results of any experiment will be the same regardless of how the laboratory is moving, so long as there is no force acting on the laboratory to accelerate it. As a consequence, we cannot in any way distinguish a particular *frame of reference* (the laboratory, for example) as being absolutely at rest.

This being so, then in the case of

Esher Foundation/Haags Gemeentemuseum

Above: 'Relativity', a lithograph by M. C. Escher, illustrates the way in which circumstances appear to change when viewed from different positions. Each element of the picture appears to be geometrically correct only when viewed from the right angle and considered in isolation from the others. The relativistic concepts of the space-time continuum pose similar intellectual problems; space and time, considered locally, appear quite straightforward, but viewed on a universal scale they become much more complex and confusing, and may even appear to be in direct contradiction to everyday common sense.

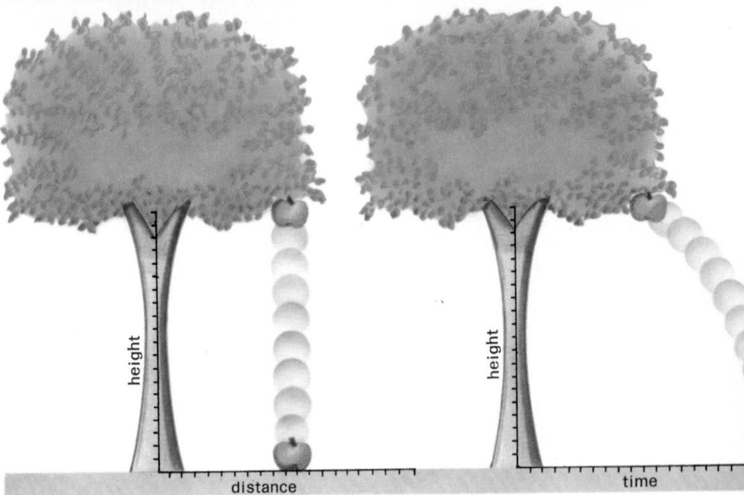

Above: These two diagrams, based on the graphs that would be obtained by plotting the height of a falling apple against horizontal distance and against time, represent the idea of the curvature of space-time. The apple's path is straight in (local) space, but *curved* in space-time.

Below: One of the predictions of the General Theory was that light is deflected by gravity, and so starlight passing near the Sun on its way to Earth would be deflected by the Sun's gravity and appear to be coming from a different angle. This was confirmed during a solar eclipse in 1919.

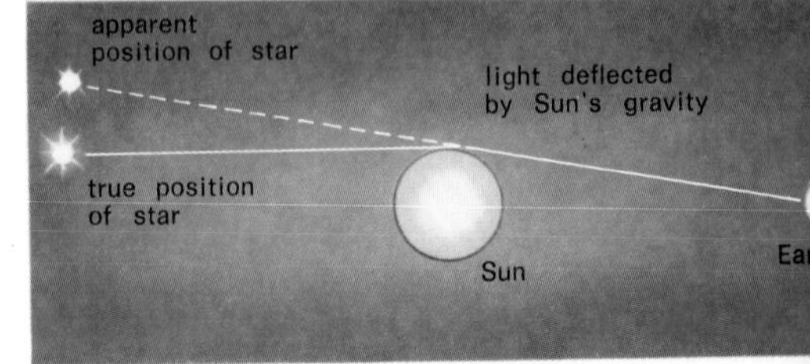

British Transport

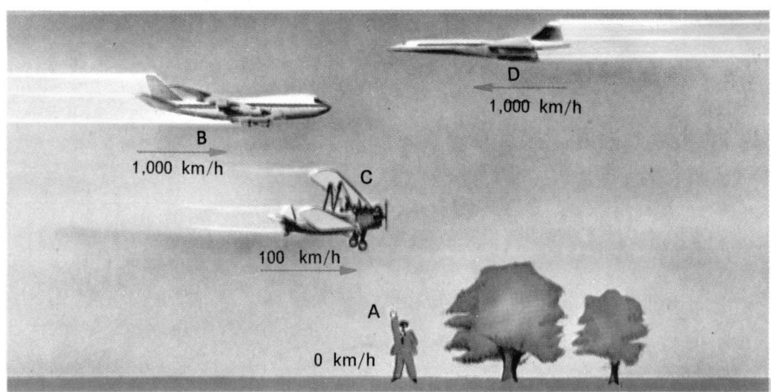

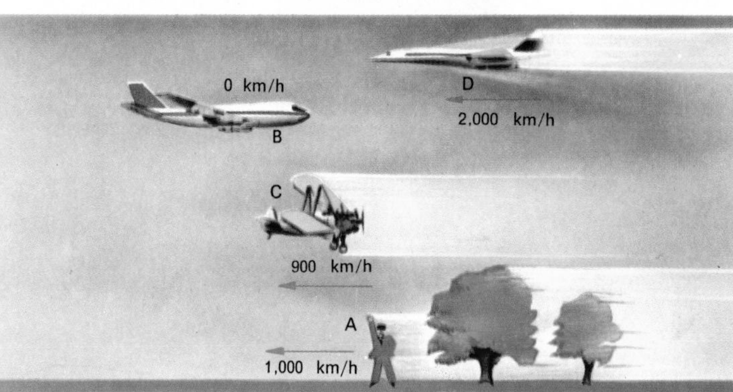

Above: If two trains stand side by side in a station, and one begins to move, passengers in the stationary train often think that it is *their* train which is moving. In fact, the two trains can *both* be considered as moving relative to each other, although only one is moving relative to the Earth.

Right: These two diagrams illustrate how observed motion is relative to the motion of the observer. In the upper diagram, the observer is stationary on the ground. Ground features are stationary, and the aircraft are moving at the speeds and in the directions shown. In the lower diagram, however, the observer is moving along with aircraft B. From this viewpoint, aircraft B could be considered to be stationary, with the ground and aircraft C and D moving from right to left at the speeds shown. Nothing can be *absolutely* at rest or in motion, only at rest or in motion *relative* to something else.

CEGB

CEGB

Left and above: One aspect of the Special Theory was the equation $E = mc^2$: the total energy in a piece of matter equals its mass multiplied by the square of the speed of light. A nuclear power station, such as the one above, operates by converting some of its fuel's mass into energy. This yields much more energy from a given mass of fuel than would be obtained by burning it. The heap of coal on the left is capable of producing about 2.2 million MWh of electricity when burnt in the power station; if all its mass could be converted to energy, about 34.3 million million MWh could be produced.

electromagnetism the electrical properties of a vacuum must be the same in all laboratories. Since the speed of light is related to these properties, it too must also be the same in all reference frames. This is where the difference with the ether theory arises. The older theory had light moving at a constant speed in a medium at rest, and hence one could measure the *absolute* velocity of one's laboratory. In Einstein's theory, light travels at a constant speed *relative to whoever is observing it*. For example, if two spaceships were travelling at 200,000 km per second, one towards the Sun, and the other away from it, they would *both* measure the velocity of sunlight to be 300,000 km per second (and *not* 500,000 and 100,000 km per second, respectively).

The result of the Michelson-Morley experiment follows quite naturally from the Principle of Relativity, because the two light beams actually travelled at the same speed relative to the apparatus, and hence returned at the same instant.

To understand the other results of Relativity we can consider two rockets passing each other at high speed. Each flashes a light bulb the instant they pass. The light from each bulb travels at the same speed regardless of the speed of the bulb itself (Einstein's second postulate of Relativity). So both flashes expand in all directions as a *single* sphere of light. Now, an observer in rocket A must remain in the centre of the expanding sphere from his own flash bulb, and hence he is also at the centre of the sphere from rocket B's flashbulb. He sees rocket B travelling away from the centre, so to him, B is no longer centrally placed within the sphere. To an observer in rocket B, on the other hand, he (B) is always at the centre of the spheres, and A is moving away; to him, *A* is *not* at the centre.

To resolve this apparent contradiction, we must admit that the distance between B and the sphere as measured by A is *not the same* as that measured by B himself. In other words, distances appear to alter when the object under study moves relative to the observer. From this it can be shown mathematically that the physical length of a body always appears to decrease with increase of speed, and becomes zero if the moving object approaches the speed of light. This effect is often known as the *Lorenz-Fitzgerald contraction*, after the two physicists Hendrik Lorentz (1853-1928) and George Fitzgerald (1851-1901) who proposed it as an explanation of the result of the Michelson-Morley experiment.

Similarly, experiments have shown that a moving clock always goes more slowly than one which is fixed relative to the observer, and would appear to stop altogether if it could travel near the speed of light. In addition, it can be shown that the *mass* of a body *increases* with velocity, and becomes infinitely large for

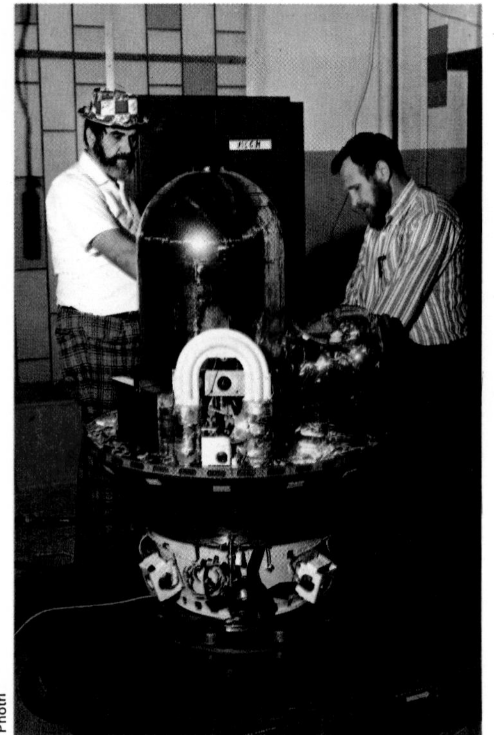

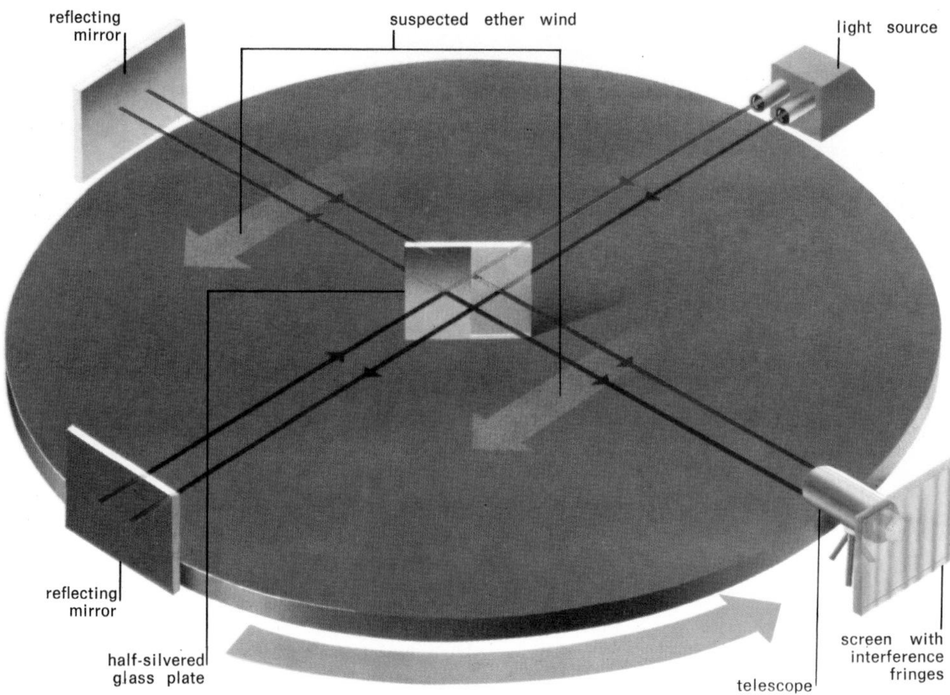

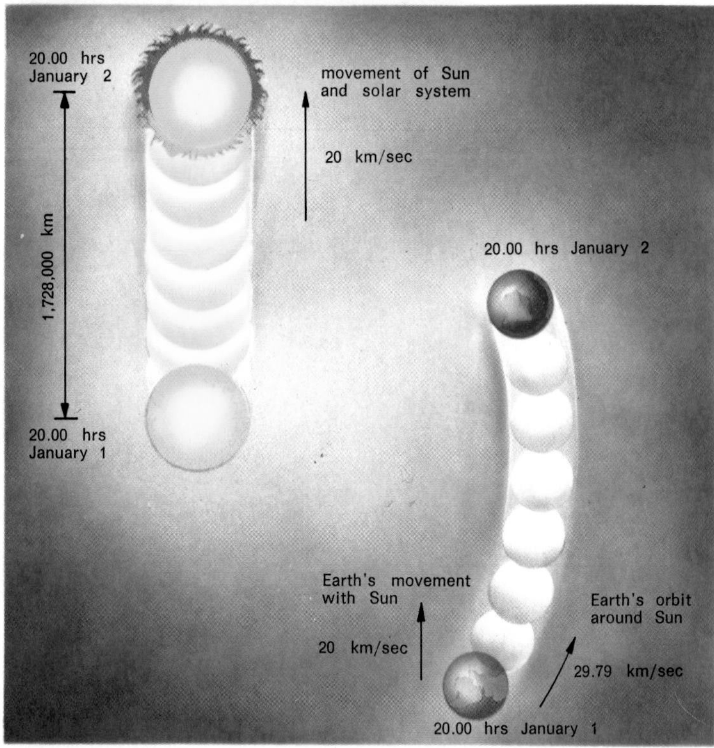

Above left: One of the atomic clocks used in experiments which have tested Einstein's theories concerning the effects of speed, acceleration and gravity on time. This one went on a 2-hour rocket flight, during which its timekeeping was compared with that of similar clocks on Earth.

Above: The Michelson-Morley experiment of 1887 set out to detect the 'ether wind' which was supposed to be passing over the Earth as it moved through space. It hoped to show that the speed of light was affected by the ether wind; its failure resulted in the rejection of the ether theory, and led Einstein to his ideas about relativity.

Left: If you stay at home for 24 hours you will not normally feel that you have travelled anywhere. Taking the Earth as your frame of reference, this is quite true, but taking a larger area of space as your reference frame you find that you have, in fact, travelled millions of kilometres during that 24 hours.

speeds near that of light. Since more force is required to speed up a more massive body, it is never possible to accelerate a particle until it actually moves at the velocity of light. The latter thus constitutes a natural 'speed limit' for the Universe.

This slowing of time and increase in mass have both been verified for sub-atomic particles, the only objects that can be made to reach speeds approaching that of light. At these speeds, fairly appreciable relativistic changes can be observed.

Another way of looking at the increase of mass with speed is to say that when a body is given energy of motion (*kinetic energy*), this energy is converted into extra mass. In 1907, Einstein realized that the converse must also be true: the normal 'at rest' mass of a stationary body must be convertible to energy. The exact amount of energy (E) is calculated by multiplying the mass (m) by the speed of light (c) squared: in symbols, $E = mc^2$. This prediction was not verified for another 25 years, but it led eventually to the atomic bomb, a development which Einstein himself opposed strenuously.

The General Theory

After the Special Theory, Einstein started work on a General Theory of Relativity which would hold for accelerating laboratories as well as for those moving at constant speed. The Principle of Relativity does not hold here: we all know that acceleration can be felt by the human body, and an experiment does not give the same result on an accelerating train as it does on a constant-speed train. Einstein realized, however, that (in a small laboratory where the force of gravity is constant) it is impossible to tell the difference between the effects of acceleration and those of gravity. The inmates of an enclosed rocket, for example, cannot tell whether it is at rest on Earth, or in free space and accelerating at a rate of 9.81m per second. In either case they are pressed against the floor with the same force.

With this *Principle of Equivalence*, and the requirement that Special Relativity shall hold good when no accelerations or gravitational effects are present, Einstein built up the mathematical structure of the General Theory. It is too complex to describe accurately without complex mathematical formulae, but roughly speaking it combines time and the three dimensions of space into a four-dimensional 'space-time continuum'. This is impossible to visualize, but its geometry can be described mathematically just as the geometrical theorems of Euclid can.

The Principle of Equivalence shows that matter changes this geometry in a subtle way (somewhat analogous to curvature in ordinary geometry). Objects passing through this 'curved space-time' have their motion affected by it—they are *gravitationally deflected*. Einstein changed the concept of gravity from a force to being an alteration of the basic background of space-time.

This mathematical formulation of space and time also allows the properties of accelerating systems to be predicted. Acceleration is found to slow time, for example, so a space traveller who experiences accelerations as he leaves Earth, changes course at his destination and eventually lands again on Earth will find that he has aged less than his twin who has remained on Earth. This 'twins paradox' has now been confirmed experimentally by flying extremely accurate atomic clocks around the world. They ran more slowly, by an infinitesimal amount, than identical clocks kept on the ground.

Astronomy and Astrophysics

About 18,000,000,000 years ago, all the matter in the universe seems to have been contained in a small region. Just how small, and precisely how long ago, are debatable points; neither can we say what happened before that. Ever since then, however, the material has been expanding outwards, possibly as a result of an enormous explosion which has been nicknamed the 'Big Bang'.

The main component of the material which expanded out of this Big Bang was hydrogen, each atom consisting of a nucleus with a single proton, and a single electron. About 10 per cent of the atoms, however, were formed by the Big Bang into helium atoms consisting of two protons, two neutrons and two electrons. Since that makes them four times as heavy as hydrogen, some 28% of the *mass* of the early universe was helium. From this hydrogen and helium, all the other elements that we know today were formed.

How do we know all this? As we look at the universe, we can see distant objects such as galaxies. The fainter these objects are, the more their light appears to be shifted to the red end of the visible spectrum. This is not quite the same thing as saying that they are reddened: that would mean that something is filtering out the blue light, as happens to sunlight at sunset. What is actually happening is that their spectral lines—the wavelengths in the spectrum caused by, say, hydrogen, calcium or other elements—are further to the red than they ought to be.

What interpretation is put on this finding is crucial to our whole understanding of the universe. The most familiar way in which spectral lines can be shifted is by the *Doppler effect*, the change in wavelength due to a source's motion. On this interpretation, which is generally accepted, all objects are moving away from all others, and the universe is expanding. The rate at which this Doppler shift takes place is the same wherever we look.

By searching for objects of known brightness or size, a value can be put on the expansion rate, and the most recent figure is 55 kilometres per second for every *megaparsec* (Mpc) of distance. (A parsec is an astronomical unit of distance, and is equal to 30.857 x 10^{12}km). This rate is called the *Hubble Constant*, H, after the American astronomer Edwin Hubble (1889-1953) who first investigated the subject. So if an object has a redshift of 1100 km/sec, it is about 20 Mpc away (although random motions also have to be taken into account). The value of 1/H now gives a figure for the time elapsed since the Big Bang—that is, the age of the universe in seconds. It works out to be some 18,000,000,000 years.

As we search to greater distances, so we are in effect looking back in time. Light and radio waves travel at nearly 300,000 km/sec, but the most distant objects are so far away that the radiation now reaching *us* left *them* several thousand million years ago—when the universe was very much younger. Much interest centres on looking as far as possible, to try to discover whether the universe looked any different then. The signs are that it did. Objects seem to have been closer together, as one would expect with an expanding universe.

Gerry Clyde/Michael Holford

Left: The observatory built in the eighteenth century at Jaipur, India, by Sawai Jai Singh. Much early astronomy was devoted to studying the motion and measuring the positions of the Sun, stars, Moon and planets. In the West, including the Arabic countries, one of the main uses of astronomy was to produce tables of astronomical data for use in navigation. Serious studies of the actual nature of the universe did not begin properly until telescopes came into general use.

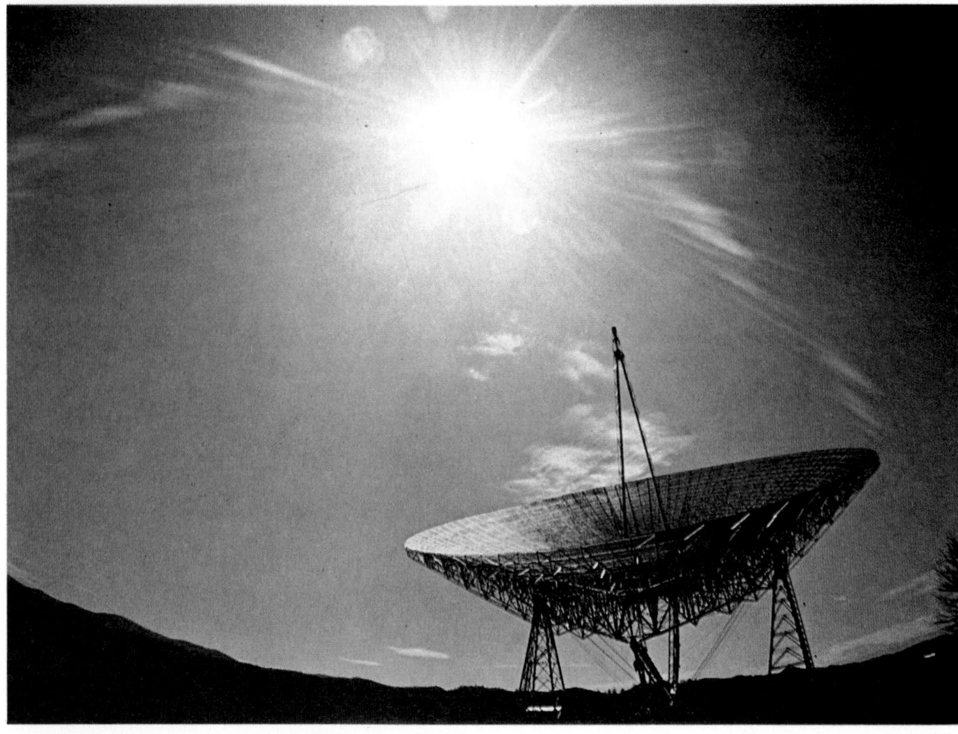

Photri

Below: Stars emit electromagnetic radiation covering a very wide spectrum. Ordinary telescopes are used for observing the visible light emitted by stars, but radio telescopes, such as this one in the US, detect the longer-wavelength radio emissions from stellar objects.

Below: The radio source Cassiopeia A is the remnant of a supernova, a star which exploded in about 1700. Its radio intensity has been measured by the 5 km radio telescope at Cambridge, England, and has been converted into this 'radio photograph'.

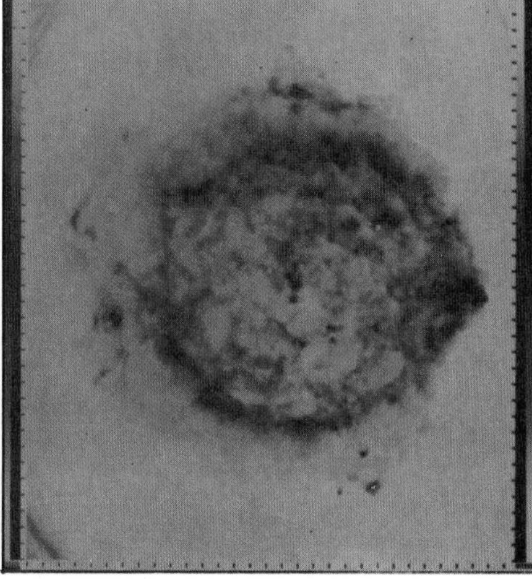

Cambridge 5km Telescope

Another piece of evidence in favour of the Big Bang hypothesis is the discovery that wherever we look in the universe, there is a background glow, a sort of very dull warmth. This is at a temperature of only 2.76 K—just above the absolute zero of temperature—but even so it represents a challenge to astronomical theory. It seems to be the residual heat of the later stages of the Big Bang itself, spread out in every direction equally. Its temperature agrees with what we should now expect from an original fireball temperature of over a million degrees, which in turn would create the observed ratio of hydrogen to helium.

Quasars

The objects with the greatest redshifts, and which are therefore assumed to be

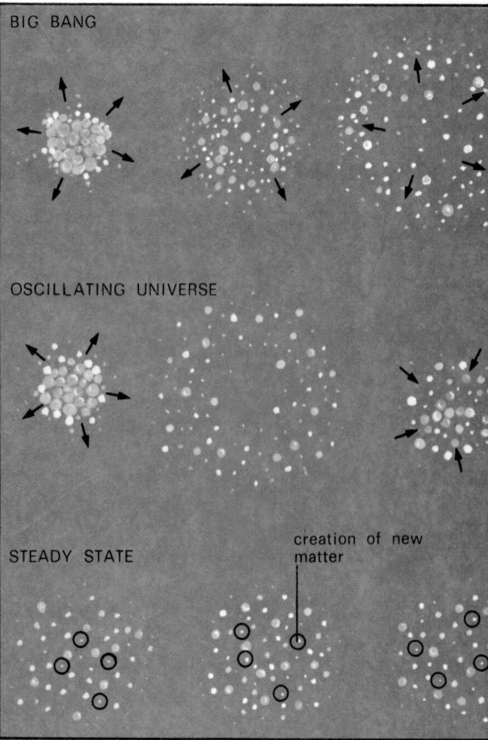

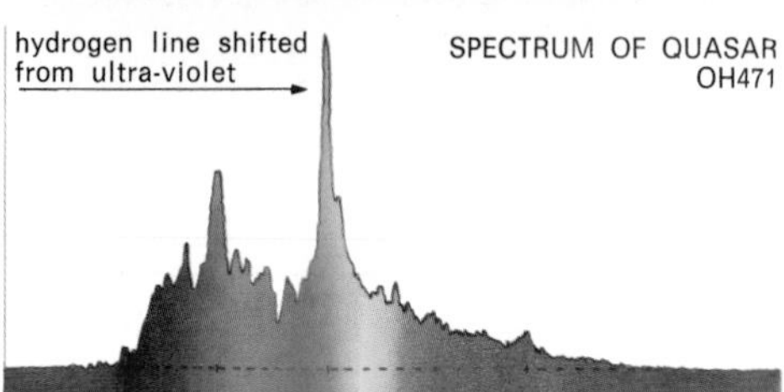

Left: The spectrum of one of the most distant observable objects—the quasar OH471. This object is about 10 billion light years away, which means that what we see of it now is in fact that way it looked 10 billion years ago. The graph shows the intensity of its light at each wavelength. The tallest spike represents the emission due to its hydrogen; this spike would normally be in the far ultraviolet region to the left of the spectrum, but the Doppler effect due to the quasar moving rapidly away from us has shifted the spike towards the 'red' end, so it appears in the visible region.

Above left: The 'Milky Way'. The brightest part is obscured by gas clouds which are in the spiral arms of the galaxy, and the glowing red areas are clouds of hydrogen from which stars are formed. The white streak is the track of an Earth satellite crossing the sky when the picture was taken.

Above: Three theories of the origin of the universe. The 'Big Bang' theory, top, says the universe expanded out from a condensed mass of matter. A second theory, centre, says that the universe is continually expanding and contracting, while a third, bottom, says that matter is being created continuously.

the most distant, are the *quasars*. The name comes from 'quasi-stellar radio sources', and they were first identified in 1963 as sources of radio waves which looked like stars. Their properties include a very high redshift, measured from strong bright lines in their spectrum; they generally look bluer than ordinary stars, and they flicker in brightness slightly on a time scale as short as a few months. Nowadays, any star-like object with these properties is classed as a quasar, though many of them are not radio sources. Observations indicate that quasars are fairly small, and so they must be exceedingly bright to be visible at these enormous distances.

Galaxies

Closer at hand, and more familiar, are the galaxies. These are giant star systems, each containing as many as a million million stars and which come in a variety of types—spiral, elliptical, irregular and so on. Our own Milky Way is one fairly typical spiral galaxy. As we look to greater distances, we find curious things happening in the centres of some galaxies. These may have bright centres or nuclei; in some cases there are signs that explosive events have taken place.

The nuclei of such galaxies behave in many ways like mini-quasars—they are bright and blue, they flicker, they have the same bright lines, and they may be radio sources. In recent years, new detection techniques have revealed that some comparatively nearby objects once thought to be quasars are actually *N-galaxies*, consisting of a bright nucleus with a surrounding 'fuzz'; the underlying fuzzy area, previously hidden in the glare,

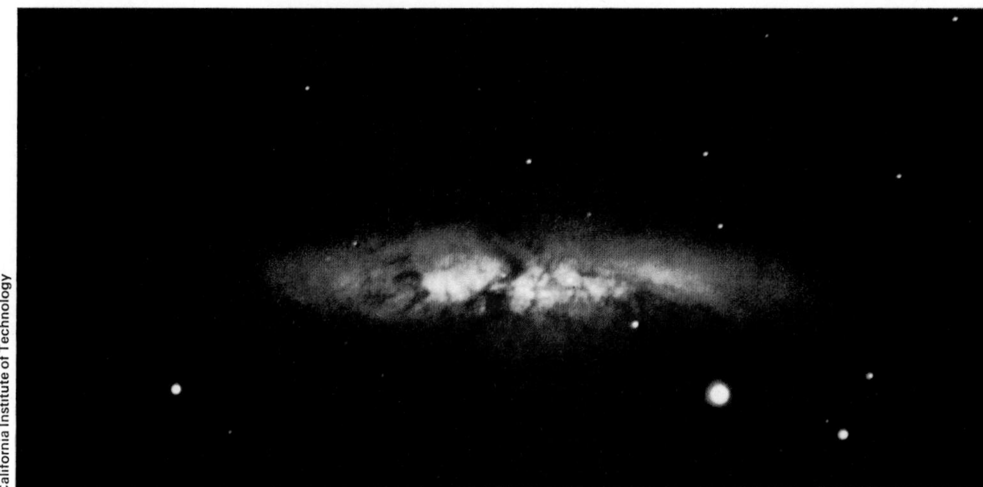

Above: The galaxy M82, in the constellation of Ursa Major. Signs of explosive events can be seen in the nucleus of the galaxy, and it appears reddish in the central region because the stars there are old. The blue colour of the outer regions is due to the stars there being newer ones.

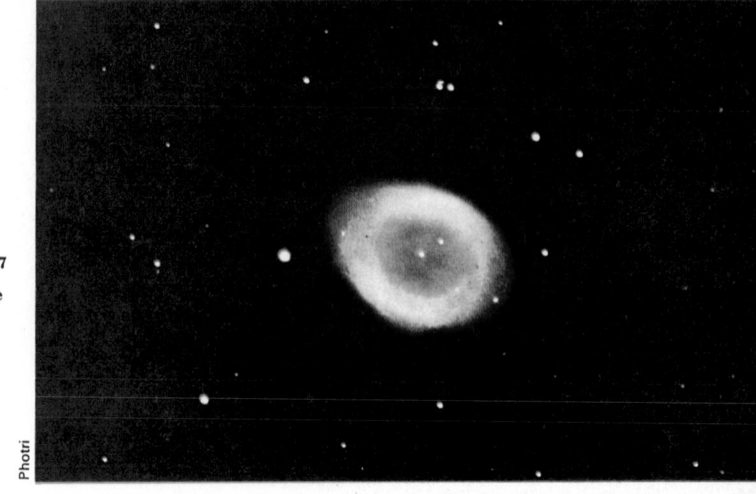

Right: A planetary or ring nebula within our own galaxy, number M57 in the constellation of Lyra. Planetary nebulae may be glowing shells of material thrown off by dying stars. In this picture, the material appears to be spreading outwards from the bright star at the centre of the ring. Alternatively, a dying star may flare up and become a nova.

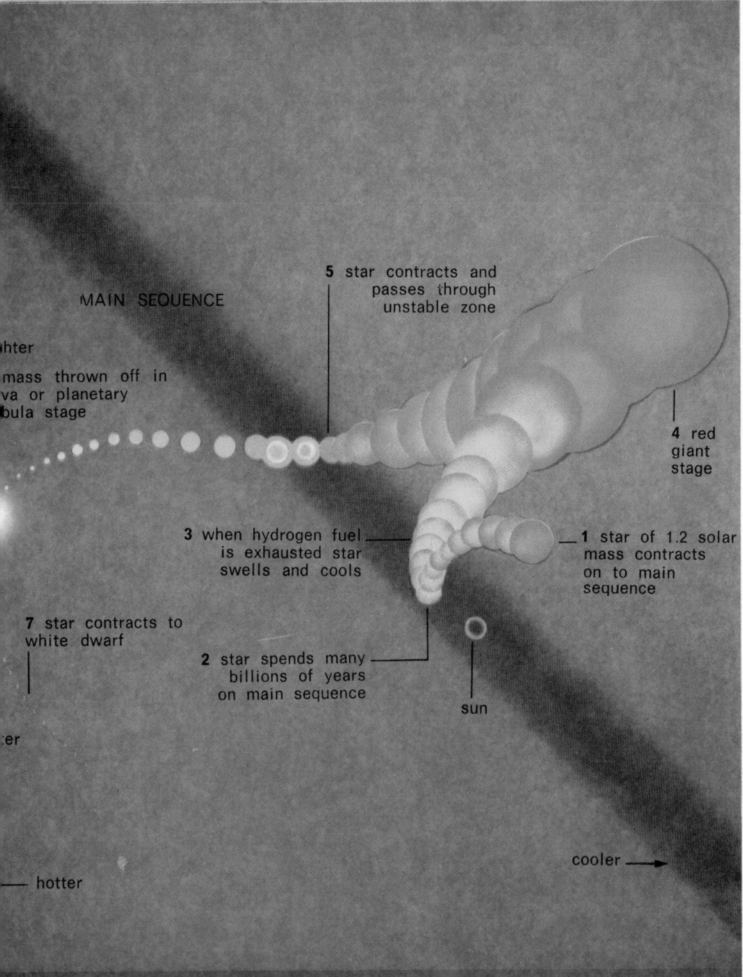

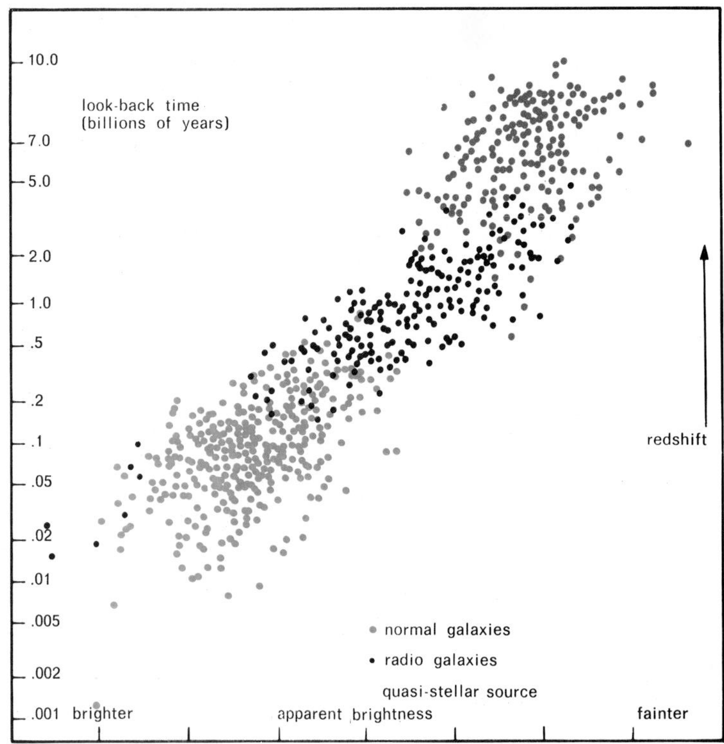

Left: The Hertzsprung-Russell diagram represents the relationship between the temperature and brightness of a star at different stages in its life cycle. Stars usually spend most of their lives at some point along the main sequence, which is where our own Sun is at present.

Above: The Hubble diagram is produced by plotting the red shifts of objects (vertical axis) against their apparent brightnesses (horizontal axis). The faintest objects have the greatest redshifts; they are also the oldest, the furthest away and the fastest-moving. The 'look-back time' scale represents how far back into the history of the universe we are looking when we observe an object, and the diagram suggests an evolutionary pattern of quasar into radio galaxy, and then radio galaxy into normal galaxy. Normal galaxies appear brighter in the sky than do quasars, but only because they are nearer.

Mount Wilson/Palomar Observatory/Alphabet & Image

Left: A nearby spiral galaxy, number NGC2841, in the constellation of Ursa Major. The round objects in the picture are stars in our own galaxy, which itself is similar in shape to this one although its spiral arms are not so tightly wound. This picture was taken with a 200 inch telescope.

Sky & Telescope

Above: The upper object is Comet West, which appeared in March 1976, and the lower is the track of a meteor—a tiny piece of rock which entered the Earth's atmosphere and burned up while the picture was being taken. Comets are members of the solar system, travelling in orbits around the Sun.

has now been seen. Efforts are being made to study more distant quasars, in the hope of proving that they, too, are really the very bright cores of galaxies.

Most galaxies occur in clusters, ranging in size from a couple of dozen to thousands of members. Our Milky Way is in a small cluster which contains about 24 members, called the Local Group. The largest galaxy in the Local Group is not our own but the Andromeda Galaxy, also called M31, which can be seen as a misty patch with the naked eye on a clear night. This is perhaps twice as large again as our own Galaxy, which ranks second. A galaxy called M33 is third, while fourth and fifth are the Magellanic Clouds, two fairly large misty patches visible from the Earth's southern hemisphere. These appear to be satellites of our own Galaxy.

Our own Galaxy is a fairly typical one. There is an important difference between the spiral arms or disc and the central hub, a difference found in other galaxies too. If you could take the disc away, the hub would look like a small elliptical galaxy—a flattened globe of stars, with almost no gas or dust mingled in. All the stars have the appearance of being old.

Around the outside of the hub, like moths round a street light, are a couple of hundred *globular clusters*. These too are globes of stars, but are much smaller than galaxies—each contains up to a million stars only. These globular clusters contain very old stars, distinguished by their red colour. Again, there is an almost complete absence of dust and gas.

The spiral arms, however, are quite different. They contain a large number of blue, white and yellow stars, as well as copious amounts of dust and gas. In the

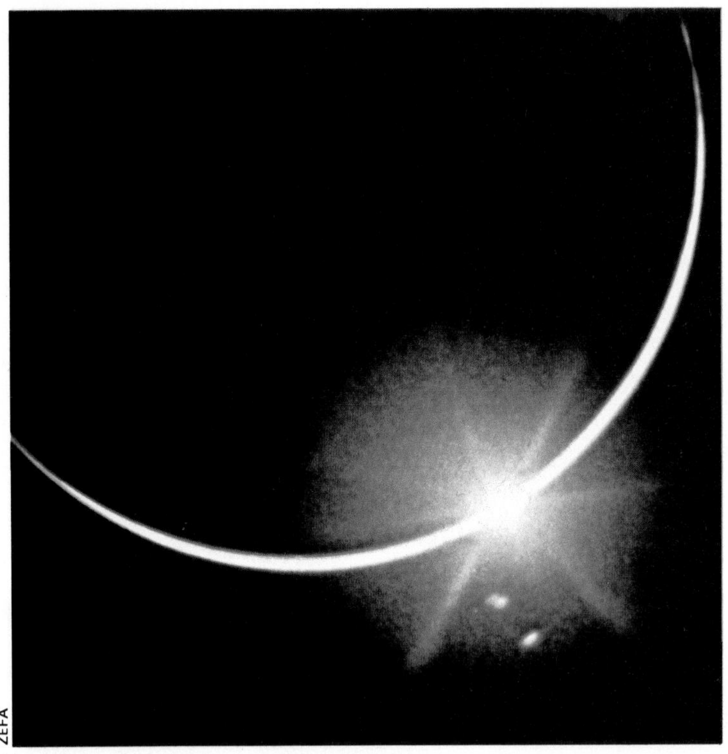

ZEFA

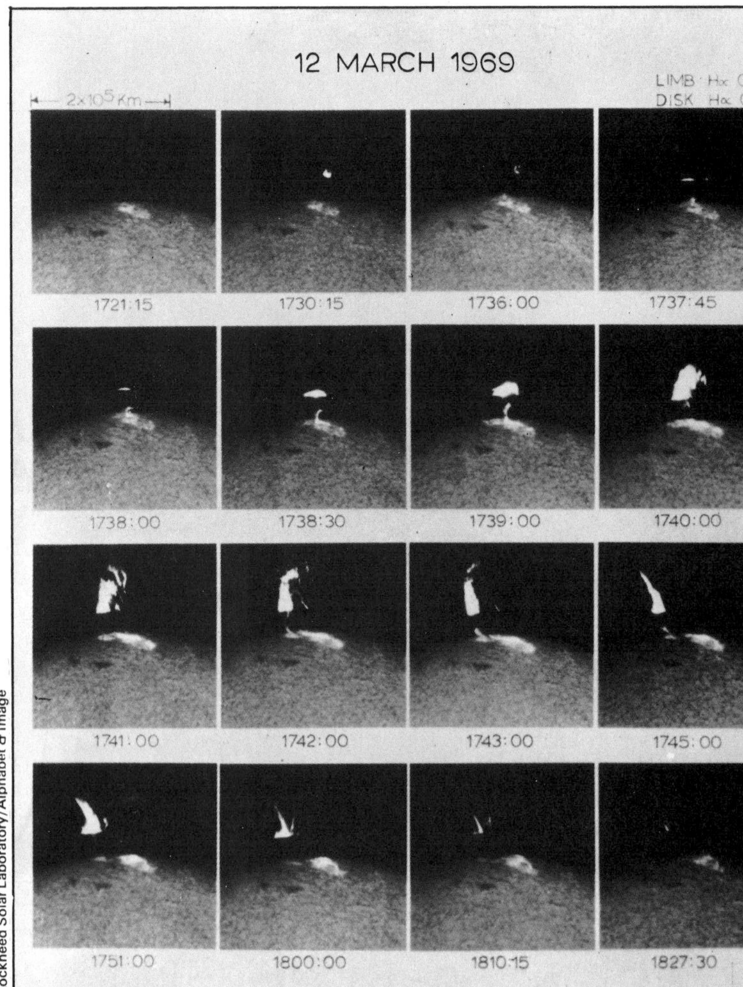

Lockheed Solar Laboratory/Alphabet & Image

Above: A solar eclipse occurs when the Moon moves directly between the Earth and the Sun, and briefly obscures the view of the Sun from the Earth. The bright flash is caused by more of the Sun being visible at that point because of a large lunar valley at the rim of the Moon's disc.

Below: A diagram, not to scale, of the principal members of our solar system. The asteroids are small lumps of rock which circle the Sun in a large range of orbits, but most of them are concentrated in a belt of orbits between Mars and Jupiter. The largest is Ceres, 955 km in diameter.

Right: A sequence of photographs showing the eruption of a flare of gas from the surface of the Sun. Particles and radiation thrown off by these solar flares interact with the charged layer in the Earth's atmosphere known as the *ionosphere*, and this can often be a source of radio interference.

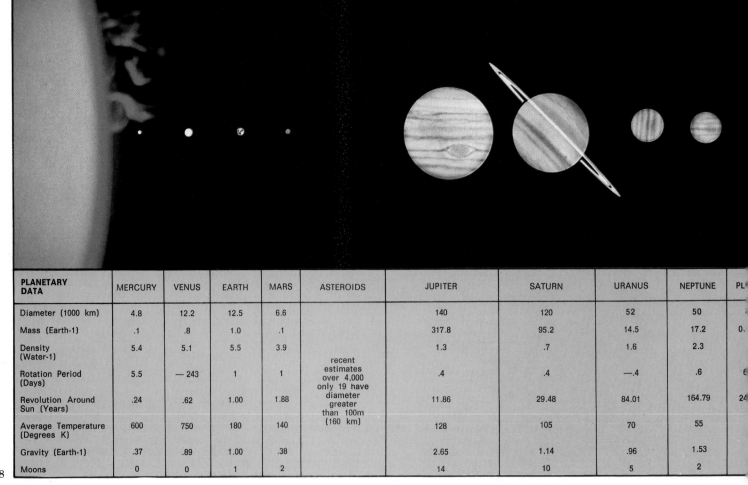

PLANETARY DATA	MERCURY	VENUS	EARTH	MARS	ASTEROIDS	JUPITER	SATURN	URANUS	NEPTUNE	PL
Diameter (1000 km)	4.8	12.2	12.5	6.6	recent estimates over 4,000 only 19 have diameter greater than 100m (160 km)	140	120	52	50	
Mass (Earth-1)	.1	.8	1.0	.1		317.8	95.2	14.5	17.2	0.
Density (Water-1)	5.4	5.1	5.5	3.9		1.3	.7	1.6	2.3	
Rotation Period (Days)	5.5	— 243	1	1		.4	.4	—.4	.6	6
Revolution Around Sun (Years)	.24	.62	1.00	1.88		11.86	29.48	84.01	164.79	24
Average Temperature (Degrees K)	600	750	180	140		128	105	70	55	
Gravity (Earth-1)	.37	.89	1.00	.38		2.65	1.14	.96	1.53	
Moons	0	0	1	2		14	10	5	2	

Bavaria

Left: A star track picture taken with a time exposure of about four hours. The tracks show the motion of the stars around the sky during the exposure period, and this kind of picture can be taken with almost any camera. The thick track near the centre of the tracks is that of the Pole Star.

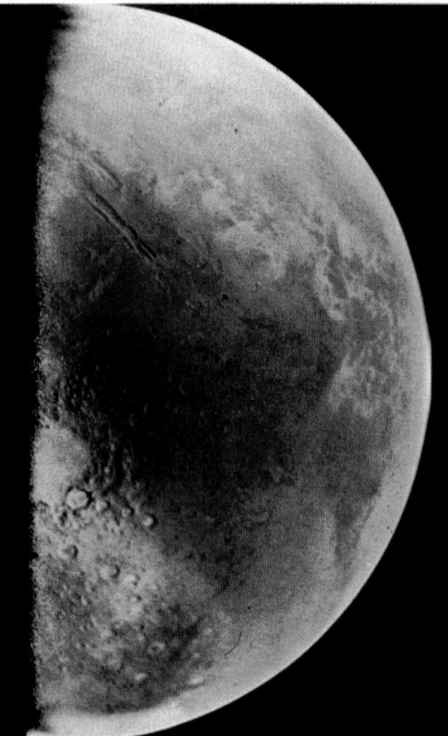

Space Frontiers

Above: A picture of Mars taken from the Viking I spacecraft. Just above the centre, at the top of the darker region, are the Valles Marineris—an enormous system of valleys and ravines that might have been caused by water flowing on the surface or by a fracturing of the surface.

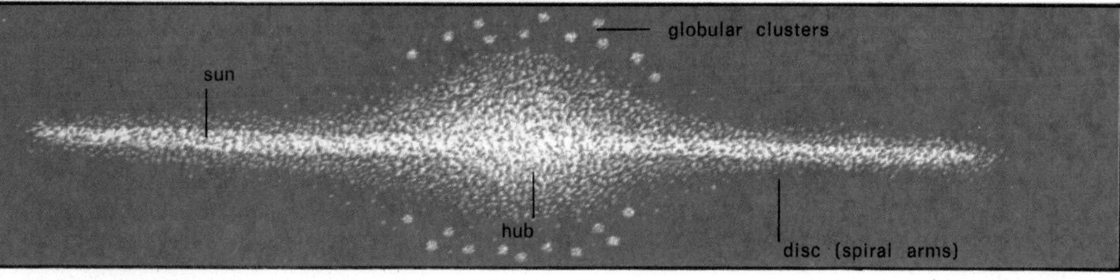

Above: This diagram represents an edge-on view of our own galaxy, which has a thick central hub and spiral arms. The Sun is situated about two thirds of the way out from the central hub. The total diameter of the galaxy is about 30,000 parsecs, which is about 100,000 light years.

Below: Saturn is unique in being circled by a series of rings consisting of billions of ice-covered rock particles. The rings are only a few kilometres thick, and the particles range in size from about 1 metre down to a few centimetres. Saturn also has 10 known satellites.

Lunar & Planetary Laboratory/University of Arizona

disc, stars seem to be forming and dying all the time. All around us we can see clouds of dust and gas, some of it obscuring the stars behind and producing dark lanes in the sky, where no stars appear. In other cases, the material is illuminated by nearby stars to produce glowing clouds in the sky, such as the Orion Nebula.

Stars

It is from such clouds that stars are born. Some of the material will begin to collapse on itself, just as on a larger scale the Galaxy itself once formed. As it does so, it attracts nearby material and after a while enough mass has formed to generate heat in the densest regions of this *protostar*, simply by virtue of the gravitational contraction. Eventually the central regions become sufficiently hot and dense for the atoms, already stripped of their electrons, to combine and release energy in a process which results in the formation of helium, and the star begins to shine.

If the original material has been rotating rapidly, it will probably form a disc around itself as it contracts. This disc in turn gathers into small bodies, which then accumulate to form the solid bodies called planets, all orbiting the star in the same plane and in the same direction.

A star which happens to be particularly massive—say 20 times the mass of the Sun—will become very hot in its interior, where the nuclear reactions go on, and will squander its hydrogen fuel at a great rate. Such stars shine brilliant blue-white, and can be many thousands of times as bright as the Sun. They go through their life cycle much more rapidly and within a few million years they have used up all their fuel. By contrast, yellow, orange and red stars are normally much less massive and longer lived.

In their later stages, massive stars use up first their hydrogen, then their helium, then progressively heavier elements, each one formed in turn by the previous nuclear reactions. Eventually, however, these stars are no longer able to support the pressure of the overlying material by the outward flow of energy produced. After undergoing further collapse, they may undergo a cataclysmic explosion, throwing off much of the material. This is the rare event known as a *supernova*—rare because only three have been observed in the Galaxy in the last thousand years.

The heavy elements produced in the star are now scattered throughout the surrounding regions of space, where they will become fixed with the interstellar gas and may eventually become part of new stars and planetary systems. All the elements on Earth, other than hydrogen and helium, are thought to have been formed long ago within massive stars.

The remains of the star itself are probably what radioastronomers observe as a *pulsar*—a pulsating radio source. These strange objects send out a stream of radio pulses, rather like the ticking of clocks, every second or so with great regularity. They are best explained as being rotating *neutron stars*—objects so dense that all the electrons and protons are forced together to form neutrons, all very densely packed.

The whole thing is so compact that material with the mass of the Sun may be squeezed into a globe no more than a few kilometres across. Such an object is able to rotate very rapidly, and as it does so it sends out the stream of pulses, rather like the flashes from a lighthouse as its machinery rotates.

Black holes

Some objects may be so massive that they form *black holes*. The existence of such objects has not been proven, but they seem theoretically quite likely and their existence was suggested as long ago as the eighteenth century by the French mathematician Pierre Laplace (1749-1827). What happens, astronomers ask, when an object has so great a mass that nothing, not even light, can escape from it? Since Einstein's theory of relativity states that nothing can exceed the velocity of light, once material enters a black hole it can never be accelerated fast enough to escape. There are a few candidates for black holes in the heavens—the signs are that in some systems there are objects of comparatively small size with considerable mass but which are quite invisible.

Most stars, however, are never likely to become black holes, and may end their lives by simply shedding mass, as *planetary nebulae*, *novae* or *white dwarfs*. White dwarfs are fairly numerous, and are about the same size as the Earth.

Paranormal Phenomena

Along with the recent upsurge of interest in the occult there has been a corresponding rise in scepticism about the validity of *paranormal* events, that is events that defy normal scientific explanation. Some of the scepticism is as irrational as is the level of belief on the other side of the fence. The belief in some paranormal phenomena does give cause for concern, however; cases have been reported where people have committed murder or suicide out of fear of spirits supposedly controlling them or communicating to them.

There is also the possibility of the abuse of psychic powers, if they exist, for military purposes. The US Department of Defense, for example, is believed to spend at least five-figure sums annually on research into various aspects of the paranormal, and Soviet interest appears to be at least as high. If psychic abilities are real then indeed they could be misused in both times of war and peace. Telepathy and clairvoyance could both be used for surveillance purposes as well as for long distance communications, such as communication with nuclear-armed submarines.

The basic question still at issue in the paranormal is the validity of the phenomena. This problem has to be investigated with great care to avoid bias on the part of subjects and observers involved leading to distorted reporting of cases. There is also the problem of fraud, conscious or unconscious, practised by the subject ('medium' or 'psychic') or even by the investigator. Cases of the exposure of conscious fraud abound in the history of the subject since its beginnings around the middle of the last century.

The ideal evidence for a psychic event would involve a phenomenon which could be made to occur again and again, and under a variety of conditions. This criterion of repeatability is a prerequisite of scientific respectability. Without it there would seem to be little hope of authenticating a phenomenon or, as importantly, of understanding it. The level of repeatability seems to have improved somewhat for psychic phenomena in the last few decades, but there is still a great deal to be desired. No truly repeatable psychic phenomenon is presently known.

Scientifically impossible phenomena

Into this category fall life after death, precognition and materialization. The first of these would require the persistence of a high level of information after the death of a highly organized brain. Such persistence would require energy, and therefore matter, and would be impossible to organize under earthly conditions without a structure like a brain. Precognition would contradict the notion of *causality*, that cause must come before effect. Materialization, along 'Star Trek' lines, would require millions of times more energy than is naturally available to the human body. And such a feat has never been demonstrated scientifically, even at the microscopic level involving atoms and molecules.

The evidence for life after death in-

Below: A sequence of photographs showing the supposed materialization of an Indian girl during a seance. Materialization was once a popular spiritualist trick, but is now so discredited that it is rarely performed today.

Below right: A pair of witches demonstrating some of their rituals. The circle laid out on the floor is to protect the witches from the demons that they claim they can summon by constant incantation of their names. There are a number of varieties of witchcraft practised today, and the main attraction of many of them is probably the sexual and sado-masochistic nature of their rituals.

TABLE OF PARANORMAL PHENOMENA

PHENOMENON	ENERGY REQUIRED	FEASIBILITY (from 1 = feasible to 4 = impossible
life after death	?	4
precognition	?	4
materialization	megajoules	3
spoon bending	joules	2
levitation	joules	2
poltergeists	joules	2
Bermuda Triangle	kilojoules	2
UFOs	kilojoules	2
ball lightning	megajoules	1
faith healing	millijoules	1
dowsing	millijoules	1
ghosts	millijoules	1
astrology	millijoules	1
ley lines	millijoules	1
meditation	millijoules	1

Left: A table showing the energy levels that would be required to activate some well-known paranormal phenomena, and their scientific feasibility. The feasibility of each phenomenon is determined by the amount of energy that it would require; the classification of a phenomenon as 'feasible' does not imply that the phenomenon actually exists, only that its existence would not be beyond the limits of the laws of nature as we know them. It has been suggested that the increasing interest in the paranormal is symptomatic of a psychological need formerly catered for by traditional religions, now in decline.

Syndication International

Psychic News

Below: One dowsing method involves the use of a forked rod, which supposedly twists downwards when the dowser walks over an underground water source.

Right: In the 1920s Alfred Watkins suggested that ancient sites such as prehistoric earthworks, stone circles, and early churches, were sited so as to form a network of straight lines, which he called *ley lines*, that possibly marked out travel routes. Since then some people have claimed that ley lines possess some mysterious psychic energy detectable by sensitive individuals such as dowsers.

John Goldblatt

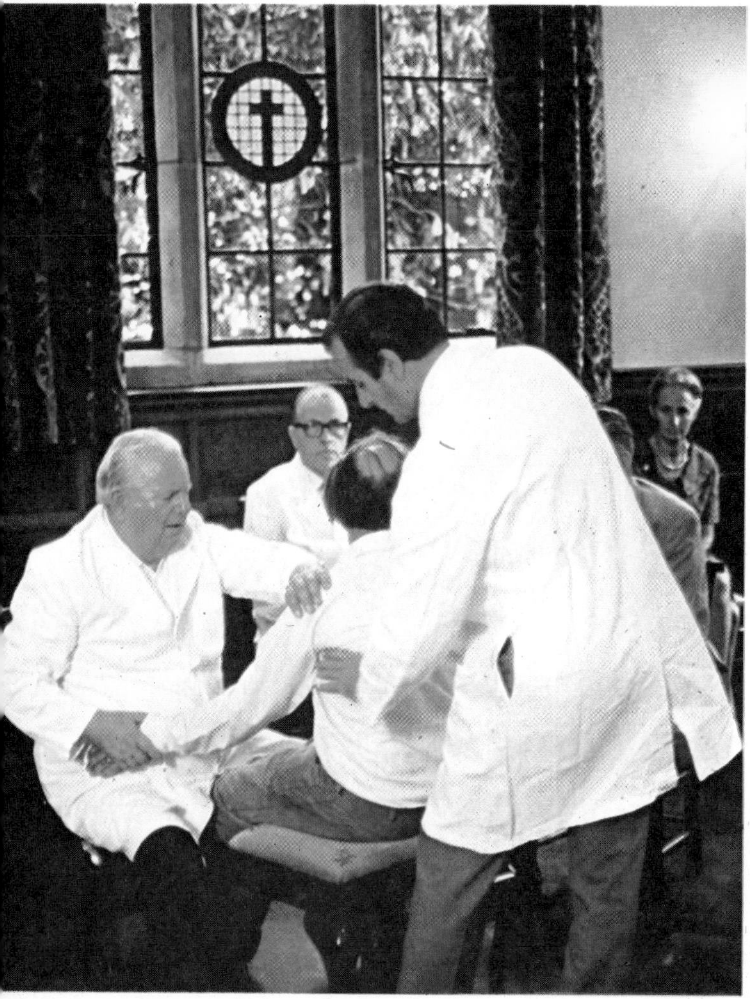

Daily Telegraph Colour Library

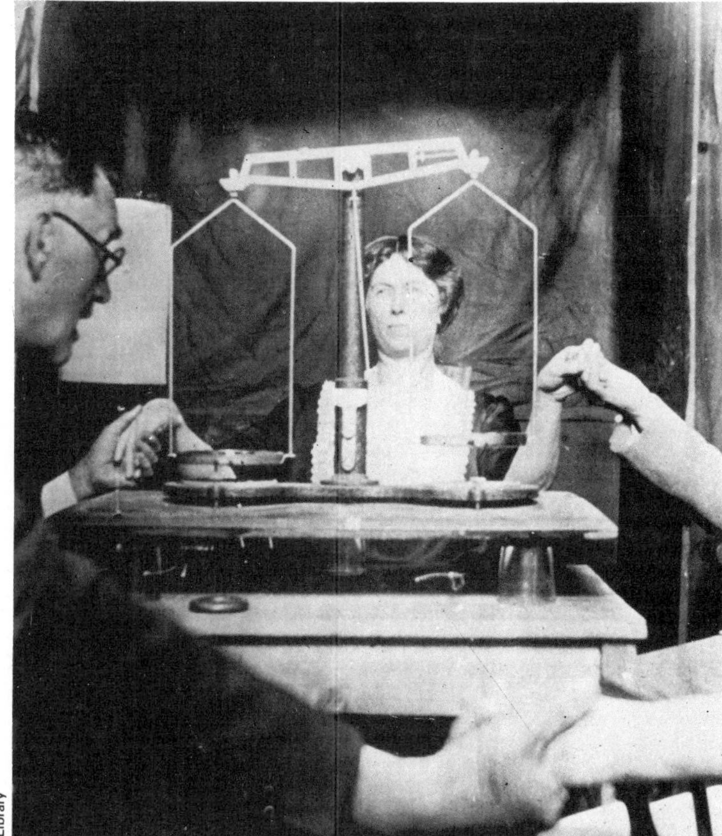

Harry Price Library/University of London

Left: Faith healer Harry Edwards, right, treating a patient at a healing session. Faith healing undoubtedly works for many patients if they have absolute faith in the healer; the healing process may be initiated by the mind of the patient, just as psychosomatic illnesses are caused by emotional disturbances.

Above: A medium apparently tilting a balance by means of psychokinesis; this may be possible, but it is not necessarily a psychic effect.

THAMES ESTUARY
Isle of Grain
Medway
Leysdown-on-Sea
Isle of Sheppey
bridge
The Swale
crossing
points
Sittingbourne
Faversham
church
Doddington church
KENT
Lenham church
railway

cludes messages from the dead or claims of the knowledge of earlier lives by those presently living. The information coming from the dead is mainly very naive, though there are a few items told which appear unlikely to have been learnt by normal means by the medium who is transmitting the message. Information on earlier lives is quite extensive in certain cases, but very few of these bear up under more careful examination. Thus a man who claimed to have lived an earlier life, being killed at the Battle of Sedgemoor in 1685, gave a great deal of seemingly authentic historical data relating to that period, but it was subsequently found that the eight dates of births, marriages and deaths associated with his supposed former family were not recorded in the local parish church register.

Materialization, involving either the appearance of solid objects inside boxes or completely closed rooms, or its converse of dematerialization, has been reported as an adjunct to poltergeist ('noisy ghost') phenomena. It was also very popular at seances in the last century, though is not currently demonstrated. The complete appearance or disappearance trick involves so much energy as to be physically impossible, as was noted earlier, but a more tenuous form is feasible. This might even be explained in terms of the well-documented but poorly understood natural electrical phenomenon of ball lightning. However, very strong electric fields would be required to produce such an effect in psychic events, and since they have not been noted in materialization seances of the past such a possibility is not likely to be correct.

Faintly possible events

This category includes spoon bending, poltergeists, levitation and more general *psychokinesis* (the willed moving of objects). All of these involve energies which are naturally available to the human body. There are many people who claim to be able to cause various items of cutlery to bend or break by gently stroking them, and some have claimed the ability to cause such items to bend without actually touching them.

The validation of spoon bending by direct contact has proved very difficult. Many anecdotal reports support the authenticity of the phenomenon, but no subject able to perform the feat repeatably and under perfect conditions has come forward. The criteria for scientific validation require at least that the mechanical pressure being used by the subject be monitored all the time the test occurs, and that videotape records be taken simultaneously to ensure that fraud be demonstrably absent. No evidence has been produced at this level. Validation of indirect bending has been attempted by setting 'impossible' tasks, such as the distortion of pieces of metal in sealed glass tubes or globes. Some progress has been made in this, but again without the desired level of validation.

Poltergeist cases are, by their nature, far less repeatable than other psychic events, and also less accessible to scientific investigation. Many cases have been reported, some of which appear to have been carefully witnessed by respectable members of the community, although they are not completely fraud-proof.

Levitation has been witnessed numerous times in the past, the most famous medium to demonstrate it being D. D. Home, who supposedly floated out of a second floor window to return through another one. There have not been any detailed tests of such an ability, and the evidence is too imprecise to support the authenticity of the phenomenon at any real level. It is just feasible on scientific grounds, the most reasonable suggestion being that it is achieved by means of some electric field effect. If the medium had electrically charged himself then he might be repelled upwards by the electric field near the Earth's surface. However, there should be various clues that such electricity was involved, such as the medium's hair standing on end; photographs of levitators never show this.

The willed movement of objects has been performed by many subjects, notably two Russian women, Kulagina and Vinogradova. Some of these have used trickery such as 'invisible' threads, though others, very likely including the Russians, are clearly authentic. Indeed, there are various cases of intensive investigation of willed object movement where fraud can be completely ruled out. Thus various cases are known of subjects moving a small item, such as a needle, hung by a thread inside a plastic or glass container, or rotating straws on a disc floating on water in a beaker inside a glass jar. Yet all these instances can be explained either in the known terms of electrostatics or heating effects; none of them can be regarded as paranormal, though at first sight they look as if they are so. Such explanations may also be relevant to the powers of the two Russian women mentioned earlier.

Just possible events

Such phenomena as faith healing, dowsing, telepathy, clairvoyance, ghosts, astrology, plant intelligence and UFOs (unidentified flying objects) are classified under this heading. If they occur at all they would be expected to be activated either by energies naturally accessible to the human body (for the first seven phenomena in the above list) or, in the case of UFOs, by natural phenomena. Ghosts and hauntings have only anecdotal evidence to support them, and so will not be considered further here.

Faith healing has a venerable tradition; for example, it was mentioned in the Bible as one of the powers of Jesus Christ. Many cases of miraculous cures of diseases, from arthritis to cancer, have been reported, some of them extremely well documented. Fraud may well be practised in 'psychic surgery', where the healer's hands are supposed to enter the patient's body and remove diseased tissue without the use of any surgical instruments, the hole in the patient's body closing up without a scar immediately the healer's hands are removed. But the cases remarked on above, and associated with the 'laying-on of hands' are undoubtedly authentic. Yet there are hundreds of cases of spontaneous regression of cancer, so that it is difficult to disentangle the psychological effect the healer has on the patient from anything deeper.

Dowsing has also been practised for a long time, a forked twig or a pendulum being the usual tool used to detect water or buried objects. In spite of many anecdotes of successful dowsing, careful tests have not uncovered any ability to

Syndication International

Above: An example of the early 1970s spoon bending craze. In November 1973 the Israeli entertainer Uri Geller, during a British radio broadcast, invited listeners to concentrate on metal objects such as keys or spoons to see if they could bend them. This lady, Dora Portman of Harrow, near London, reported the bending of a ladle that she was using at the time, and many other listeners phoned in to report the bending of cutlery, keys, nails and jewellery, and the stopping or starting of watches and clocks. No cases of metal bending have yet been scientifically verified.

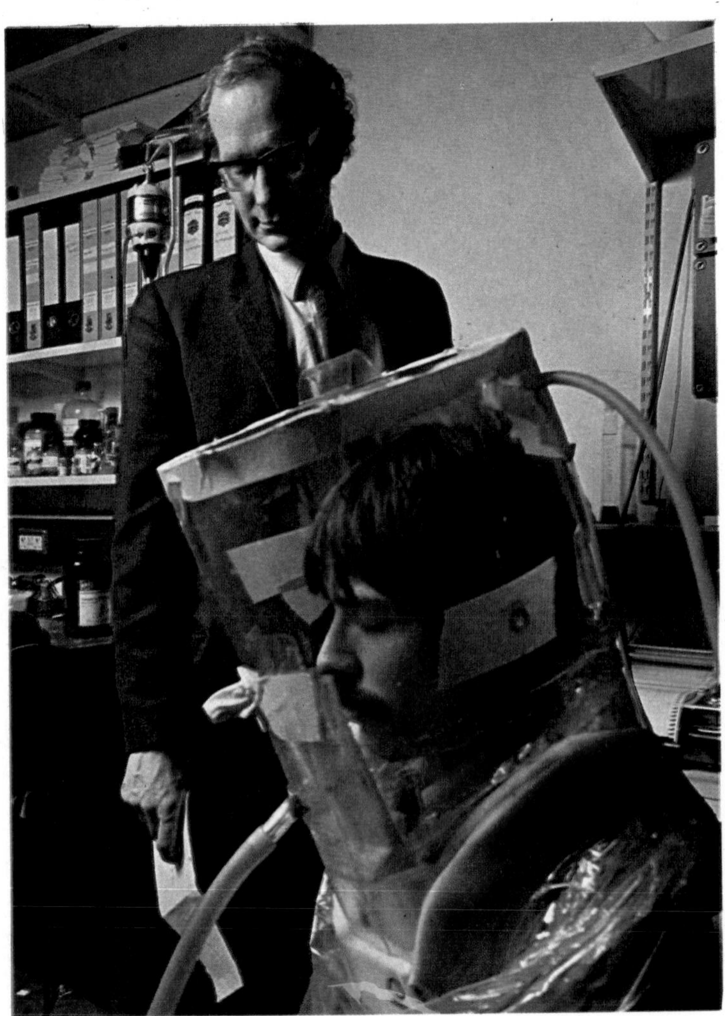

Left: The study of the brain and body functions of people in altered states of consciousness, for example during meditation, may prove of great value to the study of many psychic phenomena such as faith healing and telepathy.

Above and right: A Soviet *Vostok* rocket, and (right) a picture of a cylindrical object bearing the name 'Vostok'. The picture on the right is one of many claimed to have been produced by the American Ted Serios, who can apparently project images psychically on to photographic film. Most of Serios's pictures have been produced on Polaroid film in a Model 95 camera.

Psychic News

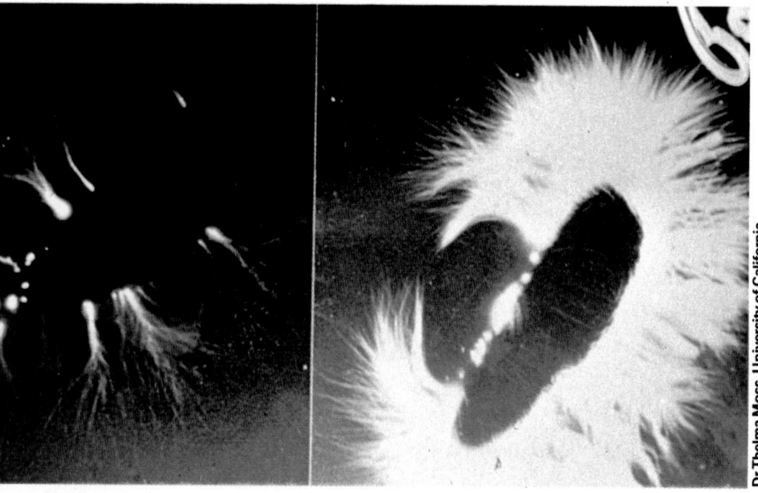

Left: Kirlian photographs of the 'aura' around the fingertip of a patient before (left) and after treatment by a faith healer. Kirlian photography, which involves the use of a high voltage, high frequency electric field, is claimed to show the supposed aura of the subject. The size and shape of the aura is said to be indicative of the health of the subject, but variations in the aura (probably just the electrical phenomenon known as a *corona discharge*) are due to variations in the moistness of the finger and other unmysterious factors.

Dr Thelma Moss, University of California

Below: The principles of Kirlian apparatus.

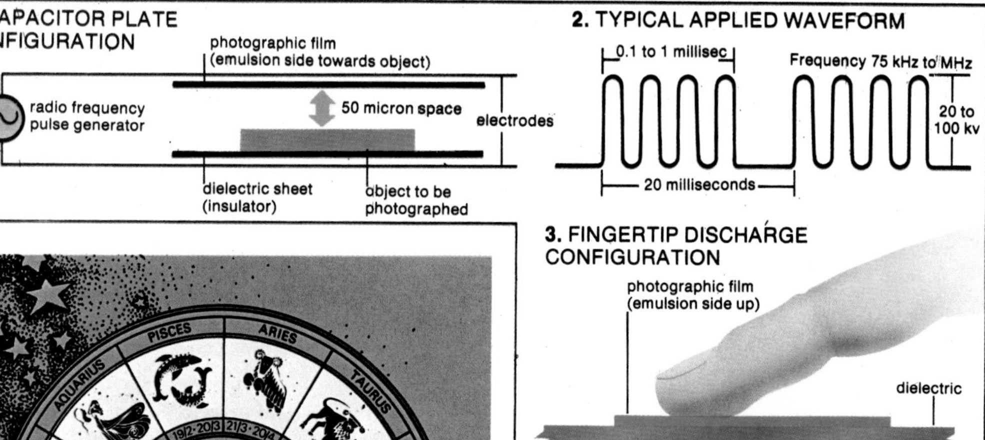

detect hidden objects, and many of the successes are now ascribed to the fact that a dowser gives the confidence to go ahead and dig in otherwise unpromising locations.

Telepathy also has its stores of anecdotal cases supporting its authenticity, and also has a considerable wealth of more carefully controlled tests. Most of these have involved various types of card guessing in which a long series of cards would be transmitted from a 'sender' to a 'receiver'. The test is successful if the receiver guesses the cards significantly more than would be expected on pure chance alone. Some tests of this type have been remarkably good, such as that of Dr. B. F. Riess and a young woman with a distance of a quarter of a mile between them.

Of the 1,850 guesses 73 per cent were successful, whereas the chance level of success should have been 20 per cent; the odds against this being pure chance are astronomical. However, this and other similar tests have been strongly criticized, and have not been accepted by many. There have also been attempts to see if telepathy is greater in young children than adults, or enhanced during dreaming or in altered states of consciousness. There have been encouraging results on these problems, but telepathy has still failed to prove as repeatable as hoped.

Clairvoyance testing has had a similar history, with some remarkable successes obtained by Dr J. B. Rhine and his colleagues during the 1930s and 1940s. These have all been strongly criticized by certain sceptics, as have the apparently highly successful tests at the Stanford

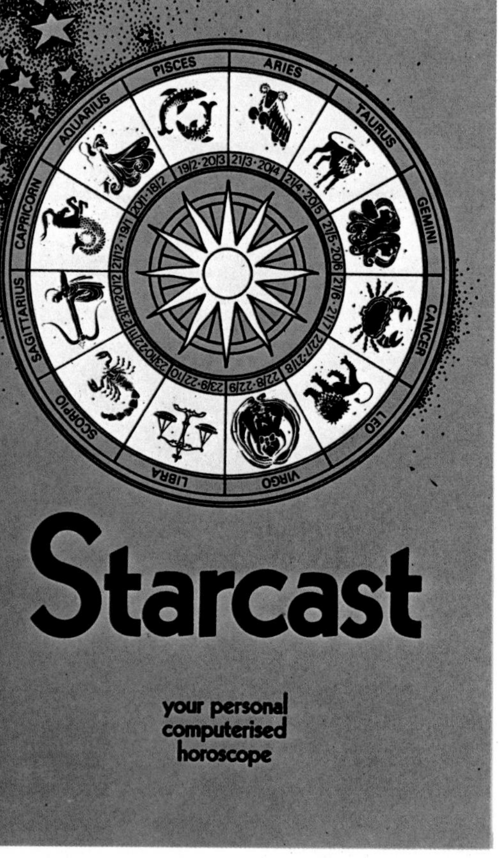

Above: Astrology has become one of the most popular aspects of the paranormal, but studies claiming to have verified its effectiveness by statistical means have been disputed by other researchers. Many serious astrologers feel that the subject has been trivialized by the generalized horoscopes published in the popular press, which make vague predictions about the whole population of the world; horoscopes, they claim, can only work on an individual basis.

Right: The unidentified flying object (UFO) controversy began in June 1947, when Kenneth Arnold, piloting a private plane from Chehalis to Yakima in Washington, US, saw nine saucer-shaped objects flying in formation near Mount Rainier. Since then there have been thousands of reports of UFO sightings and hundreds of photographs of them. Many of the photos are fakes; this one is of a model, made of a pair of car hubcaps, thrown into the air.

John Cutten

Photri

Below: The so called 'Bermuda Triangle', an area in the western Atlantic in which it has been claimed an alarming number of ships and planes have disappeared in mysterious and terrible circumstances. The books and articles which have been written by advocates of the phenomenon consist of ludicrous but very entertaining (and lucrative) combinations of fiction, supposition and distortions of known facts. For example, their accounts of the disappearance in 1945 of a flight of Avenger aircraft, plus a Mariner aircraft sent to look for them are completely at odds with the known facts.

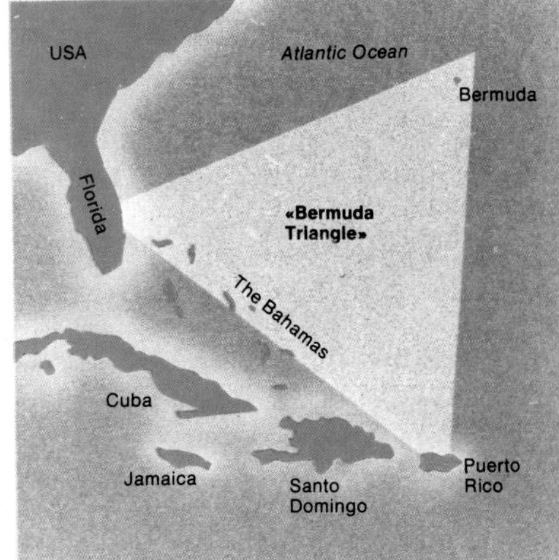

Research Institute by Drs Puthoff and Targ with several subjects. These results have been published in the British journal *Nature*, though with an accompanying editorial strongly criticizing the experimental procedure.

A certain amount of statistical investigation has been carried out to test the validity of astrology. Recent work by two French psychologists has claimed to show a relationship between the date and time of birth of a person and their later career, though since there are apparently more births in late summer such analysis has to be done with great care.

Many UFO cases have been reported, but since there is no unequivocal evidence such as a piece of an alien spacecraft or being, the 'alien' interpretation of such events is less likely than one of the many normal ones, such as planets, noctilucent (luminous) clouds, or ball lightning. Plant intelligence is unlikely, but response of plants to external human body fields is possible. There is not yet enough evidence to show whether this occurs or not.

Finally, it must be pointed out that the only *scientific* explanation of paranormal events can be in terms of electromagnetism, since the other three forces of nature (nuclear, radioactive, gravitational) can be excluded as being impossible for humans to activate at the required levels. A radiowave hypothesis had been proposed for telepathy in the 1920s by the Italian Cazzamali, but doubt was cast on it by experiments with subjects in shielded rooms.

More recently, a series of tests performed by Professor J. G. Taylor and E. Balanowski failed to discover *any* radiowave emission associated with psychic phenomena over the whole range of possible wavelengths, other than that naturally emitted by humans. Since at least a millionfold higher level of such waves would have been needed to achieve the various phenomena it is very doubtful that electromagnetism can explain the paranormal (excluding ball lightning and perhaps UFOs).

Top: The summer of 1952 was a peak period for UFO sightings in the United States and elsewhere. This picture was taken at a coastguard station at Salem, US, on 16 July 1952, and shows what seems to be four objects flying in formation. Visual sightings by military personnel are often reported, and there are many instances of strange objects being detected by radar. The great majority of UFO sightings have been explainable in terms of known natural phenomena such as optical illusions created by temperature inversions, or as mistaken identification of objects such as aircraft, meteors and weather balloons. Some sightings remain inexplicable, however, but there is no evidence at all that UFOs are alien spacecraft. The ideal evidence for this would be a well-observed landing of such a craft and contact with its occupants. Contacts have been claimed, but never proven.

Above: Some of the main areas of UFO sightings in England and Wales. One of the most intriguing periods of UFO activity in England was in the mid-1960s, around the town of Warminster. Phenomena reported included UFOs, strange noises and vibrations, and birds falling dead from the sky.

Part II

Technology Today

John Moss/Colorific

Chapter 1
Materials

Warp knitting machines. Using interlocking loops, each machine may have as many as 2,500 needles and form over 1,200 rows of stitches – a total of over 3 million loops per minute.

Leather

Leather has many uses and has been employed by man for many thousands of years. Prehistoric man took skins (pelts) from the animals he hunted for food and used these as rough clothing wrapped around the body and feet. Skins were sometimes worn to denote rank and were also used as bedding and building materials in the construction of huts and shelters.

Early man must also have learned fairly quickly that unless the skins were treated or cured, their useful life would be limited once putrefaction or rotting began. The earliest methods used to *tan* or preserve skins as leather were probably smoking, dry salting and vegetable tanning in bark extracts.

Curing

The hide from the slaughtered animal is rarely processed directly into leather, but usually held in a state of preservation until tanning can be carried out. The three main methods used to preserve hides prior to tanning are *air drying, wet salting* and *dry salting*.

Most reptile, goat and fur skins are dried, care being taken to dry them slowly so that the centre of the skin is preserved. Most of the skins from the tropics of Asia, Central and South America and Africa are air dried before shipment to the tannery. Wet salted hides are preserved by soaking in brine after being refrigerated or chilled, cleaned and trimmed. Dry salted hides are taken straight from the animal and covered with salt before being placed in large piles.

Bovine leather is normally sold as *hides* (whole skins); *sides*, which are skins cut down the backbone; or *bellies*, which are hides cut into two parts—the *shoulder* (front) and *butt* (rear). The butt contains the best quality leather.

Leather processing

Before tanning, the *epidermis* (a thin outer layer of tissue) and any unwanted hair must be removed. After dehairing the skins are washed and treated with dilute acid. Normally *bating* follows, the hides being treated with enzymes which remove or modify some of the fibre bundles (*collagen*) which make up the skin, giving softer leathers. Firm leathers, such as shoe sole leathers, are rarely bated. Following bating the hide may be pickled in salt (sodium chloride) or dilute sulphuric acid.

There are two main methods of tanning, namely *vegetable tanning* and *mineral tanning*. Several other less widely used processes include *oil tanning*, *aldehyde tanning*, *syntanning*, and *retan* or *combined tanning*.

Vegetable tanning was the main method used until about 1850, when *chrome tanning* (mineral) was developed. Vegetable tanning can take up to six weeks, with the skins being soaked in progressively stronger solutions of tanning liquor, although light tannage can take as little as 12 to 18 hours. The liquors are made from vegetable extracts derived from various trees and shrubs, the most common being quebracho wood and mimosa bark.

Others used are made from the wood of

Spectrum

Above: Leather dyeing pits at Fez, Morocco, where vegetable-tanned goatskins are dyed with a crimson dye obtained from locally-grown berries to make Morocco leather.

U.N.F.A.O.

Right: The traditional method of curing and tanning in the Yemen is to sew up the hides, stuff them with pomegranate and acacia bark chips, and hang them to cure and dry in the sun.

Below: The main sources and uses of leather. East India (EI) tannage is a traditional vegetable tanning process used in India and Pakistan for sheep, goat and kip (immature cattle) leather. The tanning liquor is based on avaram bark.

	CATTLE HIDES		CALF, VEALS, KIPS AND SMALLER HIDES			SHEEP			GOAT		
						WOOLLED TYPES	HAIR TYPES				
SOURCES	Europe, N. and S. America, Austra-lasia	S. America, Central America, India, Africa Asia	Europe America Austra-lasia	India Asia	Africa	Europe, America, New Zealand	Cape, Ethiopia, N. Africa	India Nigeria	India, Middle East, Brazil, Nigeria	India Nigeria	E
USUAL TYPE OF PRESERVA-TION	Wet-salted, brined	Sun-dried dry-salted	Wet-salted brined	Dry-dry-salted, rough-tanned	Dry and dry-salted	Usually pickled	Dry-salted or pickled	Rough-tanned	Dry and dry-salted	Rough-tanned	W sa
PRINCIPAL USES	*Veg. Tan:* Sole leathers; saddlery, upholstery, strap, bag and case leathers; mechanical leathers *Chrome Tan:* Water-proof chrome sole leathers; mechanical leathers *If Split:* Grain or suede shoe upper leathers; upholstery		*Veg. Tan:* Shoe linings, bag leathers, book-binding *Chrome Tan:* Shoe upper leathers, grain or suede *Semi-chrome:* Shoe upper leathers			*Veg. Tan:* shoe linings, bag linings, fancy goods, roller leathers *Chrome* or *Semi-chrome:* Gloving, clothing	*Chrome Tan:* Gloving, clothing	*Veg. Tan:* Shoe linings *Semi-chrome:* Gas meter diaphragms, gloving, clothing, as suede or Nappa	*Chrome Tan:* Glacé kid and suede for shoes	*Veg. Tan:* shoe linings, Morocco and fancy leathers, book-binding *Semi-chrome:* Gloving, clothing	S s' g a c le

Hides drying in Alaska. Air drying preserves the hide, before it goes on to the processes of tanning, splitting and stretching, which loosen up the leather fibres.

Above: In a modern tannery the main processes, such as washing, hair removal, degreasing and chrome tanning, are carried out in large drums which revolve to ensure that the processing chemicals are distributed thoroughly throughout the hides. After tanning the hides are usually split.

Below: Split hides are shaved to produce an even thickness, dyed, and then dried. This picture shows a vacuum dryer; the hide is spread on a heated plate, a perforated metal plate is lowered on to it, and a vacuum is applied to draw excess moisture from it, leaving it ready for *staking*.

chestnut and oak trees, the fruit from myrobalans (nuts) and valonia (acorn cups), and also the shrubs sumac and gambier. These liquors all contain tannic acid and are sometimes supplemented with animal (for example sheep) dung.

Chrome tanning is the major method of mineral tanning, being much quicker than vegetable tanning. The discovery of chrome tanning is usually attributed to Knapp in about 1858. The process gives a more durable, perspiration-resistant leather, although it tends to be stiff and harsh. Chrome tanned leathers are normally characterized by their blue or blue-green colour before dyeing.

The process of chrome tanning can be carried out in either a two-bath or, more commonly, a single bath process, using an acid solution of sodium dichromate into which an agent such as sugar is added to reduce the dichromate prior to introduction of the hides.

Once tanned, the hides or skins are often split to provide two or sometimes three layers (*splits*). Following splitting the leathers are drum-dyed. The percentage of dye used varies, being as much as 15 per cent for some suedes and as low as 1 per cent for side leathers intended for shoes. During dyeing the leather may be *fat-liquored* or, alternatively, fat-liquoring is carried out separately, This step is essential to replace the natural oils which have been removed during the processing, otherwise the leather would dry to a hard inflexible mass.

Fatty esters, mineral oils and triglycerides are the three types of fat liquors used. These can be introduced into the leather from solvent solution (*solvent fat-liquoring*), by putting them into a drum with molten oils (*stuffing*), or more commonly by drum treatment with oil emulsions. Heavy, water resistant leathers are often produced by stuffing.

Once dyed and fat-liquored the leather must be dried. Tanning is not complete until drying has been finished. Drying is done carefully to avoid 'baking' the outer surfaces. The easiest method is to air-dry by hanging the leather on hooks or horizontal racks, often using fans to circulate the air. Other systems of drying include vacuum drying, and *toggling* in which the leather is stretched over a screen before being placed in a drying tunnel.

Quite often leathers are *staked* (stretched) after drying to further loosen up the fibres. Finally the leather is ready for finishing, usually on the grain surface. The leather is given a light buff before the finishing solution is either sprayed or mopped and padded into the leather. The most common finish used is acrylic resin, often with a final very thin nitrocellulose top film for the desired surface shine or gloss. Other finishes include anilines, patents and 'wet looks' (which are predominantly polyurethanes) and for fine leathers casein glazes.

The grain can also be embossed, using heat and pressure to reproduce reptile prints or the hair follicle pattern of, say, calf on cheaper bovine splits. Suede effects are produced by buffing on an abrasive wheel to bring up a nap. The finished leather has many uses, such as footwear, clothing, baggage and upholstery.

Below left: A staking machine, which works the leather to loosen the fibre structure and spread the natural lubricants in it throughout its thickness to make it supple. The staking machine achieves this by beating the leather with blunt knives which are driven by a reciprocating arm.

Below: Leather is sold by area, and because the skins have variable and irregular outlines complex machines are necessary to enable the surface area of a skin to be measured accurately. This automatic machine uses a system of lights and photoelectric cells to measure the areas of the skins to within 230 cm² (0.25 ft²).

Synthetic leather

The supply of natural leather is largely governed by the world demand for beef (and other meats), and by economic and political factors. Irrespective of the world distribution of leather, the consumer demand for leather has outweighed supply for many years and so synthetic materials have been developed to fill the gap.

In the early 1940s pvc (polyvinyl chloride) was first used to coat plain woven cotton fabrics, producing materials which were certainly a big improvement on the earlier oilcloths in their resemblance to leather. However, these early vinyl fabrics were impermeable to water vapour and also tended to become stiff and crack when cold. They were almost always made up of a solid layer of pvc laminated to the base fabric, which meant that they lacked the soft, supple handle and feel associated with natural leather.

Following the remarkable post-war advances made with pu (polyurethane)

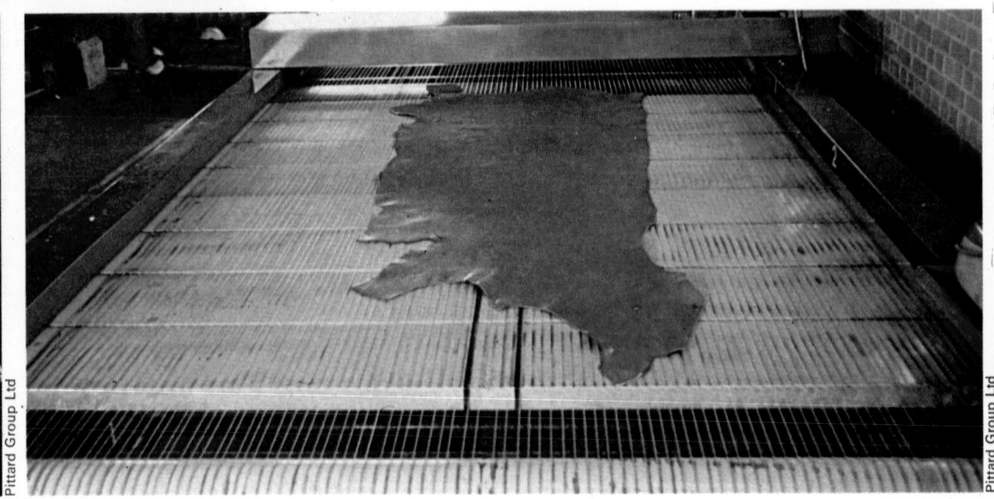

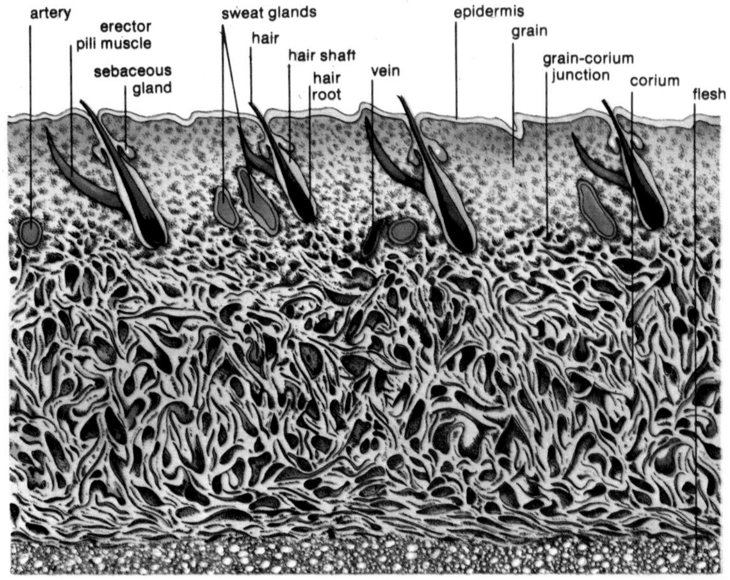

British Leather Manufacturers Research Association

Left: The cross-section of a typical animal skin. The *epidermis* is an outer layer of tough keratinous cells which is removed before tanning. The *sweat glands* discharge sweat through pores in the grain, and the *sebaceous glands* produce protective oils for the hairs. The sebaceous glands are controlled by the *erector pili* muscles, which also make the hair stand upright. The main section of the skin is the *corium*, which consists of tightly entangled *collagen* fibres.

Right: A magnified view of a section of cattle hide sole leather.

Below: The porous structure of Porvair, a poromeric consisting of a microporous polyurethane foam with a thin top skin of much finer pore structure. Porvair does not have a felt or fabric base.

polymers these materials have been increasingly used to produce synthetic leathers. Today more pu than pvc is used in synthetic leather production, and in terms of the coating or main layer these two polymers dominate.

Current synthetic leathers can be classified either as *poromerics* (in which properties such as permeability or breathability and a leather-like feel are built into the material) or as polymer-coated fabrics.

Poromerics

The major outlet for poromerics is in footwear, where permeability to moisture is most important to ensure foot comfort and hygiene. Other uses include belts, baggage, footballs, fancy goods and a small amount of upholstery.

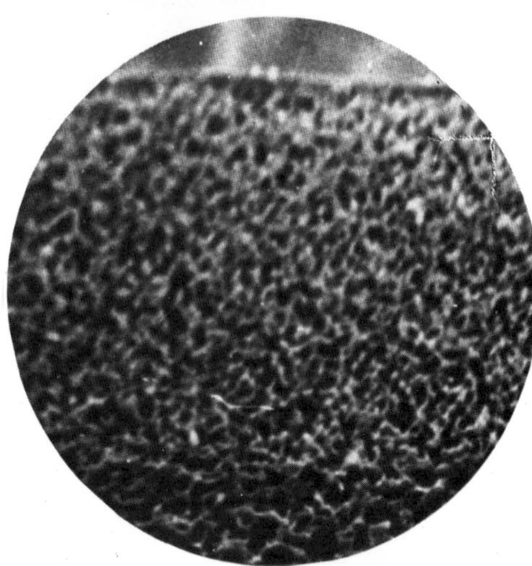
Porvair Ltd

The first poromeric to be introduced commercially was *Corfam*, produced by the Du Pont Corporation in the USA in about 1962. The original material, although having excellent qualities, did not prove viable due to the high initial development costs. However, production of Corfam has recommenced in Poland under a Du Pont licence.

Corfam has a complex structure designed to resemble leather. The outer surface is microporous polyurethane with a top skin on to which the finish is applied. This pu layer allows the passage of water vapour through the porous cell structure, but is sufficiently water resistant to prevent excess water entering shoes in wet weather. Beneath the pu layer is a woven fabric (nylon in the original American Corfam) to prevent excessive stretch of the poromeric, and laminated to the woven cloth is a non-woven felt.

Clarino and *Cordley* (both of Japanese origin) resemble Corfam in construction except they do not have a woven interlayer. *Porvair*, the only British-produced poromeric, has no fabric or felt base, but is comprised of a microporous homogeneous pu foam with a thin top skin. The density of the foam varies, the outer surface having much finer pores to give a pleasing surface or 'grain' after finishing.

The interconnecting pores in Porvair are produced by mixing salt (sodium chloride) with the isocyanate and polyol used to produce the polyurethane. The whole mix, which is held in a solvent such as dmf (dimethyl formamide) is spread on to a moving, continuous wire mesh belt. As the pu is formed by chemical reaction between the isocyanate and polyol the solvent is removed. The salt is leached out as the polyurethane is passed through tanks of water.

Attempts have been made to produce porous or permeable materials from pvc using sintered powder coating layers, and by the use of very fine perforations in solid coatings. To date none of these approaches have proven commercially viable, so at present all poromerics are polyurethane based. One major drawback with all pu poromerics (yet to be overcome) is that they become brittle and crack when contaminated by sweat. This can lead to a short service life in some types of footwear.

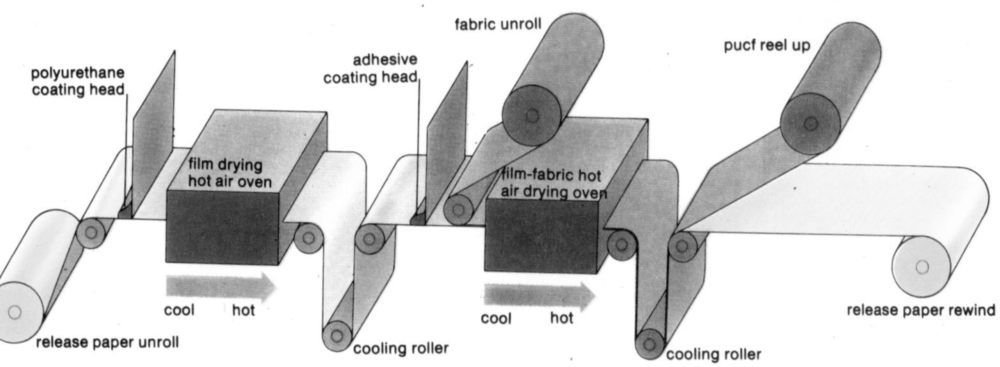

Above: A process for the manufacture of polyurethane-coated fabric (pucf). A film of polyurethane is cast on a sheet of *release paper*, and then the film is coated with adhesive and the fabric bonded to it. The adhesive solvent is dried off in an oven, and after cooling the pucf is separated from the release paper and is ready for surface finishing processes such as embossing and lacquering.

Daily Telegraph Colour Library

Left: The *Brendan*, the leather boat which was sailed across the Atlantic in 1977 to demonstrate that such a voyage could have been made, as has been suggested, by medieval Irish monks sailing similar craft.

Adhesives

Although adhesives in one form or another have been in use for thousands of years, the exact physical and chemical nature of adhesive bonding is still not clearly understood. Several theories have been proposed to explain adhesion, describing it in terms of various mechanical, chemical and electrical phenomena, but no completely satisfactory explanation has yet been devised.

One of the more recent theories involves the *van der Waals' forces*, weak attractive forces which exist naturally between molecules and are due to the distribution of positive and negative electric charges within the molecules. These forces give molecules a natural tendency to stick firmly together, and vary in strength according to the shape and structure of the molecules concerned and the distances between them.

The van der Waals' forces have a much shorter range than ordinary electrostatic forces. Doubling the distance between two molecules reduces the force between them to 1/128 of its previous value, and so very close contact is needed between two molecules before they will stick together. The short range of these intermolecular forces explains why two objects will not normally adhere to one another. Their surfaces, however highly polished, are so rough that the molecules of one can contact those of the other at only a relatively small number of points, and the resulting force of attraction between the two is insufficient to cause adhesion.

An adhesive must therefore be capable of contacting the maximum possible number of molecules on each of the surfaces to be joined, and the surfaces should be free from dirt or grease otherwise the adhesive will stick to the dirt rather than to the surfaces. Optimum contact between the adhesives and the surfaces of the objects to be joined (the *adherends*) is usually achieved by applying the adhesive in a liquid form which then sets into a solid.

The adhesive itself must have good *cohesion* if it is to make a serviceable joint between two solids, that is, it must

BASF

Left: Adhesives are often used to fix floor coverings in place. This picture shows a polymeric dispersion—made of a finely-divided polymer distributed in a liquid carrier medium—being used to bond a felt floor covering to a concrete floor.

Right: Some of the enormous number of uses for which adhesives and sealants (which are similar to adhesives in many respects) are employed. Modern adhesive formulations are being used increasingly as alternatives to more traditional methods of fixture; in joining metal components, for example, adhesives are frequently used instead of welding or riveting.

Samuel Jones & Co Ltd

John Dickinson & Co

Above: One of the most important uses of adhesives is for labelling, for instance for sticking the labels on to matchboxes.

Right: A high-speed labelling machine sticking the labels on to beer bottles with a *high tack* adhesive, one which sticks strongly to the adherends while it is still liquid.

Left: A machine applying gum to envelopes. The gum is dispensed from the vertical bottle and applied to the envelope flaps by a series of rollers. Although most envelopes use a water-soluble adhesive for the flap seal, self-sealing types using pressure-sensitive elastomeric adhesives are becoming increasingly popular. These do not require wetting to make them stick, and so are more hygienic and convenient to use.

Samuel Jones & Co Ltd

1 vehicle body and window sealants
2 structural adhesives
3 adhesives for tiles, flooring and decorative laminates
4 wall insulation and cladding panel adhesives
5 window sealants
6 adhesives used in clothing and footwear

7 self-adhesive letters
8 movement joint sealants
9 fuel tank and pump sealants
10 adhesives for bonding brake linings
11 vehicle badge adhesives
12 resin mortar for kerb stones

13 adhesives for roofing materials
14 sealants for electronic equipment
15 aircraft window sealants
16 adhesives used in printed circuit board manufacture
17 sealants for galley equipment
18 adhesives for non-slip stairway sheeting

19 adhesives for vehicle and aircraft interior trim and flooring
20 synthetic rubber adhesives for liferafts and lifejackets
21 wing de-icer systems bonded with synthetic rubber adhesives
22 body panel adhesives
23 headlight sealants
24 adhesives for sports equipment

Courtesy Bostik Ltd

stick firmly to itself as well as to the two adherends. The cohesion of an adhesive depends to some extent on the way in which it changes from liquid to solid form. The most obvious way to turn a liquid into a solid is to freeze it, and this is what happens with *thermoplastic* or *hot melt* adhesives. These adhesives, as their name implies, are solid at normal temperatures and are heated to melt them into liquids. The hot liquid adhesive is applied to the joint and then allowed to cool and harden.

Some adhesive materials, however, cannot be melted into a thin enough liquid without breaking down into chemically different substances which do not revert to their original form when they cool. This problem can be overcome by dissolving the adhesive in a suitable solvent solution and spreading this solution over the joint surfaces. The solvent then evaporates, and the adhesive sets solid.

Sometimes the solvent is a simple one—the adhesives used on postage stamps, for example, are water-soluble and can be activated simply by licking them. Other adhesives must be dissolved in more complex liquids such as benzene or toluene. Dissolved adhesives are not entirely satisfactory for all purposes because as the solvent evaporates the adhesive tends to shrink away from the surfaces of the joint.

A third method of forming a solid from a liquid is that employed by the *thermosetting* resin adhesives. These are formed by mixing together two separate liquids whose molecules react chemically with each other and undergo irreversible physical and chemical changes. The earliest thermosetting resins were formed from *phenol* and *formaldehyde*. When these two liquids are mixed together and heat and pressure are applied, the molecules can combine in a number of different ways. There are two points on the formaldehyde molecule at which the phenol molecule can form a strong covalent chemical bond, and there are three points on the phenol molecule where such a bond can be made.

As the mixture 'cures', more and more of these bonds are made and the final result is a complex interlocking network, in which each phenol molecule is attached to two or three formaldehyde molecules, each of which is in turn linked to other phenols. The component molecules of the resulting structure have very little freedom of movement, and the fully cured resin is thus a rigid solid. This means of forming a solid is known as *chemical crosslinking*.

Glues

Although the word 'glue' is often used to mean any kind of adhesive, it strictly applies only to adhesives made from animal or vegetable protein. *Animal glue* is an impure form of gelatin, which is formed from the protein *collagen* found in bones and connective tissues. This type of glue is produced by heating animal bones with high pressure steam, so that they are reduced to a sticky liquid which sets solid when cooled, and is used as a hot melt adhesive. One of the chief disadvantages of animal glues is their low water-resistance, but they are one of the most popular glues used in woodworking.

Casein glue, which was first used in ancient Egypt, is less easily penetrated by water than are animal glues. It is made from the milk protein casein, which can be precipitated from milk by the action of weak acids such as acetic acid or citric acid. A simple glue can be made by dissolving casein in slightly alkaline water, and if lime is added to this solution a more waterproof adhesive is formed because the casein becomes converted into insoluble sodium caseinate. Casein glue has many uses in the woodworking and paper industries, but it is susceptible to attack by various micro-organisms and chemicals which cause it to degenerate.

Another class of natural adhesives, used mainly where convenience is more important than strength, are derived from starches. The starches may be unprocessed, as in simple flour-and-water paste, or they may be converted into related substances known as *dextrins* and then mixed with water. There are also natural re-moistenable adhesives, such as *gum arabic* which is obtained from acacia trees and was formerly used for postage stamps. It has now become too expensive for this purpose and has been replaced by synthetic adhesives, but it is still used for many paper-bonding applications.

Synthetic adhesives

Synthetic adhesives fall roughly into three main categories: *thermoplastics*, which soften when heated; *thermosetting* resins, the chemically crosslinked resins described earlier, and *elastomers*, which have long, coiled molecules which enable them to stretch easily when pulled and regain their original shape when released.

Thermoplastics are relatively tough materials which, if subjected to excessive stress, tend to stretch permanently rather

Left: The arched concrete beams of the Olympic Stadium and Velodrome in Montreal were built up from segments weighing up to 65 tonnes each, which were bonded together with epoxy resin adhesives. Special fast-curing versions of the adhesive were developed to enable joints to be made during the winter when temperatures were as low as —18°C (0°F).

Above: An arched wooden footbridge which was bonded with a resorcinol adhesive.

than break apart completely. The most important of this type are the *polyvinyl* adhesives, which are used for bonding plastic sheet to metals, for joining wood, and for sticking upholstery materials (particularly vinyl cloths which they closely resemble) to furniture. *Polystyrene cement*, widely used in plastic model kits, consists of polystyrene dissolved in a volatile solvent. *Cellulose acetate* and *cellulose nitrate* are thermoplastics formed by regenerating natural cellulose, and are used in quick-drying solutions as general-purpose household adhesives.

Thermosetting adhesives are much stronger than thermoplastics, though they are more brittle. They can withstand much higher stresses, but when over-stressed fail suddenly and completely. For all but the most demanding applications this is no problem, because the stresses they have to take are normally well below their breaking point. The phenol-formaldehyde resins have now been largely superseded by *resorcinol-formaldehyde* complexes, which are cold-setting and do not require a corrosive catalyst to make them set. They are widely used for bonding wood, leather and rubber, as are the *amino resins* such as *urea-formaldehyde*.

The strongest of all the two-part thermosetting resins are the *epoxy resins*, polymeric derivatives of epichlorhydrin (derived from glycerol) and bisphenol-A (2,2-Bis(4-hydroxyphenyl)-propane). Their behaviour differs from that of phenolic and amino resins in one important respect. Each time a crosslink is formed in a phenolic or amino resin, a molecule of water is also formed, and since this water must escape from the

Right: Smoothing down the edge of the joint between the upper and lower halves of a glass fibre car body. The joint was bonded with an epoxy resin adhesive, a type of adhesive that has a wide range of applications, both industrial and domestic. Epoxy resins do not shrink on setting, and are waterproof.

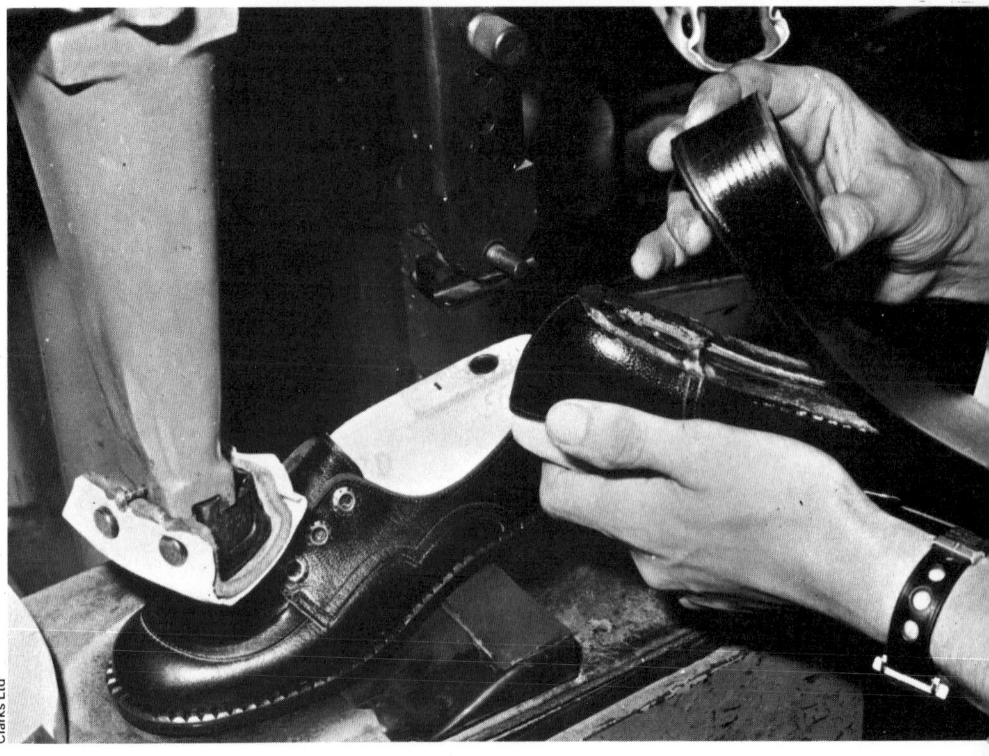

CIBA-Geigy Co.

CIBA-Geigy Co.

CIBA-Geigy Co.

Clarks Ltd

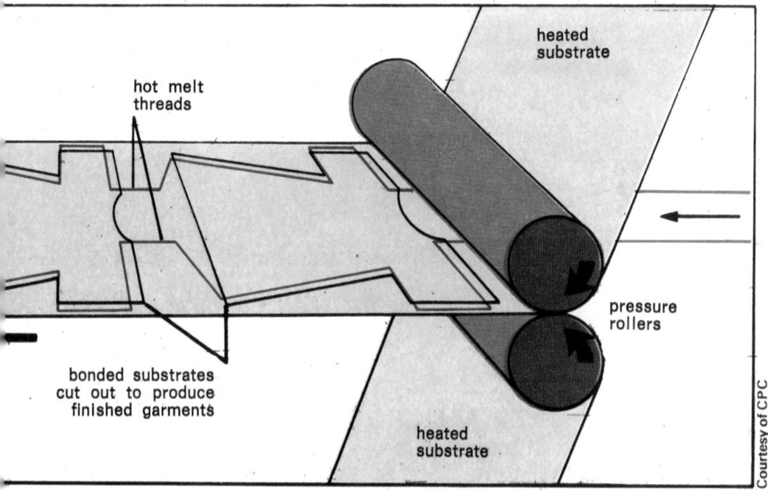

Left: A recent development in adhesives is the hot melt adhesive-coated thread, which consists of a central core of thread covered with a sheath of hot melt adhesive. The adhesive is activated either by heating the coated thread or, as shown in this suggested method of making disposable surgical gowns, by heating the materials to be bonded. This type of adhesive thread has many uses in the packaging industry.

Below: Filling grooves cut into the frame for a fire-resistant door with a sealant which swells when subjected to heat, preventing flames and hot gases passing round the edges of the door.

Courtesy of CPC

Evode Ltd

Left: Bonding soles and heels to shoe uppers on a *sole-laying* machine, which applies pressure and heat to cure the adhesive used to join them.

Below right: Some typical uses of adhesives in footwear manufacture. The use of adhesives means that shoes can be made more quickly and cheaply than they can when only the traditional stitching methods are employed. The adhesives are based on natural rubber or synthetic polymers.

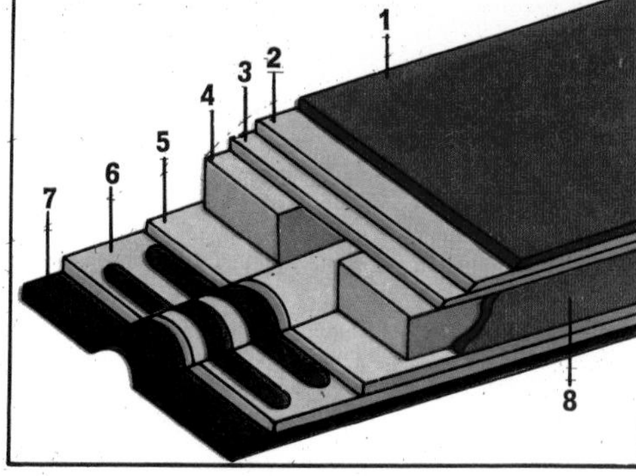

Left: The composite structure of a seven-layer bonded ski. The component layers are bonded together by a thermosetting resin adhesive.

1 phenolic fibre top
2 high-carbon spring steel camber stabilizer
3 high-tensile aluminium
4 wood-particle board dampening core
5 high-tensile aluminium
6 slotted high-carbon spring steel sole
7 textured phenolic fibre running surface
8 phenolic fibre panels

1 topline folding—polyamide hot melts
2 linings—acrylate-ethylene/vinyl acetate (eva) natural rubber
3 toe puff—heat activated eva
4 stiffener—heat activated eva
5 lasting—neoprene-urethane solvent or polyester-polyamide hot melts
6 shank—hot melt polyamides
7 sole attaching—polyurethane solvent
8 insock—acrylate or natural rubber latex

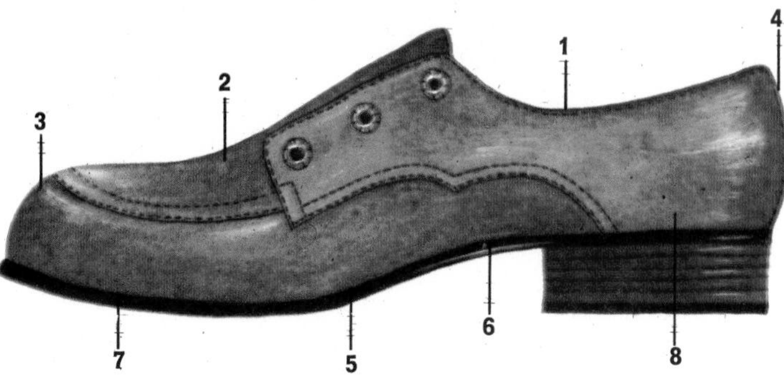

Courtesy of Satra

resins by evaporation or absorption they are best suited to use with porous materials which can absorb the water. When an epoxy resin cures, no such waste water is formed and there is no shrinkage of the adhesive, which makes these resins very suitable for bonding non-porous materials such as metal or glass.

Elastomeric adhesives are used for many applications where their ability to stretch is essential, for example in bonding the felt covers to tennis balls, but their main uses are in *pressure-sensitive* adhesives. Their coiled molecules can be compressed as well as stretched. Two surfaces coated with elastomerics do not bond very tightly if they are simply brought into contact with each other, because their molecules do not contact each other at very many points. When pressure is applied, however, the molecules are brought into close contact and they are also compressed, bringing their atoms closer together. This closer contact results in firmer bonding. Elastomeric adhesives are nearly always solutions of either natural rubber (*isoprene*) or synthetic rubber (*polychloroprene*, also called *neoprene*).

For applications such as the construction of aircraft frames, where the highest standards of strength and durability must be met, the so-called *structural adhesives* are employed. These are blends of thermosetting resins, which provide strength, and thermoplastics or elastomers, which provide toughness and flexibility. Several different combinations are used, most of which need heat and pressure to make them set. An exception is the very popular mixture of epoxy resin and *polyamide* (nylon), which sets at room temperature and atmospheric pressure.

The two largest areas of use for adhesives are in packaging and labelling, for example in the manufacture of corrugated cardboard, and for making and sealing cartons and bags. A variety of adhesives are used for labelling and packaging, including hot melt and pressure-sensitive types, and silicates (such as sodium silicate) which are unusual in that they are inorganic whereas most other adhesives are based on organic compounds.

Adhesives have long played an important role in the woodworking industries. Although the traditional animal and casein glues are still used, they are being replaced by newer synthetic adhesives such as the thermoplastic *polyvinyl acetate* resin. In the furniture industry, thermosetting resins are commonly used in conjunction with *radio frequency* (rf) *heating* systems, which use high-frequency radio waves to heat the glued joints and so reduce the curing time.

In a typical rf heating system, the assembled and glued components are held firmly in a jig or press while an rf field of, for example, 6 kW at 13.56 MHz, is applied to the joint. The curing time depends on the type and thickness of the wood and the type of adhesive used, but is commonly between about 5 seconds and 2 minutes.

There are now a considerable number of adhesives available for household use, and the range of industrial adhesives is even greater. Domestic adhesives include simple pastes and gums for sticking paper, 'cements' for plastics, rubber and leather, and resin adhesives for joining non-porous materials such as ceramics and metals.

Detergents

The oldest type of detergent is soap—made by reacting a fat with an alkali—which was first made in the Middle East over 5,000 years ago. The first synthetic soapless detergent was not invented until 1916, but since then the manufacture of non-soap detergents has become a major sector of the petrochemical industry.

The most important constituents of detergents are complex molecules known as *surface active agents* or *surfactants*, so named because of their effects on the *surface tension* which exists at the surface of a liquid, and on the *interfacial tension* which exists at the interface between two different liquids or between a liquid and a solid.

Within a liquid, such as water, there are strong inter-molecular forces acting in all directions to bind the molecules together, but at its surface these forces act only in an inward direction. The result of these inward-acting forces is a curvature of the surface of the liquid, which accounts for the near-spherical shape of a drop of water at the end of a tap.

The elastic-like force at the surface of a liquid which tends to pull it into a spherical shape is what is known as the surface tension, and it is this which prevents water from being, on its own, a truly effective cleaning agent. When it comes into contact with, for example, a particle of dirt on the surface of a fabric, its surface tension prevents it from making really intimate contact with either the fabric or the dirt, and this prevents it from washing the dirt particle from the material.

The function of a surfactant is to break down the surface tension of the water—making it effectively 'wetter'. Surfactant molecules can be thought of as tadpole-shaped, having a water-loving or *hydrophilic* head attached to a long water-hating or *hydrophobic* tail. When a surfactant is mixed with water, the surfactant molecules at the surface arrange themselves with their hydrophobic tails sticking up through the 'skin' of water molecules at the surface. This destroys the continuity of the water surface and greatly reduces the surface tension.

The hydrophobic tails of the surfactant molecules dispersed within the water will also take any opportunity to pull themselves out of it, and will readily attach themselves to any particle of grease that they encounter. A grease particle thus becomes covered with surfactant molecules, firmly fixed to it by their hydrophobic (also called *lipophilic* or fat-loving) heads. If the grease is stuck to a fabric or other material being washed, a combination of this surfactant action and the mechanical agitation provided by the washing action will dislodge the grease, producing minute droplets of surfactant-coated grease which are dispersed through the water as an *emulsion*.

Surfactants can be divided into three main groups: *anionic*, which become negatively charged *negative ions* when in solution; *cationic*, which form positive ions in solution; and *non-ionic*, which do not become ionized. Soaps are anionic; sodium laurate, for example, has a tail

DETERGENT ACTION

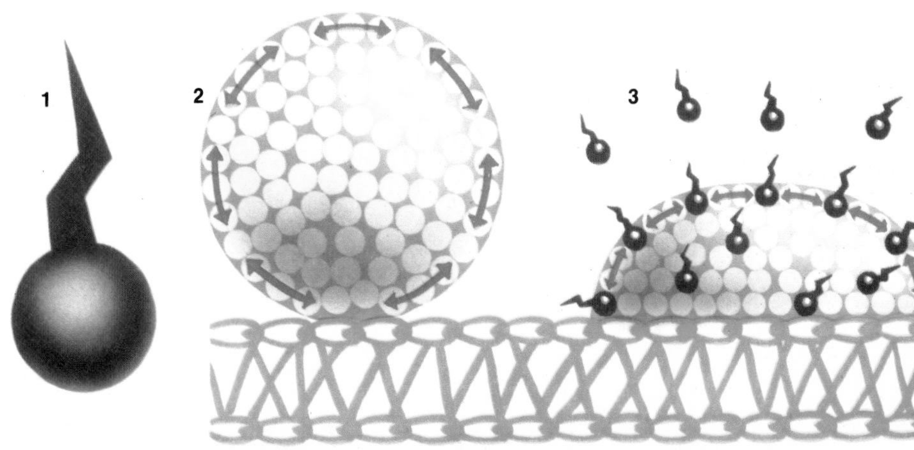

Courtesy Unilever

Lever Bros

Shell Photo Service

Left: A 1903 soap advertisement. Soap consumption rose rapidly during the second half of the 19th century, increasing during that period from under 90,000 tonnes per year to over 300,000 tonnes per year. Toilet soaps, soap powders and soap flakes were introduced around the turn of the century.

Above: Testing a dishwashing liquid in a laboratory. Dishwashing liquids usually contain both anionic and non-ionic surfactants, and produce a thick lather.

Below: Tests with live fish help determine the toxicity of detergents. Most household detergents are relatively harmless.

Lever Bros

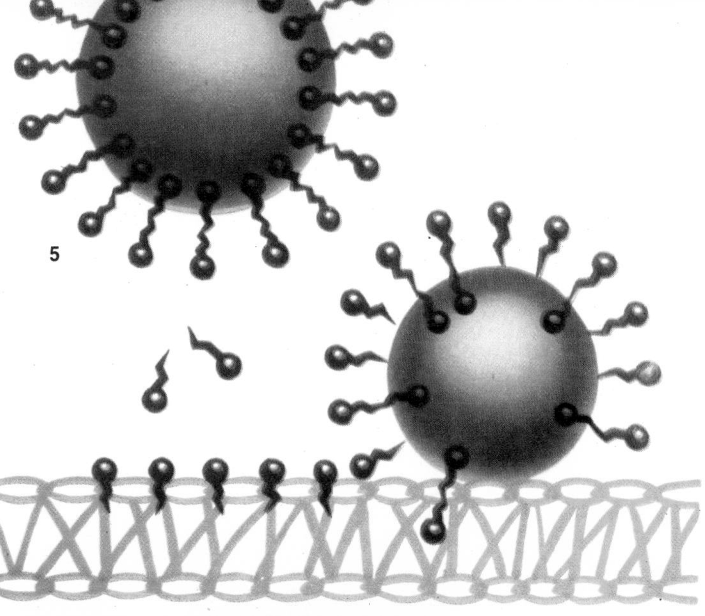

Left: A typical surfactant molecule, 1, has a tadpole-like structure with a hydrophilic head and a hydrophobic tail. Surface tension pulls a drop of water into a near-spherical shape, 2, but when a detergent is added to it the surfactant molecules reduce its surface tension so that it collapses, and spreads over the surface with which it is in contact, 3. Detergents remove grease from fabrics by breaking it into droplets coated with surfactant molecules, 4. Other types of dirt, such as rust particles, attract the heads of the surfactant molecules, and become coated with a double layer of them joined tail-to-tail, 5.

Albright & Wilson

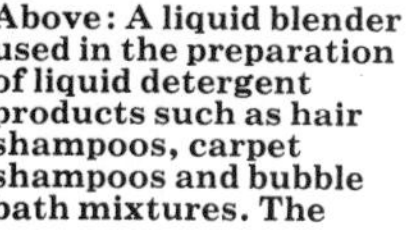

Above: A liquid blender used in the preparation of liquid detergent products such as hair shampoos, carpet shampoos and bubble bath mixtures. The blender mixes the surfactants with the hydrotopes and the colourants, perfumes, preservatives and other ingredients to produce the finished products.

Lever Bros

Above: Early synthetic detergents contained surfactants which could not be broken down by bacteria, and this caused foaming on rivers. Modern domestic detergents are *biodegradable*, which prevents this happening.

Below: Testing the effects of a detergent on skin.

Procter & Gamble

comprising a straight chain of eleven carbon atoms linked with 23 hydrogen atoms, and a head comprising a carbon atom and two oxygen atoms, one of which carries a net negative charge when in solution. Non-soap detergents may be anionic, cationic or non-ionic, or a mixture of two or more types of surfactant.

Soaps

Soaps are made by reacting fats, of both animal and vegetable origin (for example tallow, coconut oil and palm kernel oil), with an alkali such as caustic soda (sodium hydroxide, $NaOH$) or caustic potash (potassium hydroxide, KOH). In a modern continuous soap-making plant, this *saponification* is carried out by mixing the fats and the alkali and heating them, under pressure, to about 130°C (266°F). The reaction produces glycerine as well as soap, and this glycerine is removed by mixing the soap and glycerine with hot brine. The glycerine dissolves more readily in the brine than the soap does, and the soap is separated from the glycerine and brine by centrifugal extractors. The molten soap then undergoes further processing to produce the type of finished product required.

Hard soaps are produced by spray-drying the molten soap, adding other ingredients such as colourants and perfumes, and forming it into bars. *Toilet soaps*, which are made from higher quality fats than those used for hard soaps, are heated after drying to reduce their moisture content to about 10 per cent, compared with the 28 per cent moisture content of hard soaps.

Soap flakes are formed by spreading molten soap over a revolving, water-cooled drum. The solidified soap is scraped from the drum in the form of thin ribbons of soap, which are passed into a drying chamber to reduce their moisture content to about 7 per cent. Perfumes and preservatives are added, and the soap is rolled thin and cut into flakes before packing.

Soap powders are produced by spray-drying, but a variety of additives are mixed with the molten soap before it is dried, the finished product containing about 50 per cent soap. The additives used in soap powders are also used in many non-soap detergents, and are formulated to assist and improve the cleaning action of the product.

A *builder*, such as sodium tripolyphosphate, 'builds up' the detergent action of the soap. It combines with the calcium and magnesium ions present in hard water which impair the action of the surfactant, forming soluble complexes which do not interfere with the cleaning action. It also assists in the removal and dispersal of solid, non-greasy dirt particles.

Conditioners such as sodium silicate or sodium sulphate keep the powder free-flowing and maintain the alkalinity of the washing solution. Stain removal is enhanced by the addition of a chemical bleach such as sodium perborate, and *optical brighteners* are added to improve the 'whiteness' of white cellulosic fabrics such as cottons. These brighteners or *fluorescers* adhere to the surface of the fabric, and emit a bluish-white light which gives a whiter appearance to it.

The redeposition of dirt on to fabrics is prevented by the addition of *anti-redeposition agents* which give the fabrics an electrical charge that repels the similarly-charged dirt particles suspended in the water. Sodium carboxymethyl cellulose, for example, protects cotton fabrics from redeposition by giving them a negative charge. Other washing powder additives include *ethanolamides*, which stabilize the lather and disperse scum, and perfumes. Blended detergents, containing both soap and non-soap surfactants, are also produced.

Non-soap detergents

A wide range of non-soap detergents are now manufactured, in both powder and liquid form. The most common synthetic surfactants used in domestic detergents are the anionic alkylbenzene sulphonates. These are produced by the *sulphonation* of an alkylbenzene such as dodecyl benzene ($C_{12}H_{25}.C_6H_5$). The alkylbenzene is reacted with oleum ($H_2S_2O_7$, also known as fuming sulphuric acid or pyrosulphuric acid), to give the sulphonated alkylbenzene and sulphuric acid (H_2SO_4). The sulphuric acid is diluted with water and separated from the sulphonate, which is then neutralized with caustic soda.

Non-soap detergent powders, which contain 20-25 per cent surfactant, are manufactured by spray-drying a mixture of surfactant paste and the other ingredients such as builders and anti-redeposition agents. *Protease enzymes*, which catalyze the breakdown of protein-based stains such as blood or egg, are included in some brands of washing powder.

Liquid non-soap detergents are produced by mixing the ingredients, in liquid form, together with a *hydrotrope* such as sodium xylene sulphonate or potassium toluene sulphonate which ensures that the ingredients do not separate out of the mixture.

Non-ionic surfactants are becoming increasingly important in detergent manufacture, particularly in washing powders designed for use in washing machines (such as front-loaders) which require a low-foaming detergent. The commonest non-ionic surfactants are the ethoxylated alkylphenols. These are made by heating ethylene oxide and an alkylphenol to a temperature of 180°C (356°F) in the presence of an alkaline catalyst.

Detergents, both anionic and non-ionic, are also used in other cleaning products such as scouring powders and creams. Typical scouring powders contain an anionic detergent, a finely ground mineral powder such as felspar, and a chlorine bleach. Scouring creams are more complex, often consisting of a mixture of anionic and non-ionic detergents, a finely ground mineral such as calcite, a polyphosphate to maintain alkalinity, and ammonia to assist the cleaning action.

Special detergent formulations are manufactured for a wide range of industrial cleaning purposes. For example, food processing machinery and dairy equipment, which must be cleaned to the highest possible standards, are cleaned with special formulations of non-ionic and cationic surfactants.

Fabric conditioners are a blend of cationic and non-ionic surfactants, plus preservatives, colourants and perfumes. The conditioning is done by the cationic components, which are adsorbed on to the surfaces of the fabric fibres. They lubricate the individual fibres so that they do not cling together, and this makes the fabric feel softer and restores its original bulk.

Albright & Wilson

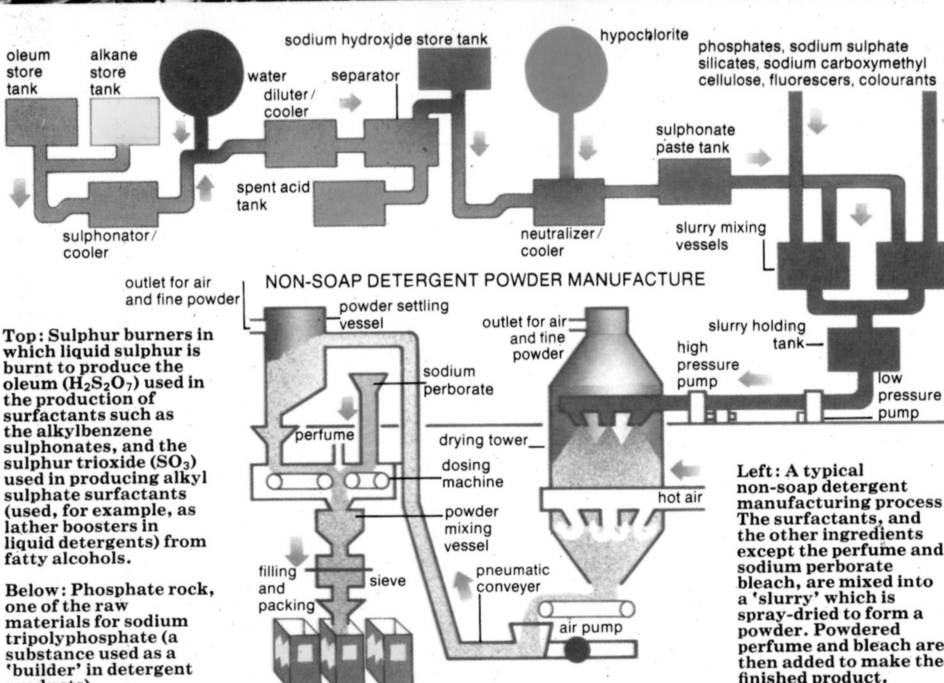

Courtesy Unilever

Top: Sulphur burners in which liquid sulphur is burnt to produce the oleum ($H_2S_2O_7$) used in the production of surfactants such as the alkylbenzene sulphonates, and the sulphur trioxide (SO_3) used in producing alkyl sulphate surfactants (used, for example, as lather boosters in liquid detergents) from fatty alcohols.

Below: Phosphate rock, one of the raw materials for sodium tripolyphosphate (a substance used as a 'builder' in detergent products).

Left: A typical non-soap detergent manufacturing process. The surfactants, and the other ingredients except the perfume and sodium perborate bleach, are mixed into a 'slurry' which is spray-dried to form a powder. Powdered perfume and bleach are then added to make the finished product.

Albright & Wilson

Dyes, Paints and Varnishes

The world today is a much brighter and more colourful place than it was 100 or even 50 years ago, partly because of changes in fashions and tastes but mainly because of technical advances which have vastly increased the range of coloured paints and dyes available. Even in the 1950s, for example, most cars were painted black; alternative colours were either unavailable or expensive options. Today, black cars are very much the exception rather than the rule.

The use of dyes and paints to brighten and decorate clothing, buildings and other artifacts dates back to the very beginnings of civilization. Cave paintings found in France and Spain, for example, were produced some 17,000 years ago, and the dyeing of textiles has been practised for well over 4,000 years.

Dyeing

Until the middle of the last century, the only dyes available were natural products obtained mostly from plants and flowers, and so the range of colours was restricted by the relatively limited range of sources of dyes. These natural dyes included *woad*, a blue dye obtained from a plant of the same name, *indigo*, another blue dye of plant origin, other plant dyes such as *madder* (red), *safflower* (yellow) and *turmeric* (yellow), and the expensive and highly-prized *Tyrian purple*, extracted from certain kinds of sea snail (the *Muricidae*).

The most important advance in the technology of dyeing came in 1856 with the discovery of the first synthetic dye. This was *mauviene*, a bluish-purple dye discovered accidentally by William Perkin during experiments intended to synthesize the drug quinine (obtained naturally from the bark of the cinchona tree) from aniline ($C_6H_5NH_2$), a coal tar derivative.

Mauviene, although initially expensive, was an immediate success, and this success, coming at a time when research into organic chemistry was just getting into full swing, triggered an intensive search for other synthetic dyes based on coal tar derivatives. These dyes, being the salts of organic bases, are known as *basic dyes*. Several thousand such dyes were subsequently synthesized.

Although these synthetic dyes were satisfactory when used on animal fibres such as wool, they were easily washed out of vegetable fibres like cotton. This difficulty was overcome by treating the fibres with metal salts or with solutions of these salts in tannic acid before they were dyed, a process known as *mordanting*. The dyes react with the mordants to form insoluble compounds which are retained with the vegetable fibres and are not easily worked out of them.

The *azo dyes* are a large and important group of dyes formed by linking together organic molecules with an *azo bond*, which comprises a pair of nitrogen atoms arranged as —N—N—. The azo dyes include *acid dyes*, acidic dyes which combine chemically with proteins and so form very stable dyes when used on animal fibres such as wool, and *direct dyes* which

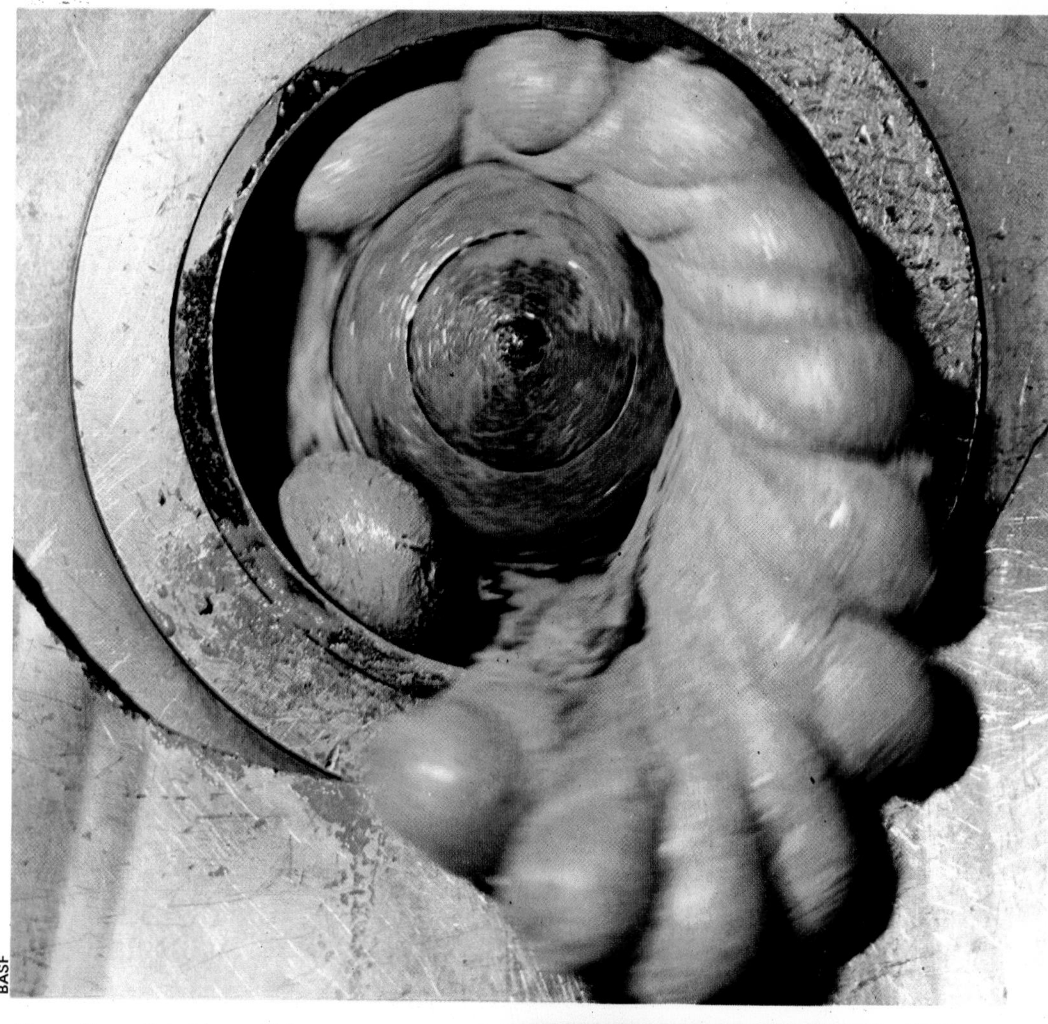

BASF

Above: The outlet of a machine used in dye manufacture.

Below: Man-made fibre being fed from a dyeing container into a dryer. Many man-made fibres are dyed with *disperse dyes*, which are insoluble in water but will dissolve into the fibre when heated to about 80°C (176°F).

Right: A researcher mixing pigments to formulate new shades of lipstick. Lipsticks are basically mixtures of high quality waxes (such as beeswax or carnauba), oils (castor oil, for example) and fats. The dyes used in cosmetics must be carefully chosen to ensure that they are not harmful to health.

BASF

Courtaulds

form insoluble compounds with a high affinity for cellulose fibres when hydrated sodium sulphate (Glauber's salt) or sodium chloride (common salt) is mixed with them in the dyeing solution. The direct dyes can be made even more stable by treating the dyed material with metal salts which combine with the dye, forming larger molecules which are much less soluble.

Azoic dyes are two-component dyes used for cellulosic fibres. The material is first treated with one of the components, and then put into a solution of the other so that the two compounds react to produce the dye within the fibres themselves. This type of dye is highly resistant to washing.

Another group of very stable dyes used for cellulose fibres are known collectively as *vat dyes*. These dyes, which include the

Above: The main stages in the production of a typical gloss paint. Linseed oil and alkyd resin are blended to make the *binder* or *medium*. This is thinned with white spirit and left in a tank for about five months so that impurities settle out of it, and then it is filtered to remove any remaining impurities. The next stage is the *pre-mixing*, when the pigments are added to form a thick paste that is thinned down to the required consistency. In the next stage, the paint is passed through a mill containing steel balls; the pigment and binder are mixed and ground, ensuring that each pigment particle is thoroughly wetted with binder. The paint is now ready for the *make-up* stage, where dyes and thinner are added to adjust the colour and consistency.

Right: A row of mixers in which pigment, binder, thinner and drier are mixed.

Below: Enamel paint leaving a roller mill which grinds it to eliminate lumps and ensure that the pigment is thoroughly wetted.

synthetic indigo used for dyeing blue denim, are mixed with chemicals which make them soluble for the dyeing process. After the material has been dyed it is dried or treated with other chemicals to render the chemical additives inactive and make the dye insoluble again.

When rayon (regenerated cellulose) was introduced at the turn of the century it was found that it could be dyed easily with the same dyes that were used for cotton, which is a natural form of cellulose. Cellulose acetate and triacetate, however, proved difficult to dye until the *disperse dyes* were developed in the 1920s.

These dyes are water-soluble azo and anthracene dyes which will dissolve in the acetate fibres at high temperatures. They are prepared by dispersing very fine particles of the dyestuff in an aqueous base, the particles being held in suspension by means of surface-active ingredients in the base. The dispersion is heated to about 80°C (176°F), at which temperature the dye particles dissolve into the fibres.

Polyester fibres are also dyed with disperse dyes, and these dyes can also be used for polyamides although acid dyes are more often used. Acrylics, another important group of synthetic fibres, are usually dyed with basic dyes.

Paints

A paint consists basically of a finely-powdered, solid *pigment*, suspended in a liquid *vehicle*, also known as a *binder* or *medium*. The pigment (or mixture of pigments) provides the colouration of the paint; the vehicle enables the paint to be spread or sprayed over a surface, and when it dries, by evaporation or oxidation, it forms a film which binds the particles of pigment together and to the painted surface.

The enormous range of pigments used in the manufacture of paints includes both natural and synthetic materials. Natural pigments include *ochres*, which are natural earths containing hydrated iron oxide and which range in colour from pale yellow to orange or red, and *umber*, a brown earth containing oxides of iron and manganese. Manufactured pigments include *carbon black*, made by burning oil or natural gas with insufficient air so that a finely-divided amorphous carbon soot is formed, and oxides of lead, zinc and titanium which are white pigments.

Rolls-Royce Motors

Left: Testing samples of paints used on Rolls-Royce cars in a machine which simulates the effects of weather on them.

Right: The stator coil of a 1,000 kW electric motor being lowered into a tank of polyester varnish. The varnish, two coats of which are applied, forms a tough film over the coil windings and the steel core, which protects them from moisture, chemical contamination and dirt. The varnish is cured by baking the coil for eight hours at 150°C.

Below: Paints based on polymer resins are widely used in the motor industry because of their toughness and deep gloss.

Parsons Peebles Motors & Generators Ltd

Organic *pigmentary dyestuffs*, based on materials developed originally for textile dyes, are becoming increasingly important to the paint industry. One of the most widely used of these is the blue copper phthalocyanine.

There are many types of medium employed in modern paintmaking, based on both natural and synthetic ingredients. The type of medium used determines the physical properties of the paint.

Gloss paints were formerly based on a blend of a natural resin, such as Congo copal, with a *drying oil* such as linseed or soya bean oil, plus a *thinner* such as turpentine or white spirit and additives to promote faster drying, enhance the gloss and make the paint easier to apply. Modern gloss paints, however, generally use synthetic instead of natural resins. These resins are synthetic polymers, the most important being the alkyd resins made by reacting glycerol with phthalic anhydride. Enamel paints, which dry to a tough, high-gloss finish, consist of very finely ground pigment in a varnish binder.

Many of the synthetic resins now used give a very high gloss and form a tough coating with excellent wear and corrosion resistance. Paints used by the motor industry, for instance, are often based on alkyd-melamine copolymers or on acrylic polymers such as polymethyl methacrylate. Epoxy resin based paints have very good resistance to corrosion, while the polyurethane resins confer toughness and heat resistance to gloss paints.

In emulsion paints, the vehicle is in the form of tiny particles of a pigmented polymer, such as polyvinyl acetate, suspended in water. These paints, which are popular for domestic decoration such as the painting of interior walls, are water-thinnable. Thixotropic or 'non-drip' paints have a viscous, jelly-like consistency, the viscous medium being produced from a blend of a polyamide (nylon) resin and an alkyd resin.

The principle additives used in paints are *driers*, *dispersing agents* and *extenders*. The drying oils used in oil-based paints react with atmospheric oxygen, after the paint has been applied, and oxidize into a solid film. This oxidation can be made more rapid if driers, compounds formed from metals and organic oils, are included in the paint.

Dispersing agents help to keep the pigment in suspension in the medium and stop it from settling into a hard mass at the bottom of the can. Many dispersing agents are forms of detergent, such as sulphonates, stearates or oleates, which ensure that the pigment is thoroughly 'wetted' by the medium.

Extenders also help to prevent the settling of the pigment, give the paint more 'body' and viscosity, and contribute to the hardness of the paint film. Materials used as extenders include finely-divided china clay, silica and asbestos.

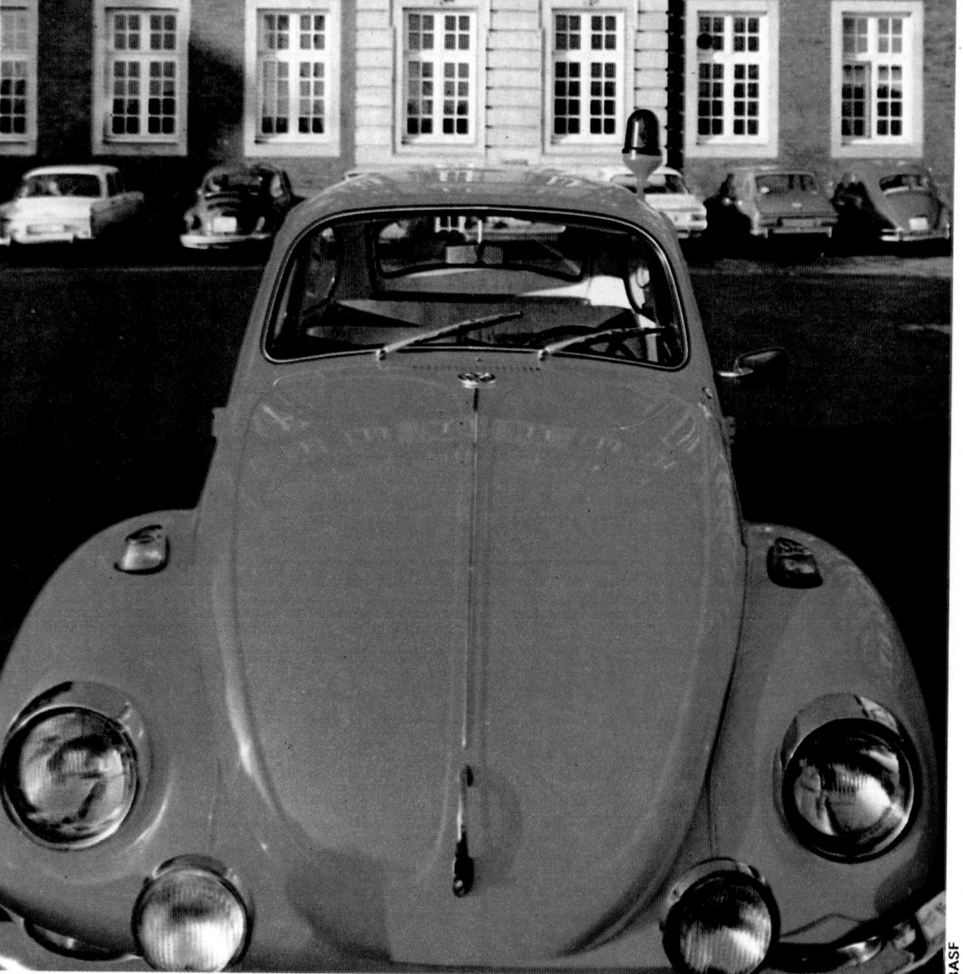
BASF

Varnishes

A varnish is basically a paint without pigment; many paints, in fact, are blends of varnish and pigment. The main types of varnish are *oil varnishes*, made from natural or synthetic resins combined with a drying oil; *spirit varnishes*, which are oils and resins dissolved in volatile solvents; and *water varnishes*, made from emulsions of resins and oils in water.

The resins used include natural varieties, such as copal, and synthetic varieties, such as alkyd, phenolic, vinyl, acrylic and epoxy resins. Drying time is reduced by the addition of small quantities of driers such as salts of cobalt or manganese. Suitable thinners are added to adjust the varnish to a usable consistency.

Apart from their traditional uses, varnishes and *lacquers* (varnishes which dry by solvent evaporation only, without oxidation) have many other important applications. These include the lining of food and drink cans to prevent corrosion or the formation of undesirable metal compounds which might contaminate the contents, and the coating of electrical windings with protective varnishes.

Polymers

Polymers are substances whose molecules consist of long chains of atoms or groups of atoms known as *repeating units*. To many people, the word 'polymer' implies a synthetic substance such as polyethylene (polythene) or nylon, but there are in fact a great many natural polymers, some of which are essential components of living creatures. Cellulose, for example, occurs in the cell walls of plants and is the main constituent of wood. Its complex chain structure is made up of repeating units consisting of groups of carbon, hydrogen and oxygen atoms, each repeating unit having the formula $C_6H_{10}O_5$.

Other natural polymers include proteins, starches and resins, and natural polymers form the basis of materials such as wool, cotton, rubber, leather, silk, asbestos and fur. Most polymers are organic (carbon-based), but there are also inorganic polymers; asbestos, for example, is a polymeric silicate.

The roots of the modern plastics industry can be traced back to the middle of the nineteenth century. The earliest plastics were made not by *polymerization*, the joining together of small molecules to make polymer chains, but by modifying cellulose, which is already a polymer.

The first of these cellulosic plastics was Parkesine, introduced in 1862 by an English chemist called Alexander Parkes. The process devised by Parkes was based on that used for the production of the explosive guncotton, a form of cellulose nitrate made by treating cotton with nitric and sulphuric acids. Parkes' process worked very well on a small scale, but he was unable to achieve the same success on a commercial level and the company which he set up to manufacture Parkesine went bankrupt in 1868.

The problems which Parkes had encountered were overcome two years later by John Wesley Hyatt in the United States. Parkes had used castor oil as a softening agent for his material, and it was this aspect of the process which had caused the most serious technical problems. Hyatt discovered that these problems could be avoided by using camphor as a softener, and his product, which he called Celluloid, was soon being used to make hundreds of items such as knife handles, billiard balls and photographic film.

Celluoid was, however, extremely flammable, and the search for a safer type of material led to the use of cellulose acetate in place of cellulose nitrate as the basis for cellulosic plastics.

The first successful truly synthetic polymer was produced in 1908 by Leo Baekeland in Belgium. This plastic, known as Bakelite, was made by reacting

British Industrial Plastics Ltd

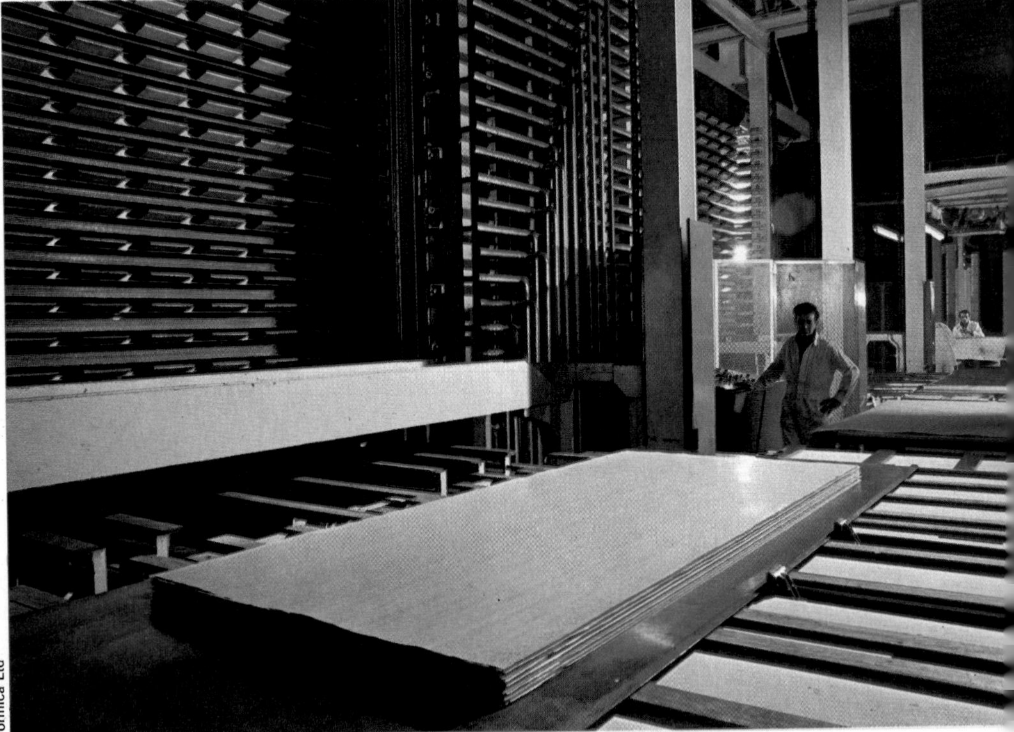
Formica Ltd

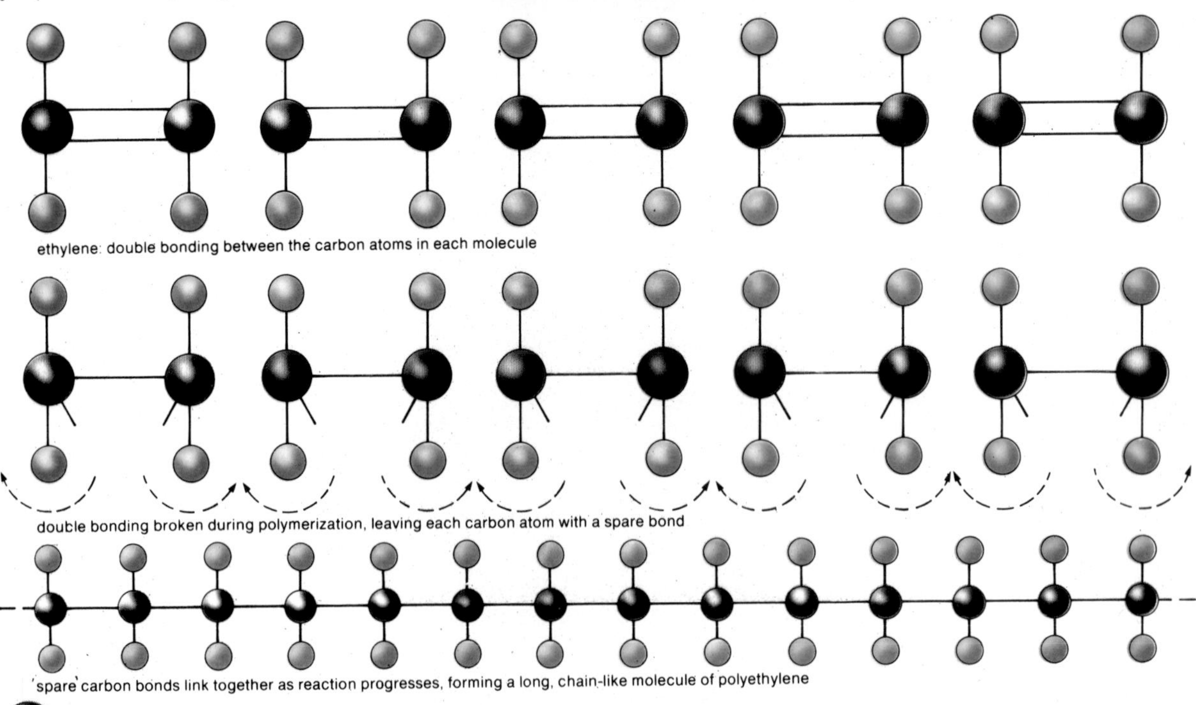

ethylene: double bonding between the carbon atoms in each molecule
double bonding broken during polymerization, leaving each carbon atom with a spare bond
'spare' carbon bonds link together as reaction progresses, forming a long, chain-like molecule of polyethylene
carbon
hydrogen

POLYMERIZATION of ethylene to polyethylene

Top: Some plastic products of the 1920s and 1930s. The lamp and the bowl are of urea formaldehyde; the fuse box, the plug and the socket are of phenolic resins.

Above: Plastic laminates are made from layers of resin-impregnated paper that are subjected to high temperatures and pressures which fuse them into rigid sheets. Decorative laminates, for example, consist of base layers impregnated with phenolic resin, a white or coloured layer impregnated with melamine-formaldehyde, and a top layer, also impregnated with melamine resin, which becomes tough and transparent when cured. This picture shows a laminate about to enter a curing press.

Left: During the polymerization of ethylene into polyethylene, the double bonds between the CH_2 groups in the ethylene molecules are broken into single bonds, and the 'spare' bonds this produces join together to link the CH_2 groups into long chains.

phenol (carbolic acid, C_6H_5OH) with formaldehyde (H.CHO) under carefully-controlled conditions.

Despite the success of materials such as Celluloid and Bakelite, plastics technology could make little real progress until the structure of polymers, and thus the polymerization processes themselves, had been properly understood. The modern understanding of the nature of polymers is based on the work of the German chemist Hermann Staudinger who, during the 1920s, explained the structure of polymers in terms of molecules consisting of hundreds, thousands or even hundreds of thousands of atoms linked together in chains.

This understanding of the nature of polymers gave a great impetus to the development of synthetic polymers, and the 1930s saw the advent of the large-scale production of some of today's most important plastics, namely polystyrene, polyvinyl chloride (pvc), polyethylene (polythene) and polyamide (nylon). Polystyrene and polyvinyl chloride were both known in the nineteenth century, but had not been commercially developed because they were not properly understood.

Direct polymerization

Polymerization involves the linking together of reactive molecules of relatively low molecular weight, known as *monomers*, to form polymers. In the manufacture of polyethylene, for example, the monomer is ethylene, $CH_2{=}CH_2$. During the polymerization the double bond (=) between the two CH_2 groups becomes a single bond (—), and the CH_2 groups then have 'spare' bonds which they use to link up with each other to form a polymer chain in the form $—CH_2—CH_2—CH_2—CH_2—CH_2—$. Polyethylene is therefore built up from repeating units which each comprise a carbon atom and two hydrogen atoms; the polythene molecule consists of a long chain of about 25,000 carbon atoms, each of which has a pair of hydrogen atoms attached to it.

Polymerization is initiated by the application of heat, pressure or mechanical agitation, or by the action of suitable catalysts. In many cases a combination of two or more of these is necessary to promote polymerization. Polymer chains begin to grow as activated monomer molecules within the *reaction medium* (for example the ethylene used in making polyethylene) react with unactivated monomer molecules.

Each activated monomer links up with an activated molecule two monomers long. This activated molecule then reacts with another unactivated monomer to form an activated molecule three molecules long. This process repeats itself over and over again, building up a long chain of monomers. Chain growth eventually terminates when the activated end of a chain combines with the activated end of another chain or with a free activated monomer.

In *bulk polymerization* the reaction medium consists of only the monomer and a catalyst, but in other types of polymerization the monomer may be dissolved in a solvent or suspended in water. In *precipitation polymerization* the monomer is soluble in the solvent but the polymer is not, and so it precipitates out of the

Left: Roller shutters made from extruded polyvinyl chloride (pvc). Polymerization of vinyl chloride monomer ($CH_2{=}CHCl$) to polyvinyl chloride was first noted by the French chemist Henri Regnault (1810-1878) in 1838, but large-scale pvc production did not begin until 1931, in Germany.

Below: One advantage that plastics have over metals is that they do not corrode. This factor, together with their lighter weights and the ease with which they can be moulded, has led to the use of plastics in place of metals for an increasingly large number and variety of applications.

Hoechst UK Ltd

Shell Photo Service

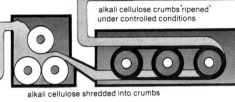

CELLOPHANE PRODUCTION

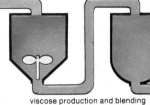

alkali cellulose crumbs 'ripened' under controlled conditions

wood pulp mixed with caustic soda to form alkali cellulose

alkali cellulose shredded into crumbs

viscose production and blending

Below: A gymnasium roofed with glass reinforced polyester (grp) sheet. The polyesters used for this type of material are usually cross-linked; the polyester is heated together with styrene and a peroxide initiator, and the styrene molecules form cross-links between adjacent polyester chains. Other uses for the type of grp shown here include claddings for exterior walls and storage tanks, housings and cabinets for electrical equipment, and body and roofing panels for vehicles.

Right: A high roof conversion for a Ford van, moulded in glass reinforced polyester.

BP Chemicals Ltd

British Industrial Plastics Ltd

Below: One of the most important processes in the manufacture of plastics is *extrusion*. Granular polymer is driven through the heated cylinder of the extruder by the rotating screw, and forced, in molten form, through a die which forms it into rods, tubes, ribbons, sheets or profiled sections.

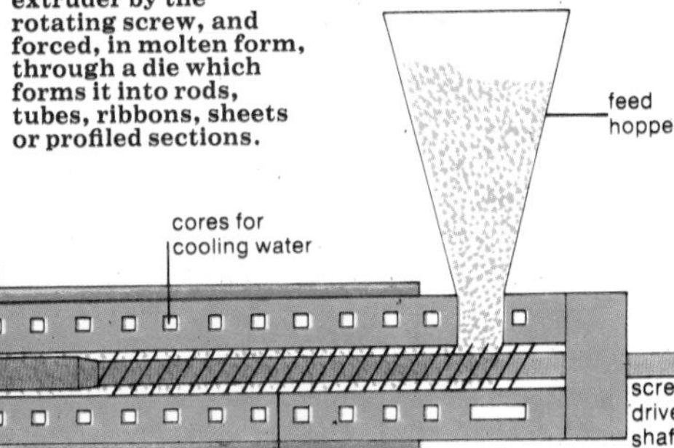

solution when it is formed. If the polymer is also soluble, however, the reaction produces a polymer solution, and so a process of this type is known as *solution polymerization*.

In *suspension polymerization* the monomer is in the form of tiny droplets suspended in water, and the activated monomer molecules are formed within them. In the case of *emulsion polymerization*, the monomer is finely dispersed throughout the aqueous phase (the water) by an emulsifier, which is a kind of detergent. The activated monomer molecules are formed within the aqueous phase rather than within the monomer particles.

Bulk, precipitation, solution, suspension and emulsion polymerization processes are all forms of *direct polymerization*. Materials made by direct polymerization include low density polyethylene (bulk polymerization), high density polypropylene (precipitation), polyvinyl chloride (emulsion or suspension), and polystyrene (bulk).

Copolymerization is the process of making a polymer from two or more different types of monomer, the polymer chain, known in this case as a *copolymer*, being a combination of the different monomers.

Hoechst UK Ltd

Right: Four common processes used in plastics production. In *injection moulding*, a hydraulic plunger forces the polymer through a heated barrel and into a die or mould, which forms it into the required shape. Articles such as plastic bottles are often made by *blow moulding*, in which a length of molten plastic tubing (known as a *parison*) is forced against the walls of a mould by compressed air or steam. In *compression moulding*, a version of which is used for making records, the polymer is compressed between two halves of a heated mould. *Calendering* is a method of making plastic sheet or film by passing polymer through a series of heated rollers.

Left: Bottles made from high density polyethylene. This is more rigid than low density polyethylene because it has straight polymer chains which can pack closely together, whereas the branched polymer chains of low density polyethylene cannot pack as closely.

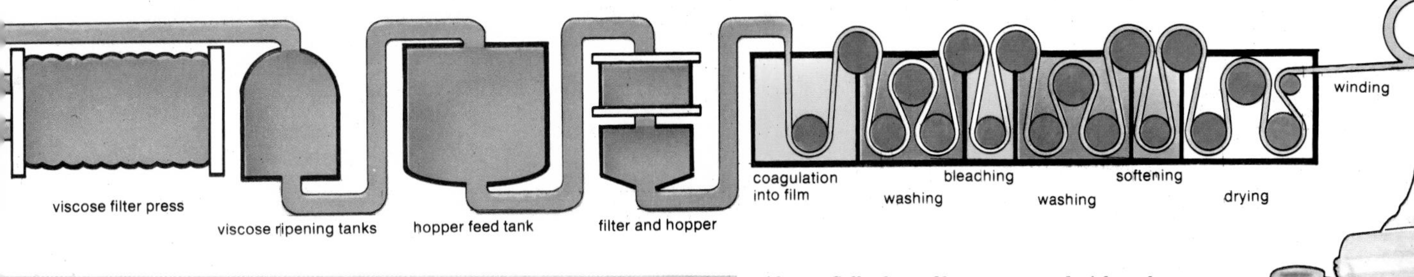

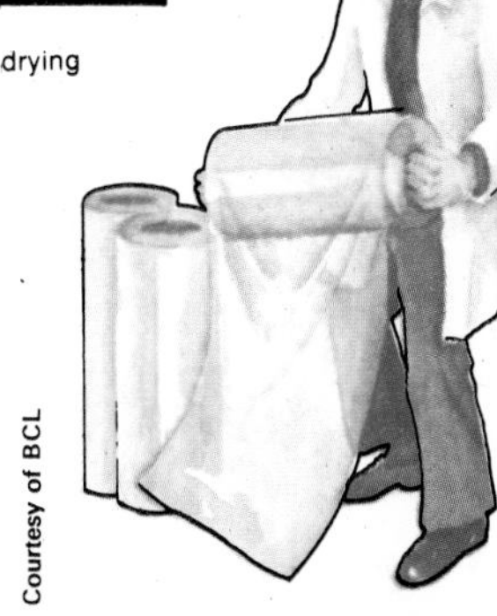

Above: Cellophane film is made from *regenerated* cellulose, produced by making natural cellulose into a soluble chemical compound, and then treating this compound to recover the cellulose in a more usable form. Wood pulp is mixed with caustic soda to form alkali cellulose, which is reacted with carbon disulphide to make cellulose xanthate. This is dissolved in caustic soda to form *viscose*, and when this is *ripened* the cellulose begins to reconstitute. The ripened viscose is passed through sulphuric acid, where the cellulose coagulates and is made into a film.

Courtesy of BCL

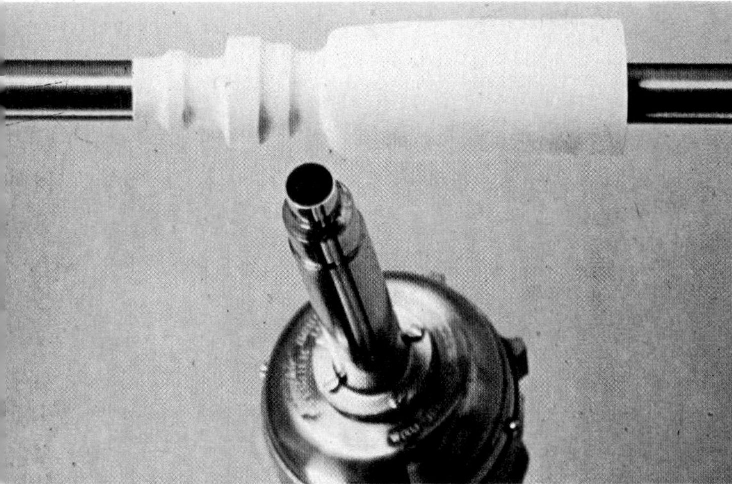

Raychem Ltd

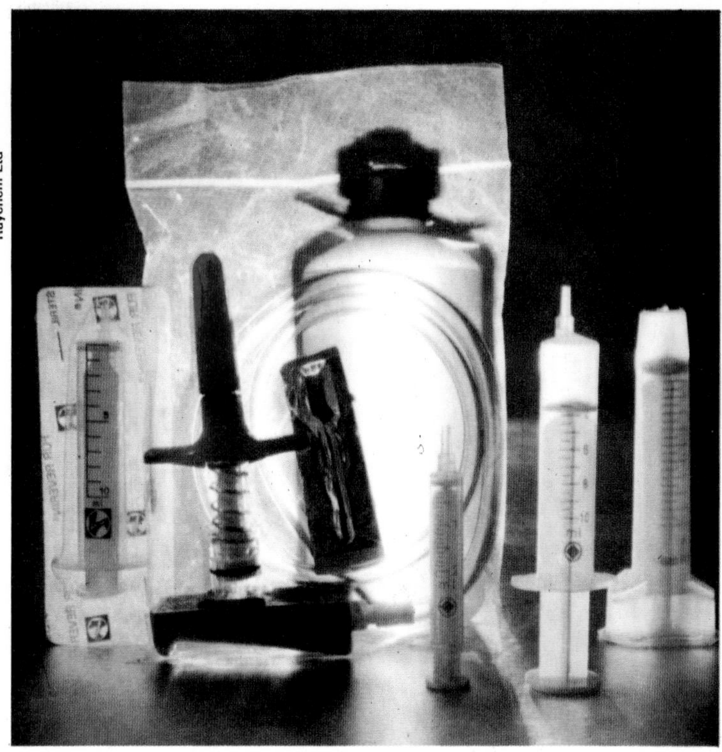

Hoechst UK Ltd

Above: Flexible tubing which shrinks when heated is ideal for covering joins in pipes and cables. This particular polymer is a polyolefin. It is irradiated by high energy electrons during manufacture to cause cross-linking between the molecular chains and so prevent melting. On heating to about 120°C (250°F) the tubing shrinks to half its original diameter.

Right: The development in the 1950s of organometallic catalysts for the polymerization of olefins led to improved processes for making polyethylene and polypropylene. Medical equipment made from polypropylene is relatively cheap and can be heat sterilized.

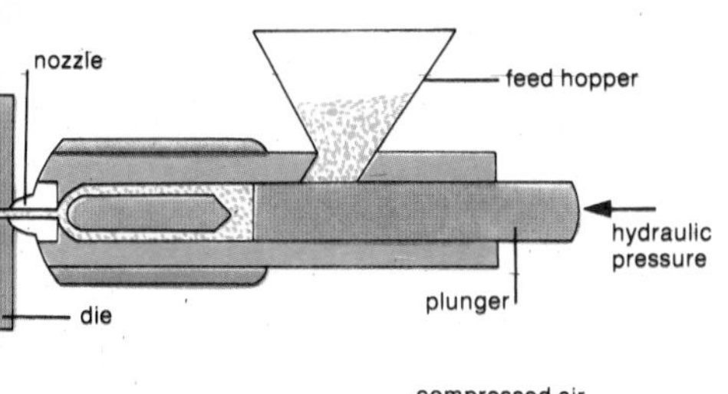

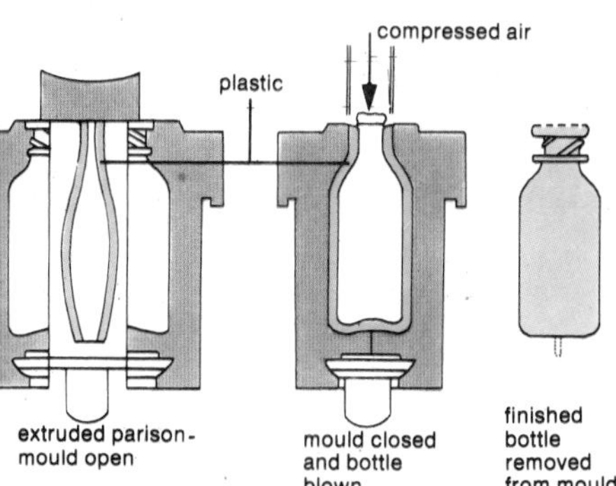

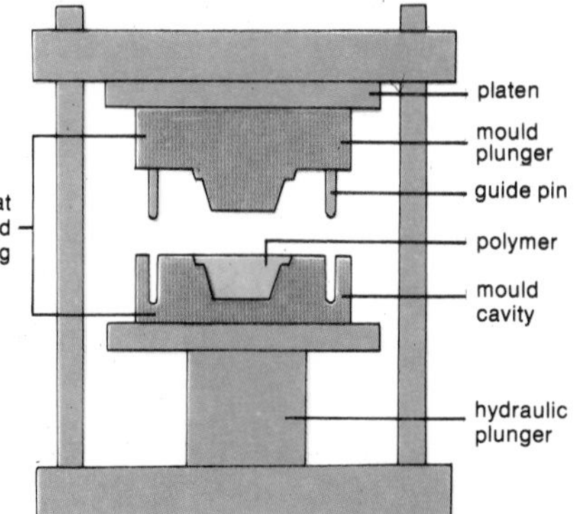

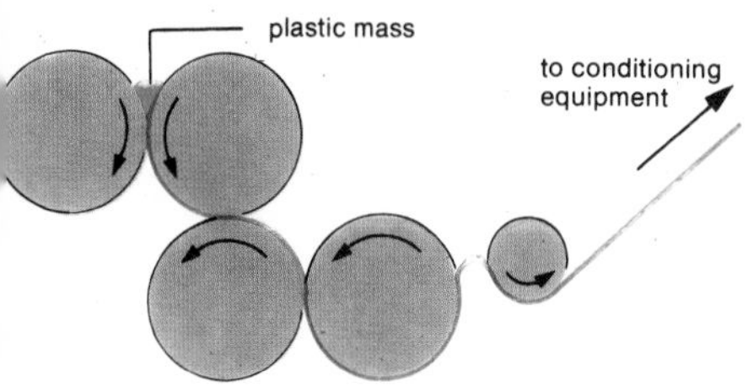

Condensation polymerization

Condensation polymerization is a more complex process than direct polymerization, and it is the method by which many important synthetic polymers are made. The reaction involves the combining of two substances which each contain more than one reactive *functional group*. A molecule of one of the substances reacts with a molecule of the other to form a larger molecule, and in the reaction a smaller molecule such as water, containing atoms from each of the parent molecules, is eliminated.

Each of the parent molecules uses one of its functional groups to carry out the reaction; the other remains intact and ready to react with another molecule. This means that another pair of parent molecules can react with the new molecule in the same way to produce an even larger molecule, and the process can continue in this manner and build up long polymer chains.

One of the commonest polymers produced in this way is the polyester *polyethylene glycol terephthalate*, which is used in the manufacture of synthetic fibres such as Terylene or Dacron. It is made by reacting terephthalic acid, which has a pair of reactive carboxyl (—COOH) groups attached to a benzene ring, with ethylene glycol, which has two reactive hydroxyl (—OH) groups, one at each end of its molecule.

When these two molecules react they give off a molecule of water and form a large molecule which has a carboxyl group at one end and a hydroxyl group at the other. These groups can then react with another molecule of ethylene glycol and terephthalic acid respectively, producing an even bigger molecule with similarly reactive ends which continue the process so that a long chain is built up.

Another important group of polymers produced by condensation polymerization are the polyamides (nylons). Whereas the polyesters are made by reacting an acid with a glycol, the polyamides are made by reacting an acid with an amine. The first nylon to be produced was the type known as nylon 6,6, which is so named because both the acid and the amine involved (adipic acid and hexamethylene diamine) contain six carbon atoms.

Another form of nylon, called nylon 6, is made by reacting molecules of caprolactam with each other, each of these molecules having an amine group at one end and an acid group at the other.

The formaldehyde-based resins, such as

ICI

Vickers

phenol-formaldehyde (Bakelite), urea-formaldehyde and melamine-formalidehyde, are also formed by condensation.

Rearrangement polymerization

The third important polymerization process, used chiefly for the production of polyurethane, also involves the reaction of monomers containing two or more reactive functional groups. Unlike condensation polymerization, however, it does not involve the elimination of by-product molecules of low molecular weight. During the reactions between the monomers there is a rearrangement of the atoms present and of the bonds between the molecules.

Polyurethane plastics are made by reacting a monomer containing two or more reactive isocyanate (—NCO) groups with one containing two or more reactive hydroxyl (—OH) groups. One of the isocyanate groups reacts with one of the hydroxyl groups to form a link between the two monomers, leaving the other isocyanate and hydroxyl groups free to react with other molecules to form a chain.

Plastics

Synthetic polymers can be divided broadly into three classes, namely *thermoplastic* polymers, *thermosetting* polymers, and *elastomers* such as synthetic rubbers. Thermoplastic polymers are so called because each time they are heated they become soft, and harden again when they cool. This is because the individual polymer chains are able to move relative to one another, and this ability increases as the temperature rises.

When a thermosetting polymer is heated for the first time, it softens and can be moulded but cross-linking occurs between its chains. These cross-links hold the chains permanently in place, and so any subsequent heating which takes place after the polymer has cooled will not soften it. Unlike the thermoplastics, which can be repeatedly heated and softened and then cooled again, once a thermosetting polymer has been heated and then cooled it cannot be reshaped by heating.

Above: Acrylic plastics such as the Perspex used for these yacht hatches are made from polymethyl methacrylate.

Above right: The second of the world's first glass reinforced plastic submersibles, pictured during testing in the North Sea. This one can operate at depths of about 460 m (1,500 ft), and is designed for operation in the North Sea oil fields.

Below: The performance of radar equipment in World War II was improved by the use of Teflon (ptfe) wiring insulation, whose excellent insulating and thermal properties enabled the wiring to carry heavier currents than were possible when other insulants were used. The ptfe chain consists of a string of tens of thousands of carbon atoms, each of which has two fluorine atoms attached to it.

Du Pont

The molecules of the elastomers are randomly coiled and behave rather like springs, straightening out when they are stretched and coiling up again when released. Relative movement of the chains is restricted by cross-linking, the cross-links being introduced during the *curing* or *vulcanization* process. The greater the amount of cross-linking produced, the harder and less flexible the rubber becomes.

The thermoplastics include polyolefins (polymers made from olefins, hydrocarbons of the ethylene series) such as polyethylene and polypropylene; polyvinyl chloride, polystyrene, polyvinyl acetate, cellulose acetate, polytetrafluoroethylene (ptfe) and the polyamides. Important thermosetting polymers include the formaldehyde condensates such as urea formaldehyde and phenol formaldehyde, and the epoxy resins. Polyesters are produced in both thermoplastic and thermosetting forms.

There are many basic types of synthetic rubbers, and a large number of versions of each of these types. The most important is styrene-butadiene rubber, a copolymer of styrene and butadiene, which is produced in over 500 different grades.

A polarised light micrograph of fibricated *polypropylene* cord. *Polypropylene* is manufactured by *precipitation* polymerization, one of the *direct* forms of the process.

Paul Brierley

Textiles

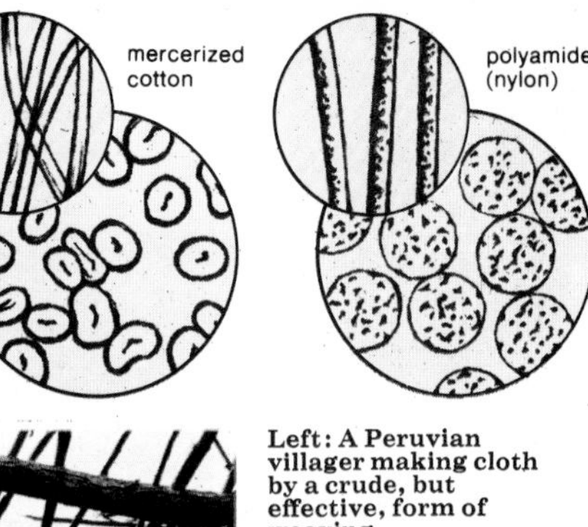

The perishable nature of fabrics has made it difficult for archaeologists to determine exactly when and where the making of textiles originated. However, artifacts which were probably used for spinning thread have been found on several Neolithic (New Stone Age) sites, indicating that the practice of spinning, and thus by implication weaving, dates back at least to this period.

Pieces of woven woollen cloth have been found at Bronze Age sites in northern Europe, and samples of linen dating from around 5000 BC have been discovered in Egypt. Cotton has also been used for textiles for a considerable time; cotton cloth was being produced in India at least 5,000 years ago.

Although the majority of the world's textiles are still made from natural fibres such as cotton or wool, man-made fibres are taking an increasingly large share of the market. The first man-made fibres, based on natural cellulose, were introduced at the end of the nineteenth century. Other man-made fibres, made from synthetic polymers (for example nylons, polyesters, acrylics and acetates), were introduced more recently but now account for the bulk of man-made fibres.

Natural fibres

Natural fibres can be divided into two main groups, animal fibres and vegetable fibres, all of which are composed of

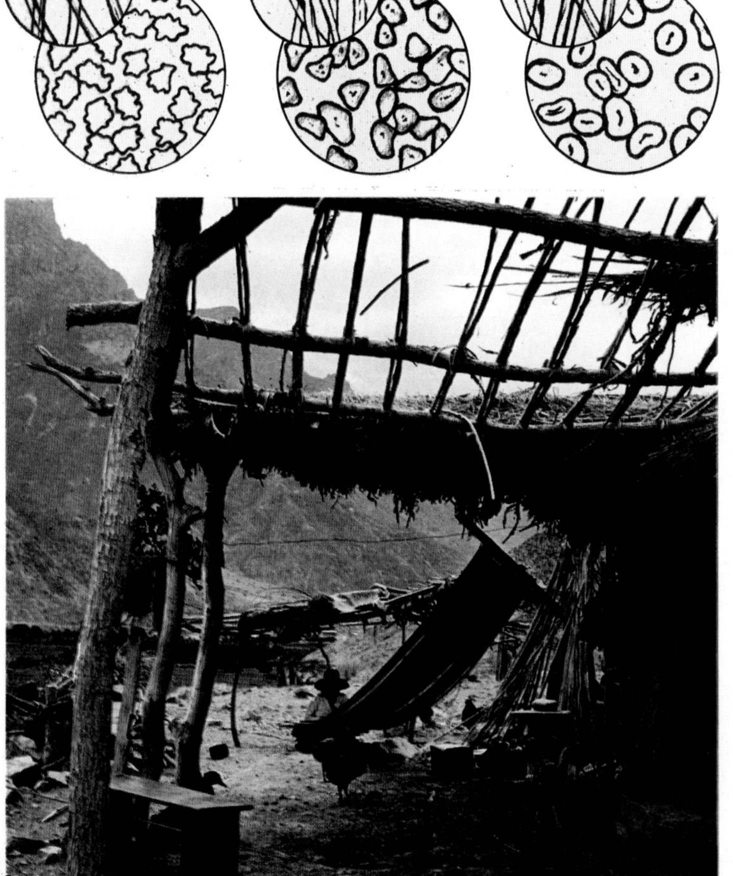
Picturepoint

Left: A Peruvian villager making cloth by a crude, but effective, form of weaving.

Right: A crofter on the Isle of Lewis, off the coast of north-west Scotland, weaving Harris tweed on a hand loom. Harris tweed is one of the most famous types of tweed cloth, and the word 'tweed' is a corruption of 'tweel', the old Scottish word for 'twill'. As the name implies, these fabrics are based on the twill weave. There are many different tweeds, woven from wool and varying in weight, quality, weave and colour pattern, and they are often named after the area in which they originated. Apart from Harris, other well-known varieties include Scottish, Irish, Saxony, Cheviot, Yorkshire and West of England tweeds. Tweed is a very versatile material, its wide range of textures, patterns and weights enabling it to be used for coats, jackets, trousers, skirts and hats. The heavier versions are especially strong and hard-wearing.

Below: *Bicomponent* fibres are made by combining two separate polymers. The two components may be arranged side-by-side in the fibre, as in the one shown here, or one may surround the other like a sheath. In a third type, fibrils of one component are distributed throughout the other.

Right: In a simple loom, the *warp* threads are separated into two groups by the *heddle*, which pulls one group upwards and the other downwards. The *weft*, carried by the *shuttle*, is fed through the gap between the two groups of warp threads, and pushed tightly into the weave by the *reed*. The positions of the warp threads are then reversed by operation of a pair of treadles, and the shuttle is passed back through them again.

Below: Six different types of fabric weave. The different weaves are characterized by the ways in which the weft threads are interlaced with the warps.

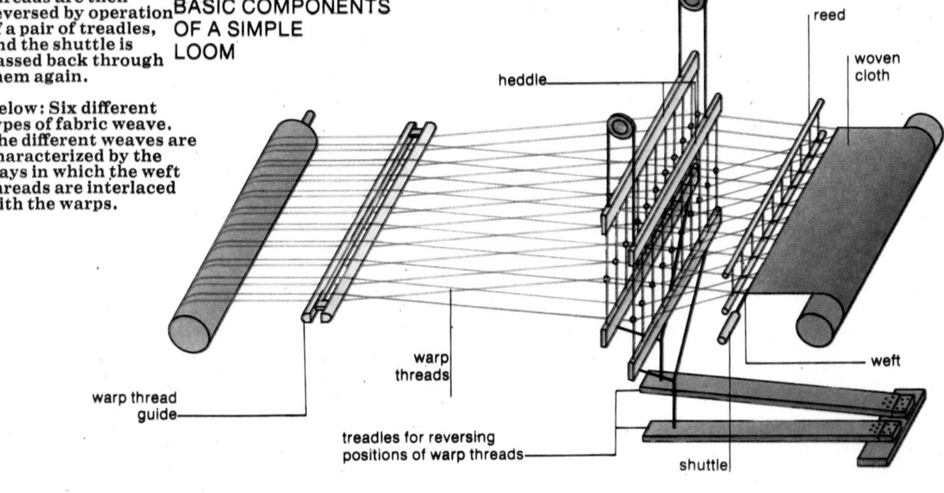

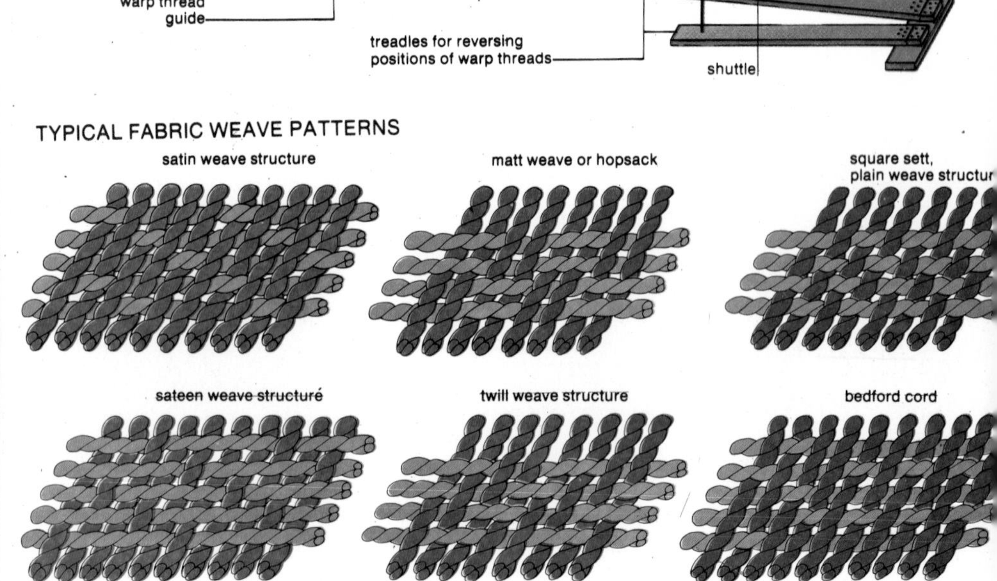

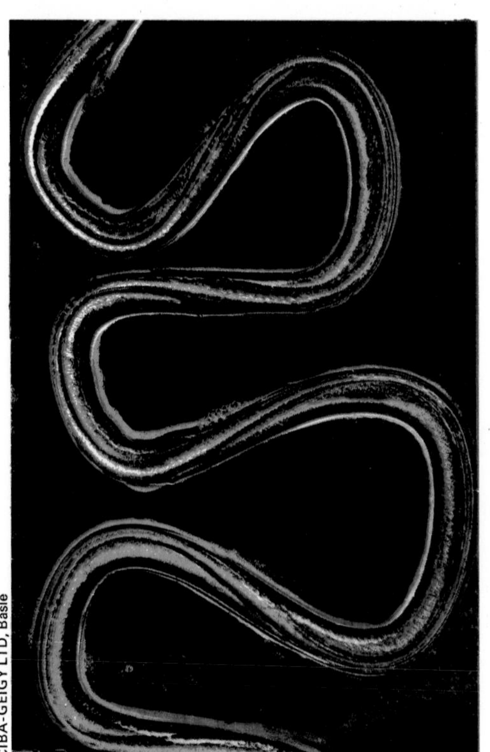
CIBA-GEIGY LTD, Basle

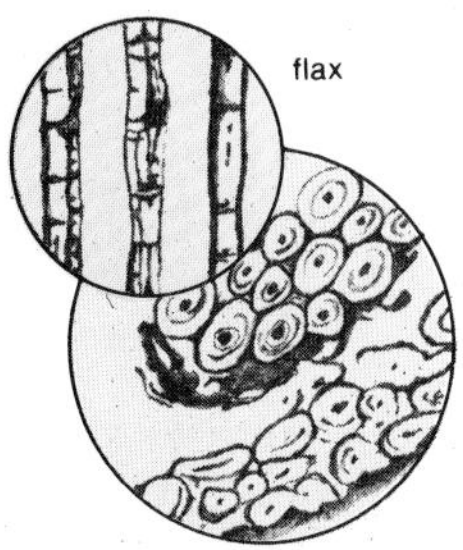

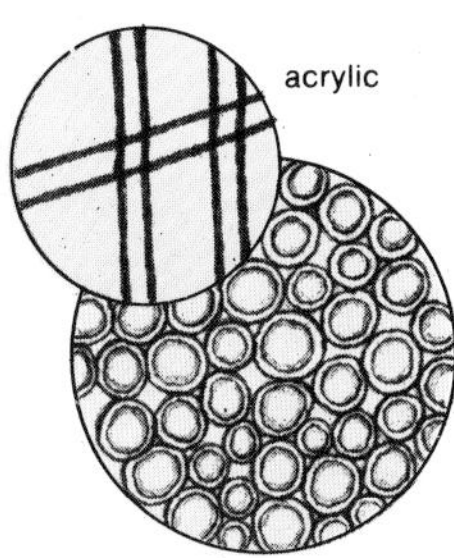

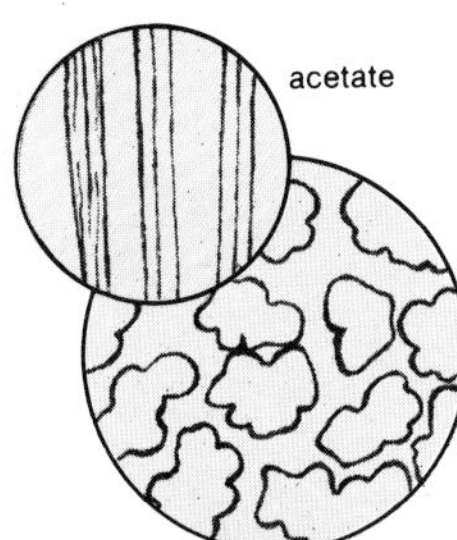

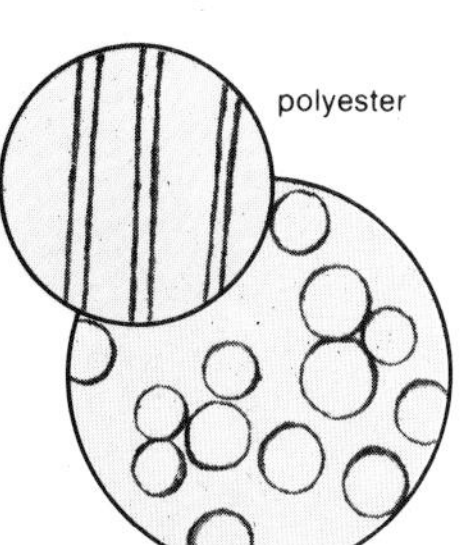

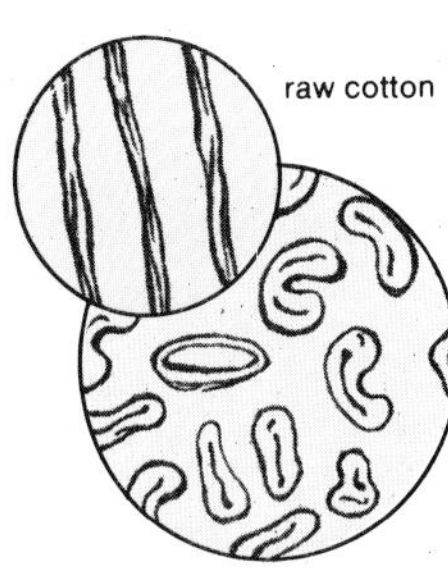

Left: The appearance of different types of fibres and their cross-sections when viewed under a microscope. The difference between cotton, which consists of tube-like cellulose cells, and flax, which is thicker and stiffer because the cells are bound together with lignin, can clearly be seen in these pictures.

Below: Rolls of yarn (spun thread) on a loom used for making plain and striped towelling material. These yarns form the warp threads of the loom, the coloured stripes being produced by coloured threads. The upper beam of this loom holds one tonne of yarn, which is sufficient for four weeks' weaving.

Spectrum

Above right: The first successful man-made fibres were the rayons, artificial silks made from regenerated natural cellulose obtained from cotton or wood pulp. Cellulose acetate and cellulose triacetate are two other important man-made textile fibres derived from natural cellulose.

Radio Times Hulton Picture Library

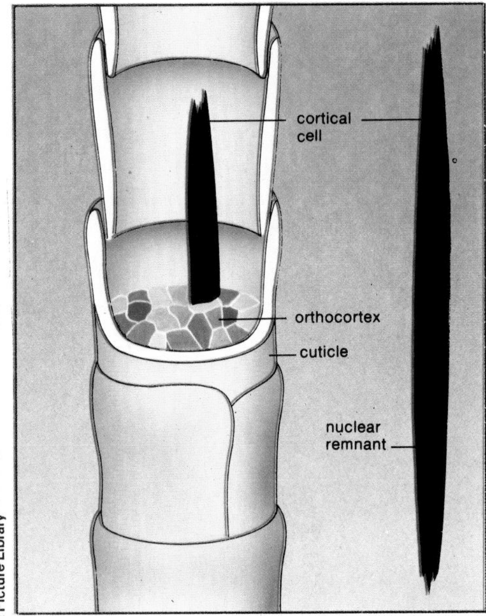

Above: The structure of a single fibre of wool. The spindle-shaped cortical cells, (the orthocortex), and the outer layer of overlapping scales (the cuticle) are composed primarily of keratin. Keratin is one of the proteins, which are formed by biological polymerization of amino acids.

Courtaulds

natural polymers. The principal animal fibre is sheep's wool, which consists of a substance called *keratin*. Keratin is one of the many types of protein, complex natural *polyamides*. Each wool fibre consists of a central core or *cortex* of spindle-shaped cells, which is covered by an outer layer of thin, overlapping scales called the *cuticle*.

Other animal fibres have a similar structure, and those used for textiles include mohair (from the Angora goat), cashmere (from the cashmere goat), common goat hair, and hair from camels, llamas, horses and rabbits.

Silk is obtained from the cocoons spun by the larvae of the moth *Bombyx mori*. The larva or *silkworm* extrudes a liquid protein known as *fibroinogen*, which denatures and hardens on exposure to the air to become *fibroin*. The worm produces a continuous filament of this fibroin several kilometres in length, and winds it around itself to form the cocoon in which it can metamorphose into an adult moth. In silk production the cocoon is unwound before the moth has been able to emerge from it, as this would split the cocoon and break the continuity of the thread.

The vegetable fibres consist of various forms of *cellulose*. The most important of these is cotton, each cotton fibre being a single, long, tube-like cell whose walls are made of cellulose. The fibres are produced by the seed pods of the cotton plant, each pod producing clusters or *bolls* of thousands of cotton fibres.

Linen, another important fibre used in clothing textiles, is obtained from the stems of flax plants. Fibres made from the stems of other *dicotyledonous* plants such as jute and hemp have many important uses, for instance for making sacking and rope. The fibres made from plant stems consist of bundles of overlapping cellulose cells bound together by *lignin*, and they are thicker and stiffer than cotton.

The fibres made from the leaves and stems of *monocotyledonous* plants, such as sisal and abaca (Manila), have a similar structure, and have many important industrial uses.

Man-made fibres

The first man-made fibres were artificial silks, later named *rayons*, made from regenerated cellulose. The two main processes by which rayon is made, the *cuprammonium* and the *viscose* processes, were developed in the late nineteenth century. Both processes involve the treatment of a natural cellulose source such as wood pulp with chemicals that dissolve the cellulose out of it.

In the cuprammonium process the cellulose is dissolved in cuprammonium hydroxide, and in the more important viscose process it is treated with caustic soda and carbon disulphide to form a solution of sodium cellulose xanthate in caustic soda.

In both methods, the cellulose solution is further treated so that the cellulose precipitates out of solution in a pure and usable form.

Two other important man-made fibres are made from wood pulp cellulose, namely *cellulose acetate* and *cellulose triacetate*. Cellulose triacetate is made by reacting cellulose with acetic acid in the presence of sulphuric acid, which acts as a catalyst. Cellulose acetate is made by diluting triacetate solution with water and allowing it to stand, so that some of

Radio Times Hulton Picture Library

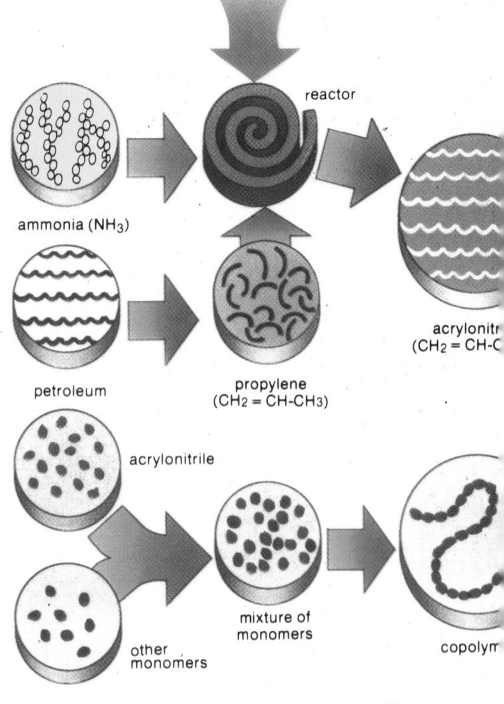

Left: In conditions such as those encountered in the Malaysian jungle, natural materials may deteriorate much sooner than synthetics. For example, the leather of a boot might rot away, but nylon laces are rot-proof.

Right: Acrylic fibres are made by the copolymerization of acrylonitrile with various other monomers. After polymerization, a solution of the material is extruded through a spinneret into a coagulating bath which precipitates the polymer from the solution, so that the acrylic material solidifies and can be drawn into filaments. These filaments are then made into fibre.

Below: The circular knitting head of a machine making tights from nylon 6, a polyamide produced by the polymerization of caprolactam.

Courtaulds

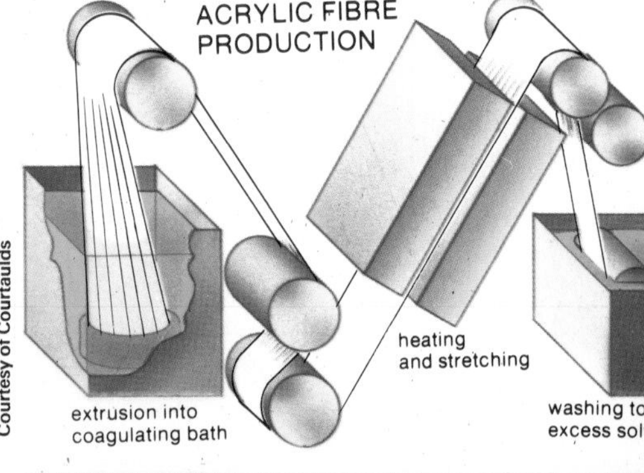

Courtesy of Courtaulds

ICI Plastics/Belfast Ropework Co

the acetyl (CH_3CO—) groups of the triacetate molecules are replaced by hydroxyl (—OH) groups.

Fibres are produced by dissolving the cellulose acetate in acetone, and the cellulose triacetate in methylene chloride. In each case the thick solution obtained is extruded into a stream of hot air, so that the solvent evaporates and the fibres form and harden.

The numerous types of *nylon*, such as nylon 6 and nylon 6,6, are synthetic polyamides, simpler versions of proteins, the natural polyamides. The numbers used to identify the different types of nylon indicate the numbers of carbon atoms in the compounds which are polymerized to make them.

Nylon fibres are produced by *melt spinning*, melting small pieces or 'chips' of the polymer, and extruding the resulting liquid through a nozzle called a *spinneret*. The long filaments of nylon emerging from the spinneret cool and solidify and are then stretched and spun into yarn.

In terms of annual production, the largest group of synthetic fibres are the *polyesters*, fibres made from polyethylene glycol terephthalate. The fibres are produced in a similar way to those of nylon; the polymer is cut into chips, melted, and then extruded through a spinneret.

Acrylic fibres, based on polyacrylonitrile, are widely used for making clothing and many other types of textile including carpets and imitation furs. *Modacrylics*, copolymers of acrylonitrile with vinyl chloride, vinylidene chloride or vinylidene dinitrile, are similar to acrylics in most respects, but many of them have the additional advantage of being flame-resistant.

Fabrics

The three principal types of fabric are *knitted*, *woven* and *non-woven* (or 'fibre'). The production of knitted or woven fabrics requires the fibres to be first spun into threads, which are then interlaced to form the fabric. Spinning basically involves the drawing out of a mass of unspun fibres into a continuous, loosely-joined length, which is then twisted to make the fibres bind together and form a strong thread.

Woven fabrics are produced on machines called *looms*. The basic design of the loom was evolved at least 6,500 years ago, and the looms used today for the mass-production of woven textiles work on essentially the same basic principles as

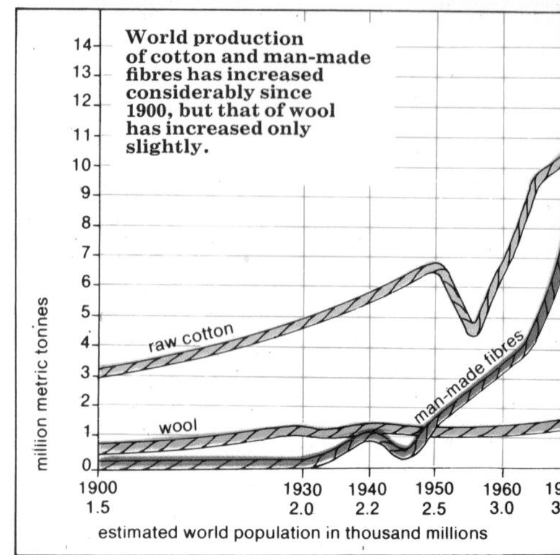

World production of cotton and man-made fibres has increased considerably since 1900, but that of wool has increased only slightly.

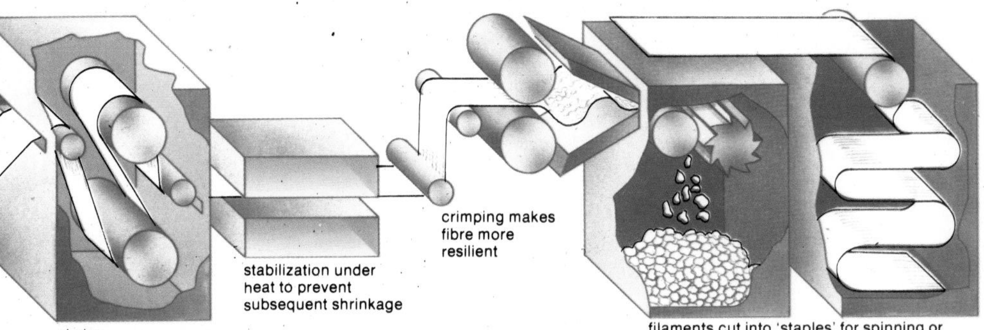

Left: Making rope from extruded and spun polypropylene fibre. Synthetic fibres made from polypropylene, polyester, polyethylene and polyamide are increasingly replacing natural fibres in the production of ropes, twines and cords. Natural rope and twine fibres include flax, jute, sisal and Manila.

Below: The workers making and packing these nylon knickers wear dark glasses to protect their eyes from the glare of the brilliant colours. Nylon (polyamide), discovered in 1935, was first used commercially (for toothbrush bristles) in 1938, and nylon stockings were introduced in 1939.

Top: Some of the 130 circular knitting machines used for producing double jersey cloth at a modern textile factory. Circular machines knitting single jersey use one set of vertical needles, arranged in a circle; double jersey knitting requires two sets of needles. The circular machines produce a tube of fabric, which is then slit lengthwise to form a sheet that is wound into a roll. The fabric is subsequently cut and stitched to make garments. The knitting of jersey fabrics is one of the main uses of circular knitting machines, and they can produce a variety of stitches.

the simple, hand-operated machines which differ little from the early designs.

In the simplest forms of woven fabric, a series of threads running from front to back in the loom (the *warp*) are interlaced by threads running from side to side across the loom (the *weft*). The warp threads are held in tension in the loom, and divided into two; alternate threads are pulled upwards, the rest being pulled downwards.

The weft thread is passed across the loom between these two sets of threads, and pushed tightly into the point of the horizontal 'V' formed at the front of the loom by the diverging threads. The positions of the two sets of warp threads is then reversed, so that the weft thread is locked into them. The weft is then passed back through the warp threads and the process is repeated over and over again to build up a length of woven cloth.

The way in which the warp and weft threads are interlaced can be varied to an almost unlimited extent, and so an enormous range of different fabric textures can be produced. Coloured design effects are produced by introducing different coloured threads or groups of threads into the warp and the weft.

Knitted fabrics are made by forming interlocking loops in a thread or threads. This can be done by hand, using pointed needles to form and hold the loops, but knitted fabrics are produced commercially on machines which use sets of hooked needles. These machines vary in size and speed of operation, and in the types of fabric that they can produce. *Circular* knitting machines, in which the needles are arranged in a circle, are used for making rolls of such fabrics as single or double jersey.

Flat knitting machines use a similar knitting action to the circular types, but the needles are arranged in an inverted 'V'. These machines can produce a wide range of fabrics, and can knit garment sections to shape so that subsequent cutting is not needed. In *warp* knitting machines, parallel threads are looped together to form the cloth, and such machines may have as many as 2,500 needles and form over 1,200 rows of stitches, a total of over three million loops, per minute.

Non-woven fabrics are formed from a sheet of fibres, often called a *batt* or *web*, the fibres being consolidated into a fabric by mechanical or chemical processes or by a combination of both. In the production of *felts*, for example, use is made of the ability of certain types of fibre to *mat* together under the action of moisture, heat and pressure.

Wool is a good example of a fibre of this type, its ability to felt being largely due to the rough, scaly nature of the cuticle of each fibre which helps the fibres to cling together. Other fibres used in felt production include cotton, jute, fur, hair, asbestos (a fibre of mineral origin), rayon, nylon and glass fibres.

Non-woven fabrics are also produced by binding a web of fibres together with stitching, or by laying one set of fibres across another and binding them together with a third set which is pushed into them.

Fabric printing

Two of the earliest methods of printing a coloured design on to a fabric were by means of a stencil or by a block cut to the shape of the design. These manual methods are still employed in many areas, but the bulk of textile printing is now mechanized.

The principal method uses engraved rollers to apply the dye to the cloth, the dye being carried in the engraved recesses of the roller. Another important method, still carried out manually in some cases, is *screen printing*. This process uses a stencil formed from a strong, fine-mesh material carried on a rectangular frame. The screen is placed on top of the cloth, and the colour is forced through the open parts of the design by a squeegee.

The screen material is usually made of nylon, polyester or metal, but it was formerly made of silk and for this reason the process is often referred to as *silk screen printing*. Some machines use cylindrical screens, the screens being in effect hollow rollers with fine mesh surfaces through which the colour is forced by internal squeegees.

The newest method of textile printing uses paper transfers, on which the design is printed with a dye that vaporizes when heated to about 200°C (390°F). The cloth and the transfer are brought together in a hot press, so that the dye vaporizes and transfers to the cloth.

Glass

Glass is one of the oldest of man-made materials. Although the actual date of its introduction is not known, there is evidence that it existed some 5,000 years ago in the eastern Mediterranean region. It is also known that it was used by prehistoric man in its natural form of *obsidian* (which is of volcanic origin) for making arrow heads and various other implements.

There is a very plausible (but fictitious) story describing its accidental discovery. Pliny, the Roman historian of the first century AD, describes how Phoenician merchants transporting a cargo of *natron* (crude soda) stopped overnight on a beach. Being unable to find suitable stones for supporting their cooking utensils, they used blocks from their cargo for this purpose. The heat of the fire melted the soda which then combined with the beach sand to form glass.

This story of an accidental discovery, though not based on fact, fits in well with the basic composition of glass, which consists of *silica* (sand), *sodium oxide* (derived from sodium carbonate) and *calcium oxide* (derived from calcium carbonate or limestone). In Pliny's story the three essential constituents were present. The beach sand would contain shell particles made of calcium carbonate and the soda was, allegedly, provided by the natron blocks. Glass of only very poor quality could have been produced, as the temperature available from a camp

Mansell Collection

Left: The Portland Vase, now in the British Museum, was made by Roman craftsmen in the first century BC or AD. It was made by a technique developed by the Alexandrian Greeks: a vase of blown blue glass was dipped into white, opaque glass which formed a coating on it. The coating was then cut away to leave the design in relief.

Right: An ornament made of Egyptian *faience*. This material was made by heating a mixture of silica sand and an alkali, such as soda or potash, to a temperature high enough to make the sand grains fuse and form a glassy surface film. Glass was probably discovered as a result of overheating the mixture.

Below: The stained glass south rose window of Notre Dame cathedral in Chartres, France. Glasses are coloured or 'stained' by the inclusion of various metal oxides or other compounds during manufacture. For example, compounds of iron give a green tint, while those of cobalt give the glass a blue colour.

Michael Holford

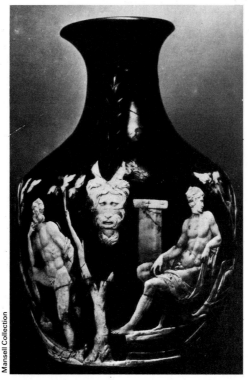

Below: A Neolithic arrowhead, made of natural glass, found in Algeria. Natural glasses, impure forms of fused silica (silicon dioxide, SiO_2), occur in areas where molten rock has cooled rapidly, for example near volcanoes. Ancient natural glass artifacts have been found all over the world.

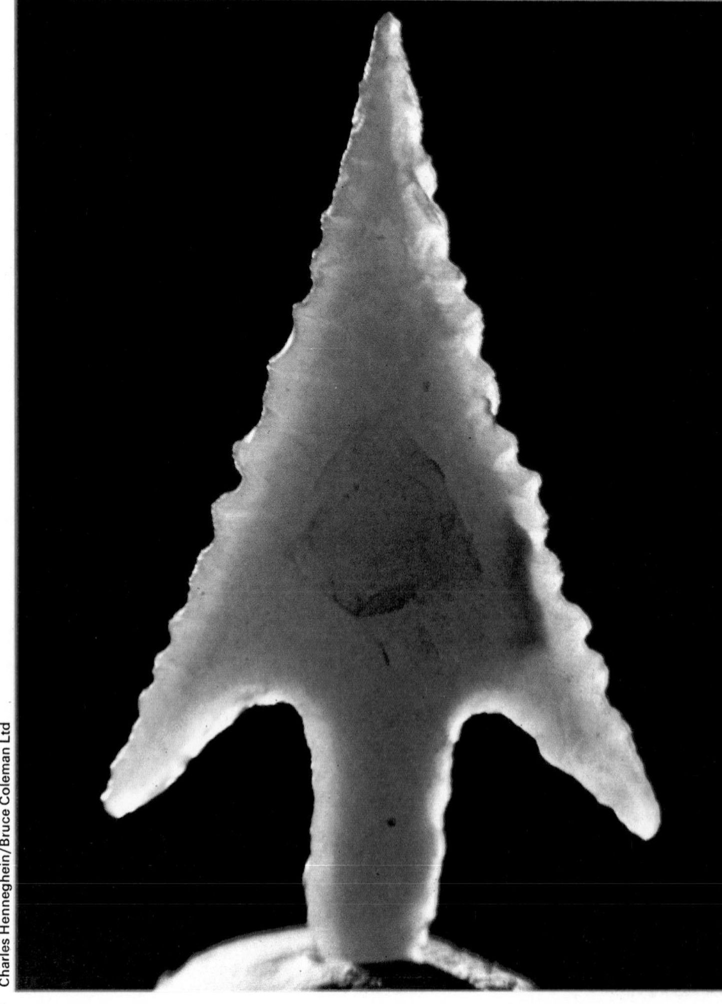

Charles Henneghein/Bruce Coleman Ltd

Toni Schneiders/Bruce Coleman Ltd

Below: The production of glass yarn, which is woven into glass fabrics used for making such items as curtains, laminates, insulating tapes and protective clothing. Boro-silicate glass is formed into marbles, which are subsequently remelted in an electric furnace. The molten glass passes through small holes in the bottom of the furnace, emerging as filaments which are coated with a lubricating binder that protects them from abrasion.

Right: The roof of St Pancras railway station, London, was one of the first to be constructed of glass panels—in 1868-74.

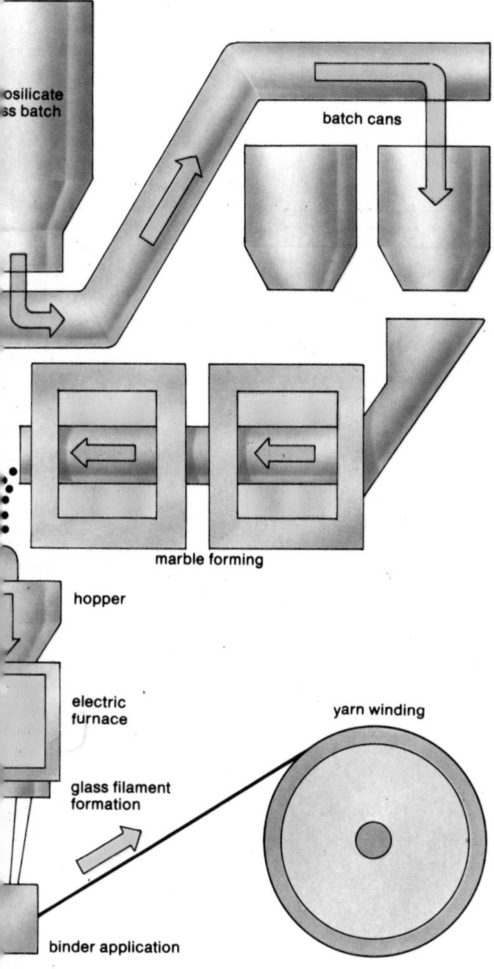

fire would produce a low melting point glass of high soda content which would be very different from the glass known today.

It is known that glass was melted in furnaces some 3,500 years ago in Egypt and that small vessels were made from it. These were made by winding threads of coloured glass around a sand core or by dipping the core in molten glass. The sand core was then scooped out and the result was a transparent bottle or vase of many colours.

At some unspecified date, believed to be about 100 BC, glass making was revolutionized by the invention of the *blowpipe*. The iron rod, which was previously used for dipping the core into the molten glass or for producing glass threads was replaced by a pipe at the end of which molten glass could be *gathered* from a pot and then blown into almost any shape. Glass blowing by mouth or by more sophisticated mechanical methods has been practised ever since.

Glass is a *supercooled* liquid, formed by the fusion of inorganic materials such as the oxides of silicon, calcium and sodium, which has cooled at a fast enough rate to prevent crystallization. If it were allowed to cool down slowly from its molten state, crystals would be formed and its transparency would be lost. It has no definite melting point, but there is a temperature at which flow begins to take place and this is known as the *softening point*.

In the developed countries the largest use of glass is for containers. In the UK, for example, 1.825 million tonnes of container glass were melted in 1975, representing some 66 per cent of the total UK production for that year. Flat glass accounted for 19.5 per cent, domestic glassware for 4 per cent, and glass fibre for 3.2 per cent. UK sales of glass containers in 1976 amounted to 6,546 million units, some 120 containers per head of population.

Glass containers

The average composition of container glass (which is a *soda-lime-silica* glass) is 72.3 per cent silica (SiO_2), 14.8 per cent sodium oxide (Na_2O), 10.2 per cent calcium oxide (CaO), 1.8 per cent alumina (Al_2O_3), 0.5 per cent magnesia (MgO), and 0.4 per cent minor constituents. This is obtained from the following proportions of raw materials: 50 per cent sand, 16 per cent soda ash (sodium carbonate), 12 per cent limestone (calcium carbonate), 4 per cent other materials, and 18 per cent *cullet* (crushed scrap glass).

The raw materials used must be of a very high purity. For example, the presence of small amounts of iron or chromium oxides can give the finished glass a pronounced green tint. The basic raw materials are comparatively plentiful and cheap; sand and limestone are widely distributed, and the sodium carbonate is made by reacting common salt (sodium chloride, NaCl) with carbon dioxide (CO_2). Cullet is obtained from factory rejects, or from discarded bottles and jars.

The raw materials are accurately weighed, mixed thoroughly, and then fed into a large furnace. The glass is melted in a tank, lined with refractory bricks, which can hold several hundred tonnes. The raw materials are known collectively as the *batch*.

The furnace is heated by firing fuel oil or gas across the top of the glass. This is a very inefficient way of heating, but

Royal Doulton

Royal Doulton

MAKING A GLASS JUG BY HAND

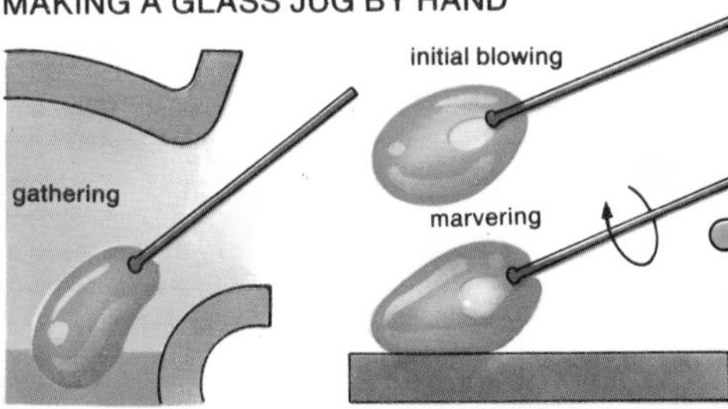

Courtesy Glass Manufacturers' Federation

Far left: Gathering molten glass on the end of a blowing iron.

Left: Blowing a gather of glass into a hollow shape which can then be modelled into, for example, a jug or vase.

Above: Making a glass jug. After initial blowing, the glass is *marvered* (rolled on a slab), blown again and shaped. A *pontil* (rod), by which the glass is held when the blowing iron has been removed, is attached to the base, and the jug is cut and shaped. The handle is fitted, and then the pontil is removed and the jug is annealed to relieve any internal stresses.

Right: Stages in the making of a glass.

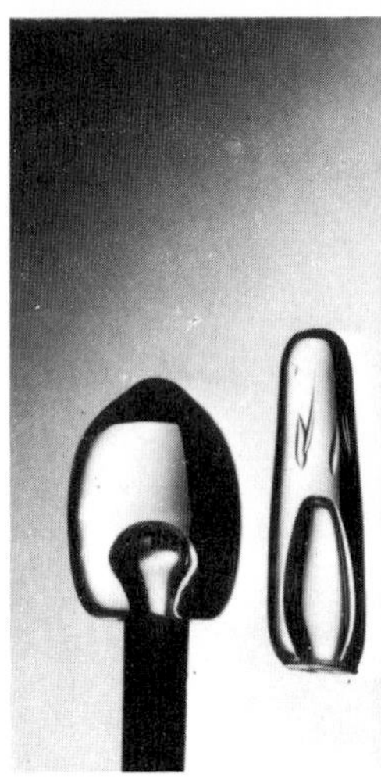

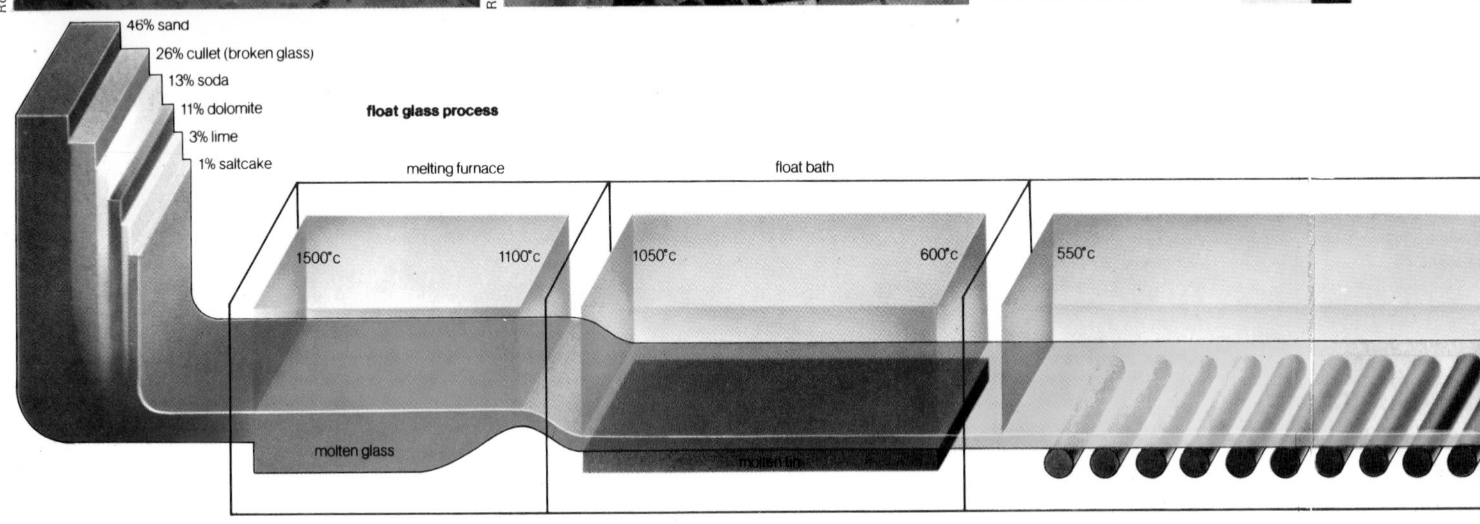

unfortunately there are no refractory materials which could be heated like a kettle to give a temperature of 1,500°C (2,730°F) to the melt. Recently, however, a method of melting glass by electricity has been developed. In its solid form glass is a very good electrical insulator, but in its molten form it becomes a conductor. By passing a current through the molten glass heat is created inside the melt, thus allowing raw materials to be melted.

By this method the heat is applied exactly where it is wanted; unfortunately, however, electrical energy is too expensive to make all-electric melting a commercial proposition. Electricity is therefore used for boosting the output of a furnace which is already fired by oil or gas. Such a temperature is obtained by a process of recovering and re-using waste heat. The two methods used are *regeneration* and *recuperation*.

In the regeneration method, the outgoing waste gases heat a honeycomb of brickwork for 20 minutes as they leave the combustion zone, and then the direction of firing is reversed and the combustion air is pre-heated by extracting the heat previously deposited in the brickwork by the outgoing waste gas. In a furnace using the recuperation method, the outgoing waste gases heat the tubes which carry the combustion air into the furnace, thus pre-heating the air.

When the batch of raw materials is melted, it is further refined by passing from the main tank by means of a narrow channel at the base of the end wall into a *conditioning bath*. From the conditioning bath the glass is conveyed along long channels, called *feeders*, to a feeding mechanism. This extrudes *gobs* of molten glass which fall into a bottle-forming mould on a machine. The gobs must be of the correct shape and weight, and they are made into containers at speeds of about 200 per minute, although much higher speeds can be achieved.

There are three methods of bottle production: the *blow and blow* process, the *press and blow* process, and the *suck and blow* process. In the first process the gob is dropped into a *blank* or *parison* mould, which is the pre-forming mould. A puff of compressed air then blows a bubble into the parison. The parison or *blank glass* is then inverted and transferred to the final mould. The mould closes around the parison, and a blow head comes down and compressed air blows the glass against the sides of the final mould. The bottle is then removed

Below: Production of a glass bottle by the *blow and blow* process. A gob of glass is dropped into the *blank mould*, and pushed down by air pressure so that the neck is formed. Compressed air is blown through the neck so that the glass is blown to the shape of the blank mould, and the blank or *parison* is then *blow moulded*.

Right: High speed automatic machines making glass bottles. The streams of hot glass are cut into gobs, which are automatically placed in the moulds and blown.

BOTTLE PRODUCTION

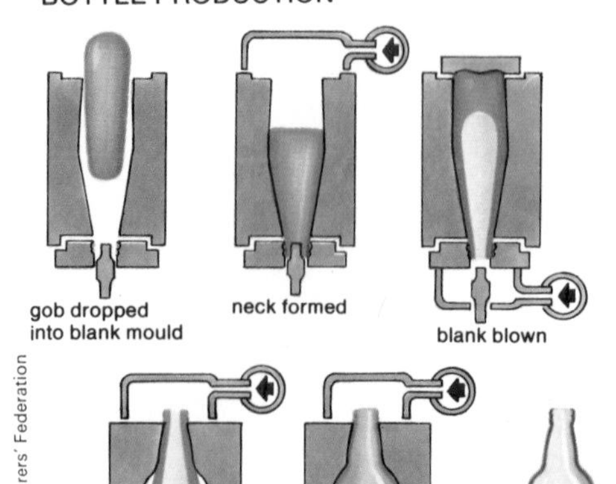

Glass Manufacturers' Federation

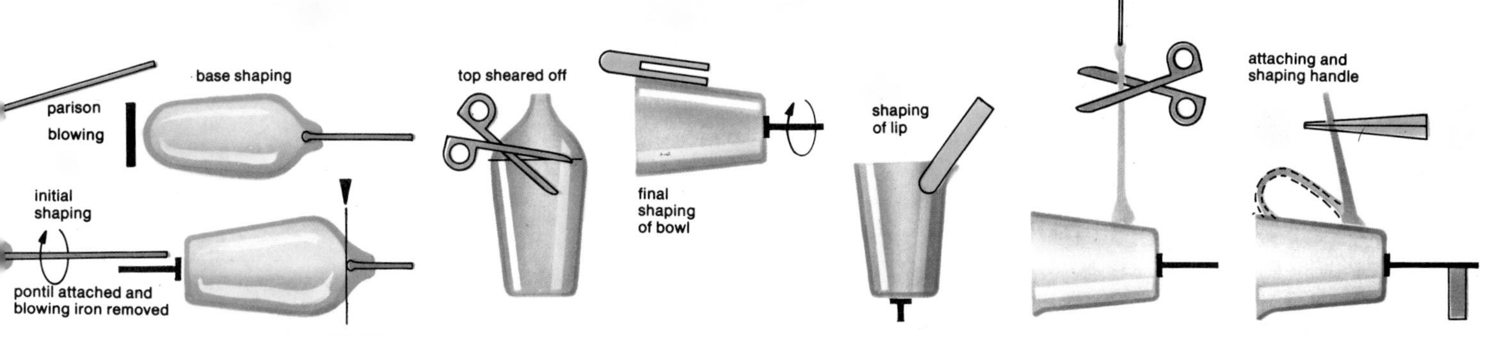

Courtesy Glass Manufacturers' Federation

Right: A sheet of float glass on a conveyor. The float glass process was introduced in 1959, and it produces high quality, distortion-free glass sheet that does not require the grinding and polishing needed by other types of sheet glass. It is now the principal method of making flat glass.

Below: Two methods of making flat glass: the float glass process, and the older sheet glass process in which a metal 'bait' is dipped into molten glass and raised so that it draws a ribbon of glass up between the rollers. A typical float glass plant is about 200 m long, with a melting tank capacity of over 2,000 tonnes.

Glass Manufacturers' Federation

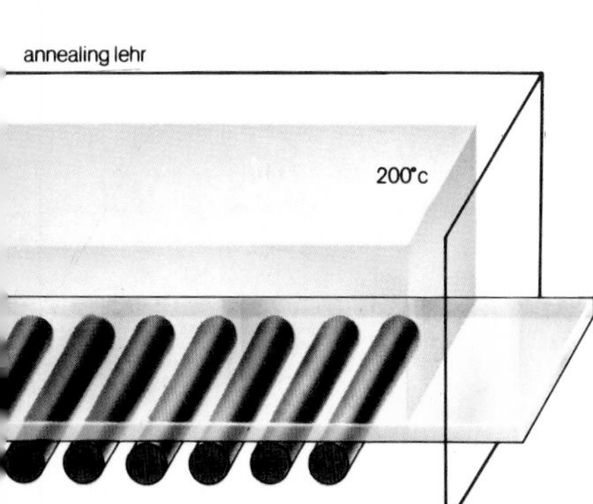

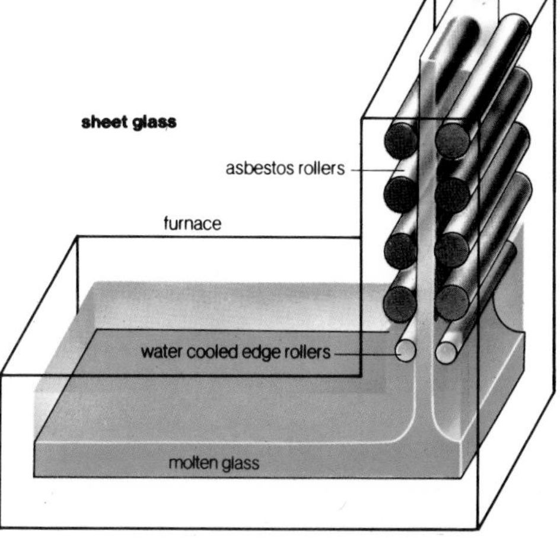

Glass Manufacturers' Federation

from the mould and conveyed into a cooling tunnel known as the *lehr*.

In the second process the parison is pressed instead of being blown, and then transferred to the final mould and blown out in the same way as in the first process. The press and blow process is used mainly for the production of wide mouth jars. In the suck and blow process, the parison is formed by sucking the glass into a parison mould, and the final blowing is done as in the other two methods. This process is not now used extensively.

The lehr is an essential part of any glass production. If glass is allowed to cool in the atmosphere, severe stresses develop within it. These stresses have to be relieved by reheating the glass to a temperature of about 600°C (1,110°F), when flow can take place without physical deformation of the product, and then cooling it slowly to a point where no further flow occurs. The finished bottles or jars are then automatically inspected, packed and despatched.

Flat glass

A typical flat glass, such as window glass, is very similar in composition to the average container glass, but it has a higher (3.5 per cent) magnesia content. The same raw materials as for container glass are used, and they are melted and refined by the same method except that flat glass furnaces tend to be larger than those used for containers.

The earliest example of flat glass goes back to the seventh century AD, when the *crown glass* process was developed by the Syrians. This process utilized the blow pipe. A bubble of glass was blown and then spun rapidly. Centrifugal force did the rest, producing a flat piece of glass with a 'bull's eye' in the centre. Such discs could be as large as 1 m (3 ft) in diameter.

The next stage in the development of flat glass manufacture still relied on mouth blowing. An elongated bubble was blown, which was then cut open along one side and flattened out to give a sheet of glass. Special pits were used to enable

Above: A test rig for simulating head impacts on vehicle windscreens. The screen under test here is made of a type of laminated glass, which has a highly-stressed inner sheet that breaks down into small, blunt granules on impact to minimize facial lacerations and eye injuries.

Below: The production processes for vehicle windscreens. The flat glass blanks for toughened screens are heated and curved to shape, then a double bank of air jets cool the surfaces rapidly. When the inside of the glass cools and contracts it exerts a compressive stress on the already-cooled surfaces. This toughens the glass, and makes it fracture into small, relatively harmless pieces when broken. Laminated glass is made by sandwiching a layer of polyvinyl butyral between two sheets of glass. The *interlayer* holds the glass in place when it is broken, and inhibits the spread of cracks.

Above: Tinted, double-glazed windows reduce solar glare and heat during the summer, and reduce heat loss from the building during winter.

Right: A cat's-eye reflective roadstud has a heavy cast iron base, and a highly resilient rubber insert holding the glass reflectors.

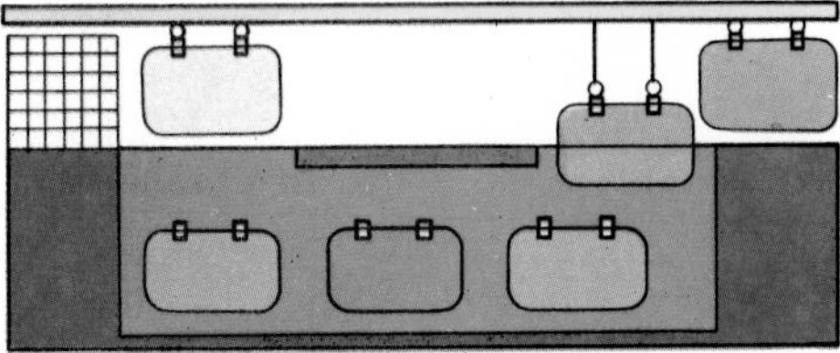

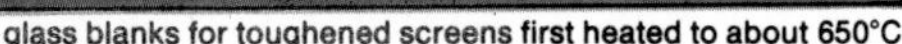

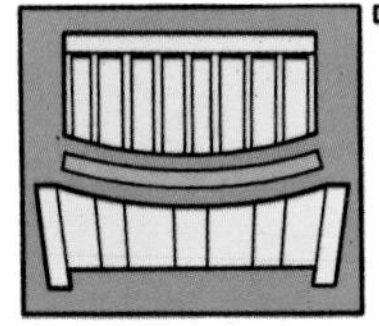

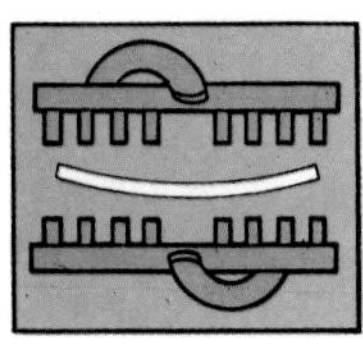

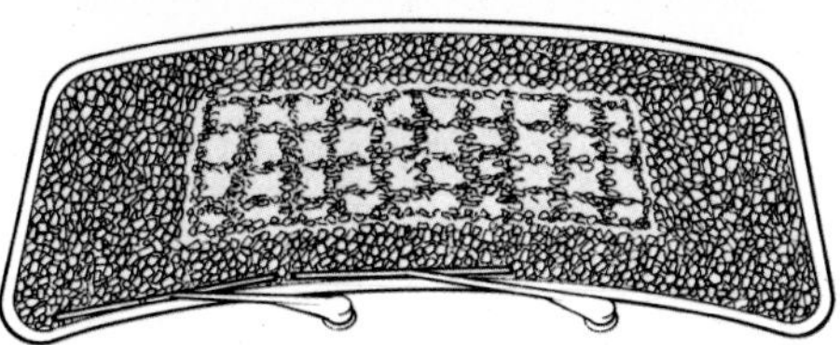

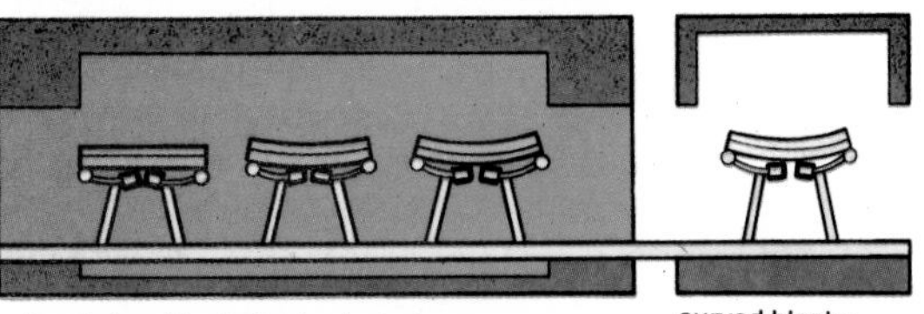

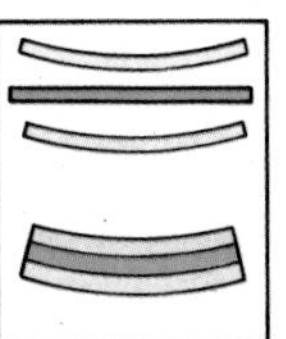

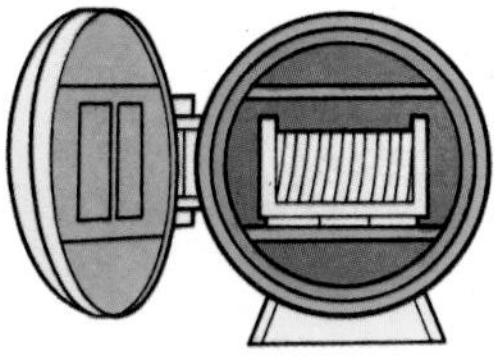

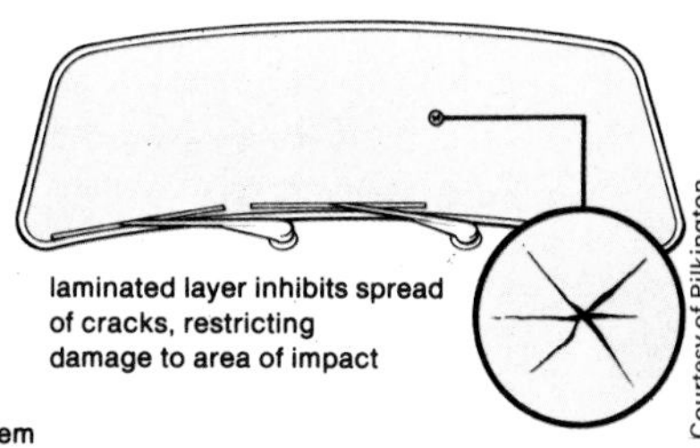

the glass blower to achieve a long bubble.

toughened glass breaks into tiny pieces when fractured

pairs of glass blanks for laminated screens heated to about 600°C so that they curve

curved blanks cooled slowly

screen assemblies heated to 100°C in a vacuum to remove trapped air, then to 150°C under pressure to bond them

laminated layer inhibits spread of cracks, restricting damage to area of impact
Courtesy of Pilkington

In 1903 this method was mechanized, and long, large cylinders were drawn which were then cut into smaller sections, cut open and flattened. It was not until 1913 that flat glass was drawn automatically. This was done by drawing the glass vertically upwards from a bath of molten glass between refractory rollers. Much better quality sheet was being achieved, but since the glass was not ground and polished it still had a wavy surface.

Until the invention of *float glass*, by Pilkington Brothers Ltd in 1959, plate glass was cast in large sheets. It was then ground and polished simultaneously on both sides. Float glass is made by floating a ribbon of molten glass on a bath of molten tin, so that a perfectly flat sheet of glass is formed. The float process was the most significant step forward in flat glass manufacture.

Domestic glassware

Most of the glassware in everyday domestic use, such as jugs and drinking glasses, is made of a glass which is similar in composition to container and window glass. These types of glassware are usually made on high speed, automatic machines.

Lead crystal glass, however, is still hand made by highly qualified craftsmen, and hand cut and polished. It was invented by George Ravenscroft in England in 1675. By the addition of lead oxide and replacement of sodium oxide by potassium oxide, a glass of a much higher refractive index was produced, giving it more brilliance and beauty. The lead content can vary from just a few per cent to over 30 per cent. Lead crystal glass is melted in refractory pots rather than in a tank.

Other glasses

There is an almost infinite variety of *optical glasses*, which are used for lenses, prisms, filters and other optical components. Complicated compositions are used involving varying percentages of oxides of barium, lead, zinc and titanium. The purity of materials needed for optical glass is of utmost importance, and so are the melting techniques required to produce a homogeneous melt.

Large quantities of glass are melted to produce *glass fibres*, which are used mainly for heat insulation. These are produced by extruding very thin threads of molten glass through tiny holes in the base of a platinum alloy crucible. Glass fibres are also used to make glass fibre reinforced plastics, composite materials comprising glass fibres embedded in a matrix of, for example, polyester.

Heat-resistant glass is made by the addition of boric oxide to the melt, to produce what is known as *boro-silicate glass*. A typical boro-silicate glass may contain between 10 and 13 per cent of boric oxide in place of some of the calcium oxide and sodium oxide.

Container (and window) glass is not heat-resistant because its coefficient of expansion is sufficiently high to create a breaking strain on the outer surface when there is a temperature differential between the surfaces. A heat-resistant glass is one which has a greatly reduced coefficient of expansion. The lower the percentage of sodium and calcium oxide the lower the expansion coefficient.

Unfortunately, a low coefficient of expansion is coupled with high melting temperatures, and thus higher production costs are incurred by the extra fuel needed to melt the glass as well as by the use of costly boric oxide. Boro-silicate glasses are more resistant to chemical attack than are other glasses, and are therefore used for chemical plant and special pharmaceutical applications where corrosion resistance is important.

Baccarat glass. The Baccarat factory, France's most important maker of crystal glass, was founded near Luneville in 1764. The making of coloured glass was introduced in the mid 19th century.

Sygma/John Hillelson Agency

Ceramics

The use of clay, from which most ceramics are made, is as old as civilization itself. Its water-resistant qualities, its relative ease of use and its general availability, have made it a useful building material since prehistory, a role that it still fulfils today. Primitive man discovered quickly that, when exposed to the heat of the sun, clay undergoes a dramatic change, becoming solid and brittle.

He also discovered that this natural change could be brought about artificially by the controlled application of fire. Clay is thus in many ways the most natural material available to man, its use being wholly dependent upon the four elements, earth, fire, air and water.

Since prehistory the use of clay has developed in many ways. From the production of sun-dried mud bricks has grown the 'heavy clay' industry, responsible for the production of bricks, tiles, and other building materials, and the malleable quality of the material has given rise to the gradual development of table, ornamental and sanitary wares, the production of which is now a huge industry that has developed directly from the crudely-modelled beakers and urns that were first made in the late Stone Age. The last three hundred years have seen the development of the scientific and industrial applications of ceramics, based on the resistance of the material to high temperature, thermal shock, corrosion and abrasion.

THE STRUCTURE OF KAOLINITE

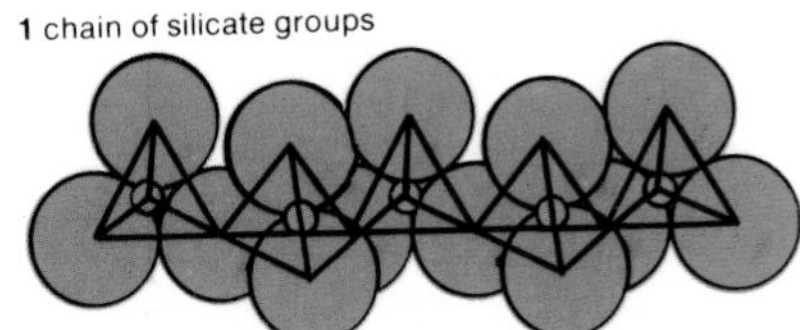

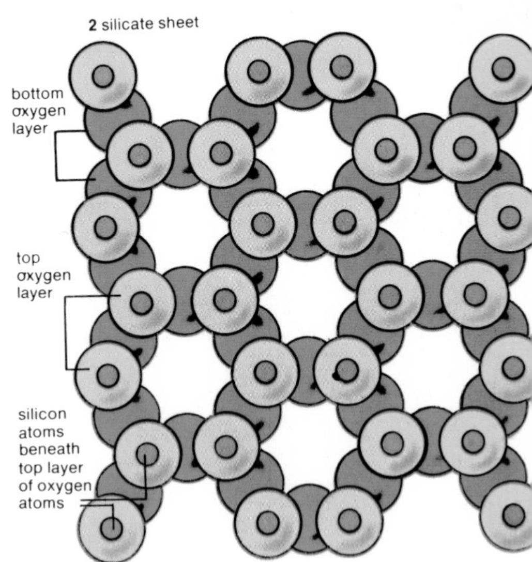

Above and right: China clay (kaolin) consists primarily of *kaolinite* ($Al_2O_3.2SiO_2.2H_2O$), a hydrated alumino-silicate. Silicate groups, consisting of silicon atoms each surrounded by four oxygen atoms, combine to form chains, 1, which link together to make sheets, 2. Aluminate sheets, 3, consist of aluminium ions surrounded by hydroxyl (—OH) groups and kaolinite is a kind of 'laminate' of silicate and aluminate sheets, 4. Kaolinite is formed by the natural decomposition of *igneous* rocks, such as granite, which were produced as a result of the cooling of molten rock masses.

English China Clays Group

Above: High pressure water jets, operating at pressures of up to 24 bar (350 psi), are used to wash china clay deposits out of the ground. The water jets produce a slurry of water, clay, and the particles of quartz and mica that are present in the clay. The slurry is pumped to a separation plant where the quartz and mica are removed, and dewatered to recover the clay which is then pressed and dried. Although china clay is an important material for the ceramic industry, over three quarters of the world's output is used in papermaking; a high quality paper may contain 30 per cent china clay by weight.

BRICK MANUFACTURE

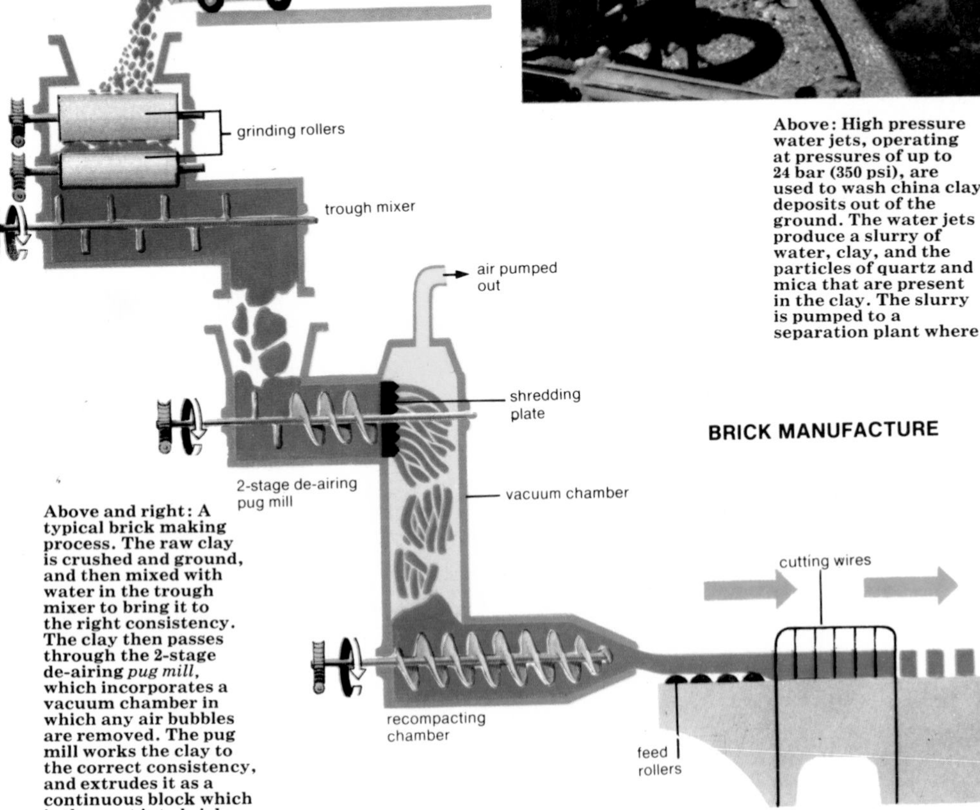

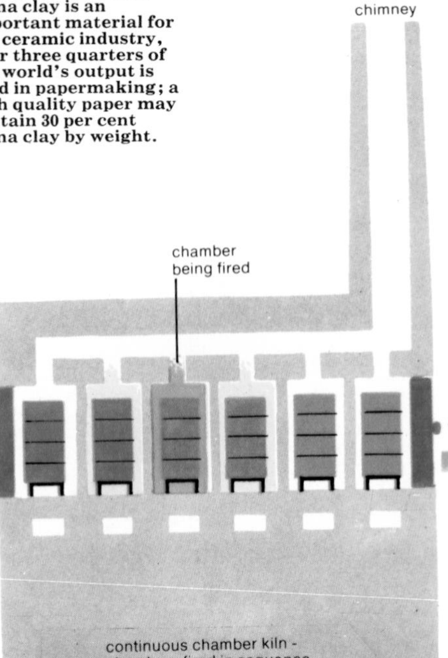

Above and right: A typical brick making process. The raw clay is crushed and ground, and then mixed with water in the trough mixer to bring it to the right consistency. The clay then passes through the 2-stage de-airing *pug mill*, which incorporates a vacuum chamber in which any air bubbles are removed. The pug mill works the clay to the correct consistency, and extrudes it as a continuous block which is then cut into bricks. The bricks are dried and then fired.

aluminate sheet

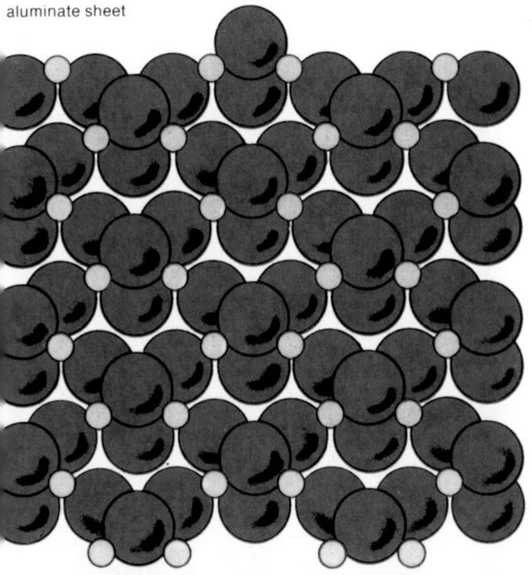

4 kaolinite sheet: laminate of silicate and aluminate sheets

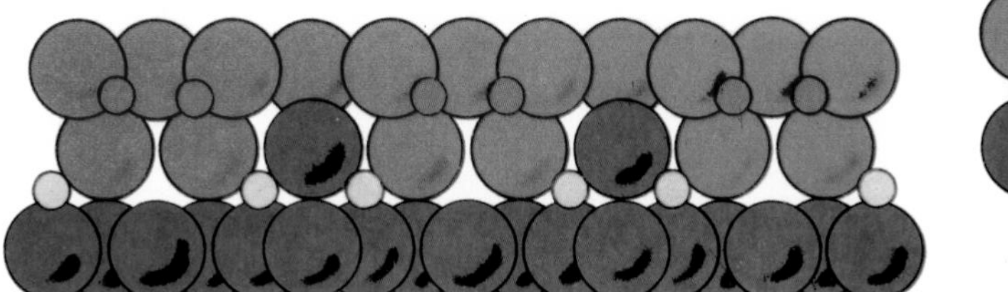

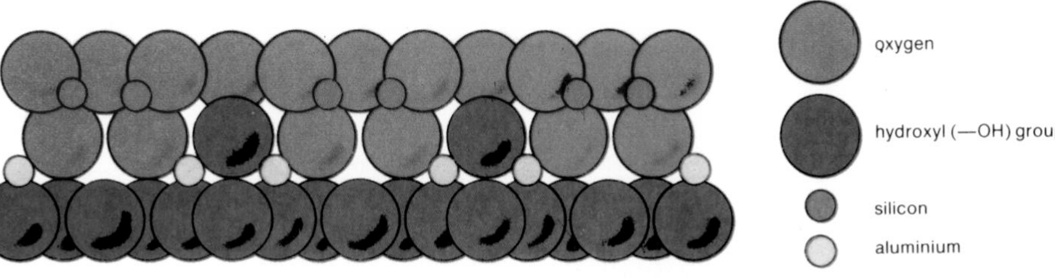

The main stages in the production of tableware are clay preparation, shaping, the first or *biscuit* firing which hardens the clay, the application of decoration and glaze, and the *glost* firing which turns the glaze into a hard, glassy coating.

Left: English bone china clay emerging from the pug mill which works the clay to remove the air from it and make it pliable.

Left, below: Making cups on a machine called a *jolley*. A ball of clay is put into a plaster mould, which is rotated at high speed while a metal shaper is lowered into it to form the clay into shape.

Left, bottom: Tableware being loaded on to a truck ready for biscuit firing, which takes 60 to 70 hours at temperatures of up to 1,120°C for earthenware or 1,250°C for bone china.

Right: Applying colour with a spray gun, a convenient method of applying solid bands or areas of colour.

Royal Doulton

Wedgwood

Royal Doulton

Wedgwood

Clay-based products now have many important applications not based on the material's ability to be shaped, for example in the papermaking industry, while many other industries, such as iron and steel, are dependent upon the heat-resisting properties of ceramic refractory products.

The widespread use of ceramics today is based on several factors. The material is cheap to produce because the basic ingredients are readily available and do not require chemical extraction. It is easy to shape in the unfired state, and after firing becomes hard, durable, stable, resistant to chemicals and oxidization, and has high electrical resistivity. On the negative side, ceramics are inflexible, brittle and have a low resistance to shock.

Ceramic production

There is a wide variation in the properties of ceramic products, partly because so many factors are involved in their making. After firing, most ceramics are composed of one or more crystalline *phases* and a glassy phase in variable proportions and not in equilibrium, plus pores which form a large part of the total volume.

The endlessly variable properties of the product partly explain the relatively late development of industrial ceramics; the traditional description of the manufacturing process, 'materials of dubious composition heated to an unknown temperature for an indefinite time', while being a simplification, nonetheless still has a ring of truth when related to much ceramic production, especially that of the past.

Although ceramic products are extraordinarily diverse, certain basic principles apply to the production processes. Clays, usually composed of small particles of alumino-silicates, are extracted from the ground, purified or blended with other materials, and are then shaped into the desired form by moulding or casting when in a wet or *plastic* state. Bricks and tiles can be made from raw clay as it comes from the ground, while clay for products such as tableware requires elaborate blending, purifying and filtering before use.

After shaping, the products are allowed to dry until they are firm to touch. Then they are fired in a kiln, a process that converts the malleable clay into a brittle and porous crystalline form. The length of firing and the temperature will vary according to the type of clay being used, but the temperature range will normally be between 600°C and 1,600°C (1,100 and 2,910°F).

The production process for heavy clay products such as bricks and tiles will now be complete, but more sophisticated ceramics will undergo one or more further firings, their surfaces will be made non-porous by the addition of a glassy layer of glaze, and any required decoration will be applied.

Domestic ceramics

The best known ceramic products are domestic items such as tableware and sanitary fittings. These products are made from earthenware clays, or, in a more developed form, from stoneware or porcelain clays. All clays used today for domestic products require elaborate preparation in order to achieve greater strength, consistency and durability.

It will be obvious that a delicate translucent teacup in porcelain is made from a

Royal Worcester

U.K.A.E.A.

Left: An automatic glazing machine. The glaze is a mixture of water and finely-powdered *frit* (a glass-like substance), clay and flint. The water dries out, leaving a thin film of the powdered ingredients on the surface. When the glazed article is fired these ingredients fuse into a glassy coating.

clay radically different to that used for a heavy casserole or a hand basin. Until this century the preparation of clays was a rather arbitrary process, with considerable inconsistency in the results. Most potters had their own closely-guarded recipes, and always prepared their own materials. Today, clay preparation is a complex, computer-controlled operation.

Clay on its own is rarely pure or strong enough for industrial production, and so various ingredients such as powdered flint or calcined bone ash are added to it. Most basic clays are *red-firing*: the clay turns reddish-brown when fired. Porcelain therefore requires white-firing clays, the most important of these being *china clay* (*kaolin*), large deposits of which are found in south-west England and in the US, USSR, France, Germany and Czechoslovakia. The standard English porcelain is *bone china*, made from china clay, china stone (felspar), and bone ash.

Earthenware is made from blends of white-firing *ball clays* and china clays together with china stone and calcined (roasted) flint. *Stoneware* is made from mixtures of ball clays and other clays which fire to a brown or grey colour rather than white, and it contains little or no china clay.

After blending and purifying, the air is removed from the clay mechanically and it is then ready for shaping. The traditional idea of pottery making is of someone 'throwing' the clay into shapes on a wheel. Although picturesque, in developed countries this technique is today only practised by craft and amateur potters, and has had no real industrial significance since the eighteenth century.

Most ceramics today are shaped either by *slip-casting* or *press-moulding*. In the former process, liquid clay (*slip*) is poured into plaster of Paris moulds, which are then left for a period of time to absorb much of the water in the clay. When the clay is sufficiently dry the moulds are removed, leaving the cast ware to be taken to the drying sheds. In the latter process, clay is forced into shape by mechanical means. In general, moulding is used for flatware, such as plates, while more complex shapes, such as teapots, require slipcasting, often in more than one mould. Complex pieces cast in several moulds are assembled before firing.

Most domestic ceramics are then *biscuit-fired:* the clay is transformed by the fire into a brittle but permanent form and the remaining water is driven out. Considerable shrinkage takes place during this first firing, and so pieces are generally made larger than they will be in their final form. Firing today generally takes place in a *continuous tunnel kiln* fired by gas or oil. The products, stacked on trolleys, pass slowly through a continuously-burning tunnel in which the fiercest heat is at the centre. For smaller-scale production *intermittent kilns* are used, which are often heated by electricity.

Until the 1950s, many potteries still relied on intermittent 'bottle-oven' kilns, fired by coal. These kilns were loaded with ware when cold, and were then sealed when full. Coal fires were lit beneath the oven and were fed until the heat had reached the required temperature which was then maintained until the firing was complete. The oven was then left to cool, at which point the seal was opened and the ware removed. It could

Above: A selection of components made from a silicon carbide (SiC) ceramic originally developed as a cladding material for the nuclear fuel elements used in gas-cooled reactors. This material is strong, impermeable, resistant to oxidation and abrasion, and it retains its physical properties at very high temperatures. Its uses, apart from those in the nuclear industry, include rocket nozzles, furnace tubes, gas turbine components, bearings, and chemical plant components.

Right: Average firing temperatures for some typical ceramic products and the glazes and colours used on domestic goods such as tableware.

2,000°C
special refractories
alumina refractories
silica refractories
1,500°C
high grande porcelain
ordinary porcelain
soft porcelain
fireclay drainpipes
common glazes
1,000°C
red clay tiles and pots
gold colours
painted colours on top of glaze
500°C

CAP-AND-PIN INSULATOR UNIT

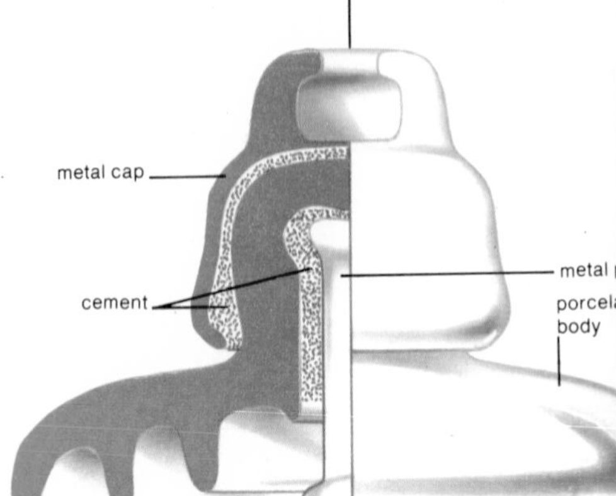

then be prepared for the next firing.

After the biscuit firing, most products are covered in glaze, either by dipping or spraying, and are then given a second or *glost* firing to seal the glaze into a non-porous, glassy outer coating. Most domestic ceramics are decorated, a process that can occur at various stages in the manufacture depending on the type of ware and the type of decoration required. Painted decoration and colour staining can occur either before or after the glost firing.

Painting, usually in enamel colours on top of the glaze, requires one or more lower-temperature firings to fuse the colours into the glaze. The most common method of decoration in use today, however, is by applied transfer, printed either from engraved copper plates or by lithography; this usually occurs before the glaze is fired.

Wedgwood

Morganite Ceramic Fibres Ltd

Above: The glost firing, which hardens the glaze, typically takes about 30 hours at temperatures of 1,000 to 1,100°C. Decoration is applied either before the ware is glazed, or on top of the fired glaze, in which case additional firing is necessary to fuse the colour into the glaze.

Below and below left: One very important engineering application of ceramics is for making electrical insulators. The photograph shows insulators ready for glazing, and the diagram shows a suspension unit of the common cap-and-pin type. These suspension units are strung together to make up the long insulators used on high voltage overhead transmission lines, and consist of a brown glazed porcelain body with a metal cap on top and a metal pin in the base; the pin is shaped to fit into the recess in the cap of the unit below it. Toughened glass is also often used for insulators.

Above: A furnace interior lined with ceramic blanket instead of refractory firebricks. The texture of ceramic fibre blanket is similar to that of glass fibre, but finer and softer. It is an alumino-silicate, made from china clay, and can withstand temperatures of up to 1,260°C.

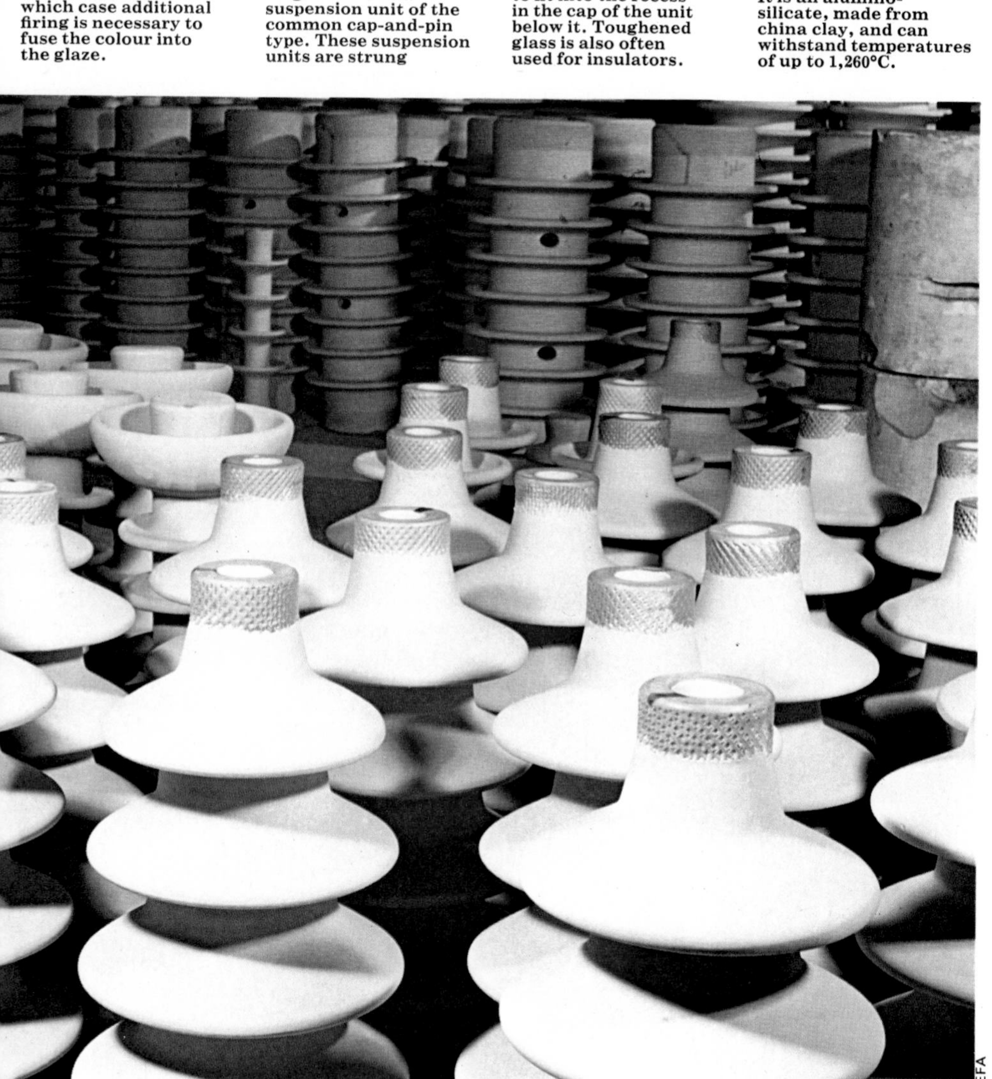

ZEFA

Technical ceramics

The production processes used in domestic ceramics also apply to many scientific and industrial wares, but many others are highly specialized and require different treatment. For these, shaping may also be achieved by extrusion, injection moulding, vibratory processes, or by compressing dry powder in a die. Intermittent kilns are often used for firing, as the control of factors such as shrinkage has to be far more precise.

Many of the specialized industrial and scientific ceramics require complex additional ingredients to make them suitable for their allotted purposes. Some are based on metal oxide compounds; such ceramics include refractories, and electrical porcelains which are used for insulator stacks, bus bar mountings and switchgear bushings. Common refractory materials include magnesia (MgO), zirconia (ZiO_2) and thoria (ThO_2).

A particularly important group are the alumina ceramics, which include sparking plug insulators, components for textile machinery, and products for the aerospace industry where high temperature resistance is critical. Space capsules, for example, are protected from the heat of re-entry into the atmosphere by a ceramic coating.

Other ceramics contain graphite and various carbon compounds, and are used in nuclear power station equipment and in gas turbines. There are also non-oxide ceramics, based on compounds such as borides and carbides, used for the manufacture of resistors, semiconductors and abrasives. Specialized ceramics include the magnetic ceramics used on transformers, alternators and loudspeakers.

Glass ceramics, used in heat exchangers and electronic circuit boards and substrates, can be made by heating glass in such a way that a crystalline structure develops within it. Alternatively, a conventional clay can be converted into a glass ceramic by heating it to 1,700°C (3,100°F) so that it melts and becomes a glassy liquid that is then crystallized.

Ceramic-based products play a part in almost every aspect of present-day industrial, scientific and domestic life. Indeed many industries, such as electricity and aerospace, could not exist in their present forms without them. At the same time, many industrial applications of ceramics have still to be explored, for it is a relatively recent science likely to play an even greater role in the future.

Timber and Paper

Wood, one of the most plentiful and versatile natural materials, has been used since prehistoric times, and today it still plays an important part in everyday life. Although the world's largest single use for wood is as a fuel, in most industrialized countries its many other uses are of far greater importance.

These uses include timber for such applications as building, furniture, packing cases, boatbuilding, pit props, railway sleepers and poles for carrying telephone and electricity cables; wood pulp for the manufacture of paper, board, cellulose film and regenerated cellulose fibres; wood chips which are mixed with resins and converted into manufactured board such as chipboard; and thin sheets of wood used as decorative veneers and, in the case of lower quality woods, for the manufacture of plywood.

Wood pulp is the principal raw material for paper, although a variety of other plant fibres may be used. Wood pulp for papermaking is obtained from a wide variety of trees, both coniferous and non-coniferous, including spruce, pine, eucalyptus, poplar, birch and chestnut.

Reed Group

Bruce Coleman

Right: Trees provide the raw material for most papermaking pulp, but many other plant fibres are used either for making particular types of paper or in areas where wood pulp is not readily available. These other fibres include esparto, straw, cotton, flax (linen), hemp, jute, manila and bagasse.

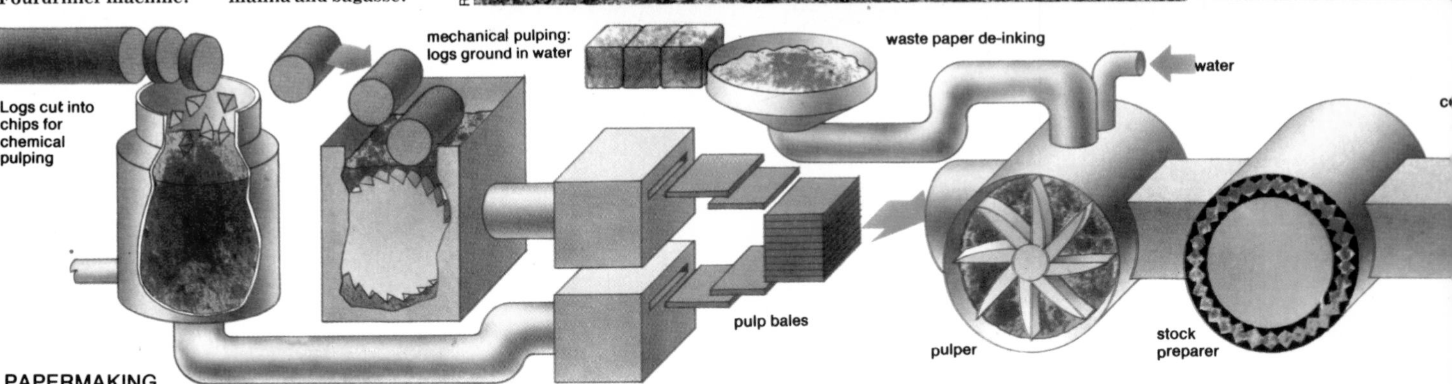

Below: A simplified flow diagram of a typical papermaking process. The bark is removed from the logs, which are ground or cut into chips and 'digested' to make pulp. Bales of dried pulp are taken to the paper mill, where they are broken up in water and made into paper on a Fourdrinier machine.

Development of papermaking
The first paper was made in China some 2,000 years ago, although *papyrus*, a writing material similar to paper in many ways, was first made in the Middle East before 3500 BC. Papyrus, made from the outer layers of the stem of a reed of the same name, remained in use in the Mediterranean area for about 4,000 years, until it was superseded by parchment (made from animal skins) in about the first century BC in most countries except Egypt, where papyrus was still in use until the Middle Ages.

Papermaking began in the Arabic countries in the eighth century AD, and the technique spread to Europe when the Moors invaded Spain in the eleventh century. The basic principles of modern papermaking are essentially the same as those developed by the Chinese, although the process has been developed considerably since then and the raw material is usually wood pulp instead of rags or plant stems.

Pulp
There are two main types of wood pulp: *mechanical pulp* which is produced by grinding logs and mixing the particles of wood with water, and *chemical pulp* which is made by cutting the logs into small chips which are heated under pressure in a chemical solution. An alkaline solution is used for most types of wood, although spruce may be processed in an acidic solution. Mechanical pulp is not as strong as chemical pulp, and its largest use is for short-lived paper such as that used for newspapers. Chemical pulp is used for better grades of paper, such as those used for brochures, books, glossy magazines and strong wrapping papers. Pulp intended for making white paper is bleached.

Papermaking
Before leaving the pulp mill the pulp is washed and filtered to remove any impurities, bleached if necessary, and dried and formed into sheets so that it is easier to handle. The sheets are packed into bales for delivery to the paper mill.

At the paper mill, the sheets of pulp are fed into a *pulper*, a machine which disintegrates them and mixes them with water. Cleaned and de-inked waste paper is often mixed with the pulp at this stage.

The mixture of water and fibres leaving the pulper is known as the *stock*, and the

Keystone

Bowater Paper Sales Ltd.

Above: Stacks of timber in a London wood yard. Felled timber is cut into planks in sawmills, and then it must be dried to reduce its moisture content to less than 24 per cent before it can be used, for example for making furniture. The drying may be done in special kilns, or else the timber may be stacked in such a way that the air can circulate through the stack and dry it. The stacks shown here weigh about 4,000 tonnes each.

Left: Logs awaiting transport to a pulp mill, near Kviteseid in the Telemark region of Denmark. Large quantities of logs can be transported easily by floating them down inland waterways, often by tying them together to make huge rafts that can be pulled by tugs. The main producers of wood for pulping are the United States, Canada, Scandinavia and the Soviet Union.

Wiggins Teape

Above: A de-barking machine which removes the bark from logs before they are pulped. The machine consists of a large, revolving, slotted drum. The rotation of the drum tumbles the logs together so that the bark is knocked off them, and a stream of water washes the pieces of bark out through the slots. The bark is usually disposed of by burning it as a fuel to raise steam in the mill's power station.

Left: Wood chips produced by the chipping machine are blown on to stock piles to await chemical pulping. The chips are about 25 x 25 x 5 mm in size. Logs used for making mechanical pulp do not have to be cut into chips, as the pulp is made by forcing the logs against a large grindstone and mixing the ground fibres with water. Mechanical pulp is coarser than that made chemically.

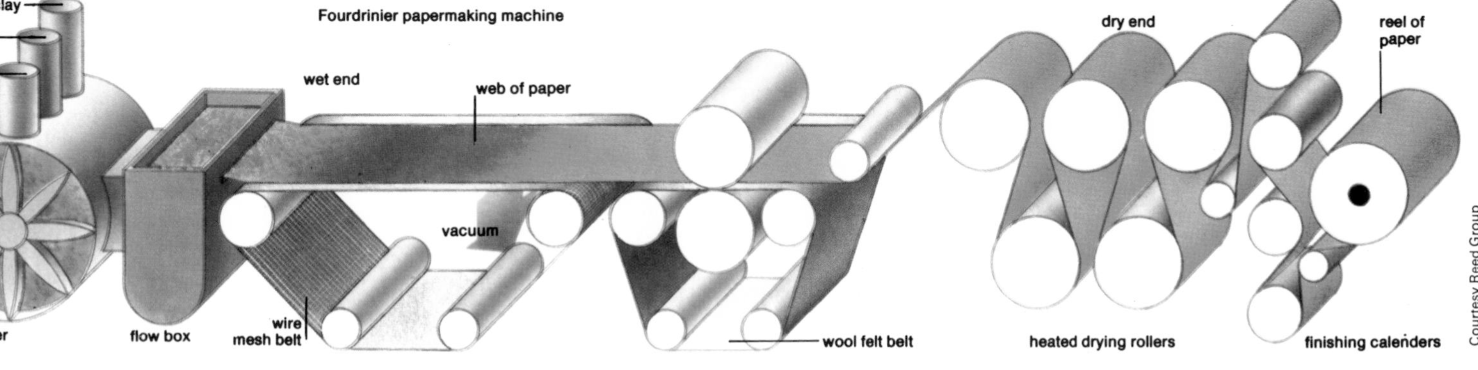

Courtesy Reed Group

next stage in the process is the mechanical treatment of the stock to alter the size and texture of the fibres according to the type of paper being produced. The stock then passes into a mixer where it is mixed with other ingredients such as china clay, size and pigments. The china clay improves the opacity and surface finish of the paper, and makes it more white. Titanium oxide and finely powdered chalk are also used for this purpose.

Sizes, usually resins, make the paper resistant to water penetration (but not waterproof) so that when it is written on with water-based ink the ink does not spread through the fibres and make the writing illegible. Paper to be used for printing does not require as much sizing as writing paper because printing inks are not water-based and spread less.

Pigments, such as various coloured clays, are finely powdered so that the particles coat the fibres and fill the spaces between them to give the finished paper the required colour. Paper may also be coloured by the addition of dyestuffs to the stock.

The commonest type of papermaking machine is the *Fourdrinier*, the first of which was built by Henry and Sealy Fourdrinier in Hertfordshire, England in 1803. The stock enters the *wet end* of the machine and flows on to a moving, continuous belt of phosphor bronze wire mesh or plastic mesh. This belt, known as the *wire* or *cloth*, may be up to 9 m (30 ft) wide, and moves at speeds of up to 1,000 m (3,280 ft) per minute. The weight and thickness of the paper are regulated mainly by the amount of stock that is allowed to flow on to the wire.

As the stock is carried along by the wire, the water begins to drain out of it through the spaces in the mesh and the fibres begin to intermesh. At the end of the wire, more water is removed from the *web* of fibres by the suction created by vacuum boxes positioned beneath the wire. The consolidation of the fibres is assisted by gentle pressure from a *dandy roll*, an open cylinder covered in wire mesh. A design may be wired or soldered on to the wire mesh of the dandy roll, so that it impresses a *watermark* into the fibres.

The consolidated sheet of fibres then passes on to a wide continuous belt of woollen felt, which carries it through a series of heavy rollers that squeeze out more water and press the fibres more

Wiggins Teape

Above: Preparing wood pulp for papermaking. Most paper is produced on a continuous papermaking machine called a *Fourdrinier*, named after the two brothers, Henry and Sealy Fourdrinier, who with John Gamble and Bryan Donkin produced the first one in 1803. Modern machines may be over 100 m long.

Below: Reels of *paperboard*, a packaging material made up of layers or *plies* of fibre. The majority of paperboard is made on *cylinder-mould* machines, developments of the machine built by John Dickinson in 1809, which use a wire-covered cylinder in place of the wire belt of the Fourdrinier.

Right: The pulp mill in Bratsk, Siberia. Bratsk is one of the rapidly-developing towns of Siberia, a heavily-forested area which, in addition to timber, is also rich in oil, gas and many other important minerals, and has large rivers such as the Angara which provide hydroelectric power.

Novosti

Imperial Group Ltd

firmly together. The web continues on through the *dry end* of the machine, where it passes around a series of steam-heated metal cylinders which evaporate the majority of the remaining water.

After drying, the paper is fed through a series of *calenders*, highly polished iron rollers which smooth the surface of the paper. The drying and calendering processes generate a great deal of static electricity in the paper, which must be eliminated otherwise it may cause the paper to stick to itself when cut into sheets, or make the layers of a reel of paper stick together making it difficult to unreel without tearing.

The static electricity can be removed by thin copper wires, connected to earth, which are arranged so that they brush the surface of the paper as it leaves the calenders.

After the calendering, the paper is wound into large reels. These reels are subsequently slit into smaller reels if required, and if the paper is to be supplied to the customer in sheet form it may be slit to width and cut into sheets on an automatic cutting machine.

A variety of finishing processes are employed to produce the required finished surface of the paper. The paper for high-quality magazines, for example, is coated with a layer of finely-divided white mineral pigment, which fills in the tiny irregularities in the surface and gives it a smooth, glossy appearance. The pigments, such as china clay or a mixture of alumina and calcium sulphate known as *satin white*, are mixed with an adhesive such as casein or polyvinyl acetate which binds them to the paper.

Waxed papers can be divided into two main groups: those which have the wax impregnated into them, and those which have a surface layer of wax. The first type, which can be printed on, are made by coating one side with wax and then passing the uncoated side over a heated roller so that the wax is drawn into the fibres of the paper. The second group, which must be printed before waxing, are made by passing the paper through a bath of molten wax. A set of rollers removes any excess wax, and then the paper is sprayed with or passed through cold water to set the wax. The wax used is based on paraffin wax, with additives that improve its flexibility.

Board

Boards such as cardboard are made mostly by processes based either on the Fourdrinier machine or else on the *cylinder-mould* machine. The cylinder-mould machine was invented in 1809 by John Dickinson, and it uses a large, revolving cylinder in place of the continuous belt of mesh used by the Fourdrinier. The wire mesh surface of the cylinder picks up stock from a vat, and the water is drawn away through the wire. The fibre web is transferred from the cylinder to a felt belt which then carries it through a drying arrangement similar to that of the Fourdrinier machine.

Paper consumption

One of the factors which has made paper invaluable in hundreds of industries is that the nature of the product is basically simple, and a great body of technology has been developed to provide the means by which its properties can be adjusted to give precisely the characteristics required by the user.

In general terms, the primary use of paper is, as it was originally, as a medium of communication. This is, however, only one of its innumerable uses in commerce, industry and in the home. Its wide range of uses has encouraged a steady growth in paper production and consumption. Between 1954 and 1974, for instance, the annual consumption of paper and board

Wiggins Teape

Peter Grugeon/Portals Ltd

Left: Paper emerging from a bath of molten wax. Waxed paper and cardboard are useful packaging materials, particularly in the food industry. For example waxed cartons, often lined with foil, are used for milk, fruit juices and other liquids, and waxed paper is often used for wrapping bread.

Above: Almost all high security paper—like that for banknotes—is made on cylinder-mould machines. Using such machines it is possible to create the watermark at exactly the same time as the paper web is being formed, and this results in the watermark having a multi-tone appearance as seen here.

The History of Papermaking

100 BC/AD	Paper already being made in China
105	Ts'ai Lun 'invented' paper
610	paper used in Japan
794	paper made in Baghdad
875	toilet paper used in China
900	paper made in Egypt
1035	paper used to wrap vegetables in Egypt
1150	paper made in Spain
1269	paper made in France
1276	paper made in Italy
1309	paper used in England
1390	paper made in Germany
1465	blotting paper in use
1494	paper made in England
1576	paper made in Russia
1650	about 50 mills in England
1692	paper made in America
1696	108 mills in England
1724	Portals' monopoly of Bank of England paper starts
1758	first English banknote forgery
1799	French patent on paper machine
1801	English patent on same machine
1804	first book printed on machine-made paper
1805	six paper machines in UK produce 557 tonnes of paper
1806	carbon paper patented
1816	first paper machine in USA
1824	cigarette paper made
1827	transparent paper patented
1830	sandpaper in use
1840	first adhesive postage stamps
1846	paper made from wood pulp
1848	253 paper machines in England
1851	cartridge paper in use
1856	corrugated paper patented
1862	tracing paper made
1871	rolled toilet paper patented
1873	asbestos paper patented
1876	first paper-bag machine built
1889	1 million tonnes of paper made in US
1891	paper used for electrical insulation
1906	photocopier patented
1919	first airmail flight
1930	international 'A' paper sizes first introduced
1933	aerogramme introduced
1939-45	straw widely used in paper making
1947	Formica first made in UK (2 resin-impregnated types of paper bonded to melamine)
1955	carbonless copy paper first made in UK
1974	world production 8½ million tonnes

Courtesy of Colin Cohen

Dickinson Robinson Group

Right: Paper and board have innumerable uses in packaging. One of the most important types of paper used in this area is known as *kraft* paper ('Kraft' is the German word for 'strength'), which is made from a chemical pulp.

Below: One of the commonest forms of *carbonless copy paper*, widely used for business forms. The back of the top sheet is coated with tiny capsules of a colourless chemical; when the sheet is written on, the pressure breaks the capsules and the dye reacts with chemicals in the clay coating of the sheet below to form a blue or black image on it.

top sheet
capsule coating
bottom sheet
image formation
reactive clay coating

Courtesy Wiggins Teape

in the United States rose from 27 million tonnes to 56 million.

During the same period, annual consumption in Japan rose from under 2 million to over 15 million tonnes. The same general pattern was repeated in most other countries—for example, in West Germany consumption rose from 2.5 million to 8.1 million tonnes, in France from 1.6 to 6.2 million, in Sweden from 0.6 to 1.8 million, and in the United Kingdom from 3.7 to 7.9 million tonnes.

On a per capita basis the US leads the world's big consumers with 265 kg (564 lb) per year. The United Kingdom heads Western European consumption at around 140 kg (309 lb). In contrast, Sudan has an annual per capita consumption of only about 6 kg (13 lb).

The bulk of the wood from which paper is made comes from the forests of North America, Scandinavia, the Soviet Union, Japan and West Germany. A small, but important, proportion of pulp is made from straw and from special grasses such as esparto and albardin, and banknotes are usually made from cotton or cotton and linen fibres. Methods of making a suitable pulp from alternative types of fibre are being introduced in many developing countries. *Bagasse*, for example, the fibrous residue left when the sugar has been extracted from sugar cane, is proving to be a useful source of pulp.

The increasing costs of wood and pulp, plus a growing awareness of the need for careful management of natural resources (including renewable ones such as trees), have accelerated the use of waste paper as a source of pulp. Waste paper has long been used in the production of boards and low grade paper, but since the 1960s the range of papers using waste as a raw material has been greatly increased. This has been helped by the development of de-inking processes for removing the ink from printed paper, enabling a cleaner and more useful pulp to be produced.

Rubber

The Indians of South America were the first people to make use of the milky fluid, known as *latex*, which is produced by the tree *Hevea brasiliensis* and is the raw material for natural rubber. The latex occurs beneath the bark of the tree and acts as a protective substance, for if the bark is damaged or cut, the latex seeps out of the damaged area and dries to form a protective coating over it.

The Indian name for the tree was *cahuchu*—'the weeping tree'—and this name is the origin of the French and German words, 'caoutchouc' and 'Kautschuck', for rubber. The Indians made primitive rubber footwear by spreading layers of latex over clay formers and smoking them over a fire to dry the latex into a crude rubber, and waterproof sheeting for tents and cloaks was made by sandwiching a layer of latex between two layers of cloth. The English name 'rubber' was first used in the middle of the eighteenth century, when it was discovered that the material could be used to rub out pencil marks on paper.

The potential usefulness of rubber, particularly for such purposes as waterproofing, was initially recognized in the first half of the nineteenth century by such men as Charles Macintosh and Thomas Hancock in Britain and Charles Goodyear in the United States. Macintosh dissolved solid, dried rubber in coal tar naphtha, and used the resulting solution for impregnating fabrics to make them waterproof and for making dipped goods such as gloves and galoshes. The rubber, although providing excellent waterproofing, was however sensitive to heat: the garments became brittle during cold weather, and in warm weather they were sticky and smelly.

This heat-sensitivity of rubber also caused problems for the many other early manufacturers of rubber goods, and a great deal of effort was expanded in attempts to overcome it. Several people, including Macintosh, Hancock, Nathaniel Hayward and Alexander Parkes, tried to make the rubber more stable by treating it with sulphur in various ways, but it was Goodyear, in 1839, who first discovered a successful process.

Hayward had developed a partially successful method of treating rubber with sulphur to stabilize it, and Goodyear had bought the rights to the process and was trying to perfect it. He accidentally spilled some rubber and sulphur mixture on to a hot stove, and when he later examined the hardened scrap he found that the effect of the heat on the rubber and sulphur had made the rubber strong, pliable and relatively unaffected by changes in temperature.

He had discovered what later came to be known as the *vulcanization* of rubber, during which atoms of sulphur combine chemically with the molecules of rubber. Rubber is a *polymer*, the rubber molecule consisting of a chain of carbon atoms which each have hydrogen atoms attached to them. The basic formula of rubber is $(C_5H_8)_n$, where *n* is in the region of 3,000. The repeating unit of the polymer chain is derived from *isoprene*, $CH_2{=}CH{-}C(CH_3){=}CH_2$, which also occurs, in unpolymerized form, in terpentine.

Malaysian Rubber Producers Research Association

Above: The seedlings used to start the rubber plantations of South-East Asia were grown from seeds collected in Brazil in 1876 by Henry Wickham. He collected about 70,000 *Hevea brasiliensis* seeds, of which 2,600 germinated at Kew Gardens and were later planted in Ceylon (Sri Lanka).

Malaysian Rubber Producers Research Association

Right: John Boyd Dunlop (1840-1921), who in 1887 invented the first successful pneumatic tyre. The first pneumatic tyres were in fact made in 1845 by R. W. Thomson, but the rubber then available was not satisfactory and Thomson did not develop the idea. This photograph was taken in July 1918.

Malaysian Rubber Producers Research Association

Left: The traditional method of processing latex is to coagulate it and then dry it in smoke-houses, but the latest techniques involve breaking the coagulated latex into *crumb*, which is loaded into metal trays (shown here) and put into drying ovens. The dried crumb is then compressed into bales.

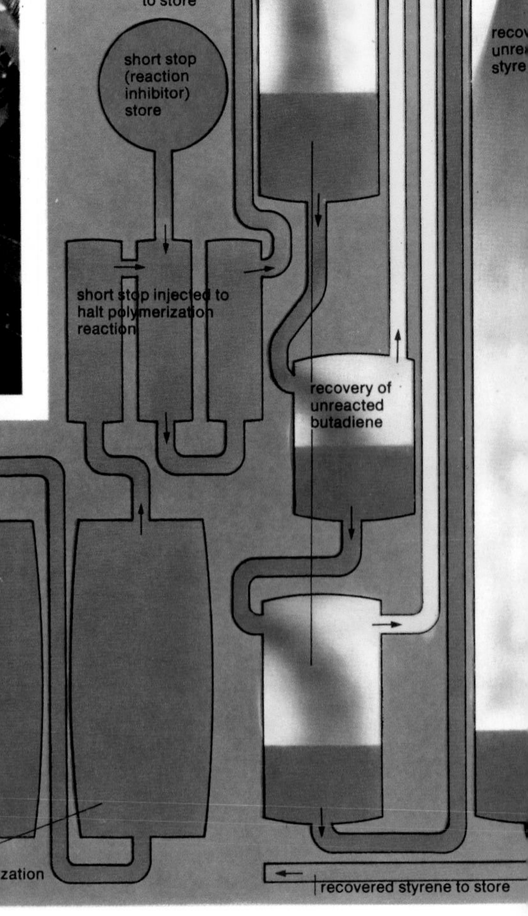

Below: A typical styrene-butadiene rubber (SBR) production process. The butadiene and styrene are pumped into the reactors with catalysts and a soap solution. The rubber is formed as an emulsion in the soap solution, then separated from it, dried, and compressed into bales for shipping.

International Synthetic Rubber Co.

Malaysian Rubber Research and Development Board

Above: Bales of synthetic rubber leaving the production unit. This rubber is a styrene-butadiene rubber to which carbon black has been added. Carbon black, a finely-powdered form of carbon, is used as a *reinforcing pigment* which stiffens and strengthens the rubber and colours it black.

International Synthetic Rubber Co.

Left: A large synthetic rubber production plant at Grangemouth in Scotland. This plant produces synthetic rubbers by *solution polymerization*; the monomers and the catalysts are dissolved in solvents before being brought together in the reactors where polymerization occurs.

Above: *Dipped goods* such as rubber gloves are made by dipping formers into baths of latex. When the formers are withdrawn, a layer of latex adheres to them, and the required thickness is obtained by repeated dipping to add further layers to the original one. The gloves are then heated to vulcanize them.

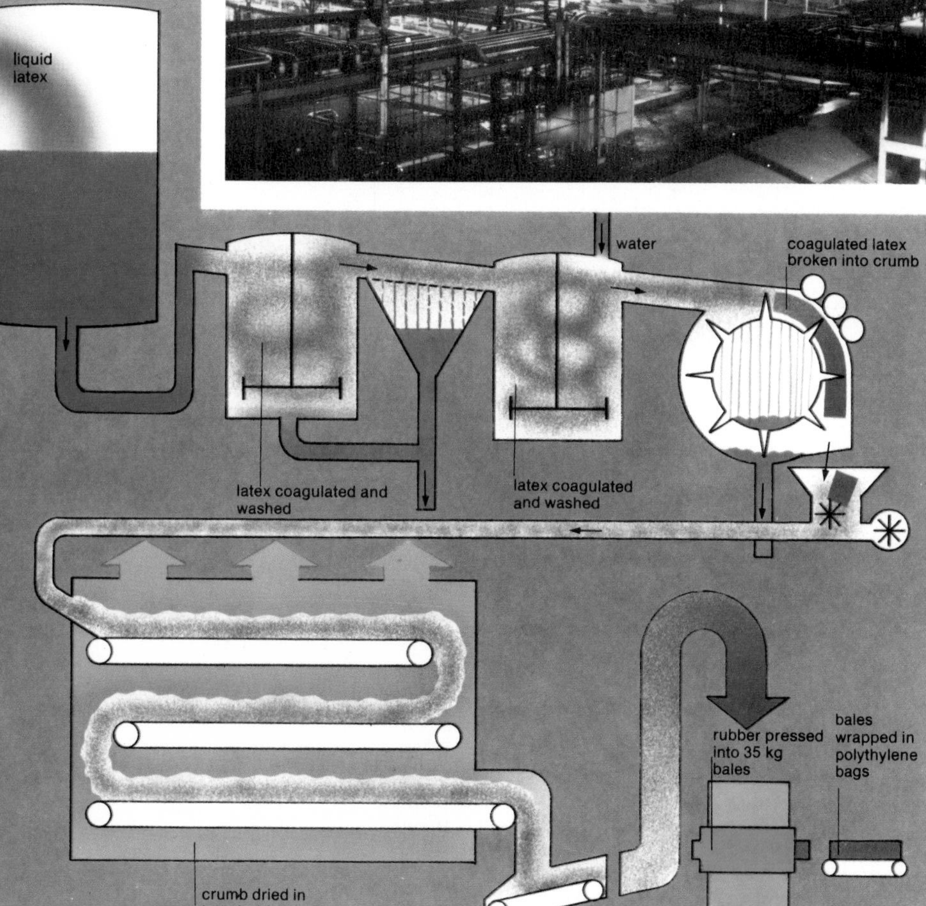

Before vulcanization, the polymer chains in the rubber are capable of considerable elastic deformation, but if the stress is too high the chains begin to slide over each other and plastic deformation occurs. During vulcanization, sulphur atoms combine with adjacent rubber molecules, forming *cross-links* between the chains which resist this plastic deformation.

Increasing the number of cross-links formed makes the rubber harder and more rigid and less affected by changes in temperature. Vulcanization is achieved by mixing sulphur or sulphur compounds with the raw rubber before it is formed into finished articles, the heat necessary for the vulcanization being applied during the forming of the articles, for instance in a heated mould, or by heating them after they have been formed.

The first stage in making a rubber article is the *mastication* of the raw rubber in a machine which 'chews' it thoroughly to shorten the molecule chains and make it soft. The masticated rubber is then compounded with the other ingredients necessary to produce the required type of rubber, for example the sulphur for vulcanization and carbon black to make the rubber more resistant to wear.

Various processes are used for forming the rubber into shapes, including extrusion, moulding, calendering (passing it between heavy rollers to produce sheeting), and the production of *dipped* goods such as rubber gloves by dipping shaped glass, metal or ceramic formers into liquid latex to which the other ingredients have been added. The latex used in the dipping process is treated soon after collection so that it does not coagulate during shipping.

Left: A rubber boot production line, where the main components of the boots, such as the uppers, soles and insoles, are joined together to make the finished boots.

Right: Rubber mouldings for gas masks. Rubber, especially some types of synthetic rubber, is a valuable material for the manufacture of protective equipment.

Below: The main stages in tyre manufacture. The raw rubber is masticated (chopped into small pieces) and then compounded (mixed) with other ingredients such as sulphur compounds (for vulcanization) and carbon black (which gives it its black colour and makes it more resistant to wear). The *plies* of the tyre are built up from cords, and wound around the tyre-building drum. The sidewall and tread rubbers are stuck on to the plies, and then the cylindrical structure is pressed into a 'raw' tyre shape ready to be moulded into its final shape. Vulcanization takes place while the tyre is in the heated mould.

The annual production of natural rubber is more than three million tonnes, the great majority of which comes from Malaysia, Thailand, Sri Lanka and India. Many countries in Africa (such as Liberia and Nigeria) and South America (for instance Brazil) are also important sources of natural rubber.

Synthetic rubber

The ratio of carbon atoms to hydrogen atoms in natural rubber (5:8) was determined by Michael Faraday in 1826, and in 1860 Greville Williams succeeded in isolating a liquid with the same carbon to hydrogen ratio—which he called 'isoprene'—by the dry distillation of rubber. Several chemists subsequently found that a number of resinous materials could be made from isoprene, and in 1892 William Tilden discovered that isoprene (which he had synthesized from turpentine) could be polymerized into a synthetic rubber. At that time, however, the mechanism of polymerization was not understood, and large-scale production of the material was not possible.

As the main source of isoprene in those days was natural rubber, there was little point in turning rubber into isoprene and then turning it back into rubber again, and so experiments into the production of isoprene from other sources were carried out by many researchers. Tilden had succeeded in making isoprene from turpentine, and F. Hofman, in Germany, produced isoprene from mineral substances.

The substance which formed the basis of the early synthetic rubbers, however, was not isoprene but dimethyl butadiene, whose molecule is similar to that of isoprene except that one of the hydrogen atoms is replaced by a methyl (CH_3—) group. The polymerization of dimethyl butadiene was first achieved by the Russian chemist Kondakov in 1900, and in 1910 C. D. Harries (in Germany) and E. H. Strange and F. E. Matthews (in England) discovered that the process could be speeded by the use of metallic sodium as a catalyst.

The rubber produced by this process,

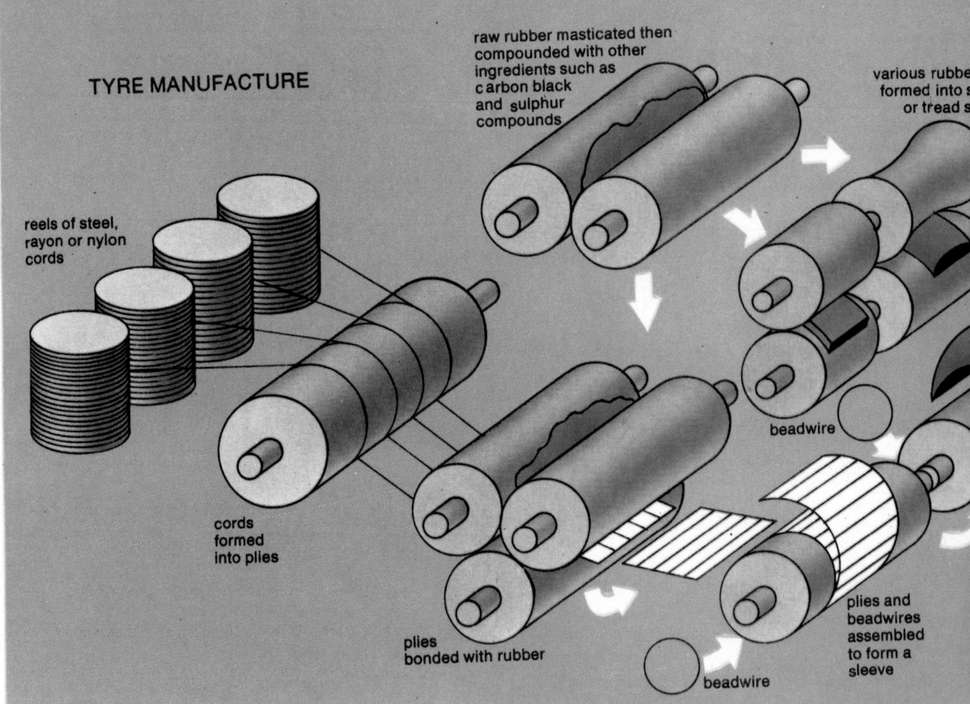

known as *methyl rubber*, was used by the Germans as a replacement for natural rubber during World War I, and during this period they produced some 2,500 tonnes of it. During the 1920s the price of natural rubber began to rise rapidly, and this provided another incentive to the German synthetic rubber industry.

Hermann Staudinger had by then produced his theory of polymerization, and this new insight into the formation of giant molecules was of great benefit in the research into synthetic rubbers. Two important new rubbers were developed, both based on butadiene ($CH_2{=}CH{-}CH{=}CH_2$) and using sodium as a catalyst. One, which was known as *Buna-N* (the name 'Buna' being derived from the first two letters of butadiene and the chemical symbol for sodium, Na), was made by

polymerizing butadiene with acrylonitrile, and the other, *Buna-S*, was a copolymer of butadiene and styrene.

The Japanese occupation of the rubber-producing areas of South-East Asia during World War II led the US and Canada to invest heavily in plant for the production of Buna-S, more commonly known as *styrene-butadiene rubber* (*SBR*), and by the end of the war the North American factories were capable of producing over a million tonnes of SBR a year. One of the main uses of SBR was for tyres, and another synthetic rubber, *butyl rubber*, was developed for inner tubes. Butyl rubber, made by polymerizing isobutylene, $CH_2{=}C(CH_3)_2$, retains air better than natural rubber does.

SBR is still one of the most important synthetic rubbers, accounting for over half of the world's total synthetic rubber production. It has good mechanical properties and resistance to ageing, and its many uses include vehicle tyres, belting, footwear and electrical insulation.

Another important synthetic rubber is *Neoprene*, which was introduced in 1931 by the Du Pont company in the United States. Neoprene (polychloroprene) is made by the polymerization of chloroprene, $CH_2{=}CCl{-}CH{=}CH_2$, which is made by reacting acetylene with hydrochloric acid. It is more resistant to oil, solvents and the effects of sunlight and ageing than are natural rubber and SBR, and so it has many industrial applications among its wide range of uses.

Polyurethane rubbers, whose molecules contain the characteristic —NHCOO— linkage found in polyurethane, are strong and have very good resistance to abrasion, oils and oxidation. In solid form they are often used for roller coverings, solid tyres and many engineering components, but the main use of polyurethane rubbers is as foam for upholstery, bedding and heat insulation. Many polyurethane rubbers do not require vulcanization.

The molecules of natural rubber and of almost all synthetic rubbers have 'backbones' consisting of chains of carbon atoms. *Silicone rubbers*, however, have backbones made up of alternating silicon and oxygen atoms. They are chemically unreactive, have very good electrical insulating properties and retain their electrical, mechanical and chemical properties over a broad temperature range.

One of the difficulties of producing a synthetic rubber based on isoprene is that the isoprene molecule has a three-dimensional structure which can take one of two forms, each of these forms being a mirror image of the other. In natural rubber, nearly all of the molecules are of the same form, but in synthetic rubber based on isoprene both forms are present in equal numbers, and this makes the material inferior to natural rubber. This problem was overcome during the 1950s by the use of specially-developed metallic catalysts. Modern synthetic *isoprene rubbers* are practically identical to natural rubber, except that they have slightly lower tensile strengths.

The principal synthetic rubbers presently available include, apart from those already mentioned, *acrylate*, *chlorosulphonated polyethylene*, *fluorocarbon*, *ethylene-propylene* and *ethylene-vinyl acetate* rubbers. Most synthetic rubbers are made in a range of different grades; there are, for example, over 500 different grades of SBR.

Lockheed-Georgia Co.

Right: The world's largest aircraft, the Lockheed C-5A Galaxy transport. Aircraft tyres are subjected to enormous loads, especially during landing, and they can get very hot, reaching temperatures well in excess of 100°C. Aircraft tyres are usually made of natural rubber, which is superior to synthetic rubber in its ability to handle the stresses experienced by modern aircraft tyres. Natural rubber is also used for large vehicle tyres such as those used on earthmoving machinery, but normal vehicle tyres usually contain both natural and synthetic rubbers.

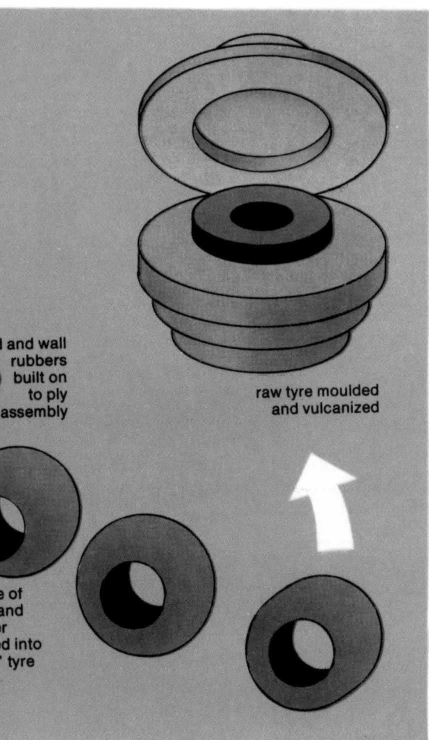

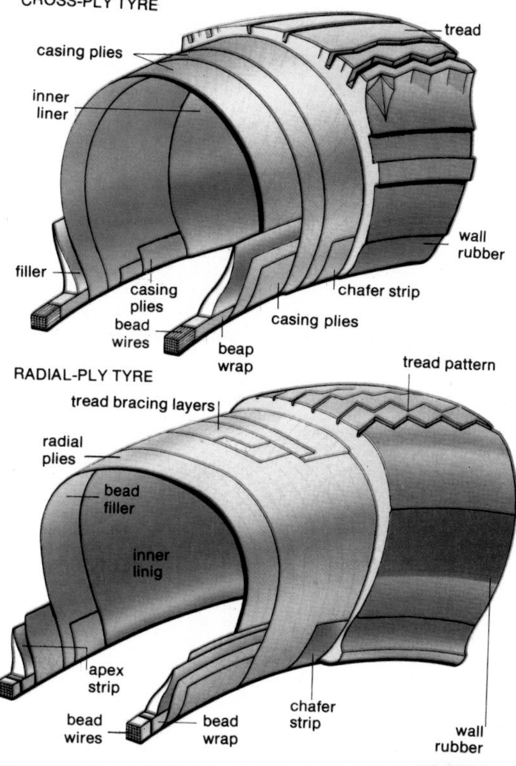

Below right: Cross sections of the two commonest types of road vehicle tyre, the *cross-ply* tyre and the *radial ply* tyre. In the cross-ply tyre, the cords in the casing plies run at an angle from one bead wire to the other, but in the radial ply tyre they run radially between the wires, making an angle of 90° with a circumferential line through the middle of the tread.

Left: A large roll of rubber belting used for conveyer belts. Rubber belting is made by *calendering*, passing the rubber mix through a series of heavy metal rollers so that it is formed into a continuous strip of the required thickness. The belting can be vulcanized by passing it through a set of heated rollers, or by heating it with hot air or radiant heat.

BTR Ltd

Right: The flexible rubberized skirting in the stern wall of a fixed-wall air cushion vehicle, a form of marine hovercraft in which the supporting air cushion is created in a space beneath the hull bounded by thin fixed sidewalls and flexible end walls.

Iron and Steel

Iron, and its principal alloy, steel, are the most important and widely used of all the metals. Iron is the second most common metal in the Earth's crust (the most common being aluminium), occurring in several types of commercially-important ore. The chief iron ores are *magnetite* (Fe_3O_4), *haematite* (Fe_2O_3), *limonite* (which has no definite formula) and *siderite* ($FeCO_3$), and the main producers of iron ores are the USSR, Brazil, Australia, and the US. The majority of the deposits are close to the surface of the ground, and so are fairly easily extracted by open-cast mining methods.

Iron is obtained from the ores by heating them, together with carbon in the form of coke, in *blast furnaces*. A blast furnace is a tall steel tower, water-cooled and lined with heat-resistant refractory bricks. The *charge* or *burden* of ore and coke, together with limestone which helps to remove impurities such as sand or clay, is loaded into the top of the furnace, and pre-heated air is blown in through the bottom. Alternatively, many modern furnaces are charged with *sinter* and untreated ore. Sinter is made by crushing iron ore, coke and limestone together and then roasting them, producing lumps of sinter which have a relatively high iron content.

As the charge drops down the furnace it meets the blast of hot air being blown up from the bottom, the air being at a temperature of around 1,000°C (1,800°F). The chemical reactions which occur when the charge meets the air are quite complicated, but in essence the carbon in the charge reacts with the oxygen in the air to form carbon monoxide; this carbon monoxide in turn reacts with the oxygen in the iron ore, reducing the iron oxide to iron and forming carbon dioxide.

The exhaust gases from the reaction, which contain about 25 per cent carbon monoxide and can thus be used as a low-grade fuel gas, are extracted from the top of the furnace. After being mixed with richer fuel gases, the furnace gas is burnt in the plant that heats the blast air.

The molten iron collects at the bottom of the furnace. The limestone, having combined with the impurities in the ore, forms a *slag* consisting mainly of calcium aluminium silicate which floats on the top of the molten metal. The iron-making process is a continuous one, with fresh batches of charge being loaded in at regular intervals. The metal and the slag are tapped off separately, also at regular intervals.

In some modern blast furnaces the process is made more efficient by the use of *supplementary fuel firing*. This involves the addition of extra *reducing gases* (which will again combine with the oxygen in the ore) to the blast, these gases being produced by burning a fuel such as oil or pulverized coal.

The molten iron tapped off from the furnace, typically about 2,000 tonnes every six hours for a large furnace, is either cast into large ingots (*pigs*) or carried in molten form to a steelmaking plant. This iron contains various impurities, depending partly on the composition of the original ore but mainly upon the proportion of limestone used in the charge.

Radio Times Hulton Picture Library

British Steel Corporation

Above: The Eiffel Tower, Paris, during its construction. It was built of *wrought iron*, which is made by keeping pig iron molten so that impurities oxidize out of it, and then mechanically working the resulting spongy iron into a usable metal by means of heavy duty hammers or presses.

Below: Lumps of iron ore about 50 mm (2 in) across are used in blast furnaces without any prior treatment. Larger pieces are crushed and mixed with smaller lumps to be made into *sinter*, a roasted mixture of ore, coke and limestone, pictured here leaving the sinter machine where it is roasted.

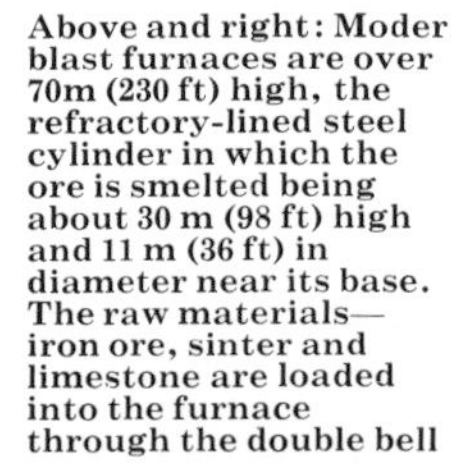

Above and right: Modern blast furnaces are over 70m (230 ft) high, the refractory-lined steel cylinder in which the ore is smelted being about 30 m (98 ft) high and 11 m (36 ft) in diameter near its base. The raw materials—iron ore, sinter and limestone are loaded into the furnace through the double bell charging arrangement at the top, which prevents hot gases escaping when the charge drops into the furnace. As the charge passes down the furnace, the hot air blast blown in through the bottom reacts with it to reduce the ore to molten metal. The impurities in the ore react with the limestone to form a slag.

British Steel Corporation

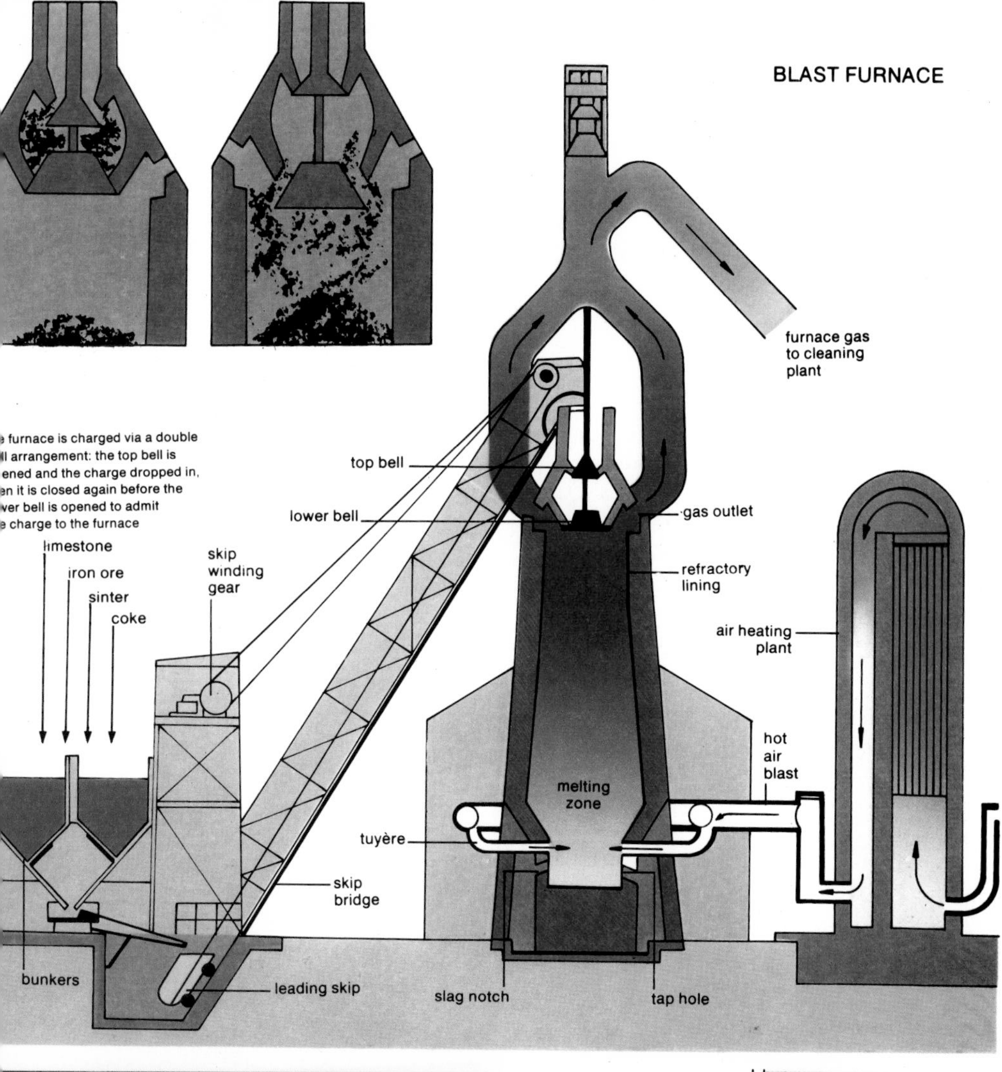

When a minimum amount of limestone is used, so as to produce a slag with a low melting point which gives the furnace a higher themal efficiency, the iron produced is known as *basic iron*. Basic iron contains sulphur, either in the form of iron sulphide or, if the ore has a high manganese content, as manganese sulphide.

Acid iron is formed when the charge contains a high proportion of limestone, which results in a slag of higher melting point than that used for basic iron. The higher temperature involved means that some of the silica present in the ore is not drawn into the slag, but reduced to silicon which becomes dissolved in the molten iron.

White cast iron, so called because when fractured it has a bright, whitish appearance, is a basic iron containing less than 1.5 per cent silicon and about 3.5 per cent carbon in the form of iron carbide. This iron carbide makes iron hard, brittle and difficult to machine, and so it is less widely used than the far more machineable *grey cast iron*.

Grey cast iron has a silicon content of between about 2 and 4 per cent, and the carbon present in it is in the form of flakes of graphite. The graphite makes the iron brittle, and gives it its characteristic dull grey appearance when fractured. Grey cast iron is extensively used for vehicle components such as cylinder blocks and for many other heavy castings.

White cast irons are often modified by heat treatment to produce *malleable irons* which are much less brittle and thus more useful. *White-heart malleable iron* is produced by heating white cast iron in such a way that the carbon near the surfaces is oxidized away. This makes the iron less prone to fracture because its surface layers, being largely freed of iron carbide, are more ductile.

By heating white cast iron in such a way that the iron carbide in it is decomposed into particles of graphite, an iron with mechanical properties close to those of mild steel is produced. This iron is known as *black-heart malleable iron*. The main difference between this iron and grey cast iron is that the graphite does not form as flakes, which act rather like tiny cracks within the grey cast iron, but as 'rosettes' which do not have such an adverse effect on the strength of the metal.

The addition of small amounts of elements such as calcium or magnesium to molten acid iron causes the graphite to precipitate as irregular, rounded nodules, rather than as the flakes typical of grey cast iron. The iron thus produced, *nodular cast iron*, has similar properties to black-heart malleable iron, but the production process is much simpler,

Above and above right: Most of the steel produced today is made in basic oxygen converters. During the 'blow' the converter is in its vertical position and covered by a fume-collecting hood (through which the oxygen lance is inserted) which carries away the exhaust gases and dust.

Below: The main stages in the production of basic oxygen steel. The converter is charged with scrap and then molten iron, then brought into the vertical position for the blow. When the metal is ready it is poured off into a ladle, then the converter is tipped over and the slag is removed.

THE BASIC OXYGEN PROCESS

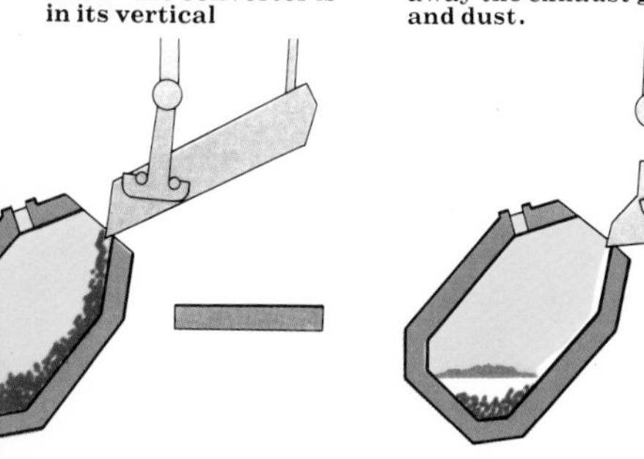

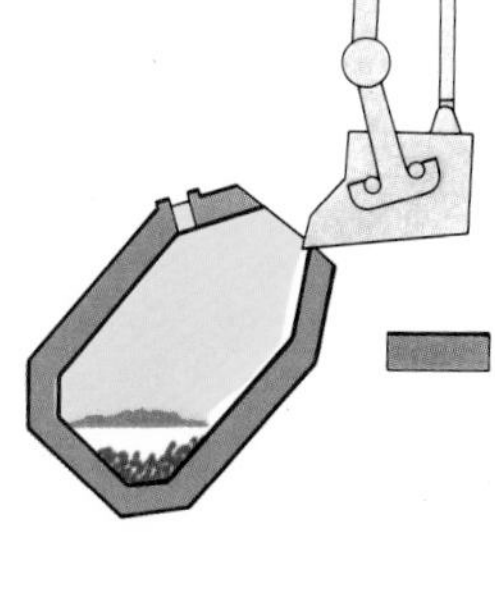

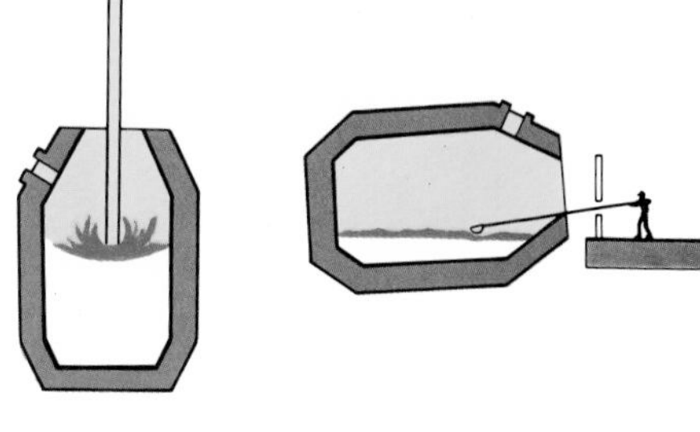

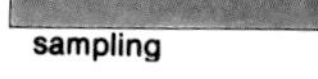

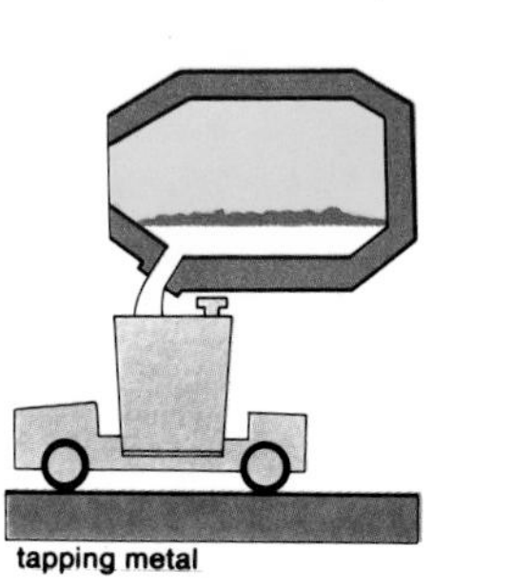

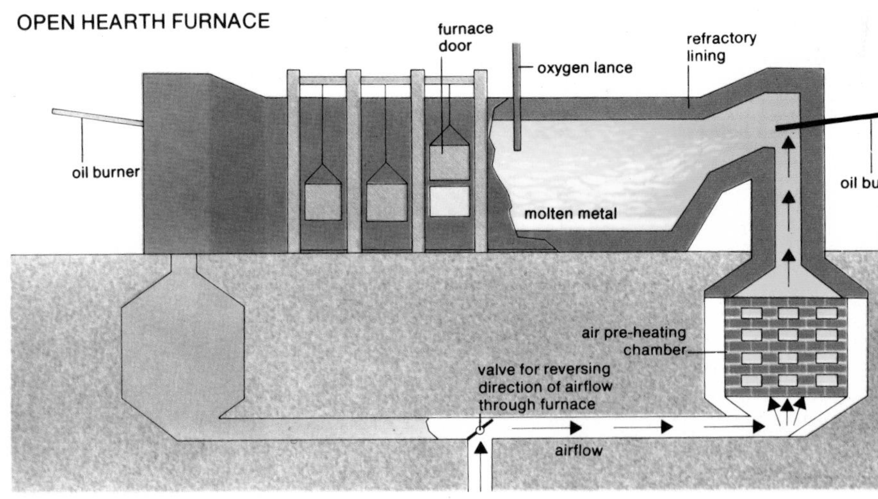

Above left: Charging an open hearth furnace with hot metal after the 'solid charge' of scrap and limestone has been put in.

Above right: In an open hearth furnace the charge is melted by burning a fuel, such as oil or gas, in a stream of pre-heated air. The process is speeded by the use of oxygen blown in through lances.

Left and right: The electric arc furnace uses electric arcs to melt the charge. To charge the furnace the electrodes are withdrawn and the roof swung clear, allowing the charge to be dropped in. The molten metal is tapped off by tilting the whole furnace.

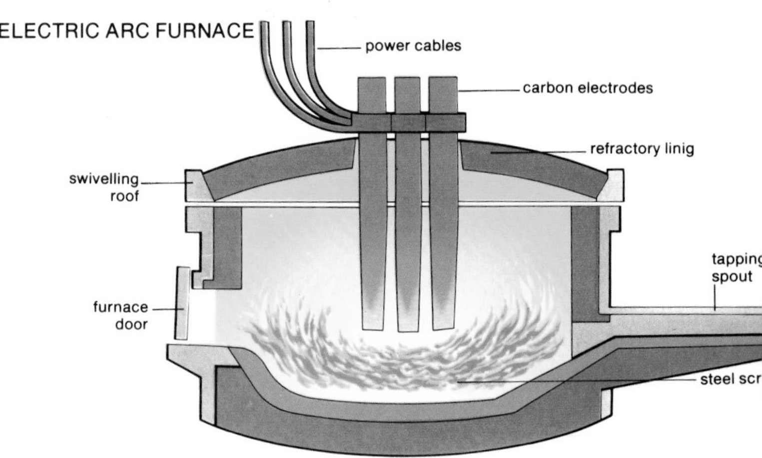

merely requiring the addition of extra elements to the molten iron rather than a period of carefully-controlled heat treatment.

Steelmaking

Steel is basically an alloy of iron and carbon, the carbon content being carefully controlled and much lower than that of cast iron. The carbon content is usually well under 2 per cent, most steels containing around 0.25 per cent. A wide range of other elements, such as chromium, manganese, nickel and vanadium, may be added to produce *alloy steels* with enhanced properties such as hardness or corrosion resistance.

In essence, steel is made by removing the carbon and other impurities from iron, and then adding precise amounts of carbon and other elements to turn the iron into steel.

The first successful method of producing steel in large quantities was devised in England by Henry Bessemer (1813-1898) in the middle of the nineteenth century. Bessemer's *converter* was a large iron barrel lined with refractory bricks and mounted on a pair of pivots so that it could be tilted from a horizontal to a vertical position.

With the converter in the horizontal position, molten iron, scrap iron and limestone were charged into it, and it was then tilted into its vertical position. Powerful blasts of air were blown through the bottom of the converter and up through the charge. The oxygen in the air combined with the carbon in the iron to form carbon monoxide, thus removing the carbon from the iron. The oxygen also reacted with the other impurities present, such as silicon and manganese, to form oxides which combined with the limestone *flux* to form a slag. The 'blow' took about 15 minutes, after which the converter was carefully tilted so that the metal was poured into a ladle and the slag was left behind in the converter to be removed separately.

As the metal was poured into the ladle, controlled amounts of ferro-silicon, aluminium, and a special alloy of manganese and iron known as *spiegel* were added to remove any oxygen and iron oxide from the metal. The iron was then made into steel by the addition of precise amounts of carbon, usually in the form of coke or anthracite.

The Bessemer process remained in use for over 100 years, but it is now obsolete, having been supplanted by a more efficient version known as the *basic oxygen* process. Instead of blowing air up through the charge, a water-cooled lance is inserted into the mouth of the converter so that its tip is just above the surface of the charge, and then oxygen is blown through it at very high speed. In a typical converter the lance delivers some 860 m^3 (30,000 ft^3) of oxygen per minute.

The oxygen oxidizes the impurities in the charge, and the turbulence that it creates in the metal ensures that all the impurities are oxidized. The process is termed 'basic' because the refractory lining of the converter is made of *basic* refractory materials composed of oxides of metals such as magnesium or calcium. *Acid* refractories, made of silica, would be chemically attacked by the lime in the flux, this lime being necessary for the removal of phosphorus from the iron.

Below: Pouring molten steel from a ladle into a *tundish*, a pre-heated refractory-lined trough which carries it to the top of a *continuous casting machine*. In this machine the steel passes through a water-cooled mould, emerging as a continuous length of metal which is then cooled and cut into slabs.

Right: A continuous casting machine. The molten steel is brought from the converter or furnace in a ladle, and *teemed* (poured) into the tundish. It flows from the tundish into the mould, then through a cooling chamber where it is sprayed with water to solidify it ready for straightening and cutting.

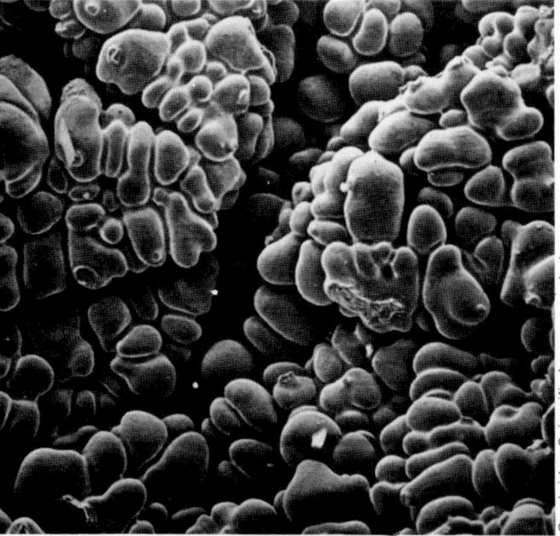

Above: An electron microscope photograph of the surface of a cast steel containing 0.1 per cent carbon. Most of the carbon in a steel is present as iron carbide (Fe_3C), which occurs either as distinct globules called *cementite*, or as *pearlite*, an intimate mixture of almost pure iron with iron carbide.

Right: Slabs of cast steel, up to 10 m (33ft) long and 250 mm (10 in) thick, are heated to about 1,300°C (2,370°F) and then passed through a series of rollers which make them progressively longer and thinner. They are then ready to be made into plates, sheets, or large coils of strip steel.

Above right: Coils of hot-rolled steel are treated with dilute acid to remove surface scale, cold-rolled to reduce them to the required thickness, then annealed and rolled again to optimize their mechanical properties before being wound into coils such as the ones shown here.

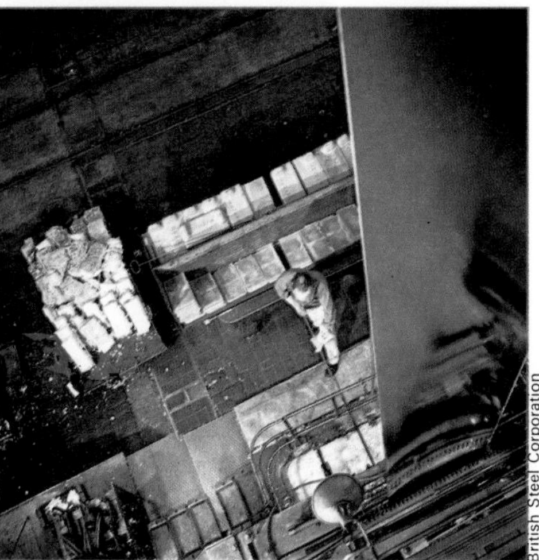

Right: Iron and steel are often *galvanized*, coated with a thin layer of zinc to protect them from corrosion. This picture shows a *hot dip* process, in which a strip of steel, cleaned with acid and coated with zinc ammonium chloride, is dipped into a bath of molten zinc to galvanize it.

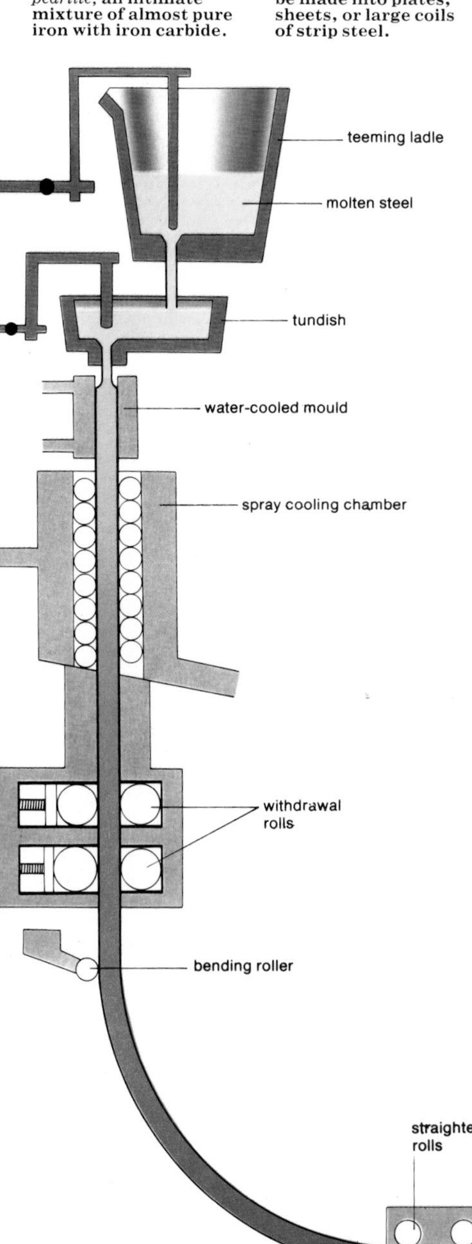

The basic oxygen process accounts for the bulk of the world's steel production, its advantages over other methods including its speed (a typical basic oxygen converter can make 350 tonnes or more of molten iron into steel in about 40 minutes) and its relative cheapness. It requires no fuel, because the reactions which occur between the charge and the oxygen are *exothermic*, that is they produce heat.

The other principal steelmaking processes, however, require fuel or electricity to provide heat and have much lower output rates. In the *open hearth process*, developed by Dr Charles Siemens in the 1850s, fuel oil or gas is burnt in preheated air above the surface of the charge, which consists of molten iron, scrap iron, fluxes such as limestone, and oxygen-rich materials such as iron ore which together with the oxygen in the furnace gases supply the oxygen needed for the reaction.

Most alloy steels, such as stainless steel, are made in electric furnaces such as the *electric arc furnace*. This type of furnace is loaded with cold metal such as scrap steel or cast iron, then the roof is swung closed and three large carbon electrodes are lowered through it. A voltage is applied to the electrodes and electric arcs are struck between them and the charge, creating intense heat which melts it. Alloying metals, and fluxes such as lime, fluorspar and iron oxide, are added through a door in the side of the furnace, and an oxygen lance is often employed to speed the reaction.

Electric induction furnaces also use a cold charge, but in these the heat is generated by the use of electric coils, arranged outside the furnace, which induce currents to flow within the charge itself. These induced currents heat and melt the charge. Induction furnaces have relatively low capacities, ranging from a few kilogrammes to about 20 tonnes.

Refining

Although the steel produced by the three main processes (basic oxygen, open hearth and electric arc) is of high quality, it still contains certain amounts of trapped gases and solid impurities. There are numerous specialized applications which require steels of very high purity, for example in the aerospace, nuclear and chemical industries, and the steels used for these purposes must first be *refined*.

There are a number of different processes by which steel can be refined, such as *vacuum remelting* and *electroslag refining*. Vacuum remelting involves melting the steel in a vacuum, the gases given off from the molten metal being drawn off by the vacuum pumps.

In electroslag refining, the end of the bar of steel to be refined is immersed in a pool of molten slag and melted by an electric arc. Droplets of metal melted from the bar pass through the slag, which removes the impurities from them.

Non-ferrous Metals

The term 'non-ferrous' describes all metals other than iron, and is also applied to alloys which contain no iron. The number of different metals is very large—some two-thirds of all the chemical elements are metals. These range from the well-known and widely-used metals such as aluminium (and iron) to the less common elements such as the 'rare earth' metals (for example europium and yttrium).

The most important non-ferrous metals are aluminium, copper, zinc, lead, tin, and nickel, which are essential to industry; and to a lesser extent the precious metals gold, silver and platinum which have many important industrial and engineering uses in addition to their decorative and commercial roles. Two metals which have come to prominence during the last 40 years or so are uranium, a natural element, and plutonium, which does not occur in nature. These metals have an ambiguous and controversial nature, offering on the one hand the prospect of plentiful supplies of energy, and on the other the threat of nuclear warfare and the danger of lethal pollution.

Keystone

Above: The statue of Eros in Piccadilly Circus, London, designed by Sir Alfred Gilbert and unveiled in 1893 as a memorial to Lord Shaftesbury, the reformer and philanthropist. The statue is made of cast aluminium, which at the time was a very expensive and uncommon metal.

British Aluminium Co. Ltd.

Above: Removing blocks of aluminium from a casting pit at a smelter in Invergordon, north-east Scotland. The blocks weigh 6 to 8 tonnes each, and are supplied to rolling mills where they are rolled to various thicknesses ready for shaping processes such as pressing, stamping or extrusion.

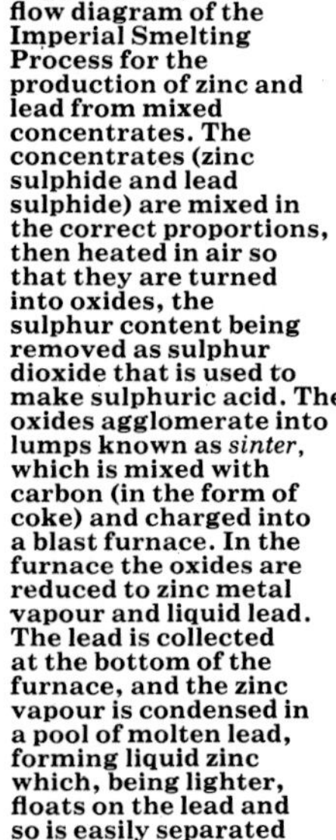

Right: A simplified flow diagram of the Imperial Smelting Process for the production of zinc and lead from mixed concentrates. The concentrates (zinc sulphide and lead sulphide) are mixed in the correct proportions, then heated in air so that they are turned into oxides, the sulphur content being removed as sulphur dioxide that is used to make sulphuric acid. The oxides agglomerate into lumps known as *sinter*, which is mixed with carbon (in the form of coke) and charged into a blast furnace. In the furnace the oxides are reduced to zinc metal vapour and liquid lead. The lead is collected at the bottom of the furnace, and the zinc vapour is condensed in a pool of molten lead, forming liquid zinc which, being lighter, floats on the lead and so is easily separated from it.

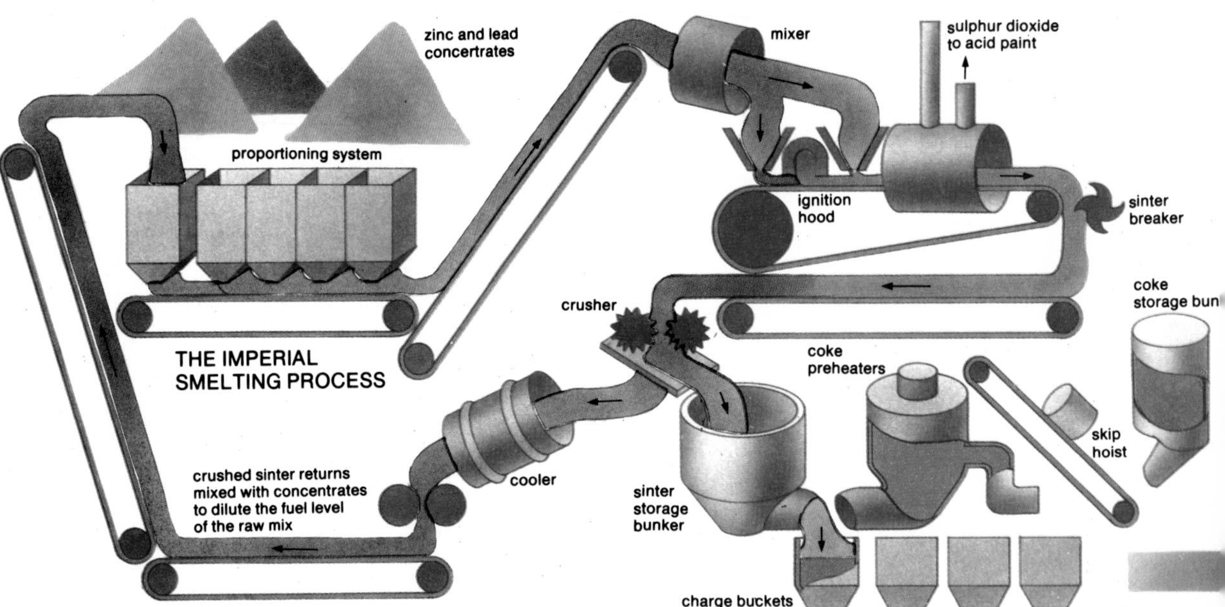

Aluminium

Aluminium is the most abundant metal in the crust of the earth, accounting for about one-twelfth of its mass. Not all of this is easily accessible for use as a metal: a large part of it exists in chemical combination with other elements from which it cannot easily be separated. Clay, for example, contains about 25 per cent aluminium, but the extraction of pure aluminium from it is far too expensive to be of any use.

The ore from which aluminium is extracted is known as *bauxite* ($Al_2O_3.H_2O$ or $Al_2O_3.3H_2O$), a hydrated form of aluminium oxide formed by the weathering of clays. Large deposits of bauxite occur in many parts of the world, including Australia, Jamaica, Guinea and the USSR.

The principal method of extracting the metal from its ore is by electrolysis. The bauxite is first crushed and mixed with hot, strong caustic soda. This produces a solution of sodium aluminate in caustic soda, and insoluble impurities which are then filtered off. The sodium aluminate is further processed to obtain anhydrous *alumina* (Al_2O_3).

The alumina is dissolved in molten *cryolite* (Na_3AlF_6), and this solution is electrolyzed at a temperature of about 1,000°C (1,830°F) to obtain the aluminium. The electrolysis takes place in large metal *pots* which can hold about 20 tonnes each, and a modern smelter may have several hundred such pots. Each pot has a carbon cathode in its base, and the anodes, massive carbon blocks, are lowered into the electrolyte from above.

The process operates at a low voltage but enormous currents are used, and so one of the main considerations involved in the siting of aluminium smelters is the availability of large amounts of cheap electricity, for instance from a hydro-electric power station. A typical smelter requires about 18 kWh of electricity to produce 1 kg (2.2 lb) of aluminium.

Aluminium is a light metal, having about one-third the density of steel, and it is more resistant to atmospheric corrosion than most other metals. This is because a thin but tough film of oxide forms on its surface to resist further corrosion. For increased corrosion resistance, some aluminium products are *anodized* by an electrolytic process that creates a much thicker and tougher oxide coating than that which forms

Hoechst UK Ltd.

Above: Electricity cables with aluminium conductors are now replacing those with copper conductors (such as the one in the background) because, for a given current-carrying capacity, although somewhat bulkier they are cheaper and lighter. Those shown here are insulated with pvc.

Consolidated Gold Fields Ltd.

Above: A scoop tram carrying tin ore at the Wheal Jane tin mine in Cornwall, England. Cornish tin has been mined since before 500 BC, and Cornwall was one of the sources of tin for the ancient Mediterranean civilizations. The Cornish mines produced about 3,330 tonnes of tin in 1976.

Below: Pouring molten zinc at the United Kingdom's sole producer of primary zinc metal at Avonmouth, near Bristol. This zinc is produced by the Imperial Smelting Process, which was developed at Avonmouth after the Second World War and as now used, under licence, by about a dozen countries.

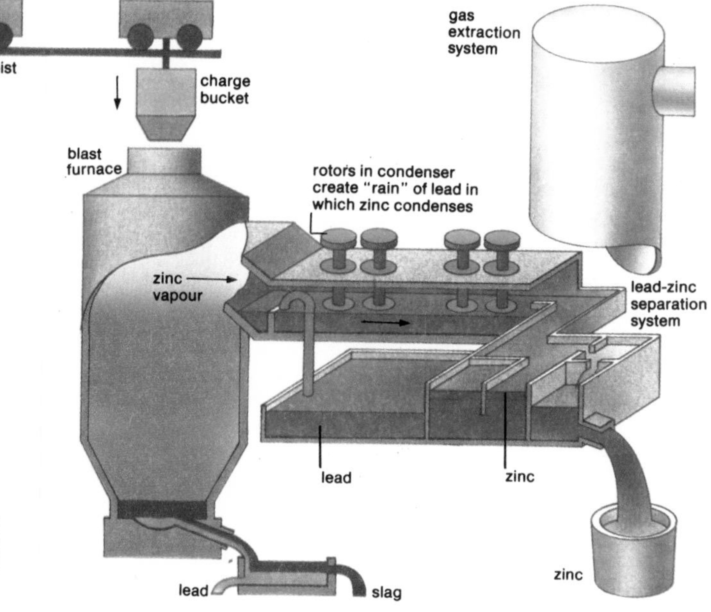

RTZ

naturally. This coating is also able to absorb dyes, and so the metal can be given a coloured surface.

Aluminium and its alloys have a great many uses, ranging from aluminium foil and cooking utensils to window frames, building cladding panels, and alloys for the aerospace industry. In electrical engineering, aluminium is increasingly replacing copper as the metal used for the conductors of power cables and domestic wiring. Although its conductivity is only about two-thirds that of copper, an aluminium cable of given current-carrying capacity is lighter and cheaper than an equivalent copper one.

Copper

Copper was one of the first metals used by man, because small amounts of metallic copper occur naturally and so the fabrication of copper artifacts was possible before the techniques of smelting the metal from its ores were discovered. The use of natural copper marked an intermediate stage between the Neolithic and the Bronze Ages, and this period is sometimes referred to as the Chalcolithic or Copper Age. The Chalcolithic Age evolved into the Bronze Age in about 3000 BC, when the first bronze, an alloy of copper and tin, was produced in Anatolia (Turkey).

The principal copper ores are *copper glance* (copper sulphide, Cu_2S), *chalcopyrite* or *copper pyrites* (copper iron sulphide, $CuFeS_2$) and *cuprite* (cuprous oxide, Cu_2O). The major sources of copper ores are the USA, the USSR, China, Zambia, Chile, and Canada.

The two main areas of use for copper are for electrical wiring, contacts and connectors and for making alloys such as bronzes, brasses (based on copper and zinc) and cupro-nickel alloys. In addition to its very high electrical conductivity, copper is an excellent conductor of heat, and so has many uses in heat exchangers.

Zinc

The first use of zinc was for making brass, although at the time its existence as a separate metal was not appreciated. The first brass was made in about 1000 BC by the Mossynoeci people in north eastern Turkey, and subsequently by the Persians and the Romans. It was thought to be a form of bronze, and was made by heating copper with charcoal and powdered *calamine* (zinc carbonate, $ZnCO_3$), an ore of zinc. During the primitive processes

INCO Europe Ltd.

Bank of England

Above: Many 'silver' coins nowadays contain little if any silver, and are made of cupro-nickel alloys or, in the case of the Canadian coins, pure nickel. Canada is the world's largest producer of nickel, producing twice as much as any other country. Its output in 1976 was about 239,000 tonnes.

Right: Casting gold bars at the West Driefontein mine in South Africa, one of the richest gold mines in the world. Total gold production in the non-communist countries in 1976 was 955 tonnes, of which 709.1 tonnes were produced by South Africa, 52.8 tonnes by Canada, and 32 tonnes by the United States.

Above: Some of Britain's gold reserves, in the vaults of the Bank of England. Apart from its monetary role, the most important use of gold is for jewellery, which accounts for about 90 per cent of the non-monetary use of the metal. Other important uses include dental and electronic applications.

Below: An important modern use of lead is for radiation shielding in nuclear power stations and laboratories and in X-ray and gamma ray equipment. The laboratory cells shown here have walls of cast lead bricks, and windows made of glass containing a high proportion of lead.

Consolidated Gold Fields Ltd.

UKAEA

used, any zinc metal formed that did not combine with the copper would have vaporized away, and so its presence went undetected.

Zinc was first isolated in the late Middle Ages in China and Sumatra, and the first zinc known in the West was imported from these countries in the early seventeenth century. The first commercial zinc smelter in the West was built by William Champion of Bristol in 1740.

The chief zinc ore today is *sphalerite* or *zinc blende* (zinc sulphide, ZnS), large deposits of which are found in North America, the USSR, Australia, Peru, Japan and Poland. Zinc can be recovered from its ores by electrolytic processing, but most processes involve heating, first (in the presence of air) to convert the sulphide into zinc oxide, and then (in the presence of carbon) to reduce the oxide to the metal. The metal appears as a vapour and is condensed to form solid zinc.

About a fifth of all zinc produced is used for making brass, and a similar proportion is used for *galvanizing* iron to protect it from corrosion. Like aluminium, when zinc is exposed to air a film of oxide forms on its surface and protects it from further oxidation. Galvanization is the coating of an iron or steel article with a thin coating of zinc, either by dipping the article into a bath of molten zinc, or by electroplating.

Zinc alloys are widely used for such items as vehicle components (for instance carburetter bodies) and toys. Such items are usually *diecast* by forcing the molten alloy into a steel mould or die. Zinc sheeting is often used for roofing, and other uses of sheet zinc include lithographic printing plates, dry battery casings and coffin linings.

Lead

The first large-scale consumers of lead were the Romans, who used it for their water and drain pipes, although the metal was known to the Egyptians in the Bronze Age. The main source of lead is *galena* (lead sulphide, PbS), which frequently occurs in association with zinc blende. To obtain the metal from the galena, the ore is concentrated and then roasted to convert it to lead oxide (PbO). The lead oxide is reduced to lead in small blast furnaces, and the lead thus obtained is further refined to remove impurities such as arsenic, tin, antimony, copper and silver which were present in the original ore and not removed during the smelting.

The traditional uses of lead, for plumbing and roofing, are now of comparatively little importance. It is, however, widely used in accumulators, many types of alloy such as pewter, leaded bronzes and solders, and radiation shields. Its high resistance to attack by sulphuric acid makes it very useful to the chemical industry. Lead is also used for cable sheathing, and lead compounds are used extensively in anti-corrosion paints, explosives and glass. Lead tetraethyl ($Pb(C_2H_5)_4$) is used as an anti-knock additive in some grades of petrol, though it does give rise to atmospheric pollution.

Tin

Tin, first used for making bronze, is one of the more expensive of the common non-ferrous metals. One of the reasons for its high cost is that its principal ore, *cassiterite* (tin oxide, SnO_2), is only found in very low concentrations; a tonne of earth may have to be mined in order to recover 200 g (7 oz) of ore. Extensive concentration of the ore-bearing material is therefore necessary before the ore can be smelted into tin. The smelting is achieved by heating the concentrated ore in a furnace together with anthracite and fluxing materials such as limestone and sand. The anthracite (a form of carbon) reacts with the oxygen in the ore, forming carbon dioxide and reducing the tin oxide to tin.

The most important use of tin, accounting for about 40 per cent of tin consumption, is for the coating of steel to make tinplate. The chief use of tinplate is for food and drink cans, the tin protecting the steel from external corrosion and from internal attack by the contents of the can. The tin coating also enables the steel can to be soldered together.

1 aluminium
2 copper
3 zinc
4 lead
5 tin
6 nickel
7 magnesium
8 chromium
9 silver
10 gold
11 mercury (vapour)
12 tungsten

Left: Some common uses of non-ferrous metals. Aluminium is used extensively in aircraft, for radio and tv antennae and for electricity cables. Copper's uses include plumbing and central heating fittings, and electricity and telephone cables. Lead has been used for water pipes since Roman times, and other common uses including roofing, cable sheathing and battery plates. The largest single use of magnesium is in Volkswagen engines, and it is also used in flash bulbs. Zinc, tin, nickel and chromium are used for plating and in many alloys, such as bronze, brass and stainless steel. Silver is an important ingredient of photographic materials and, like gold, a popular metal for jewellery.

Tin is an important constituent of many alloys, chiefly the bronzes and the solder alloys. Tin compounds have many applications, and are used in fungicides, anti-fouling paints (used on boat hulls), catalysts and electronic components.

Nickel

The most important use of nickel is for the production of alloys, its largest single application being in the making of stainless steels. Its principal ore is nickel sulphide (NiS), which is usually found mixed with other ores such as those of copper or iron. After it has been separated from the other ores, the sulphide is roasted to produce nickel oxide, which is then reduced to nickel by heating it to about 350°C (660°F) in an atmosphere of *producer gas*, a mixture of hydrogen and carbon monoxide.

The nickel at this stage is in an impure form, and so a refining process is necessary. This may be an electrolytic process, or else the refining may be by the *Mond process*, developed in 1889 by Ludwig Mond and Alfred Langer. In this process the nickel powder is again exposed to producer gas, but at a temperature of about 50°C (122°F) instead of 350°C, so that it combines with the carbon monoxide to form nickel carbonyl ($Ni(CO)_4$). This is a volatile compound, which passes as a vapour into a decomposition tower where it is heated further (to about 180°C) so that it breaks down into pure nickel metal, which is deposited as pellets, and carbon monoxide gas.

Pure nickel has important uses as a catalyst, and is often electroplated on to other metals to give them a corrosion-resistant coating. This coating may have a further layer, of chromium, electroplated on to it to give it a brighter appearance; 'chromium plated' articles are, in fact, plated with nickel and then chromium, the chromium being too brittle to give adequate protection on its own.

Below: Drums of uranium oxide concentrate being delivered to a processing factory which produces uranium fuel for nuclear reactors. The principal sources of uranium are the United States, Canada, France and several African states including South Africa, Niger and Gabon.

Below: Pellets of uranium-plutonium oxide which are used as fuel in *fast breeder* nuclear reactors. The fissile plutonium in the fuel is consumed during the reactions, but the fast neutrons given off by it convert the uranium into plutonium; more than one plutonium atom is created ('bred') for each one destroyed.

UKAEA

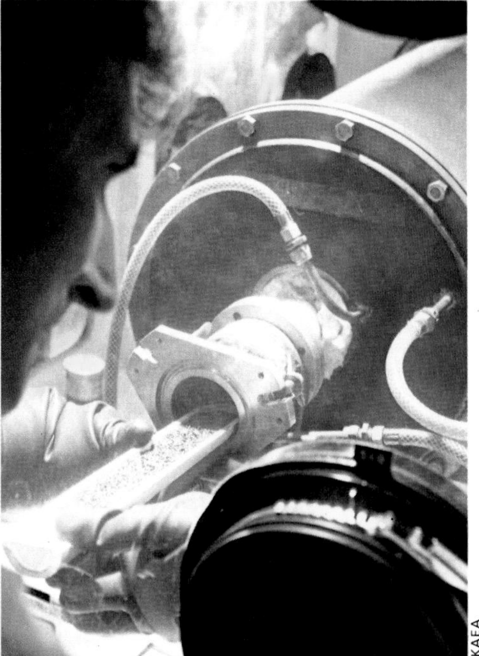

UKAEA

Alloys

An alloy is an intimate mixture of two or more substances, at least one of which is a metal. Almost all alloys are made by mixing the constituent elements in the required proportions in the molten state. There are three ways in which the elements can combine to form an alloy, and in practice an alloy may contain elements combined in more than one of these ways.

The three ways in which metals combine with each other (or with other elements) to form alloys are as *substitutional* or *interstitial solid solutions*, or as *intermetallic compounds*. In the two forms of solid solution, the metals are effectively dissolved in one another. In a substitutional solution, the crystal lattice of one metal contains atoms of another, these atoms occupying normal atomic sites (which would otherwise be occupied by atoms of the parent metal) at random points within the lattice. In an interstitial solution, on the other hand, the atoms of the second metal occupy spaces between the atoms in the crystal lattice of the first.

Intermetallic compounds are formed when two different metals combine chemically, in definite proportions, to form crystalline compounds with lattice structures containing atoms of each metal arranged in a regular pattern. Copper and aluminium, for example, can form an intermetallic compound with the formula $CuAl_2$.

The physical properties of a metal, such as its strength, ductility, hardness, melting point and electrical conductivity, depend upon its crystalline structure. When two metals are alloyed, the resulting alloy has, in the case of a substitutional solution or an intermetallic compound, a regular crystal lattice containing two different types of atom. In an interstitial solution, the basic crystal structure is that of the parent metal, but the lattice is distorted by the presence of atoms of the other squeezed into the spaces within it.

In either case, the structure of the alloy is different from that of either of the metals from which it is formed, and consequently its properties are different. The majority of metal articles in use today are made of alloys rather than of pure metals.

Copper-based alloys

The copper-based alloys include *bronze* (the oldest man-made alloy), *brass* and the *cupro-nickel* alloys. Bronze was originally an alloy consisting of about three parts copper and one part tin, but the name now refers to an extensive range of copper-based alloys containing a variety of metals and sometimes little or no tin.

Among the most important bronzes are the *phosphor bronzes*, made by adding up to 0.5 per cent of phosphorus to a copper-tin bronze containing 85 to 90 per cent copper. When the phosphorus content is less than 0.3 per cent the alloy is springy, and since it is also non-magnetic it is very useful for such items as relay contacts. When the phosphorus content is higher, the alloy is made much harder by the formation of copper phosphide (Cu_3P) within it. This harder form is widely used as a bearing metal, and its usefulness is further enhanced by the addition of about 3.5 per cent lead. The leaded phosphor bronzes are particularly useful for bearings which are exposed to high speeds and pressures.

Another example of bronzes containing lead are the *leaded tin bronzes*, which contain amounts of lead ranging from as little as 0.5 per cent to as much as 20 per cent. These low-lead alloys are used in components for oil pumps and carburettors, for steam and water pipe fittings, and for ornamental bronzes. The high-lead tin bronzes, like the leaded phosphor bronzes, find many uses in high-performance bearings.

Lead, in proportions of up to 5 per cent, is also used in some types of *gunmetal*, a bronze containing zinc which, as its name implies was originally used for making gun barrels. The traditional gunmetals contain about 88 per cent copper, with about 8 to 10 per cent tin and between 2 and 4 per cent zinc. Nickel gunmetals contain up to 5 per cent nickel. Gunmetals are now used for many engineering purposes, including bearings, pumps, gears, valves and castings.

Aluminium bronze is an alloy of copper and aluminium, often containing

Picturepoint

Picturepoint

Inco Europe Ltd

Above: A bronze casting from Nineveh, made over 4,000 years ago. Bronze, the oldest alloy, is made basically from copper and tin, although some modern 'bronzes' may contain no tin.

Left: An ornamental dish made from pewter, an alloy of tin and lead.

Above: A modern Japanese temple roofed with black stainless steel (the blue appearance is a reflection of the sky), which is made by treating the metal with hot chromic and sulphuric acids.

Below: A large ship's propeller made of high tensile brass.

Copper Development Association

small amounts of other metals such as nickel, iron or manganese, but although it is called a bronze it usually contains no tin at all. It is as strong as mild steel, and has a good resistance to corrosion and attack by dilute acids. It has many uses, including ship's propellers, hydraulic equipment components and chemical engineering equipment such as acid-resistant tanks and pumps.

Brass is basically an alloy of copper and zinc, combined in a wide range of proportions and often alloyed with other metals including tin, lead and aluminium. *Cartridge brass*, originally developed for cartridge cases and still used for this purpose, is made from about 70 per cent copper and 30 per cent zinc. Other uses include valves and plumbing fittings and the base caps of electric light bulbs.

Cartridge brass is very ductile, but this property is offset by its relatively low tensile strength. *High tensile brass* is harder and stronger, and is made by alloying copper and zinc with manganese, iron, tin, lead and aluminium. It is easily worked and very suitable for casting, and typical uses include marine equipment such as propellers.

There are many other types of brass, and the metal has a wide spectrum of applications including engineering components, domestic fittings, gears, ornaments and electrical components such as connectors, plug pins and cable terminations. *Nickel silver*, an alloy of copper, nickel and zinc (but containing no silver), is best known for its use in domestic cutlery, for which purpose it is usually plated with silver and known as *electroplated nickel silver* (EPNS).

Left: A pure metal (top diagram) bends easily because its atoms are arranged in straight rows, but the presence of dislocations between rows leads to splitting (centre). In a solid solution alloy (bottom) the rows of atoms of the parent metal are distorted by the presence of the atoms of the alloying metal, resulting in a much stronger and tougher structure.

Right: The changes in the composition of British bronze coins since 1860 and silver coins from 1921 to 1947. The 'silver' coins today contain no silver.

Below: A shop in Park Lane, London, fitted out in stainless steel.

COMPOSITION OF BRITISH BRONZE COINS

date	copper %	tin %	zinc %
1860-1923	95	4	1
1923-1942	95½	3	1½
1942-1945	97	½	2½
1945-1959	95½	3	1½
1959-to date	97	½	2½

COMPOSITION OF BRITISH SILVER COINS

date	silver %	copper %	nickel %	zinc %
1921	92½	7½	0	0
1922	50	50	0	0
1927-1947	50	40	5	5

British Steel Corporation

Aluminium alloys

Compared with the copper-based alloys, the production of aluminium alloys is a recent development and most of the alloys now in use were developed within the last 50 years. Aluminium alloys suitable for casting usually contain up to about 15 per cent silicon, plus small amounts of, for example, copper, iron, nickel, magnesium and zinc.

Cast aluminium alloys have many uses, including engine cylinder blocks and components for aircraft engines and airframes. Aluminium alloys suitable for other types of shaping processes, such as forging, rolling or drawing, contain up to about 7 per cent magnesium plus around 1 per cent manganese. Very strong aluminium alloys of this type, widely used in the aircraft industry, are made with about 5 per cent zinc and smaller amounts of copper, magnesium and manganese.

One of the most important discoveries in the development of aluminium alloys was that of the phenomenon known as *age hardening*. This was discovered by the German metallurgist Dr Alfred Wilm in 1909. Wilm was experimenting with an aluminium alloy containing about 3.5 per cent copper and 0.5 per cent magnesium, attempting to make it harder by various methods of heat treatment, including heating the metal to about 500°C (900°F) and then plunging it into water to cool it.

This treatment did not harden the metal as much as Wilm had hoped, but when he tested it again after a period of several days he found it had somehow become very much harder although it had had no further treatment. This alloy, which became known as *Duralumin*, was soon being used in the Zeppelin airships and in aircraft, but it was some time before the reasons for the hardening were understood.

When the alloy was heated, the copper in it entered the aluminium as a solid solution. At room temperature, however, aluminium can only hold about 0.5 per cent of copper in solid solution, and so after the alloy had been cooled in water the copper began, slowly, to come out of solution. Immediately after heat treatment the alloy was little harder than it was before, and most of the copper was still in solution. After four or five days, however, most of the copper had come out of solution and formed minute particles of the intermetallic compound $CuAl_2$ dispersed throughout the alloy. These particles gave the 'aged' alloy its hardness by straining its crystal lattice in such a way as to inhibit the *slip* (or *dislocation*) mechanism by which the crystals, and thus the metal, could be deformed.

Duralumin has many uses, for example in the aerospace industry and for making radio and tv antennae. Its typical composition is an aluminium base containing 3.5 to 4.5 per cent copper, 0.4 to 0.7 per cent each of magnesium and manganese,

A. M. & S. Europe Ltd

Above: If two different metals are immersed in salt water, electrochemical reactions will be set up which cause corrosion of the metal which has the higher *electrode potential*. The corrosion of ships' hulls can be reduced by the use of 'sacrificial' zinc alloy anodes; these have a higher potential than the steel of the hull, which means that they corrode away rather than the hull. This picture shows anodes being fitted.

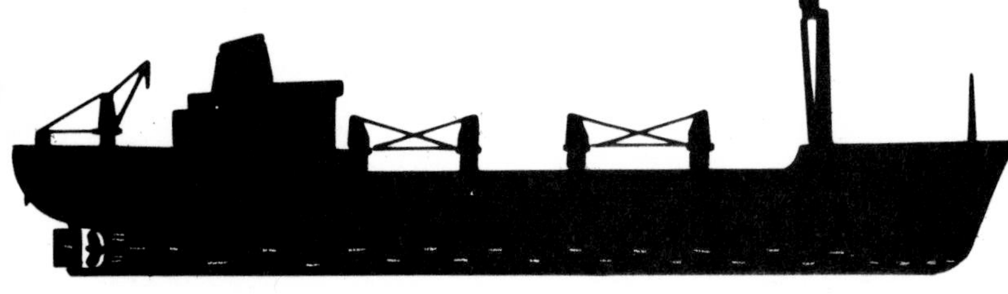

Below: Typical sacrificial anode positions for a general cargo vessel.

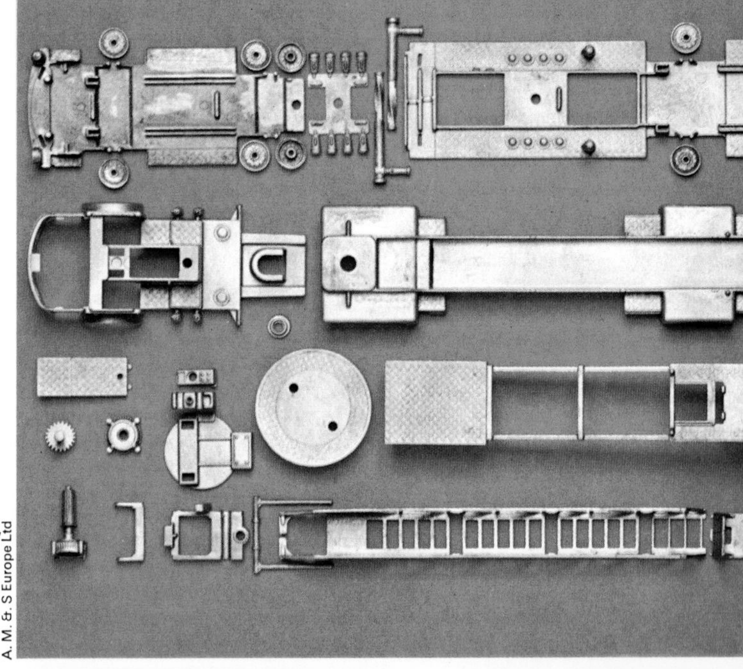

A. M. & S Europe Ltd

Right: The diecast zinc alloy components of a toy fire engine.

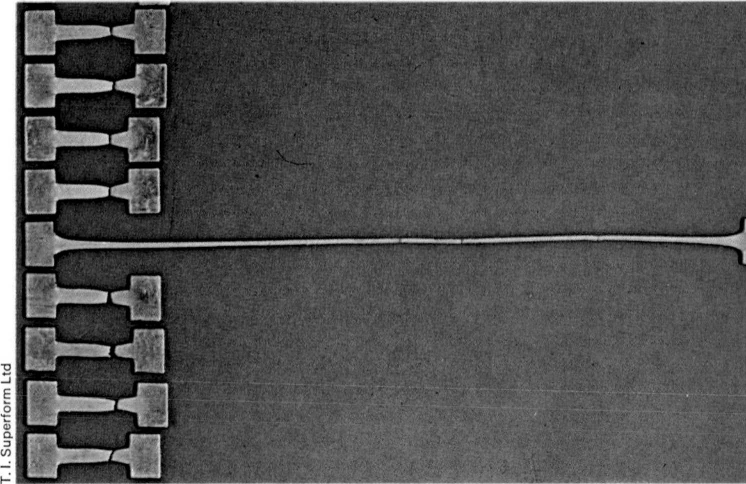

T. I. Superform Ltd

Right: A sample of a *superplastic* aluminium copper alloy compared with samples of conventional aluminium copper alloy. The samples, originally all the same length, were all subjected to tensile stress until they fractured. The superplastic alloy sample was capable of eighteen times more elongation before fracture than were the normal alloy samples. The first practical superplastic aluminium alloy was produced in 1969, and superplastic alloys based on other metals, such as zinc, are now available. The high plasticity of these alloys means that they can easily be pressed into complex shapes without danger of fracturing.

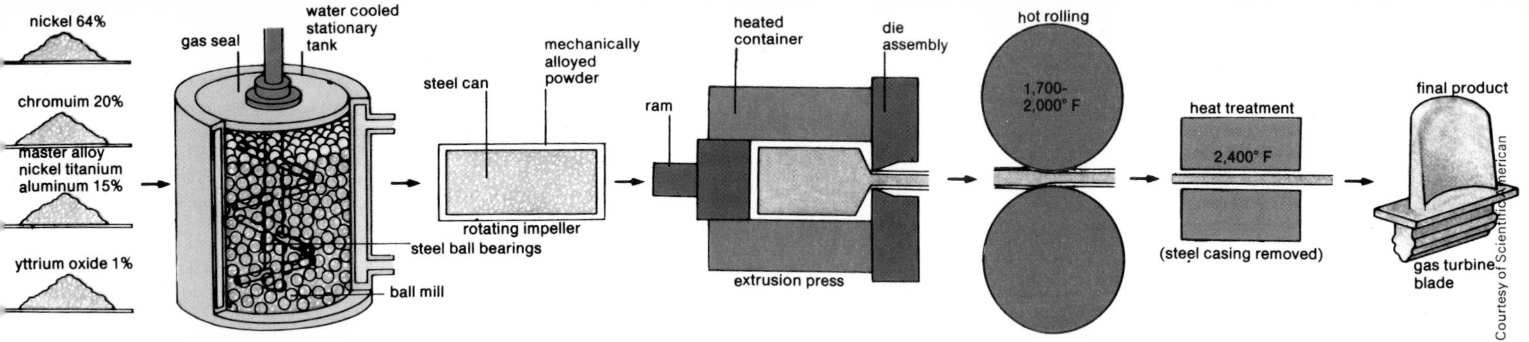

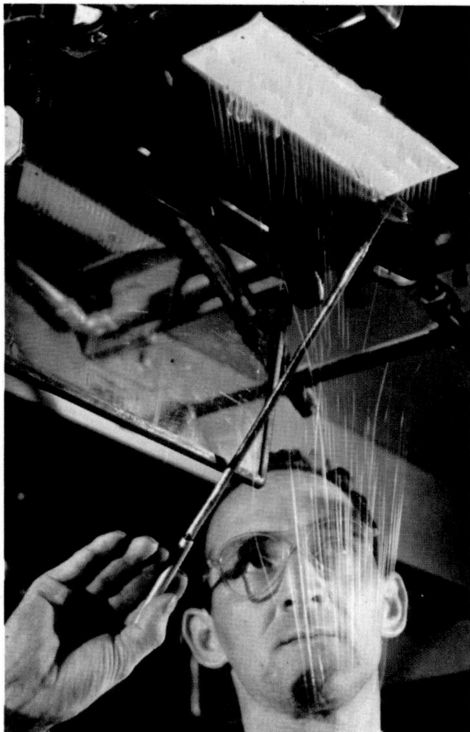

Above: When normal alloying techniques are employed, some metals may form a solution when liquid but separate again when the solution is solidified. This can be overcome by *mechanical alloying*, in which finely-powdered metals are ground together in a high-energy steel ball mill so that the particles of the different metals become welded together, producing a powdered alloy. The alloy powder is sealed in a steel can, then heated and extruded so that the powder consolidates into a solid metal bar. The steel is removed after a hot-rolling process, leaving a bar of strong, hard alloy. The process shown here is used for making gas turbine blades.

Left: Glass fibres being extruded through a perforated plate of platinum-rhodium alloy.

Right: Superplastic zinc alloy wall panels.

Below: The use of alloys in the Olympus 593 turbojet. The *Waspaloy* is made of nickel, chromium, cobalt, molybdenum, titanium and aluminium.

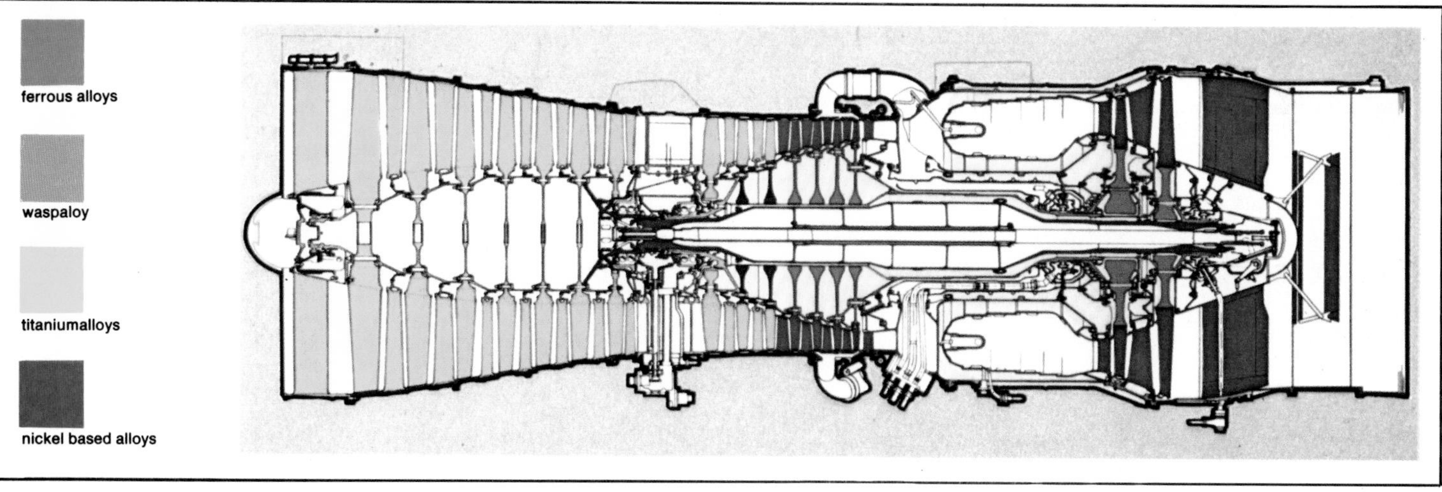

and up to 0.7 per cent silicon.

A development of the age hardening process, known as *precipitation hardening*, involves speeding the formation of the intermetallic compound by reheating the heat-treated alloy to about 175°C (345°F). By this means the hardening occurs in a matter of hours rather than days. Precipitation hardening is also used to harden alloys based on many other metals, including many alloys which will not form intermetallic compounds and harden by means of age hardening.

Alloy steels

Alloys steels are steels to which additional alloying elements, such as nickel, silicon, manganese or chromium, have been added. These additional elements alter the basic structure of the steel, and make the metal more amenable to the various forms of heat treatment employed to make the steel harder, softer, springier or tougher.

The alloying elements used alter the structure of the steel in various ways. Silicon and manganese, for instance, harden the *ferrite* (iron) phase of the steel by going into solid solution in it, while many other elements, including tungsten, chromium, molybdenum and vanadium, harden the steel by combining with the *cementite* (iron carbide globules) within it to form more complex carbides.

The range of alloy steels which can be produced by different combinations of alloying elements and forms of heat treatment is enormous, and these steels play a vital role in modern engineering. Manganese steel, for example, is used for components which are subjected to intense wear, such as the teeth of excavator buckets or the points and crossings at busy railway junctions.

This type of steel, containing about 1 per cent carbon and 11 to 14 per cent manganese, has, when cast, a crystal structure known as *austenite*. When the steel is in use, however, the mechanical effects of impact and abrasion convert the steel at the affected surface into the extremely hard form known as *martensite*.

Certain metals, such as chromium and aluminium, are often added to steel to make it resistant to corrosion. The stainless steels, containing from 12 to 30 per cent chromium, plus in many cases smaller amounts of other metals such as nickel, molybdenum or copper, are common examples of this.

Nicholas Devorre/Bruce Coleman Ltd.

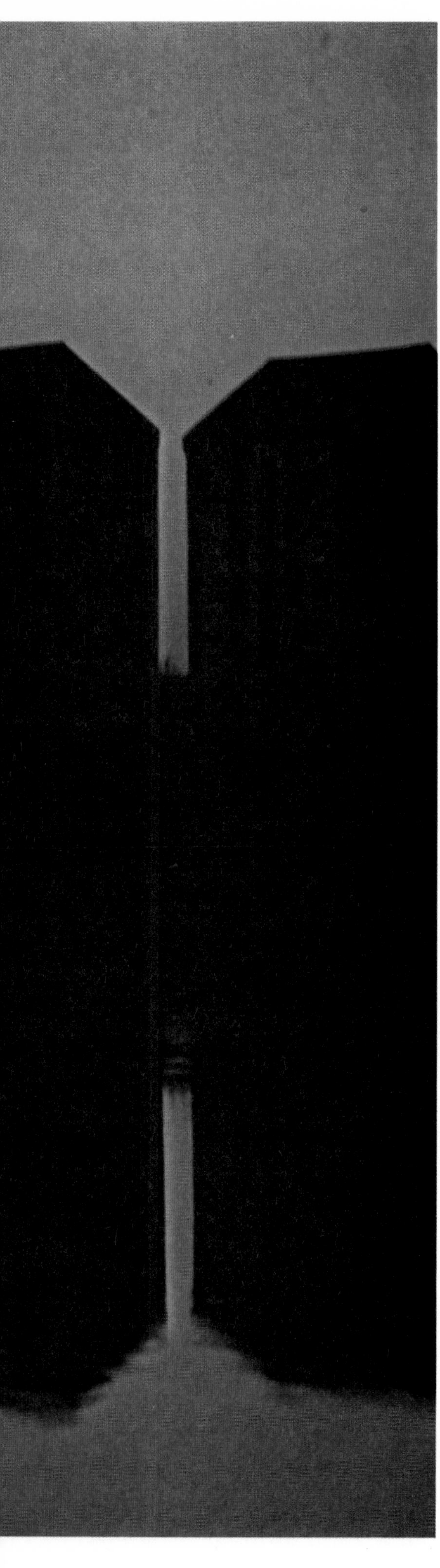

Chapter 2

Consumer and Service Technology

Grain harvest in Montana. The U.S.A. produces over 13% of the world's total supply of wheat. Large scale grain farming is comparatively new, generally occurring in regions settled within the last 150 years.

Fishing and Whaling

Modern fishing and whaling techniques are basically no more than up-dated, large-scale versions of the fish hunting methods used since the Stone Age. Fish remains the only major source of food which is not, on any appreciable scale, produced by farming.

The earliest method of catching fish was by some form of direct attack, such as spearing or clubbing. Whaling is still based on direct attack, the animals being hunted with explosive grenades attached to harpoons fired from guns, but the modern fishing industry catches fish by trapping them in nets or by luring them on to baited hooks.

The world's major fishing areas are in the northern Atlantic and Pacific Oceans, and large fishing fleets are operated by many countries including Japan, the USSR, the USA, Norway and the United Kingdom. The principal methods used are *trawling*, *seining*, and *drifting*, all of which use nets, and *long line* fishing in which lines as long as 120 km (75 miles) and carrying thousands of baited hooks are used.

Toni Schneiders/Bruce Coleman

Left: A fleet of crab fishing boats in the harbour of Greetsiel, West Germany. Shellfish, such as shrimps, prawns, crabs, lobsters and oysters, form an important part of the modern fishing industry. Quick-freezing methods allow locally-caught shellfish to be transported all over the world.

Specturm

Below: A trawler returning from the fishing grounds. Drawn up to the sides of the ship, near the stern, are the *otter boards*, which act like rudders to keep the mouth of the bag-shaped trawl net open as it is drawn through the water. Smaller trawl nets are sometimes kept open by a beam rather than otter boards.

Net fishing

The sea fish hunted by the fishing industry can be divided broadly into two groups, namely *pelagic* fish, which live near the surface of the sea, and *demersal* fish, which live on or near the seabed. Some of the most important pelagic fish are herring, mackerel, tuna, pilchard, anchovy and salmon, and the demersals include cod, plaice, sole, hake and halibut.

Trawls are large, tapering, bag-shaped nets which are towed behind *trawlers*, the fish being swept into the open mouth of the net and trapped at the closed end, which is known as the *cod end*. The *beam trawl*, used by small trawlers, has a rigid beam across the mouth to keep it open, but this arrangement is impractical for large trawls because the beam would be too long to handle easily.

Most trawlers use the *otter trawl*, a large net whose mouth is kept open by floats attached to the top rope or *headline*, weights attached to the bottom rope or *footrope*, and a pair of *otter boards*, one on each side of the mouth, which are made of wood or metal and are pushed outwards as the trawl is towed forwards through the water. The towing lines or *warps* are attached to each side of the trawl mouth. The otter trawl is the chief method of catching demersal fish.

Trawls are operated at depths of up to 900 m (3,000 ft) or more, the warp length being generally 2.5 to 3 times the trawling depth. Large trawl nets may be over 100 m (330 ft) long. When full, the nets are pulled up to the side of the trawler, or, on the more modern vessels, to a ramp at the stern, by powerful winches.

One of the most effective forms of capturing demersal fish from areas where the seabed is smooth is by the use of a *bottom seine*, also called a *Danish seine* after its country of origin. The bottom seine is similar to a large trawl, but it has no otter boards. Two ropes are laid out on the seabed to form a large circle, with

Novosti

Left: A seine net is supported on the surface of the water by a row of floats. Seine nets are used to catch both pelagic (shallow water) and demersal (deep water) fish. They are, however, difficult to use in rough weather for they are often several hundred metres long and so easily fall foul of the ship.

British Trawler Federation

Below: A modern British stern trawler, the 'Northella' from Hull. Stern trawlers are much more efficient than traditional trawlers—not only do they haul the catch up a ramp at the stern of the ship rather than lifting it over the side, but also they are equipped to process and store a huge quantity of fish.

Shoaling species of fish are caught in trawls – large, tapering bag-shaped nets towed behind the boat. Swept into the open mouth of the net, the fish are trapped at the closed 'cod' end.

British Trawler Federation

Picturepoint

Left: A mixed catch nears the ramp of a stern trawler. The trawl net is divided into two sections in order to save half of the catch if the net is holed. Among the fish caught are redfish or ocean perch, coalies and cod. The cod has long been one of the most important commercial fish. It is found throughout the north Atlantic and Arctic Oceans living in deep water down to about 500 m (1,600 ft). About 90 per cent of the cod landed in Britain is caught by trawling.

Right: The covered quayside at a British fishing port. Once a catch has been landed it is auctioned to a processing firm at the port. After filleting (which is often done by hand) the fish is sent to retailers or further processed, usually by smoking or freezing.

Below: A selection of different kinds of fishing vessels and their nets, from the small Pacific shrimp boat (bottom left) to the huge Russian factory ship (top right).

the ship on one side of the circle and the open net on the other. The ship then winches the ropes in, and as they are drawn in they move closer together and draw the net forward. The moving ropes drive the fish towards the centre of the diminishing circle, where they are eventually trapped in the advancing net and drawn up to the ship.

Purse seining is the chief method of capturing shoals of pelagic fish. When a shoal of fish has been located, it is surrounded by a circular wall of net which is supported on floats at the top and weighted down at the bottom. Once the shoal has been encircled, the bottom of the net is drawn closed, preventing the fish from escaping. The net is then drawn to the side of the ship and the fish are taken out.

Drifting is used exclusively for pelagic fish, especially herring and mackerel. Flat, rectangular nets, about 50 m (165 ft) long and 13 m (43 ft) deep, are strung out end to end in the water to form a vertical wall of net which may be up to 5 km (3 miles) long. The nets are suspended from floats, the tops of the nets being at a depth of about 3 m (10 ft) below the surface.

Once the nets have been set in the water, they are allowed to drift with the wind and tide, together with the floating buoy or the ship (*drifter*) to which they are attached. The fish which swim into the net, providing they are not too large or too small, become trapped in it because the size of the holes allows the head and gills to pass through, but not the body. The fish cannot back out of it, however, because their gills act like barbs and trap them securely in the net. For this reason, the nets are often known as *gill nets*. The nets are subsequently winched in to the boat and the fish are removed.

Line fishing

Long line fishing is a development of *hand line* fishing, in which lines carrying one or more baited hooks are cast into the water and then drawn in by hand when a fish swallows the hook. Long lines may be anchored to the sea bed for

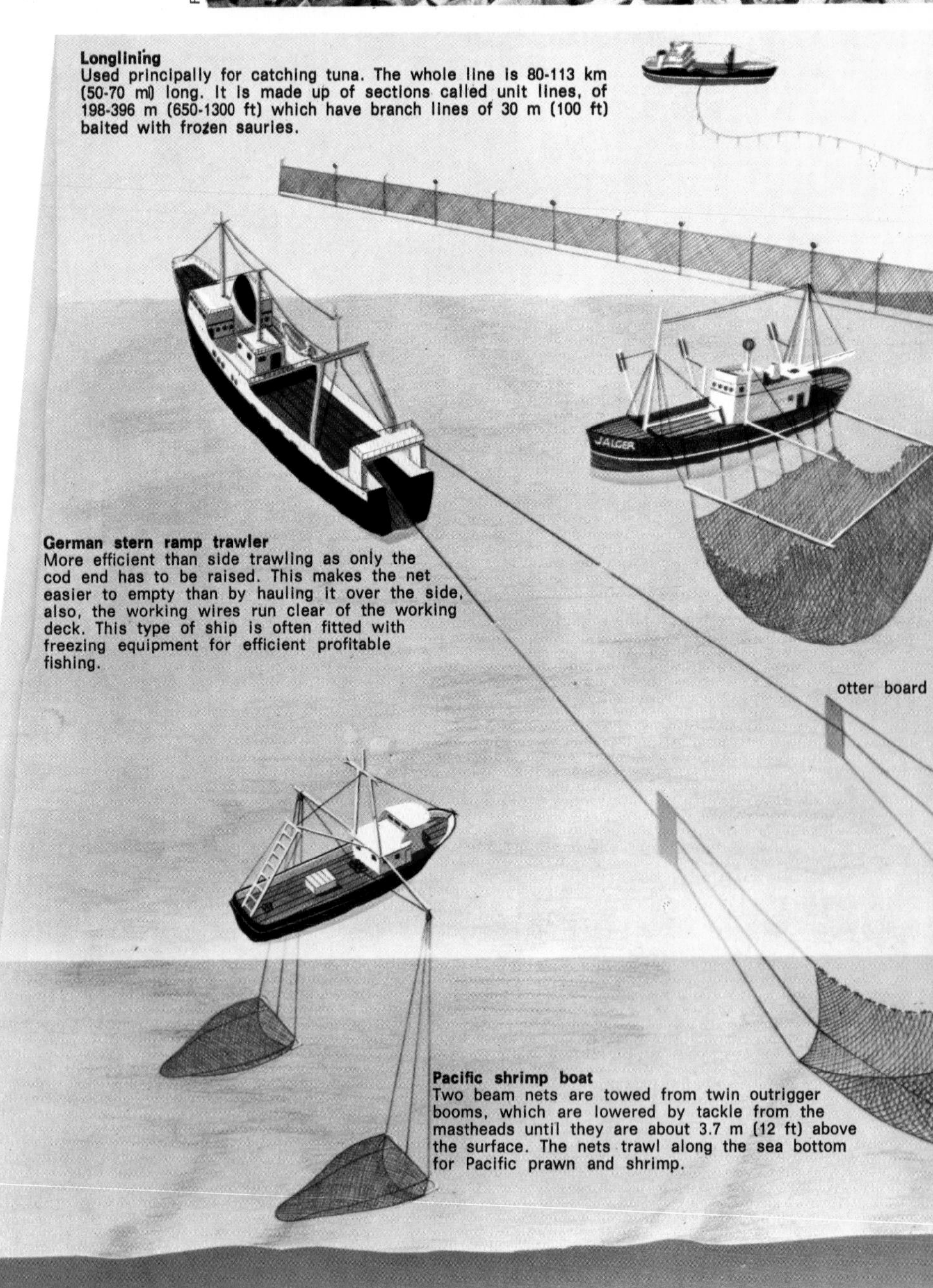

Longlining
Used principally for catching tuna. The whole line is 80-113 km (50-70 mi) long. It is made up of sections called unit lines, of 198-396 m (650-1300 ft) which have branch lines of 30 m (100 ft) baited with frozen sauries.
JALGER
German stern ramp trawler
More efficient than side trawling as only the cod end has to be raised. This makes the net easier to empty than by hauling it over the side, also, the working wires run clear of the working deck. This type of ship is often fitted with freezing equipment for efficient profitable fishing.
otter board
Pacific shrimp boat
Two beam nets are towed from twin outrigger booms, which are lowered by tackle from the mastheads until they are about 3.7 m (12 ft) above the surface. The nets trawl along the sea bottom for Pacific prawn and shrimp.

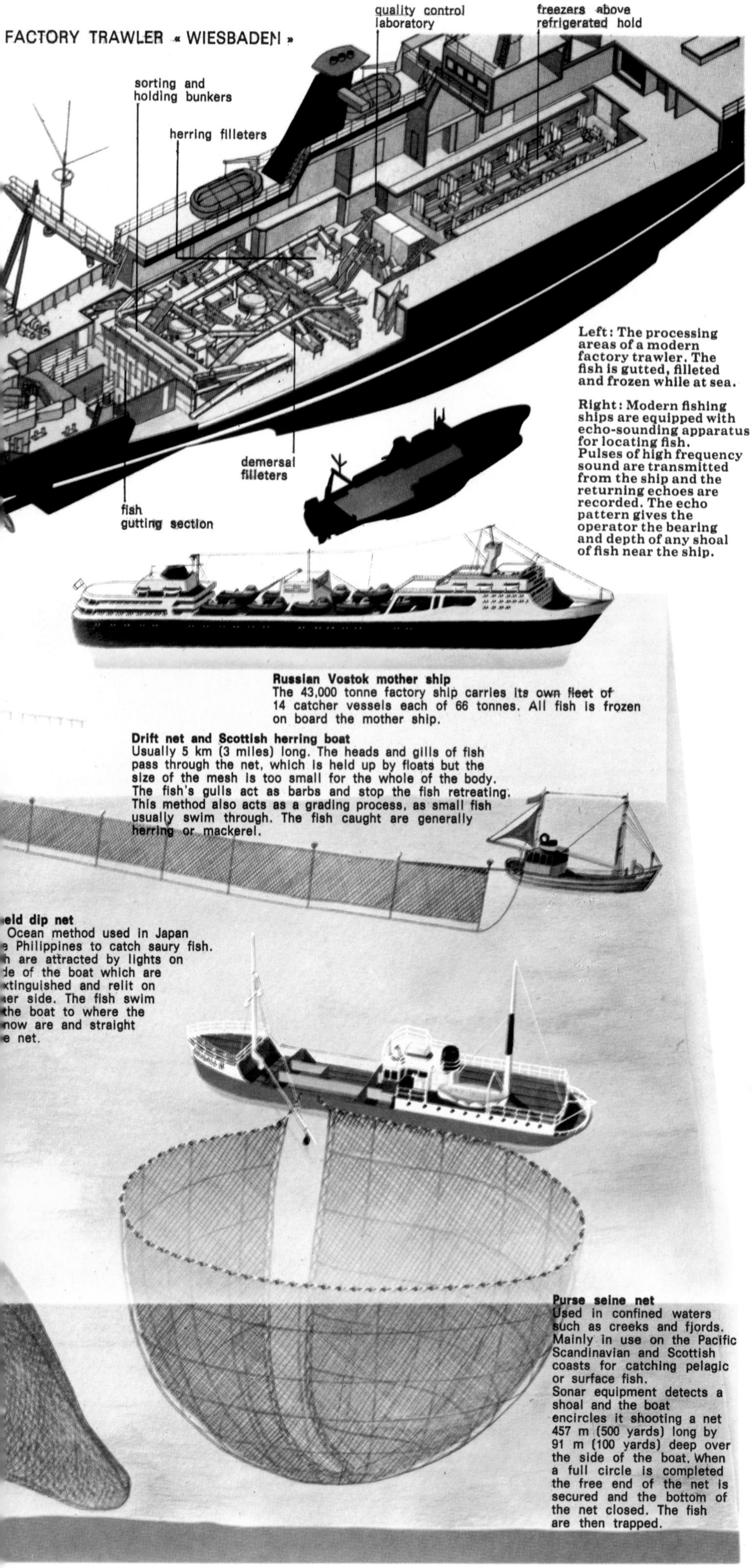

FACTORY TRAWLER « WIESBADEN »

quality control laboratory

freezers above refrigerated hold

sorting and holding bunkers

herring filleters

demersal filleters

fish gutting section

Left: The processing areas of a modern factory trawler. The fish is gutted, filleted and frozen while at sea.

Right: Modern fishing ships are equipped with echo-sounding apparatus for locating fish. Pulses of high frequency sound are transmitted from the ship and the returning echoes are recorded. The echo pattern gives the operator the bearing and depth of any shoal of fish near the ship.

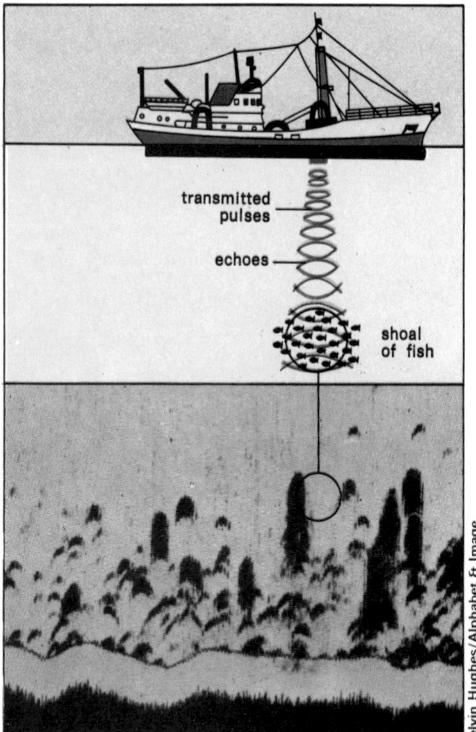

Russian Vostok mother ship
The 43,000 tonne factory ship carries its own fleet of 14 catcher vessels each of 66 tonnes. All fish is frozen on board the mother ship.

Drift net and Scottish herring boat
Usually 5 km (3 miles) long. The heads and gills of fish pass through the net, which is held up by floats but the size of the mesh is too small for the whole of the body. The fish's gills act as barbs and stop the fish retreating. This method also acts as a grading process, as small fish usually swim through. The fish caught are generally herring or mackerel.

eld dip net
Ocean method used in Japan
e Philippines to catch saury fish.
h are attracted by lights on
de of the boat which are
xtinguished and relit on
er side. The fish swim
the boat to where the
now are and straight
e net.

Purse seine net
Used in confined waters such as creeks and fjords. Mainly in use on the Pacific Scandinavian and Scottish coasts for catching pelagic or surface fish.
Sonar equipment detects a shoal and the boat encircles it shooting a net 457 m (500 yards) long by 91 m (100 yards) deep over the side of the boat. When a full circle is completed the free end of the net is secured and the bottom of the net closed. The fish are then trapped.

catching demersal fish such as cod, halibut and hake, or floated near the surface for catching pelagic fish such as tuna. Another form of line fishing used for catching tuna, and also for salmon, is *trolling*. Troll lines, which are drawn along behind the boats, are long single lines carrying one or more baited hooks. Hand lines and troll lines are both drawn in when they have hooked a fish, but long lines are left unattended for periods so as to get as many fish as possible on to the hooks before they are drawn in.

Fish farming

Although freshwater fish, such as carp, have been reared in captivity in China and other Asian countries for thousands of years, it is only recently that any thorough research has been carried out into the possibilities of raising large numbers of edible fish in captivity.

In the wild, less than one per cent of all fish eggs spawned survive to grow into mature fish, and so the potential yield from eggs hatched in a protected environment is enormous. Farmed fish are hatched in large tanks, and when they have matured they are transferred to larger areas of water to grow to market size. Freshwater fish are often transferred to lakes, and sea fish to netting enclosures in sheltered coastal areas. Shellfish such as oysters and mussels are also cultivated in tanks and then later transferred to the seabed.

Warm water is best for the rearing of fish which are grown to market size in large tanks. Fish bred and matured in this manner include clams, prawns, plaice, sole and turbot.

Whaling

The first people to hunt whales were probably the Alaskan Eskimoes and the North American Indians living on the coast of the north-east Pacific in the late Stone Age. In Europe, small Norwegian and Flemish whaling operations were active by the ninth century, but the first significant whale fisheries were those

Keystone

CEGB

Above: Heavy fishing has led to a serious depletion of fish in the once popular fishing grounds around the coasts of northern Europe. As a result, many countries have set up fishing limits in order to protect their own industries. This photograph, taken in 1972, shows an Icelandic gunboat inspecting an unmarked trawler fishing inside Iceland's newly established 50-mile fishing limit.

Left: Grading rainbow trout at a hatchery in Wales. This particular hatchery makes use of the slightly warm, spent cooling water from a nearby nuclear power station to hasten the growth of the fish before they are released into local rivers.

Keystone

established, in about the eleventh century, by Basque fisherman in the Bay of Biscay.

The Basque whalers spread their activities as far as the north-west Atlantic. and by the seventeenth century the seas around Iceland, Greenland and Newfoundland were being used for whaling by several other nations, including Norway and Iceland. Until the middle of the eighteenth century, the whale carcasses had to be brought back to shore stations for processing, and so whaling voyages were comparatively short.

Longer (and thus more profitable) voyages were made possible by the forerunners of modern factory ships in the 1760s. These were American vessels equipped with brick ovens called *try-works*, in which the whale meat or *blubber* could be melted down to make oil. The oil did not deteriorate as the blubber did, so there was no need for the ships to return to shore soon after the whales had been caught to prevent their catch from spoiling.

The whales were pursued in small, open boats, and captured with small, hand-thrown harpoons. Although this was, by modern standards, a slow and inefficient way of killing whales, it did not prevent the serious depletion of the whale populations in some of the most popular whaling areas. The introduction of steam-powered whaling vessels, together with the development of more deadly forms of harpoon, further reduced the chances of a whale escaping its hunters once it had been spotted.

Harpoons

The first harpoons were barbed spears which had lines attached to their shafts, so that a harpooned whale could be secured to prevent it escaping. This basic design was improved by the invention of the swivelling barb in 1848. This type of barb was mounted on a pivot at the end of the shaft, and held in line with the shaft by a wooden peg. When the barb entered the whale, a pull on the line sheared the peg and allowed the barb to turn sideways and anchor itself firmly in the animal's flesh. Harpoon guns, which could fire harpoons further and with greater accuracy than was possible by hand, were first introduced by the Dutch in about 1731, but most of the major advances in whaling technology were introduced by a Norwegian sealing captain called Svend Foyn, in the second half of the nineteenth century. Foyn introduced the first steam-driven whaling boat in 1863, the bow-mounted harpoon gun capable of firing explosive harpoons in 1868, and the first true factory ship in 1890, this last innovation leading to the first Antarctic whaling expedition in 1893.

Modern explosive harpoons have iron shafts about 1.5 m (5 ft) long and weigh around 75 kg (165 lb). The end of the

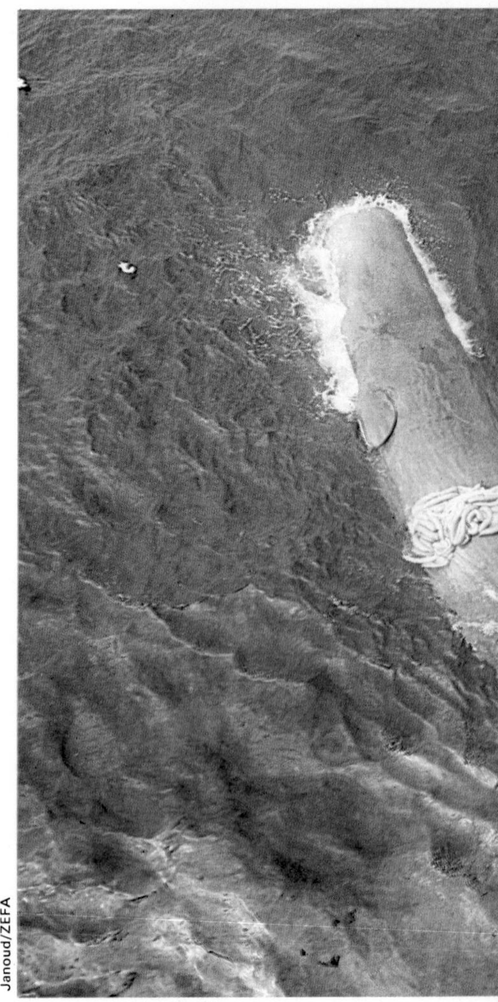

Janoud/ZEFA

Left: The harpoon from a whaling ship strikes home. Modern whaling techniques are so effective that they have brought several species, notably the blue whale, to the brink of extinction.

Below: The USSR has one of the world's largest whaling fleets. Here, a huge factory ship, the 'Sovetskaya Ukraina', is serviced at sea. On her port side a refrigerator ship takes off frozen whale meat and bone meal. On her starboard side a tanker loads blubber and unloads fuel. Whale carcasses are towed behind the ship before being drawn up a ramp in her stern for processing. A hunting ship keeps station a short distance astern.

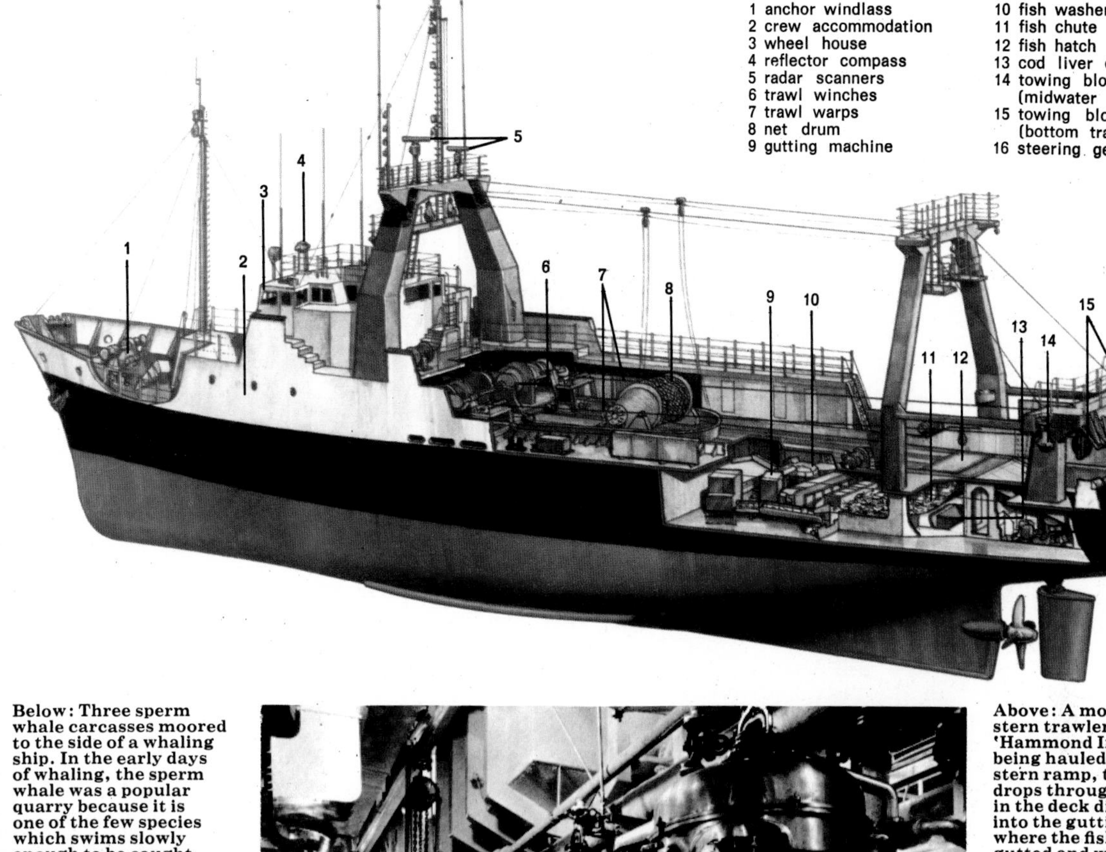

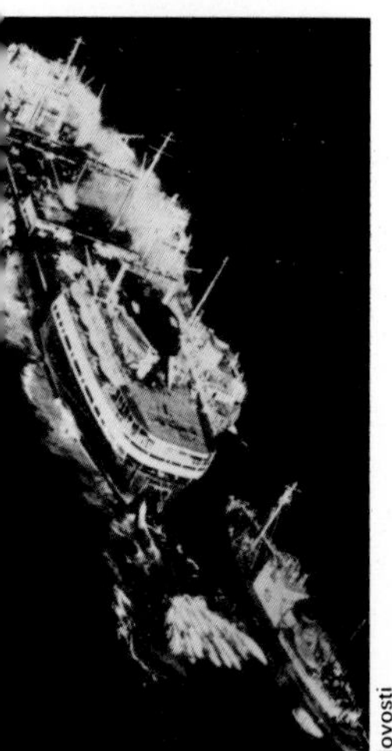

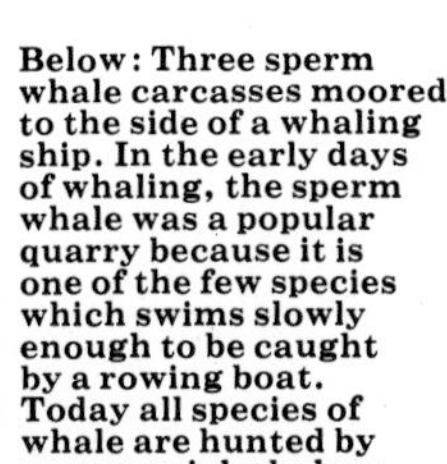

Below: Three sperm whale carcasses moored to the side of a whaling ship. In the early days of whaling, the sperm whale was a popular quarry because it is one of the few species which swims slowly enough to be caught by a rowing boat. Today all species of whale are hunted by commercial whalers.

Above: A modern British stern trawler, the 'Hammond Innes'. After being hauled up the stern ramp, the catch drops through a hatch in the deck directly into the gutting room where the fish are gutted and washed by machine. Then they are conveyed to a 550 cu m (19,500 cu ft) fish room which is situated beneath the net drum and maintained at a constant temperature of 0°C (32°F). This is a 'wet fish' trawler—the fish is not frozen on board.

Left: Many processes which were once carried out on land are now done on board ship. This picture shows whale blubber being extracted on the factory ship 'Sovetskaya Ukraina'.

harpoon carries a four-pointed barb, and a pointed, explosive head containing about 8 kg (17.6 lb) of explosive. The impact of the explosive stuns or kills the whale, which is then winched back to the whaler by means of a line attached to the harpoon. If the whale has not been killed outright by the harpoon, it may take as long as two hours to die unless several more harpoons are fired into it. Many whalers now use electric harpoons, which carry a cable along which an electric current is passed to kill the whale more humanely.

The gun itself weighs about 450 kg (1,000 lb), and its charge of black powder explosive which propels the harpoon is ignited by a blank 8 mm (0.32 in) pistol cartridge loaded into the breech and fired by a trigger.

Whaling ships

The principal vessel of a whaling fleet is the factory ship, a large vessel which processes the carcasses brought to it by the catcher boats. These catcher boats are small, fast and manoeuvrable, usually about 60 m (200 ft) long and capable of speeds of up to 20 knots. The whales are located by helicopter patrols, or by underwater echo-sounding equipment. Once located, the whales may be driven towards the catchers by scaring them with ultrasonic devices, or else these devices may be used to chase the whales until they are exhausted and confused and thus easy to catch. When a whale has been caught and killed, its carcass is inflated with air to keep it afloat, and marked with a flag or a radio beacon so that it can be collected later and towed to the factory ship.

At the factory ship, the carcasses are dragged up a ramp or slipway at the stern and on to the main deck. Here, the blubber is *flensed* (stripped) from the bones, and dropped, through holes in the deck, into high-pressure steam cookers which separate the oil from it. The oil is then purified and stored in large tanks to await collection by tanker ships. The bones, which also contain oil, are similarly treated, the residue being converted into bone meal.

A small proportion of the edible whale meat is converted into oil, but most of it is frozen or canned for human consumption (whale meat is popular in Japan). Flesh not suitable for human consumption is processed to remove the oil, and the residual solids are dried for use as animal foods.

Dairy Products

Dairying, the rearing of animals for their milk and the use of this milk for drinking, or for making milk products such as butter, cheese and yogurt, probably originated in south-west Asia at the end of the Stone Age. Since these early beginnings, when most of the milk was obtained from sheep and goats, the dairy industry has become a major source of food, particularly in Western countries. Although the cow is the chief source of milk in developed countries, this is not always the case in less developed areas where the climate may not be suitable for cattle rearing. Other animals used as sources of milk include sheep, goats, buffalo, reindeer and camels.

Milk is the only natural food which contains, to a greater or lesser extent, most of the essential nutrients. Proteins, principally *casein* (which gives milk its characteristic white colour), *lactalbumin* and *lactoglobulin*, account for about 3.75 per cent of the weight of milk. Fats, in the form of tiny globules which are lighter than the water in the milk and so float to the top as cream, constitute about 3 to 5 per cent of milk.

Another constituent of milk is the carbohydrate *lactose* or milk sugar. Lactose, which accounts for about 4.75 per cent of the weight of milk, is easily digested by most people, and in addition to its value as an energy source it also promotes the growth of *Lactobacillus* bacteria in the intestines. The lactobacillus bacteria create acidic conditions in the intestines, and this inhibits the growth of certain harmful bacteria there.

Calcium is one of the most important minerals contained in milk, whose mineral content is about 0.75 per cent by weight. Other important minerals in milk are phosphorus and potassium, and small amounts of iron are also present. The principal vitamins in milk are vitamin A (*retinol*) and vitamin B_2 (*riboflavin*), plus some vitamin C (*ascorbic acid*) and vitamin D (*calciferol*).

Milk production

One of the most important advances in dairy farming was the invention of the milking machine, which allowed large herds to be milked quickly, hygienically, and with a minimum of labour. The forerunners of today's machines appeared in the late nineteenth century, and all the basic features had been established by the 1920s. The vacuum-operated milking machine uses a combination of sucking and squeezing on the cow's teats to make the milk flow, and the milk is drawn into a calibrated container so that the yield from the cow can be measured and recorded. A good cow on a modern farm may yield as much as 4,100 litres (900 gal) of milk per year.

When the milk has been collected, it must be cooled to below 10°C (50°F) to inhibit the growth of the bacteria which are found in fresh 'raw' milk. The traditional way of storing the milk for collection and delivery to the dairy is by putting it into metal churns, but many farms are now equipped with refrigerated milk tanks. These tanks cool the milk to 4.4°C (40°F) and keep it at that temperature, until it is collected by a refrigerated milk tanker.

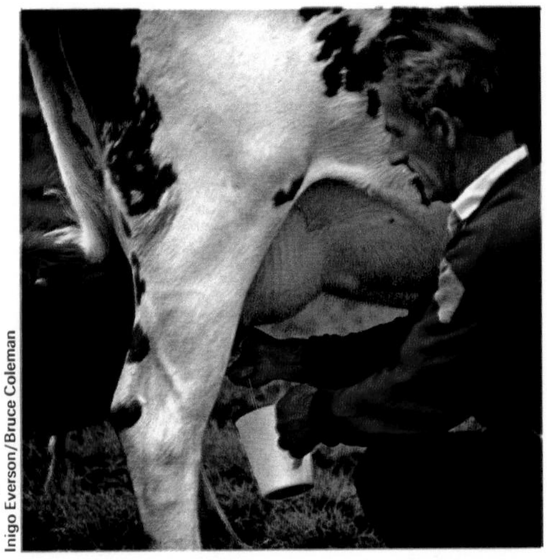

Inigo Everson/Bruce Coleman

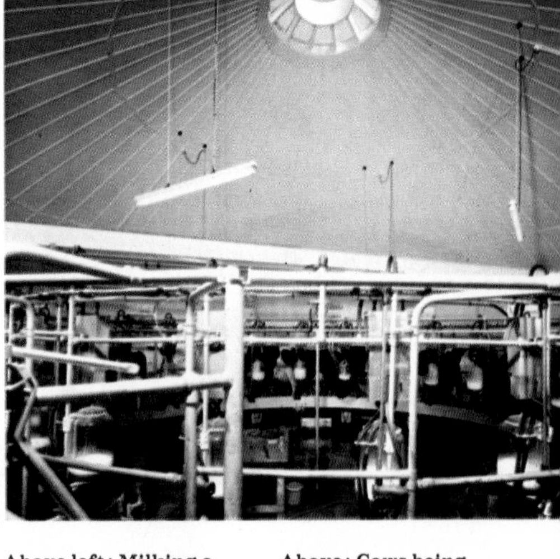

Alfa-Laval

Above left: Milking a cow by hand. Cows begin producing milk when they have calves, at about 2 years old, and to ensure a regular supply of milk they are usually mated or artificially inseminated about every 12 months. This means that they can be milked for about 9 or 10 months in each year.

Above: Cows being milked by machine in a modern *rotary herringbone* milking parlour. The milking stalls are arranged in a herringbone pattern around a platform which rotates around the operator's work area, so that, for example, up to 180 cows can be milked in an hour by only two operators.

Milk processing

Nearly all the milk sold to the public has undergone some form of processing to destroy the bacteria which cause souring by converting the lactose into *lactic acid*. This processing is designed to extend the keeping life of the milk. One of the commonest forms of treatment is *pasteurization*, named after the French chemist and bacteriologist Louis Pasteur (1822-95) whose work led to the development of the process.

Pasteurization is carried out prior to bottling, and most dairies now use the HTST (high temperature, short time) process. This is a continuous process, in which the milk is heated to over 72°C (161°F) for at least 15 seconds, then cooled rapidly to about 3°C (38°F) and bottled. Pasteurized milk will keep well in a refrigerator for about three days, but then it begins to go off because of the action of *proteolytic* bacteria which attack the milk proteins.

These proteolytic bacteria can be destroyed by *sterilization*. The milk is first pasteurized, and then *homogenized* by forcing it through very small openings so that the fat globules are broken up. The fat then remains thoroughly dispersed throughout the milk and does not separate out and float to the top. Pasteurized milk is often homogenized before bottling, and sold as pasteurized homogenized milk.

In the sterilization process itself, the pasteurized, homogenized milk is bottled and then steam-heated for between 20 and 30 minutes at least at 100°C (212°F). Sterilized milk will keep well, even without refrigeration, for several weeks.

The most effective form of milk treatment is the UHT (ultra heat treatment) process, of which there are several versions. In one of these, milk is preheated to 75 to 80°C (165 to 175°F). Then steam is injected into it to raise its temperature rapidly to about 150°C (300°F) and keep it at that temperature for about three seconds to kill off all the bacteria and mould spores present. The milk is then passed into a vacuum chamber, where the water which condensed into it from the steam evaporates again and cools the milk as it does so. The milk is then homogenized, and packed into sterile, foil-lined cartons. It will keep for several months without refrigeration.

Two other forms of liquid milk which

Edouard Rousseau/Snark

Above: The traditional way of taking milk from the farm to the dairy is in churns, which are collected from the farm and taken to the dairy by truck. This picture shows samples of milk being taken for quality checks after delivery to a French dairy. France has the largest dairy industry in Europe.

Below: The pasteurization section of an automated dairy. Milk is delivered to the dairy by tanker, tested for quality, then passed through the pasteurization plant and filled into bottles or cartons. Strict standards of quality and hygiene are maintained throughout the process.

County Dairies Ltd

milking line

ernsey

Friesian

Jersey

Ayrshire

farm milk storage

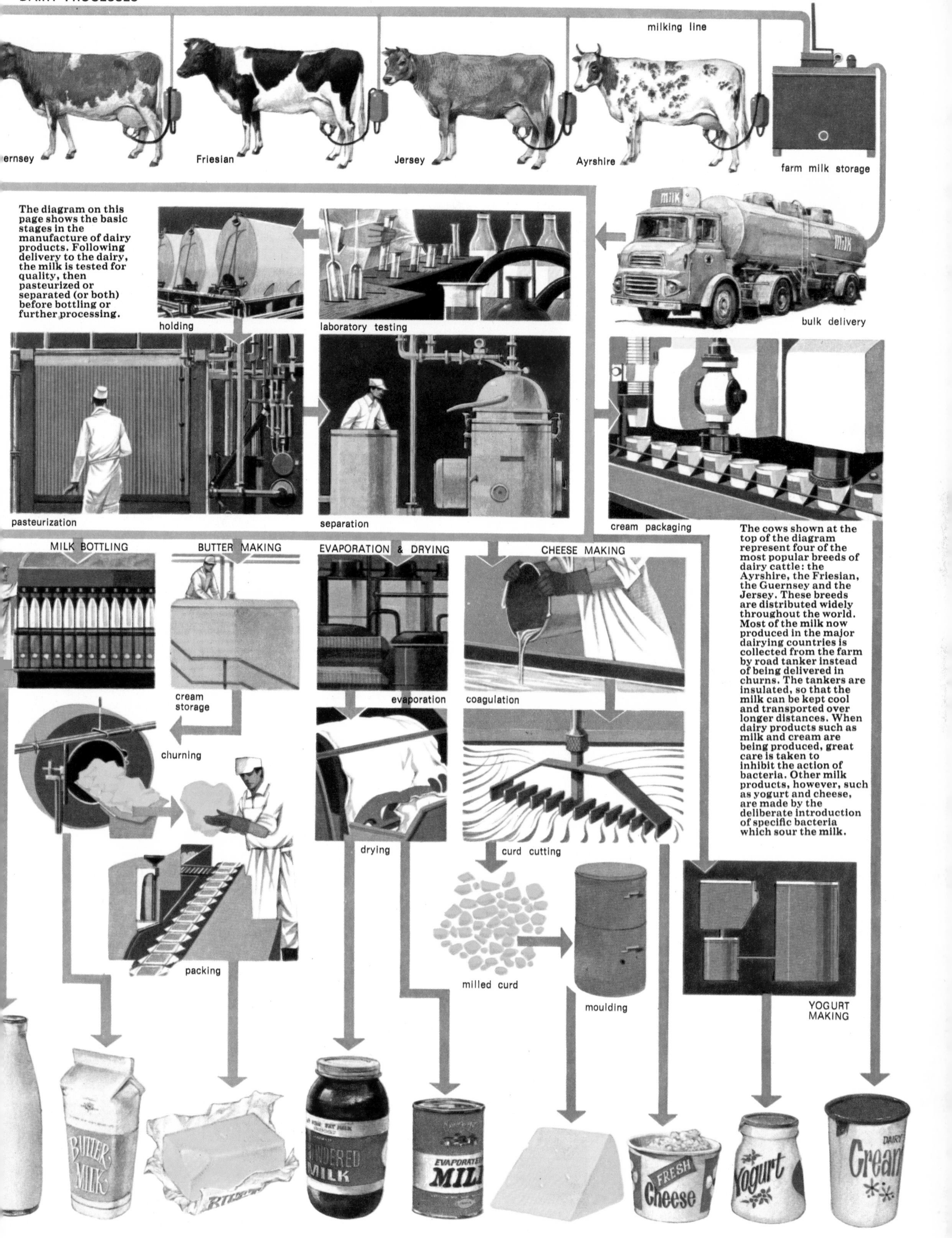

The diagram on this page shows the basic stages in the manufacture of dairy products. Following delivery to the dairy, the milk is tested for quality, then pasteurized or separated (or both) before bottling or further processing.

holding

laboratory testing

bulk delivery

pasteurization

separation

cream packaging

The cows shown at the top of the diagram represent four of the most popular breeds of dairy cattle: the Ayrshire, the Friesian, the Guernsey and the Jersey. These breeds are distributed widely throughout the world. Most of the milk now produced in the major dairying countries is collected from the farm by road tanker instead of being delivered in churns. The tankers are insulated, so that the milk can be kept cool and transported over longer distances. When dairy products such as milk and cream are being produced, great care is taken to inhibit the action of bacteria. Other milk products, however, such as yogurt and cheese, are made by the deliberate introduction of specific bacteria which sour the milk.

MILK BOTTLING

BUTTER MAKING

EVAPORATION & DRYING

CHEESE MAKING

cream storage

evaporation

coagulation

churning

drying

curd cutting

packing

milled curd

moulding

YOGURT MAKING

BUTTER MILK

EVAPORATED MILK

FRESH Cheese

Yogurt

DAIRY Cream

Right: Removing butter from a churn at an automated butter factory in New Zealand. The butter produced in New Zealand is made from pasteurized cream and it is salted. This means it has good keeping properties under refrigeration, which is an advantage because most of New Zealand's butter has to be shipped long distances to overseas customers such as the United Kingdom.

Below: Blocks of Cheddar cheese ready to be cut, weighed and packed. Cheddar cheese, made from pasteurized milk, is ripened for up to 9 months at a temperature of about 10°C (50°F) and a relative humidity of 80 to 90 per cent.

keep well for long periods are *condensed* milk and *evaporated* milk. Both of these products are basically milk which has been concentrated by having the water removed from it by evaporation in a vacuum. The temperature at which water boils is reduced when the surrounding air pressure is low, and so when milk is heated in a vacuum the water will boil away at less than 54°C (130°F). At such temperatures, the nutritious constituents of the milk are practically unaffected, whereas they would be if the milk were concentrated by prolonged boiling at 100°C (212°F).

Above: One of the causes of milk spoilage is the action of *proteolytic* bacteria which attack the milk proteins. These bacteria can be destroyed by sterilization. In this process, pasteurized, homogenized milk is bottled and then steam-heated to 100° C (212°F) for up to 30 minutes.

Below: Rows of Emmenthal cheeses ripening under conditions of controlled temperature and humidity. The length of the ripening time depends upon the type of cheese. Many soft cheeses need no ripening, but hard cheeses may require months of ripening before they mature.

Dried milk

Dried milk may be made either from whole fresh milk or from *skim milk*, milk from which most of the cream has been separated. Most dried milk is made by *spray drying*, although milk intended for use as baby food may be dried by passing it over heated rollers. Milk to be spray dried is first concentrated by vacuum evaporation to reduce its water content to about 60 per cent. It is then preheated to about 65°C (150°F), and sprayed into a large chamber into which air at a temperature of about 190°C (375°F) is blown. The water is driven out of the milk droplets, leaving particles of dried milk solids which contain less than 5 per cent moisture.

Butter and cream

The simplest way of separating cream from milk is simply to leave the milk to stand undisturbed, so that the cream floats to the top and can be merely skimmed off. A quicker and more effective method is to heat the milk to about 49°C (120°F), and pass it through a *centrifuge*. The centrifuge is basically a rapidly-rotating bowl, and when the warm milk is put into it the heavier part of it, the skim milk is flung out to the edge by centrifugal force. The lighter part, the cream, remains near the centre of the bowl, and the skim milk and cream are discharged from the centrifuge through separate outlets.

New Zealand Dairy Board

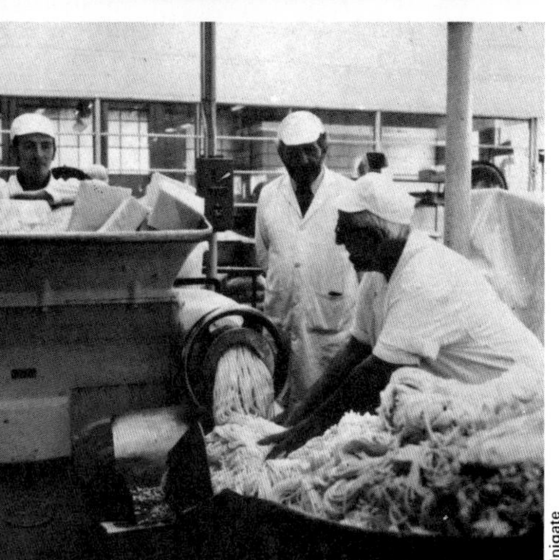

Unigate

Above: The first stage in the manufacture of processed cheese is to extrude a hard cheese, such as Cheddar, into this spaghetti-like form. It is then emulsified with salts (such as citrates or phosphates), water and whey powder, and heated and mixed to give it the required consistency.

Below: Yogurt is made from whole, evaporated, partly skimmed or dried milk, to which is added a 'culture' containing bacteria which converts the lactose to lactic acid. In this picture, a culture is being prepared from a 'mother culture'. One type of bacteria commonly used is *Lactobacillus bulgaricus*.

Alfa-Laval

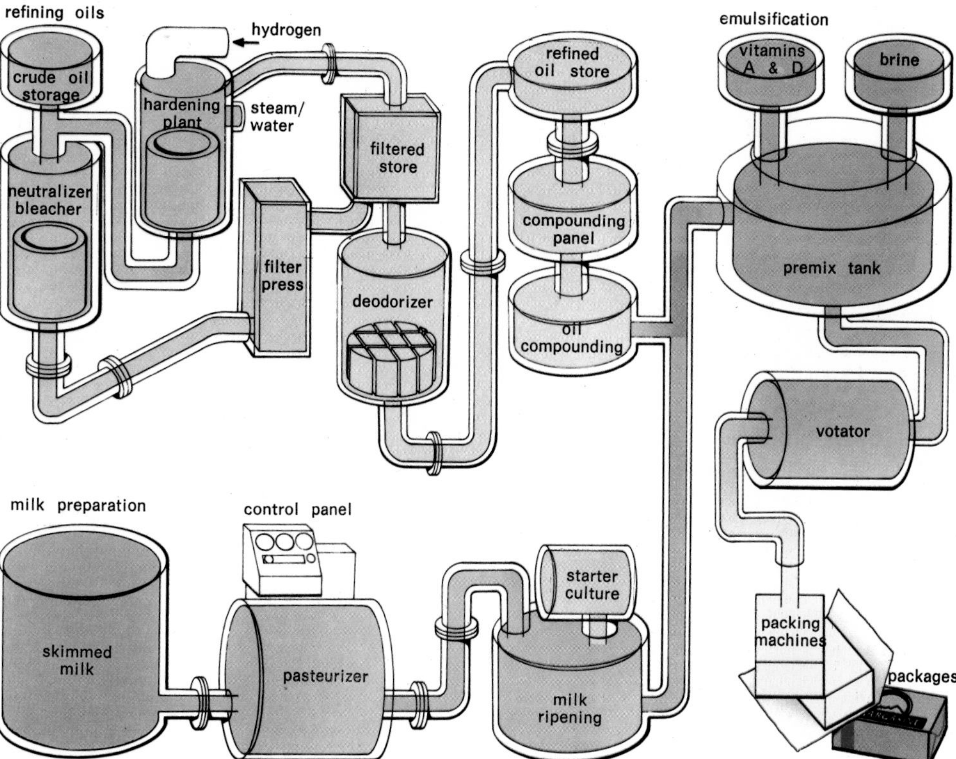

Above: Ordinary margarine is made by emulsifying blended vegetable and animal oils with ripened skimmed milk. The oils used, which include palm, sunflower, coconut and groundnut oils, fish oils, and animal fats such as lard, are bleached, hardened and deodorized and then blended before entering the premix tank. In the premix tank the blended oils are mixed with the milk which has been ripened to give it flavour and acidity, and vitamins are added. This mixture is solidified in a machine called a *votator*, which chills and mixes it to produce the required texture and consistency.

Dairies produce many types and grades of cream. In Britain they range from *half cream*, which must contain at least 12 per cent milk fat (also known as *butterfat*), to *clotted cream*, which has a minimum fat content of 55 per cent. Creams may be pasteurized, sterilized or ultra heat treated, and some are also homogenized. A small amount of untreated cream is also produced.

Butter may be made either from plain pasteurized cream, known as 'sweet cream', or from cream which has been 'ripened' by bacteria cultures such as *Streptococcus paracitrovorus* to enhance its flavour. Sweet cream butter, such as New Zealand butter, has very good keeping qualities. Butter is made in large churns, stainless steel barrels which are rotated mechanically so that the butter-fat particles in the cream cling together to form grains of butter. The churning continues until the butter grains are approximately pea-sized, then the liquid residue or *buttermilk* is removed.

Next, the butter is rinsed with water, and if a salted butter is to be produced the salt, up to about 5 per cent of the butter weight, is added at this stage. Salting gives the butter a stronger flavour and prolongs its storage life. The churning is then continued to work the butter into a single mass of the required consistency and to remove excess moisture. Finally, the butter is removed from the churn and packed.

Cheese

There are hundreds of different types of cheese produced throughout the world, but they can be divided roughly into two groups, 'hard' cheeses and 'soft' cheeses. Hard cheeses, such as Cheddar, are made from pasteurized whole milk which has been ripened with a culture of lactic acid bacteria, which converts some of the lactose into lactic acid.

The milk proteins are then coagulated into a *curd* by the addition of *rennet*, a substance containing the enzymes *rennin* and *pepsin* which is obtained from the stomachs of young calves. The curd is next cut into cubes to allow the liquid residue or *whey* to separate out. The curd is heated to 38°C (100°F) to drive out the whey, which is drained off, and then cut into blocks which are pressed to remove the last of the whey.

The blocks of dry curd are *milled* (cut into small pieces) and then salt is added to improve the flavour and act as a preservative. The final cheese is produced by pressing the salted curd in moulds for about 48 hours, then ripening it under conditions of controlled temperature and humidity for three to six months. The ripening is a result of bacterial and enzyme action.

Soft cheeses are made in a similar way, except that the whey is left to drain from the curd by gravity, without the application of pressure or heat. The resulting cheese has a high moisture content, between 50 and 70 per cent, and so has a soft texture. Certain soft cheeses are inoculated with mould cultures that excrete enzymes which give them characteristic flavours. Camembert, for example, is treated with *Penicillium camemberti*, and blue-veined cheeses are pierced with wires to allow air into the interior so that the growth of the mould used, *Penicillium roqueforti*, is encouraged along the wire holes.

Lactic acid cheeses are produced by the action of lactic acid on the milk protein. The acid coagulates the protein into a soft curd, which is then simply drained of whey and salted. Cottage cheese is made in a similar way, but it is made from pasteurized fat-free milk and the curd is washed with skim milk, often containing skim milk powder, to give it its characteristic texture.

Food Processing

Erich Hartmann/John Hillelson Agency

Above: Salting cod. The fish is split, headed and cleaned, then packed between layers of pure salt. Eventually, the salt content of the fish reaches a concentration of about 18% of the weight of the fish, and then the surplus is washed off and the fish is dried to reduce its moisture content to less than 15%, which prevents mould growth.

Interpress/John Watney

Right: Gherkins are pickled in brine, which reduces their moisture content and creates a chemical environment which inhibits the growth of decay-producing organisms. Here, Polish gherkins are being pickled in barrels of brine kept in pools of slightly salted water.

Techniques of food preservation derive from the historical need for man to preserve surplus food produce in times of plenty to allow for seasonal variations and famines. When plant or animal tissue is harvested, the food immediately becomes subject to spoilage attack by enzymes, bacteria, moulds and yeasts.

Enzymes are proteins which catalyze biochemical reactions within the food tissue. The browning of apples, for example, is caused by the oxidation of the amino acid *tyrosine* by the enzyme *phenolase*. Enzymes in harvested fruits and vegetables are normally made harmless by steam or water blanching at temperatures from 90°C to 100°C (194 to 212°F) for 3 to 5 minutes.

Bacteria are micro-organisms varying in size from 0.001 mm to 0.003 mm. Frequently, bacteria cause only food spoilage, as in the case of the lactic acid bacteria which sour milk. But much more serious are the bacteria which excrete a toxin—a type of spoilage termed *pathogenic*. The best-known pathogenic bacteria is *Clostridium botulinum* and it has been estimated that one teaspoon of the toxin from this micro-organism would be sufficient to poison a large urban water supply. To destroy the spores of a pure culture of *Cl. botulinum* requires 2.5 minutes at 121.1°C (250°F), and canning processes are always designed so that all the food within the can has adequate heat treatment to kill this and other pathogenic organisms. Equivalent processing times at 121.1°C are sometimes of the order of 10 minutes to take account of the thermal protection afforded to the micro-organisms by the food.

Moulds are filamentous micro-organisms. *Byssochlamys fulva* is a particularly heat-resistant variety which attacks the *pectin* in the tissue cell walls of fruit, causing disintegration, for example, of canned strawberries. It can be inactivated by heat treatment at 91°C (196°F). *Yeasts* have a low heat resistance and can be eliminated by a few minutes' exposure at 74°C (165°F).

An important parameter determining the susceptibility of a processed food to spoilage is its *water activity*. This is the ratio of the pressure of the water vapour in the food to the vapour pressure of pure water at the same temperature. Most foods will be free from spoilage at a water activity below 0.62. It is this principle that gives the long shelf life of comparatively moist foods such as dried fruits (15-20 per cent moisture) and cakes.

Additives such as glycerol and salt are frequently used in small quantities (such as 0.5 per cent salt and 1.6 per cent glycerol) to lower the water activity of cakes and thus extend their shelf life. These additives, or *humectants*, are frequently employed because there is a limit to the amount of moisture which can be removed from a cake without significantly altering its freshness and 'mouthfeel'.

Low temperature processing

Low temperature food processing can be divided into two main categories: *chilling* and *freezing*. Chilling does not involve crystallization of the water in the food, and occurs within the temperature range 0°C (32°F) to 8°C (46°F), the upper figure being typical of a domestic refrigerator. Fruits such as apples and pears, for example, can be preserved for about one year by storage at temperatures of between 1.5°C and 3.0°C (35 and 37°F).

The preservation of meat involves both chilling and freezing. Typically, a 164 kg (360 lb) carcass of high-quality beef is chilled to 12°C (54°F) in 25 hours using air at —1°C (30.2°F) circulated in the chiller at a speed of 2 m/sec (6.7 ft/sec). Further chilling and freezing is then completed by using air at —10°C (14°F). Both stages of the operation are completed within approximately 5½ days of slaughter.

The rate of beef freezing can be increased by butchering it into smaller portions and *blast freezing* it. For example, beef quarters can be frozen to —20°C (—4°F) in 21 hours by passing the meat from the slaughtering and dressing line into an air-blast freezing tunnel. Within the tunnel, fans circulate the air at 5.1 m/sec (16.7 ft/sec) at —40°C (—40°F).

Fluidized bed freezing is a method which can be applied to small food particles such as peas. Air at —23°C (—9.4°F) is blown through the underside of a continuous stainless steel mesh belt so that the peas become suspended in the air and the mixture of peas and air behaves rather like a fluid. The *Reynolds Number* (air density x pea diameter x air velocity/air viscosity) has to be greater than 100 for this fluidization to occur. Peas can be frozen in three minutes in this type of unit. Hygienic standards are met by passing the steel belt through a sanitizer and a water wash spray before it returns to the freezer to be loaded with more peas.

Liquid nitrogen spray freezing is now being more widely adopted in the food industry. Higher priced commodities such as scampi and pre-cooked dishes are ideal for this method. The boiling point of liquid nitrogen is —196°C (—321°F) and, since the nitrogen gas that is formed when the liquid vaporizes as it is sprayed on to the food is also initially at —196°C, it is used to pre-cool the food material on entry to the freezing tunnel. In this way, maximum utilization of liquid nitrogen is achieved and thermal stresses within the food, which could easily cause cracking, are minimized. The manufacture of frozen foods is now a major industry producing an enormous range of goods.

Interpress/John Watney

Left: Burning the bristles from a pig carcass after slaughtering. An alternative method of removing the bristles is to pass the carcass through a tank of water at 60°C (140°F), which loosens the bristles, and then through a machine which removes them mechanically.

Right: This sequence of four pictures shows some of the stages in the production of canned processed peas. The first picture is of the soaking tanks in which dried peas are rehydrated before being put into storage tanks to await processing. From the storage tanks, the peas pass along a conveyer belt where they are inspected visually and any bad ones are removed (second picture). The third picture shows the filler heads which fill the sterile cans with peas and brine. The cans are then sealed and conveyed into the oven, shown in the fourth picture, where they are cooked for over twenty minutes. After they have cooled, the cans are labelled and then packed for delivery.

Batchelors

Batchelors

Batchelors

Batchelors

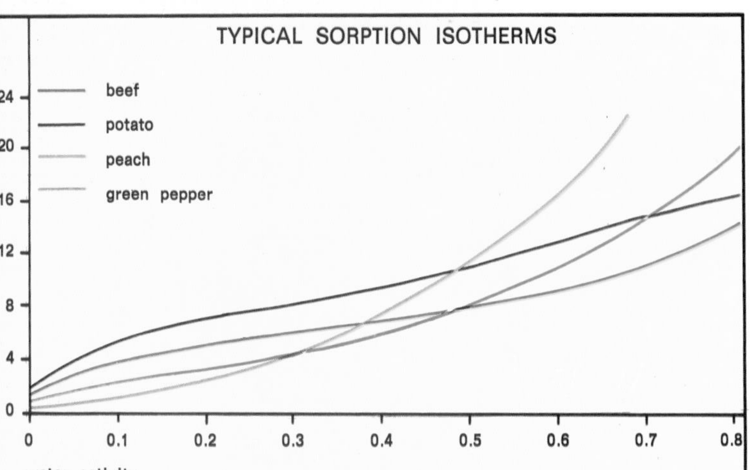

Above: This diagram shows the *sorption isotherms* for some popular foods. The isotherms show the relationship between the moisture content and the water activity of the foods. This type of graph is used to determine to what level the moisture content of a food must be reduced in order to bring its water activity to below that at which it will be free from spoilage: most foods will be free from spoilage below a water activity of about 0.62. Thus beef, for example, could be free from spoilage if its moisture content were reduced to below about 10 per cent.

Imperial Foods Ltd

Left: A cold storage warehouse containing meat and poultry. These warehouses are designed for storing frozen food for long periods, and are rather like enormous refrigerators. They are heavily insulated, and designed in such a way as to avoid heat entering through the doors. The temperature inside cold stores is usually maintained at less than —18°C (0°F) to minimize any deterioration of the stored food.

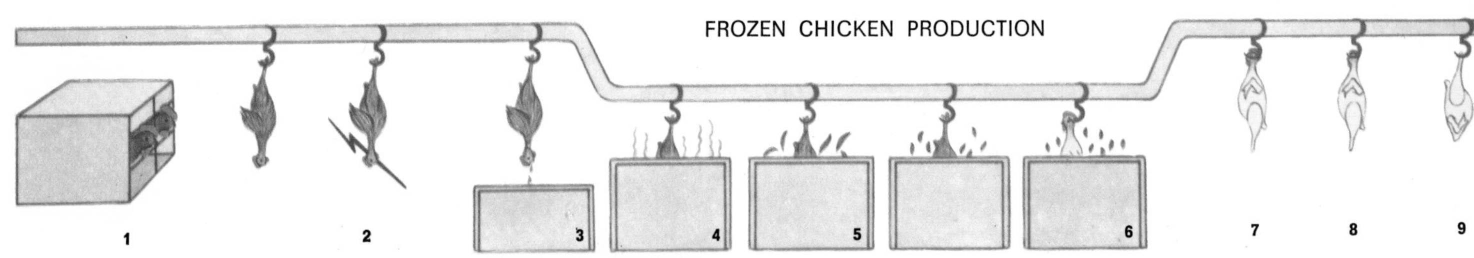

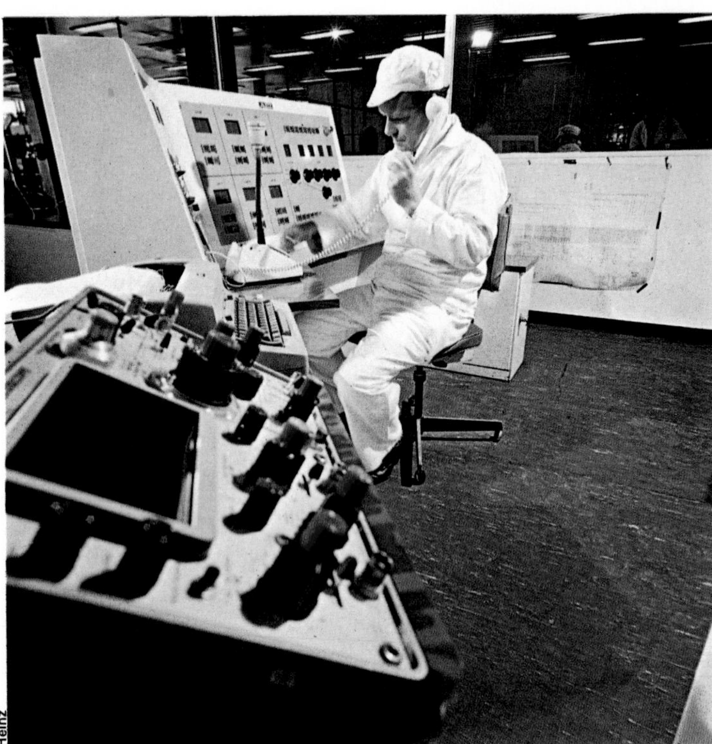

Left: The production control room at a modern soup factory. In this factory, the production process is controlled by a computer, which selects the raw materials for 40 different soups from stocks of 44 separate ingredients. The computer selects the required quantities of ingredients for each type of soup and controls their delivery to the production lines, which can produce up to 68,000 litres (15,000 gallons) of soup per hour.

Right: The food industry uses a wide range of flavourings and colourings, particularly in the manufacture of convenience foods such as desserts and savoury snacks. Although there are many synthetic flavourings in use, a large proportion of the flavourings used are concentrated from natural sources.

Below: This chart shows the effects of the main food preservation methods on the various organisms and chemical conditions which cause food spoilage.

High temperature processing

There are three main categories of high temperature processing: *pasteurization* at temperatures below 100°C (212°F); *steam retorting* (after canning) at 121.1°C (250°F); and *ultra heat treatment*, also called ultra high temperature (UHT) processing in the region of 180°C (356°F).

Most canned fruits can be preserved by pasteurizing between 90°C (194°F) and 100°C (212°F) because their pH (a measure of their acidity) is in the range 3 to 4. This is a sufficiently low pH (high acidity) to prevent the growth of pathogenic organisms. Grapefruit segments can be prepared by removing the outer membrane in a 2 per cent sodium hydroxide solution at 98°C (208°F) with a 10-second immersion time. The sodium hydroxide is neutralized by a further immersion in citric acid, and then the peeled segments are pasteurized at 100°C for 20 minutes in a can containing a sucrose syrup of 30 per cent weight concentration.

Food commodities of lower acidity (higher pH) such as soups, meat, fish and vegetable products require a more severe heat treatment. An example of this type of food is canned baked beans, a popular commodity consisting of pea or navy beans in tomato sauce.

The dried beans are first sieved to grade them for size, and any discoloured beans are removed by a photo-electric sorter. Other foreign material sinks out when the beans are *flumed* over a series of waterfalls. Moisture is re-absorbed by the beans by soaking in cold water for 12 to 18 hours, and the enzymes are destroyed by blanching at 88°C to 99°C (190°F to 210°F). At this stage the beans have approximately

	enzymes	bacteria	fungi	oxygen	water	ph control	ionic
cooking	destroys above 80°C	most destroyed	some destroyed				
gas & vacuum packing		prevents growth	inhibits	removes or excludes			
canning or bottling	destroys	destroys	some destroyed	removes and excludes			
chilling	slows up	inhibits					
freezing	lowers reaction	kills 50-80%	inhibits		removes		
dehydration	destroys	inhibits	inhibits		removes		
curing	inhibits	inhibits	inhibits	partly replaced by CO_2			alters
pickling	inactivates	inactivates	inhibits			reduces	alters
irradiation		destroys	destroys				

Right: Spaghetti is a form of *pasta*, which is made of durum semolina (which comes from a variety of hard wheat) and water, often with other ingredients such as eggs or spinach. The ingredients are mixed into a dough, which is extruded through a die to form long strands of spaghetti that are then cut into lengths and dried.

Below: The principal stages in the making of Kesp, a textured vegetable protein meat substitute made from soybeans. The beans are processed into isolated soya protein, which is then mixed with oils, flavourings and colourings before being spun, formed into shape, dehydrated and packed.

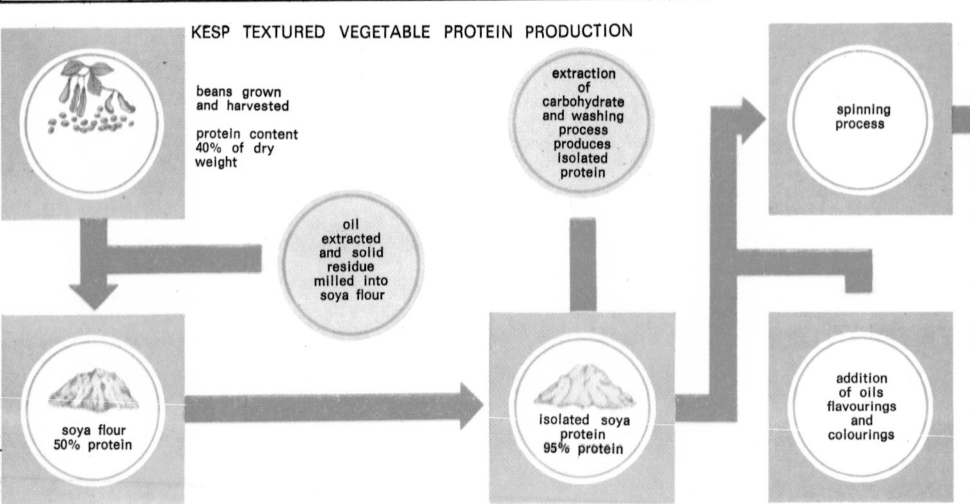

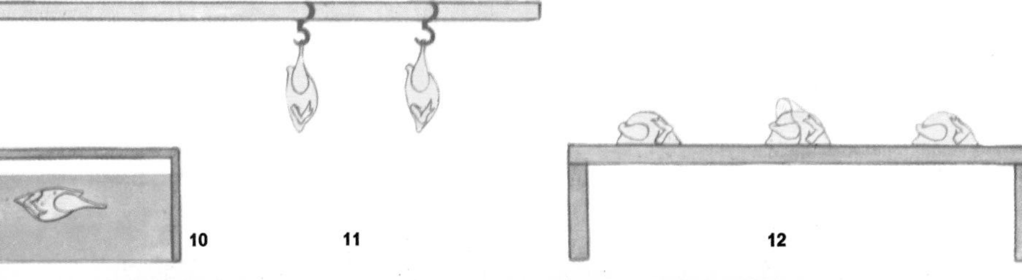

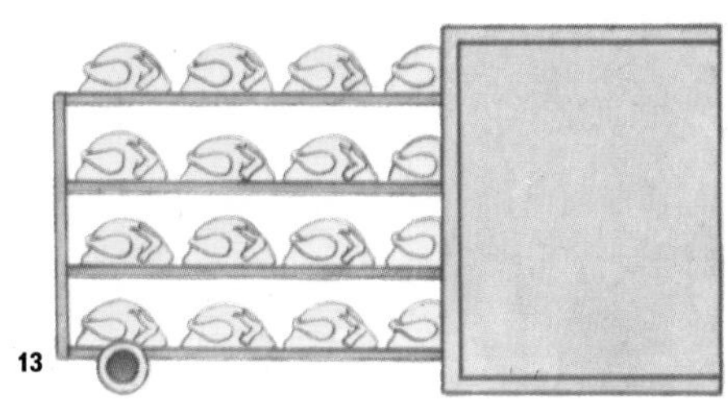

Golden Wonder Ltd

Above: This diagram shows how frozen chickens are produced. The live chickens (1) are stunned electrically (2) then killed by having their throats cut (3). The carcasses, drained of blood, are scalded to loosen the feathers (4) and then passed through machines which pull out the quills (5) and feathers (6). The feet, innards and heads are then removed (7, 8 and 9) before the carcasses are chilled (10), dried (11), trussed and vacuum-packed (12), and finally frozen (13).

Left: Potato crisps emerging from the cooker. To make potato crisps, the potatoes are first put into a machine which peels and washes them. They are then graded for size and inspected for blemishes, and passed through machines which cut them into slices about 1.4 mm (0.056 in) thick. After washing to remove the surface starch, the slices are drained of excess moisture and cooked in hot groundnut oil, then sprinkled with salt or flavourings such as 'cheese and onion' or 'salt and vinegar'.

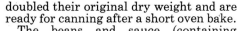

Pasta Information Centre

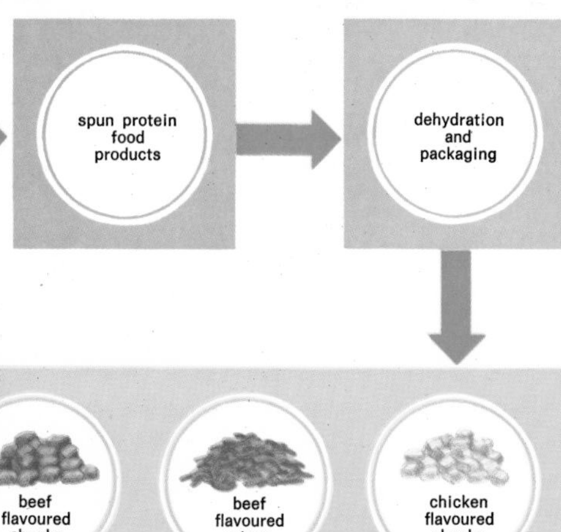

doubled their original dry weight and are ready for canning after a short oven bake.

The beans and sauce (containing tomato puree, sugar, salt, flour and spices) are machine-filled into cans. The filling temperature must be about 80°C (176°F) in order to give a high final vacuum in the can after closure and retorting. The vacuum is necessary because the product is corrosive and a significant amount of oxygen in the head-space of the can (between the product and the lid) would cause extensive damage to the tin-plate walls of the container. The ends of the can are made from lacquered tin-plate and, after filling and seaming on the lid, the cans are processed in steam retorts at 115°C (240°F). Since the product is viscous, the rate of heat penetration would normally be very slow and result in overcooking. Therefore, it is the usual practice to agitate the cans in a rotary steam retort, particularly when large catering packs are being processed.

With the UHT process, the destruction of micro-organisms in milk is accomplished in approximately three seconds. The familiar tetrahedral and brick-shaped packs are constructed from an aluminium foil-lined waxed sheet which is sterilized by passing it through a solution of hydrogen peroxide (H_2O_2) before filling it with the heat-treated milk. This technique of sterilizing the food and container separately is known as *aseptic processing*. It has also been applied to yogurts, fruit purees and baby foods.

Dehydration processing

Peas can be dried by a *fluidized-bed* technique. Before drying they are washed, graded for size, and then pricked with needles on a rotating drum so that the rate of rehydration in subsequent home preparation is improved. The enzyme *peroxidase* is inactivated by blanching at about 95°C (203°F), and then the peas are treated with a sodium bicarbonate solution to retain their colour and improve their tenderness. A dilute sodium metabisulphite ($Na_2S_2O_2$) solution is used to inhibit non-enzymic browning and prolong the storage life of the peas.

The first stage of drying is carried out in a series of seven fluidized-bed dryers throughout which the air temperature is gradually raised from 40°C (104°F) to 55°C (131°F). The temperature is lower in the first bed because the moisture evaporates rapidly from the surface of the peas and too high a temperature would cause the sugars to ooze out of them, forming a sticky skin on the surface. Higher temperatures are needed in the later stages of fluidization because moisture is now migrating from the interior of the pea against a greater resistance to drying. By the time the last stage of fluidization is completed, the moisture content has fallen from 80 to 50 per cent by weight.

The second stage of drying reduces the moisture content to 20 per cent, but the drying rate is so slow that fluidization offers no advantage, and so the air velocity is reduced to give thorough drying with a minimum of fluidization. A final moisture content of 5 per cent is achieved in bin dryers after a total drying time of about 16 hours. The peas are packaged inside a plastic laminate to prevent oxidation of the fat content and the absorption of moisture.

Freeze drying is a process in which the food is frozen at —18°C (0°F), or lower, and then placed in a vacuum chamber at a pressure of 0.0025 bar (0.036 psi). Under these conditions the ice into which the moisture in the food has turned reverts directly to water vapour, which is condensed out on to the coils of a refrigerator.

Powdered foods are frequently prepared by *spray drying*. The sprays are formed either by a high pressure nozzle or by a vaned-disc atomizer rotating at speeds of up to 40,000 rpm. A unique method for producing dried tomato powder has been developed, in which tomato paste (containing 33 per cent tomato solids) is pumped through a vaned-disc atomizer into a drying chamber fed with filtered air at 80°C (176°F). Nodules of dry powder are formed on the sloping walls of the chamber. Because tomato powder is hygroscopic (water-absorbing) it is packaged in a room of low relative humidity (approximately 60 per cent RH) to prevent the absorption of moisture from the air.

Another product commonly made by spray drying is instant coffee. Coffee is brewed from roasted, ground coffee beans and then sprayed into a chamber through which hot air is blown. The hot air turns the coffee into powder.

Beers, Wines and Spirits

The production of alcoholic drinks is a craft as old as civilization itself. Archaeological evidence suggests that wine-making began in the Middle East over 10,000 years ago, and gradually spread westward to the Mediterranean countries then up into Europe. Ancient Egyptian wall paintings depict the harvesting of grapes and the making of wine, and also show small stills which indicate that the art of distillation was known to the Egyptians.

Beer is known to have been made by the Egyptians and the Babylonians at least 6,000 years ago, and there is evidence that barley, the raw material for beer, was cultivated in Britain and northern Europe some 5,000 years ago. There is every likelihood that these early Europeans were capable of making the barley into a fermented drink.

Wines can be made from a wide range of fruits and vegetables, but true wine is made from grapes. The juice of the grape is mostly water, but it also contains sugar, fruit acids, and many trace elements which contribute to the distinctive flavour of the final wine. On the outside of the grape skin are millions of tiny living organisms, primarily yeasts, but including a number of moulds and bacteria which are of little importance to the winemaking process.

It is the yeasts on the skin of the grape which, having been brought into contact with the juice when the grapes are crushed, are responsible for the chemical reactions which turn the juice into wine. The yeasts contain enzymes which break down the molecular structure of the grape sugar (mainly *dextrose*, $C_6H_{12}O_6+H_2O$) and re-arrange the atoms into molecules of alcohol (principally *ethyl alcohol*, C_2H_5OH) and carbon dioxide gas (CO_2). During this fermentation process the grape juice loses some or all of its sweetness as its sugar is turned into alcohol, and becomes wine, with an alcohol content in the region of 10 to 14 per cent. The rest of the wine consists of water containing traces of acids, sugar and other substances which give it its flavour and colour.

The vines which provide the grapes are hardy, long-living and fast-growing plants which fruit once each year, in the autumn. For commercial wine production, the vine plant is pruned back to little more than a bush, and its life span limited to about 30 years. The vine is best suited to the temperate zones between latitudes of approximately 30 and 50°, both north and south of the equator. Within these zones it does best where the soil and the local climatic conditions most suit it.

The nature of the soil is very important. It should be well drained and never waterlogged; some of the finest wines are produced from grapes grown on poor, stony, chalky soils. The local mini- or micro-climate also influences the growth of the vines, and those grown on slopes which face the sun do better than those grown on slopes which receive less direct sunlight.

The variety of vine predominant in a wine-producing region depends on the prevailing soil and climate conditions. Thus the Riesling grape does well in Germany, the Cabernet grape thrives in Bordeaux, and the Pinot grape is widely grown in Burgundy.

Spectrum

Above: A vineyard in the famous French wine region of Burgundy. This region, which produces a wide range of fine red and white wines including Chablis, Beaujolais, Mâcon and Nuits St George, is situated in eastern central France to the south of Champagne, another famous wine region.

Wine & Spirit Education Trust

Above right: Bottles of Champagne are stored for two or three months as the sediment settles. The bottles are initially stored on their sides, then every day they are given a light shake and twisted slightly. They are gradually moved into an upright position so that the sediment settles on to the cork.

Distillers Co. Ltd.

The colouring matter that gives red wine its colour is contained in the skins of black grapes, and so to make a red wine it is necessary that the fermentation takes place with the skins still in the grape juice. White wine, on the other hand, can be made from either black or white grapes as the juice is white in both varieties. Providing that fermentation takes place in the absence of the skins, white wine can be made from black grapes.

Champagne, and some other sparkling wines, are made by the *méthode champenoise*. The wines are given a second fermentation in the bottle by the addition of a little sugar and yeast, and the bottles are stored upside down so that the sediment produced settles on the cork. The carbon dioxide formed during the fermentation dissolves into the wine, giving it its sparkle, and when the fermentation is complete the necks of the bottles are frozen, so that the sediment freezes on to the corks and can be removed by drawing the corks. Some sugar is added to give the wine the required sweetness, then the bottles are re-corked.

In the *transfer method* of making sparkling wines, the wine is removed from the bottles after the second fermentation and put into a large vat. It is then filtered to remove the sediment, and re-bottled. Sparkling wines can also be made by the *cuve close* method, in which the second fermentation takes place in a

Distillers Co. Ltd.

Left: Malt whisky is made by distilling the alcoholic liquid obtained by fermenting malt sugar. This sugar is produced by the action of enzymes on the starch in barley, these enzymes being formed in the barley when it is malted. Here, malted barley is being spread in a kiln for drying.

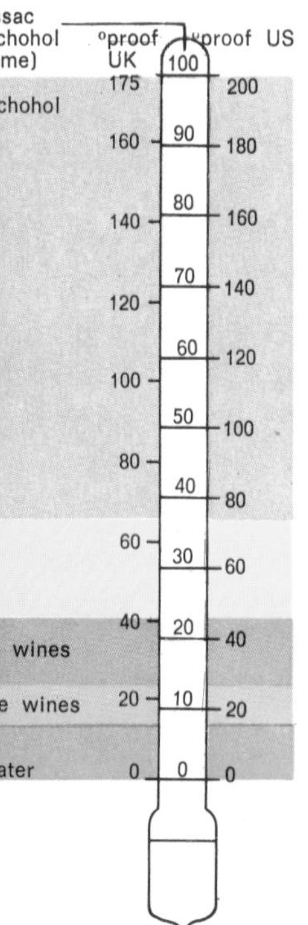

Below left: The alcohol content of a drink is generally expressed in terms of *degrees proof*. There are three main proof scales in use: the Gay-Lussac scale, used on the European continent (which directly indicates the percentage of alcohol in the drink), the US proof scale, and the British (Sikes) scale.

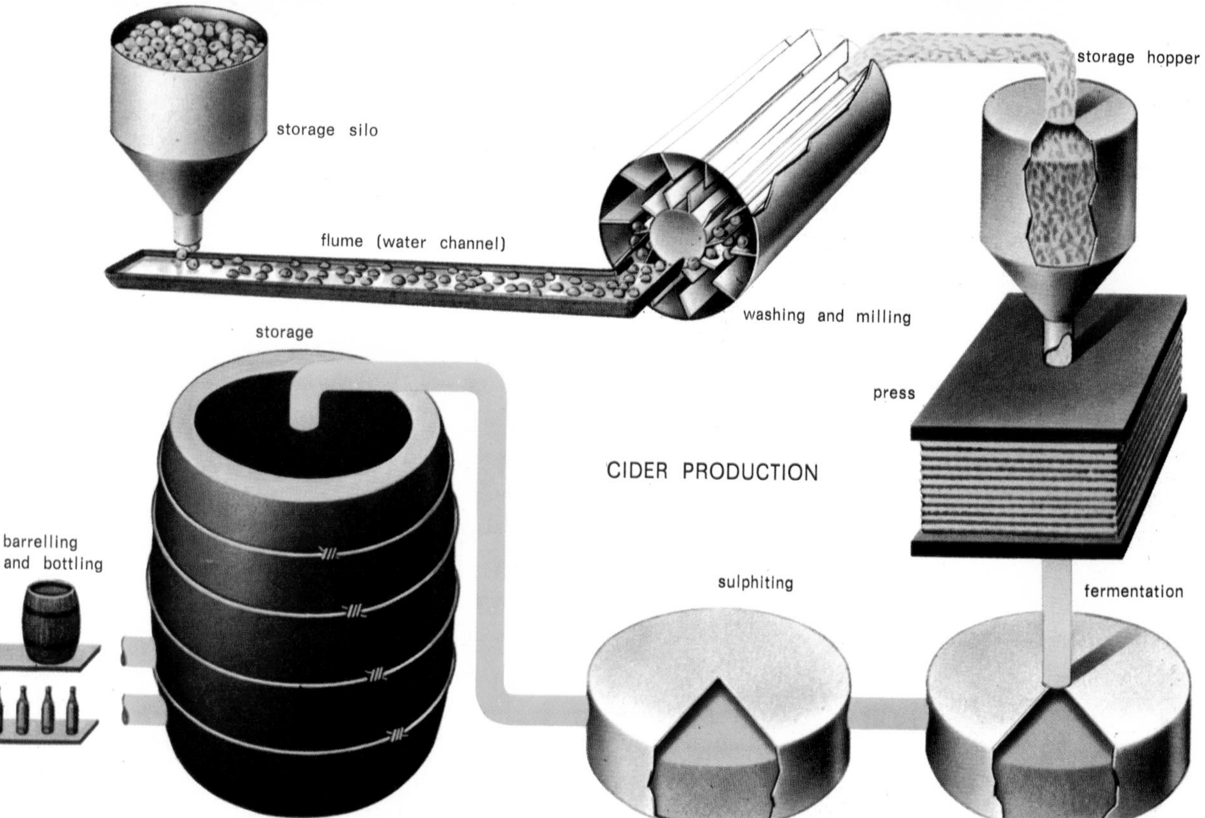

Above: Cider is made by fermenting apple juice. The apples are washed and milled, then the juice is pressed out of the pulp and fermented. The sulphiting process kills off the yeasts to prevent any secondary fermentation. Cider must be matured for about 6 months before it is ready for consumption.

Below: A *spirit still* at a malt whisky distillery, in which the second stage of the distillation is carried out. In the first stage, the 'wash' of fermented malt sugar is distilled in a *wash still*. The distillate obtained is then put into the spirit still for a second distillation.

Left: Filtering a sample of the alcoholic wash produced by the fermentation of malt sugar during whisky production. The *specific gravity* of the sample, the weight of a given volume of it compared with that of an equal volume of water, indicates the amount of alcohol being produced.

vat and the wine is filtered before bottling. The cheapest method of making sparkling wine is to inject carbon dioxide gas into chilled wine and bottle it under pressure so that the gas dissolves into the wine, but sparkling wines made by this *carbonation* method soon go 'flat' after the bottle is uncorked as the gas rapidly bubbles out.

Another important group are the *fortified* wines. These include port, sherry and madeira, and are fortified by the addition of extra alcohol, usually in the form of brandy, which gives them an alcohol content of between about 16 and 24 per cent. The extra alcohol inhibits further fermentation, and so these wines usually have a comparatively high sugar content and are thus sweeter than non-fortified wines.

Spirits

Spirits are made by the distillation of alcohol which has been produced by a fermentation process. True brandy, for example, such as Cognac, is made by the distillation of wine made from grape juice. The wine is heated in a *still*, and the alcohol which evaporates out of it is condensed and collected. Alcohol has a lower boiling point than water, about 78.4°C 173.12°F) as opposed to 100°C (212°F), and so if the still is heated to just over the boiling point of alcohol, the alcohol will evaporate out leaving most of the water behind (some of the water will evaporate out, even at this temperature).

Apart from alcohol, other substances are given off during distillation, and many of these are poisonous and must be removed. The initial flow of condensed liquid from the still contains the more volatile of these substances, those such as *acetaldehyde* (CH_3CHO) which have a lower boiling point than alcohol. This initial flow is collected in a separate tank from that into which the purer alcohol will be run when it starts to flow from the still.

Towards the end of the distillation, other impurities begin to appear in the alcohol as those with higher boiling points begin to evaporate. These include

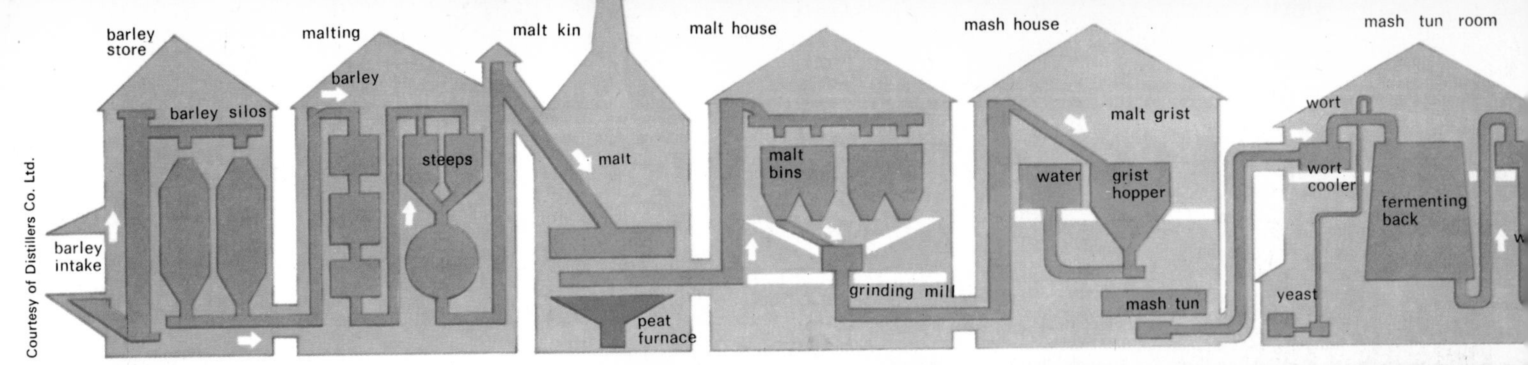

Courtesy of Distillers Co. Ltd.

Below: Most whiskies sold are blends of many different 'single' whiskies, and the blender assesses each sample by its aroma, not its flavour. Malt whiskies are made from malted barley, and grain whiskies from malted barley plus unmalted barley and maize. Both are used in blended whiskies.

Distillers Co. Ltd.

ZEFA

Above: The part of the hop used in brewing is the female flower cone. It contains oils and resins which impart flavour to the beer and act as preservatives, and tannin which precipitates protein matter out of the wort during boiling and so helps to clarify the beer. The spent hops are sold as fertilizer.

Bass Worthington

Right: One of the first stages in the brewing of beer is the mashing of the malted barley. After the barley has been milled, it is put into one of these *mash tuns* where it is mixed with hot water. This activates the enzymes in the barley that turn the starch into sugar, which dissolves in the water.

fusel oils, which consist mainly of *amyl alcohol* and *isoamyl alcohol*, and when these appear in the distillate the flow is diverted once more into the tank containing the impurities given off in the beginning.

Spirit distillation is usually done in two or more stages, and some spirits may be re-distilled to make them more pure. The flavour of a spirit is derived from substances formed during the original fermentation which are retained in the spirit during the distillation process, or from flavourings added after distillation.

An enormous range of spirits are produced from many different source materials. Whiskies are made from grains such as barley, rye and corn (maize); rum is made from molasses, a syrup obtained from cane sugar; brandies can be made from virtually any fermentable sweet fruit (for example Kirsch is made from cherries and Slivovitz from plums). Tequila, the strong Mexican spirit, is made from a form of cactus.

Gin, which originated in Holland, is usually made from grain or molasses spirits flavoured with juniper berries, and often other ingredients such as coriander, orange peel, liquorice and anise.

Liqueurs can be made from any spirit by the addition of flavourings and sweetenings. Cherry brandy, for example, is not a brandy made from cherries (as is Kirsch), but a blend of brandy, cherry essence and sugar. Many other fruits, as well as chocolate, coffee and mint, are used in making liqueurs.

Some of the most famous liqueurs, such as Drambuie, Benedictine and Chartreuse, are blended from spirits and mixtures of herbs and essences whose ingredients are

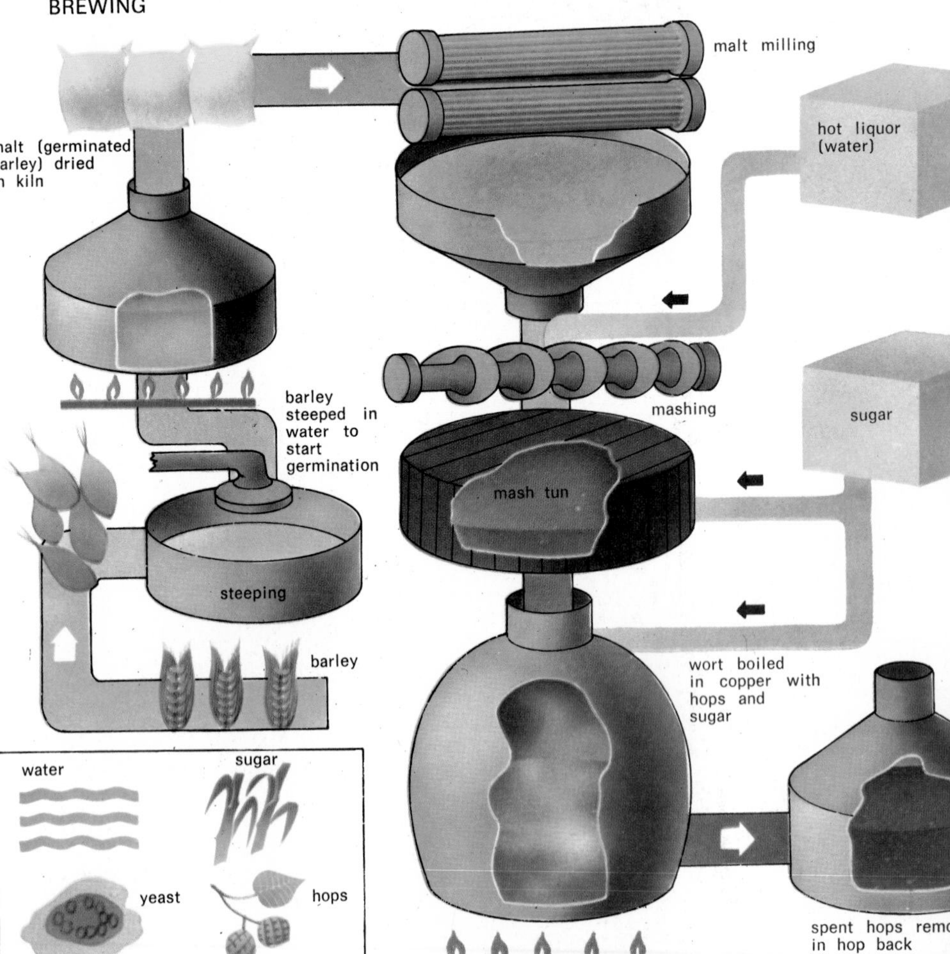

Courtesy of Youngs Brewery

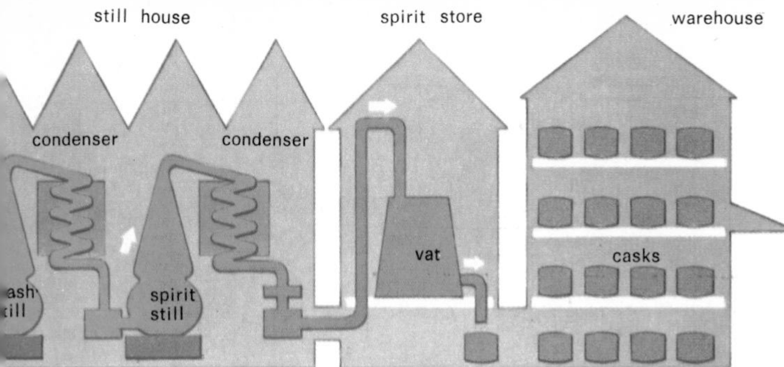

Bass Worthington

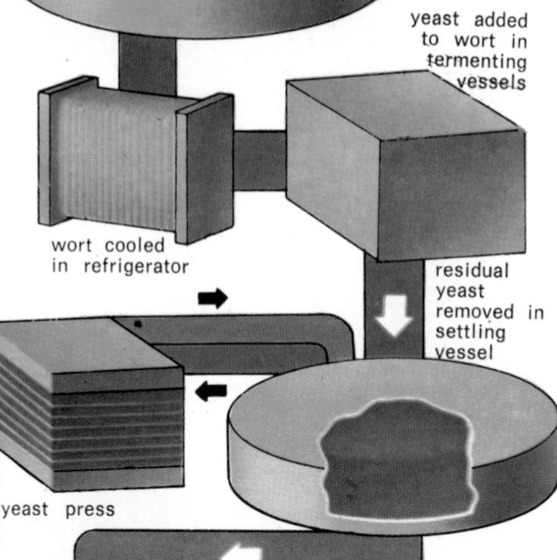

Youngs Brewery

Left: This diagram shows how malt whisky is produced. The barley is malted by soaking it in water and then allowing it to germinate in a warm, damp atmosphere. After the barley has germinated, further growth is stopped by drying it in a peat-fired kiln, the smoke from which contributes much to the flavour of the whisky. The malt is ground and mixed with warm water to make a sugary solution (wort) which is cooled and mixed with yeast in a vessel called a *fermenting back*, where the yeast converts the sugar to alcohol. The resulting wash is distilled in a copper *pot still* known as the *wash still*, and the distillate is given a second distillation in another pot still, the *spirit still*. The spirit is diluted in the spirit store vat, then put into oak casks to mature for several years. The spirit from the still is colourless and harsh-tasting, and during maturation it absorbs flavour and colour from the casks, which are often casks that have previously contained sherry.

Left: The traditional type of vessel used for fermenting beer is a large, fairly shallow vat, but many modern breweries use large cylindrical fermenting vessels such as those shown here.

Below: Filling barrels with beer, an operation which is known as 'racking'.

Left: A typical brewing process. Milled malted barley, hot liquor (water) and sugar are mixed in the *mash tun* to produce the sugary liquid known as *wort*. The wort, plus hops and sugar, is boiled in a large 'copper', then discharged into the *hop back* where the spent hops are extracted from it. The wort is cooled and put into the fermenting tanks, where the yeast is added and the sugar is converted into alcohol. Fresh beer from the fermenting tanks is put into settling vessels, where the residual yeast is removed and pressed dry. After a period of storage, the beer is put into barrels or bottles.

closely-guarded secrets. Benedictine, for instance, is still made to a secret recipe invented by a Benedictine monk, Dom Bernardo Vincelli, at the abbey at Fécamp, France, in the early sixteenth century.

Beer

Beer is usually made from barley (although other grains can be used), hops, yeast and sugar. The barley corns consist largely of starch, which will not ferment, and so it must first be converted into sugar, which ferments readily. This is brought about by *malting* the barley. During the malting process, the barley is soaked and then kept in a warm atmosphere so that it begins to germinate. As the barley germinates, it produces an enzyme called *diastase* which will convert the starch into malt sugars (chiefly *maltose*, $C_{12}H_{22}O_{11}+H_2O$), which in turn are then converted to alcohol by the yeast enzymes during the brewing.

After malting, the barley is milled and then mashed together with hot water and sugar. The resulting liquid, known as *wort* (pronounced 'wert'), is pumped into large copper vessels where it is boiled with hops and sugar. The hops act both as a flavouring and as a preservative. Next, the spent hops are separated from the boiled wort, which is cooled and put into the fermenting vessels. The yeast is now added, and fermentation begins.

British beers begin fermentation at a temperature of about 15.6°C (60°F), and fermentation takes from five to seven days. These beers are top-fermented, that is, the type of yeast used floats on the top of the liquid. The beer, after fermentation, is drawn off into settling tanks where any residual yeast is removed, and then stored for a time (from a few days to a few weeks, depending on the type of beer) at around 0°C (32°F) to allow it to mature before it is *racked* (filled) into casks, bottles or cans.

Lager beers are bottom-fermented, the yeast used settling at the bottom of the vessels during fermentation, which begins at a temperature of from 6 to 10°C (43-50°F) and takes about eight days. Lager beers are matured for up to three months at 0°C (32°F) before racking (the name 'lager' is the German word for 'store'). During the maturation period a second fermentation takes place which clears the beer and improves its flavour and strength.

The term 'ale' originally applied to un-hopped beers, but it is now widely used as a general name for top-fermented beers. The amount of hops used depends upon the type of beer being produced. A strong top-fermented beer may be made with about eight times the amount of hops used in making a light lager.

Another factor which varies according to the type of beer being produced is the malting process. For example, the barley for a top-fermented beer may be germinated for 11 days and then dried at 107°C (225°F) for three or four days, but barley for a lager may only be germinated for seven or eight days and then dried at a temperature of about 55°C (130°F). When dark beers such as brown ales and stouts are to be made, the barley is also highly roasted. The rootlets which sprout from the barley during germination shrivel and drop off when it is dried, and they are usually collected and sold for use in animal feeds.

Farm Technology

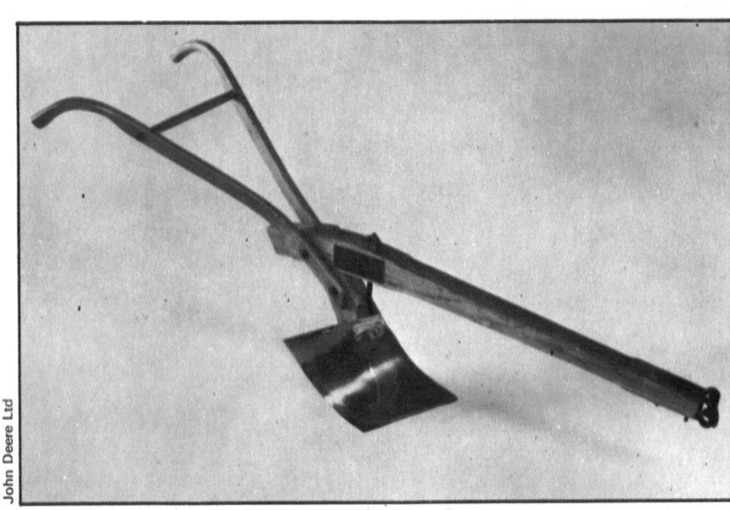

Right: The steel plough invented in the US by John Deere (1804-1886) in 1837. This one was tougher than the iron or iron-faced wooden ploughs then available, and it made an important contribution to the development of agriculture on the American prairies.

John Deere Ltd

Below: A replica of the reaper designed by Cyrus McCormick in the US in 1831. The reaper cut the crop and laid it on the ground, and then it was tied into bundles by hand and taken away for threshing (separating the grains from the stalks). Reapers were succeeded by reaper-threshers, the forerunners of the combine harvester.

International Harvester

Modern agriculture makes extensive use of many forms of technology, and the wide range of machines that till the soil, plant the seeds and harvest the crops make a vital contribution to the production of the world's food supplies. With the aid of these machines, one man can do as much work in one day as a team of men could do in a week before the introduction of mechanization.

The best-known piece of farm equipment is probably the tractor, first developed around the turn of the century as a replacement for the horse. Tractor design has improved considerably since the 1950s, not only in performance but also in the amount of comfort and safety provided for the driver.

The early tractors gave the driver no protection from the weather, and the only concessions to comfort were footrests and a hard metal seat. The next step was to mount the seat on springs, and to provide crude mudguards to give the driver a certain amount of protection from the mud, dust or water thrown up by the large driving wheels. One result of this lack of attention to the driver's comfort was that tractor drivers were liable to back injuries and a variety of muscular ailments because of having to spend so much of their working lives being bumped around in the cold and wet. In addition, the drivers obtained less output from the tractors than they were capable of giving because they drove them relatively slowly to minimize the discomfort.

Massey Ferguson

Left: A Massey-Ferguson MF 1505 tractor pulling an MF 23 cultivator. The tractor is a large, four-wheel-drive machine, powered by a 134 kW (180 bhp), 10.4 litre V-8 diesel engine, and the cultivator is a heavy-duty model designed for clearing stubble after harvesting and for deep seed bed preparation.

International Harvester

Right: A twenty-row seed drill, the International 511. This machine can sow a wide variety of crop seeds, such as grass or wheat, planting twenty rows at a time at a constant, pre-set depth and depositing the seeds at pre-determined intervals to obtain uniform spacing between the plants.

Another danger faced by the driver was that of being killed or severely injured if the tractor overturned when working on sloping ground or by the side of a ditch.

In the early 1960s, cushioned seats and rudimentary 'weather cabs' were fitted to tractors to improve the comfort and weather protection. These early cabs, however, gave rise to another form of discomfort—noise. The sheet-metal panelling acted as a soundbox, amplifying the noise from the engine, gearbox and hydraulic system so much that the drivers were exposed to damaging levels of noise.

A British survey in the 1960s showed that potential increases in productivity due to improved driver comfort had been offset by losses due to noise. Instead of slowing their tractors to speeds that their bodies could stand, drivers now had to slow them to keep the noise down to a level that their ears could tolerate. The survey estimated that this slowing down reduced output by about 20 per cent.

Since then, tractor cab design has been greatly improved, and the latest cabs give complete protection against the weather, overturning, and noise. Nearly all modern cabs are fitted on rubber mountings to insulate the driver from vibration, and they incorporate sound insulation, comfortable seating, heating and ventilation systems, windscreen wipers and washers, and power-assisted controls.

Most tractors are constructed so that the engine and transmission form a rigid backbone for the whole machine, so that a separate chassis is not needed. Engine powers range from about 15 kW (20 bhp) for small horticultural machines up to 186 kW (250 bhp) or more for the largest heavy-duty models, but most general-purpose farm tractors use engines delivering between about 22 kW (30 bhp) and 89 kW (120 bhp).

The engines themselves are usually diesels, driving the rear wheels or, on some models, all four wheels. The engines also drive the *power take-off* shafts which provide the drive for implements towed by or mounted on the tractor, and the hydraulic systems which are used for controlling these implements.

Ploughing and seeding

The *plough* is the most basic tool of agriculture, and it has been in use in one

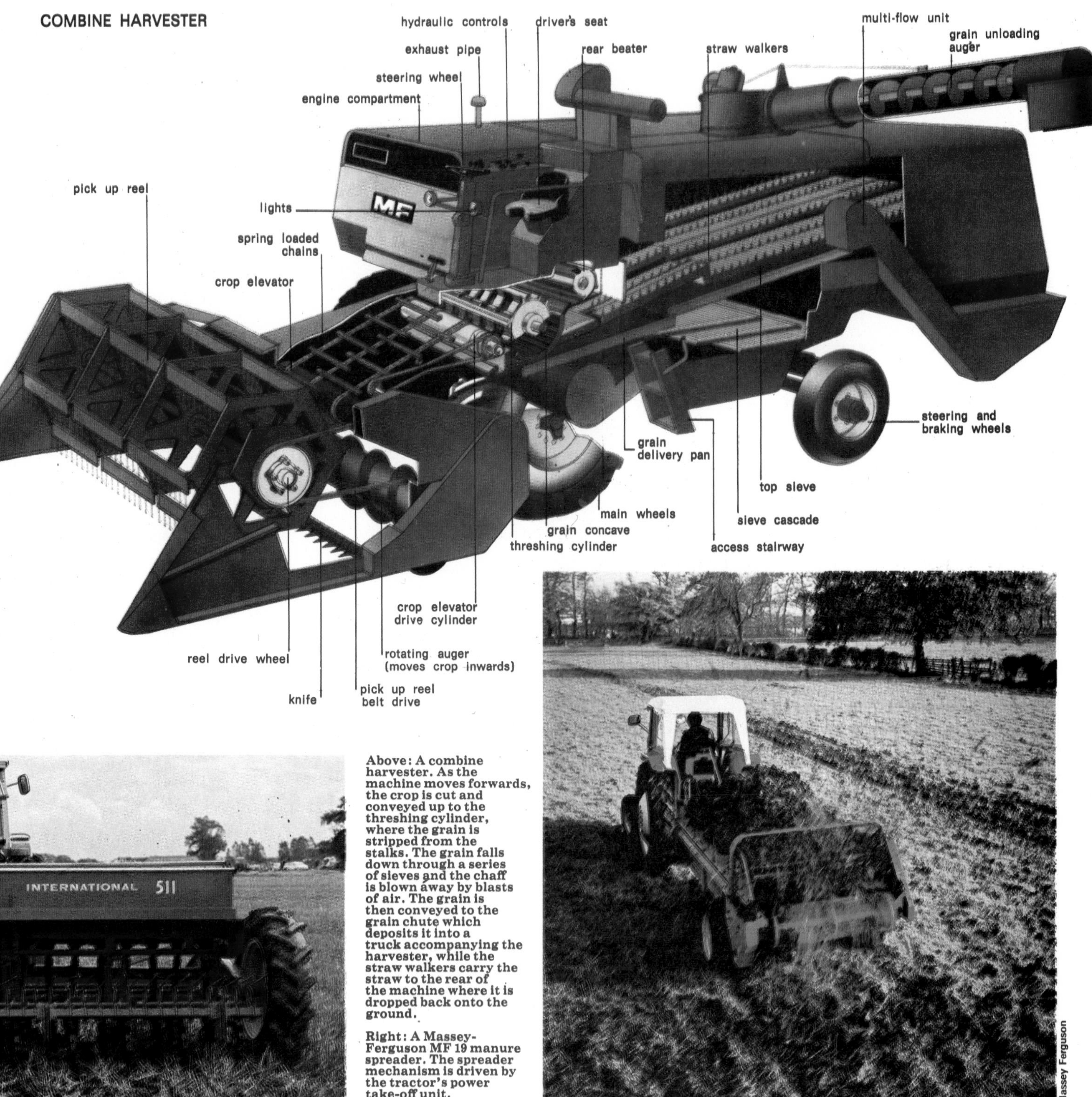

Above: A combine harvester. As the machine moves forwards, the crop is cut and conveyed up to the threshing cylinder, where the grain is stripped from the stalks. The grain falls down through a series of sieves and the chaff is blown away by blasts of air. The grain is then conveyed to the grain chute which deposits it into a truck accompanying the harvester, while the straw walkers carry the straw to the rear of the machine where it is dropped back onto the ground.

Right: A Massey-Ferguson MF 19 manure spreader. The spreader mechanism is driven by the tractor's power take-off unit.

form or another since Neolithic times. Its function is similar in many ways to that of a spade—it turns the topsoil over, loosening it and breaking it up and at the same time burying any trash and weeds. In modern mechanized farming the plough, like many other agricultural implements, is pulled by tractor, although simple ploughs pulled by animals such as horses or oxen are still in use in many countries.

Before crops can be planted in ploughed land, a certain amount of final ground preparation is usually necessary. Just as the gardener uses a rake to prepare soil for planting, the farmer uses a tractor-drawn harrow to level the ploughed soil and destroy any new weeds that may have started to grow. Another type of machine used for soil preparation and weed destruction is the *cultivator*, which uses steel spikes or blades to break up the soil. *Rotary cultivators*, which use spikes or blades mounted on a revolving, power-driven shaft, can often be used to prepare ground that has not previously been ploughed.

The planting of many crops can now be carried out mechanically, using machines which open up the ground, deposit the seeds at pre-determined intervals and depths, then cover them over. Such machines plant a number of rows at a time, and many also apply fertilizer as they plant the seeds.

Harvesting machinery

A wide range of crops, including root crops such as potatoes, and fruits such as grapes and cider apples, are now harvested by machines. One of the first and most important of these machines was the *combine harvester*, used for grain crops such as wheat. The combine is a self-propelled machine which cuts the crop, separates the grain from the straw and removes the husks, transfers the grain into an accompanying truck, and deposits the straw on to the ground for later collection.

Until recently, straw was regarded mainly as a waste product, useful at best only as bedding for cattle or for providing some roughage in their feed. Consequently, little effort has been put into removing it from the field, especially by arable farmers; it is often simply burnt away. A new process is being developed, however, which may enable straw to be converted economically into animal feed.

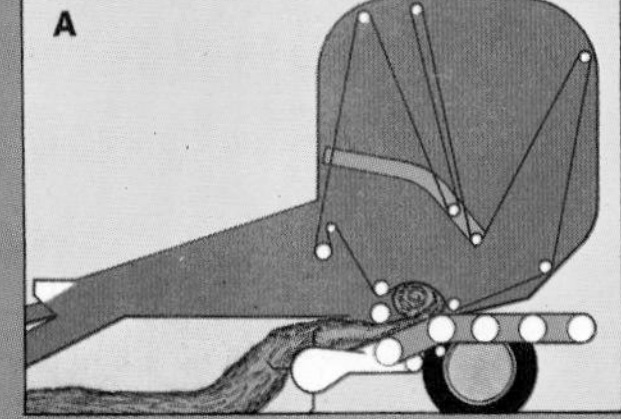

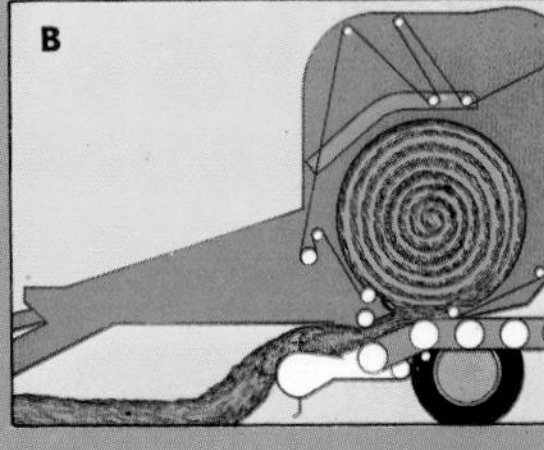

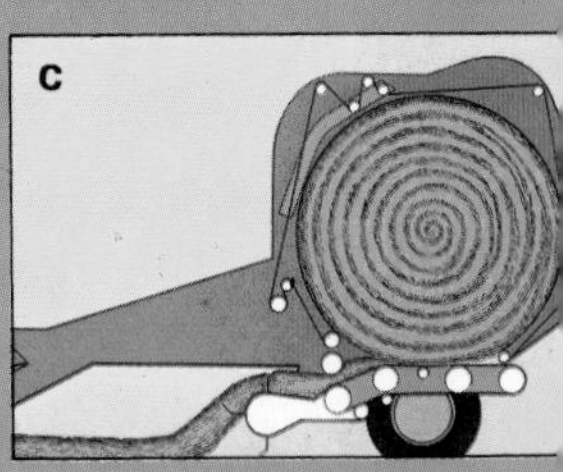

A Baler picks up hay and draws it into baling chamber

B Hay rolled into bale

C Completed bale bound with twine prior to ejection from machine

Above: The International 241 big roll baler. The mown hay is collected by the white-painted unit just in front of the baler's wheels.

Below: Potatoes, like any other crop, are susceptible to attack by insects and fungus diseases, and potato fields need to be kept free of weeds which could hinder the growth of the plants. This diagram shows the types of pest likely to afflict potatoes, and some of the chemicals used to combat them: herbicides to kill the weeds without harming the potatoes, and insecticides and fungicides to kill the insects and fungi. The fertilizers enrich the soil and promote the growth of the potatoes.

Left: Kolos combine harvesters being built at the Taganrog works, Rostov, Russia. The Soviet Union produces about one sixth of the world's total cereal output, and plans to have its annual output running at over 235 million tonnes in the early 1980s. Output in 1976 was more than 220 million tonnes.

Above: These three diagrams show the way that round 'big bales' of hay are produced. After the grass has been mown, the baler, drawn by the tractor, picks up the crop and feeds it back into the baling chamber where it is rolled into a bale. When the bale is complete it is bound with twine and ejected.

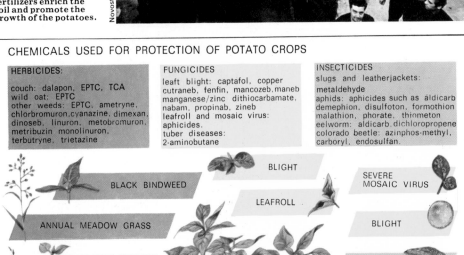

Above: One of the many types of harvesting machine now in use. This one is harvesting spinach in Sweden. The tractor-drawn harvester picks the crop and conveys it through a delivery chute into the trailer travelling alongside.

Right: Spraying a field of wheat with Calixin, a brand of *tridemorph* fungicide used to combat the fungus disease known as 'mildew' which affects cereal crops. Mildew in cereals is caused by the fungus *Erysiphe graminis*, which attacks the leaves and root system of a plant. This results in a reduced grain yield, which may be as much as 40% below normal in severe cases of infection.

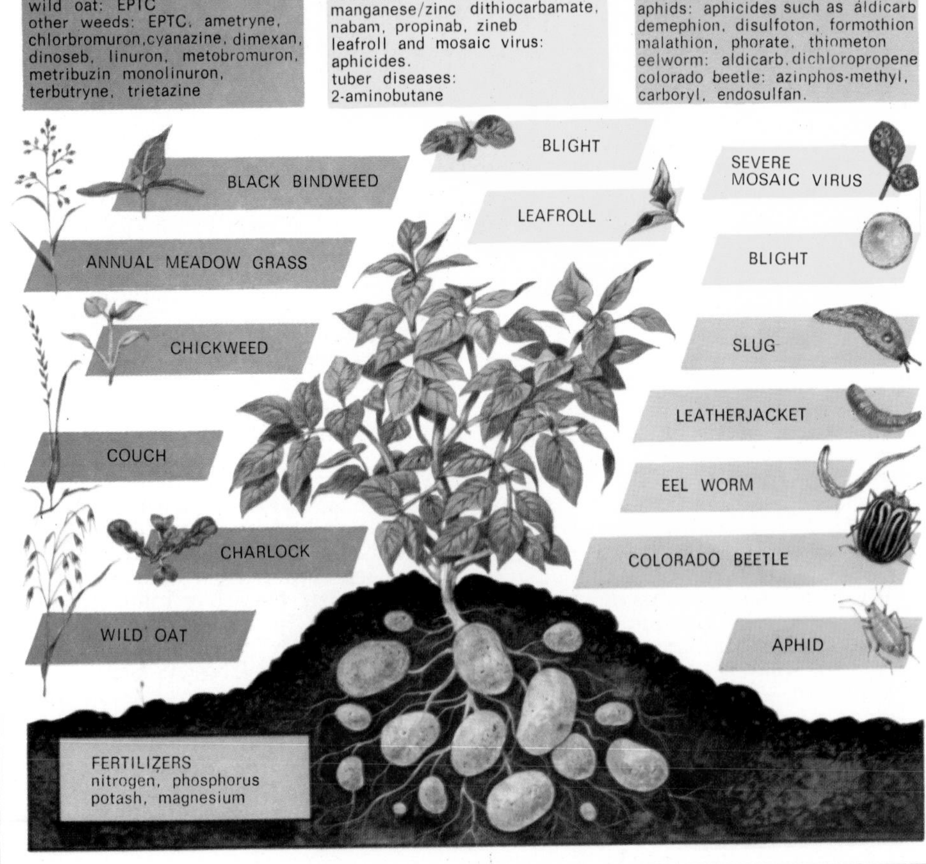

Daymond Ltd

Above: Good drainage and irrigation are essential to agriculture. This picture shows a crawler tractor fitted with a pipe-laying plough which opens up the ground and lays continuous flexible piping. The tractor is guided along the required route by a laser beam system.

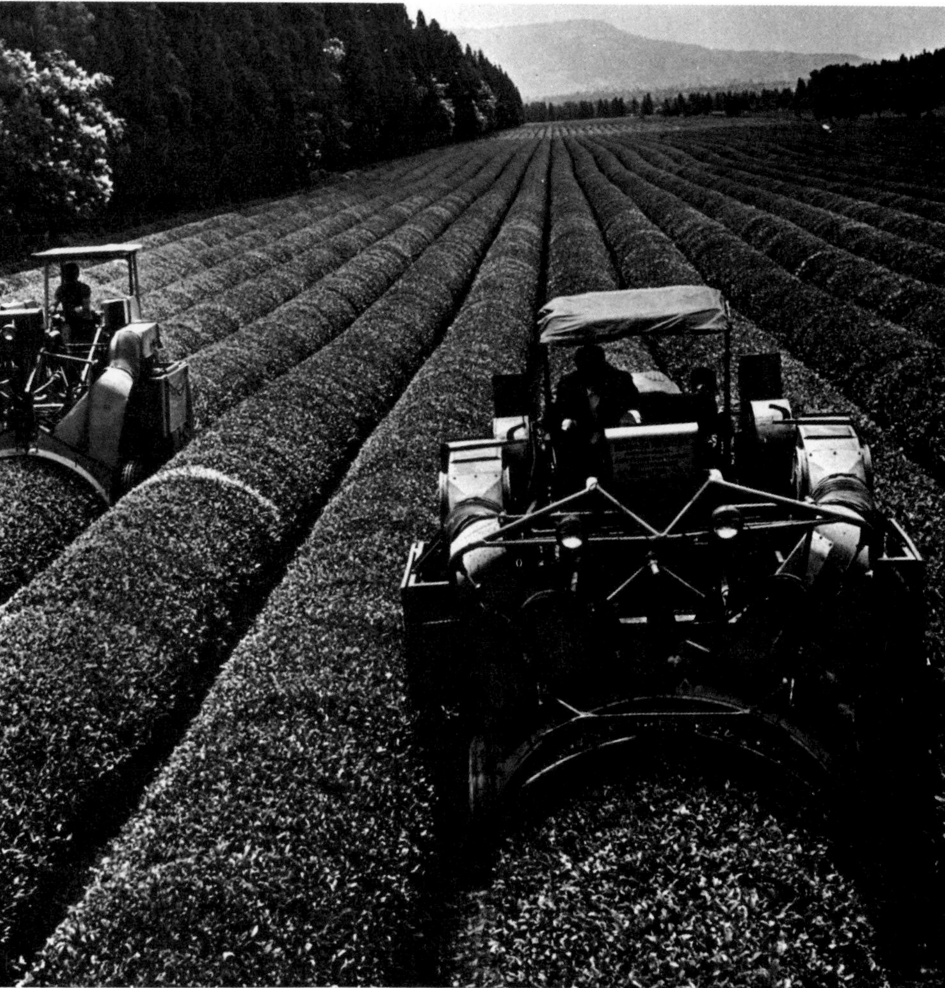

Novosti

Right: Harvesting tea on a plantation in Georgia, where 96% of the Soviet Union's tea is grown. The machines straddle the rows of tea bushes, and travel along trimming off the outermost leaves and sucking them back into hoppers. Most of the world's tea, however, is still picked by hand.

Paolo Koch

BASF

One of the main constituents of straw is cellulose, which can be used as a food by ruminant (cud-chewing) animals such as cows. The cellulose in straw, however, is enclosed in an indigestible substance called lignin, which must be removed before the straw can be used as feed. The German chemist Ernst Otto Beckmann (1853-1923) developed, during the First World War, a method of soaking straw in caustic soda (sodium hydroxide, $NaOH$) to dissolve away the lignin. Beckmann's process needed about 50 cubic metres of water per tonne of straw to wash away the dissolved lignin and any excess soda, and this washing also removed all the water-soluble substances from the straw. Without these water-soluble substances, the food value of the straw was considerably reduced, and so the process was never adopted.

In the latest version of the Beckmann process, the straw is first chopped into pieces about 3.75 cm long. A controlled amount of caustic soda solution, about 90 litres per tonne of straw, is then sprayed on as a fine mist and the straw is tumbled around by augers and paddles to ensure that every piece is evenly coated with soda.

The treated straw is then blown into a heap and left for three days, during which time it 'cooks' as the chemical reactions take place between the soda and the lignin. The straw heats up slowly to about 90°C within about 20 hours, and then slowly cools again. During this time the lignin is dissolved away, leaving the cellulose and the water-soluble substances available for cattle feed.

Cattle are usually fed considerable quantities of rolled or crushed barley, but with the high price of cereals this is increasingly regarded as wasteful, particularly when these cereals could be processed directly into human food at a lower cost than is involved in converting them into meat by feeding them to cattle. The chemically-processed straw has about two thirds of the food value of barley, and so it could replace the barley constituents in cattle feed, thus releasing the barley for human consumption.

Balers

Straw, the stalks of grain crops such as wheat, and hay, grass which is cut and stored for cattle feed, are usually packed into bales for transport and storage. This baling is done by *balers*, tractor-drawn machines which pick up the straw left by the combines or the hay left on the ground by mowers and compress it into bales bound with twine.

One of the biggest revolutions in materials handling on the farm in recent years has been the 'big bale', which weighs about half a tonne whereas the conventional bale weighs only about 27 to 30 kg. Conventional bales measure about 1 m x 45 cm x 35 cm, and after baling they are left in the field in stacks of eight, which in turn are loaded on to trailers and taken to the storage building. All this is wasteful of effort because the bales are handled several times before they reach their destination.

With half-tonne packages there are only about seven bales per hectare of field, compared with about 138 small bales. Consequently there is far less handling involved and the time taken to collect and transport the bales to the store is halved. The cost of the twine

BASF

Dr. A. Cooper/G.C.R.I.

Above: The greenhouse of the herbicide laboratory at the BASF research station at Limburgerhof, Germany. The research station develops and tests a wide range of pesticides and fertilizers.

Left and below: The *nutrient film technique* is a new method of rearing crops without soil. The plants are grown, either outdoors or in greenhouses, by planting them in plastic gullies through which a nutrient solution is circulated. The technique was developed by the Glasshouse Crops Research Institute in Surrey, England, and is now being used successfully in many parts of the world.

needed for tying the bales is also reduced.

Big bales come in two shapes, oblong and round. Oblong bales measure 1.5 x 1.5 x 2.4 m, and bale density is about 64 kg per cubic metre. The bales are made in the same way as conventional bales; the baler collects the crop and pushes it into a chamber the same shape as the bale. Once the correct size has been reached, the twine is tied round the bale and it is ejected into the field.

Round bales are about 1.2 m in diameter and 1.8 m wide, and are made by a machine that rolls the crop between belts until the density is about 144 kg per cubic metre. Their main advantage over oblong bales is that they can be stored in the open without serious deterioration. Because of their formation, the outer layers of round bales act like the thatch on a thatched roof, and rain water runs off them, being able to penetrate, and so damage, only the outer five centimetres of the straw.

Rain will penetrate both the oblong big bale and the conventional bale, and reduce them to waste material within a few weeks. The water-repellent outer layer of the round bale means that it does not need to be stored in a barn; instead, it can be stored in the field in long lines, thus reducing storage costs and eliminating the risk of losing a whole crop of hay or straw, plus a barn, because of fire.

Crop handling

After a crop has been harvested, more equipment is needed for handling and storing it before it goes to market. This equipment includes items such as trailers, fork lift trucks and conveyers, but a number of rather more sophisticated devices are coming into use on the modern farm.

One example of this type of equipment is the device used for separating soil and stones from harvested potatoes. Potatoes are often harvested when the ground is wet, and if the crop is grown on stony land, quantities of stone and soil may be collected with the potatoes. Wet soil can cause rotting, and stones can cut, scuff and bruise the potatoes. Soil and stones must therefore be removed from the crop to prevent damage to the potatoes.

Soil can be separated from potatoes by passing them over a sieve and letting the soil fall through, but separating stones is more difficult. It can be done by having several pickers standing at either side of a conveyer belt and removing the stones by hand as the crop passes by them, but this is expensive in terms of labour and time. One solution is to use X-rays to differentiate between the stones and potatoes. The crop passes along a conveyer and falls off the end through a series of X-ray beams.

The beams detect the difference in density between a stone and the potatoes, and when a stone has been detected, rubber-coated fingers flick out to remove it while allowing potatoes to fall through. The fingers are operated by compressed air, and the system is about 95 per cent accurate. There is no radiation danger from the X-ray units as they are totally enclosed.

The X-ray sorter has yet to gain widespread acceptance on farms, mainly because of its cost compared to other systems, but as labour costs increase and labour becomes more difficult to recruit for farm work, it is likely to become much more common.

NUTRIENT FILM TECHNIQUE

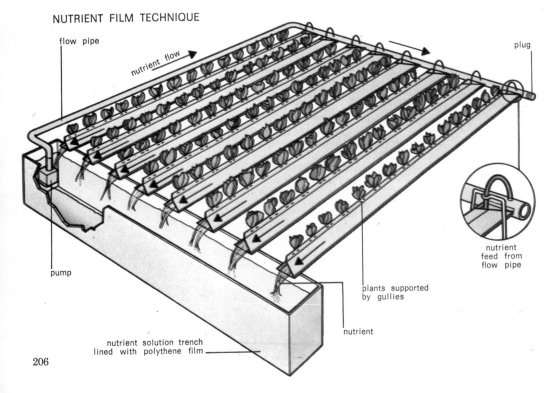

flow pipe

nutrient flow

plug

pump

nutrient feed from flow pipe

plants supported by gullies

nutrient

nutrient solution trench lined with polythene film

Domestic Appliances

The tremendous growth in the production and use of domestic appliances has been one of the characteristic features of industrialized societies in the twentieth century. Although their impact on society is, perhaps, more subtle than that of some other forms of modern technology—motor vehicles, aircraft, radio and tv for instance—they have had a significant effect on daily life, and what were once luxury goods are increasingly being regarded as essentials. To people accustomed to the convenience of, for example, refrigerators, vacuum cleaners and washing machines, the prospect of having to go without them is not a pleasant one.

The variety of domestic equipment now produced is enormous, ranging from the large appliances such as cookers and freezers to the small ones such as irons, toasters, electric kettles and the more exotic gadgets like egg boilers and shoe polishers.

Cookers

The earliest method of cooking food was to heat or roast it over an open fire, and the first ovens and stoves were heated by burning solid fuels. Solid fuel cookers are still available today, but the majority of cookers are now gas or electric. The commonest types of cooker have an oven, hob (gas burners or electric hotplates or radiant rings) and grill incorporated in a single, free-standing unit, but an increasing number of manufacturers are offering these as separate components which can be built-in to the kitchen furniture.

This arrangement, apart from providing greater flexibility in the positioning of the equipment, also makes it easier to use a gas hob in conjunction with an electric oven. This combination offers the controllability and economy of the gas hob with the even heating of the electric oven, particularly when it is fitted with a fan that circulates the warm air so that the whole of the oven is kept at the desired temperature.

When a fan is not used, there may be differences in temperature between the top, middle and bottom parts of the oven, the middle section being at the temperature set on the thermostat control while the top and bottom sections are hotter and cooler respectively.

'Self-cleaning' ovens work on either the *catalytic* or the *pyrolytic* principle. Catalytic ovens have their internal panels coated with a special enamel which encourages any splashes of fat or food that fall on it during cooking to vaporize away. Any splashes not vaporized away during the cooking can be removed simply by wiping with a damp cloth, or by leaving the oven on until they are vaporized.

The pyrolytic ovens clean themselves by burning away the dirt. This process is carried out at a very high temperature, much higher than the highest cooking temperature, and the dirt is reduced to a small amount of ash which can be brushed out later.

Refrigerators

The basic principle behind refrigeration is that a fluid absorbs heat when it changes from a liquid to a gas, and releases this heat when it changes back from a gas to a liquid. In a refrigerator a fluid, the *refrigerant*, is passed through an *evaporator* placed within the refrigerated compartment. As it enters the evaporator its pressure is reduced and it evaporates from a liquid to a gas, absorbing heat from the refrigerated compartment in the process.

The gas then passes to a *condenser* situated outside the refrigerated compartment, where it condenses back into a liquid and gives off its heat to the atmosphere. The liquid refrigerant from the condenser, having given up the heat it absorbed from the refrigerated compartment, then returns to the evaporator to continue the cycle.

In a typical domestic refrigerator the

Ronan

Above right: A late nineteenth century dishwasher. The dishes were placed in the machine together with hot, soapy water, and when the handle was turned the water was flung against the dishes by the paddles.

Right: In a modern dishwasher, very hot water containing detergent is sprayed on to the dishes by sets of rotating and fixed spray jets. The spray angles and pressures are designed so that all parts of the load are cleaned, and even microscopically small particles of food are removed. On the machine shown here, the temperature and pressure of the water can be varied to suit the type and number of dishes to be washed and their level of soiling.

Below: The first electric vacuum cleaners were large machines mounted on horse-drawn carts. They were parked outside the building in which the cleaning was to be done, and the suction hoses were led into the building through doors and windows. This one is in Paris in 1904.

Robert Bosch Ltd

Ronan

Below: The cleaning action of an 'upright' vacuum cleaner. The agitator loosens the dirt in the carpet and sweeps it back into the machine, where the suction created by a fan draws it into the dustbag.

Right: A modern upright cleaner which works on this principle.

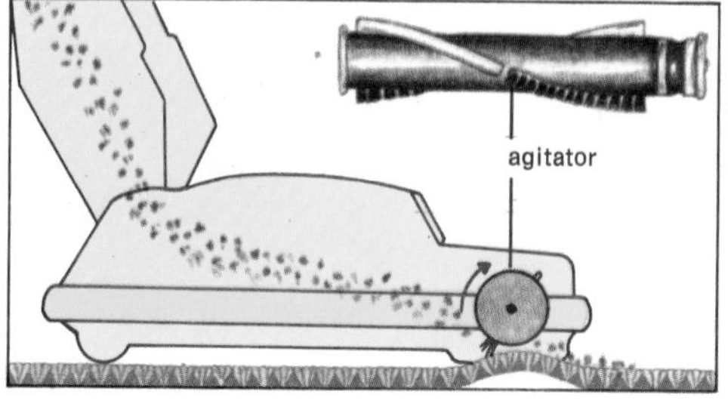

Hoover Ltd

refrigerant is pumped around the system by a motor-driven compressor, which draws the low-pressure gas from the evaporator and passes it at high pressure into the condenser. The refrigerant is usually one of the halogenated hydrocarbons known as *Freons*, such as Freon-12 (dichlorodifluoromethane, CCl_2F_2) and Freon-114 (dichlorotetrafluoroethane, $C_2Cl_2F_4$). Carbon dioxide (CO_2) and sulphur dioxide (SO_2) can also be used as refrigerants.

An alternative to this compression system is the *ammonia absorption system*. In this system there are no moving mechanical parts, the cycle being maintained by heat from an electric element or from a gas or oil burner. There are four main components in this system: an evaporator, which is within the refrigerated area, and a condenser, a *boiler* and an *absorber*, which are all outside it. A strong solution of ammonia (NH_3) in water is heated in the boiler so that it gives off ammonia vapour.

As the pressure of this ammonia vapour builds up it is driven into the condenser, where it condenses into a liquid. This liquid passes into the evaporator, where it evaporates and absorbs heat. From the evaporator, the ammonia vapour passes down into the absorber where it is absorbed by a trickle of weak ammonia solution produced in the boiler when the ammonia is driven out of the strong solution. The resulting solution produced in the absorber returns to the boiler to continue the cycle.

Hydrogen gas circulates through the absorber and the evaporator at a lower pressure than that at which the ammonia condenses in the condenser. This means that when the liquid ammonia enters the evaporator it has to evaporate to make up the difference between these two pressures. By using hydrogen in this manner the need for an expansion valve in the evaporator is eliminated, and as the total gas pressure remains effectively constant throughout the system there is no need for pressure reduction valves.

Freezers

Freezers operate on the compression system, but their cabinet temperatures are much lower than those of refrigerators, having a maximum temperature of —18°C (0°F) as opposed to the usual refrigerator main cabinet temperature of between 0 and 7°C (32 and 45°F). In addition, freezers must be capable of freezing fresh food or cooked food rapidly

Above: A combined refrigerator and freezer. The refrigerator section, which is the upper half of the machine, has a capacity of 225 litres (about 7.9 ft³), and the capacity of the freezer section, the lower half of the machine, is 160 litres (about 5.6 ft³). Each half has its own door.

Below: Built-in electric oven, grill and hob units. The oven unit has a large fan-assisted oven, with a smaller combined oven and grill beneath it. The hob unit, to the left of the oven, has four rings, and when not in use it can be retracted below the working surface and covered with a lid.

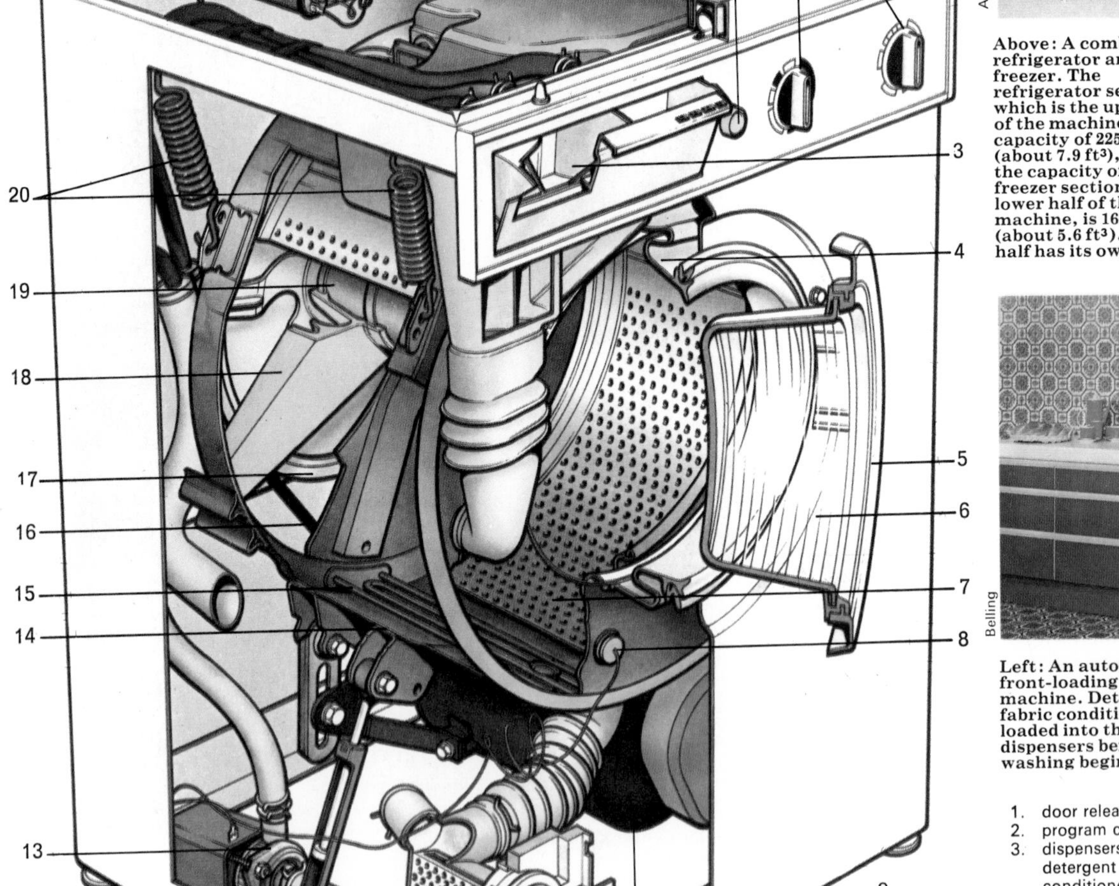

Left: An automatic front-loading washing machine. Detergent and fabric conditioner, loaded into the dispensers before washing begins, are automatically drawn into the drum when required. Ten different programs can be selected to suit various types and colours of fabrics.

1. door release
2. program controls
3. dispensers for detergent and fabric conditioner
4. door seal
5. door
6. door glass
7. revolving inner drum
8. thermostat sensor
9. motor
10. filter access panel
11. lint filter
12. shock absorber
13. drain pump
14. fixed outer drum
15. 3 kW heater
16. drive belt
17. drum pulley
18. drum support
19. drum bearings
20. outer drum suspension springs
21. control circuits

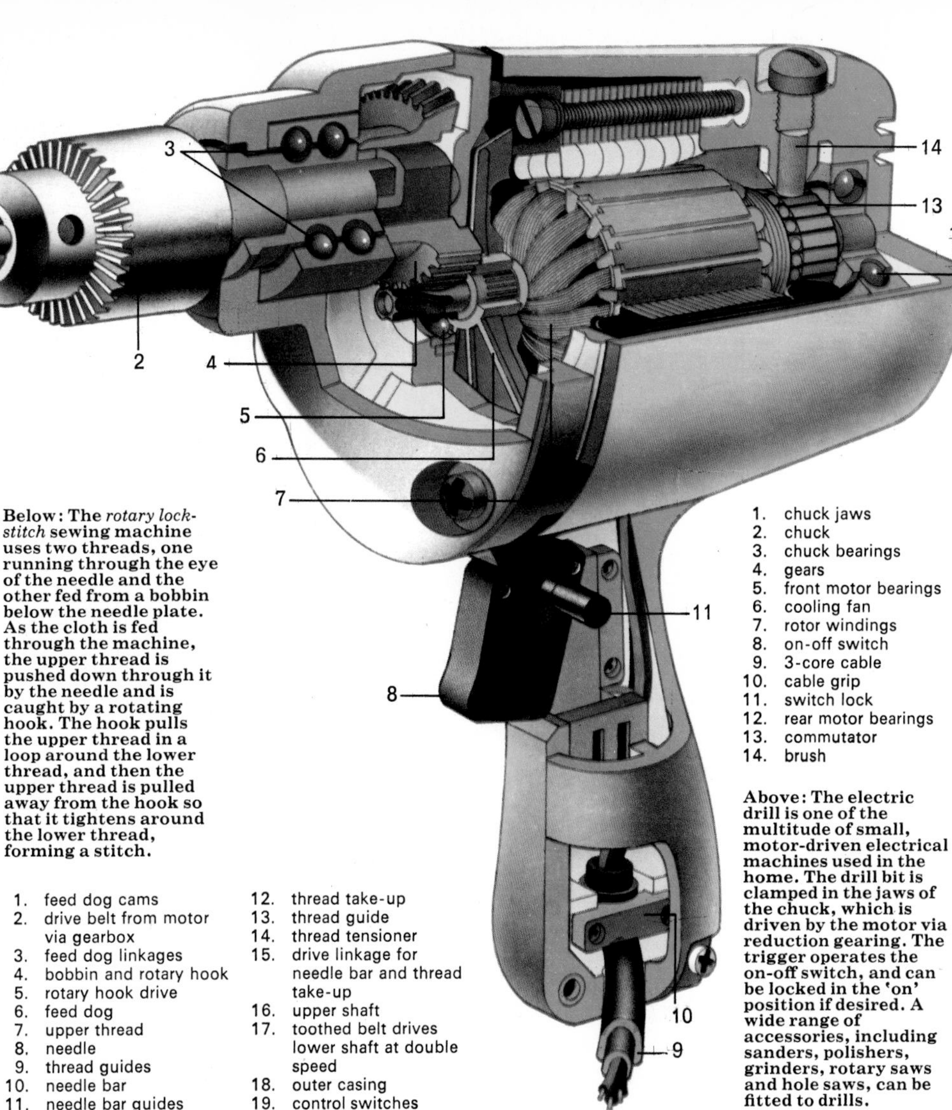

1. chuck jaws
2. chuck
3. chuck bearings
4. gears
5. front motor bearings
6. cooling fan
7. rotor windings
8. on-off switch
9. 3-core cable
10. cable grip
11. switch lock
12. rear motor bearings
13. commutator
14. brush

Above: The electric drill is one of the multitude of small, motor-driven electrical machines used in the home. The drill bit is clamped in the jaws of the chuck, which is driven by the motor via reduction gearing. The trigger operates the on-off switch, and can be locked in the 'on' position if desired. A wide range of accessories, including sanders, polishers, grinders, rotary saws and hole saws, can be fitted to drills.

Below: The *rotary lock-stitch* sewing machine uses two threads, one running through the eye of the needle and the other fed from a bobbin below the needle plate. As the cloth is fed through the machine, the upper thread is pushed down through it by the needle and is caught by a rotating hook. The hook pulls the upper thread in a loop around the lower thread, and then the upper thread is pulled away from the hook so that it tightens around the lower thread, forming a stitch.

1. feed dog cams
2. drive belt from motor via gearbox
3. feed dog linkages
4. bobbin and rotary hook
5. rotary hook drive
6. feed dog
7. upper thread
8. needle
9. thread guides
10. needle bar
11. needle bar guides
12. thread take-up
13. thread guide
14. thread tensioner
15. drive linkage for needle bar and thread take-up
16. upper shaft
17. toothed belt drives lower shaft at double speed
18. outer casing
19. control switches

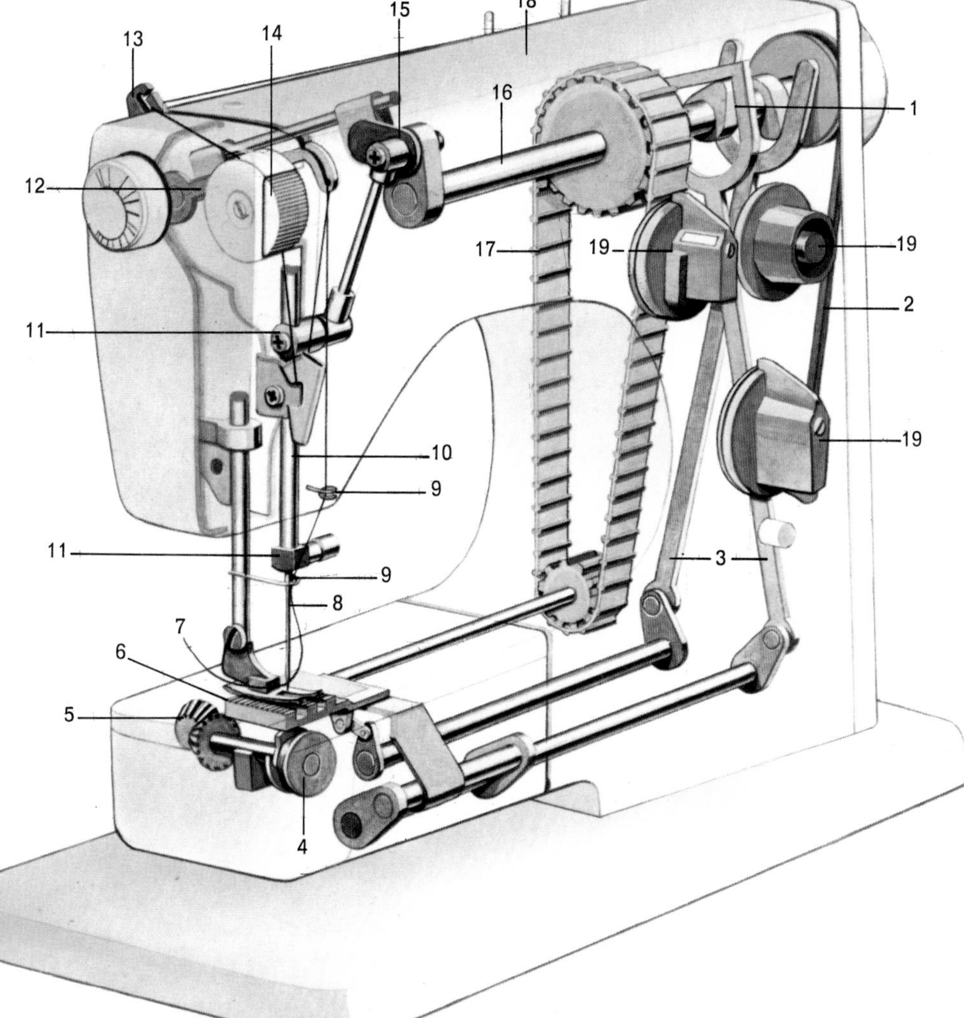

so that its quality and flavour are maintained. This can be done by setting the cabinet temperature to a much lower level than that used simply for storage, but many models have one or more separate fast-freeze compartments, operating at temperatures down to about —35°C (—31°F), in which food can be frozen rapidly.

Good cabinet insulation is essential for freezers, and this is usually provided by a layer of polyurethane a few centimetres thick, equivalent in insulating value to about 5 m (16 ft) of concrete. This level of insulation enables a freezer to maintain its low temperature for more than 24 hours in the event of a power failure.

Washing machines

Washing machines range broadly from the basic single-tub machines, controlled by simple timer and temperature controls, to the automatic machines controlled by programming units, which perform the entire wash/rinse/spin-dry sequence completely automatically. Most washing machines use one of three types of washing action: *agitator*, *pulsator* or *tumble* action. The agitator and the pulsator are both used in conjunction with vertical washing tubs, whereas tumble action requires a horizontal drum.

The agitator, which is mounted in the centre of the bottom of the tub and projects upwards towards the top, swirls the clothes back and forth in the water. The pulsator, mounted on the side or bottom of the tub, is a ridged disc which rotates at several hundred rpm to create a vigorous turbulence in the water. Machines using agitators or pulsators are *top-loaders*, that is, the clothes are loaded into the vertical tub through a lid on the top of the machine.

Tumble-action machines, on the other hand, are *front-loaders*. The clothes are loaded through a watertight door, usually circular with a glass window set into it, in the front of the machine. The drum of a front-loader is made of perforated enamelled or stainless steel, and it rotates within an outer, unperforated steel container. During washing, the drum rotates at about 50-55 rpm, tumbling clothes around in the water. On many models the rotation of the drum is reversed at intervals to give a more thorough washing action and prevent tangling of the clothes.

Automatic machines wash the clothes, then discharge the dirty water and rinse the clothes with clean water one or more times. When the rinsing is completed and the last of the rinsing water has been discharged by the drain pump, the machine spin-dries the clothes. The tub or drum rotates at high speed, usually 800-1,000 rpm, so that centrifugal force throws the clothes against the walls of the drum and draws most of the water out of them.

After spin-drying, the clothes can be air-dried, or dried in a *tumble-dryer*, a machine similar in appearance to a front-loader, in which the clothes are tumbled around in a perforated steel drum through which hot air is blown.

Spin-dryers, for drying clothes not washed in an automatic machine, are available as separate units. *Twin-tub* washing machines, having a vertical wash tub and a spin dryer mounted side by side, are another popular type of washing machine.

Electricity Supply

The first public electricity supply systems came into operation in the late nineteenth century. They were owned and operated by private companies or by local authorities such as city councils. There was little co-ordination between these individual undertakings; inter-connection between these many different systems was often economically impractical because they operated not only at different voltages but also at different alternating current (ac) frequencies, and in fact many were direct current (dc) systems.

As the use of electricity grew, it became obvious that voltages and frequencies should be standardized on a national level. This would not only permit the easy transmission of power from one part of a country to another, but it would also simplify the design and construction of electrical equipment. With a wide range of supply voltages in use, any electrical apparatus had to incorporate circuitry which enabled it to be adjusted to accept as many different supply voltages as possible.

In many countries, such as Britain and France, the establishment of national supply networks was followed by state ownership of the supply companies. In others, for example the USA and Switzerland, the national network interconnects a mixture of private and public systems.

The largest power system under centralized control anywhere in the world is in England and Wales. Operated by the Central Electricity Generating Board, this system supplies power to local Electricity Boards who in turn supply nearly 19 million consumers.

At present, the system comprises 168 power stations with a total of 785 generators, which are able to meet a simultaneous demand of 58,523 MW (millions of watts). These are all interconnected by means of nearly 18,000 kilometres (over 11,000 miles) of high voltage transmission lines—the Grid system.

Power is transmitted over the Grid at three different voltages. More than 4,350 km of transmission lines operate at 400 kV, over 2,300 km at 275 kV and nearly 11,000 km at 132 kV. The 400/275 kV network, often referred to as the Supergrid, will remain adequate for system loads up to at least 110,000 MW, that is, roughly to the end of the century.

Using high voltages for power transmission has two advantages: firstly it reduces the power loss along the cables, and secondly it increases the amount of power that a given size of conductor can carry. For example, a 400 kV line has three times the power-carrying capacity of a 275 kV line and eighteen times the capacity of a 132 kV line.

Circuit breakers

Three-phase electricity is usually produced in the stator windings of large modern generators at up to about 25 kV, and this is directly connected by heavy cables to a generator transformer in the adjoining main Grid substation. This steps up the voltage to 132 kV, 275 kV or 400 kV. From here conductors carry it to

power station
22 kv
transformer
275 kv or 400 kv
transformer
grid system
transfo

Above: A diagram showing how electricity is brought from the power station to the consumer. The windings of the power station alternators are arranged so that they produce three separate alternating voltages, which are out of step with each other by 120° of rotation of the alternator rotor. One end of each of these phase windings is connected to a common point, the neutral point, which is connected to earth. The voltage between any two of the phases is about 1.73 times the voltage between any one of them and earth. Large consumers are provided with a three phase supply, but small ones, such as houses, are supplied with one phase and a neutral line. This carries the return current to the substation where the transformer secondary windings have an earthed neutral point. In this diagram, these local low-voltage systems provide 415 V phase to phase, and 240 V phase to neutral or earth.

ASEA

Right: An 18/400 kV transformer at a power station in Venezuela.

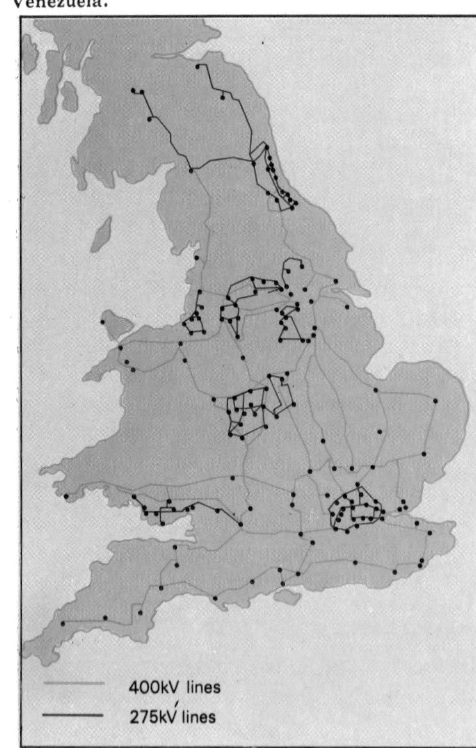

Above: The 400-275 kV main transmission network operated by the CEGB in England and Wales. The CEGB generates power and transmits it over 400 kV, 275 kV and some 132 kV circuits to the 12 Area Electricity Boards. It is then distributed to the consumers at voltages down to 415/240 V.

John Topham

Above right: The cable ship *Dame Caroline Haslett* laying the cable which links the CEGB network with that of Electricité de France.

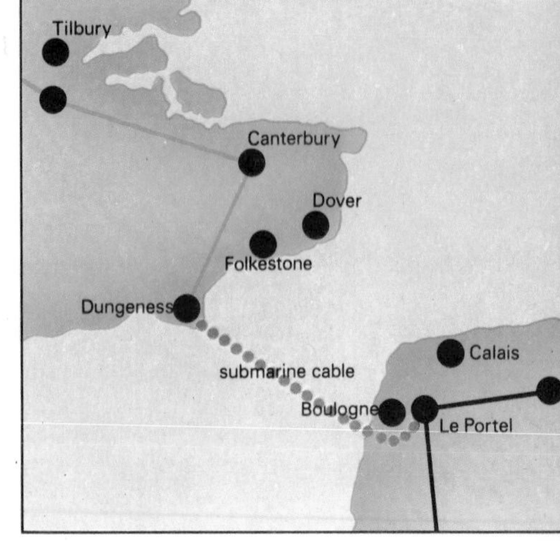

Right: The approximate route of the ±100 kVdc submarine cable which can transfer up to 160 MW of power either way between England and France.

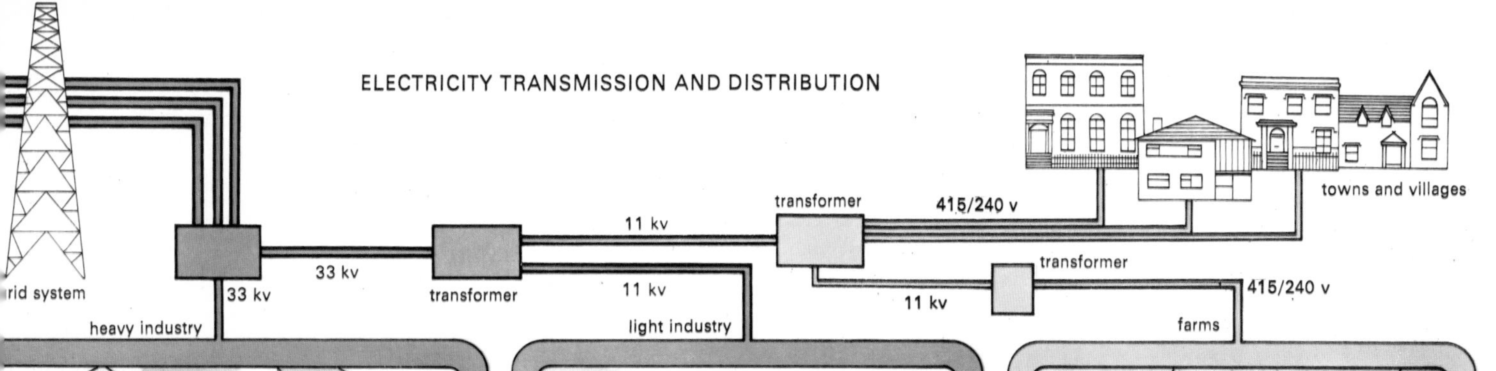

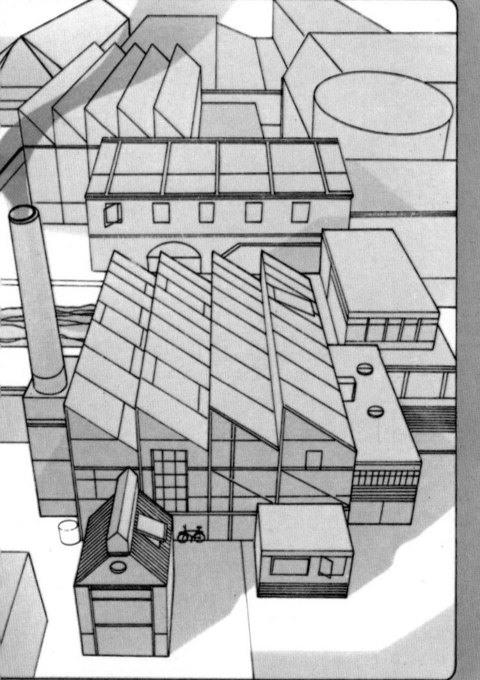

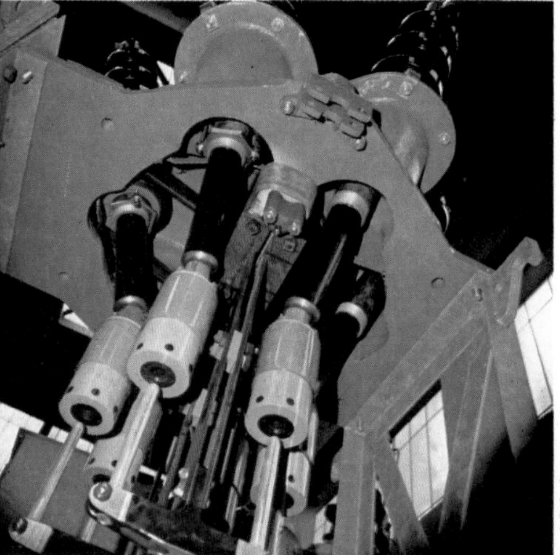

Paul Brierley

CEGB

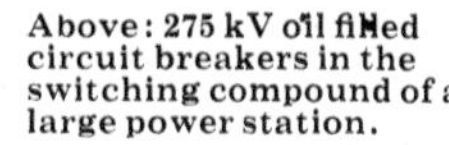

CEGB

Above: 275 kV oil filled circuit breakers in the switching compound of a large power station.

Above left: Many circuit breakers can be isolated from the supply by lowering them so that they 'unplug' from the circuit. This picture shows the spiked connectors on the top of a circuit breaker, and the sockets they plug into. The breaker can only be isolated after it has switched off the circuit it controls.

Left: The control room of the CEGB's National Control Centre in London. This control centre supervises the seven Area Control Centres of England and Wales, and plans the transfer of power from one area to another.

a series of three switches, comprising an *isolator*, a *circuit-breaker* and another isolator, which are used to connect or disconnect the transformer with the transmission lines. There are three groups of such switches for each generator transformer—one for each of the three phases of the power supply.

The circuit-breaker is a heavy-duty switch capable of operating in a fraction of a second, and is used to switch off the current flowing to the transmission lines. Once the current has been interrupted the isolators can be opened. These isolate the circuit-breaker from all outside electrical sources, so that there is no chance of any high voltages being applied to its terminals. Maintenance or repair work can then be carried out in safety.

From the circuit-breaker the current is taken to the *busbars*—conductors which run the length of the switching compound —and then to another circuit-breaker with its associated isolators before being fed to the Grid. Each generator in a power station has its own transformer, circuit-breaker and isolators but the electricity generated is fed onto a common set of busbars.

Circuit-breakers work like combined switches and fuses, but they have certain special features and are very different from domestic switches and fuses. When electrical current is switched off by separating two contacts, an arc is created between them. At the voltage used in the home, this arc is very small, and only lasts for a fraction of a second. At the very high voltages used for transmission, however, the size and power of the arc is considerable and it must be quickly quenched to prevent damage.

One type of circuit-breaker has its contacts immersed in insulating oil so that when the switch is opened, either by powerful electromagnetic coils or mechanically by springs, the arc is quickly extinguished by the oil. Another type works by compressed air which operates the switch and at the same time 'blows out' the arc. These *air-blast* circuit-breakers are almost universally employed on 275 and 400 kV circuits.

Control centres

Power stations generate electricity most economically when they operate 24 hours a day, but as the demand for electricity is never constant, changes in consumption have to be balanced by starting or shutting down some of the generators in the power stations. The cost of generation is the main factor that guides the control engineers in deciding which power stations to operate. Large modern stations have the lowest running costs, while the older, smaller ones away from fuel sources are the most expensive to operate.

The operation of power stations must therefore be co-ordinated on both a regional and a national basis. In England and Wales there are seven areas, each with its own control centre, which are co-ordinated by the National Control Centre in London. These control centres, in conjunction with the engineers in the power stations, are also responsible for ensuring that the supply frequency, which is 50 Hz in Britain, is maintained at all times.

Distribution

The main 400/275 kV transmission system of the CEGB is connected to a total of 190 *grid sub-stations*, which together accommodate 519 transformers and associated switchgear. These, in turn, are connected via 132 kV lines to more than 750 *bulk supply points*, large substations again incorporating transformers and switchgear. From these substations, bulk supplies of electricity at 33 kV are taken for primary distribution in the towns and to industrial areas, groups of villages and similar concentrations of consumers. The lines are fed into numerous intermediate substations where transformers reduce the voltage to 11 kV.

The transformers in these substations are usually equipped with automatic or remotely operated *tap changing* gear to ensure that consumers always have the correct supply voltage, within the statutory limits of plus or minus 6%. As the load on the system increases, the voltage tends to drop. The tap changers compensate for this by changing the ratio between the primary and secondary transformer windings to keep the supplied voltages within the legal limits.

Secondary distribution lines radiating from these substations carry the power into the areas to be supplied, and terminate at local distribution substations. Here the voltage is reduced to its final level of 415 V three phase (the voltage between any two phase lines) and 240 V single phase (the voltage between a single phase and earth) for use in small factories, shops, offices, schools and homes.

Some consumers use electricity in such large quantities that they are supplied at a higher voltage than that used in the home. Heavy industries may have their own connections direct to the grid, taking power at 33kV or even higher,

Picturepoint

Above: The copper conductors which route the power around this 400/275 kV substation are hollow tubes. There is no need for them to be solid, because at these voltages electromagnetic effects cause the current to flow near the surface of a round conductor, and very little flows through the centre.

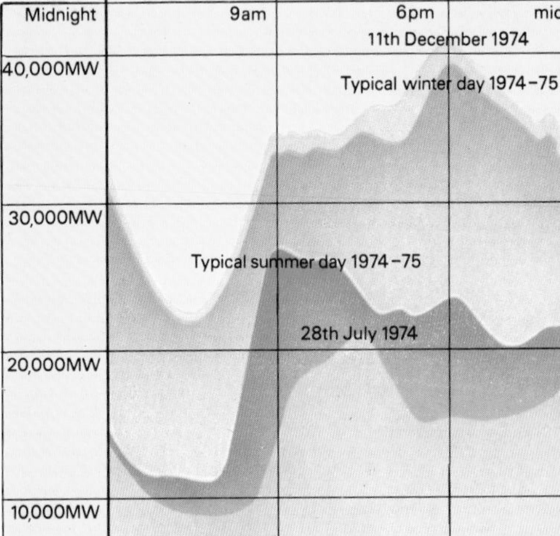

Right: The demand for electricity varies throughout the day, and the year. This graph shows the average demands during winter and summer in England and Wales, plus the days of maximum and minimum demand during 1974. Peak daily demand in summer is at about 9 am, and in winter at about 6 pm.

CEGB

Above: To avoid any interruption of electricity supplies a great deal of repair work and routine maintenance is carried out without switching off the power. This picture shows men working on a live high voltage line, using insulated glass fibre equipment to handle the conductors.

CEGB

Right: Live line repairs can be carried out on lines operating at as much as 400 kV. The linesman wears an electrically conducting protective suit, which dissipates any electric charges, such as static electricity, which may occur. The sling carrying him is insulated from the tower.

SWEB

Above: This local substation consists of a transformer, switchgear and fuses, enclosed in a module of aluminium slats coated with coloured pvc. This type of substation is an alternative to the ordinary 'outdoor' substation, which has the equipment mounted on a concrete plinth and surrounded by a fence.

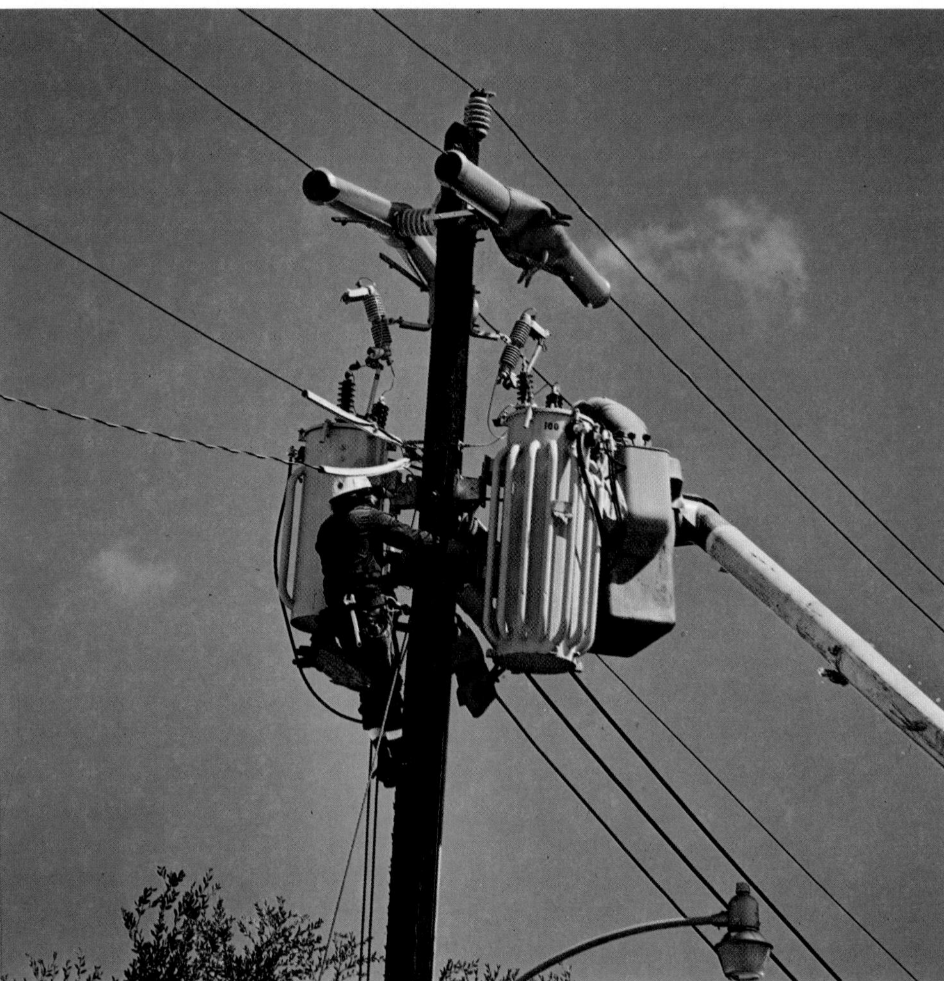

Picturepoint

Right: Pole-mounted transformers are widely used on overhead distribution systems. They are connected to the high voltage lines, and the low voltage supply to the consumers is taken from them either by overhead lines or underground cables. Fuses and isolators may also be mounted on poles.

Paul Brierley

Above: This old type of underground power cable has conductors made of copper wire, with rubber insulation. Rubber has been replaced by special oil-impregnated paper on modern cables. These are often enclosed in a lead sheath, protected by steel wire or tape and a canvas outer layer impregnated with pitch.

Below: Copper wire conductors are not always used on modern cables. This one has solid aluminium conductors, which are lighter and cheaper than copper although they have to be larger in cross-section to provide the same current-carrying capacity. This one uses a plastic insulating material.

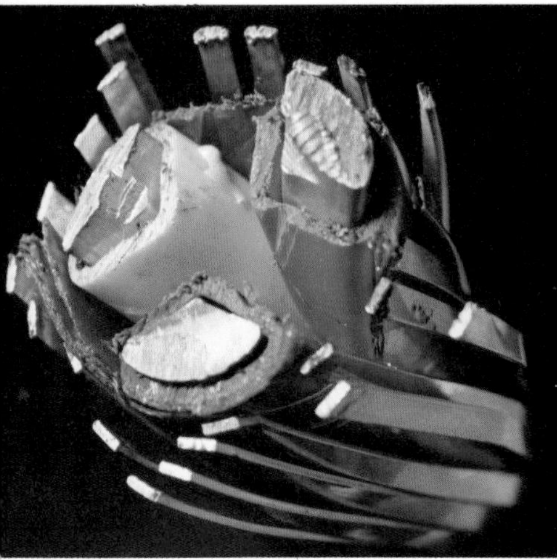

Paul Brierley

while hospitals, factories and large office buildings are often supplied directly from intermediate substations at 11 kV.

Railways have special substations alongside the tracks, drawing electricity directly from the Grid; the latest rail electrification schemes work at 25 kV.

Where existing power stations are already close to consumers, as in London, the power is often fed into the local primary distribution network at 66 kV or 33 kV, connections to the Grid system also being made in case of breakdown

The distribution of electricity is arranged so that, as far as is practicable, supplies are not interrupted if there is a fault in one section of the system. In a typical case this is done by running separate 33 kV lines from the Grid supply point to the intermediate substation feeding the town and the substation serving heavy industry. A further 33 kV line connects these two points together to form a ring so that if the direct connection to either substation breaks down, supplies can still be maintained through this connecting link. This arrangement for ensuring the security of supplies is in widespread use throughout all transmission and distribution networks.

There is no fixed pattern for local distribution, the arrangement of substations and transmission lines being developed as a result of the particular requirements of the area. Sometimes an intermediate substation may be built alongside a bulk supply point, and occasionally, even the bulk supply point may be in the town centre.

The above survey necessarily presents a rather simplified view of the power distribution system. As can be imagined an enormous amount of equipment and resources are employed to ensure that a reliable supply of electricity is available to all consumers. At present, the final distribution network operated by the Electricity Boards in England and Wales comprises no less than 390,000 substations and well over half a million kilometres of mains. These mains are operated at voltages ranging from 132 kV down to the 415/240 V of the local low-voltage distribution networks.

The whole network is fully protected by automatic circuit breakers, lightning arresters, fuses and other devices to prevent overloads damaging the system. In the event of a fault, the line or equipment concerned can usually be isolated and power routed over alternative lines, so that interruptions to consumers are kept to the minimum.

This vast network of overhead and underground cables, substations, transformers and switchgear represents a considerable financial investment and it must all be kept in working order to ensure continuity of supply. At the same time, modifications are continuously being made to reinforce supplies to particular areas, such as new housing estates, office buildings, and expanding or new factories. All this must be done with the minimum of interruption to supplies.

In fact, a great deal of work is carried out without switching off the power. Techniques of live-line working using special insulated tools have been developed in recent years which enable modifications, repairs and connections to be made to overhead lines while they are on load.

Water Supply

As soon as men began to settle into large communities they were faced with the problems of ensuring an adequate fresh water supply. The small settlements of the Neolithic age had successfully relied on natural springs and simple wells, but such sources were simply not capable of satisfying the towns and cities which began to develop about 4000 BC. At first, as in the cities of Mesopotamia, open conduits were used to channel water from distant springs and lakes. The ruins of Mohenjo-Daro in the Indus Valley, which date from about 2500 BC, boast the earliest known enclosed system.

The ancient Greeks made considerable use of conduits, pipes and tunnels to supply water to their cities, and their techniques were refined and developed by the Romans. Imperial Rome enjoyed a water system unrivalled at the time and unsurpassed for many centuries after. It has been estimated that enough was supplied by the Roman systems to give every urban inhabitant some 225 litres (50 gallons) per day. This is as much as many modern municipalities provide.

Water quality

Groundwater sources are usually less contaminated than surface waters because they have had less contact with possible impurities. Surface water may have flowed through hundreds of kilometres of stream and river before it reaches the lake or reservoir from which a public supply is taken. In the course of its journey it will have picked up a quantity of minerals, some of which may be poisonous industrial waste, and an assortment of plant and animal matter, including sewage, in various states of decomposition. In addition, lakes may become infested with algae, which give the water an unpleasant taste and smell.

A water treatment works aims to supply water that is safe and pleasant to drink. A number of simple tests are performed on the treated water to ensure that this is the case. Perhaps the most important of these is the *coliform bacteria count*. Coliforms, such as *Escherichia coli*, which is also widely cultivated for use in research, live naturally in human intestines and are excreted in large quantities into sewage. In themselves they are harmless, but the presence of such bacteria in a water sample indicates that other, more dangerous bacteria and viruses may also be present.

The *biochemical oxygen demand* (BOD) test is a useful measure of the amount of decomposing organic material present. Decomposition uses up oxygen, and the BOD test measures the amount of oxygen used up in this way by a sample of water which is maintained at 20°C (68°F) for five days.

The total amount of solid matter suspended in a water sample, which also includes inorganic matter such as clay, can be estimated by measuring the *turbidity* (cloudiness) of a sample. This can be done quite simply by shining light through the water and measuring the proportion of light scattered by the suspended particles.

The presence of an appreciable quantity of nitrogen in water is a good indica-

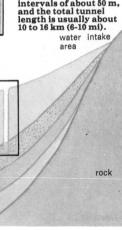

Bruce Coleman

Above: A Roman aqueduct at Segovia in Spain, built during the reign of the Emperor Trajan (53-117 AD) and still in use today. It carries water from the Rio Frio for about 823 m (2,700 ft) to the old town, its maximum height being about 28.5 m (93.5 ft).

British Steel

Above right: Laying a pipeline to carry water from a reservoir to a treatment works. The pipes are made of iron lined with concrete.

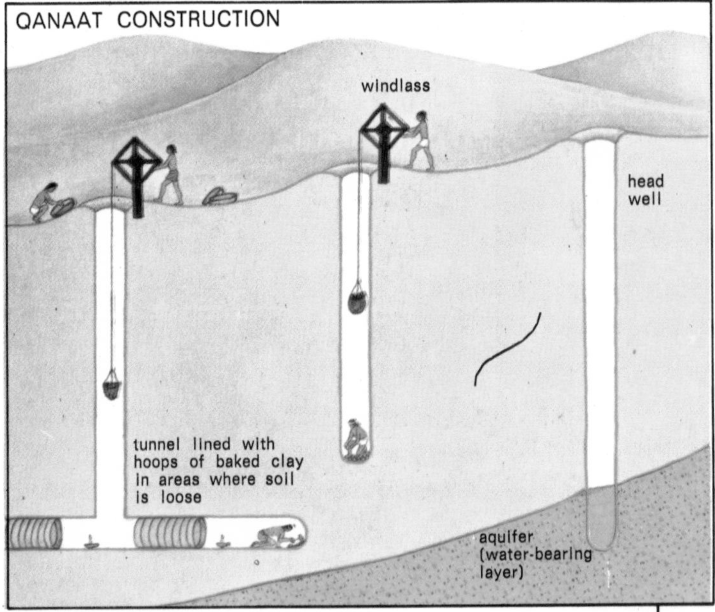

Israel Information

Left: The first step in building a qanaat is the digging of a head well down into the water-bearing strata in the hills, and then the tunnel is dug from the downhill end up to the head well. Ventilation shafts are dug at intervals of about 50 m, and the total tunnel length is usually about 10 to 16 km (6-10 mi).

Qanaats, widely used in Iran and other Middle Eastern countries, are inclined irrigation tunnels which carry mountain groundwater to arid plains.

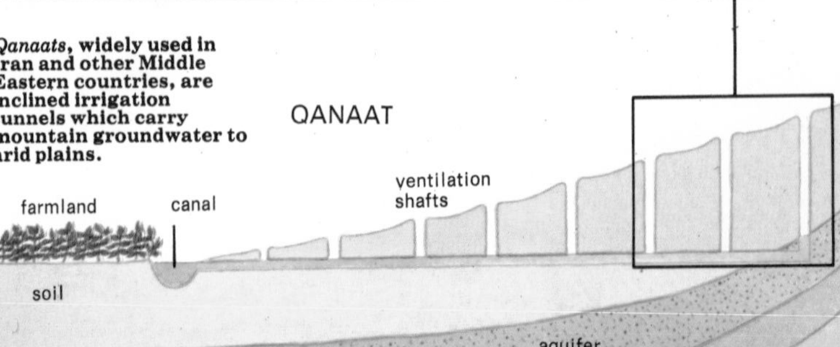

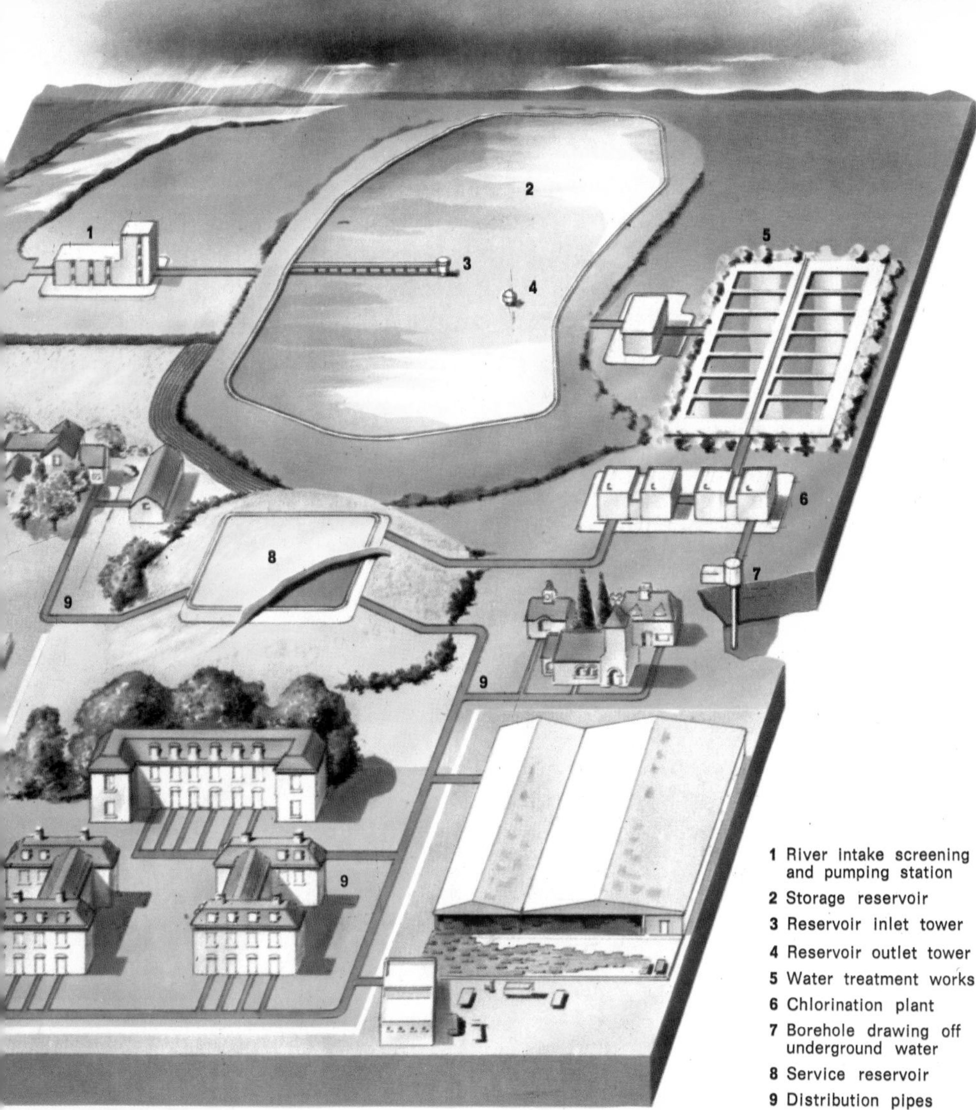

1 River intake screening and pumping station
2 Storage reservoir
3 Reservoir inlet tower
4 Reservoir outlet tower
5 Water treatment works
6 Chlorination plant
7 Borehole drawing off underground water
8 Service reservoir
9 Distribution pipes

Above: A typical water supply system. Here, water taken from a river is screened to remove debris and pumped into a storage reservoir. It is then filtered, purified and chlorinated before distribution to the consumers. Water pumped up through boreholes drilled into underground water sources needs only chlorination before it is distributed.

Left: Part of Israel's National Water Carrier, which carries water to the Negev desert.

Weir Pumps Ltd

Above: Three *pumpsets*, each consisting of a pump and an electric drive motor, at the Ross Priory pumping station in Scotland. These pumpsets, which have a total capacity of 227 million litres (50 million gallons) of water per day, pump water from Loch Lomond for distribution to reservoirs and treatment works supplying central Scotland.

Picturepoint

Left: A reservoir in North Wales. Reservoirs play an important part in the purification of water. While the water is standing in the reservoir, the larger solid impurities settle to the bottom, the large surface area allows the oxygen in the air to attack other impurities, and the various physical, chemical and biological conditions set up within the water during storage have a destructive effect on any harmful bacteria.

tion of possible contamination. Combined with hydrogen (forming ammonia, NH_3), it indicates pollution by organic matter. In the form of nitrites and nitrates, it points to inorganic pollutants such as fertilizers and chemical wastes.

Water treatment

Before it can be distributed to consumers, water must undergo a series of physical and chemical treatments to remove the impurities. The number and nature of the cleaning processes varies from one works to another, because some sources of raw water are much cleaner than others. The following is an exhaustive series of treatments, not all of which will be necessary in every case.

The first treatment is quite simple—the water is stored in large reservoirs or settling basins for several weeks. This allows the larger particles to sink to the bottom of the basin. During this period chemical reactions, which take place naturally and slowly in the water, tend to neutralize any acidity or alkalinity. The most important advantage of storage, however, is that the number of toxic bacteria in the water is strikingly reduced. Shortage of suitable food, a low temperature in the depths of the storage basin, the effects of sunlight, and the competition from harmless micro-organisms all contribute to the decline in the bacterial population.

The next stage in the treatment is to pass the water through a fairly coarse screen which removes leaves and other debris. At this stage chlorine is usually added to kill off the remaining bacteria. Chlorine is not the only possible disinfectant. Some European countries use ozone (O_3), which is rather more expensive, and in some small plants the water may be sterilized by irradiating it with ultra-violet light. A second screening usually follows, which removes algae and small particles. This is done by a *microstrainer*, a rotating filter drum covered with a very fine stainless steel mesh. The holes in the mesh are less than one micron (one millionth of a metre) in diameter, and the water passes through them from the inside of the drum outwards.

Even after passing through the extremely fine mesh of the microstrainer, water still contains many small suspended particles. Some of these are insoluble minerals, others are dead bacteria, and all make the water look cloudy and sometimes discoloured. They can be trapped by a process known as *coagulation and flocculation*.

In cloudy water the suspended particles are in continuous rapid motion and are never in close contact with each other for long enough to stick together. If a chemical coagulant such as aluminium sulphate ($Al_2(SO_4)_3 . 14H_2O$) or ferric sulphate ($Fe_2(SO_4)_3 . H_2O$) is added, the particles can be trapped by it so that they slowly aggregate together and eventually form a single, amorphous mass, leaving the water clear. This coagulated mass has a woolly appearance and settles in a sort of blanket about halfway down the tank; it is called a *flocculent precipitate* or *floc* for short. A small residue of the coagulant remains dissolved in the water and may make it harder and more corrosive.

By this stage the water is considerably purer than it was at its source, but it

Weir Westgarth

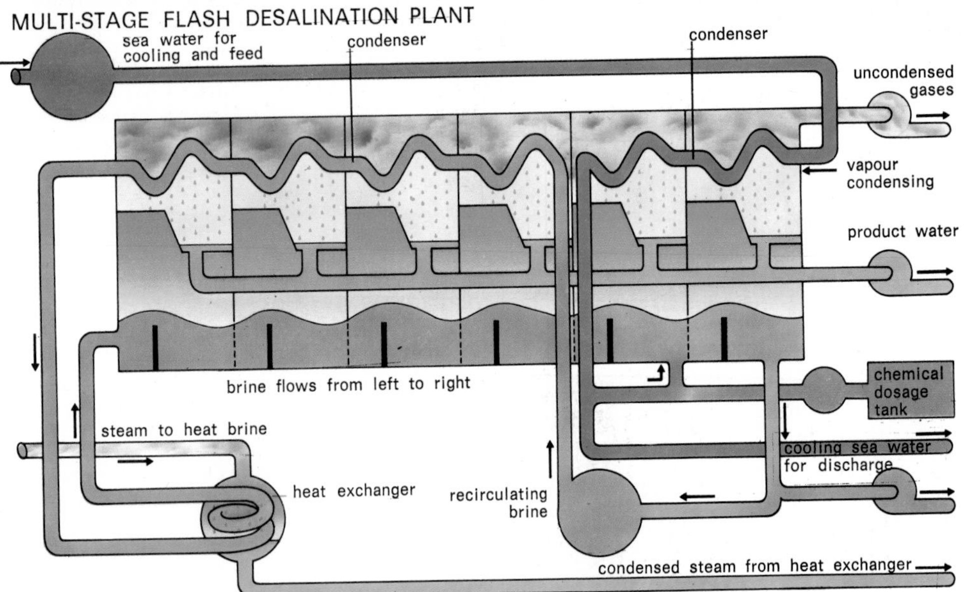

UKAEA

Top: A *multi-stage flash desalination* plant in Abu Dhabi, capable of producing over 9 million litres (2 million gallons) of fresh water per day.

Above: The multi-stage flash desalination plant distils fresh water from salt water by heating it and then reducing the air pressure around it. Sea water is heated by steam, and then passed through a series of chambers in which its pressure is progressively reduced. This causes fresh water to 'flash' (evaporate because of the low pressure) out of it and condense onto the condenser tubes.

Left: The *reverse osmosis* process is a potentially important desalination method. In this process, salt water is forced against a *semi-permeable membrane*, one which allows the solvent of a solution to pass through it but not the dissolved substances, in this case pure water and salt respectively. The membranes are made from suitable polymer materials such as cellulose acetate.

must still undergo further cleaning in filter beds. Filtering is one of the most important processes of all. There are two main methods of filtration. *Slow sand filtration* may be used for water which comes from a relatively pure source and has not undergone any previous treatment. The water flows into beds of fine sand, and seeps through the sand and an underlying bed of gravel into an underground drainage system.

Rapid sand filters are filled with coarser sand, often with a layer of crushed anthracite below and sometimes with a layer of fine sand above. Rapid sand filters are the most commonly used because they allow faster rates of flow, but they are generally suitable only for water that has been previously cleaned to some extent by coagulation and flocculation. Rapid filters are cleaned daily by *backwashing*, passing water through them in the opposite direction to the normal flow. Slow filters are cleaned about once every two months by removing the top layer of sand and replacing it with clean sand.

After filtration, water is usually *aerated* to increase the amount of dissolved oxygen it contains. This improves the colour and freshness of taste as well as reducing acidity by eliminating dissolved carbon dioxide. There are several different types of aerator. One, the *spray aerator*, forces the water through fine nozzles into the air. Another, the *cascade aerator*, has a series of steps over which the water falls.

No amount of filtration, sedimentation or coagulation, however, will rid water of substances that are completely dissolved in it, and a large group of such substances—the salts of calcium and to a lesser extent magnesium—are responsible for the 'hardness' of water. Hard water makes washing with soap more difficult, hinders the extraction of meat and vegetable juices in cooking, and deposits scale in kettles, boilers and pipes, and chemical treatment is often necessary to reduce hardness to an acceptable level. In areas where the water is exceptionally hard, a softening process may be carried out at the treatment works if costs permit, but it is usually left to individual consumers to install their own softening units if they require soft water. There are two kinds of hardness, *permanent* and *temporary*.

Temporary hardness is due to calcium bicarbonate ($Ca(HCO_3)_2$) and magnesium bicarbonate ($Mg(HCO_3)_2$), and causes scale when the water is heated because the bicarbonates break down into insoluble carbonates which settle out of the water and stick to the surface of the container. This kind of hardness can be removed by treating the water with lime (calcium hydroxide, $Ca(OH)_2$), which reduces the bicarbonates to carbonates, so that they precipitate out without the need for heating.

Permanent hardness cannot be removed by boiling. It is caused by sulphates and chlorides of calcium and can be reduced by treatment with sodium bicarbonate ($NaHCO_3$). This leads to an *exchange reaction*, in which the carbonate group of atoms is transferred from the sodium to the calcium atoms to make an insoluble compound which settles out of the water. The sodium atoms receive in exchange the chloride and sulphate groups, making salts which do not contribute to hardness.

Firefighting

A fire is basically a chemical reaction, or a combination of reactions, during which heat and light are emitted. Three factors are necessary for these reactions to occur—heat, a fuel (any combustible material), and an oxidizing agent. The oxidizing agent is usually oxygen, supplied by the air around the fire, but certain other elements can act in a similar way. For example, hydrogen will burn explosively with oxygen to form water (H_2O), but it can also be burnt with chlorine to form hydrochloric acid (HCl). The oxidizing agent may, in some cases, be contained within the fuel itself; nitrates and chlorates, both rich in oxygen, are good examples of this type of material.

Heat, fuel and oxygen together form what is known as the *triangle of combustion*. The removal of one or more of these factors from a fire will result in the collapse of the triangle, and combustion will cease. Firefighting is based on the simple principle of breaking the triangle.

Fire brigades

The earliest known organized fire fighting force was set up by the Romans. This was the *Familia Publica*, slaves who were stationed around the walls and at the gates of Roman cities to watch for, and deal with, any fires that might break out. It was not an efficient organization, and it was eventually disbanded by the Emperor Augustus who replaced it with a new force, the Corps of Vigiles, which performed the combined duties of police and fire brigade and was in existence for about 500 years.

In Rome, which was divided into 14 administrative regions, there were seven *cohorts* of Vigiles. Each cohort consisted of 1,000 men, and was divided into ten *centuries* each commanded by a *centurion*. The ranks and titles of the Vigiles included *aquarius*, whose duties included organizing the supply of water to the pumps, *siphonarius*, who was in charge of the pumps, and *uncinarius*, who carried a pole with a hook on it which he used for pulling down or moving burning thatch or furnishings.

The equipment used by the Vigiles included thick blankets to protect them from radiated heat, plunger-operated pumps, ladders, buckets, brooms, sponges for mopping up, and pickaxes. Similar equipment can be found on modern fire appliances, which shows that many of the basic principles of firefighting and salvage have changed little since those early days.

Following the collapse of the Roman Empire, organized firefighting forces ceased to exist, and the knowledge and experience of the Vigiles was lost. It was not until the late Middle Ages, when more stable and effective civil administrations became established, that properly-organized firefighting procedures were set up again. Parishes, villages and small communities started to provide buckets, hooks and ladders, which were usually kept in the local church.

As towns became larger it soon became apparent that these provisions were inadequate. Some towns still provided equipment, but communications were

Ronan

Above: Early oxygen breathing apparatus designed by Commandant Giersberg in France in about 1904. Breathing apparatus is an important item of firefighting equipment, enabling firemen to work safely in dense smoke and also protecting them from any toxic fumes given off by burning materials.

MERRYWEATHER'S

"KIT-BAG" PORTABLE FIRE-ESCAPE

(J. C. Merryweather's Patent No. 2765.)

As Supplied to H.H. the KHEDIVE of EGYPT.

The Best Traveller's Fire-Escape.

No visitor to South of France or other Continental Hotels should be without one.

FIG. Nº 1396

A. Kit-Bag Escape, for use when travelling. B. Kit-Bag Escape, in ca e, for fixing in Mansions, Hotels, &c.

ADVANTAGES.—(1) Absolutely safe for any weight up to 20 stone. (2) Light and portable. (3) Has no pulleys to stick or jam the rope. (4) Brake is entirely automatic, thus insensible or invalid persons can be easily lowered. (5) Can be used from any window, and requires no hooks or fastenings to be fixed before use. (6) It is carried in an indispensable article for travellers, and is therefore not likely to be out of reach when required.

Prices on application. Escape can be seen in action at 63, Long Acre, W.C.

MERRYWEATHER'S,

63, LONG ACRE, W.C., and GREENWICH, S.E., LONDON.

Illustrated London News

Above: An advertisement of 1895 for a portable fire escape, which consisted of a large bag and a rope by which means people could lower themselves from burning buildings. Also advertised is a fixed version, mounted in a glass case, which could be installed in premises such as hotels or houses.

SUN

ROYAL

ALLIANCE

Merseyside Fire Brigade

Right: Three examples of the 'fire marks', which insurance companies fixed to the walls of buildings insured by them, in the days when they operated their own fire brigades. When a fire broke out the insurance company brigades went to the scene, but if the premises were not insured by them they left the fire to burn. They eventually began to co-operate with each other, and early in the nineteenth century many combined their resources into single brigades.

Below: The Rangoon Fire Brigade, 1894. The fire engine is horse-drawn with a steam-powered pump, and the men's helmets are of brass.

Illustrated London News

Left and above: The three factors necessary for combustion are a fuel, oxygen (or other oxidizing agent) and heat. These three together constitute the 'triangle of combustion', and a fire can be extinguished by the removal of one or more of these. The three main ways of putting out a fire are thus *starvation*, which is the removal of the fuel; *smothering*, which is the exclusion of oxygen from the fire; and *cooling*, which is the removal of heat. The most common method of extinction is cooling by the application of water, but often, for instance when the fire involves electrical equipment, other media must be used to smother it.

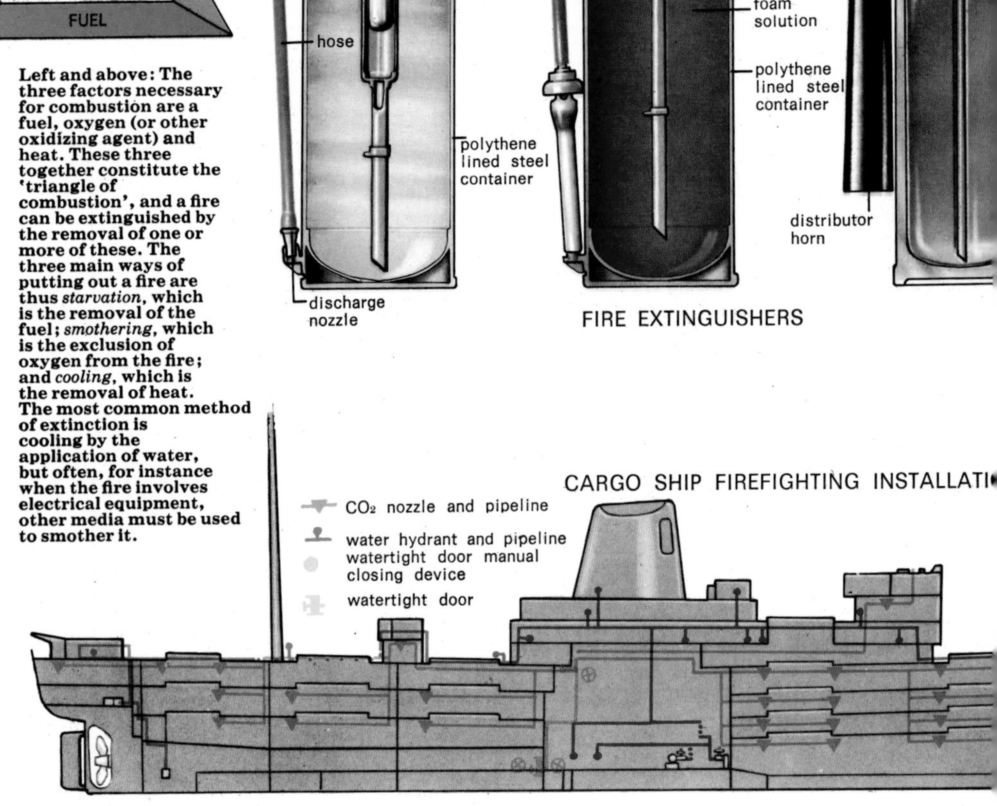

Above: A typical firefighting installation on a cargo ship consists of pipelines carrying water to hydrants, and a system of pipes and nozzles through which carbon dioxide gas can be injected into a hold to put out a fire by smothering it.

Below: The former passenger liner *Queen Elizabeth* (85,016 tonnes) is destroyed by fire in Hong Kong harbour in 1971.

Right: The *Forties Kiwi* is a tanker which has been converted into a firefighting ship for the protection of North Sea oil platforms.

Keystone

poor and distances were increasing. Equipment, when provided, often fell into disrepair or was not returned after use.

Following the Great Fire of London, which began on 2 September 1666 and burned for five days, property owners began to take out fire insurance on their buildings. This led to the development of numerous private fire brigades, operated by the insurance companies to fight fires in premises they insured. The insurance company brigades operated alongside the various voluntary and municipal brigades, where these were provided, but they would not normally attend to fires in buildings not insured by their company.

By this time, most fire engines were horse-drawn and fitted with hand-operated pumps. When a fire occurred, volunteers were required to man the pumps and to fetch water. It was usual to pay them for their services, sometimes in cash but often in beer. A large fire in the late eighteenth century created intense excitement. Large crowds were attracted to the scene, and there was often intense rivalry between the various brigades. People fought for the job of manning the pumps, and when they were paid off in beer they often fought again.

Eventually, the insurance companies realized that their interests would be better served if they pooled their resources, and these combined forces were the ancestors of the modern brigades operated by the public authorities.

Modern firefighting

The main weapon of the fireman has always been water, and most fire appliances are basically designed to carry and pump water. The first fire engine to use a steam-powered pump was built by Braithwaite and Ericsson in 1829, and the use of steam to drive the vehicle as well as to

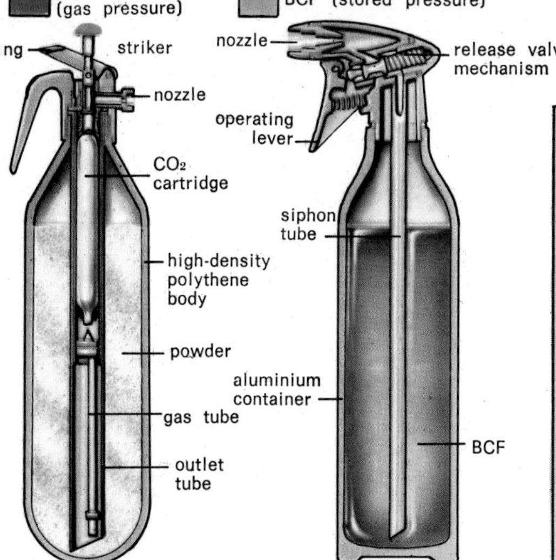

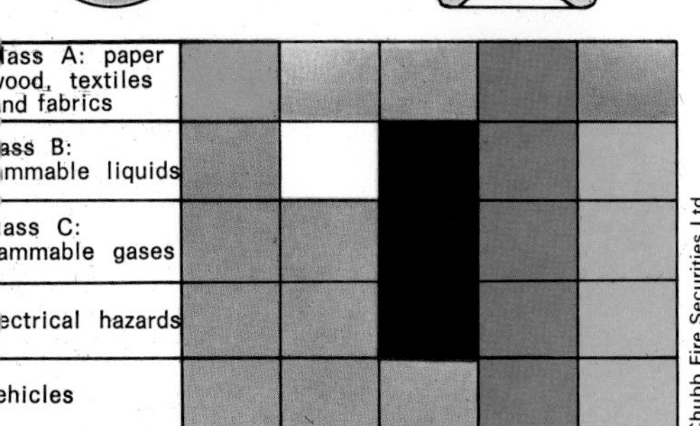

Chubb Fire Securities Ltd

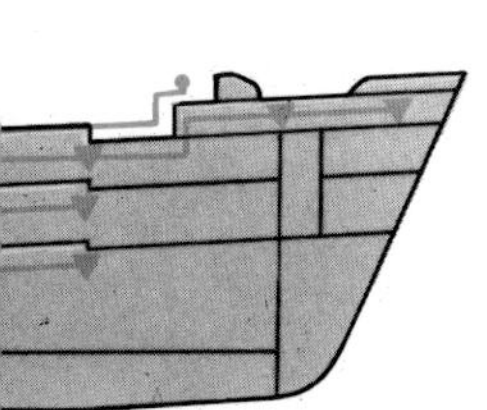

Above: The main types of fire extinguisher—water, foam, carbon dioxide, dry powder and vaporizing liquid (BCF)—and the types of fire on which they can be safely and effectively used. No fire extinguisher should ever be used on a class of fire for which it is not recommended by its manufacturer.

UNISAF

Above: Forest fires pose many problems for firefighters, as they can rapidly spread over a wide area of inaccessible forest.

This picture shows a Lockheed Hercules dropping 13,640 litres (3,000 gallons) of fire-retarding liquid on to a forest fire.

BP

power the pumps was introduced by Paul Hodge in 1840. Steam-powered pumps, both horse-drawn and self-propelled, remained in use well into the twentieth century until they were finally replaced by petrol and diesel-powered machines.

Another very important piece of fire brigade equipment is the ladder. There are several basic types in use, including the wheeled, telescopic *escape ladder* which can be extended to about 15 m (50 ft) or more, and the larger *turntable ladder* which is power-operated and carried on a specially-built appliance. The largest turntable ladders can be extended to about 45 m (150 ft). As well as providing a useful position from which water can be directed onto a fire, ladders are essential equipment for rescuing people from burning buildings, the saving of life being the most important function of the fire services.

The principal effect of water on a fire is to cool the burning material, thus removing the heat, one of the factors without which combustion cannot continue. It can be applied in a variety of ways, such as by flooding the fire with water at low pressure, or by using smaller quantities of water at pressures as high as 41 to 55 bar (600-800 lb force/in^2). Jets of water are used to knock down the flames of a fire, and sprays are used to absorb heat and drive back smoke and gases.

Although water can be used to good effect in the majority of cases, there are other ways of dealing with a fire. In fact, there are some types of fire in which the use of water may actually make things worse. If water is used on burning oil, for example, the oil simply floats on top of the water and carries on burning, and as the water flows away it can carry the oil with it and so spread the fire.

Such fires are usually dealt with by

the application of *foam*, which floats over the surface of the burning liquid rather like a blanket of soap bubbles and extinguishes the fire by excluding air from it, thus depriving it of the oxygen it needs in order to burn. There are several types of foam available to the fireman. The ordinary foam has an *expansion ratio* of approximately 8:1; that is, a litre of water, when mixed with the protein-based foam compound and aerated, will froth up to produce 8 litres of foam. In recent years, following the development of higher expansion foams, this type of foam has come to be known as *low expansion foam.*

Equipment is now available which, using a detergent-based foam concentrate, produces very light foams with medium or high expansion ratios. A *medium expansion foam* has an expansion ratio of approximately 150:1, and a *high expansion foam* has one of about 1,000:1. Medium expansion foam flows freely, especially over liquid surfaces. It cannot be projected well over a distance, but it is useful for dealing with outdoor fires at ground level involving either liquids or solids. Since the foam cannot be projected very far, the branchpipe (delivery nozzle) is best used at the fire itself rather than at a distance from it, and this means that protective clothing such as an aluminized suit may be necessary.

High expansion foam is generated by spraying a mixture of water and foam concentrate through a series of nozzles into the airstream from a fan, which blows it on to a fine mesh. The effect of this is to produce a mass of air-filled bubbles which cannot be projected any useful distance but can easily be blown along trunking, usually polythene tubing, on to the fire. High expansion foam is ideal for extinguishing fires in enclosed areas such as basements or the holds of ships. The fire is extinguished mainly by being starved of air. The high expansion foam generators used by fire brigades are readily portable, and can produce up to 140 cubic metres (5,000 ft^3) of foam per minute. Fixed foam installations in buildings may have even higher output rates.

Another type of foam is known as *light water foam*. It has been found that foam produced from water mixed with certain synthetic detergents (*surfactants*) made from fluorocarbon compounds has a greater imperviousness to flammable vapour than does protein-based foam. It is a much looser foam, and it flows easily across burning liquids and leaves a vapour-proof film on the fuel, which makes re-ignition difficult even after the foam has broken down.

Fire extinguishers

The exclusion of air from a fire can be achieved in other ways than by the use of foam. The more common methods are by means of vaporizing non-flammable liquids such as fluorocarbons, or by means of carbon dioxide (CO_2). The fluorocarbons used for extinguishing fires vaporize readily when heated. They form a dense, heavier-than-air cloud of non-flammable vapour which not only excludes air from the fire, but also inhibits the chemical reactions which are responsible for the propagation of flame in the burning material. This property can be measured scientifically for individual vaporizing liquids and is

Right: The hydraulic platform, a relatively recent type of fire appliance, is used for both firefighting and rescue work.

London Fire Brigade

Above: This diagram shows the operating range of extensions and heights for a typical hydraulically-powered turntable ladder.

Right: Heat resistant, non-flammable suits protect firefighters from the heat when they are working in close proximity to a fire.

Bristol Uniforms Ltd

Chubb Fire Securities Ltd

The Port Authority of New York & New Jersey

Above left: The rugged chassis and suspension of a Chubb 'Pathfinder' airfield crash truck.

Above: The 'Pathfinder' can discharge over 61,370 litres (13,500 gallons) of low expansion foam per minute over a distance of up to 91 m (300 ft), and has a top speed of over 96 km/h (60 mph).

London Fire Brigade

Above: A London Fire Brigade *pump escape*, equipped with a built-in pump and carrying an escape ladder.

Left: A large fire at a London hospital. Two turntable ladders and an escape ladder can be seen in use, and the firemen in the foreground are standing next to a *control unit*, a vehicle equipped to serve as a mobile administrative and communications headquarters. Special rescue and salvage vehicles are also in attendance. The pumps used by fire brigades may be either built into the appliances and driven by their engines, or self-contained units with their own engines.

Below: A typical wheeled escape ladder. The telescopic sections of the ladder are extended by means of a manually-operated winch and cable system, the overall extended length being about 15 m (50 ft). Chocks are placed under the carriage wheels to keep it firmly in place while it is in use.

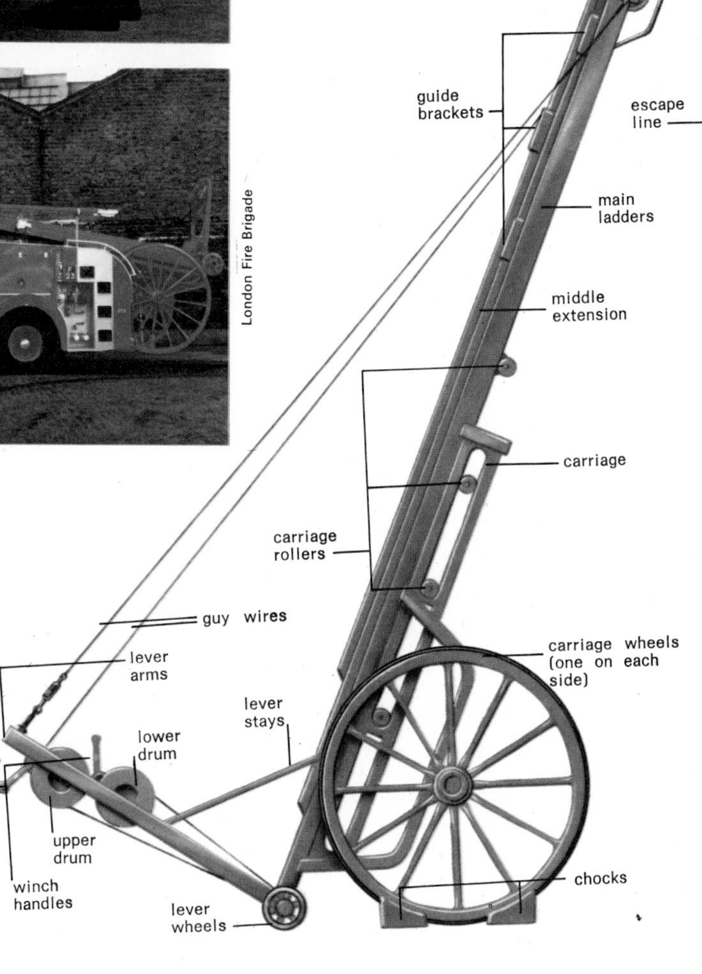

known as the *inhibitory factor* of a liquid.

Vaporizing liquids are particularly useful for extinguishing fires in electrical equipment as they are non-conducting, which means that there is no risk of electric shock for the user of the extinguisher, and they do not damage sensitive electronic equipment. Vaporizing liquid extinguishers are also suitable for extinguishing fires in the engines of motor vehicles.

Chlorobromomethane ('CBM'), bromochlorodifluoromethane ('BCF') and bromotrifluoromethane ('BTM') all have high inhibitory factors and are replacing carbon tetrachloride ('CTC') and methyl bromide ('MB') as fire extinguishing media because the latter have a higher toxicity. The toxicity of vaporizing liquids used for fire extinction has always been a matter of concern, although there would probably be a greater danger from carbon monoxide produced as a result of a fire than from the toxicity of the vaporizing liquid. Care must be taken, however, when any vaporizing liquid extinguisher is used, and none should be used in a confined space.

CBM, BCF and BTM extinguishers are usually operated by the pressure from a gas cartridge, although some may be pump-operated. The vapour-forming spray should be directed straight at the fire so that it is rapidly converted into a dense vapour.

Carbon dioxide extinguishers are carried on some fire brigade appliances, but they are more often found in commercial or industrial premises and in electricity supply installations. They are often installed in the kitchens of hotels and restaurants, and they are especially useful in fish-frying establishments because the carbon dioxide does not contaminate the frying oil.

Dry powders are also used to exclude air from a fire, and they are particularly suitable for extinguishing running fires involving highly flammable liquids and for open surface fires on such liquids. Many powders used are based on sodium bicarbonate mixed with a metallic stearate, and others, based on materials such as graphite or talc, are very good for dealing with burning metals such as magnesium, titanium and beryllium.

Although dry powders do not have a cooling effect, they do provide a certain amount of heat-shielding which protects the person operating the extinguisher from radiated heat. Dry powders have also been developed for use on fires involving radioactive metals such as uranium.

Drainage and Waste Disposal

The disposal of surplus rainwater, sewage, and household and industrial rubbish has been a problem for towns and cities ever since the Industrial Revolution began increasing urban populations. Once, sewage farms—growing crops on land fertilized by a town's wastes—plus open drains and rubbish tips were the most efficient way of disposing of wastes. Today, much more sophisticated methods are needed.

Sewage presents different disposal problems from those of the water which runs off streets after a rain shower. So in some countries it is still common for towns to have completely separate drainage systems for the two. One set of pipes takes the surface water run-off from street drains and house gutters, while another set conveys the discharges from domestic sinks and lavatories. But today a partially separate system is more common. In this, the street gullies empty into one set of drains, while a second set takes the sewage and the run-off from roofs. In this way the roof water helps to dilute the sewage and flush out the pipes to prevent noxious accumulations of *sludge* (sewage solids).

The combined system, where one set of pipes carries away both surface water of all kinds and sewage, has the same advantage of regular flushing. During heavy storms, however, the flow of liquid in the pipes sometimes becomes too high for the size of the sewers or the capacity of the treatment works. Stormwater overflows must therefore be provided to empty the excess flow directly into rivers or the sea. (In storm conditions the sewage is so diluted by rainwater that there is no danger to public health in dumping it like this.)

Rainwater drains can discharge into rivers, lakes and seas with no health risk, but sewage is usually treated before disposal to destroy its offensive or unhealthy content. This is not always the case, however. Many coastal towns still discharge raw, untreated sewage directly into the sea. The theory is that the sewage is rapidly diluted by the seawater to such an extent that organisms naturally present in the sea can digest and neutralize it faster than it is discharged. The solids are often chopped into small pieces by the rapidly revolving blades of a *comminutor* to aid this dispersal. However, unusual conditions of wind and tide may inhibit dispersion; the natural ecology of the sea bed may be disturbed and valuable seafood harvests may be destroyed. So the treatment of sewage by simple dilution in this way has only cheapness to recommend it.

Inland communities have to divert their sewage through a treatment works before it can be finally disposed of. There are generally two distinct stages in the treatment. *Primary* treatment involves removal of the sludge from the remaining liquid, which is known as *effluent*. *Secondary* treatment involves an artificial acceleration of natural biological processes of decay, ridding the effluent of its remaining impurities.

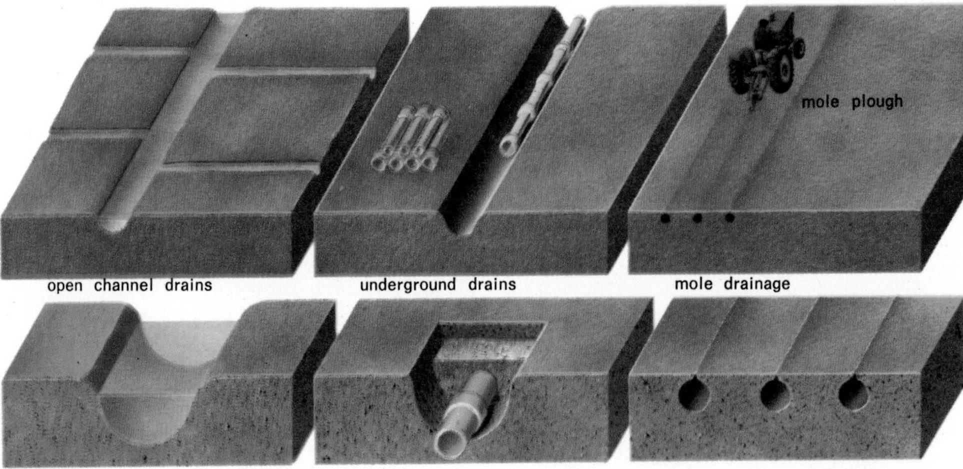

Above: Three methods of draining land. The simplest and oldest form of drainage consists of a network of channels which lead the surplus water to a nearby river. Underground drains usually consist of clay pipes laid in a trench or tubular channels cut in the earth by a mole plough.

A. F. Trenchers Ltd

Left: A small tracked trenching machine. The trench-cutting boom (left) and the dozer blade (right) can be raised or lowered hydraulically. The latter is used for filling in trenches after pipe sections have been laid.

Below: A trenching machine at work. In ideal conditions it can cut a trench to a depth of 1.1 m (45 in).

Primary treatment

In a modern works, the first stage is to remove the coarse solids. The larger particles are caught by screens of parallel bars spaced about 2.5 cm (1 in) apart, or by lattice screens with apertures of the same size. Screens are raked mechanically, or in smaller works manually, to remove the accumulated solids which may be either incinerated or broken up and returned to the flow of sewage. Next, any grit is settled out in *grit chambers*, which consist basically of U-shaped open channels through which the sewage flows at a speed of a little more than 30 cm/sec (1 ft/sec)—just fast enough to avoid organic materials also settling out. The grit is cleaned out of the channels periodically and disposed of.

Floating solids are removed in *skimming tanks*—saucer-shaped concrete tanks which are fed from beneath with the sewage. A rotating arm skims off the scum and floating particles, and the effluent spills over the lip of the tank into a surrounding collection channel. The finer suspended solid particles are extracted either by means of fine screens with a mesh of 1-2 mm ($\frac{1}{32}$ - $\frac{1}{16}$ in) or by sedimentation; sometimes both methods are used. In a well-designed sedimentation tank up to 60 per cent of the suspended solids may settle to the bottom within a two-hour period. This is generally the last of the primary treatments, but occasionally the sewage may also undergo *chemical precipitation*. In this process, a chemical such as alum or ferric sulphate is added to the sewage to encourage the smallest suspended particles to aggregate together into a single mass which sinks to the bottom.

A. F. Trenchers Ltd

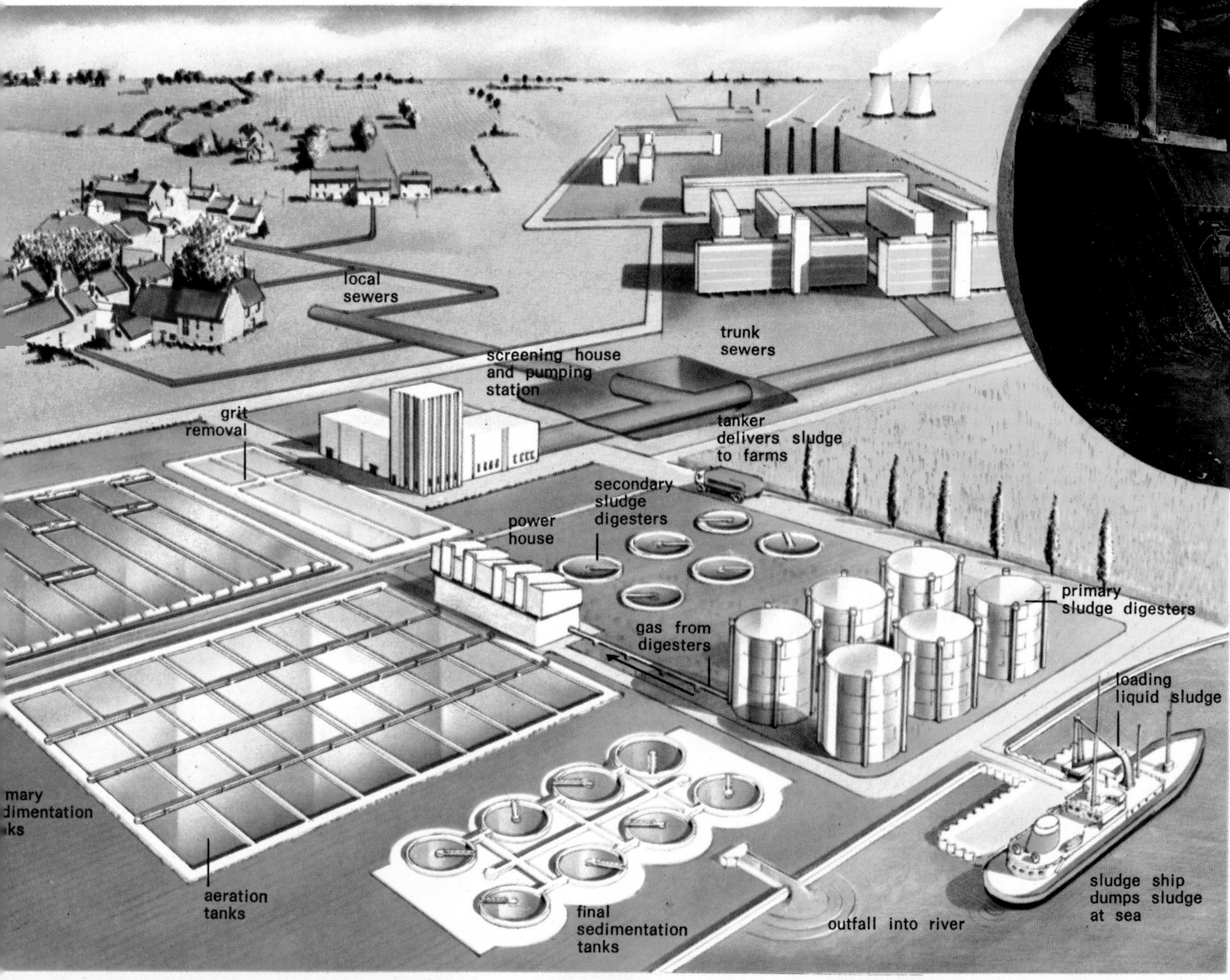

Above: A junction in one of London's largest sewers.

Left: On arrival at a treatment works, solid objects such as planks of wood and sand are first removed from the sewage. Then sludge is separated from the more liquid sewage in primary sedimentation tanks. The sludge is transferred to digesters where it is used to produce methane, the chief fuel for the works' power house. The digested sludge is dried and used as a soil conditioner. The liquid sewage is aerated to allow micro-organisms to grow and break down the harmful chemicals. After about eight hours the liquid is clean enough to be discharged into a river.

Courtesy of Thames Water Authority

Anderson Mavor

Above: A tracked 'roadheader'. This type of machine is used for cutting the tunnels needed for large sewers. The cutting boom is hydraulically operated and it is telescopic. Cut material is carried away from the front of the roadheader by a conveyer. The machine is powered by two 90 kW electric motors.

British Steel Corporation

Right: Laying a new main sewer in a town is a major operation. This picture shows concrete pipe sections 1.4 m (54 in) in diameter being laid. The amount of sewage that has to be disposed of each day in a city is enormous. In greater London, for example, some 4,300 million litres are treated daily.

Left: One method of disposing of domestic refuse. A special receiver fitted to each kitchen sink outlet accepts most items of rubbish, including cans and bottles. By lifting a waste tube these are flushed into an underground collection chamber, which is periodically emptied by a tanker.

Right: A tanker for emptying cesspits or clearing gullies. The tank is divided into two compartments, one being filled with fresh water when the machine is used for clearing drains. The suction pipe, on a counterbalanced arm, is powered by a pump located under the chassis and is fitted with a control valve.

Fergussons Tankers Ltd

Whale Tankers Ltd

Above right: This tanker operates on the same principle as the one shown above, but it is designed for heavy duty work in hilly areas. The 5,500 litre (1,200 gal) tank is mounted on a strong six-wheel-drive chassis.

Right: Aeration tanks at a modern sewage works. To enable the micro-organisms which break down the sewage to thrive, the liquid sewage must be oxygenated. In these tanks compressed air is blown into the liquid through submerged tiles, called diffusers, which produce streams of very tiny bubbles. Another method of aerating the sewage is to spray it on to a bed of clinker or gravel where it takes up oxygen.

Courtesy Matthew Hall

Thames Water Authority

Secondary treatment

The sludge which has been collected in the various primary treatments may be dried and chemically sterilized, but it is more usual to treat it biologically. The raw sludge is mixed with a quantity of previously-treated sludge containing a large number of micro-organisms which are *anaerobic* (that is, able to thrive in the absence of oxygen). They live and breed in the mass of sludge, feeding on it and breaking down the offensive organic compounds into simpler chemicals. This *digestion* of the sludge may be carried out slowly at normal temperatures, in which case the methane and other combustible gases given off are collected and sold. More commonly, the gases are used to heat the sludge and accelerate its digestion. The treated sludge can be used as a fertilizer.

The sewage effluent from which the sludge has been extracted is also treated biologically, but in this case the organisms involved are *aerobic*—that is, they need oxygen to live and carry out their function. All secondary treatments consist essentially of establishing a colony of the right sort of micro-organisms, feeding this colony with the effluent and making sure that plenty of oxygen is available. The first method developed—one which is still widely used all over the world—was the biological filter. This consists of a basin with side walls from 1.5 to 1.8 m (5 to 6 ft) deep and a slightly sloping floor to permit free drainage. The basin is filled with a durable material, preferably containing pores to help give the largest possible surface area. Clinker, coke and blast-furnace slag are all ideal for this. Such a filter may be dosed inter-

Thames Water Authority

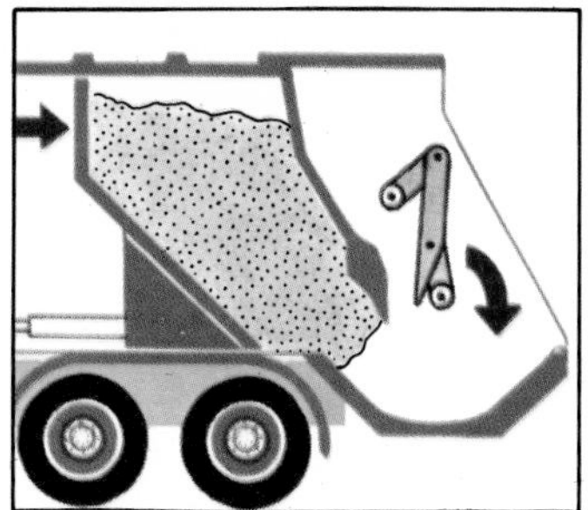

Left and below: A modern refuse collecting truck equipped with a hydraulically operated compacting mechanism. Material is constantly pressed into the body of the truck by a moving 'comb' in the loading compartment. The front of the refuse chamber is bounded by a moving bulkhead, and as more refuse is received it automatically moves forward, maintaining a constant pressure on the refuse. The process continues until the body is completely full with evenly compacted refuse. The loading comb normally operates four times a minute, and a relief valve on the hydraulic motor prevents any undue build-up of pressure.

GLC

Shelvoke & Drewry Ltd

Left: The primary sedimentation tanks at a sewage works. Sludge settles to the bottom of the tanks where it is removed by rotating scrapers. Liquid sewage flows over the rim of each tank into an outer channel which conducts it to aeration tanks like those shown above right. The sludge is pumped to a digester.

Above: In large cities refuse often has to be transported for a considerable distance before it can be dumped. Here, barges loaded with rubbish pass the Houses of Parliament in London on their way to the Essex Marshes where the material is used to fill and reclaim low-grade land for agricultural use.

mittently and drained completely before being used again, or may be fed with a continuous trickle of effluent. By either method, up to 95 per cent of the putrefying matter is oxidized into harmless compounds.

Recirculation is the basis of the *activated sludge* process, which was developed in 1916 and is now probably the most widely used secondary sewage treatment. Activated sludge is sludge in which the necessary organisms are already well established. It is mixed with the settled sewage (effluent) and aerated in a variety of ways to provide the necessary oxygen. The air may be blown through thousands of small apertures spaced out on the bottom of the tank, or the liquid may be agitated by rotors to mix in air from the surface and distribute it throughout the mixture. Between four and 10 hours' aeration is necessary to degrade the sewage, which is then drawn off and left to stand in a sedimentation tank. About 30 per cent of the sludge which settles in this final sedimentation tank is returned to the aeration tank to be mixed with another batch of sewage.

In thinly populated areas, it is sometimes uneconomical to pump sewage to a treatment works. In such areas it is common for each house's sewage to be stored in either a *cesspool* or a *septic tank*. The cesspool is a watertight tank buried in the ground, which is emptied every two weeks or so; even this simple storage helps decompose the sewage a little. More degradation is achieved in the septic tank, where anaerobic bacteria feed on the sewage, which takes about a day to seep slowly through the tank. When the tank is half to two-thirds full, most of the sludge is sucked out, but about a third of it is left to maintain the population of bacteria.

Refuse disposal

Solid waste presents the sanitary engineer with a different set of problems. Unlike sewage, it cannot be pumped along drains, although a few housing projects have their own waste-disposal works to which rubbish is conveyed along pneumatic tubes. Usually, the cost of collecting rubbish from individual houses and business premises is the most expensive part of the whole waste disposal operation because it entails so much manual labour.

Once the garbage has been collected there are three ways of disposing of it. The easiest solution is simply to dump it directly on tips or use it to fill in land which has been excavated in (say) mining operations, but this is rather unsightly and often unhealthy. A better alternative is *controlled tipping*, which involves spreading the waste in layers which are then overlaid with a layer of soil, then another layer of waste, then another layer of soil and so on. Small organisms in the soil help to decompose the rubbish.

Large towns and cities often do not have enough spare land within easy reach for them to tip all their rubbish untreated; something must first be done to reduce its volume. The two methods of doing this are *pulverization* and *incineration*.

Pulverization is a simple mechanical process whereby the rubbish is pounded into small particles by sheer force. Magnetic separators may be used beforehand to sort out steel cans and so on which can be sold as scrap and recycled. Two methods of pulverization are possible. *Wet pulverizers* use less energy, because water is sprayed on to the waste to soften and lubricate it. A wet pulverizer typically consists of a rotating inner drum which is fitted with deflector plates and baffles to pound down the rubbish. This inner drum is constructed of a grid of alloy steel bars and, once the rubbish has been ground small, it passes between the bars into an outer drum. This drum, which is covered with thick steel sheet, also rotates and grinds the rubbish yet smaller. Although wet pulverization decreases the volume of waste, the added water increases its weight—and this raises the cost of transport. So the system is economical only when the pulverizer is sited at the rubbish tip itself.

Dry pulverizers are fitted with rotating or reciprocating hammers to crush brittle materials, and with rotating steel teeth to shred the softer materials such as cardboard. They have the advantage that they can reduce glass to a fine powder. They may be vast machines, capable of dealing with over 50 tonnes of rubbish an hour.

Incineration—high temperature burning—is the most effective way of reducing the volume of rubbish. It is also the most efficient in terms of the energy which has to be supplied, since much of the energy required comes from the rubbish itself as it burns. Before it reaches the main incineration chamber the waste is dried by means of the hot gases produced by the combustion. Inside the main chamber the rubbish is tipped on to sloping grates where it burns at a temperature between 750°C and 1000°C. The ash falls through the gaps in the grates and is conveyed away. The main disadvantage of burning rather than pulverizing waste is that a considerable amount of soot and smoke is released as a result of combustion. Various methods of cleaning the incinerator exhaust gases must therefore be employed to minimize air pollution.

Lighting

The use of artificial lighting is almost as old as man himself. One of the things that distinguished him from the apes was the use of fire—and this must soon have developed from its original purpose of a means of defence, first to its use for cooking, and then to the employment of burning branches or splinters of wood to provide illumination.

How long ago man first hit on the idea of using a wick on the edge of a stone bowl filled with animal fat to provide light, it is impossible to say, but primitive lamps hollowed out of chalk or sandstone have been found in such places as the Lescaux caves, and must date from about 80,000 BC. The basic principles remained the same for thousands of years; the lamps used in medieval Europe were much the same as those found in the ruins of Pompeii or the tombs of the Pharaohs.

Candles, still used today in religious ceremonies, as decorations and for emergency lighting, have been in use for at least 5,000 years. Modern candles are usually made from paraffin wax, although beeswax is used for higher quality candles such as those used in churches.

The first notable advance in the technique of producing light from an open flame was the invention of the Argand lamp (by Ami Argand) in 1784. This lamp used a tubular wick, and air was drawn up through its centre as well as from the side, so that it burned brightly with very little smoke. The introduction first of

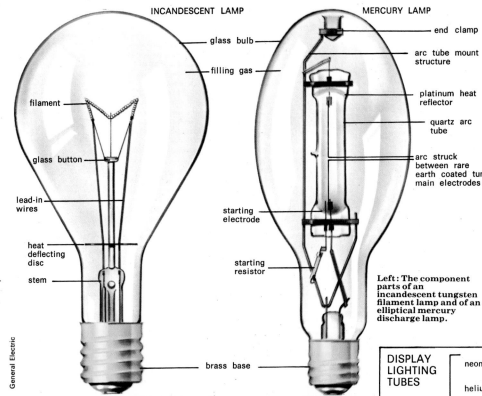

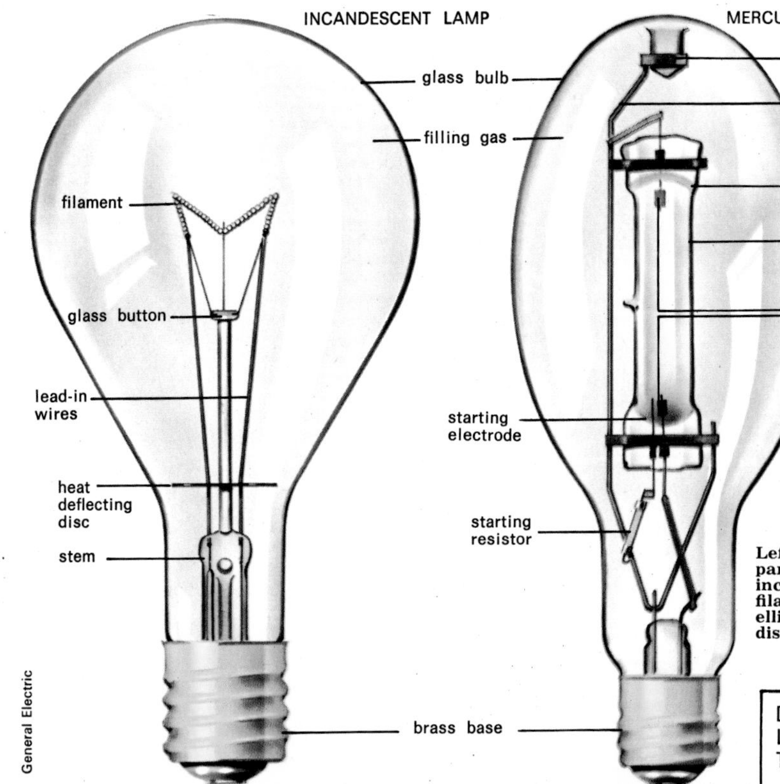

General Electric

Left: The component parts of an incandescent tungsten filament lamp and of an elliptical mercury discharge lamp.

DISPLAY LIGHTING TUBES

- GASES
  - neon
  - helium
  - nitrogen
  - carbon d
- METAL VAPOURS
  - mercury
  - sodium
  - magnesiu

Above: The colour of a discharge tube light is basically determined by the gas with which it is filled, although neon- and mercury-filled tubes can be coated internally with fluorescent powders which can produce a wide range of colours. This chart shows the colours produced by some of the discharge tubes commonly used in advertising signs. These signs are popularly known as 'neon signs', although in many cases they may not be using neon tubes at all.

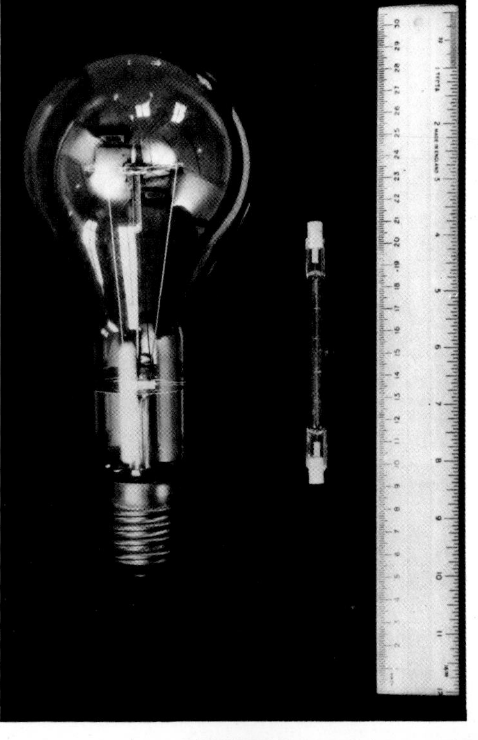

Thorn Lighting Ltd

Left: A 500 W linear tungsten-halogen lamp is much smaller than a conventional tungsten lamp of the same power, and its bulb is made of quartz instead of glass.

Snark

Below: A gas street light in Paris in 1890. The first gas lights used fairly simple burner nozzles, and their light output was low. The illuminating power of gas lights was considerably increased when the *incandescent mantle*, made of 99% thoria and 1% ceria, was developed late in the 19th century.

Tilley Lamp Co.

Above: Lamps used for street lighting include incandescent and fluorescent lamps (which give a white light), mercury lamps (white or greenish light) and sodium lamps (orange light).

Right: Advertising lights in Tokyo, Japan.

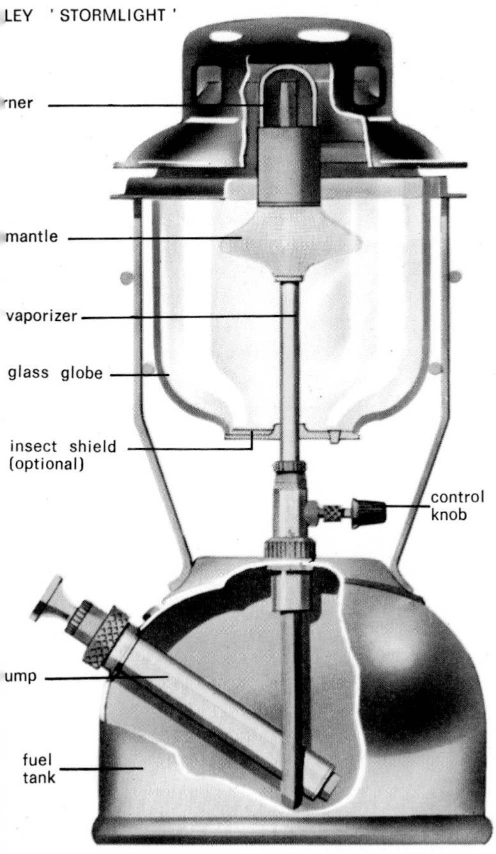

Left and above: The Tilley 'Stormlight' is a powerful modern oil lamp in which the paraffin fuel is vaporized and burnt at an incandescent mantle. The fuel tank is pressurized by pumping air into it, so that fuel is sprayed into the burner as a vapour.

colza oil (made from rape seeds) and then of paraffin in the nineteenth century brought still further improvements, and today the pressure lamp with an incandescent mantle gives a strong white light.

The first really spectacular advance, however, was the invention of gas lighting. The first large scale experiments were made by William Murdoch in the late eighteenth century, and in spite of difficulties in eliminating impurities, and of the rather feeble flame emitted by the early 'cockspur', 'batswing' and 'fishtail' burners, gas street lighting was well established in London, Paris and other large cities by the second decade of the nineteenth century. The introduction of an efficient incandescent mantle by Baron Carl Auer von Welsbach of Vienna in 1893 gave considerable impulse to its domestic use, and in many places it remained a serious rival to electric light right up to the beginning of the Second World War.

The earliest electric lamps were carbon arcs, the first of which was exhibited to the Royal Society by Sir Humphry Davy in 1810. He used an enormous battery to supply the arc, and it was not until Faraday's work on generators in the succeeding decades had provided a plentiful source of power that they became a practical source of light. By the late 1850s, a number of temporary street lighting installations had appeared in London, Paris, Berlin and New York, and in 1862 the first permanent carbon arc was installed in Dungeness lighthouse.

Carbon arcs give a very powerful light, but they are clumsy, dirty and need constant attention, so from about 1840 onwards, a number of people started to experiment with the idea of producing light from an electrically-heated filament operating in a vacuum. Pioneers such as Grove and de Moleyns made lamps with platinum filaments, but were unable to obtain a satisfactory vacuum and it was not until Sprengel invented a really efficient vacuum pump that the first practical lamps were produced.

The first successful filament lamps were produced (independently) by Sir Joseph Swan in England in 1878, who used carbonized cellulose filaments, and by Thomas Edison in the United States in 1879, who used filaments made from carbonized bamboo.

Incandescent lamps

An incandescent lamp is essentially a coiled tungsten filament contained in a glass bulb and heated to incandescence by passing an electric current through it. The amount and colour of light emitted depend upon the operating temperature of the filament, the light becoming stronger and whiter as the temperature is raised to about 2,700°C (4,890°F).

The light emitted from a lamp is measured in units called *lumens* (lm), and the ratio of the number of lumens produced to the number of watts of electricity consumed by a lamp is known as its *efficacy*. The efficacy of a tungsten filament lamp is about 12 lumens per watt; it is in fact a very inefficient light source as almost all the energy radiated by the filament is in the infra-red, only a very small proportion being in the visible part of the spectrum.

The 'life' of a lamp is also directly related to its filament temperature.

Atoms of tungsten escape from the surface of the hotter parts of the filament and settle on the inside of the glass bulb. These parts of the filament gradually become thinner, while the inside of the glass is gradually blackened, reducing the light output of the lamp and changing the colour of the light.

Eventually, part of the filament becomes so thin that it cannot support its own weight, and it breaks and the lamp fails. The rate of 'evaporation' of the filament can be reduced by filling the bulb with an inert gas (usually a mixture of argon and nitrogen), but it cannot be eliminated and mains voltage lamps are usually designed to fail after 1000 hours of use.

Tungsten halogen lamps

At temperatures between about 300°C (570°F) and 1,500°C (2,730°F) tungsten will combine with certain halogens, such as iodine or bromine, to form an unstable gaseous halide. If a lamp is made with a small quartz bulb, the surface of which is maintained at about 250°C (482°F), and a very small quantity of a halogen is added to the gas filling, the tungsten atoms ejected from the filament will combine with the halogen, and so never reach the bulb wall. The tungsten halide is carried back into the filament by convection and the two elements dissociate, the tungsten being deposited back on to the filament and the halogen released to repeat the cycle.

Because the halide is deposited upon the cooler parts of the filament, its attenuation is not directly affected, but the smaller, stronger bulb allows a considerably higher vapour pressure so that the rate of evaporation can be reduced, and the filament can be run hotter, giving a brighter and whiter light without shortening its life.

Discharge lamps

The earliest discharge lamps used for lighting used sodium or mercury vapour to carry an electric discharge which was struck between a pair of electrodes. Both these types were introduced in the early 1930s and were extensively used for street lighting. The sodium lamp, operating at a low vapour pressure, produces virtually monochromatic yellow light. The efficacies of the first sodium lamps were in the region of 70 lm/W; today efficacies of 200 lm/W can be obtained, but objects seen in the light of these lamps appear in tones of yellow and black, and it is impossible to distinguish colours in it.

Mercury lamps, with efficacies of about 45 lm/W, have a discontinuous spectrum consisting of strong lines in the green and yellow regions, a slightly less marked purple line and two strong lines in the near ultraviolet and far ultraviolet regions. Some colours, notably reds which tend to appear brown, are much distorted, but colours can be distinguished in the light from mercury lamps. By the late 1930s fluorescent phosphors were being used to add some of the missing red light to the mercury spectrum, but the advent of the fluorescent tube at the beginning of the Second World War put a temporary stop to this development.

Fluorescent tubes

A fluorescent tube is a mercury discharge

Thorn Lighting Ltd

Above: Measuring the light output from fluorescent tubes inside a sphere in which the surface reflections are known and constant.

Below: A graph showing the increase in lamp efficacies between 1920 and 1975.

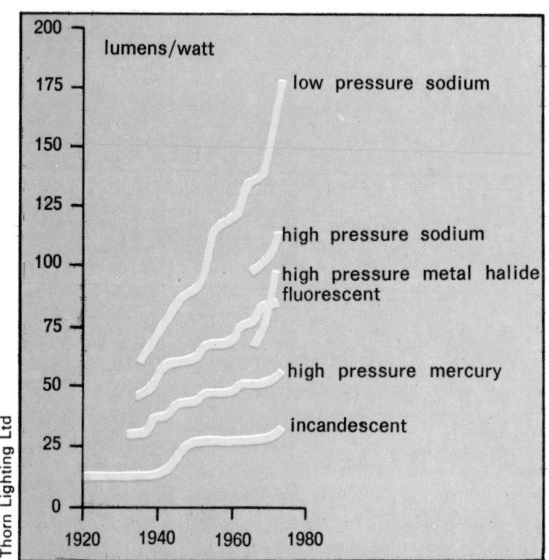

Thorn Lighting Ltd

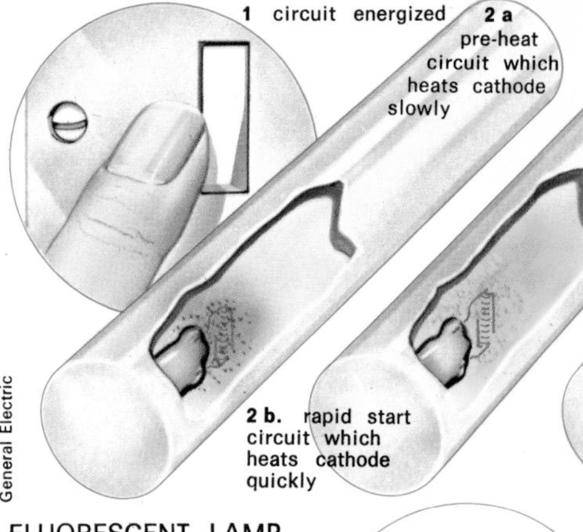

General Electric

FLUORESCENT LAMP OPERATION

2 electrons released from cathode by one of three methods:

3 electrons ionize starting gas which reduces its resistance and an arc is formed. Electrons in arc excite mercury atoms which give off radiation

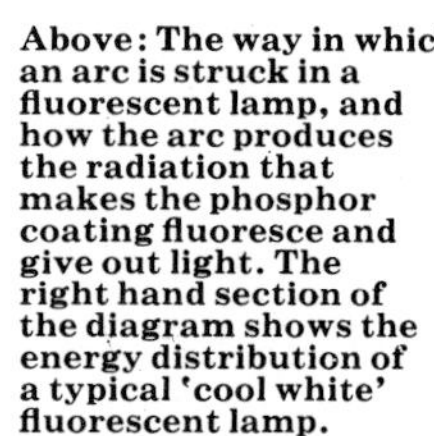

Picturepoint

Above: The way in which an arc is struck in a fluorescent lamp, and how the arc produces the radiation that makes the phosphor coating fluoresce and give out light. The right hand section of the diagram shows the energy distribution of a typical 'cool white' fluorescent lamp.

Left: A lighthouse uses an elaborate revolving array of reflectors and lenses to focus its light into a powerful, rotating beam. The light is produced by electric lamps (filament or xenon discharge) or sometimes by gas or oil burners.

Below: The photo-engraving department of a printing works, lit by sodium lamps which give adequate illumination but, because of the colour content of their light, do not 'fog' the sensitive plates used in the engraving.

Thorn Lighting Ltd

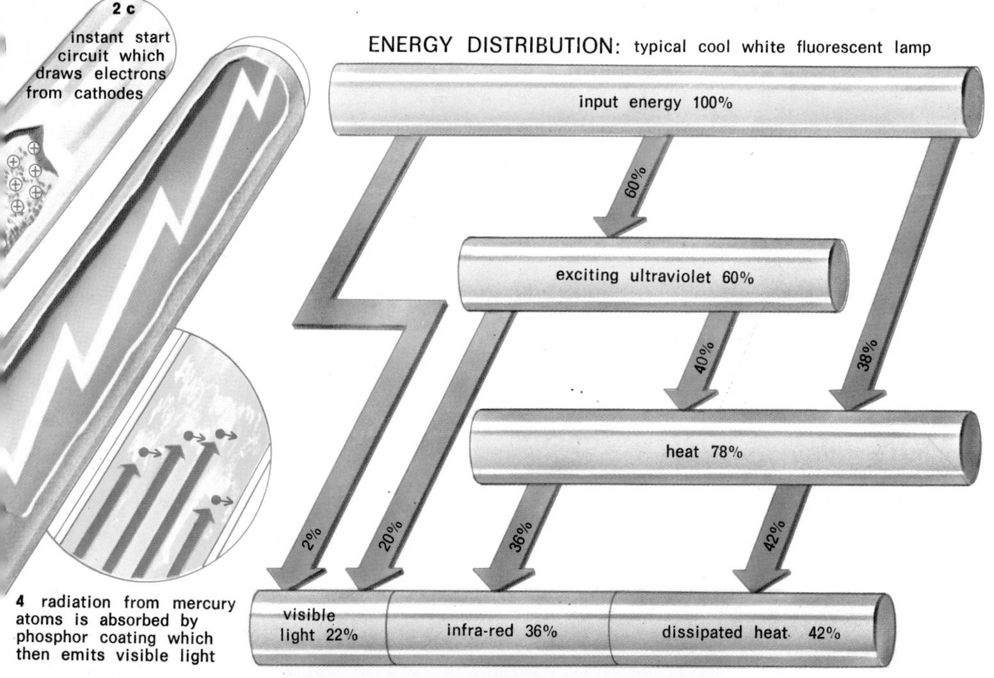

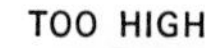

TOO HIGH

TOO LOW

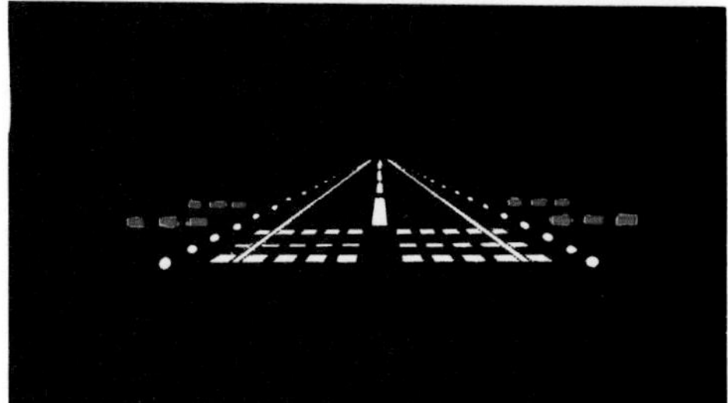

CORRECT

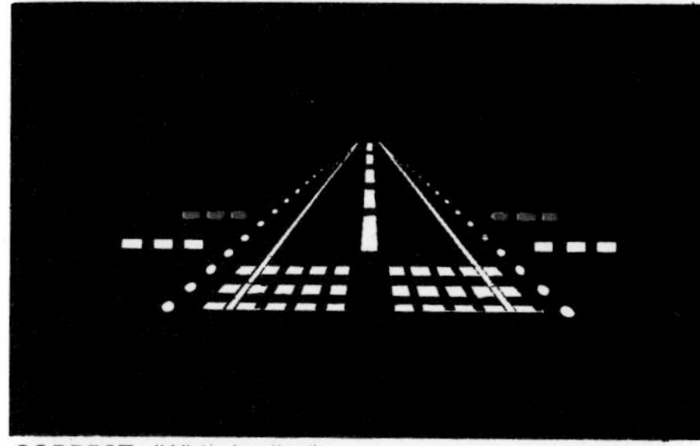

CORRECT (Wide-bodied)

British Airways

Left: The navigation and warning lights on a Boeing 747 include a red light on the port wingtip, a green light on the starboard wingtip, rotating anti-collision beacons on top and beneath the fuselage, and a pair of white runway turnoff and taxi lights on the tailplane.

Right: The VASI (*visual approach slope indicator*) consists of sets of lights, each of which produces an upper beam of white light and a lower beam of red light, which are carefully positioned at the sides of airport runways to guide incoming planes along the correct approach slope. Two sets are used for conventional aircraft, and three for wide-bodied jets. The combination of colours seen by a pilot depends on the aircraft's angle of approach, and shows if the angle is too high, too low or correct.

Thorn Lighting Ltd.

lamp (which also contains a small amount of argon) in which the vapour pressure is kept deliberately low, so that a higher proportion of ultraviolet radiation is emitted than of visible light. This powerful uv component is used to excite phosphors coating the inside of the arc tube, which *fluoresce* (absorb the energy of the uv light and re-emit it as visible light) to produce light of almost any desired colour or mixture of colours.

High pressure discharge lamps

In the mid-1960s, interest in high-pressure mercury discharge lamps revived with the use of a rare earth, yttrium vanadate, which gave a strong red fluorescence and much improved their colour rendering. These lamps are much more compact than fluorescent tubes, and if provision is made within them for housing the choke and capacitor, they can be used in fittings designed for filament lamps. They are especially suitable for use in bulkhead fittings because they use only a quarter of the power of a filament lamp of equivalent light output, thus reducing the heat in the enclosure.

A more fundamental way of producing white light is to modify the spectral characteristics of the discharge itself, and this can be done by adding other metals such as thallium, dysprosium, indium and sodium to the original mercury arc.

Metal halide lamps give white light with good colour-rendering properties at efficacies in the region of 80-85 lm/W. They are made with large outer bulbs (with or without a fluorescent coating) similar to those used for mercury lamps, and in double-ended tubular form for use in floodlight projectors. A very compact 1000 W metal halide lamp, sealed in a pressed glass reflector bulb, is used for floodlighting football stadia, and for outdoor television lighting where it has virtually superseded the large carbon arc lamps.

Sodium lamps with the discharge operating at low pressure are extremely efficient, but their monochromatic yellow light is unsuitable in many situations. It had long been known that increasing the vapour pressure would cause improved colour-rendering, producing light in which colours could be distinguished at an efficacy of about 100 lm/W.

The main technical difficulty was to produce an arc tube that would stand up to the chemical attack of ionized sodium vapour, at temperatures of about 700°C (1,290°F). An aluminium oxide ceramic tube made of a material called 'Stellox' was found suitable, but since it cannot be softened and worked like glass, it presented serious problems of sealing the electrodes. These have now been overcome, and high-pressure sodium lamps are being used for an increasingly wide range of applications.

Three types of high-pressure sodium lamp are available: one in which the outer jacket is elliptical, and is internally coated with a diffusing powder; a single-ended lamp with a cylindrical clear glass jacket 53 mm (2.1 in) in diameter designed for use in floodlights; and a very slender double-ended lamp in which the arc-tube is enclosed in a 24 mm (0.95 in) quartz tube, designed to be used in the enclosed floodlights originally made for tungsten halogen lamps, and made the same length and with similar caps as the 1500 W and 1000 W lamps of this type.

High pressure sodium lamps must be operated with a choke, capacitor and igniter to provide a high voltage starting pulse. They are made in sizes ranging from 70 W to 1000 W and are finding applications in industrial and commercial situations as well as for street lighting.

Heating and Ventilation

The purpose of a heater or of a heating system is to produce heat and transfer it to areas where warmth is required, preferably at the highest possible efficiency and the lowest possible cost. Heat can be transmitted by *conduction*, *convection*, *radiation*, or by a combination of any or all of these.

The conduction of heat from one object to another takes place when they are in direct contact, the heat 'flowing' from the hotter object to the cooler one. In an electric iron, for example, the heat produced by the heating element is conducted through the sole plate of the iron, and from there to the material being ironed.

Convection is the movement or circulation of air, or of a liquid, created and sustained by the application of heat. When air comes into contact with a hot surface, such as a heating element, it absorbs heat by conduction and in doing so it becomes warm and expands. Having expanded, the air is now less dense and so it begins to rise through the cooler, denser air around it.

As the warm air rises away from the heating element its place is taken by cooler air, which in its turn is heated and rises. Meanwhile, the air already heated is gradually losing its heat to its surroundings and so it contracts, becomes more dense again, and begins to fall. This continuous cycle of heating, rising, cooling and falling results in circulating currents of air termed *convection currents*.

Convector heaters are designed to heat the air in a room by means of this type of convection. Typical modern convector heaters are slim, rectangular units containing a heat source, with an inlet at the base for the incoming cold air and an outlet grill near the top for the outflow of warm air. Some convector heaters are fitted with fans, which draw air over heating elements and expel it through a grill. This method is termed *forced convection*.

Radiant heat is a form of electromagnetic radiation which is emitted when the atoms of an object, which contain electrically-charged particles, vibrate due to the object being heated. The more an object is heated, the faster its atoms vibrate, emitting more radiant heat as they do so. Many substances, such as air, are effectively 'transparent' to radiant heat, that is, very little of it will be absorbed when it passes through them.

Other objects, however, such as furniture or people, absorb the heat and so become hotter. The amount of heat absorbed by an object depends upon its colour and texture as well as on the type of material from which it is made. Dark or rough surfaces absorb radiant heat more readily than do light or polished surfaces, which tend to reflect most of the heat.

The most important example of radiant heat is that radiated to the Earth by the Sun, without which life on Earth would cease. Central heating radiators are designed to emit radiant heat, and they also heat the air in a room by convection.

Michael Holford

Left: The large, open fireplace at the palace of the Counts of Poitou, in Poitiers, France, built by Guy de Dammartin in the late 14th century.

Right: A modern solid fuel room heater with a built-in boiler that provides a hot water supply and hot water to run one radiator and a heated towel rail. Larger models can supply enough hot water to run as many as ten radiators.

Below: The first central heating system was the Roman *hypocaust*. The heat from a fire circulated beneath the floors of a house and up through hollow walls. Hot water was provided by a boiler situated above the fire. A modern method of underfloor heating uses insulated electric warming elements embedded in a concrete floor, the floor itself acting as a heat storage medium. Another form of concealed electric heating employs heated ceiling panels which have an insulating layer above them to prevent heat escaping upwards.

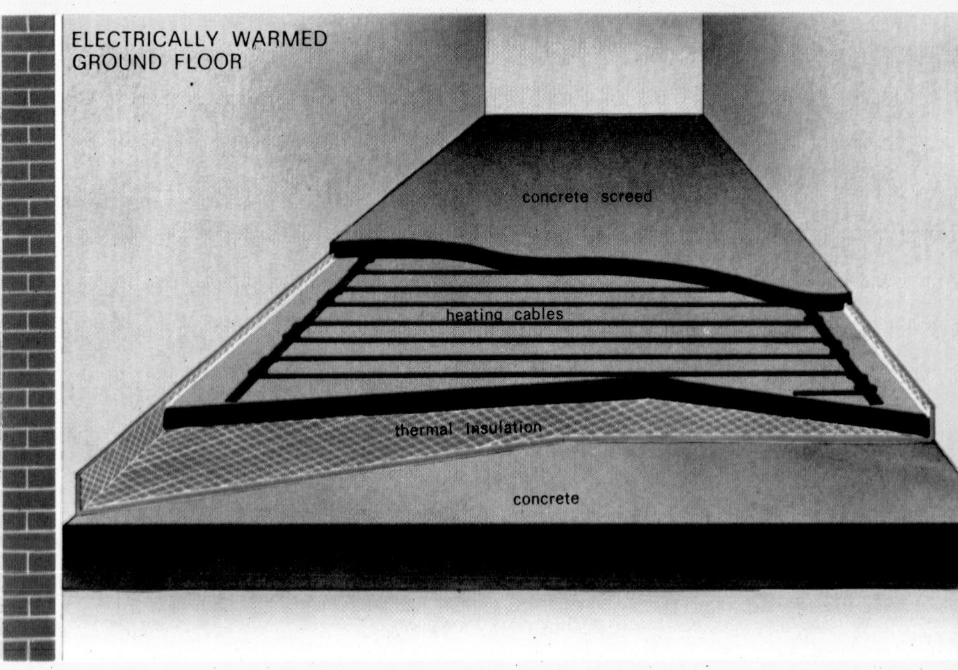

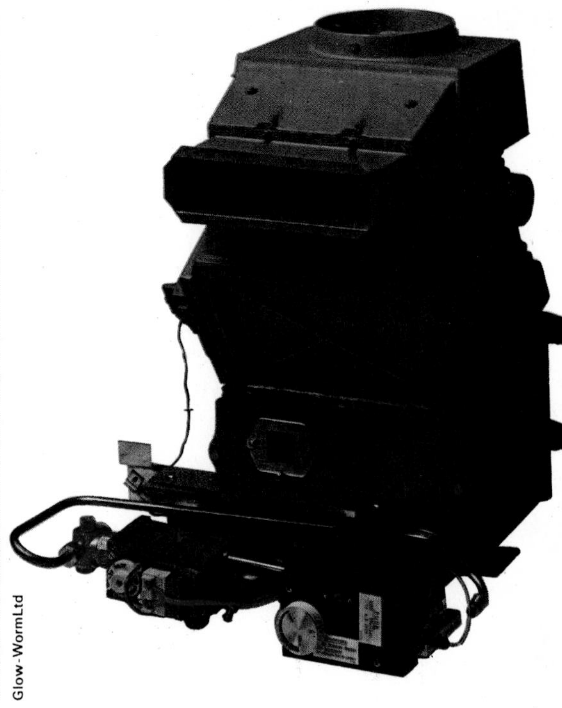

Left: A modern gas-fired central heating boiler, to the right of the sink, which can supply all the hot water and heating requirements of a four-bedroom house.

Above right: A *back boiler* unit which can be fitted into a fireplace behind a gas fire. The boiler provides enough heat to run a full central heating and hot water system in a three- or four-bedroom house.

Right: The layout of a typical central heating and hot water system. The domestic hot water is heated by a heat exchanger which is fed with hot water from the boiler.

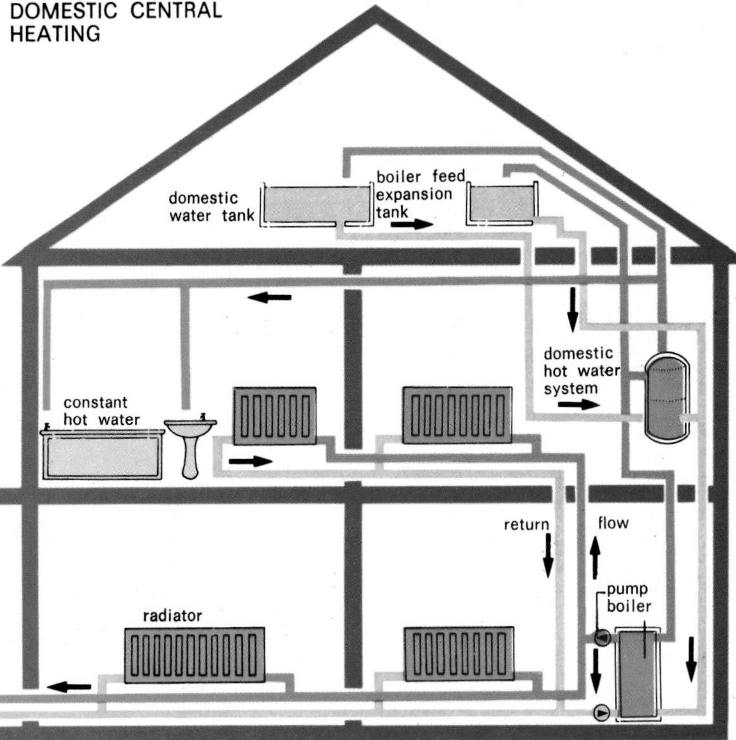

Radiant heat itself can only indirectly heat the air in a room, by heating the walls and the objects within the room so that they in turn heat the air which is in contact with them.

Heaters

The heat used for warming buildings is normally produced by burning a suitable fuel, such as coal, wood, peat, gas or oil, or by passing an electric current through a heating element. This length of resistance wire becomes hot when the current is passed through it, the heat being generated because of the wire's resistance to the flow of current.

Many of the older designs of solid-fuel fire are very inefficient, only about a quarter of the heat produced by the burning fuel being passed into the room as useful heat. With the increased use of smokeless fuels, however, more efficient grates were developed which deliver a much greater proportion of the heat into the room.

There is an extensive range of gas heaters, including radiant heaters, convectors, combined radiant and convector heaters, and gas-fired central heating boilers. In many countries, natural gas (composed primarily of methane, plus small amounts of other gases including ethane, propane, butane and nitrogen) has replaced coal gas (mainly hydrogen, methane, nitrogen and carbon monoxide) as the primary source of gaseous fuel. Liquefied gases, including propane and butane, are supplied in cartridges and containers of various sizes for use with portable heaters and in areas where there is no mains gas supply.

A gas fire usually needs a flue, which can mean a drop in efficiency as convected currents of warm air are expelled via the flue, but flueless models are available for use in rooms which have no suitable outside wall through which a flue could be installed.

Room heaters burning paraffin oil are mainly of the portable type. These range from the simple but effective cylinder-shaped unit, which is primarily a convector although it does emit a certain amount of radiant heat from its casing when hot, to the more modern designs fitted with a sophisticated burner and a parabolic reflector. In another type of oil heater, also burning paraffin, the fuel is sprayed under pressure into a mantle-type burner situated in front of a highly-

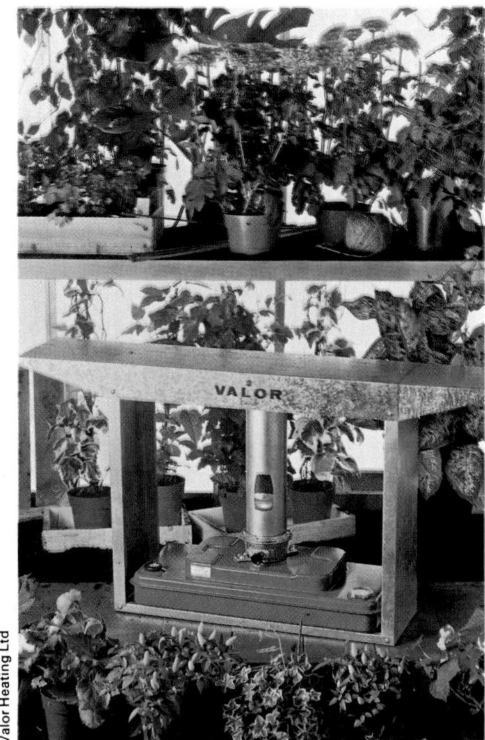

Valor Heating Ltd

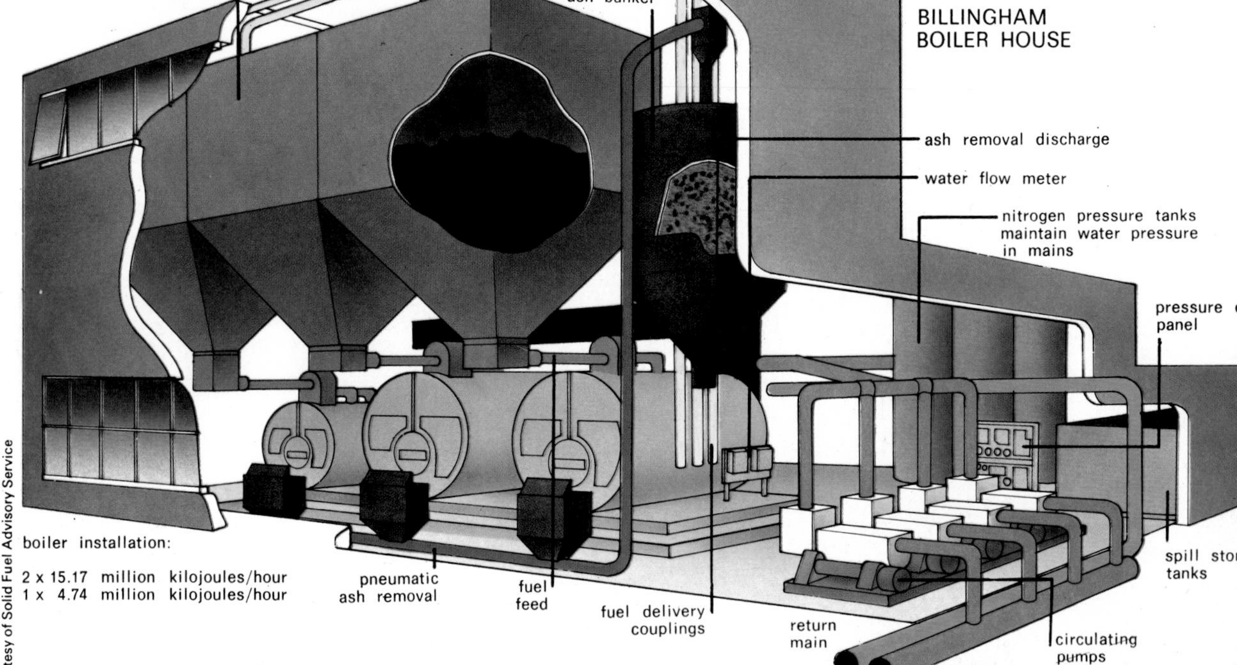

Courtesy of Solid Fuel Advisory Service

Above: A greenhouse paraffin heater, with a maximum heat output of nearly 2 kW.

Right: The town centre of Billingham in north-east England is heated by a *district heating scheme*. District heating schemes are in effect large-scale central heating systems. Hot water from a boiler house is piped around the area to all the buildings involved in the scheme, providing them with central heating and a constant supply of hot water. In the Billingham scheme, which uses three solid fuel boilers, the water leaves the boiler house at a temperature of 149°C (300°F) and returns at 93°C (200°F). The water is distributed by 20 cm (8 in) diameter steel pipes in brick ducts insulated with glass fibre. District heating schemes can also be run on the surplus heat produced by power stations, which would otherwise be wasted.

Below right: This *wind tower* in Bahrain provides ventilation by funnelling any breeze through ducts into the house below.

polished parabolic reflector.

Electric heaters are also made in a wide range of models, including radiant 'fires', convectors, fan heaters, storage radiators, wall-mounted panel heaters, oil-filled radiators and combined light and heat units.

It is current practice to divide electric heating into two classes: *direct* heating, where heat is given out only when the electricity is being used, and *storage* heating, where cheaper off-peak electricity is used to produce heat which is stored in the heater and gradually released from it when the current is switched off.

Direct heaters include all types of radiant and convector heaters. Storage heaters are self-contained units, containing electric elements enclosed within a thermal storage material such as high-density refractory clay blocks. The blocks are surrounded by a layer of thermal insulating material and an outer metal casing. The thickness of the insulating layer determines the rate of radiant heat output of these units, which are termed *storage radiators*. The amount of heat stored while the unit is consuming current can be varied by means of a thermostatic input control, but the rate of heat output cannot be controlled.

Another form of storage heater is the *storage fan heater*, which contains a fan that draws air over the storage blocks, thus warming it, and expels it through a grille. The fan circuit is energized from the 24-hour electricity supply, instead of the separate off-peak circuit to which the heating elements are connected, and so it

Picturepoint

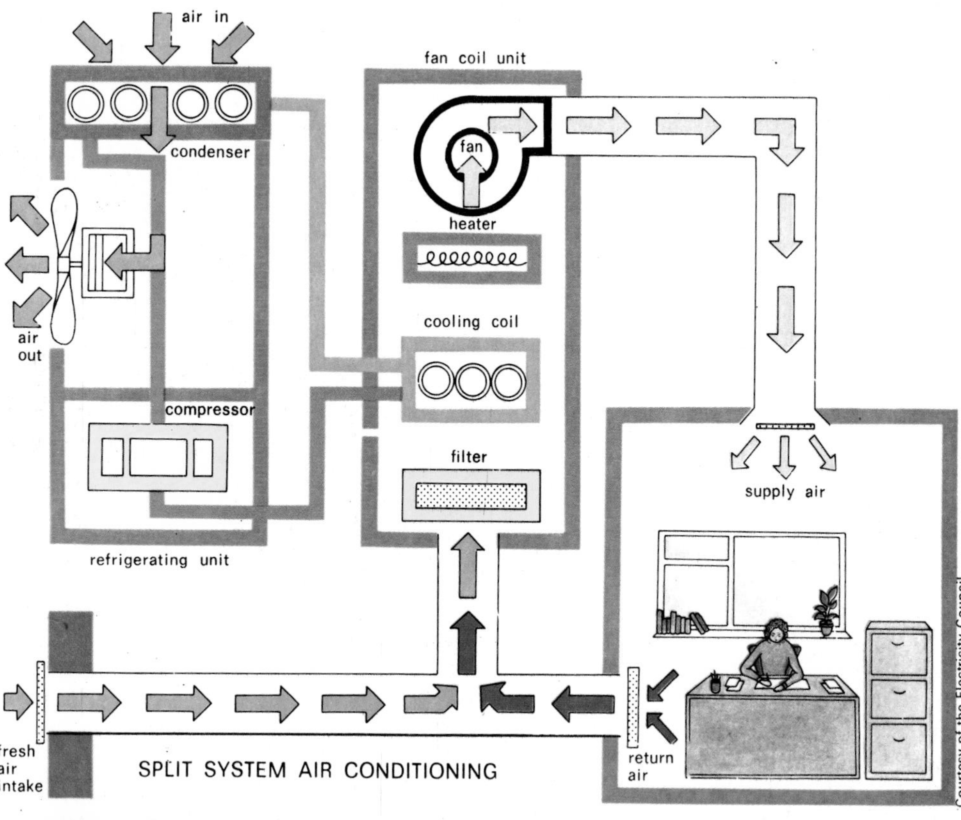

Above left: An air conditioning unit installed above the door of a butcher's shop.

Above: A 'split' air conditioning system consists of two parts, a refrigerating unit and a fan-coil unit. The refrigerating unit is connected to the cooling coil of the fan-coil unit by a pair of pipes which carry the refrigerant. The compressor drives liquid refrigerant through the coil, where it evaporates and absorbs heat from the coil before returning to the condenser, where it condenses and releases this heat. The fan-coil unit extracts stale air from the room, mixes it with fresh air and filters it, then passes it over the cooling coil where moisture condenses out of it as its temperature is reduced. The air may then be heated to bring it up to the required temperature before being returned to the room via ducting and a ceiling vent.

Left: Assembling the impeller of a large, variable-pitch ventilation fan.

can be switched on whenever heat is required.

Central heating

A central heating system consists basically of a boiler or other heat source from which heat is taken and distributed throughout a whole building or a substantial part of it. The heat is distributed either through hot water pipes to radiators, or as warm air through a system of ducting with outlet grilles situated in the rooms and service areas.

In hot water ('wet') central heating systems, the water is heated by a boiler burning solid fuel, gas or oil. The hot water may be pumped around the system, giving up its heat to the radiators before returning to the boiler for re-heating, or else it may simply circulate around the system by gravity, the heated water rising to the top of the system and slowly descending to the boiler again as it cools and becomes more dense.

Warm air central heating systems use fans to blow air through a heater unit and into the ducts which carry it around the building to the outlet grilles. The heater unit may be a solid fuel, oil or gas burner, or a large electric storage heater unit.

Central heating systems are controlled by thermostats and time switches, and these may be combined into sophisticated *programmers* which enable the heating of different sections of the building to be controlled independently.

Ventilation

Although most buildings have a certain amount of natural ventilation, with air flowing in or out through doorways and windows, this ventilation may not always be adequate or sufficiently controllable. One of the simplest methods of controlled ventilation is the electric *extractor fan*, the smallest useful size having a blade diameter of 15 cm (6 in.)

Ventilation requirements are usually expressed in terms of the number of *air changes per hour* that are needed. A room of 1,000 m^3 volume requiring 5 air changes per hour would thus need a total air movement through it of 5,000 m^3 per hour, and so an extractor fan capable of moving air at that rate would be required in order to ensure adequate ventilation.

For example, a domestic kitchen when in use requires about 15 air changes per hour, so a kitchen measuring around 3.7 x 3 x 2.4 m (12 x 10 x 8 ft) would require a total air movement of 400 m^3 (14,400 ft^3) per hour. This could be provided by a 19 cm (7.5 in) fan, which would have a capacity of about 425 m^3 (15,000 ft^3) per hour.

Air conditioning systems not only provide proper ventilation, but also clean the air and maintain its temperature and humidity within specified limits. Air conditioning may be provided by centralized units which supply conditioned air to various parts of a building through systems of ducts, or by individual units fitted into windows or against outside walls. A typical system works by extracting the stale air from the room via return air grilles, mixing it with fresh air, and then filtering the mixture to remove any dirt or dust in it.

The filtered air then passes through a cooling unit, where it is not only cooled but also de-humidified as moisture condenses out of it as its temperature drops. The air may now need to be heated to bring it up to the required temperature, and in some cases it may also be passed through a humidifier to give it the desired moisture content. The conditioned air is then blown into the room at slightly above atmospheric pressure, so that it drives the stale air out through the return air grilles.

Barnaby's Picture Library

Chapter 3 Building Technology

The Ouse Bridge over the M62 motorway, near Goole in Yorkshire. A mile (1.5km) long, its 29 spans are of composite plate girder construction.

Building Materials

The earliest building materials were, by necessity, those which were readily available and which could easily be cut and shaped with primitive tools such as stone axes and knives made from sharpened bones. These materials included branches, turf, suitably-sized stones, and mud—hand shaped, sun-dried mud bricks were being used for building in the Near East by about 6000 BC.

The introduction of metal tools, such as axes, saws and chisels, in the Bronze Age enabled builders to make more use of the materials available to them. They were able to fell mature trees and cut them into planks and beams, instead of just using branches or the trunks of smaller trees. The metal tools also enabled them to quarry stone and cut, shape and polish it. This ability to cut and shape stone had a profound effect upon the development of the early civilizations, as it permitted not only the building of permanent dwellings but also of large and impressive palaces, temples and monuments and the carving of the ornamental stonework and the statues with which they were decorated.

Another important advance, which occurred in about 2500 BC in Mesopotamia, was the spread of the art of kiln-firing from pottery to brickmaking. The kiln-fired bricks were harder and more durable than the sun-dried variety because of the higher temperatures to which they had been exposed, and such bricks were usually shaped in wooden moulds which led to greater consistency in size and shape, making them easier to use.

The Mesopotamians used bitumen as a mortar for their larger buildings, but the Egyptians used a mortar based on *gypsum* ($CaSO_4.2H_2O$), a hydrated form of calcium sulphate. Plaster of Paris, which is used for making plaster casts, is a partly dehydrated form of gypsum. The original mortar used by the Greeks and Romans was based on *slaked lime*. The lime (calcium oxide, CaO) was made by heating limestone (calcium carbonate, $CaCO_3$), which reacted with the water when the mortar was prepared to form slaked lime (calcium hydroxide, $Ca(OH)_2$).

This type of mortar is not very resistant to weathering, however, and the Greeks and Romans later adopted a mortar based on a *hydraulic cement* (one which will set under water) which the Romans called *pozzolana*. This cement was made from finely-ground lime, sand, and a volcanic ash which was first found at a town called Pozzuoli, near Naples.

This good quality cement enabled the Romans to make concrete, which they used extensively in their building. Concrete is made by mixing cement with sand and small stones or gravel, and whereas the Greeks built with solid stone or marble the Romans used concrete walls which were faced with these materials.

Stone, timber and brick remained the dominant construction materials until the Industrial Revolution brought cheap and plentiful supplies of iron and steel. The use of large amounts of iron was made possible by Abraham Darby's discovery, in 1708, that the efficiency of blast fur-

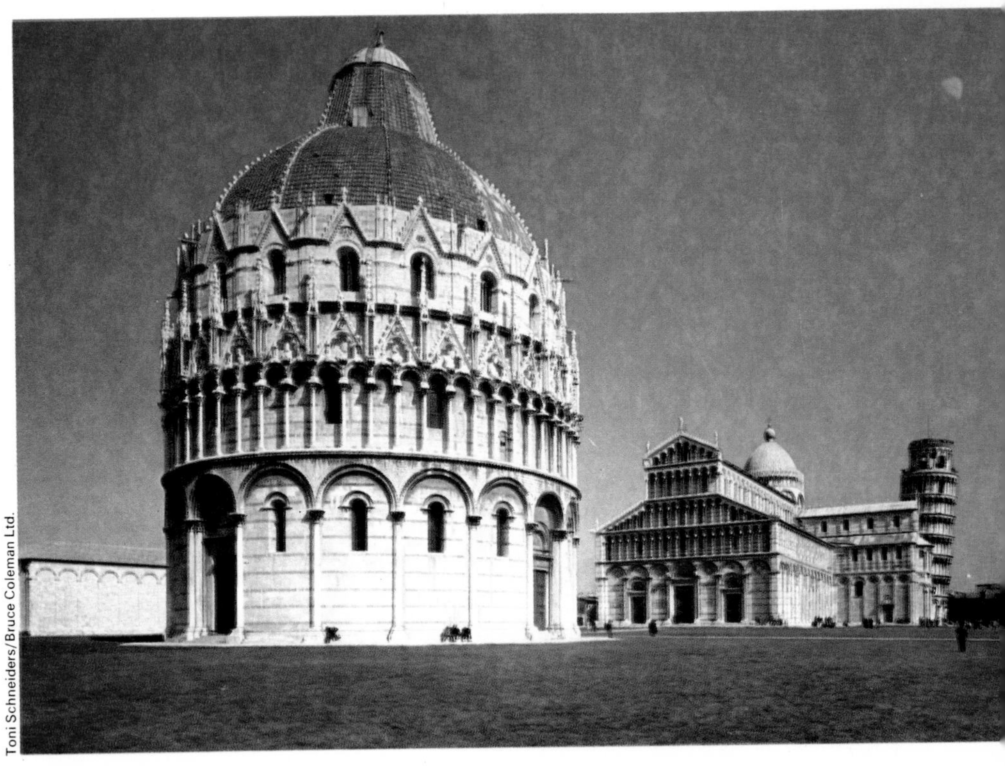

Toni Schneiders/Bruce Coleman Ltd.

Above: The baptistry, cathedral, and the famous 'leaning tower' at Pisa, Italy, fine examples of building in stone. They were built during the eleventh and twelfth centuries. Stone is one of the most durable and attractive of building materials, but unfortunately also one of the most expensive.

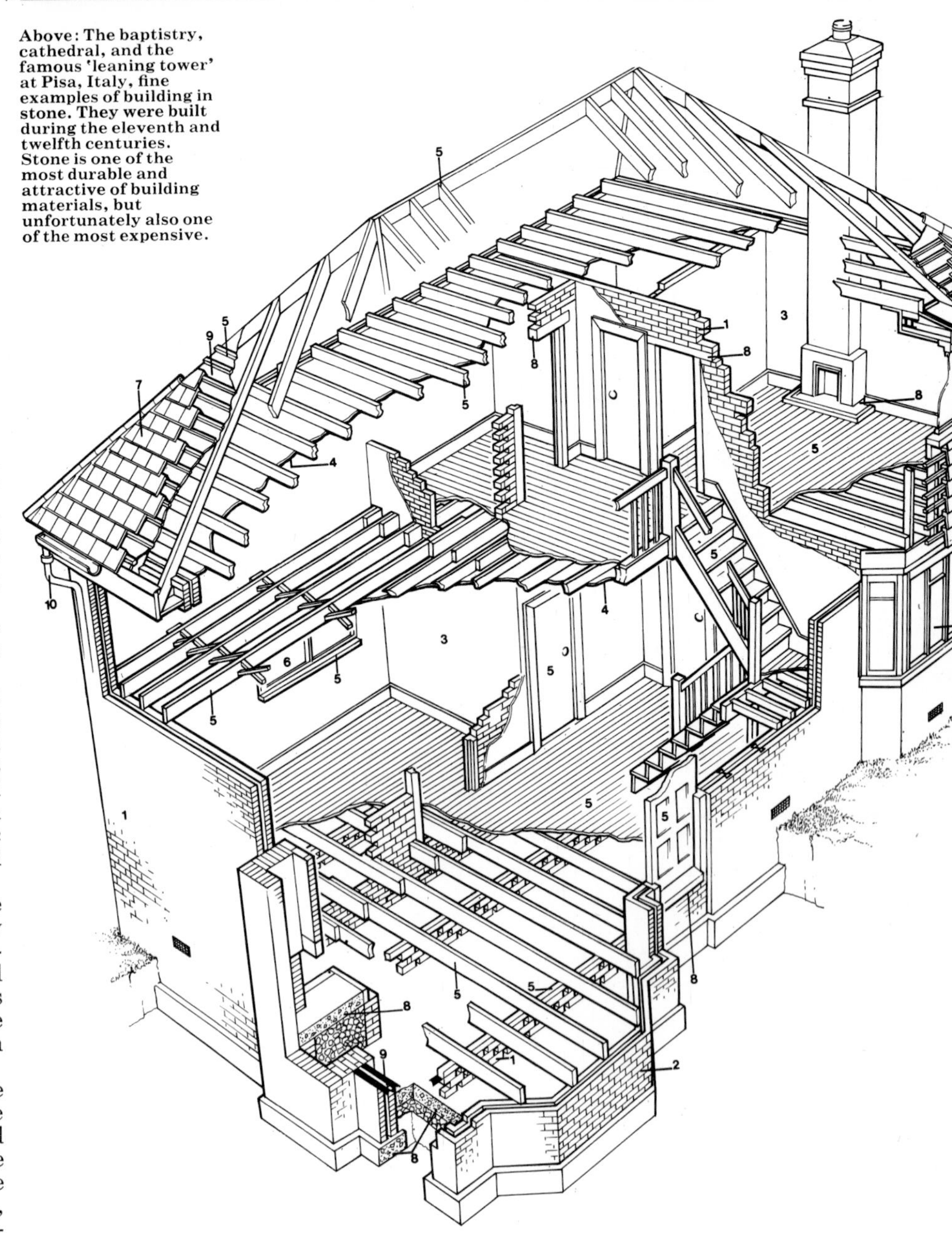

Redlands Ltd.

Cement & Concrete Assoc.

Left: Checking the verticality of a brick wall with a spirit level. Bricks are made of clay and fired in kilns to harden them. The mortar which is used to join them together when they are laid is usually made from cement, lime and sand mixed with water, although sometimes the lime is omitted.

Above: Cement kilns, long inclined cylinders which are slowly revolved as the mixture of raw materials passes down them and is turned into *cement clinker* by heat blown up through them. After cooling, the clinker is ground into cement powder. The raw materials used include chalk, clay, shale and limestone.

British Gypsum Ltd.

Above: Lining an interior brick wall with *plasterboard*, a useful building material consisting of an aerated gypsum core encased in thick paper. Plasterboard is widely used for ceilings, and partition walls are easily made by fixing plasterboard to a framework of wooden battens. The ceilings and walls of a building can be thermally insulated by the use of plasterboard laminated with an insulating layer of, for example, expanded polystyrene.

The materials in the ...ruction of a ...tional brick-built ...h house. The ...bearing external ... are *cavity walls*, ...sting of two layers ...ckwork with a ... or cavity between ... The cavity ...des a certain ...nt of thermal ...ation, but much ... effective ...ation can be ...ned by filling the ...y with an insulant ...as polyurethane ... Newer designs of ... commonly use ...us other ...rials, such as ...ete blocks for the ... layers of the ...y walls and for ...artition walls ...en the rooms, ...c drainpipes, and ... window frames.

...ck
...rtar
...ster
...sterboard
...od
...ss
...s
...ncrete
...uminized felt
...st iron

Picturepoint

Left: Re-thatching the roof of a cottage. Thatch is one of the oldest of roofing materials, its use dating back to ancient Egyptian times. Straw and reeds are the traditional thatching materials, although imitation thatch made of glass fibre is now available. More common roofing materials for houses include slate, and tiles moulded from clay or pigmented concrete; roof frames are usually of timber.

...s could be greatly increased if the ...ge of iron ore was reacted in the fur... with coke instead of the charcoal ...h had been used until then. The first ... structure to be made from iron in...d of the traditional materials was the ... Bridge over the River Severn at ...brookdale in Shropshire, England. ... bridge, completed in 1779, was de...ed, cast and built by Darby's grand... also called Abraham.

...e use of iron as a structural material ... steadily during the nineteenth cen..., and it was widely used for railway ...ges and stations. The latter half of ... century saw the emergence of steel ...building material, following the intro...ion of the Bessemer and Siemens-...in steelmaking processes. The cheap, ...-quality steels produced by these ...esses had almost completely replaced ... for building by the end of the century, ...at about this time a new and very im...nt use for steel was being developed —as a reinforcement for concrete. Concrete and steel are now the most important building materials, although timber and brick still play a very important role in building, particularly in the housing sector.

Bricks

Bricks, which are available in an enormous range of colours and textures, are normally made by shaping clay into blocks which are then fired in kilns to harden them. Not all bricks are made in this way, however; *calcium silicate bricks*, for example, are made from hydrated lime mixed with such materials as sand and crushed flint, pebbles or rock. The mixture is moulded under pressure into bricks, which are hardened by exposure to high-pressure steam. These bricks, also called *sandlime* or *flintlime* bricks, are usually smooth-textured and vary in colour from white or cream to light pink, although they can be produced in other shades and textures if required.

Bricks can be divided into three main types: *facing bricks*, which are coloured and textured to give exposed brickwork an attractive appearance; *engineering bricks*, which are hard, strong bricks suitable for heavy-duty applications such as power stations; and *common bricks*, used for general construction work where appearance is of secondary importance.

Cement and concrete

Up to the end of the eighteenth century, the most common form of cement in use was basically the same as the pozzolana used by the Romans and Greeks. One of the first to produce an improved cement was John Smeaton, who devised a cement made by heating limestone and clay for use in building the Eddystone Lighthouse in the English Channel in 1759. Smeaton's cement was superior in many ways to pozzolana, especially for underwater use.

The next significant step in the develop-

Left: The foundations for large buildings are often constructed on *piles*, steel or concrete columns driven into the ground to carry the weight of the building. This is a stack of reinforced concrete piles.

Below: Concrete is strong in compression but weak in tension. When a load is applied to a plain concrete beam, 1, the tension set up in the lower part of it may be sufficient to crack it. Steel reinforcement, 2, resists this tensile force and prevents cracking. Pre-tensioned concrete beams are cast around reinforcing wires held in tension, 3, and when the concrete has set the tensioning force is removed and the wires hold the beam in compression, 4. In post-tensioning, the beam is cast, 5, and when it is set steel bars are inserted into ducts in it and tensioned, 6. Concrete is made by mixing aggregates, 7, adding cement, 8, and then water, 9, so that the cement particles form crystals which bind the aggregate particles together, 10.

ment of cement came in 1824, when Joseph Aspdin patented his Portland cement, so called because when set the cement was similar in colour to Portland stone. The higher strength of this cement compared with that of Smeaton's was due to the higher temperatures used in the manufacturing process.

The raw materials used today for cement manufacture are calcium carbonate ($CaCO_3$), in the form of chalk or limestone, and aluminium silicates in the form of clay or shale. Other materials, such as low-grade iron ore or blast furnace slag, may also be used where they are readily available. A recent development, which could be of great value in many developing countries, is the production of cement from a mixture of ground rice husk ash (which has a high silica content) and lime.

Cement is made by one of two main processes, the *wet process* or the *dry process*, according to the raw materials being used. In the wet process, used when the ingredients have a high moisture content as is the case when chalk and clay are used, the raw materials are first mixed with water to form a slurry. The slurry is then fed into a kiln, a long cylinder up to about 120 m (400 ft) in length which is inclined at a slight angle and slowly rotated.

The slurry is fed into the upper end of the kiln and heat, produced by burning oil, gas or pulverized coal, is blown up through the kiln from the bottom end. As the slurry passes down the kiln its temperature is raised to about 1,500°C (2,730°F) and it fuses into lumps of *cement clinker*. This clinker is then cooled, and made into cement powder by grinding it finely with about 2 per cent gypsum, which prevents the cement from setting too quickly in use. The cement clinker can be stored easily for long periods, even in the open air, but once it has been ground into cement it must be stored carefully away from moisture.

When cement is made from harder, drier materials, such as limestone and shale, the dry process is employed. In this process the raw materials are ground together in a ball mill to form *raw meal*, and before being fed into the kiln this raw meal is pre-heated (using the hot gases from the kiln) so that it requires less time in the kiln. This means that a shorter kiln can be used. The clinker produced is then made into a powdered cement by the same method as that used in the wet process. Both processes employ filters and electrostatic precipitation systems to remove dust from the kiln gases and so minimize air pollution around the plant.

CEMENT AND CONCRETE

CONCRETE BEAM
1.
tension
reinforced concrete beam
2.
steel rod
pre-tensioned concrete beam
3.
wire under tension
cut ends of tensioning wire
4.
concrete cast around wires
post-tensioned concrete bear
cast conc
ducts
5.
tensioning bar
6.

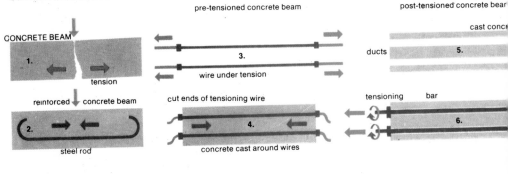

sand
gravel
7.

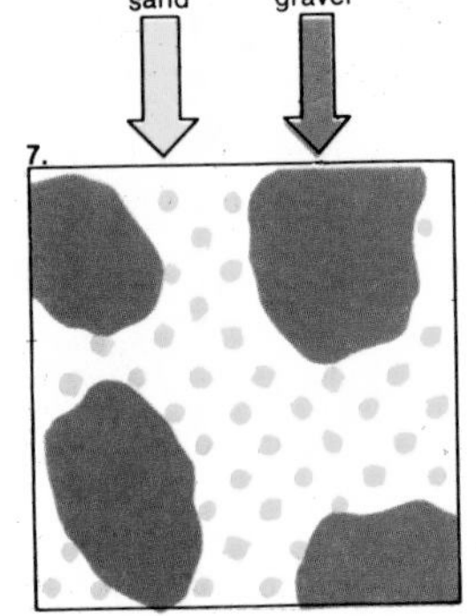

cement
concrete: a coarse aggregate such as gravel is mixed with sand and the cement powder is added to the mixture
8.

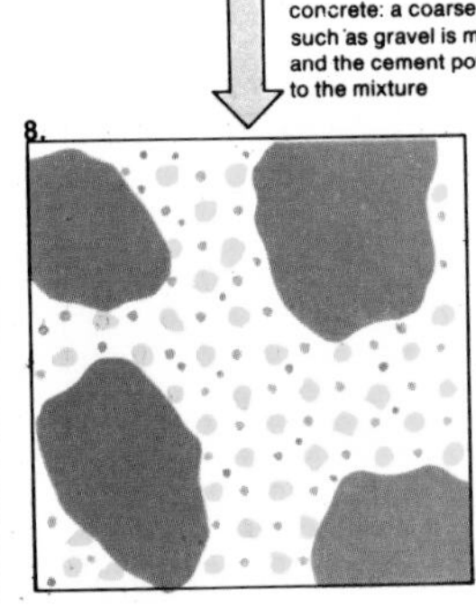

water
when water is introduced the cement particles grow into crystals which finally surround the sand and gravel, binding them together
9.

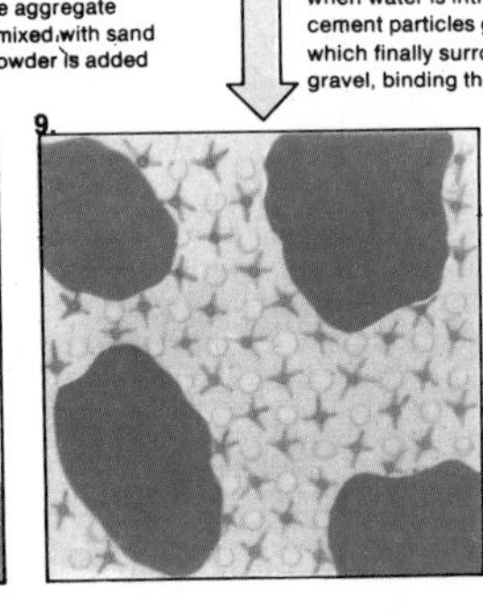

10.

Cement is a complex mixture of silicates and aluminates, the four principal constituents being tricalcium silicate ($3CaO.SiO_2$), tricalcium aluminate ($3CaO.Al_2O_3$), dicalcium silicate ($2CaO.SiO_2$) and tetracalcium aluminoferrite ($4CaO.Al_2O_3.Fe_2O_3$). When water is added to the cement, the chemical reactions which occur result in the formation of a complex matrix of long, interlocking, needle-like crystals which give the set cement its hardness and strength.

Cement is one of the principal ingredients of mortar. A basic mortar is made simply by mixing cement, sand and water, but the addition of lime to the mixture improves the adhesion of the mortar and prevents it from drying out too quickly. Coloured mortars are obtained by using cement which has been ground together with 5 to 10 per cent of a suitable pigment.

Mortars used for bricklaying are commonly made up of cement, lime and sand in proportions (by volume) ranging from 1:0:3 to 1:3:12, while those used for plastering may contain the ingredients in the proportions 1:1:6 or 1:2:9. *Plasticizers*, which trap air in the mixture and help the cement and lime mix more thoroughly

Pilkington Bros. Ltd.

Thyssen

Left: A spiral staircase at the Susqueda hydroelectric station in Spain. The staircase, which is made of prestressed concrete, needs no supporting columns and sweeps through a full 360°, rising a vertical height of 6 m (19.7 ft). The walls, floors and supports are also made of concrete.

Above: A house in Abu Dhabi, clad in *glass reinforced concrete* (GRC). The glass fibres used for GRC are an alkali-resistant type which are not prone to chemical attack by the cement, and the concrete usually consists of about 5 to 6 per cent (by weight) of fibres mixed into a cement-sand mortar.

Right: The decorative finial being lowered into place on top of the dome of the new London Central Mosque. The finial is moulded glass reinforced concrete and the dome is clad in a copper-zinc alloy, covered with a protective coating of transparent plastic to prevent discolouration.

with the sand, are used in many plaster and mortar formulations to make the mixture more workable and reduce the possibility of it cracking when it dries. Plasters based on gypsum, with or without lime and sand, are often used for interior plastering.

The largest use for cement is for making concrete, which is basically a mixture of cement, solid *aggregates* such as sand and small stones or gravel, and water. Typical general-purpose concretes contain 5 or 6 parts of aggregate to each part of cement, the proportion of fine aggregate (such as sand) to coarse aggregate (such as stones) being between 3:7 and 4:6. The water content is normally 45 to 50 per cent by weight.

Concrete is very strong in compression but comparatively weak in tension, and so it is often reinforced by embedding steel rods or bars in it, the reinforcement supplying the necessary tensile strength to the material. *Prestressed* concrete is an improved form of reinforced concrete; the steel rods are held in tension, so that they stretch slightly, before the concrete is poured around them. When the concrete has set, the tensioning force is removed from the rods and they try to contract back to their original lengths. Being firmly embedded in the concrete they cannot contract, and as a result they exert a compressive force on the concrete. Any tensile load applied to the concrete must therefore overcome this compressive force before it can exert any tensile stress on the concrete, and this makes the material more able to withstand tensile loads than ordinary reinforced or unreinforced concrete.

Another way of reinforcing concrete is by *post-tensioning*. In this method the concrete is cast, into a beam for example, and allowed to harden. Steel rods or bars are inserted into longitudinal ducts cast in the beam, and placed under tension by hydraulic jacks. The tensioned rods are then firmly anchored to each end of the beam, so that when the tensioning jacks are removed the rods exert a strong compressive force on the beam.

John G. Ross/Robert Harding Assoc.

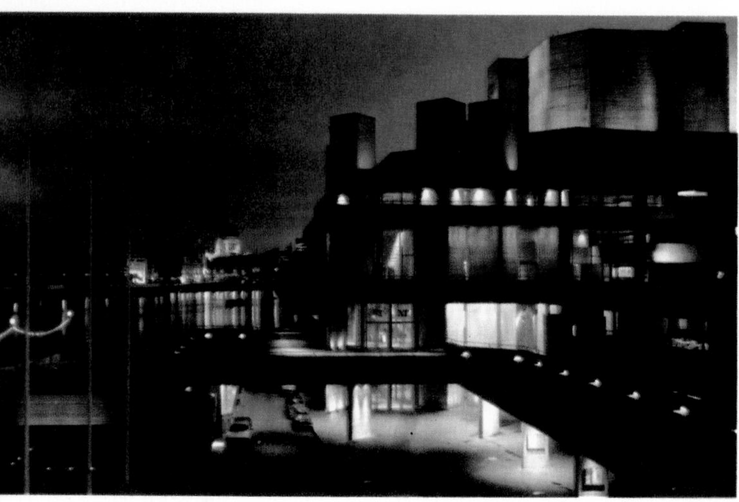

Cement & Concrete Assoc.

Above: An unusual design for an office block, with outer walls of plate glass. The greatest use of glass in building is for windows, doors, skylights, decorative blocks and internal fittings, but research into the use of glass as a structural material may produce types of glass suitable for use in load-bearing structural components. Glass fibres and glass reinforced concretes, composite materials containing glass, already have many uses in building, for example as roofing and cladding materials.

Left: The new National Theatre, London, a good example of the use of concrete, steel and glass in building.

Building Techniques

During the last 200 years the introduction of new construction materials, such as iron, steel and reinforced concrete, has necessitated the development of new techniques and machinery with which to handle them. The traditional crafts, such as bricklaying, joinery and scaffold erection, still play a vital role in modern building, but they have been joined by a wide range of newer skills such as excavator operation and those needed for building with concrete and for the assembly of prefabricated structures.

House construction
Two of the principal traditional types of house are the brick house and the timber-framed house. The brick house is popular in Britain and many other European countries, while the timber-framed house is more common in the US, Canada, Scandinavia, Australasia and many other parts of the world.

Picturepoint

Caledonian Mining Company

Redland Ltd.

Above: A stonemason at work during renovation of Bayonne Cathedral in France. Stonemasonry is one of the oldest building crafts, and in the Middle Ages masons were often responsible for the design and construction of buildings as well as for the cutting and working of the stone. The name 'freemason' is derived from 'freestone mason', a mason who worked with the type of stone known as *freestone* that was widely used in the construction of the cathedrals of the Middle Ages.

Left: Covering the roof of a house with interlocking concrete tiles. These are nailed to the horizontal softwood battens fixed to the roof on top of the waterproof underlay.

Right: A hydraulic excavator digging the foundation trenches of a house. The introduction of machinery, such as excavators, dump trucks, concrete mixers and powered hand tools, has helped to make the construction industry much more efficient.

Picturepoint

The brick-built house is built on concrete foundations, and a layer of concrete, the *oversite concrete*, is spread over the levelled ground within the foundations. The flooring at ground level is made either of concrete slabs or of wooden floorboards laid across stout timber beams called *floor joists*. Concrete floors are made by spreading a thick, level layer of concrete on top of the oversite concrete. This layer may be given a smooth top surface at the time of laying, or else it may be covered with a finishing layer or *screed* of finer concrete after it has hardened.

The ends of wooden floor joists may be fitted into the brickwork of the walls, or supported on metal *joist hangers*. The joist hangers, made of mild steel plate which is galvanized or coated with bitumen to prevent corrosion, are cemented into the brickwork and the ends of the joists are slotted into them. The joists are, where necessary, supported at intervals along their lengths by *sleeper walls*, low brick walls built on the oversite concrete and topped with a timber beam, the *sleeper plate*, on which the joists bear.

The floorboards, laid across the joists at right angles to them and nailed to them with rectangular-section *flooring nails*, are usually 25 mm (1 in) thick and have either plain edges or interlocking *tongue and groove* edges.

The *ceiling joists*, also fitted into the brickwork or carried on joist hangers, have the ceiling boards (usually made of plasterboard) nailed to their lower edges, and the floorboards for the upper floor (if there is one) are nailed across the top of them.

The timber frame of the roof is supported by the main load-bearing walls of the building. When the frame has been constructed, it is covered with a waterproof material such as bituminized felt and then horizontal rows of softwood strips or *battens*, to which the slates or tiles are nailed or clipped, are laid on top of the waterproofing and nailed to the *rafters* (the sloping members) of the roof frame.

The *partition walls*, walls which divide the structure into separate rooms but do not carry any of the structural load, may be made of brick, concrete blocks, or plasterboard fixed to timber battens. Door frames are generally made of wood, and window frames of wood, steel or aluminium. The apertures in the brickwork into which the doors and windows are fitted

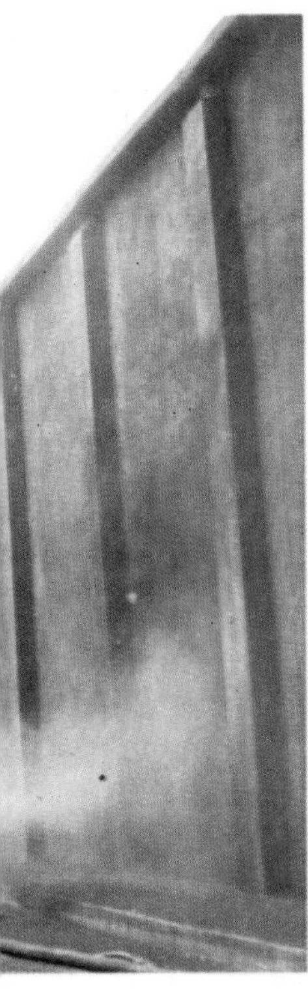

British Gypsum Ltd

Left: One way of constructing a concrete wall is to erect wooden *formwork*, which acts like a mould, and then pour concrete into it. A newer method, shown here, is to erect a lightweight metal framework, and then build up a wall by spraying it with a suitable concrete mixture.

Above: Another spraying technique. This picture shows plaster being sprayed on to a ceiling. After the ceiling has been covered with plaster, it is smoothed down in the normal way to produce an even surface. This system, *projection plastering*, is also used for plastering walls.

Below left: A layout for the plumbing and electrical systems in a small two-storey house. The pipes and wiring are ideally installed before the walls are plastered, so that they can be concealed under the plaster. In a modern house the pipes are made of copper, and the wiring has aluminium conductors.

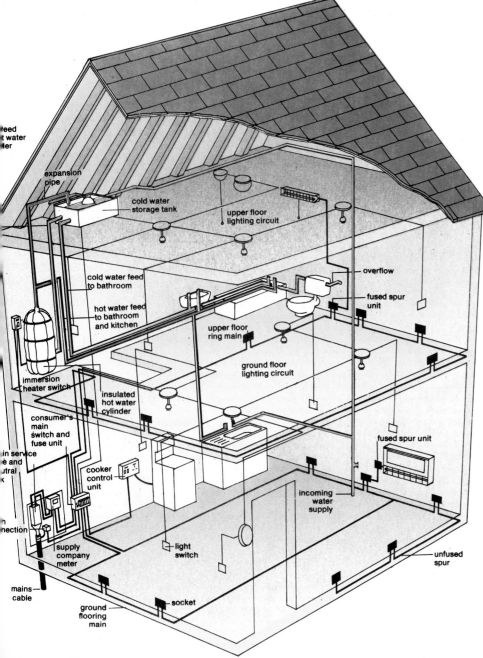

expansion pipe
cold water storage tank
upper floor lighting circuit
overflow
cold water feed to bathroom
hot water feed to bathroom and kitchen
fused spur unit
upper floor ring main
ground floor lighting circuit
immersion heater switch
insulated hot water cylinder
consumer's main switch and fuse unit
cooker control unit
fused spur unit
incoming water supply
supply company meter
light switch
unfused spur
mains cable
socket
ground flooring main

are spanned by *lintels*, beams of concrete, reinforced concrete, or galvanized steel. The lintels prevent the brickwork above the apertures from sagging or collapsing.

The traditional timber-framed house consists of a strong wooden framework constructed on concrete foundations, clad externally with timber or asbestos cement boards and panelled internally with timber or plasterboard. Many modern timber-framed houses, however, are finished externally in materials such as brick, stone and tiles, and the fact that they are timber-framed is not apparent from their appearance.

Timber-framed houses are no more of a fire risk in themselves than are brick or stone houses, and nowadays the timber used is often treated chemically to give it a certain amount of resistance to burning. When timber-framed construction is used for terraced rows of houses, however, there is a greater danger of a fire spreading from one dwelling to the next, and so adjacent houses are usually separated by continuous brick or concrete block walls to minimize this danger.

Timber-framed construction is well suited to prefabrication techniques; standardized components, such as frame subassemblies and cladding panels, are fabricated in a factory rather than on the construction site. This permits better control of the component quality, and reduces the actual construction time since most of the on-site work consists of simply assembling the prefabricated components. Timber-framed construction is used for industrial and commercial buildings as well as for housing, and structures three or four stories high are easily built by these techniques.

A recent development, used for both domestic and non-domestic buildings, is the use of *sprayed concrete construction* systems. In one such system a lightweight, prefabricated, galvanized metal framework is erected in concrete foundations, and mobile spraying equipment is used to spray a special lightweight concrete mixture on to the framework to form a strong, reinforced concrete structure.

In another spraying system, the concrete used contains tiny steel fibres which give it a very high impact strength, more than twice that of ordinary reinforced concrete. The first houses built by this particular system, in Nottinghamshire, England, have main load-bearing walls of sprayed concrete 115 mm (4.5 in) thick, covered with 40 mm (1.6 in) of polyurethane foam for heat insulation and a 40 mm sprayed concrete outer skin.

The concrete is mixed in a mobile machine which has an output of about 40 tonnes per hour, and the spraying machines used can each handle about 5 tonnes per hour. The total spraying time required for average-sized house is about 2½ days.

System building

The terms 'system building' and 'industrialized building' are widely used to describe building methods, particularly those used for high-rise developments, which are based on the use of standardized, factory-built components. The use of prefabricated building components is a major feature of the modern building industry, but it is not a new technique; prefabrication was being employed as long ago as the middle of the nineteenth century, notable examples from this period

Cement & Concrete Association

Cement & Concrete Association

BSC

Above left: Laying the reinforced concrete foundations for a large building. The steel reinforcement for the concrete has been positioned, and the concrete, brought to the site by mobile concrete mixers, is being poured in via chutes.

Above: Forming the floor slabs of a greenhouse with *no fines* concrete, a relatively lightweight concrete which contains coarse aggregates, such as stones, but no fine aggregates such as sand. The lack of fine aggregates means that empty spaces are left between the coarse aggregate particles, making the concrete lighter and improving its thermal insulation properties.

Left: The steel framework of the new wholesale flower market at Nine Elms, London. The high strength to weight ratio of steel makes it very useful for wide, unsupported spans such as those used in buildings of this type. The roof of this building was clad in glass reinforced plastic mouldings.

being Joseph Paxton's design for the Crystal Palace in London, and Isambard Kingdom Brunel's 1,000 bed prefabricated hospital for use in the Crimean War.

Extensive use is now made of standardized structural components made of timber, concrete and steel for both high-rise and low-rise buildings. One of the most important materials used in system building is prestressed concrete, and components made from this material include structural beams and columns, floor and roof slabs, stairways, wall cladding panels, and precast load-bearing wall units, which, in some systems, support the weight of the building without the need for a structural framework of columns and beams. Prefabricated external wall panels are supplied from the factory complete with decorative facings and, in many cases, with the windows already installed.

One of the most common forms of construction for high-rise buildings is the *core structure* type, in which the building is cantilevered out from a vertical central core of reinforced concrete. The foundations for this type of building usually take the form of a massive slab or *raft* of reinforced concrete.

The concrete core, which is hollow and is often used to house the lift shafts of the building, is then built up on the foundation slab. The steel or concrete structural frame of the building is then constructed on massive horizontal beams cantilevered out from the central core, and prefabricated wall and floor sections are fitted into the framework to complete the main structure.

Concrete structural components are often cast at the construction site. They may be cast at ground level, and then put into position on the structure when they have hardened, or else they may be cast *in situ*, that is, in the position in which they are to be used. The concrete, which may be freshly mixed on site or delivered 'ready mixed', is poured into moulds known as *formwork*, usually built up from wooden boards which are coated with a *release agent* that prevents them from sticking to the concrete.

A recently-developed alternative to wooden formwork is the use of glass reinforced concrete *permanent formwork*, which becomes the outer surface of the finished component. The permanent formwork is moulded to the required shape, size, colour and surface texture as specified by the customer, this work being carried out in a factory. The formwork is then delivered to the site, put into position, and the concrete is poured into it. Typical applications for permanent formwork include bridge parapets, columns, floors and structural beams.

Structural steel

The improved steel production methods introduced during the latter half of the nineteenth century made cheap, good quality steel available in sufficient quantities to make it a useful building material. By the end of that century steel had almost completely superseded cast and wrought iron for structural purposes, and its use was leading to the development of completely new concepts in building design.

Engineering works such as bridges were the first major applications of structural steel, notable early steel bridges being the Eads Bridge (1874) over the Mississippi River and the Glasgow Bridge (1878) over the Missouri. The concept of using a metal skeleton to carry the structural loads of a building, which made it easier to construct large buildings and meant that the windows in the outer walls (which were no longer load-bearing) could be made bigger, had been patented in 1848 by James Bogardus in the United States.

Bogardus used cast iron, but when steel became available it was soon being used for this type of construction by the builders of the first American skyscrapers in the late nineteenth century. One of the best-known examples of these early steel structures is Louis Sullivan's Guaranty Building (which later became the Prudential Building) in Buffalo, New York State, which was built in 1894.

Steel structural members are usually rolled girders, typically of 'I'-shaped cross-section. Prior to World War I the steelwork was connected together by means of bolts or rivets. During the war, however, the technique of electric arc welding was developed. The joints produced by welding are smaller and more efficient than those made by bolts or rivets, and arc welding is today the most important method used for joining steel in the construction industry.

The chief uses of steel in the building industry are for reinforcing concrete, for the construction of large steel structures such as bridges, and for the steel frames of buildings such as high-rise apartment or office blocks. The use of structural steel framework is not, however, restricted to large buildings. It is widely used for smaller buildings, including houses, small industrial and commercial premises, and low-rise apartment blocks.

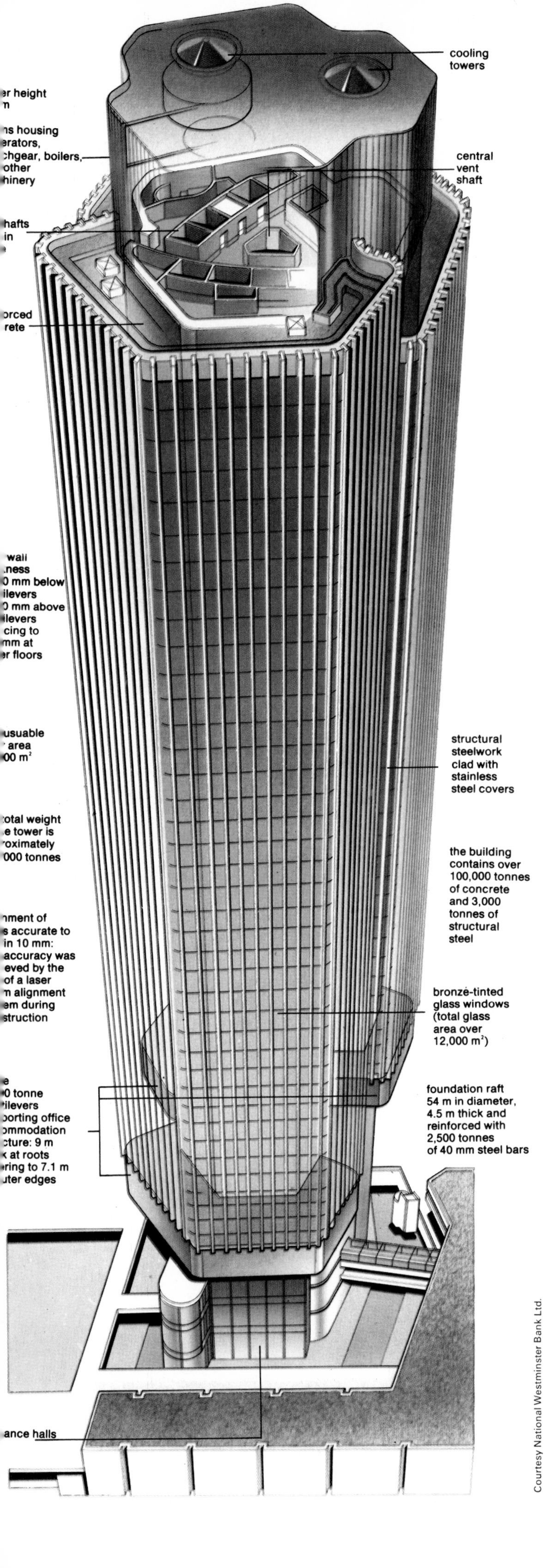

er height
n

ns housing
erators,
chgear, boilers,
other
hinery

hafts
in

orced
rete

wall
ness
0 mm below
ilevers
0 mm above
ilevers
cing to
mm at
er floors

usuable
area
00 m²

otal weight
e tower is
roximately
000 tonnes

nment of
s accurate to
in 10 mm:
accuracy was
eved by the
of a laser
n alignment
em during
struction

e
0 tonne
ilevers
porting office
ommodation
cture: 9 m
k at roots
ring to 7.1 m
uter edges

ance halls

cooling
towers

central
vent
shaft

structural
steelwork
clad with
stainless
steel covers

the building
contains over
100,000 tonnes
of concrete
and 3,000
tonnes of
structural
steel

bronze-tinted
glass windows
(total glass
area over
12,000 m²)

foundation raft
54 m in diameter,
4.5 m thick and
reinforced with
2,500 tonnes
of 40 mm steel bars

Courtesy National Westminster Bank Ltd.

National Westminster Bank

Redpath Dorman Long Ltd

Left: The structure of the new National Westminster Bank tower in Old Broad Street, London. The tower is 183 m (600 ft) tall, built around a central core of reinforced concrete, erected on a massive reinforced concrete foundation raft approximately 54 m (177 ft) in diameter and 4.5 m (14.8 ft) thick. The office floors are made of lightweight concrete built on a structural steel frame, the three linked wings of the office structure being supported by the cantilever structures at the bottom.

Top: Constructing the foundations of the tower in 1972. The reinforcement is in place, and the concrete is being poured in.

Above: An early stage in the construction of the tower, in February 1974. The supporting structure for the construction of the first cantilever is in place.

Right: A view from the base of the tower, showing two of the three supporting cantilevers.

Road Building

The invention of the wheel and the establishment of stable civilizations led to the development of the first paved road systems, the forerunners of our modern road networks. Although the great caravan routes between Europe and Asia and the system of roads that helped hold China together were older than the Roman Empire, it is the Roman roads that are best known. The Romans were first-class engineers and pioneered most of the elements of modern road construction: efficient drainage, a good foundation, an even surface, a planned network with well-sited 'service areas', and regular maintenance. When this regular maintenance ceased in the turbulent decline of the Roman Empire, the roads fell into decay and disuse. It is even claimed by some that the neglect of this vital road system contributed to the decline of that empire. Much of Europe, though, including England (but not Scotland) owes the outline of its road sýstem to the Romans.

The Middle Ages were a time of great neglect of the roads, but in the wake of the Renaissance and the voyages of discovery, however, came a new need for travel and for better roads. Towards the end of the eighteenth century the science of road building flourished in Britain as a result of the work of two Scottish engineers, Thomas Telford (1757-1834) and John Loudon McAdam (1756-1836), the latter giving his name to a system of road building ('tarmacadam', 'tarmac' or 'coated macadam') still the basis of most modern road construction. In Scotland earlier in the eighteenth century, General Wade had laid the foundations of today's Scottish road network in order to open up and pacify the Highlands.

This development in Great Britain was interrupted by the (historically speaking) brief interlude of the railway age, but the invention of the internal combustion engine late in the nineteenth century, and the advent of the motor car, created a great demand for good roads. Today an extensive and well-maintained road network is a basic necessity of life for every civilized community.

As we have seen, in European countries such as Britain the road networks acquired their present shapes over the centuries. However, the British *motorway* network, now over 2,500 km (1,550 miles) long, was not begun until the 1950s. The construction of a motorway is, therefore, a good example of all stages of modern road building.

Planning

Once the need for a particular motorway has been established, the precise route has to be mapped out. First a general survey is taken to avoid wherever possible centres of population, good agricultural land and areas of outstanding beauty, as well as areas of vital industry such as coal mining. Often the engineers will plot a number of alternative routes and examine each for the various advantages and disadvantages they present. Once the route has been chosen, a more detailed survey is made and the provisional line of the road is determined. This becomes the basis for the publication of a *draft scheme*, and it is at this stage that

Right: A road under construction near Nairobi, Kenya. The construction principles being used for this road are similar to those developed by the French engineer Pierre Trésaguet (1716-1796) and by Thomas Telford. A foundation of heavy stones is laid on to the levelled topsoil, and this is covered by a layer of smaller stones and a wearing surface of gravel.

Picturepoint

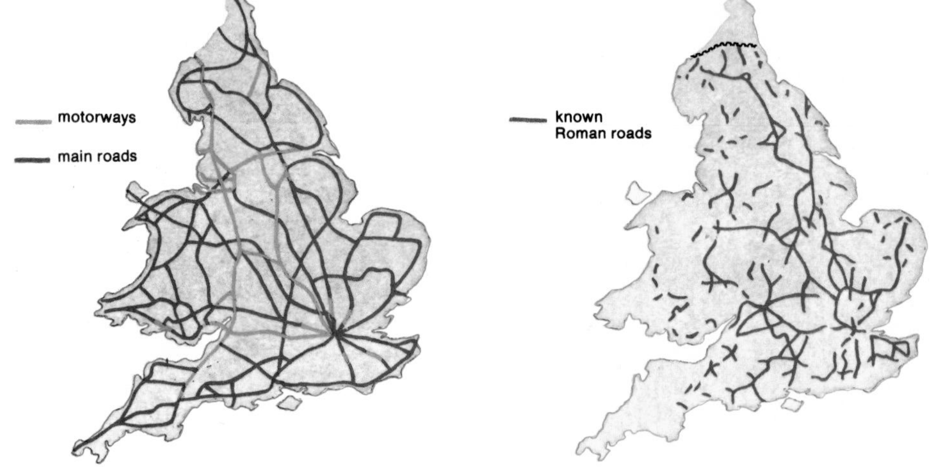

Below: The principal Roman roads of England and Wales, compared with the modern network of motorways. The motorway network serves the same purpose as did its Roman predecessor: to facilitate rapid travel between important locations.

Bottom: An early stage in the construction of the first section of the M1 (London to Leeds) motorway, the first road of its type to be built in Britain. This section, 88 km (55 miles) long, included 134 bridges and was completed in 1959. The construction time for this section was 19 months. Britain now has well over 2,500 km of motorway.

John Laing & Son Ltd.

objections may be lodged by parties affected. In some cases a public inquiry may be held, which can—and often does—bring about changes in the draft scheme.

Many hundreds of detailed working plans are now prepared, and the engineer in charge will have to co-ordinate these for the construction of the road itself, for the junctions and slip roads, and the bridges, underpasses, culverts and other structures needed. Indeed, the organization of this work is now so complex that special computer programs have been developed to handle it.

Earthworks and drainage

Depending on the type of terrain, site clearance may involve the removal of many obstacles or simply consist of the cutting of the original construction 'scar' across the countryside. This is followed by what is perhaps one of the biggest and least appreciated tasks of the road builder: the physical movement of enormous quantities of earth. Over 16 million tonnes of earth and rock were shifted, for example, in the construction of the first 88 km (55 miles) of the M1 motorway.

Valuable topsoil is always removed and saved for covering verges, slopes and central reservations. These areas, on modern motorways, have provided a new type of nature reserve for plants and wild life. In order to provide as even a profile as possible for the road, much 'muck shifting' consists of excavating earth from some parts of the line and shifting it to other parts to form embankments. This kind of working is called *cut and fill.*

Very early in the design of the road, consideration is given to the important subject of drainage. *Primary drainage* takes care of the run-off water from the entire pavement structure, and an extensive system of drains is laid well before the *formation level*—the platform of subsoil on which the road pavement is laid—is built up. Surface water from the pavement, once the road is built, is conducted to the sides of the road and thence into the drainage system by means of the *camber* of the road—its curved profile. The Romans ensured good drainage (and provided against flooding) by always raising their roads high above the ground on either side—possibly the origin of the word 'highway'.

The pavement

The road pavement is the actual structure of the road, built up on the subsoil which is usually called the *subgrade*. It consists of three principal parts—the *sub-base*, the *roadbase* and the *surfacing*. The primary purpose of the pavement is to distribute the traffic loads in such a way that the subgrade is not *deformed* (damaged). Permanent deformations would lead to unevenness in the road and therefore detract from its usefulness for fast and heavy traffic. A great deal of attention is, therefore, given to pavement design so that the right structure can be selected for each class of traffic and the anticipated traffic density. An additional function of

Top left: A heavy *bulldozer*, one of several types of earthmoving machinery used in road construction. These machines are driven by large diesel engines, and the blade position is controlled by hydraulic rams.

Left: A large *motor scraper*, which scrapes up earth and carries it away in the large scraper box mounted between the axles. As the vehicle is driven forward, the leading edge of the open-fronted box is pushed a little way into the ground so that earth is scooped up into the box. The original type of scraper, the *scraper trailer*, consists of a scraper box mounted on wheels and pulled along by a tractor.

Below left: Laying concrete pavement by means of *slip form machines*. The first machine in the 'train' (not shown here) spreads the concrete on the roadbase, and the second machine, the one in this picture, compacts it into a firm slab.

Below: Laying the wearing course of coated chippings on top of the base course of a flexible pavement. The wearing course is the road's surface.

Richard Costain Ltd.

John Laing & Son Ltd.

Asphalt & Coated Macadam Association

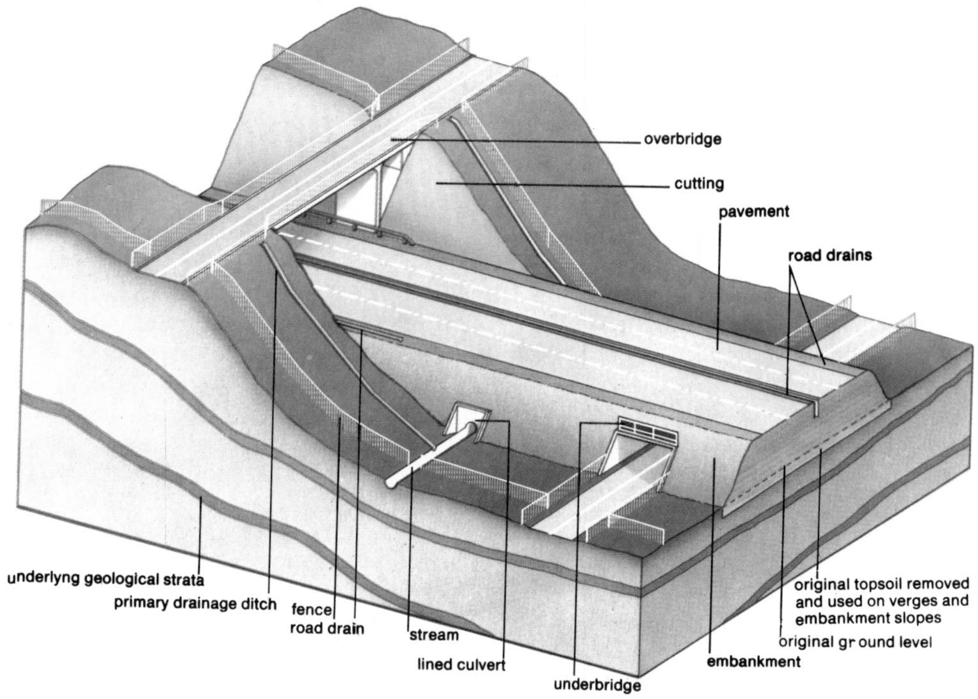

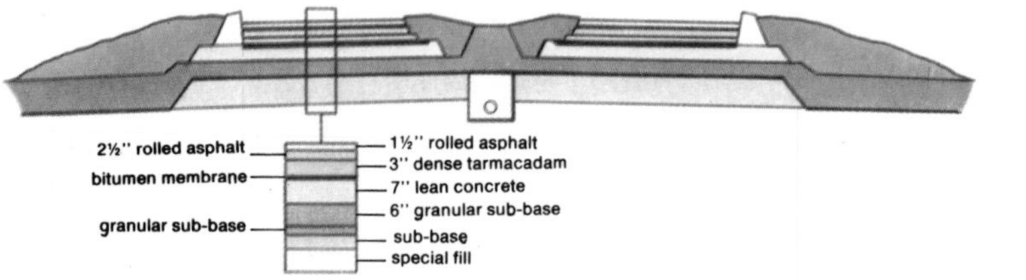

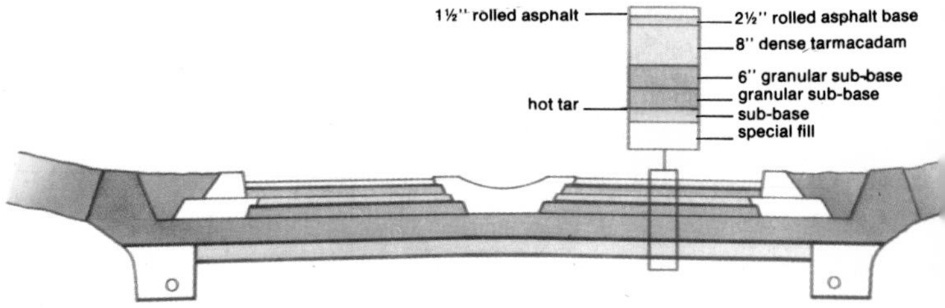

overbridge
cutting
pavement
road drains
underlyng geological strata
primary drainage ditch
fence
road drain
stream
lined culvert
underbridge
embankment
original topsoil removed and used on verges and embankment slopes
original gr ound level

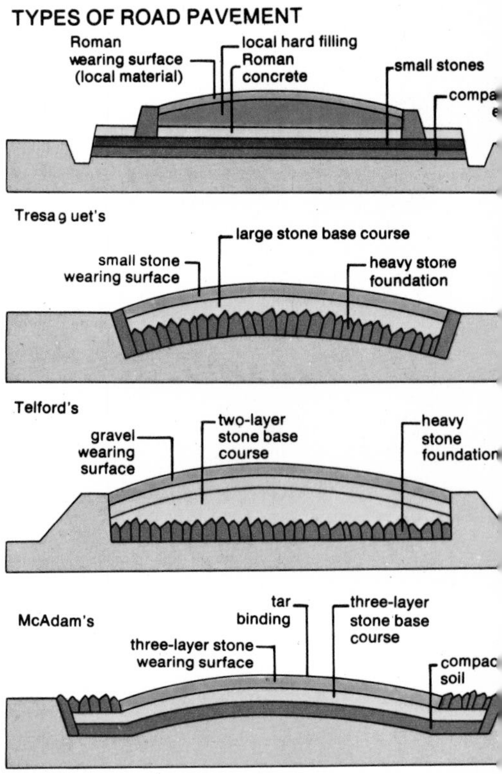

TYPES OF ROAD PAVEMENT

Roman wearing surface (local material)
local hard filling
Roman concrete
small stones
compa...

Tresag uet's
large stone base course
small stone wearing surface
heavy stone foundation

Telford's
gravel wearing surface
two-layer stone base course
heavy stone foundation

McAdam's
tar binding
three-layer stone base course
three-layer stone wearing surface
compac... soil

2½" rolled asphalt
bitumen membrane
granular sub-base
1½" rolled asphalt
3" dense tarmacadam
7" lean concrete
6" granular sub-base
sub-base
special fill

1½" rolled asphalt
hot tar
2½" rolled asphalt base
8" dense tarmacadam
6" granular sub-base
granular sub-base
sub-base
special fill

Courtesy of Michael Overman, *Roads, Bridges and Tunnels.* /Aldus Books

the surfacing is to prevent the entry of water to the road structure, allowing traffic to run smoothly in all weathers.

There are two types of pavement: *rigid*, consisting of concrete, and *flexible*, consisting of layers of various types of *coated materials*. These are composed of aggregates such as stone and sand, mixed with varying percentages of *tar* (extracted from coal) or *bitumen* (derived from oil), and are delivered hot to the site. They are variously known as *tarmacadam*, *bitumen macadam*, *hot rolled asphalt*, and *dense tar surfacing*; all are often referred to as *black top*.

For both types of pavement the sub-base is much the same: a layer of granular material such as stones or gravel laid upon the compacted formation and then itself compacted to form a firm base for the next stage. This, in the case of rigid construction, is a roadbase of *lean cement concrete*, a concrete containing a relatively small percentage of cement. The same material is sometimes used to provide the base for flexible surfacing, but fully flexible construction calls for a roadbase of coated materials, laid (often in several layers or *courses*) by a mechanical finisher and compacted by rollers. In some instances a roadbase of coated materials is also used for rigid pavements: this is known as *composite construction* and has been used on many motorways and airfield runways in Europe. The base is a vital part of the pavement, and it is rightly said that 'a road is only as good as its base'.

For rigid construction the final slabs of concrete are now laid. The roadbase is covered with plastic sheeting, steel mesh reinforcement is laid on top (this may be omitted if the concrete road is not carrying heavy traffic), and the concrete is poured to a thickness of at least 250 mm (10 in). Although the concrete, to allow for expansion and contraction, is poured in sections called *bays*, and the joints are then filled with a flexible and waterproof bituminous compound, the whole operation is highly mechanized, using a complex *concrete train* proceeding slowly along the road.

Flexible pavements can use the principle of *stage construction*. Relatively thin layers of coated materials are laid down as and when traffic conditions demand, the whole becoming one strong and homogenous pavement. Normally, the surfacing laid on the roadbase will consist of a *base course* averaging from 45 to 60 mm (1.8 to 2.4 in) thickness, followed by a final *wearing course* which may be between 25 and 40 mm (1 and 1.6 in) thick. Both are prepared to stringent specifications, and laid with a mechanical finisher to closely controlled levels. The stone for the wearing course is carefully selected to ensure a skid-resistant surfacing and, especially on motorways, coated chippings (hard stones with a coating of bitumen) are applied for extra resistance to skidding. Various types of road rollers (smooth-wheeled, pneumatic-tyred or vibrating) are used to compact each layer while it is hot.

The finishing touches

Before the motorway can be opened to traffic the lane markings, signs, barriers, emergency telephones and other equipment have to be installed. White lane

Top: A sectional drawing of a short length of completed road, showing some common construction features, and cross-sections of some important types of pavement structure from Roman times to the present day. The composite pavement shown here is similar to a flexible pavement but incorporates a lean concrete roadbase like that of a rigid pavement. Other composite types use a roadbase of coated materials with a concrete surface.

Right: The bridge over the River Avon near Bristol, England, carrying the M5 motorway which runs from Birmingham to Exeter.

Picturepoint

C.O.I.

Redland Ltd.

Left: The M62 motorway in northern England divides into two to bypass a farm in the Pennine hills. The 53 km (33 mile) long M62 connects the busy industrial regions of Lancashire and Yorkshire.

Above: Applying an anti-skid road surface. The road is first coated with a binder consisting of bitumen and epoxy resin, and when the binder has cooled to road temperature an aggregate of calcined bauxite is spread over it. The coating takes between two and five hours to set hard enough to be driven on. It has a very high skid resistance even when wet, and is often used at junctions and other hazardous sites.

Consulting Engineers: Howard Humphreys & Sons

Braham Millar Group Ltd.

Above: The M56/M63 motorway interchange near Manchester, England. The design of interchanges such as this one is nowadays aided by the use of specially-developed computer programs.

Left: A *road planer*, a machine which strips off the worn surface layer of a road when a new wearing course is to be laid. The road surface is heated to about 1,000°C (1,830°F) by a propane-fired heater unit, and broken up by rotary cutters. The loose material is scraped up and conveyed to the truck backed up behind the planer. The machine is self-propelled, and is powered by a 56 kW (75 bhp) four cylinder diesel engine.

markings on British motorways are generally provided with reflecting road studs known as 'cat's eyes' and these may be coloured red, yellow or green for special purposes. A variety of directional and warning signs must be provided, and many of the latter are now centrally controlled and can display electronically a range of appropriate warnings and instructions.

Metal crash barriers are erected along the central reservations and at other critical points. On urban stretches motorway lighting is installed. Emergency telephones are spaced at reasonable intervals, and all the appropriate wiring has to be accommodated in waterproof conduits along or under the sides of the road. At the same time, the slip roads have to be similarly fitted out and advance directional signs pointing to the motorway have to be erected over a wide area of the feeder road network.

Maintenance

The opening of the motorway is by no means the end of the story; in some ways the highway engineer's work has only just begun. Planned regular maintenance of both the fabric of the road and the many ancillary installations is essential to protect the original investment and to give a long and useful life to the road.

Maintenance includes such items as grass, tree and bush cutting to keep the line of the road clear and visible, the cleaning and repair of signs and lamps, and the general cleaning of the road. Winter maintenance includes snow clearing, gritting and salting. The maintenance of the actual road structure may consist of simple patching, or of *surface dressing* whole stretches to restore skid resistance. This is done by spraying tar or bitumen on to the road, spreading stone chippings, and then rolling it. For more lasting maintenance, the road is provided with a relatively thin overlay of coated materials (sometimes the existing surface is heated or burned off), which renews the surface and adds strength to the whole of the road structure.

Tunnels

Some of the earliest tunnels constructed were those connected with supplies of water. Long before the birth of Christ *qanaats* were used in many Middle Eastern countries to supply water for irrigation and domestic purposes. The qanaat system of winning water (still in use today) employs a tunnel driven more or less horizontally into a wadi bed or similar formation until it encounters water-bearing strata. The first such tunnels were, however, relatively short, and it was not until Roman times that tunnels of any appreciable length were engineered. These formed part of the aqueduct systems that carried water from distant springs to Rome and other cities of the Empire.

The development of tunnelling

Modern tunnelling owes its conception and birth to the canal era that began with the commissioning of the Duke of Bridgewater's canal in northwest England in 1761. The great problem that all canal engineers, from James Brindley (1716-72) onwards, had to face was the lack of water at the summit where a canal passed from one catchment to another. Seldom was the amount available sufficient for the operation of the long chain of locks that would have been needed to carry it over the top. At the start of the era, experience in the construction of tunnels was very limited and consequently the early canals tended to follow the contours of the countryside.

Howard Humphreys & Sons

Thyssen

Left: The cutting head of a Thyssen FLP 35 full face hard rock tunnelling machine. The 4.2 m (13.8 ft) diameter head rotates at 4.5 rpm, and the machine has a forward thrust of 400 tonnes. The machine is guided with the aid of a laser unit positioned 150 to 300 m (492 to 984 ft) from the cut face.

Above: The tunnelling shield used in driving one of the twin tunnels on the Newport to Monmouth trunk road in Wales. The tunnel face was blasted out 1.2 m (4 ft) at a time; after each blasting the shield was moved forward to support the roof, then the concrete lining was put into place behind it.

Below: The rotating cutting head, mounted on a hydraulically-controlled, movable boom, of a Thyssen Titan roadheader tunnelling machine. The machine moves forward on crawler tracks, and the boom moves the cutting head across the entire area of the tunnel face. The water jets suppress the dust.

Thyssen

This meant that routes were long and circuitous, and as competition between canal companies increased so did the need to provide shorter and more economical routes. This required the increasing use of tunnels, and as experience was gained so construction methods and techniques improved. The old Harecastle tunnel built by Brindley on the Trent and Mersey Canal in England, for example, took 11 years to construct, but when the second Harecastle tunnel was built some 60 years later only three years were needed.

But even before that tunnel was completed, in 1827, there was evidence that the days of the canal were numbered. In 1825 the opening of the Stockton and Darlington Railway heralded the dawn of the railway age, and in the following 25 years, in a great explosion of activity, the old canal system was reduced to obsolescence by this new and exciting form of transport. The 'navigators' who had built the canals were transformed into the railway 'navvies' of the nineteenth century, bringing with them the skill and experience in the construction of tunnels which was as essential to the railways as it had been to canals.

In the construction of these early tunnels there was little in the way of machinery available and most of the excavation was done by hand, the spoil being loaded into skips and hauled from the tunnel by ponies. If the tunnel was long, a number of shafts would be sunk so that extra faces could be opened up and the rate of progress increased. Spoil was hauled to the surface by horse *gins* (hoists) and removed by horse and cart. At Box tunnel, on the Paddington to Bristol railway line, I. K. Brunel used a force of over 4,000 men and 300 horses working night and day. The cost was high even by modern standards, amounting to some £6.5 million.

Another railway tunnel constructed at about the same time was the Woodhead tunnel through the Pennines, which is

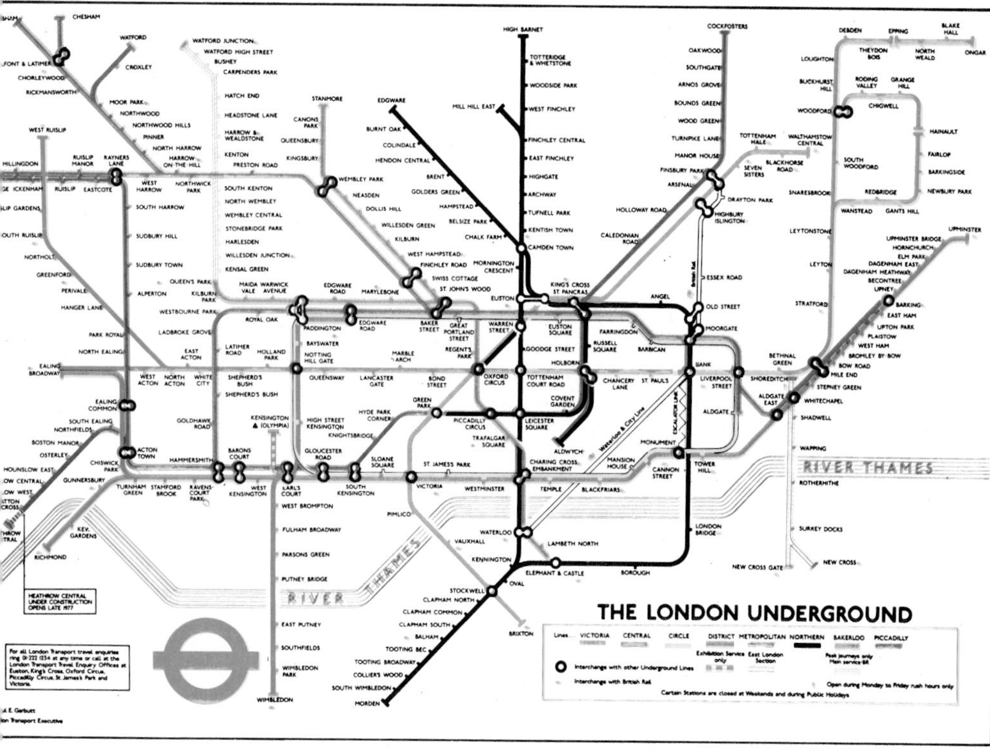

Markham & Co Ltd

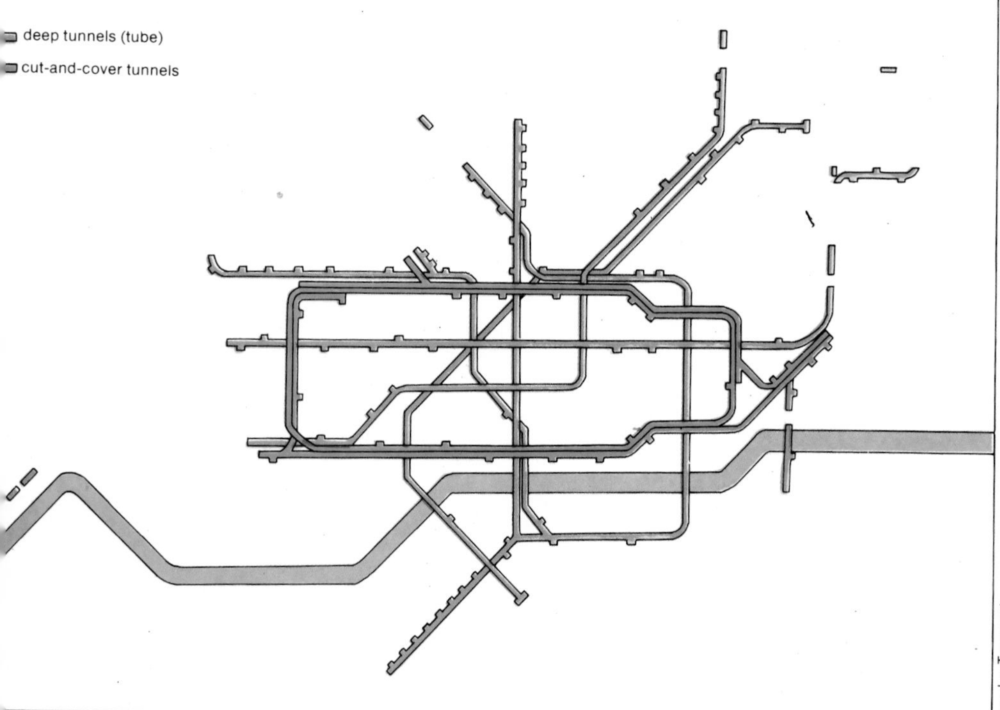

London Transport

London Transport

Thyssen

Left and below left: In 1977 London Transport was operating over 400 km (250 miles) of railway, of which some 122 km (76 miles) were in bored tunnels. 35 km (22 miles) were in sub-surface tunnels built by 'cut-and cover' tunnelling, which involves digging a large trench and then roofing it over.

Above: A Markham soft-ground tunnelling machine.

Below: The charges used in blasting a tunnel face are sealed in place with gel-filled ampoules. These retain the blast within the rock, and the explosion atomizes the gel into a fine mist which absorbs the dust and fumes.

more than twice the length of the Box tunnel. At one time nearly 1,500 labourers were employed on the project, driving the tunnel through the treacherous millstone grits, shales, soft red sandstones, slate and clay that were encountered. In these circumstances injuries and deaths were frequent occurrences.

One of the first tunnels to be built under a river was constructed between Rotherhithe and Wapping in London. In 1805, the Thames Archway Company first proposed the tunnel, but the venture did not develop and was abandoned in 1808. However, it was revived in 1823 following the invention by Marc Isambard Brunel, the father of Isambard Kingdom Brunel, of the first ever *tunnelling shield* in 1818. The tunnelling shield supports the surrounding earth during excavation, and is moved forward as work progresses.

For a while good progress was made, but in 1827 a great inflow of mud and water occurred, bringing construction to a halt. By the end of 1827, as the result of great determination and unremitting labour, the problems were overcome and work restarted. To celebrate this triumph over disaster, in the true spirit of the age, a banquet was staged under the river at which a company of 50 dined and listened to music provided by the Coldstream Guards. Unfortunately, mounting costs and further trouble led to more delay and the tunnel was not completed until 1843.

The idea of a tunnel beneath the English Channel to link England and France was first proposed in 1802 by a French engineer called Albert Mathieu, but little happened until 1865 when Sir John Hawkshaw carried out borings and took samples in St Margaret's Bay and at sea. Further sampling from the seabed was carried out in 1875-76, and in the late 1870s pilot headings, each a mile long, were driven out to sea on both sides of the channel using Colonel Beaumont's newly-invented mechanical tunnelling machine. In 1882, however, British fears that the French would use the tunnel to mount an invasion brought work to a halt, and although various studies were made subsequently at different times no further work was undertaken until 1973. Further exploratory drives were then again made from each shore but rapidly escalating cost estimates led in 1975 to a further cessation of work. A new proposal, put forward in 1977, suggested that the tunnel should be funded by the European

CONSTRUCTION OF HONG KONG CROSS-HARBOUR TUNNEL

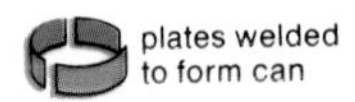

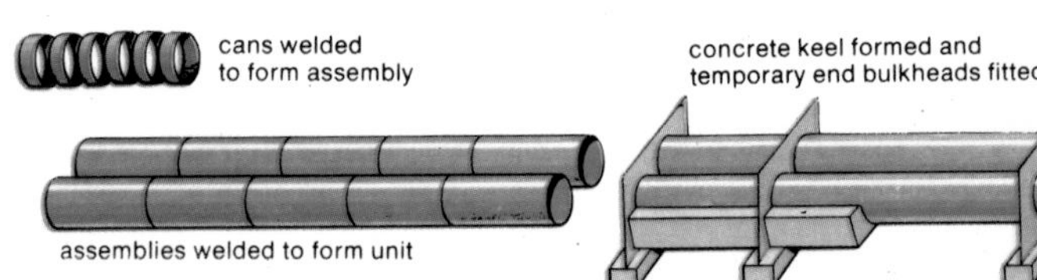

Richard Costain Ltd

Courtesy of Richard Costain Ltd

Thyssen

Economic Community.

By the end of the nineteenth century construction techniques had improved immeasurably, helped greatly by new machinery then becoming available. Sweden in particular pioneered the use of compressed air tools and excavators which could be used underground where ventilation was poor.

Above: The Hong Kong Cross-Harbour Tunnel, which was built by the *immersed tube* method. The twin-tube tunnel sections, which were up to 114 m (374 ft) long and made of steel lined with reinforced concrete, were fabricated on shore, floated out into the harbour, and then sunk into place on the harbour bed. The ends of the tubes were sealed with steel plates, which were cut away when the sections were joined together.

Above right: A tunnel driven under the North Sea during exploration of the coal deposits off the coast of north-east England.

Right: The entrance to one of the two tunnels of the 28 km (17 mile) Chesapeake Bay bridge-tunnel scheme linking Virginia with Maryland. The scheme consists of a raised causeway incorporating two bridges and two tunnels that provide navigation channels for shipping.

Below: Two of the fan units which provide ventilation for the tunnels of the Naples ring road system.

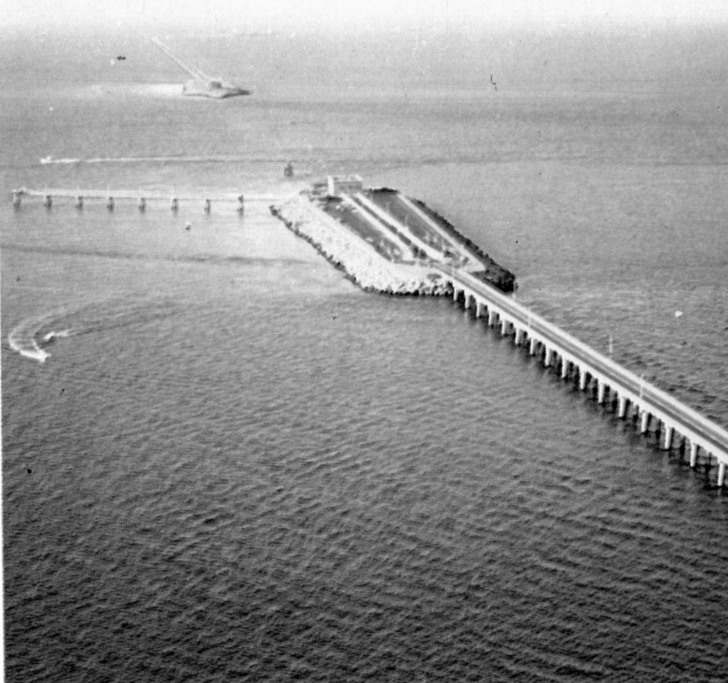
Photri

Modern tunnelling

Most of the hazards encountered in tunnelling arise because the ground conditions encountered have not been predicted. Before a tunnel is built, detailed geological surveys are carried out by means of boreholes and trial excavations, but as the samples obtained by such methods are minute compared with the volume of material which can affect the tunnel, difficult ground conditions are not always revealed. Typical problems include areas of broken and shattered rock in an otherwise unbroken rock formation due to folding or faulting. The presence of water in such faults is a further hazard which may lead to sudden and uncontrollable inflows, especially if the tunnel is deep or subaqueous.

Sometimes small-size pilot tunnels are driven so that the strata can be examined at first hand, but the driving of such a tunnel can itself be a hazardous undertaking. Nowadays the use of pilot tunnels is less frequent but some indication or warning of dangerous conditions can be obtained by probing ahead of the face.

For construction purposes tunnels can be divided into two types, those in rock and those in soft ground. Tunnels in rock are generally excavated by drilling and blasting. At one time, in the case of tunnels with a large cross-sectional area, a top heading was often driven both to provide a working platform and to permit the placing of roof support with the minimum lapse of time after excavation. Even in badly-jointed rock the roof will stand unsupported for a while, but if support is not provided quickly rock falls are bound to occur. This is because the excavation of a tunnel leads to some readjustment of the stresses in the rock that are caused by the weight of the material above it.

Woods of Colchester

Support is generally provided by means of steel arches and timber lagging, but reinforced concrete arches are also used. A recent development is the use of *shotcrete*. This is a carefully-graded concrete sprayed, at high pressures, onto the exposed faces of the formation as soon as possible after excavation. Many tunnels in sound rock, however, require no support at all for much of their length, even in some cases for all of it, and in such cases *full face* work is now adopted.

This method of tunnelling has been made possible by improvements to the lighting and ventilation of tunnels so that heavy excavators and dump trucks can be used. Drilling is carried out from hydraulically-controlled rigs and blasting is

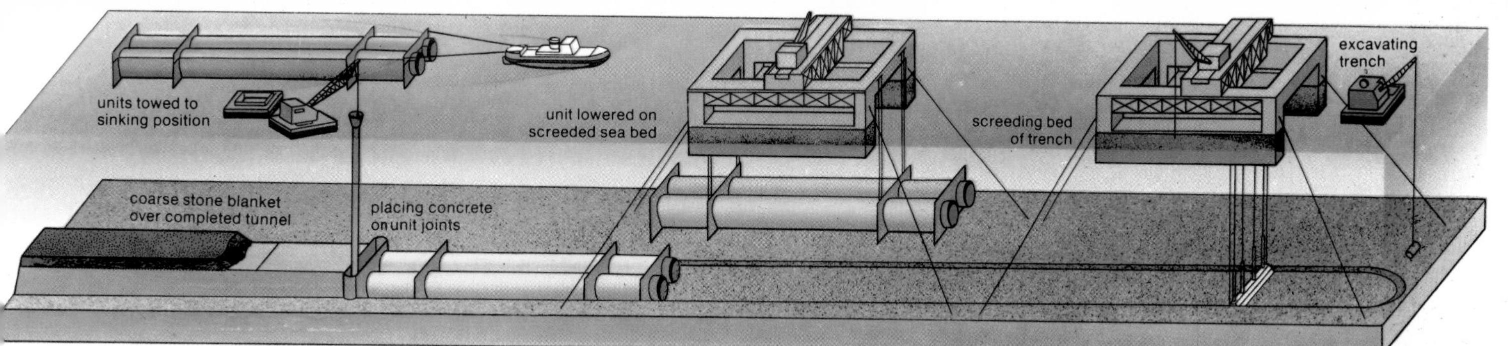

Above: The construction of the Hong Kong Cross-Harbour Tunnel. The prefabricated steel tube sections of the tunnels were sunk on to a bed consisting of a screed of crushed granite laid in a trench dredged across the harbour bed. The construction began in 1969, and the tunnel was opened in 1972.

Below: An artist's impression of the construction of the proposed rail tunnel under the English Channel, and (bottom) the likely route and section of such a tunnel. The proposal envisages three parallel tunnels; two single-track railway tunnels with a smaller service tunnel linked to them every 250 m (820 ft). The tunnels would be some 98 km (32 miles) long, about 70 km (23 miles) being below the sea.

Right: The British end of the Channel Tunnel workings. Work was halted in 1975 because of escalating costs, but may be restarted with EEC funding.

Courtesy of Channel Tunnel Association Library

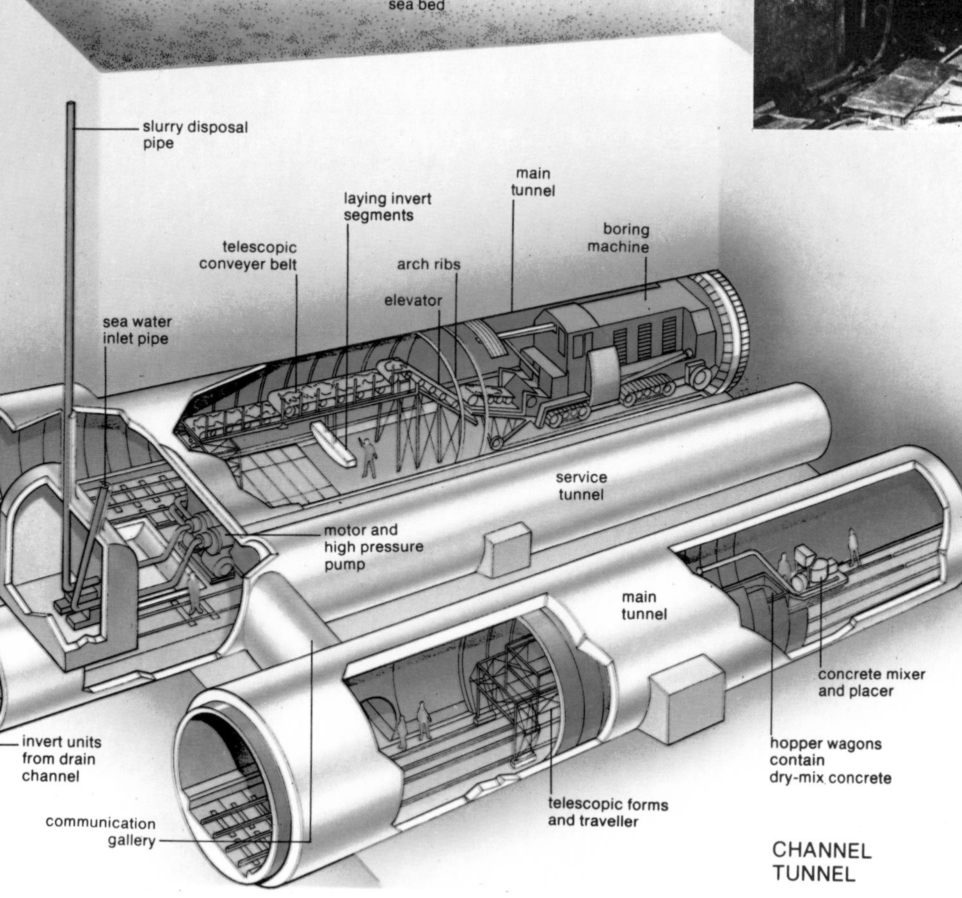

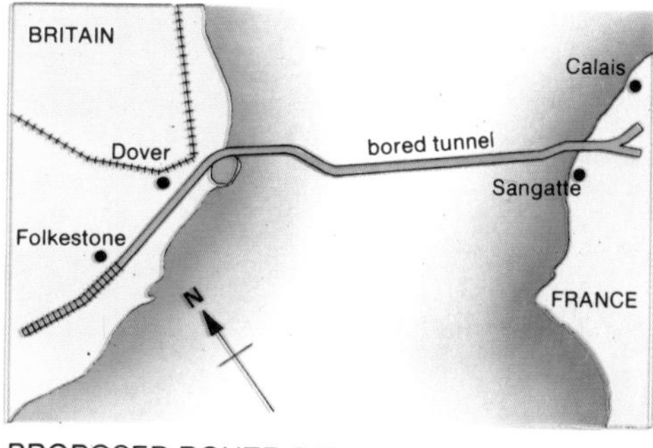

PROPOSED ROUTE OF CHANNEL TUNNEL

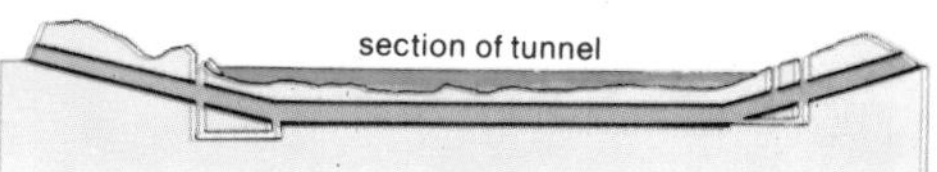

now a well-developed and very accurate operation. A thin cover of shotcrete is frequently applied to prevent surface deterioration due to weathering and to reduce the risk of accidents.

Tunnels in soft ground require a different technique. In the past, excavation has been carried out by using hand-held pneumatic tools, and the spoil loaded mechanically on to railway skips. The tunnel must be supported as close to the face as possible, and segmental cast iron or precast concrete rings are used for this. The face is advanced by, for instance, about 60 cm (2 ft), and a ring erected before further excavation is undertaken. These methods are now however being replaced by the use of tunnelling machines. In the case of smaller tunnels such machines frequently have a single, large, rotating head equipped with cutters, but for larger tunnels a *roadheader*, a machine with a rotating cutting head mounted on a movable, hydraulically-controlled boom, is used.

In situ concrete provides a frequently-adopted alternative to the use of precast segmental rings. Specially-made steel formwork is used in such cases, but temporary support may still have to be provided by means of steel rings. After erection or placing, both precast and in situ linings are 'tightened' by injecting cement grout between them and the formation so that all voids are filled. This is done to prevent deterioration and loosening of the strata which might impose a high loading and lead to failure of the lining.

In very bad ground such as silty gravels, and especially if the tunnel is below water, compressed air may have to be used to prevent inflows and to support the face. Alternatively, the formation may be sealed with cement or chemical grouts.

Another method of construction, especially for subaqueous tunnels in soft material at comparatively shallow depths, is the *immersed tube* method. It was first suggested at the end of the eighteenth century by Trevithick, but has only recently become practical. It involves the construction on dry land of sections of tunnel, which are then floated into position and sunk into a dredged trench which is subsequently backfilled with sand. When all the sections are in position and the ends are above water level, the joints between the sections are sealed and the tunnel is pumped dry ready for internal finishing.

So the science of tunnelling has advanced from the early qanaats, using lining rings of baked clay, to the elaborate structures of today. The Seikan railway tunnel in Japan, linking two of Japan's larger islands, is probably the most notable currently under construction. On completion, scheduled now for 1982, it will be nearly 54 km (33.6m) long and 9.6 m (31.5 ft) in diameter, and will be up to 100 m (328 ft) beneath the seabed with a depth of water of up to 140 m (460 ft).

Bridges

Modern industrial and developing economies depend upon increasingly sophisticated overland transport systems, in which bridges play a vital part. Bridge builders have always been faced with the same set of basic questions. Will the span be great enough? Will the structure be economical and durable enough? Will it bear the loads of the prevailing transport system? The answers to these questions can only be reached after computing many complex equations in which the main variables are the bridge types, the differing materials available and their relative abilities to withstand the differing types of stress that they encounter during use.

The *beam bridge*, basically a flat beam supported at each end, is the simplest type of bridge. Each end of the beam exerts a force directly downwards, and in the beam itself the *bending moment* (weight x distance from support) increases towards the middle of the span. The upper surface of the beam will be *compressed*; the lower surface will be in *tension*, or stretched. The strength of a beam will depend on its ability to withstand these opposing forces created by its own weight plus any applied load. Within certain limits, the deeper the beam is, the greater its strength will be.

Cantilever bridges work like a pair of springboards facing each other. The shore ends are anchored down and the main weight is carried by supports placed a certain distance from each anchored end. The bending moments in the projecting parts increase towards each tip. The forces in the cantilevered part are thus in *tension* on the upper surface and in *compression* in the lower zone of the material. If the tips cannot be made to meet because the distance to be spanned is too great, they may be linked by a short *suspended span*.

The *arch* works by converting the *downward* force of gravity acting on the material into an *outward* thrust at each end. The forces within the arch 'ring' are thus exclusively those of compression, and the *abutments* must be strong enough to maintain this force by holding the end of the arch in. In multi-span arches, some of the outward thrust of each arch may be taken up by the opposing thrusts from the arches on either side.

The converse of the arch is the *suspension* principle, where the road is hung from cables which are exclusively in *tension*. The weight of the bridge is taken by the towers which hold the cables aloft. The extreme ends of the cable have to be anchored to maintain a downward and outward force. Much attention has been paid to the problem of stiffening the roadway itself to counteract the effect of wind-induced oscillations and of *torsional* (twisting) forces caused by uneven loading of the deck.

Few modern bridges are built using only one of these basic forms. New combinations are always being sought—the great Swiss designer Robert Maillart, for example, integrated the concrete beam and arch in original and complex ways. *Cable-stayed* bridges combine the cantilever and the girder principles. The *box girder* principle used in this type of bridge has also found wide application in

G. F. Allen/Bruce Coleman Ltd

Above: The Postbridge, an ancient bridge over the East Dart River on Dartmoor in southwest England. This bridge, which possibly dates back to the thirteenth century, is a *clapper bridge*, consisting of several slabs of granite resting on heavy stone piers. The basic design is of prehistoric origin.

Below: A primitive form of suspension bridge, made from cane and liana, spanning the Tsau River in the Central Highlands of New Guinea. Suspension bridges made from these and similar materials are to be found in many parts of the world, including South America, Africa and South-East Asia.

Right: Many of the bridges built by the Romans are still standing today. This is the Ponte Sant' Angelo over the Tiber in Rome, built in AD 136 during the reign of the Emperor Hadrian. It is one of the eight masonry bridges (of which six remain) built in Rome between 179 BC and AD 370.

Michael Holford

Brian Coles/Bruce Coleman Ltd

Michael Holford

continuous beam bridges (where each span of a multi-span beam bridge acts with a cantilever effect on its neighbours), and also in providing the roadway deck for suspension bridges.

Bridge development

From Roman times to 1779 (the date of the world's first iron bridge at Coalbrookdale in Shropshire, England), the development of bridges had been the story of the masonry arch. The main improvements over that period included the use of ribbed arches, a progression from semicircular shape to shallower, segmental and elliptical profiles, and the lightening of the *spandrels* (the areas above each 'shoulder' of an arch) by pierced channels. Iron worked well enough in compression for several notable arches of 60 m (200 ft) and more to be built, such as Rennie's Southwark Bridge (1819) over the Thames. Telford even proposed a single 183 m (600 ft) span of cast iron to replace the ancient London Bridge.

The advent of steel, however, offered much greater possibilities, both for the creation of much larger spans and for the use of the cantilevering method of construction. The first great steel arch bridge was the celebrated Illinois and St Louis bridge of 1874, which was designed by Captain James Eads. The *fixed end* principle used by Eads, however, was superseded by the *two-hinged* arch pioneered by Gustave Eiffel in his wrought iron Barabit Viaduct of 1884. The hinges at abutments allow the slight temperature-induced movements in the bridge to take place without causing extra stresses. The greatest such arch is

Above: The Pont Valentré which spans the River Lot at Cahors in southwest France. This bridge, a good example of a medieval fortified bridge, was completed in 1355 after almost 50 years of building. A large number of fortified bridges were built in Europe during the Middle Ages.

Below left: The Iron Bridge over the River Severn at Caolbrookdale in Shropshire, England, the first large iron bridge in the world. The original design for the bridge was prepared by Thomas Farnolls Pritchard, but this was modified by Abraham Darby, who built it in 1779.

Below: London Bridge since 1500. The first three drawings show the bridge in the sixteenth, seventeenth and eighteenth centuries; the fourth shows John Rennie's London Bridge, built in 1831 about 55 m (180 ft) upstream from the old bridge, and the fifth shows the present bridge, which was opened in 1973.

the 503 m (1,650 ft) span Syndey Harbour Bridge, opened in 1932, itself modelled on the 1916 prototype *through arch*, the Hell Gate in New York.

Concrete, with its enormous strength in compression, also offered possibilities for the construction of arches, though their construction usually required more *falsework* or *centering* (temporary supporting framework) than did steel arches. Maillart pioneered the delicate and economical *stiffened slab arch*, using very thin reinforced concrete for the arch-ring. Freyssinet in France applied pre-stressing techniques to through arches, for example over the Seine at St Pierre de Vouvray and in a design for a 1,000 m (3,281 ft) structure over the Hudson river. Interestingly, one of the most recent concrete arches, the 305 m (1,000 ft) Gladesville Bridge in Sydney, Australia, was built by the ancient construction technique of centering, though with sophisticated precast hollow box *voussoirs* (wedge-shaped sections put together to form an arch) post-tensioned together.

In the development of beam bridges the designers' main concern was to evolve beams and girders of sufficient depth with the least possible weight. The *truss*, an open framework of short struts, was first developed in timber, though early designs often incorporated an arch rib. Development was particularly rapid in eighteenth and nineteenth century America where designs were rapidly modified in iron, then steel, to provide the many short-span bridges required by the burgeoning railway systems.

Two British beam bridges by Robert Stephenson are of particular interest. The High Level Bridge across the Tyne at Newcastle, opened in 1849 and still in use, is a fine example of the *bowstring girder* principle. Though the main structural element in each of the six spans is a wrought iron arch, the outward thrust at each end is taken up by members tensioned betweem them like the string of a bow. The complete unit thus rests directly downwards on its piers, a principle later employed in many steel and concrete bridges.

The Britannia Bridge, opened in 1850, was the prototype box girder bridge. Though Stephenson only had rivets and 46 x 13 cm (18 x 0.5 in) wrought iron strips as basic materials, he planned four spans, each composed of twin rectangular boxes, through which the London to Holyhead railway would run over the Menai Straits. The complete spans were constructed on shore then floated out and hoisted into place. The spans, once in position were further locked together so that the bridge became a continuous structure.

The continuous box girder has come into prominence as the most important structural principle of recent years. Modern box girders, however, differ from Stephenson's in that they are made of steel plate, are welded together, use the top of the box as the running surface and are often aerodynamically shaped. Since the strength of the box girder derives principally from its shape, any buckling of the thin steel plate used would be dangerous, and stiffening *stringers* are welded inside the sections to prevent distortion. The box girder concept allows the engineer to work economically by designing much closer to the maximum possible stresses of steel, though the collapse of the West Gate Bridge in Mel-

Science Museum

Left: Isambard Kingdom Brunel's wrought iron railway bridge across the River Tamar at Saltash in Cornwall, completed in 1859. This picture, taken in 1858, shows the second of the two 142 m (465 ft) main spans being raised into position. The outward thrust of the arched top tube of each span is contained by the curved suspension chains below it.

Spectrum

Below: The Forth Railway Bridge, a steel cantilever bridge designed by Benjamin Baker and Sir John Fowler. The bridge, which was opened in 1890, has three main towers carrying the cantilevers, with a short section called a *suspended span* between each of them.

Picturepoint Ltd

Left: The Nosslach Bridge in Austria, a reinforced concrete arch road bridge. The first concrete bridge was built in 1840 over the Garonne Canal in France, and other early concrete bridges were built in Germany, Switzerland and the US during the second half of the nineteenth century. Concrete is strong in compression but weak in tension, so until the advent of steel-reinforced concrete at the end of the century the arch was the only feasible form of construction for concrete bridges. The first large reinforced concrete bridge was built by Francois Hennebique over the River Ourthe in Belgium in 1905.

Right: The Europe Bridge near Innsbruck, Austria, is a steel box girder bridge carried on reinforced concrete piers. There are six continuous spans, of 81 m (266 ft), 108 m (354 ft), 198 m (650 ft), 108 m, 81 m and 81 m, and the tallest pier is 160 m (525 ft) high. Europe's highest bridge, the Lao Bridge in Italy, is 260 m (853 ft) high.

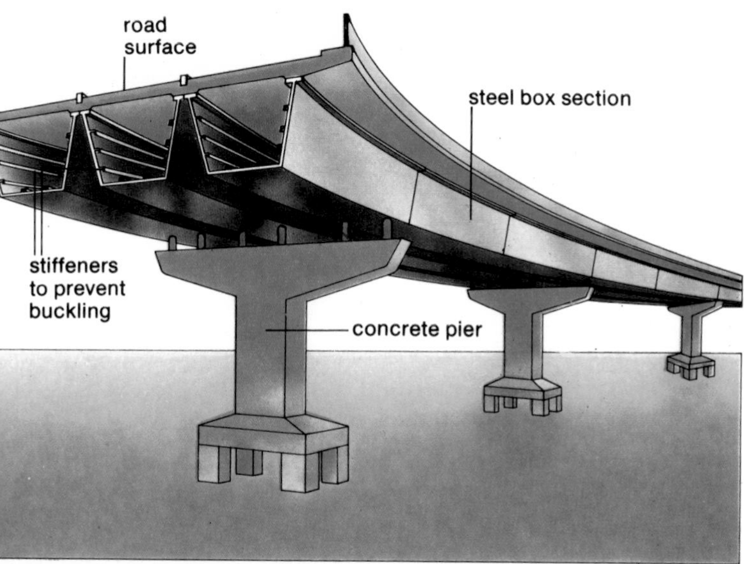

Above left: The structure of a steel box girder bridge with three trapezoid sectioned box girders. Box girder bridges generally have one, two or, more rarely, three girders, which may be of either rectangular or trapezoidal cross-section.

Above: The Ponte Presidente Costa e Silva bridge over the Rio Niteroi, Brazil, during construction in 1973. The centre section of the bridge (shown here) over the navigation channels of the river, is a cantilevered steel twin box girder structure; the approaches to the centre section are of reinforced concrete box girder construction. The bridge, opened in 1974, is over 8 km (5 miles) long.

Left: The Severins Bridge over the Rhine at Cologne is a *cable-stayed* bridge, the bridge deck being supported by cables attached to a tower. The bridge is assymetric, having one span of 151 m (495 ft) and one of 302 m (991 ft), and it was opened in 1959.

bourne and the Milford Haven Bridge in Wales highlighted the dangers of too narrow margins.

Cantilever bridges have been built on traditional patterns from wood and stone since time immemorial, particularly in Asian regions such as China and Kashmir. However, modern cantilevers date from the advent of steel, and the Forth Railway Bridge (1890) remains one of the greatest and earliest examples.

A reaction against the 'unnecessarily' high safety margins of the Forth Bridge caused the principle to be more economically tried in the Quebec Bridge. During construction in 1907, however, a lower main compression chord buckled and the bridge collapsed. The modified design called for the central suspended span to be completed and then hoisted into position. Quebec's second disaster occurred when the 5,000 tonne section dropped into the river during lifting operations.

Other notable steel cantilevers include the Viaur Viaduct (on the Toulouse to Lyons railway line in France) where the deck runs flush with the level (tensioned) upper chords of the structures; and the New Howrah Bridge over the Hooghly River in Calcutta, where the roadway runs flush with the level (compression) lower chords.

Concrete has also been used in several cantilever structures, notably in Riccardo Morani's Maracaibo Lake Bridge in Venezuela. The principle used in the five central spans is very similar to that of the Forth Bridge, though each lower, compression member is formed by the horizontal roadway slab. Each cantilever tower is independent from its neighbour (though linked by a suspended span) to minimize damage caused by the regular earth tremors experienced in the area.

Though many so-called 'primitive' suspension bridges were (and still are) built with considerable sophistication, the use of the suspension principle in European bridges required the development of materials strong and reliable in tension. The first notable spans in Europe were constructed with wrought iron chains. Telford's Menai Bridge (1826) was one such, in which each of the 15 chains for the central span were hoisted, complete, into position.

In the US, John Roebling developed an alternative method of constructing weight-bearing suspension cables. Working first with iron wire he devised a system of travelling *sheaves* (pulleys) which could cross and recross the opening between the two towers of the bridge, on each passage

Bay Bridge, completed in 1936, is over 8 miles long, spanning San Francisco Bay. A double-deck road bridge, it has 2 suspension spans, 20 arches and a tunnel.

Penny Tweedie/Colorific

Department of Public Works, Canada

Society for Anglo-Chinese Understanding

Above: The Nanking Bridge over the Yangtze River, China, opened in 1968, is a continuous truss double-deck bridge. The upper deck carries two lanes for vehicles, two for cycles, and two footpaths, and the lower carries a double track railway.

Left: Completed in 1956, the Richmond-San Raphael Bridge across San Pablo Bay, California, is a two-deck road bridge over 6 km (4 miles) long.

Below: The Severn Bridge, England, is a suspension bridge with a steel box girder deck. The main span is 988 m (3,240 ft) long, and the side spans are each 305 m (1,000 ft) in length.

Michael Holford

laying down a single strand. When sufficient strands had been strung, they would be gathered then clamped together into a thick cable. Using steel wire, this method of *cable spinning* has since become standard for virtually all suspension spans. Among early bridges thus constructed was Roebling's Niagara Railway Bridge of 1855.

Roebling used deep trusses and radial cables to add stiffness to the roadway, though later US refinements progressively lightened the trusswork and heightened the towers to create longer and longer spans. Successes include the George Washington Bridge, 1931 (1,067 m, 3,500 ft) and the Golden Gate Bridge, 1937 (1,280 m, 4,200 ft). The light plate girder stiffening and narrow roadway of the Tacoma Narrows Bridge, 1940 (853 m, 2,800 ft), however, led to its collapse from progressive harmonic oscillations brought on by a moderate wind.

Subsequent intensive research into the effects of wind on suspended decks highlighted the need to reduce *vortex shedding* (the creation of severe air turbulence) by the decks, and later suspended spans (for instance the Verrazano Narrows and the Forth Road Bridges) featured more open trusswork and longitudinal vents in the roadway to prevent the build-up of air pressure above and below.

A more original solution, however, was used for the Severn Road Bridge in England, 1966 (988 m, 3,240 ft), which incorporates aerodynamically-shaped trapezoidal box sections for the road deck. This relatively light structure has also been adopted for the construction of the world's longest span (1,410 m, 4,626 ft), the bridge over the River Humber in northeast England.

Fixed bridges are often not feasible over busy shipping channels flanked by low-lying banks, and so movable bridges are often necessary. *Bascule* spans hinge at the landward end on *trunnion bearings* or rock upwards on *Scherzer rolling bearings*. Tower Bridge in London is the best known example of a *double-bat bascule*. *Vertical lift* Bridges usually consist of a trussed deck with each end supported at the base of a tower. The bridge is opened by hydraulically raising the ends up the towers. Other types of moving bridge include the *swing bridge*, pivoted for horizontal rotation, and the *transporter bridge*. In this rare type a short section of roadway is suspended from a wheeled trolley running along a high truss, and pulled to and fro from bank to bank.

Daily Telegraph Colour Library

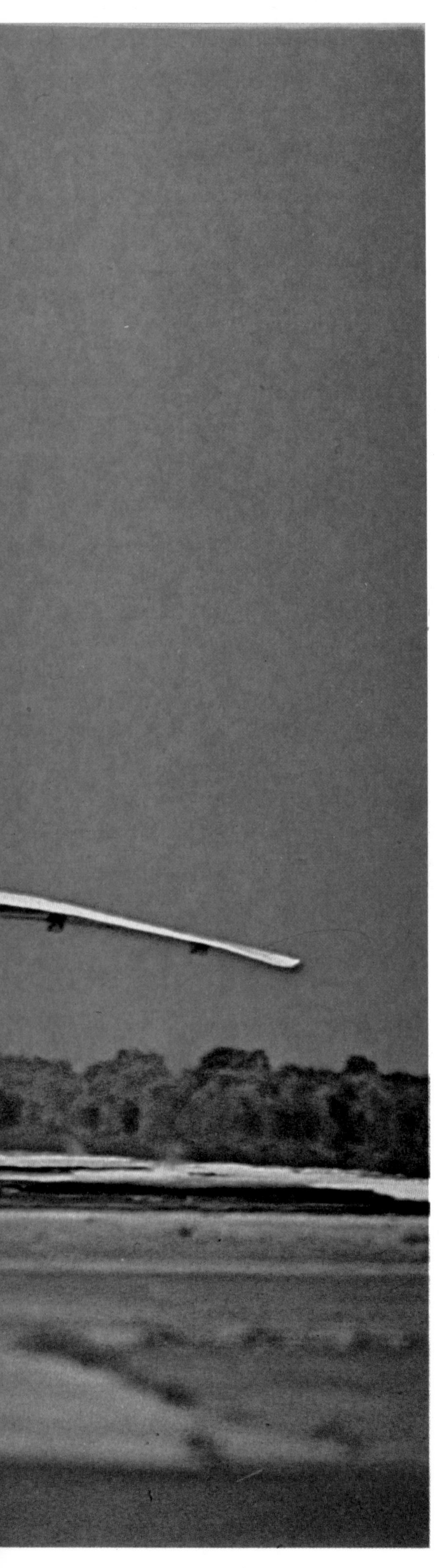

Chapter 4

Transport Technology

Concorde is capable of speeds of Mach 2 (1,354m.p,h.). It is powered by 4 Rolls-Royce engines, situated in ducts under the wings, giving 38,050lbs (17,260kg) of thrust.

Aircraft

To defy the force of gravity and take to the air was for many centuries one of man's greatest ambitions. From the end of the eighteenth century, there were a number of successful attempts at flight —in balloons, gliders and a variety of strange flying machines—but in 1903 the dream finally seemed to have come true. In that year the Wright brothers made the first-ever 'sustained' flight in a powered airplane. The freedom of long distance flight, and ultimately space-travel, was then only decades away.

The essential principle involved in flight is the need to create enough force to overcome gravity and lift a craft into the air. Then this force must somehow be maintained, otherwise the aircraft will sooner or later be pulled back to earth.

An airplane which is unpowered, like a glider, is given the initial force required to launch it by the pull of a towing truck or light aircraft. This gives it sufficient *lift*, the force which keeps it in the air, until it picks up a rising air current or 'thermal' upon which it can soar. Without this fresh impetus from air currents, the glider will slow down and sink because of the combined effects of air resistance, or *drag*, and gravity.

Powered aircraft, however, can overcome drag and gravity through the force of their engines. It is these that provide the necessary forward motion to generate lift on the wings.

Hit a ball into the air with a racket and it climbs for a while before gradually falling back to earth. In so doing it is obeying Newton's first law of motion, which states that an object stays still or continues to move in a straight line at a constant speed unless it is interfered with in some way by an external force. In other words, the ball would not have climbed into the air spontaneously. It required an initial external force from the movement of the racket by the arm to launch it. Once in the air, in the absence of any external forces, the ball would continue on and up along its original course. Instead it follows a smooth curve because the invisible force of the earth's gravity pulls it down all the time while the air friction slows it. The action of these external forces constantly and subtly modifies the direction and speed of the ball, eventually bringing it back to earth. When the ball is given a light tap with the racket it does not travel as high or as far as when it is

Newton's laws of motion

The laws of motion, first formulated by Sir Isaac Newton in the seventeenth century, explain why a lifting force is necessary for flight. The first law of motion states that a force must be applied to any object before it will change its position, its speed or its direction of travel; thus an object will remain quite still or continue moving in a straight line at a constant speed unless some external force acts upon it. This tendency to oppose any change in its state of rest or motion is called the object's *inertia*.

The second law of motion states that, providing the *mass* of a body remains constant, a force acting on it will produce an *acceleration* which is proportional to that applied force. The mass of a body is a measure of the amount of matter it contains. This is not necessarily the same as a body's weight, which is a measure of the pull exerted on it by the force of gravity. The difference is easily demonstrated in space flight, where a body becomes increasingly weightless the further it travels into space, as the force of the earth's gravity gets weaker; the body's mass, however, remains constant.

The third law of motion states that action and reaction are equal and opposite. According to this law, when an aircraft is standing on the ground the ground is providing an equal and opposite reaction to its weight—otherwise it would either sink into the ground or rise into the air. In flight, however, the air itself must be made to provide the necessary reaction to the action of the aircraft's weight. This reaction or upward force is provided by the lift, a force created largely by the wings as the aircraft is pushed or pulled through the air by its engines.

Any structure, such as an aircraft wing or tailplane, which is shaped to produce aerodynamic lift is known as an *aerofoil* (airfoil). Looking at an aircraft wing in cross-section, the upper surface is curved slightly upwards, while the lower surface is almost flat. As it moves through the air, the wing's rounded front or leading

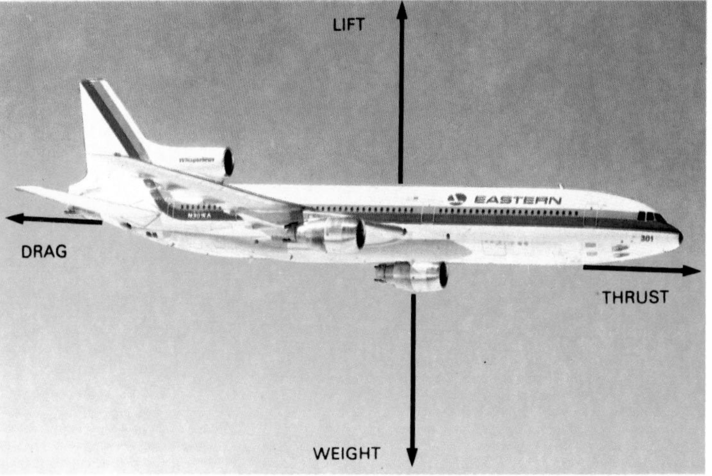

Left: The way an aircraft moves in the air depends upon the action of four basic forces. When an aeroplane is flying at a constant speed along a perfectly straight course these forces are in equilibrium. The lift from the wings exactly matches the weight; the forwards thrust balances the air resistance or drag.

Below: A model of an aeroplane in a wind tunnel shows the formation of turbulence. A swirling mass of air is created when the smooth airflow breaks away from the wings. Wind tunnels are used to test the airflow over new aircraft designs. Smoke is introduced into the tunnel to make the airflow visible.

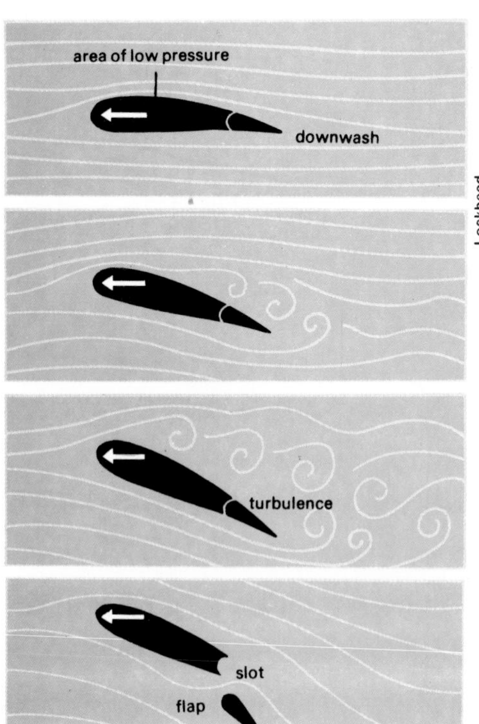

Left: The airflow over a level wing or aerofoil is smoothly curved downwards, giving good lift. Tilting the wing up slightly boosts its lift. At larger angles the airflow starts to break away from the wing. As it is tilted further the turbulence moves forwards so that less of the wing gives lift. Eventually a critical angle of attack is reached when the airflow separates from the wing completely. Then so little of the aerofoil is creating lift that the aircraft 'stalls' and drops sharply.

Bottom left: Lowering the flaps on the wing exaggerates the profile of the whole aerofoil, increasing its lift and the critical stalling angle.

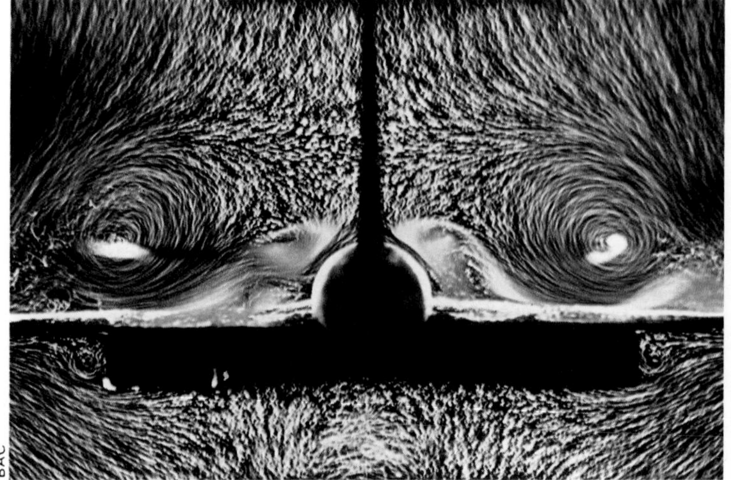

given a much stronger hit. According to the second law of motion, provided the mass of an object is kept constant, the force applied to it is proportional to its acceleration. While the mass of the ball is the same, the force applied by the racket in each case is different. The greater the force, the further the ball flies because of its greater acceleration.
When the ball lands, it bounces up again in accordance with the third law of motion. This states that to every action there is an equal and opposite reaction. As it hits the ground, the ball depresses the earth fractionally, but because the earth is so much larger than the ball, this dent is invisible to the naked eye. The earth reacts, however, by pushing back with exactly the same force as the force of impact, trying to return to its original shape. If the ground is soft, a slight depression might be visible where the ball landed because the soil was not strong enough to resist the sudden rapid acceleration of impact.

edge deflects the air into two streams, one of which passes over the wing and the other under it. Early attempts at heavier-than-air flight used wings with a flat cross-section, but designers soon realized that much more lift could be obtained if suitably curved aerofoil surfaces were used.

The shape is specifically designed to create lift, and is effective for two reasons. Firstly, as the aircraft moves forward, air has to rush in behind it to prevent a vacuum forming. Secondly, because the curved upper surface of the aerofoil is longer from front to back than the relatively straight lower surface, the upper airstream must travel faster than the lower airstream, in order to reach the trailing edge of the wing at the same time. That these actions create lift is explained by a principle discovered by the eighteenth-century Swiss scientist Daniel Bernoulli.

According to Bernoulli's principle, if the speed at which a *fluid*—that means a gas or a liquid—flows across a surface is increased, the pressure which it exerts on that surface will decrease. The faster airstream over the top of the aerofoil therefore exerts a much lower pressure than the slower one under it. This situation of reduced pressure above a wing creates a very powerful upward force, or lift.

The flow of air over the curved wing surface is known as *laminar flow;* it is made up of successive layers of air flowing smoothly over each other. The layers next to the surface of the wing, known collectively as the *boundary layer,* travel more slowly than the rest of the laminar flow, because of the friction between them and the wing. This boundary layer is very thin, less than a fraction of a millimetre thick.

The *angle of attack,* that is the angle at which the wing meets the airstream, has an important bearing on the amount of lift the wings generate. The wing meeting the air at a slightly up-turned angle gives a slightly increased pressure on the underside, which backs up the effects of the low pressure above the wing in creating lift. Increasing the angle of attack increases lift—up to a certain critical angle of about 15°. After that point, lift falls off sharply and the result can be a *stall.*

Turbulent air

The fall-off in lift is caused by *turbulent* air. At small angles of attack the boundary layer leaves the upper surface of the wing at or near the trailing edge; this is the *separation point.* Behind the separation point, the air flowing over the wing is no longer streamlined—in line with the direction of the wing—but *turbulent,* breaking up into swirling vortices. Turbulent air creates a lot of drag but very little lift. As the angle of attack increases, the separation point moves further and further forward on the wing, so that an increasingly small area of the wing is producing lift. Finally when the critical angle is reached, so little of the wing is contributing lift that the aircraft stalls and drops sharply. Similarly, when a plane runs into weather conditions that are causing turbulent air, this disruption of the smooth airflow can produce the same stalling effect. To correct a stall in mid-air the pilot needs to level-off the angle of attack and increase lift; the usual manoeuvre is a shallow dive, which will help the aircraft pick up speed and generate more lift.

Alternatively the lift of a wing can be increased at low speeds by extending different types of slats and flaps that effectively change the whole profile of the aerofoil. A small, adjustable aerofoil, or *slat,* positioned in front of the main wing with a small gap, or *slot,* between the two

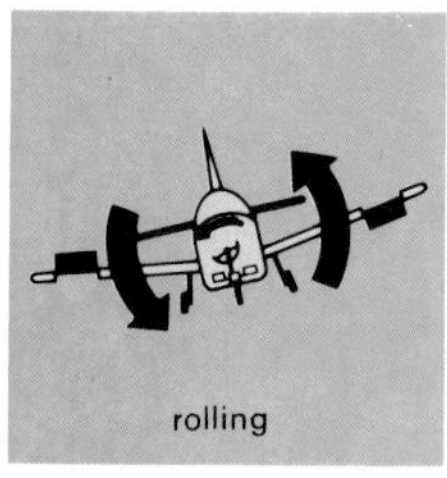

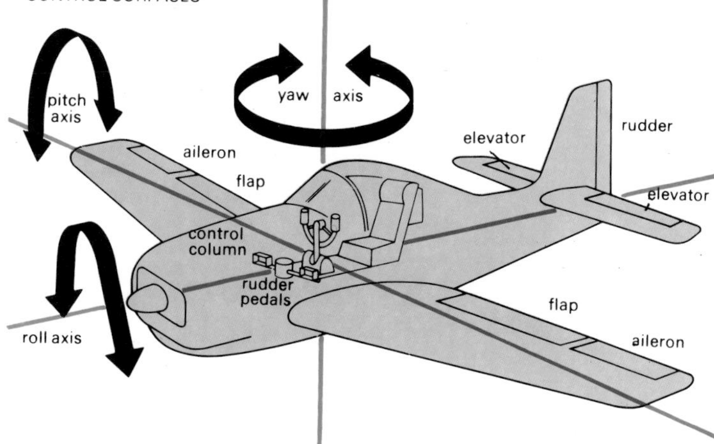

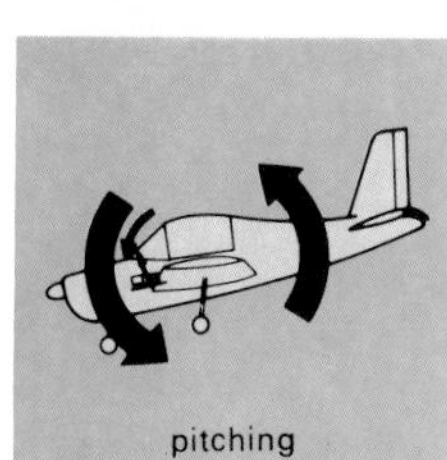

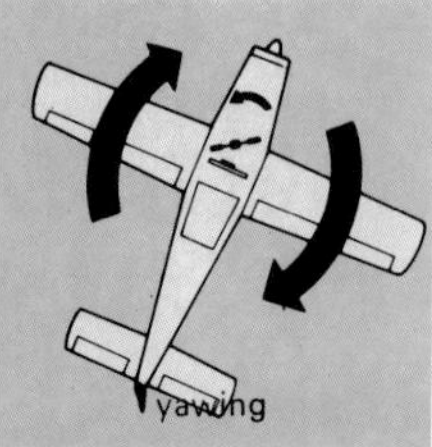

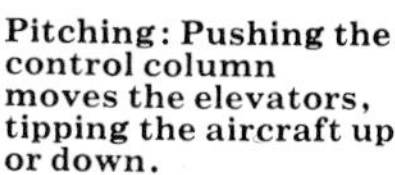

normal turn

Above and left: A normal aircraft is manoeuvred about three axes by three sets of control surfaces.

Rolling: Turning the control column in the cockpit moves the ailerons, causing the aircraft to roll. When an aileron is lowered the wing creates more lift and rises. Raising the aileron on the other wing reduces its lift.

Pitching: Pushing the control column moves the elevators, tipping the aircraft up or down.

Yawing: Turning the rudder makes the aeroplane yaw, or turn. A normal banking turn combines yawing the aircraft and rolling it in to the turn.

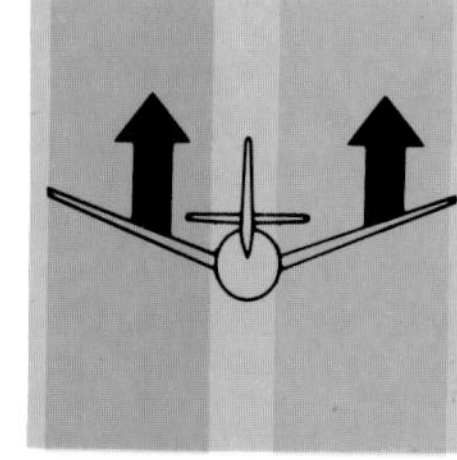

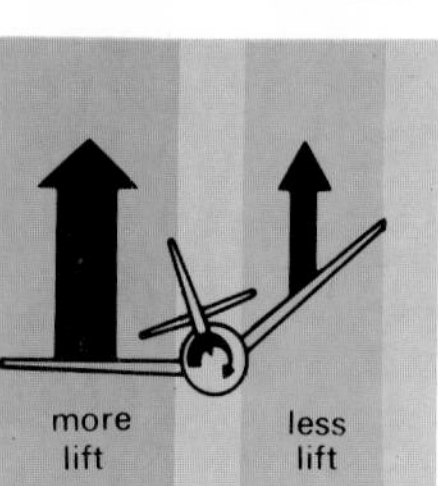

Left: The upwards tilting, or dihedral, of the wings stabilizes the aircraft. When equally inclined to the horizontal, both wings create equal lift. As the aircraft rolls, a sideways airflow hits the lower wing at a larger angle than the upper wing, so that it generates more lift, righting the aeroplane.

Saab

Right: A delta winged aircraft has no separate tailplane. The wings are swept back so far that the control surfaces, or elevons, on the trailing edges can serve as both elevators and ailerons. To roll the aeroplane, one elevon is raised and the other is lowered. For a climbing turn, one elevon is raised while the other remains level.

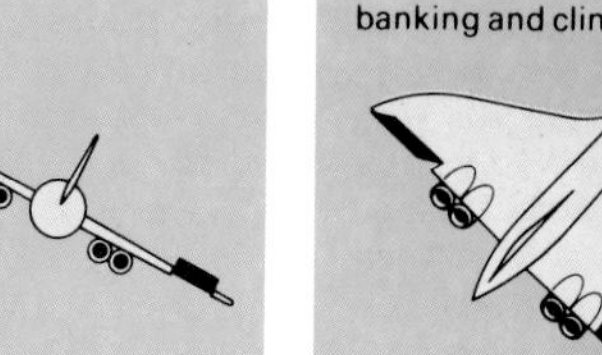

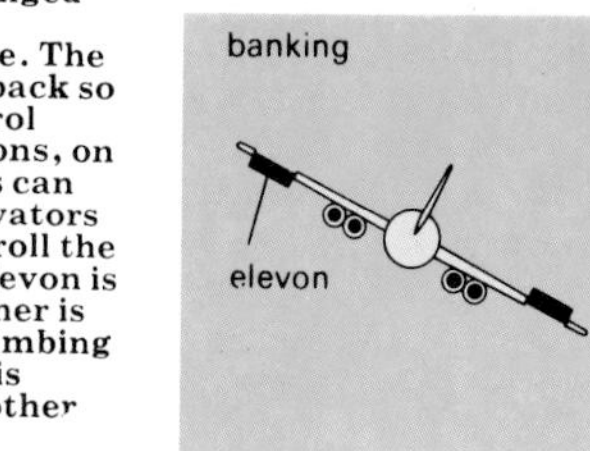

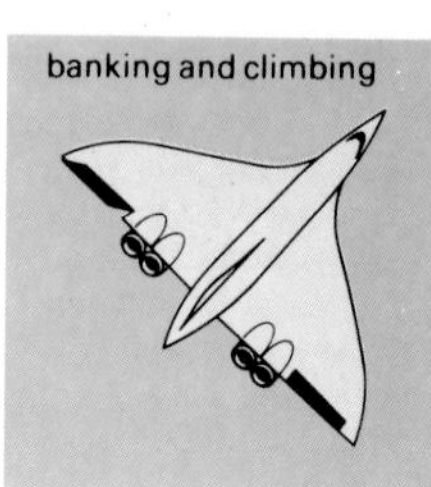

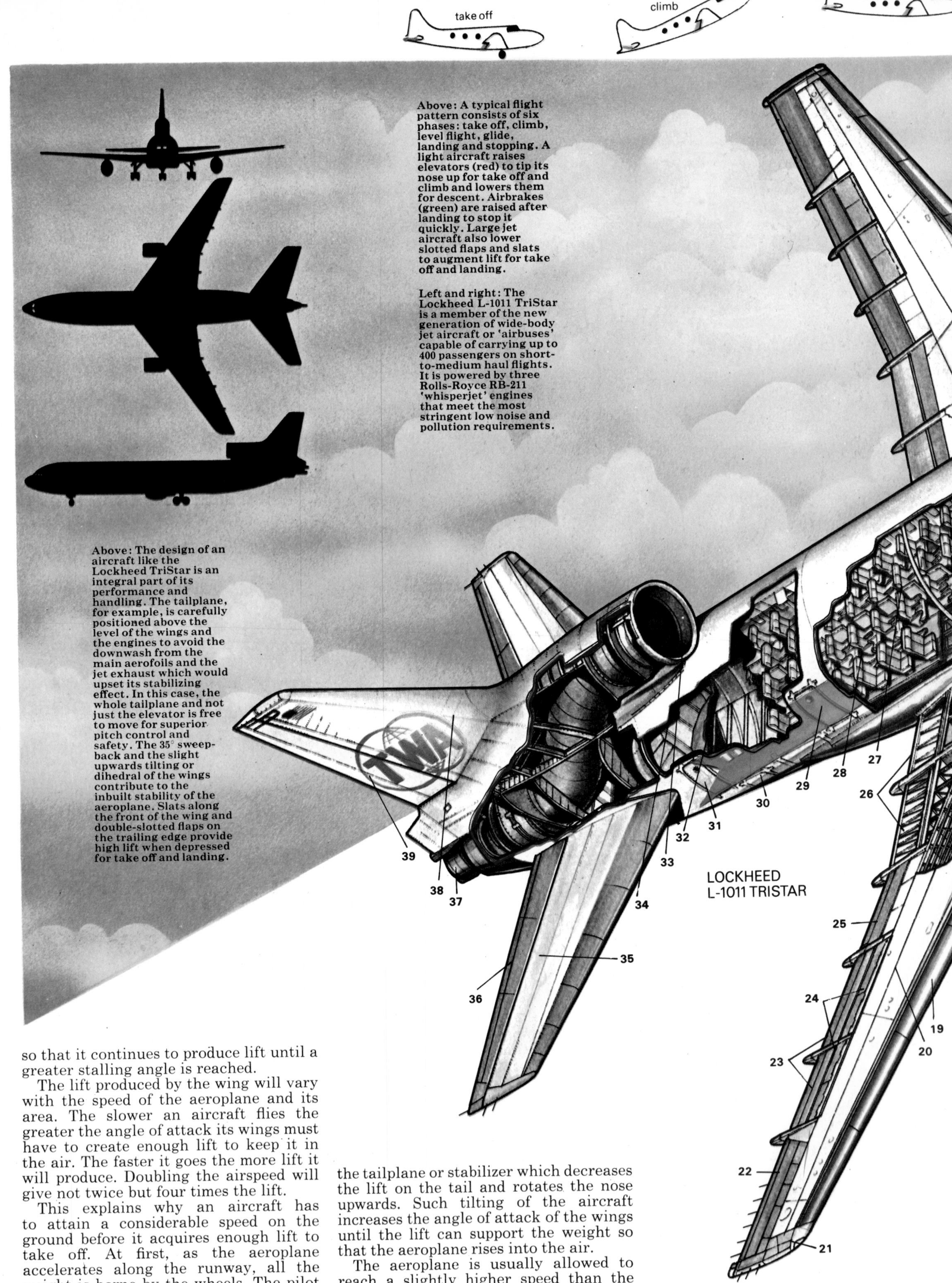

Above: A typical flight pattern consists of six phases: take off, climb, level flight, glide, landing and stopping. A light aircraft raises elevators (red) to tip its nose up for take off and climb and lowers them for descent. Airbrakes (green) are raised after landing to stop it quickly. Large jet aircraft also lower slotted flaps and slats to augment lift for take off and landing.

Left and right: The Lockheed L-1011 TriStar is a member of the new generation of wide-body jet aircraft or 'airbuses' capable of carrying up to 400 passengers on short-to-medium haul flights. It is powered by three Rolls-Royce RB-211 'whisperjet' engines that meet the most stringent low noise and pollution requirements.

Above: The design of an aircraft like the Lockheed TriStar is an integral part of its performance and handling. The tailplane, for example, is carefully positioned above the level of the wings and the engines to avoid the downwash from the main aerofoils and the jet exhaust which would upset its stabilizing effect. In this case, the whole tailplane and not just the elevator is free to move for superior pitch control and safety. The 35° sweep-back and the slight upwards tilting or dihedral of the wings contribute to the inbuilt stability of the aeroplane. Slats along the front of the wing and double-slotted flaps on the trailing edge provide high lift when depressed for take off and landing.

so that it continues to produce lift until a greater stalling angle is reached.

The lift produced by the wing will vary with the speed of the aeroplane and its area. The slower an aircraft flies the greater the angle of attack its wings must have to create enough lift to keep it in the air. The faster it goes the more lift it will produce. Doubling the airspeed will give not twice but four times the lift.

This explains why an aircraft has to attain a considerable speed on the ground before it acquires enough lift to take off. At first, as the aeroplane accelerates along the runway, all the weight is borne by the wheels. The pilot watches the airspeed indicator and when the aeroplane is travelling fast enough he pulls back on the control column. This raises the elevators on the trailing edge of the tailplane or stabilizer which decreases the lift on the tail and rotates the nose upwards. Such tilting of the aircraft increases the angle of attack of the wings until the lift can support the weight so that the aeroplane rises into the air.

The aeroplane is usually allowed to reach a slightly higher speed than the minimum required for flight so that it does not have to be tilted to the maximum angle of attack before lift off. This would leave little margin for early flight

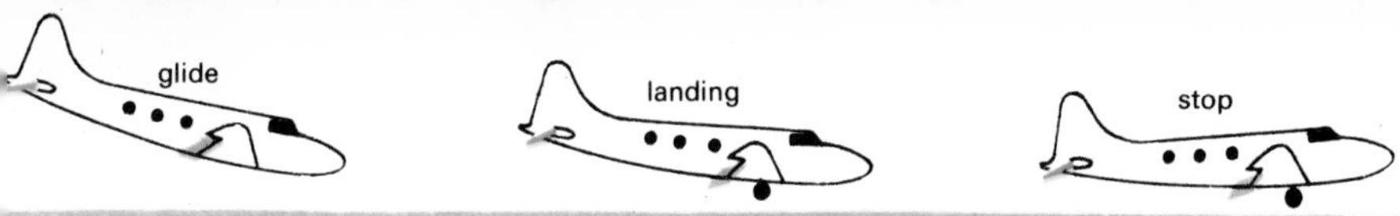

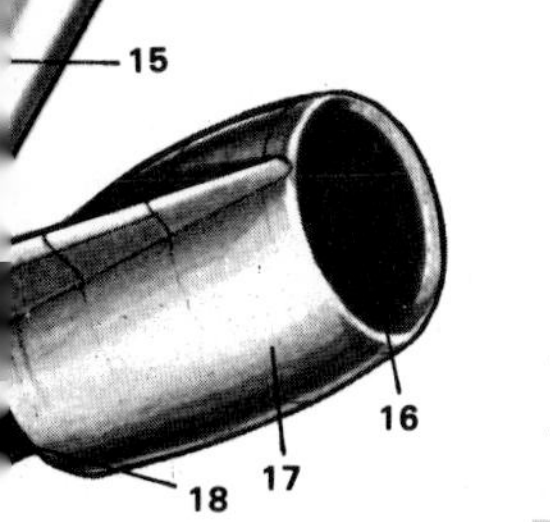

glide landing stop

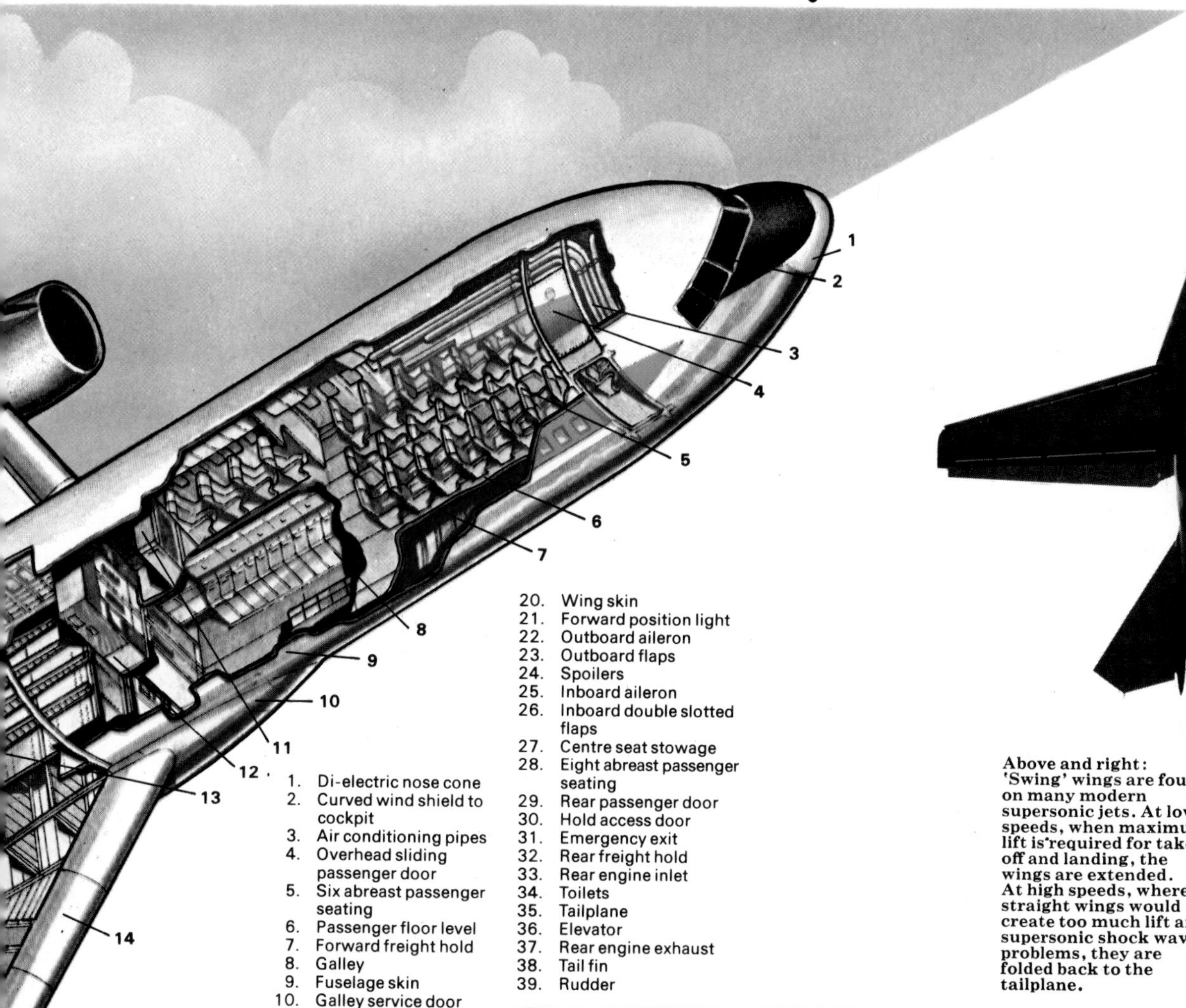

1. Di-electric nose cone
2. Curved wind shield to cockpit
3. Air conditioning pipes
4. Overhead sliding passenger door
5. Six abreast passenger seating
6. Passenger floor level
7. Forward freight hold
8. Galley
9. Fuselage skin
10. Galley service door
11. Overhead coat stowage
12. Galley elevator
13. Floor support members
14. Inboard leading edge slat
15. Fuel tank
16. Engine inlet
17. Rolls Royce RB-211 Turbofan engine
18. Variable nozzle exhaust outlet
19. Outboard leading edge slat
20. Wing skin
21. Forward position light
22. Outboard aileron
23. Outboard flaps
24. Spoilers
25. Inboard aileron
26. Inboard double slotted flaps
27. Centre seat stowage
28. Eight abreast passenger seating
29. Rear passenger door
30. Hold access door
31. Emergency exit
32. Rear freight hold
33. Rear engine inlet
34. Toilets
35. Tailplane
36. Elevator
37. Rear engine exhaust
38. Tail fin
39. Rudder

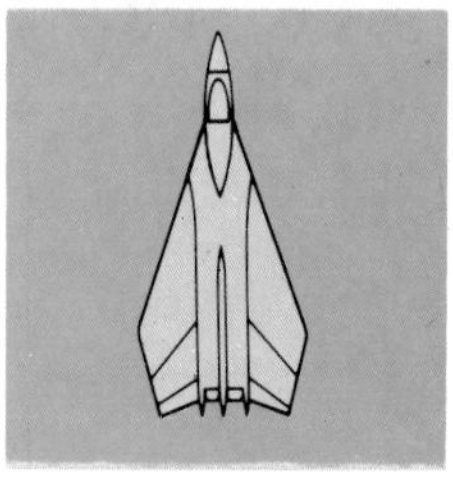

Above and right: 'Swing' wings are found on many modern supersonic jets. At low speeds, when maximum lift is required for take off and landing, the wings are extended. At high speeds, where straight wings would create too much lift and supersonic shock wave problems, they are folded back to the tailplane.

Left: The almost rocket-like Lockheed Blackbird supersonic reconnaissance aircraft has flown the Atlantic in less than two hours. The flanged body acts as a 'wing' in flight. It is painted black to resist the intense heat generated by skin friction during sustained flight at twice the speed of sound.

Left: The Russian Tupolev Tu-144 has a pair of retractable foreplanes behind the cockpit to improve its stability at low speeds.

Right: The streamlined Concorde is designed to cruise at supersonic speeds. The droop nose is lowered for landing to increase the pilot's visibility.

manoeuvres. Sometimes in large jet aircraft flaps are lowered for take off to increase the lift of the wings and enlarge the angle of attack the aeroplane can reach safely before stalling.

Raising these flaps prematurely after take-off can have tragic consequences. For if the aeroplane is still climbing steeply when the flaps are raised, the wings may be inclined at an angle of attack greater than the critical stalling angle. In which case the aircraft stalls and, because it may not have gained sufficient height to give the pilot time to correct the situation by tilting the nose down into a glide until it has picked up enough airspeed to restore lift, it plummets to the ground out of control. Fortunately the chances of this error occurring are extremely slight because of the numerous warning systems built into the control panel in the cockpit.

Since lift also depends on the mass or density of the air, airports at high altitudes and in tropical countries where the air pressure is lower than at sea level or in temperate regions have longer runways. This allows the aeroplane more room to build up the slightly higher speed it needs before it can generate an equivalent amount of lift. Similarly, after take off, as the aeroplane climbs into thinner air at high altitudes, it must either go faster or fly at a greater angle of attack to maintain lift.

For landing, the elevators are lowered to tip the nose down into a gradual descent to the runway. On the final approach, the aeroplane adopts an increasingly nose-up posture, giving the wings a high angle of attack to sustain lift at the reduced speed. Flaps are also lowered during landing to boost lift. One potential danger in landing is that the nose will tip back so far that the aeroplane will stall and drop on to the runway. Depressed flaps help to minimize this risk of stalling by increasing the operative angle of attack of the wings.

Landing transfers the lift from the wings to the ground again. The pilot aims to bring the aeroplane into contact with the runway at the slowest possible vertical velocity and a low ground speed. Aircraft usually land into the wind in order to cut their ground speed. After landing, the aeroplane is slowed rapidly by raising air brakes or *spoilers* to increase drag and cut lift and by reversing the engine thrust to stop it as quickly as possible.

Helicopters and Autogyros

A conventional fixed wing aircraft is able to fly because of the lift generated on its wings as they move forward through the air. On a helicopter or autogyro, however, the fixed wings are replaced by a set of thin wings called *blades* attached to a shaft. The rotation of this set of blades, or the *rotor,* through the air creates the lift necessary for flight.

An autogyro or a helicopter will climb when the total lift of the rotor exceeds the weight of the machine. The helicopter will hover when the sum of all the lift forces on the rotor blades is equal to the weight of the machine.

A helicopter has a rotor which is driven by an engine, but an autogyro has a rotor which gets its power from the motion of the airstream blowing through it, rather like a windmill. Thus the autogyro needs some other device, usually an engine-driven propeller, to pull or push it through the air horizontally.

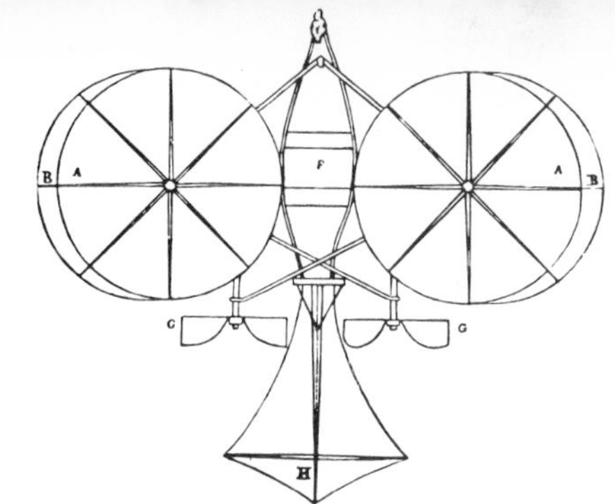

Right: Designed by Sir George Cayley in 1843, this early idea for a vertical take-off and landing aircraft used two sets of rotors to provide lift, and two propellers to provide forward thrust. It was intended that the fan-like rotors would fold flat to form circular wings to create lift during forward flight.

Below: This helicopter was built in France by Paul Cornu in 1907 and during several short flights in November of that year it reached a height of almost 2 m (6 ft). It was powered by a 24 hp Antoinette engine driving a pair of rotors mounted in a tandem configuration, and the pilot sat next to the engine.

Radio Times Hulton Picture Library (above also)

Hovering and climbing

As the rotor turns, it traces out a circle in the air which is known as the *rotor disc.* The total lift generated by the rotor acts through the centre of this disc and at right angles to it. This means that when a helicopter is hovering the lift forces are acting vertically upwards through the centre of the rotor. To make the machine climb, the lift generated by each blade must be increased. This is done by increasing the *angle of attack*—the angle at which the leading edge meets the airstream—of each blade equally, thus increasing the total lift without changing the direction in which it acts. The pilot controls this by means of a lever known as the *collective pitch control.*

In order to make the helicopter fly forwards the rotor disc must be tilted forwards slightly, so that part of the rotor acts to pull the machine in that direction. The rotor disc is tilted forwards by increasing the angle of attack of each blade as it travels around the rear of the disc, and decreasing the angle as each blade travels around the front of the disc. As a change in the angle of attack means a change in lift, the lift is increased at the rear of the rotor disc and decreased at the front, causing the disc to tilt forwards.

These changes in the angle of attack of the blades can be made to occur at any point around the rotor disc, tilting the disc accordingly. This enables the helicopter to fly in any direction. The pilot controls the tilt of the rotor disc by means of the *cyclic pitch control lever.*

Russ Kinne, Photo Researchers

Above: The helicopter produces the vertical force needed to lift it from the ground by forcing air downwards, creating the down draught which is making the circular ripple patterns on the surface of the water. When a helicopter is hovering, about 70 per cent of its power is used in creating this force.

Left: The down draught is strongest beneath the points on the rotor at which the most lift is generated, shown here by the arrows above the rotor blades. The sea directly below the helicopter fuselage is relatively calm, as it is shielded from the down draught by the body of the helicopter and by the tail.

The importance of blade speed

When a helicopter is hovering, the speed of the blades through the air is due to their speed of rotation and is constant at all points around the rotor disc. When the helicopter is moving forwards, however, the speed of a blade through the air changes as it travels around the disc. When a blade is travelling towards the front of the disc, its air speed is its speed due to its rotation plus the speed of the aircraft (just as a bullet fired forwards

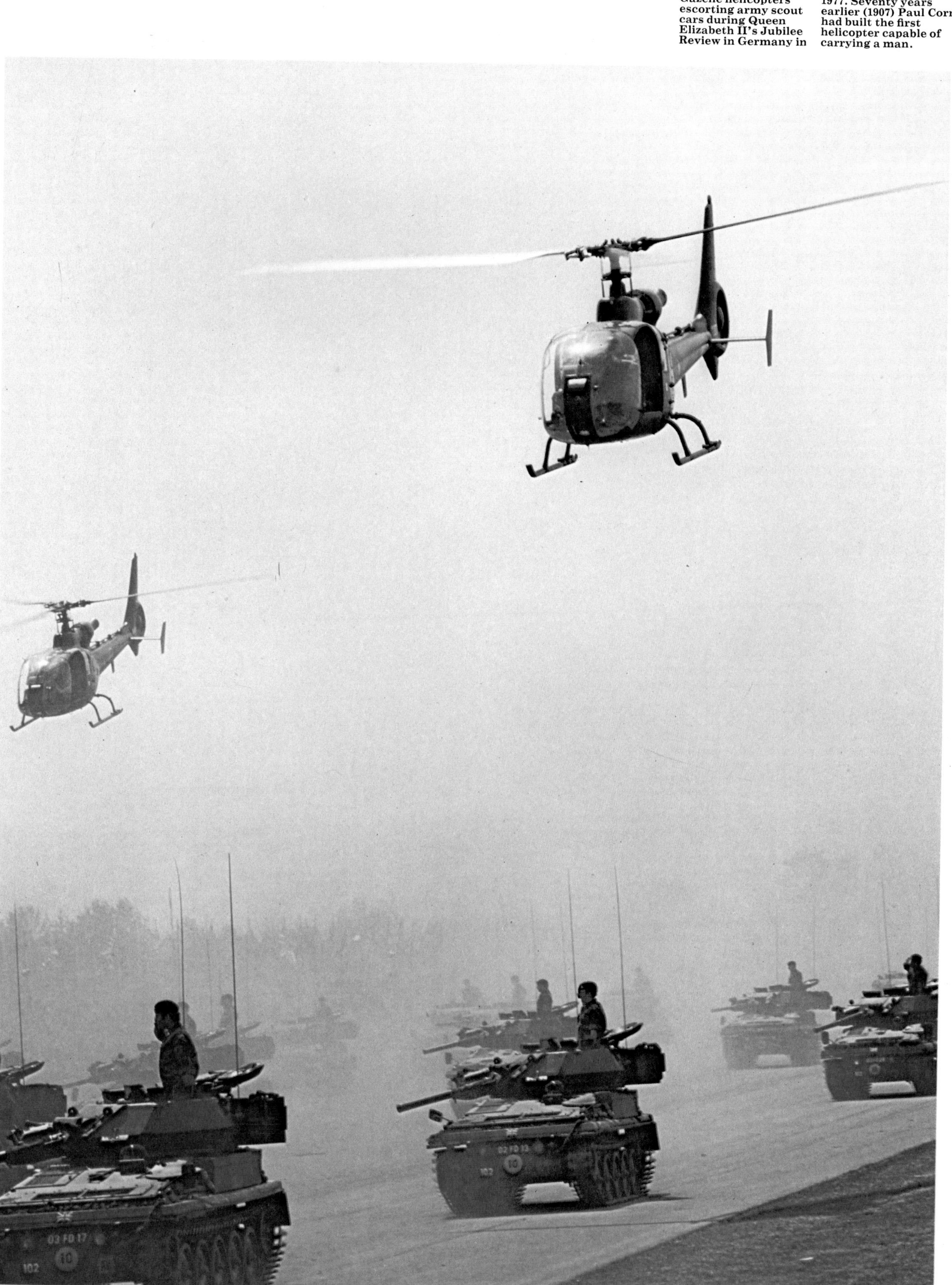

Gazelle helicopters escorting army scout cars during Queen Elizabeth II's Jubilee Review in Germany in 1977. Seventy years earlier (1907) Paul Cornu had built the first helicopter capable of carrying a man.

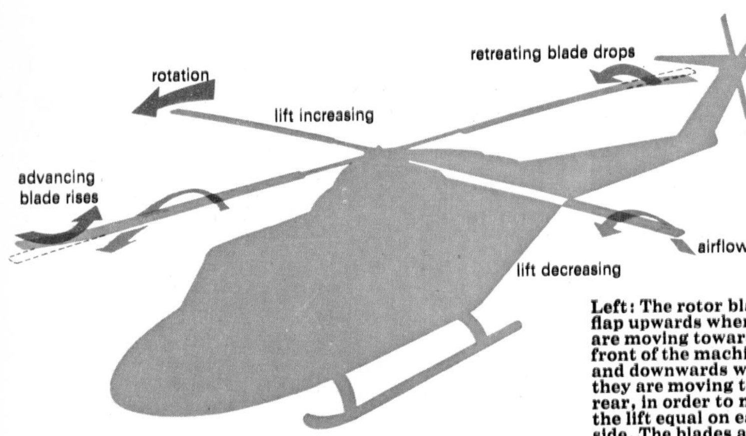

Left: The rotor blades flap upwards when they are moving towards the front of the machine, and downwards when they are moving to the rear, in order to make the lift equal on each side. The blades are at their highest flap position when pointing forward and at their lowest when they point to the tail.

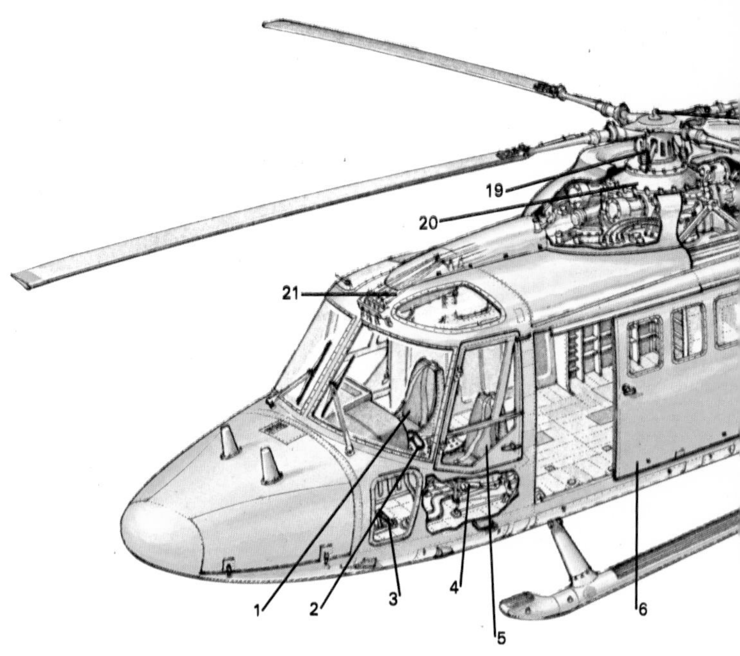

Right: The Westland/Aérospatiale Lynx has hingeless rotor blades and is powered by two Rolls-Royce BS-360 Gem turboshafts which give it a top speed of 160 knots at sea level. Main rotor diameter is 12.8 m (42 ft), and the overall length of the aircraft is 15.2 m (49.75 ft). The army version is shown here.

from a gun on a moving train will travel at the speed at which it left the gun plus the speed of the train on which the gun was travelling).

When a blade is travelling towards the rear of the disc, however, its air speed is reduced by the speed of the aircraft, which at that point is effectively travelling in the opposite direction to it. As the lift on a blade varies according to its speed through the air, the forward-moving blade has more lift than the rearward-moving one.

If the rotor was a completely rigid structure, these differences in lift would cause it to tilt towards the rearward-moving side, and the helicopter would tend to fly sideways instead of straight ahead. To overcome this problem, the rotor blades are hinged at the roots to allow them to flap up and down a certain amount. This allows the forward-moving blade to rise slightly, in effect reducing its lift. The blades thus rise when moving forwards and drop again when moving backwards in order to keep the actual lift on them constant.

Certain helicopter designs, such as the Westland/Aérospatiale Lynx, have replaced the flapping hinge with a controlled stiffness, or flexible, section near the root of the blade. The blade moves in a way which is broadly similar to that of the fully articulated blade described above but the control power at the pilot's command is greatly increased, allowing a number of flexible manoeuvres.

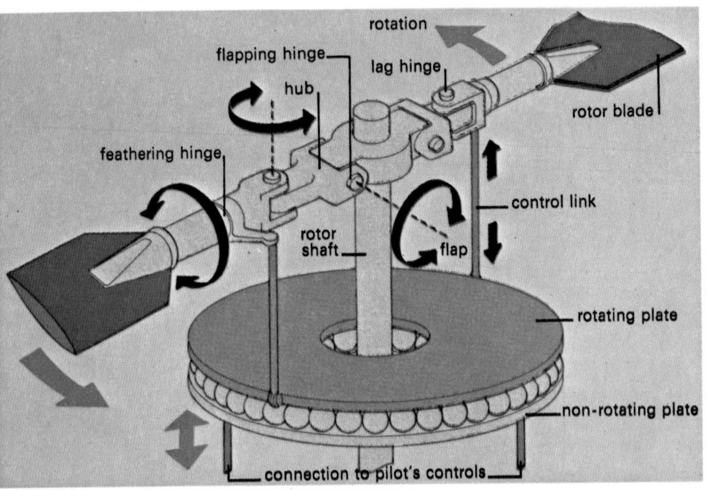

Left: Changes in rotor blade pitch angle are transmitted by the swash plate which moves up or down for collective pitch changes, and tilts to give cyclic pitch changes. Blade pitch angle depends on the swash plate height. If it is tilted the pitch of a blade is increased as it passes the high side.

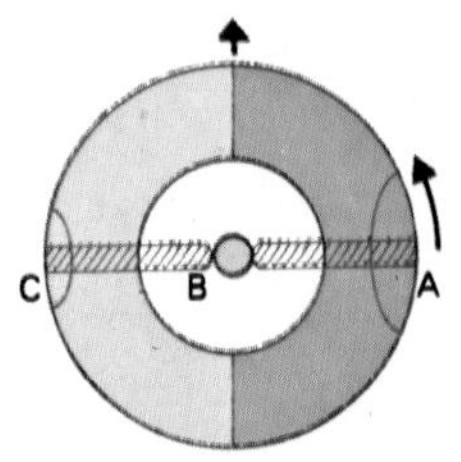

Above: A plan view of a rotor shows the points at which problems can occur when travelling at speed. At point 'A' the blade speed nears the speed of sound and drag is high; at 'B' the airspeed is too low for useful lift; and at 'C' the blade tip stalls as the pilot increases blade pitch to maintain lift.

Changing direction

Newton's third law of motion states that every action produces an equal but opposite reaction. In other words, if a body exerts a force on another in one direction, it will itself be subject to an equal force acting in the opposite direction. Thus a main rotor which is rotated by an engine in the fuselage will set up a reaction which will result in the fuselage rotating in the opposite direction. To prevent this, a torque, or twisting force, compensating system is installed, such as the small anti-torque rotor at the tail of single main rotor helicopters.

Directional control can be achieved by varying the amount of torque compensation applied. Over-compensating turns the fuselage in the same direction as the main rotor, and under-compensating allows it to turn in the opposite direction. Where compensation is by means of an anti-torque rotor, the amount of compensation is controlled by varying the *pitch*, or angle of attack, of the blades.

Right: A tandem rotor helicopter can move sideways by tilting both rotors towards the appropriate side. In order to turn the helicopter, the rear rotor is tilted to one side and the forward rotor to the other, so that the nose and tail of the craft are moved in opposite directions, causing it to turn.

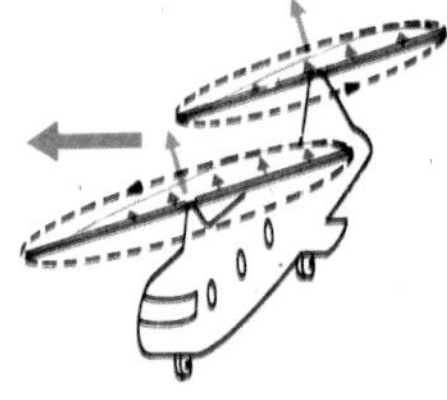

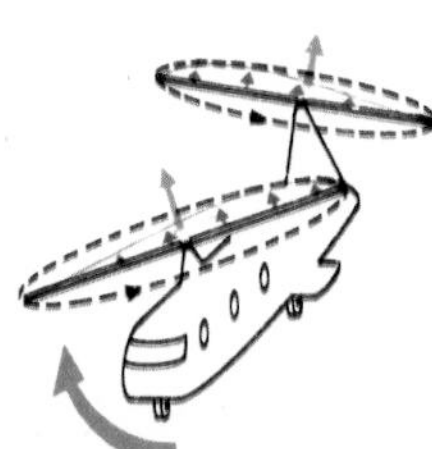

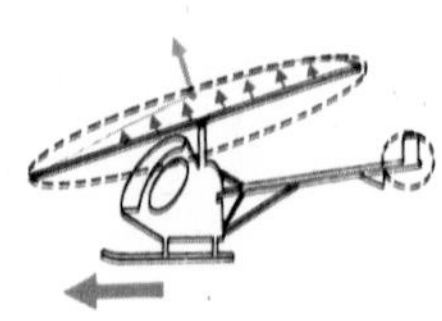

Left: Forward flight is achieved by tilting the rotor forwards. Then the lift from the rotor acts at an angle which provides forward thrust as well as the vertical lift. If the load of a helicopter is towards the front, the fuselage will tilt to keep the centre of gravity beneath the centre of the rotor.

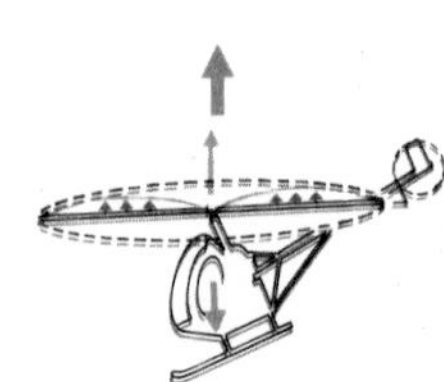

Right: With helicopters like the Lynx, which have a semi-rigid rotor construction without blade hinges, greater control is available. This makes it possible to fly upside down and to perform many other manoeuvres that were impossible with other less flexible craft using the conventional hinged rotors.

Westland

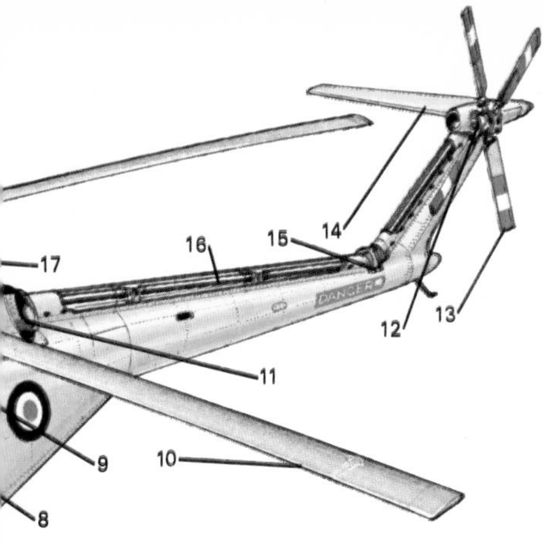

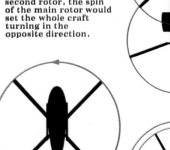

WESTLAND/
AEROSPATIALE LYNX

1. pilot's seat
2. cyclic pitch stick
3. tail rotor control pedals
4. co-pilot's collective-pitch lever
5. co-pilot's seat
6. main door
7. wheel attachments
8. forged frame
9. Rolls-Royce BS.360 gas turbine engines
10. rotor blade
11. exhaust outlet
12. tail rotor power unit
13. tail rotor
14. tailplane
15. intermediate gearbox
16. tail rotor drive
17. rotor hub
18. drag hinge damper
19. pitch control rod
20. main gearbox
21. collective pitch linkages

Below and right: These four illustrations show how helicopters overcome the effects of torque - without a second rotor, the spin of the main rotor would set the whole craft turning in the opposite direction.

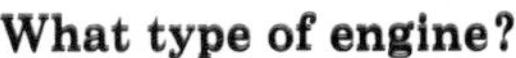

A small tail rotor is the most common anti-torque device (above). The reaction torque can also be cancelled out with two main rotors turning in opposite directions (top and bottom right). The co-axial layout has two rotors, one turning above the other (centre right).

What type of engine?

Helicopter rotors are usually driven through a shaft fitted to the rotor hub (shaft drive), but some have been built with small jet thrust units fitted at the rotor blade tips (tip drive).

Shaft drive rotors can be driven by any form of aero engine. Originally all helicopters were powered by piston engines, but the *turboshaft*, or gas turbine, engine is now used on all but the smallest machines. Rotary engines, like the Wankel engine invented in Germany, are being considered for these small machines.

Dealing with engine failure

In the event of engine failure, the rotor rapidly slows down and loses lift, but it is possible for the pilot to land safely by use of *autorotation*. By rapidly lowering the collective pitch lever the pilot can set the blades so that their leading edges are pointing slightly downwards from the horizontal. As the aircraft is descending, the new position of the blades means that a positive, or upwards, angle of attack is maintained against the upward flow of the airstream. This generates forces on the blades to keep them spinning, and as the helicopter nears the ground the pilot raises the collective pitch lever slightly, so that the spinning rotor provides enough lift to slow down the machine before it lands.

Helicopter speed limits

The conventional helicopter cannot fly at more than about 400 km/h (250 mph) because at high speeds the air speed of the forward-moving blade approaches the speed of sound and that of the rearward-moving blade is very low. The result of this is that the drag on the forward-moving blade is greatly increased and it begins to lose lift because of the break-up of the airflow over it. The rearward-moving blade loses lift because of its low air speed. At a critical speed, when pointing directly to the tail of the aircraft, the blade stalls, because air is flowing from the rotor hub to the blade tip—not across the blade to give lift.

A partial solution to this problem has been put forward by the Sikorsky Company. This is the Advancing Blade Concept (ABC) which uses two identical rotors, positioned one above the other and turning in opposite directions. The system balances the forces on the advancing side of each rotor, thus balancing the helicopter by cancelling out the loss of lift on the rearward-moving side of each rotor.

Textron's Bell Aerospace Division, N.Y.

Left: The Sikorsky Skycrane can carry a heavy load of up to 9,072 kg (20,000 lb). The anchor points for the load are directly below the rotor hub, so that the centre of gravity of the load is below the centre of the rotor. This prevents the helicopter from becoming unstable when fully laden.

Above left: Helicopters are often used as air taxis, linking a city's airports with each other and with the city centre, or ferrying passengers to and from remote areas. They can take off and land in such confined or rough places as the roof of a skyscraper, or an off-shore oil rig or in a field.

Above: The Bell X-22A experimental vertical take-off aircraft. For take-off and landing the ducted propellers were tilted into the horizontal position, as shown in the upper picture; for forward flight they could be tilted forwards as in the lower picture. Its highest speed was 518 km/h (325 mph).

Russ Kinne, Photo Researchers

Left: The rotor of an autogyro is turned by air blowing through it. Lift is only created when the rotor is spinning, and so an autogyro must be moving forwards before it can take off.

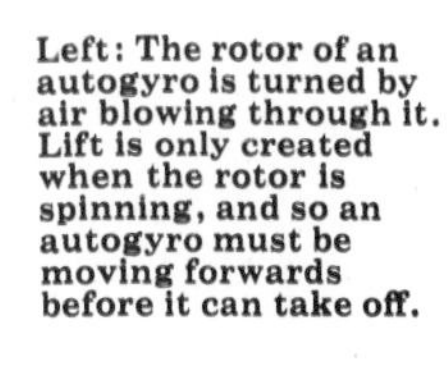

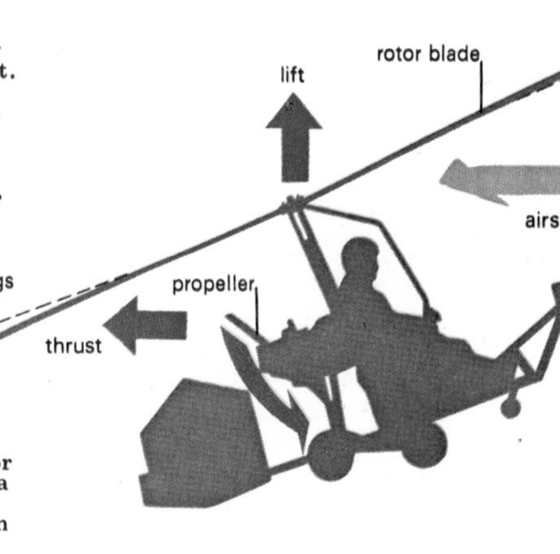

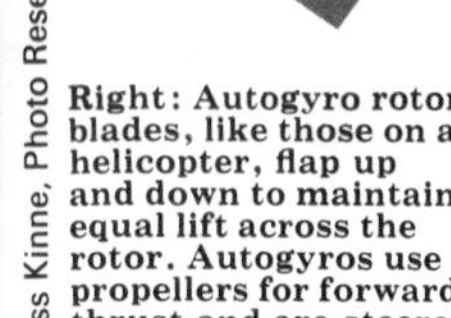

Right: Autogyro rotor blades, like those on a helicopter, flap up and down to maintain equal lift across the rotor. Autogyros use propellers for forward thrust and are steered by rudders.

Hovercraft and Hydrofoils

In 1953 the British inventor Christopher Cockerell began investigating methods of making boats go faster. It was one of his successful experiments that gave the first real impetus to the development of vehicles supported by a layer of air. A number of names are used to describe air cushion supported craft, including *hovercraft, air cushion vehicles* (ACV), *ground effect machine* (GEM) and *surface effect ships* (SES).

Cockerell's idea was to trap air beneath the hull of a boat, thereby eliminating the friction between the hull and the water which slows down conventional craft. Originally this was achieved by blowing air into a shallow upside-down hull at a pressure slightly higher than atmospheric and trapping it by means of a curtain of very high pressure air around the edge of the hull. This *air cushion* trapped within an *air curtain* provided two to three times more lifting force than if the same air was simply directed downwards as an even jet of air. Cockerell produced a free-flight model using this system, followed by the construction of a full-scale manned hovercraft.

Flexible skirts

One of the disadvantages of the early system was that it required an excessive amount of power to generate the air curtain. The next important step in the development of an economic hovercraft was the introduction of a *flexible skirt system* in 1961. This is a rubberized material fringe that hangs down around the edge of the vessel. The skirt serves the same function as the air curtain in containing the air cushion.

In marine vehicles the air cushion permits speeds three times faster than a ship, with relatively low water resis-

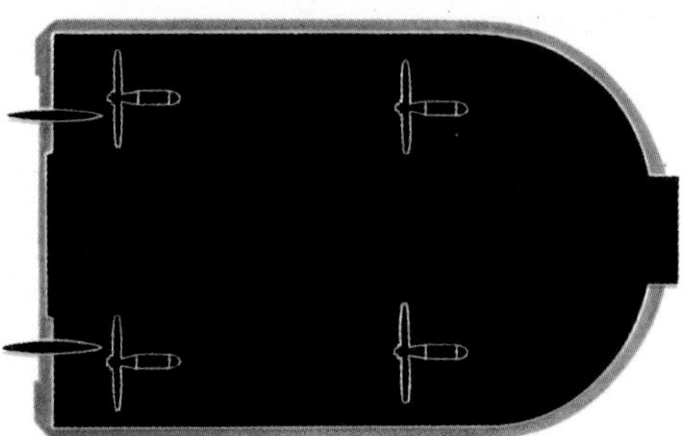

Above and right: The SR.N4 hovercraft travels on a 2.5 m (8 ft) deep cushion of air and is powered by four Rolls-Royce Marine Proteus gas turbine engines. The SR.N4 is 39 m (130 ft) long with a beam (width) of 24 m (78 ft). Overall height on its landing pads is 11.5 m (38 ft), and it weighs 160 tons.

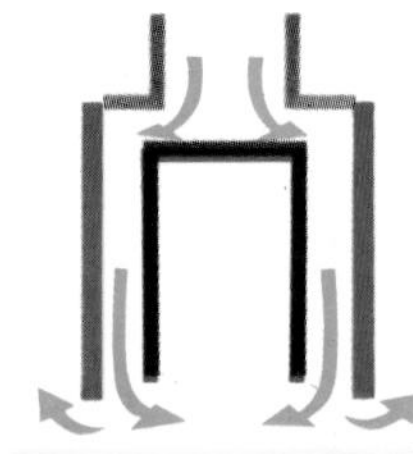

Below and right: Air blown into the space between two cans creates a curtain of air around the lower rims. This traps a cushion of air below the inner can which gives the needed lift. On measuring the pressure on a scale Cockerell proved that the force of lift was greater than that achieved by one can.

National Research Development Council

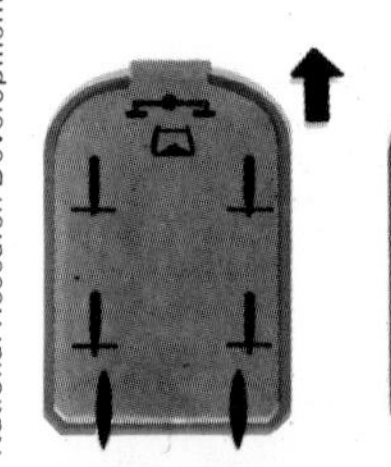

Below: Directional control of the SR.N4 is determined by the angle of the fins at the rear of the craft and of the pylons, the propeller mounts, on the roof of the craft. These are controlled by the rudder bar, shown at the top of the diagram, and the handwheel just below it.

Popperfoto

Left: The world's first hovercraft, the SR.N1, was built by aircraft makers Saunders-Roe and financed by Britain's National Research Development Corporation. SR.N1 made the first hovercraft crossing of an open body of water when it crossed the English Channel from Calais to Dover in 1959.

British Hovercraft Corporation

Right: Hovercraft are used to provide ferry services in many parts of the world. SR.N4s, the world's largest amphibious hovercraft, operate a regular service across the English Channel, each carrying 254 passengers and 30 vehicles. Larger passenger-carrying hovercraft are being developed.

TYPES OF HOVERCRAFT

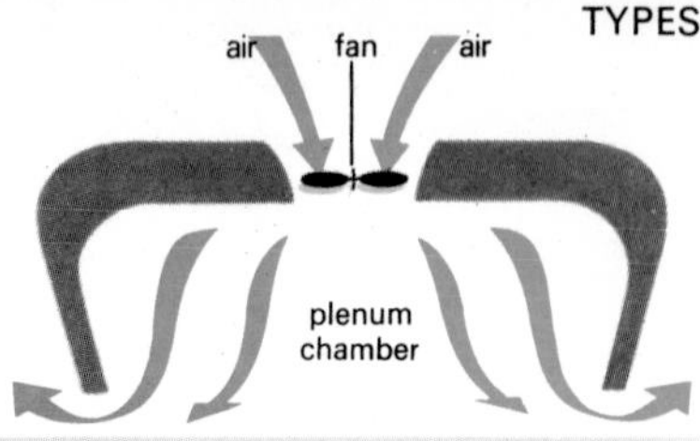

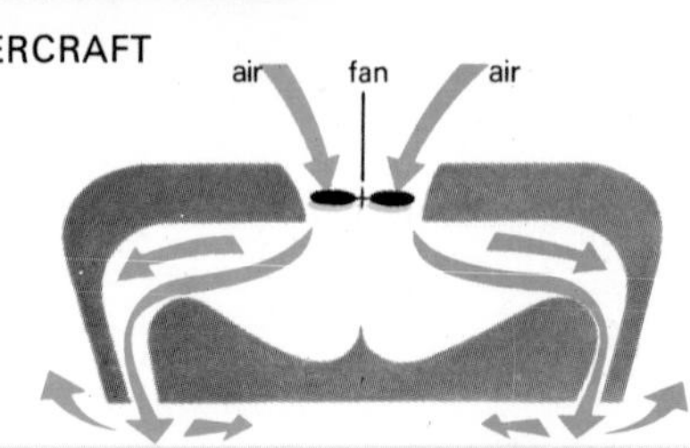

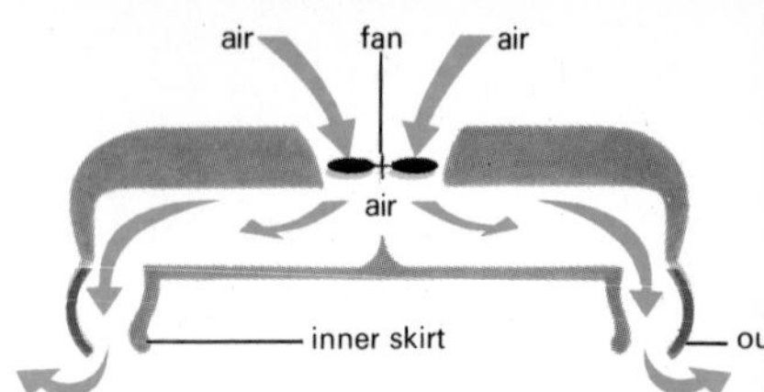

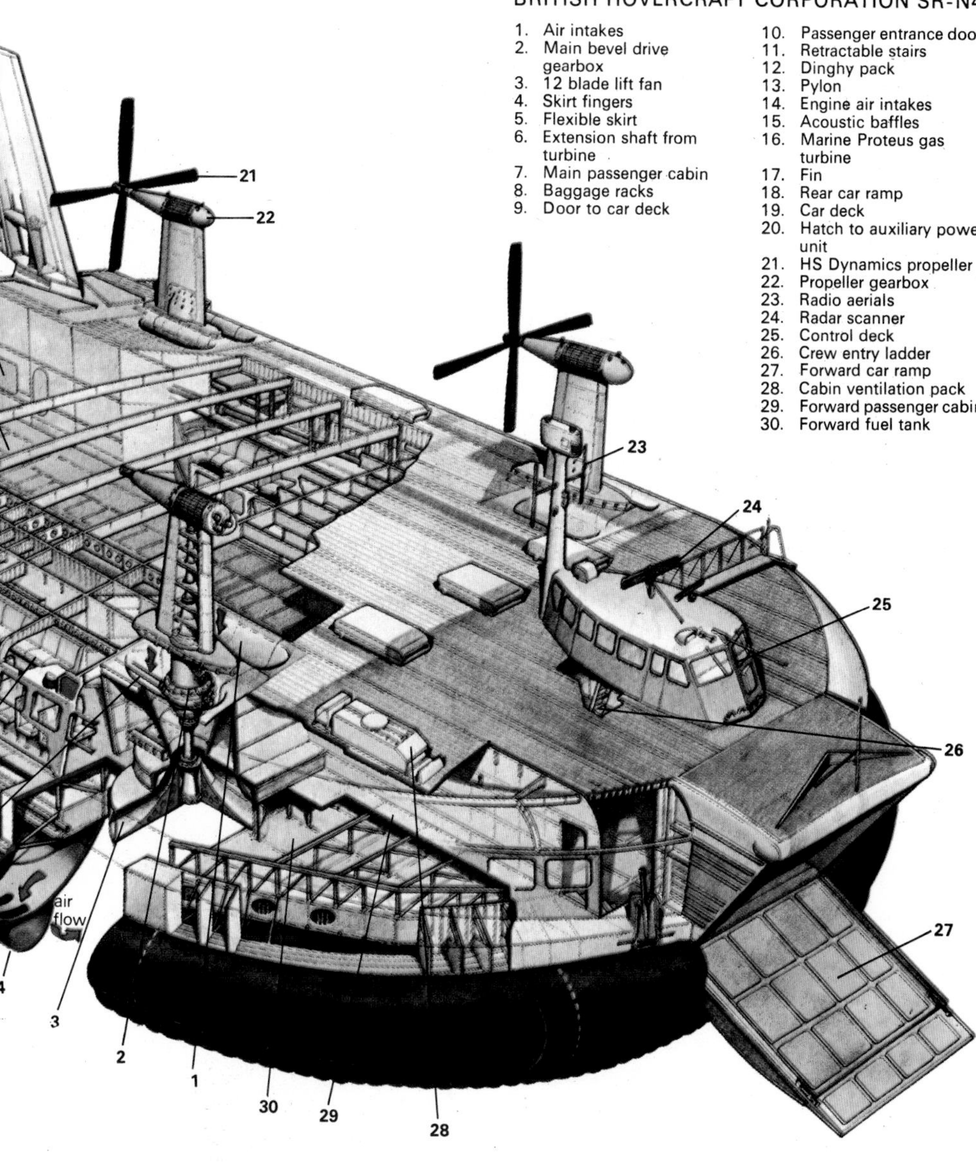

BRITISH HOVERCRAFT CORPORATION SR-N4

1. Air intakes
2. Main bevel drive gearbox
3. 12 blade lift fan
4. Skirt fingers
5. Flexible skirt
6. Extension shaft from turbine
7. Main passenger cabin
8. Baggage racks
9. Door to car deck
10. Passenger entrance door
11. Retractable stairs
12. Dinghy pack
13. Pylon
14. Engine air intakes
15. Acoustic baffles
16. Marine Proteus gas turbine
17. Fin
18. Rear car ramp
19. Car deck
20. Hatch to auxiliary power unit
21. HS Dynamics propeller
22. Propeller gearbox
23. Radio aerials
24. Radar scanner
25. Control deck
26. Crew entry ladder
27. Forward car ramp
28. Cabin ventilation pack
29. Forward passenger cabin
30. Forward fuel tank

tance. Craft using a full peripheral skirt can travel from one kind of surface to another with little perceptible change in the craft's motion. This means that amphibious movements — travelling from land to sea — and over-ice operations are possible. Non-amphibious marine hovercraft have been developed with side walls or keels immersed in the water, sealing the sides of the cushion, with the ends sealed by flexible curtains. These craft offer greater economy of power as far as the cushion is concerned but require relatively higher driving power because of the sidewall resistance in the water.

Moving forwards

Hovercraft can be propelled by a variety of means, including ducted or unducted propellers, with low tip speeds for quietness, and centrifugal fans. Propulsive devices which operate by contact with the ground are being considered for use in Arctic regions where the sloping terrain demands substantial side forces to control the craft effectively.

Redirection of the propulsive thrust is one common steering method. Many craft employ rudders operating in the fan or propeller slipstream to swing the craft into a turn. Sideways facing air nozzles are also used on some designs to help turn the craft at low speeds. For purely marine hovercraft, control can be very effectively obtained by the use of conventional rudders, and craft with immersed sidewalls can be steered by turning the sidewalls.

Braking of amphibious hovercraft is not as effective as for wheeled land vehicles unless a surface contacting device is used. Cutting off the lift-creating air to stop the craft by letting it settle on the surface is only advisable over water or smooth surfaces. Drawing to a halt is thus a very gradual process for amphibious craft — reverse thrust of the propellers is used, which provides only about one third of forward thrust.

Hovercraft are now used quite extensively as passenger and cargo ferries, and many are now in military use as patrol craft and troop carriers. *Hovertrains,* running along concrete tracks, are under development in several countries, including France where design projects by companies such as Bertin and SEDAM are quite well advanced. Another Bertin proposal is the use of air cushion landing gear for heavy freight aircraft, and SEDAM are building 225-ton air cushion ferry craft.

Rapid progress has been made in the development of air cushion platforms and strap-on skirt systems for the movement of large, heavy items such as oil storage tanks and electrical transformers. Air cushion platforms range in size from small ACV pallets a few feet square to large ACV platforms capable of handling loads weighing hundreds of tons. Basically these consist of flat boxes, sealed except for an inlet at one edge which is connected to an air pump and vents in the bottom through which the air escapes to form the air cushion. The use of these ACV pallets hovering a few inches above the ground means that heavy items like aero-engines or large castings can be easily be moved around by hand.

Ice-breaking is another dramatic role for ACV platforms. The reasons why ice-breaking occurs beneath an air cushion are not yet fully understood, but in

Beken of Cowes

Left: Fixed sidewall hovercraft ride on 'captured air bubbles' and are nicknamed CABs. Thin but solid sidewalls extend into the water to block air leakage from the chamber beneath the hovercraft deck. Increasing the air pressure lifts the craft, thus reducing water drag.

Below: ACV pallets are used to move heavy loads. Air is pumped into the pallet and, as pressure builds up, escapes through thin lubricating seals. This creates an air cushion between the pallet and the ground, making the pallet and its load airborne. It can then be moved with little effort.

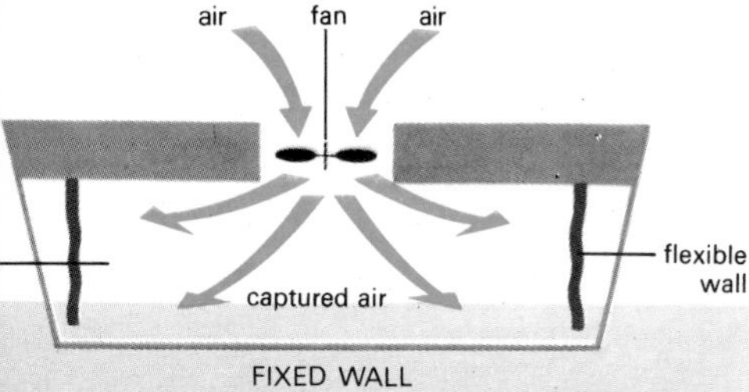

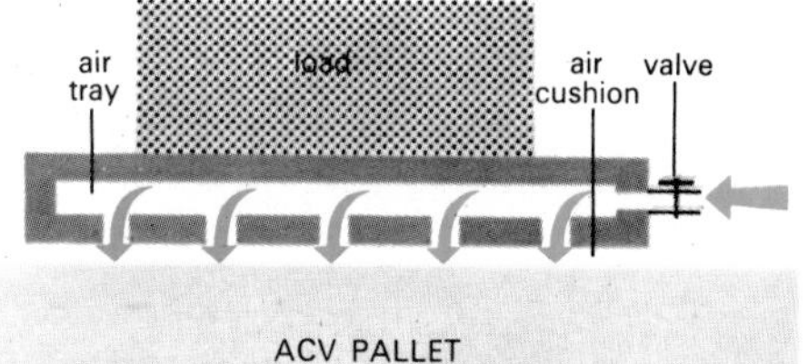

Canada 69 cm (27 in) thick ice has been broken by the passage of a 220-ton ACV.

Hydrofoils

A hydrofoil boat works on the same principle as an aircraft. It has a boat-shaped hull to which 'wings', or *hydrofoils,* are attached at the front and back by means of vertical, leg-like struts. As they travel through the water these hydrofoils produce lift in the same way the aerofoil shape of an aircraft wing provides lift in the air.

A stationary hydrofoil boat floats on the surface of the water like a conventional boat. As it gathers speed it begins to rise in the water until, when it is travelling fast, the lift created by the flow of water over the hydrofoil is sufficient to raise the hull clear of the water. A hydrofoil boat in full flight looks rather like an ordinary boat on water skis. Once out of the water the hull no longer suffers resistance from friction between the hull and the water or from waves in rough water and therefore gives a faster, smoother ride.

Water wings

The thicker the medium through which a foil is travelling, the more lift it can produce. As water is several hundred times denser than air, hydrofoils can be much smaller than an aircraft's wings and yet still create considerable lift. An aircraft's wings, however, operate in air whose density changes little over the range of altitudes at which they fly. The hydrofoil boat's 'wings' are working very close to the surface of the water where there is a massive and abrupt change in density between air and water. If the foils break through the surface a large drop in lift occurs because the pressure difference between its upper and lower surfaces is destroyed when the water no longer flows over the top.

The upper and lower limits of the depth within which the foils must operate are too fine to be controlled by hand. To ensure a nearly constant flying height, the foils need some form of automatic control. This in-built stability is achieved differently by the two principle types of hydrofoil design.

Surface piercing hydrofoils

In the *surface piercing* hydrofoils, the foils actually break the surface of the water as the craft moves forward. When lift is lost due to the hydrofoil breaking through waves, the craft sinks deeper into the water, thereby immersing a greater foil area which in turn creates more lift. This very simple design is used in almost all the commercial hydrofoil ferries in the western world.

Fully submerged hydrofoils

In the *fully submerged* hydrofoils, the foils are completely immersed in water all the time. The amount of lift produced is controlled by altering the angle of attack of the foils with hydraulic rams. These are rods moved by liquid under pressure which press down on or pull back from the hydrofoil to change its angle of inclination.

The movement of the hydraulic rams themselves is directed by signals from a sonic device in the bow which sends out pulses of high-frequency sound waves and listens for echoes from on-coming waves in order to assess the wave's height. It then automatically instructs the hy-

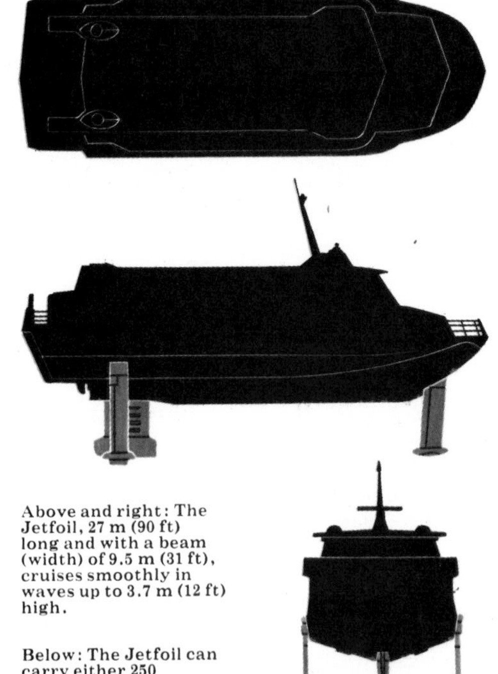

Above and right: The Jetfoil, 27 m (90 ft) long and with a beam (width) of 9.5 m (31 ft), cruises smoothly in waves up to 3.7 m (12 ft) high.

Below: The Jetfoil can carry either 250 commuter passengers or 25,000 kg (25 tons) of cargo.

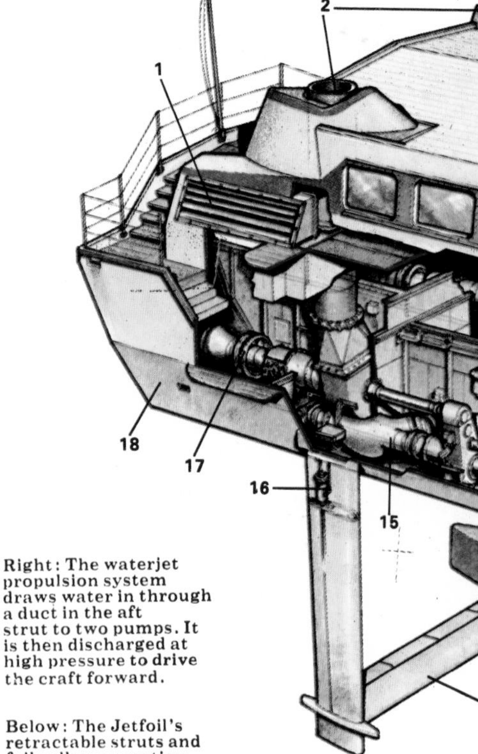

Right: The waterjet propulsion system draws water in through a duct in the aft strut to two pumps. It is then discharged at high pressure to drive the craft forward.

The Boeing Company

Below: The Jetfoil's retractable struts and foils allow operation in shallow water.

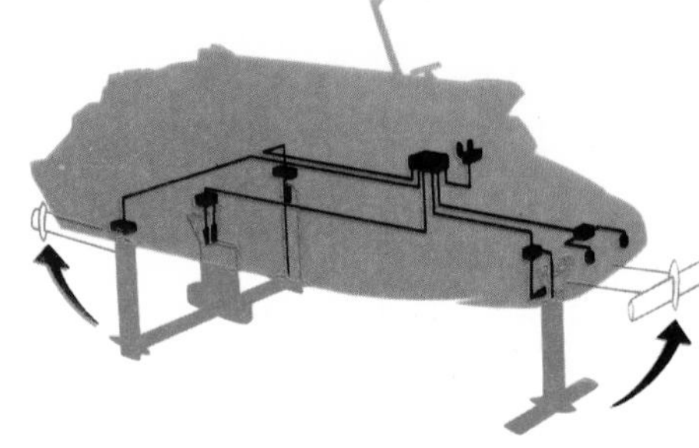

Below: The torpedo-shaped HD4 hydrofoil boat was designed by Alexander Graham Bell and Casey Baldwin. Nicknamed the 'Water Monster' and weighing over 5,100 kg (5 tons), it achieved lift even at low speeds. In 1918 it reached a world speed boat record of 114.4 km per hour (70.86 mph).

Right: The Tucumcari, a Patrol Gunboat Hydrofoil, was designed to United States Navy specifications under a programme initiated in 1965. Its maximum foilborne speed of 50 knots made it ideally suited to Vietnam war service. The craft was scrapped in 1972 after running aground in the Caribbean.

Gilbert H. Grosvenor/National Geographic Society

The Boeing Company

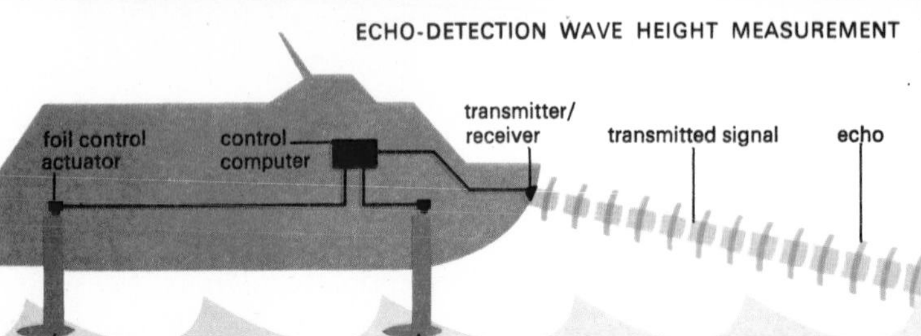

Left: Sonic sensors assess the height of oncoming waves and the tilt of the foils is adjusted automatically to hold the craft level in choppy water.

draulic system to make the appropriate adjustments to the angles of the hydrofoils so that the hull is held steady. Gyroscopes in the hull which sense the craft's pitch, roll and heave motions also feed information into this control circuit and help to keep the hydrofoil boat level. These systems are very expensive; the principal user of fully submerged hydrofoils is the US Navy.

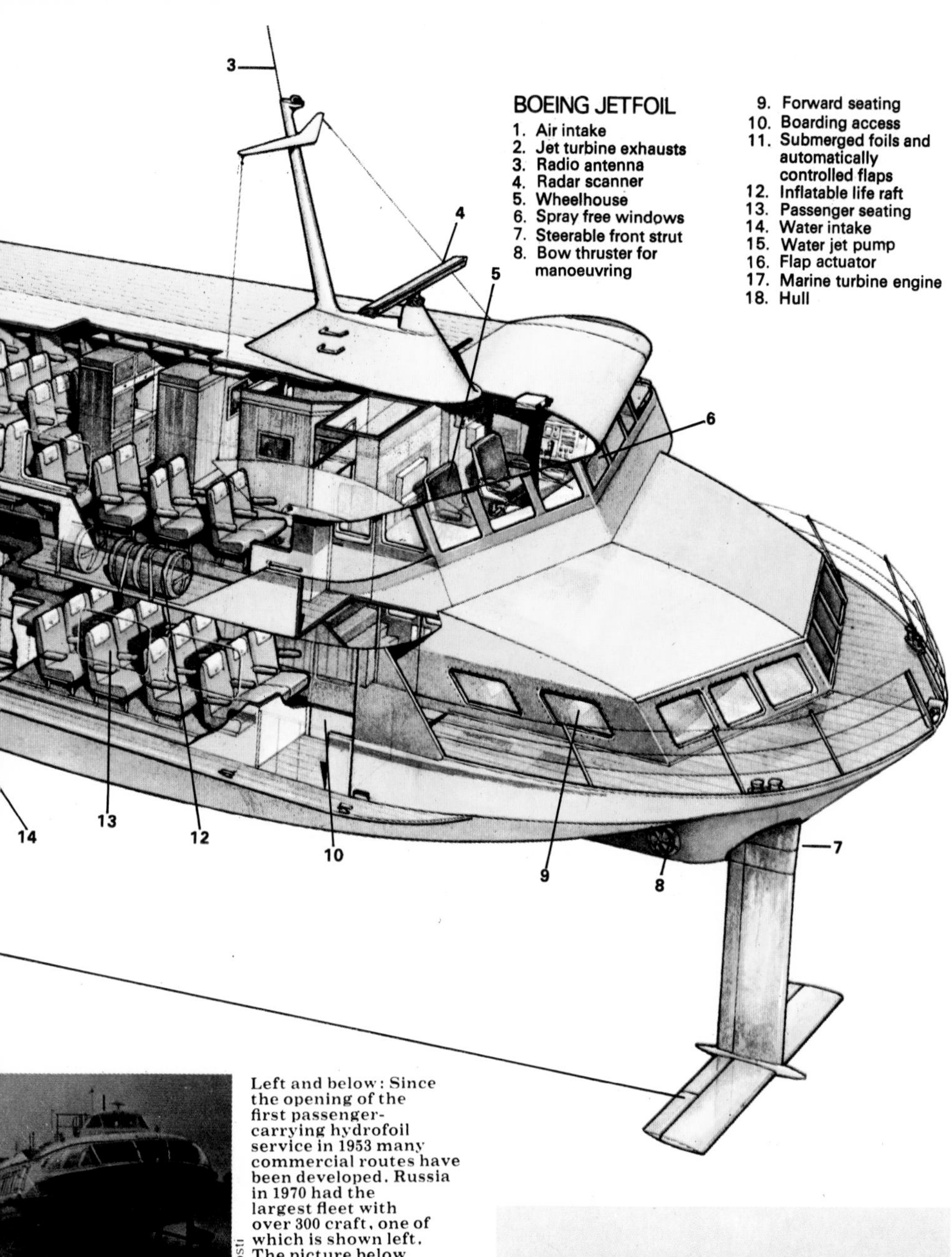

Propulsion systems

An early type of hydrofoil arrangement was the 'ladder' type, in which the amount of lift generated depends on the number of rungs immersed — the greater the number of rungs covered, the greater the lift.

Some designs of either type of hydrofoil have most of the weight carried by a large foil or foils at the front while on others the main foils are placed towards the rear. The smaller foil which carries the remaining weight is usually pivoted for steering the craft.

Commercial hydrofoil boats are usually powered by marine diesel engines, but high speed military craft often use gas turbine engines. There may be two separate propulsion systems, one for use when the craft is being carried by the foils and another for when it is moving very slowly and floating on its hull.

Problems at high speed

At speeds above 50 knots, hydrofoils can suffer from the effects of *cavity flow*. As a result of increasingly turbulent water flow across the top of the foil, cavities are formed along the foil surface which cut its lifting force. These cavities subsequently fill with air or water vapour.

When the craft is travelling very fast, the water pressure on the upper foil surface may drop below atmospheric pressure. Under such circumstances, air from above the surface of the water may be sucked down the strut and along the foil to fill the cavities. This effect is called *ventilation* and again causes a variation in lift.

If the pressure across the top of the foil falls low enough, the water will vaporize, forming bubbles of water vapour which break up the smooth flow of water over the upper surface, thereby reducing lift. This phenomenon, known as *cavitation*, not only upsets efficient lift production but can also seriously erode the foil over a period of time. As the bubbles burst they smash minute jets of water against the foil surface with sufficient force to damage the metal.

Left and below: Since the opening of the first passenger-carrying hydrofoil service in 1953 many commercial routes have been developed. Russia in 1970 had the largest fleet with over 300 craft, one of which is shown left. The picture below shows a Swedish ferry to Oland.

Novosti

Above: FRESH 1 (foil research experimenting super cavitating hydrofoil) holds the hydrofoil speed record of 84 knots. When foilborne the craft is powered by a fan jet producing 8,200 kg (18,000 lb) of thrust. The craft has a catamaran hull linked with a bridge to which test foils are fitted.

Picturepoint

The Boeing Company

Right: The Little Squirt in full flight can do 50 knots. Built in 1962 as a research vessel it was the first craft to be fitted with a waterjet system of propulsion. Trailing edge flaps were fitted to the foils and foil controls introduced—both features used in later hydrofoil designs like the Jetfoil.

The Boeing Company

TYPES OF HYDROFOIL

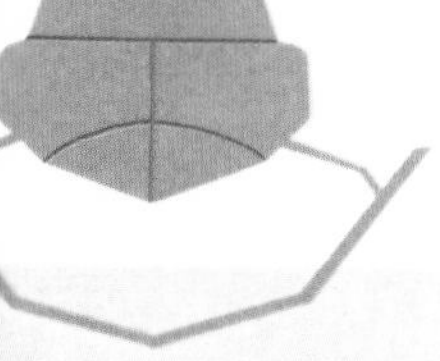

SURFACE PIERCING

SHALLOW-DRAFT

SUBMERGED

LADDER

Ships and Boats

The ability of a ship or boat to float, even if it is made of a heavy material such as steel, is due to the relationship between its weight and the volume of its hull. A solid object will float if it is lighter than an equal volume of the fluid in which it is floating. If it has the same weight as an equal volume of the fluid it will float with its top just level with the surface, and if it is heavier it will sink.

When an object is put into water, as when a boat or ship is launched, a certain volume of water must move aside or be *displaced* to make room for it. The weight of water displaced by a ship is equal to the *upthrust,* an upward force which the water exerts on the ship. If the weight of the ship were greater than the upthrust, then it would sink.

A solid block of steel does not float in water, but that block of steel can be made into a ship which will float although it weighs the same as the block. This is because the hull of the ship has a large volume for its weight and so it can displace a sufficient amount of water to produce an upthrust equal to its own weight. The upthrust exerted on the ship by the water is termed the *buoyancy.*

The volume of water displaced by the ship is equal to the volume of the part of the ship which is below the surface of the water. If a load is added to the ship it sinks lower so that more water is displaced, increasing the upthrust to support the extra weight. If the load is too heavy the ship will sink so low that water will come over the sides, fill the ship, and make it sink completely.

Stability

The stability of a ship or boat depends on the relative positions of three imaginary points known as the *centre of gravity, the centre of buoyancy,* and the *metacentre.* The total weight of a ship, which is of course spread throughout its structure, can be thought of as a single force acting downwards through a point called the centre of gravity.

Similarly, the buoyancy of a ship, which is distributed all around the hull, can be considered to be a single force acting upwards through a point called the centre of buoyancy. When the ship is upright, the centre of buoyancy is vertically below the centre of gravity, both points being on an imaginary line, the *centreline,* drawn down through the middle of the ship.

If the ship leans over to one side, because of wind or wave action for example, the centre of gravity remains at its fixed position on the centreline but the centre

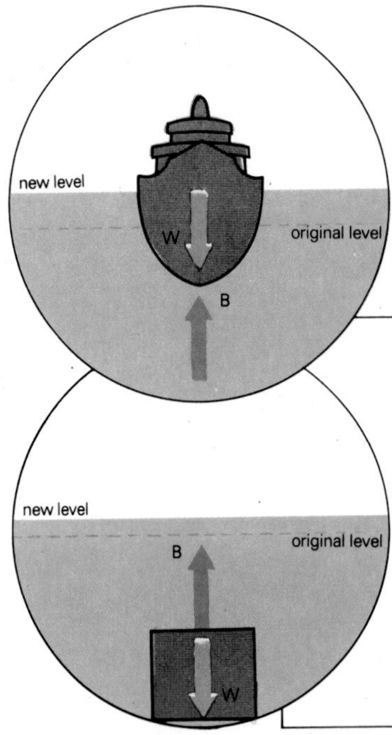

FLOTATION
The upthrust is equal to the weight of the water displaced

new level
original level
W
B

LOAD LINES

TF F T S W WNA L R

Left: A ship floats because it displaces its own weight of water, but a solid steel block displaces only a fraction of its weight so it sinks.

Right: Load lines or Plimsoll lines painted on the sides of ships show the depth to which they can be loaded in different climates and seas. The numbers on a ship's bow show its draught.

Below: The underwater volume of the hull equals the volume of water displaced.

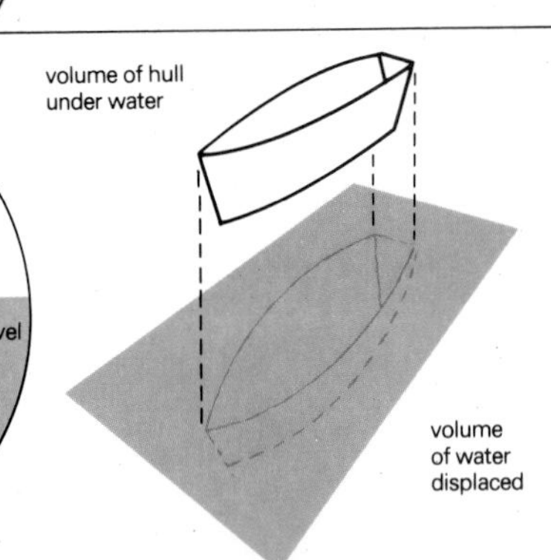

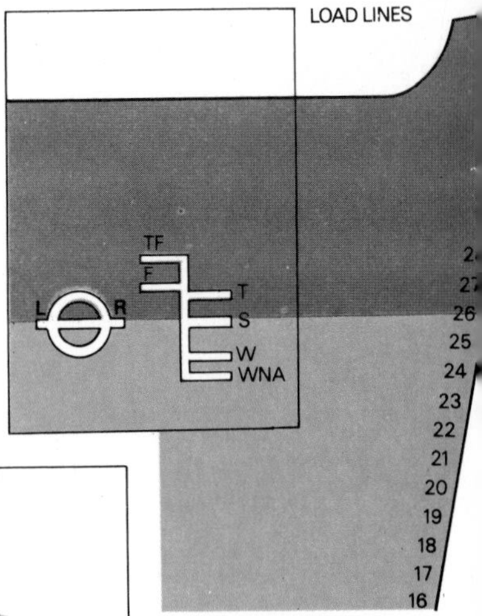

Below: Lifeboats have watertight cabins and compartments which create strong buoyancy forces if the boat capsizes, so that it rolls back upright again. The top picture shows a boat righting itself after being deliberately capsized. Modern lifeboats are almost unsinkable unless badly damaged.

Right: Special boats for lifesaving were first used by the ancient Chinese on large rivers such as the Yangtze. Attempts at making unsinkable lifeboats began in Europe in the late eighteenth century, using airtight compartments in the hulls to keep the boats afloat. A variation of this type was the 'hydrogen lifeboat' design first built in the USA in 1816, which gained extra buoyancy from tanks of hydrogen fitted in the bottom of the hull. Most lifeboats are between 7.6 and 15.8 m (25 to 52 ft) long, the larger versions being capable of carrying up to 100 people at a speed of 9 knots.

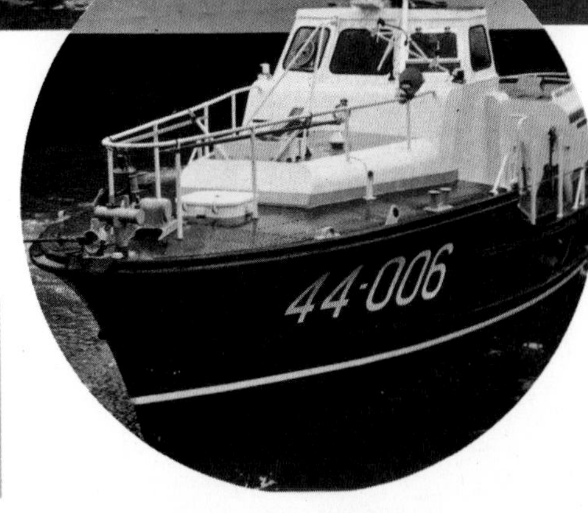

CENTRES OF BOUYANCY AND GRAVITY

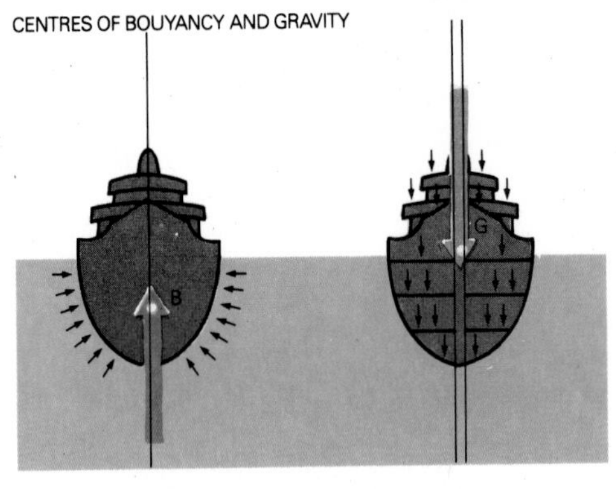

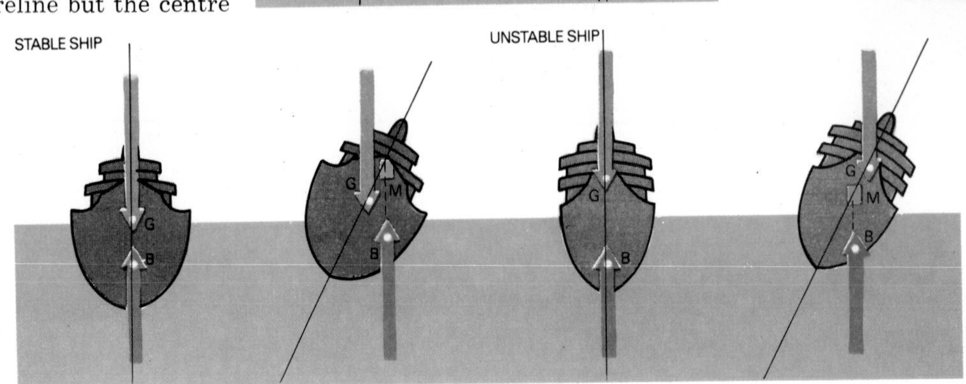

Above right: Buoyancy forces act at all parts of the submerged area of the hull, but they can be thought of as a single force acting up through the centre of buoyancy, B. Similarly, the weight of a ship, which is spread throughout the structure, may be considered as a single force acting down through the centre of gravity, G. The positions of these two points determine the stability of the ship, which is its ability to remain upright in the water.

Left: When a ship is heeled over, the line of action of the buoyancy moves to the side, and meets the centreline at a point called the metacentre, M. In the case of a stable ship, when it leans over G pulls down at the centre and B is pushed up to one side, so the two will combine to right the vessel. On an unstable ship G is further to the side than B is, and they combine to capsize the vessel. A ship is stable when M is above G, unstable when it is below G.

The *Spirit of London* (17,370 tons) in dry dock. Renamed *Sun Princess* in 1974, she is based on the west coast of the U.S.A. and cruises to Alaska, Mexico and the Caribbean, carrying 874 passengers and 322 crew.

photo courtesy P & O Lines

of buoyancy moves away from the centreline and towards the side of the ship which is lower in the water. The weight of the ship and the buoyancy force are still equal but they are no longer vertically in line. The weight of the ship acting down through the centre of gravity works together with the upward buoyancy force to pull the ship back to its upright position.

When the ship leans over, the line of action of the buoyancy force meets the original centreline of the ship at a point called the metacentre. As long as the metacentre is above the centre of gravity, the ship is stable and will return to the upright position when the force causing it to lean over is removed.

If the metacentre and the centre of gravity coincide, the buoyancy and weight forces will be acting directly against each other and so will cancel each other out. This means there will be no turning motion to bring the ship back to its upright position, and in this situation the ship will tend to remain leaning over.

More seriously, if the metacentre is below the centre of gravity then, when the ship leans over, the weight and the buoyancy will act in such a way as to lean the vessel over still further and possibly even to capsize it completely.

The positions of the centres of gravity and buoyancy and of the metacentre are carefully calculated by the ship's designers before it is built, so as to ensure a safe and stable design.

Hull strength

Ships, especially longer vessels such as oil tankers, must be strongly built to prevent them bending in the worst wave conditions.

The conditions which create the highest stresses in the hull occur when the vessel is sailing into waves where the distance between successive wave peaks is equal to the length of the ship. The worst situations are when there is a wave trough at the middle of the ship and a peak at each end, and when there is a wave peak at the middle and a trough at each end.

There is a relatively high buoyancy force on any part of the hull passing through a wave peak because more of it is under water, and a relatively low buoyancy force on any part of the hull passing through a wave trough because less of it is under water. This means that with a wave peak at each end the ship will tend to sag in the middle; with a peak at the middle and a trough at each end it will

Queen Elizabeth 2
1 Propeller
2 Safety control room
3 Fresh water tanks—evaporators convert sea water to fresh water
4 Oil fuel tanks
5 Machinery room
6 Steam turbines
7 Stabilizers
8 Steam turbine control room
9 Main control and computer room
10 Boilers
11 Hospital
12 Swimming pool
13 Refrigerated stores
14 Passenger cabins
15 Bridge and chartroom with officers' cabins below
16 Bow thrusters for easy berthing

Right: The 'Queen Elizabeth 2' is one of the most modern passenger ships in service. Commonly referred to as the 'QE2', she went into service at the end of the 1960s and is used on the Southampton – Cherbourg – New York run and for cruising. The ship is powered by two steam turbines which produce a total of 110,000 hp. The steam for the turbines is produced by three huge oil-burning boilers and the two six-bladed propellers, made of a bronze-based cast alloy, weigh 32 tons each.

Left: A ship is designed to move through the water as smoothly as possible. A vessel that pushes up huge waves from the prow puts an extra strain on the engines that reduces its performance.

Photo Researchers

Spectrum

Top: The icebreaker 'Manhattan' in action. Icebreakers have strengthened bows to enable them to smash through the ice.

Above: The 'Bosanka', a general dry cargo vessel. These ships carry a wide range of cargoes, whereas bulk carriers usually carry only one type.

tend to bend up in the middle. In extreme cases these effects could even break the ship in half.

Small ships are not likely to suffer so much from high bending stresses as long super tankers or bulk carriers, and this is one reason why the large ships are very broad, as this gives the required cargo capacity without increasing the length so much as to make the ship dangerously vulnerable to bending stresses.

The *draught* (the vertical distance between the bottom of the hull and the surface of the water) may be large, and it affects the strength of the hull because the pressure of the water on it increases uniformly as the draught increases. The pressure on the hull of a deep draught ship may be considerable, and if the hull is not strong enough this pressure can crush it.

Panting, pounding and racking

In addition to the pressure of the water on the hull, there are other important forces acting on it due to its motion through the waves. The three main effects of these forces are known as *panting, pounding* and *racking*.

As the vessel moves up and down in the sea, the steel plates of the hull near the bow undergo a pressure variation which tends to push them inwards when the bow pushes down into the sea, and then as the bow lifts they are released again. This in and out motion of the plates is called panting and the hull is stiffened near the bow to resist this effect. Panting also occurs along the sides of the ship and at the stern, but the most severe effect is at the fore (front) end.

When a ship is heading through the waves the fore end may leave the water and then an instant later slam hard down on to the sea surface. This is known as pounding. Not all vessels suffer from a bad pounding force, as it depends on the draught at the fore end of the ship when it is travelling without cargo or passengers, ships with shallow draughts being more likely to suffer from pounding. Ships which are prone to pounding are usually stiffened for approximately 30% of their length from the fore end.

When the waves are approaching a ship from the side, the depth of water on one side of the ship may be greater than that on the other as a wave passes it. This creates unequal forces across the width of the ship which tend to distort the hull. To help the ship resist this racking effect the internal framework is reinforced at the points where the vertical side frames join the horizontal beams running across the ship. The divisions across the vessel, called *bulkheads*, also help to prevent racking.

Barnaby's

Above: A great deal of cargo is carried in containers, which are loaded on specially designed container ships either by dockside cranes or by cranes mounted on the ship. The containers must be carefully loaded for even weight distribution. This is an American ship, the 'Transidaho'.

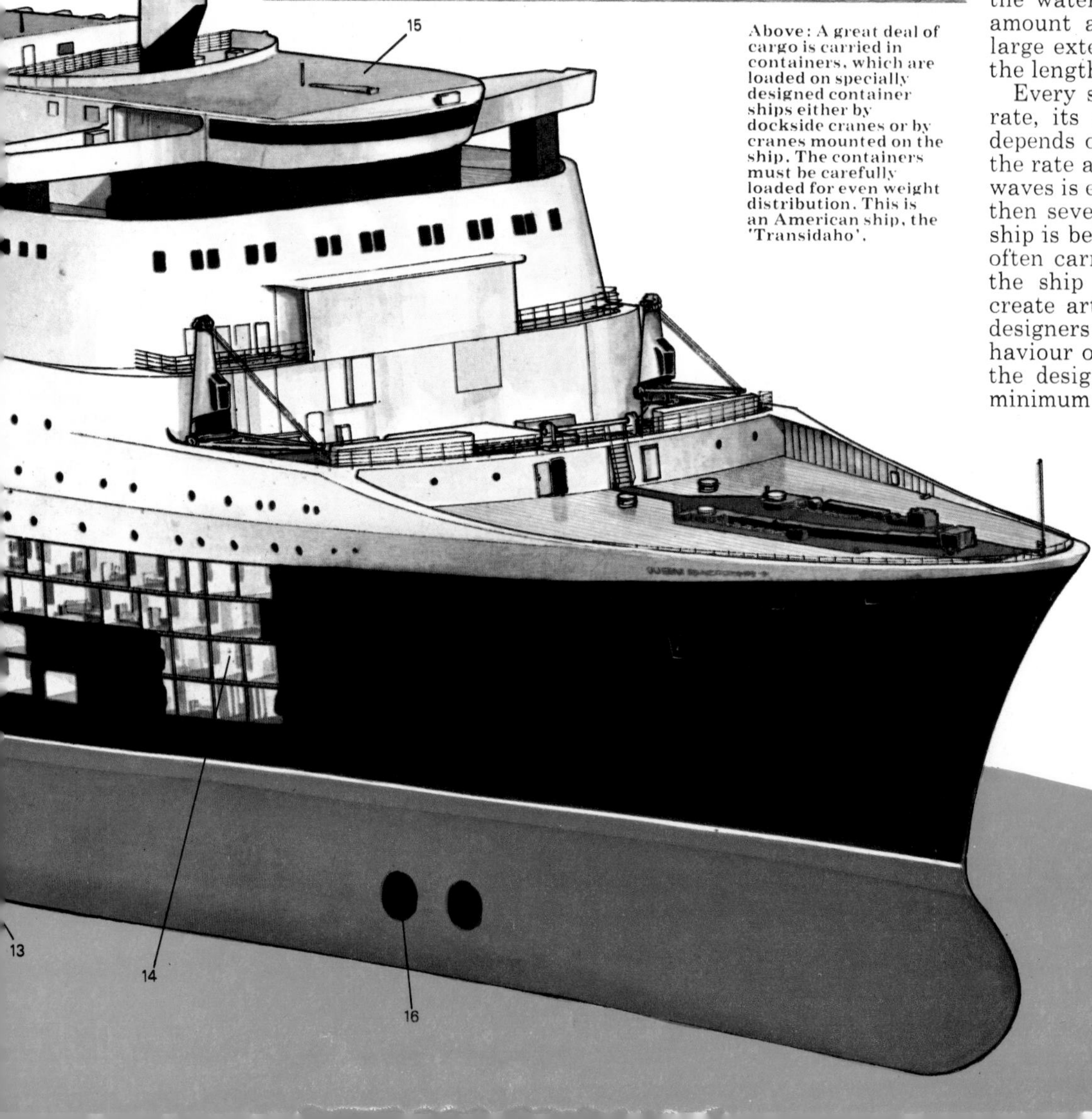

Pitching and rolling

Pitching, a kind of see-saw motion of a vessel, can reduce its performance when moving through waves, and ships that pitch badly may dip their bows beneath the water when they meet a wave. The amount a ship will pitch depends to a large extent on its speed, its length, and the length of the waves.

Every ship tends to pitch at a certain rate, its *natural pitching period*, which depends on its size, shape and weight. If the rate at which the ship encounters the waves is equal to its natural pitching rate then severe pitching will occur. When a ship is being designed, a series of tests is often carried out using a scale model of the ship in a testing tank which can create artificial waves. This enables the designers to predict the probable behaviour of a ship in waves and to amend the design so as to keep pitching to a minimum.

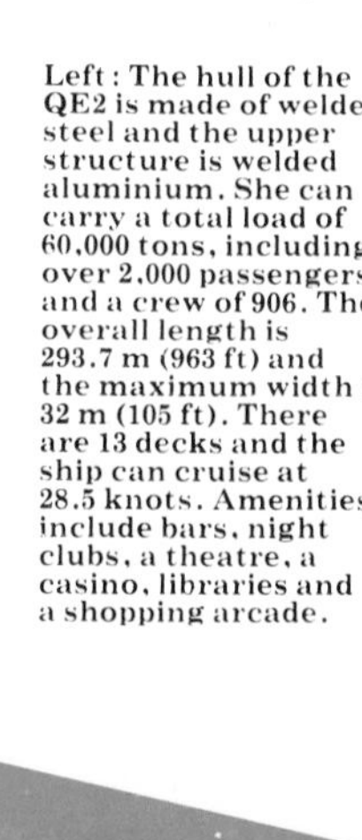

Left: The hull of the QE2 is made of welded steel and the upper structure is welded aluminium. She can carry a total load of 60,000 tons, including over 2,000 passengers and a crew of 906. The overall length is 293.7 m (963 ft) and the maximum width is 32 m (105 ft). There are 13 decks and the ship can cruise at 28.5 knots. Amenities include bars, night clubs, a theatre, a casino, libraries and a shopping arcade.

Left and below: A new development in cargo shipping is the LASH (Lighter Aboard Ship) vessel. The lighter is a floating container which is towed by a barge to the stern of the LASH vessel, where it is loaded into the hold of the ship by a gantry crane which runs along rails on the deck of the ship.

T. E. Czerski, Bavaria

Rolling is a side to side motion caused by wind and waves. This action can set up stresses in the structure and may increase operational costs. It is also unpleasant for the passengers and crew, and this has led to efforts to reduce rolling to a minimum.

The most critical factors are the weight distribution of the cargo and structure, and the distance between the centre of gravity and the metacentre. If this distance is large the ship will be very stable, but the ship will roll from side to side very quickly and it is said to be 'stiff'. Ship stabilizers are now used on many vessels to reduce the roll and give greater passenger comfort.

Ship resistance

As a ship moves it meets a certain amount of resistance from the water, and some of the ship's power must be used in overcoming this resistance.

The resistance is made up of a number of separate components, including *frictional drag, wavemaking resistance, form drag, eddy-making resistance,* and the resistance caused by attachments such as the rudder or propeller. Once the total resistance is known then the power needed to propel the vessel can be estimated. This is done by making a scale model of the ship and measuring its resistance in a testing tank. The power needed for the full-sized ship can then be calculated from the figures obtained from the model tests.

Frictional drag, as its name implies, is caused by friction between the hull and the water, and wavemaking resistance is the amount of energy expended by the ship in creating bow and stern waves as it moves.

At the bow a wave crest is formed, and at the stern a wave trough. As the bow waves reach the stern they interact with the stern waves, and if a bow wave crest coincides with a stern wave trough the resulting pattern of waves leaving the ship will be almost damped out.

The naval architect aims to achieve this result because it gives minimum resistance; if the troughs of the bow waves coincide with the stern wave troughs the two reinforce each other resulting in a pronounced wave pattern behind the ship and maximum resistance. Some modern vessels are fitted with a submerged bulbous bow section which modifies the height of the bow waves and helps reduce wavemaking resistance.

As the ship moves forwards a low pressure area is created in the water

Photo Researchers

Picturepoint

Far left: If ships encounter severe bending forces they can be broken in half.

Left: There can be a considerable difference between the draught of a loaded ship and its draught when not loaded. The red part of this ship would be underwater if it was fully loaded.

Oil Tanker
1 Mooring winches
2 Boiler
3 Crew mess and cabins
4 Radar
5 Engine rooms
6 Water inlet pipes
7 Wheel house, chartroom and radio room
8 Oil fuel bunker
9 Ballast tank
10 Pump room
11 Fire tower
12 Fire hydrant
13 Cargo tank
14 Mooring winches
15 Access for tank cleaning machinery
16 Tank hatches
17 Steam pipes for cleaning tanks
18 Derricks for lifting pipes on board
19 Discharge and loading points
20 Anchor winches
21 Mooring winches

behind it, and this tends to hold the ship back. This resistance to forward motion is known as form drag. Eddy-making resistance occurs when water particles are made to whirl by the action of the hull, because the energy needed to cause the whirling must be supplied by the ship.

The effective power needed to drive the ship at a certain speed is found by multiplying the overall resistance by the speed. The engine power output required to produce this effective power is determined by calculations involving the performance of the propeller and the efficiency of the propeller and its drive system. Once the power requirements have been estimated the engine builder is informed and then the engine design can be started.

Ship engines

The first engine-driven ships were built in the nineteenth century, and were powered by steam engines. Steam turbines were introduced at the end of that century, and today most large ships are driven by them. The marine diesel engine is widely used in smaller ships and in many types of boat, and marine gas turbine engines, often based on aircraft engines, are used on many high speed naval craft, where their high cost is less prohibitive.

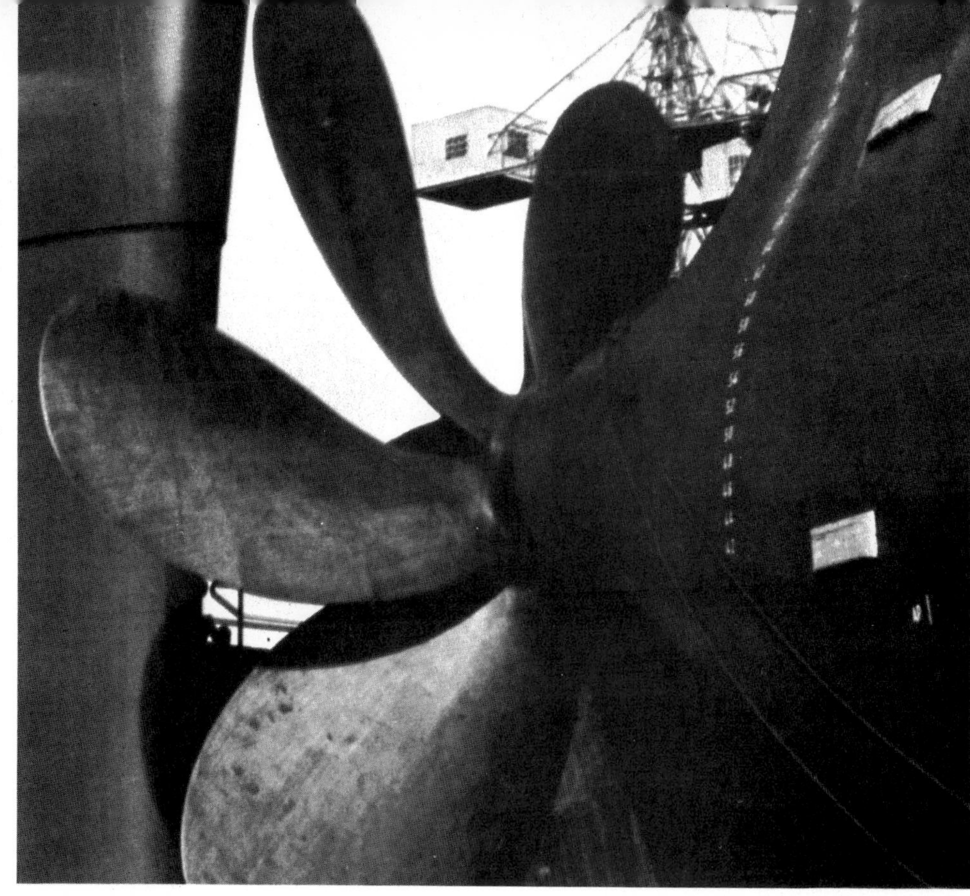

Above: this is the largest propeller in the world, weighing 72 tons and measuring 9.4 m (31 ft) across its diameter. It is fitted to the 386,000 ton tanker 'Ioannis Colocotronis'. Most of the big tankers are driven by a single large propeller.

Below: A modern oil tanker has engines, bridge and crew accommodation at the stern, and most of the hull is divided into tanks for the oil. There are store rooms and water tanks at the bow and pump rooms at each end of the oil storage section.

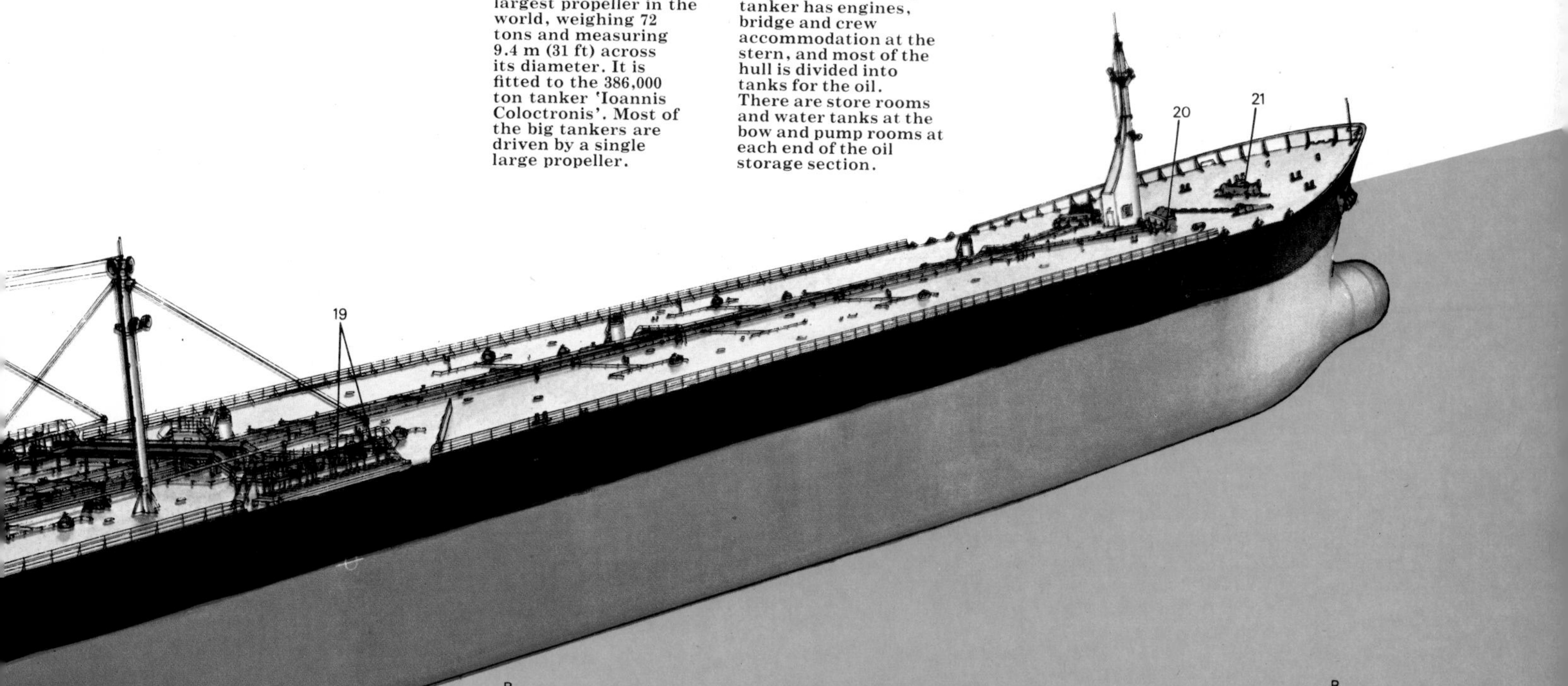

LONGITUDINAL BENDING

Left: Wave conditions can create severe bending forces on the hull of a ship. The upper diagram shows the buoyancy (B) and weight (W) forces when there is a wave peak at each end of the ship, and the lower diagram shows the forces when there is a peak at the middle and a trough at each end.

Balloons and Airships

The balloon, a thin 'envelope' containing hot air or a light gas, was the means by which man was first able to achieve sustained flight.

Following the discovery of hydrogen gas in the eighteenth century the building of balloons for flight, although not strictly a new idea, became a practical proposition. The main problem was to find a material for the envelope which was thin, light and strong but did not allow the gas to leak.

After experimenting with hydrogen balloons, Joseph and Etienne Montgolfier of France concluded that, as they could not prevent the hydrogen from leaking, the only practical solution was to provide a continuous supply of gas to make up for the loss.

As hydrogen was difficult to produce they decided to use what they assumed to be a similar light gas, which was given off when anything burned. They made an envelope, open at the bottom, from cloth-backed paper, and lit a fire of straw and rags below the opening. The 'gas' from the fire (consisting mainly of hot air, which is lighter than cold air and so rises) filled the envelope and the balloon rose successfully into the air.

After a series of experiments with unmanned balloons, including one carrying a sheep and two birds, preparations began for the first manned balloon flight. On 21 November 1783, a balloon was launched from the Bois de Boulogne in Paris, carrying Jean Pilâtre de Rozier and the Marquis d'Arlandes. It crossed the River Seine at a height of about 300m, landing 25 minutes later at the Butte aux Cailles just over 8 km (5 miles) away.

Ten days later, also in Paris, the first manned hydrogen balloon flight was made by Jacques Charles and M. N. Robert, with a balloon made of rubberized silk. Their two hour flight took them to the town of Nesles, 43 km (27 miles) away.

These flights started a craze for ballooning, but hot-air balloons, which had a tendency to catch fire, were soon superceded as the design of gas balloons improved. The modern hot-air balloon is the result of development sponsored by the US Navy in the late 1950s, and the first commercial design went into production in 1963.

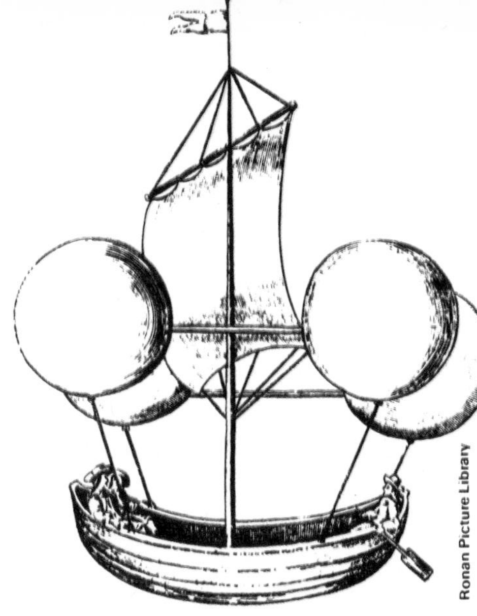

Ronan Picture Library

Left: A design for a flying ship by Lana di Terzi in 1670. The four spheres were to have been made of thin copper: to make them lighter than air, it was intended to pump all the air out of them. This would not have worked, however, as without the air inside, the spheres would have collapsed.

Mary Evans Library

Right: The first men to make a balloon flight were the Frenchmen Jean Pilâtre de Rozier and the Marquis d'Arlandes, in a Montgolfier hot-air balloon. The twenty-five minute flight took place in Paris on 21 November 1783, from the Bois de Boulogne to the Butte aux Cailles.

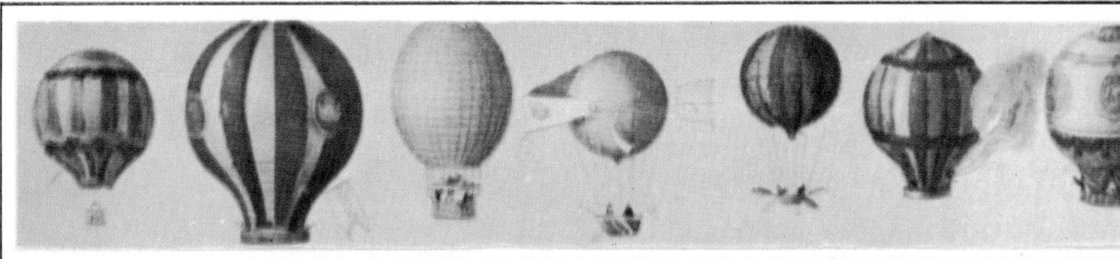

Bulloz

Above: A series of illustrations from a French encyclopedia, showing some of the balloons which flew between September 1783 and September 1784. The series shows three hot-air balloons, two gas balloons filled with hydrogen, two more hot-air balloons, and four more hydrogen balloons.

Photri

Right: Inflating the hydrogen balloon 'Intrepid' during the Battle of Fair Oaks, 31 May-1 June 1862, in the American Civil War. This balloon was used by Thaddeus Lowe, Chief Aeronaut of the Army of the Potomac, for spying on the Confederate lines. Later he used it to make aerial maps of Virginia.

Daily Telegraph Colour Library

Right: A modern hot-air balloon in flight. The weight of a hot-air balloon, including the envelope, basket and burner, is about 180 kg (400 lb), plus about a ton of hot air inside the envelope. The light, hot air displaces well over a ton of heavy, cold air to produce the force to lift the balloon.

Tim Graham/Transworld

Diana Hunt/Colorific

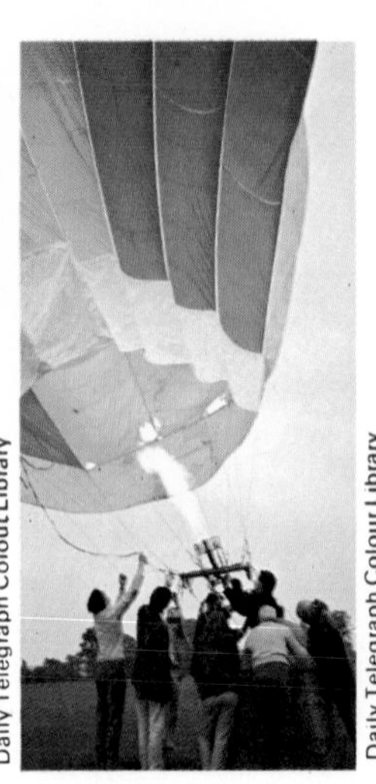

Daily Telegraph Colour Library

Left, above and right: Inflating a hot-air balloon. The envelope is laid out on the ground and hot air is blown through the open neck. As the envelope fills with hot air it rises into its upright position. A balloon can be unpacked, inflated and launched in about 15 minutes.

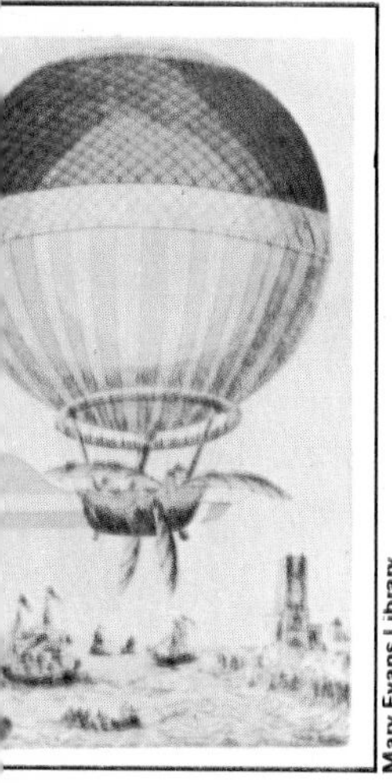

Left: The first flight across the English Channel was made on 7 January 1785 by Jean-Pierre Blanchard and Dr John Jeffries in a gas balloon. In recognition of this achievement, King Louis XVI of France granted Blanchard a pension, which he drew until his death in 1809.

Mary Evans Library

Bulloz

Right: A painting showing the French statesman Leon Gambetta about to escape by balloon from the siege of Paris, during the Franco-Prussian war in 1870. During the siege, 68 balloons were made in a factory at the Gare du Nord, and they were used to carry people out of the city.

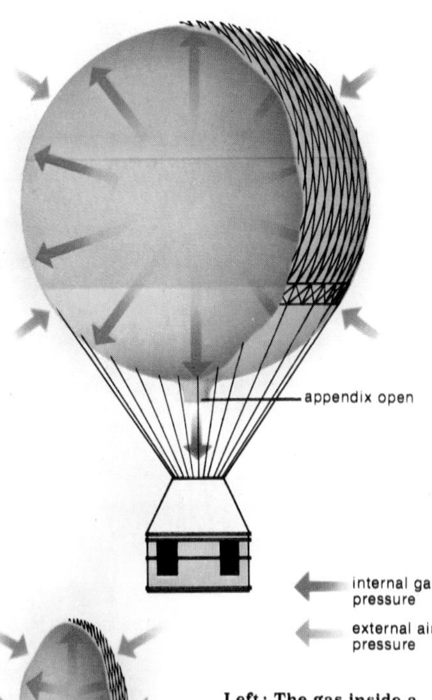

Left: The gas inside a balloon expands or contracts to keep its pressure the same as that of the air outside. At ground level the air pressure is relatively high, but it decreases steadily the further it is from the ground. Balloons meant to fly to high altitudes may be only partially inflated at ground level so that they do not burst as the gas expands when they rise. Most hydrogen balloons have an opening called an appendix at the bottom to allow the gas to escape if the pressure inside gets too high. When the pressure of the gas is the same as the air pressure the appendix closes, which prevents air entering the envelope.

Bubbles in the air

A balloon floats in the air in a similar way that a ship floats on water, following a basic principle first realized by Archimedes in the third century BC. In essence, Archimedes' principle states that if an object is wholly or partially immersed in a fluid (a liquid or a gas) its weight decreases by an amount equal to the weight of the fluid it has displaced. This loss in weight is an upward force which the fluid exerts on the object.

One example of this effect is the behaviour of a bubble of air in a jar of water. The bubble rises to the surface, because the weight of air forming it is far less than the weight of the volume of water it has displaced.

In the same way a balloon, which is in effect a bubble of light gas, rises through the relatively heavy air. For example, air is approximately 14 times heavier than hydrogen, and so 1 kg (2.2 lb) of hydrogen will displace about 14 kg (31 lb) of air, which means that there will be an upward force on it of 14 kg.

A balloon will rise if the weight of air displaced by the gas-filled envelope is greater than the total weight of the envelope, gas, fittings and occupants. If these two weights are the same the balloon will remain at the same height; if the balloon is heavier than the displaced air it will descend.

Gas balloons

Most gas balloons are filled with hydrogen, which is very light, but great care must be taken in handling it as it is highly inflammable. Modern balloons have spherical envelopes made of fabric impregnated with rubber or neoprene. The envelope is enclosed in a net of thin rope secured to a load ring, below the envelope, to which the basket carrying the crew and equipment is attached.

The pressure of the earth's atmosphere decreases the further it is from the surface, so as a balloon rises the gas within the envelope expands because its pressure is greater than that of the surrounding air. To prevent the balloon bursting when the gas expands, there is a long narrow tube at the bottom of the envelope through which the gas can escape. This tube, the *appendix*, acts as a one-way valve allowing gas to escape but preventing air from entering the envelope.

A gas balloon is made to ascend by reducing its weight, and this is done by discharging ballast, usually in the form of sand bags. As weight cannot be added to the balloon once it is airborne, gas must be released in order to descend. The gas is released through a small valve in the top of the envelope, operated by a cord leading down into the basket.

Once the balloon has landed it is necessary to deflate it as soon as possible, otherwise it could act like a sail and drag the basket and crew along the ground. To achieve this, a small panel near the top of the balloon, the *ripping panel*, is pulled open to deflate the envelope quickly.

Unmanned gas balloons are widely used for scientific research and weather studies, carrying sets of instruments which either transmit the data back to the ground or record it for analysis after the balloon has been recovered. These balloons are only inflated to a small portion of their full size at ground level; they expand to full size as they ascend to their working altitude.

Hot air balloons

The increase in the popularity of ballooning as a sport has been mainly due to the development of the modern hot-air balloon. These are cheaper, easier to operate and safer than gas balloons.

The envelope, wide at the top and tapering towards the bottom, is usually a nylon-based material with nylon tapes sewn into it to support the burner and the basket. Modern burners use propane gas, blowing the hot air up into an opening in the bottom of the envelope.

The balloon is made to ascend by turning on the burner to heat the air, and to descend by turning off the burner and allowing the air in the envelope to cool. The hot air makes the balloon rise because

Imperial War Museum

Left: Tethered or 'captive' balloons were first used for military observation in 1794, but the streamlined shape was not properly developed until 1916. During the Second World War they were used as 'barrage balloons' to prevent enemy bombers from flying low over their targets.

Below: On the evening of 6 May 1937 the German airship 'Hindenburg' burst into flames as it was landing at Lakehurst, New Jersey, after a flight from Frankfurt. Of the 36 passengers and 61 crew on board, 61 people escaped alive. The Hindenburg was the largest airship ever built.

Popperfoto

Popperfoto

Right: The airship 'Graf Zeppelin' in August 1931, during a tour of Britain. The Graf Zeppelin was grounded after the Hindenburg disaster and it was eventually dismantled during the Second World War. Like the Hindenburg, the Graf Zeppelin was used for passenger flights across the Atlantic.

air expands when it is heated, and so the hot air inside the envelope weighs less than the cold air which it has displaced. This gives the same effect as having the envelope filled with a light gas, although it does not create nearly as much lift.

The lifting power available from a hot-air balloon, with the air at a temperature of 100°C (212°F) when the surrounding air is 16°C (61°F), is only about a quarter of the lift that would be available from a similar volume of hydrogen.

Hot-air balloons also have ripping panels, but whereas on a gas balloon these must be sewn and gummed in place to prevent gas leakage, on a hot-air balloon they are fixed by a self-adhesive strip.

Airships

The first design for a powered, steerable balloon or *dirigible* was published in France in 1784 by Jean Baptiste Marie Meusnier. Although it was never built, it contained many features which were to become part of the basic design of subsequent dirigibles, more popularly known as airships.

The first reasonably successful design was Henri Giffard's airship, filled with coal gas and powered by a steam-driven propeller, which flew 27km (17 miles) on 24 September 1852. This airship was a non-rigid type, having no form of framework to strengthen or help to retain the shape of the gas envelope. Many non-rigid airships were built during the late nineteenth century, some of the most successful being those built by Alberto Santos-Dumont, a Brazilian.

Despite the success of the Santos-Dumont airships, however, it was realized that large, efficient airships could not be built without some form of framework to maintain the shape of the envelope. *Semi-rigid* designs with a rigid keel and some additional strengthening were built, mainly in Italy, but this development was eventually abandoned in favour of the *rigid* airship. The rigid airship had a light alloy framework, covered in a thin fabric skin which contained the gas bags.

The development of the rigid airship

Rigid airship

1 gondola
2 separate gasbags in nets slung between frames
3 engines
4 vertical stabilizer
5 horizontal stabilizer
6 flap valves for releasing gas in order to descend

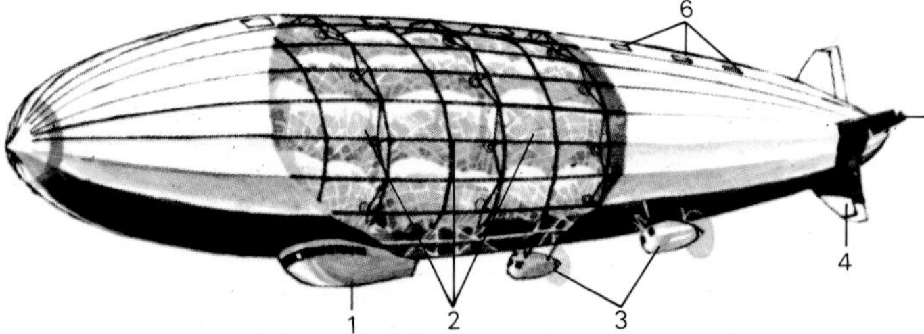

Left: The rigid airship had a light alloy skeleton which contained the separate internal gasbags and carried the engines.

Right: The non-rigid airship or 'blimp' has no internal framework, and its shape is maintained solely by the gas pressure inside the envelope.

Goodyear

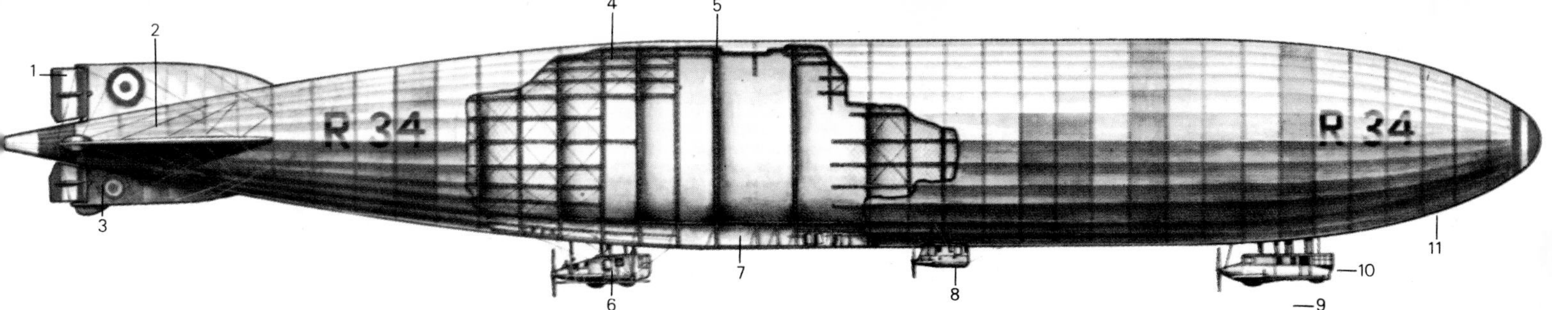

Below: The British airship R34 on a trial run in 1919. On 2 July 1919 the R34 left East Fortune, Scotland, and set out across the Atlantic to New York, arriving on 6 July. It arrived back in Britain on 13 July, the first ever double Atlantic crossing by air. The R34 carried a crew of 30.

Above: A cutaway drawing of the R34. Its overall length was 196 m (643 ft) and its maximum diameter was 24 m (79 ft). It was powered by five Sunbeam 'Maori 4' engines, and its maximum speed was probably about 88 kph (55 mph). The R34 was destroyed in a storm in January 1921.

R34 airship

1 vertical stabilizer
2 horizontal stabilizer
3 landing skid
4 aluminium alloy framework
5 gasbags
6 rear car
7 corridor inside framework connecting front and rear cars and crew accommodation (not shown)
8 starboard power car (port car not shown)
9 radio aerial
10 front power car and control cabin
11 fabric outer skin
12 propeller
13 compressed air landing bag
14 engine oil cooler
15 handling rail
16 access ladder

Popperfoto

Above: The rear car of the R34. The single propeller, 5.9 m (19.5 ft) in diameter, was driven by two engines coupled together. This car carried a set of steering controls which could be used in the event of a failure of the controls in the main control cabin at the front.

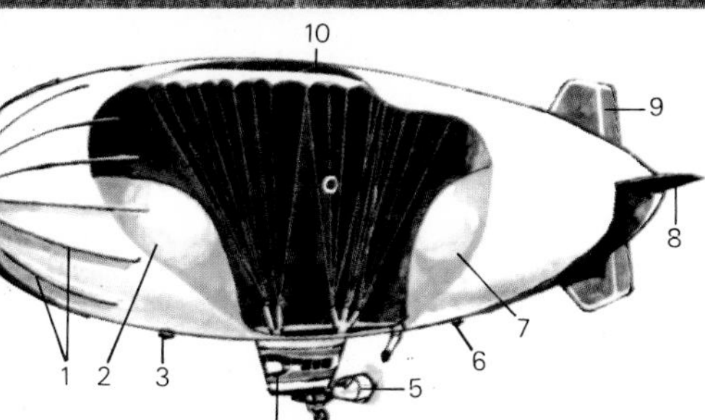

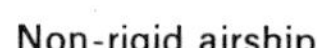

Non-rigid airship

1 nose cone battens
2 forward ballonet
3 ballonet air valve
4 gondola
5 engine
6 ballonet air valve
7 aft ballonet
8 horizontal stabilizer
9 vertical stabilizer
10 catenary curtain

Far left: The Goodyear blimp 'Europa', one of the few airships now in existence, on a flight over Rome. The Europa was built at Cardington, England, in 1972.

Colorific

Left: Another blimp, also a Goodyear, being used to publicize a water-saving campaign in New York City.

Left: The 'Skyship', a model of a proposed cargo-carrying airship which was built at Cardington in 1975. This model is powered by a set of small electric motors, driving propellers. It is filled with helium gas which is light and does not explode or burn.

was primarily the work of the German Count Ferdinand von Zeppelin, whose first craft flew from Lake Constance on 2 July 1900. The First World War provided a great impetus for rigid airship design, particularly in Germany, and after the war designers turned their attention to huge, long-distance airships.

Many of these were produced, with the intention of setting up regular inter-continental flights, but the development of airliners, and a series of tragic crashes, brought an end to the use of large airships in the 1930s.

Several countries continued to build small airships, usually non-rigid, for such military purposes as naval observation, and there has recently been renewed interest in the possible use of airships for cargo carrying.

Airship construction

Semi-rigid and non-rigid airships are also known as pressure airships because their shape is largely maintained by their internal gas pressure. They consist basically of an elongated gasbag from which are suspended the engines and propellers and the crew accommodation. Control surfaces such as rudders and elevators may be mounted on the tail of the gasbag itself or on the suspended structure.

The earliest airships, like the first aircraft, provided no weather protection for the crew, but on later models the 'gondola' in which the crew travelled was fully enclosed like an aircraft cabin.

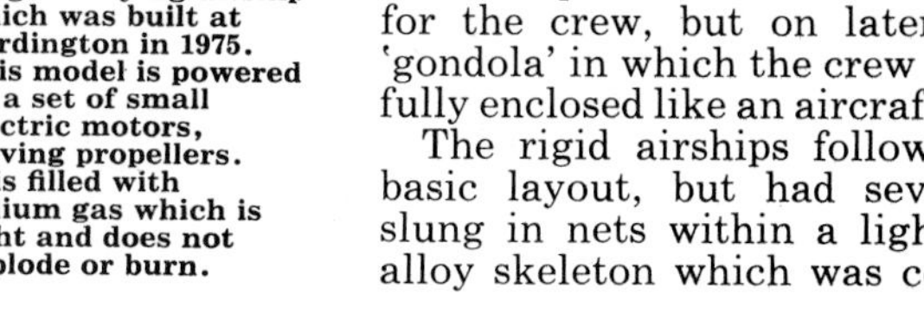

The rigid airships followed the same basic layout, but had several gasbags slung in nets within a light aluminium alloy skeleton which was covered by an outer skin of cotton. The gasbags were made of cotton lined with a material called 'goldbeater's skin'. This material, prepared from the outer membrane of the large intestines of cattle, made the bags gas-tight, and was so called because it was used to separate sheets of gold leaf when they were being beaten.

Nearly all airships used hydrogen gas despite its inflammability, because helium, an inert gas which does not burn, was expensive and scarce. The main world source of helium, the USA, decided after the First World War to use only helium in its airships and banned its export. This forced the large German and British passenger airships to use hydrogen.

Control of the ascent and descent of the early airships followed ordinary ballooning practice, jettisoning water ballast to gain height and releasing gas to descend. This system was augmented on later airships by the use of *ballonets*, collapsible air bags placed within the envelope of a pressure airship or inside the skeleton of a rigid airship. By pumping air into the ballonets to inflate them, the volume of the gas within the envelope is effectively reduced, making it heavier and reducing the lifting force produced. When the air is pumped out of the ballonets the gas expands again and the lift increases.

The use of a ballonet at each end of the envelope means that the amount of air in each one can be varied separately to raise or lower either end of the craft.

Future airships

Only a handful of modern airships exist, and these are small non-rigid craft often known as 'blimps'. However, many new designs have been suggested for rigid-construction airships, filled with helium, capable of carrying containerized cargoes and perhaps even passengers.

Using modern alloys and synthetic fabrics in their construction, and shaped to give good aerodynamic performance, they would be faster, safer and more reliable than their ancestors and capable of carrying far greater loads.

Bicycles and Motorcycles

Science Museum

Above: An 'ordinary' or 'penny-farthing' bicycle, built in 1878 by Bayliss Thomson.

Left: The first pedal-driven bicycle, built in 1839 by Kirkpatrick Macmillan. He was also the first person to be fined for a cycling offence, after knocking over a child in Glasgow in 1842.

The bicycle is a very efficient form of personal transport. Its history dates back over 200 years to the early designs of the second half of the eighteenth century. The most famous of the early machines was the 'Célerifère', later named the 'Vélocifère', built by the Comte de Sivrac in France in 1791. This was a two-wheeled wooden horse, propelled by the rider pushing his feet against the ground, and it must have been difficult to steer as the front wheel was not pivoted.

The first machine with a steerable front wheel was demonstrated by the German Baron von Drais de Sauerbrun in 1818. Known as the Draisienne or 'hobby-horse', it had a simple wooden frame and two large, spoked wooden wheels fitted with iron tyres. The hobby-horse was enormously popular during the following 20 years, but interest declined and production ceased about 1830.

The next development was the pedal operated bicycle invented in 1839 by Kirkpatrick Macmillan, a Scottish blacksmith. The pedals were fitted to the ends of two levers pivoted at the front of the frame above the front wheel, and the forward and back motion of the levers was transmitted by connecting rods to cranks driving the rear axle. Little progress was made in the development of drive mechanisms until the 1860s, when Pierre and Ernest Michaux of Paris fitted pedals and cranks to the front wheel of a hobby-horse type machine, which they called a 'vélocipède'.

During the 1860s, wire-spoked wheels and rubber tyres were introduced, and this led to the evolution of the 'Ordinary' or 'Penny-farthing' bicycles of the 1870s. This type of bicycle had a large front wheel, driven by pedals and cranks fitted to its axle, and a small rear wheel about half the diameter of the front one. The frame was a single metal tube and the saddle was mounted on it above the front wheel, close to the handlebars.

The forerunner of the modern design was the 'Safety' bicycle developed between 1870 and 1890. This type of cycle had two wheels of approximately equal diameter, with wire spokes and rubber tyres and a chain drive to the rear wheel. By 1895 the diamond-shaped frame was standard, as were pneumatic (air filled) bicycle tyres which had been patented in 1888 by J. B. Dunlop. Pneumatic tyres had, in fact, been invented in 1845 by R. W. Thompson, but were not adopted at that time and were forgotten.

The basic design of bicycles changed little during the first quarter of the twentieth century, but in the late 1920s improvements in materials and construction methods permitted the development of lightweight sports and touring machines.

One of the most radical changes in bicycle design came in 1962, with the introduction of the small-wheeled Moulton cycle and its many successors. These small-wheeled machines soon became popular, and contributed to the general revival of interest in cycling during the 1960s and 1970s.

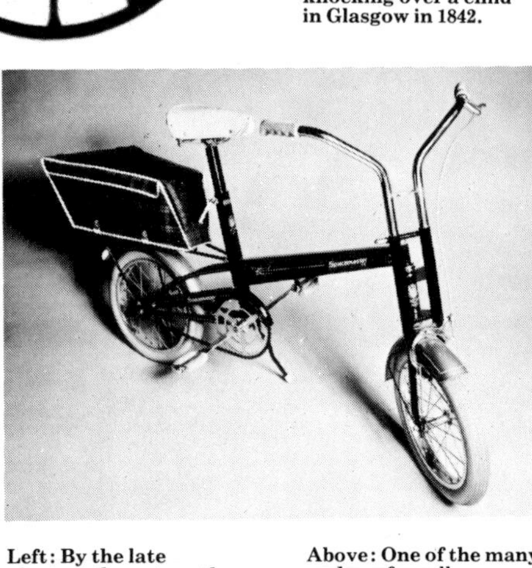

Left: By the late nineteenth century the 'safety' type of bicycle was the standard design. This picture shows Charles Terront of France with the bicycle he rode to win the 1,185 km (736 mile) race from Paris to Brest and back, in September 1891. He completed the course in under three days.

Above: One of the many makes of small-wheeled bicycle built since 1962 when Alex Moulton designed the first of this type. Unlike most of its successors, the Moulton cycle had a suspension system, using a coil spring on the front and a rubber shock absorber at the rear.

Ronan

Below: A derailleur gear mechanism. Operating the hand lever moves the change mechanism towards or away from the wheel. As it moves, it transfers the chains from one sprocket to another. The system shown has a double chainwheel, which doubles the number of gear ratios available.

Right: A modern lightweight sports bike. Competition cycles can be very expensive, due to the high standards of workmanship employed, the small numbers produced and the use of expensive materials such as titanium. The frames are usually made of manganese-molybdenum steel.

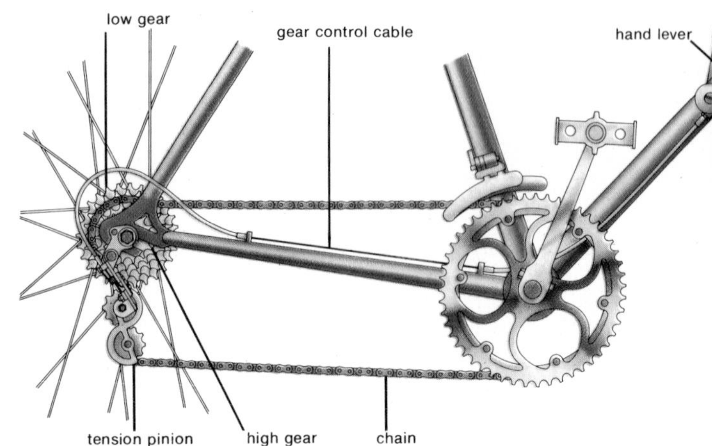

The inner wheel of the Yamaha RD 50 motorbike. The design is deliberately simple – adjustment of the drive chain, for example, is made easy by reference marks.

Steve Bicknell

Left: The motorcycle built by Gottlieb Daimler in Germany in 1885. The drive from the single cylinder petrol engine was transmitted to the rear by a belt and pulley arrangement. A small gear fixed to the driven pulley turned the ring gear attached to the spokes of the rear wheel.

Bildarchiv

Right: Early machines were basically strengthened pedal cycles fitted with engines. This 1903 Triumph has an ordinary pedal drive on one side for starting and to assist the engine on uphill runs, and the belt drive from the engine on the other side.

Motor Museum

Above: One of the most powerful road bikes built, the 903 cc (55 in^3) four cylinder Kawasaki 900 Z1. The engine produces over 60 kW (80 hp) at 8,500 rpm, giving it a top speed of 200 kph (125 mph). Its basic weight is 232 kg (511 lb). Braking is by a front disc brake and a rear drum brake.

Right: This unusual motorcycle and sidecar combination was photographed in Berlin in 1928. The bike is an NSU, and the sidecar carries a duplicate set of controls and handlebars so that the combination can be driven from the sidecar or from the bike itself.

Bildarchiv

Syndication International

Above: Speedway bikes are single cylinder, single gear machines. They have no brakes or gearchange, the only controls being the clutch and throttle.

Below: Cross-country racing is a popular sport in many countries, using tough, purpose-built bikes. This one is a Spanish Bultaco.

Modern mass-produced bicycle frames are made from high-quality lightweight steel alloy tubing, with steel or light alloy handlebars. The wheels have steel or alloy rims and hubs, with steel wire spokes.

The pedals and cranks are fitted to a short axle running through the bottom bracket of the frame; this axle also carries the chainwheel. The chain is made of steel and connects the chainwheel with the rear drive sprocket mounted on the hub of the rear wheel. Except for track racing bikes, this rear sprocket incorporates a freewheel mechanism which allows the rear wheel to turn freely, enabling the rider to coast downhill without having to keep pedalling.

Many bicycles are fitted with gears, either the fully-enclosed type built into the rear wheel hub or the derailleur type comprising a set of rear sprockets of different sizes. The enclosed type is a miniature form of the epicyclic gearbox, the type of gearing used on many vehicle transmission systems, and gearchanges are accomplished by engaging different combinations of gear wheels within the hub.

Gear changing on a derailleur system is achieved by shifting the chain from one sprocket to another, the smallest sprocket giving the highest gear ratio.

Motorcycles

The first motorcycle was built in Germany in 1885 by Gottlieb Daimler, but the motorcycle industry did not really begin until the end of the nineteenth century. Early motorcycles were modified bicycles fitted with engines, but manufacturers were soon designing and building frames especially for motorcycles.

Most modern bike frames are made of steel tubing, with the engine mounted on twin tubes which form the bottom section of the frame. Suspension is provided for both wheels to give greater comfort to the rider and to improve the roadholding of the machine. The front suspension is by coil springs and telescopic hydraulic damper units incorporated in the front fork legs. The rear suspension uses a pair of spring and damper units. With one on each side, the upper ends are fixed to the frame below the saddle and the lower ends to the rear fork. The rear fork extends back almost horizontally from the frame, and it is pivoted to allow it and the wheel to move up and down under the control of the spring units.

The hydraulic damper units, or shock absorbers, regulate the up and down motion of the suspension. For example, when the wheel hits a bump in the road it is pushed upwards, compressing the spring. The spring pushes it back down on to the road again and it then tends to rebound back up, starting the whole process over again. If no dampers were fitted, this wheel bounce would make the machine uncomfortable to ride and difficult to control, especially at high speeds. The dampers smooth out these unwanted oscillations of the suspension by resisting the up or down movement of the spring.

The upper part of the damper is in effect a cylinder of oil, fixed to the frame in the case of rear dampers or to the upper part of the forks in the case of front dampers. The lower part, which moves up and down with the wheel, is connected to

Syndication International

Picturepoint

Above: 250 cc (15.25 in^3) racing bikes at the Daytona racetrack in Florida, USA. The technical experience gained from racing is of great benefit to the designers of ordinary machines.

Below: Competitors in a sidecar race at Brands Hatch racetrack in England.

Syndication International

a piston within the oil cylinder. This piston has small holes drilled through it and as it moves the oil has to pass through these narrow holes. This means that the speed at which the piston can move is limited by the speed at which the oil can pass through the holes.

The speed at which the suspension unit can be compressed or expand again is thus limited to that of the piston, and this prevents the oscillations of the spring that could cause wheel bounce.

The wheels themselves have steel rims and spokes, except for motor scooter wheels which are usually made of pressed steel. Aluminium alloy rims and cast magnesium alloy wheels are also now available.

Engines and transmissions

Modern motorcycle engines range in capacity from just under 50 cc (3 in^3) to over 1200 cc (73 in^3). They may be two or four-stroke petrol engines or rotary Wankel-type engines, either air cooled or water cooled. Some small electrically-driven machines have been produced for town use.

The crankshaft motion is transmitted to the gearbox via the primary drive, which is either a chain drive or a set of gears, and the clutch. The final drive from the gearbox to the rear wheel is usually by chain, but some of the more expensive machines use a drive shaft.

Most two-stroke bikes have magneto ignition systems, self-contained units driven directly from the engine that generate the power to run the ignition, lighting and horn circuits. The ignition coil and the contact breaker are built in to the unit.

Four-stroke machines use battery and coil ignition systems, with either a dc dynamo or an ac alternator, driven by the engine, to keep the battery charged and provide electrical power when the engine is running. Many bikes now use electronic ignition systems in place of the conventional mechanical contact breaker sets.

Brakes and controls

Motorcycles may be fitted with either drum or disc brakes, or have a disc brake on the front wheel and a drum brake on the rear. The drum brake consists of a brake drum built into the wheel hub and a pair of brake shoes lined with an asbestos-based material, which press against the inside of the drum when the brake is applied.

The disc brake is a steel disc mounted on the wheel hub, with a pair of brake pads which are pushed against the disc from either side to grip it as the brake is applied.

The front brake is operated by a lever mounted on the right of the handlebars, the rear brake by a foot pedal, on the right hand side on modern machines. Drum brakes are usually operated mechanically, by cable on the front and by a rod on the rear, but disc brakes use hydraulic systems.

Engine speed is controlled by a twist-grip control on the right hand side of the handlebars, connected to the carburettor or carburettors by a cable. The clutch is operated by a lever on the left of the handlebars and smaller machines and motor scooters often use a twistgrip control, also on the left, to operate the gearchange.

Below right: the BMW R90 S, a large, luxurious touring bike. The 898 cc (55 in^3) horizontally-opposed twin cylinder engine develops 50 kW (67 hp) at 7,000 rpm, and the transmission is by fully enclosed drive shaft. Top speed is 200 kph (125 mph), and it weighs 215 kg (474 lb).

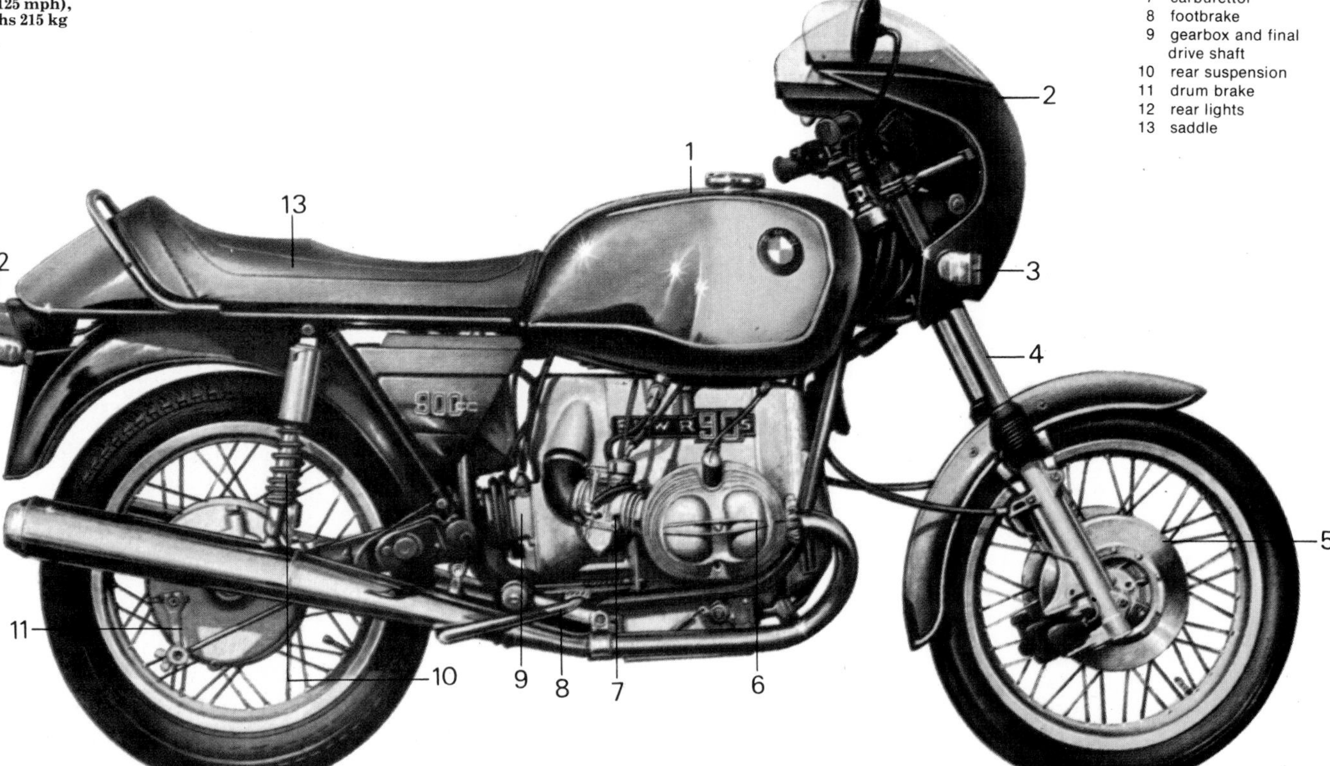

Cars, Trucks and Buses

1875 Marcus

1886 Benz

1902 Wolsely

The idea of using an engine to drive a wheeled road vehicle first became a practical reality in Paris in 1769, when Nicolas Cugnot built a steam powered carriage that ran at about 4 kph ($2\frac{1}{2}$ mph). Many steam cars and trucks were built during the following 150 years, and in 1906 a steam car designed by the Stanley brothers in the USA reached a speed of 204 kph (127 mph).

By this time, however, the more efficient internal combustion engine was rapidly taking over as the source of power for road vehicles. Steam vehicle building had virtually ceased by the middle of the 1920s. Despite the overwhelming dominance of the internal combustion engine, however, a few people are still designing steam cars and indeed steam-powered vehicles may yet come back into use.

Battery powered vehicles have been somewhat more successful than steam vehicles, but the main limitation is the size and weight of the batteries. In practice a great deal of the vehicle's power is used up simply carrying the batteries around, and this means that its range and speed are restricted. Until sufficiently light and powerful batteries have been developed, electric cars are unlikely to become a viable alternative to conventional vehicles.

Yet there are some applications of battery power which are possible even now. Large numbers of battery vehicles are in use, for example, performing duties such as milk or mail delivery which do not involve high speeds or long distances. They are quiet and pollution-free, and ideal for work involving a lot of stopping and starting which would soon wear out a diesel or petrol engine.

Mains-type electric vehicles, such as trolley buses and tramcars, do not have the problem of carrying their energy around with them since they pick it up as they go. Many cities are now building tramway systems again, in some cases less than 30 years after abandoning trams in favour of ordinary buses.

Cars

Although the credit for the building of the first automobiles powered by internal combustion engines is usually given to Karl Benz and Gottlieb Daimler, several such machines were built during the previous 60 years. Benz and Daimler produced their first cars in 1885 and 1886 respectively, but a car running on hydrogen gas had been built by Samuel Brown in London in the early 1820s. The Belgian engineer J. J. E. Lenoir built a car in 1862, and this was followed by the two built by Siegfried Marcus in Austria in 1864 and 1875.

The achievement of Daimler and Benz, however, is important because they envisaged the use of the car as a popular means of transport, and their efforts led directly to the creation of the motor industry. The earlier pioneers appear to have had little real interest in the future possibilities of their inventions, and did not persist in their development.

The drawings above and at the bottom of the page show how the shape of car bodies has evolved since the nineteenth century. Top row: Early cars were open vehicles with no weather protection, but body design progressed rapidly during the 1900s. The mass-produced Model T Ford was introduced in 1908 and over 15 million were built in its 19-year production run. The move towards fully enclosed designs continued during the 1920s, and in the 1930s body lines became more graceful and flowing. Bottom row: Designs changed little during the 1940s, but the introduction of unitary construction in the 1950s allowed designers to produce longer, lower and more adventurous shapes. Small cars like the Mini became very popular in the 1960s, and during the 1970s the clean, efficient 'wedge' shape evolved.

Right: A drawing of a 1903 Mercedes.

Below: A 1909 Buick, with a front-mounted engine driving the rear wheels through a chain and sprocket final drive.

Photomedia/Bavaria

Photri

Above right: The 1955 Lincoln is a good example of American car design of that period. The body is long and low, and the large windows and windshield give the driver excellent visibility.

Photri

Right: During the 1920s mass production techniques enabled manufacturers to build large numbers of cheap and reliable cars. The relative affluence of the period provided them with large sales, particularly in the US and western Europe, until the economic collapse of the early 1930s.

1948 Vauxhall

1954 Oldsmobile

1908 Ford

1922 Austin

1937 Rolls-Royce

Michael Holford

Right: The operation of a four-speed manual gearbox. The gear lever moves the yokes to lock the required gears to the drive shaft. Here only one of the two yokes is shown at a time, and the line of power transmission is shown in red. The drive from the engine enters the box through the clutch shaft which drives the layshaft. First, second and third gears are selected by locking the required gear to the transmission shaft, taking up the drive from the layshaft. Top gear is selected by locking the clutch shaft directly to the transmission shaft. Reverse gear, not shown, is selected by connecting the transmission shaft to the layshaft via a separate idler gear.

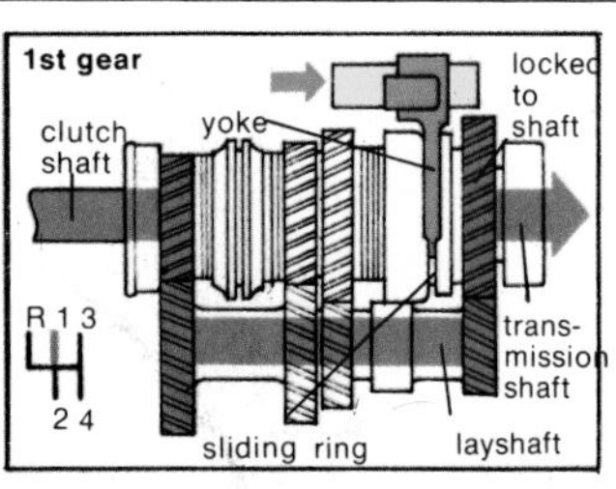

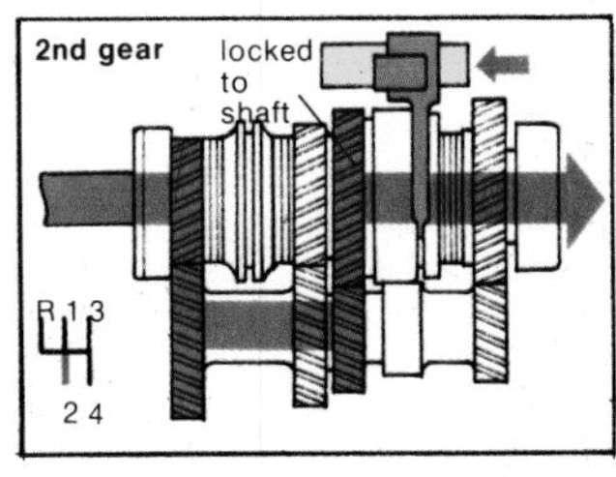

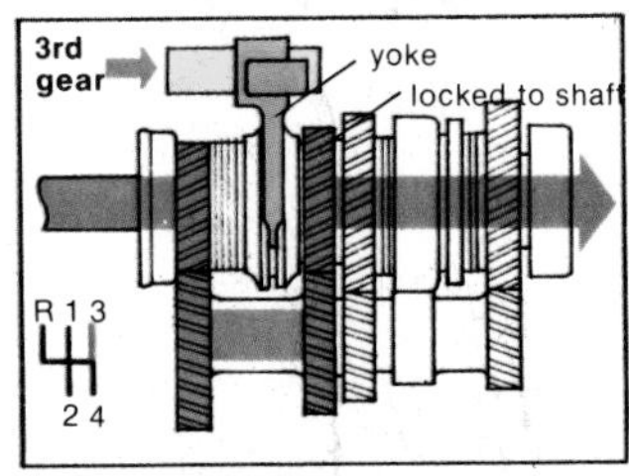

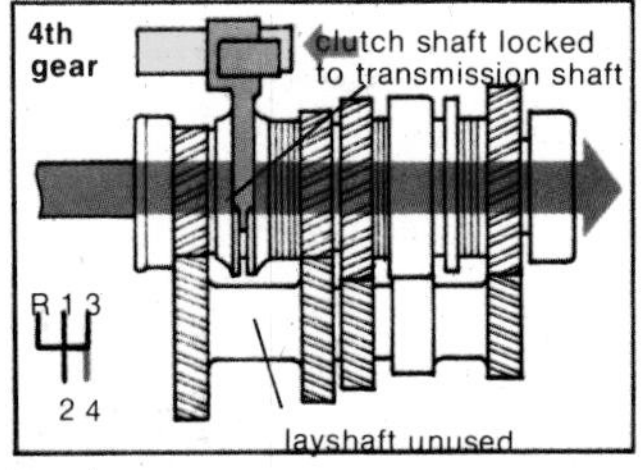

Michael Holford

Daymark

Left: Racing cars have evolved into highly specialized designs. On this one the engine is sited between the driver and the rear wheels. The cowling above and behind the driver's head is the air intake for the carburettors. Aerofoils at the front and back keep the wheels firmly on the ground at high speeds.

Top: Most car suspensions use coil springs, as in this example, but hydraulic or pneumatic systems are also used. The horizontal rod with the rubber dust seal is one of a pair linking the front wheels to the steering mechanism. When the steering wheel is turned the rods move sideways to pivot the front wheels.

Above: The rear suspension and drive shafts of a Lotus car.

Right: A cutaway of a Chevrolet Stingray, a powerful American sports car which has a lightweight body built on to a steel girder chassis. The use of chassis-type construction has continued for a number of sports cars despite the use of unitary construction for most modern cars.

CHEVROLET STINGRAY
1 gearshift
2 engine
3 cooling fan
4 lightweight body
5 gearbox
6 chassis
7 drive shaft
8 differential

1955 Citroen

1959 Mini

1975 Vauxhall

The early Benz and Daimler cars used single cylinder engines. But engine design progressed rapidly and by 1900 multi-cylinder engines were well established. During the first decade of the twentieth century, the design practice of putting the engine at the front of the car and taking the drive from there to the rear wheels was adopted by most manufacturers. This is still the most widespread layout, but the trend towards smaller cars has made other layouts, such as front engine, front wheel drive and rear engine, rear wheel drive, common.

The drive from the engine is taken via the clutch to the gearbox, and from there by drive shafts to the driving wheels. The clutch used with manual gearboxes has three main components: the clutch plate, the pressure plate and the flywheel on the end of the engine crankshaft. When the clutch is engaged, the pressure plate presses the clutch plate against the face of the flywheel. As the flywheel turns, the clutch plate turns with it, and so the drive is transmitted into the gearbox.

When the clutch pedal is depressed, the pressure plate is forced away from the clutch plate by hydraulic pressure. The clutch plate is then no longer being pressed against the flywheel and turned by it, and so the drive from engine to gearbox is disconnected.

Automatic transmission systems use hydraulic couplings in place of the friction type clutch. The flywheel drives a saucer-shaped impeller which is enclosed within a casing full of oil. As the impeller turns, oil is flung outwards by radial vanes on its inside face. The oil is deflected against similar vanes on the inside of another saucer-shaped unit, the turbine, which faces it. The force of the oil turns the turbine, which is connected to the gearbox by a shaft.

The various combinations of gears within an automatic gearbox are selected by clutch mechanisms within it. The clutches are activated hydraulically or electrically by devices which sense the engine and car speeds, and the position of the accelerator pedal, to determine the correct ratio required. These devices can be over-ridden by the driver, using the gear selector lever, so that the car can be held in any particular gear or put into reverse or neutral.

Cars use disc or drum brakes, or a combination of both with discs on the front and drums at the rear. The brake pedal operates all four brakes via a hydraulic system, but the handbrake operates only the brakes on the two non-driving wheels. The handbrake lever is linked to the brakes by steel cables or rods, and as it is independent of the hydraulic system it can provide some braking if the main brake system fails.

Until the 1950s, almost all cars had a steel girder chassis on to which the pressed-steel body was built, but during this period mass-produced cars were beginning to be built without a chassis. This method is called *unitary construction*.

The body and chassis parts are built together as a single unit from welded steel pressings. The method is lighter and cheaper than chassis type construction, and better suited to mass production techniques. Apart from this and styling considerations, body designers also have to take into account such factors as passenger safety and the aerodynamics of the body shape.

National Motor Museum

Fodens

Above: The petrol-engined Albion of 1914. The development of trucks was stimulated by their use during the First World War. After the war the large numbers of surplus military trucks which were sold did much to encourage the spread of motor transport in Europe and the US.

London Transport

Right: This ancestor of the modern double-decker bus is a 1910 type 'B' which belonged to the London General Omnibus Company. There is no roof to the upper deck and the wooden seating accommodates thirty passengers. The tyres are solid rubber, and its speed was 20 kph (12 mph).

Fodens

Top: A large articulated truck with a twin-axled semi-trailer.

Above: A heavy duty articulated low-loader carrying a motor grader, a large earthmoving machine. Special low-loaders have been built which can carry loads of over 400 tonnes.

Right: A cutaway drawing of a three-axle rigid truck, showing the strong ladder-type steel chassis, the engine, the transmission and suspension. The drive is transmitted to both rear axles, and the use of double wheels on these axles allows heavier loads to be carried.

FODEN TRUCK
1 driver's cab
2 engine and gearbox
3 fuel tanks
4 drive shaft
5 final drive gearboxes
6 frame chassis
7 brake drum
8 rear suspension
9 front suspension
10 steering box

Japanese Tourist Board

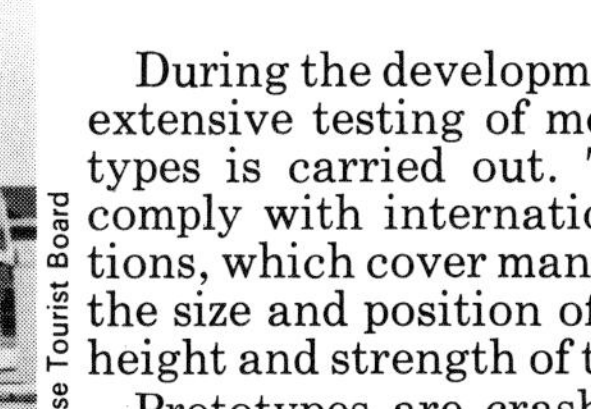

Above: A rear-engined tour bus. Bus safety is improved by using multiple braking circuits. Many buses are also fitted with electro-magnetic retarders which exert a strong magnetic force on the vehicle's drive shaft to slow it down, thus supplementing the action of the brakes.

Below: A one-man-operated London bus. The driver collects the passengers' fares as they enter, and it has seats for 68 passengers with room for 21 standing. The six-cylinder 114 kW (153 hp) diesel engine and the four-speed gearbox are mounted across the rear chassis.

London Transport

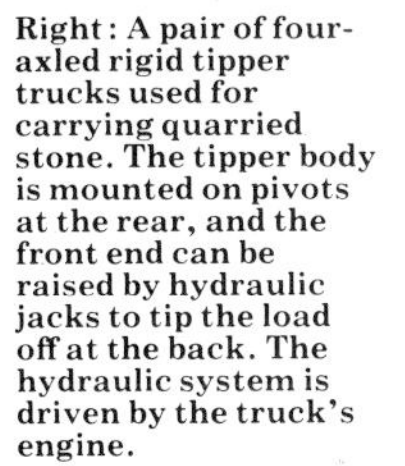

Right: A pair of four-axled rigid tipper trucks used for carrying quarried stone. The tipper body is mounted on pivots at the rear, and the front end can be raised by hydraulic jacks to tip the load off at the back. The hydraulic system is driven by the truck's engine.

Fodens

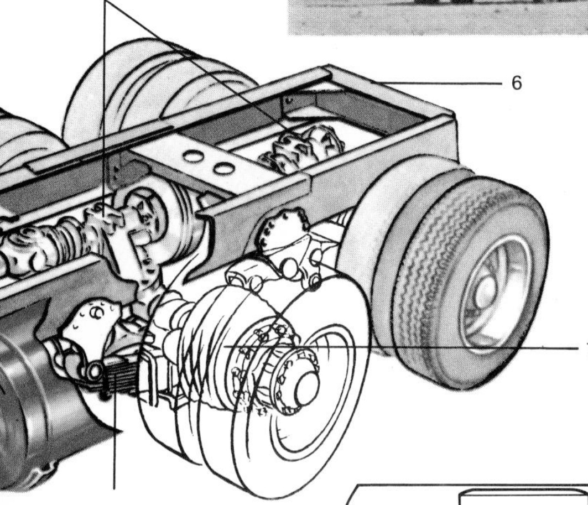

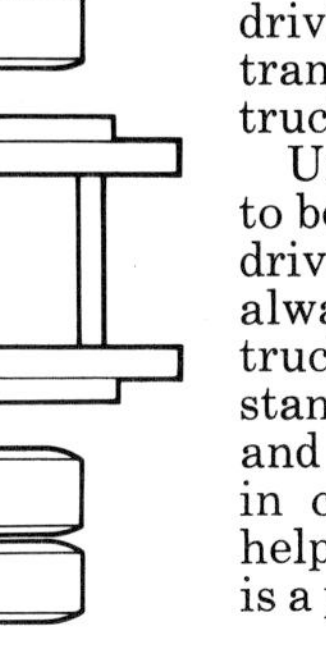

Below: The triple-circuit braking system of an articulated tractor unit. The tractor and semi-trailer brakes are independently operated by compressed air from a compressor driven by the engine.

During the development of a new model, extensive testing of mock-ups and prototypes is carried out. The design has to comply with international safety regulations, which cover many aspects including the size and position of the lights and the height and strength of the bumpers.

Prototypes are crashed into walls and other vehicles in order to evaluate the strength of the passenger compartment, and the ability of the front and rear body sections to absorb the impact created by a collision.

Wind tunnel testing is also used to improve the aerodynamic qualities of the body shape. This leads to better road-holding and acceleration, higher top speeds and greater fuel economy.

Commercial vehicles

Commercial vehicles are an important part of the transport systems of most of the countries of the world, particularly since the comparative decline of the railways. Early commercial vehicles were powered by steam, electricity or petrol engines, but most are now diesel powered.

The diesel engine was invented by Rudolf Diesel in Germany in 1897. Despite its success in marine propulsion, however, satisfactory road vehicle versions did not appear until 1922. On most commercial vehicles today the engine is mounted at the front, ahead of or beneath the driver's cab. Some manufacturers fit the engine beneath the chassis, and many buses and coaches use this layout or have the engine at the rear.

There is a wide range of commercial vehicle diesel engine, both two-stroke and four-stroke. Most are water-cooled, the main exceptions being the air-cooled engines produced by Magirus Deutz in Germany.

Light vans and some buses are often of unitary construction, without a chassis, but larger vehicles usually have a ladder-type frame chassis on to which an enormous variety of bodies can be built. Trucks may be either rigid or articulated. The rigid type has a single chassis carrying the cab, engine and body or load platform, and can have from two to four axles.

The articulated truck consists of a short tractor unit comprising the cab, engine and transmission. There is a 'fifth wheel' or turntable on top of the chassis, above the rear axle or pair of axles, to which the trailer is attached. The articulated trailer unit, called a semi-trailer, has no wheels at the front, being supported by the tractor, but one or more axles at the rear. Rigid units are often used for drawbar operation, towing trailers which are linked to them by a steel towing bar.

Most truck gearboxes are manually operated, and the number of gears available from the main gearbox can be doubled by means of an extra set of gears called a 'range splitter', or by using a two-speed driving axle. Automatic or semi-automatic transmissions are used on some heavy trucks and many buses.

Until recently, truck cabs were designed to be purely functional, unlike cars where driver comfort and convenience have always been carefully considered. Modern truck cabs, however, incorporate similar standards of seating, sound insulation and easily operated controls to those used in cars. This type of ergonomic design helps to reduce the driver fatigue which is a potential cause of accidents.

Railways

On August 31, 1975, a grand cavalcade of locomotives was held to mark 150 years of rail travel in Britain. Since the opening of the Stockton and Darlington Railway in 1825, railways have become one of the most widespread forms of transport, serving almost every country in the world.

At the beginning of the nineteenth century Britain was still in the throes of the Industrial Revolution. Manufacturing industry, with its demand for power and raw materials, and its output of mass-produced goods, was altering the pattern of life. Not only merchandise but people also needed to be transported all over the country to help weave the web of commerce. The rutted and muddy roads were totally unable to meet this demand, while the canals were handicapped by the need for locks to overcome changes in water level. But by 1800 the public was already familiar with the two elements that were to combine to make the steam railway the transport of the future.

Railways had already existed in Britain for over 200 years, the first examples being wooden trackways along which horses could haul wagons of coal from the mines to the nearest water transport—canal, sea or navigable river. In time the wooden rails changed to iron, and the flat 'plateways' changed to edged rails along which flanged wheels were guided.

The other vital element was steam power, the moving force. This too had been developed as an adjunct of the mining industry, where low pressure steam engines were used to pump water from the underground workings. The Cornish mining engineer, Richard Trevithick, was the first to conceive the idea of building a high pressure engine and mounting it on wheels.

Trevithick's first two steam locomotives were in fact road vehicles: the idea of a steam engine running on rails only came about as the result of a wager. Much impressed by the potential of this new invention, Samuel Homphray, a South Wales iron master, bet a friend that a railway engine could be built to haul a ten ton load along the newly opened Penydarren Tramway at Merthyr Tydfil, a feat which Trevithick's specially built locomotive duly performed on Tuesday February 21, 1804.

In the years that followed, experimental railway engines were tried on various mineral railways. George Stephenson, the giant among the early railway builders, was, like Trevithick, a mining engineer. His particular achievement was to synthesize the best available knowledge and thus develop not only a serviceable and reliable locomotive but also the concept of the steam-worked railway.

1825 was the year of his first great triumph, the opening of the Stockton and Darlington Railway, the first public railway to be worked by steam traction. The opening train was hauled by Stephenson's *Locomotion*, preceded by a mandatory horse rider bearing a red flag.

Such exploits were at first regarded as highly dangerous by the general public, but in spite of widespread suspicion the construction of new railways proceeded apace and by 1841 the skeleton of Britain's railway network was already in existence.

Above: These drawings show how steam locomotives developed from 1803 to the beginning of the twentieth century.

Adam Woolfitt/Susan Griggs

Left: The *Locomotion* was built in 1825 by George Stephenson, and in that year became the first steam engine to haul a train on a public railway, between Stockton and Darlington.

Ronan

Right: The Furness Railway's locomotive number 9, built in 1855 by Fairbairn and Company. Steam engines can be classified by their wheel layouts; this one is an 0-4-0, having no wheels in front or behind its four driving wheels. These classifications do not include the wheels of the tender.

American History Library

Below: Steam engines at a depot in West Germany. Steam engines are sturdy and reliable, but of the total heat energy supplied to them from the burning fuel only about six per cent is converted into useful mechanical energy. The unused energy escapes as heat in the exhaust steam and smoke.

Below right: A cutaway drawing of a steam engine. The steam from the boiler passes into the steam chest, and when the valve is opened it enters the cylinder. In the cylinder it expands, forcing the piston along. The piston's motion is transmitted to the driving wheels by the connecting rod.

ZEFA

STEAM LOCOMOTIVE
1. Cylinder
2. Smoke deflectors
3. Steam chest
4. Piston
5. Chimney
6. Valve gear
7. Connecting rod
8. Coupling rods
9. Sanding pipes
10. Water injector
11. Safety valve
12. Boiler tubes
13. Fire box
14. Regulator
15. Steam brake lever
16. Whistle
17. Vacuum brake lever
18. Reversing gear
19. Sand lever

The Stirling 1870

Midland 4-4-0 compound 1902

Right: The *Dolbadarn*, a small, narrow-gauge locomotive on the Llanberis Lakeside Railway, Wales. Steam engines need to take on water frequently, either from trackside tanks, as in this case, or by scooping it up from troughs—between the rails at intervals along the track—as they travel.

Below: Southern Pacific locomotive number 2372 was the first of the twelve Class T-32 4-6-0 engines which were built at Sacramento, California, during the First World War. This particular locomotive was completed in 1918 and remained in use until it was scrapped in 1956.

Picturepoint

11 12 13 14 15 16 17 18 19 8 9 10

The Mallard 1935

Stanier Coronation class 4-6-2 1938

Picturepoint

Above: Three twentieth-century steam engines. The streamlined *Mallard* set the world steam engine speed record of 202.8 kph (126 mph) in 1938. *Evening Star* was the last steam locomotive to be built by British Railways.

Left: The A-3 class *Flying Scotsman*, built in the 1920s and now restored. The extra tender was added to carry water, as watering facilities no longer exist on the British Rail network.

Right: A powerful diesel locomotive used for hauling trains along the line from Whitehorse in the Yukon Territory, Canada, to the port of Skagway in Alaska.

Railway construction had by this time spread to Europe and North America. The first lines on the continent were built by British engineers and used British-built locomotives. In France the first public steam railway was the 61 km (38 mile) long Lyons and St. Etienne line, opened in 1828. Germany followed a few years later with a short line from Nuremberg to Furth. Its first locomotive, Der Adler, was delivered complete with a British driver, William Wilson, who had been one of Stephenson's pupils.

British engineers later pioneered lines in many other European countries. Thus the 1.435 m (4 ft 8½ in) gauge adopted by Stephenson eventually became standard in most of the world.

Railways in the Wild West

In the United States and Canada, railways were built largely across virgin territory, where few restrictions of private ownership applied. North American railways were thus built to one of the most generous loading gauges in the world, even though the track was the standard 1.435 m (4 ft 8½ in). In the West, lines were built to open up the country, the towns arriving after the railway rather than vice versa. Many such lines converged on Chicago, which became the greatest railway town in the world. On May 9, 1869, a golden spike was driven to mark the completion of the first transcontinental railroad.

By 1850 some 10,460 km (6,500 miles) of line were in operation in Great Britain. Subsequent lines were generally of lesser importance, being either branch lines or competing routes. The working life of many of these has been relatively short, the rule of 'last opened, first closed' seeming to apply.

On the continent the railways were generally state owned rather than under private ownership. Lines were built for strategic or economic reasons, and on the whole a less dense but more efficient network has resulted.

The First World War left the European railways battered, and it was some time before pre-war standards were regained. However, the war had also encouraged the mass production of motor vehicles, and for the first time the dominance of the railway was challenged. During the depression of the 1930s there was little money available to carry out much-needed modernization plans and in only a few countries such as Switzerland and France was progress made with electrification. Experiments were made with diesel traction, including the high-speed *Flying Hamburger* from Hamburg to Berlin, but steam remained the dominant form of power.

The Second World War once again put enormous strains on Europe's railways, which suffered severely from bomb damage. In the post war era, car ownership came within the reach of most families, while an increasing proportion of freight traffic was carried by road. British Railways were nationalized and subsequently modernized. Many branch lines were closed and steam was replaced by diesel and electric traction.

The handling of individual wagon loads of freight began to be phased out in favour of bulk train loads, with automatic loading and unloading at terminals. Freightliner container trains now travel at speeds of 113 kph (70 mph) between most parts of the country. On the passenger side the emphasis is on fast and frequent services linking major cities, while suburban and minor cross-country trains are given lower priority.

Rolling stock

Steam power was the force that made the railways great, even though it has now been almost entirely replaced by diesel and electric traction. Steam locomotives can still be found at work in South Africa, India and China and eastern Europe, while in Britain various branch lines such as the Severn Valley Railway have been reopened by railway enthusiasts in order to run steam trains.

The steam locomotive is a robust and simple machine. Steam is admitted under pressure from the boiler to the cylinders.

Tom Browne

Above: *Venus*, a British Railways 'Britannia' class steam engine, number 70023. The 4-6-2 Britannia class locomotives, which were introduced in 1951, were the first express passenger steam engines to be built by British Railways after they were nationalized on 1 January 1948.

Below: A French electric locomotive. The power is picked up from the overhead cable by the pantograph on the top of the locomotive. The voltages used by electric trains vary from one railway system to another, from 600 V (direct current) to 25,000 V (alternating current).

Roger Viollet

Evening Star — Last British Steam Locomotive 1960

Picturepoint

ZEFA

Above: Mountain railway cars may be self propelled, the driving wheel being a large cog that engages with a toothed rack between the rails, or they may be pulled along by a cable from a fixed winch.

Left: Monorail trains, running on single overhead rails, are used in some cities as an alternative to underground railways.

Below: British Rail's Advanced Passenger Train, designed to run at 240 kph (150 mph) on existing tracks. Its unique suspension system enables it to travel at 200 kph (125 mph) around bends which would limit ordinary trains to 130 kph (80 mph).

British Transport

In the cylinder, steam expands and pushes a piston to the other end. On the return stroke a port opens to clear the exhaust steam. By means of mechanical coupling rods, the travel of the piston turns the driving wheels of the locomotive.

Diesel locomotives are of three main types: diesel-electric, diesel-hydraulic and diesel-mechanical. In the diesel-electric locomotive, the diesel engine drives a dynamo, and the electrical output from the dynamo powers electric motors which drive the wheels. In the diesel-hydraulic, the engine drives a hydraulic transmission, which turns the wheels by a form of miniature turbine, while in the diesel-mechanical locomotive the transmission is by a gearbox, just as in a diesel road vehicle. Diesel-electrics are by far the most common type, although diesel-mechanical locomotives are often used for shunting.

The third main form of motive power is electric traction. The first electric locomotives were powered by batteries, but modern locomotives take current from overhead wires or from a third rail. On the third rail system the current is supplied via the third rail and returned via the running rails. Four-rail systems are also used, on underground railways for example, which have two conductor rails for the supply and return of the current. Modern transmissions and traction motors are small enough to be housed in the bogie of the locomotive, rather than above footplate level as in older designs. Electric locomotives have a very high power-to-weight ratio as they do not have to generate their own power or carry fuel.

The design of railway rolling stock has undergone a development parallel to that of the locomotive. The latest passenger carriages are air-conditioned and are designed to travel at speeds in excess of 161 kph (100 mph). Freight vehicles show a tremendous variety in shape and size, depending on the type of load they have to carry. Modern freight trains are fitted with continuous brakes and can travel at much higher speeds than the old loose-coupled freights.

The track and signalling of modern railways has undergone a similar improvement to cope with faster and more frequent train services. Lengths of continuously welded rail (CWR) a quarter of a mile long considerably reduce the number of rail joints in comparison with standard 18.28 m (60 ft) rail lengths, and most main lines are now laid with CWR. Coloured lights have now largely replaced the old crank-operated semaphore signals and a single control box can now operate a section of line that was formerly controlled by numerous signal boxes.

Before modernization the railways were extremely labour-intensive, but rationalization is now the rule. It is even possible to do away with train drivers altogether, and one-man, semi-automatic trains have been in use on London Transport's Victoria Line since its opening in 1968.

Earl Young/Colorific

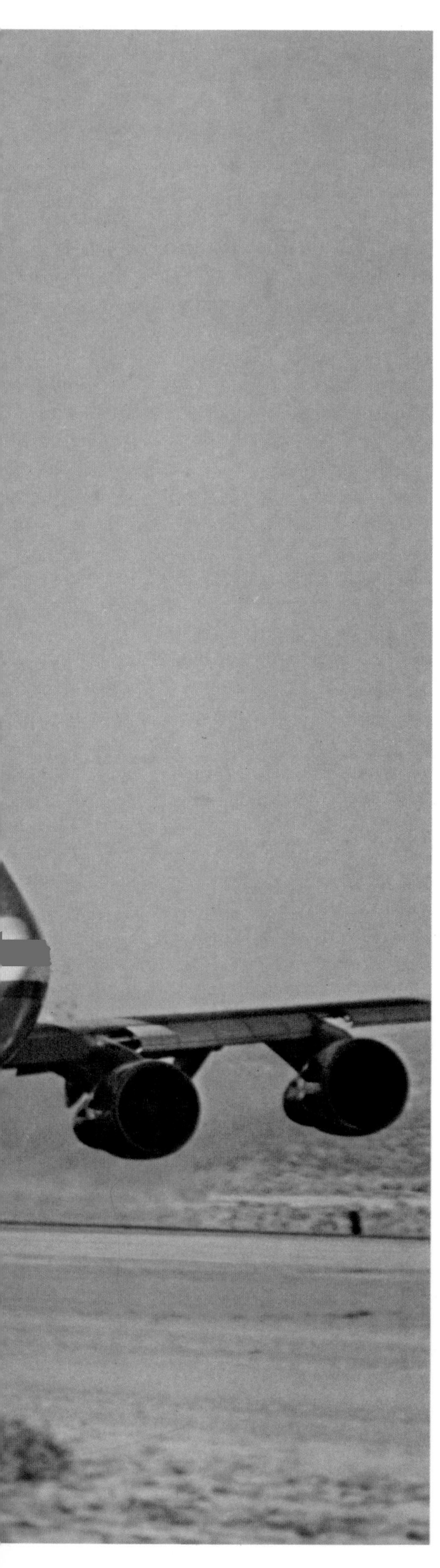

Chapter 5

Military and Space Technology

The space shuttle, a re-usable manned aircraft, is launched like a rocket from the parent 'plane, and returns unpowered to a runway landing. The liquid-fuel tank is discarded after use.

Guns

Although the Chinese were using *gunpowder* in rockets and fireworks almost a thousand years ago, there is no hard evidence to show that it was used as a propellant in firearms until the formula reached Europe some time in the thirteenth century. The reason for this lay in the level of technology necessary to construct a suitable barrel, which only existed in the Western world. By the end of the fourteenth century the knowledge of guns was widespread.

Early guns were shaped like flower vases and shot arrows. Arrows were quickly replaced by bullets of metal or stone, although some muskets were still being loaded with arrows at the time of the Spanish Armada. From the very beginning, guns were made in two sizes, the larger for bombardment and the smaller for carrying and firing by hand.

Early hand guns were about 30cm (12in) long, made of iron or bronze and mounted on a long stick so that they could be held in one hand and pointed at the target with the stick tucked under the arm for steadiness. The other hand wielded a glowing match and the charge was ignited through a touch-hole. The cannon were larger and were given pivots or trunnions. They were mounted on wooden carriages derived from farmcarts and dragged by horses. Although they were heavy and cumbersome, needing a large crew to service each gun, they were effective and heralded the end of the mediaeval castle. For over 300 years the design of such guns hardly changed and improvements were only made to ancillary items, not to the overall weapon.

Firing mechanisms

Things went differently for the handguns, which developed rapidly. The first improvement was the firing mechanism. Carrying the match in one hand was impractical for general use, and the match was soon put into an S-shaped metal lever pivoted on the side of the stock. Pulling the lower end of the lever pushed the match into the touchhole.

The next improvement was to make the match holder in two parts with a finger-lever, or 'tricker' to operate it. The whole mechanism was known as the *matchlock*, and it was used, with very few exceptions, on shoulder arms, muskets and Hackbuts or Arquebus as they came to be known. Pistols were not made with matchlocks, although oddly enough they appeared later on in China and Japan.

Early in the sixteenth century the *wheel-lock* was invented. This used the principle of flint and tinder to produce a spark to ignite the powder. The wheel-lock was far more practical for ordinary use and many were produced, particularly in Germany where the clockmaking industry was ideally suited to making the mechanism required. The successor to the wheel-lock was not long in appearing, and before the end of the sixteenth century the first *flintlocks* were in use.

The flintlock proved to be the most durable and widespread of all the early forms of ignition for it remained in general use for almost 350 years. The flintlock used the same principle of flint and steel as the wheel-lock, but it employed it in a

Photoresources

Above: The 'Tsar's Great Cannon'. This is the largest cannon in the world. It is 5.7 m (17.5 ft) long with a bore of 91.7 cm (36.1 inches) and weighs 40 tonnes. Made from cast iron, it was cast by Andrey Chokhov in 1586 in Moscow.

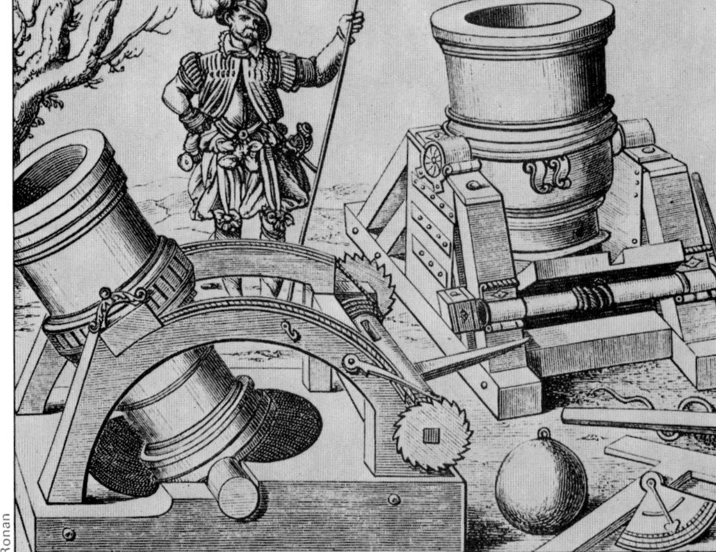

Ronan

Right: Bombards on portable gun carriages—from an engraving published in 1575. The mobility of artillery pieces had become an important feature by the end of the fifteenth century; previously the emphasis had been placed on size.

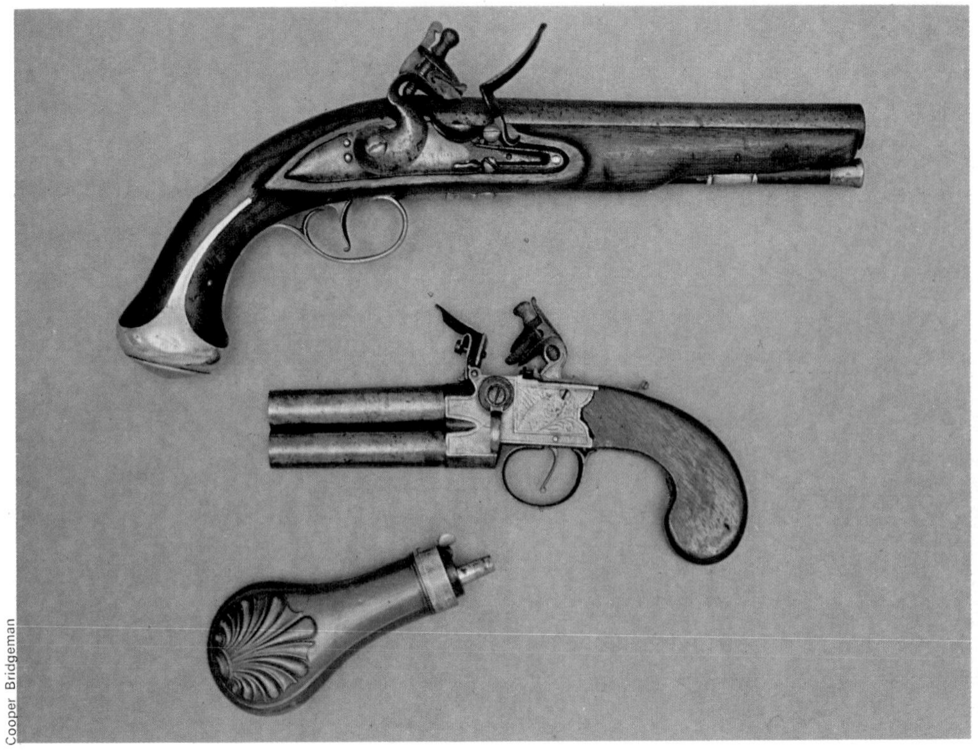

Cooper Bridgeman

Below: (Top) A brass-mounted flintlock pistol manufactured by Twigg and Bass of London in the late eighteenth century. (Centre) Tap action, boxlock, flintlock pistol. (Bottom) Metal powder flask of the size usually associated with pistols.

Until the 15th century the barrels of portable firearms were fixed to long, straight wooden hafts. Later these were shortened, broadened and curved, so that the recoil was directed upwards instead of straight back against the user.

WHEEL-LOCK MECHANISM

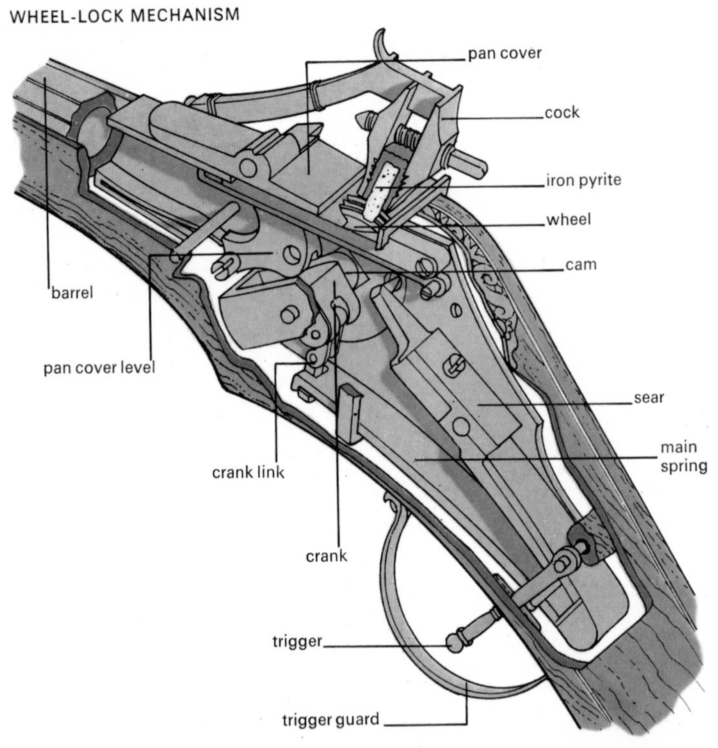

FLINTLOCK MECHANISM

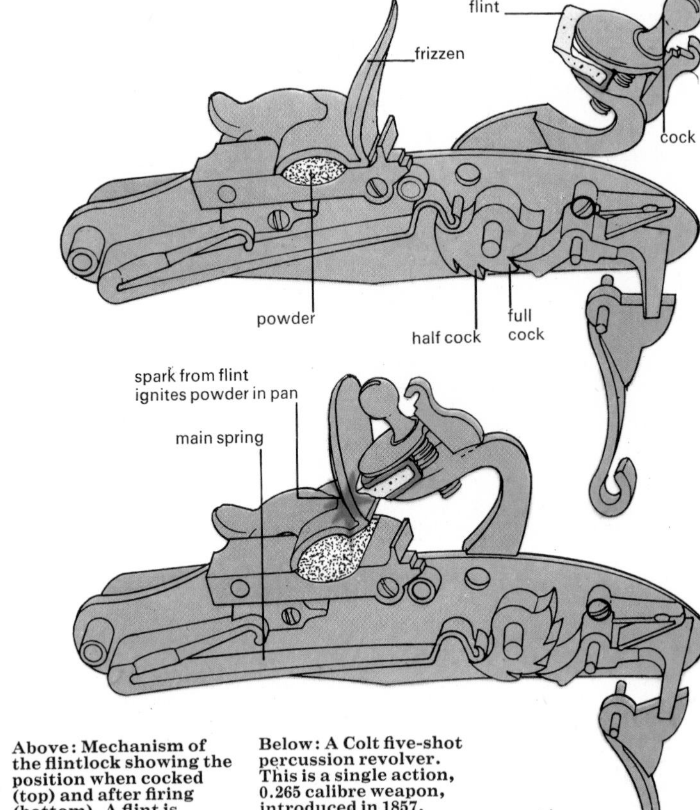

Above: The wheel-lock mechanism. This involves a steel wheel which is wound up using a winding spanner. A piece of iron pyrite is clamped in the cock which is held under spring tension. A small pan surrounding the wheel contains the primer. Sparks shower onto this when the cock hits the moving wheel.

Above: Mechanism of the flintlock showing the position when cocked (top) and after firing (bottom). A flint is clamped to the cock which is pulled back against a spring prior to firing. On pulling the trigger, the cock is released and the flint strikes the steel, showering sparks into the pan.

Below: A Colt five-shot percussion revolver. This is a single action, 0.265 calibre weapon, introduced in 1857. Revolvers were simple, cheap and robust devices with high firing rates but they were slow to reload. Many armies used this weapon until the 'automatic' pistol had proved itself as a reliable device.

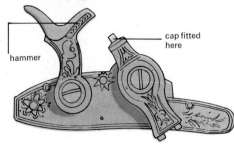

Cooper Bridgeman

Above: A wheel-lock pistol from about 1640. The barrel is 36 cm (14 inches) long and has a bore of 1.1 cm (0.45 inch). Although a more complex mechanism than the matchlock, the wheel-lock needed no lighted match and gave a more consistent firing action. The priming powder was ignited by a spark.

Cooper Bridgeman

FORSYTH PERCUSSION

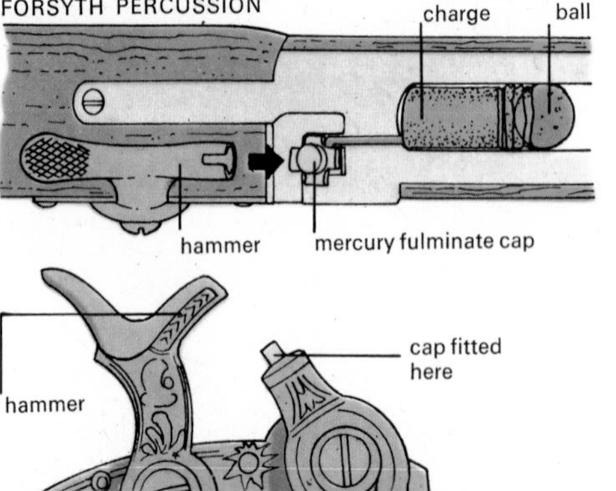

Left: The percussion-cap mechanism. Mercury fulminate was used as the detonating compound and contained in a small inverted cup. This was placed over a narrow steel tube connected to the main chamber containing the charge. On release, the hammer struck the cap and the flash passed down to the main charge.

Right: The Colt revolver mechanism. This is the single-action type which means that the chambers are advanced by the action of cocking the hammer; pulling the trigger only releases the hammer. To ensure exact alignment of chamber and barrel, a catch engages with a recess in the cylinder.

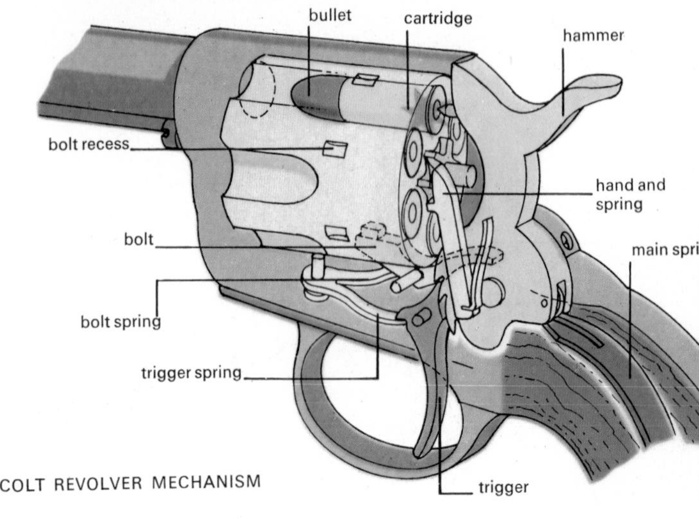

COLT REVOLVER MECHANISM

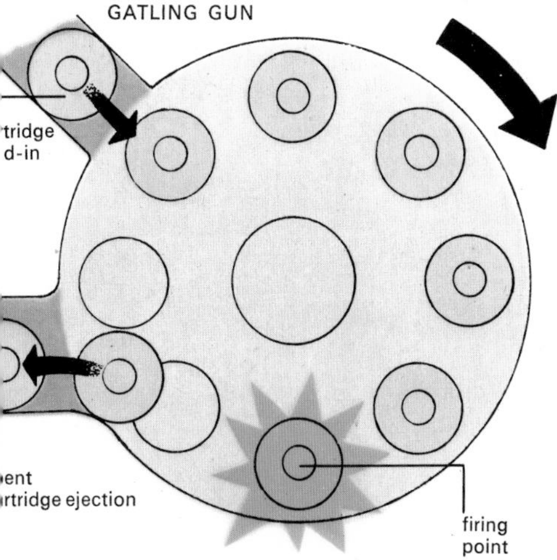

Above: Operation of a multi-barrel Gatling gun. The cartridges were gravity-fed from a hopper above the gun and fired when the barrel reached its lowest position. The cartridge was then ejected. The Gatling gun could fire up to six rounds a second, but modern aircraft types can exceed this.

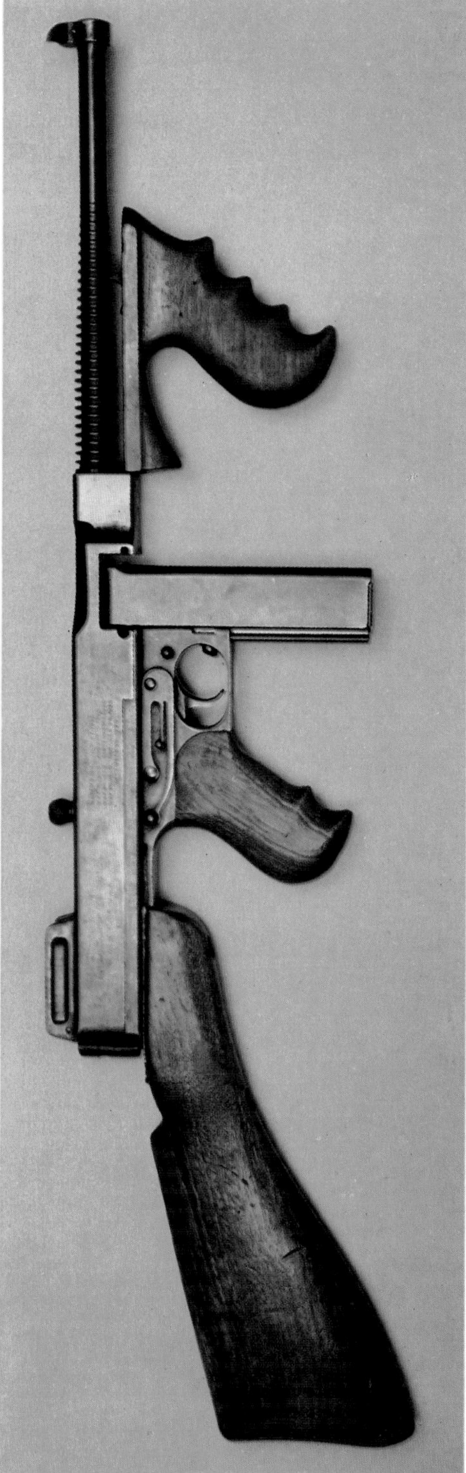

Right: The 1921-model Thompson sub-machine gun with a 20-round box magazine of .45 inch cartridges. The firing rate of this weapon was so great that it could discharge its magazine in less than two seconds. Sub-machine guns are lighter than machine guns with a limited supply of ammunition stored in the magazine.

Cooper Bridgeman

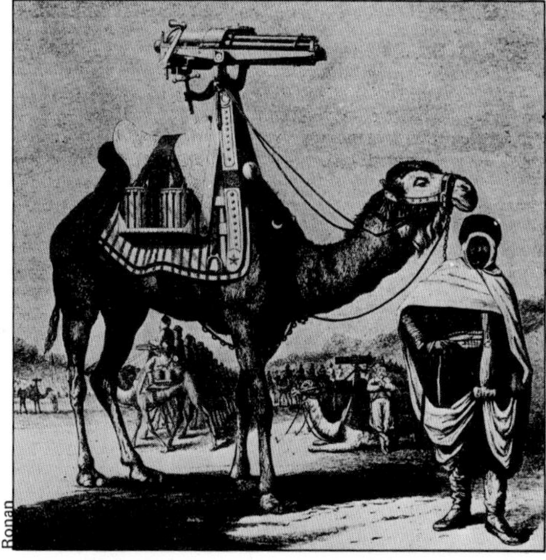

Ronan

Above: A Gatling gun fitted to a camel saddle, from an engraving published in 1872. As the first practical machine gun, the Gatling gun was used in the American Civil War and some were issued to the British Army. Its size and weight, however, limited its potential and it was soon replaced by other designs.

Below: The new British 105 mm light field gun shown here with the one tonne 4x4 Land-Rover. It is undergoing acceptance trials (1973) and is currently entering service, replacing the Italian designed 105 mm pack howitzer. Light field guns can be dismantled for transportation over rough terrain.

Peter Russell/Spectrum

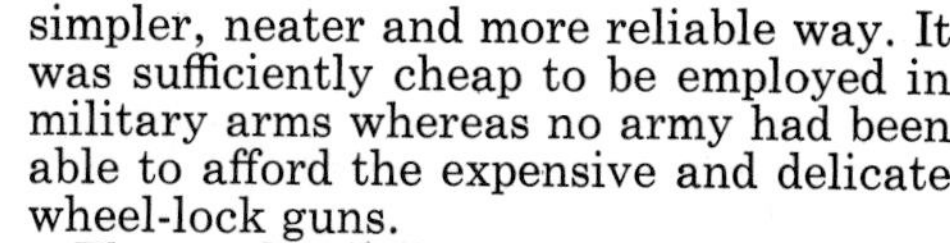

simpler, neater and more reliable way. It was sufficiently cheap to be employed in military arms whereas no army had been able to afford the expensive and delicate wheel-lock guns.

The end of the flintlock era came through the activities of a clergyman. It had been known from the seventeenth century that certain metallic salts such as mercury fulminate would explode if struck sharply and in 1800 the Reverend Alexander Forsyth used these compounds to ignite the main charge. Thus was introduced the last form of the muzzle-loaders, the *percussion cap* gun. They did not last for long.

Breech-loading guns

About 12 years after the first percussion cap gun was made, a Paris gunmaker, Pauly, made a gun which was loaded at the breech end using a paper cartridge with a metal base. Few were made and an improvement soon appeared. This was the needle gun, using a long needle which travelled through the length of the paper cartridge and struck a percussion cap on the base of the bullet. It was an instant success and led directly to the German victories in the Danish and Austrian wars of the 1860s. But another feature of the needle gun was even more successful: this was the breech mechanism. The breech was closed by a rotating bolt, not unlike a door-bolt. It was strong, simple and highly reliable, and rapidly became the most widely used rifle mechanism of all time. Within a hundred years many millions of bolt action rifles had been made.

Rifles, as opposed to smooth bore guns, were made from the earliest times. Some matchlock guns from about 1500, for example, had *rifling* grooves cut into the barrel, to give the bullet a spin and thus greater accuracy. Others soon followed this example. The difficulty with muzzle-loaded rifles was that they soon became blocked, preventing the bullet from being loaded. Breech loaders had no such trouble, and progress in rifling forms and bullet shape was rapid with the cartridge-loaded weapons. By the middle of the nineteenth century all-metal cartridges had replaced the earlier paper and metal ones, and design was rapidly becoming standardized.

The cartrigdes were detonated by one of two methods: *rim-fire* or *centre-fire*. In rim-fire cartridges the detonator compound was contained in a thin ring around the inside of the cartridge rim. The striker crushed a small portion of the rim against the breech and so ignited the charge. The advantage of this method lay in the fact that the case could be in one piece and the cost was therefore reasonably low. The centre-fire cartridge, on the other hand, had a percussion cap let into a hole in the centre of the base of the case, which was struck by a pin or hammer to fire the charge. The centre-fire cartridge was more expensive to make, but it withstood greater pressures and gave a more even ignition. Today only very small cartridges, such as the 0.22 inch target and sporting ammunition, use rim-fire detonation. Centre-fire is used in all others.

Many of the first breech loaders used a hinged block to close the breech but these were only suitable for firing single shots. With the introduction of the metal cartridge case, however, designers devised

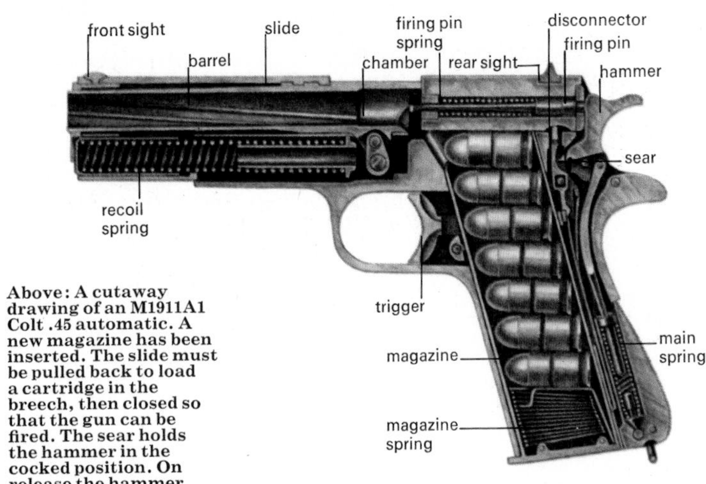

Above: A cutaway drawing of an M1911A1 Colt .45 automatic. A new magazine has been inserted. The slide must be pulled back to load a cartridge in the breech, then closed so that the gun can be fired. The sear holds the hammer in the cocked position. On release the hammer strikes the firing pin.

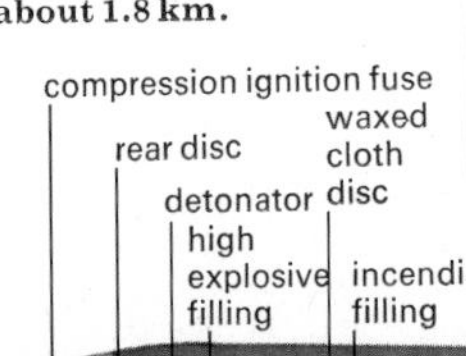

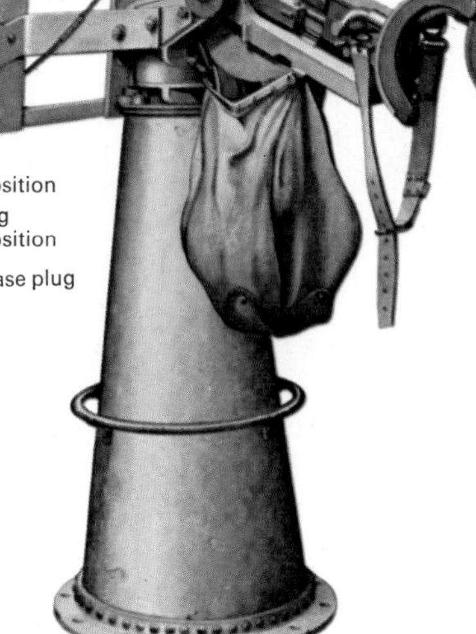

Right: The Oerlikon MkII anti-aircraft machine gun. A MkII shell with high explosive, incendiary and tracer components is shown below. The gun had a length of 2.4 m and weighed 67 kg (gun only). Its rate of fire was 465 to 480 rounds per minute. Maximum range at 45° elevation was about 1.8 km.

repeating action mechanisms where the cartridges are loaded and fired successively using some hand-operated lever to work the system. One of the earliest of these was the Winchester under-lever repeater so well known from cowboy books and films.

The Winchester rifle carried its ammunition in a tube under the barrel, from where it was fed backwards by spring pressure to a point under the breech. Working the under-lever downwards opened the breech, ejected the empty cartridge case and placed the loading platform opposite a fresh round. The spring pushed the round onto the platform and the action of closing the lever brought the platform up to the breech and pushed the round in, all in one movement. The breech then closed. The mechanism was somewhat complicated, but it was enormously successful and remained in manufacture for over 50 years.

The popular bolt action was made into a hand-operated repeater by placing a magazine beneath the bolt and allowing the bolt to strip a fresh round off the magazine platform as it went forward, pushed by the firer's hand. This was far simpler than the Winchester system and better suited to long, powerful cartridges.

Revolvers

Wheel and flint-lock mechanisms enabled practical pistols to be made and with the arrival of percussion ignition multi-barrel pistols became fashionable. From these the *revolver* was quickly developed. In this, the rounds are stored in the chambers of a cylinder which line up in turn with a single barrel.

The automatic pistol was not invented until the end of the nineteenth century, and the first practical one was made in Germany by Borchardt. This pistol used the force of recoil in the firing of a 9 mm round to push the barrel backwards and operate a mechanism which ejected the spent case, cocked the hammer and fed another round into the breech. The Borchardt was followed by the Mauser and Luger which were derivatives of it, and at the same time a flood of other designs poured out from factories all over the world.

In 1900 in Belgium, the firm of Fabrique Nationale made a compact automatic pistol to the design of the American gunsmith John Browning. This pistol operated by a combination of recoil and blowback, in which the force on the cartridge case actually pushed the bolt backwards.

Peter Russell/Spectrum

Left: An M109 155 mm SP gun at maximum elevation. Note the narrow track and large rear entry doors. These SP (self propelled) guns come into the medium-sized artillery range, with a firing range of between 16 and 24 km (10-15 miles) depending on the size of the shell—usually between 25 and 50 kg.

Below: 35 mm twin anti-aircraft field gun. This is one of the most modern all-weather, medium-range anti-aircraft guns with fully automatic control equipment. It has an effective range up to 4000 m and a firing rate for each gun of 550 rounds per minute. The ammunition is fed automatically.

Oerlikon

Below: A German MG 42 machine gun which operates on the recoil system, with a simplified representation of the gas operated and blowback systems. In the MG 42, the bolt is driven forward by the recoil spring when the trigger is depressed. The bolthead drives a cartridge into the barrel chamber and is locked in position by the locking piece. A further small movement forward by the bolt (red arrow) fires the round. The barrel and the bolt recoil and the locking piece releases the bolthead. The cycle is then repeated. A flash hider is fitted to the barrel and, for stability, the gun is mounted on a bipod.

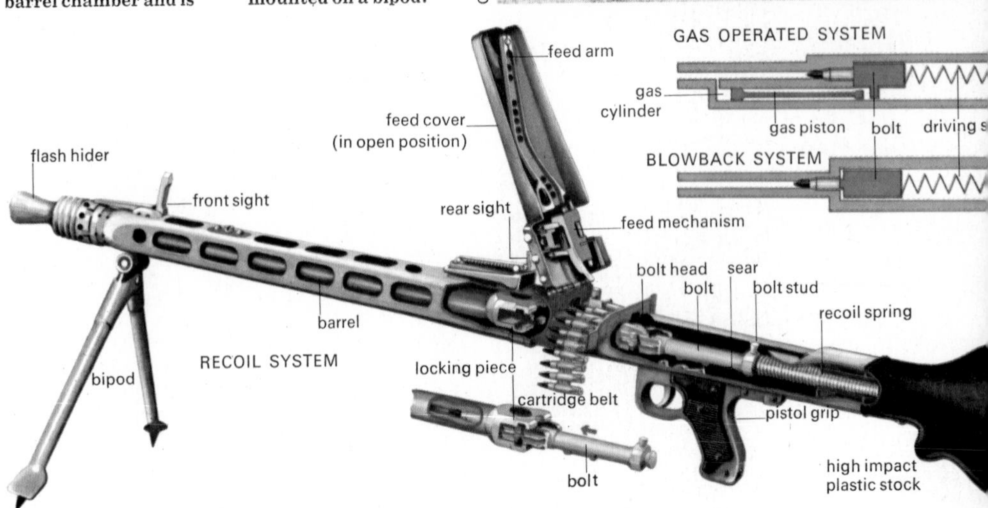

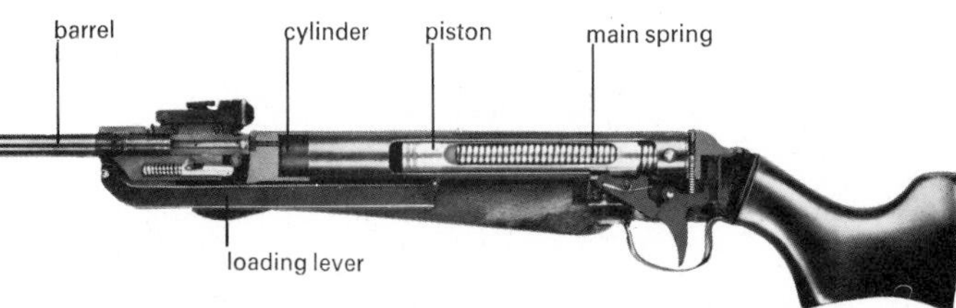

Cooper Bridgeman

Left: A Russian designed AK Assault rifle. These can also be classed as light machine guns as they combine the rapid fire capability of the machine gun with the mobility and accuracy of the rifle. All Soviet rifles fire a 7.62 mm bullet. This particular type weighs about 6 kg and has a curved box-type magazine.

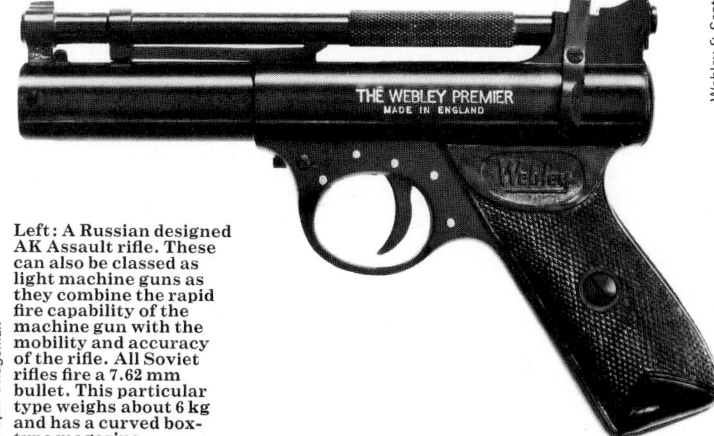

Webley & Scott Ltd

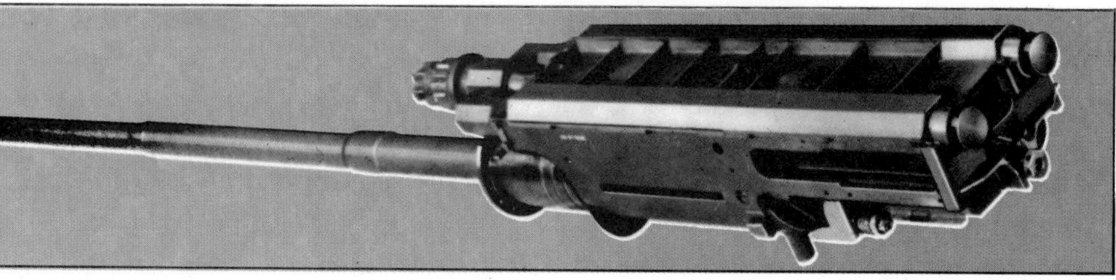
Oerlikon

Top left: A cutaway diagram of an air rifle. Air guns are weapons in which the force for propelling the bullet (or pellet, as it is more commonly called) is derived from compressed air or gas. The gun is 'primed' by compressing the main spring. This is attached to the piston which fits snugly into the cylinder.

Above: An air pistol. With air pistols, a more compact design is required. Here, the barrel is mounted above the piston and cylinder arrangement. To prime the pistol, the barrel is released at the rear and pushed round in an arc. The barrel is connected to the piston via a linkage arm and compresses the spring.

Above: An Oerlikon 30 mm aircraft cannon. This is a high-performance cannon which operates on the revolver principle. It is basically designed for installation in tactical aircraft and has an effective range of about 2000 m. Its rate of fire is 1,350 rounds/minute and it has a high muzzle velocity of 1,050 m/sec.

Below: An 81 mm Mortar. These have a range exceeding 1.6 km (one mile) although they are usually used for lobbing shells over hills and other obstacles at close quarters. The barrel is smooth and they are muzzle loaded with finned projectiles. As such, mortars stand in a class of their own but are related to artillery.

Peter Russell/Spectrum

The magazine was in the butt and the whole weapon was light and handy, and it set the pattern which has been followed by most manufacturers since.

Machine guns

Towards the end of the First World War the Germans produced the first *sub machine gun,* a two-handed, light shoulder gun which fired pistol ammunition from a box magazine containing 30 or more bullets. The Italians did the same in a slightly different and less practical way, and the Americans followed with a larger and heavier version which became the famous, or infamous, 'Thompson' sub machine gun.

From the very beginnings of gunmaking there were dreams of a gun that could fire continuously. This could never be done with muzzle-loaders, and it was not until the metal cartridge case came into general use that inventors got to work to make the first *machine gun.* Doctor Gatling produced the first practical model to be made in quantity, a gun consisting of six rifle barrels grouped around a spindle and rotated by hand. Each barrel had a bolt which was opened and closed by a cam-way as the barrels turned. Ammunition dropped in at the top of the circle from a gravity hopper. As the barrel went round the bolt closed, fired when at the bottom and opened again to eject the spent case on the way up.

The Gatling gun was heavy and clumsy and it was not long before single-barrelled machine guns appeared. The best was the invention of another American, Hiram Maxim. He used a single water-cooled barrel and fed the ammunition in with a long cloth belt, each round in a pocket sewn into the belt. His mechanism was complex, but immensely robust. The system used the force of recoil to provide the energy, as in the Borchardt pistol. Maxim's design first appeared in 1882 and was instantly successful. It was adopted all over the world and used by both sides in both World Wars. The British Army, for example, changed it slightly and called it the Vickers gun, and it is still in service with many armies.

In France, a machine gun was developed which used the pressure of the propellant gas to drive the mechanism. This was the Hotchkiss gun, and the principle of gas operation is the most popular today in all countries. A small hole about half-way down the barrel taps off a little of the propellant gas and conducts it through a tube to a piston. This piston is connected to the bolt and a suitable delay is arranged so that the bullet has left the barrel before the breech opens. Most machine guns fire at about 600 rounds per minute, or 10 shots per second.

Machine guns generate enormous quantities of heat when they are fired and the chief difficulty for the designer is cooling the barrel. Maxim and some others used a water jacket, but this is heavy and vulnerable and modern guns are all cooled by air. This often means having a removable barrel, which can be taken off to cool down while another is fitted.

Field guns

As the rifles and pistols improved and advanced, so also did the cannons and heavy guns. Breech-loaded field guns gave immensely greater power to any army, and rifled guns enabled cylindrical, pointed shells to be fired. These shells carried a far greater load of explosive than the old circular ball. Smokeless powders appeared in the 1880s and 1890s and these were so much more powerful than gunpowder that it became necessary to use some sort of recoil absorber, otherwise the guns could not be restrained when they fired. This gave rise to a completely new technology of buffering heavy shocks and in its turn enabled yet more powerful guns to be built.

Modern field guns weigh about four tonnes, fire a shell weighing around 20 kg (40 lbs), and have a range of about 16 km (10 miles). They have complicated firing mechanisms and recoil-absorbing gear. The barrels are made from the very highest grade of steel, and they are very expensive.

Explosives

When wood is burnt on a fire, compounds in the wood slowly combine with oxygen and release heat, light and gases. This process is known as *combustion.* With some substances, however, this combustion takes place very rapidly with the sudden release of heat, light and gases and this is called an *explosion.*

The destructive effect of explosives is largely attributable to the rapid and violent release of gases and where this occurs in a confined space, such as in a bomb, the effect is greatly increased. Thus, a small quantity of petrol vapour and air does not produce much of an explosion when it is ignited in the open, but within the cylinders of an internal combustion engine these gases are produced at a pressure of about one million newtons per square metre (several hundred pounds per square inch) and so drive the piston down. Yet even these explosive forces within an internal combustion engine are trivial compared with those produced by modern high explosives. For example, some of the bombs dropped during the Second World War generated at the moment of detonation a pressure of about 3,500,000,000 N/m² (500,000 psi).

Left: Preparing charges for blasting at a quarry face. The holes are drilled deep and positioned along the line of the required fault. Firstly, a detonator is placed at the bottom of each hole and then black powder is poured into the holes. Finally, a small amount of sand is carefully placed in the hole to act as a plug. Because the charges must be detonated simultaneously, electrical fuzes are used and these are connected together in series.

Right: With the charges prepared, the detonator leads are taken to this generator.

Below: An explosion in a stone quarry using the benching technique.

V-DIA

Classification of explosives

Explosives are broadly defined as substances which can undergo rapid combustion, and may be in either solid, liquid or gaseous form. But there are basically two classifications: 'high' and 'low'.

With the *low* explosives, combustion spreads through the material at relatively slow speeds up to 400 m/sec (1,300 ft/sec). With these types of explosives, however, the burning speed increases with pressure which is why their destructive power is enhanced when they are placed in a confined space. This relatively slow combustion is often termed *deflagration* and low explosives are sometimes referred to as *propellant explosives* because they tend to push or propel objects rather than shatter them. They are useful as propellants for shells and rockets.

High explosives, on the other hand, undergo extremely rapid combustion and in a completely different way to low explosives. When a high explosive is set off, the combustion sets up a supersonic shockwave or *detonating wave* that travels through the material at between 2,000 and 9,000 m/sec (approximately one to six miles per second). The shockwave disrupts the chemical bonds of the substance, and so initiates combustion as it proceeds—this rapid reaction is known as *detonation.*

High explosives need no container as the shockwave velocity is independent of pressure. The shockwave pressure is, however, extremely high—up to 100 tonnes/cm² (600 tons/sq inch)—and tends to shatter anything in its path. Consequently, they are used in bombs and artillery shells and for blasting in mines.

There are three factors which determine the effectiveness and safety of an explosive: power, velocity of detonation and sensitivity to detonation.

Power is measured by the quantity of gas produced by a given weight of the explosive. This is compared with the volume produced from the same weight of picric acid (picric acid is an explosive used as a standard) which is given a rating of 100. Thus, if the relative rating of the test sample is over 100 it is a more powerful explosive than picric acid. For example, PETN, the high explosive in *cordtex* (a detonating cord with industrial and military applications), has a power rating of 166.

Speed of detonation is measured directly as a speed (in metres per second or feet per second, for example). Nowadays, this is measured electronically.

Measuring an explosive's *sensitivity to detonation* is based on the fraction of material that will explode when struck and how this relates to the force which is applied. Some extremely insensitive materials will only explode locally and not propagate through the whole explosive when struck. Again, picric acid is used as the standard and given a sensiti-

K. Hackenberg/ZEFA

Dr. W. C. G. Baldwin

Left: The operating panel of the Biazzi-type glycerine nitrator. Glycerine is fed from the extreme right into the large nitrating vessel (centre right) where it is added to a mixture of *oleum* (super-strong sulphuric acid) and nitric acid. The mixture is stirred mechanically by paddles powered from above. The nitro-glycerine is then fed to the mushroom-shaped gravity separator in the middle. The nitro-glycerine floats above the acid, is collected at the top and fed to the three washers further to the left.

Right: One type of machine used for packaging nitro-glycerine powders.

Dr. W. C. G. Baldwin

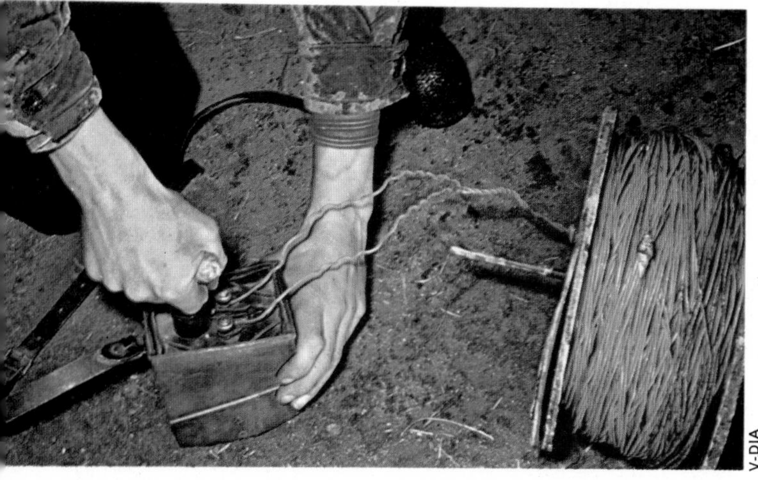

V-DIA

V-DIA

Above: Where sequential blasting is required it may be advantageous to use slow-burning time fuzes. Such a fuze is shown here. Where several are to be lit in sequence, some warning must be given to the operator when the detonation is due. To achieve this, an ingredient is added to the fuze which produces a red flash one minute before the explosive is detonated.

Dr. W. C. G. Baldwin

Left: A lorry for the transportation of *prilled* ammonium nitrate (in the form of ball-bearings about 2 mm in diameter). This is mixed with about 5% oil and fed by pump to the required location such as the shot holes drilled into the ground in quarry blasting.

RYING

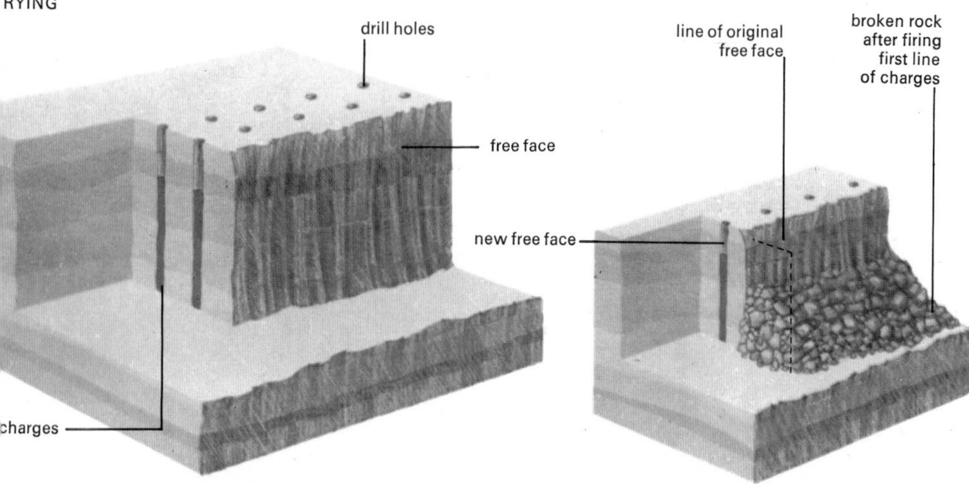

Above: How drill-holes are positioned for blasting in a stone quarry. The method is known as benching. Each bench may be 15 to 20 m high. The holes are placed about 4 m back from the face and spaced about every 4 m. The exact positioning will depend on the nature of the rock and its intended purpose. This will also determine the type of explosive used. High explosives will fragment rocks suitable for road chippings. Low explosives are used for large masonry blocks.

Novosti

Left: Explosives are often used in civil engineering. This explosion near Kazakhstan in the USSR helped to excavate a basin for an ice-skating rink.

vity rating of 100. Explosives with a sensitivity rating of less than 100 are more sensitive, unstable and unsafe.

Types of explosive

Gunpowder was the first of all explosives and is still used in many types of fireworks. Although gunpowder had been used by the Chinese for thousands of years in fireworks and as a propellant in a primitive type of military rocket fired from a leather launcher, it was unknown in Europe until the mid-thirteenth century. The first European to make written reference to gunpowder was the English monk Roger Bacon who described its potentialities as a military weapon in his book *De Secretis Operibus Artis et Naturae* (The Secret Works of Art and Nature) published in 1245.

Today, gunpowder consists of 75 per cent potassium nitrate (saltpetre), 15 per cent charcoal and 10 per cent sulphur and when burned it releases about 3,000 times its own volume in gases. Its explosive action is due to the charcoal and sulphur burning in the oxygen released by the saltpetre. Gunpowder is classified as a low explosive.

Black powder, or blasting powder as it is often called because of its early use in quarries, is really a minor development of gunpowder. By reducing the saltpetre content, the rate of combustion is slowed down thus making it more suitable for quarrying building-stone where shattering is not required. It was once used as a propellant in firearms and artillery pieces, but it suffered from the disadvantage that it released enormous amounts of thick smoke which not only betrayed the position of the gunner but also interfered with his aim. Gunpowder and black powder ceased to be used as military explosives with the invention of the smokeless powders based on nitro-cellulose.

One of the landmarks in the development of explosives was guncotton—the first useful high explosive. It was compounded by the German chemist Christian Schönbein in 1845. Guncotton was originally made by treating cotton fibre with strong sulphuric and nitric acids, but this was found to be a rather unstable compound. Today, it is made by treating paper or wood shavings with sulphuric and nitric acids and for that reason is generally called nitro-cellulose. Nitro-cellulose has a sensitivity rating of 23 when dry and about 120 when wet. Depending on its preparation, its final state (for example, whether it is wet or dry) and its blending with other ingredients, nitro-cellulose can be used as either a high or low explosive. As a low explosive it was once used as a propellant for artillery shells.

In 1846, Ascanio Sobrero, Professor of Chemistry at Turin Institute of Technology, discovered nitro-glycerine. This is an extremely powerful explosive—it releases 12,000 times its own volume of gas when exploded, has a power rating of 160 and a detonation speed of 7,750 m/sec (25,426 ft/sec). Nitro-glycerine is made by dripping glycerine slowly into strong sulphuric and nitric acids. For some years after it was first compounded, it was too dangerous to handle as it could be set off by mere shaking or rough handling. It had a sensitivity rating of only 13.

In 1886, the Swedish chemist Alfred Nobel discovered that if nitro-glycerine was mixed with a kind of clay called kieselguhr it became a semi-solid substance with the consistency of cheese which could be rolled into sticks. Nobel named his improved nitro-glycerine *dynamite*. Although dynamite is a less powerful explosive than the original nitro-glycerine, it is relatively safe to handle and responds only to sharp and heavy impact. In much of the dynamite used today, ammonium nitrate replaces a large proportion of the nitro-glycerine, while in place of the absorbent kieselguhr, wood-pulp mixed with sodium nitrate is used as a safety factor. Because of dynamite's convenience and cheapness, it is extensively used for quarrying.

Picric acid was first prepared by Woulfe in 1771 by the nitration of phenol. Although it is a powerful explosive comparable with nitro-cellulose and nitro-glycerine, it is much less sensitive and for over a hundred years it was found difficult to detonate. By 1888, however, it had replaced gunpowder as a shell-filling with a mercury fulminate cap as a detonator. Picric acid is of little use today except as a standard.

Because of their devastatingly shattering effects, high explosives constitute the explosive elements in the shells and bombs used in warfare. The high explosive most commonly used in both world wars, for example, was trinitrotoluene, better known as TNT. This has a power rating of 95, a detonation speed of 7,000 m/sec and a sensitivity rating of 110. Another important explosive is pentaerythritol tetranitrate or PETN. This has a power rating of 166, a detonation speed of 8,100 m/sec and a sensitivity rating of 40.

RDX, also called *Hexogen* or *Cyclonite*, is a very powerful explosive (power rating 167) discovered by a German called Henning in 1899. It also has one of the highest detonation speeds at 8,400 m/s, and a sensitivity rating of 55.

Detonators

One of the characteristics of high explosives is that they are not easily set off or exploded by themselves, either by heat, flame, friction or impact. Indeed, some explosives merely burn fiercely when ignited but do not explode.

Consequently, high explosives need some method or substance to initiate their explosion. These initiators are called primary explosives or *detonators* and work by creating a high pressure shockwave which triggers the main explosive. Examples of primary explosives are mercury fulminate, lead azide, copper acetylide, silver acetylide, nitrogen sulphide, fulminating gold, nitrogen chloride, tetracene, lead styphnate and mixtures of chlorates with red phosphorous or sulphur.

To obtain complete combustion of the main explosive and consequently the maximum destructive effect from it, a quantity of a powerful but moderately sensitive high explosive is used to boost or reinforce the detonating or primary explosive. This booster is called an *intermediary charge*. The more sensitive explosives, with values around 20 are used as the primary charge. The impulse from this can set off the intermediary charge (with a sensitivity of about 60) which in turn will initiate the shockwave in the main (high) explosive. For example, to detonate TNT (sensitivity 110), a detonating cap with a mercury fulminate primary (sensitivity 8) and a tetryl intermediary charge (sensitivity 70) may be used.

How explosives work

Although the mechanisms of combustion differ widely between deflagrating and detonating explosives, the chemical processes involved are essentially the same. During an explosion, oxygen is rapidly consumed and because this cannot be readily obtained from the air the explosive

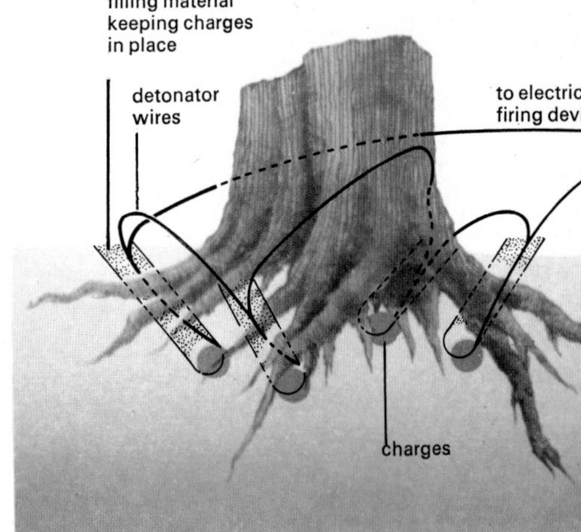

Above: Positioning charges to remove a large tree stump with laterally spreading roots. The charges are usually placed under the largest roots. Electrical fuzes are used because the charges must be detonated together.

Right: Demolishing a tall factory chimney with explosives. If correctly placed, only a small amount of explosive is required.

Below: A general purpose bomb designed to explode after penetrating the upper floor of a building. The firing pin and primer are screwed into contact with the booster charge by the propeller as the bomb falls through the air.

stabilizing fin
tail fuze
primer
detonator
booster charge
high explosive main charge
bomb casing
booster charge
nose fuze

Above: Unblocking a canal with explosives. Unlike quarry explosions, which are accompanied by large amounts of dust which hide the hot expanding gases, in this photograph the fireball can be clearly seen. It gives an impression of the temperature of the liberated gases. Much of an explosion's destructive effect, however, is due to the inrush of air immediately after detonation.

Right: The British Army demolishing Gillhall House—a seventeenth century stately home. The charges are placed at the base of the house and ignited simultaneously using electrical fuzes for maximum effect.

Scotsman

Spectrum

must incorporate its own supply. For this reason explosives include chemicals such as ammonium nitrate which are rich in oxygen.

Nitrogen compounds are used extensively in explosives because of their chemical instability. Indeed, an explosive might be described as an unstable substance which undergoes a complete transformation within a very short period of time—in other words, a mixture of substances which are in unstable equilibrium. This equilibrium is upset when the mixture is ignited or detonated.

As combustion proceeds through the material, the originally large molecules of the explosive are converted into a large number of smaller molecules (gases) and heat is released. Initially, these gases are confined in a small volume at a high temperature and therefore exert a tremendous pressure.

In low explosives, combustion takes place throughout the whole material but not instantaneously. The hot gases under high pressure that are generated accelerate the total combustion until the container ruptures. With high explosives, however, no container is required. Nearly all the combustion takes place on the front of the detonating wave as it travels through the material. Thus, the combustion *spreads through* the material, albeit in a very short time—no more than a few millionths of a second.

Above right: East German border guards placing explosives along the East/West border in the Harz mountains. Although explosives are the stock-in-trade of all modern armies, more are used for peaceful purposes. It is also true, however, that many of the major advances in explosives technology throughout the centuries have resulted from military experience.

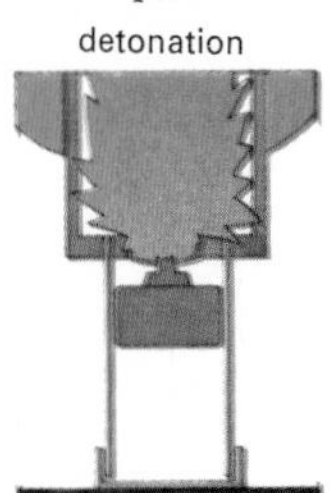

Left: A percussion fuze with mercury fulminate primary and a booster (or intermediary) charge. Detonators are classed as either *igniferous* (heat producing) or *disruptive* (producing shockwaves) depending on which initiates the main explosion.

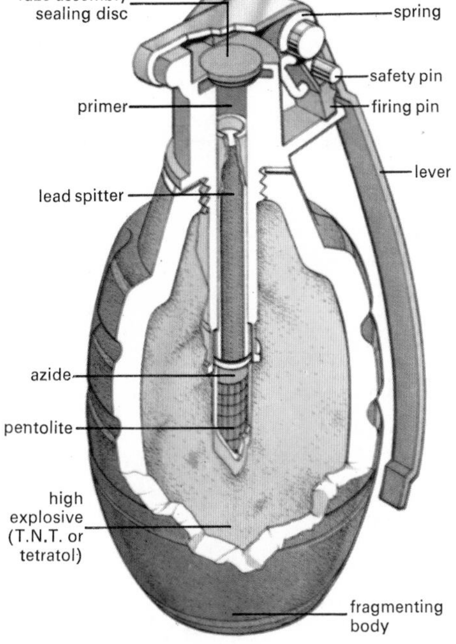

The blast wave

As the gases expand into the air they set up a blast or pressure wave that travels in all directions at speeds up to 335 m/sec (1,100 ft/sec). This pressure wave forces away the surrounding air and any other objects in its path. There is, however, a secondary effect. In the vicinity of the explosion, where the air has been displaced, a partial vacuum is created into which air rushes to reestablish normal atmospheric pressure.

Although the pulling effect of the vacuum is weaker than the pressure wave, it lasts longer. As a result, objects which have been merely weakened by the initial pressure wave are further damaged and sometimes completely demolished by this secondary effect. That is why windows some distance from a blast may actually be sucked towards the source of the explosion rather than away from it.

Applications

Rather unexpectedly, figures show that more explosives are employed for peaceful purposes than were ever used in warfare. For example, vast quantities are used in mining, quarrying and demolition. Without explosives to cut through or loosen rock and hard ground, the boring of tunnels and the building of canals would be almost impossible.

Carefully controlled explosions of small charges are used for cutting heavy steel and for forming metals into required shapes. In this latter application, called *explosive forming*, the sheet of metal is placed over the open end of a die mould and together they are enclosed in a sealed chamber containing an explosive charge. When the explosive is detonated, the gases force the metal into the die where it is shaped. A similar technique is used for the cold-welding of dissimilar metals. Explosive forming can also be used for compressing powdered metals into dies to form solid shapes.

Sam Contractors

Above: The basic mechanism of a hand grenade. When the lever is released, the spring tensioned firing pin strikes the time fuze primer. This triggers the time fuze which finally sets off the primer, intermediary charge and main explosive. Time fuzes or an electric current are the main methods for setting off detonators.

Left: This lump of iron, left at the bottom of a demolished blast furnace, is to be fragmented using explosives. Holes are being cut in the iron with a thermic lance into which the explosive charges can be placed. In this particular case, high explosives are necessary.

Armour and Armoured Vehicles

The first wheeled vehicles designed to increase mobility on the battlefield were the chariots, but they not only lacked the manoeuvrability of the horsed soldier, they could operate only on firm ground and were effective only against infantry unprotected by cavalry. Above all, the chariot provided no protection for its crew. What was required was an assault vehicle that would enable its crew to bring their weapons to bear on an enemy and at the same time give them some degree of protection.

No serious attempt was made to solve the problem until about 1420, when John Zizka, one of the Bohemian leaders in the Hussite revolt, converted a heavy, four-wheeled farm cart into what he called a 'battle waggon'. Zizka's battle waggon carried a crew of 18 crossbowmen who were protected by walls of thick timber built round the sides of the vehicle. The battle waggon was drawn by a team of a dozen horses which were also protected by planking.

Zizka further developed his battle waggon idea by designing and building a waggon protected by wooden walls and mounting a light cannon called a 'snake'. This was quite an advance in artillery tactics as it enabled guns to be moved about in battle instead of being confined to the static role of a siege train.

The limiting factor in the employment of battle waggons was reliance on the horse as their means of propulsion. Numerous efforts were made in the nineteenth century to use steam power to propel mobile gun-platforms. One example was the Cowan 'battle car'. This had a helmet-shaped steel body, mounted two

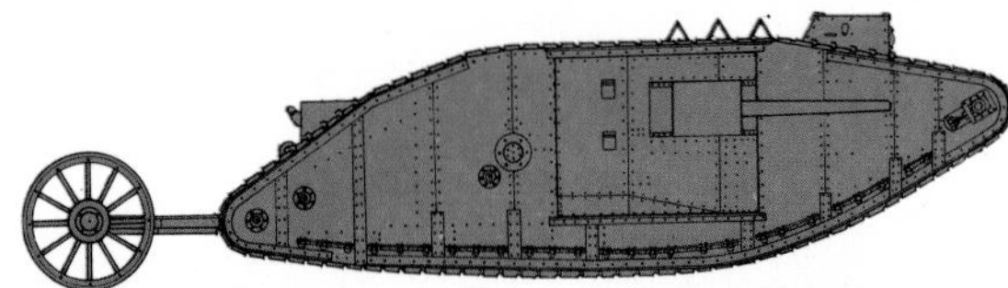

Big Willie (Mother) Mk I 1916

Medium 'A' Whippet 1917

Vickers M

Above: These drawings show how British tanks evolved from 1916 to 1943. The 'Mother' tank, the first ever used in a battle, had a 78 kW (105 hp) engine and a top speed of 6 km/h (3.7 mph), very slow compared with the 1943 Cromwell whose 447 kW (600 hp) engine gave it a top speed of 64 km/h (40 mph).

Mansell

Left: A model of a Roman cart covered with leather armour.

Below: An increasingly common non-military use of armour. Armoured vehicles like this, used to carry valuable loads such as payrolls and bullion, are designed to withstand likely forms of attack such as ramming, and to protect their crews from bullets or chemical sprays such as ammonia or acid.

Novosti

Above: The KV-85, a Russian tank first introduced in 1942 and used extensively during the Second World War. One of a series of tanks derived from a 1939 prototype named after Kliment Voroshilov, the Soviet defence minister, it was armed with an 85 mm gun and carried a crew of four.

Securicor

Below: These drawings show seven types of armour in use between 1100 BC and 1700 AD.
1. An Assyrian archer wearing armour made of metal plates.
2. A Greek infantryman wearing bronze armour.
3. A Norman infantryman wearing armour made of leather covered with metal plates.
4. A Mongol warrior wearing leather armour.
5. A medieval suit of armour, which gave complete protection from head to foot.
6. A Japanese Samurai warrior wearing armour made from lacquered wood and metal.
7. A later form of European armour, with a leather tunic, gloves and boots, and a metal breastplate and helmet.

Assyrian 1100-612 BC

Greek 600-300 BC

Norman 1066

Light Tank Mk I 1930

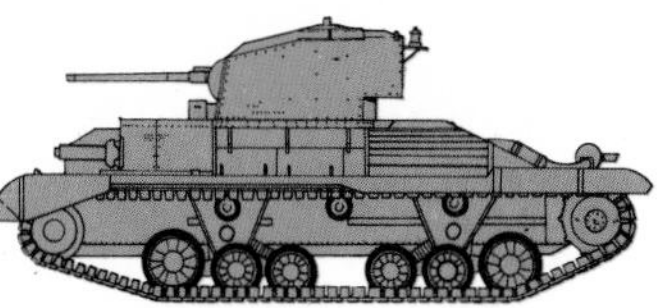
Cruiser Mk I A9 1938

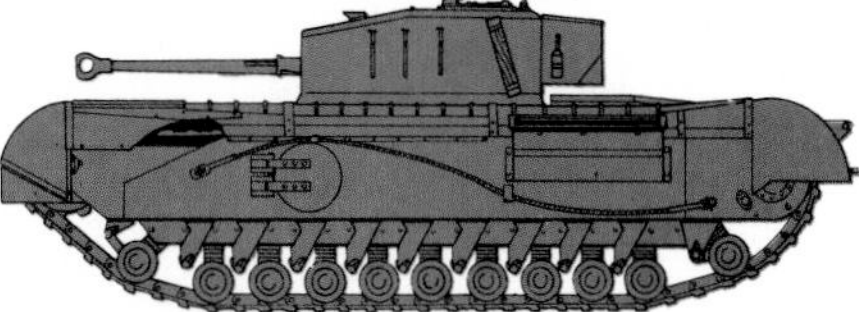
Churchill Mk VII 1941

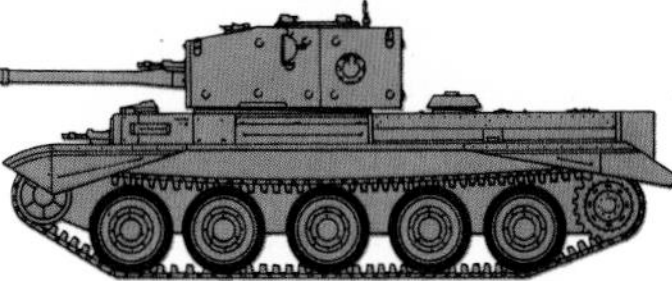
Cromwell 1943

Novosti

Left: Russian armoured personnel carriers at a miltary base in eastern Russia. These vehicles carry 14 troops, and are armed with 14.5 mm and 7.62 mm machine guns.

Right: The American M-4 'Sherman' tank was the most widely used Allied tank of the Second World War. First produced in 1942, over 49,200 were made. The standard armament was a 75 mm gun.

Mansell

three-pounder guns and was driven by a steam engine. It was far too heavy for its motive power and was never tested in battle.

Armoured cars

With the development of efficient internal-combustion engines, an entirely new and revolutionary era opened for the armoured fighting vehicle. This was the advent of the armoured car. At the outbreak of the First World War in 1914 all the contending armies had squadrons of armoured cars.

Protected by steel plating and armed with one or more machine-guns, armoured cars were designed chiefly for employment in a cavalry and scouting role. They also proved of value for fast and sudden raids into enemy territory. Initially, the armoured car and its crew constituted an independent fighting unit.

When a squadron was operating together, the commander of the group transmitted his orders by a system of flag signals. The introduction of radio greatly simplified the control by commanders of their squadrons.

Today the armoured car is an essential arm in many military operations and has entirely superseded horsed cavalry. Armoured cars are now in fact cavalry on wheels. With powerful engines to give them a high speed, a heavy armament of machine guns, steel plating to protect their crews, and bullet-proof tyres for their wheels, they are ideal for patrolling and spearheading attacks on lightly-defended positions.

Closely related to the armoured car is the armoured personnel carrier. Under the protection of armoured cars, the personnel carriers can bring into action infantry who are fresh and not loaded with equipment.

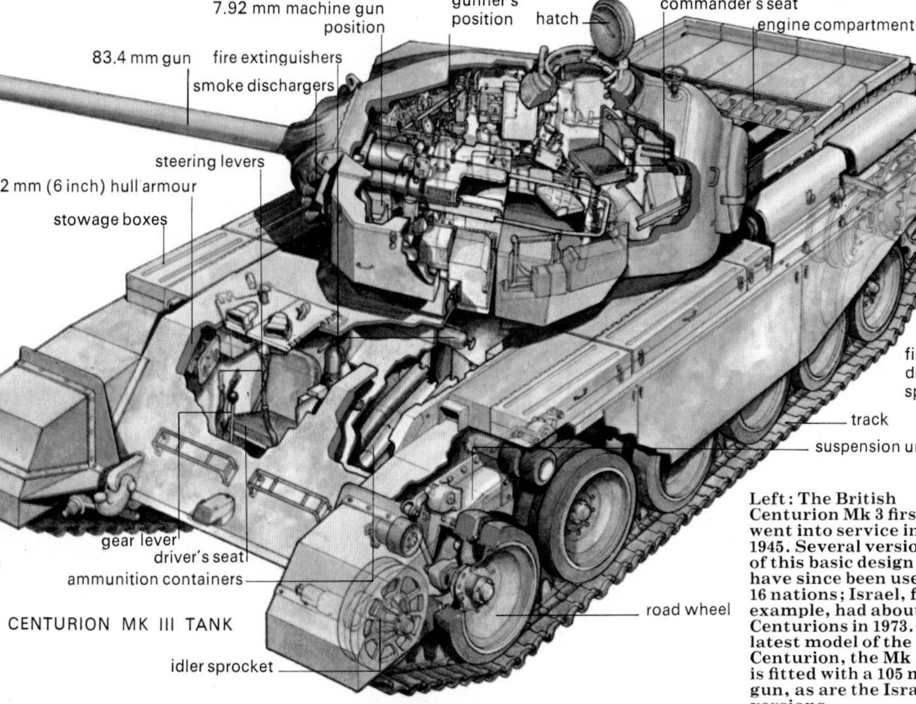

CENTURION MK III TANK

Left: The British Centurion Mk 3 first went into service in 1945. Several versions of this basic design have since been used by 16 nations; Israel, for example, had about 850 Centurions in 1973. The latest model of the Centurion, the Mk 10, is fitted with a 105 mm gun, as are the Israeli versions.

Mongol 1225-1400

European 1450-1500

Japanese 1150-1550

European 1650-1700

The first tanks

In spite of its speed, armour and armament, the armoured car labours under one great disadvantage. Being a wheeled vehicle, its movement is limited to roads or to relatively smooth country. That is why the armoured car was unable to play any significant part in the Western Front campaigns of the First World War.

The only answer to the problem of capturing well-defended trench systems was to design a heavily armed and armoured vehicle that could move across rough ground and in and out of deep shell-holes. In other words, the vehicle would have to carry some kind of road with it. So why not do that by taking away the wheels and substituting a caterpillar track?

The caterpillar track had been invented as long before as 1882, when John Fender, an English engineer working in the Argentine, built a steam traction-engine with caterpillar tracks instead of wheels. Each track consisted of a series of rectangular metal plates, each plate being joined to its neighbour by a flexible link to form a continuous chain of plates. Each plate on the underside of the track was fitted with a shoe to give a good grip on the ground. The upper side of the track had flexible and continuous rows of sprockets which passed over teethed wheels driven by a steam engine. The vehicle was steered by a single wheel mounted in front.

Eventually, production of tracked fighting vehicles began. The first of these was known as 'Little Willie', but it was dropped in favour of the design known as the Mk 1 or 'Mother'. The Mk 1 weighed 28 tons, was 8 m (26 ft) long, 4.3 m (14 ft) wide, and 2.4 m (8 ft) high. Its 78 kw (105 hp) Daimler engine gave it a top speed of about 6 km/h (3.7 mph), and it carried sufficient fuel for a range of 37 km (23 miles). It was armed with two 6-pounder guns and four machine guns. There was a crew of eight, and the vehicle could cross a gap or trench 2.4 m (8 ft) wide. It was steered by altering the relative speeds of its tracks.

To maintain the secrecy of the new weapons, they were packed in wooden crates marked 'TANKS' for the journey from the factory to the front. It was because of this that the name 'tank' has persisted for all types of tracked armoured fighting vehicles.

Baptism of fire

Tanks had their baptism of fire on September 15, 1916, when a force of 49 were sent to the battle of the Somme. The vehicles advanced in small detachments and their appearance took the Germans completely by surprise. In a few cases heavily defended trenches were overrun, but in general the debut of the first tanks was not particularly successful. This disappointment was due in large measure to the terrible state of the ground which even bogged down tracked vehicles.

Germany countered the British and French tanks with a vehicle of her own design, but it was a clumsy and extremely unreliable weapon and built too late to make other than a brief appearance on the Western front. By the closing stages of the First World War, however, the British and French armies had many hundreds of tanks in action.

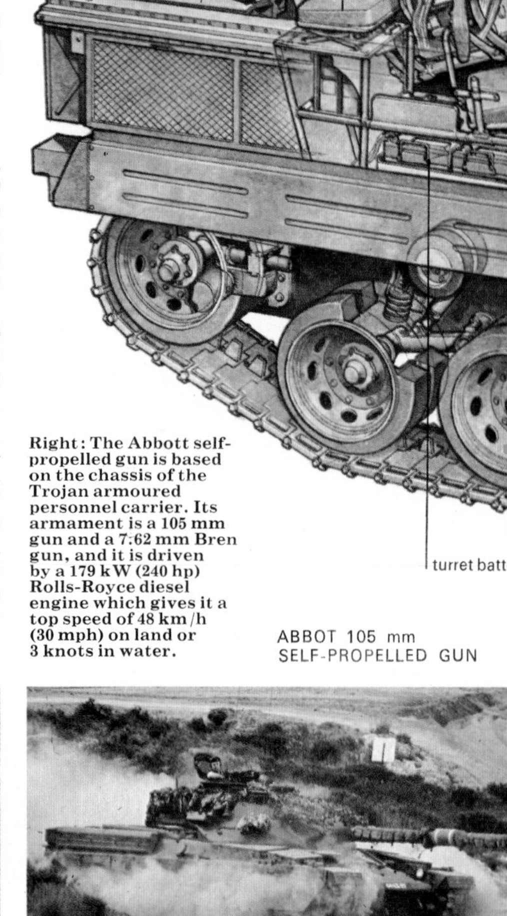

Right: The Abbott self-propelled gun is based on the chassis of the Trojan armoured personnel carrier. Its armament is a 105 mm gun and a 7.62 mm Bren gun, and it is driven by a 179 kW (240 hp) Rolls-Royce diesel engine which gives it a top speed of 48 km/h (30 mph) on land or 3 knots in water.

ZEFA

Left: A modern form of personal armour, used by troops and police for riot control work. The shield and helmet visor are made of an almost unbreakable plastic, and the bullet-proof body armour is made from a fibre-reinforced composite plastic material. The helmet is made of glass fibre.

Right: The Shorland armoured patrol car is built on a Land Rover chassis. It can be armed with a 7.62 mm machine gun, tear gas equipment or a water cannon.

Far right: The interior of an SB.301 armoured personnel carrier, which is also based on a Land Rover chassis.

Spectrum

Above: A British Chieftain Mk 3 main battle tank. The 120 mm gun is aimed by means of a laser rangefinder, which is accurate to within ±10 m (33 ft) at a distance of up to 10,000 m (33,000 ft).

Right: The FV4205 bridgelayer version of the Chieftain carries a small bridge section which it can lay across streams, ditches or trenches.

Left: An eight-wheeled armoured reconnaissance vehicle about to cross a river.

Shorts

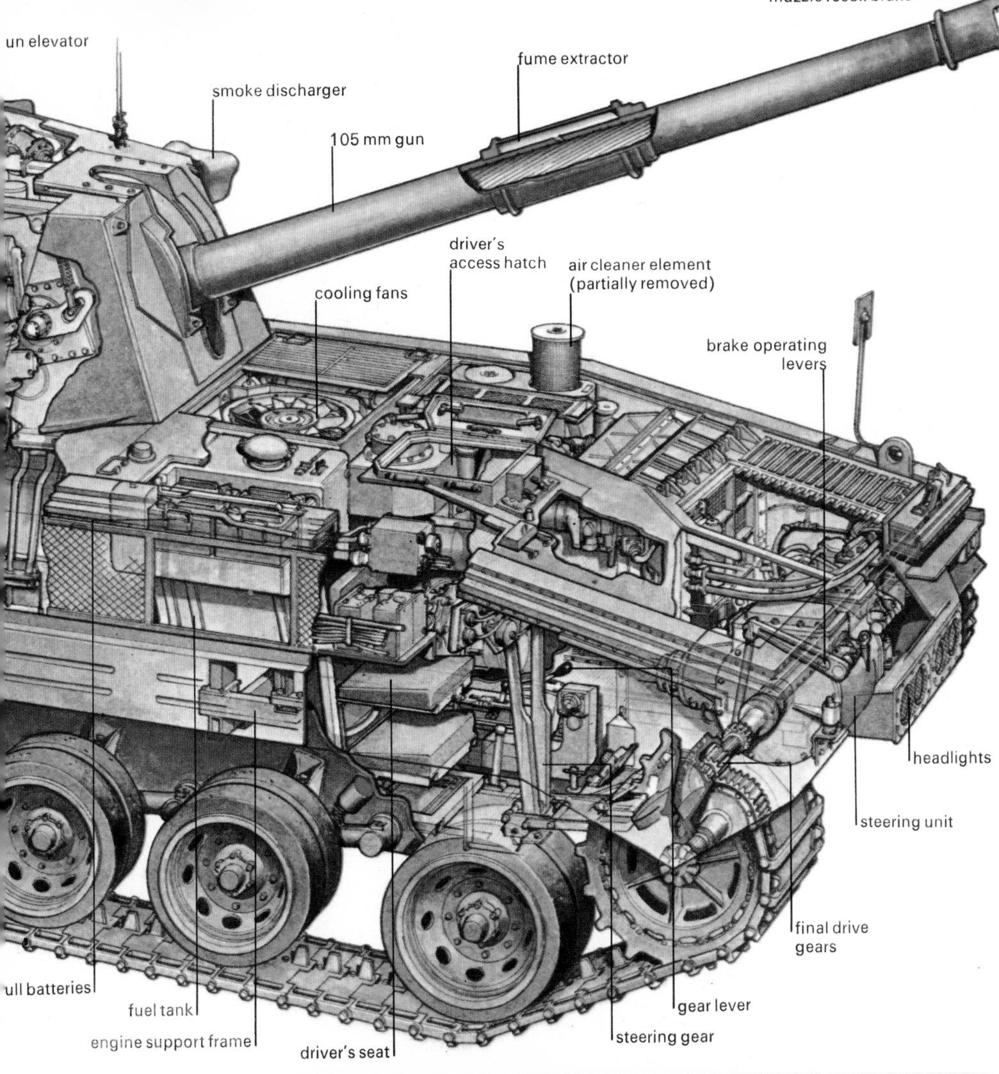

Second World War tanks

That Germany had profited from her lessons of the First War was more than proven when her brilliantly led Panzer divisions swept through Poland in a few days and later defeated France in six weeks. To their cost, the British appeared to have learned very little about the tactical use of tanks. What little and inadequate armour their armies possessed was frittered away, in futile but gallant forays by a few tanks at a time against the faster and better armed and armoured Panzer units. Practically all the British Army's tanks were lost in the retreat to Dunkirk. When the troops had been successfully evacuated back to England, the army in Britain was virtually without armour to face an expected German invasion.

Happily the invasion never came, and Britain was able to use the unexpected breathing space to accelerate the production of improved tanks and to perfect plans for their proper tactical use. The first of the new British tanks was the Crusader.

Classed as a medium cruiser tank, the Crusader weighed about 19 tons, had a top speed of 43 km/h (27 mph), a radius of action of 177 km (110 miles), carried a crew of five and was armed with one 7.92 mm gun and one 40 mm gun (later replaced by a 57 mm gun) in a revolving turret. Large numbers were in service in 1941, and the Germans soon had to contend not only with the new British tanks but also with the powerful tanks of Russia and America. One of the best tanks of the war was the Russian T-34, a fast 28 ton vehicle armed with a powerful 76.2 mm gun. The German Tiger tank was based on this design, but it was introduced too late in the war to have much effect.

A number of special-purpose tanks were developed, including flame-throwing tanks, bridging tanks, tanks fitted with flails for clearing a path through anti-tank minefields, tanks carrying batteries of rocket-launchers, amphibious tanks, and tanks specially designed to be dropped from aircraft by parachute in support of airborne forces.

Right: A German Leopard tank chassis fitted with twin 35 mm Oerlikon-Contraves anti-aircraft cannons. The vehicle carries a radar control system for aiming the cannons, which have a range of 4,000 m (13,120 ft) and a firing rate of 550 rounds per minute each. It is driven by a 10 cylinder, 620 kW (830 hp) diesel engine, and has a top speed of around 65 km/h (40 mph). The version shown here is the GDP-BO3. The guns can also be used against targets on the ground.

Peter Russell/Spectrum

Shorts

Oerlikon

Modern tanks

Modern tanks can be grouped into two basic categories: *battle tanks* and *reconnaissance tanks*. The battle tanks are heavy and well armed, and this group includes the German Leopard, the British Chieftain, the American M60, the Russian T-70 and the French AMX 30. The basic armament of the NATO countries' tanks is a 105 mm gun, although larger guns are used on some tanks such as the Chieftain, which has a 120 mm gun. Russian tanks also use large guns, for example the T-70 uses a 115 mm weapon. The Swedish Stridsvagh 103A ('S' tank) is an unusual design of battle tank which has no turret, the gun being fixed in the hull. The gun is elevated or depressed by tilting the hull with the vehicle's adjustable suspension.

Reconnaissance tanks, such as the British Scorpion, the American M551 Sheridan and the Russian PT-76, are fast and lightly armed and armoured. The Scorpion, for example, has aluminium alloy armour and a 76 mm gun, and can travel at up to 80.5 km/h (50 mph). Reconnaissance tanks, in common with battle tanks, can be armed with guided missile launchers in place of their guns.

Warships and Submarines

The development of the modern warship began in the middle of the nineteenth century, when the first steam-driven, armour-plated warships went into service. Until this time, the navies of the world were equipped with wooden-hulled sailing ships armed with rows of cannon. Ships of this type had ruled the seas for centuries, but they became obsolete in a matter of only a few years.

Armour-plated ships were first developed in response to the use of explosive shells. In November 1853, in a naval battle between Russia and Turkey, Russian ships destroyed seven Turkish frigates in the Black Sea, and attacked the town of Sinop. Three thousand Turks died in the battle, but only 40 Russians. The Russian success was largely due to their use of explosive shells instead of the ordinary solid cannonballs.

This dramatic demonstration of the ineffectiveness of unprotected wooden hulls caused a major change in warship design. Armour plating was now essential and the new ships were fitted with steam engines as well as sails to compensate for their greatly increased weight.

The first armoured warship was the French frigate *La Gloire*, designed by Dupuy de Lôme and built in 1859. It had a wooden hull protected by 120 mm (4.72 in) thick iron armour plate. Its displacement was 5,600 tonnes. At the same time the British Royal Navy was building the warship *Warrior*, under the direction of Isaac Watts, which was the first armoured warship built entirely of iron. Construction began in 1859 and it was launched in 1861. Soon after completion the *Warrior* was fitted with two of a new type of naval gun which had a rifled bore for greater accuracy.

Breech-loading guns, which could be re-loaded and fired more quickly than the muzzle-loading guns, were installed on the *Hercules* in 1867, a vessel which had armour from 152 to 248 mm (6 to 9.75 in) thick. After the *Warrior* and the *Hercules* came a long contest between advances in the effectiveness of guns and advances in armour design, from which the 'belt and battery' system evolved. This system used thick armour to protect a battery of heavy guns placed amidships, but allowed the 'belt' of armour around the hull to be reduced in thickness at the less vulnerable regions near the ends of the ship.

As naval guns became larger and more powerful, the armament of the ships was concentrated in this central battery. However, it was later decided that it was better to place the large guns on revolving turrets, widely separated around the vessel, so that a single shell could not put all the guns out of action, as was possible when they were all grouped together. The rotating turrets enabled the guns to be fired to either side of the vessel and, in addition, the guns could be aimed without have to turn the whole ship. HMS *Devastation*, 1873, was the first turret battleship without sail, laying down the design principles for the future battleships.

On 28 May 1905, the Japanese navy

Imperial War Museum

Above: The *Dreadnought*, launched in 1906, which set new standards of armour and fire power. It was also the first turbine-powered battleship; the 18,420 kW (24,700 hp) produced by its four Parsons steam turbines gave it a speed of over 21 knots. Its displacement was 22,500 tonnes.

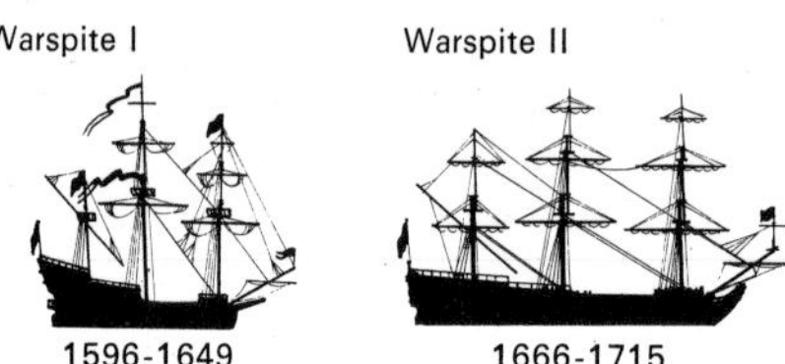

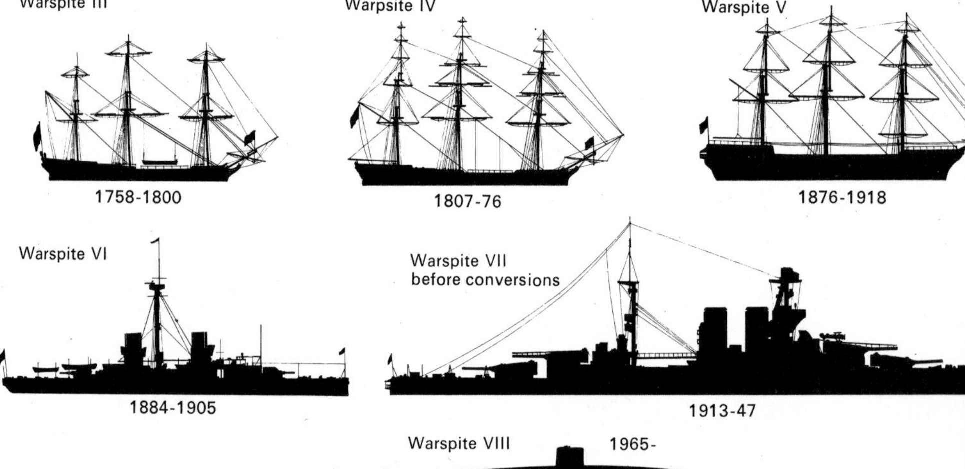

Warspite VIII 1965-

The eight Royal Navy ships that have had the name *Warspite*. The first, launched in 1596, displaced 648 tonnes and was armed with 36 guns. The first steam-powered *Warspite*, launched in 1884, displaced 8,400 tonnes, followed in 1913 by a 27,000 tonne ship. The eighth is a nuclear submarine.

COI

Left: The commissioning ceremony of the nuclear powered fleet submarine HMS *Warspite*, when it formally went into service with the Royal Navy. It is 87 m (285 ft) long and 10 m (33 ft) wide, and displaces 4,500 tonnes when submerged. Its underwater speed is 30 knots and it is armed with torpedoes.

Right: A guided missile cruiser of the Russian Navy, now possibly the most powerful navy in the world. The first guided missile cruisers were converted from conventionally-armed ships, the first purpose-built guided missile cruiser being the 14,000 tonne, nuclear-powered, USS *Long Beach*, launched in July 1959.

E. Hummel/ZEFA

K. Scholz/ZEFA

Left: The American warship USS *Alabama*.

Above: The Type 82 guided missile destroyer HMS *Bristol*, which displaces 6,000 tonnes and is 154.5 m (507 ft) long and 16.8 m (55 ft) wide. It is driven by steam and gas turbines, and is used to test Sea Dart and Ikara missile systems. The Sea Dart is radar-guided, with a range of over 30 km (19 miles); the Ikara is a kind of small, radio-controlled plane that carries a homing torpedo. The Ikara flies near its target, and then releases the torpedo, which homes in on the sounds made by the target.

defeated a Russian fleet at the Battle of Tsushima Strait. An analysis of this battle led Admiral Fisher to design a new type of battleship for the British Navy. He concluded that what was needed was a heavily-armoured ship, armed with large guns capable of accurate fire over a long distance. The ship he designed was the *Dreadnought*, fitted with ten 305 mm (12 in) guns and 280 mm (11 in) armour. The *Dreadnought* was launched in 1906, having been built in only a year, and its armour and fire power set the pattern for the battleships of other nations.

The Washington Naval Treaty of 1921, which limited the displacement of capital ships to 35,000 tonnes, had a great effect on warship design. It meant that Britain could no longer build massive warships like the *Hood*, completed in 1920, which had a displacement of 42,000 tonnes and carried eight 380 mm (15 in) guns. This restriction on the size of warships, together with limitations of the numbers of warships each nation was allowed to have, effectively prevented Britain from being the dominant naval power in the world.

The major naval powers continued building battleships, subject to the treaty limitations, but the Second World War showed that such ships were no longer really effective, as their big guns were no defence against torpedoes and aircraft. The last British battleship was the *Vanguard*, completed in 1946, and the principal ships of the Russian and American navies are now the aircraft carriers.

Another class of warship, similar to the battleship but smaller, is the cruiser. Cruisers are fast and were used to patrol

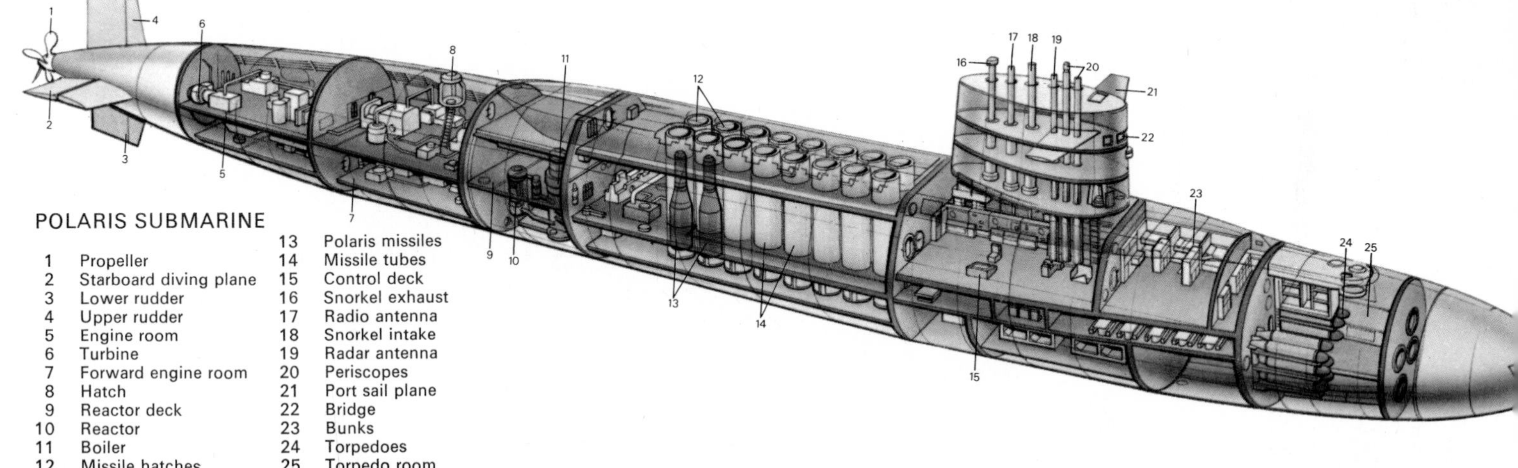

Above: A cutaway of a nuclear submarine equipped with Polaris nuclear missiles. The Polaris missiles can be launched from under the water, and have a range of 4,500 km (2,800 miles). The latest versions carry multiple warheads. This submarine is also armed with conventional torpedoes.

Left: A royal Navy task force on manoeuvres in the English Channel in 1975. The vessels shown here are, from left to right, the frigates *Tartar, Londonderry, Rothesay* and a Leander class frigate. The helicopter on *Tartar* is a Westland Wasp, which is an anti-submarine helicopter.

Below: The Lockheed Corporation are building Deep Submergence Rescue Vehicles (DSRVs) for the US Navy. These vehicles are designed to rescue crew members from damaged submarines at depths of about 1,220 m (4,000 ft). Operated by a crew of two, they can rescue 24 men at a time.

shipping routes, typical armament being 152 mm (6 in) or 203 mm (8 in) guns and displacement ranging from 4,000 to 12,000 tonnes, with thinner side armour than that used on battleships. Modern cruisers are armed with guided missiles.

Destroyers

Destroyers are smaller than cruisers, but fast and well-armed. In the First World War they were used to attack the enemy battle fleets with torpedoes and to prevent the enemy flotillas from attacking merchant convoys or naval vessels. They also acted as a screen against possible submarine attack. In the Second World War destroyers were fitted with anti-aircraft guns, anti-submarine depth charges and greatly improved submarine detection equipment.

The thinly-armoured guided missile destroyer (GMD) has become one of the most important surface vessels. The British 'County' class destroyers are typical of this kind of warship. They have a displacement of over 6,000 tonnes and are powered by both steam turbines and gas turbines. Their armament consists of four 114 mm (4.5 in) guns, plus Seacat and Seaslug guided missiles which can be used against aircraft or surface targets. In addition, each ship carries a Westland Wessex helicopter, armed with homing torpedoes, for anti-submarine work.

Modern destroyers such as these are very expensive because, as well as having costly propulsion and weapons systems, they also have many features not fitted to earlier types. These features include reversible-pitch propellers, stabilizers, and the special closing and washing-down facilities needed for protection against nuclear fall-out. A modern destroyer can provide long and close range anti-aircraft cover for the fleet, and it can defend surface forces against a ship attack. They may also act as radar stations to direct aircraft attacks and they can be used to hunt and destroy submarines.

Frigates

Frigates are fast vessels originally used for fleet reconnaissance work. The frigates used in the Second World War for convoy escort were characterized by a single gun main armament, with no torpedo tubes but with a powerful battery of anti-aircraft guns. Corvettes, smaller than frigates but with anti-submarine weapons and detection equipment, were also used for convoy escort. Post-war development was aimed at producing three principal types of frigate, namely anti-submarine, anti-aircraft and aircraft direction. Designs capable of fulfilling all of these roles, the general purpose frigates, were later introduced.

Modern frigates, such as the British 'Leander' class, often have a greater displacement than the destroyers used in the Second World War and may carry more hitting power than some battleships of that period. The armament used on the new frigates includes surface-to-air, surface-to-surface and anti-submarine missiles, anti-submarine mortars, guns, and torpedo-carrying helicopters.

Aircraft carriers

The idea of using a ship as an aircraft carrier began before the First World War —the first aircraft take-off from a ship happened on 14 November 1910, when Eugene Ely flew a Curtiss biplane from a platform built on the bows of the USS *Birmingham.* In January of the following year, Ely was the first to land a plane on a ship, in this case on a platform on the after-deck of the USS *Pennsylvania.*

During the Second World War the aircraft carrier took over from the battleship as the heart of the naval battle force. After the war the introduction of jet aircraft resulted in several modifications to carrier design. The higher take-off and landing speeds required by jet aircraft led to the introduction of steam-powered catapults to accelerate the jets along the deck at take-off. The carriers were fitted with angled flight decks to enable aircraft to take-off along the angled section while others were landing on the straight section.

Britain has stopped building any aircraft carriers as such, but the *Ark Royal* was put back into service after modernization. The carriers *Albion* and *Bulwark* have been converted to commando ships, carrying helicopters, vehicles and landing craft assault vessels. The US Navy, however, has a fleet of modern carriers, including the nuclear-powered *Enterprise,* which has a displacement of 83,350 tonnes and a flight deck measuring 335.6 m (1,101 ft) by 76.8 m (252 ft).

Fast patrol boats

The first coastal motor boats (CMBs), were developed by Thorneycrofts in England in 1916, and were powered by petrol engines which gave them a speed of over 30 knots. They were armed with torpedoes and later versions were equipped for minelaying work. American motor launches developed during the First World

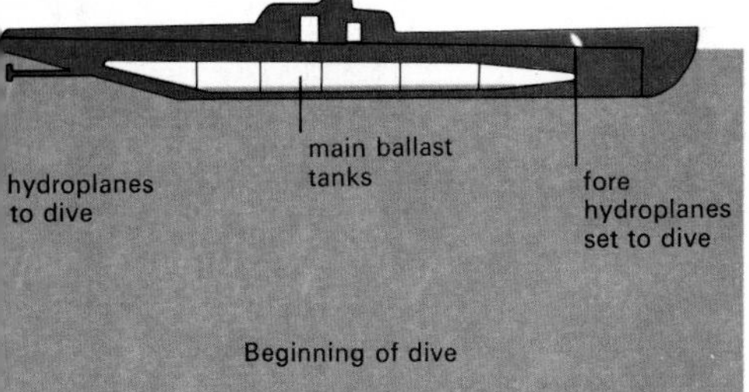

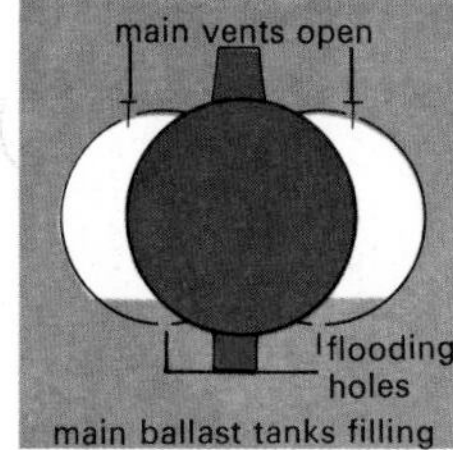

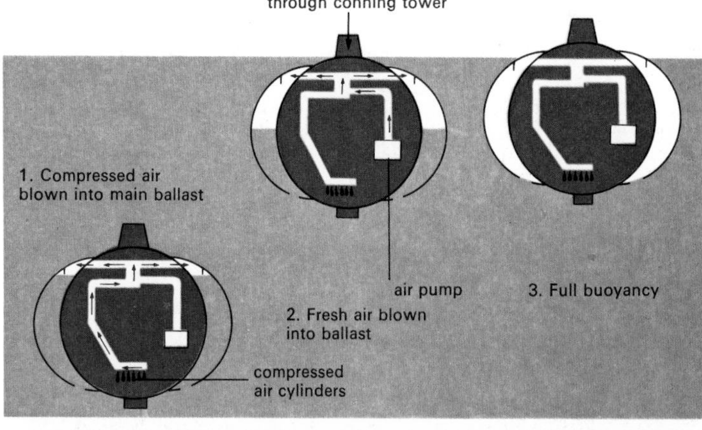

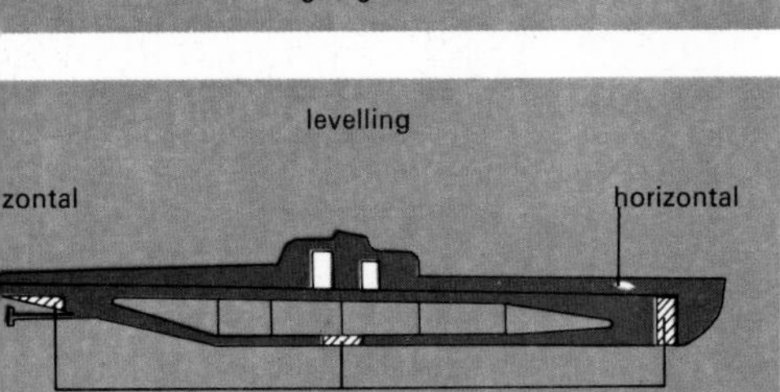

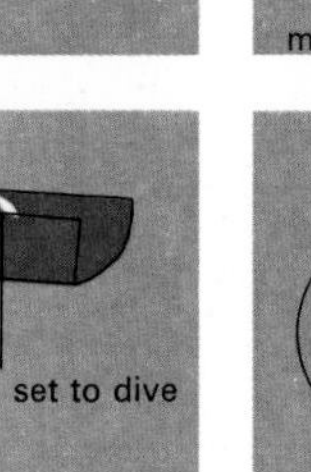

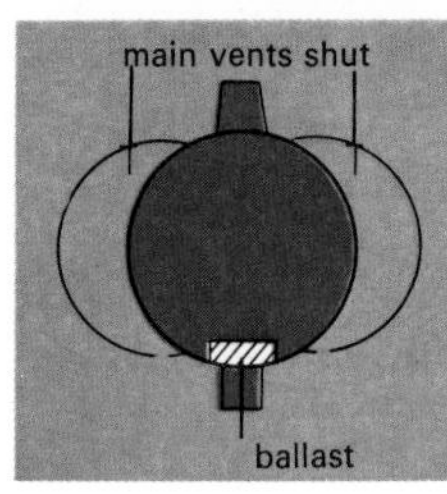

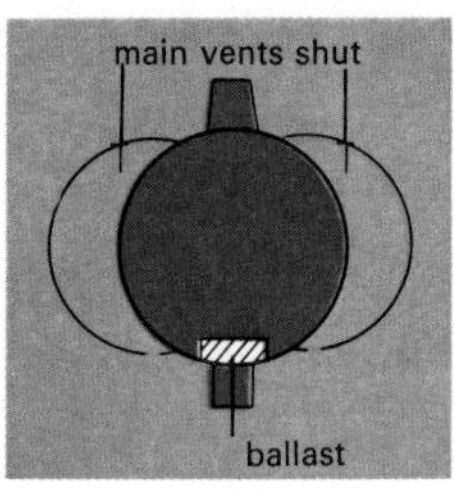

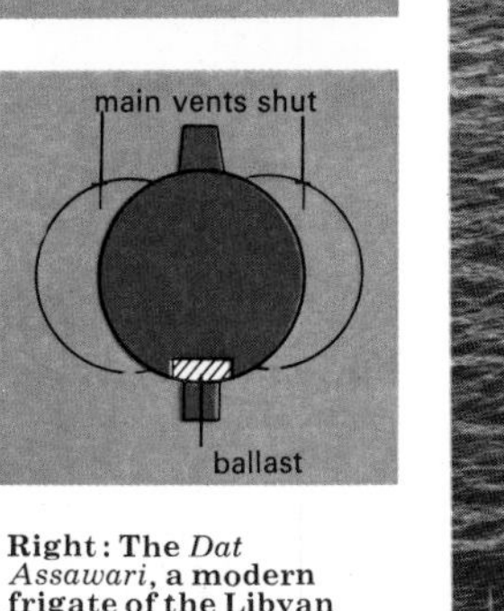

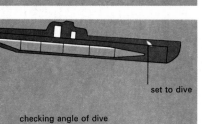

Above: Submarines dive by flooding the main ballast tanks with water and setting the hydroplanes to the 'dive' position. Once a sub is submerged, the rear hydroplanes are re-set to control the dive angle, and when it is at the desired depth it is levelled by flooding small internal ballast tanks.

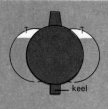

Above right: A submarine surfaces by using its hydroplanes to bring it close to the surface, then following the procedure shown here. It begins blowing the water out of the ballast tanks with compressed air, and as the conning tower leaves the water it sucks in fresh air to finish the process.

Vosper Thorneycroft

Right: The *Dat Assawari*, a modern frigate of the Libyan Navy built by Vosper Thorneycroft in Britain. Modern frigates have displacements of up to about 5,000 tonnes.

Below: The Polaris missile room in the nuclear submarine HMS *Resolution*.

Keystone

War were used for anti-submarine work.

During the Second World War, small, fast coastal craft were widely used as harbour defence launches, motor torpedo boats and motor gun boats. Modern patrol boats are powered by gas turbine engines and are capable of speeds of over 50 knots, some of the faster craft being hydrofoil boats.

Minesweepers

Minesweepers have non-magnetic hulls built from glass-reinforced plastic, aluminium or wood—this means they do not trigger off mines which are activated by the magnetic disturbance caused by a metal hull passing near them. Magnetic mines are exploded by trailing a cable, carrying a pulsating electric current, from the stern of the minesweeper. Acoustic mines, triggered by sound waves created by the engines and propellers of a nearby ship, are detonated by a noise generator which is towed behind the minesweeper.

Submarines

Despite many attempts to build submarines, from the seventeenth century onwards, real naval interest in submarines did not begin until the early twentieth century, but submarine development proceeded rapidly once the major navies began to build them. Most early subs used battery-powered electric motors to propel them while submerged, with petrol or steam engines to drive them on the surface and generate power to recharge the batteries. The role of the petrol and steam engines was soon taken over by the diesel engine, and the diesel/electric system is still used on all sub-

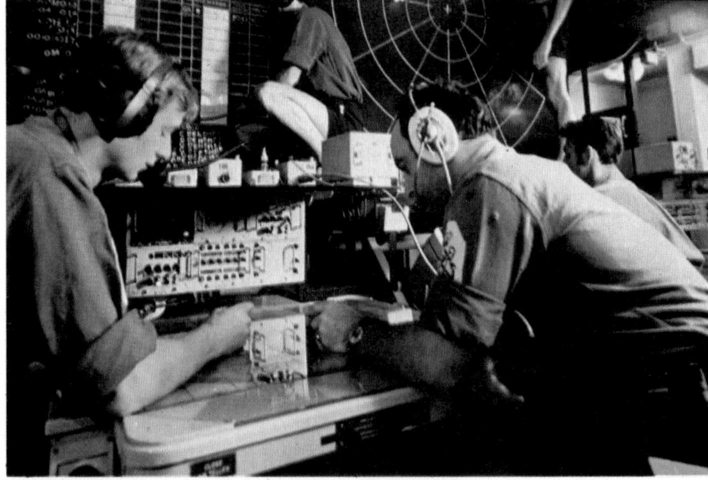

COI

John Watney

Above: The Aircraft Direction Room of the aircraft carrier HMS *Ark Royal*.

Right: The US Navy's *Enterprise*, the world's first nuclear-powered aircraft carrier, which was launched on 24 September 1960. The ship's turbines produce about 223,710 kW (300,000 hp), giving it a cruising speed of about 33 knots. The larger aircraft are F-4 Phantom fighter-bombers and the smaller ones are A-4 Skyhawk light attack bombers. The aircraft are kept in hangars below the flight deck, and their wings can be folded so that they take up less space in the hangars. The ship is armed with anti-aircraft missiles instead of guns.

Jack Novak/ZEFA

Above: Assault vessels leaving the dock at the stern of an assault ship. These vessels are used for ferrying troops and light equipment ashore.

Below: A Boeing Sea Knight anti-submarine helicopter lands on the helicopter deck of an assault ship, as a light assault vessel enters the dock below it. Assault ships can also carry Harrier vertical take-off jets, and large assault vessels capable of carrying tanks, self-propelled guns and other heavy equipment. The ships themselves are armed with guided missiles and anti-aircraft guns for self-defence.

Vosper Thorneycroft

Above: HMS *Brave Borderer*, a fast patrol boat of the Royal Navy, travelling at over 50 knots. The first fast patrol boats, built in 1916, were coastal motor boats and had a speed of about 30 knots. They were armed with torpedoes, as is the modern boat shown here, and later versions were equipped for minelaying work. During the Second World War small, fast coastal craft were widely used as harbour defence launches, motor torpedo boats and motor gun boats. Modern patrol boats are powered by gas turbine engines and some of them are fitted with hydrofoils. Many are equipped with anti-aircraft and anti-ship missiles as well as guns and torpedoes.

John Watney

marines except nuclear vessels.

Submarines are fitted with pairs of *hydroplanes*, horizontal rudders rather like small wings, whose angles can be altered so as to direct the vessel upwards or downwards as it moves forwards under the thrust from its propeller. When a submarine dives, it opens valves which admit sea water into its *ballast tanks*, thus reducing its buoyancy, and the hydroplanes are angled to direct it downwards. To surface again, the hydroplanes are angled so as to direct it upwards, and when it is just below the surface the water is blown out of the ballast tanks by compressed air to restore its buoyancy and enable it to float normally on the surface.

The development of the *periscope* enabled submarines to travel inconspicuously just below the surface yet still see what was going on there. Another development which aided this was the *schnorkel* (also called a *snorkel* or *snort*), a retractable arrangement of vent pipes which allowed the vessel to draw in fresh air while at periscope depth. This allowed the sub to run at periscope depth on its diesel engines, the schnorkel system supplying the engines with air and removing their exhaust fumes.

The first nuclear-powered submarine was the USS *Nautilus*, which made its first run under nuclear power on 17 January 1955. The nuclear power plant uses heat from a nuclear reactor to raise steam to drive its propulsion turbines, and also to drive a turbogenerator which generates the electricity needed by the vessel. Exhaust steam from the turbines is condensed, and the water is returned to the reactor for re-use.

U.S.S. *Will Rodgers* (dived displacement 8,250 tons) was commissioned in April 1967. The 41st Fleet Ballistic Missile submarine authorised by U.S. Congress, she is 425 feet long and manned by two crews alternating every two months.

Dirck Halstead/Contact/Colorific

Rockets and Missiles

Of all those confusing and remote doctrines of the classroom, Isaac Newton's Third Law of Motion must surely rank among the most well remembered. This 300-year-old law stating that 'every action must have an equal and opposite reaction' has maintained a dramatic significance on world events through its most direct application—the rocket.

A rocket is simply a device or vehicle propelled by the expulsion of a stream of matter (usually gas) from it. The emerging surge of matter imparts an equal and opposite force to the vehicle itself. The inflated balloon or the garden hose nozzle are everyday examples of the principle—both come to rather eccentric (unguided) life when released. The escaping jet of air or water generates a *reactive thrust*.

A rocket vehicle does not fly, but maintains travel under impetus. A thrown ball continues until air resistance (or *drag*) and gravity overcome its projected force. Likewise, a rocket will continue to ascend for a little while after its engine cuts out, and then the combination of drag and gravity will slow it so that it falls back to Earth in an arc corresponding to that of its ascent. This is called a *ballistic* course or trajectory and can be used as a means of delivering a warhead from one part of the Earth to another in the shortest possible time.

The more a rocket accelerates and the higher the speed attained, the farther it will be 'thrown' before it falls back to Earth. Eventually it will reach a speed where its fall will take it constantly beyond the Earth's curvature and it will continue to fall around the Earth for ever, or until slowed by rocket thrust or fringe atmospheric particles. It is then in orbit. The minimum speed necessary for this is nearly 7,925 metres per second (26,000 ft/sec.). In this application the rocket is usually called a *launch vehicle.*

Rocket development

The rocket owes its development largely to the needs of war. Its first known use was to provide power assistance to the arrows and spears of the thirteenth century Chinese against the Mongols who, in turn, developed it for use against the Arabs, who then introduced it warmly to the French Crusaders. Brought to Europe, the rocket was used by the French against the British at Orleans in 1429.

The emergence of the more accurate cannon reduced the rocket's military value for 300 years until the late eighteenth century, when British troops fighting in India found themselves once again on the receiving end of fiery salvos. This time they took notice, and the early nineteenth century saw extensive efforts, notably by Sir William Congreve and later by William Hale, to produce effective war rockets. Their work led to a naval bombardment weapon, to marine distress and rescue rockets, and to the

Novosti

Above: The Russian rocket pioneer Konstantin Tsiolkovsky (1857-1935), working on a model of one of his rocket designs.

Below: A model of the West German ORTAG rocket, a low-cost vehicle designed to burn diesel oil and nitric acid.

Dpa

Photri

Left: A Titan/Centaur rocket of the kind used to carry the Viking missions to Mars. The rocket is 48.8 m (160 ft) tall, and consists of two solid-fuel boosters, a US Air Force Titan III, and a NASA high-energy Centaur final stage. The lift-off thrust of the boosters is 2.4 million pounds.

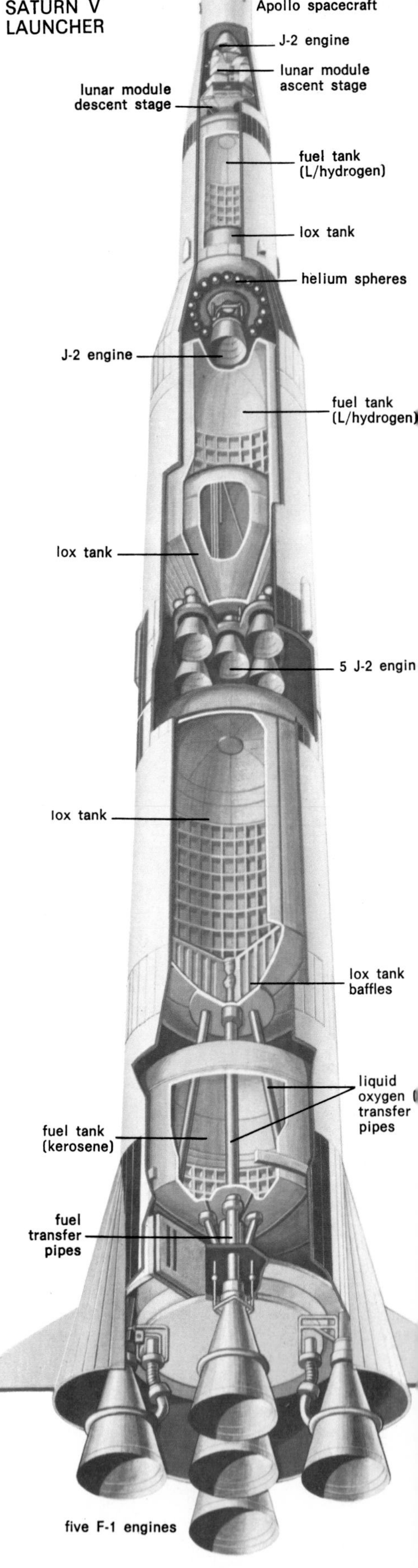

Above: The Saturn V rocket which was used by the Apollo Moon missions. The first stage was powered by five kerosene/liquid oxygen (lox) F-1 engines, and the subsequent stages, including the Apollo spacecraft itself, were powered by liquid oxygen/liquid hydrogen J-2 engines.

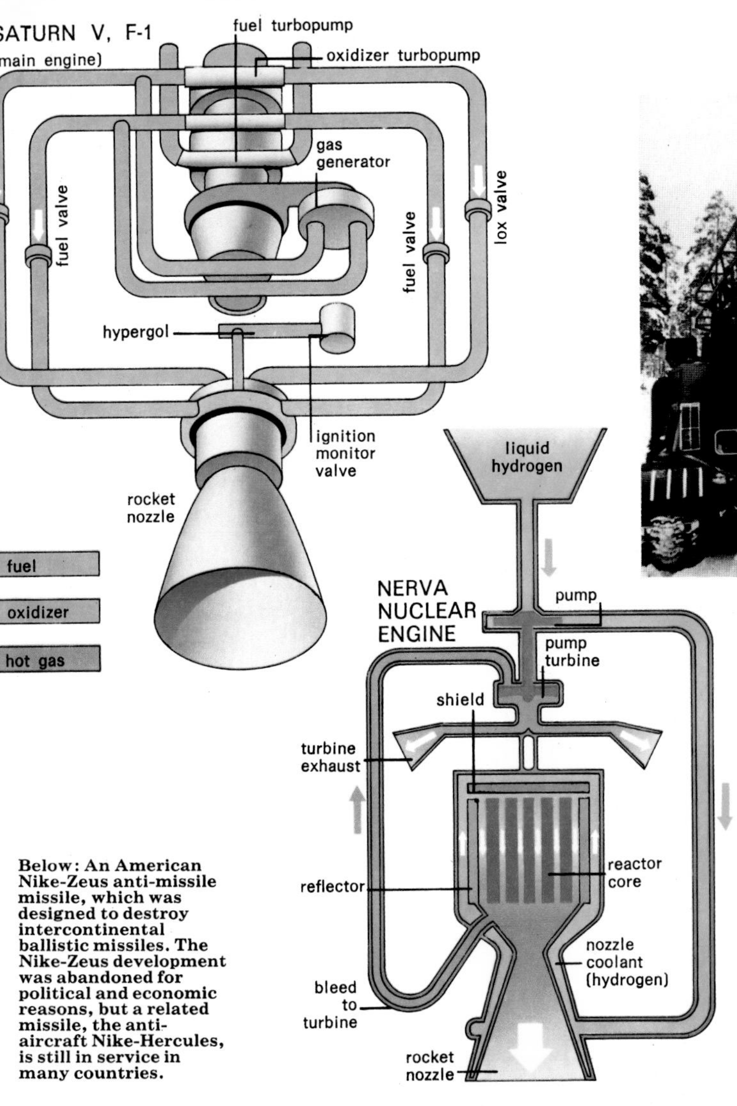

Novosti

Above: A Scud-A surface-to-surface tactical missile in service in the Soviet Union. It has a range of about 130 km (80 miles), and can be equipped with either a nuclear or a high-explosive warhead.

Left: The F-1 engine uses kerosene fuel oxidized by liquid oxygen. The engine is ignited by mixing the kerosene with a *hypergol*—a chemical that causes it to ignite spontaneously. The gas generator produces a stream of hot gas which drives the turbopumps. The Nerva nuclear engine, not yet in use, uses the heat from a nuclear reactor to expand hydrogen out through the thrust nozzle.

Below: An American Nike-Zeus anti-missile missile, which was designed to destroy intercontinental ballistic missiles. The Nike-Zeus development was abandoned for political and economic reasons, but a related missile, the anti-aircraft Nike-Hercules, is still in service in many countries.

crude anti-airship missiles of the First World War.

The birth of modern rocketry, however, is generally associated with Russia's Konstantin E. Tsiolkovsky (1857-1935) who, as early as 1883, began expounding on the potential and means of using rockets as launch vehicles. In 1929 Russia became the first nation to offer official, albeit military, status to rocket research. In Germany the theories of Hermann Oberth stimulated the formation of the celebrated Society for Space Travel (VfR), itself succumbing in the mid-1930s to the opposition of the Nazi party. Military work absorbed some of its members, notably Wernher von Braun, whose efforts led to the world's first ballistic missile—the V-2. In the US, Robert Goddard independently covered much pioneering work in practical research.

As well as the V-2, used against Britain in 1945, small tactical missiles, fired by aircraft or from ground batteries, were used with reasonable effect in the Second World War. Since then the missile has really come into its own. The growth of the Cold War in the 1950s gave rise to the *strategic* missile, the intercontinental carrier of nuclear bombs. America delayed its development programme slightly to await the perfection of the compact hydrogen bomb, and the consequent reduction in launcher size. Russia, however, went straight ahead with the construction of large missiles to carry the massive atom bombs. Soviet scientists saw, too, that the same missile could place a smaller payload in orbit—and in October 1957, Sputnik 1 soared into space.

Photri

Photri

Left: A battery of Nike surface-to-air missiles erected and ready to be fired. Nike missiles can be deployed either at fixed launch sites, as they are here, or carried on mobile launchers.

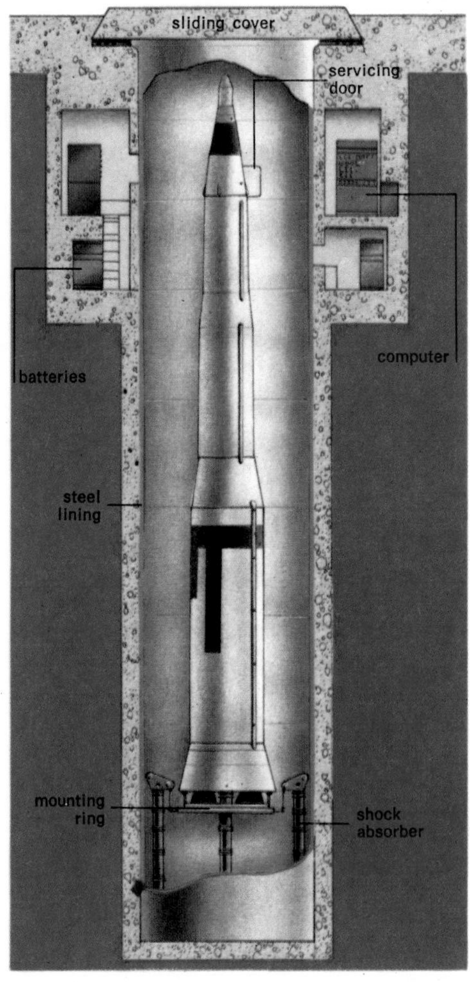

Right: Many long-range missiles are launched from underground 'silos'. The US, for example, houses its Minuteman III intercontinental ballistic missiles in silos 24.4 m (80 ft) deep. The Minuteman III can be equipped with MIRV (multiple independently-targetable re-entry vehicle) warheads, which contain several separate nuclear warheads that spread out to attack several targets at once.

America's belated response four months later was due not just to the deliberate 'missile lag' but also to an inter-service rivalry over launch vehicle development, of which the winner, the US Navy, had far from the best programme in hand. Later, as the Thor, Atlas and Titan missiles became obsolete they formed the core of the development of 'medium' launchers, while the diminutive Scout and the mighty Saturn rockets were civilian programmes.

Specific impulse

The fundamental key to rocket propulsion is still Tsiolkovsky's *Ideal Rocket Equation* ('Ideal' because it ignores atmospheric drag) which says that total increase in vehicle velocity is equal to the exhaust velocity times the natural logarithm of the *mass ratio* (launch weight divided by empty weight). The greater the required acceleration, the higher must be either or both of the exhaust velocity and the mass ratio. Mass ratio can be improved by minimizing structural weight so that fuel burn-off plays a maximum part in allowing speed to increase. The exhaust velocity can be improved by increasing the efficiency of the *propellant* (fuel mixture).

Propellant efficiency is defined as the number of pounds of thrust that can be developed per second out of each pound of fuel (using a maximum efficiency engine). It is called the *Specific Impulse* (Isp) and the units in which it is measured are called *seconds*. Obviously, the faster the gases are emitted the greater the value of thrust per second, so that high speed/low volume tends to be more efficient than the reverse. There is thus a direct relationship between Isp and exhaust velocity, and an Isp of about 102 seconds provides an exhaust velocity of 1 km/sec. As a result, the higher the rated Isp, the lower the fuel mass needed for any specific acceleration, or the greater the acceleration obtainable from any given fuel mass.

Today's chemical propellants have a relatively low Isp and therefore present a severe weight penalty. Without the techniques of *staging* it would be impractical to accelerate a payload to orbital velocity. Any increase in propellant mass to prolong acceleration reduces the *rate* of acceleration—and therefore cancels out the value of the extra propellant. The extra mass can be used more effectively, however, if it is placed in separate tanks and given its own engine, forming an upper stage. It then becomes an extra rocket launched at altitude. In the vacuum of space, the Isp is measurably increased and the smaller mass needs only a small and less thirsty engine to maintain acceleration.

Guidance systems vary according to the degree of accuracy required. A general environment-measuring satellite intended for an orbit of 560 km (350 miles) will not suffer from a moderate variation from its course, provided that it can be accurately tracked. A pre-programmed autopilot would probably provide adequate positioning, while engine cut-out at the required velocity is obtainable by radio signal or pre-determined fuel supply. For pin-point aiming of a missile, or the injection of a deep-space probe into interplanetary trajectory, a very much higher degree of accuracy is required. A sophisticated

BAC

Above: The BAC Rapier is a close-range surface-to-air missile system. The missile is guided to its target by radio signals from the tracker's computer.

Photri

Right: The US Army's Davy Crockett is one of the growing number of portable battlefield missiles now coming into use, and it can be equipped with either a nuclear or a high-explosive warhead.

Below: A Polaris A-3 strategic nuclear missile launched from a submarine. The Polaris has a range of 4,630 km (2,875 miles), and is equipped with multiple nuclear warheads. It has two stages, each of which is powered by a solid-propellant rocket motor.

Photri

Boeing Aerospace

Right: A prototype Air Launched Cruise Missile (ALCM) being launched from the weapons bay of a B-52G bomber. The ALCM is a new breed of small, cheap and very accurate nuclear missile.

Below: One of the most widely-used forms of rocket is the *sounding rocket*, a small, lightweight vehicle, usually solid-fuel propelled, used for scientific experiments in the upper atmosphere. This diagram shows some of their many uses.

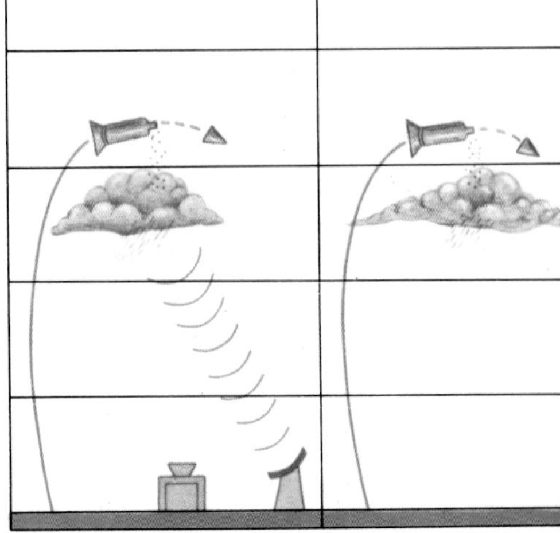

Wind measurement: clouds of alkali metals are released in the atmosphere and tracked by radar.
Rainmaking: clouds are « seeded » with dry ice make them release their moisture.

Flight International

Above: The Russian Mig-25 Foxbat, equipped with AA-6 Acrid air-to-air missiles mounted under its wings.

ION ENGINE

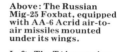

neutralizer cathode supplies electrons to neutralize the ions

electromagnet producing magnetic field

electrons

of neutralized

discharge chamber

keeper anode

plasma arc

mercury atom

hollow cathode

mercury ions

accelerator grid

main anode

electron trajectories

mercury vapour feed

main ionization region

Left: The T4 ion engine designed for use on a European satellite. Its thrust is obtained from the stream of neutralized ions expelled through the accelerator grid.

Hughes Aircraft Co.

Above: The US Navy's F-14 Tomcat fighter is equipped with the Phoenix air-to-air missile system, which can track up to 24 separate targets at once, and attack six of them simultaneously. The radar-guided missiles have a range of over 160 km (100 miles).

Atmospheric temperature pressure information beamed to ground station by instruments in the rocket and in separated instrument package.

Electrical and magnetic properties of the upper atmosphere measured by instruments in nose cone.

Cosmic rays detected by geiger counters.

Atmospheric absorption of solar radiation measured by infra-red spectrometers.

altitude in kilometres

250

200

150

100

50

0

inertial guidance system is now usual in which gyroscopes sense minor variations from the programmed path and correct them by vectoring the main thrust.

This can be backed up by ground-based navigation and control. A short-range combat missile may often be wire-guided, an operator 'flying' it by sending corrective signals along a wire that is drawn out behind. Others are controlled by radio signals, with visual directions supplied to the operator by a television camera in the nose of the missile. Still others have automatic homing devices using radar, infra-red or visual contact.

Rocket engines

A basic characteristic of the modern rocket is its ability to operate independently of atmosphere. Rocket propulsion consists of burning a chemical in a confined space and allowing the gases to escape through a restricted nozzle. As oxygen must be present for combustion, a large supply of oxidizer must be carried. In modern liquid-fuel engines the fuel, such as kerosene or liquid hydrogen, and the oxidizer, now often liquid oxygen, are pumped separately into a small combustion chamber.

Solid-fuel rockets are also in common use for their simplicity and reliability, powering most missiles and acting as auxiliary boosters and integral stages on many launch vehicles. Solids are basically power-packed squibs, the charge being a mixture of a dry fuel and a dry oxygen-rich chemical (polyisobutane, for example, and ammonium perchlorate). Disadvantages include high weight—the rocket is, in effect, one large combustion chamber; the fact that the fuel has a lower Isp than liquids; and a lack of controllability except in burn rate, which is determined by the shape of the propellant grain or of the core cavity.

Many other means of generating thrust are now being identified, some within technology's present grasp, others merely options for the future. Much work has been done in Russia and America on nuclear engines which, if unsuitable for Earth launchings because of contamination risks, could at least provide the hard acceleration needed for a quick orbital insertion or fast interplanetary flight.

In a very different category are low-thrust systems which develop minute thrust in relation to engine weight and are therefore suitable only for overcoming inertia, rather than gravity. They do, however, offer extremely high Isp ratings. Already test flown is the *electrostatic* or *ion* engine which isolates ions from the fuel (mercury or caesium) and accelerates them electrically to produce thrust. The thrust is tiny (about 1/1,600 lb), but the fuel consumption is very low and the craft could attain otherwise impossible speeds merely by accelerating slowly for months on end.

Still on the drawing boards is the electromagnetic or *plasma* rocket, in which an electric arc is used to convert hydrogen to a charged plasma (a gas-like stream of particles) which can then be accelerated out by a magnetic field. Even more exotic is the idea of the *photon* rocket which, in theory, will provide thrust from a concentrated beam of light—the exhaust velocity being, of course, the speed of light.

Satellites

Between 1957 and the end of 1975, approximately 17,500 different payloads were lofted into space from the surface of the Earth. A few made headlines, notably those carrying men to the Moon and back. Others sped quietly off to other worlds, expanding the frontiers of human contact. The majority, all but about 250 of those payloads, were dispatched unobtrusively into Earth *orbit* to serve a considerable variety of purposes.

An orbit is merely a track along which one body travels around another, be it a planet around the Sun, or a moon or artificial satellite around the planet. The primary properties of orbital mechanics were identified as early as the seventeenth century by the German astronomer Johannes Kepler (1571-1630) who formulated them into three laws: 1, the orbit of each planet is an ellipse, with the Sun at one focus; 2, the line joining the planet with the Sun sweeps over equal areas in equal periods of time (so that the planet moves faster when close to the Sun and slower when further away); 3, the square of the time taken for a planet to complete one revolution around the Sun is directly proportioned to the cube of its mean distance from the Sun. In other words, planets farther from the Sun take longer to complete each revolution, and travel at lower speeds.

In his work on gravity, Sir Isaac Newton also formulated a relationship between the orbit speed and its height. These laws are still used as the basis for calculation of the main parameters of a particular orbit.

In concise terms, an orbit is achieved when a satellite body's centripetal (outward) acceleration exactly balances the gravitational (inward) force at a particular height. Up to a certain speed, objects thrown into the sky will fall back to Earth. The harder and more horizontally they are thrown the farther they will travel before falling back. An object thrown horizontally at 7,800 m/sec (25,600 ft/sec) would, in fact, fall back at an angle matching the curvature of the Earth. Without the braking friction of air it would continue 'falling' around the Earth indefinitely. Lifted above the atmosphere it does just that—in orbit. The forces inherent in an 'ideal' or circular orbit compare with those acting on a ball whirled at the end of a piece of string.

Increasing the velocity increases the height of the orbit until, given an initial speed of 11,125 m/sec (36,500 ft/sec) the object will range far enough to take it out of the Earth's sphere of influence and it will break free.

Novosti

Above: One of the first living creatures to orbit the Earth and return alive, the Russian space dog Belka together with its companion Strelka was launched into orbit on 19 August 1960. Another dog, Laika, had made the first spaceflight by a living creature in the Russian satellite Sputnik 2 in 1957.

Below: The first satellite to go into Earth orbit was 'Sputnik 1', launched by the Russians on 4 October 1957 from their launch site at Tyuratam in Kazakhstan. Sputnik 1 carried a radio transmitter which transmitted a series of 'bleeps' so that the satellite could be tracked.

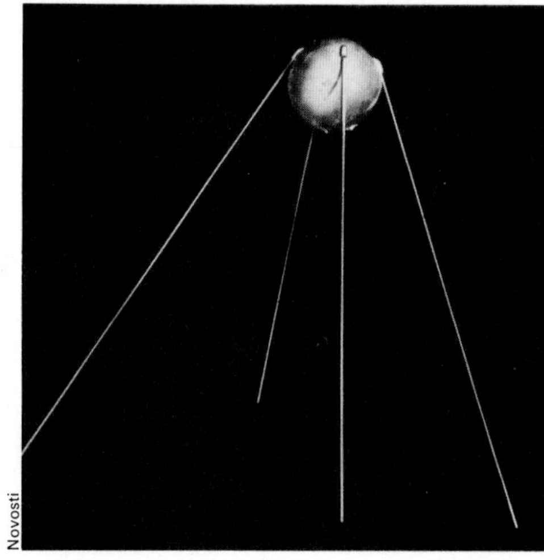

Novosti

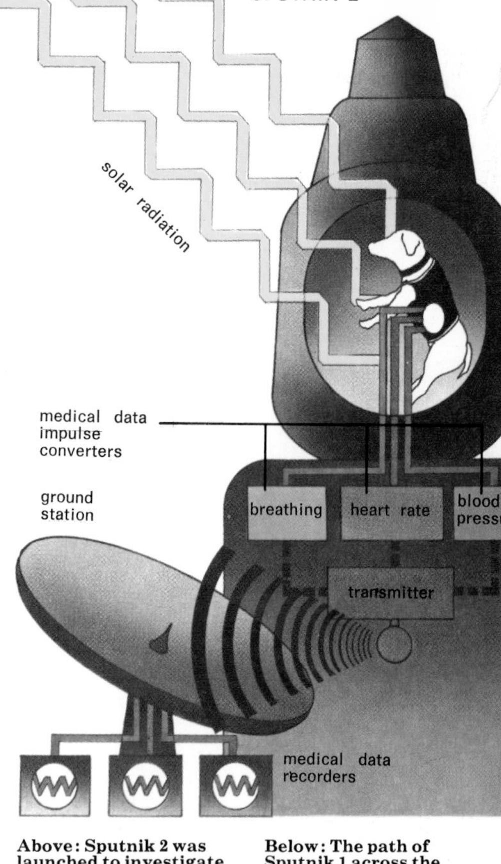

Above: Sputnik 2 was launched to investigate the effects of solar and cosmic radiation and weightlessness on living creatures. Its occupant, the dog Laika, was connected to instruments which monitored its breathing, heartbeat and blood pressure.

Below: The path of Sputnik 1 across the face of the Earth during a 24-hour period. The lines of the path are the result of the rotation of the Earth and the orbital direction of the satellite. Sputnik 1 burned up on 4 January 1958.

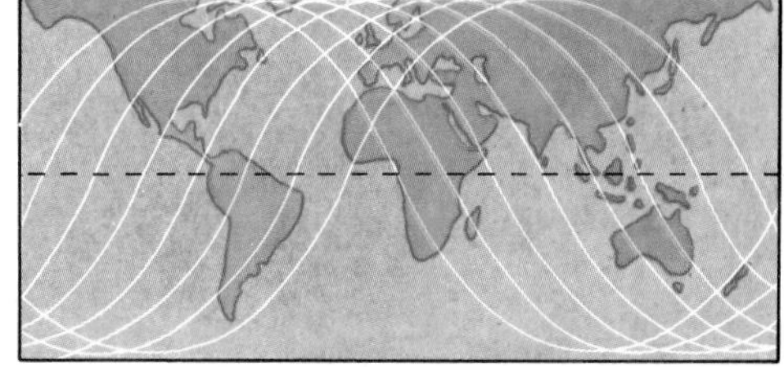

Orbits

As the gravitational force decreases with distance, so the necessary speed decreases. And with increasing height the circumference of the circular track, and therefore the time taken to complete one orbit, also increases. A circular orbit at about 160 km (100 miles) altitude requires a speed of about 7,800 m/sec (26,000 ft/sec) and a revolution time or *period* of about 90 minutes. If the orbit is raised to 386,250 km (240,000 miles) a speed of only about 1,000 m/sec (3,300 ft/sec) will be required, and one orbit will take 28 days. These are, in fact, the parameters of the Moon. At a height of 35,900 km (22,300 miles) the speed is about 3,350 m/sec (11,000 ft/sec), giving a period of 24 hr, the speed of rotation of the Earth at the equator. A satellite at this height, aligned with the equator and travelling in the same direction as the earth's rotation, will parallel the same spot on the Earth's surface, effectively remaining fixed in the sky as seen from Earth. Such an orbit is termed *geostationary* or *synchronous*.

If a satellite has a horizontal attitude at *orbit injection* (engine cut-off point) but is travelling too fast, the injection point will become the *perigee* (or lowest point) of the orbit. Conversely, insufficient speed will make it the *apogee* (highest point). If the attitude is off-horizontal, then the injection point will remain somewhere in between apogee and perigee.

Elliptic orbits, usually termed eccentric orbits, can range from 160 km (100 miles) to tens of thousands of kilometres from the Earth between perigee and apogee. The velocity of the satellite varies according to Kepler's Second Law. Gravity accelerates the craft as it approaches Earth, then hurls it far out into space again until the speed drops off and, at apogee, it turns back towards the Earth.

The most serious effect on a satellite is, strangely, atmospheric drag. Even at heights of 480 km (300 miles) and more, a perceptible if extremely thin atmosphere can be found. This sparse scattering of air molecules imparts a slow drag on to the spacecraft. Even if the erosion of speed occurs only at the perigee, the momentum of the entire orbit is affected and slowly the apogee is lowered until it too comes under the influence of the peripheral atmosphere. This is known as *orbital decay* and inevitably results in the re-entry and destruction of the satellite. The length of orbital life depends on perigee height and can range from a few months at 130 km (80 miles) to 20 or 30 years at 480 km (300 miles).

Uses of satellites

In the years since Sputnik 1 ushered in the space age in 1957 a huge variety of spacecraft have been dispatched into Earth orbit by several nations. Generally speaking they fall into three main categories—*scientific*, *applications* and *military*.

NASA/Alphabet & Image

Spectrum

Left: A multiple exposure picture showing the movement of a 9.14 m (30 ft) diameter tracking antenna at a ground station.

Right: The Russian satellite tracking ship *Yuri Gagarin*. NASA operate a similar rocket and satellite tracking ship, the *SS Vandenberg*.

Below: The European Space Agency's GEOS scientific satellite undergoing tests at the BAC Electronic and Space Systems facility at Bristol, England. GEOS carries seven separate experiments designed to investigate the *magnetosphere*, the area of space influenced by the Earth's magnetic field.

BAC

Below: Three types of orbit. In a *polar synchronous* orbit the satellite appears to follow a figure-of-eight path over the Earth and can observe most of it over a period of time. Satellites in *retrograde* orbits travel against the Earth's spin, those in *direct* orbits with it.

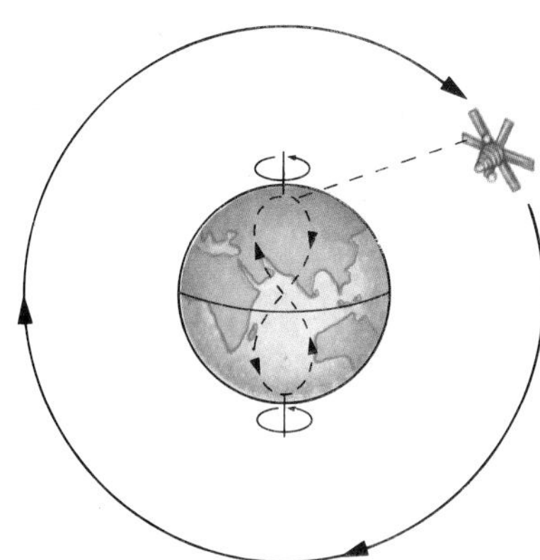

polar-synchronous orbit

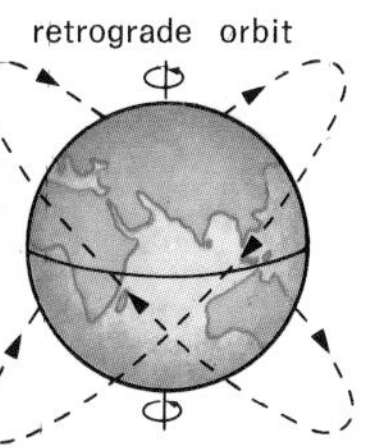

retrograde orbit

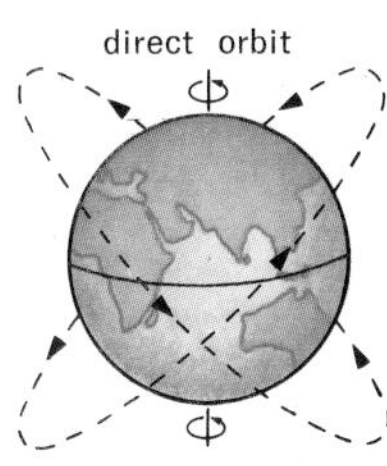

direct orbit

Right: This picture shows how communications satellites have grown in size and complexity. The larger one is Intelsat IVA (1975), and the smaller one is a model of 'Early Bird' (Intelsat 1, 1965). The outer surface of each is covered in solar cells which produce its electrical power.

Hughes Aircraft Co

The use of spacecraft has produced a whole new scientific arena of space physics. Where the early craft made revolutionary discoveries, the latest are developing and refining our knowledge of these discoveries. Studies of the composition of near-Earth space, and of solar emissions and their interaction with the terrestrial environment, involve the use of numerous low-orbiting and Sun-orbiting scientific satellites, and satellites with highly eccentric orbits.

Meanwhile, astronomers are reaping the benefit of looking at the stars free, for the first time, of the 'dirty window' of the Earth's atmosphere. Not only are they provided with optical telescopes in orbit, but many satellites have been equipped to examine the sky at radio, X-ray and gamma-ray wavelengths and, as the latter two cannot readily penetrate the atmosphere, such satellites have already contributed as much to celestial knowledge as all previous ages together. In this category, too, are technology satellites: spacecraft equipped purely or partially to test operational and engineering techniques for application to other craft.

While scientific satellites look out to the stars, applications satellites look inward at the Earth. Applications satellites are considered one of the most important developments of the century and concern spacecraft which provide a direct practical and financial service to humanity. Improved communications were the first real benefit to be demonstrated. Networks of satellites chasing each other around the same orbit or fixed in geostationary orbit serve as active repeaters to relay large numbers

Aerospatiale

Above: The French 'Starlette', designed for use in *geodetic* (Earth-measuring) experiments, is covered with 60 laser reflectors. By studying the reflections of laser beams transmitted to the satellite from Earth, researchers can make accurate measurements of distances and angles.

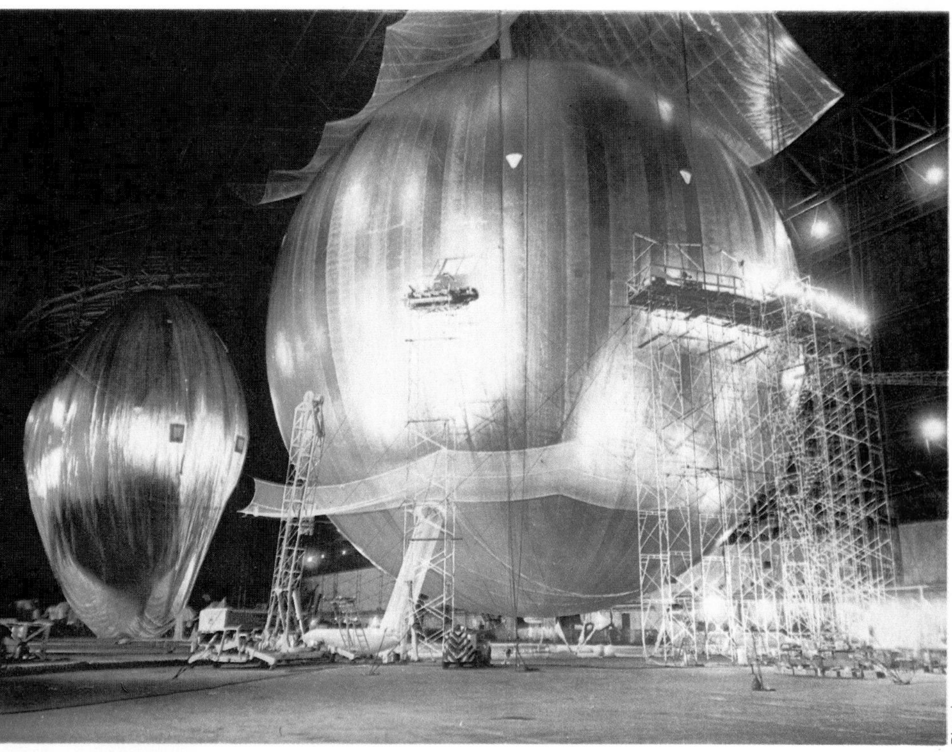

Photri

Right: A simpler form of geodetic satellite, the Echo II was a 41 m (135 ft) diameter aluminized plastic balloon, carried into orbit by rocket and inflated automatically as it separated from the launch vehicle. It was used for reflecting communications signals as well as for geodetic surveying.

Photri

Left: An applications technology satellite in the Space Environment Simulation Laboratory of the Johnson Space Center, Houston, Texas. This part of the laboratory is a huge vacuum chamber in which the performance and structure of space vehicles and satellites can be checked out in space-like conditions.

Below: The European Space Agency's METEOSAT, ready to form part of a system of five geostationary weather satellites spaced around the Earth to provide global weather observations. The other satellites are being provided by the US (2), Japan and the USSR. The satellite's total weight when launched is 697 Kg (1537 lb).

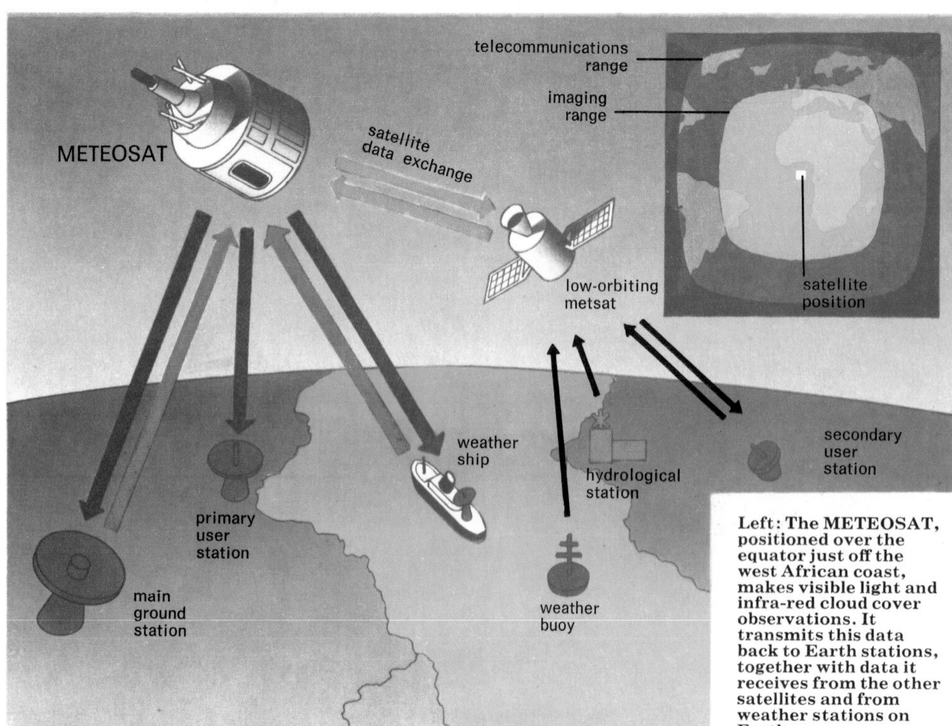

Left: The METEOSAT, positioned over the equator just off the west African coast, makes visible light and infra-red cloud cover observations. It transmits this data back to Earth stations, together with data it receives from the other satellites and from weather stations on Earth.

of telephone and television channels around the curvature of the Earth or distribute them economically over wide or remote areas.

The multi-nation Intelsat consortium has been running a global network of geostationary satellites since the mid-1960s. Increasingly, countries are finding such satellites useful for local use, and regional *comsats* (communications satellites) are being operated or planned by developing as well as advanced countries, serving educational as well as entertainment purposes. A new communications application is the maritime or aeronautical satellite which provides vhf radio links for ships and aircraft when far from land.

Weather forecasting has long been a regular satellite activity, using low-orbiting spacecraft which photograph cloud patterns by day and night.

The latest development in applications is the earth resources survey satellite, represented largely by America's Erts or Landsat craft in polar orbit. Continuous infra-red photography of the ground tract has produced unprecedented information on our use and abuse of the Earth. Data on crop disease, pollution, mineral and forestry resources, fish movements and many other subjects can be obtained from these photographs. This programme has been hailed as the most important in the history of spaceflight, and it appears to have enormous potential.

Many military requirements are not applicable to civilian activities, although most provide comparable support roles. America, Russia, Britain and Nato all have their own military comsat networks and the US Defense Department operates its own *metsat* (meteorological satellite) system. In addition, however, it has satellites equipped to detect nuclear tests on Earth or in space, and others to detect missile launches and provide early warning of attack. Satellites are used as navigational aids by submarines, ships and land forces, which calculate their own positions from time and ranging measurements of the satellite's signal.

Spaceflight

Space activities are generally divided into two categories: manned and unmanned spaceflight. Major design differences as well as different operational roles distinguish the two categories. Unmanned craft, such as Earth satellites, also fall into various subgroups according to their intended purpose. The main groups cover space sciences, space applications, military support and interplanetary exploration. Manned craft have, to date, been devoted to such a limited range of objectives that they cannot be compared operationally with the unmanned vehicles, although most tasks performed by unmanned craft have at times been attempted on manned missions.

The majority of space activities have been confined to a small sphere of space enclosing the Earth and broadly termed Earth orbit. Orbit is achieved when the speed of a body produces a momentum that balances the force of gravity and therefore continues literally to fall round the Earth. An almost infinite variety of orbits is obtainable from a permutation of factors such as the *altitude*; the *velocity*, which, by Kepler's laws, is dependent on the altitude; the *inclination*, which is the angle the orbit makes with the equator; and the *eccentricity* or *ellipticity* which is the degree by which the shape of the orbit differs from circular. All these factors can be adjusted to give the right orbit for the particular scientific mission.

Orbital speed at low altitudes of about 190 km (120 miles) is about 4,755 m/sec (15,600 ft/sec). Acceleration pushes the orbit higher and, if speed is increased to about 10,670 m/sec (35,000 ft/sec) it will raise the orbit to the distance of the Moon. This is the method used for lunar travel. Arrival speed is invariably too high for orbital capture by lunar gravity, and so a braking rocket must be fired to slow the craft and achieve orbit, and then fired again if a soft landing is required, there being no atmosphere to slow the craft.

Return flights require an escape velocity of only about 2,377 m/sec (7,800 ft/sec) to overcome the low gravity. Apart from landing missions, lunar orbit has also been used for lunar surface photography as an 'anchor' for a few satellites devoted to certain types of cosmic science.

For interplanetary travel, a spacecraft must break out of Earth orbit and enter an elliptical orbit around the Sun which will intersect with that of the destination planet. Initial speed required for this is about 11,580 m/sec (38,000 ft/sec). Missions to Venus are launched 'backwards' in relation to the Earth's motion around the Sun, so that their relative speed is slower and they drop towards the Sun. Missions to Mars and the outer planets are launched ahead of the Earth for the opposite effect.

Known as a *Hohmann ellipse*, this technique reduces the power required from the launch vehicle, and so although it is not the fastest route, it permits the use of much smaller and cheaper launch vehicles. It also requires specific positioning of the departure and destination planets at launch, usually near the period of closest approach. Such approaches occur at short and infrequent intervals, and the associated launch opportunities are called 'launch windows'. For Venus this occurs every 583 days, and Mars every 280 days.

Journeys to the more remote planets have been shortened by a *gravity swing-by* technique. America's Mariner 10 reached

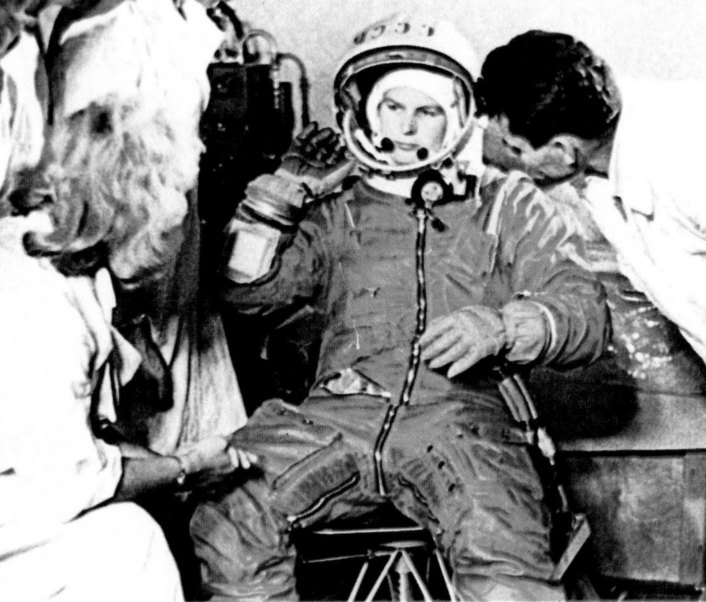

Novosti

Left: Valentina Nikolayeva-Tereshkova, the first woman to make a spaceflight. Her Vostok-6 spacecraft, launched from Baikonur cosmodrome in Central Asia on 16 June 1963, made a total of 48 orbits during its 70 hour 50 minute flight, covering a distance of 1,970,990 kilometres (1,224,084 miles).

Novosti

Below left: The first man in space was the Soviet cosmonaut Yuri Gagarin (1934-1968). His 108 minute flight, during which he made one complete orbit of the Earth in his Vostok-1 spacecraft, took place on 12 April 1961. In this picture, Gagarin is talking to Soviet rocket designer Sergei Korolyev.

Photri

Below: This multiple exposure shows the launch tower dropping away as the American Gemini-10 lifts off on 18 July 1966. Gemini-10, which used a Titan launch vehicle, was crewed by John Young and Michael Collins, and successfully docked with an Agena target vehicle orbiting at 298 km (185 miles).

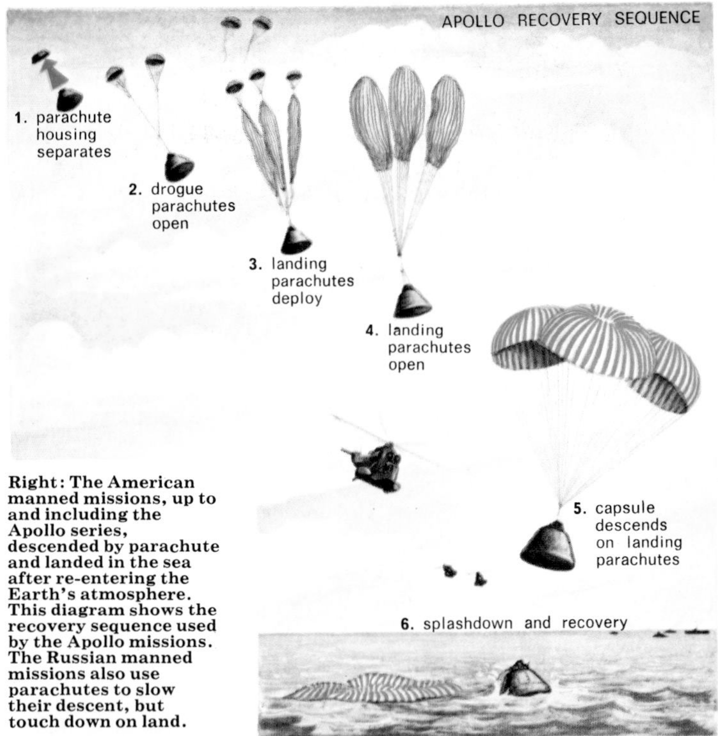
APOLLO RECOVERY SEQUENCE
1. parachute housing separates
2. drogue parachutes open
3. landing parachutes deploy
4. landing parachutes open
5. capsule descends on landing parachutes
6. splashdown and recovery

Right: The American manned missions, up to and including the Apollo series, descended by parachute and landed in the sea after re-entering the Earth's atmosphere. This diagram shows the recovery sequence used by the Apollo missions. The Russian manned missions also use parachutes to slow their descent, but touch down on land.

Novosti

Above: Russia's Luna 16, an unmanned vehicle which in September 1970 travelled to the Moon, collected samples of soil, and returned them to Earth for analysis.

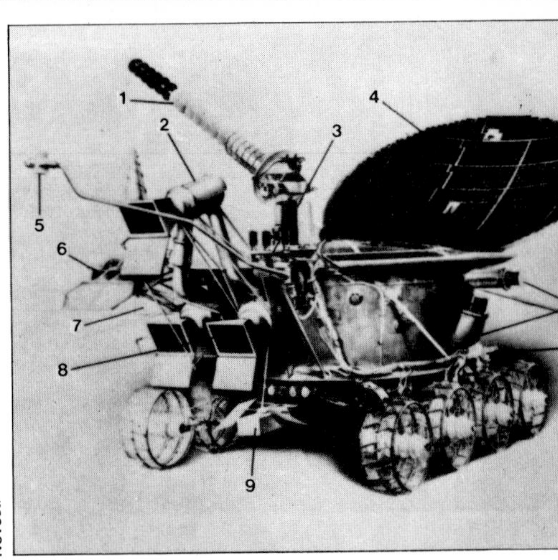
Novosti

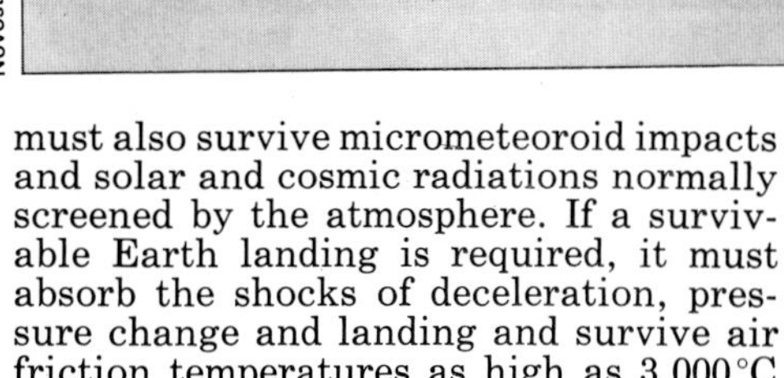

Right: Lunokhod 2, the second of Russia's remotely-controlled lunar exploration vehicles, was landed at the edge of the Sea of Serenity on 16 January 1973. Lunokhod 2's equipment included: 1, directional antenna; 2 and 8, tv cameras; 3, photoreceptor; 4, solar panel; 5, magnetometer; 6, laser reflector; 7, astrophotometer; 9, soil analysis unit; 10, telephotometers; 11, soil mechanics probe. The vehicle covered a total distance of 37 km (23 miles). It is planned to send a similar machine to explore the surface of Mars.

Photri

Left: Apollo 15 astronaut James Irwin with the electrically-driven Lunar Roving Vehicle, which enabled the astronauts to explore a wider area of the Moon than they could cover on foot. In the background is Mount Hadley.

Mercury in 1975 by flying close to Venus and using the force of that planet's gravity to accelerate and re-direct the spacecraft to its destination. Likewise Pioneer 11 was boosted by Jupiter's gravity as it flew by on its way to Saturn.

Spacecraft

The term 'spacecraft' usually applies to any self-sustaining, active device operating for extended periods beyond the Earth's atmosphere. Spacecraft designed to leave Earth orbit and explore planets or adopt solar orbits of their own are known as *space probes*. Their designs vary considerably according to their particular destination, duration of mission and objective—whether they are supposed to fly-by, enter orbit or release a landing craft. The operational and environmental demands placed on these craft has led to their development into some of the most sophisticated robots yet devised.

The general design of a spacecraft is dominated by three main considerations —intended purpose of the mission, launch vehicle compatability and, usually most important, weight reduction. The peculiarities of its operational life require a spacecraft to protect and support its payload over a wide range of extreme conditions. At launch it may experience acceleration forces 10 to 15 times that of gravity, atmospheric pressures which fall rapidly from that at sea level to a vacuum, plus heavy vibration.

In space it meets a considerable range of temperatures according to its position and attitude in relation to the Sun, and must also survive micrometeoroid impacts and solar and cosmic radiations normally screened by the atmosphere. If a survivable Earth landing is required, it must absorb the shocks of deceleration, pressure change and landing and survive air friction temperatures as high as 3,000°C (5,400°F).

The conditions of spaceflight dictate a basically common complement of subsystems. Unmanned craft consist of a simple open-frame structure to which subsystems are individually attached in separate boxes, or a sealed container enclosing most of the systems together. Manned spacecraft, with their need for living and working quarters for their crews, demand a very large sealed structure, usually large enough for the subsystems to be distributed widely in and around it.

The basic elements of any spacecraft consist of power supply, temperature control, communications, data-processing, stabilization and attitude control equipment and, if required, navigation and propulsion systems and even a computer. Power is usually supplied by panels of solar cells which convert the Sun's energy to electricity. As far from the Sun as Mars, solar arrays are efficient

Photri

Left: Testing one of the Surveyor lunar landing probes, which made soft landings on the Moon and sent back television pictures and scientific data. The first of the seven Surveyor probes was launched on 30 May 1966, and landed on the Moon on 1 June. The final one was launched on 7 January 1968.

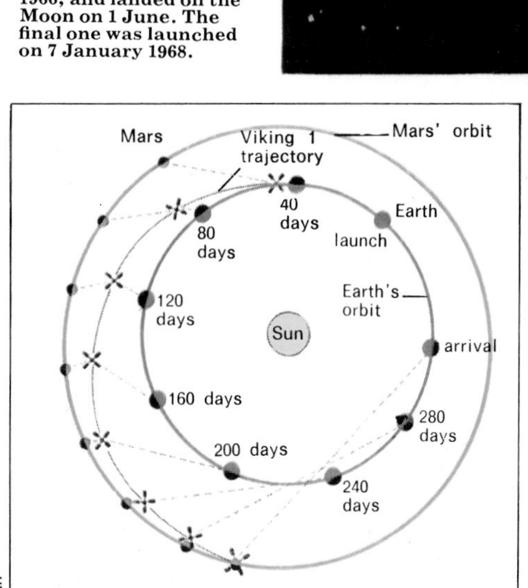

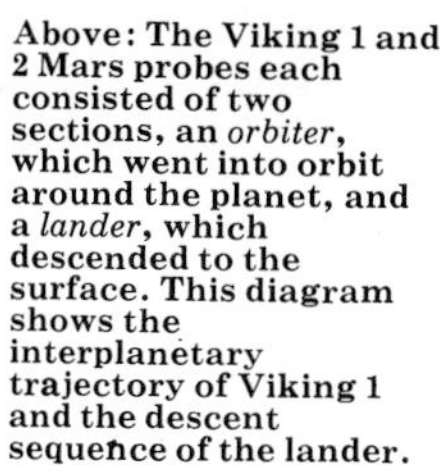

Above: The Viking 1 and 2 Mars probes each consisted of two sections, an *orbiter*, which went into orbit around the planet, and a *lander*, which descended to the surface. This diagram shows the interplanetary trajectory of Viking 1 and the descent sequence of the lander.

Photri

Left: David R. Scott standing in the hatch of the Apollo 9 command module. The Apollo 9 mission, from 3 to 13 March 1969, was an Earth-orbital mission designed to test the rendezvous and docking procedures of the command/service module and the lunar module. This picture was taken from the lunar module.

enough to be kept manageably small, but beyond Mars the Sun's strength attenuates to unusable levels and radioactive isotope-powered thermoelectric generators (RTGs) were used on the two Pioneer probes to Jupiter.

Short-life craft, notably the early satellites and some of the Soviet lunar probes, carry only simple chemical batteries. In all other cases, however, the generated raw power is conditioned and stored in batteries before delivery to components. Most spacecraft require between 100 W and 500 W. Large solar arrays developed for high-power comsats (communications satellites) can produce 1.5 KW. Some US manned spacecraft—the Apollos and later Geminis—depended on fuel cells in which hydrogen and oxygen were processed to generate electricity, supplying drinking water as a by-product.

Temperature control is often the most challenging element of a spacecraft, involving the appropriate distribution of cooling and heat with minimal power use. Some craft now use controllable louvres to exploit the Sun's heating. Rotation of the craft, or positioning of reflective thermal blankets and sunshields, keeps temperatures down.

Photri

Below: A simulated picture of a Pioneer probe passing the Moon on its way from Earth to the outer planets. The first Pioneer programme was a series of probes intended to investigate the Moon, but it was not a success. The second, successful, series has been investigating the solar system.

Numerous techniques, some ingenious, include relative positioning of hot- and cold-running components, heat sinks and direct electric heating.

Communications involve several essential links between controllers and craft, each link operating at a different frequency through its own type of aerial. One receives commands from Earth, while another feeds out telemetry data reporting on the condition of the various subsystems. Finally there is the mission data, the information which the spacecraft is sent to collect. Most Earth satellites use simple non-directional aerials, but at planetary ranges, and even from the Moon, probes must concentrate the available power into highly directional signals if they are to be readable on arrival, hence the large, parabolic

Below: The type of spacesuit worn by astronauts during the Apollo Moon missions. The suit comprises over twenty layers, which provide cooling, pressurization, and protection against micrometeoroids and radiation. The backpack contains the oxygen and cooling liquid supply equipment and a radio.

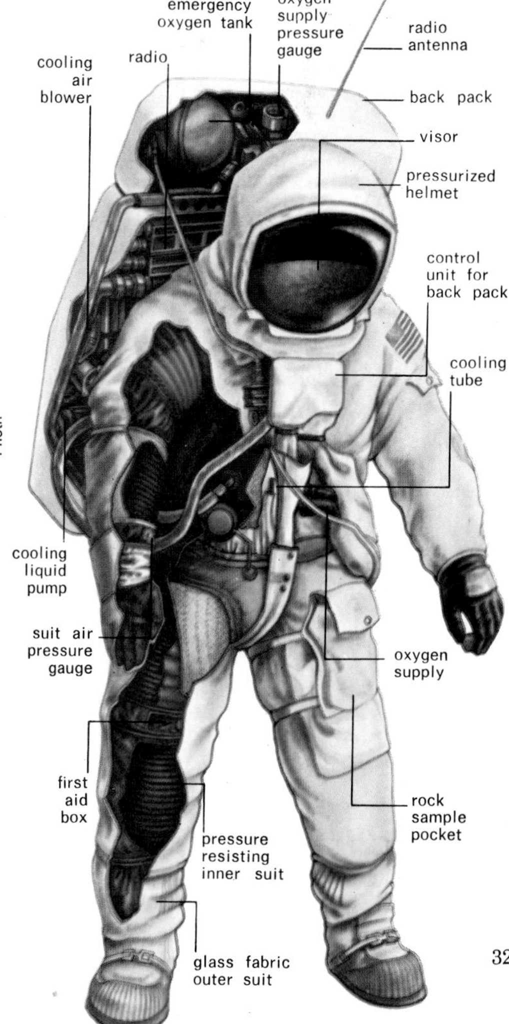

Photri

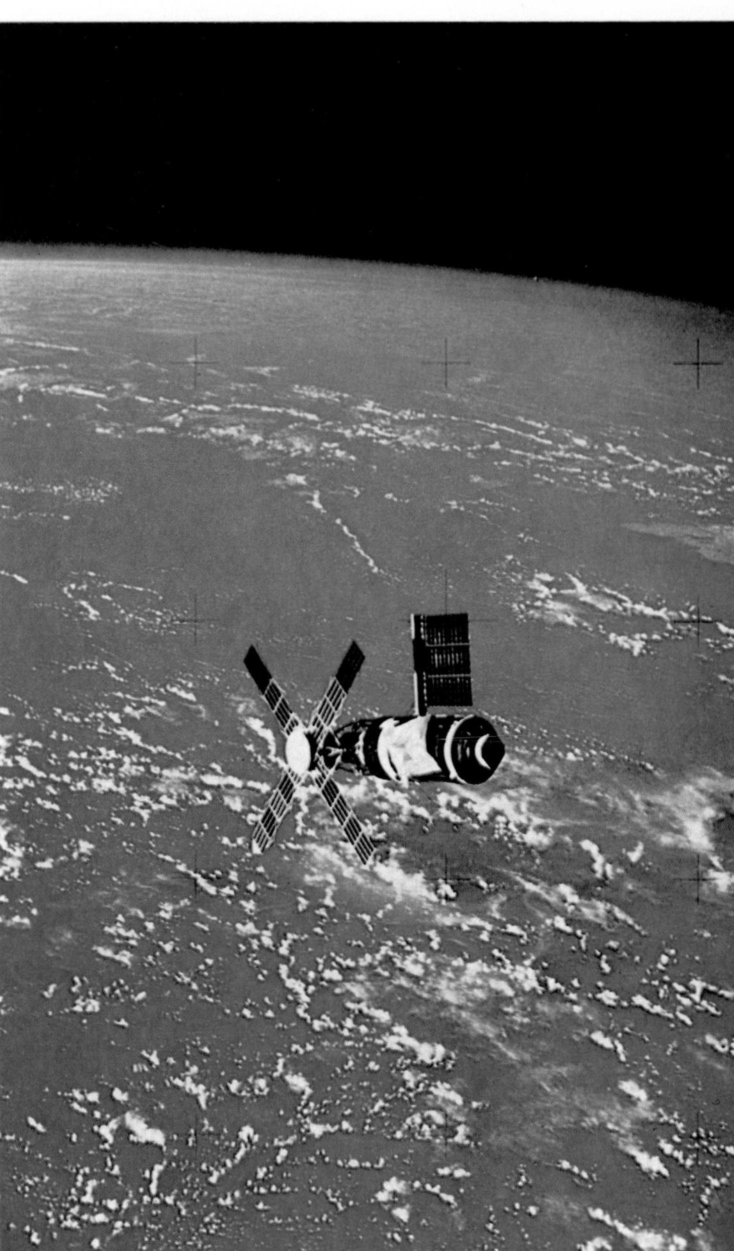
NASA

Above: During the Apollo-Soyuz Test Project (ASTP) in July 1975, an American Apollo spacecraft docked in Earth orbit with a Russian Soyuz vehicle. This picture shows one of the American astronauts, Vance D. Brand, in the docking passage connecting the two vehicles.

Above right: Skylab, the American space station which was put into Earth orbit on 14 May 1973. Shortly after lift-off, Skylab's meteoroid shield and one of its solar cell arrays broke away, and the damaged area was covered with aluminized plastic by the astronauts who docked with the station on 25 May.

dish-shaped aerials which characterize most interplanetary craft.

Even then there is such a heavy flow of information that some form of data processing becomes necessary. Normally this involves equipment which can selectively sample the telemetry or payload data on a command from Earth or from an on-board sequencer. Earth satellites often have to select data and store it on tape recorders while out of sight of a control station, and transmit it all on the next pass.

Like an aircraft, most spacecraft need to be able to change attitude at will and to keep stable at any particular attitude. Attitudes and navigational positions in space are identified by light sensors graded to specific objects such as the Sun, the Earth's horizon or, for interplanetary craft, the conveniently positioned bright star Canopus. Attitude is changed either by small gas jets or inertial wheels aligned along all three axes, both methods using reaction to turn the craft. Stabilization can be maintained most simply by spinning the entire spacecraft to create gyroscopic forces which keep it stable. For more accurate stability a system of three gyroscopes is required.

Many satellites spend their operational lives in the orbits into which they were first launched. Any manoeuvring, however, means that a rocket motor must be carried. For example, if recovery is intended, then the craft must have a braking rocket. Geostationary satellites are first launched into elliptical orbit with apogee (highest point) at 35,900 km (22,300 miles). On board is a solid-fuel *apogee-motor* which is fired at apogee to

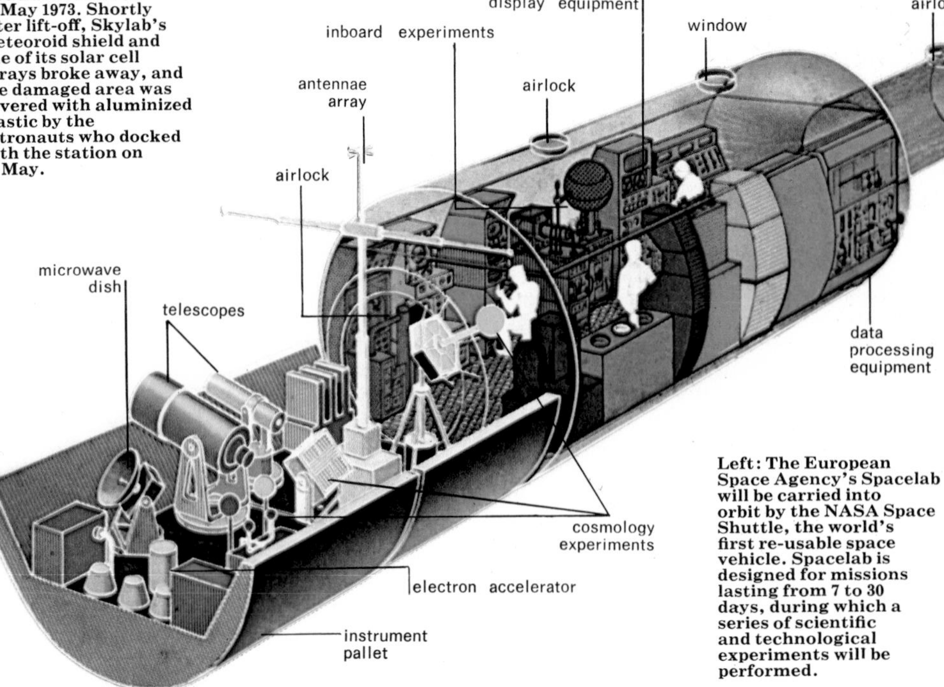

European Space Agency

Left: The European Space Agency's Spacelab will be carried into orbit by the NASA Space Shuttle, the world's first re-usable space vehicle. Spacelab is designed for missions lasting from 7 to 30 days, during which a series of scientific and technological experiments will be performed.

circularize the orbit. Missions that might require numerous manoeuvres must carry a liquid-fuel engine which can be stopped and started at will.

A few satellites and most modern probes have some form of automatic control system. Generally this is just a simple sequencer which converts particular signals into necessary sequences of actions. More sophisticated craft have varying sizes of computer. At their most advanced level, such as those used by Mariner 10, these are programmed not only to correct minor faults but also to perform the entire planned mission without reference to Earth should command reception fail.

Photri

Above: Examples of the packages of food carried on spaceflights, and their equivalent in conventional food. The dehydrated foods are reconstituted by means of a water gun.

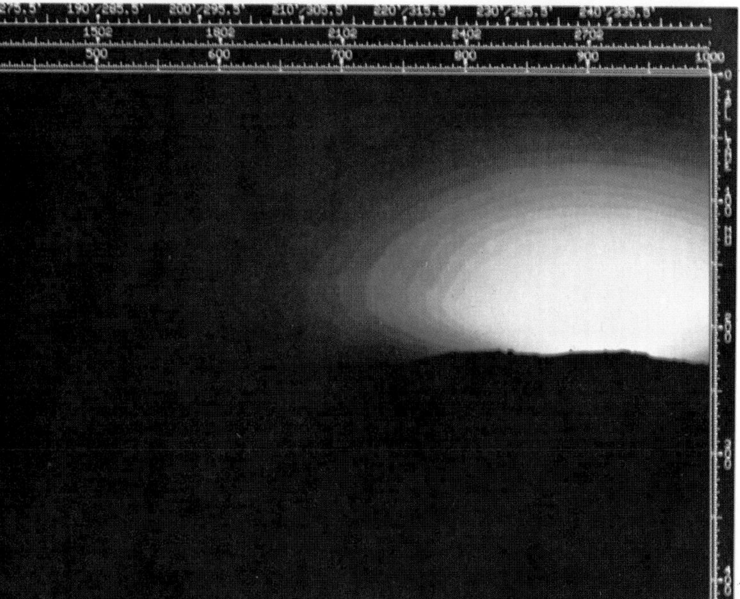

Left: Sunset on Mars, 20 August 1976, photographed by the Viking 1 lander. The layered effect of the light is due to the camera scanning action.

Photri

Below: The proposed Spacelab mission cycle. The Shuttle Orbiter, carrying the Spacelab, takes off using its three main engines and two boosters. At 43 km (27 miles) the boosters separate and return to Earth by parachute for re-use. At 113 km (70 miles) the external fuel tank separates and burns up in the atmosphere. The Orbiter then remains in orbit while the experiments are performed, and finally re-enters the atmosphere and glides back to Earth.

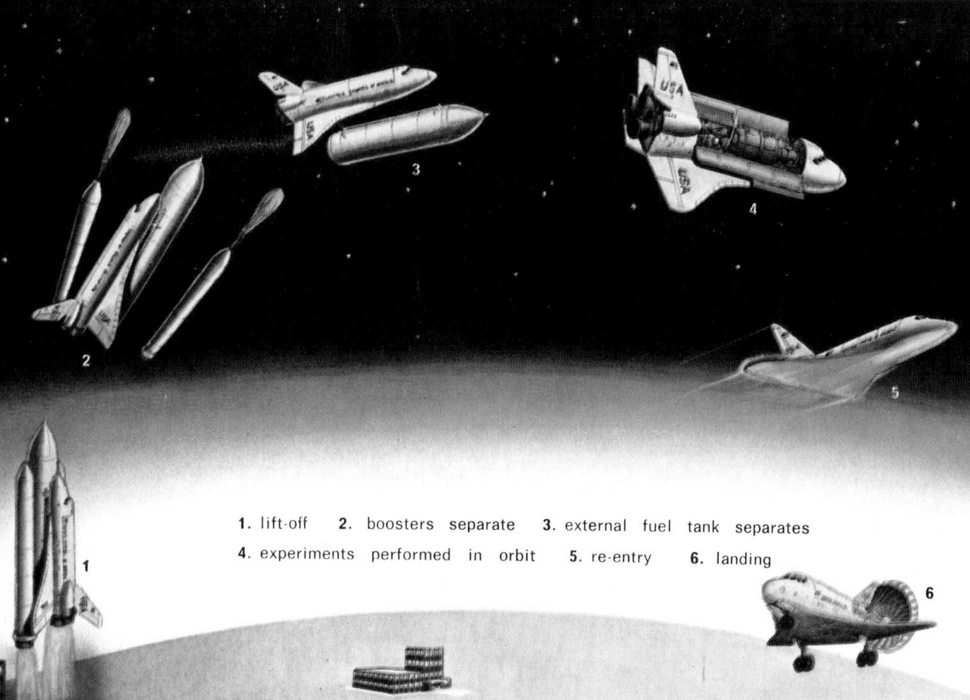
1. lift-off 2. boosters separate 3. external fuel tank separates
4. experiments performed in orbit 5. re-entry 6. landing

Manned flights

Manned spaceflight has a number of special features. Crew safety requires systems to be duplicated or triplicated to ensure against failure. All craft to date have been fully controllable from Earth, but later craft, particularly the Apollo series, also used automatically-sequenced control commanded by the crew. Manual controls were used for fine manoeuvres such as docking.

Life support systems—the supply of air, water and heating/cooling—chiefly characterize manned craft. Consumption of a basic store is sufficient for most flights, but recycling of air and water may be required for long duration flights in the future.

Re-entry problems are solved by presenting a blunt face forward for braking, and covering it with *ablative* materials, materials which dissipate the intense friction heat simply by burning and melting away. The next generation of manned craft, America's aeroplane-like 'Space-Shuttle', will have its entire undersurface coated with a re-usable covering of ceramic and carbon materials. US craft have traditionally landed on water for the sake of simplicity and safety, whereas the Russians have preferred land touchdowns, cushioned by terminal braking rockets. The early Vostok cosmonauts ejected at altitude and descended separately by parachute.

Space suits

Such is the protective and support capability of the average spacesuit that these are sometimes known as 'man-powered spacecraft'. In addition to their use for extra-vehicular activity, spacesuits are worn ready for instant pressurization during critical phases of flight, such as launch and transfer between craft.

The basic pressure garment of the suit used on the Apollo missions, including Apollo 11 when Neil Armstrong and Edwin Aldrin became the first men to land on the Moon, comprised five airtight layers threaded with tubing for cooling water circulation. In addition, the lunar surface explorers wore an 18-layer *integrated thermal-meteoroid suit.* All this was covered with a two-layer abrasion-proof outer garment. Umbilical tubes connected the suit with the air, water and power supplies of the mother craft, except for lunar surface excursions when limited supplies were carried in a back-pack or *Personal Life Support System.* The entire assembly added up to an Earth weight of 25.85 kg (57 lbs) and earned the title of *Extravehicular Mobility Unit.*

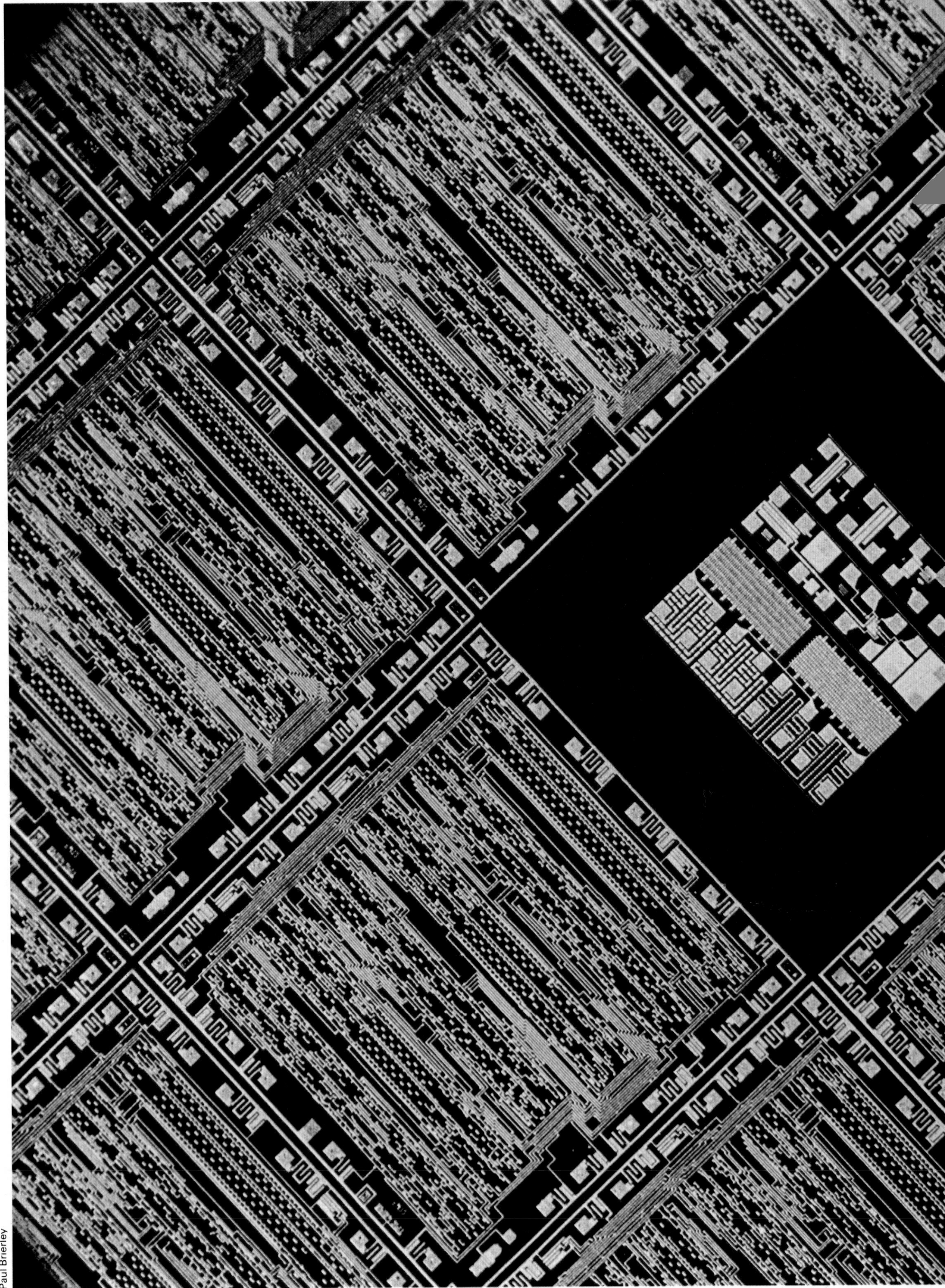

Paul Brierley

Chapter 6
Applied Technology

Tiny chips of crystalline silicon (the central test chip is 4mm square) are used as semiconductors, such as transistors, rectifiers and solar batteries. Silicon can deal with large amounts of power without overheating.

Mechanics

The science of mechanics deals with the effects of forces—anything from the force needed to make a knife cut an apple to the massive forces of gravity which keep the planets in orbit around the sun. A force is an influence which acts on an object to alter its position, its speed or its direction of travel, or to create pressure or stress within it. Forces themselves are invisible, but their effects can be measured and so their size and direction can be calculated.

One of the most important natural forces is the force of gravity, and the weight of an object is a measure of the downward pull exerted on it by the earth's gravity. The mass of an object, which is often confused with its weight, is a measure of the amount of matter it contains and is independent of the earth's gravity.

When more than one force acts on an object, the overall effect or *resultant* of these forces can be calculated by drawing a *vector* diagram. Each force is represented by a line called a vector, which is drawn in the direction in which the force acts and whose length is proportional to the size of the force. The vector diagram is drawn in such a way that a resultant line is produced, whose length and angle represent the size and direction of the resultant force.

There is often no resultant force, however, even with several forces acting on the object. This happens when the forces are balanced or cancel each other out, for example when two equal forces are pulling in opposite directions. When there is no resultant force the object is said to be in *equilibrium*.

Stress and strain

When a force is applied to an object which is moving or free to move, it will try to alter the object's motion in some way. If the object is fixed, however, the force will try to deform it in some way (stretch it or compress it, for instance), a situation which the object will naturally try to resist.

Internal resisting forces are set up within the object, acting in the opposite direction to the applied force to counteract it. The object is then in a state of *stress*; this will be *tensile* stress if the external force is pulling on the object, *compressive* stress if the load is pushing on it, or *shear* stress if there are two or more external forces acting on it in opposite directions but not in line with each other.

Stress is calculated by dividing the value of the external force by the area of the cross-section of the object. *Strain* is a numerical ratio which gives an indication of the effect of such a force on an object. It is found by dividing the change in the length of the object (when subject to the stress) by its original length.

Up to a certain point, this change in length is directly proportional to the size of the force or load producing it, and when the load is removed the object will return to its original length. This ability of an object to return to its original length is known as its *elasticity*—all materials have some degree of elasticity.

The relationship between load and deformation was first demonstrated by Robert Hooke in 1667. The behaviour of a spring is a good example of what is known as Hooke's Law (which applies to all materials, and not just springs). If a weight is hung on a spring it will stretch by a certain amount, and if the load is doubled the spring will stretch twice as much. The stretching is proportional to the load; in other words strain is proportional to stress.

The spring continues to stretch until a point is reached where it has been stretched so far that it will not return to its original length when the load is removed. This point, where strain is no longer proportional to stress, is known as the *elastic limit*.

Once the elastic limit has been passed, the spring will stretch further and further until it eventually breaks.

Hooke's work was taken a step further in 1807 by Robert Young, who found that provided the elastic limit is not exceeded, stress divided by strain gives a certain value or *constant*. The value of this constant, known as Young's Modulus of Elasticity, varies from one material to another. Flexible materials, for example, have lower values than rigid ones.

Pressure

Pressure is the amount of force acting on each unit of area, and so it is expressed in terms such as kilograms per square metre (km/m^2) or pounds per square inch (lb/in^2 or psi). Reducing the area on which a force acts increases the pressure it exerts; increasing the area reduces the pressure. A knife needs less force to make it cut if it is sharp than if it is blunt, because the area of the cutting edge is smaller and so the pressure required to make it cut can be produced with a smaller force.

In the case of a knife, the area on which the force acts is kept as small as possible so that the maximum pressure can be obtained. On the other hand it is sometimes necessary to increase the area to minimize the pressure. For instance, vehicles designed to work over soft sand or marshy ground have wider tyres than road vehicles, so that by spreading the weight of the vehicle over a larger area the pressure exerted on the ground is lower and the wheels will not sink in.

Speed, velocity and acceleration

Forces not only produce stress and pressure. They may also act on an object to make it move, or to alter its motion if it is already moving.

The speed at which an object is travelling is the distance it travels in a specified time, such as the number of miles per hour or metres per second. The measurement of speed does not involve consideration of the direction of travel, but any measurement of velocity does. Velocity is the speed of an object in a specified direction.

Acceleration is defined as the rate of change of velocity with time and, as velocity involves both speed and direction, a change in either or both of these is an acceleration. A train increasing its speed as it travels along a straight length of track is accelerating, and so is a train moving at a constant speed as it goes around a curve.

If an object is increasing its velocity by, for example, 10 metres per second

Right: A spring balance gives a direct measurement of weight and it will show a different weight for the same object at the top of a mountain than at sea level. This is because at the mountain top the object will be further from the centre of the Earth, so the pull of gravity will be less than at sea level—as predicted by the universal law of gravitation.

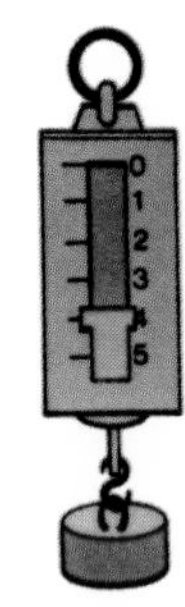

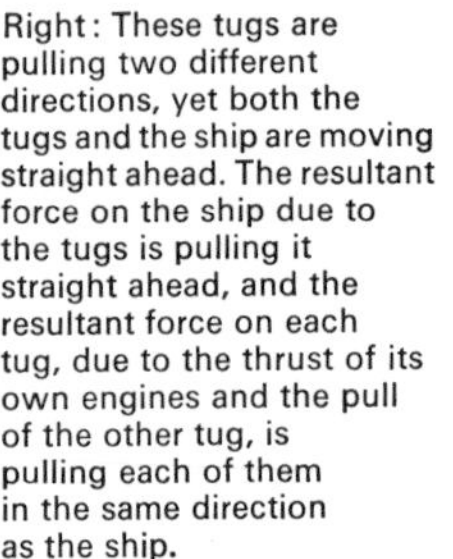

Left: The pull of gravity acts on every particle within an object, and if a the tiny weight forces of these particles were replaced by one large force it would act down through a point called th centre of gravity. This point is not necessarily within the material of the object. In the case of this vase, for example it is a point in the space inside it.

Right: These tugs are pulling two different directions, yet both the tugs and the ship are moving straight ahead. The resultant force on the ship due to the tugs is pulling it straight ahead, and the resultant force on each tug, due to the thrust of its own engines and the pull of the other tug, is pulling each of them in the same direction as the ship.

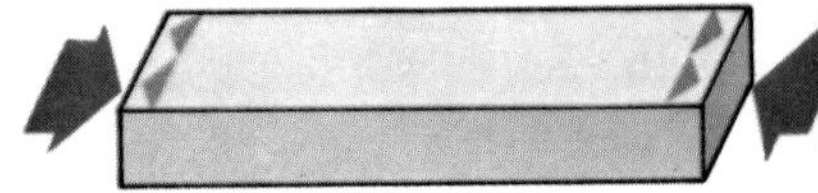

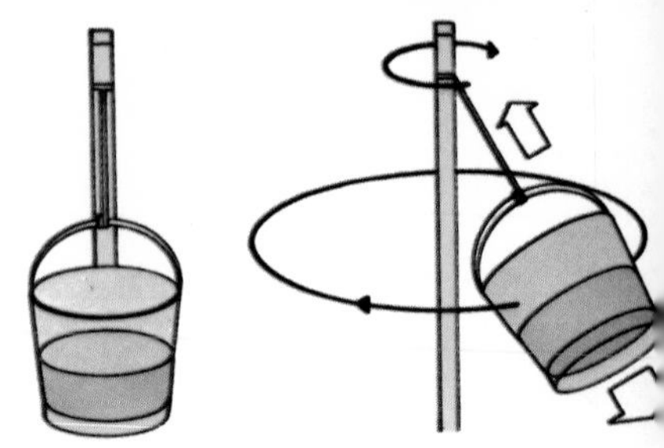

Weight is a measure of the ɔull of gravity on an ɔbject. This pull was explained by Newton in his universal law of gravitation. It states that the force between two bodies (such as the Earth and an object on it) is directly proportional to the product of their masses and inversely proportional to the square of the distance between them.

Left: Unlike the spring balance, which measures a weight by the extent to which it stretches the spring, the beam balance compares the unknown weight with a known weight or weights. It will give the same measurement at a mountain top as it will at sea level because the change in the pull of gravity affects both weights equally. They still balance despite their change in weight.

Spectrum

Left: This weightlifter is lifting a bar carrying 80 kg (176 lb) of weights. In lifting the weights he is doing work against gravity. If he lifts them 2.2 m (7.2 ft), he will have done 80 x 2.2= 176 m.kg (1269 ft.lb) of work. This is in addition to the work done in lifting the bar itself and in raising the weight of his own body from a crouched position.

Photri

Left: The load hook is positioned so that the load's centre of gravity is in line with the helicopter's. If it was in front or behind it would tend to tilt the craft.

Right: A tower crane can lift a greater weight when the load trolley is near the tower. This is because the load is then exerting less leverage than it would at the end of the jib.

Photri

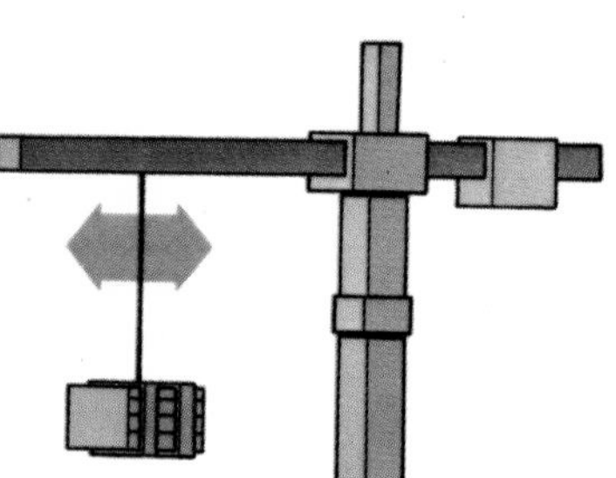

ght: When a barge is eing towed along a canal y two ropes, one on ther side, the resultant rce can be calculated by awing a parallelogram, vo adjacent sides of hich represent the size d direction of the two ılling forces. The size and ection of the resultant found by measuring the ngth and angle of e diagonal of the rallelogram.

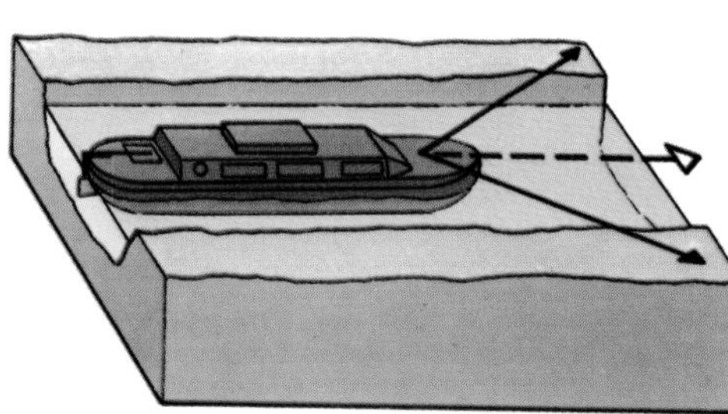

Terence Le Goubin, Colorific

Left: The geodesic dome is made up of metal tubes arranged in triangles. The triangle was chosen as the basic unit of the framework because its shape cannot be altered without physically bending any of the tubes. Other shapes, such as squares or pentagons, can be altered by changing the angles between the tubes, so they are more liable to collapse.

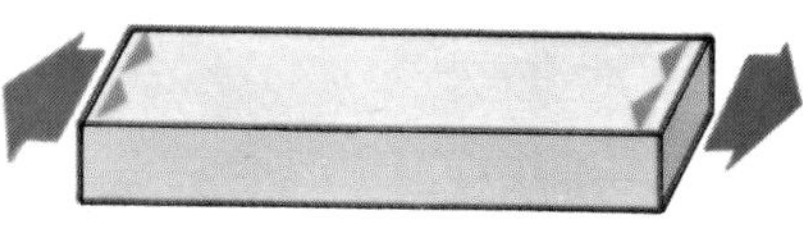

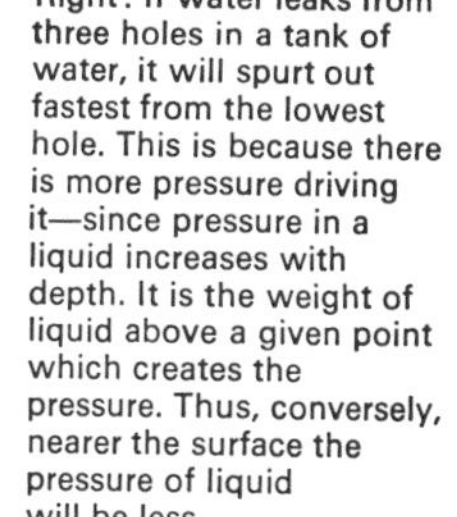

Far left: When an object such as a bar is subject to forces pushing in from each end, internal forces are set up to resist them and the bar is then said to be in a state of compression.

Left: When the applied forces are pulling on the bar, the internal forces act inwards to resist the pull, and the bar is then in a state of tension.

Right: If water leaks from three holes in a tank of water, it will spurt out fastest from the lowest hole. This is because there is more pressure driving it—since pressure in a liquid increases with depth. It is the weight of liquid above a given point which creates the pressure. Thus, conversely, nearer the surface the pressure of liquid will be less.

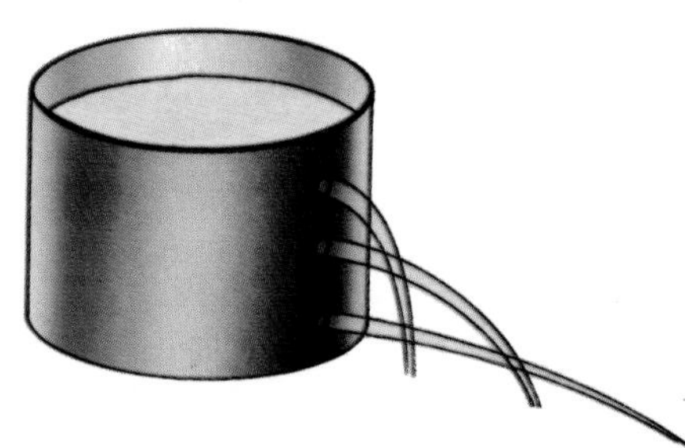

ft and Right: Two amples of friction, the istance force which poses the motion of two faces sliding over each ıer. The scorched paint- rk of the Apollo capsule the result of the heat nerated by air friction en the craft entered the nosphere. The smoke m the car's tyres is due friction caused by eelspin during eleration.

Photri

Transworld

Left and right: A rocket taking off illustrates Newton's laws of motion. First, it will not move or change direction unless acted on by a force, in this case the reaction to the engine thrust; second, its acceleration is proportional to the force applied; third, every action (the engine thrust) produces an equal but opposite reaction (the motion of the rocket).

Transworld

t: A bucket of water, ung round on a rope, avelling in a circle and continuously changing ection. It is said to be elerating all the time, ause acceleration is a nge in either speed or ction. The force ducing this acceleration ne tension in the rope ch is preventing the ket from flying off straight line. is called the centripetal force. The value of this force is the square of the speed of the bucket divided by the radius of the circle around which it is travelling. The tendency of the bucket to fly off in a straight line is the centrifugal force, equal in size but opposite in direction to the centripetal force. This is holding the water in the rotating bucket despite it being almost horizontal.

Photri

Left: A picture of a hurricane in the South Pacific taken from the Skylab orbital laboratory. The rotation of the earth causes a deflection of the winds blowing over it—to the right in the northern hemisphere and to the left in the south. This effect (known as the Coriolis force) makes hurricanes spiral clockwise in the south and anti-clockwise in the north.

(m/sec) every second, its acceleration is written as 10 m/sec/sec or 10 m/sec^2.

Velocity, acceleration, time and distance are brought together by the three equations of motion, providing the acceleration remains constant during the specified time. These deal with initial velocity (u), final velocity (v), acceleration (a), distance travelled (s) and time (t).

The first equation, $v = u + at$, enables us to calculate the final velocity from the initial velocity, the acceleration, and the length of time the object was accelerating. The second, $s = ut + \frac{1}{2}at^2$, gives the distance travelled when the initial velocity, the acceleration and the time are known.

The third equation, $v^2 = u^2 + 2as$, allows the final velocity to be calculated from the initial velocity, the acceleration, and the distance travelled. In each of these equations, of course, any one of the quantities involved can be calculated if all the others in the equation are known.

Acceleration due to gravity

The force of gravity causes falling objects to accelerate as they drop, and in theory this acceleration is approximately 981 cm/sec^2 (32 ft/sec^2). In practice, however, falling objects are slowed down by air resistance and so a steel ball falls much faster than a feather.

An object falling freely from a great height does not continue accelerating until it hits the ground, because it eventually reaches a speed at which the upward force of the air resistance equals the downward pull of gravity. When this happens the object stops accelerating and falls at a fairly constant velocity known as its *terminal velocity*.

The terminal velocity an object can attain depends on its size and shape. A person falling from an aircraft without a parachute is unlikely to achieve a terminal velocity greater than about 225 kph (140 mph). In a vacuum, of course, there is no air resistance and so any falling object will continue accelerating until it hits something.

Momentum and inertia

The inertia of an object is its reluctance to move when it is stationary, or to change its direction or speed once it is moving. The amount of inertia a body possesses depends on its mass, the larger the mass the greater the inertia. In the case of a rotating object such as a flywheel, it is a quantity called the *moment of inertia* which must be considered.

The moment of a force is its turning effect about a given point. This is found by multiplying the size of the force by the perpendicular distance between its line of action and the point.

For example, a girder projecting from a wall, has a weight of 4 kg hanging on it at a distance of 2 metres from the wall. The moment of the weight about the point where the girder is fixed to the wall is $4 \times 2 = 8$ kg.m (kilogramme-metres).

The moment of inertia therefore takes account of not only the mass but also its distance from the point about which it is rotating. The further the mass is from its centre of rotation, the larger its moment of inertia. This means that a flywheel has a larger moment of inertia if it is made with a thick rim and thin spokes than if it were a solid disc of the same weight and diameter, because most of its mass is at the edge, away from the centre of rotation.

The *momentum* of an object is the product of its mass and its velocity, and a small, fast-moving object may have the same momentum as a large, slow-moving one. For example, a mass of 1 kg moving at 100 m/sec has the same momentum as a mass of 100 kg moving at 1 m/sec. In both cases the same amount of force would be required to change the momentum of each one equally.

The momentum of an object due to its rotation, its *angular momentum*, is found by multiplying its moment of inertia by its *angular velocity*. Angular velocity is the angle the object rotates through in a given time, and is commonly measured in radians per second. A radian is approximately 57.3°.

Potential and kinetic energy

Work is performed when a force acts on something to produce motion, and it is defined as the product of the force and the distance moved. The capacity to do work is termed *energy*. There are two kinds of energy in mechanics which are called *potential energy* and *kinetic energy*.

An object possesses potential energy because of its position, and kinetic energy because of its velocity. If a stone weighing 2 kg is lifted to a height of 10 metres, the work needed to do this (force × distance) is 20 m.kg (metre kilogrammes); this is stored in the stone in the form of potential energy, also 20 m.kg. When the stone is allowed to drop, this energy can be turned back into work by, for example, dropping the stone on to a stake to drive it into the ground.

When the stone is half way to the ground (at a height of 5 metres), its potential energy (weight × height) is now only 10 m.kg, half what it was before. As it has not yet done any work, its total energy must still be the same, and so half its original potential energy must have been converted into another form of energy. This other form is kinetic energy, which it now possesses because it is moving.

When it reaches the ground all its potential energy will have been converted into kinetic energy and when it hits the stake this energy will be released as work, to push the stake into the ground. The kinetic energy of an object of a mass m travelling at a velocity v is $\frac{1}{2}m \times v^2$.

The conversion of potential energy into kinetic energy follows the *Law of Conservation of Energy*, which states that energy cannot be created or destroyed, only converted from one form into another.

The uses of mechanics

The study of machines is an essential part of many areas of science and technology. In civil engineering, for example, before a building or a bridge can be built the designers must calculate the stresses likely to occur within the structure, to ensure that the materials used will not be overloaded and collapse during use.

When a vehicle is being designed—whether it is a car, a locomotive or a space rocket—its weight, its planned top speed and the acceleration required must be decided so that the power needed from the engine can be calculated. In fact the basic principles of mechanics are involved in any consideration of the design or performance of any kind of structure or machine.

K. E. Deckart, ZEFA

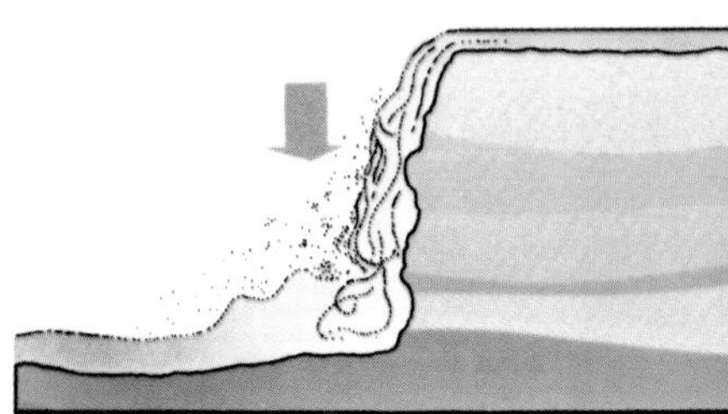

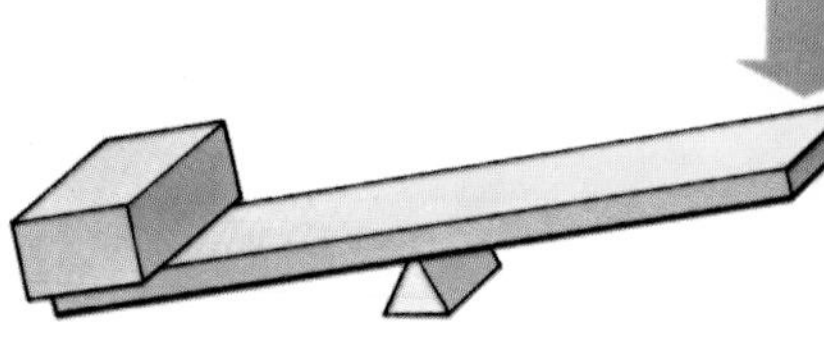

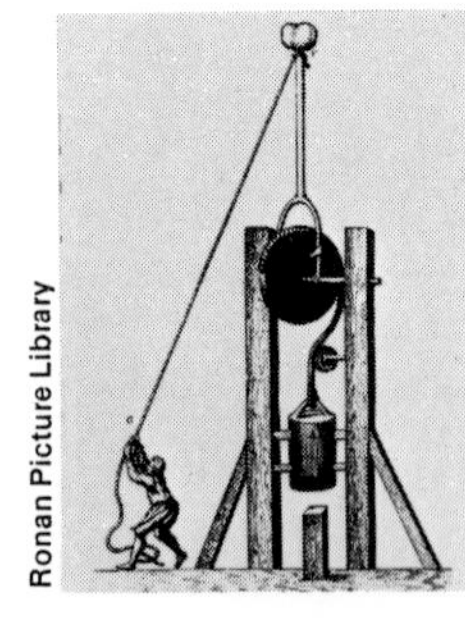

Ronan Picture Library

Left: A seventeenth-century piledriver. Pull on the rope G drew th lever E downwards, turning the pulley whe This wound up the rop lifted the block A, givi potential energy. Whe rope was released the block fell back down, turning its potential en into kinetic energy, w was released as work to drive the pile into the ground.

Ronan Picture Library

Right: Steam engines have large flywheels to keep them going when the piston changes its direction of travel at each end of its stroke. The inertia of the flywheel, its reluctance to stop once it is moving, keeps it turning when the piston stops momentarily at these two points (known as the top dead centre and the bottom dead centre). This is a single cylinder engine.

Left: This waterwheel is turned by the force of the water flowing under it. This force acts near the edge of the wheel and produces a turning effect called a torque. Multiplying the value of the force by the distance between its point of action near the edge of the wheel and the centre of rotation at the axle, gives the value of the torque.

Spectrum

Left and right: The force of the wind pushes the sails of a windmill round, producing four torques on the shaft carrying the sails. This mill has four sails, the torques on each opposing pair of sails combining to form what are known as couples. A couple is formed when two forces, acting in opposite directions, act on directly opposite points about an axis.

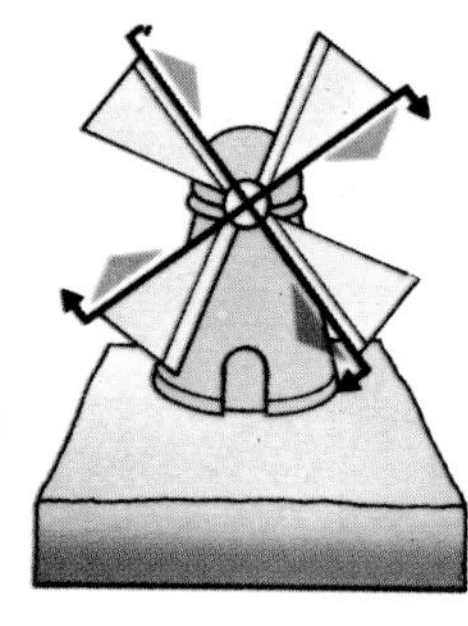

Left and right: The water at the top of a waterfall has a certain amount of kinetic energy because it is moving. It also has potential energy because of its height from the bottom of the fall. As it drops over the edge it starts losing potential energy because its height is decreasing, and gaining kinetic energy as it picks up speed. At the bottom, all its energy is kinetic.

Spectrum

Left: The effect or moment of a force acting at a distance from a pivot is the product of the size of the force and the distance from the pivot. Thus a force of 10 kg exerted on the handle of a crowbar, 0.5 m from the pivot, will produce a force of 100 kg at the other end of the bar if it is 0.05 m from the pivot. The total moment on each side of the pivot is always equal.

eft: If an effort of 2 kg xerted on one side of a ver lifts a load of 4 kg n the other, the lever has mechanical advantage of (calculated by dividing ne load by the effort). The ork done by each side of e lever is the same ecause the effort moves vice as far as the load; us the lever has a velocity tio (distance moved by fort divided by that oved by the load) of 2.

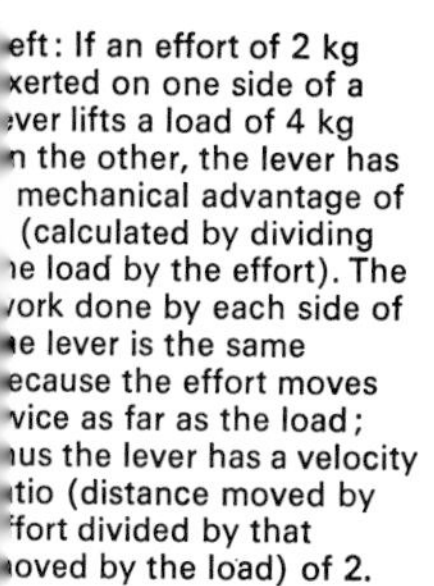

Left: A simple lever which has the load and effort on opposite sides of the pivot or fulcrum is called a first order lever. A lever which has both load and effort on the same side of the pivot is a second order lever. A pair of nutcrackers is in fact a pair of second order levers joined at a common pivot. In both orders the effort is further from the pivot than the load.

Left: Sugar tongs are third order levers, the load being further from the pivot than the effort. The load is therefore less than the effort.

Right: An example of seventeenth-century mechanical engineering. This machine for raising water from a well uses several basic mechanical devices, such as levers, gears and cranks.

Ronan Picture Library

eft: Gears are devices hich are used to transmit tational motion. If a gear as twice as many teeth as e one it is driving, the iven gear will turn twice s fast as the driving gear. other words the gear tio is 2:1. The driven gear rns in the opposite irection to the driving ear. For example, in this ustration the large gears rn the opposite way to e small one.

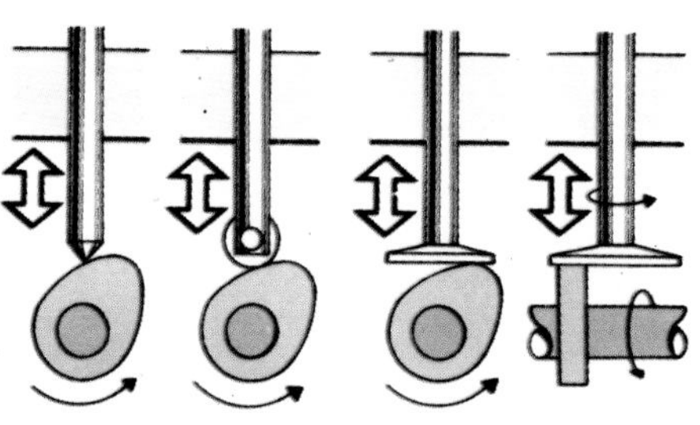

Left: Cams are used to turn rotational motion into reciprocating motion—that is up and down or back and forward. Cams are mounted on shafts and act upon cam followers. These follow the profile of the cam rising as the high point of the cam comes round and falling back as it passes. Shown here are four common types of cam follower in general use.

Ronan Picture Library

Left: A machine, designed by Sir Marc Isambard Brunel in the late eighteenth century, for cutting slots in blocks of wood used in ship-building. Born in France in 1769, Brunel was a prolific inventor and a civil engineer, as was his son Isambard Kingdom Brunel who designed railways, ships and bridges. Sir Marc died in London in December 1849.

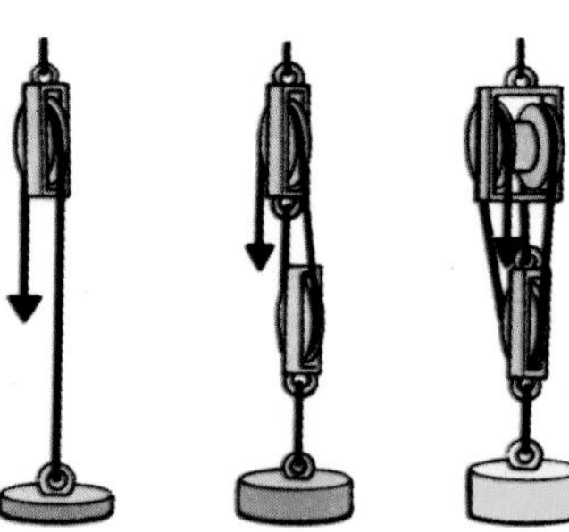

Left: In a pulley system the velocity ratio is equal to the number of pulleys, providing all pulleys are of equal diameter. 'Work' must be done to overcome friction and lift the lower pulley block itself, and the efficiency of a system is work output divided by work input. The efficiency equals the mechanical advantage divided by the velocity ratio.

Right: The crank is a means of converting reciprocating motion into rotary motion. As the piston moves to the right the connecting rod, which is attached to the wheel, moves down and to the right and turns the wheel clockwise. When the piston moves to the left the wheel end of the rod moves up and then to the left, so keeping the wheel turning.

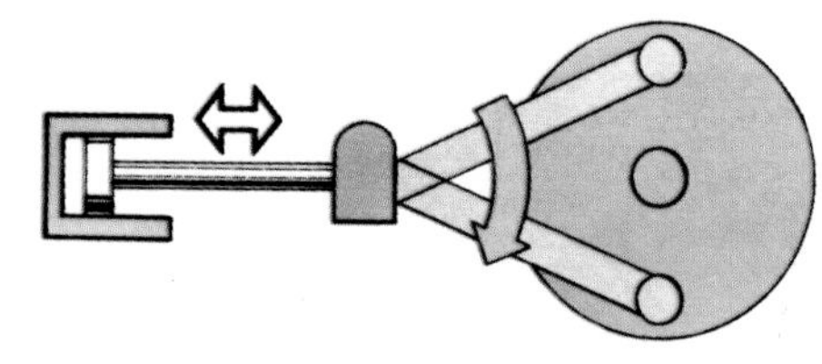

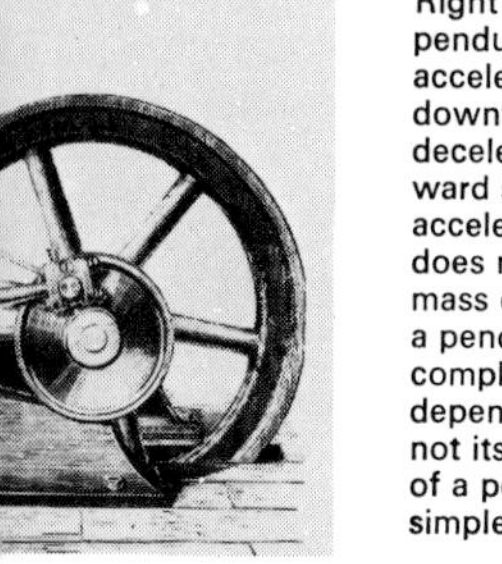

Right: The swing of a pendulum is due to gravity accelerating it on its downward swing and decelerating it on its upward swing. Because acceleration due to gravity does not depend on the mass of an object, the time a pendulum needs to complete one swing depends on its length and not its mass. The motion of a pendulum is called simple harmonic motion.

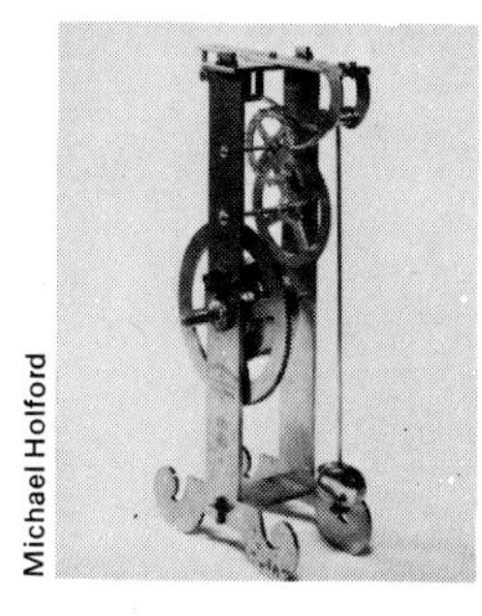

Michael Holford

Photri

Left: The collapse of the Tacoma Narrows bridge, Washington, in 1940. Gusts of wind started it swinging, and it reached such a rate that it tended to keep moving even when the wind dropped. At this rate of swing, which is called the resonant frequency of the bridge, such severe stresses were set up within it that it literally shook itself to pieces.

Strengths of Materials

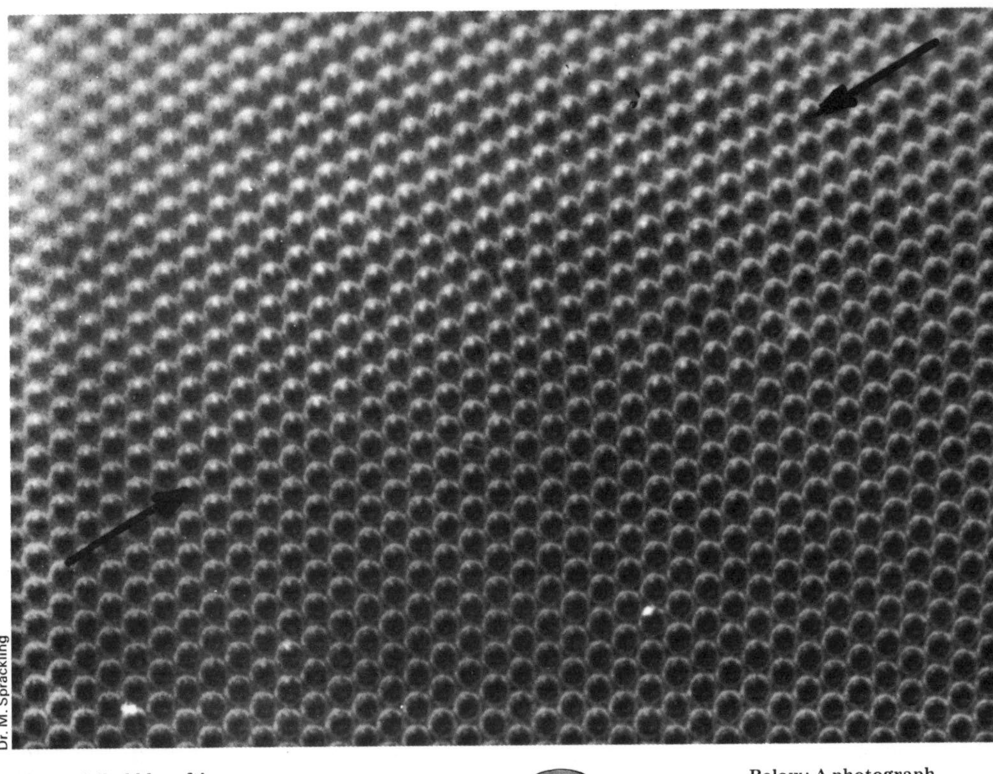

Above: A 'bubble raft', uniformly-sized bubbles spread over a sheet of wet glass, behaves in some ways like metal atoms when they form into crystals. The bubbles arrange themselves into a close-packed structure, some areas of which are perfectly regular (like perfect crystals) while others, one of which can be seen by looking along the arrows in the picture, are irregular and correspond to the dislocations found in metal crystals. The bubbles used here were of about 1 mm diameter.

The materials used in engineering can be divided into three general groups: *metals*, such as iron, copper and aluminium; *ceramics*, such as stone, bricks, concrete and glass; and *organic* (carbon-based) materials, which include natural substances such as rubber and synthetic materials like polythene and other plastics.

All materials possess, to a greater or lesser extent, the property known as *elasticity*. This property enables them to return to their original size, shape or volume after being *deformed* by the application of an external force, provided that this force does not deform them beyond what is known as their *elastic limit*. If the elastic limit of a material is exceeded, *plastic deformation* occurs and the material will not return to its original state when the force is removed, and if the force is high enough the material will fracture.

A stress acting on, say, a steel rod, in such a way as to stretch it longitudinally, is known as a *tensile stress* and it puts the rod into a state of *tension*. The strain produced by such a stress is called *tensile strain*. A stress tending to compress the rod longitudinally is called a *compressive stress*, and it creates *compressive strain* and puts the rod in a state of *compression*. *Shear stress* and *shear strain* occur when a material is subjected to bending.

The structure of materials

Most solid materials, and all solid metals, have a crystalline structure, their atoms or molecules being arranged in regular three-dimensional groups. In a metal, the outer or valence electrons of the atoms dissociate from their parent atoms, which thus become positively-charged ions, and permeate the space within the crystal lattice as a kind of 'cloud' of (negatively-charged) electrons which holds the ions together.

The commonest ceramic materials have predominantly crystalline structures, consisting of a matrix of oxygen atoms enclosing atoms of metals such as aluminium or magnesium, or atoms of semi-metals such as silicon. Each oxygen atom, having two vacancies in its outer electron shell, 'borrows' electrons from adjacent metal atoms to fill these vacancies. This results in the oxygen atom having a net negative charge, and leaves the metal atoms with net positive charges. The oxygen and metal atoms are thus ionized, and being oppositely-charged are held together by strong electrostatic attraction.

Glasses, although ceramics, do not have a crystalline structure. When they solidify from the liquid state they do not form crystals; their atoms do not arrange themselves in orderly, geometrical patterns but remain in the disordered state that they were in when liquid.

Polymers, whose molecules are joined together in long chains, may be of natural origin, such as cellulose or rubber, or be synthetic, such as polythene or polystyrene. Natural polymers contain both crystalline and non-crystalline (*amor-*

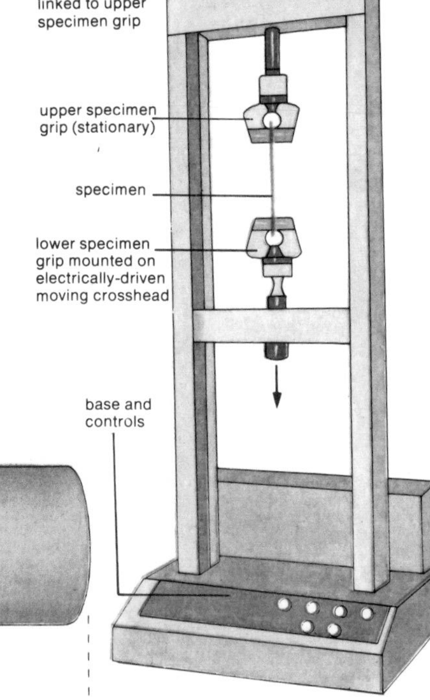

Right: A machine for measuring the strength of a specimen bar or rod of a material by stretching or compressing it with loads of up to 100 kg.

Above left: The *glide* or slip which occurs when a single crystal is plastically deformed under tension. When a crystal is stretched within its elastic limit, the amount of *strain* produced (change in length divided by original length) is proportional to the applied *stress* (the applied force divided by the cross-sectional area of the crystal) and the crystal will return to its original size when the stress is removed. If it is stressed beyond this limit it will deform plastically and remain permanently deformed.

Left: The 'necking' that occurs in ductile crystals prior to fracture under large tensile stresses.

Below: A photograph, taken through a microscope, of a crystal of leucite ($KAlSi_2O_6$) embedded in a piece of lava from Mt Vesuvius. Most minerals have a crystalline structure, although there are also non-crystalline (amorphous) minerals and others which occur in both crystalline and amorphous forms.

UKAEA

Left: A picture of a deformed magnesium oxide crystal taken under polarized light. The colours indicate the direction and magnitude of the internal stresses set up within the crystal as a result of the external stress applied to it to deform it. Magnesium oxide is a ceramic, and so when it is increasingly stressed it undergoes a certain amount of elastic deformation, but then fractures suddenly without plastic deformation.

Right: Core drilling with a diamond-tipped drill. Diamonds are very hard because their crystal structure is extremely strong and resistant to deformation.

Atlas Copco Craelins Ltd, Daventry

UKAEA

Left: When a component fails in service it is often important to know the cause of the failure, so that action can be taken to prevent similar components from failing. This ruptured superheater tube was sent to a laboratory where its fracture surface was examined to determine the origin of the failure.

E. Leitz

phous) components, those which are predominantly crystalline being comparatively strong and rigid while the predominantly amorphous types are relatively soft and elastic.

Synthetic polymers are made to be more or less crystalline according to the properties required of them. The crystallization may involve lining up individual chains in parallel so that they bond together, or folding or coiling chains back on themselves so that they bond to themselves. An alternative method of making polymers stronger and more rigid is to add a suitable chemical, such as sulphur, which links the chains together side by side. This is known as chemical *cross-linking*.

Dislocations

A great deal of force is required to deform a single, perfectly-formed crystal, because deformation involves making whole planes of atoms slide over each other, and this means overcoming the very strong forces which bind them together. Ordinary metal crystals, however, are not perfect—they contain imperfections known as *dislocations*. Dislocations are irregularities in the crystal structure, for example a *vacancy* where an atom is missing from its place in the lattice, or an *interstitial* dislocation where an extra atom has been squeezed in. These dislocations occur when the metal crystallizes on solidifying from the molten state, and they are also formed when the crystals are subjected to mechanical stresses.

The presence of a dislocation weakens the crystal structure, and so it will deform under a lower stress than that needed to deform a perfect crystal. The plastic deformation of a metal begins when the applied stress is sufficient to cause slip or *glide*, in which sheets of atoms slide over each other, in the direction of a row of atoms, by one or more complete interatomic distances. The surface over which the glide has taken place is the *glide surface*; this surface is often flat or planar, in which case it is called a *glide plane*.

Glide is not achieved by the simul-

Right: Representative values of tensile strength and Young's modulus. The tensile strengths are determined by dividing the maximum tensile load that a sample can withstand by the cross-sectional area of the sample. The Young's modulus (or modulus of elasticity) of a material is the ratio of applied tensile or compressive stress to the amount of strain it produces. Young's modulus gives an indication of the hardness and elasticity of a material.

Below: The deck of a transporter bridge, suspended on steel cables. Steel is one of the strongest and most important materials used in engineering.

TENSILE STRENGTHS OF VARIOUS MATERIALS	
MATERIAL	kgf/m
iron, "whiskers"	1400
carbon filaments	320
glass filaments	100-
steel, piano wire	200
viscose rayon, tyre cord (cellulose)	100
nylon, high tenacity	100
flax (cellulose and lignin)	90
cotton (cellulose)	50
mild steel	46
viscose rayon, textile fibre	30
wool	20
aluminium	17
acrylic, oriented	16
nylon, undrawn	8
acrylic	8
urea-formaldehyde resins	4-8
rubber	3

Above: No matter how well a structure is built, or how carefully the materials are chosen, there is always a danger that unexpected conditions will arise that stress it beyond its limits. In 1963 the huge Vaiont Dam, in northern Italy, was destroyed when part of a nearby mountain collapsed on to it.

Below: Air friction generates a great deal of heat at supersonic speeds. At speeds over Mach 2.5 this heat can soften and weaken aluminium alloys, necessitating the use of heavier and costlier steel and titanium. Concorde was designed to fly at around Mach 2 so that it could be built from aluminium.

taneous movement of all the atoms on the glide plane, but by the consecutive slipping of atoms over each other along the glide plane. The boundary between the slipped and unslipped regions is the dislocation, and slip therefore involves the movement of the dislocation along the glide plane.

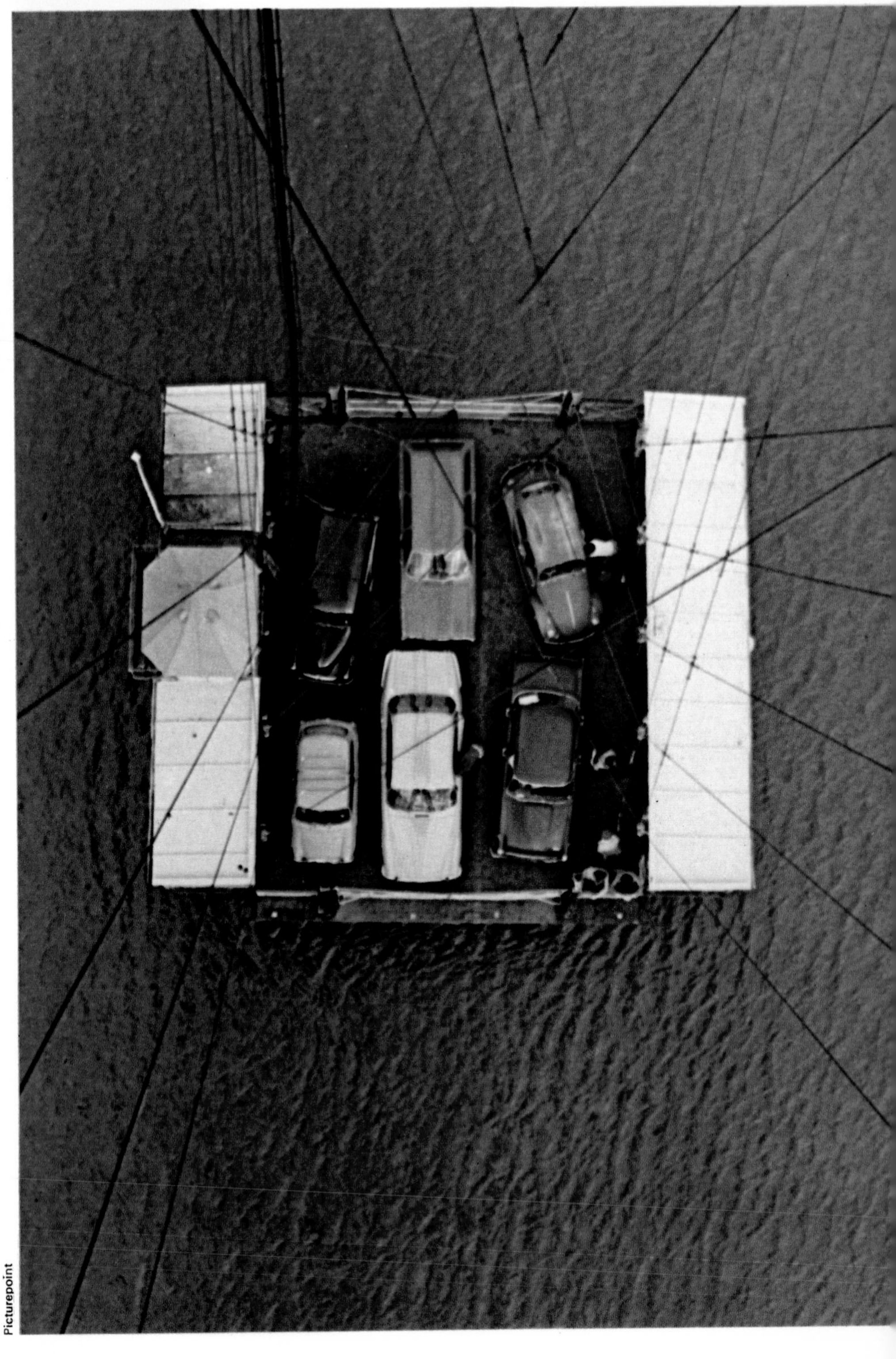

The presence of large numbers of movable dislocations is what gives metals their *ductility*, their ability to be mechanically shaped by hammering, rolling or drawing without fracturing. When a metal is stressed within its elastic limit, the bonds holding its atoms together 'stretch' to accommodate the stress and then pull the atoms back to their original positions when the stress is removed. When the stress exceeds the elastic limit, however, the dislocations move to allow the metal to deform plastically without fracturing.

The ductility of a metal can be reduced, making it harder and stronger (but more brittle), by obstructing the movement of

Picturepoint

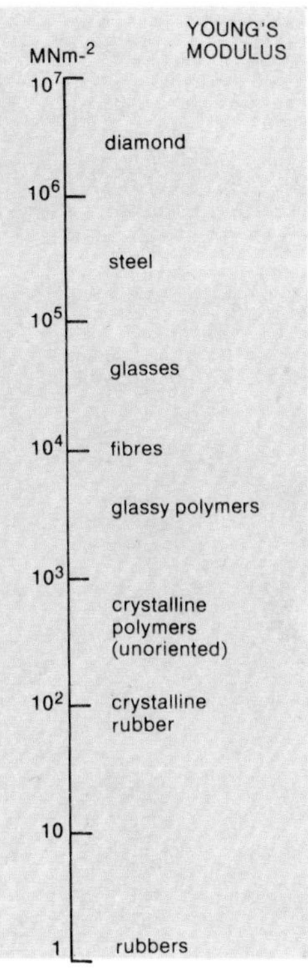

Bristol Composite Materials Engineering Ltd

UKAEA

Below: Four equally-sized bars, of rubber, polythene, acrylic and steel, would require different loads to bend them through a given distance. If the polythene bar required 1 kg, the acrylic bar would require 15 kg as its Young's modulus is fifteen times greater. The rubber would bend under its own weight.

Above: A bullet-resistant clipboard made from a fibre-reinforced plastics composite material. The material will stop shotgun pellets or a 9 mm pistol bullet fired from point blank range. Similar materials are used in making lightweight body armour and protective helmets.

Right: Following the breakdown of the clock on the Houses of Parliament in London (which includes the famous bell popularly known as 'Big Ben'), the components of the mechanism were tested for defects, such as cracks or casting flaws, which could have led to further breakdowns.

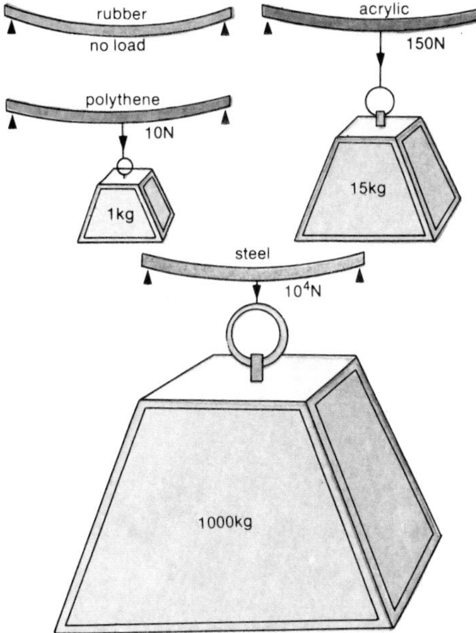

the dislocations within it. When examined under a microscope, metals can be seen to have a grainy structure, each grain being a single crystal. The boundaries between the grains obstruct the movement of dislocations, and so if the metal is made to solidify in such a way that the grain size is small there will be a large number of grain boundaries and therefore a large number of obstructions to dislocation movement.

Another method of hardening a metal is to create so many dislocations within its grains that they obstruct one another's movement. The number of dislocations can increase considerably when a metal undergoes plastic deformation, and this is the cause of the *work-hardening* which occurs during metalworking processes such as hammering or rolling.

The presence of atoms of another element within the crystal lattice of a metal will also impede the movement of dislocations. This is what makes many alloys harder than the pure metals from which they are made.

Non-crystalline materials such as glass, and ceramics which may be completely crystalline or contain both crystalline and glassy components, do not possess these easily movable dislocations which would enable them to deform plastically. After their elastic limit has been exceeded, they fracture suddenly with no plastic deformation. Even though crystalline ceramics do contain dislocations, these are usually prevented from moving by the presence of impurities in the material.

Cracks

The movement of dislocations also makes metals more resistant to fracture due to crack propagation than are non-metals. If a material in tension has a small surface crack, for example, the stress will not be evenly distributed throughout it; there will be a localized concentration of stress at the tip of the crack. The smaller the radius of the crack tip, the greater the concentration of stress there. In a metal, this concentration of stress will cause a movement of dislocations and plastic deformation in the area of the crack, leading to a blunting of its tip which reduces the local stress.

In a glass or a crystalline non-metal, however, this blunting effect is not possible, and the crack may spread rapidly and cause a fracture. In such cases the crack may spread extremely rapidly; the deeper it goes, the higher the concentration of stress, which in turn drives it deeper into the material.

Metal fatigue arises when a component is subjected to a static load over a long period of time, or to a large number of stress oscillations. Fatigue cracks begin at points within the metal where there is a concentration of stresses, but where the total stress is not sufficient to cause enough plastic deformation to relieve the local concentration. Dislocations gradually move into the stressed area, but they accumulate in such a way as to prevent one another from moving any further. When this occurs the metal hardens and becomes brittle in the area around the original stress concentration, and this allows a crack to form.

The crack spreads through the brittle region until it reaches a more ductile area of the metal, at which point it draws more dislocations to it and the process of hardening begins again, with a subsequent further spread of the crack. The crack eventually spreads through so much of the component that there is insufficient unaffected metal left to support the load, and the component snaps.

Composite materials

Composite materials are made up of two or more different materials, put together in such a way that the finished product has superior mechanical properties to any of its components. There are many natural composite materials; wood, for example, consists of strong, flexible cellulose fibres bound together with harder, more brittle lignin which imparts stiffness.

Man-made composite materials are commonly made of thin fibres of a material having a high tensile strength, which are embedded within a matrix of a softer material. For example, glass fibres have an extremely high tensile strength, much higher than the best steels, but the tiniest surface scratch will cause them to crack under comparatively light loads. By embedding them in a suitable matrix, such as an epoxy or polyester resin, they are protected from serious scratches. If a fibre breaks under load, the matrix holds the two halves in place and distributes the load between them, and the complex structure of the composite impedes the propagation of cracks through it.

A special advantage of composite materials is that they provide a practical method of using the strongest forms of material known—short, single-crystal filaments called 'whiskers'. Among the types of whiskers with great potential for use in composites are glass, carbon fibres (tiny fibres of graphite) and many types of strong, stiff ceramics such as silicon carbide, boron carbide and aluminium oxide.

Machine Tools

Machine tools, power-operated machines which shape articles to any desired form by the action of mechanically-controlled cutting tools, played an essential part in the Industrial Revolution and are vital to modern industry. As well as greatly simplifying the manufacture of individual items, the use of machine tools permits the making of large numbers of identical articles at a low cost.

The earliest machine tool was the lathe, which is known to have been used by the Egyptians in the third century BC, by the Etruscans in about 700 BC, and possibly in Mycenae in around 1200 BC. Water-driven saws, boring machines and hammers were invented in the Middle Ages, and Leonardo da Vinci produced designs for several types of machine tool.

The machine tools in use in the late eighteenth century were essentially little different from those of the Middle Ages, but by 1850 their designs had improved radically and they were, in principle, the same as their modern counterparts. As the Industrial Revolution progressed, the need for more and better machine tools to facilitate the manufacture of such items as textile machinery and steam engines grew considerably. In their turn, machine tools benefited from the new technologies they helped to create.

For example, James Watt was able to develop his improved steam engine because John Wilkinson's cylinder-boring machine, invented in 1775, was capable of boring cylinders to the close tolerances required by the design. Watt's engines could drive rotating shafts, which earlier steam engines could not do satisfactorily, and this rotary motion was soon employed to drive, via belts and pulleys, new forms of machine tools.

By far the greater part of machine tool development in the first half of the nineteenth century took place in England and the US. Most of the general-purpose machine tools of the present day, such as boring, planing and shaping machines, the powered lathe, and tooling such as taps and dies for cutting screw threads, were developed in England during this period. By the middle of the century, however, the US had become the world leader in machine tool design.

The rapid expansion of the US economy created a scarcity of skilled labour, and this prompted the production of machine tools capable of high output rates which needed a minimum of labour to operate them. Among these were the automatic lathe, and the turret lathe which had several tools mounted on a rotatable turret, so that a series of machining operations could be carried out on a workpiece simply by rotating the turret to bring the appropriate tool into operation. This meant that a sequence of operations could be performed on a single machine without the need to replace the cutting tool between each operation.

The interchangeable system of manufacture, known in the nineteenth century as the 'American System', was pioneered in the US by Eli Whitney and others. This system was the origin of today's mass-production techniques, and it was based on the idea of assembling articles from standardized components.

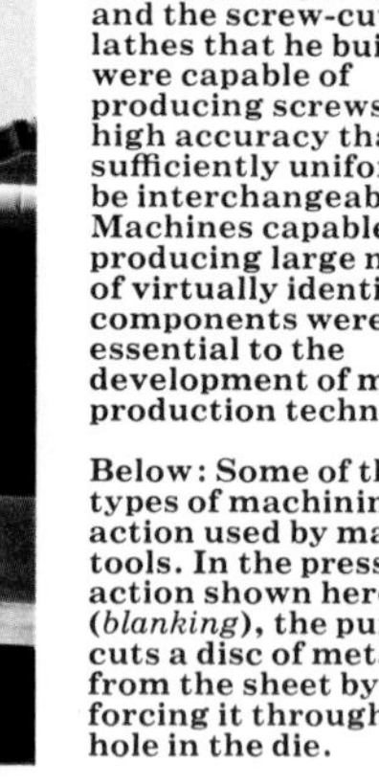

Michael Holford

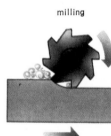

Left: A lathe built in 1810 by Henry Maudslay (1771-1831). Maudslay was a pioneer of precision engineering, and the screw-cutting lathes that he built were capable of producing screws of high accuracy that were sufficiently uniform to be interchangeable. Machines capable of producing large numbers of virtually identical components were essential to the development of mass production techniques.

Below: Some of the types of machining action used by machine tools. In the pressing action shown here (*blanking*), the punch cuts a disc of metal from the sheet by forcing it through the hole in the die.

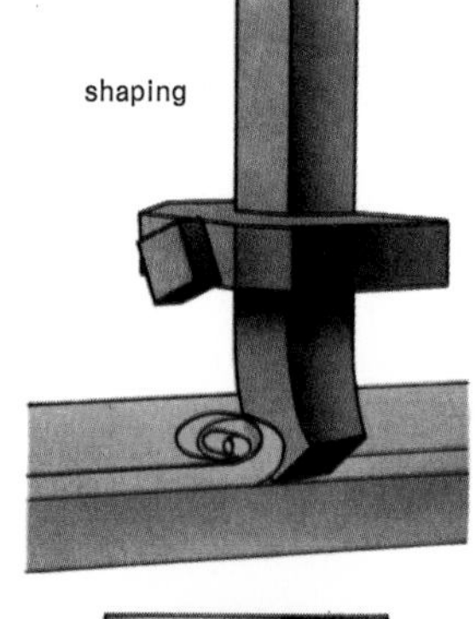

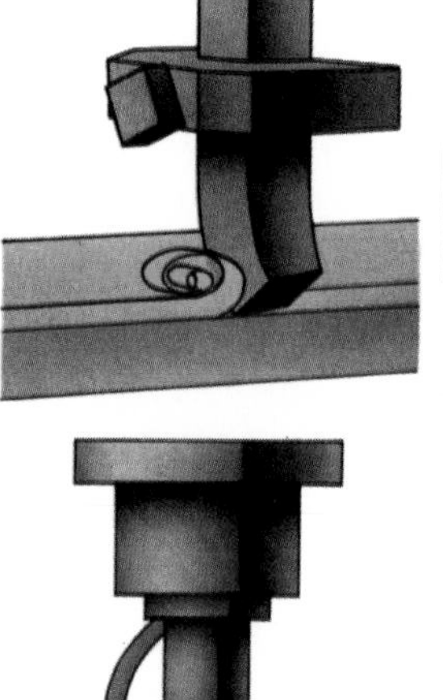

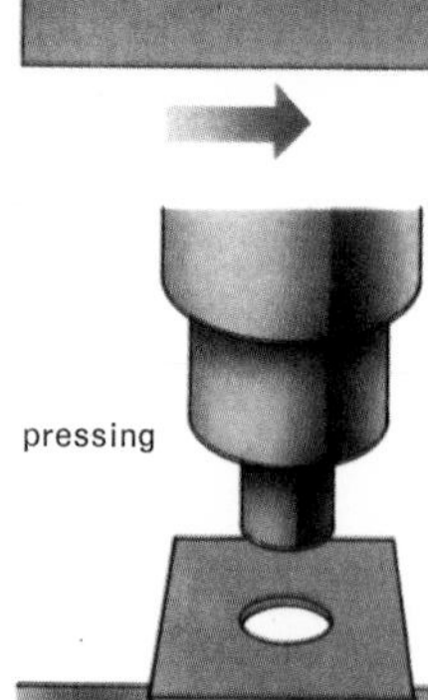

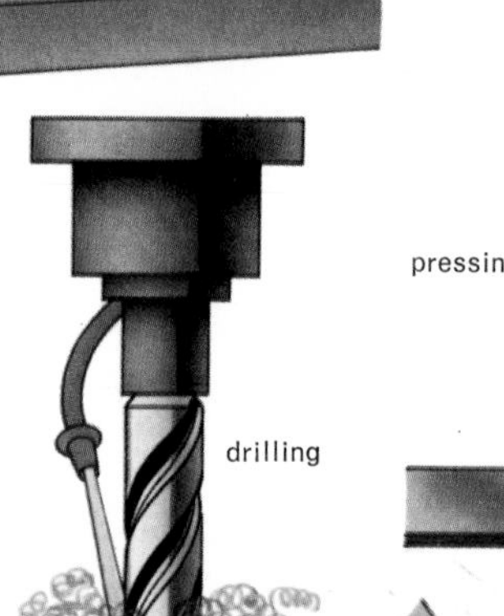

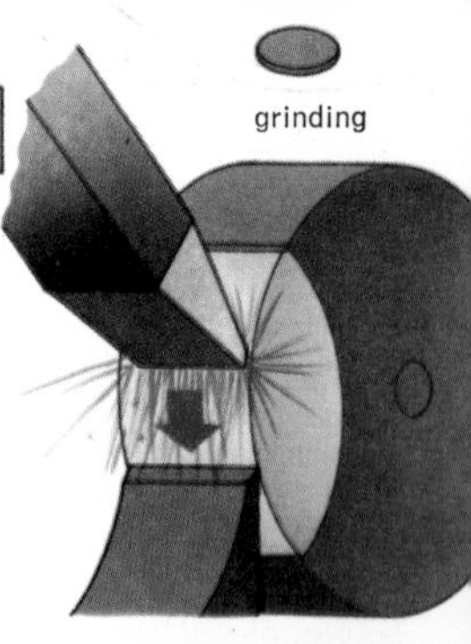

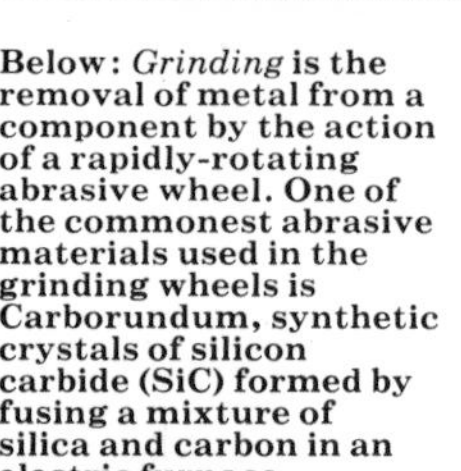

Alfred Herbert Ltd

Above: When metal parts are being machined, as on this turret lathe, streams of *cutting fluid* are directed on to the cutting points to dissipate the heat generated and provide lubrication. This protects both the tools and the machined part and reduces the chance of breakage. The fluids are usually oil-based.

Below: The mass production of cluster gears for automobile gearboxes. At the top of the picture a gear has just been cut by a rapidly-rotating cutter, which is itself shaped like a large gear. This type of machine, known as a *gear shaper*, is widely used for rapid and economic gear production.

Alfred Herbert Ltd

Below: *Grinding* is the removal of metal from a component by the action of a rapidly-rotating abrasive wheel. One of the commonest abrasive materials used in the grinding wheels is Carborundum, synthetic crystals of silicon carbide (SiC) formed by fusing a mixture of silica and carbon in an electric furnace.

Rolls Royce

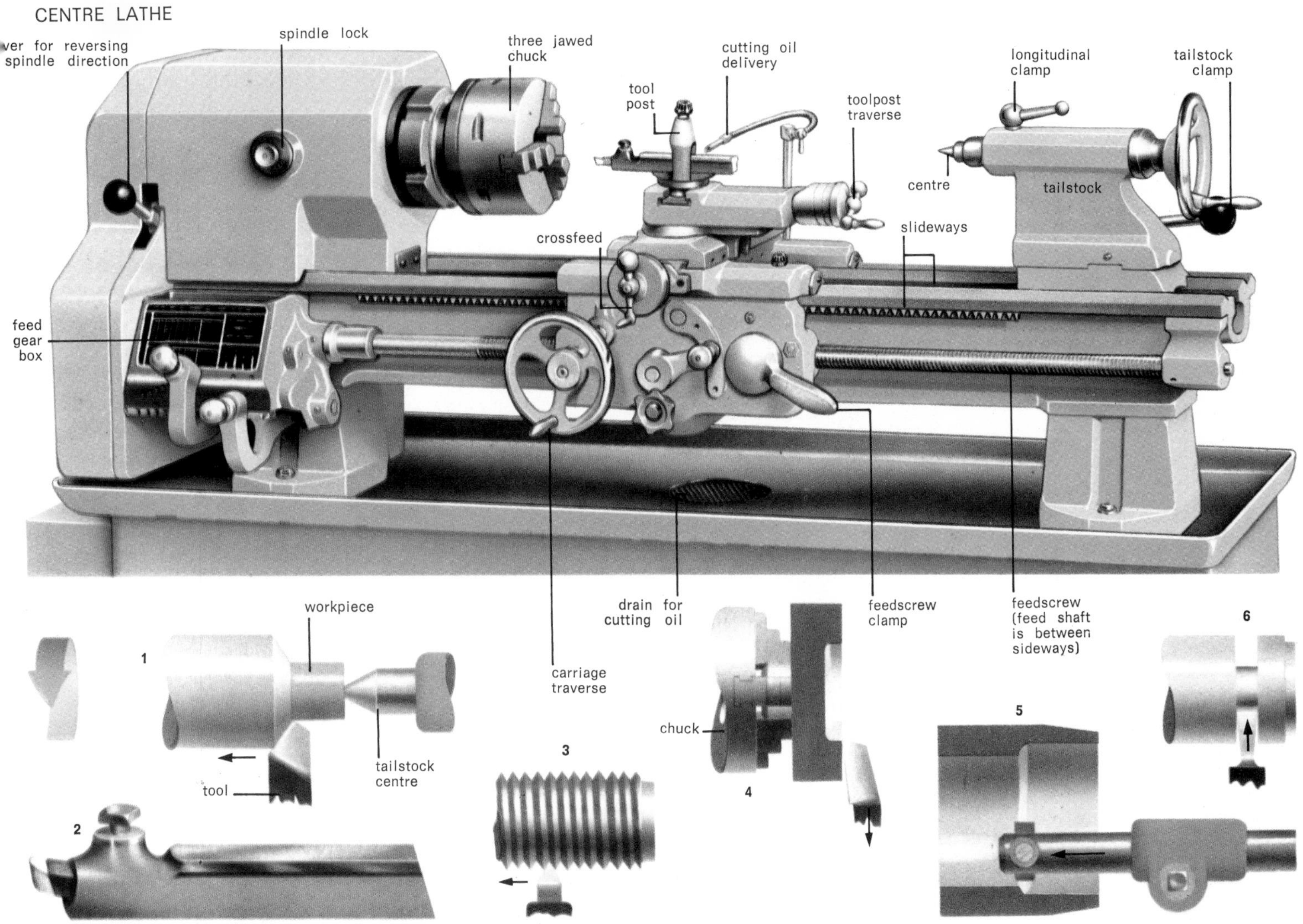

CENTRE LATHE

ver for reversing spindle direction
spindle lock
three jawed chuck
tool post
cutting oil delivery
toolpost traverse
longitudinal clamp
tailstock clamp
centre
tailstock
slideways
crossfeed
feed gear box
workpiece
drain for cutting oil
feedscrew clamp
feedscrew (feed shaft is between sideways)
carriage traverse
chuck
tool
tailstock centre
1
2
3
4
5
6

Above: A centre lathe, and some of the cutting operations that can be done on it: 1. straight cutting; 2. a tool holder and cutting tool; 3. thread cutting—speed of workpiece and motion of tool determine thread pitch; 4. facing off—cutting a flat face on the end of the workpiece; 5. boring—tool advances within rotating workpiece, cutting inner surface; 6. cutting a machined component from the unmachined bar. A lathe of this type, in common with most other machine tools, would be driven by an electric motor.

Below: Turning the barrel of a large gun.

Keystone

Lathes

The basic type of lathe is the *centre lathe*, which is used for operations such as machining or *turning* cylindrical components and for cutting screw threads on them. The workpiece is rotated horizontally while the cutting tool is drawn along it by the *feed* mechanism of the machine.

On a typical centre lathe, the workpiece is held in a chuck mounted on the *headstock* at the left-hand end of the machine. The headstock contains the gearing which transmits the drive from an electric motor to the chuck. At the other end of the machine is an adjustable *tailstock* which can be used to support the right-hand end of a long workpiece during turning.

The cutting tool is clamped in a *toolpost* mounted on a *carriage* assembly, which moves on slideways along the *bed* of the lathe between the headstock and the tailstock, and is driven along the bed by a *leadscrew*. A workpiece can be drilled longitudinally by fitting a drill bit to the tailstock in place of the pointed *centre* which it normally carries.

On *turret lathes* and *capstan lathes*, the tailstock is replaced by a turret assembly, usually hexagonal, to which several different tools can be fitted. This means that several operations, such as drilling and thread-cutting, can be performed in sequence by *indexing* (rotating) the turret to bring each tool on it into operation in turn. The turret of a capstan lathe is mounted on a short slide, which is carried on a base that can be positioned at a convenient point on the bed. On a turret lathe, however, the turret is mounted directly on a saddle which moves along the bed itself.

Other types of lathe include the *vertical borer*, a large machine which operates vertically instead of horizontally and is used for boring and turning large castings, and the *automatic bar lathes*, which machine components from long bars of metal fed in through the hollow chuck spindle of the headstock and held in place by the chuck. As each component is finished it is separated from the bar, which is then fed forward into the machine ready for the next component to be machined from it.

Milling machines

Milling machines are used for metal-shaping operations such as cutting grooves and slots. Unlike a lathe, on which the workpiece is rotated while a stationary tool is brought into contact with it, a milling machine uses a rotating tool which cuts the metal away while the workpiece is moved beneath it. When the workpiece is moved in the opposite direction to that in which the teeth of the cutter are moving when they contact it, the action is known as *up-cutting*. If the teeth and the workpiece are moving in the same direction, the milling action is *down-cutting*.

Milling machines can be divided into two general classes: those on which the cutter is mounted on a horizontal spindle and is shaped rather like a wheel with cutting teeth around its edge, and those on which the spindle is vertical and the cutter is roughly cylindrical with teeth cut into its sides and often on its end. Some of the vertical machines have an *offset* milling head which can move the spindle in an arc while it is rotating the

Right: The motor industry is one of the largest users of machine tools, and a high degree of automation is used in the production of the components.

Below: This press can exert a pressure of up to 60,000 tonnes, and can be adapted to a variety of production processes. This type of press was originally designed for the production of synthetic diamonds, a process requiring high pressure and temperature, but its applications now include the pressing of complicated sheet-metal components, and the production of special steels for high-speed cutting tools by the compaction of powdered metal. This technique, known as *powder metallurgy*, can produce tool steels of a very high quality.

Ford Motor Co Ltd

ASEA

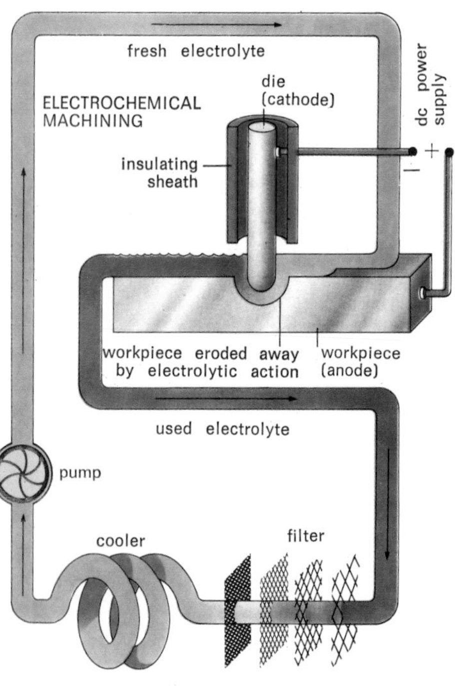

Above: In the *electrochemical machining* (ECM) process a current is passed between a die and the workpiece through a suitable electrolyte. Metal from the workpiece combines with the electrolyte to form ions, which are carried away by the electrolyte. The workpiece is thus eroded away, the shape of the eroded area corresponding to the profile of the die.

Below: A complete ECM machine.

Healy of Leicester Ltd

tool. This means that the machine can cut irregularly-shaped holes if required.

Jig bores, also known as *mill bores* or *boring mills*, are large, versatile milling machines. The horizontal spindle can be moved up or down and in or out, and the workpiece can be moved in the same way as on an ordinary milling machine. They are used for machining large workpieces, such as heavy machinery castings.

Shapers and planers

Shapers and planers are used to remove metal from flat surfaces. On a shaper, the workpiece is held stationary, and the cutting tool is driven across it by a mechanical or hydraulic ram. The tool is lifted clear of the workpiece during the return strokes. Planers are much larger than shapers, and so can handle larger workpieces. On a planer, the tool is stationary and the workpiece is held on a reciprocating table that moves it backwards and forwards beneath the tool.

Other machine tools

The machine tools mentioned above are only a few of the multitude now in use. Others include drills, grinders, machines for cutting gears, and *machining centres*. A machining centre is a machine tool which carries a wide range of tools that enable it to carry out, under automatic control, a sequence of operations such as drilling, thread-cutting and milling.

Many specialized machines have been developed for production-line work where high output rates are required. These units comprise a series of *machine stations*, each of which is tooled up to perform a specific machining function such as drilling or milling. The component to be machined, such as an engine's cylinder block, is passed automatically to each station in turn until the complete sequence of operations has been completed.

One of the automatic control systems for machine tools is known as *numerical control*. The instructions for the machine tool, such as tool positions, cutting speeds and operating sequences, are recorded as numerical and symbolic codes on a storage medium such as paper tape, punched cards or magnetic tape. The coded instructions are read by a control unit, which activates the machine functions in accordance with the instructions. The use of numerical control means that machine tools can be programmed to operate at their most efficient, with a consequent reduction in production times and cost.

A simpler form of automatic control is *plugboard control*. The plugboard consists of a grid of holes in a circuit board, each horizontal row representing a particular machine function. The control unit scans the plugboard one vertical column at a time; if a plug has been inserted into one of the holes, the function that the hole represents will be activated when the column is scanned.

A further type of control, *tracer control*, involves the use of a template or a three-dimensional model of the component to be produced. A mechanically or electrically driven probe is moved around the template or model, following its contours. As the probe moves, a servomechanism makes the cutting tool move in exactly the same way, so that the workpiece is machined to the same shape as the model or template.

Welding

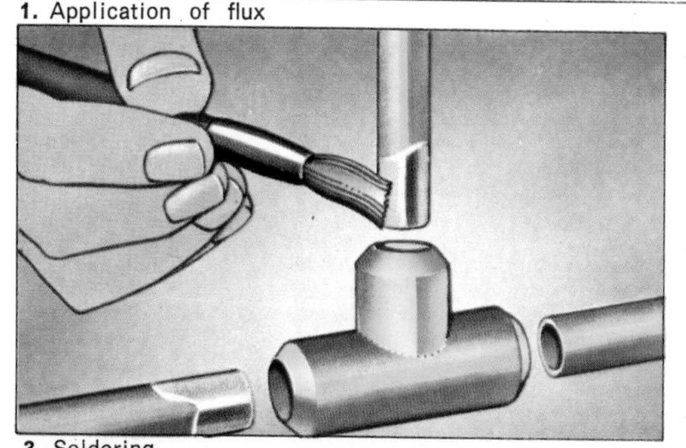

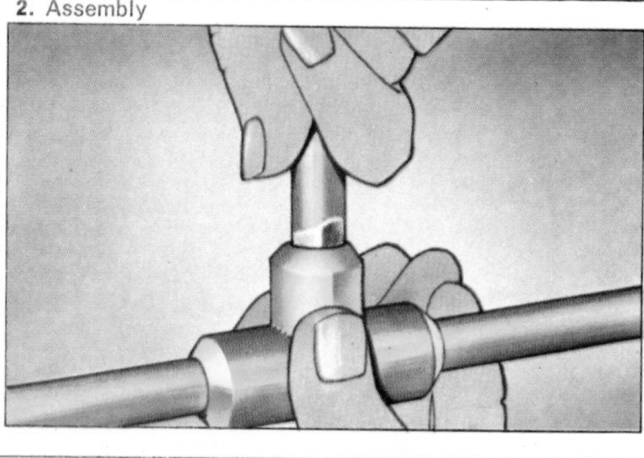

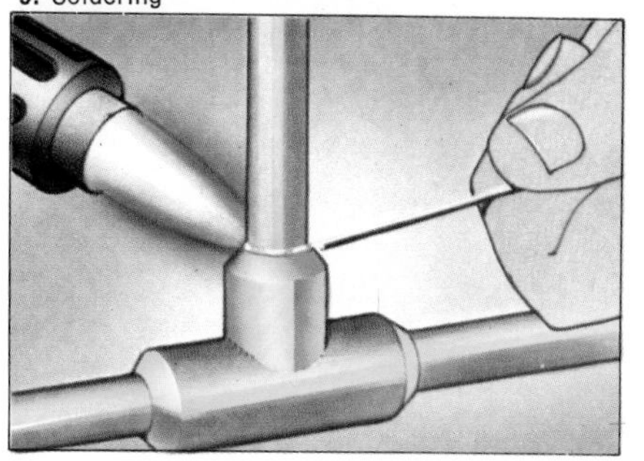

Welding is the joining together of two pieces of metal by means of heat, pressure, or by a combination of both. Early examples of welding include a forge-welded headrest which belonged to the Pharaoh Tutankhamun and was made in about 1350 BC, and a hammer-welded gold sheet produced in Ireland in about 1000 BC. An early example of a joint made by brazing, which is a similar process to welding, is a decorated copper panel made in Mesopotamia before 3000 BC.

Gas welding and cutting

Gas welding is a common form of welding in which the surfaces to be joined are melted, usually together with a *filler metal*, by the flame from a torch burning a mixture of oxygen and a fuel gas such as acetylene or propane. The oxygen and the fuel gas are fed to the torch from separate cylinders, and flame temperatures of around 3,000°C (5,430°F) are produced.

Oxy-acetylene torches are also used for cutting through materials, particularly ferrous metals such as steel or cast iron. When ferrous metals are being cut, the cutting process involves not only a melting away of the material by the high temperature of the flame, but also a certain amount of actual burning of the metal because of its strong chemical affinity for the oxygen in the gas jet. In addition to this chemical reaction there

Above: Soldering three copper tubes to a tee-joint. The ends of the tube are coated with flux, and then the tubes and joint are assembled. Each tube is then soldered into place by heating with a blowtorch and applying the solder wire, which melts and is drawn into the join.

Right: In *reflow soldering*, an electrode is placed on either side of the joint, then an electric current is passed between them and through the joint, heating the joint so that the solder melts. The third probe in this picture is a thermocouple that controls the current flow.

Below: Four important welding processes: gas, submerged arc, plasma-arc and laser welding.

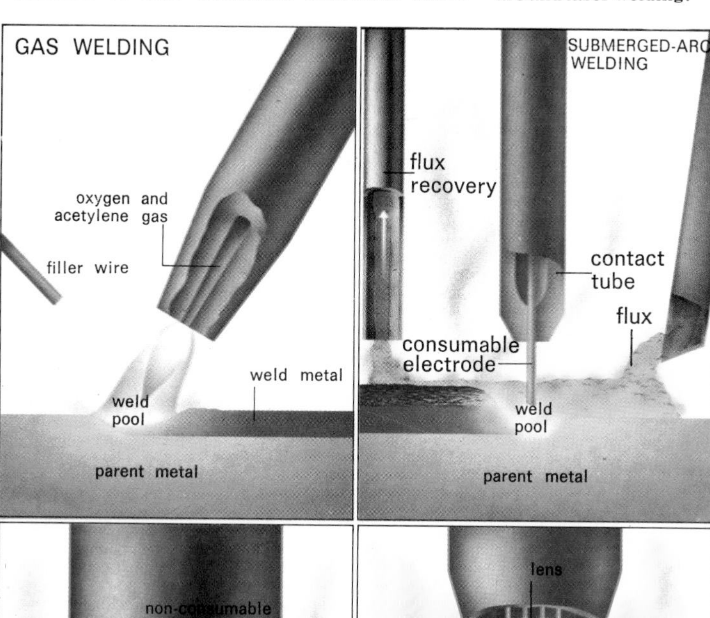

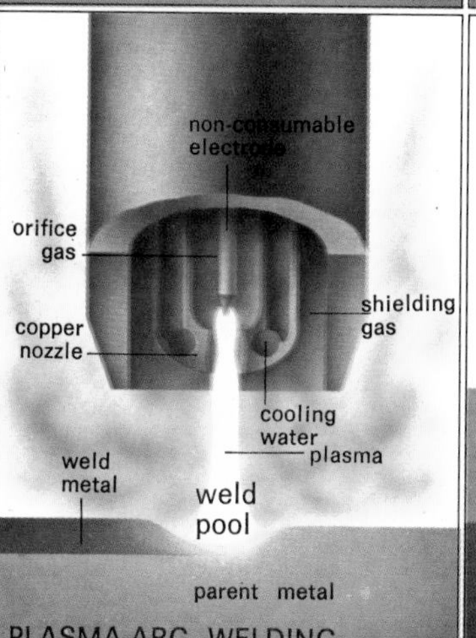

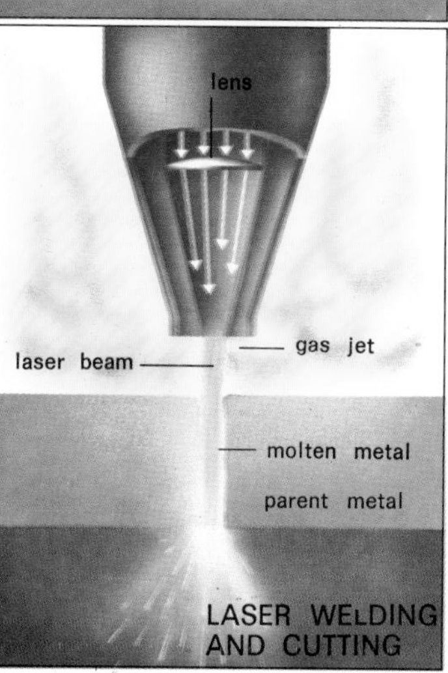

Below: Repairing the bucket of an excavator by gas welding.

Welding Institute

Above: Two cylindrical components being joined by *friction welding*. One component is rotated at high speed, and then pressed against the other, which is held stationary. The resulting friction generates a great deal of heat, which melts the ends of the components. When sufficient melting has occurred, the fixed component is released so that it can rotate with the moving one, and the joint then cools and solidifies.

Right: A joint produced by *explosive welding*, in which components are forced together by explosives and the heat and pressure of the impact welds them together.

International Research & Development Co. Ltd.

Above: Electron beam welding, which is carried out in a vacuum chamber, uses the energy contained in a beam of electrons to generate the heat required to melt the metal. This picture shows a 25 kW beam melting through a 3.8 cm (1.5 in) thick tube made of stainless steel.

Below: An electron beam welding unit. Electrons from an electron gun, 1, pass through a focusing system, 3, on to the workpiece, which is carried on a servo-controlled trolley, 5. A vacuum system is connected to the side of the chamber, 4, and the operator can view the workpiece through an optical system, 2.

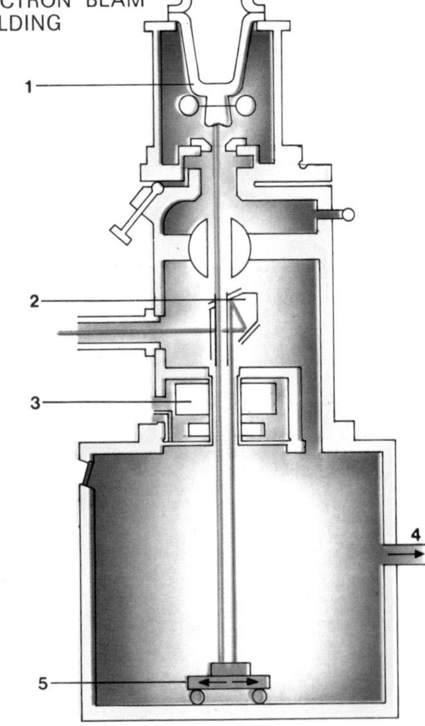

is an extremely important mechanical eroding effect produced by the kinetic energy of the flame, which blows molten material and oxidized metal away from the cut.

Brazing

Gas torches are also used in *brazing*, a process in which the metals to be joined are heated to above about 400°C (750°F) and a non-ferrous filler metal is melted into the junction between them. The filler metals used in brazing have lower melting points than those of the metals that they are used to join.

Brazing in its simplest form is carried out using an oxy-fuel gas torch similar to that used for oxy-acetylene welding. *Silver-alloy* brazing, one of the most common forms, is used in the silverware industry and for making joints where strength and resistance to shock are required, such as in the joining of band-saw blades. The filler metals used contain from 10 to 80 per cent of silver, with 50 to 15 per cent copper and 40 to 5 per cent zinc. They are often known as *silver solders*, but they should not be confused with the metals used for *soft soldering*, the type of soldering used for making connections in electronic circuits. The silver solders melt at between about 700 and 875°C (1,290 and 1,600°F), whereas soft solders melt at around 200°C (390°F) or even less.

Brazing can also be carried out by heating the workpieces, together with the filler metal, in a gas-fired or electrical furnace, or by immersing them in a bath of molten salt. Whichever method is used, however, it is imperative that the surfaces to be joined are completely clean. They must be degreased, and any oxide or scale must be removed chemically or mechanically. The cleaned surfaces must then be protected by a film of *flux*, a material which prevents the formation of a film of oxide on the surfaces during the brazing. One of the oldest and most commonly used flux materials is *borax*, which is hydrated sodium borate ($Na_2B_4O_7.10H_2O$). In certain instances the filler metal must also be protected by a coating of flux.

Arc welding

In *arc welding* the heat required is produced by an electric arc struck between an electrode and the workpiece. One of the most versatile forms of this is *manual arc welding*. The electrode holder is connected to one terminal of a power source, such as a motor-driven generator, a transformer or a transformer-rectifier, and the workpiece is connected to the other terminal. The electrode is typically about 36 or 46 cm (14 or 18 in) long, consisting of a filler metal wire core coated with a layer of flux.

The power is turned on, and the end of the electrode is brought to the workpiece so that an electric arc is struck between them. The heat generated by the arc melts at the join and at the tip of the electrode, and metal and flux from the electrode are drawn across the arc to the workpiece.

Manual arc welding equipment is, in general, inexpensive and portable, and can be used in a workshop or out of doors, for example in a shipyard or on a construction site. It is, however, limited in some respects; for instance, because each electrode is relatively short, only small lengths of weld can be made with each one, necessitating frequent stopping and starting.

A process designed to overcome many of the limitations of manual arc welding is the *gas metal arc* process, which includes CO_2 welding and *metal inert gas* welding. Instead of using a short length of wire coated with flux, the electrode wire is fed from a continuous roll, and the join is shielded from the oxidizing effects of the atmosphere by surrounding it with a suitable gas or gas mixture.

In this process, the electrode wire passes through a heavy-duty welding gun and is surrounded by gas supplied from a cylinder. An arc is then struck between the wire and the workpiece, and a droplet of molten metal forms on the end of the wire. This drop is detached

Rolls Royce Ltd

Plascut Ltd

Above: In plasma-arc welding, the arc ionizes a jet of gas to form a very hot stream of *plasma* that is directed on to the workpiece. The nozzle of the gun concentrates the arc and plasma into a very narrow stream, and this results in very high arc temperatures of up to 30,000°C (54,000°F).

Above right: A plasma-arc cutting machine. Two arcs are produced by plasma-arc cutting and welding torches: one, the *non-transferred* arc, is within the nozzle and creates the initial ionization of the gas; the other, the *transferred* arc, is carried in the plasma jet to the workpiece.

power source for transferred arc
power source for non-transferred arc
PLASMA CUTTING TORCH
carbon electrode
gas
torch body
ionized gas stream
non-transferred arc
transferred arc

FLAME CUTTING TORCH
heating oxygen inlet
inlet
cutting oxygen inlet
injector
mixing chamber
heating jet
cutting jet

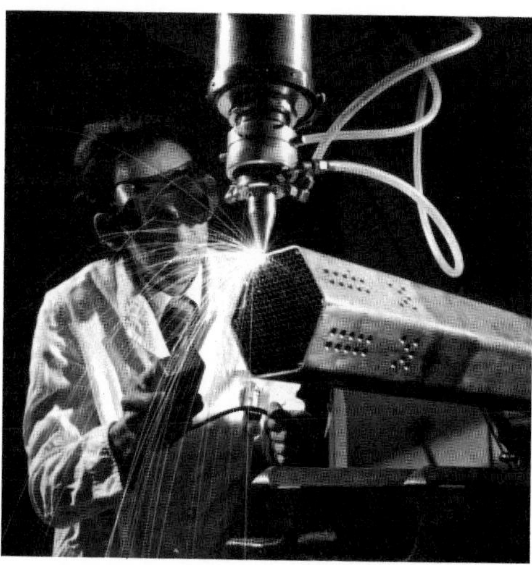

UKAEA

Left: Using a laser beam cutter to trim the outer skin of a nuclear fuel canister without damaging the interior structure.

Above: Sectional drawings of the nozzles of a plasma-arc cutting torch, left, and an oxygen-fuel gas cutting torch.

from the electrode and transferred to the workpiece by the arc, drops of metal being formed and transferred at a rate of about 200 times per second.

The gases used include argon, helium, and argon-helium mixture (for metal inert gas welding) and carbon dioxide for CO_2 welding. The inert gases give a better weld finish than that produced with a carbon dioxide shield, but their cost is much higher. This difference can be overcome by using a tubular electrode filled with flux instead of a solid electrode wire. This flux-cored wire can be used, depending on the composition of the flux, with a carbon dioxide shield or with no gas shield at all.

The flux-cored wire enables higher rates of metal deposition to be achieved with a lower heat input, thereby reducing the risk of distortion of the workpiece. A further advantage of these 'gasless' flux-cored wires is that when welding in exposed positions, such as on a bridge or on the top of an oil rig, there is no gas shield to be blown away.

Another process using a continuous wire electrode is *submerged arc welding*. This process is carried out with one or more welding heads mounted on special carriages, and a hopper placed just in front of the electrode deposits a layer of flux on the workpiece. The arc is struck beneath this loose blanket of flux, hence the name of the process.

Other important forms of arc welding are *tungsten inert gas* welding and *plasma-arc* welding. In tungsten inert gas welding, heat is produced by an arc struck between a non-consumable tungsten electrode and the workpiece. The electrode, arc, weld pool, and the adjacent heated areas of the workpiece are protected from contamination by a stream of gas such as argon or helium.

The process is best suited to the welding of thin materials, and although many of its applications are for the production of *autogenous* welds (where the workpiece is welded by melting together just the two abutting surfaces without a filler), some now involve the use of a separate filler wire which is fed into the weld pool by hand. Tungsten inert gas welding is finding an increasing number of applications in areas such as nuclear engineering and the aerospace industry.

Plasma-arc welding is similar to tungsten inert gas welding, but the arc used is constricted by a narrow nozzle just beneath the electrode. This has the effect of concentrating the arc and of increasing the velocity of the gas flow, which also passes through the nozzle. The gas becomes a stream of electrically-charged atoms (or *ions*) which is known as a *plasma*, and temperatures as high as 30,000°C (54,000°F) may be reached. The process can be used with very thin as well as thick materials, and the high arc temperatures allow a wide range of metals to be welded, including stainless steel, aluminium and titanium. The plasma-arc principle is also used for the cutting of sheet metals.

Resistance welding

The heat for *resistance* welding is produced by an electric current which is passed through the workpiece. Much of the heat generated is dissipated by the water-cooled electrodes used, so that the melting is confined to the area of the joint. Major applications of *resistance spot welding* include the production of car bodies and of domestic equipment such as washing machines.

Resistance seam welding is an extension of spot welding, but the pieces to be welded are joined by continuous seams of welding rather than by a series of spot-welds. The electrodes which pass the current through the workpiece are in the form of a pair of wheels, as opposed to the two rods used in spot welding. Typical applications include the welding of the gutter channels on to car roof panels, and the production of tubes.

Telephone and Telegraph

Michael Holford

The technology of telecommunications is concerned with the transmission and reception of information using electricity and electromagnetic waves (such as light and radio waves). It involves many different disciplines from electrical engineering to electronics, signal analysis and information theory. The information itself may be printed news, speech, television pictures or telegraphic messages.

The early telegraph

The basic components of a telegraphic system, such as sources of direct (dc) current (batteries), electromagnets (solenoids) and current-carrying metal wires, all existed by about 1830. Of the numerous designs invented during this period, many were concerned with methods for displaying the characters (letters, numbers and punctuation) at the receiver after their transmission in an electrical form.

One of the most important telegraph systems of the nineteenth century was that invented in America by an artist called Samuel Morse. The Morse telegraph was attractive because of its simplicity—requiring only one wire (and a return) for the transmission of any character. Each character was represented by a combination of two simple signals: a dot (short burst of current) and a dash (a current of longer duration). The complexity of each coded character was chosen according to its frequency of use. Thus, for example, the most common English letter, 'e', is a single dot, while an 's' is three dots and an 'o' three dashes. The international distress call 'SOS' is simply · · · – – – · · ·.

Automatic telegraphy

The speed and accuracy of the Morse system was determined by the operator's skill rather than any technical limitations of the apparatus itself, and with the growth of telegraphic traffic, ways of using existing telegraph lines more efficiently were sought.

Frequency division multiplexing

Top: A replica of a 19th-century Morse telegraph receiver.

Above: *Frequency division multiplexing,* a method of sending more than one message simultaneously down a single wire by superimposing each one on to a different carrier frequency, was first suggested by Elisha Gray in the late 19th century. These diagrams show a carrier wave (top) and a carrier wave modulated by a Morse code signal of one dot and three dashes; this gives one short and three long pulses.

Bell Labs

Above: Bell's telephone transmitter (left) and receiver (right) which on 10 March 1876 carried the first sentence ever spoken over a telephone. The sentence, spoken by Bell to his assistant Thomas Watson, was 'Mr Watson, come here; I want you.'

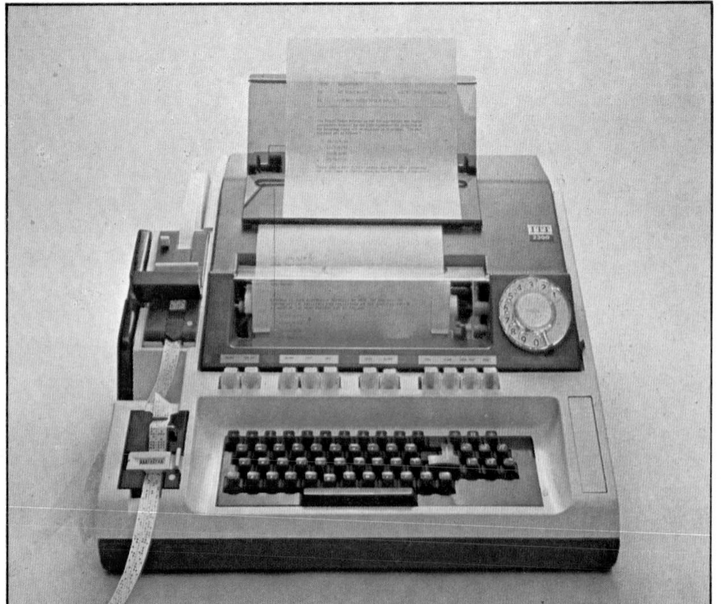

ITT

Left: A teleprinter produces electrical pulses, based on a 5-unit code, which represent the various characters typed by the operator. These pulses are transmitted to the receiving teleprinter, which decodes them and types out the message.

Right: This chart shows the international code used for punched paper tape telegraphy, plus the Morse code. The patterns of holes in the tape code mean either letters, or other characters and instructions, depending on whether they were preceded by a 'letters' or a 'figures' code.

combination nos	Figures & symbols	tape channels 5	4	3		2	1	letters	Morse Code
1	—				•	•	•	A	● –
2	?	•	•		•		•	B	– ● ● ●
3	:		•	•	•	•		C	– ● – ●
4	who are you		•		•		•	D	– ● ●
5	3				•		•	E	●
6	(optional)		•	•	•		•	F	● ● – ●
7	(optional)	•	•		•	•		G	– – ●
8	(optional)	•		•	•			H	● ● ● ●
9	8			•	•	•		I	● ●
10	bell		•		•	•	•	J	● – – –
11	(		•	•	•	•	•	K	– ● –
12	)	•			•	•		L	● – ● ●
13	.	•	•	•	•			M	– –
14	,		•	•	•			N	– ●
15	9	•	•		•			O	– – –
16	0	•		•	•	•		P	● – – ●
17	1	•		•	•	•	•	Q	– – ● –
18	4		•		•	•		R	● – ●
19	'			•	•		•	S	● ● ●
20	5	•			•			T	–
21	7			•	•	•	•	U	● ● –
22	—	•	•	•	•	•		V	● ● ● –
23	2	•			•	•	•	W	● – –
24	1	•	•	•	•		•	X	– ● ● –
25	6	•		•	•		•	Y	– ● – –
26	+	•			•		•	Z	– – ● ●
27	carriage return		•		•				
28	line feed				•	•			
29	letters	•	•	•	•	•	•		
30	figures	•	•		•	•	•		
31	space			•	•				
32	all space				•				

Punched paper tape code and Morse code

Telephone exchange systems, showing the transition from hard wired stage (left) through integrated circuits (mid 1970's) to large scale integration (late 1970's). The exchange on the right has a capacity 16 times greater than the hard wired circuit.

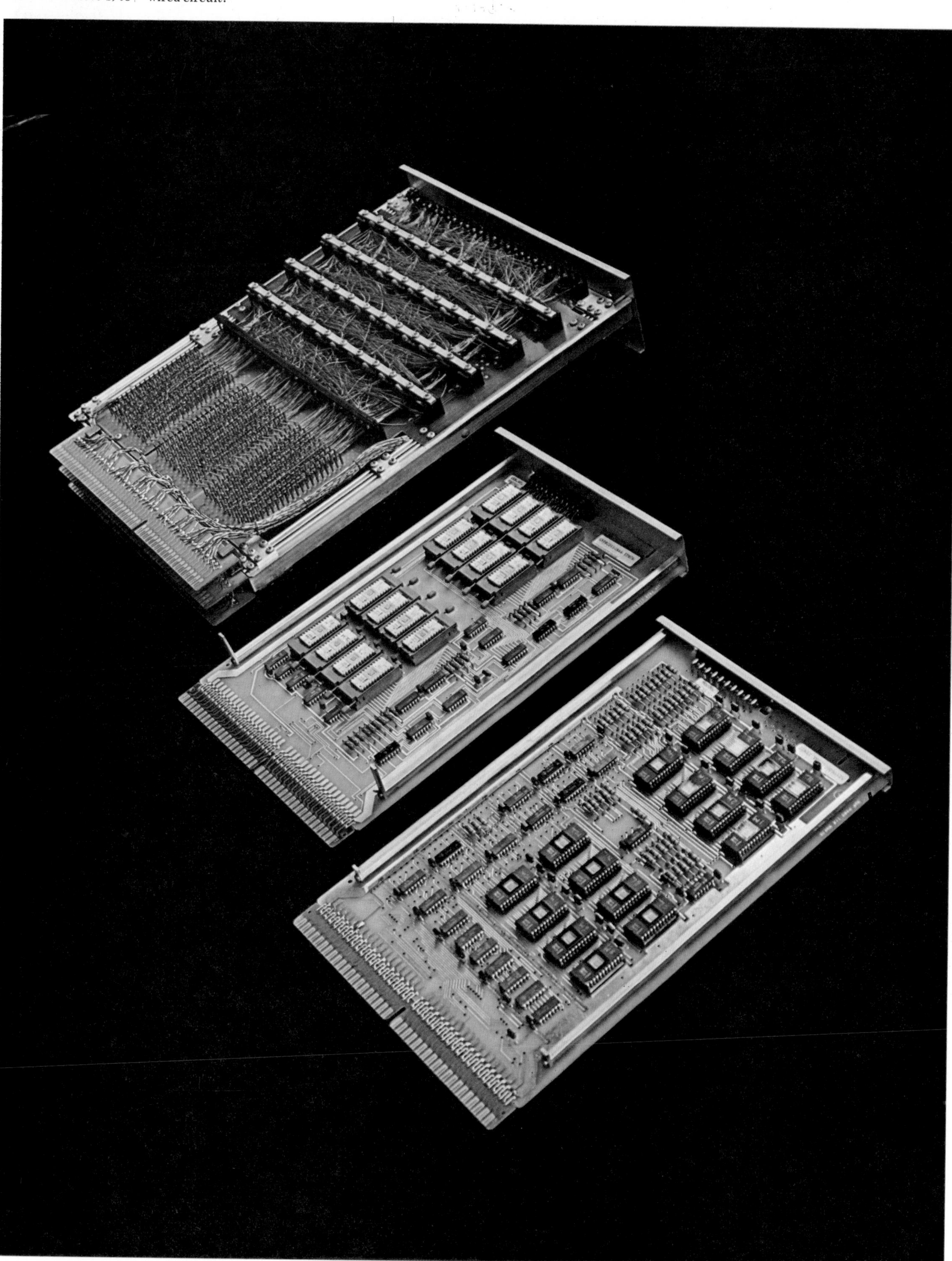

Paul Brierley

Charles Wheatstone provided a simple solution to this problem by designing a mechanical Morse sender which converted messages, stored in the form of holes punched in paper tape, into electrical pulses. At the receiver, an inker recorded these pulses on another reel of paper. The speed limitation of this device was determined solely by the reading and recording speeds of the terminal equipment. Whereas an expert Morse operator could send only 30 to 35 words a minute, the paper tape system could transmit at speeds up to 600 words per minute.

Above: A telephone with its casing and handset removed. One of the two bell gongs, and part of the electromagnet that operates the hammer which strikes the gongs, are visible below the dial.

Right: These diagrams show a simplified telephone mouthpiece and earpiece, and an exploded view of a dial mechanism. The cam opens and closes the dial contacts to produce the dialling pulses as the dial returns to its rest position.

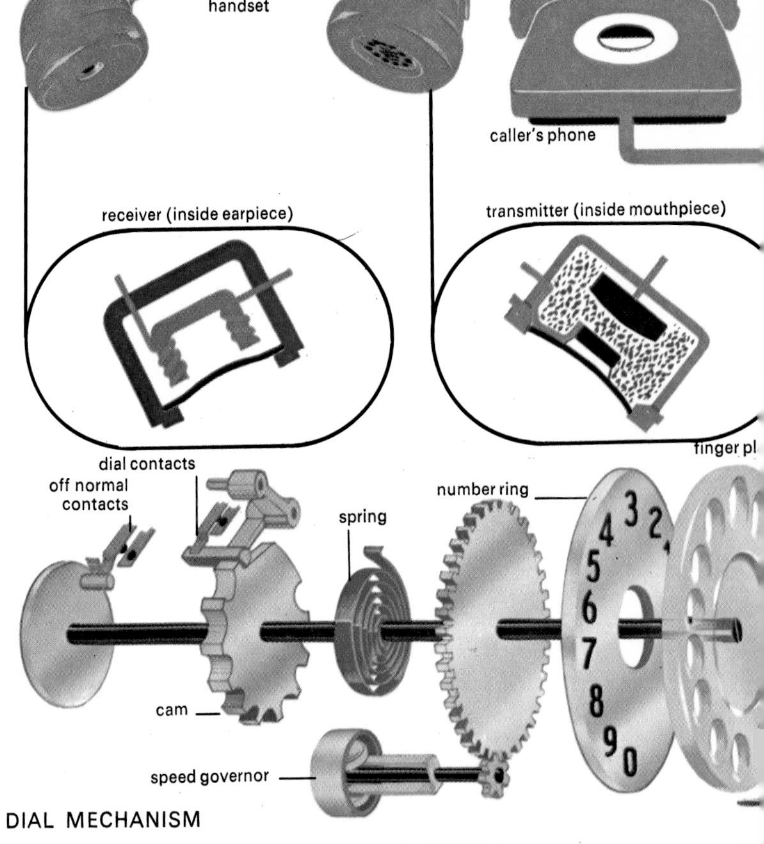

The telephone

Although others before him had succeeded in using electricity to transmit sounds and musical notes over a wire, in 1876 Edinburgh-born Alexander Graham Bell was the first to patent a device capable of sending and receiving recognisable words. While the device worked well as a receiver, its performance as a transmitter was less successful.

An improved transmitter was developed almost simultaneously by Edison and Hunnings in 1878. This was the *carbon granule transmitter*. The modern version consists of an aluminium alloy diaphragm which is attached to a dome-shaped piece of carbon, anchored in such a way as to be free to move in and out of another cup-shaped piece of carbon, filled with carbon granules. Electrical connections are made to the carbon electrodes at the front and back and the current flows from one, through the granules, to the other. The rapid changes of air pressure set up by speech cause the granules to be alternately compressed and released, so altering their electrical resistance. The current flowing through the granules thus fluctuates in the same way as the air pressure, so that the original sound can be faithfully reproduced at the distant end.

Bell's original earpiece worked on the principles of a combined permanent magnet and electromagnet acting on an iron diaphragm. A similar system is used in modern receivers, in which a thin metal diaphragm is made to vibrate by variations in the magnetic field of an electromagnet. These variations are set up by the varying electrical current carrying the incoming voice signal.

Telephone exchanges

The first telephone exchange opened in Connecticut, USA, in 1878, followed a year later by the first European exchange in Coleman Street in the City of London. The earliest exchanges were all manual, with operators physically placing and removing plugs to complete circuits. The first automatic telephone exchange was installed at La Porte, Indiana, USA, in 1892. It was based on a system invented in 1889 by Almon B. Strowger, an irascible American undertaker irritated by inefficient operators.

An automatic exchange is simply a set of apparatus to which all the telephones in a neighbourhood are connected, with a switching network that will interconnect any two of them. Interconnection is achieved by a series of signal pulses, transmitted by the dial mechanism of the sender's telephone, which control the switching network.

Strowger's invention consisted of a metal arm, rather like a windscreen wiper, which was driven around a series of numbered contacts (arranged in a semicircular form) by the dial pulses. The modern version of this *selector* is a two-motion type which first moves the wiper vertically to select one of ten sets of contacts, and then sweeps it in a horizontal arc to select one of the ten individual contacts in that set.

When dialling the first digit of a telephone number, say six, six pulses are sent to a *first selector* in the exchange. This makes the wiper move vertically to the contacts on the sixth level—corresponding to all telephones beginning with the number six. At this point it is necessary to find a *second selector* for handling the second telephone digit. To do this, the first selector wiper moves in a horizontal arc 'searching' for a free contact (and thus a free second selector). If the next digit dialled is 'two' the second selector wiper moves up to level two and then sweeps horizontally until a free third selector is found (corresponding to all telephone numbers beginning with 62). This third selector deals with the third digit (vertical

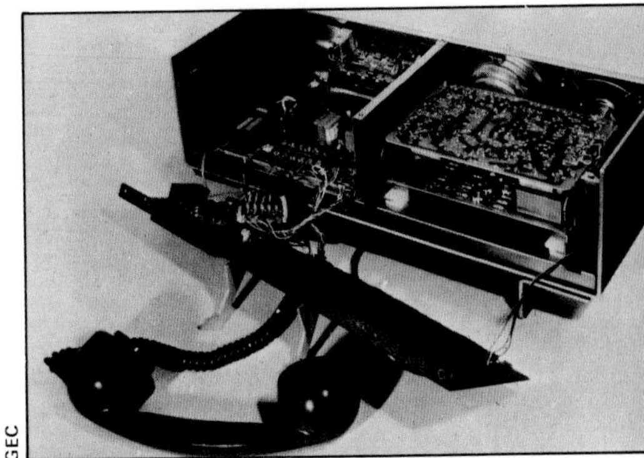

Above: A rear view of the inside of a loudspeaking telephone unit. This type of telephone puts the incoming speech through an amplifier and loudspeaker, and has a microphone at the front to pick up the user's voice. The handset is provided for use when confidential calls are being made.

Below: A telephone with a pushbutton dial instead of the conventional rotary type. The electronic unit shown next to it is the circuitry which produces the dialling pulses and transmits them to the exchange, leaving a pause between each set of pulses to allow the exchange equipment to operate.

cal exchange

international trunk exchange

repeater

multipair cable

air cable

The series of drawings along the top of this page and the following pages shows the route taken by an overseas telephone call, and details of some of the types of telephone cables used.

The local exchange (left) puts the call through to the trunk exchange (right) to which the international circuits are connected. The trunk exchange then routes the call to its destination country.

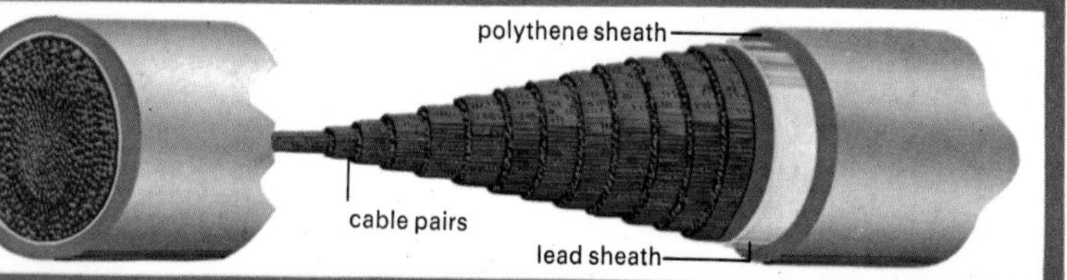

Above: The cables to which individual telephones are connected, and some connecting small local exchanges, are of the *multipair* type. Large multipair cables serving an area's telephones may contain up to 4,800 pairs of wires. The large cable is successively split off into smaller ones serving smaller groups of subscribers, and these smaller cables eventually terminate at *distribution points.* From these points, single-pair cables run to the subscribers' telephones. Multipair cables have aluminium or copper alloy conductors, insulated with paper or polythene.

Cable & Wireless

Right: Submarine telephone cable stored in the cable tanks of the cable-laying ship the CS *Mercury,* operated by Cable & Wireless Ltd. Fully laden, the *Mercury* can carry up to 1,930 km (1,200 miles) of cable, plus submarine repeater units. It can lay the cable at speeds of up to 5 knots.

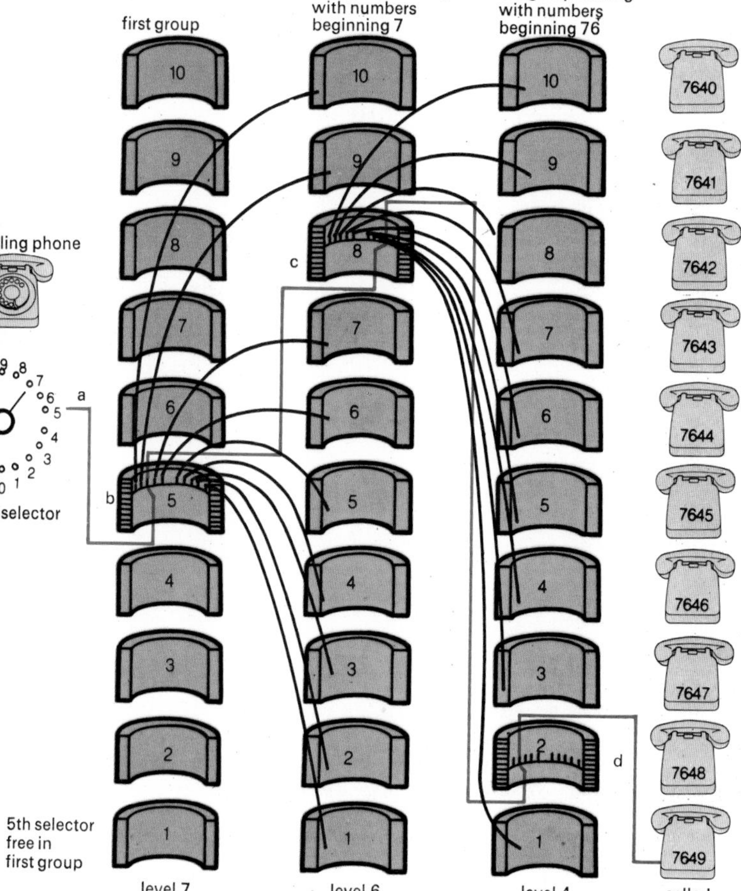

Above: The operation of a Strowger exchange. When a caller lifts the handset, the uniselector to which the phone is connected *a*, finds a free first selector, *b*. Other equipment then sends a dialling tone back to the phone, and the number required can then be dialled. If the first digit dialled is a '7', the first selector steps up to level 7, to which a 2nd selector group, which deals with all numbers beginning with 7, is connected. In this case, it finds that the 8th selector in that group, *c*, is free, and connects the call to it. When the '6' is dialled, this selector steps to level 6, which is connected to a 3rd group that deals with numbers beginning '76'. Finding the 2nd selector of this group, *d*, free, selector '*c*' connects with it. Dialling the final two digits steps selector '*d*' up to level 4 and round to contact 9, which is connected to the wires leading to phone 7649.

Plessey

Right: A uniselector switch used in Strowger exchange equipment. Each subscriber's phone has its own uniselector in the exchange; when the subscriber picks up the handset of the phone, the central part of the selector rotates so that the contacts it carries step around the fixed contacts, which are connected to other sets of selectors in the exchange, until it finds a set which is not in use. When a free set has been found, the dialling tone is transmitted to the subscriber's phone.

Below: Some of the complex wiring used in telephone exchanges to link up the various sections of the equipment. The wires are made of copper, with plastic insulation which is colour-coded. This makes it easier to identify a particular circuit when equipment is being installed, tested or repaired.

Plessey

international trunk exchange

repeater

coaxial cable

submarine coaxial cable

fibre optic link

Left: At the country of destination for an overseas call, the trunk exchange linked to the international cable routes the call to the local exchange (right) serving the called number.

The groups of digits dialled by the caller route the call as follows: dialling the USA from London, for example, '010' connects the caller (via the local exchange) with the international trunk exchange. A further '1' routes the call to the USA, and the next three digits route it to the city required, such as '305' for Miami. The remaining digits set up the final connection via the local exchange.

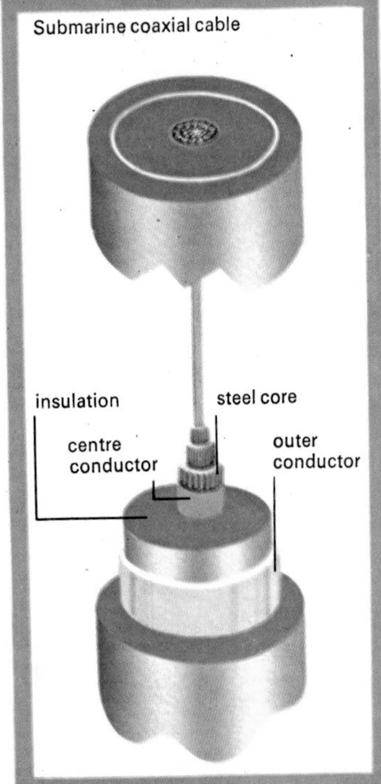

Multicore coaxial cable

coaxial core:
centre conductor
insulation
outer conductor
control pair
steel screening tape
lead sheath
polythene sheath

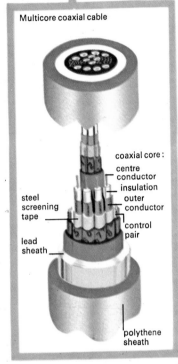

signal
modulator
laser source
optical fibre diameter 0.1 mm core diameter 0.05 mm
signal
demodulator
modulated light beam
photodiode

This diagram shows the principles of a new telecommunications technology called *fibre optics*, in which information is modulated onto a light beam transmitted along thin glass fibres.

Above: Light is a form of electromagnetic radiation. It has a very much higher frequency than radio or microwaves, but it can be modulated in a similar fashion. In a fibre optic system, the light from a laser is modulated by an information signal such as a telephone conversation. The modulated light is beamed into the inner core of the fibre, which has a higher refractive index than the outer cladding layer. The light is reflected from side to side along the fibre by the core/cladding interface which acts as a sort of pipe to carry the light along. At the receiving end, a photodiode produces an electrical output signal when the light strikes it, and this signal is demodulated to reproduce the original signal.

Below: This experiment simulates the passage of a laser beam along a fibre optic link, so that its attenuation can be measured.

movement) and fourth digit (horizontal movement) and at this point the required telephone is interconnected.

A *uniselector* precedes the first selector, and this hunts for a free first selector. Consequently, no selector 'belongs' to a particular telephone but can be allocated to one for the duration of the call. This reduces the amount of equipment necessary in an exchange—the only equipment which does belong to each telephone is the uniselector, and this is relatively simple and cheap. If at any stage a free selector cannot be found, or if the telephone sought is in use, an 'engaged' tone is transmitted to the sender.

Since Strowger's invention, other switching systems have been developed, some of them electro-mechanical and others electronic. In the electronic exchanges the switching is performed by electronic circuits which are faster, more compact and less prone to failure than electro-mechanical systems such as Strowger or the 'crossbar' system widely used in many countries.

Multiplexing techniques

If one pair of wires were necessary for every telephone conversation going on in the world then we would either be queuing to use the phone or the world would be a veritable maze of copper wires. These problems are avoided by the use of transmission methods known as *multiplexing*. These methods allow us to transmit hundreds and sometimes thousands of conversations along one pair of wires.

One common multiplexing method, *frequency multiplexing*, uses a similar technique to that used in radio transmission, where it is necessary to be able

Above left and above: Drawings of submarine and land *coaxial* cables. Coaxial cables can carry signals of a much higher frequency than can multipair cables, so multiplexing techniques employing high frequency carrier waves can be used on coaxial circuits. A submarine cable such as this one would be capable of carrying up to 4,000 simultaneous telephone calls. The multicore land coaxial cable shown here could carry up to 16,200 telephone circuits, using carrier frequencies of up to 12.5 MHz with repeaters spaced at intervals of 2 km (1.24 miles). The paper-insulated control pairs are used for system control purposes.

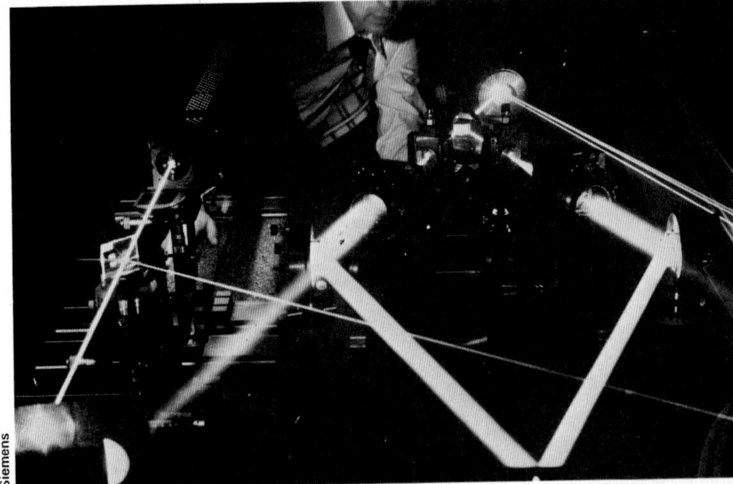

Siemens

Julian Barnard/John Watney

Left: One of the services provided by most telephone systems is the 'speaking clock'. The time announcements are put together from phrases recorded in tracks on a rotating, magnetically-coated drum. The drum is 'read' by sets of pick-up heads controlled by timing cams.

Right: The Transaction Telephone is used for automatic verification of credit card transactions. Two cards are inserted into the machine: a dialling card which instructs it to dial the computer at the credit company's data centre, and the customer's credit card. The amount of the transaction is entered via the keyboard.

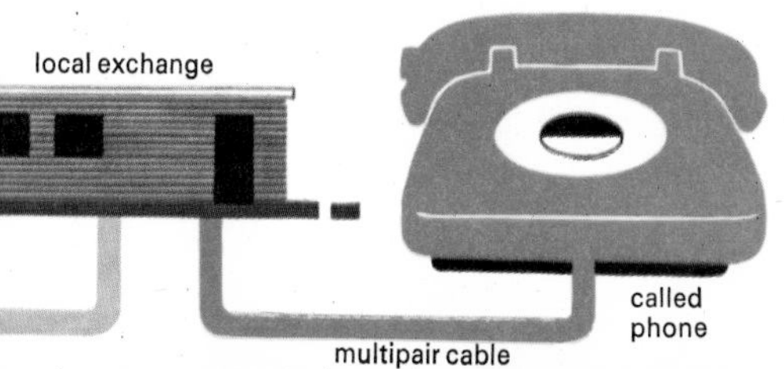

Below: The crossbar system, like Strowger, is electro-mechanical, but faster and more reliable. Crossbar switches have contact assemblies arranged in a grid pattern. Connections are made by electromagnets which make a row of input contacts intersect with a column of output contacts.

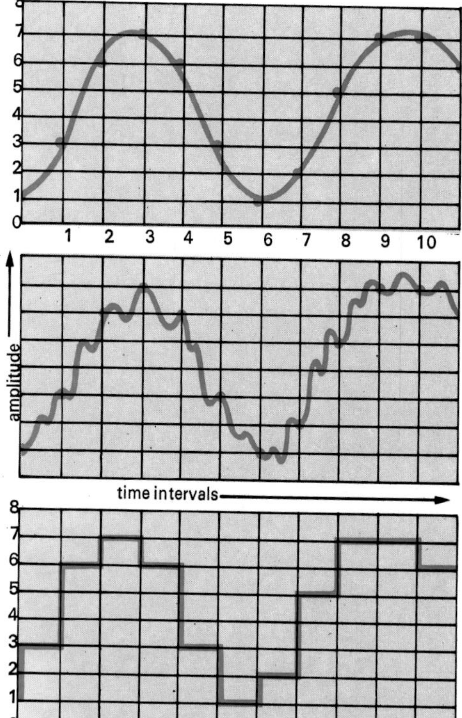

Left: The principles of *pulse code modulation* (PCM). This is a system for transmitting information so that it arrives with a minimum amount of distortion caused by electrical 'noise'— unwanted voltages picked up as it passes through the system. The first graph shows the waveform of the original signal.

This is how the original wave might look after being transmitted in an unmodulated form. The instantaneous values are the same, but it is very distorted. A wave reconstructed from a PCM signal would be free from this distortion, being based only on the instantaneous values.

This graph shows how the modulator measures the amplitude of the wave at regular intervals, and then produces electrical pulses whose amplitudes correspond to those of the original wave at those intervals. At the receiving end the demodulator uses these pulses to reconstruct the original wave.

GEC

Left: A communications station in the United Arab Republic. A large number of information channels can be carried by microwaves, and they are widely used instead of cable transmission systems. Because microwaves travel in straight lines and cannot bend around obstructions or over the horizon, the transmitter and receiver must normally be in 'line of sight' of each other. This can be overcome by beaming them up to a satellite, which then re-transmits them to distant stations, or by *tropospheric scatter*, bouncing them off the layers of air in the lower atmosphere. The large dish shown here is for satellite communications.

Cable & Wireless

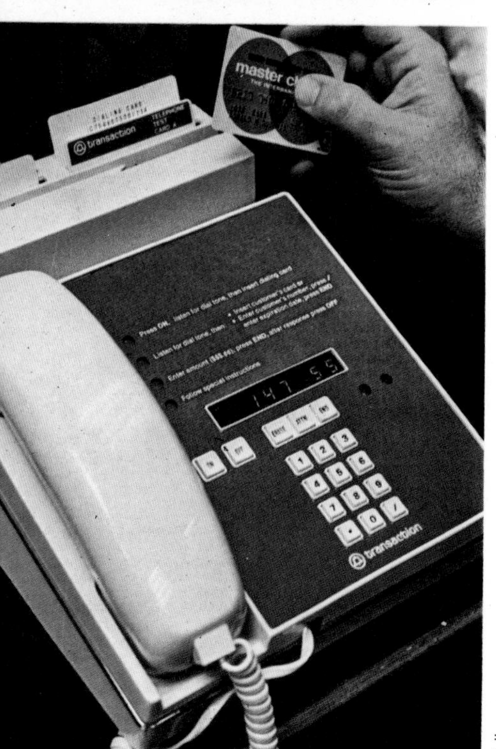

Bell

to distinguish one signal from the hundreds of radio signals received by an aerial. This is achieved by a process known as *modulation*, whereby every broadcast is superimposed on a unique 'signature tone' or *carrier frequency*. At the radio receiver, a particular broadcast is obtained by selecting its associated carrier frequency and *demodulating* the incoming signal.

The use of carrier frequencies enables the capacity of a telephone network to be greatly increased. Between exchanges, for example, where the communications traffic is most dense, each conversation to be transmitted can be modulated on to a unique carrier frequency and at the receiving end a demodulater can extract any one of the conversations to the exclusion of all the others.

Frequency and bandwidth

The most important frequencies making up speech lie between 400 and 4,000 Hz, and if these are present the words and the person speaking them are recognizable. Thus a telephone line (and the associated transmitter and receiver) must be capable of handling these frequencies without losing too much of their strength (amplitude).

Unfortunately, a simple pair of telephone wires impedes high frequency alternating currents more than lower frequencies—a situation exacerbated by long distances. Consequently, the frequency bandwidth which the wires can handle decreases with distance. With a simple telephone conversation, this can be overcome by attaching inductive filters to the line which 'boost' the higher frequencies of the electrical signal. When, however, a modulated signal is transmitted down a telephone line other techniques must be sought.

When a speech signal, with frequencies from 400 to 4,000 Hz, is modulated on to a carrier frequency (which is much higher and beyond the audible range), the whole signal is moved up to the region of the carrier frequency. For example, if the carrier frequency is 100,000 Hz then the modulated signal occupies a bandwidth of 8,000 Hz about the 100,000 Hz mark (that is from 96,000 to 104,000 Hz). This presents a problem in telecommunications because ordinary wires will not handle such high frequencies.

Two inventions eventually came together to overcome the problem of transmitting high frequency modulated signals over long distances—these were the *coaxial cable* and the *telephone repeater*.

Modern coaxial cables will handle frequencies up to 10 MHz (10 million Hertz). If each signal occupies a bandwidth of 8,000 Hz about its own carrier frequency then approximately 1,000 different conversations can be transmitted along it.

However good a cable is, it will still attenuate (reduce) signals over long distances. To overcome this, amplifiers were developed which could be placed periodically along the cable to boost the signals—these are called *repeaters*. As low frequency currents (and especially dc) are attenuated less than high frequency ones, it was found to be possible to power all the repeaters on a cable from the terminal exchanges by passing direct current along the cable.

Radio

The invention of radio, at the end of the nineteenth century, marked the beginning of the era of mass communications. It was soon possible to broadcast the details of events, as they happened, directly to people's homes, and to communicate directly with ships at sea or moving aircraft. The development of radio also paved the way for the advent of television, which has had an even greater impact on home entertainment. Military operations have been affected by radio, and space exploration, both manned and unmanned, would be impossible without it.

Radio waves are a form of *electromagnetic radiation*, which consists of a combination of alternating electric and magnetic fields. Radio waves travel at the same speed as light, and the peaks of the waves are the points at which the values of the electric and magnetic fields are at their maximum.

The *frequency* of a radio wave is the number of times per second that these fields reach a maximum in one direction, reverse to a maximum in the other direction, and then return to the original maximum. The distance between two successive maximum values in the same direction is known as the *wavelength* of the wave, and the higher the frequency of a wave the shorter its wavelength.

Radio waves range from the very low frequency (VLF) waves having wavelengths of between 1,000 km and 10 km, up to the very high microwave frequencies which have wavelengths of from 1 m down to less than 1 mm.

The invention of radio

The existence of electric and magnetic fields was first recognized by Michael Faraday in 1845. Faraday's concepts were taken up by James Clerk Maxwell, who went on to predict the existence of electromagnetic radiation and calculated that electromagnetic waves could travel through space at the speed of light.

The German physicist Heinrich Hertz devoted much time to the study of Maxwell's theory—although it was generally not accepted by other scientists at that time—and in 1887 he succeeded in demonstrating the generation, transmission and reception of electromagnetic waves. He produced his waves by making a spark jump across a small gap in a loop of wire. A similar loop, with a small gap in it, was placed nearby, and when the spark was created in the first loop, a spark also appeared at the gap in the second. The current flowing in the first loop had created electromagnetic waves, which radiated away from the loop and were picked up by the second loop, causing a current to flow in it.

The work of Hertz was studied by researchers in many countries. Sir Oliver Lodge in England, Alexander Popov in Russia, Edouard Branly in France and Augusto Righi in Italy are among the most notable of these. Their work on methods of generating and detecting radio waves was studied by Guglielmo Marconi, who took out the first patent for wireless telegraphy in June 1896.

Marconi began his experiments in 1894, constructing a transmitter and receiver

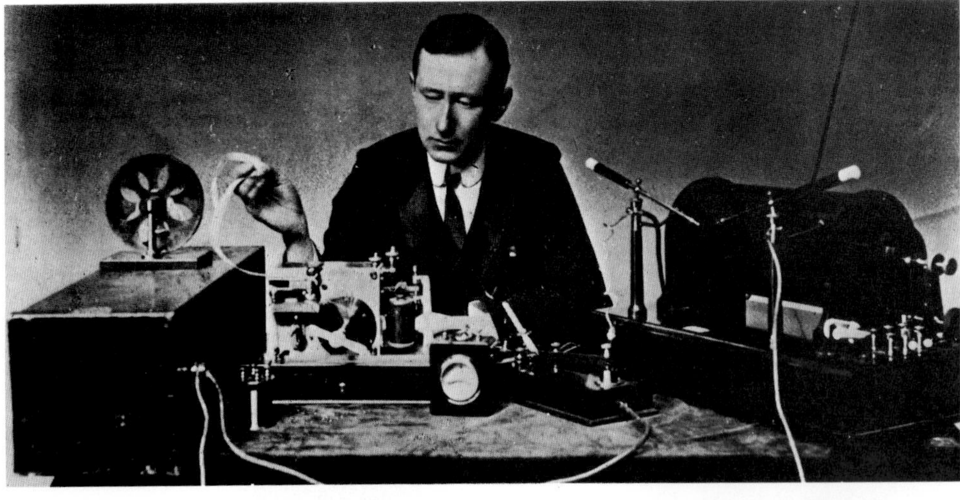

Marconi

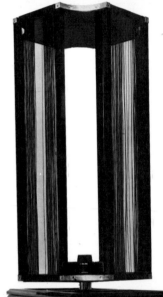

Above: Guglielmo Marconi (1874-1937), the son of an Italian father and an Irish mother, was only 22 years old when he patented the first wireless telegraph in 1896. He was a joint recipient of the Nobel Prize for physics in 1909, and received other honours from both Britain and Italy.

Science Museum

Right: This 1927 radio is a *superheterodyne* receiver. It contains circuits which mix the modulated signal with an unmodulated one to produce a lower, intermediate frequency signal. This signal is then demodulated to produce the audio frequency signal that is used to drive a speaker or headphones.

Radio Times Hulton Picture Library

Above: George Bernard Shaw broadcasting from a studio in Plymouth, England, in 1929. The microphone is contained within the 'meat safe' housing; it comprised a flat aluminium coil mounted within the field of an electromagnet and held in place by cotton wool pads covered in petroleum jelly.

Below: A 'crystal set', a popular form of cheap radio during the 1920s. The crystal set had a coil and a variable capacitor for tuning, and a silicon or germanium crystal which, when contacted with a wire probe called a 'cat's whisker', demodulated the signal by rectifying it.

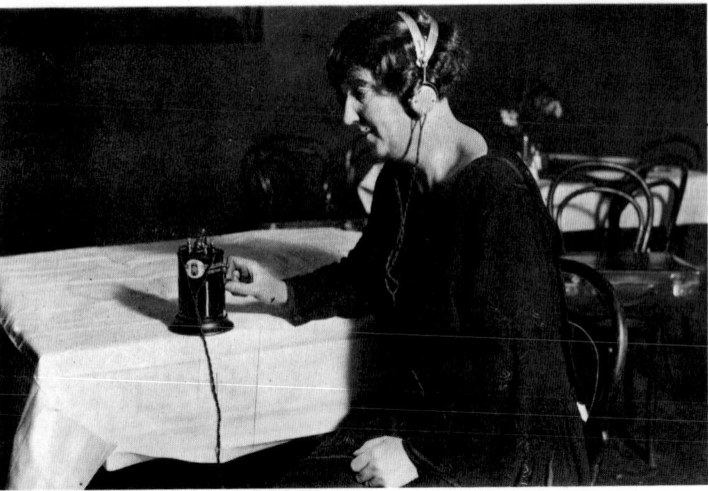

BBC

Right: Radio waves can be transmitted considerable distances around the earth because the electrically-charged layers in the upper atmosphere, known collectively as the *ionosphere*, reflect them back down to distant receivers. The ionosphere is a series of layers, known as D, E, F_1 and F_2, consisting of ionized gas molecules with free electrons which were liberated when the molecules were ionized by the action of solar radiation. The height at which radio waves are reflected depends on their frequency, and the highest frequencies are not reflected at all. At night, the F_1 layer merges with F_2.

Heinzelmann

Left: The 'Heinzelmann' radio of 1948 was the German Grundig company's first product. It was supplied initially in kit form, but no valves were provided; customers were advised to buy the valves from army surplus stores.

Right: Low and very low frequency radio waves can travel around the earth in the region between the earth's surface and the ionosphere. This region acts as a kind of natural waveguide for waves of these frequencies. Short wavelength, high frequency waves, with frequencies up to 30 MHz, are bounced around the world between the ionosphere and the surface.

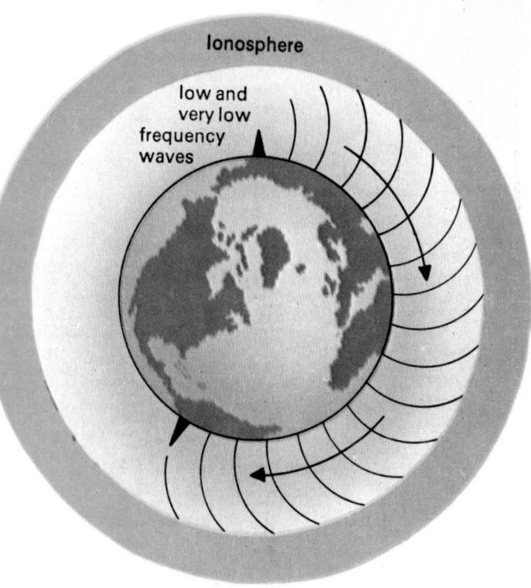

BEHAVIOUR OF RADIO WAVES IN THE ATMOSPHERE

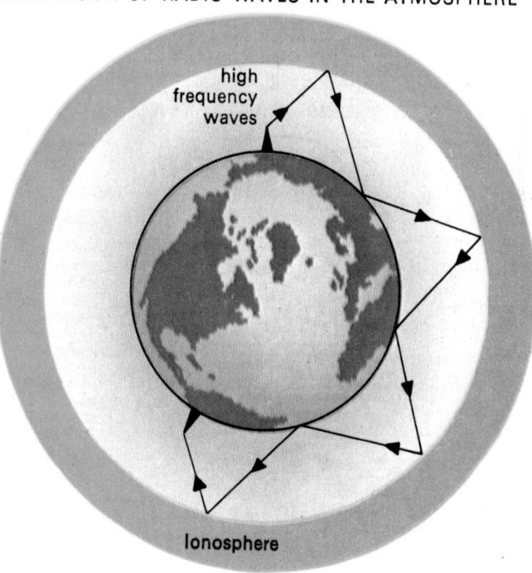

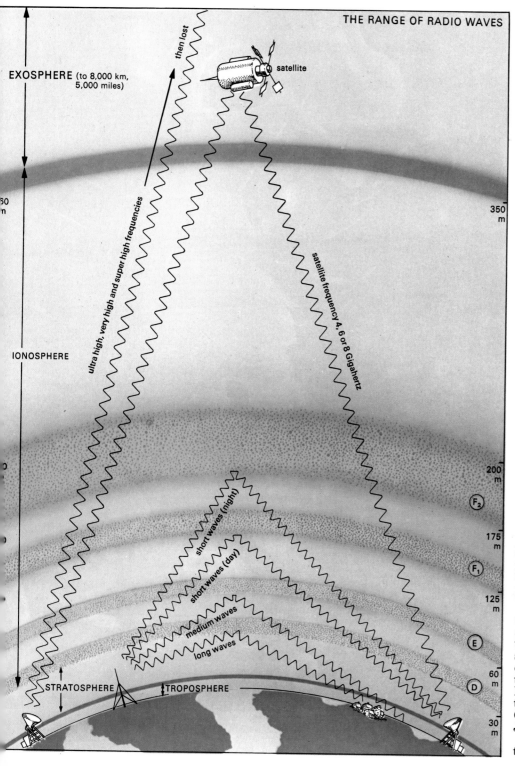

THE RANGE OF RADIO WAVES

EXOSPHERE (to 8,000 km, 5,000 miles)

then lost

satellite

ultra high, very high and super high frequencies

satellite frequency 4, 6 or 8 Gigahertz

IONOSPHERE

350 m

200 m

F2

175 m

short waves (night)

F1

short waves (day)

125 m

medium waves

E

long waves

60 m

D

STRATOSPHERE

TROPOSPHERE

30 m

at his father's villa near Bologna, Italy. His receiver was a detector of the 'coherer' type, invented by Branly, in which metal powder inside a glass tube stuck together when magnetized by a spark appearing across a gap in the adjacent aerial circuit. When the powder stuck together it allowed a current to be passed through it, and this current operated a telegraph receiver. By transmitting Morse Code signals in the form of pulses of radio waves, similar pulses of electric current were made to flow in the coherer and so the message was recorded by the telegraph receiver connected to it.

Post Office backing

Marconi approached the Italian government for backing, but they were uninterested and so he went to England, where Sir William Preece, the Engineer in Chief of the Post Office, put full facilities at his disposal. His system was successfully operated between the Post Office headquarters and the Thames Embankment in 1896, and the following year a 13 km (8 mile) circuit was set up across the Bristol Channel.

By removing the spark gap from the aerial circuit to a closed circuit—which acted as a reservoir of energy—long trains of waves were produced and very soon distances of several hundred miles could be covered. After building links to the Isle of Wight and to France, in 1901 Marconi successfully transmitted the first transatlantic signal, an 'S' in Morse Code, from Poldhu in Cornwall to St John's in Newfoundland.

The Marconi system only transmitted telegraphic messages in the form of pulses of radio waves, and it was not until 1906 that a method of transmitting speech was developed. This method was the work the Canadian physicist Reginald Fessenden, who invented the technique of *modulating* radio waves.

Fessenden used a continuous signal or *carrier*, with the speech signal superimposed on it in such a way that the amplitude of the waves varied with the variations in the speech signal. At the receiver, these variations in amplitude were used to produce a varying electrical signal which corresponded to the original signal with which the carrier was modulated. This signal was then amplified and put through a loudspeaker to reproduce the original sounds.

This method is known as *amplitude modulation* (AM), and it is the modulation technique used for long, medium and short wavelength radio broadcasts. One major drawback to AM radio, however, is that the wave can be modulated by unwanted electrical signals such as those produced by thunderstorms and some types of electrical equipment. This means that the signal can arrive at the receiver modulated not only with the original signal but also with these unwanted ones, which produce the background noise or 'static' often heard on AM radio.

A solution to this problem of static interference was found in 1939 by Edwin Armstrong in the US. Instead of using the sound signal to vary the amplitude of the carrier wave, he used it to vary its frequency. The signal produced by the receiver varied according to the variations in the frequency of the incoming carrier wave. This method is known as *frequency modulation* (FM), and it is used for transmissions in the higher frequency wavebands such as the VHF (very high frequency) band and the microwave bands.

Static interference still creates variations in the amplitude of FM signals, but as the receiver only responds to variations in the frequency of the signal these amplitude variations do not affect the reproduced sound.

Tuning

When a radio is tuned to a particular station, its tuning section is set to accept only the carrier frequency of that station. The tuning circuit contains, in its simplest form, a coil and a capacitor that together constitute a *resonant circuit*, one that offers very little impedance to a current whose frequency is the same as the *resonant frequency* of the circuit. This resonant frequency is determined by the values of the inductance of the coil and the capacitance of the capacitor.

The capacitor in a simple radio tuning circuit is variable, and when the tuning knob is turned the value of the capacitor is altered, so altering the resonant frequency of the circuit. The radio will now be tuned to the station whose frequency is the same as the new resonant frequency of the circuit.

Radio transmitters operate by amplifying the modulated signal and applying it to the transmitting aerial from which the radio waves are emitted. At the receiving end, the radio waves coming into contact with the aerial create tiny currents in it which are then passed through the tuning stage, demodulated, and amplified. Finally ,the signal is played through the loudspeaker to reproduce the

BBC

Left: Actors rehearsing an episode of a radio serial. The studio is equipped with various items for producing sound effects, including three types of stairs; two types of window; a door with a knocker, bell, latch, three types of lock and a bolt; and kitchen equipment including a stove.

Cable & Wireless

Above: A studio control booth. The signals from the studio, on the other side of the glass screen, pass through the control console before being sent to the transmitter.

Below: Radio waves are either *amplitude modulated* (AM) or *frequency modulated* (FM). In both cases, the variations in the modulated carrier wave correspond to the variations in the original sound signal. In the case of AM, the wave's amplitude varies; in that of FM its frequency varies.

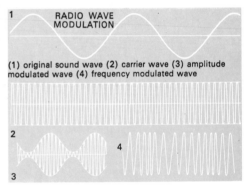

RADIO WAVE MODULATION

1

(1) original sound wave (2) carrier wave (3) amplitude modulated wave (4) frequency modulated wave

2

3

4

Below: Part of the output stage of a large radio transmitter.

Marconi

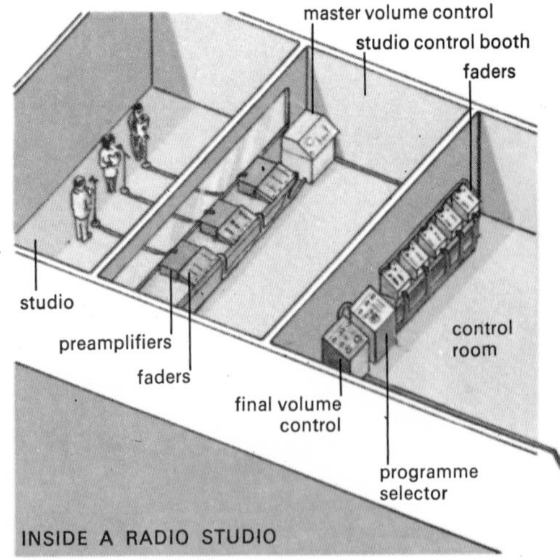

Above: A studio and control room arrangement. The studio has its own control booth where the signals from its microphones are amplified and then combined, using faders to adjust their relative volumes. The combined signal is then sent to the control room, which controls the output from several studios, before going on to the transmitter.

Right: At the transmitter, the carrier wave is modulated with the signal from the studio then transmitted. The receiver retrieves the sound signal from the modulated wave and plays it through the loudspeaker.

Left: A modern portable radio, and below it a quadraphonic receiver and its loudspeakers. Stereophonic and quadraphonic broadcast signals contain sub-signals that are used by the receiver to sort out the separate sound channels. Each channel is then amplified separately and fed to its speaker.

Grundig

Nordmende

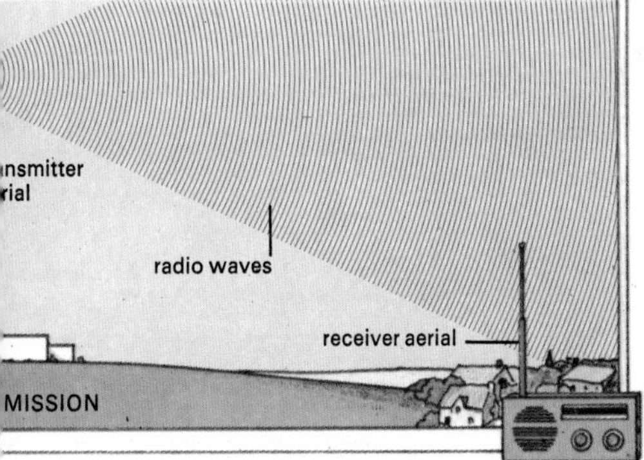

Marconi

Above: The signal applied to the transmitter aerial creates the radio waves which spread out in all directions. When they are picked up by the receiver aerial they set up a corresponding signal in it.

Right: A two-way radio.

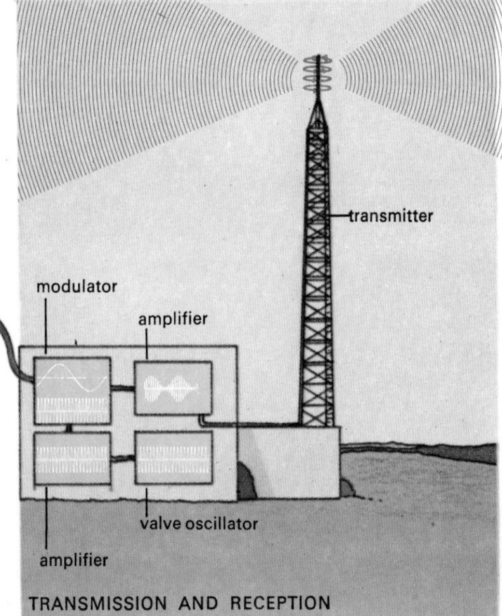

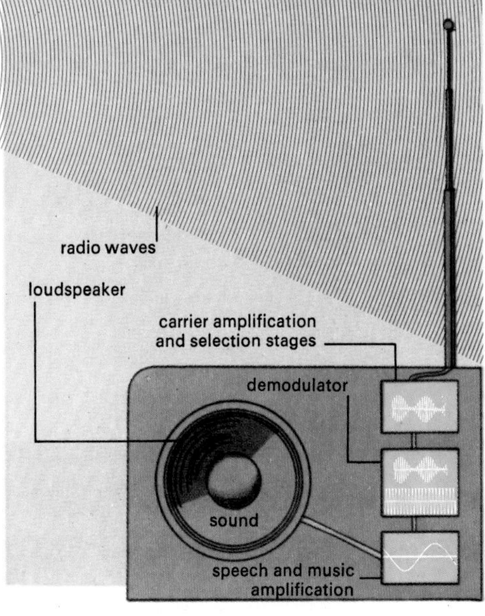

broadcast sound.

An aerial transmits and receives radio waves most efficiently when its length is the same as the wavelength of the waves it is handling. This is usually quite feasible with a single frequency radio transmitter or receiver using the shorter wavelengths. An aerial will also operate quite effectively when its length is an even sub-multiple, such as a half or a quarter of the wavelength, and in many cases this may be more convenient. However, aerials designed to handle a wide range of wavelengths, such as those in domestic radio sets, cannot be accurately matched to all the wavelengths and so a loss of efficiency is unavoidable.

Broadcasting

The wavelengths of all radio stations are determined in accordance with the rules laid down by the International Telecommunications Union. These rules are intended to prevent transmissions from one station interfering with those from another. For stations not transmitting to other countries, the most widely used frequencies are between 150 and 550 kHz (long wave), 550 and 1660 kHz (medium wave) and 87.5 and 100 MHz (VHF). Most overseas broadcasts use the 2.2 to 30 MHz region of the short wave band. Amplitude modulation is used for long, medium and short wave broadcasts, and frequency modulation for the VHF transmissions.

The VHF frequencies (30 to 300 MHz), together with the UHF (ultra high frequency, 300 to 3,000 MHz) band, are also used for two-way radio systems such as those used by aircraft, ships, the armed forces, the police, and other operators such as taxi services.

The lower end of the long wave band, below about 100 kHz, plus some of the very low frequency band (3 to 30 kHz), is used for marine communications, radio navigational aids, and for long-range military communications.

Microwaves are radio waves with frequencies between 1,000 MHz (or 1 gigahertz, abbreviated 1 GHz) and 300 GHz. They are widely used in telecommunications because they can be modulated in such a way as to enable them to carry, for example, up to about 1,000 simultaneous telephone conversations on a single carrier wave.

Microwaves cannot be handled in the same way as lower frequency radio waves, because at frequencies above 1 GHz a current cannot be passed along a cable from one point to another, such as from the modulator to the transmitter, without it radiating all its power away or losing it due to capacitive effects. Instead of using cables, microwave transmitters use *waveguides*, hollow tubes which channel the microwaves from their source to the aerial. The aerial is a dish-shaped structure, and the microwaves are beamed into the centre of it so that it reflects them away in a narrow, straight beam.

Microwave receiver aerials are of similar construction, with the dish serving to reflect the incoming beam into the open end of a waveguide situated at the focus of the dish. In addition to their use in ordinary telecommunications networks, microwaves are used for space vehicle communications links and are the type of radio waves employed by radar systems.

Electronic Devices

The development of electronic devices, such as valves and transistors, has had a tremendous impact on life in the twentieth century. For example, without these devices there would be no radio, television, hi-fi systems or computers, to name but a few of the many types of equipment which depend on electronic components to control or amplify the voltages and currents within them.

One of the first major steps in the evolution of these devices and the equipment based on them came in 1900, when Sir John Fleming (1849-1945) invented the *thermionic diode*. This device acts as a sort of one-way valve, allowing current to pass in one direction but not in the other, hence the general term 'valve' which is often applied to thermionic devices.

In its simplest form, the thermionic diode has two electrodes which are called the *cathode* and the *anode*. These are sealed within a glass tube, from which the air has been removed to prevent current passing from one electrode to the other by conduction through the air molecules. The cathode is heated, either by a heating current which is passed through it or by an adjacent heater filament, so that it emits electrons. The emission of electrons from a heated surface is called *thermionic emission*. These electrons form a cloud or

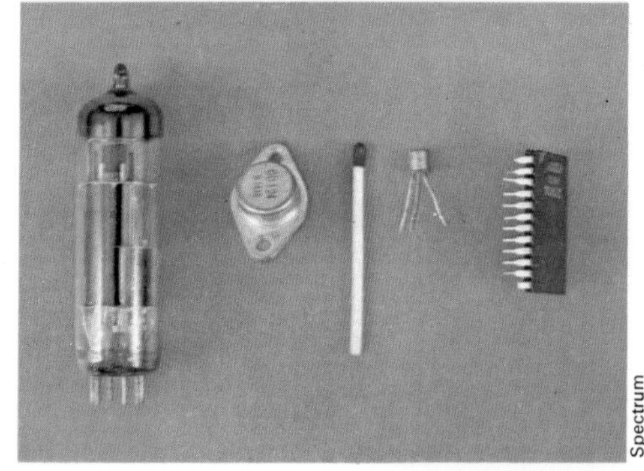

Spectrum

Left: Three types of electronic device—a small thermionic valve (left), a pair of transistors, and an integrated circuit (right), shown beside a matchstick to give an impression of their sizes. An integrated circuit can contain the equivalent of thousands of transistors, built into a chip of silicon measuring from 1.27 mm (0.05 in) to 6.4 mm (0.25 in) square.

Right: This chart shows the symbols used to represent some common electronic components.

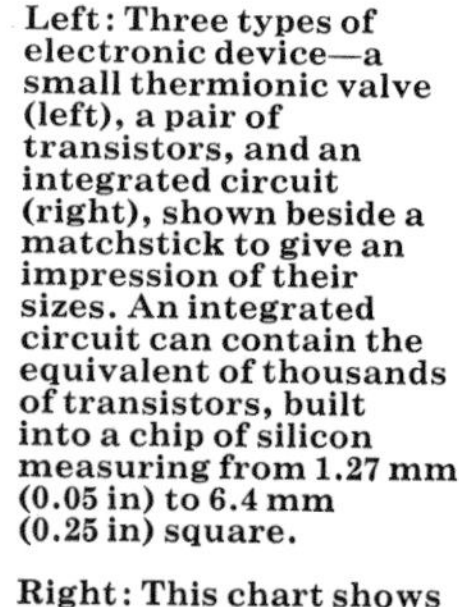

PREFIX	SYM
tera	T
giga	G
mega	M
kilo	K
milli	m
micro	µ
nano	n
pico	p

Mullard

Right: A strip of subminiature Zener diodes. These have operating voltages of from 5.1 to 75 V, and can handle up to 400 mW of power.

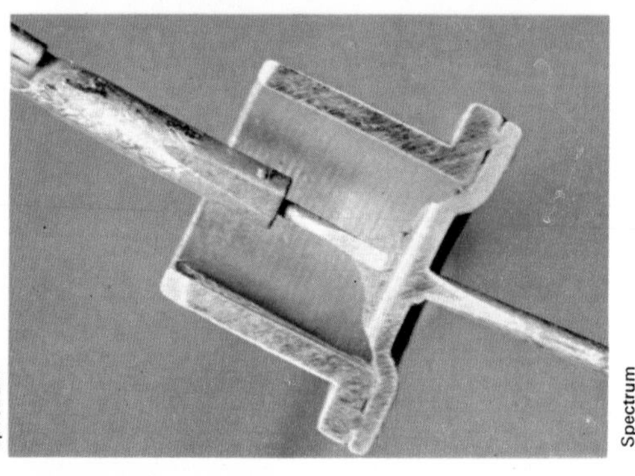

Spectrum

Below right: A semiconductor diode, cut in half to show its internal structure. The pn junction is on the inside face of the base of the device. During manufacture, this junction, comprising a layer of p-type material on top of a layer of n-type material, is soldered on to the base. The connecting wire is then soldered on, and the device is sealed within its protective metal can.

Spectrum

Below: The inside of a portable transistor radio. The components are mounted on an epoxy resin circuit board, which has strips of copper bonded to its lower side to make the connections between the components.

Dave Hoskings

1-8 transistors
9 variable tuning capacitor
10 loudspeaker
11, 12 transformers
13-18 capacitors
19 resistors
20-22 tuning coils
23 diode
24 capacitor
25 waveband selector switch
26 telescopic aerial
27 internal aerial
28-29 capacitors
30-33 intermediate frequency transformers

John Watney

Left: A germanium junction transistor, with its case removed. The actual germanium chip, with its emitter, collector and base regions, is at the top of the structure. All the early transistors used germanium, but modern ones use a silicon chip instead. Silicon can operate at higher temperatures than germanium, and so it can handle larger amounts of power without risk of failure due to overheating.

Mullard

Below: Three stages in the assembly of a silicon transistor. The silicon chip, doped with impurities to produce its p- and n-type regions, is soldered on to the terminals, and then sealed within a can.

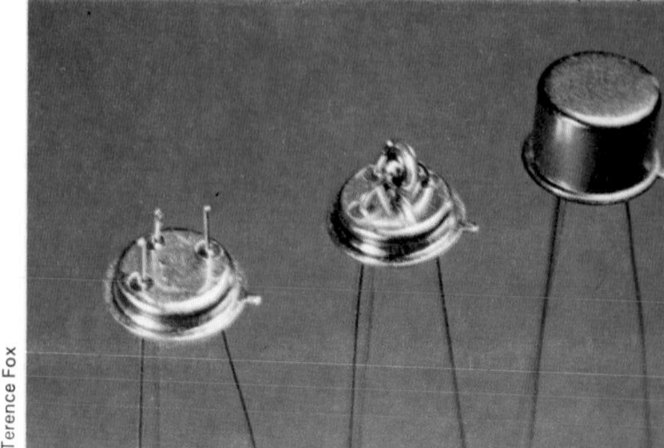

Terence Fox

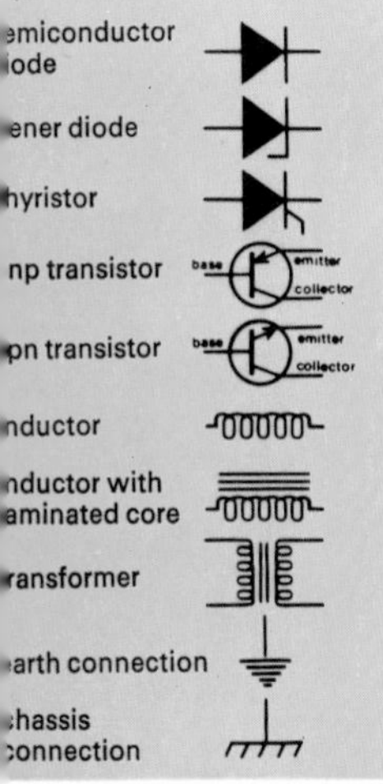

TIPLICATION FACTOR	
,000,000,000,000	(10^{12})
1,000,000,000	(10^{9})
1,000,000	(10^{6})
1,000	(10^{3})
0.001	(10^{-3})
0.000001	(10^{-6})
0.000000001	(10^{-9})
0.000000000001	(10^{-12})

Left: Some of the prefixes used to denote multiples and submultiples of electrical units, for example kilovolts (kV, thousands of volts).

Right: A diagram of a thermionic triode, the arrangement of its contact pins, and the way in which it amplifies voltage.

THERMIONIC TRIODE

input, V_G, I_A, V_A, output

mica disc, heater, anode (cut away), grid, cathode, anti-interference screen, glass envelope, valve base, connecting pins

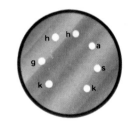

VALVE BASE

a anode
g grid
h heater
k cathode
s screen

Left: A selection of semiconductor diodes, showing some of the different types of protective encapsulation such as metal cans, glass, and epoxy resin. In the larger diodes, the threaded stud forms the cathode connection.

Right: The inside of a power transistor, one which is designed to handle large amounts of power in the final stages of an amplifier. The large area of metal helps to dissipate the heat produced during operation.

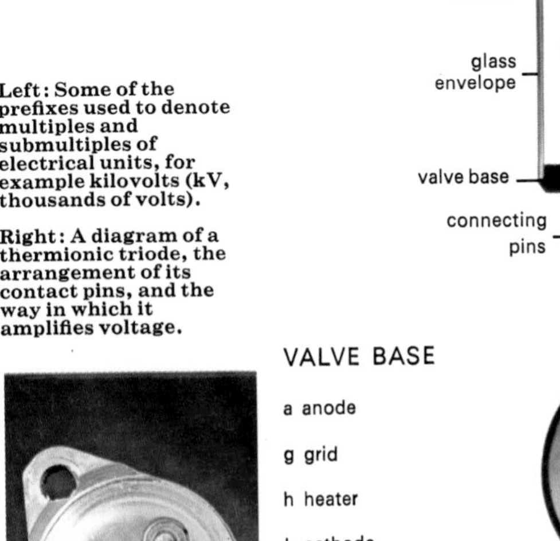

Spectrum

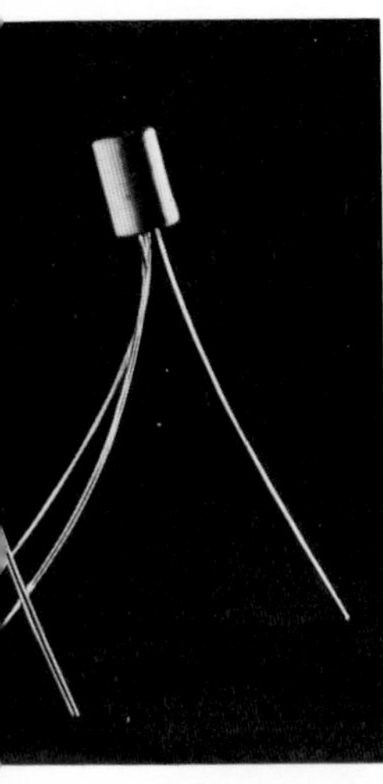

Left: Medium power germanium transistors, designed for use in audio equipment such as record player amplifiers and the audio frequency amplifiers of transistor radios.

Below: Silicon semiconductors are made by 'doping' wafers of pure silicon with small amounts of other elements such as gallium. This process involves hermetically sealing them within a glass tube, and then heating them in an oven. In this picture, an operator is using a flame torch to seal a tube of wafers. The wafers are sliced from a rod of silicon, and are about 3 cm (1.2 in) in diameter and 0.3 mm (0.012 in) thick.

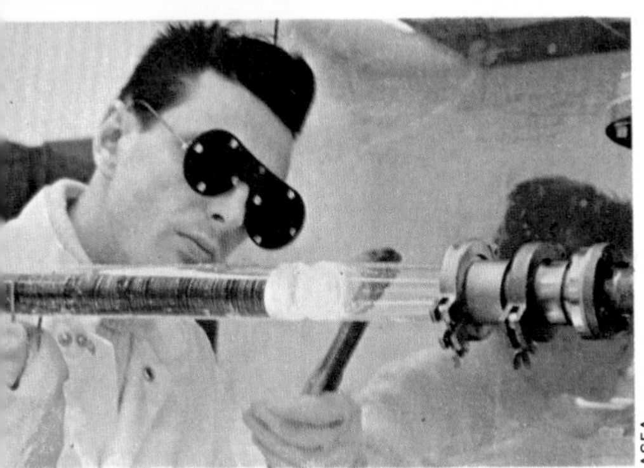

ASEA

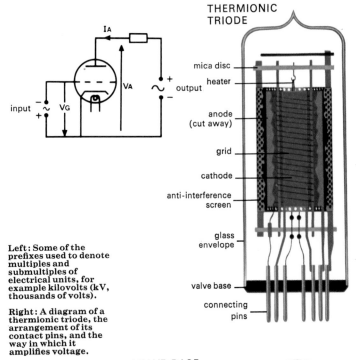

space charge around the cathode.

With the diode connected to an external circuit so that the anode is made positive and the cathode negative, electrons from the space charge will be drawn across from the cathode to the anode. They then flow through the external circuit, constituting an electric current, and back to the cathode.

If the connections to the external circuit are reversed, however, making the anode negative and the cathode positive, the electrons in the space charge will be repelled by the anode (like charges repel). No electrons will then pass from the cathode to the anode, and so no current will flow through the external circuit via the diode. Current can thus flow through a diode in one direction only, making it a useful device for controlling the flow of current around a circuit.

The next major development in electronics came in 1904, when Lee de Forest (1873-1961) added a third electrode, the *control grid*, to a diode, thus making a *triode*. The control grid takes the form of a spiral or open mesh of wire placed close to the cathode, between it and the anode. If the grid is made more negative than the cathode, it will partially neutralize the positive potential of the anode. Consequently, fewer electrons are attracted to the anode, and the size of the anode current is reduced as the grid is made more negative. Because the grid is in close proximity to the space charge around the cathode, only a small change in the grid voltage is needed to produce a large change in the number of electrons passing from the cathode to the anode. In other words, a small change in grid voltage produces a large change in anode current.

The triode can thus be used as an amplifier. The signal from a record player pick-up, for example, is too small to drive a loudspeaker. The pick-up signal can be fed to the grid of a triode, and the resulting changes in the anode current constitute a much larger version of the original signal, which can then be used to drive a loudspeaker.

Tetrodes (four electrodes) and *pentodes* (five electrodes) are valves with additional grid electrodes which refine the basic operation of the triode.

Semiconductors

The electrical characteristics of a material are determined by its atomic structure, in particular by the outermost or *valence* electrons of its atoms. An atom has a central core or nucleus, consisting of positively-charged protons and uncharged neutrons, around which the negatively-charged electrons orbit. In isolated atoms, each electron orbit corresponds to a permissible discrete energy level in accordance with the quantum theory.

In solids, where the atoms are in close proximity, the valence electrons of an atom are shared with neighbouring atoms to form *covalent bonds* which hold them all together. As a result, the previously permissible discrete energy levels of the valence electrons become a relatively wide band of permitted energies. The electrons forming the bond can reach higher energies without breaking free because the task of holding them in place is shared by two atoms.

By supplying energy, such as heat, light or electricity, to these electrons in this *valence band* of energies, their energy levels can be increased sufficiently to free them from their atoms and allow them to wander through the material. An orderly flow of free electrons (as opposed to random movement) through a material constitutes an electric current, and such electrons have energies which fall into the *conduction band*.

If the valence band and the conduction band overlap, the material will be a good conductor of electricity because little energy is required to produce the free electrons and an electric current is easily established. Metals such as silver and copper are good examples of such a material.

Where there is a small *forbidden energy gap* between the valence and conduction bands, the material will offer greater resistance to the flow of current than a good conductor. Nickel-chrome alloys, carbon and tungsten are some of the materials which have this property and are called *resistors*. As the temperature of resistors is raised, their atoms vibrate more, causing more electron-atom collisions which reduce the number of free electrons available. This results in an increase in their *resistance*, their opposition to current flow.

Glass, ceramics, plastics, mica and rubber are non-conductors or *insulators*. The gap between their valence and conduction bands is large, and even moderate amounts of energy are insufficient to detach electrons for conduction.

Between conductors and insulators there are other solid elements and compounds which have intermediate electrical properties. Of these, quite a number exhibit decreasing resistance with increasing temperature. These materials,

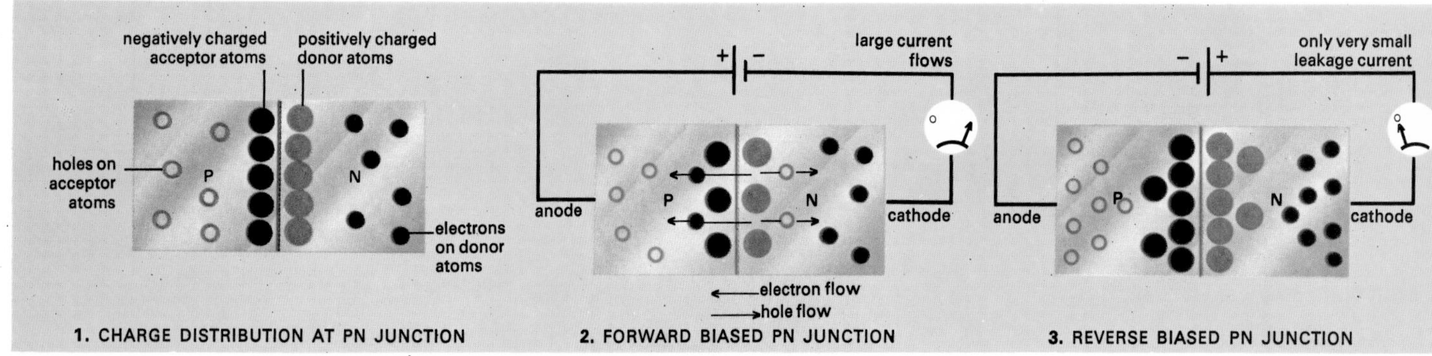

Above: This series of diagrams shows the operation of junction diodes and transistors. 1. In a pn junction, electrons diffuse from the n-region to just inside the p-region, and holes from the p-region to just inside the n-region. Forming ions on either side of the junction, this prevents charge flow. 2. Forward biasing the junction breaks down the voltage barrier caused by the ions, and current flows. 3. Reverse biasing reinforces the voltage barrier; only a tiny leakage current flows. 4. In a transistor, when the emitter-base junction is forward biased electrons can cross it. As they do so they are swept on into the collector by the collector-base reverse bias voltage, creating a collector current. Small changes in emitter-base bias create large changes in collector current. 5. By using a small input signal to create changes in the emitter-base bias, a large output signal can be obtained from the collector. This is the basis of transistor amplifiers.

Left: Semiconductor devices used in electrical power control systems. The devices on the right are diodes, and on the left are thyristors. A thyristor is a sort of electronic switch. It has two p- and two n-type regions, arranged $P_1N_1P_2N_2$. P_1 is the anode, N_2 the cathode, and P_2 is called the 'gate', and the device can be thought of as two interconnected transistors, formed by $P_1N_1P_2$ and $N_1P_2N_2$. If the gate is made more positive than N_2, $N_1P_2N_2$ will be switched on, and this will switch on $P_1N_1P_2$, so that current flows from P_1 to N_2. The thyristor will continue to conduct after the voltage applied to P_2 has been removed.

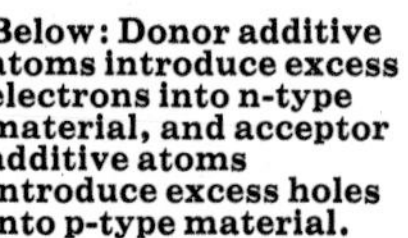

Below: Donor additive atoms introduce excess electrons into n-type material, and acceptor additive atoms introduce excess holes into p-type material.

N-TYPE SILICON OR GERMANIUM

excess electron

covalent bond

pentavalent donor additive atom

tetravalent silicon or germanium atom

hole

incomplete bond

P-TYPE SILICON OR GERMANIUM

trivalent accept[or] additive ato[m]

which include silicon and germanium, are known as *semiconductors*.

In a semiconductor, when a valence electron is excited into the conduction band, it leaves behind a net positive charge on the atom and a 'hole' in the structure of bonded atoms. This hole or incomplete bond may be filled by an electron moving in from a neighbouring atom. This results, of course, in the formation of a 'hole' in that atom, which in its turn can be filled by yet another electron moving in from another atom. Thus as the current of negatively charged electrons flows in one direction, there is a corresponding 'flow' of positively-charged holes in the opposite direction.

This ability to conduct electricity is small in pure semiconductors, but it can be increased by *doping* the pure semiconductor with materials known as *additives* or *impurities*.

Donor pentavalent (having five valence electrons per atom) additives, such as phosphorus, arsenic, antimony and bismuth, introduce extra electrons when added to *tetravalent* (four valence electron) silicon or germanium, producing *n-type* semiconductor material. Four of the valence electrons in each additive atom form covalent bonds with neighbouring silicon or germanium atoms, leaving the fifth electron easily detachable for conduction.

Similarly, *acceptor trivalent* (three valence electrons) additives such as gallium and boron introduce extra holes when added to silicon or germanium, producing *p-type* semiconductor material.

Semiconductor diodes

For many applications the thermionic diode has now been replaced by the semiconductor *junction diode*, because of its greater reliability, more compact and robust construction, and the fact that it requires no heater power.

The basis of the junction diode is a *pn junction*—a junction between p-type and n-type materials—formed within a single piece of semiconductor material. Free electrons, which exist in large numbers in the n-type material, diffuse across the pn junction to just inside the p-region. Similarly, holes from the p-region diffuse across the junction to just inside the n-region. With no external voltage applied across the pn junction, these holes and free electrons create charged additive atoms (ions) on either side of the junction until, because like charges repel, further charges are prevented from crossing. To obtain a steady flow of charges (an electric current) across the junction, this voltage barrier must be reduced.

This is achieved by applying an external voltage which makes the p-region (cathode) positive with respect to the n-region (anode). This is known as *forward biasing*. Charges which have crossed the pn junction are now attracted

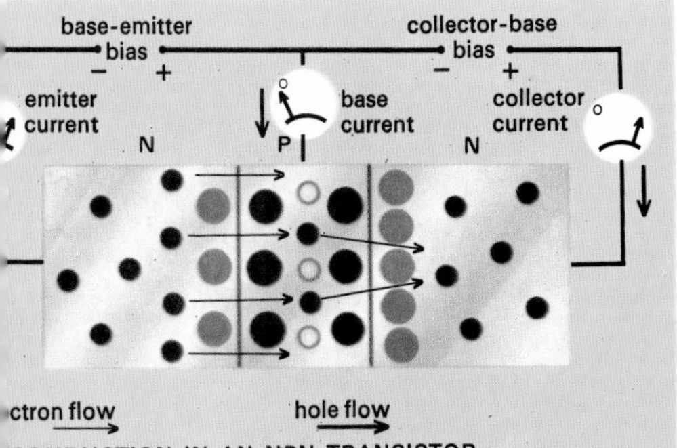

CONDUCTION IN AN NPN TRANSISTOR

Left: Thyristors can be used to convert alternating current to direct current. This is a 125 MW, 125 kV unit installed in a converter station in Denmark, which converts ac into dc for long distance transmission.

Below: These diagrams show how a thyristor can be considered as two interconnected transistors. When the thyristor is used as a switch, the circuit it controls is connected to the anode and cathode.

ASEA

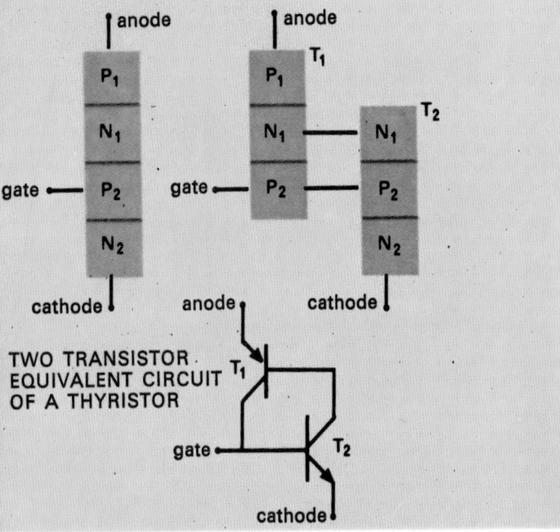

TWO TRANSISTOR EQUIVALENT CIRCUIT OF A THYRISTOR

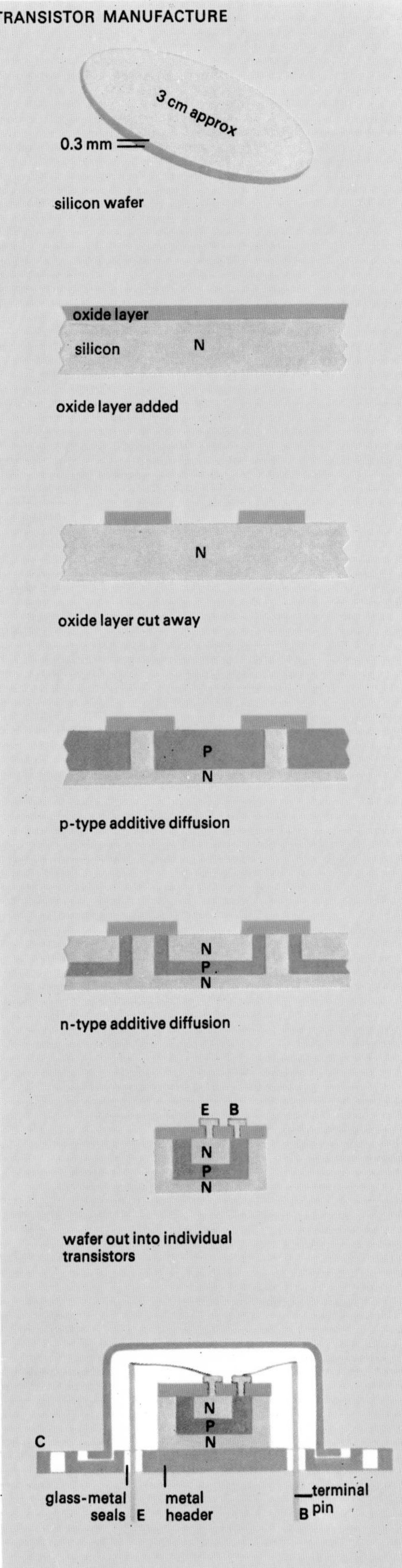

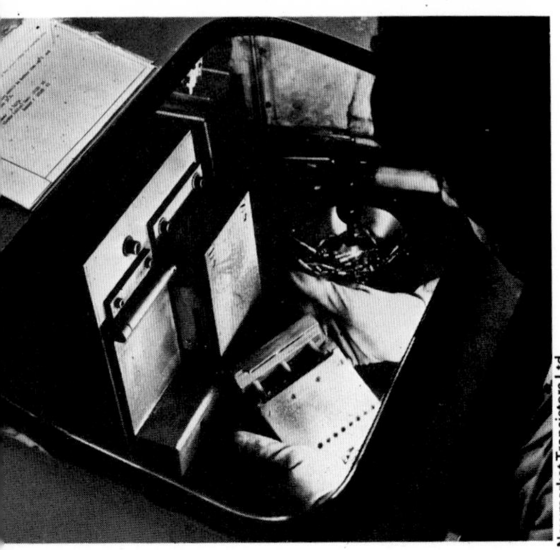

Left: 'Canning' transistors, fitting the protective metal cans, is done within a glove box to prevent any dirt or moisture contaminating them.

Above: Seven stages in the manufacture of npn transistors. N-type silicon wafers are given a coating of silicon dioxide, which is then cut away so that p-type additives can diffuse into the exposed areas to form bases. N-type material is then diffused into the base areas to form emitters. The wafers are then cut into individual transistors, the connecting wires are added, and the devices are sealed in metal cans.

Newmarket Transistors Ltd.

away from the junction electrons to the anode and holes to the cathode. This allows more charges to cross the junction and a continuous flow, an electric current, to be set up.

If the polarity of the applied voltage is reversed—making the junction *reverse biased*—holes in the p-region and electrons in the n-region are attracted away from the junction towards the anode and cathode respectively. This increases the voltage barrier to the flow of charges across the junction, and prevents the establishment of an electric current (although in fact a small *leakage current* does flow). These are the basic operating principles of signal and rectifier diodes.

Other types of diode, namely *Zener* and *voltage regulator* diodes, are operated at a critical reverse bias voltage, known as the *breakdown voltage*. At this voltage level the blocking effect of the diode breaks down and there is a sudden rush of current through the diode.

Light-emitting diodes (leds), also pn junction devices, radiate light when sufficiently biased in the forward direction. Under these conditions, high energy electrons in the conduction band diffuse from the n-region into the p-region. In doing so, they fall into the lower energy valence band to combine with a hole, giving off their surplus energy as light (in rectifier diodes, this energy is dissipated mainly as heat).

Transistors

The first transistor, called a *point contact transistor*, was invented in 1948 by William Shockley, John Bardeen and Walter Brattain at the Bell Laboratories in the USA. Its name derived from the use of two pointed electrodes, called the *emitter* and the *collector*, which were placed in contact with a block of germanium. A third contact, the *base*, was arranged so that the device was, in effect, two semiconductor diodes, one being formed by the emitter and the base, and the other by the collector and the base.

This arrangement was improved on shortly afterwards with the introduction of the *junction transistor*. This type is very widely used, and is made up of a sandwich of two types of semiconductor material, arranged either as a pnp sandwich or as an npn sandwich. The main difference between the operation of these devices is the direction in which current flows through them. The operation of an npn junction transistor is as follows.

With the emitter-base junction forward biased and the collector-base junction reverse biased, electrons from the emitter region readily cross the emitter-base junction as an emitter current (I_E). Once in the narrow base region, the electrons come under the influence of the voltage which reverse-biases the collector-base junction, and are swept into the collector region to form a collector current (I_C).

A few electrons, in passing through the base region, combine with holes. This gives rise to a small base current (I_B) which replaces the lost holes such that $I_E = I_C - I_B$. Just as small variations in the forward bias of a semiconductor diode produce large variations in the forward current, so only small variations in the forward bias of the emitter-base junction are required to produce relatively large changes in the emitter and collector currents, with corresponding small changes in the base current.

Electronic Circuits

Since the first days of radio and thermionic valves, electronic devices and their applications have become increasingly diverse. Today, solid state semiconductor devices are the principal electronic amplifying, switching and rectifying devices. Their fields of application can be generally classified as telecommunications, data processing, automatic control, instrumentation and excitation. Despite this wide spectrum of applications, however, there are a number of basic electronic circuits and fabrication techniques which are commonly employed.

Half-wave and full-wave rectifiers

Most electronic circuits require a dc voltage supply. This is usually obtained by transforming the ac mains voltage up or down and then *rectifying* it to give the required dc voltage. Where *half-wave* rectification is adequate, the transformer secondary (output) winding is connected to the electronic circuit (or *load* as it is termed) through a single diode. During each positive half-cycle of the alternating secondary voltage, when the diode anode is positive with respect to its cathode, current will flow through the diode to the load. During the intervening negative half-cycles, however, current flow to the load will be blocked by the diode. The current thus supplied to the load is in one direction only but consists of a regular succession of pulses. Since in many cases the load can be regarded as a resistor, the voltage waveform will be a similar shape.

Full-wave rectification requires two diodes connected either anode-to-anode or cathode-to-cathode across the transformer secondary: the load is connected between the point common to both diodes and a centre-tap on the secondary winding. Each diode conducts every alternate half-cycle, and since the load is common to both diode circuits, a pulse of unidirectional current flows in the load every half-cycle.

Amplifiers

Amplifiers are employed to increase the magnitude of voltage and current signals or the power in these signals. Where a transistor is used as the amplifying device, the signal to be amplified normally effects a change in the base-emitter voltage and thus base current, which produces correspondingly large changes in collector and emitter currents.

Different arrangements of transistors and biasing and coupling components are used, depending on whether voltage, current or power amplification is required; whether the signal to be amplified is dc or ac; and in the event of an ac signal, the frequency of the signal. For example, a single stage audio frequency amplifier might comprise an npn transistor, load, emitter and base bias *resistors*, and *coupling* and *decoupling capacitors*.

To prevent collector and emitter currents varying with temperature, and adversely affecting operation of the amplifier, dc stabilization is necessary. One common method employed to achieve good dc stabilization and to provide base

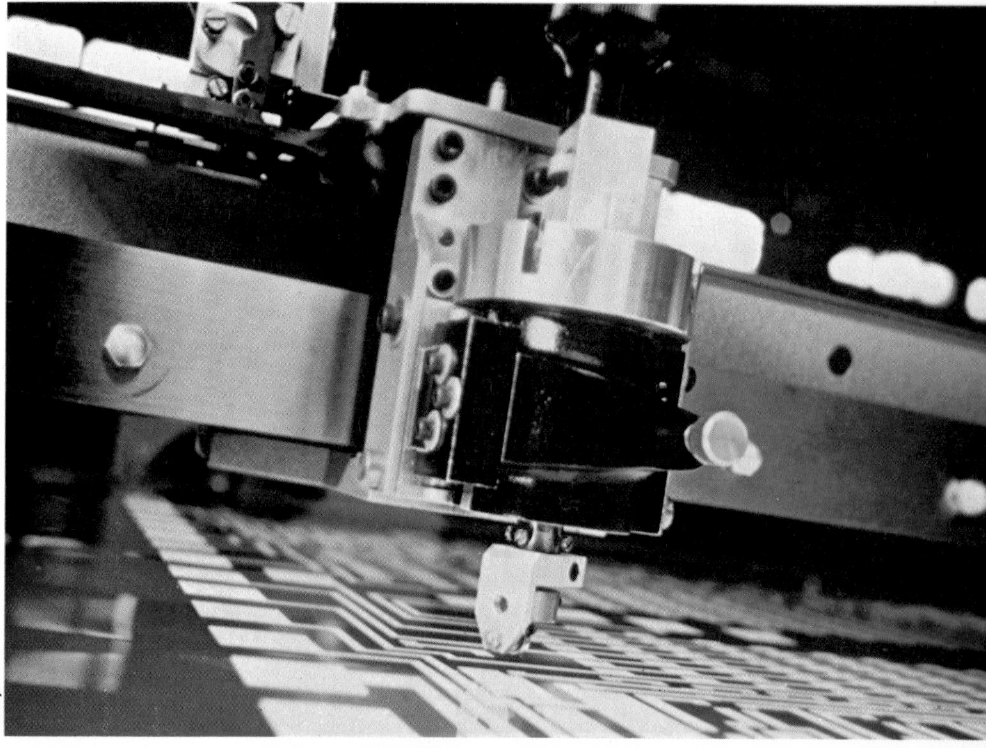
Plessey

Above: This machine is making a large drawing of the layout of an integrated circuit. The drawing will be reduced photographically to produce a set of masks which provide the pattern for the engraving of the actual circuit.

Siemens

Right: Planning the layout of a circuit with the aid of a computer.

RCA Solid State

Below: Wafers of silicon 7.6 cm (3 in) in diameter are each made into between 100 and 4,000 individual circuits.

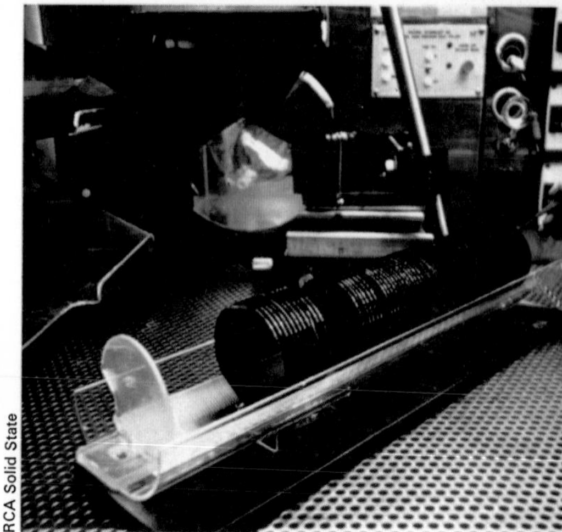
RCA Solid State

Below right: Silicon wafers about to enter the furnace where they are heated to form an oxide layer on their surfaces. After this, they are coated with a light-sensitive emulsion, the layout masks are placed over them, and a light is shone onto them to expose the emulsion to the pattern of the masks. The exposed areas are then hardened and the wafers are etched with acid, which dissolves away the oxide areas not protected by a coating of hardened emulsion.

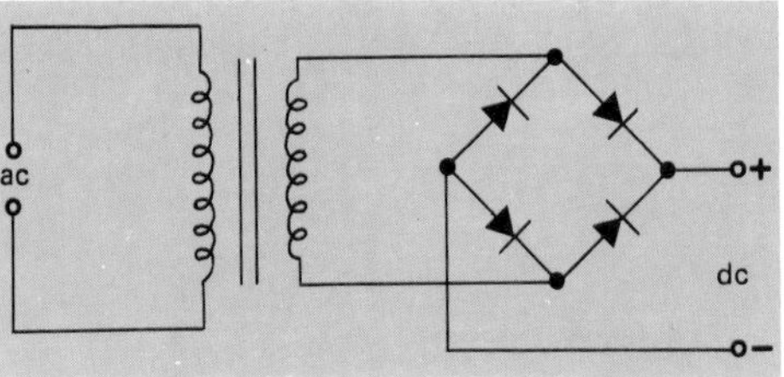

Above: The circuit diagram for a full-wave *bridge rectifier*. The ac supply is fed to the transformer, and the output voltage from the secondary winding is applied to the bridge circuit which converts it from ac to dc. The bridge rectifier is used where a centre-tapped transformer is not available.

Below: A 'push-pull' amplifier output stage of the kind often used in small audio amplifiers. The two transformer secondaries each drive a transistor which conducts on alternate half-cycles of the amplified signal. The outputs from the transistors are used to drive a loudspeaker.

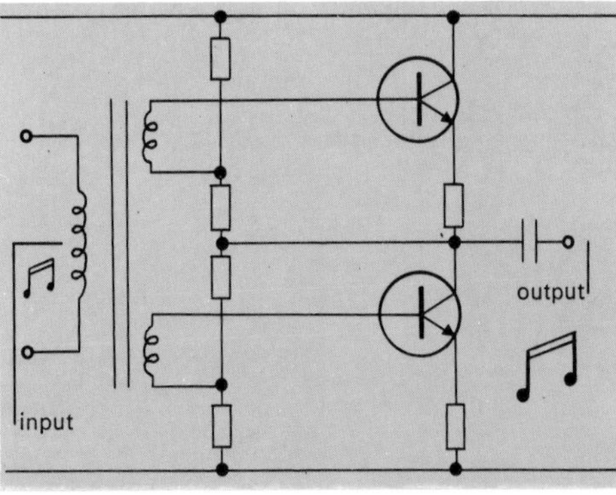

Top left: After the integrated circuits have been built into the silicon wafers, each one is tested on an automatic machine such as this one, which scans the circuits with contact probes to test their electronic functions.

Left: After testing, the wafers are cut up into individual circuits. Any circuits which fail the test are rejected, and those which pass are mounted on ceramic bases containing the external connecting leads.

RCA Solid State

Below left: After a circuit has been fitted on to its ceramic base, the connecting leads are bonded to it. It is then ready for encapsulation within a protective plastic casing.

Below: This is an enlarged picture of a *microprocessor chip*, a complex integrated circuit used in computer equipment. The circuit, which contains the equivalent of approximately 10,000 components, is built into a single chip of silicon.

bias is to use a potential divider and emitter resistor arrangement.

The emitter resistor is connected between the transistor emitter and the negative supply line, while the potential divider resistors are chosen to make the base slightly more positive than the emitter and thereby forward bias the junction. Any increase in emitter current causes an increase in the voltage dropped across the emitter resistor, which reduces the base-emitter voltage. This reduces the base current and the emitter current, thus opposing the original change. This arrangement is known as *negative dc feedback*.

To avoid amplified signal variations in the emitter current causing variations in the voltage across the emitter resistor, which would reduce the input signal voltage at the base (*negative ac feedback*), a decoupling capacitor (having little impedence at signal frequencies) is connected across the emitter resistor. Some degree of negative ac feedback is frequently employed, however, in which a fraction of the output signal is fed back over one or several stages to the input and in opposition to the input signal, so as to reduce the distortion a signal may undergo in being amplified. Although this technique involves a loss in amplification, this loss can be made up by using additional amplification stages.

Oscillators

A mechanical analogy of an electronic oscillator is a spiral spring having its upper end rigidly fixed and its lower end carrying a weight. If the weight is raised and then released, it will oscillate up and down with decreasing amplitude as energy is lost. If, however, each time the weight is moving downwards it receives a downward tap sufficient to replace the energy losses, then the oscillations can be sustained.

Electronic oscillators produce alternating output voltages at pre-determined frequencies, and are used, for example, to generate the carrier waves for radio signals and the fundamental tone signals

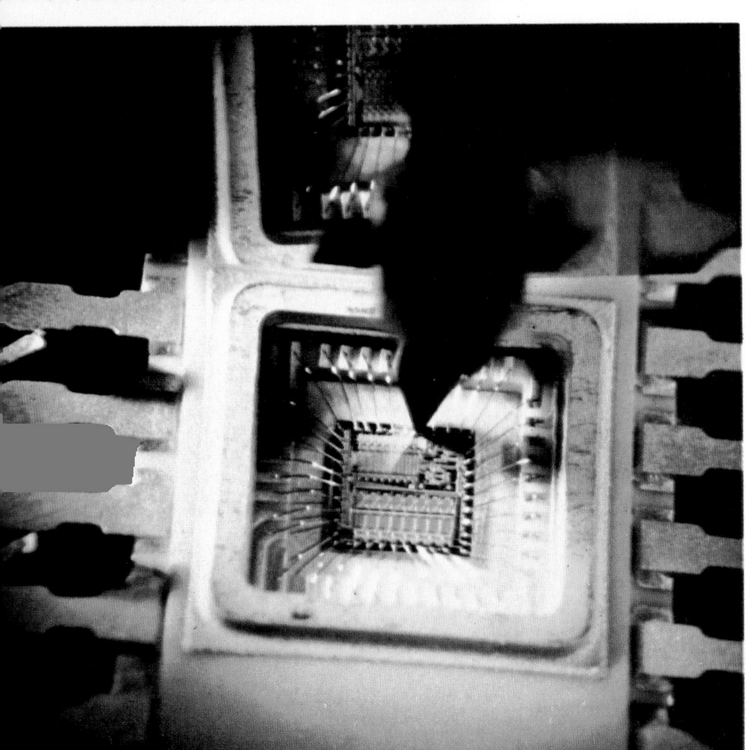

RCA Solid State

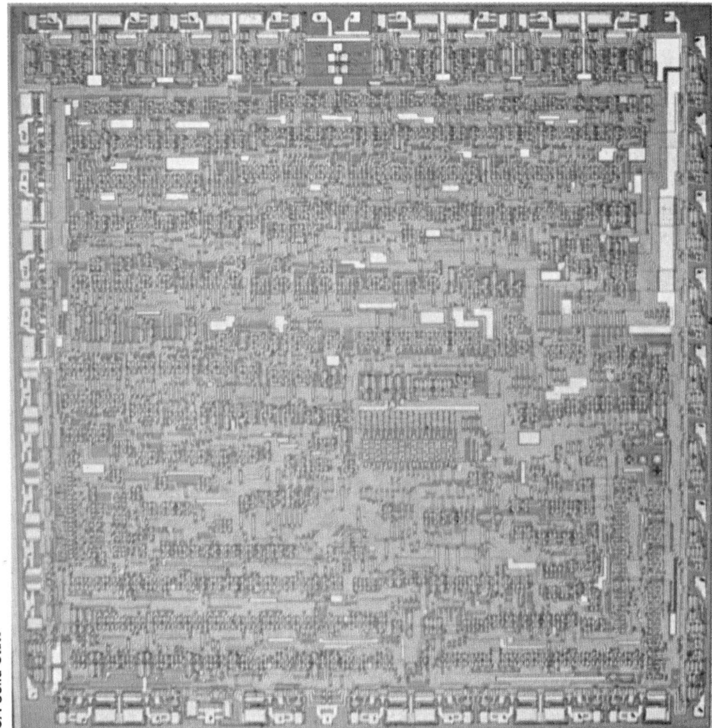

RCA Solid State

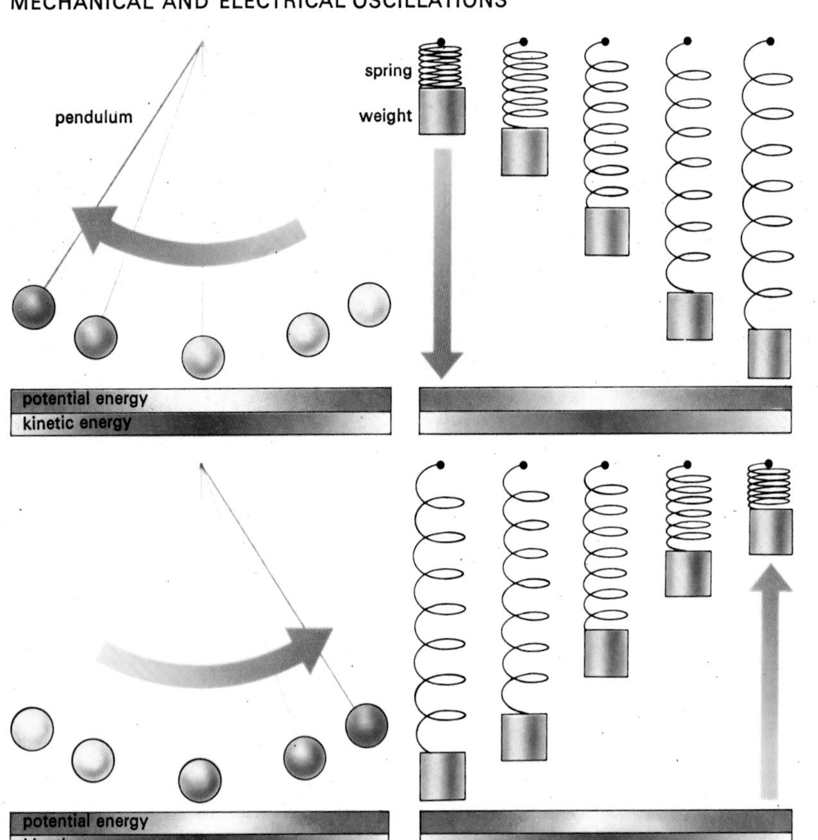

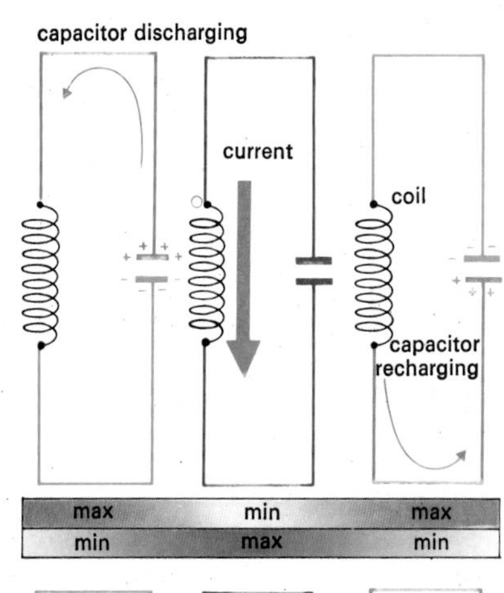

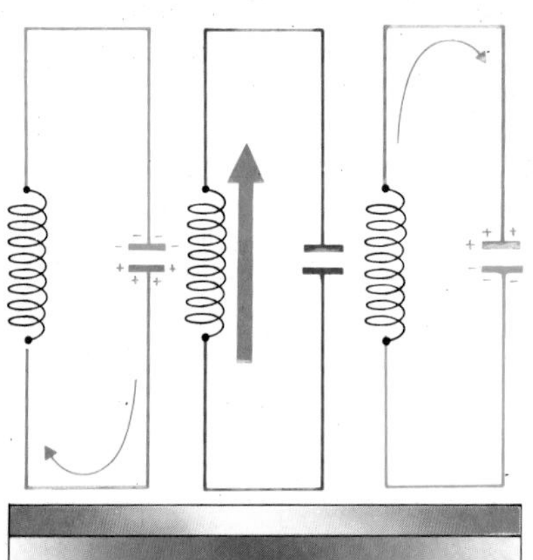

Above: A circuit diagram for a sinusoidal oscillator. The tuned circuit consists of the primary of the transformer, and a variable capacitor to allow adjustment of the oscillation frequency. The transformer secondary provides the feedback signal to the transistor base to maintain the oscillations.

Left: In mechanical oscillations, potential energy is converted into kinetic energy and back to potential energy. In electrical oscillations, these two quantities are replaced by voltage and current.

for electronic organs. As with mechanical oscillations, lost energy has to be replaced in-phase to maintain the oscillations of current and voltage in an electronic oscillator. This is usually achieved by amplifying part of the oscillating current or voltage signal and feeding it back into the original oscillating circuit in-phase with the voltage or current signal. This is known as *positive feedback*. Providing the amplification is sufficient, the energy in the feedback signal will replace the lost energy and oscillations will be sustained.

Sinusoidal oscillators, which generate a smoothly alternating *sine wave* output waveform, basically comprise a *tuned circuit*, a transistor, and a feedback circuit or element. The tuned circuit may be either the primary or secondary of a transformer connected in parallel with a capacitor, while the feedback element will be the secondary or primary of the transformer respectively.

Switching and logic circuits

Modern data processing and control equipment make extensive use of switching and logic circuits. In these, the action of the transistors resembles that of switches since their operating voltages and currents undergo rapid transitions from one level to another rather than varying continuously.

Multivibrators are one family of switching circuits which are a form of oscillator: their basic circuit comprises two transistors, (T1 and T2), each with collector and base resistors and with positive feedback between the collector of each transistor and the base of the other.

In the *astable multivibrator*, two coupling capacitors provide ac feedback between the transistors such that the multivibrator switches between T1 on and T2 off, and vice versa, thereby generating a waveform which is a suc-

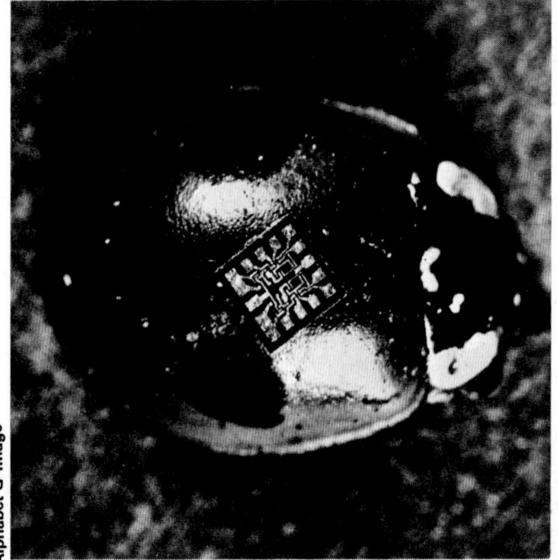
Alphabet & Image

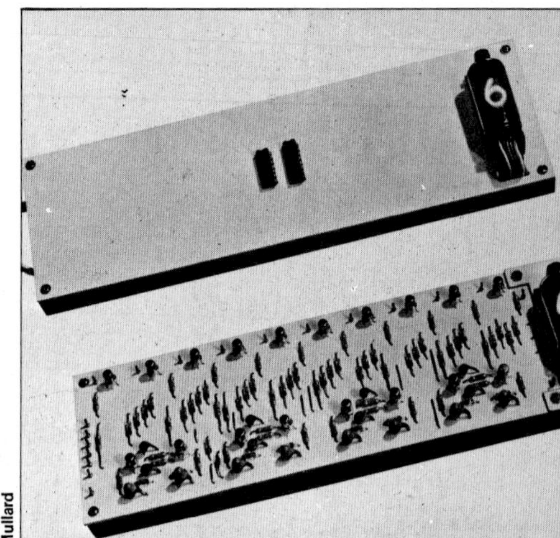
Mullard

Above: This picture shows just how small an integrated circuit can be. This one is about 1 mm (0.04 in) square, and contains thirty components, including transistors, resistors, diodes and capacitors.

Above right: An electronic counter using integrated circuits (top), compared with a similar device using discrete components.

Right: This circuit, used in televisions, is an example of a *hybrid film circuit*. These circuits are made by depositing conductor and resistor patterns on to a ceramic base or substrate, and small capacitors can also be formed on the substrate by depositing alternate layers of conductor and insulator to form a two-plate capacitor. Larger components, such as transistors and coils, are then attached to the circuit.

Erie

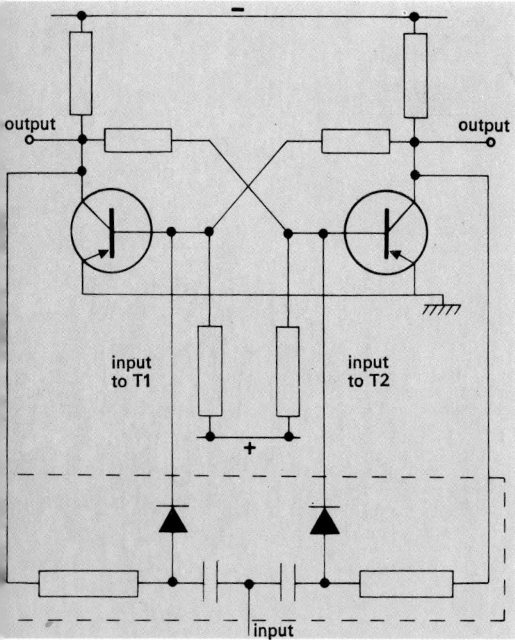

Above: A bistable multivibrator circuit. The bistable multivibrator, often called a 'flip-flop' or 'latch', has two stable states, T_1 on and T_2 off, and T_1 off and T_2 on. The circuit within the broken rectangle is the 'steering circuit' which directs the trigger pulse from the input to the transistors, causing the circuit to change its state.

Below: A thick film circuit, with discrete capacitors and a transistor added to it, ready for encapsulation in a plastic casing.

cession of square pulses. The astable multivibrator is free-running, and it is used for generating timing frequencies and for frequency division, producing a low frequency output signal from a high frequency input signal.

The *monostable multivibrator* has one stable state (T1 on and T2 off) and one unstable or quasi-stable state (T1 off and T2 on). Positive feedback between the transistors is provided by a resistor (T1 collector to T2 base) and a capacitor (T2 collector to T1 base). It is triggered by an external pulse from its stable state into its quasi-stable state, where it remains for a predetermined time before switching back to its stable state. The monostable multivibrator is used for example for pulse amplification and for standardizing pulses of random widths.

The *bistable multivibrator* has two stable states (T1 on, T2 off and vice versa). Positive feedback between the transistors is provided by two resistors. The values of the coupling resistors and the base bias resistors are chosen so that when one transistor is 'on' the other is biased 'off'. The circuit will only change state on receiving an external trigger pulse, usually applied through a capacitor to the base of the conducting transistor so as to switch it off. The bistable multivibrator is used as a logic storage unit and in tuning circuits as a frequency divider.

It can also be used as the basic unit in a counter which employs the binary system for counting. (While the *denary* or decimal system is based on the radix 10, the *binary* system is based on the radix 2). In counter applications, pulses from a single input switch off each side of the multivibrator alternately, switching the other side on at the same time.

Another switching circuit, with a single input, is the *Schmitt trigger* circuit. The circuit changes state whenever the input exceeds a critical amplitude and changes back again when the input falls to approximately the same level. The circuit is used for waveform restoration, signal level shifting, and for dc level detection.

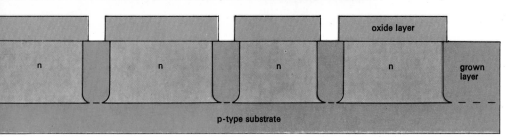

Terence Fox

Below: The manufacture of semiconductor integrated circuits. The upper diagram shows the p-type substrate which has had a layer of n-type material 'grown' on top of it. The surface of the n-type layer has been oxidized, and p-type material has been been diffused into the n-type through gaps cut in the oxide. These p-type areas separate the n-type material into isolated regions. The lower diagram shows how further diffusions of impurities form various types of semiconductor within these isolated n-type areas, which are interconnected by the aluminium metallization layer. This technique is known as *diode isolation*.

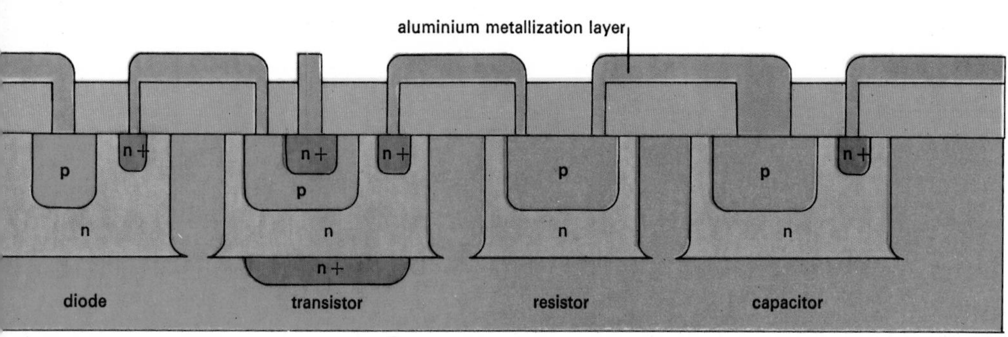

Electronic circuit construction

Prior to the 1950s the production of electronic circuits involved the mounting of electronic devices and components directly on the equipment chassis or tag-boards, followed by their interconnection using hand-wiring techniques. The advent of printed wiring boards (frequently termed *printed circuit* boards), however, radically changed the construction of electronic circuits and enabled automatic techniques to be used in their production.

Early printed wiring boards had a phenolic laminate substrate which was clad on one side with copper from which the conductor pattern was etched. Components were mounted on the non-copper side and their leads were passed through holes for soldering to the conductors. This form of circuit construction is still widely used today. The developments in recent years have been boards clad on both sides with a conductor pattern, and multi-layer printed wiring comprising conductor patterns interleaved with insulating laminates.

Following the development of the planar semiconductor manufacturing technique, where many hundreds of devices could be diffused at one time into a wafer of silicon, it was realised that the same technique could also be used to diffuse resistors and capacitors into the same wafer. Complete circuits could therefore be *integrated* into single chips of silicon.

While the most complex semiconductor integrated circuits occupy only a minute volume, they are limited in power output and by the resistor and capacitor values that can be obtained. *Thick* and *thin film circuits* are not so limited, although they do occupy larger volumes.

Thick film circuits are produced by a screenprinting technique on an alumina substrate. The substrate is rigidly supported in the printing press and covered by a fine wire mesh printing screen which carries a hardened emulsion stencil of the conductor film pattern. A squeegee is passed across the printing screen forcing conductive ink through the open mesh of the stencil onto the substrate to form the required conductor pattern. After printing, firing in a furnace bonds the film to the substrate. Resistance and dielectric inks (for making capacitors) are similarly screenprinted and fired onto the substrate.

Thin film circuits are produced by vacuum deposition onto a glass substrate. The film source material and substrate are placed in a chamber which is subsequently evacuated and the temperature of the source material raised until evaporation takes place. Deposition of evaporated film material on the substrate surface is controlled by metal masks with apertures corresponding to the film pattern required.

Optics

As you look at this page, you are actually observing a certain type of reflection. Almost everything we can see, except for actual sources of light such as the Sun or a light bulb, is visible only because of reflection. We normally think of reflection as being a property of mirrors or shiny objects, but the kind of reflections which produce images, such as those in a mirror, are really just one type, known as *specular* reflection.

Far more common is *diffuse* reflection, which causes this page to be visible. A beam of light striking the paper is reflected by it in all directions. Whichever angle you look at it from, it appears equally as bright. The printer's ink does not reflect as much light as the white paper—it absorbs some of it—so it appears darker by comparison. The coloured ink in the pictures absorbs some colours more than others, so only these others are reflected.

If you experiment by holding the page so as to catch the light from a table lamp in an otherwise dark room, you will find that at a certain angle it reflects slightly more light, as if it were behaving a little like a mirror. That is, the paper is not giving completely diffuse reflections—there is, in effect, also a slight specular component.

A mirror, however, gives purely specular reflections—the beam of light is reflected in one direction only, so that only when you are looking at the correct angle to the mirror will you see a particular object reflected in it. This, and the fact that light always travels in straight lines, accounts for the way a flat mirror produces reflections.

What makes some materials give diffuse, and some specular, reflections? The answer lies in the roughness of the material. If a light beam strikes a surface which is rough on a scale comparable with the wavelength of light (about 0.5 thousandths of a millimetre), then it may be reflected in any direction. But if the surface is within a few wavelengths of being flat, the beam will be reflected at a definite angle. The situation is comparable with throwing a tennis ball at a wall—if the wall is very rough, the ball may come off at any direction, but if it is smooth the ball will be 'reflected' at a predictable angle as long as it has no spin.

To make a mirror, therefore, one has to produce a very smooth surface. For normally rough surfaces, this can be done by applying a coating, such as the layer of varnish or wax on wood, or by including china clay in glossy paper. If the surface itself can be polished, as can glass or metal, so much the better. Glass can be made smooth fairly easily; to produce a mirror a sheet of glass is coated on the back with a thin layer of metal such as aluminium or silver, which reflects all colours equally well and therefore does not give a noticeable tint.

Specular reflection always obeys certain laws. In particular, the angle at which the beam strikes a surface (the *angle of incidence*) is always equal to the angle at which it is reflected (the *angle of reflection*). These two angles are measured from a line perpendicular to the surface, called the *normal*. The angles of incidence and reflection and the normal are always in the same plane. Using these laws, we can easily predict how a ray will be reflected, just as a billiards or pool player can predict how a ball will bounce off the cushion at the side of the table.

Refraction

Although light normally travels in straight lines, it sometimes appears to bend. This occurs when it passes from one medium, such as air or water, into another, such as glass or clear plastic, which has different optical properties. The obvious example of this is when a stick is put into water at an angle—it appears bent where it enters the water.

This phenomenon is called *refraction*, and the optical property which causes it is called the *refractive* index. We can see its effects if we watch a beam of light passing into a glass block from air. Instead of carrying on in a straight line, it deflects towards the normal as it enters the block. The refractive index is a measure of the light-bending ability of a medium, usually compared with that of air, and is expressed as a number.

When light enters a parallel-sided glass block, the refraction at the first surface deviates the beam. As it emerges from the

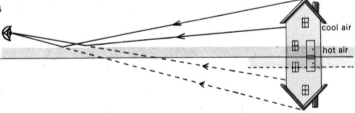

1
angle of incidence
angle of reflection
Specular
normal
Diffuse

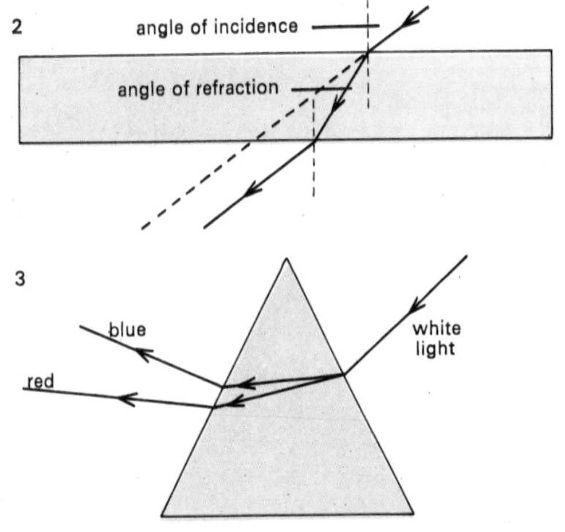

Left: These drawings show several aspects of the reflection and refraction of light.
1. When light strikes a smooth surface, such as a mirror, it is all reflected in the same direction, producing a reflected image of the object from which it is coming. This is known as *specular* reflection. If the surface is rough, the light is scattered in all directions. This *diffuse* reflection does not create a reflected image.

2. Light passing from one medium to another of different density is deflected or *refracted* slightly. Light passing through a piece of glass with parallel sides is refracted twice, by equal amounts but in opposite directions. Its direction of travel remains the same, but it is shifted slightly to one side.

3. Light passing through a prism is refracted twice in the same direction. The different wavelengths of light are refracted by different amounts, long wavelength (red) light being refracted the least and shorter wavelengths, such as blue, the most. White light passing through a prism is split into its component colours.

4. A mirage like this, an apparent reflection of actual objects, is caused by some of the light from them being refracted as it passes from cool air into hot air of lower density.

Radio Times Hulton Picture Library

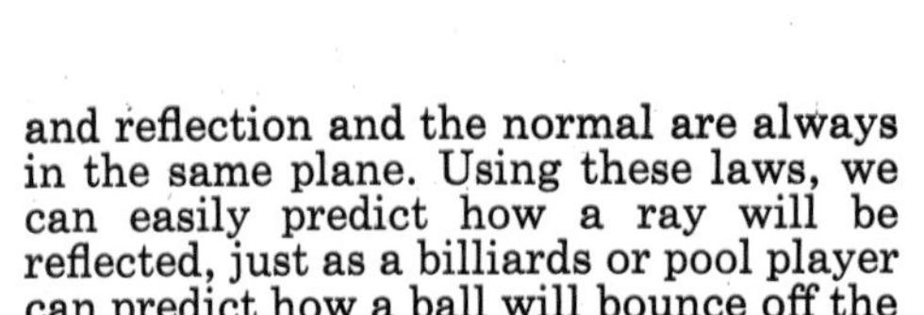

Below: 5. and 6. A convex lens is, in effect, a series of prisms, each deviating light by a different amount, arranged so that light passing through them is all deviated to the same spot. As there is a different focus for each colour of light, the image formed has coloured fringes around it.

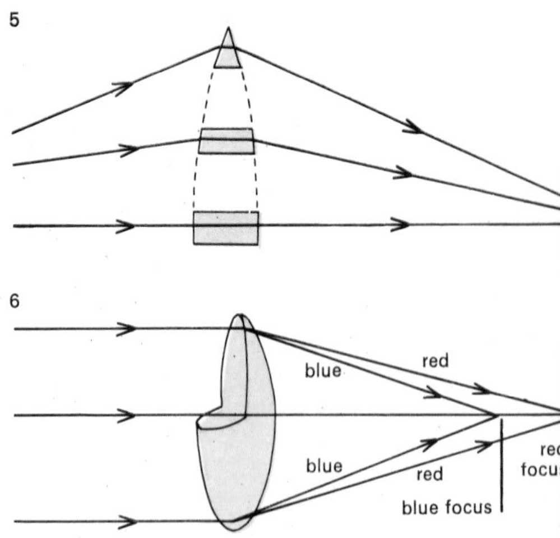

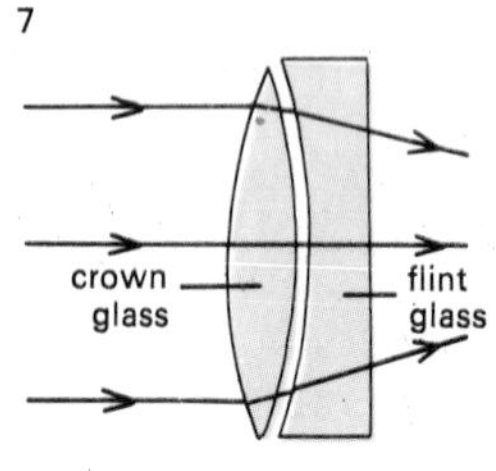

Left: 7. The *achromatic* lens produces an image with no colour fringing. The lens has two elements, made of two types of glass, and the colour dispersion caused by the first is corrected by the second. This eliminates the fringing effect or *chromatic aberration* which occurs with simple convex lenses.

other side, the beam is refracted back by an equal amount so there is no overall change in direction. But if the block does not have parallel sides, the result is an overall deviation in the light's direction. A triangular block of glass, usually called a *prism*, does this—but with one other important effect.

Unlike the law of reflection, which applies to all colours of light equally, the refractive index changes with the colour —blue light is refracted more than red when it enters a medium with a higher refractive index. For the parallel block, this *dispersion* into colours is cancelled out, just as the deviation was. But in the case of a prism, the dispersion is also increased with the result that white light is split up into all its colours, forming a *spectrum* of the colours of the rainbow. (White is simply the visual appearance of all the rainbow colours seen together). This property is exploited in *spectroscopes*, which are used to analyze the colours in a source of light.

Diffraction

There is another way in which light can be bent and split into colours—by *diffraction*, which occurs on such a small scale that we rarely observe it in everyday life. It happens more obviously with sound waves. Imagine a band marching, hidden by buildings. To start with, you hear only the bass notes. When the band emerges into full view, you can hear the high notes as well. Long waves (deep notes) can bend round corners, while short waves (higher pitched) can do so less easily.

Left: Spectacles, pairs of lenses for correcting sight defects, have been in use for over 700 years. This picture shows a 17th-century Dutch spectacle shop.

Right: A selection of high quality prisms.

Below left: The way a pair of contact lenses fit onto the eyes can be checked by dropping a special fluid into the eyes and shining ultraviolet light onto them. The fluid glows brightly and any irregularities in the fit of the lenses can easily be seen.

Below: Photo-elastic stress analysis is a method of determining the stresses within a structure subjected to a load. A model of the structure is made from clear plastic, and loads are applied to it. When viewed under *polarized* light, light in which all the waves are vibrating in the same direction, patterns are produced which correspond to the area of stress. The brightest areas of the pattern are those where the stress within the model is at a maximum.

Rank/Taylor /Hobson

Bavaria

UKAEA

TERRESTRIAL TELESCOPE

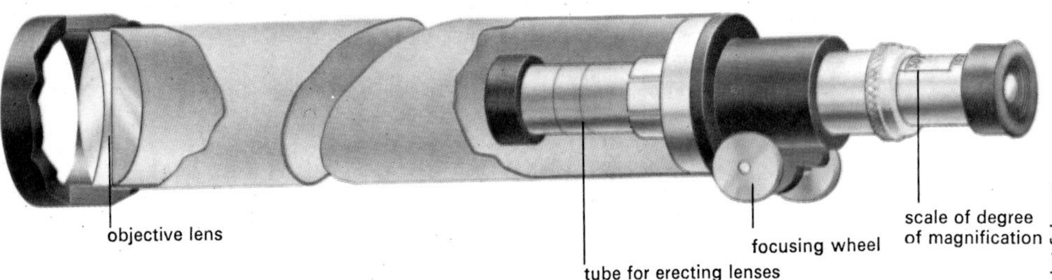

ERECTING THE IMAGE IN A TERRESTRIAL TELESCOPE

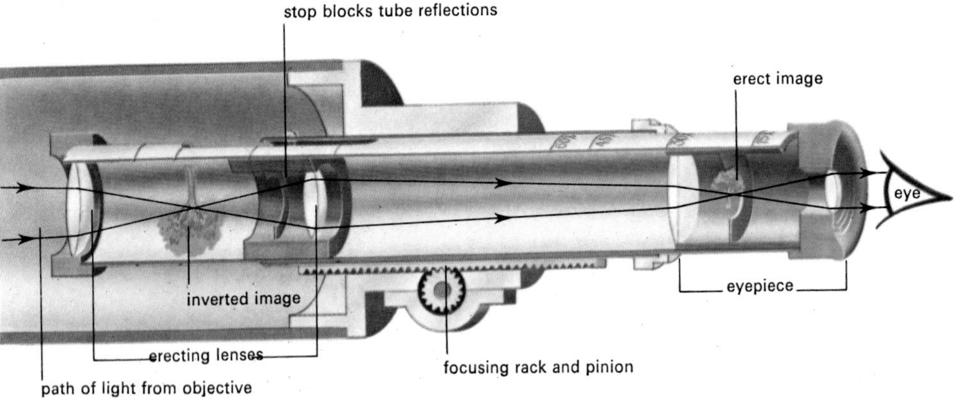

Hale Observatories/Alphabet & Image

Left and below: The large diagrams show the basic design of a terrestrial telescope and the way in which an upright image is obtained. The smaller drawings show the principles of the optical systems of four types of astronomical telescope: the refracting, Newtonian, Cassegrain and coudé.

Above: An observer sitting in the prime focus cage within the 200 inch (508 cm) telescope at the Hale Observatory on Mount Palomar, USA. The prime focus is the point where light reflected from the primary mirror first comes to a focus, and the largest telescopes have cages at this point.

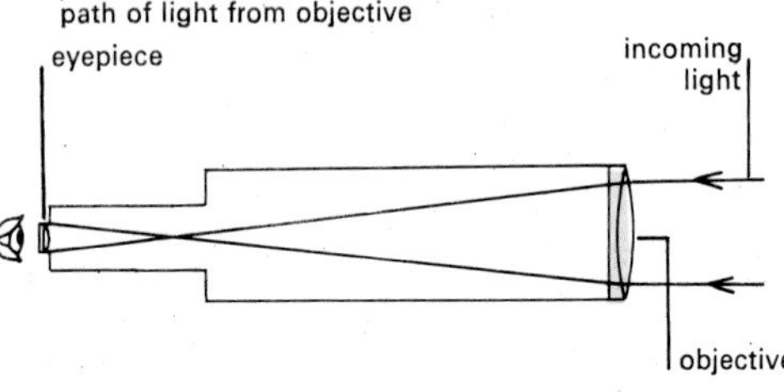

REFRACTING

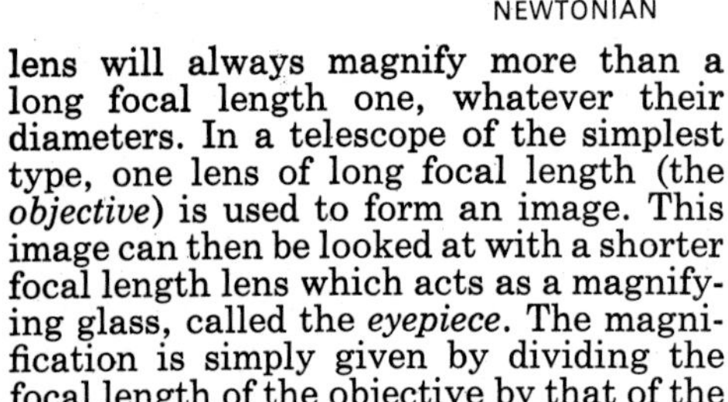

NEWTONIAN

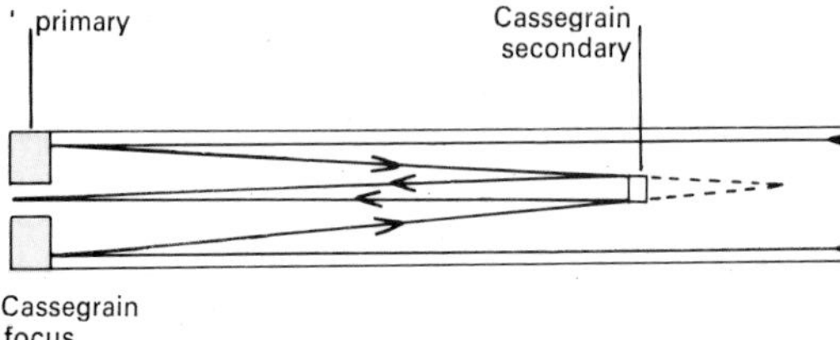

CASSEGRA

A similar thing happens with light waves. They will bend—very slightly—round obstacles, the long waves (red light) more so than the shorter ones (blue). If a regular series of obstacles is used, the effect can be seen by eye. This accounts for the colours seen in the grooves of an LP record. Lights seen through finely woven fabric also show spikes caused by this diffraction effect. A spectroscope may use a surface with finely ruled grooves, called a *diffraction grating*, in place of the prism.

Lenses

Imagine a series of prisms one on top of the other, each deviating light to a different extent and arranged so that the top one deviates the light most, while the bottom one does not deviate the light at all—that is, it is parallel-sided. Clearly it is possible to arrange the prisms in such a way that all the light coming from any particular source is deviated to the same spot.

This, in effect, is what an ordinary *convex* lens is—a series of piles of prisms, arranged in a disc so that light entering it from any direction can be deviated to one spot. This is why lenses form images. If an object is very distant—effectively 'at infinity'—its light will be refracted to form an image at a *focal point* a certain distance from the lens. This distance is called the *focal length*. A fat lens, with steeply curved sides, has a short focal length compared with its diameter while a thin one, whose sides are almost parallel, has a long focal length.

The image-forming properties of a simple convex lens allow it to be used as a magnifying glass. A short focal length lens will always magnify more than a long focal length one, whatever their diameters. In a telescope of the simplest type, one lens of long focal length (the *objective*) is used to form an image. This image can then be looked at with a shorter focal length lens which acts as a magnifying glass, called the *eyepiece*. The magnification is simply given by dividing the focal length of the objective by that of the eyepiece. Eyepieces of different focal lengths give a range of magnifications.

Astronomical telescopes

Telescopes with just two convex lenses are simple astronomical telescopes: they give upside down images, which is no great drawback in astronomy. But they have one more serious disadvantage. Just as a single prism gives colour dispersion, so a single lens has a different focal length for each colour. This results in images with coloured fringes. The longer the focal length of the lens, the less obtrusive this false colour is for a given magnification. Consequently, early astronomical telescopes had to be made impractically long to give good results.

Isaac Newton applied himself to this problem in 1668, and decided that the best solution would be to form the image not with a lens but with a mirror. A concave mirror behaves just like a lens in that it focuses light to a point—but with the advantage that since all colours are reflected equally, there is no false colour. The only drawback is that the image is formed in the path of the incoming light. To overcome this Newton placed a small flat mirror to intercept the light just before the focus and reflect it through 90° so that the image was formed outside the

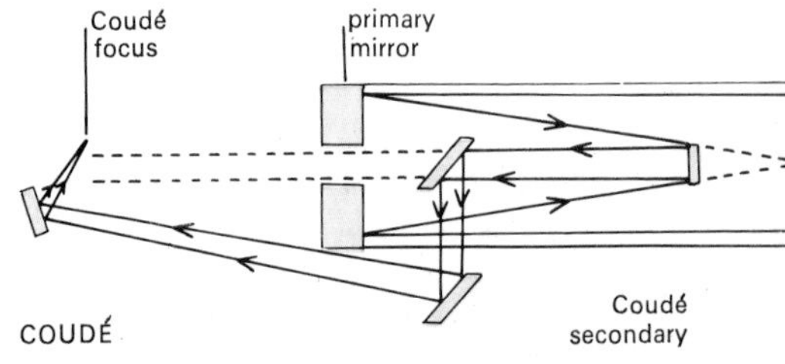

COUDÉ

Below: A Questar *catadioptric* telescope. Catadioptric telescopes use a combination of refraction and reflection to form an image. Light enters through a large concave lens, and a concave mirror at the rear reflects it on to a small reflective spot on the rear of the lens. From here, it is reflected down a central tube to a 45° prism, which directs it up to the eyepiece on top of the rear of the instrument.

Right: A pair of prismatic binoculars, which use pairs of Porro prisms to 'fold' the light path and make the system more compact.

William MacQuitty

Left: Using an optical alignment telescope to check the alignment of the bores for the main drive shafts of a light armoured tracked vehicle. The shafts pass through four bore holes in the hull, and the alignment telescope is fitted to one of the outer bores. An illuminated target is fitted into the outer bore on the other side of the vehicle, and a crossline mark on the telescope is lined up with the centre of the target by means of adjusting knobs on the telescope. The target and telescope are at the centres of their respective bores, and the adjusting knobs are calibrated to show by how much these two centres are out of alignment.

Rank Optics

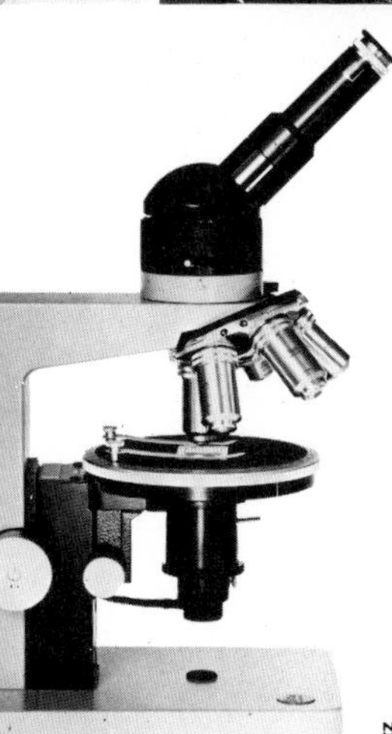
Left: A modern compact microscope designed for use by students. This one has five sets of objective lenses mounted on a revolving turret or nosepiece.

Leitz

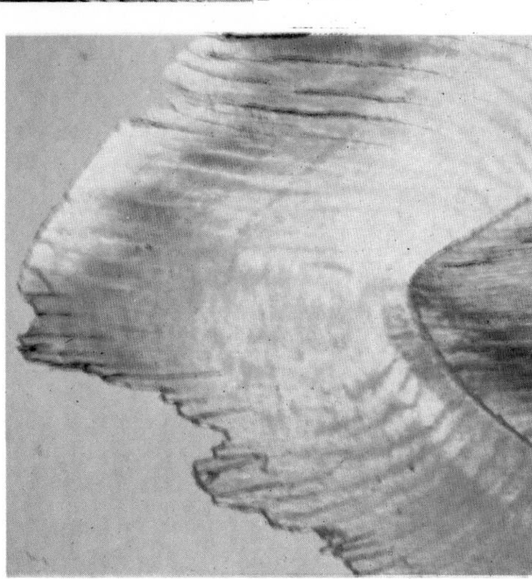
Right: This is an enlarged photograph, taken through a microscope, of a section of a porpoise's tooth. The tooth was illuminated with light polarized in one direction, and viewed through a filter polarized in another. Normally this would mean that no light could pass through the filter, but the material of the tooth has rotated the direction of polarization of the light falling on it so that some of it can pass through the filter.

Leitz

Above: The structure of the tooth is such that different wavelengths or colours of light are rotated more than others, so the original white light is split up to give a coloured image, which shows the structural detail more clearly than if it were viewed under non-polarized white light.

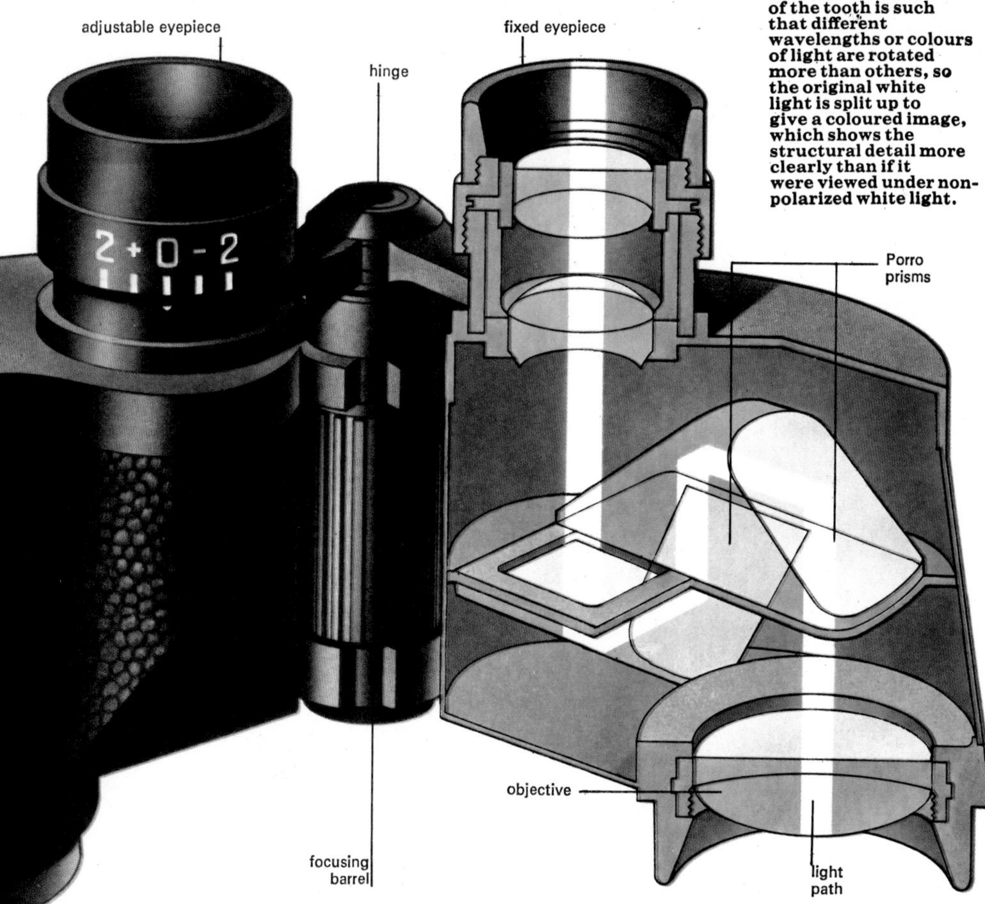

tube. There it can be viewed with an eyepiece, just as in a refractor except that the observer looks at right angles to the tube. These *Newtonian* telescopes, as they are called, are fairly easy to make and are popular with amateur astronomers.

Meanwhile, others studied the same problem and came up with the *achromatic lens*—a combination of two lenses of differing refractive index which are able to *deviate* light without *dispersing* it into colours. Achromatic lenses are now used in all high quality optical instruments.

The larger the diameter—or *aperture*—of a telescope, the more light is focused to an image and the brighter the view. For this reason, telescopes are described by their aperture rather than by their magnification (which is variable anyway). The largest telescope in the world, in the USSR, has a mirror with an aperture of 6 m (19.7 ft).

Terrestrial telescopes and binoculars

The upside down images given by astronomical telescopes are awkward when the telescope is to be used for everyday purposes. *Terrestrial telescopes*, the ordinary type used for viewing distant objects on land or sea, get over this by means of additional lenses which erect the image. Alternatively, the image can be reflected upright by a pair of *Porro prisms*, using the phenomenon of *total internal reflection*.

Because light 'bends' as it goes from a more dense medium into a less dense one, it is possible for the emergent light to be bent so much that none of it escapes from the prism at all. In this case, all the light is reflected from the surface inside the glass. In Porro prisms the light enters at right angles to one face, is totally internally reflected twice through 90° by the other two sides of the prism, and emerges at right angles to the original face, thus not suffering dispersion but turned through 180°. These prisms are used in *prismatic binoculars* to erect the image: they have the advantage over mirrors of never being able to tarnish, while their use shortens the tube length required by 'folding' the light path. Prismatic binoculars are thus two achromatic telescopes side by side, using Porro prisms to erect the image.

Simple binoculars, such as opera glasses and field glasses, are basically two-lens telescopes mounted side-by-side. These telescopes are known as *Galilean* telescopes, being based on the design invented by Galileo Galilei (1564-1642). The Galilean telescope uses a convex objective lens, but the eyepiece is *concave*. Concave lenses have one or both faces curving inwards, instead of outwards as they do on convex lenses.

Microscopes

While a simple magnifying glass can be used to give an enlarged image, it has the drawback that a high magnification would require a lens with an extremely short focal length. This would have to be so fat that it would be spherical; furthermore, it would have to be very small and it would be difficult to use. So in *compound* microscopes, the same ploy is used as in the telescope—one lens forms an image, which is then magnified by a second lens. The lenses have the same names of objective and eyepiece, but this time the objective has a short focal length and the eyepiece a longer focal length.

Cameras and Film

The first photograph was taken as long ago as 1826, by the French engineer J. N. Niépce (1765-1833). Niépce died before he could perfect his process, but his work was carried on successfully by his partner, L. J. M. Daguerre (1787-1851). Daguerre produced a photographic plate coated with light-sensitive silver iodide, and his process, known as the *Daguerrotype* process, was what made photography a commercial proposition.

The earliest cameras were very simple. A lens at one side of a box threw an image on to the box's opposite wall, where the photographer would have his light sensitive plate. The other essential was a means of controlling the exposure time. A top hat could be used just as well as any more elaborate device: it covered the lens until you wanted to take the picture. By taking it off the lens for a few minutes, you admitted light into the camera. After a suitable length of time, you replaced the top hat and the exposure was complete.

The improvement which, more than any other, brought photography within everyone's reach was the invention of film, first introduced by George Eastman in 1889. Although glass plates and single sheets of film are still used for special purposes or for studio work, the use of lengths of film, giving 12, 20 or 36 shots in rapid succession, is practically universal.

The 'top hat' aspect has also changed. Instead of many minutes' exposure, modern films usually need just a few milliseconds; but a complete range from perhaps 1/1000 sec to a minute or longer may be required. The *shutter* which achieves this has to be designed so that no part of the frame area receives more exposure than any other part.

The easiest way to accomplish this is to put the shutter at a point where it is completely out of focus—as close to the lens as possible. Most modern lenses have several components, so if a camera has a non-interchangeable lens the shutter can actually be located inside the lens, between the components. It consists of two sets of thin metal blades or leaves, which are pivoted so that one group moves out of the light beam to start the exposure and the other moves in to end it. The timing of these actions is done simply by the tension in the spring which causes them to move. The shutter is usually *cocked*—tensioning the spring—when the film is wound on.

If the camera has an interchangeable lens, however, it is most likely to have a *focal plane shutter*. This consists of a pair of blinds which move across the frame immediately in front of the film. As long as the blinds move together, all parts of the film will be exposed equally. By changing the distance separating the blinds, rather than their speed, different exposure times are possible.

Choosing the lens

Today, lenses range from simple plastic ones for mass-produced cameras to interchangeable multi-element ones costing as much as or even more than the camera they fit. A very wide range of lenses are

Radio Times Hulton Picture Library

Above: A replica of a camera used by William Fox-Talbot (1800-1877), who invented the negative/positive photographic process. His photographs were taken on paper impregnated with silver chloride, which gave negative images when developed. Positive prints were then made from the negatives.

Right: A cutaway drawing of a modern 35 mm single lens reflex (SLR) camera. These cameras have interchangeable lenses, and built-in exposure meters. The exposure meter shows the user whether or not sufficient light is entering the lens for a satisfactory image to register on the film.

Spectrum

Left: A Kodak 'Brownie' box camera, an easily-operated camera that was very popular in the 1950s. The main lens is the large one in the centre, and the two smaller ones are the viewfinder lenses, one for use with the camera upright and the other with the camera on its side. It took eight shots per roll of film.

Below: A Mamiya twin lens reflex camera, with a light meter (right) and two pairs of interchangeable lenses. Unlike an SLR, where the main lens is also the viewfinder lens, this type of camera has separate main and viewfinder lenses, so both must be changed if a different focal length is needed.

Photri

Agfa-Gevaert

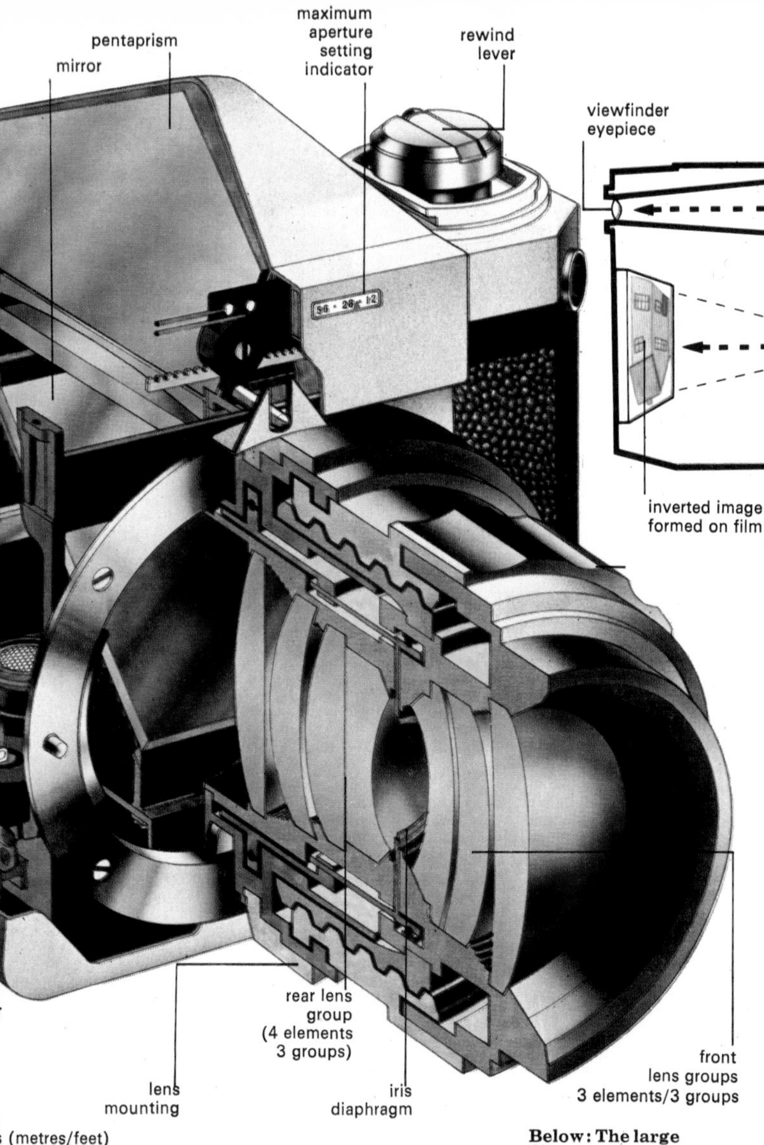

Above: This diagram shows how the image is produced within a camera. Light enters the lens, and passes through the diaphragm which controls the amount of light entering the camera. An inverted image is produced on the film when the shutter is opened, usually by a spring mechanism.

Right: A Nikkormat EL 35 mm SLR made by Nippon Kogaku K.K. (Nikon) of Japan. This camera has an electronic exposure control system, which automatically adjusts the shutter speed to give the correct exposure time for a given aperture setting. The camera shown here is fitted with a 50 mm *f*1.4 lens.

Rank Audio Visual Ltd.

Below: The large diagram is a cutaway of a 28 mm *f*4 wide angle lens used on SLR cameras. The small diagram shows the optical components of a 'fish eye' lens, which has a very wide field of view and gives a distinctive circular image. An example of such a picture is shown on the next page.

Right: This picture of a Rolleiflex SL 86 camera was taken by means of a new technique called *Neutrography*. This process is similar to X-ray photograph, but it uses beams of neutrons instead of X-rays. The image is much more detailed than those produced by X-ray photography.

General Electric Co.

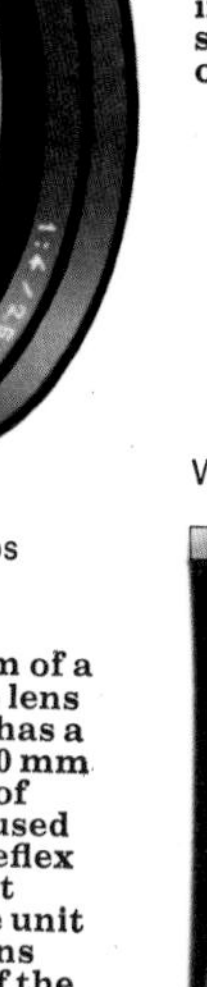

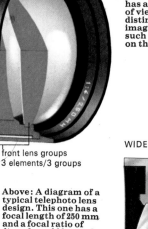

Above: A diagram of a typical telephoto lens design. This one has a focal length of 250 mm and a focal ratio of *f*4, and would be used on a single lens reflex camera. The light baffles within the unit prevent reflections from the inside of the tube, which would lower the contrast of the image.

Left: An Agfamatic 2000, one of the many simple pocket-sized cameras now available. The film is carried in a self-contained cartridge, and the flash cube has four separate flashbulbs which are rotated as the film is wound on to bring an unused bulb into position for the next shot.

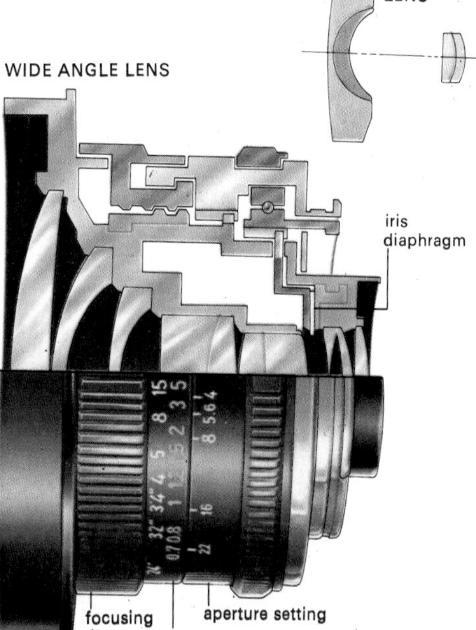

now available.

There are two factors which the photographer considers when selecting a lens. First, the *focal length*—the distance between the lens and the image it produces. It is not really so much the actual distance that is important as the scale of the image produced. For an ordinary single lens reflex (SLR) camera using 35 mm wide film, a typical standard lens has a focal length of about 45 mm to 55 mm, and produces a field of view suitable for general photography. A longer focal length—up to 400 mm is common, and press photographers may use 1,000 mm—gives a more magnified image, although taking in only a small field of view: these are called *telephoto lenses*. Lenses with shorter than standard focal lengths, say 28 mm, are called *wide angle lenses* since they give a much wider field of view. Extreme versions of these, with focal lengths of 6mm or so, are called *fish eye lenses*.

The second consideration is the *focal*

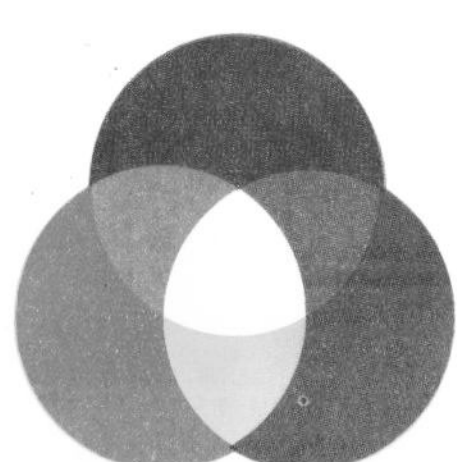

Left: This diagram shows the way in which different colours can be obtained by mixing the *primary additive colours* of light, namely red, blue and green. A mixture of red and green, for example, produces yellow, and white light is obtained by mixing equal amounts of all three primary colours.

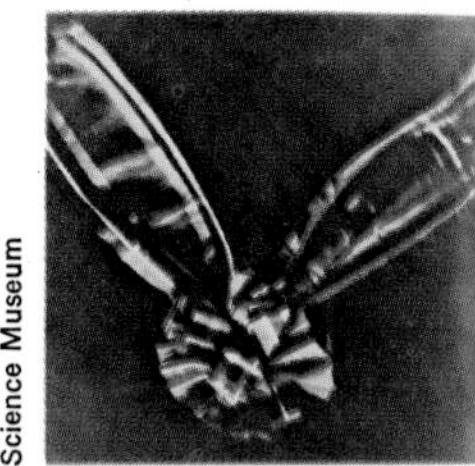

Science Museum

Left: The first colour photograph, of a piece of tartan ribbon, which was taken by James Clerk Maxwell (1831-1879) in 1861. The picture was made up of three negatives, each corresponding to one of the primary colours. Projecting these onto a screen, using coloured lights, produced a full colour image.

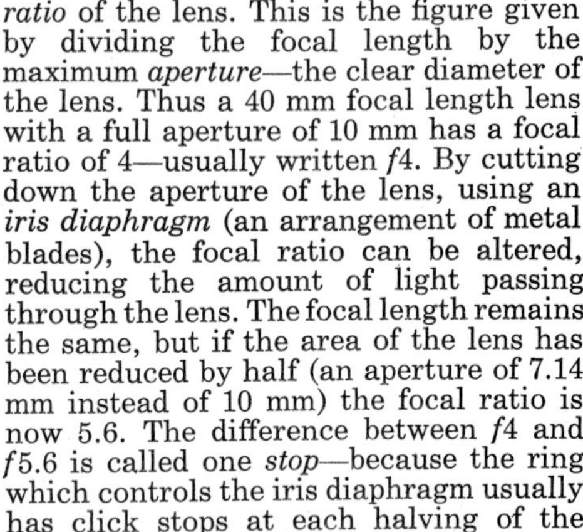

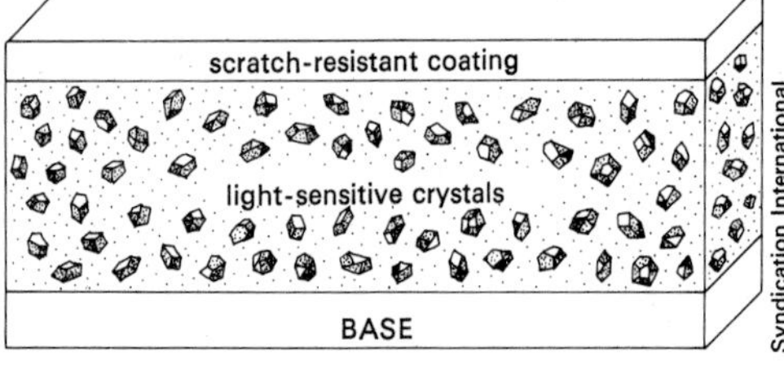

Syndication International

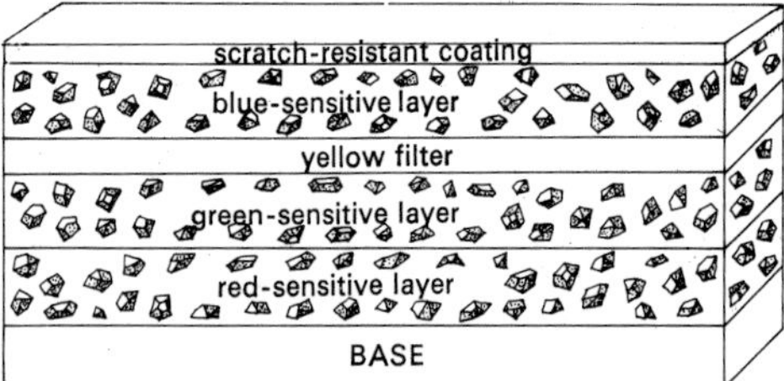

Above left: A black and white film consists basically of a layer of gelatin containing silver halide crystals, known as the emulsion, which is then coated onto a plastic base.

Left: A colour film has three separate emulsions, each sensitive to one of the primary colours.

Above: The Olympic swimming pool, Munich, taken with a fish eye lens.

Below and below left: Two pictures taken from the same position using lenses of different focal lengths. The picture on the left was taken with a normal lens, and the other with a telephoto lens.

Syndication International

Syndication International

ratio of the lens. This is the figure given by dividing the focal length by the maximum *aperture*—the clear diameter of the lens. Thus a 40 mm focal length lens with a full aperture of 10 mm has a focal ratio of 4—usually written *f*4. By cutting down the aperture of the lens, using an *iris diaphragm* (an arrangement of metal blades), the focal ratio can be altered, reducing the amount of light passing through the lens. The focal length remains the same, but if the area of the lens has been reduced by half (an aperture of 7.14 mm instead of 10 mm) the focal ratio is now 5.6. The difference between *f*4 and *f*5.6 is called one *stop*—because the ring which controls the iris diaphragm usually has click stops at each halving of the lens area. A full range of stops thus runs 1.4, 2.0, 2.8, 4.0, 5.6, 8, 11, 16, 22 and so on (some of these numbers are rounded off).

The lens' basic *f*-number is when it is wide open, letting in most light. Thus taking pictures in dim light requires a lens with a small basic *f*-number used at full aperture. But at full aperture any imperfections in the lens will be most obvious, so for perfect definition it is best to use a smaller aperture than the maximum possible on any given lens. In addition, the *depth of field* is smallest at full aperture. That is, the range of sharp focus is very small, so that only objects at the exact distance for which the lens is set will be perfectly sharp.

Shutter speeds are also arranged to vary by a factor of 2 between the click stops. So an exposure that was correct at 1/125 sec and *f*8 on a given film can be matched by one at 1/500 at *f*4, trading depth of field for a fast shutter speed which will 'freeze' movement.

If the lenses are to be interchangeable, giving different fields of view in each case, the photographer needs to know how much of the scene is appearing on the film. With non-interchangeable lens cameras, a *viewfinder* is quite adequate—a simple lens system, showing the field of view of the main lens. A development of this is the *twin lens reflex*, in which the viewfinder lens is similar to the main lens and is focused by the same mechanism. Its image is thrown on to a ground glass screen, so that the photographer can both focus up and frame the picture knowing that the main lens is seeing almost exactly the same image.

Many cameras are of the *single lens reflex* (SLR) type, where the image produced by the main lens is reflected by a mirror (placed within the camera, immediately in front of the shutter) up to a ground glass screen. The mirror swings out of the way just before the picture is taken. The photographer views the ground glass screen by means of a *pentaprism*, a prism with a pentagonal cross-section, which reflects the image so that it can be seen the right way round and in the same direction as the view being photographed. The viewfinder thus shows exactly the same scene as the lens.

Films and emulsions

The image from the lens is recorded by a light-sensitive layer called the *emulsion*, which is coated on to the film or plate material. The word 'emulsion' applies to any mixture consisting of fine particles distributed evenly throughout a liquid. The particles are thus suspended, rather than dissolved, in the liquid. In photographic emulsions, the liquid is gelatin and the particles are crystals or *grains* of silver halide. The emulsion is dried after being coated on to the film or plate, producing a solid coating of gelatin with halide grains dispersed evenly throughout.

Gelatin is made from the hooves and hides of animals. It has the almost unique property of being able to absorb water, so that it swells to several times its original size, and then dries to a solid again. It is also nearly transparent, and has chemical properties which improve the final emulsion.

Silver halides are the *salts* of silver and the *halogen* gases; chlorine, iodine and bromine are the common halogens. The grains are formed chemically in a warm solution of gelatin. The exact rate of addition of the chemicals and the temperature determine the final grain size and emulsion properties.

When a photograph is taken, there is no visible change in the emulsion's appearance. The action of light on a grain is to form a minute speck of metallic silver out of the silver halide. There is a range of sensitivity to light among the grains, so not all will be affected equally and thus subtle gradations of tone are possible. If there is a comparatively large amount of light, then a large number will be affected; if a small amount, only a few will contain the silver specks. Thus an invisible *latent image*, a pattern of halide grains containing silver specks which corresponds to the original pattern of light and shade of the image from the lens, is produced by the exposure in the camera.

This latent image is made visible by a process called *developing*. The developing agent is a chemical, such as *hydroquinone*, which will reduce silver halide to silver. The silver halide grains which have been exposed to light are more susceptible to conversion to silver, and during the carefully timed development process only the grains affected by light are converted to silver, in the form of tangled, fibre-like particles which appear black in colour. The developer is usually diluted with water, which makes the gelatin swell so that all the suspended grains are accessible to the developing agent.

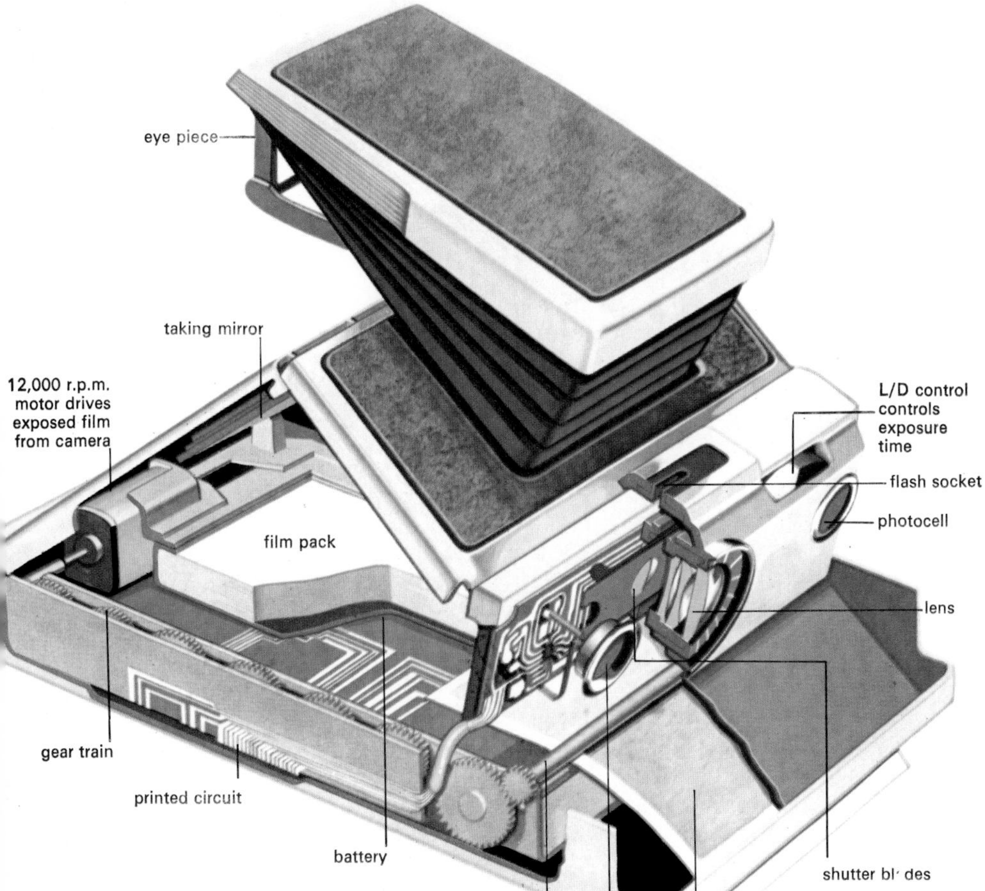

Once the development has proceeded far enough, the film is washed to remove all traces of the developing agent. The next step is to 'fix' the film by immersing it in a chemical such as *ammonium thiosulphate* or *sodium thiosulphate* ('hypo') which makes the unwanted silver halide (which has not turned black) soluble in water. The developed silver is not affected by this, so after a final wash to remove the dissolved halides the film can be dried.

The result is an image in which the brightest areas of the scene are dark, and the darkest are light—a *negative*. To make a positive print, this must be projected on to photographic paper using an enlarger. The paper is also coated with emulsion, and it is processed in the same way as film.

The sensitivity of an emulsion to light is called its *speed*. Fast films are the most sensitive, and slow films the least. There are two main systems for measuring film speed, ASA (American Standards Association) and DIN (Deutsche Industrie Normen). In the ASA system, a doubling in film sensitivity gives a doubling in the speed figure, while in the DIN system the figure increases by 3 for every stop. Thus a film of speed 200 ASA corresponds to 24 DIN, while one of 400 ASA is 27 DIN.

Colour and reversal film

A colour film is essentially three black and white emulsions together (a *tripack*), each sensitive to a different colour of light. These colours are usually red, green and blue, since by adding different amounts of these almost any colour can be produced.

An emulsion is normally only sensitive to blue light, but by adding certain dyes which absorb light of other colours, the grains can be made sensitive to other colours as well. Since they are still blue-sensitive, a yellow filter (which cuts out blue light) is deposited in the tripack above the red- and green-sensitive layers.

To make the black and white emulsion yield colour images, dyes have to be substituted for the developed silver. In the case of colour negative films, used for making colour prints, the colours opposite to the layer's sensitivity are used—that is, yellow in the blue layer, magenta (pinkish) in the green layer and cyan (bluish-green) in the red layer. When the negative is enlarged on colour paper, which also produces colours opposite to those it sees, the original colours are produced. The negative film often has an orange 'mask' or overall colouring to correct for colour bias in the printing paper.

This two-stage process is not necessary if a transparency, rather than a negative, is required. The system by which positive transparencies are produced from the original film is called *reversal processing*.

After development and washing, the film carries a developed image consisting of silver, but also a reverse image consisting of undeveloped silver halide—those parts of the image which received little or no exposure. If the negative silver image is first bleached out, these areas can themselves be developed up so as to give a positive image. In the case of colour film this image can be dyed in the original colours—blue in the blue sensitive layer, and so on.

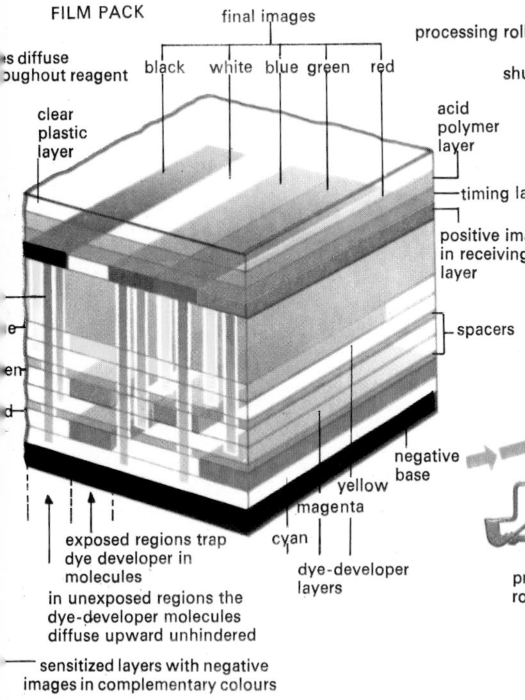

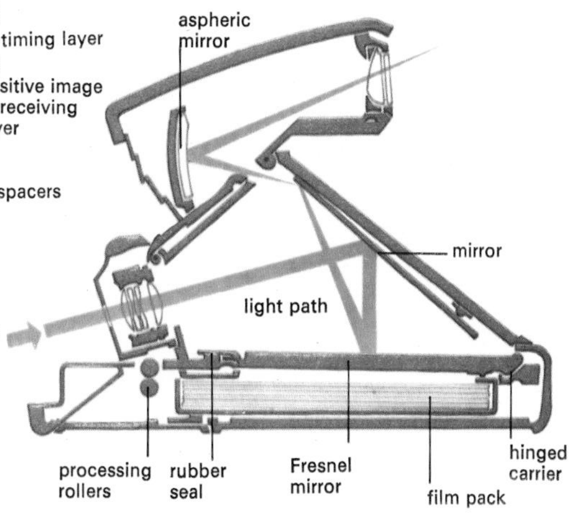

Above: The SX-70 Polaroid camera. Polaroid film contains layers of chemicals which develop the exposed film, and the image is chemically transferred onto the print paper. The exposed film is passed between two pressure rollers which burst the envelope containing the chemicals, initiating the developing and printing processes.

Left: This series of pictures shows the gradual development of an image on Polaroid colour film after it leaves the camera.

Polaroid

Sound Recording

The first recorded sounds, traditionally supposed to have been the words 'Mary had a little lamb', were made in 1877 on the *phonograph* invented by Thomas Edison (1847-1931). This device recorded sound vibrations as indentations in a cylinder covered in tinfoil, although later models used a wax surface. The next significant development was the *gramophone*, invented some 10 years later, which registered the vibrations in a spiral groove on a flat circular disc. Neither of these machines used any method of amplifying the sound before recording it, except for a resonating sound box which acted in the same way as the body of a violin or guitar, and it was mainly for this reason that their performance was relatively poor.

Good quality recorded sound only became possible in the 1920s, when the first electrically assisted recording techniques were developed. The gramophone had by then established its superiority over the phonograph, and for the next 20 years professional organisations such as radio stations recorded entirely on discs.

The possibility of using metal wire or tape to store sounds magnetically had been recognized as early as 1880 by Alexander Bell (1847-1922), the inventor of the telephone. Bell, however, abandoned the idea as impracticable with the technology then available. Then, in 1898, Valdemar Poulsen (1869-1942) demonstrated a working wire recorder which he called the *telegraphone*, and for the next 40 years work proceeded in several countries with the aim of developing a high fidelity magnetic recorder.

The big breakthrough came in Germany during the 1930s with the development of plastic tape coated with iron oxide. The process of recording on magnetic tape involves a series of conversions of the sound energy into different forms. The first of these, performed by a *microphone*, translates the fluctuating sound vibrations into an electric voltage which fluctuates in exactly the same way. Next, this signal is fed to an amplifier, which increases its strength to a level suitable for use by the recording head, which converts it once again, this time into a fluctuating magnetic field. This field aligns particles of iron oxide (or chromium dioxide in the latest tapes) on the surface of the tape (which is driven past it) to produce a pattern of magnetization on the tape which reflects the sound pattern at the microphone.

Microphones

There are several different types of microphone, each of which has its particular advantages. One of the cheapest and most robust is the *crystal microphone* which relies on the *piezoelectric effect*, whereby certain crystals generate an electric voltage whenever they are bent or twisted. This voltage is proportional to the extent of the bending. The crystal in such a microphone is firmly clamped at one end and attached at the other to a flexible diaphragm.

Sound waves make the diaphragm vibrate and in doing so it bends the crystal back and forth, giving rise to an oscillating voltage which is picked up by leads attached to the crystal surface. The

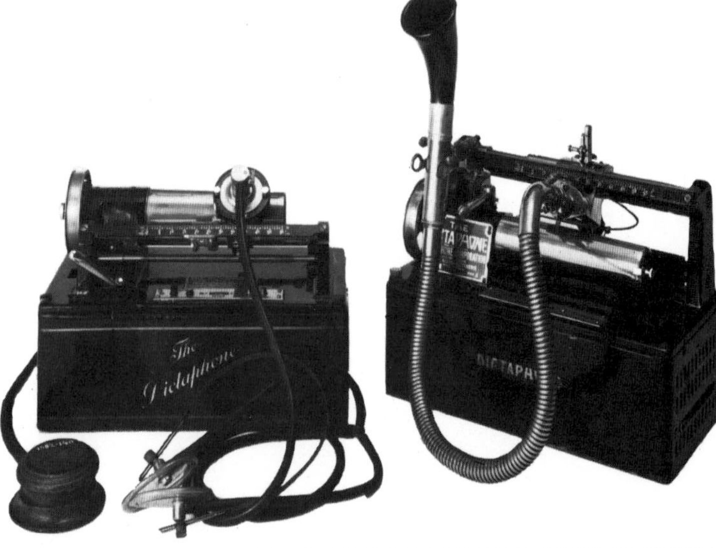

Science Museum

Left: These Dictaphone machines worked on the same principle as Edison's phonograph. The machine on the right is a Type A recorder; when dictating a letter, the user spoke into the tube and the sound vibrations moved a cutting stylus that made impressions on a wax cylinder. When the letter was to be typed, the secretary used the machine on the left, a Type B transcriber, to play the cylinder.

Right: A tape cassette. The tape is contained within the cassette, each end being fixed to a small spool. Tape speed is 4.75 cm/sec (1.875 in/sec), and a pressure pad (bottom) keeps it in contact with the heads.

Right: This recorder, invented by Valdemar Poulsen in 1900, used a steel tape wound around a cylinder. The record/replay head was driven along by the leadscrew as the cylinder was rotated, so that it tracked along the length of the tape. The microphone is on the left, and replay was via the pair of telephone earpieces on the right.

MPR

Below: One of the first tape recorders to use a non-metallic tape coated with iron oxide. The first tapes of this kind were made of paper, but were soon replaced by coated plastic tapes. The machine shown here was built by AEG in Germany in 1936, and the tape was made by BASF.

BASF

AKG/David Kelly

Above: Cutaway models of three types of cardioid microphone. These respond well to sound coming from in front of them, but less well to sound coming from the rear. They are commonly made by building a ribbon and a dynamic microphone into the same case. In such a microphone the ribbon element responds only to sounds coming from in front of it.

Science Museum

Left: A wire recorder of the 1930s. Steel wire is still used as a recording medium today, in aircraft flight recorders which record details such as the airspeed, altitude and control settings. Steel tape and ordinary plastic-based tape are also used in flight recorders.

Philips

response, however, is by no means perfect, treble (high) frequencies responding far better than any other frequencies. It is not consistent either, and tends to vary with changes in temperature and humidity.

The *moving coil microphone*, also called the *dynamic microphone*, is a far superior device. It consists essentially of a coil of wire attached to a diaphragm. As the diaphragm vibrates in response to the sound, the coil slides up and down the centrepiece of an M-shaped permanent magnet. The coil thus cuts through the magnetic field lines, which induce a fluctuating voltage in it. This fluctuating voltage faithfully represents the variations in sound pressure.

Both crystal and moving coil microphones respond equally well to sound from all directions and are consequently called *omnidirectional*, but this may not always be desirable as they tend to pick up unwanted background sounds too clearly. Often a microphone which detects better in one direction than others is more suitable, and this is a characteristic property of the *ribbon microphone*. A thin corrugated aluminium ribbon is suspended in the field of a permanent magnet and the sound arriving at the front or back of the ribbon causes it to move in the magnetic field. This induces a current along its length which is picked up by connecting leads. Sound waves impinging from the sides have little effect because they meet the thin edge of the ribbon. Strictly speaking this is a *bidirectional* microphone because it responds equally well to sound from in front or behind.

If a ribbon is combined in the same case as a moving coil the result is a *cardioid* type microphone which responds well to sound from roughly in front of it but less well to sound which approaches from the rear.

Recording

The electrical signal from the microphone is boosted by an electronic amplifier and applied to the *record head* of the tape recorder. This is basically an electromagnet, formed by a circular core of magnetic alloy in which is cut a small gap about 0.025 mm (one thousandth of an inch) wide. This is energized by the signal current from the amplifier which passes through a wire coil wrapped around the core.

The magnetic field produced in this coil is channelled around the core and can only escape at the gap. And it is just in the area of this gap that the tape makes contact with the head, so that as the tape moves past the head it cannot avoid the effect of the magnetic field. In consequence the oxide particles of the tape are magnetized either along or against the direction of tape travel according to the direction of the magnetic field when they were passing the gap. The strength of the magnetization also varies with the intensity of the field. So a small area of tape carries a complete magnetic record of the sound pressure at the instant it passed the gap.

Unfortunately the recording produced in this straightforward manner would not satisfy even the least discriminating listener. This is because the tape is not constantly magnetized in simple proportion to the magnetic field in the gap. Although for very small fields it is, as the field increases the magnetization is more nearly proportional to the square of the field. Beyond about half its maximum (or saturation) value the magnetization is once more simply proportional to the field. In short, the tape magnetization is a very poor representation of the field in the recording head gap, and hence it is a poor record of the sound and introduces frequencies which are not present in the original.

Such distortion (a form of *harmonic distortion*) must obviously be prevented and the only way to do this is to ensure that the tape magnetization is always high enough to keep it out of the region where it is not proportional to the field. One solution is to superimpose the amplified microphone signal onto a very high frequency current which is called a *bias signal*. This keeps the tape magnetization out of the danger area but still allows it to be magnetized in both directions, thereby reducing the noise problem.

The tape must of course be completely unmagnetized when it reaches the record head, because any superfluous magnetization appears as noise when the tape is replayed. This is achieved by an *erase head*, which is constructed in the same way as the record head but with a larger gap. The coil of the erase head carries a rapidly varying current of sufficient strength to magnetize the tape to saturation, first in one direction and then in the other, several times as it passes the gap. Any initial magnetization of the tape is thus completely swamped.

The large gap of the erase head allows its field to extend some distance beyond it, so that as the tape leaves the gap it still undergoes cycles of magnetization which become weaker and weaker as it

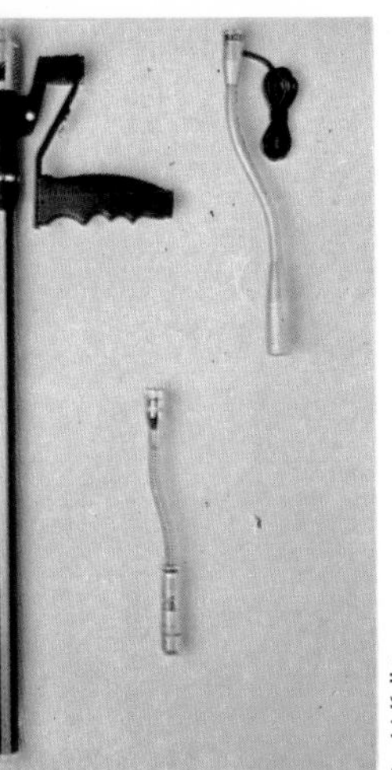

Left: A cardioid microphone (top right), an omnidirectional dynamic microphone (bottom right), and a 'rifle' type of directional microphone. The rifle microphone has a large number of narrow parallel tubes in front of the actual microphone element. Sounds entering the microphone from the front all have the same distance to travel along the tubes, and so they reach the element in phase with each other. Sounds entering from any other angle travel different distances along the tubes, and so reach the element out of phase with each other, effectively cancelling each other out. This makes the microphone highly directional.

David Kelly

EMI Ltd

Above: Magnetic tape is made in wide strips, which are then slit into single tape widths on a machine such as this one. Cassette tapes are 3.81 mm (0.15 in) wide, ordinary tapes are 6.35 mm (0.25 in) wide, and tapes for professional studio machines are up to 5.08 cm (2 in) wide.

Ferrograph

Left: A modern high-quality stereophonic tape recorder, fitted with the Dolby noise reduction system. This one is a half-track recorder; each stereo channel is recorded on half the width of the tape, or alternatively two separate mono channels may be recorded, one on each half.

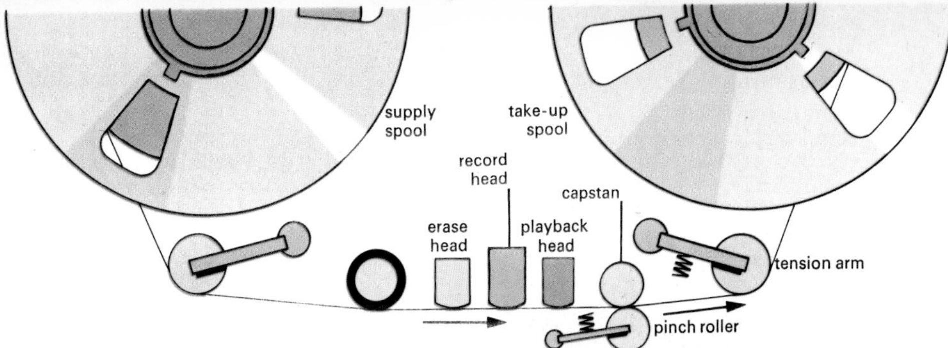

Above: The tape drive and head layout of a high quality reel-to-reel tape recorder. The tape first passes the erase head, which wipes it clean of any previous magnetism, and then passes the record head which records the signal on to it. The playback head picks up this signal during replaying of the tape.

Right: Two different ways of applying the bias signal to the tape. The conventional head arrangement feeds both the bias and the sound signals to the record head. The Akai Crossfield system uses a separate head to apply the bias in order to reduce the possibility of sound distortion.

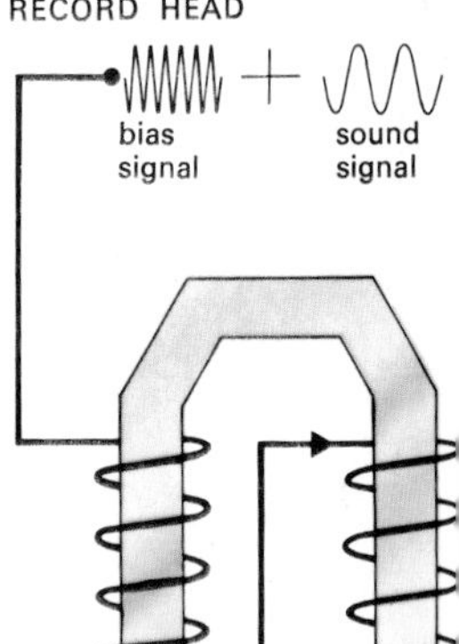

Right: The first step in record manufacture is the recording of the music. This picture shows three musicians recording at the EMI studios. Studio tape recorders use tape up to 5.08 cm (2 in) wide, and have 8, 16 or 24 tracks, compared with domestic machines which usually have only two or four tracks.

Transworld

EMI Ltd

Far left: After the recording has been completed, the *master tape* is used to drive the cutting lathe (in the background) which produces a lacquer *master disc*. This is the last time the master tape itself will be used in the record manufacturing process. Moulds can now be taken from the master disc, and these will then be used in the record presses.

Left: The next step in record manufacture is the production of a *master shell* from the master disc. This picture shows the master disc after it has been given a very thin coating of silver. This silver coating then has 0.625 mm (0.025 in) of nickel deposited on top of it, to form the master shell which is finally separated from the master disc.

Decca/Photo :John Goldblatt

Below: A master shell about to have a further nickel shell, the *positive shell*, electroplated on to its silver face. The shells are then separated, and the positive shell goes on to the next step in the process.

recedes, vanishing to zero after a short distance to leave the tape completely demagnetized.

When the tape is replayed it is run past a *replay head* (or *playback head*), which is really only a record head operating in reverse—indeed many domestic machines use the same head for both purposes. As the magnetized tape passes the gap in the replay head, the tiny magnetic field which surrounds the tape surface is channelled around the core and hence through the surrounding coil. The alternations in this field, corresponding to the recorded sounds, generate a matching current in the coil (by electromagnetic induction, the same process which on a much larger scale is used to generate current in power stations). The current in the coil is then magnified in an amplifier which is usually the same one used when recording, and fed to a loudspeaker which converts it once again into sound.

Tape drive

For faithful reproduction of the sound it is essential that the tape is played back at the same speed as it is recorded and that this speed never fluctuates. In the earliest machines one of the two spools on which the tape is wound was directly driven by a motor and dragged the tape past the heads. But this led to unacceptable variations in speed which could be heard as *wow* and *flutter*. These are the sound engineers' names for audible fluctuations in the reproduced sound, wow referring to slow and flutter to rapid fluctuations.

On all modern machines it is the tape itself that is driven, by a spindle (often called the *capstan*) which is rotated by an electric motor. The tape is squeezed between this spindle and a rubber roller and is thus driven along at constant speed. The spools are also electrically driven via friction clutches which are adjusted to slip whenever the tension of the tape rises too high. This ensures that the tape does not break from being pulled too hard onto the spool or spill out of the machine from not being pulled fast enough.

To a large extent, the speed at which the tape moves determines the quality of the recording. If the tape moves too slowly it will not record high frequencies satisfactorily because too short a length of tape passes the head to accommodate the many thousands of oscillations which occur in the space of, for example, one second, when a high-pitched note is recorded. On the other hand, if the tape moves too quickly an inconveniently large reel of tape will be required for a given length of recording. In professional sound studios this does not matter and master recordings are made with the tape moving past the heads at a speed of 79 or 38 centimetres per second (30 or 15 inches per second). For domestic recorders a compromise is sought between quality and bulk so that 19 and $9\frac{1}{2}$ cm/sec ($7\frac{1}{2}$ and $3\frac{3}{4}$ in/sec) are the common speeds.

Decca/John Goldblatt

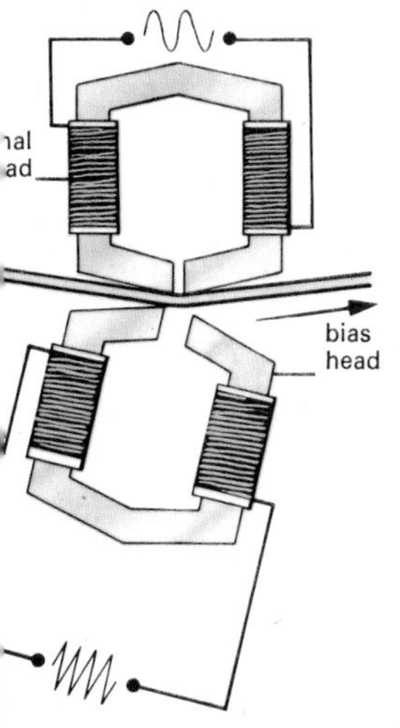
CROSSFIELD HEAD
bias
head

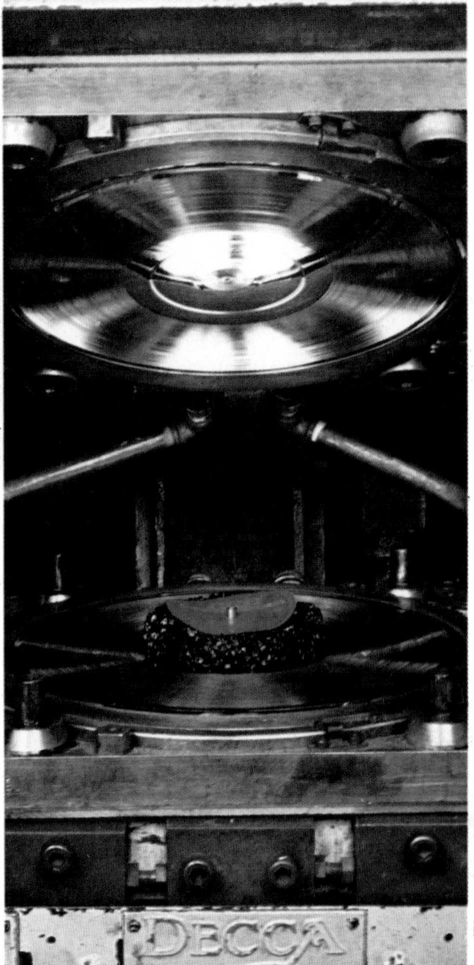

Decca/Photo: John Goldblatt

Decca/Photo: John Goldblatt

Above: One of the later stages of record making is the production of the *matrix shell*, by depositing nickel on to the positive shell. Here, the two shells are being separated. The matrix shell is the one which will be used to press the actual records, having a spiral ridge which forms the groove of the record when it is pressed.

Right: Pressing a record. A 'biscuit' of extruded pvc, with the labels in place, is squeezed between two matrix shells (or stampers), one for each side of the record. 7-inch records are usually made by injecting hot plastic under pressure into a mould, instead of by this method which is used for 10 and 12 inch LP records.

Left: This machine trims excess plastic from the edges of the records after pressing.

Below: This series of diagrams shows some of the main stages involved in the recording and manufacture of long playing records.

Decca/Photo: John Goldblatt

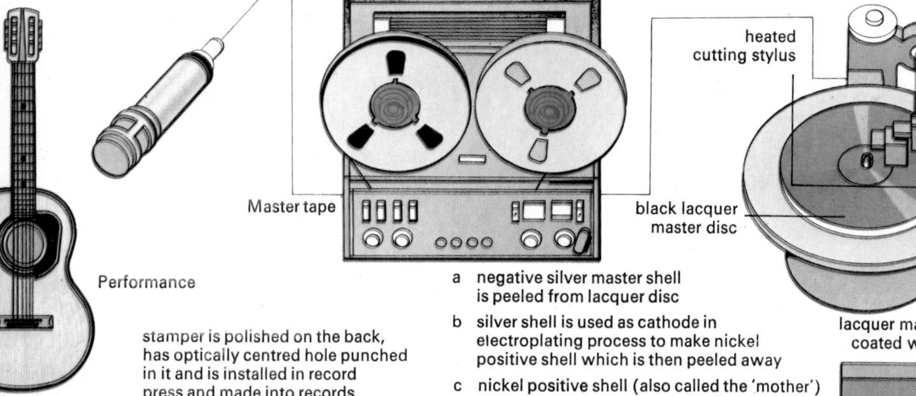
Cutting lathe
heated
cutting stylus
Master tape
black lacquer
master disc
Performance
lacquer master disc
coated with silver
a negative silver master shell is peeled from lacquer disc
b silver shell is used as cathode in electroplating process to make nickel positive shell which is then peeled away
c nickel positive shell (also called the 'mother') is used as cathode to make negative matrix shells called the 'stamper'
stamper is polished on the back, has optically centred hole punched in it and is installed in record press and made into records
ine closes, steam heat
s PVC, water cools stamper
ks, press opens
e trims excess plastic
edges of record

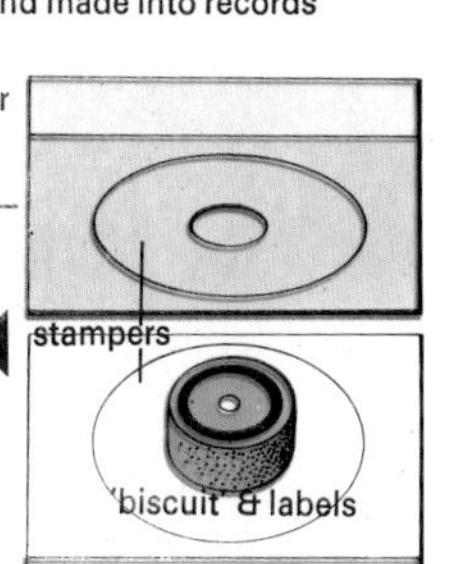

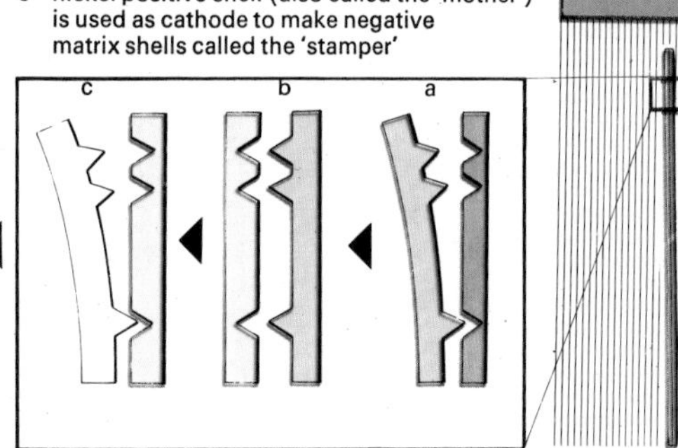
stampers
'biscuit' & labels
press
c
b
a

Cassette recorders

The major difference between cassette recorders and normal reel-to-reel machines is that the tape is permanently contained within a plastic box, the cassette, which includes both a storage and a take-up spool. The tape passes through guides along the edge of the box in which there are apertures which allow contact with the erase and record/replay heads.

Irregularities on the tape surface give rise to a slight hissing noise and if the high frequencies are boosted to compensate for loss of high frequencies due to the slow speed (4.75 cm/sec, 1.875 in/sec) of the cassette, this noise is also increased so that it tends to drown out soft passages of music or speech, particularly if they are predominantly low-pitched. There is, however, a method of overcoming this difficulty which is employed in the best cassette recorders.

It is known as the *Dolby system*, after its inventor, and relies on sophisticated electronic circuitry to detect low level passages. These are given extra amplification so that they are recorded at as much as ten times their normal intensity and when they are played back they are *attenuated* (reduced in volume) by an equal amount. The result is that these quiet passages replay at their proper level but the tape noise is only a small fraction of the total sound.

Tape cartridges also have the tape enclosed within a plastic box. In this case, however, the tape is formed into an endless loop by splicing together the two ends, and it is wound onto a single spool. It unwinds from the inside of the spool, runs past the heads, and winds back onto the outside.

Sound Reproduction

Since the 1940s the techniques of sound reproduction have developed at an amazing pace. Today's amateur enthusiast can enjoy a quality of sound which would have astonished even a professional sound engineer before the Second World War.

Sound is usually encoded in one of three forms—in the grooves of a disc, in the magnetized oxide particles on the surface of a tape, or as variations in the amplitude or frequency of a radio wave—and the first stage in reproducing it is to convert it into an electric signal whose variations correspond to those of the original sound signal. The next step is to boost this signal to a more manageable level in a *preamplifier*, which at the same time compensates for any distortion which may have been accidentally or deliberately introduced. Controls for volume and tone are usually incorporated in this section of the equipment.

The signal is then in the right form to operate a loudspeaker, but it lacks strength and must therefore be amplified once again by a *power amplifier*. The loudspeaker is the final link in the chain and serves to convert the amplified electrical signal into vibrations of the air, thus reproducing the original sound.

Most equipment made today reproduces sound *stereophonically*. Stereophonic or stereo recordings and radio programmes are designed to give a more natural effect when replayed by taking into account the ability of our ears to detect the direction as well as the intensity of sounds. If directional information is absent in the reproduced sound it appears somewhat incomplete. When a stereo recording is made, two microphones (or two sets of microphones) are used, one of which receives more sound from the left and the other more from the right. The sounds detected by each are kept entirely separate and are encoded in two completely independent 'channels' of the recording or programme. Stereo reproducing equipment is really only a duplication of ordinary single channel (*monophonic*) equipment, with independent amplifiers and speakers for each channel.

Record Players

When a disc recording is made, a master disc coated with lacquer is rotated at constant speed on a turntable. A heated cutting stylus travels slowly from the rim to the centre of the disc and cuts a spiral v-shaped groove in the lacquer. The walls of this groove are normally at 90° to each other when no sound is being recorded, as in the run-in and run-out grooves at the start and finish of every record. But the cutting stylus is also moved magnetically in response to electrical signals from the master tape recording. This leads it to cut undulations in the groove walls which encode the sound, with the left channel registered entirely on the inner groove wall and the right entirely on the outer.

The stylus moves much more for a low frequency sound than for a high frequency sound of the same intensity, so much so that it is necessary to deliberately decrease the intensity (or *attenuate*) bass

Science Museum

Science Museum

Left: A turn of the century Edison phonograph. The records were wax cylinders, rotated by a clockwork motor, and as they turned they vibrated a needle connected to a diaphragm within the unit at the bottom of the horn. The sound created by the vibrating diaphragm was amplified by the horn.

Above: The phonograph was eventually replaced by the gramophone, invented by Emile Berliner in 1887. The gramophone used flat discs instead of cylinders, and was the ancestor of today's record players. The first commercial gramophones and records were produced in Germany in 1889.

Right: An HMV Type 12 pick-up cartridge and tone arm, an example of an early magnetic pick-up. The needle was connected to a steel armature, which passed between the pole pieces of the magnet and through the centre of the coil. As the armature was vibrated by the needle, it created changes in the magnetic field which induced tiny electric currents within the coil. These were then amplified and fed to a loudspeaker.

Below right: The tone arm of a Pioneer PL-71 record deck. The small weight hanging to the right of the pivot is the bias compensation weight, which opposes the inward force on the stylus.

Science Museum

sounds to avoid wide undulations of the stylus which would lead it to cut into adjoining grooves. In the final stage, the master disc is copied and any number of records can be manufactured from it.

Playing a record on a record player attempts to reverse the process by which the master disc was produced, translating the groove wall code back into electrical signals without loss of quality. However, there are two main reasons why this can never, even in the most expensive equipment, be achieved to perfection. The first is that it is not possible to use a stylus of exactly the same shape as the cutting stylus, because it would itself cut and damage the record. So a stylus with a rounded tip must be used and this cannot follow the undulations of the walls with complete accuracy because it cannot penetrate the recesses completely.

The more important difficulty is that the stylus, unlike the cutting stylus, cannot be mechanically driven across the record as it rotates. The reproducing stylus must therefore be pulled along by the forces exerted on it by the groove, and this means that the pressure of the stylus on the groove walls will vary. It is just feasible to suspend the stylus, like a travelling crane, from a rail which it

Shriko (UK) Ltd/Varda Zisman

Below: 1. Ordinary mono records have the grooves cut in such a way that the stylus is moved from side to side by the groove.
2. An alternative to this *lateral* recording is the vertical 'hill and dale' method used originally by Edison, in which the stylus is vibrated up and down within the groove. It was originally suggested that stereo records could combine these two methods, with the left channel recorded laterally and the right vertically.
3. and 4. This led to the introduction of the 45°/45° method where the stylus is moved in two directions, each at 45° to the record surface.

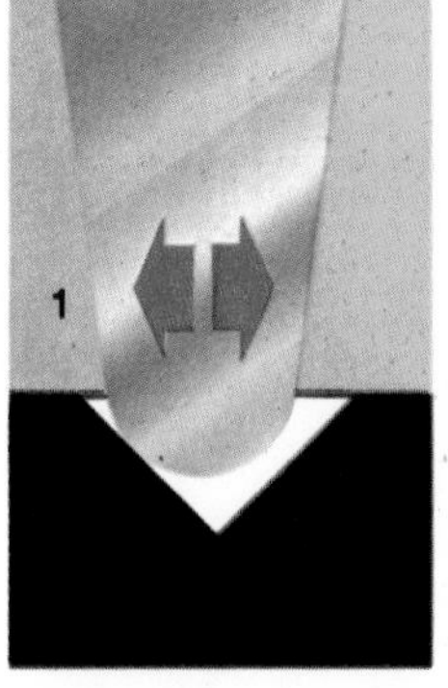

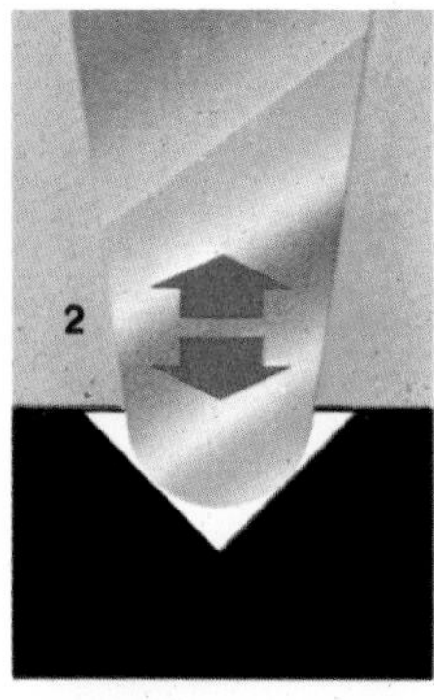

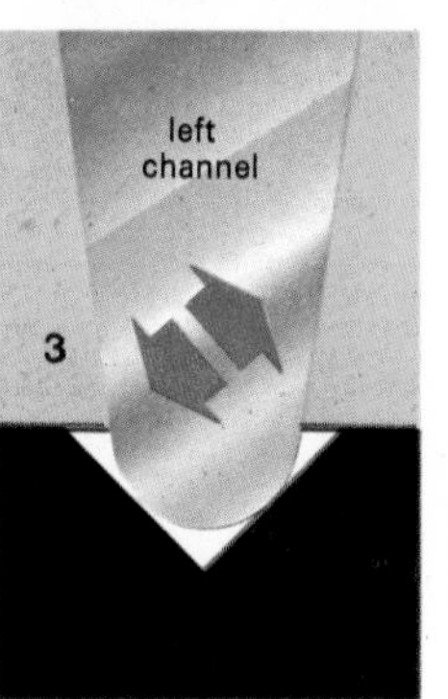

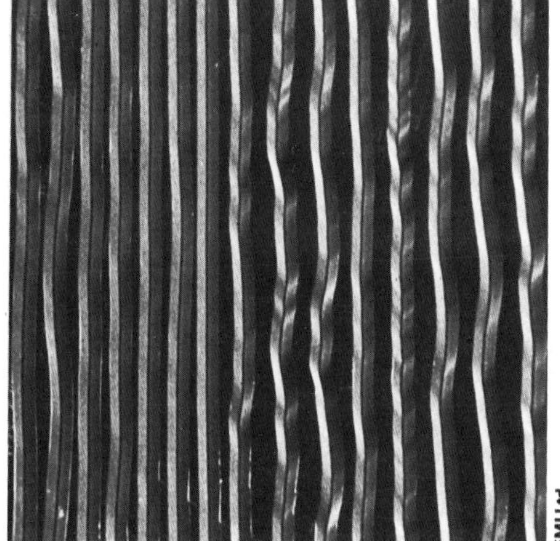

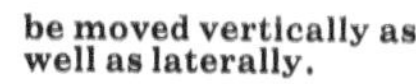

These four close-up photographs show the grooves of mono, stereo and quad records.

Above: The constant-width grooves of a mono record.

Below: A 45°/45° stereo record. The grooves are much more complicated, and their widths vary because the stylus must be moved vertically as well as laterally.

Above right: The grooves of a matrix quadraphonic disc are cut in the same way as those of a stereo disc.

Right: A discrete quadraphonic disc has a high frequency sub-signal cut on each wall of the groove.

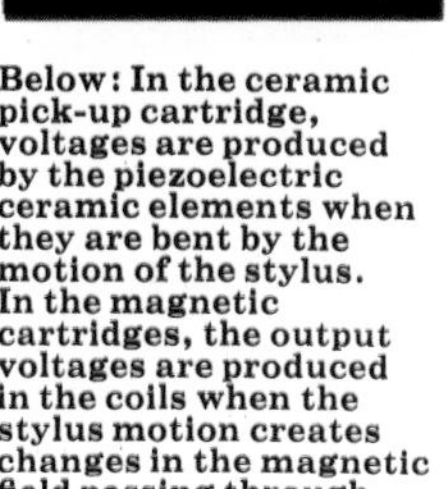

Below: In the ceramic pick-up cartridge, voltages are produced by the piezoelectric ceramic elements when they are bent by the motion of the stylus. In the magnetic cartridges, the output voltages are produced in the coils when the stylus motion creates changes in the magnetic field passing through them. This is done by moving the coils within a magnetic field (moving coil), moving an armature which links the field of a fixed magnet with a pair of coils (induced magnet), or by moving a magnet next to fixed coils (moving magnet). The photograph shows a Shure moving magnet cartridge.

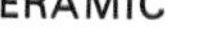

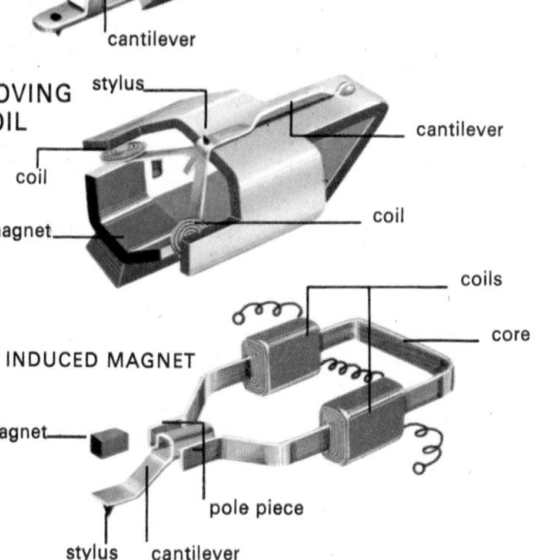

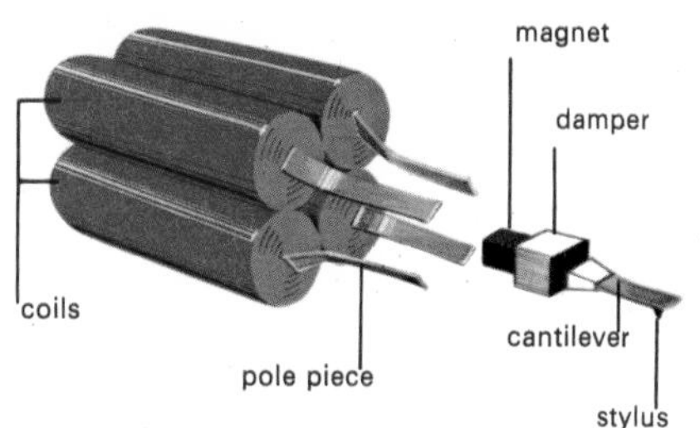

traverses from the rim to the centre of the record. This is the ideal because it ensures that the force pulling the stylus is always directed along the groove, but it is extremely costly to manufacture such a system to be neither so massive that it cannot follow the groove undulations quickly enough nor so weak that it sways and wobbles, introducing worse distortion than that which it was designed to prevent. The usual solution is to mount the stylus on a pivoted arm, known as the *tone arm*. Again, there are problems: however cunningly the tone arm is shaped it can never be exactly parallel to the groove over the whole width of the record. This introduces an unwanted force called *bias* which leads the stylus to press more against the inner than the outer wall. In practice bias can be compensated for by attaching a small weight to the other end of the tone arm in such a way that it tends to pull the stylus towards the rim.

The translation of the motion of the stylus into an electrical signal is accomplished by the *pick-up cartridge* which forms the business end of the tone arm. There are two main types of stereo cartridge, *ceramic* and *magnetic*. In the former, the stylus vibrations are transmitted by a connecting rod to two elements made of a crystalline ceramic material such as barium titanate, one of which is bent or twisted by vibrations in the plane of the inner groove wall and one by those of the outer wall. These elements thus produce, by the *piezoelectric effect*, two electrical signals which represent the left and right sound channels respectively.

In a magnetic *moving coil* cartridge the stylus is attached to two small wire coils, at 90° to each other, each of which vibrates in the field of a permanent magnet. By electromagnetic induction, this produces in each coil a voltage which represents the left or right sound channel. *Moving magnet* cartridges have this arrangement reversed, with the magnet attached to the stylus in such a way that it induces voltages in stationary coils as it moves.

Tape recordings are very easily made in stereo, because all that is necessary is to devote one half of the tape width to each channel of sound. This of course produces a tape which must be rewound after each playing, so it is common to divide the tape width into four, using the first and third quarters for the two channels of one recording and the other two for a second, which is played in the reverse direction. The output from the tape replay heads is, like that from a record player cartridge, in the form of a weak electrical signal.

Amplification

Although records, tapes and radio programmes are all translated into electrical signals these are not all of the same strength. Consequently, if the same preamplifier is to be used for all three it must be equipped to amplify each signal to a different degree. A preamplifier consists of several transistor amplifier stages in sequence, with the output of each fed to the input of the next in line. Very weak signals like those from a magnetic cartridge are switched through all the stages and the strongest, those from ceramic cartridges, perhaps only through the last stage.

The different types of input also require different degrees of *equalization* to correct for the attenuation of the bass when recording discs or replaying tapes. Radio signals do not need any equalization, nor does the output from a ceramic cartridge because the ceramic elements themselves, when connected to a suitably high impedance, produce a higher output voltage at low frequencies than at higher. Equalization is achieved by taking advantage of the properties of capacitors, which impede low frequencies more than high. If these are inserted in appropriate places in the circuit, either bass or treble can be boosted or attenuated as required.

Capacitors are also used as part of the bass and treble tone controls, which divert a fraction of the signal through a network of capacitances and resistances which attenuates either the bass or the treble. A variable resistance, whose variation is controlled by a knob on the casing, determines what fraction is diverted. Filters are included in the better preamplifiers to eliminate very low-pitched sounds, like the 'rumble' which is caused by mechanical vibrations from the turntable or drive mechanism, and the 'hum' caused by stray radiations at the frequency of the mains supply, and also the very high-pitched noise which sometimes accompanies radio programmes. These filters are like fixed versions of the tone controls, consisting of capacitive networks which effectively cut out all frequencies below about 60 Hz or above about 10,000 Hz. The filters can be switched in or out of the circuit as required.

The power amplifier is often contained in the same case as the preamplifier. Its sole purpose is to amplify the signal from the preamplifier to a level at which it can drive the loudspeakers. It usually has two or more stages to achieve the necessary amplification, and each stage consists of two transistors because one alone has not enough range to accommodate the large current difference between the peaks and troughs of the signal at these stages.

Loudspeakers

The final stage of sound reproduction is the conversion of the electrical signal into sound waves by the loudspeaker. There are two main types of loudspeaker, *moving coil* and *electrostatic*. The most common are the moving coil speakers, in which the electrical signal is passed through a wire coil attached to a paper or plastic cone. The coil is free to slide over the centrepiece of an M-shaped permanent magnet which alternately repels and attracts it as the coil becomes magnetized in one direction and then the other. The cone is thus pushed and pulled against the air, creating sound waves.

One such speaker cannot faithfully reproduce the whole spectrum of sound for two reasons. One is that the coil impedes high frequencies more than low; the other is that the cone is mechanically more efficient at producing sound whose wavelength is roughly the same as its

Below: The BSR/ADC Accutrac 4000 can automatically find and play any desired track on an LP record. A tiny unit next to the pick-up shines infra-red light onto the record, and when it is above the unrecorded space between two tracks this light is reflected back up to the unit. As the arm moves across above the record it counts the number of times the light is reflected, and thus the number of tracks, until it reaches the selected track. The machine can be remotely controlled, using the transmitter and receiver units shown in the foreground. The control signals are transmitted by an ultrasonic beam.

BSR Ltd

Right: A Quad 33 stereo control unit or preamplifier. Signals from a sound source, such as a record deck or radio, are fed into the unit. Its output is then passed to a power amplifier which amplifies it to a level which is high enough to drive a pair of loudspeakers. This unit will produce an output of 0.5 V from an input of 2 mV from a magnetic pick-up cartridge.

Below: The unit on the left is a mono valve power amplifier, which has a power output of 15 watts. The other one is a Quad 303 stereo transistor power amplifier, designed for use with the Quad 33 control unit, which produces 45 watts per channel.

Quad

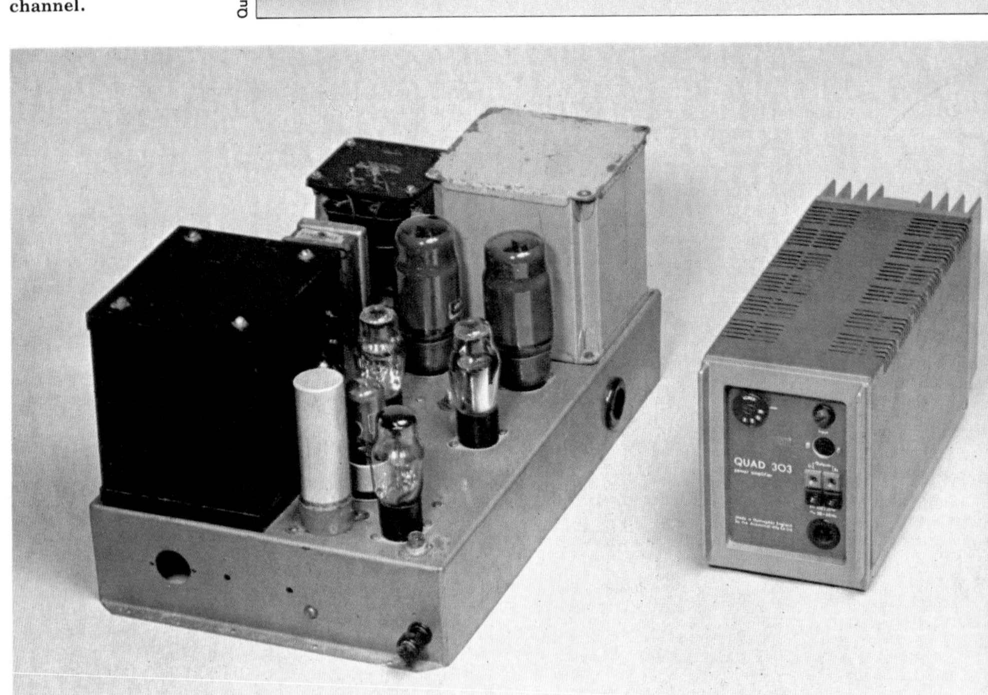

Spectrum

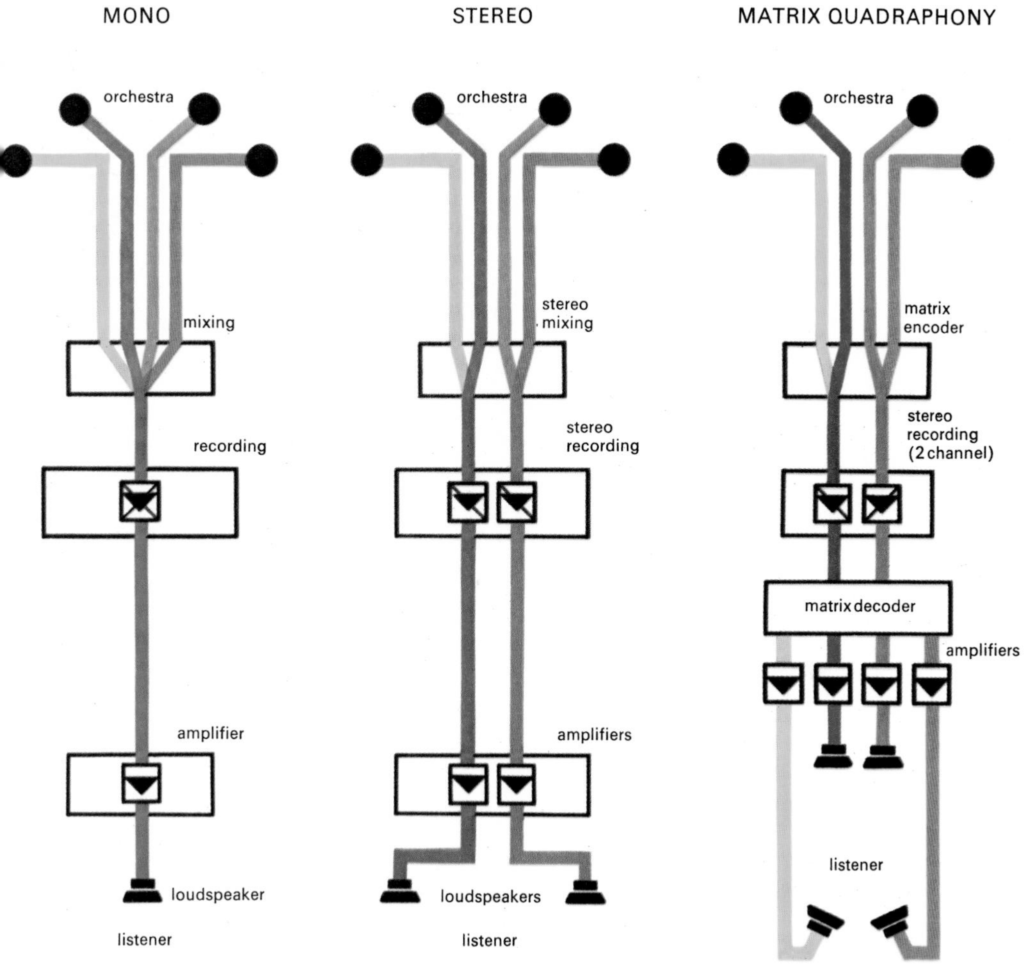

MONO

orchestra
mixing
recording
amplifier
loudspeaker
listener

STEREO

orchestra
stereo mixing
stereo recording
amplifiers
loudspeakers
listener

MATRIX QUADRAPHONY

orchestra
matrix encoder
stereo recording (2 channel)
matrix decoder
amplifiers
listener

DISCRETE QUADRAPHONY

orchestra
discrete encoder
discrete 4 channel recording
discrete decoder with demodulator
listener

Below: A Pioneer SA9900 stereo amplifier. This unit, shown with its case removed, is an *integrated* amplifier, containing both the preamplifier and the power amplifier stages. Its power output is 110 watts per channel, and it can handle sounds with frequencies ranging from 10 Hz up to 80 kHz.

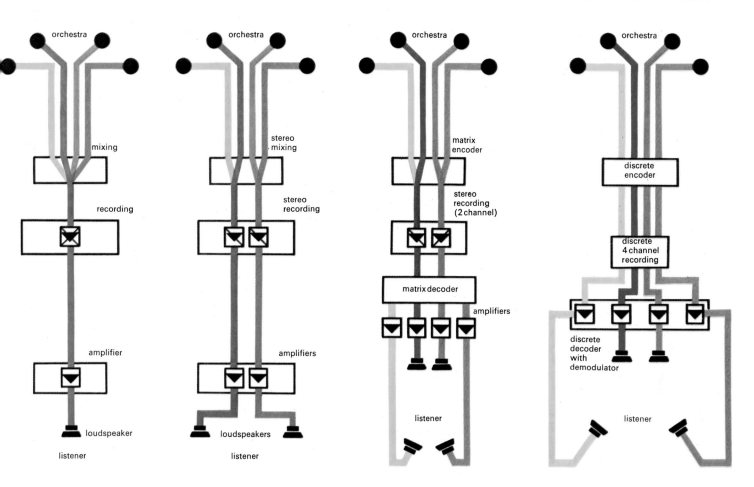

Above: This series of diagrams shows how the signals from several microphones can be combined and recorded to produce mono, stereo or quadraphonic records. Mono recordings (1) are the simplest. The microphone signals are combined into a single channel, and reproduced through a single channel. When stereo recordings (2) are being made, the microphone signals are combined into two channels, left and right, and replayed through a two-channel system. Matrix quadraphonic systems (3) encode the four channels into two, which are recorded on disc just like a normal stereo record. When a matrix disc is replayed, the decoder separates the two channels into four. Discrete quadrophonic recordings (4) are encoded together with a high frequency sub-signal, which enables the replay decoder to direct the four channels to their respective amplifiers.

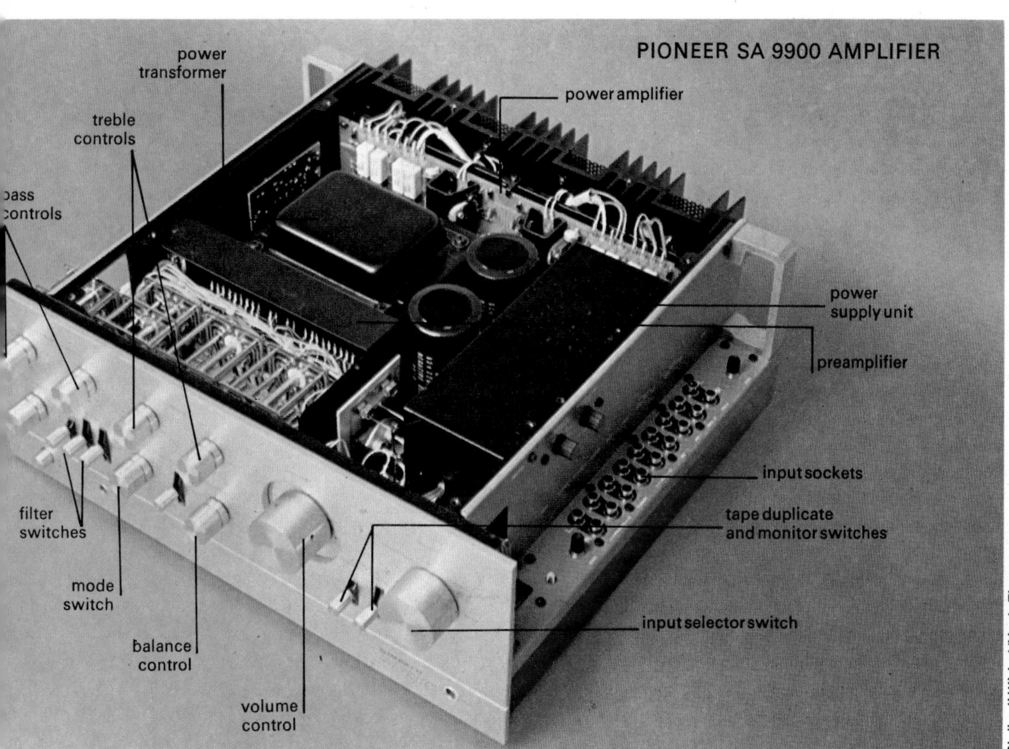

Shriko (UK) Ltd/Varda Zisman

own diameter. A small cone is better for high frequencies and a large cone for low. Thus for good reproduction two or three or sometimes more speakers of different sizes are combined for each channel. An electronic *crossover network* of capacitors, inductors and resistors splits the amplifier signal current into separate frequency ranges and feeds one to each of the appropriately sized speakers. The bass speaker is often called a 'woofer' and the treble a 'tweeter'.

Electrostatic speakers work on a different principle. They move the air by means of a flat flexible diaphragm which is coated with electrically conductive material. This is fixed at a small distance from a metal plate of the same area to which the amplifier signal is applied. A small permanent polarizing voltage is maintained between the two, which induces opposite electric charges on the surface of each (making in fact a parallel plate capacitor). Applying the amplifier signal between the two causes the diaphragm to vibrate as it is alternately attracted and repelled by the plate. This principle is widely used for tweeters and occasionally for full-spectrum speakers, in which case the diaphragm is usually fixed between two perforated plates.

Headphones, which are miniature loudspeakers mounted in a lightweight headset, may also be of the moving coil or the electrostatic type. As is the case with loudspeakers, the majority of headphones in use at present are based on moving coil drive units. Electrostatic headphones, like electrostatic speakers, give a very clean sound, but most types must be connected to the amplifier via an adaptor unit which supplies the polarizing voltage.

KEF Electronics

Left: A high quality loudspeaker system, with the cabinet cut away to show the bass speaker (bottom), mid-range speaker (centre) and treble speaker (top). The electronic crossover network is next to the treble speaker.

Below: A cross-section of a typical dual cone loudspeaker. The signal from the amplifier is fed to the voice coil, and being an alternating signal it magnetizes the coil first in one direction and then the other. This causes it to be alternately attracted and repelled by the magnet, moving the cones with it to produce sounds.

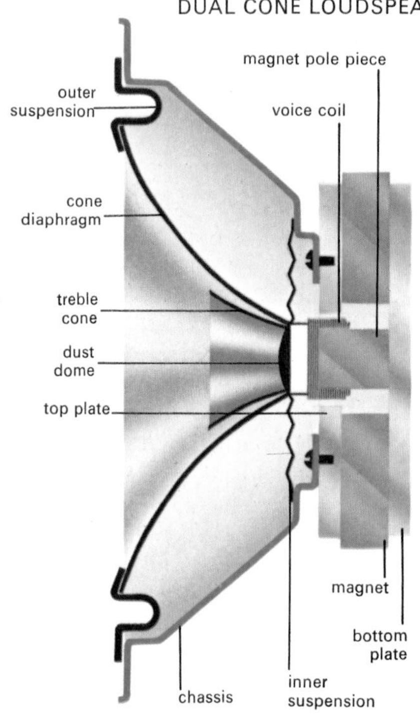

Quad

Left: The back of a Quad electrostatic loudspeaker, showing the perforations in the fixed plates which allow the sound from the moving diaphragms, which are on the other side of the plates, to be radiated from the speaker. This speaker reproduces sound frequencies from 45 Hz to 18 kHz.

Below: This Philips loudspeaker system contains its own power amplifier, mounted within a compartment at the rear of the cabinet. It has bass, mid-range and treble speakers, which give it a frequency response of 35 Hz to 20,000 Hz. The internal volume of the speaker compartment is 9,000 cc (0.32 cu. ft.).

Philips

Quadraphonic sound

In day to day life, a great deal of the sound we hear reaches our ears after being reflected by hard surfaces: indoors, for example, sounds are reflected by walls, floors and ceilings. Indeed, in a concert hall over 50 per cent of the sounds reaching the audience have been reflected. In reproducing these sounds, stereophonic equipment gives a more realistic sound than monophonic equipment because the sound 'image' is spread out instead of coming from a single point. Stereophonic reproduction, however, is still restricted by the fact that the sound reaches the listener only from one general direction.

Four-channel or *quadraphonic* sound was introduced as a means of authentically reproducing all the sounds we would hear in a concert. Quadraphonic systems use four loudspeakers, two in front of the listener and two behind, so that both direct and reflected *ambient* sounds (recorded by carefully positioned microphones) can be accurately reproduced. The use of four channels also gives record producers more scope for the use of special effects.

Quadraphonic tape systems are relatively straightforward; each channel is recorded on a separate track of the tape, using four recording and replay channels as opposed to the two channels needed for stereo. Quadraphonic disc reproduction, however, is rather more difficult. There are three basic systems in existence, known as the *discrete* or *CD-4 system* (invented by RCA), the *regular matrix system* (such as the Sansui QS) and the *SQ matrix system* (from CBS). The CD-4 discs carry a high frequency sub-signal (centred on 30 kHz) which contains information that enables the system to translate the signals cut in the two walls of the record groove into four sound channels. Because of the high frequency of the sub-signal, the pick-up cartridge used must be able to respond to frequencies of up to 45 kHz.

The matrix systems, of which the SQ system is the most popular, have the four channels combined into two channels by an encoder when the master disc is produced. When matrix discs are replayed, the signals from the pick-up (any good quality stereo cartridge) are fed to a decoder which splits them into their original four channels. Matrix systems are not quite as good as the discrete system because the separation between the four channels is less precise. They are, however, simpler and cheaper. In addition, record wear, which affects high frequency response in particular, is less of a problem because there is no high-frequency sub-signal recorded on the discs. Matrix tape systems, which encode the four channels on to two tape channels and decode them again on replay, are also available.

Quadraphonic radio signals are transmitted with additional high-frequency sub-signals, which carry the information that the quadraphonic receiver needs to enable it to route the sounds for each channel through the amplification system to their appropriate loudspeakers.

As is the case with tape and record systems, either discrete or matrix techniques can be used for quadraphonic radio broadcasts. Again, discrete systems give better channel separation, but they are more complicated than matrix radio systems.

The Hollywood Bowl has the natural accoustic quality of the amphitheatre. Seating 3,000 people, it is used mainly for musical performances – notably 'Symphonies Under the Stars' in summertime – and has its own orchestra.

Earl Young/Colorific

Musical Instruments

Musical instruments produce their sounds by creating vibrations in the air around them. With stringed instruments, for example, the vibrations in the air are created by the vibration of the strings as they are plucked, struck or played with a bow. Wind instruments, such as brass or woodwind, are so designed that when the player blows into them a vibrating column of air is set up inside them which produces the sound waves in the surrounding air.

The *pitch* of a note is determined by the frequency of these vibrations. For example, the lowest note on a piano, A_4 (the fourth A below middle C), is a result of the string vibrating 27.5 times per second; in other words the frequency of A_4 is 27.5 Hz. In comparison, the highest note on a piano, C^4 (the fourth C above middle C), has a frequency of 4,186 Hz. The systems of musical notes used by Western cultures are based on the *octave*, groups of notes in which the frequency of the highest is double the frequency of the lowest. An octave contains eight major notes, plus five minor notes (the 'sharps' and 'flats'), giving a total of twelve *semitone* steps per octave. Each step represents a frequency change of about six per cent.

Musical instruments themselves can be divided into several main groups according to their construction and the way in which they produce their sounds. The principal groups are *brass*, *woodwind*, *strings*, *keyboards* and *percussion* instruments.

Brass instruments

A brass instrument is basically a tube with a mouthpiece at one end and a flared 'bell' at the other. To produce a note, the player puts his lips against the mouthpiece and buzzes them at the correct frequency, triggering the vibrations by suddenly removing his tongue from between his lips and simultaneously blowing into the tube. On striking the mouthpiece, the air stream produces what is called an *edge tone*, which sets the column of air in the tube vibrating.

The air column vibrates with *resonant frequencies* set up by *standing wave* motions, which do not move down the tube but are a stationary pattern of vibrating air. The standing wave is set up by two waves going in opposite directions. When the edge tone is at the resonant frequency of the tube, an outgoing wave is set up, part of which is reflected back up the tube when it reaches the bell.

The lowest note available from a given tube is called the *fundamental*, and is produced by the vibration of the entire column of air. But the column vibrates in fractions of its length at the same time, giving higher pitched notes in simple ratios to the fundamental; these form the *harmonic series*. Only one series can be produced by a given length of tube; the player chooses the note by pursing his lips and altering their tension.

Simple brass instruments are not very useful; a bugle has only seven or eight notes, while there are thirty-seven notes on the piano in the same range. Brass instruments are made more versatile by providing a means of lengthening the tube, using a slide, as on a trombone, or valves, which are used on trumpets.

Woodwind instruments

The two categories of woodwind instruments are *flutes* and *reeds*. The modern orchestral flute is *side blown* (*transverse*)—the player blows across a hole near the stopped end of the tube, precisely controlling the direction of the air by the shape of his lips (known as his *embouchure*). The instrument can also be *overblown* which involves the player blowing harder so that the velocity of the air within the instrument is greatly increased.

This increases the frequency of the vibrations of the standing waves within the flute, giving a note one, one and a half, or two octaves above the fundamental. The flute also has six or seven holes which can be *cross* or *fork fingered* (raising a finger higher than the lowest one in use) to produce *semitones*.

Other woodwind instruments work on a different principle. A blade of grass or a leaf, held under tension between the palms of the hands, will produce a shrill buzzing sound if blown across. The combination of a vibrating reed with a hollow wooden cylinder has resulted in the family of reed instruments, which includes the clarinet, bassoon and oboe. Here the breath of the player causes a single or double reed to vibrate, setting up vibrations in the air column within the cylinder.

The *saxophones* were invented in the 19th century by Adolph Sax, and are single reed instruments with conical bores. They are called woodwinds although made of brass and they are especially popular in jazz and pop music.

Stringed instruments

When a stretched string vibrates, a standing wave motion is produced; between frequencies of about 20 Hz and 20,000 Hz, the displacement of air by the string is audible. The pitch depends on the

ORGAN

John Goldblatt

BASSOON

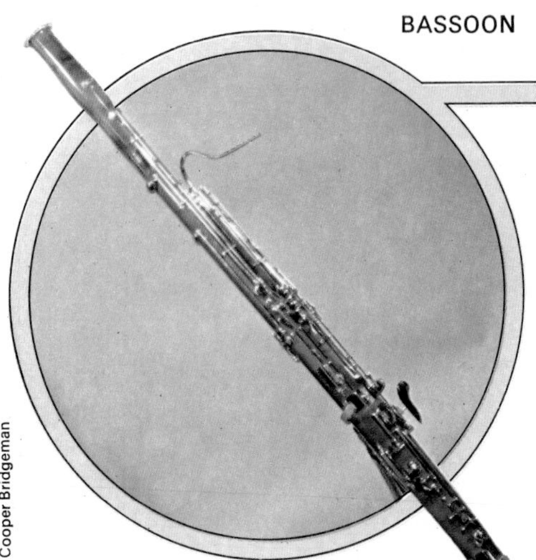

Cooper Bridgeman

Below: American jazz trumpeter Louis Armstrong. The trumpet is descended from primitive instruments such as animal horns and conch shells, which were in use thousands of years ago. The first modern type of trumpet appeared in 1815 following the invention of the valve by Heinrich Stölzel.

Above right: This chart shows the frequencies of the notes of the musical scale, and the ranges of the fundamental and harmonic frequencies produced by the major orchestral instruments and human voices. The pitchless instruments are those which do not, as a rule, produce specific notes.

Camera Press

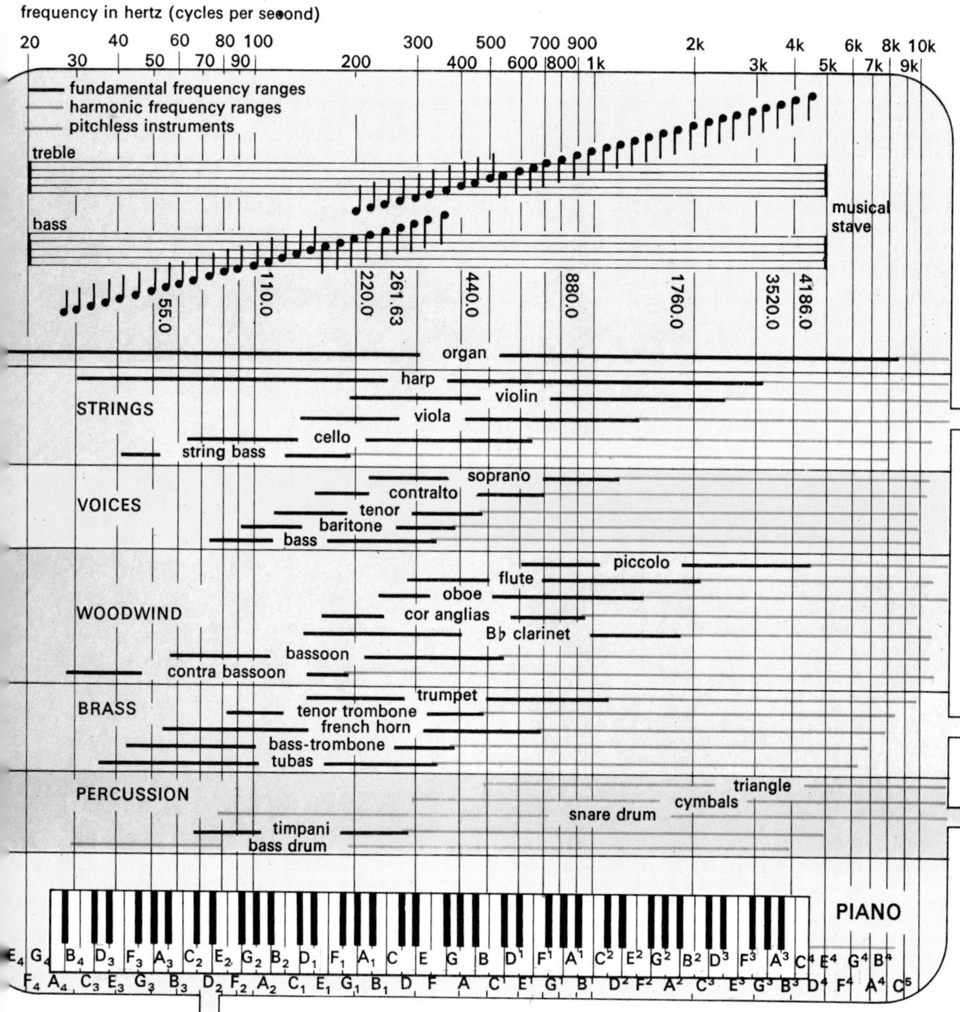

VIOLIN

Terence Spencer/Colorific

TROMBONE

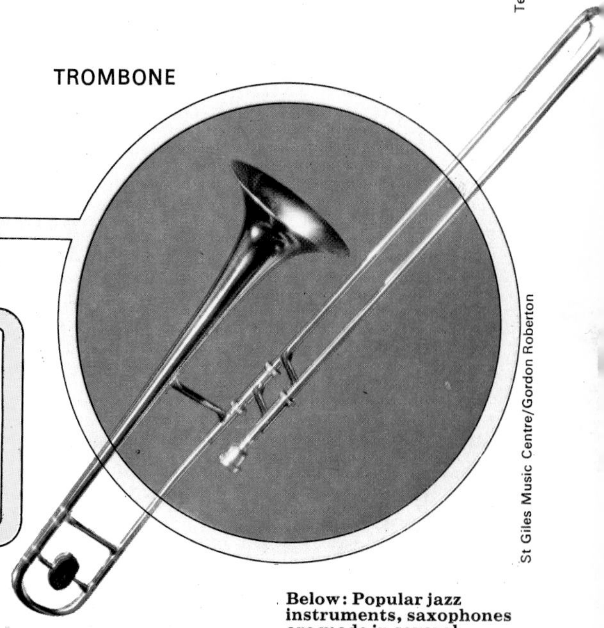

St Giles Music Centre/Gordon Roberton

PIANO

BBC

DRUMS

Above left: The fundamental frequencies of most instruments fall somewhere between 27.5 Hz and 4,186 Hz, which is the range of the piano. A few organs have been built to play as low as about 8 Hz and as high as 16,744 Hz.

Below: Popular jazz instruments, saxophones are made in several sizes, each of which has a frequency range which roughly corresponds with one of the main human singing voice ranges. The most common saxophones are the alto (corresponding to the contralto), tenor, baritone and soprano instruments.

David Redfern

length of the string and its tension; *stopping* the string mid-length gives twice the frequency, or an octave higher than the fundamental, and so forth.

The sound must be amplified, traditionally by means of a wooden *resonator chamber*. In the modern violin family, which includes the violin, viola, cello and double bass, four strings are stretched along a *fingerboard* and raised above the resonator chamber by means of a *bridge*. Each string is attached at the body end to the *tailpiece*, which is held to the body of the violin by a loop fitted over a *tail-pin*. At its other end the string is wound around a *tuning peg*.

The body of the instrument includes a *belly* or *upper* and a *back*, joined around the edge by a *rib*; inside this resonating chamber is a *sound post*, which increases the effective area of the soundboard and phases out any natural resonance of the chamber itself. The strings can be made of 'catgut' (actually sheep's intestines), but nowadays the lowest string is usually covered with a fine silver wire and the highest string is usually steel.

Fretted instruments

The guitar, as well as the banjo, mandoline, lute, balalaika and similar instruments, is *fretted*; that is, the fingerboard has metal strips (frets) attached across it at suitable intervals. Thus less precision is necessary in stopping the strings than with the violin family. The strings are stopped when they press against a fret, and so the player need only press on the string at any point between the two frets and it will be stopped accurately by the inner fret.

During the 1930s, in dance bands and jazz bands, guitar players began to amplify their instruments so that they could be heard in more than a rhythmic capacity. An electromagnetic pick-up system is placed under the strings, rather than a microphone. The pick-up consists basically of a set of small permanent magnets, one placed beneath each string, each of which is surrounded by a coil of wire. The strings must be made of a magnetic material such as steel, and the pick-up coils are connected together at the output terminals of the pick-up.

As the strings vibrate, they create disturbances in the magnetic fields around the magnets, and these disturbances cause voltages to be induced within the coils. The voltages vary precisely with the vibrations of the strings which caused them, resulting in electrical signals which, when amplified, recreate the sounds of the strings.

Keyboard instruments

Wind instruments and stringed instruments have their counterparts in the more mechanically complex keyboard instruments. The piano can be thought of as a harp with an amplifying soundboard, the strings being struck by hammers operated from the keyboard instead of being plucked by hand. Because of the hammer action the piano is usually classed as a percussion instrument.

The immediate ancestor of the piano was the harpsichord, in which a *plectrum* operated from the keyboard was made to pluck the string: the plectrum was hinged, so that after plucking the string it could return to its position of rest. This arrangement did not allow much dynamic expression; that is, the player could not vary the loudness or *dynamic level* of the sound.

Early in the 18th century, Bartelommeo Cristofori, a Paduan who was Keeper of the Musical Instruments for Prince Ferdinand dei Medici, invented the 'pianoforte' (soft-loud), in which a felt-covered hammer was thrown up at the string and rebounded immediately, regardless of the action of the player. The dynamic level of the note struck is a function of the velocity of the hammer, which is controlled by the strength of the player's touch on the key.

The intervening levers between the key and the hammer are called the *action*, and include important design features such as the *backcheck*, which catches the hammer on its return, preventing rebound which might damp the sound. Modern grand pianos have a *repetition action* or *double escapement* which stops the return of the hammer at an intermediate stage, allowing rapid repetition of the same note.

The Pan-pipe is a folk instrument found throughout the world which comprises a number of small pipes, or flutes, bound together. The pipe organ is really a kind of gigantic Pan-pipe, but the flow of air or 'wind' is produced mechanically and not by the player's lungs, and directed to the required pipe by means of valves operated by a keyboard and pedals. The wind was supplied in early times by apprentices working bellows; nowadays the wind is supplied by electric air-pumps.

An electronic organ attempts to create the *harmonics* or *overtones* of the pipe

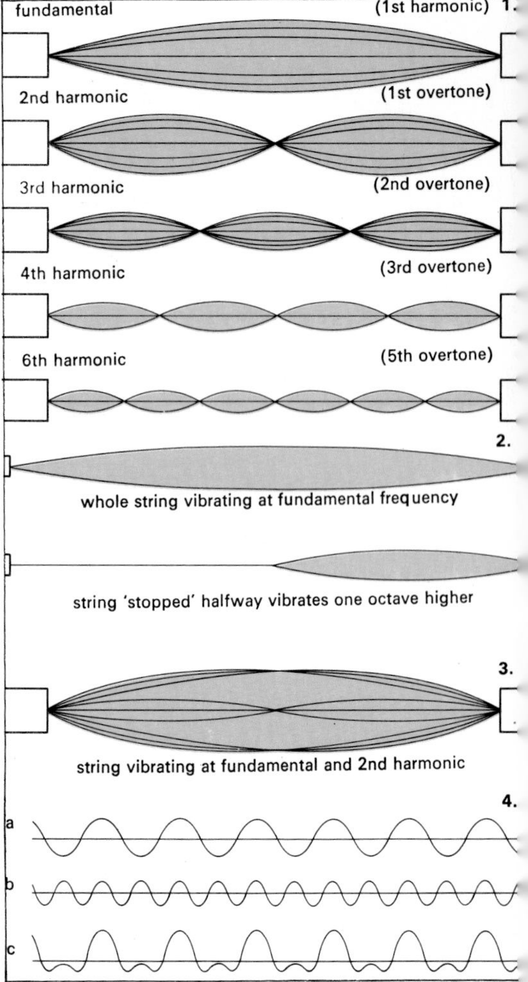

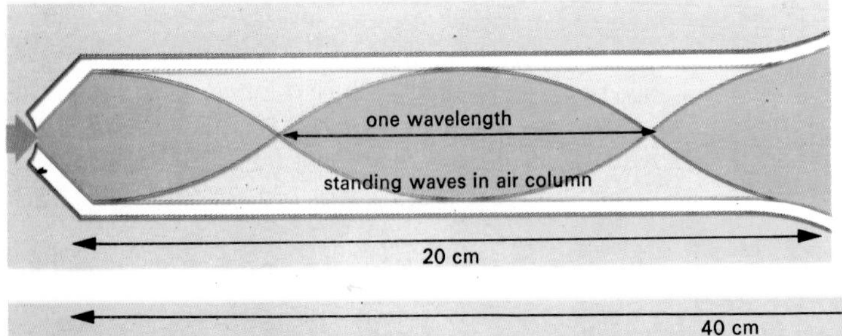

Left and below: The pitch of the sound produced by the column of air within a wind instrument depends upon its length and the velocity of the air flowing through it. Doubling the length doubles the wavelength, thus halving the frequency of the waves set up within the instrument.

CLARINET

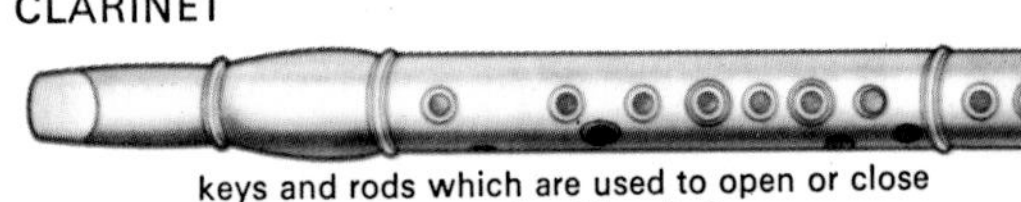

keys and rods which are used to open or close holes have been omitted for clarity

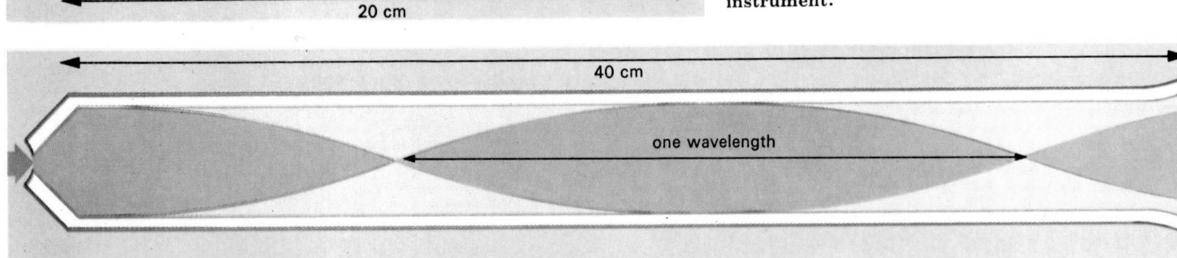

Above: The clarinet is made to produce different notes by the opening or closing of holes which alter its effective length.

Right and below right: These diagrams show how the effective length of an instrument like the clarinet is reduced by opening holes to let the air escape.

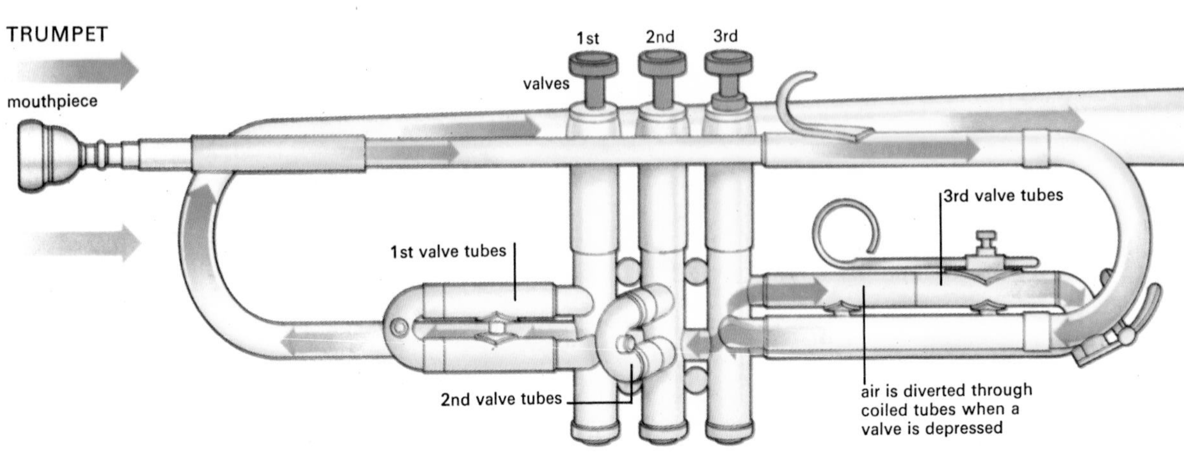

Left: The red arrows show the path of the air through a trumpet when no valves are depressed. The blue arrows show the longer route it must take when the third valve has been depressed. Because the column of air has been lengthened, it resonates at a lower frequency and so a lower note is produced.

organ using electronic *filters* to modify tones generated by either electromagnetic or electrostatic methods. From this has come the *synthesizer*, which can be operated by a keyboard or a computer tape, and which is used to imitate any instrument or just to be its electronic self.

Percussion Instruments

Percussion instruments are divided into two groups: the *membranophones* such as drums, which have skins that are struck; and the *idiophones*, such as bells, which are made of such dense, hard materials that they vibrate sonorously when struck.

Large bells are cast and tuned by cutting or grinding away excess metal until the pitch is correct. So great a mass of bronze is impractical for orchestral use; metal plates or tubes are used instead. *Gongs* are large dishes of forged bronze, originally found in Asia. *Cymbals* are forged from brass, the exact proportion of ingredients kept secret by the manufacturers, and spun and hammered so precisely that they can be produced to fit any requirement as regards quality of sound, long or short duration of vibration and so forth.

The earliest membranophone was probably the kettledrum, and as its name suggests, was a cooking vessel covered with skin. Modern kettledrums, called *timpani*, can be tuned by means of pedals as they are played enabling a range of notes to be produced. The *side* drum, or *snare* drum, is a round shell with a skin on each side. The snares are strands of wire or gut running beneath the top head, which give the instrument a dry, rattling sound. The snare is not intended to produce a definite pitch.

Spectrum

Nigel Luckhurst

Above: The strings and pick-up of an electric guitar.

Left: 1. A string vibrating at its fundamental frequency, and at its 2nd, 3rd, 4th and 6th harmonics. 2. A string, such as a guitar string, vibrating along its whole length produces its fundamental tone. If the string is 'stopped' halfway along it produces a note an octave higher. 3. A string vibrating at its fundamental and its 2nd harmonic. 4. 'a' and 'b' are the waveforms of a fundamental and its 2nd harmonic. 'c' is the waveform of these two played together.

Right: A Spanish or classical guitar.

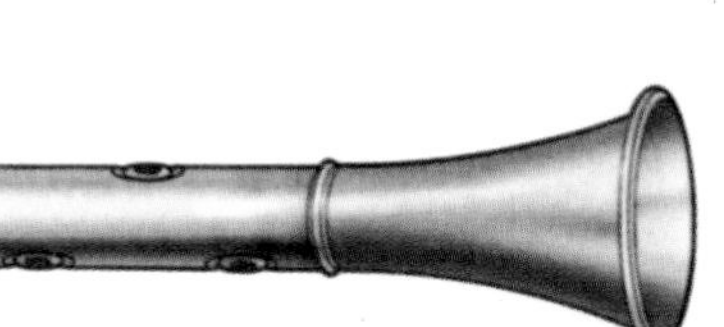

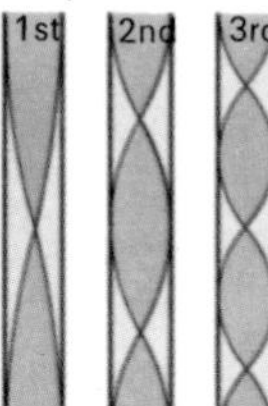

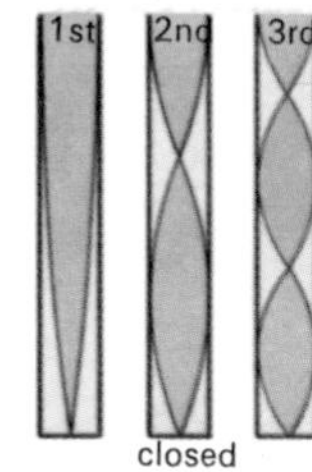

Left: Fundamental and 2nd and 3rd harmonic waves set up by air blown into open and closed pipes.

Right: Vibraphones consist of metal bars, which are struck by hammers, beneath which are resonating tubes which are alternately opened and closed to create a vibrant tone.

David Ellis/Redferns

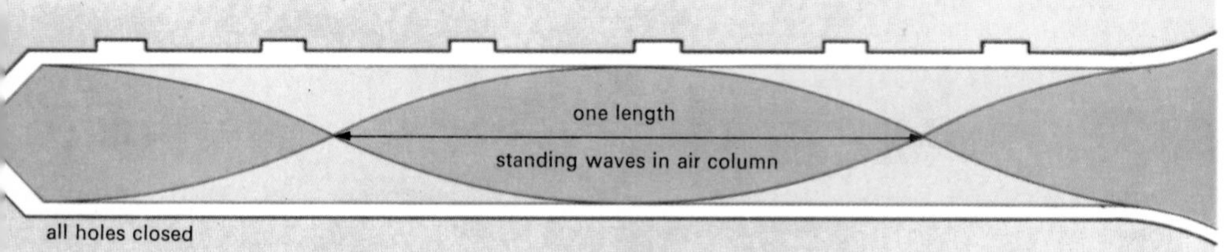

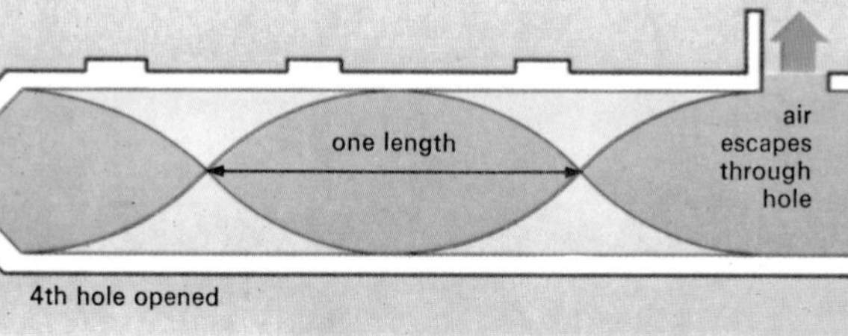

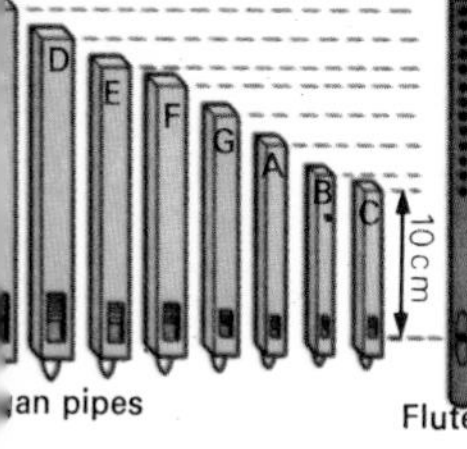

Left: The note produced by an organ pipe depends upon the pipe's length. Similarly, the notes produced by a flute are obtained by blocking off or opening holes to alter its effective length.

Right: An EMS 'Synthi 100' synthesizer, designed for use in recording studios.

EMS

Cinema

Left: An early movie camera, made in 1896. Thomas Edison, in the USA, produced the first commercial motion pictures in 1891, but these were viewed in a sort of peep-show machine rather than projected on a screen. The first motion pictures intended for viewing on a screen were produced in France by Louis and Auguste Lumière, whose camera, which also served as a projector, was patented in February 1895. This machine, called the 'Cinématographe', had its first public demonstration in Paris on 28 December that year.

Science Museum

Draw a little 'matchstick man' on the edge of a page of a book. On subsequent pages, draw similar men with slight differences, so that the movement of arms or legs is split up into individual steps. Now flick the pages so that the individual steps join up into a continuous movement and the man becomes animated.

If your eye and brain were remarkably alert, you would still be able to discriminate each individual step. But this is usually impossible as a result of *persistence of vision*. This is an effect of the eye and brain combined, and means that we do not see separate images if they occur more rapidly than about 12 times per second.

The earliest attempts at making moving pictures, during the second half of the 19th century, used the book page principle, or else consisted of a rotating cylinder with slots, each of which showed for an instant a slightly different picture on the inside of the cylinder. But the real breakthrough came in 1895, when the Lumière brothers in France demonstrated the forerunner of the modern cinema, taking photographs on a long strip of film and projecting each one for a split second.

Because each individual picture, or *frame*, needs an exposure time of about 1/50 sec, the film has to be motionless for a brief period in the film *gate*, to avoid blurring the image produced by the camera's lens. Then it must be moved on very quickly and brought to rest in time for the exposure of the next frame. This *intermittent motion*, first invented by Etienne-Jules Marey in the 1880s, was the secret of the success of the Lumière brothers' technique, and today's cameras work on the same principle. The usual method is to engage a claw in the sprocket holes of the film. This jerks the film along, then extracts itself and moves along to the next set of holes while the film remains stationary as the exposure is made. Meanwhile, a sector cut out of a disc rotating in front of the gate admits light only for a fraction of a second, cutting off the image while the film is being moved.

This procedure occurs at a standard rate. The normal shooting rate for cinema films is 24 frames per second, while amateur films are usually shot at 18 frames per second for greater economy of film.

Professional motion picture cameras generally have a viewfinder which, by a reflex system, shows the image as seen through the camera lens, rather than using a separate viewfinder system. A common way of doing this is to make the rotating shutter disc reflective, viewing the image mirrored in it except when the shutter is open.

There are four main film widths currently in use: 8 mm, 16 mm, 35 mm and 65 mm. The first is mainly for amateur film making, while the others are for professional and feature film work. Most television news or documentary films are on 16 mm film, while feature films for TV and cinema are on 35 mm. The 65 mm film size is used for major cinema films, often wide screen spectaculars, and the image is transferred to 70 mm film for projection to include the soundtrack.

Sound recording

In some 16 mm movie cameras used for TV news filming, the signals from a microphone are recorded directly on to a strip of magnetic oxide 2.54 mm (0.1 in) wide coated down one edge of the film, a method which ensures that the sound and vision are kept precisely synchronized with each other. Most professional equipment, however, does not use this system. Instead, the sound is recorded separately on a good quality tape recorder and later transferred, along with music and other effects, to the sound track of the finished film.

Editing

Film scenes are very rarely shot in the same order in which they are shown. For example, all shots made at one particular location will be taken together, even though they may appear in different parts of the finished film. Since only one camera is normally used, many sequences will have to be repeated from different angles —if two people are talking together each actor's part may be filmed separately from over the other's shoulder. For action scenes, however, another camera may be used to provide 'cuts' or alternative views, as it would be difficult to repeat the same events exactly.

The job of putting all this together in the right order, along with titles, special effects and background music, may take several months for a full length film. Much of the work is done using a machine called a *Steenbeck* or *Moviola*, which enables film and soundtrack to be run

Below: An Arriflex 35 mm movie camera, mounted on a tripod. The film is carried in the *magazine* on top of the camera body, and there are three lenses, of different focal lengths, mounted on a *turret* at the front of the camera. The turret is rotated to bring the required lens into position.

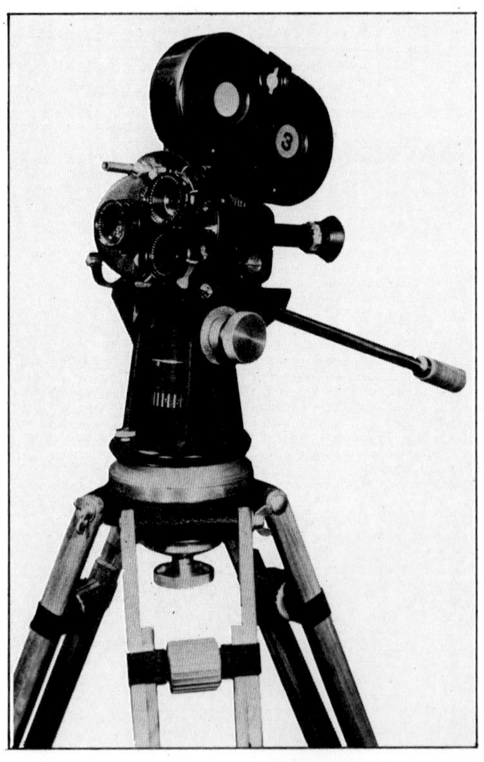

Right: A sequence of frames from a cartoon film. The amount of work involved in drawing and then photographing a cartoon film can be considerable; for example, this entire sequence would provide only about one third of a second of viewing time at a speed of 24 frames per second.

The reflex viewfinder of a movie camera uses light reflected from the shutters

Below: A cutaway drawing of a professional movie camera. The *matte* box in front of the lenses is used to hold mattes during special effects filming. The small diagram on the left shows the optical components of the reflex viewfinder system used on such a camera.

Left: An early system for producing optical soundtracks, which could also be used as a sound recorder during location filming. Some of the first 'talking pictures', introduced in the 1920s, had the sound recorded on gramophone records, but these were soon superseded by films with soundtracks.

Science Museum

Right: Special effects man Ray Harryhausen arranging a scene for the Columbia film 'Jason and the Argonauts'. The scene was shot in a large tank of water, using models for the cliffs and for the boat and its occupants. The wave effects in the water were created by a wave-making machine at the edge of the tank.

Grange Calverly/Bob Godfrey Films Ltd

National Film Archive

Picturepoint

Picturepoint

together, frame by frame, for matching and cutting purposes. The film which is used for preliminary cutting is not the original black and white or colour negative, which is unsuitable for viewing anyway. Instead, prints (positive copies) are made and the original is kept until the editing has been finalized. When the editing is completed, the original negative is cut and the final prints made. This involves *grading* the colour—making sure that the exposure and colour balance are the same from shot to shot.

Music and other sounds can now be added. Quite often it is necessary to match the music to the film, so the musicians perform in a studio with a projector so they can link the two. In many cases extra sounds are added in this *dubbing studio*, such as suitably satisfying cracks, thuds and howls during fight scenes which may well be filmed without the sound being recorded.

Finally a master soundtrack is mixed together, using multitrack facilities similar to those in recording studios. There are two ways of adding sound to a film—by *optical* or by *magnetic* soundtracks. It was the optical system which first came into general use, and is still commonly employed today. Alongside the picture area of the film are two continuous clear lines on a black area, whose width variations correspond to the soundtrack signal like the wiggles in the groove of a record. To play the soundtrack requires a photocell which responds to the variations in the intensity of light passing through the soundtrack, and produces a correspondingly varying electrical signal which is then amplified and passed to the cinema's loudspeakers.

The alternative system uses a stripe of the same type of magnetic oxide as used on recording tape. This is coated down both edges of the film, so that the extra thickness does not cause the film to wind unevenly on the spool.

Special effects

As well as the wide range of mechanical effects used to make films, such as the small explosive charges which produce realistic bullet wound effects when detonated beneath an actor's clothes, there are *optical effects* which are only possible on film. In the early days such tricks as double exposure were used, but now there are a wide range of specialized techniques, some of which require extensive laboratory facilities.

Some effects, such as the destruction of cities, are carried out using models, with no other illusion than that caused by the lack of scale. Where some monster or mythical creature is required, it will often be made as a model with flexible limbs. These are filmed frame by frame, with slight movements between each frame. Where the model is to be combined with human action, the model can be placed in front of a screen on which is projected, again frame by frame, previously-shot film of the actors. The screen may be translucent with the film projected from behind (back projection) or it may be highly reflective with the film projected from the front. The image from the projector also strikes the model, but as it is not so reflective as the screen it does not show it. These two projection techniques are also widely used at full scale with actors, for example to make it appear that they are in a moving car or perhaps in a desert.

Another method of faking a background is the *glass shot*, which uses a sheet of glass close to the camera on which details are painted. The camera views the scene through the glass, but the aperture is chosen so that both the glass painting and the scene are in focus. This may be used on location to add some landscape details or remove others by obscuring them.

One widely used method of superimposing one scene on another or achieving special effects is by means of the *matte* technique. In its simplest form, this involves masking out part of the scene being photographed by a piece of black card, the matte, right in front of the camera. Then another piece of card, which masks out the rest of the picture but leaves the originally masked area clear, is

This series of pictures shows the main stages involved in making a film.
1. Shooting a scene in a studio. The camera is mounted on a *camera crane*. The picture to the right shows a Panavision camera, mounted in an aircraft, which was used in filming aerial action for the film 'Battle of Britain', and the top picture is a set used in François Truffaut's 'Day for Night'.

2. After shooting, the film is processed in an automatic developing machine.

3. Sound recorded during shooting is transferred from tape to magnetically coated film.

4. The sound and picture are edited.

5. Music and sound effect tracks are added to the dialogue track.

6. These tracks, with the picture, are then played through the dubbing console, where the tone and volume of each track are adjusted to give the correct sound balance.

John Toward

John Toward

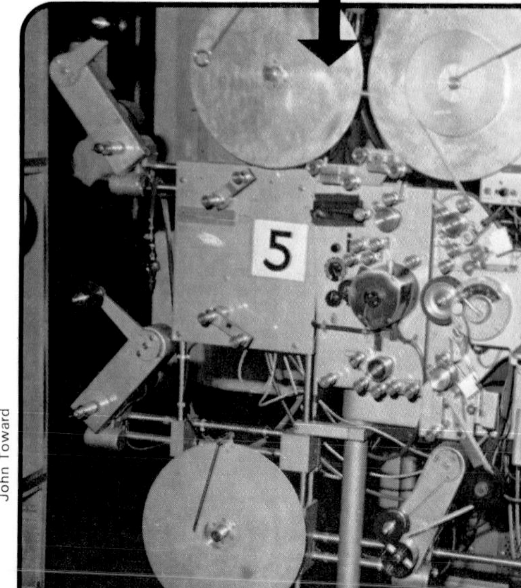

John Toward

John Toward

John Toward

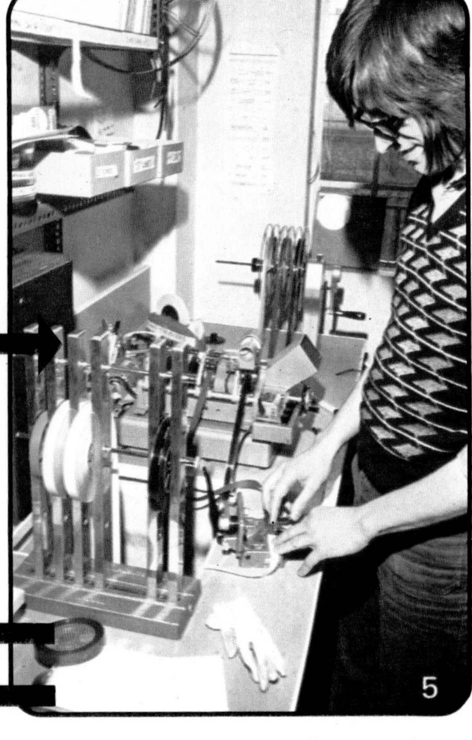

John Toward

John Toward

Ian Duff

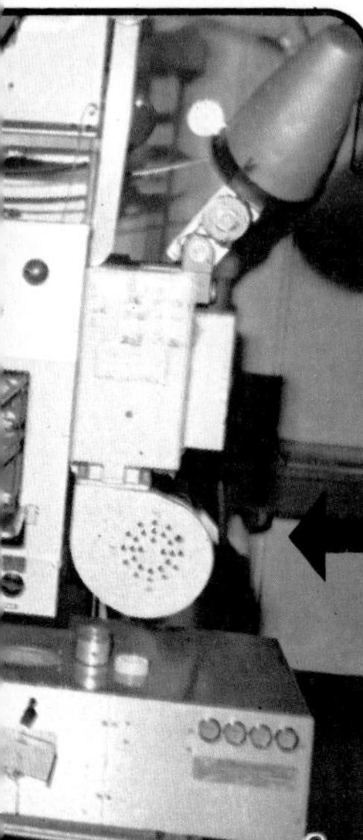

7. The magnetic recording of the mixed soundtrack is run on the *replay machine* (on the right), whose output signal drives the camera unit (left) which produces the optical soundtrack.

8. The brightness and colour balance of the picture are adjusted on a *visual colour grader*. The control settings are recorded on punched paper tape, then used to control the machine that produces the final prints.

9. The picture negative and the negative of the optical soundtrack are loaded into this printer, which produces the final combined picture and sound prints that are later distributed to cinemas.

substituted, the film is wound back in the camera and the scene is shot again to fill in the new part of the scene.

Alternatively, the new piece of action, photographed separately, is added in an *optical printer*, which enables two separate pieces of film to be photographed together on to a third. This allows the use of *travelling mattes*, which can change shape and move. Sometimes the mattes are prepared photographically by lighting the unwanted part of the film set in a hue which affects only the blue-sensitive layer of the colour film. This region can then be turned black by photographic techniques.

Cartoons are made by drawing each frame separately and projecting them in sequence, just as in the matchstick man technique. To save a lot of time the backgrounds are prepared separately and the moving characters are painted on transparent overlays called *cels*. The limbs of cartoon characters are painted on separate cels so that their positions can be changed easily. Usually the soundtrack is recorded first and the drawings made to match it.

Projectors

Projectors are mechanically quite similar to cameras—in fact, the Lumières used their cameras as projectors by placing a lamp behind the processed film as it passed through the gate. Modern projectors, however, are purpose built.

The light source used in amateur projectors is a tungsten or quartz halogen light bulb. In large cinema projectors, arc lamps, or more recently xenon discharge tubes, are used.

In order to even out the coverage of light across the film, projectors use a *condenser* system. This usually consists of a concave mirror placed behind the light source, to make use of the light given off to the rear of the lamp, and a lens in front of the source which concentrates the light on to the film area. The main projector lens, which beams the film image on to the screen, is situated in front of the film.

In the case of CinemaScope or Pana-

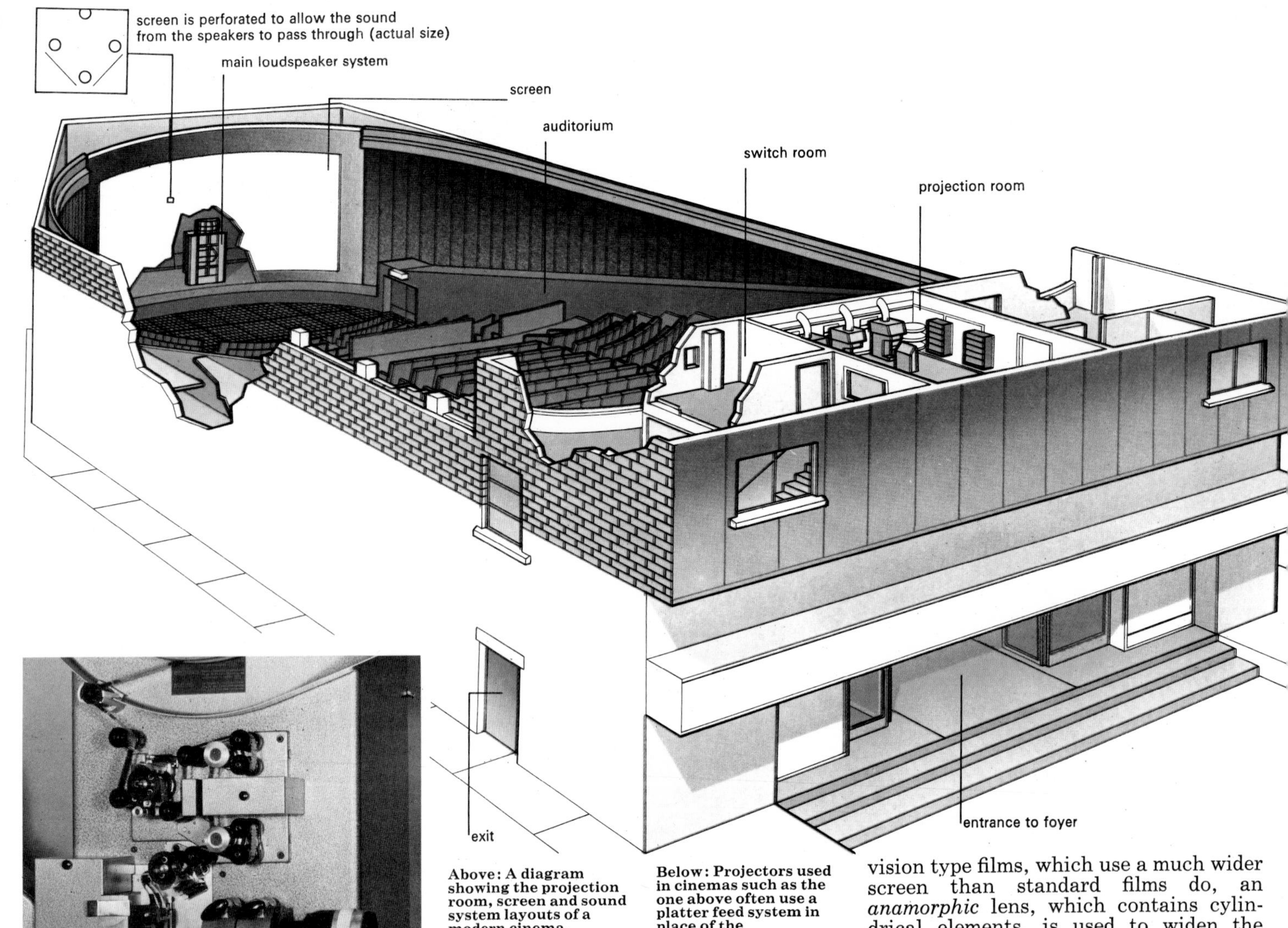

Above: A diagram showing the projection room, screen and sound system layouts of a modern cinema.

Left: This picture shows the path of the film through a modern projector. The *sound head* is housed within the casing below the body of the projection lens.

Below: Projectors used in cinemas such as the one above often use a platter feed system in place of the conventional feed and take-up reels. This arrangement permits the use of a roll of film up to about 7,500 m (24,500 ft) long, enough for a complete programme 4½ hours long.

CINEMA PROJECTOR
WITH PLATTER FEED SYSTEM

vision type films, which use a much wider screen than standard films do, an *anamorphic* lens, which contains cylindrical elements, is used to widen the image. The film will have been shot using a similar lens, and the images on the film itself appear compressed horizontally.

Just as in the camera, the film must move intermittently, and a shutter covers the image while the film is in motion. The film is moved continuously by a series of sprockets; its intermittent motion is made possible by loops of free film above and below the gate. These allow the film to be stopped and started in the gate without interfering with its continuous motion through the rest of the mechanism.

The soundtrack is recorded continuously, and not intermittently like the pictures. For this reason the part of the soundtrack which relates to a particular frame is separated from it by an exact number of frames. At the sound head itself, where the film's movement has to be completely even, it passes round a heavy 'sound drum' whose inertia damps out any remaining ripple in the motion.

The length of film on one reel is limited by bulk—a reel carrying more than about 1,800 m (6,000 ft) of film, lasting about an hour, is difficult to lift up on to the projector. Until the introduction of automated projection equipment, most films had to go on two or more reels, and cinemas needed two projectors for a continuous performance.

Modern cinemas use automated systems, which can often accommodate a whole programme of films over four hours long on a single projector, or on two projectors, operating under automatic control, which can hold about 150 minutes of film each.

Television

The first thoughts of transmitting pictures over a distance were conceived as long ago as 1880, but it was not until John Logie Baird (1888-1946) began his experiments in 1923 that any real progress was made. He successfully demonstrated his mechanically-scanned system to members of the Royal Institution in London in 1926, and in 1928 a television picture of a doll's head was sent from England to New York using Baird's apparatus. Later that year Baird even gave a demonstration of colour television.

These early television pictures were very crude and blurred compared with television as known today, but they inspired other organisations to take a serious interest in the new medium.

In 1928 Vladimir Zworykin, working in the laboratories of Westinghouse, demonstrated his 'Iconoscope', a form of electron camera embodying the principles of a cathode ray tube which made possible the modern high definition TV system.

The television camera

To televise a picture or scene it is necessary to break the picture up into numerous component parts of varying light and shade, then convert these into electrical signals. This is essentially what is done by a modern *Vidicon* television camera, which consists of three basic parts—the lens, the camera tube, and electronic circuits to operate the tube and amplify the picture signals. The image of the scene televised is focused by the camera lens on to a 'target' at the front of the camera tube. At one end of the tube is an electrode known as the cathode, which is heated by passing current through a heater element. When heated, the cathode emits electrons which are directed in a very narrow beam to the target at the far end of the tube.

Around the neck of the tube are placed two sets of *scanning coils* through which a current flows, creating magnetic fields within them. These fields have the effect of deflecting the beam of electrons as it passes through them—one vertically and the other horizontally. By applying currents of a suitable waveform to the coils it is possible to make the electron beam scan the target at the end of the tube in the same manner that we read the page of a book. The beam travels across the target, then returns rapidly to the start of the next line which is just below the previous one.

The target of the tube consists of a thin layer of photoconductive material (lead oxide) which has a very high resistance to the flow of an electric current when the intensity of light falling on it is low. When the light intensity increases the resistance of the material decreases. The target may be thought of as comprising a number of small elements, each consisting of a small resistance in parallel with a capacitor, the capacitor being formed by a transparent conductive film in contact with the target. The conductive film forms a common connection for one side of each resistive/capacitive component of the target. The camera lens focuses the scene to be televised on to the target, and as the target is scanned by the electron beam each tiny resistive/capacitive element combination is charged by electrons from

Science Museum

Above: The scanning section of Baird's original apparatus. The effect of the rotating discs was to produce a moving aperture through which light from the object passed and activated a photocell.

Marconi

Above: A 1934 Marconi television receiver, with the top lid open. When in use the lid was closed, and the image from the vertical tube was projected through the hole in the lid and viewed in the angled mirror. This set had a 50 line horizontal scan.

TELEVISION CAMERA TUBE

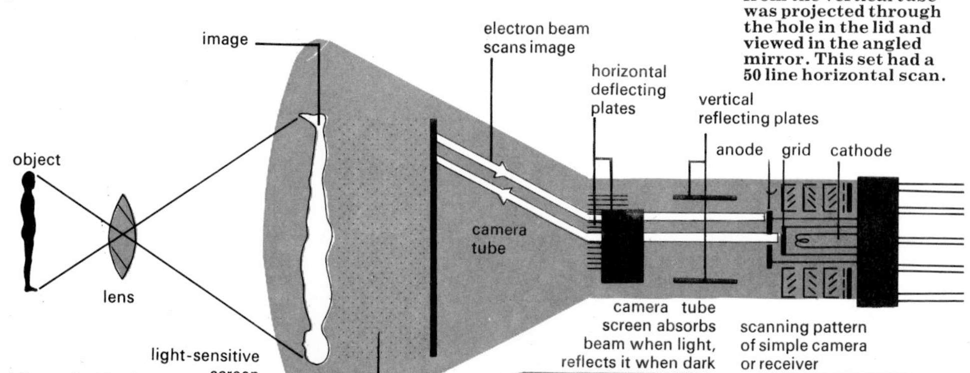

image
electron beam scans image
horizontal deflecting plates
vertical reflecting plates
anode
grid
cathode
object
lens
camera tube
camera tube screen absorbs beam when light, reflects it when dark
scanning pattern of simple camera or receiver
light-sensitive screen

Above: In the *image orthicon* television camera, the target of the camera tube has a light-sensitive layer whose electrical properties vary in proportion to the amount of light falling on it. As the electron beam scans the target, it is absorbed or reflected according to the pattern of light falling on to the light-sensitive layer.

Below: The reflected beam creates a signal which represents the image of the scene.

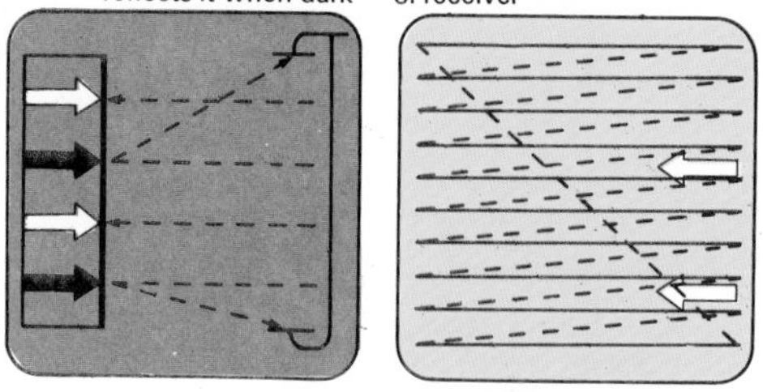

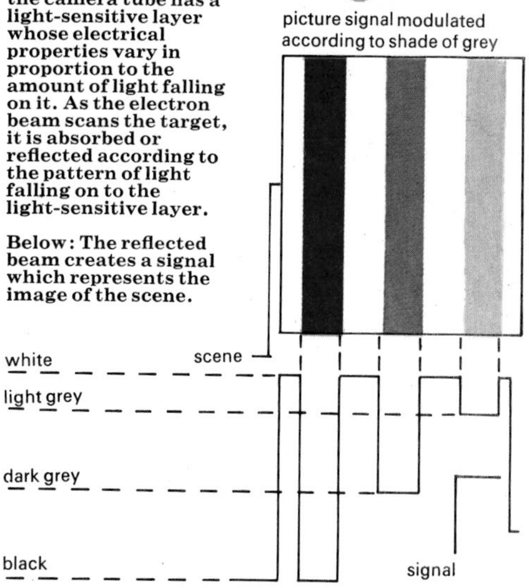

picture signal modulated according to shade of grey
white
scene
light grey
dark grey
black
signal

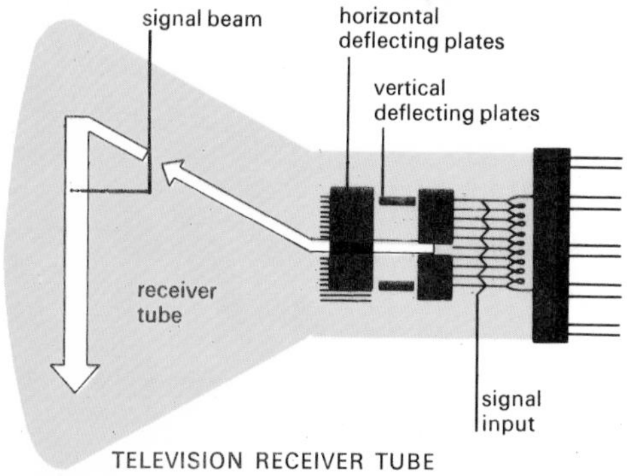

signal beam
horizontal deflecting plates
vertical deflecting plates
receiver tube
signal input
TELEVISION RECEIVER TUBE

Above: This group of three diagrams shows a basic monochrome receiver tube (top); the way in which the beam is reflected or absorbed by the target of an image orthicon camera tube (bottom left); and the basic way in which an electron beam scans either the target of a camera tube or the screen of a picture tube (bottom right).

Picturepoint

Left: This HMV set, introduced in 1938, consisted of a television with a 7 inch (18 cm) screen, a three waveband radio, and a gramophone. The television was designed for reception of the BBC's transmissions in Britain, which at that time used 405 line scanning.

the beam.

As soon as the beam passes, the charge on each capacitor begins to leak away through the resistance, the value of which varies according to the intensity of light falling on that part of the target area. On repeating the scan the electron beam supplies only a small charge to elements of the screen in areas of low light intensity, due to the high resistance, and a larger charge to areas of higher light intensity. The larger the charge supplied, the greater the flow of electrons from the gun, through the target, and out via the conductive film. This results in a current flowing through the target which varies in proportion to the picture content. The signals from the camera target, after suitable amplification, are then passed to the transmitter.

The electronic circuits that generate the waveforms applied to the scanning coils are called *timebases*. There is one for the vertical deflection of the electron beam and another for the horizontal deflection, and they are known respectively as the *field* and *line* timebases. The process of causing the electron beam to travel across and down the target is known as 'scanning'. Two methods of scanning are possible. The first, in which the beam draws a series of lines each of which is immediately beneath the previous one, is called *sequential scanning*. The second, which is the most widely used, is known as *interlaced scanning*.

In this method the beam moves across and down the target in a pattern of parallel lines, but with gaps between the lines. When the beam returns to repeat the scan, instead of drawing lines on top of the previous ones it draws lines between them. The next scan is then repeated on top of the first set of lines. Each set of lines that are traced is called a *field*, and two sets of interlaced lines completely

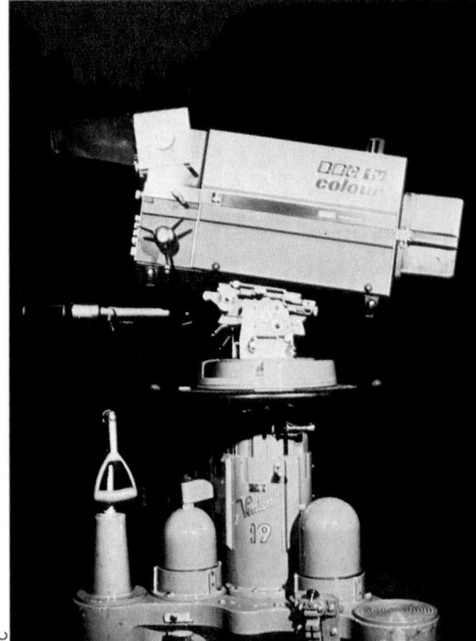

BBC

Left: An EMI colour television camera at a BBC studio. In this picture, the lens is on the right hand side. The cameraman views the scene being televised by means of a miniature television screen which is built into the rear of the camera.

Right: A television transmission tower in Hamburg, West Germany. The topmost section carries the TV antenna, and the tower also accommodates microwave radio antennae, plus a public sightseeing gallery and a restaurant.

BBC

Below: The Studio 'B' production control room in the BBC Broadcasting Centre at Pebble Mill, Birmingham, England. The studio itself is visible through the glass screen at the far end. The small monitor screens show the producer the pictures coming from each of the cameras in the studio, and the large ones show the picture which is being sent out for transmission.

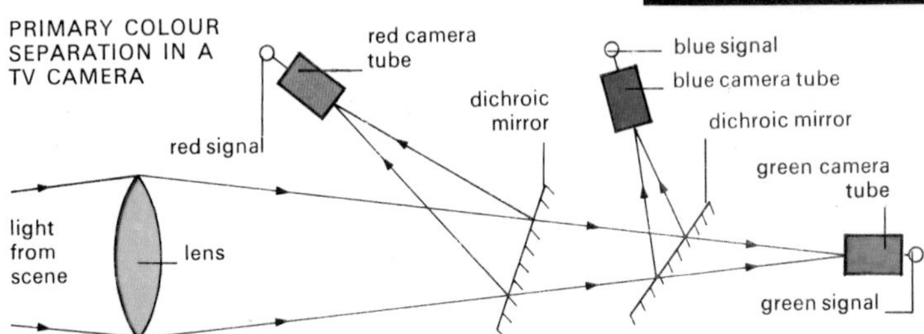

Above left: A three-tube colour TV camera has a separate tube for each of the three primary colours of light. The incoming light is split into separate colours by the *dichroic mirrors*, mirrors which reflect light of one colour but allow the others to pass through them. In the arrangement shown here, the first mirror reflects red light to the red tube, allowing the blue and green light to pass through it to the second mirror. This one reflects the blue light to the blue tube and lets the green light pass through it to the green tube.

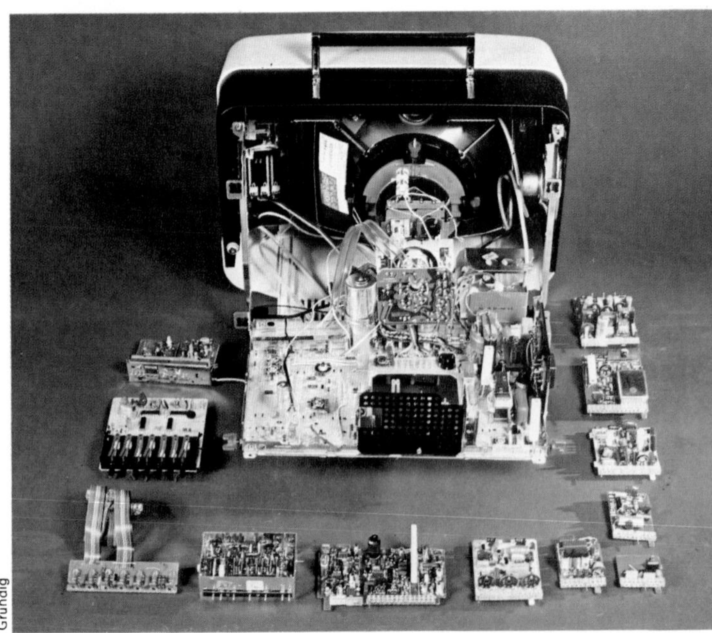

Grundig

Left: Modern colour television sets, such as this Grundig 1510, are built up from plug-in modules, each containing up to about 100 components.

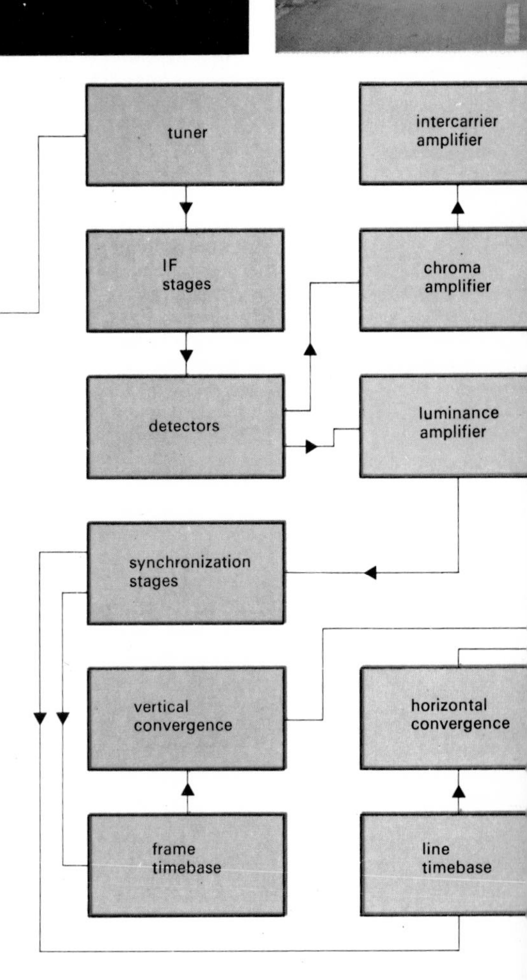

Right: A simplified block diagram of the main sections of a PAL colour receiver.

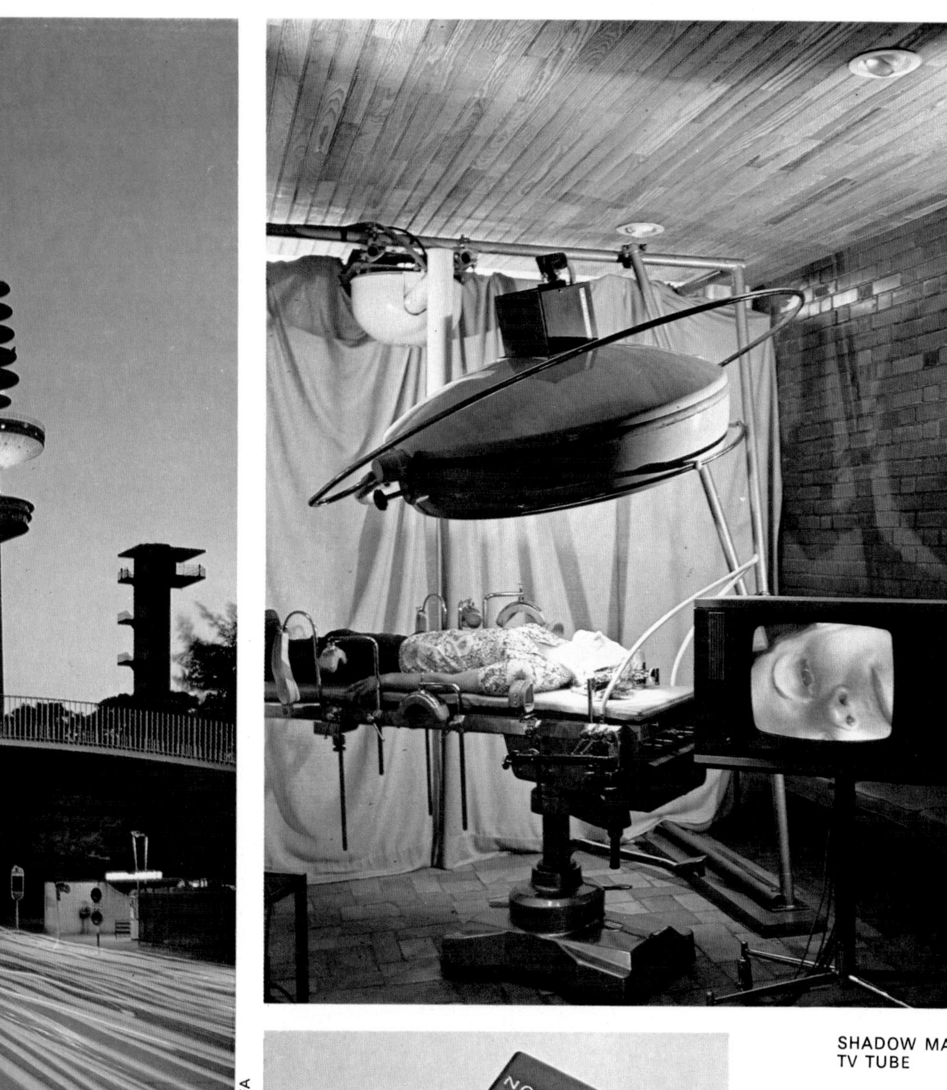

ZEFA

Snark

Left: Closed-circuit television systems, using cameras and receivers linked together by cables, have many uses in such areas as education, medicine and industry. This picture shows a closed-circuit colour system used for giving medical instruction to students during an operation.

scan the image on the target of the camera tube to produce a single *frame*.

To enable the received picture to keep in step with the picture being transmitted requires that synchronizing pulses be transmitted with the picture. In practice, at the end of each line scan a small proportion of the line is blacked out, and so are a small number of lines at the end of each frame. No picture signal is transmitted while the beam is scanning these points, so that these brief intervals can be used for transmission of the synchronizing pulses.

To enable the picture (video) and the associated sound signal to be carried by radio waves to the receiver, the signal is modulated on to a carrier wave of a much higher frequency. With the 625 line system two methods of modulation are employed, amplitude modulation and frequency modulation. Amplitude modulation is used to superimpose the video signal on the carrier, and frequency modulation is used for the sound signal. To enable sufficient picture detail to be carried the carrier frequency has to be very high, and ultra high frequencies of several hundreds of Megahertz are used for the 625 line system.

The receiver

A monochrome (black and white) receiver consists of a tuner unit, signal amplification and detector circuits, power supplies,

NORDMENDE
teleconrol IV
SOUND STOP EIN-AUS
teletimer

Nordmende

Right: Many TV manufacturers build sets which can be operated by remote control, using ultrasonic signals to carry the instructions.

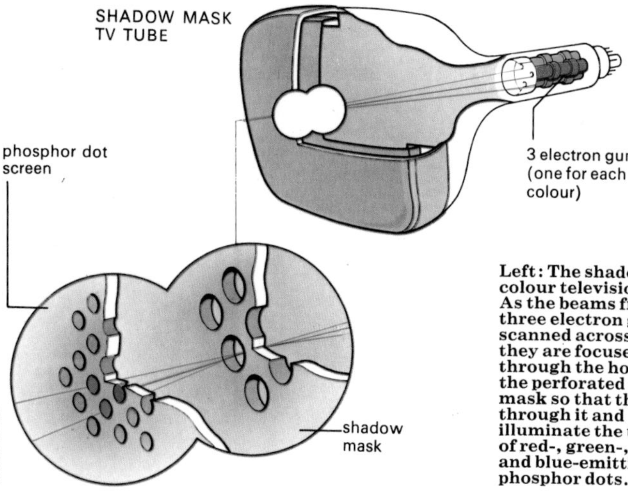

FM sound detector
colour decoder
audio amplifier
loudspeaker
power supply
picture tube
EHT tripler

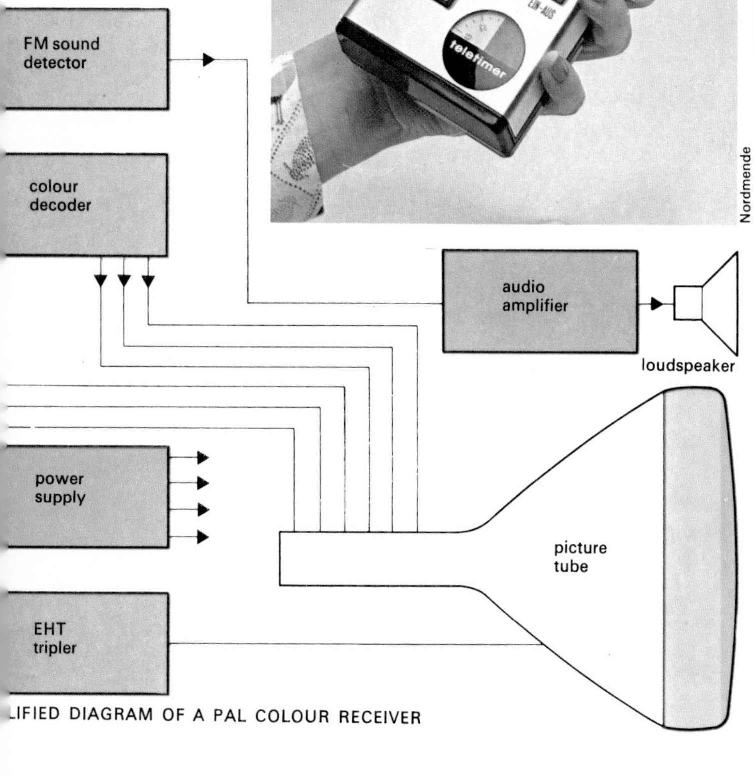

LIFIED DIAGRAM OF A PAL COLOUR RECEIVER

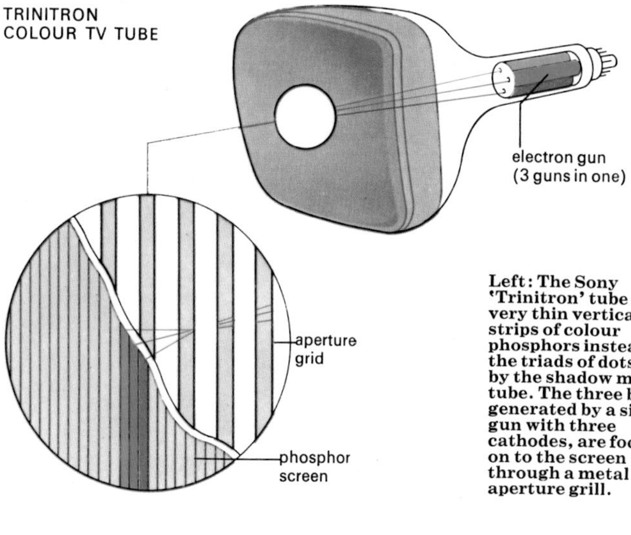

SHADOW MASK TV TUBE
phosphor dot screen
3 electron guns (one for each colour)
shadow mask

Left: The shadow mask colour television tube. As the beams from the three electron guns are scanned across the tube, they are focused through the holes in the perforated metal mask so that they pass through it and illuminate the triads of red-, green-, and blue-emitting phosphor dots.

TRINITRON COLOUR TV TUBE
electron gun (3 guns in one)
aperture grid
phosphor screen

Left: The Sony 'Trinitron' tube uses very thin vertical strips of colour phosphors instead of the triads of dots used by the shadow mask tube. The three beams, generated by a single gun with three cathodes, are focused on to the screen through a metal aperture grill.

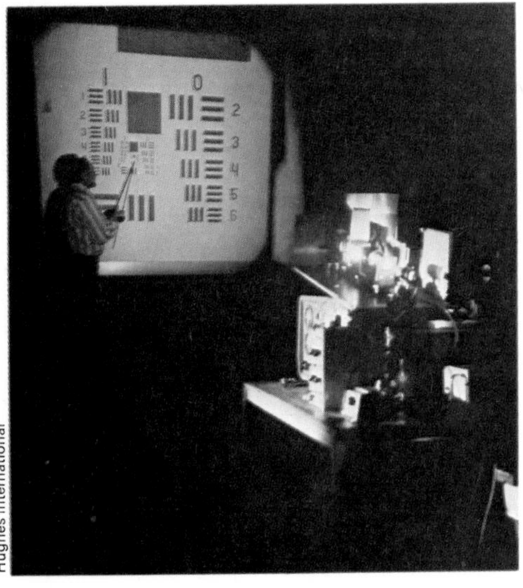
Hughes International

Left: Large-screen television systems usually have to take the picture from a normal-sized screen and project it on to the large one. The system shown here, however, uses a television picture signal to drive a cathode ray tube or a scanning laser, which in turn drives a *light valve*. This is a device that controls the projection of light on to the screen so as to form the image.

Right: The control desk of one of the first video recording systems. These systems, introduced in the 1950s, were difficult to design because of the wide range of frequencies contained in a video signal, and because of the high upper limit of these frequencies, which is about 6 MHz.

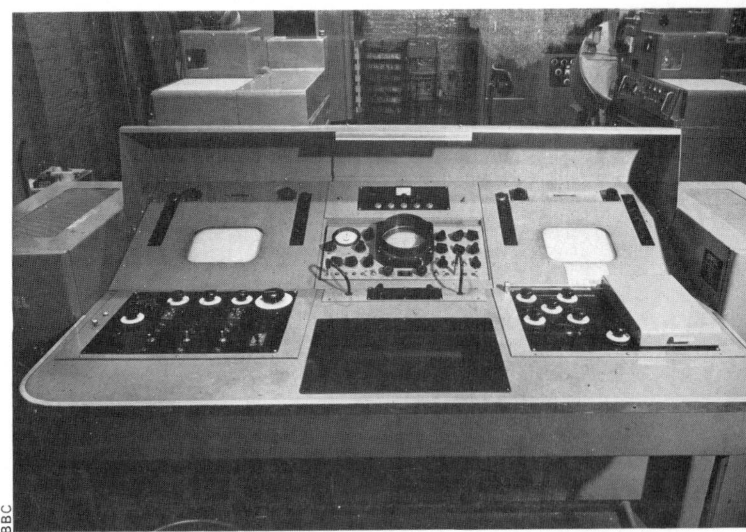
BBC

picture tube and loudspeaker. The required station is selected by the tuner unit, then amplified and passed to the detector circuits which separate the sound and video signals from the carrier. The sound signal is amplified again and fed to the loudspeaker. The video signal, after further amplification, is fed to the picture tube, which although based on the same principles as the camera tube is rather different in operation.

The glass picture tube is funnel shaped, and evacuated of air to a very high vacuum. One end of the tube is coated with a thin layer of fluorescent material to form the screen, and an electron 'gun', consisting of a cathode, grid and an anode, is mounted at the other end of the tube. When the cathode is heated, electrons are emitted and attracted at a high velocity towards the cylindrical shaped anode, which operates at a potential of several hundred volts or more above the cathode. Due to its tremendous acceleration the electron beam passes through the anode towards the fluorescent screen, and where the beam strikes the screen it causes the fluorescent material to glow.

The beam is focused to a very small point on the screen either by means of a focusing magnet fixed around the neck of the tube, or electrostatically by an internal electrode.

Many tubes have one or two additional anodes, each at potentials several hundred volts above its predecessor. The final anode may be as much as 18 kV above the cathode potential, and this results in very high acceleration of the electrons which gives a better picture image.

The electron beam is caused to scan the screen in the same manner as the beam in a camera tube, by means of scanning coils fitted around the neck of the tube and fed from the line and field timebases. Another electrode, called the grid, is mounted in front of the cathode and connected to a variable voltage source which forms the brightness control.

The amplified video signal is applied to the cathode of the picture tube, and as the video signal varies in amplitude it causes the flow of electrons to be modulated. As the cathode becomes more positive the flow of electrons to the screen is reduced. Therefore the intensity of illumination of the screen varies with the varying video signal, and as the screen is scanned an image is formed identical to that being scanned by the studio camera. The synchronizing pulses transmitted with the video signal are fed to the timebases of the receiver to ensure that the received picture is kept in perfect synchronization with that transmitted.

Decca

Nordmende

Left: The Normende 'Colorvision' (top) and 'Video-vision' units. The Colorvision machine is an electronic film scanner, which is used for playing Super 8 film cassettes through an ordinary television as an alternative to using a projector and screen. The Video-vision is a magnetic video cassette recorder which can record and replay TV programmes via an ordinary TV set.

Above and right: The video disc system developed in Germany by Teldec, a joint subsidiary of AEG-Telefunken and Decca. The discs are somewhat similar to gramophone records, but run at 1,500 rpm and have a playing time of ten minutes each.

The colour camera

A colour television camera works in a very similar way to that of a monochrome camera except that three tubes are used. The image of the scene being televised is focused on to each of the camera tubes by a system of *dichroic* and ordinary silvered mirrors. Dichroic mirrors reflect light of one colour, but allow all other colours to pass through them. The tubes are the same as those used for monochrome television but in front of each of the tubes is placed a filter of one of the three primary colours, red, blue or green. Therefore each tube will respond only to one colour. A fourth tube is sometimes used to provide a *luminance* or brightness signal, but the luminance signal can also be obtained by mixing fixed proportions of the output of each of the three tubes when a fourth tube is not used. The luminance signal, as it contains all three primary colours, is thus a monochrome signal, and a monochrome set receiving a colour transmission reproduces the luminance signal just as it would a normal monochrome signal.

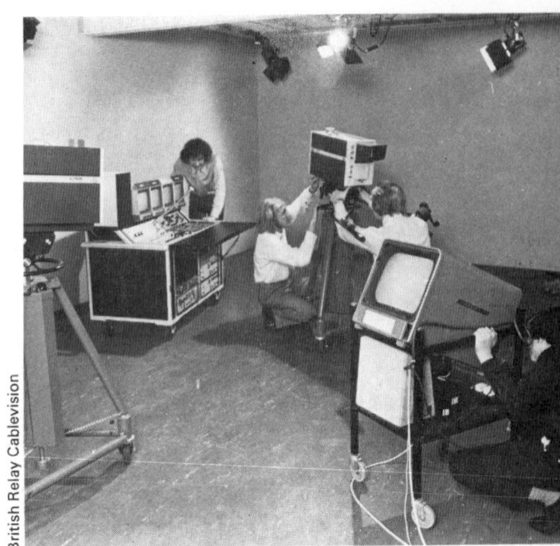
British Relay Cablevision

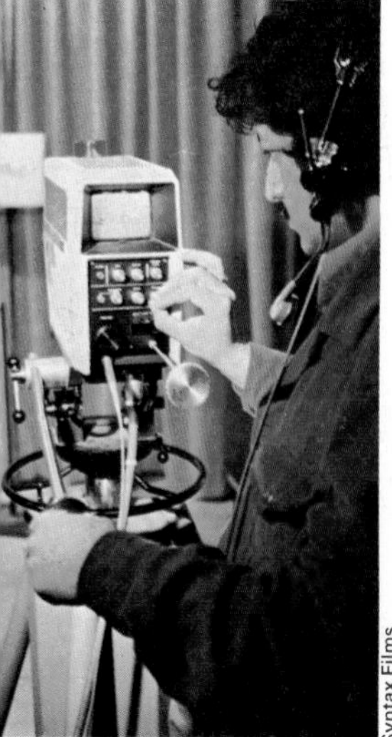

Syntax Films

Left: A small TV camera in an educational TV training studio. The miniature TV screen displays the image being produced by the camera tube.

Right: The tape head unit of a Sony video tape recorder. This machine has two recording heads, and uses 12.27 cm (½ inch) wide tape. The heads scan the tape as it passes, producing a recording which is a series of short tracks recorded obliquely across the tape. Each of these tracks corresponds to one field of the picture frame. This type of recording is known as *helical scan* recording, because the tape is wound helically around the drum containing the two video heads. The drum is beneath the U-shaped cover.

Syntax Films

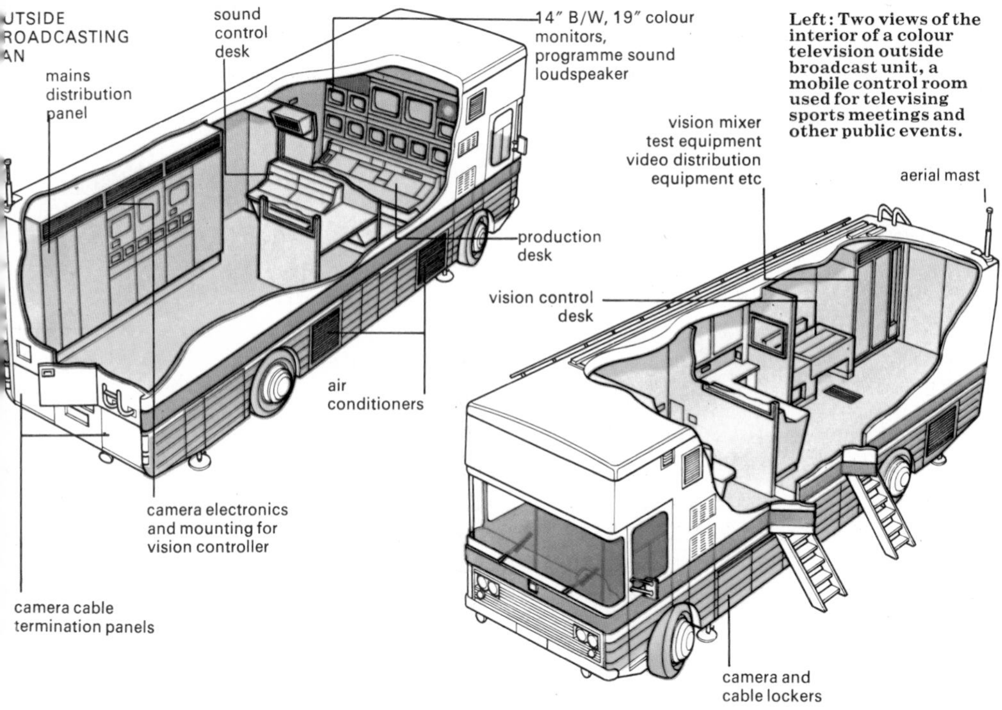

Left: Two views of the interior of a colour television outside broadcast unit, a mobile control room used for televising sports meetings and other public events.

Below left: Setting up a cablevision community television studio. Cablevision is a television service which was originally developed to relay television programmes to subscribers, by cable, from a central aerial station. But it can also be used to produce and broadcast local programmes.

Below: A 'page' from a BBC *Ceefax* broadcast. Ceefax is one of the two TV information services developed in Britain which use two of the unused lines of the ordinary 625-line transmission to carry up to 100 'pages' of news and information. These broadcasts can only be received by specially-adapted sets.

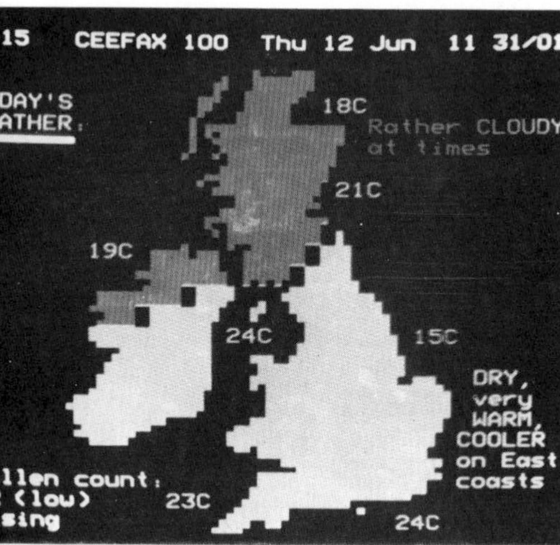

BBC

The colour camera thus produces four output signals, red (R), blue (B), green (G) and luminance (Y). These signals are not, however, the ones that are transmitted. This would mean transmitting four signals, but in practice all the information can be carried by only three. Before transmission, all four signals from the camera are put into an electronic circuit known as a *matrix*. The matrix combines the signals algebraically, and its output consists of three signals, namely the luminance signal plus two *colour difference signals*, R-Y and B-Y, and these are the signals which are transmitted.

In the receiver, a decoding matrix uses the R-Y and B-Y signals to derive a G-Y signal. The Y signal is subsequently added to each of these, thus cancelling out the -Y component of each of them and re-creating the original R, B and G signals.

The colour receiver

A colour television receiver is similar in operation to a monochrome receiver, but it has additional circuits for dealing with the colour information and of course a special tube for displaying the colour. The signal, after amplification and detection, is fed to the circuits which separate the colour information or *chrominance* signals and derive the G-Y component of the signal. The Y signal can be added at this point to recreate the original colour signals, but in most sets this process is affected at the electrodes of the electron guns of the tube.

The *shadow mask* colour television tube contains three electron guns. The screen is composed of tiny dots of three types of phosphor which emit the three primary colours when bombarded by electrons. These dots are arranged in groups of three called *'triads'*, each of which contains one dot of each colour. Behind the phosphor dot screen is a metal screen containing a large number of holes, one hole for each triad of phosphor dots. This metal screen is called the shadow mask and its purpose is to ensure that the phosphor dots of different colours are hit only by the electrons from the gun of the corresponding colour. The electrons themselves, of course, have no colour.

As the individual beams are modulated with the appropriate colour signals, the colours in each triad are proportionally illuminated. The eye sees the three colours as a mixture whose colour depends on the relative amount of illumination received by each of the primary colour dots in each triad. As the screen is scanned the colours of the original scene are therefore reproduced. The luminance signal is also fed to the tube and varies the brilliance of the colours, reproducing exactly the televised scene.

Colour systems

There are three systems of colour television in use in various parts of the world, known respectively as NTSC, PAL and SECAM. NTSC, a system recommended by the National Television Systems Committee of America and used in North America, Mexico and Japan, and PAL (Phase Alternate Line, used in most western European countries, Australia and New Zealand), are similar in many respects although PAL has some additional refinements.

The French SECAM (système en couleurs à mémoire) system differs from the other systems mainly in that the colour information is transmitted sequentially and in the method of deriving the chroma components of the signal. The SECAM receiver is simpler than that required by the other system, and this system is used by France, Russia, East Germany, Hungary and Algeria.

Radar

Radio waves, like light waves, are reflected by obstacles in their path. The detection of these reflections enables such objects to be located. This is the basis of *radar*, a word coined from Radio Detection and Ranging. The phenomenon of reflection was known from the earliest days of radio communications, but was often only regarded as a nuisance.

The development of radar in Britain arose from a suggestion by Sir Robert Watson-Watt who had been carrying out research on the ionized layers in the earth's upper atmosphere. This work involved using pulses of radio waves to measure the height of these layers and Watson-Watt saw that the same principles could be applied to the detection of distant aircraft. The outcome was the rapid development of a chain of early warning radar stations round the coasts of the British Isles. They were in operation in time for the start of World War II and contributed greatly to winning the Battle of Britain.

Having started under the impetus of a defence need, radar has developed enormously and its uses now extend to a wide range of both civil and military applications.

Basic principles

Acoustic echoes are a familiar phenomenon. Knowing the speed of sound through air one can measure the distance of a remote cliff or high building by

Below: A diagram showing the basic principles of radar. A stream of transmitted pulses are reflected by any object they encounter. The reflected pulses are picked up by the antenna when it is in the receive mode (controlled by the transmit/receive cell), amplified and displayed. Two displays are shown.

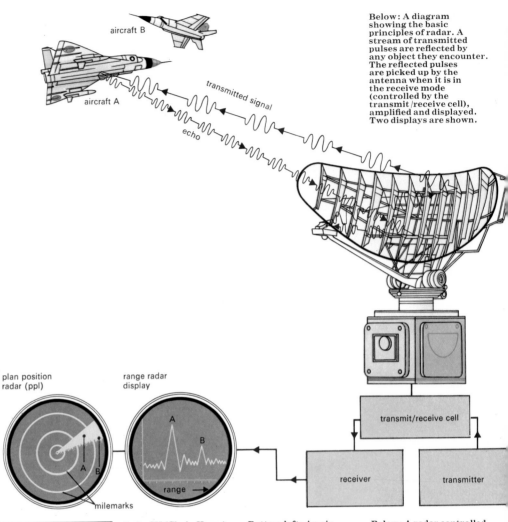

aircraft B
aircraft A
transmitted signal
echo
plan position radar (ppl)
range radar display
A
B
range
milemarks
transmit/receive cell
receiver
transmitter

Left: CH (Chain Home) towers near Dover, England. These were part of a long range, early warning system developed prior to the Second World War. By the beginning of the war the whole of the east coast of Great Britain was covered by this system. It could detect aircraft taking off in Germany.

Royal Signals and Radar Establishment Malvern

Bottom left: An air defence station used during the Second World War. The plan position indicator on the left gave the range of approaching aircraft. Aircraft altitude was determined using the right hand display by adjusting the angle of the aerial until a maximum return signal was received.

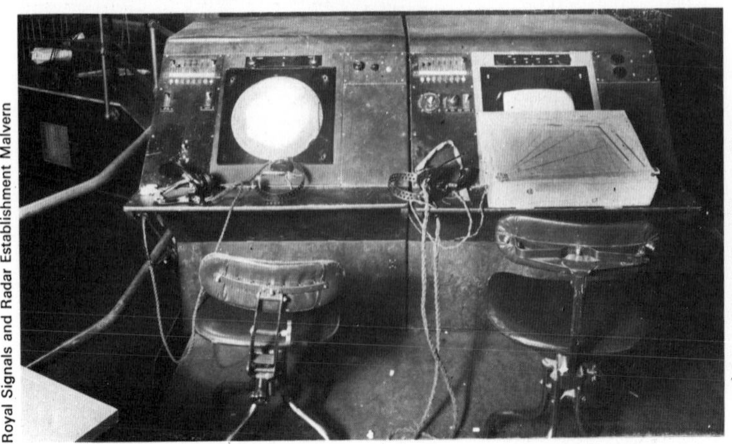
Royal Signals and Radar Establishment Malvern

Below: A radar controlled searchlight. This one was an experimental model with four Yagi receiving aerials around the searchlight and a folded dipole transmitter aerial mounted further back. This apparatus was extremely advanced for its time because it could automatically lock on to, and track, a moving target.

Royal Signals and Radar Establishment Malvern

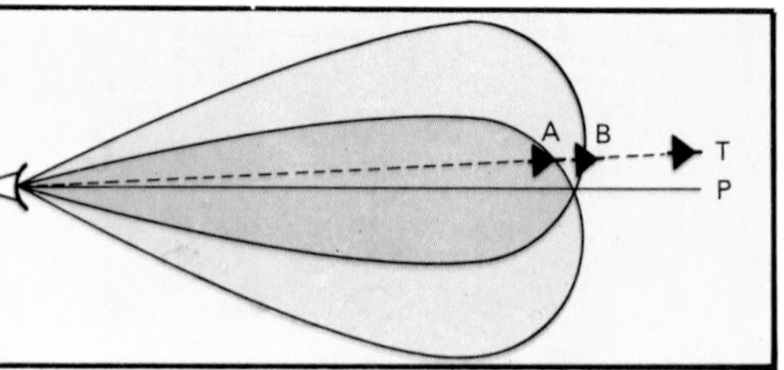

Above: Direction can be accurately determined in radar by using two partially overlapping beams. A target lying on the line of beam intersection (OP) produces an echo containing the two signals at equal strength. For a target at T, the ratio of signal strengths provides an accurate measure of the angle TOP.

Below: The Plessey ACR 430 airfield control radar system. This employs microwaves in the X-band frequency range (8,200 to 12,400 MHz). It uses a two-beam aerial system—each beam derived from a separate transmitter and fed via a waveguide to a separate horn. One of the beams is pencil-shaped for accurate surveillance.

Plessey

Below: A resonant cavity magnetron. The development of this device revolutionized radar, permitting the use of high frequency (short wavelength) radio waves at high powers. A waveguide is attached to the rectangular section on the front to channel the radio waves to the aerial. The fins cool the device.

Right: The Plessey WF-3 primary windfinding radar system. This operates in the X-band microwave frequency range. The antenna has automatic tracking facilities and a digital readout device for displaying range, azimuth and elevation. This particular version is of a portable design and is simple to instal.

EMI

ZEFA

Above: A radar tower with primary and secondary radar facilities. Secondary surveillance radar (SSR) allows extra information (such as flight data) to be returned to the flight controller along with ordinary data obtained from the primary radar system. Special apparatus is needed in each aircraft to obtain this information.

Right: A US tactical air control system with primary and secondary surveillance radar facilities. This control centre provides commanders with computerized tactical air control capability. Radar and other information can be rapidly exchanged between this and other command centres.

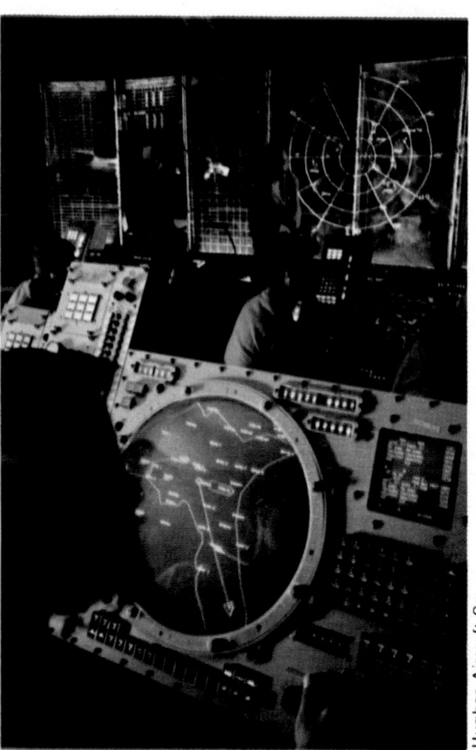

Hughes Aircraft Co.

Plessey

observing the time that an echo takes to return. This is how radar works but using radio waves which travel at a speed of 300,000 km/sec rather than sound which only travels at about 340 m/sec. If both the total time of travel of the transmitted/reflected beam and its direction are measured the position of the distant reflecting object is obtained.

Either *continuous* waves, such as are used in broadcasting, or interrupted (*pulsed*) signals can be used, but the principles of radar are easier to understand in the case of the latter. Imagine a radio transmitter sending out a train of short pulses of radio energy. Each pulse may be a few millionths of a second long; the time interval between successive pulses is arranged to be longer than it would take for radio waves to travel out to any distant object of interest and back.

If these pulses meet an object (the *target*) they are reflected and some of this reflected energy is picked up by a receiver alongside the transmitter. The train of received pulses will be slightly retarded relative to the transmitted pulses by an interval corresponding to the out and return time of the waves. If directional aerials are used for transmitting and receiving then both the distance (range) and direction of the target are obtained.

Usually the same aerial is used for transmitting and receiving. The receiver is protected against damage from the powerful transmitted pulses by being *suppressed* during the brief periods when they are emitted but *re-activated* in time to detect any reflected pulses. The rapid acting switch used for this protection of the receiver is known as *Transmit-Receive* (or *TR*) *Cell.*

The aerial directional pattern used depends on the purpose of the radar. For general surveillance as in Air Traffic Control a common pattern is the 'fan beam'. This is typically 1° or 2° wide in azimuth and 15° or 20° wide in elevation. With such a pattern, range and bearing can be measured quite accurately but no elevation information is available. This is adequate for many purposes.

It is possible to obtain full three dimensional information by using a 'stack' of beams each of which is narrow in both azimuth and elevation. The stack is arranged so that all beams lie in one vertical plane but pointing at different elevations. An alternative arrangement is to scan a narrow beam very rapidly in elevation while it scans much more slowly in azimuth. The rapid elevation scan is sometimes done by varying the frequency, the aerial having been designed so that its elevation angle is dependent upon the radio frequency.

Normally, direction is obtained as the angle at which maximum signal is received. This occurs when the peak of the aerial beam points at the target. If more accurate directional information is required the principle of overlapping beams is employed. In this arrangement the receiving aerial has two partially overlapping narrow beams. The exact direction of the target relative to the centre line of the system is obtained from the ratio of the signals in the two beams. Along the central cross-over line of the beams the signals are equal. The principle can be extended to measure two orthogonal angular co-ordinates, for example, elevation and azimuth.

ZEFA

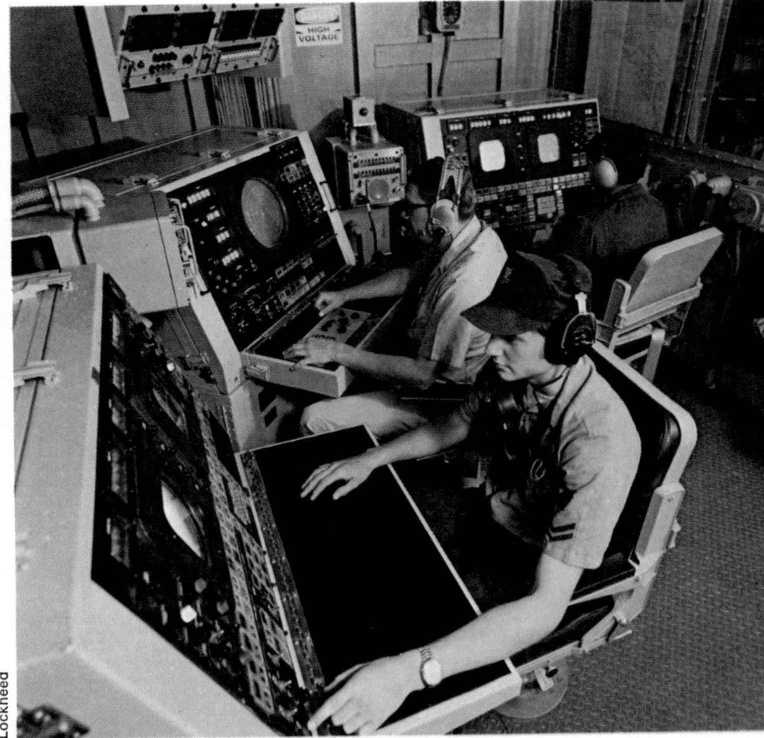

Lockheed

Syndication International

Above: The deck of the warship HMS Charybdis (a Leander Class general purpose frigate) with various radar installations for defence and attack systems.

Above right: The US Navy's newest ships are being fitted with these electronic gunfire control system consoles, shown here on the USS California nuclear guided missile frigate.

Right: The Fylingdales early warning radar system in Yorkshire, England. Vast resources have been spent on developing military applications of radar (both defence and attack systems) but there are many ways in which radar can be put to peaceful purposes.

A close relative of this form of aerial is the *conical scan* aerial in which a narrow pencil beam is caused to rotate at high speed about a line slightly displaced from the axis of the beam maximum. When a target lies exactly on the axis of spin, the echo has constant amplitude, but if it lies slightly off this axis the amplitude of the echo varies in sympathy with the rotation of the beam. Missile fire control radars use these principles.

Radar waves are essentially confined to line of sight although the atmosphere does produce a small amount of downwards bending. Thus radars do see marginally beyond the horizon. For practical purposes, however, the range of a radar is determined ultimately by geometrical considerations. High-flying aircraft can be seen at considerable range but to detect distant low targets the radar must be raised to extend the horizon.

Subject to these considerations it is possible to see aircraft up to 300 km (approx 200 miles) away. A typical modern long range air traffic control radar uses a wavelength of about 25 cm, a peak power of 2 MW and an aerial some 12 m wide by 5 m high scanning at a rate of 10 rpm.

Generation

At the heart of a radar equipment is a powerful radio-frequency generator. While radar is possible over a wide range of wavelengths, the most common lie in the range from about 25 cm to 3 cm (corresponding to frequencies of 1,200 MHz to 10,000 MHz). The most common radars are of the pulsed variety in which the transmitted signal consists of short pulses of radio-frequency energy, about 1 to 5 microseconds long, emitted in a stream at intervals of between 1 to 4 milliseconds. The peak power in the pulse may lie typically in the range of a few kW to a few MW, depending on the purpose of the radar. But the mean (average) power is less since the transmitter operates only during the short pulses. The ratio of mean to peak power is the *duty cycle* and for the figures quoted is about 1/1000.

Two types of microwave transmitting tubes are particularly important. In one, the *cavity magnetron*, a beam of electrons circulates under the influence of a powerful transverse magnetic field inside a metal structure which has cavities of a particular size. Radio energy is generated at a frequency determined by the dimensions of the cavities. The pulses are created by switching the electron beam on and off by a suitable high speed switch known as the 'modulator'. This is the commonest generator in current use.

The other important transmitting tube is the *klystron*, in which a beam of electrons passes through a series of metallic cavities 'tuned' to the required frequency. The velocity of the beam varies in sympathy with the radio frequency voltages within the cavities. The interaction between kinetic energy of the electrons and radio frequency energy in the cavities is used either to generate oscillations or to amplify oscillations already present. The tube is normally used as an amplifier, the short pulses being generated initially at quite low power.

Detection and display

The detection of the pulses returned from targets is carried out in a receiver similar to the vision receiver of a television set. Nowadays this is almost always a *solid-state* receiver. The output of the receiver is a stream of video pulses which have to be displayed suitably.

The most important display device is the *cathode-ray tube* (CRT), similar to the tube in a TV set. In the earliest radars the display tube was arranged to indicate directly the delay time of the echo pulses as follows. The cathode-ray beam is deflected across the screen of the tube at a steady rate commencing at the moment a pulse is transmitted. This produces a bright line across the tube face. Any returned pulse is arranged to cause a momentary upwards deflection of the beam thus producing a characteristic mark or 'pip'. If the speed at which the beam moves across the CRT is known, the distance of this mark from the commencement of the trace provides a direct measure of the time delay of the echo pulse and hence of the distance of the target.

In an alternative arrangement the cathode-ray beam, initially of reduced intensity so as to produce very little fluorescence on the tube face, traverses a line starting from the centre of the screen.

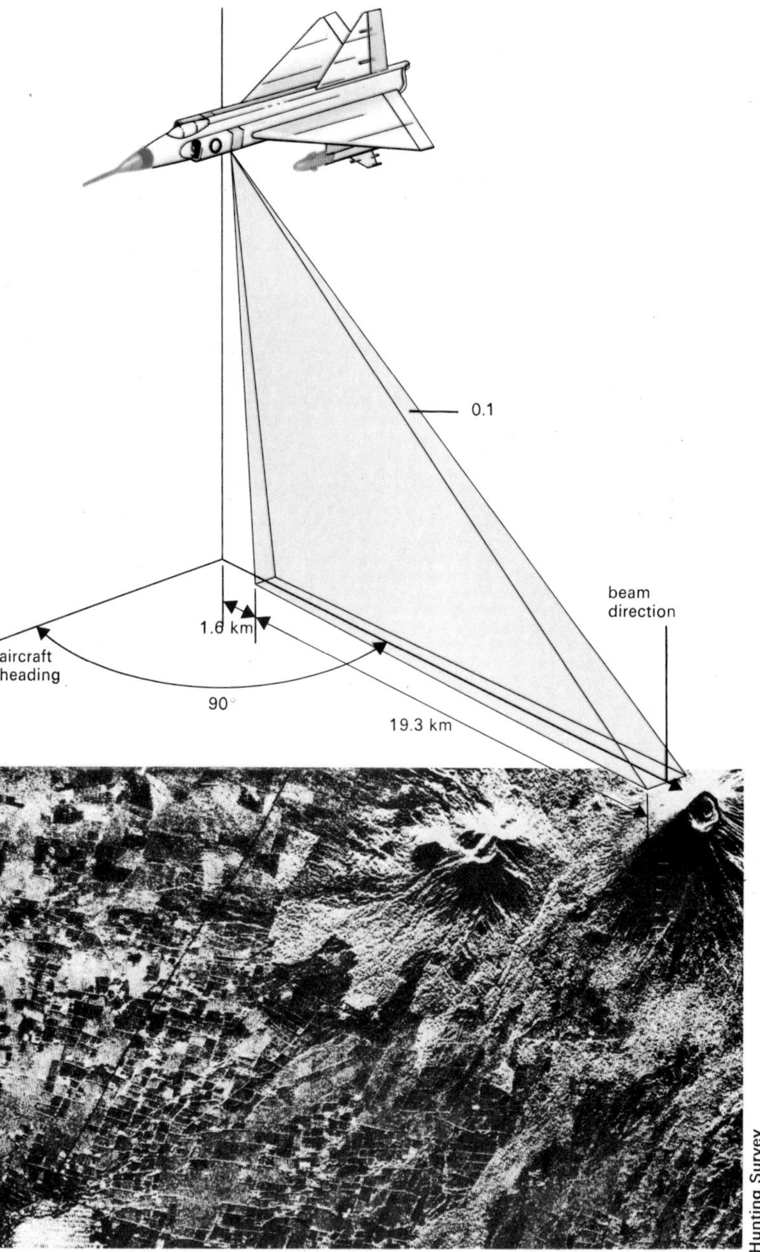

Photri

Above: An airborne radar system. Because radio waves travel in straight lines, ground radar systems are limited in range to the horizon (except for small bending effects caused by the atmosphere). To increase the range of a radar system it is necessary to use airborne radar.

Above left: A side-looking radar system for mapping ground features. This uses a sharp and highly directional beam from a fixed antenna on the aircraft. The motion of the aircraft itself provides the scan across the earth's surface.

Left: A reconstructed image of Chinandega and the San Cristobal volcano area of western Nicaragua taken by side-looking radar (SLR). This system has the advantage that it can be used at night, in fog or cloud and any adverse conditions that prevent normal photography.

Hunting Survey

Returned pulses are made to momentarily intensify the beam and so produce a bright spot on the tube face at a distance from the centre corresponding to the distance of the target. If the line across the tube face is made to rotate about the centre in sympathy with the rotation of the aerial beam a map-like picture is produced on the tube face showing the position of reflecting targets around the radar. This is the well-known *Plan Position Indicator* or PPI.

Doppler radar

When a source of sound is approaching or receding, its apparent pitch is raised or lowered. This is the *Doppler Effect*. Similarly, radio waves reflected from a moving target have their frequency raised or lowered according to whether they are moving towards or away from the observer. One important use of this is to distinguish moving from stationary objects. In air traffic control, for example, reflections from buildings, trees or high ground may obscure the returns from moving aircraft. However, the latter reflections exhibit a Doppler shift in frequency.

In *Moving Target Indication* or MTI this shift is detected, causing only moving targets to be displayed. Another important use of Doppler is in airborne navigational radar, enabling an aircraft to measure its speed relative to the ground by the Doppler shift of the waves reflected by the ground.

Applications

From its birth as an early warning device against air attack, radar has expanded to a very wide range of applications both civil and military. It is the basis of air traffic control in all areas of dense traffic and is indeed essential for safety in air transport. It is used in aircraft to detect high ground and storms and to measure relative speed over the ground. At sea, the majority of merchant ships of any size carry a navigational radar enabling them to navigate in bad visibility, while land-based radar is used in busy ports to supervise and control movements in the shipping lanes. Radar also has many meteorological uses, such as detecting and tracking storms and hurricanes.

Below: This is the Ferranti mobile X-band (that is, microwaves in the frequency range 8,200 to 12,400 MHz) target illuminating radar. This is used with surface-to-air missiles, such as the Thunderbird, in a guided weapon system. Various microwave aerials are attached to the antenna tower.

Ferranti

Right: The Ferranti Seaspray radar is in production for the naval version of the Westland Lynx helicopter. Small and lightweight, it is able to detect small targets, such as fast patrol boats, even in very rough sea conditions. The antenna waveguide, which channels the microwaves, can be clearly seen.

Ferranti

Lasers

Lasers are devices which encourage atoms to emit visible light in a regular manner, rather than the sporadic and random emission which normally occurs in nature. Masers operate on the same principles as lasers but produce microwaves rather than light. The unique properties of lasers and masers have already been applied in many fields, including industry, communications, and medicine, and new applications are continually being developed.

Light and microwaves are both forms of *electromagnetic radiation.* The only difference between them is the frequency (and hence also wavelength) of the radiation—light is of a much higher frequency (shorter wavelength) than microwaves.

Electromagnetic radiation is produced when electrons, which move in orbits or 'levels' around the nucleus of an atom, give up some of their energy. But to understand how this happens, and how lasers harness this energy into a regular, ordered form, it is necessary to explain the mechanisms of the atom.

Photri

Above: A photograph of Washington monument illuminated by lasers.

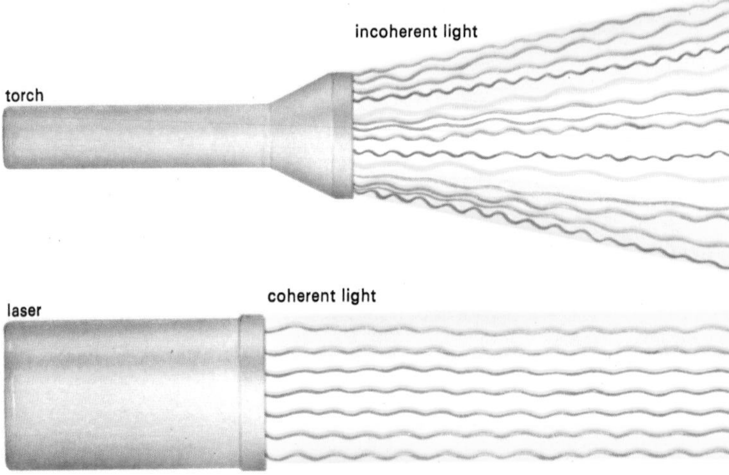

Right: The important difference between a laser and, say, an electric torch is that the laser produces *coherent* light. Ordinary light contains a jumble of light waves with different frequencies (between red and blue). These are randomly generated and scattered in all directions: it is the torch reflector that organizes these waves roughly into a beam. Such light is termed *incoherent.* With coherent light, the waves have exactly the same frequency and are in step with each other. That is, the 'crests' of the waves line up to form a *wavefront.* Laser beams are also nearly perfectly parallel.

Electrons in orbit

Whether in molecules or atoms, electrons are not free to move as they please but are confined to relatively few distinct orbits, which are always the same for any two atoms of the same element but can vary widely between elements. Electrons in each orbit have a fixed energy, those closest to the nucleus having low energies and those further out have higher. Only one electron can occupy any orbit at a time.

Electrons can move from their orbit to any empty orbit, but in so doing they must also obey the law of *conservation of energy.* So electrons wanting to move outwards from the nucleus must somehow gain enough energy to make the jump and those moving inwards must lose energy. They can do this by emitting or absorbing light in the form of small 'packets' known as *photons.* Photons are the smallest possible packets of light that can exist and the light we see consists simply of vast numbers of individual photons whose abundance gives the impression of a continuous stream of light.

Each photon has a fixed energy and a wavelength which is inversely proportional to this energy. When an electron moves from an outer to an inner orbit it emits a photon whose energy equals the energy difference between the two orbits. The reverse process, in which an electron jumps from the lower to the higher level (from the inner to the outer orbit), requires that the electron gain the same amount of energy. One way of achieving this is for the electron to absorb a passing photon of exactly the right energy and wavelength.

Spontaneous emission

The lowest energy state of an electron is called the *ground state* and all others are known as *excited states.* Electrons may be excited to higher states by several methods other than the photon absorption process just described. Heating a substance will excite the electrons of its atoms or molecules as will subjecting it to an

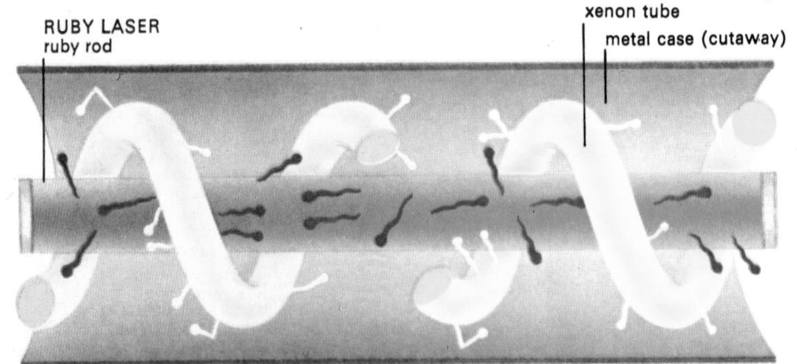

Left and below: A diagram showing the mechanism of a ruby laser. The electrons in the chromium atoms are excited into higher energy levels by the light from a powerful spiral flashtube. As these electrons drop back to their ground state (lowest energy level) they each emit a photon of light of the characteristic ruby red colour. This is spontaneous emission. To produce laser action, the crystal is cut to a special shape to enhance stimulated emission along the ruby crystal axis.

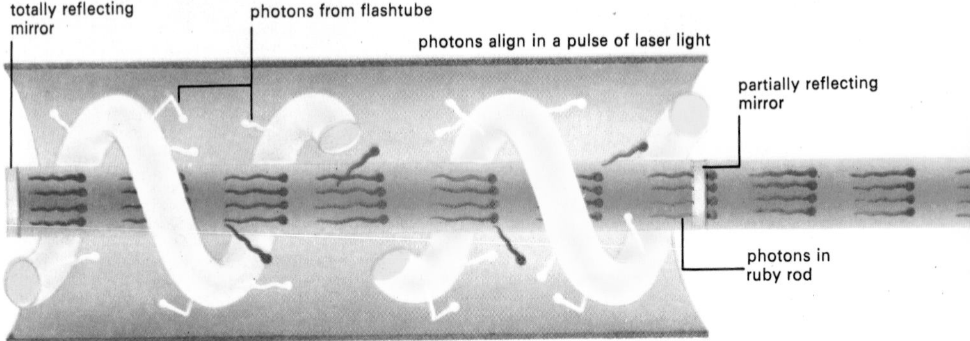

Spectra Physics

Spectra Physics

Left and right: Laser light is nearly perfectly parallel. To demonstrate this fact, a laser beam was directed from this window in a city centre (left). When viewed directly from a distant hill (right), the beam is much brighter than the surrounding street lamps even though the laser produces about 1/1000 of their power.

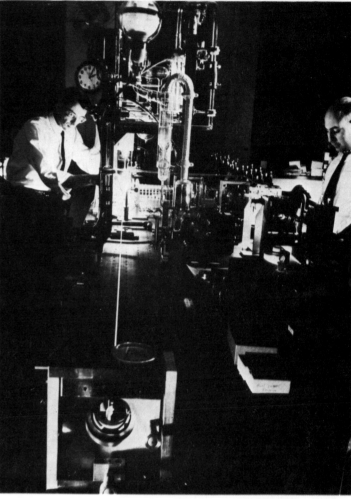

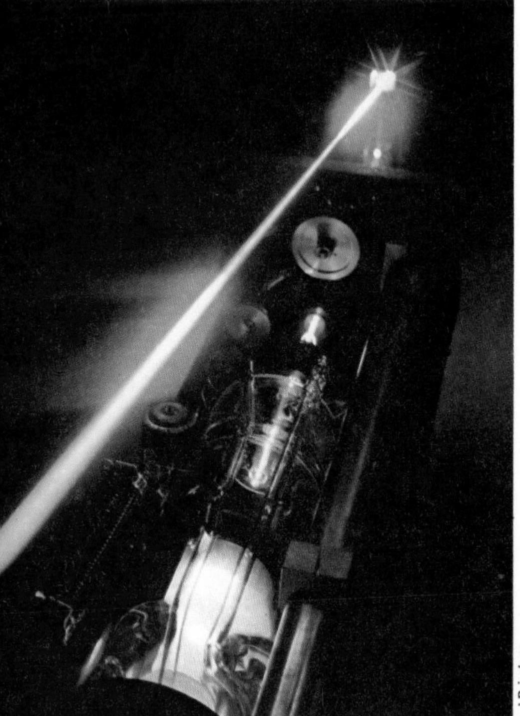

Paul Brierley

Left: This green beam of laser light is produced by an argon laser. The specific colour of a laser depends on the electron configuration of the element employed to initiate stimulated emission. The larger the energy difference between the ground state and excited state of these electrons, the higher the frequency of emitted radiation (and smaller wavelength).

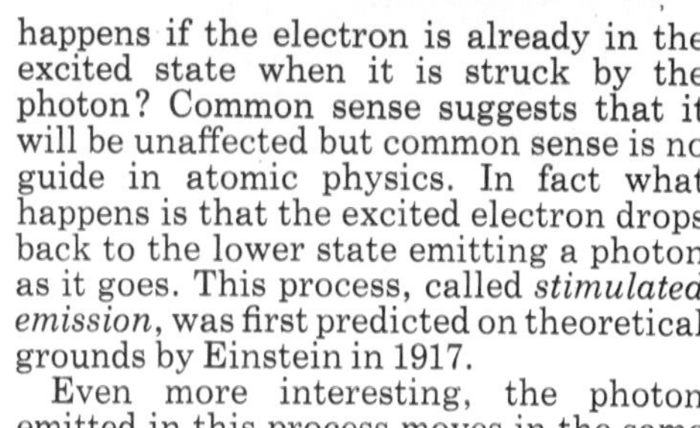

Bell Labs

Right: This was the first gas laser to produce a continuous beam of visible light. Present day lasers produce a vast range of frequencies from microwaves (masers) through infra-red and the visible spectrum to ultra-violet. Theoretically, even higher frequency laser radiation is possible. Scientists are considering the possibility of using it for X-rays and even gamma radiation.

Hughes Aircraft Co.

Below left: The inventor of the ruby laser, Theodore Maiman, with one of his instruments. The spiral flashtube can be clearly seen and inside this is the cylindrical ruby crystal with machined and silvered ends.

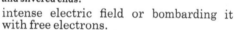

intense electric field or bombarding it with free electrons.

Electrons which have been excited to higher states by any method are, however, not stable. They spontaneously drop back to any empty lower level, emitting the appropriate photon as they do so. This *spontaneous emission* is quite random and there is no way of telling when the photon will be emitted or what direction it will move in, although for a large number of excited atoms it is possible to predict quite accurately how many photons will be emitted in a given time.

Spontaneous emission by excited electrons produces all the light that we normally see—the various light sources differ only in the method used to excite the electrons, for example nuclear heating in the sun, electric heating in a light bulb and electron bombardment in a neon tube. Because of the random nature of spontaneous emission these sources all emit light in all directions and the component photons are out of step with one another. Such light is *incoherent*.

Stimulated emission

We have seen that an electron can be excited to a higher state by the impact of a photon of the right energy. But what happens if the electron is already in the excited state when it is struck by the photon? Common sense suggests that it will be unaffected but common sense is no guide in atomic physics. In fact what happens is that the excited electron drops back to the lower state emitting a photon as it goes. This process, called *stimulated emission*, was first predicted on theoretical grounds by Einstein in 1917.

Even more interesting, the photon emitted in this process moves in the same direction and exactly in step with the stimulating photon (that is, they are *coherent*). The two identical photons are now free to stimulate further emission of photons from any other excited electrons they encounter and these photons too will match the original. Thus, if conditions are right, the original photon will be amplified again and again by each successive stimulation of an excited electron. The word laser was coined to describe this process by its initial letters which stand for Light Amplification by Stimulated Emission of Radiation.

One factor prevents laser action under normal circumstances, namely the possibility that photons, instead of stimulating emission from electrons in the higher state, will encounter electrons in the

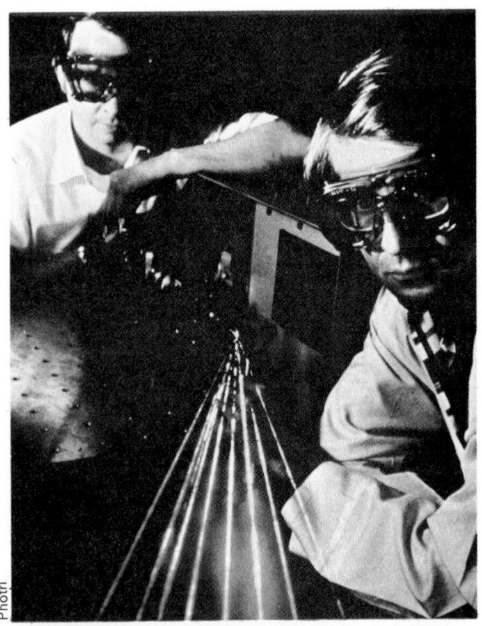

Photri

Left: This *dye laser*, produces a range of colours from ultra-violet to yellow. One device of special interest is the argon/krypton gas laser whose output of mixed radiation gives the appearance of white light.

Right: A portable laser microwelder. Because the beam from a laser is almost perfectly parallel, the focal point of the beam when focused by a lens is extremely small and distinct. Therefore the intensity of light at the focus is very high—high enough to be used in welding applications. Theoretically, a perfectly parallel beam aimed at a perfect lens will produce a *point* of light (of zero area and infinite intensity). A conventional source of light produces a large and hazy spot. More powerful types of laser, such as the carbon dioxide version, can cut through sheet metal. Such welding devices are gas jet assisted.

IRD

Howard Sochurek/John Hillelson Agency

LASER-FUSION REACTOR

high-intensity laser light

hot expanding surface of disintegrating pellet

laser beams focused onto fuel pellet

containment vessel (cutaway)

heat given off by fusion reaction is removed by heat exchangers, and used to raise steam which powers turbogenerators

'hot' electrons

alpha particles

neutrons

Scientific American

Above: Detecting an art forgery using laser techniques. One way to achieve this is by detecting the undulations of the paint surface, by which means the number and thickness of paint layers underneath can be determined. The technique employed is similar to that used in holography where the depth nature of a scene (in this case the paint undulations) modifies the laser beam reflected from the surface.

Right: Using laser light to illuminate a scene for television. The principle is not to flood the whole scene with laser light, but to scan across the scene in a manner similar to that used in a television camera and receiver.

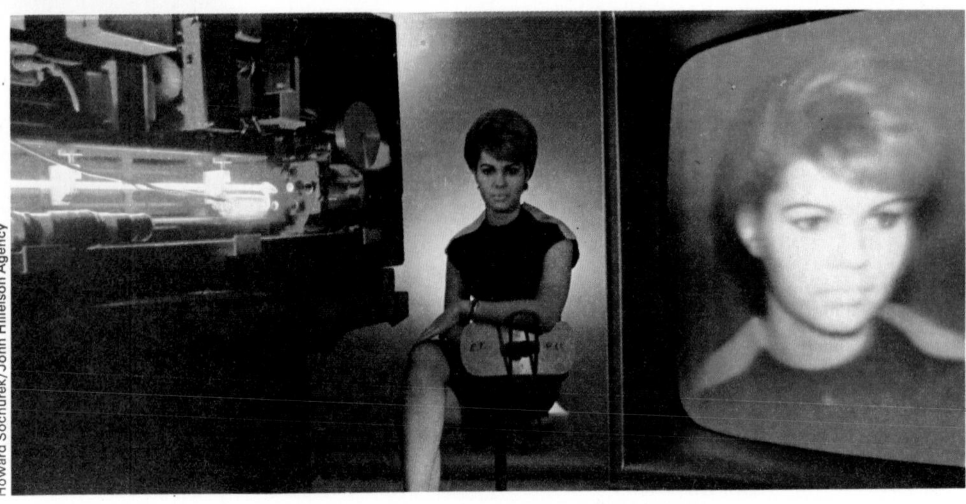

Howard Sochurek/John Hillelson Agency

Above: How lasers could be used to create the energy source of the future—nuclear fusion. If a very short but intense burst of laser light could be focused from all sides onto a frozen pellet of deuterium and tritium (isotopes of hydrogen), the nuclei would fuse together to form helium with a large release of energy. As the light strikes the pellet, the surface temperature rises and becomes ionized. 'Hot' electrons move inwards, carrying energy with them and heat the interior. As this happens, neutrons and alpha particles explode outwards causing an equal and opposite implosion of the interior which creates sufficiently high temperatures and pressures to cause fusion.

Ferranti

Above, right and below: Even if laser 'death rays' are at present confined to the realm of fiction, the uses of lasers in military applications have not been slow in developing. The apparatus above can aim a laser beam precisely at a target. The light scattered from this is registered by apparatus in the nose of the strike aircraft (right) and used to 'home in' on the target. Similar devices can also be fitted to missiles. Below the diagram shows how the apparatus is used. The aircraft receptor filters out all light except that from the laser and so this system can be used in daylight although this is much brighter than the laser light. The equipment can also be used for rangefinding. Systems such as this were used by the Americans in Vietnam. Even such sophisticated technology marks only the beginning of its military uses.

lower state and be absorbed by them. Since there are normally more electrons in lower states than higher, this means that emitted photons are annihilated more rapidly than they can breed. For amplification it is necessary to ensure artificially that the majority of electrons are in the excited state, which will tip the balance in favour of creation rather than destruction of photons. Such a situation is called an *inversion*.

The ammonium maser

The first ever maser used a very simple method of obtaining an inversion in molecules of ammonium gas. These molecules have many different energy states but the ammonium maser uses only two of these, which differ in energy such that when an electron drops from the upper to the lower it emits a photon of wavelength 1.2 cm. If ammonium gas is passed through an electric field the molecules in the upper of these two states will be deflected in one direction and those in the lower state in another, giving two beams of molecules, one predominantly upper state and the other lower. The beam of excited molecules in the upper state is then a suitable medium for laser action, until spontaneous emission degrades it once again to the lower state.

The excited beam is directed into a metal box or cavity where it is exposed to a weak microwave signal of 1.2 cm wavelength. This stimulates emission of 1.2 cm photons from some of the molecules, which quickly avalanches to full maser action. Provided a continuous supply of excited molecules is fed to the cavity, the ammonium maser will emit a continuous coherent microwave beam from a small hole in the cavity. The power is not great, being less than 1 microwatt (10^{-6} watt), but the frequency of the radiation is so stable that it is used as a standard for measuring time.

In most cases it is not so simple a matter to create an inversion as it is with the ammonium maser. The energy levels of interest cannot usually be separated by electric fields and in any case this method is obviously useless if the atoms form part of a solid. Several other methods have been developed for obtaining an inversion, each of which is appropriate for a different lasing medium.

Types of laser

The first laser (producing visible as opposed to microwave light) used a crystal of ruby as the medium and employed a process known as *optical pumping* to excite the electrons to an inverted condition. Ruby is a regular crystal form of aluminium oxide in which are embedded some chromium atoms. The chromium atoms are really only impurities in the crystal but they are responsible for the characteristic red colour light which is produced naturally by spontaneous emission from their electrons. The ruby laser produces the same colour light in coherent form by stimulated emission. To do this it makes use of *three* of the energy levels of the chromium atoms.

The middle and lower levels are those used in the laser action. The upper level really consists of a large number of levels so closely spaced that they are effectively a broad band of energy which many chromium electrons can occupy. The principle of optical pumping is to flood the crystal with light from a xenon flash lamp.

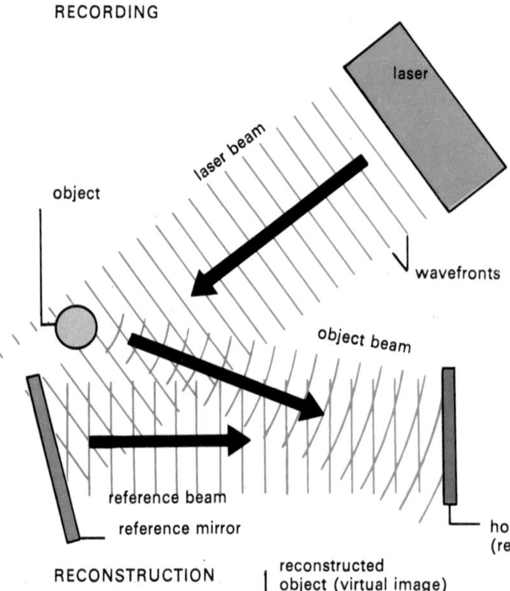

Above: How lasers are used in *holography* to record and reconstruct a 3D image. A normal photograph only records the intensity of a scene, but a holographic record or *hologram* also records phase information of the impinging light waves. This is possible because laser light is coherent. For this, a standard is necessary—achieved by directing part of the laser light directly on to the hologram (this is the reference beam). To reconstruct the image, the hologram is viewed in laser light— the image appears beyond it.

Right: A typical layout for holographic recording. On the right is the laser which floods both the scene to be recorded (bottom left) and a mirror (top left) which directs the reference beam on to the hologram.

Below: Here, the laser beam is split into two. One is aimed at the mirror, the other at the object to be recorded. The shape of an item can be checked against a standard by replacing the mirror with the standard. The hologram records the *differences* between them.

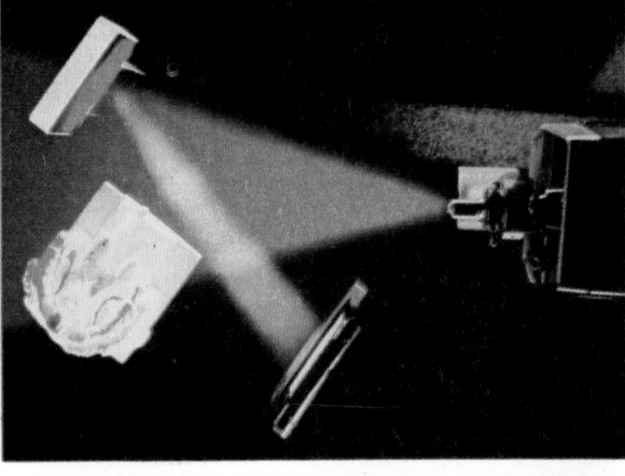
Howard Sochurek/John Hillelson Agency

Photri

Electrons in the lower level absorb photons of this light and jump directly to the upper band. Once in this band they soon lose energy to the atoms of the crystal and decay to the middle state.

If more than half the chromium electrons can be pumped like this to the upper levels, then an inversion exists with more in the middle than in the lower level. The middle level electrons will start to spontaneously emit, in all directions, photons of wavelength 0.6943 micrometres (which is 0.6943 millionths of a metre or 6943 A and corresponds to light in the red region of the spectrum).

The crystal is specially shaped to ensure that some of these cause the system to lase. It is cut in the form of a long rod and the ends polished and silvered. When a spontaneous photon is emitted along the axis of the rod it is reflected back along its path whenever it reaches one of the ends, ensuring that it travels a very long path which gives it a high probability of encountering a chromium electron in the middle state. As soon as this happens the laser avalanche is initiated. One of the ends is made less than 100% reflective so that part of the laser light can escape.

There are now many similar lasers which use a variety of crystals. One, which relies on neodymium impurities in a crystal of yttrium aluminium garnet, is of interest because its energy levels are so spaced that it can be pumped by sunlight.

Another large class of lasers uses gases as the lasing medium. Perhaps best known of these is the helium-neon laser which emits coherent neon light. The initial excitation is produced by passing an electric current through a mixture of helium and neon gas. This raises the energies of the helium electrons and as these collide with neon atoms the neon electrons are in turn raised to excited states. The gases are contained in a long tube with mirrors mounted at either end so that an initial spontaneous emission from an excited neon along the axis causes the whole system to lase back to a lower state.

Gas lasers give the most coherent light, but they are generally quite inefficient, requiring about a thousand times as much energy to be fed in as is extracted in the form of laser light. An exception is the carbon dioxide (CO_2) laser which emits up to 15% of its energy input as light. Another interesting gas laser contains a mixture of argon and krypton and is capable of lasing at several different wavelengths at the same time so that its mixed output appears as white laser light.

Applications

Because stimulated emission creates new photons which move in exactly the same direction, the beam of light from a laser is almost perfectly parallel. This means that it can be focused by a lens into an extremely small area. In this area the intensity of the light is so high (even if the unfocused beam is weak) that it can easily vaporize metals and even diamond. This has made the laser a useful tool for all sorts of cutting, drilling and welding operations, especially for small scale work where accuracy is very important. Perhaps the most spectacular application in this field is the use of a laser by surgeons to weld back a detached retina. The laser beam can be precisely aimed at the spot where the retina is detached and the eyeball itself is used to focus the beam.

The unvarying wavelength and frequency of lasers means that for the first time visible light can be manipulated in a similar way to radio waves and much research is now going on to develop a communications system based on laser light. The main advantage of using visible light is that its very high frequencies enable millions more telephone or television channels to be carried on the same beam than on a single radio wave. Also the highly directional beam means that less power is required to communicate between two points as energy is not wasted in other directions. This also means that a laser is useless for general broadcasting, which requires an aerial that will radiate in all directions. And laser light cannot penetrate cloud any better than normal light can usually.

Laser beams in Oxford St., London. A laser – the word stands for Light Amplification by Stimulated Emission of Radiation – is a powerful flash tube device to encourage atoms to emit light in a regular, coherent way, and not randomly as they do when left to themselves.

Keystone Press

Medical Technology

Doctors have always sought to use physical and engineering principles to help their patients. By their own ingenuity, or with the help of craftsmen or engineers, they have devised mechanisms like splints or 'peg-legs' which would help in times of injury or allow the patient to cope with handicap. The enormous progress made in the last few decades is, however, largely due to the emergence of a new profession, the bio-engineer or medical physicist, working in close conjunction with medical personnel to use the potential of modern technology in the fields of health care. This has led to a whole range of developments, from the most complex achievements to such simple innovations as the plastic disposable syringe—which have had a major impact on practical medicine.

X-rays and nuclear radiations

X-rays, also called Roentgen rays after their discoverer, are a type of penetrating electromagnetic radiation which is created when electrons, accelerated in a vacuum by very high voltages (20,000 to 1,000,000 volts), are suddenly arrested by impact into a target. Their extraordinary usefulness in diagnosis is due to the fact that their absorption varies from tissue to tissue, being least in air-containing structures and greatest in bone. Thus the

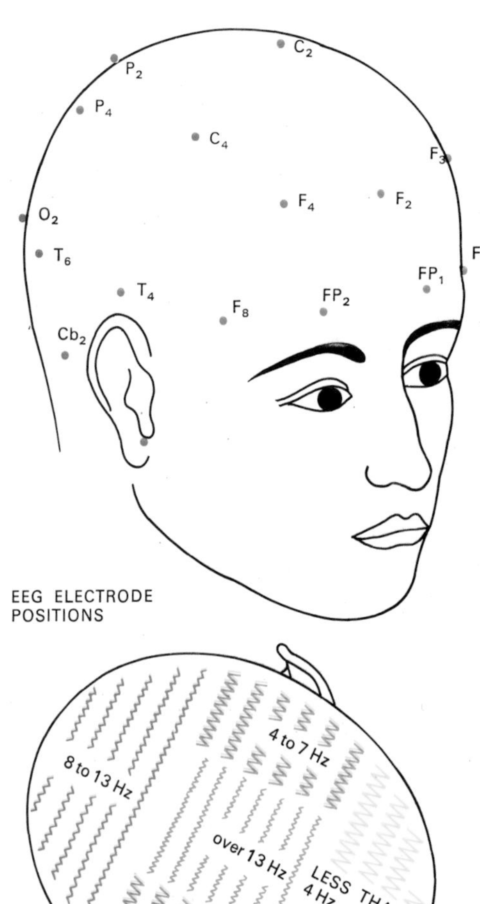

Fotogram

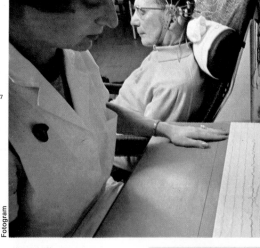

Above: The electrical activity of the brain can be examined by an electroencephalograph (eeg). The minute electrical impulses produced in the brain are picked up by electrodes attached to the scalp, and the eeg produces a chart which shows the waveforms detected from various parts of the brain.

Left: The upper diagram shows points on the scalp at which the electrodes are placed, and the lower shows the typical frequencies of brain waves detected at various areas around the scalp. If a patient's waves differ significantly from those expected, then some form of brain malfunction or damage is indicated.

bedside instrumentation
ECG pulse rate blood pressure temperature etc)

PATIENT MONITORING SYSTEM

bedside instrumentation

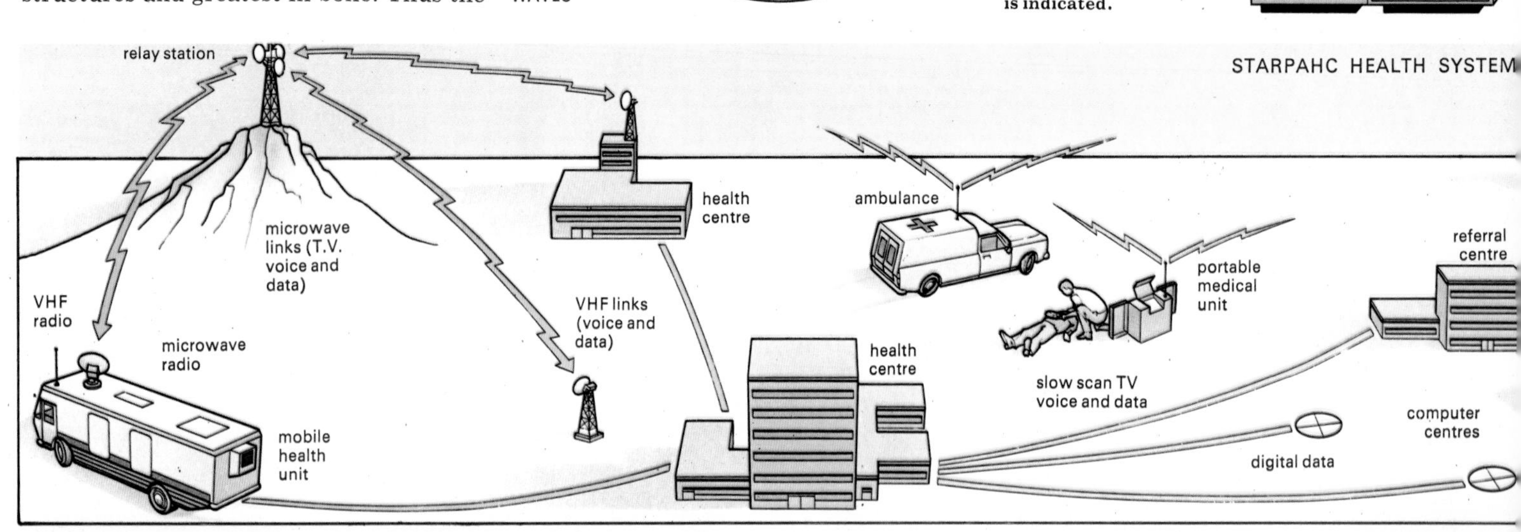

Lockheed

Above: The STARPAHC (Space Technology Applied to Rural Papago Advanced Health Care) system provides medical services to the Papago Indian reservation in Arizona, US. Mobile medical teams visit villages on the reservation. They are linked by VHF radio to health centres and computer centres which provide them with specialist information and advice. STARPAHC was developed initially by NASA and Lockheed in order to evaluate health care systems for use by astronauts during long missions.

Left: A STARPAHC Mobile Health Unit.

Right: A physician's console at one of the Health Centres.

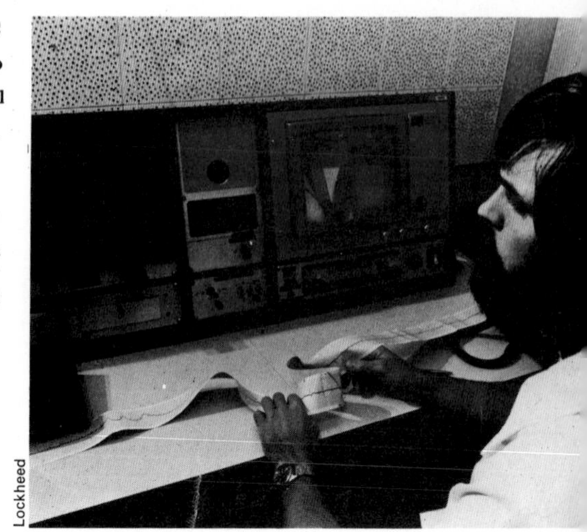

Lockheed

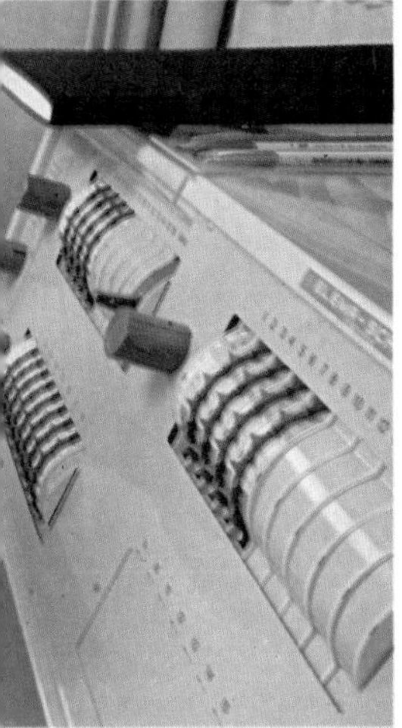

Right: A patient monitoring system in use in an intensive care unit. Patient monitoring systems contain several types of equipment, such as ecg and eeg machines, a blood gas analyzer and a blood pressure monitor, which provide continuous information about the condition of the patient's body systems.

Below: The layout of a large patient-monitoring system. This type of system, designed for monitoring five or more patients, consists of a set of instruments next to each bed, which are connected to a central station from which the condition of each patient can be supervized.

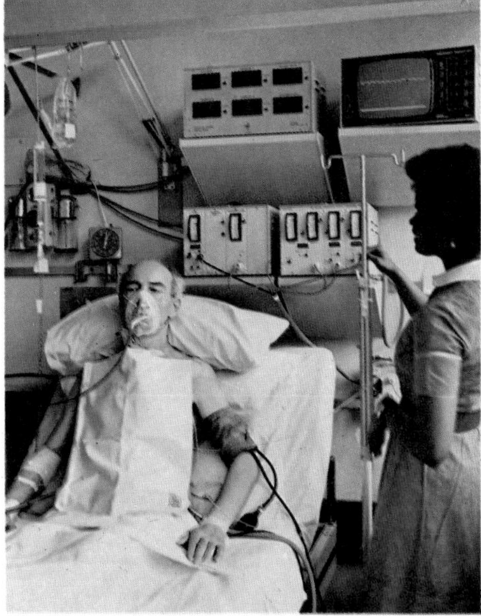

EMI

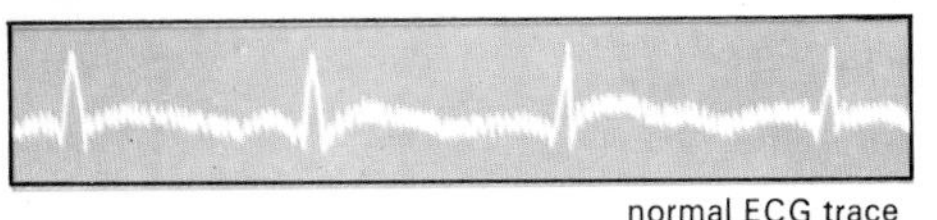

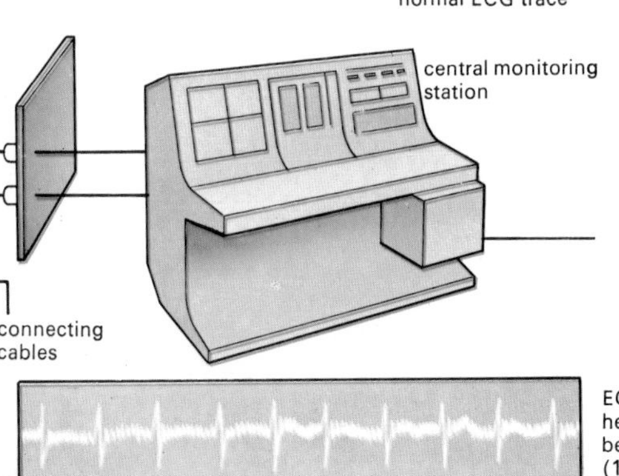

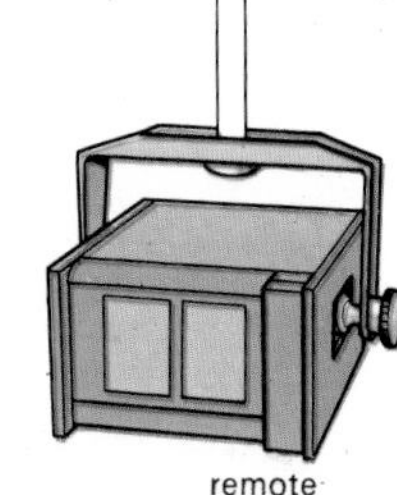

Below: An EMI-Scanner CT1010, a computer-assisted tomography unit which produces X-ray images of cross-sections of the brain and scull. The X-ray tube and detectors are mounted within the scanning gantry surrounding the patient's head, and the gantry is rotated 3° at a time. The machine produces images of two cross-sections during each scan, which takes 60 seconds. Three scans are needed to image the whole brain, which takes a total of about ten minutes.

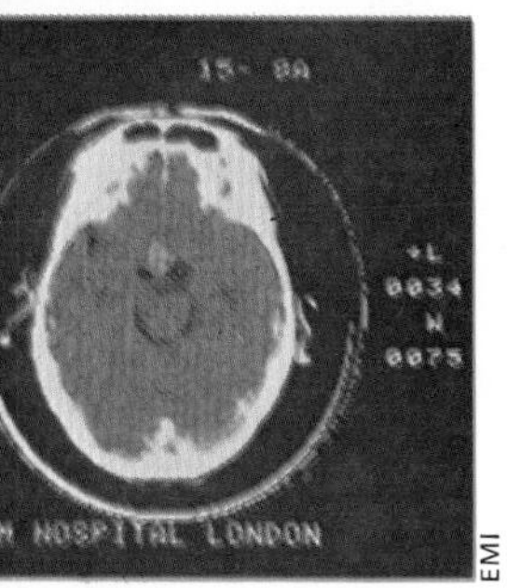

EMI

Above: A scan taken by an EMI-Scanner at the Atkinson Morley's Hospital, London.

Below: The scanning pattern and basic system of an EMI-Scanner CT1010.

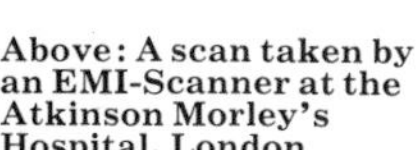

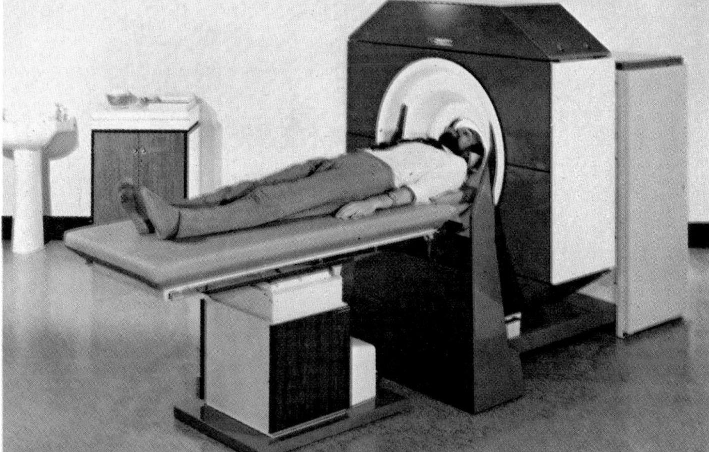

EMI

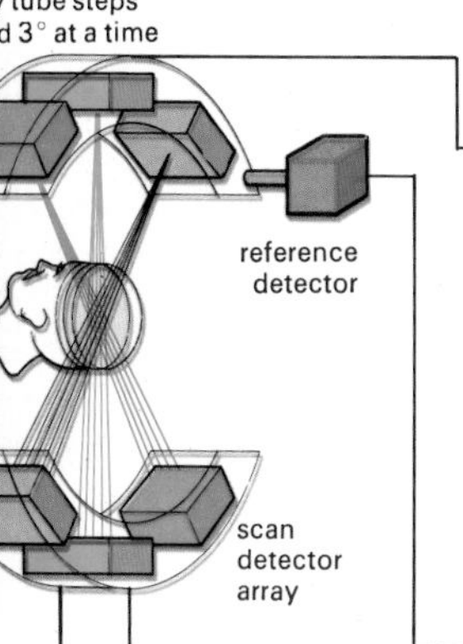

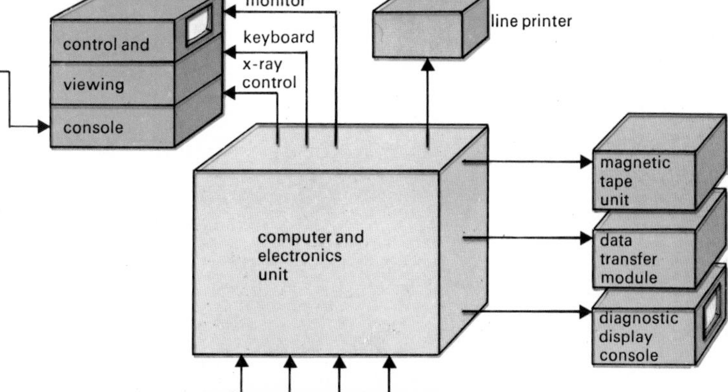

shadowgraph picture, produced by interposing part of the body between the X-ray tube and a photographic film (which is darkened by X-rays), will show fractures in bones, wear in joints or abnormalities in the lungs.

A different application of X-rays, and of the even more penetrating gamma-radiation given off by radium or artificial radioactive isotopes, is in the treatment of cancer. The destructive effect of these rays in high dosage is much greater for some tumours than for the surrounding healthy tissues. Careful adjustment of dose and concentration of the radiation in the tumour area, by the use of different but overlapping approach routes, will arrest the growth of a tumour, or destroy it altogether with minimal effect on surrounding tissue.

The equipment for generating X-rays consists of a high-voltage generator connected to the X-ray tube by heavily insulated cables. In this vacuum tube, the electrons given off by a heated filament are accelerated towards a spot on a target, where some of their energy is converted into X-radiation when they strike it. The tube is heavily shielded by lead cladding to confine the emission of X-rays to the wanted direction. Much of the bulk of modern machines is made up of equipment for adjusting the patient's position so that the beam is correctly directed and by provision for holding the photographic plates or direct-viewing devices.

To produce the most penetrating radiation, the electrons must be accelerated to energy levels greater than those which can be conveniently provided by a transformer power supply. When this type of radiation is required, the electrons are accelerated in particle accelerators such as betatrons or travelling-wave linear electron accelerators, devices in which a relatively low voltage is used over and over again in accelerating the electrons.

Computer-assisted tomography is a special X-ray technique capable of imaging cross-sections of the head or body with good contrast between tissues which cannot be visualized by conventional techniques. The X-ray source and a radiation detector, which measures the intensity of a narrow beam of X-rays as it emerges after passage through the tissues, are moved in a compound pattern so that each part of the section is traversed by the beam in several directions.

Measurements of the absorption experienced by the ray in its various directions of transit are fed into a computer which forms part of the machine. This calculates with great accuracy how much of the beam was absorbed in each minute region. The local brightness of a cathode ray tube display is then modulated so as to map the pattern of absorption in the cross-section. Organs having slightly different X-ray absorptions can be visualized and abnormalities of, say, the blood content of the different tissues noted. This powerful technique has greatly extended the range of conditions in which X-rays can give diagnostic information.

Isotope scanning is another technique used for similar purposes. Diseased tissue will often take up disproportionate amounts of compounds containing radioactive isotopes, which are introduced into the patient's circulation. As these emit X-rays or gamma-rays to the outside, regions where concentration has taken place can be detected by passing Geiger counters or other radiation-sensitive devices over the patient and noting where increased activity is present.

Ultrasonics

Ultrasound or ultrasonics, sound vibrations at frequencies beyond the upper limit of human hearing, is used in medicine in three different ways: as a therapeutic (healing) medium, for soft tissue imaging and for observing the motion of the heart or blood. Quartz or other piezoelectric materials are used to turn a high-frequency electrical oscillation (1-10 MHz) into a mechanical vibration at the same frequency. Devices such as these which convert one form of energy into another, in this case electrical into mechanical, are known as *transducers*. The beam of ultrasonic vibration is then transmitted into the body via a thin film of oil or aqueous (water-based) jelly.

In therapeutic applications, power levels of the order of a watt per square centimetre are used to produce accelerated healing of injuries, but just how this happens is still not fully understood. In the other two applications, the power levels are too low to have any effect on the tissues. The transmitting transducer, or a separate receiving transducer, translates some of the energy which is reflected by the tissues in the path of the beam into electrical waveforms.

For soft tissue visualization, the transmitting transducer is energized periodically and emits brief bursts of waves. Reflections from interfaces at increasing depths will be received with increasing delays from the time of their transmission. A map of the interfaces encountered in a section of the body is produced as follows. A spot on the cathode ray tube is deflected from a starting position, representing the position of the transducer, in the direction of the beam at a speed which corresponds to the speed of the ultrasound in tissue. The spot is brightened up whenever reflections are received. As the clinician moves the transducer so as to sweep the beam through the section, the pattern of brightness on the oscilloscope tube shows the position of organ boundaries and changes in tissue density. A common application of this technique is to follow the development of the foetus in the mother's womb.

If the reflecting interface is moving, the frequency of the reflected ultrasound will differ slightly from that of the transmitted beam. This phenomenon, the *Doppler effect*, permits the detection of moving interfaces within the body and also under favourable circumstances allows the speed of motion to be measured. The beating of the foetal heart can thus be detected by ultrasonic Doppler instruments from the tenth week of pregnancy.

An expanding use of this principle is in the measurement of the speed of blood flow in various vessels, the red blood cells acting as ultrasonic reflectors. Abnormalities of the pulsating pattern of flow in limb arteries points to the presence of obstructions. Cardiac function may also be monitored by Doppler measurements of blood velocity in the aorta, the main artery leading from the heart.

Electrophysiological instruments

Much useful information can be obtained about function in certain parts of the body

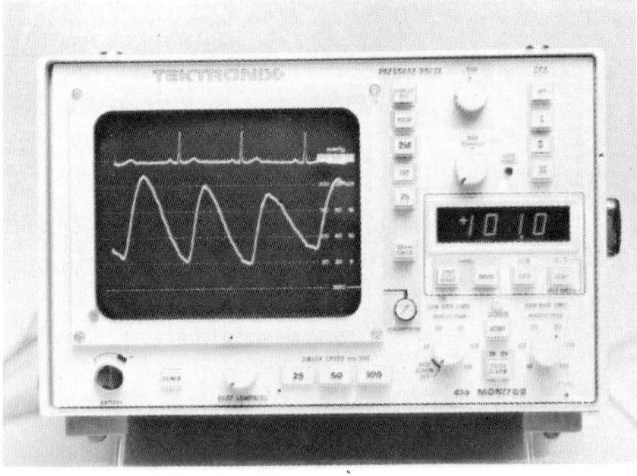

Tektronix Ltd

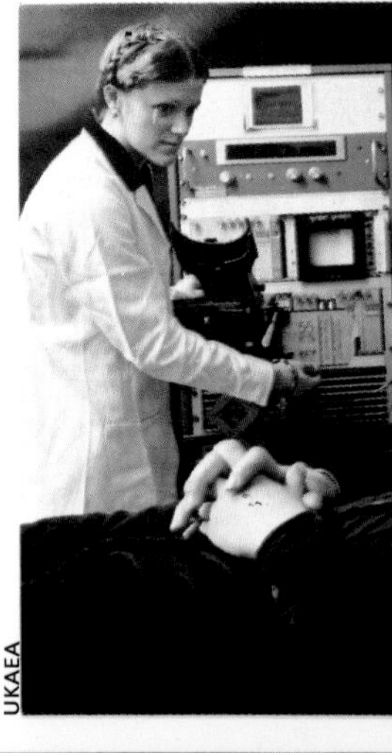

UKAEA

Left: The Tektronix 414 Portable Monitor has a dual-trace oscilloscope display which shows the patient's ecg pattern (upper trace) and blood pressure (lower trace). The digital display can show either heart rate, blood pressures or blood temperature.

Below: An MEL SL75-20 linear accelerator which produces high-intensity radiation for the treatment of cancer tumours. Many forms of tumour tissue are much more susceptible to high doses of radiation than are the healthy tissues surrounding them, and so they can often be destroyed by radiation therapy. This machine operates at an energy level of 20 million electron-volts (20 MeV).

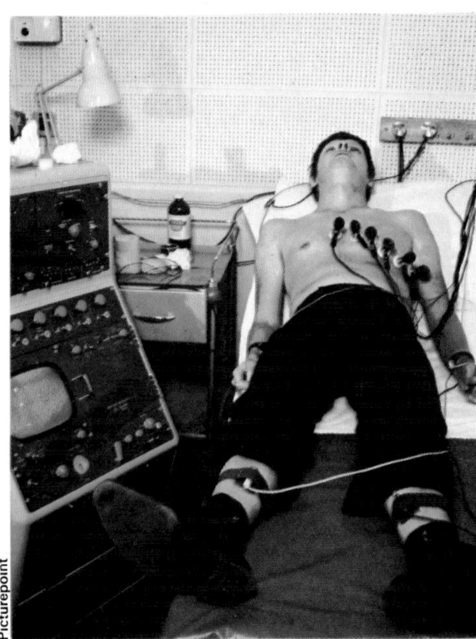

Picturepoint

Above: A patient connected to an electrocardiograph machine. The electrodes on the chest pick up the signals from the heart, and those on the arms and legs provide reference voltages that enable the heart signals to be correctly interpreted. The lead on the right leg is an earth connection.

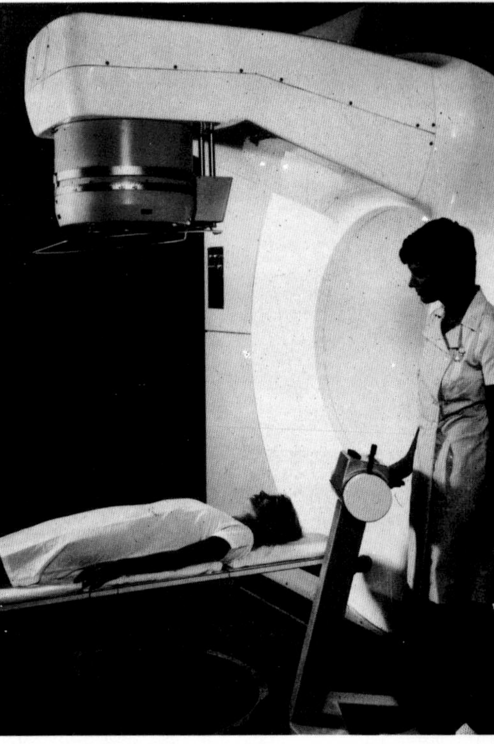

M.E.L. Equipment Ltd

Below: A diagram of a heart-lung machine, with an exploded view of the oxygenator on the left. The heart-lung machine takes over the functions of the heart and lungs during major heart surgery. The oxygenator removes carbon dioxide gas from the blood and adds oxygen to it before it returns to the patient.

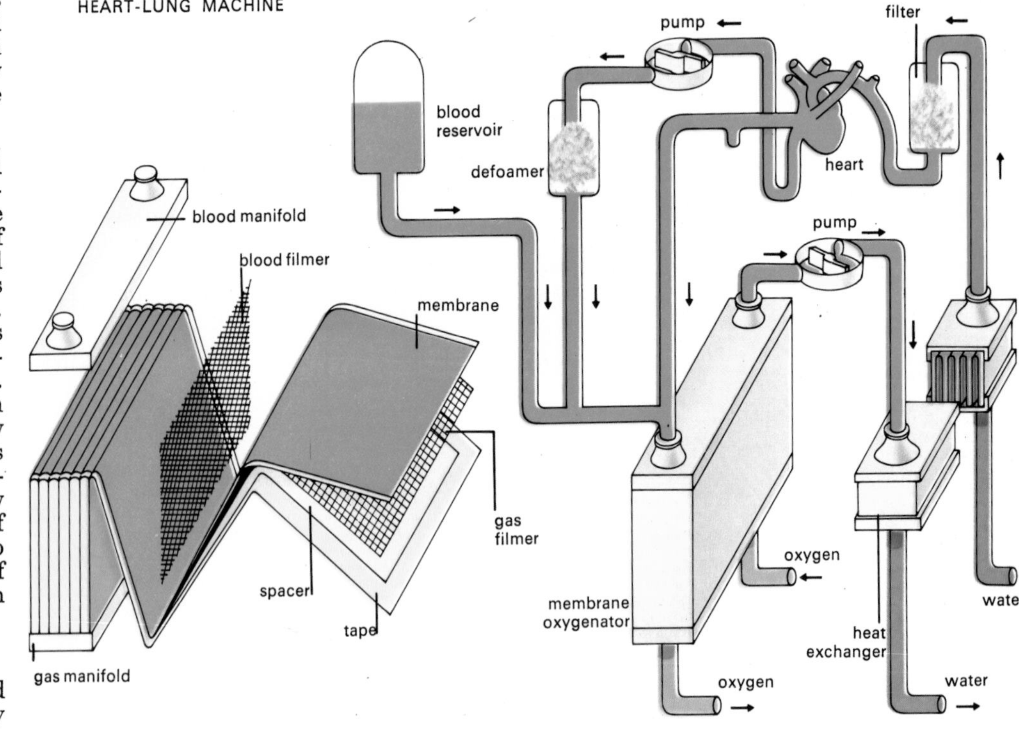

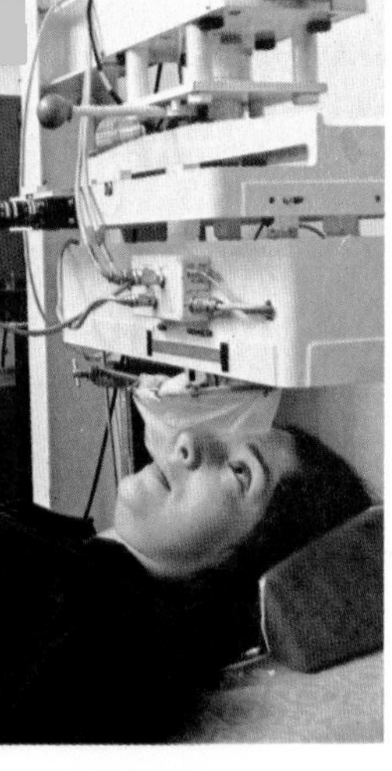

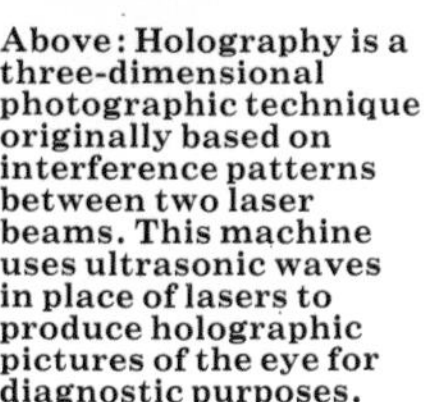

Above: Holography is a three-dimensional photographic technique originally based on interference patterns between two laser beams. This machine uses ultrasonic waves in place of lasers to produce holographic pictures of the eye for diagnostic purposes.

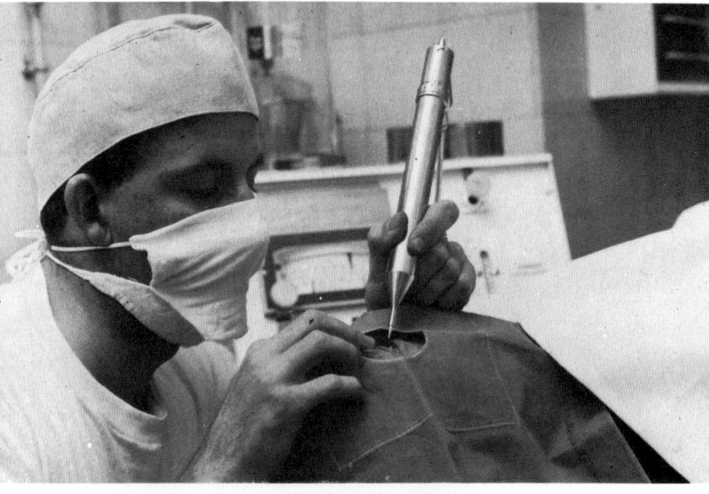

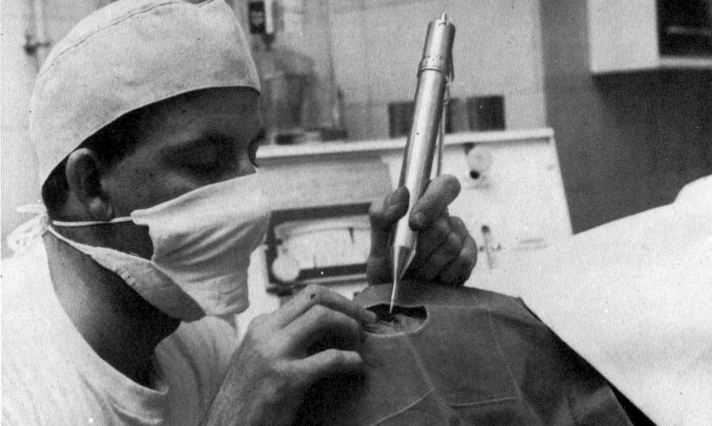

Syndication International

Above: This instrument developed for eye operations has a metal probe which is cooled by liquid helium to —120°C. Used like a scalpel, it can remove cataracts and 'weld' back detached retinas, operations which can also be performed by using heat created by laser beams.

UKAEA

Left: A heart pacemaker powered by a nuclear battery, which is implanted into the patient and maintains regular heart operation by stimulating it electrically.

Below: The Diapulse machine speeds the healing of damaged tissue by means of the energy contained in high frequency electromagnetic pulses.

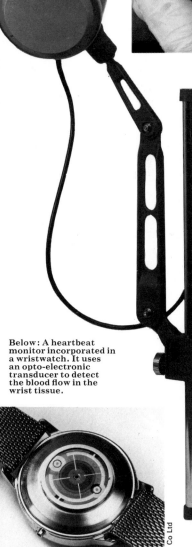

Diapulse Ltd

Below: A heartbeat monitor incorporated in a wristwatch. It uses an opto-electronic transducer to detect the blood flow in the wrist tissue.

IRD Co Ltd

by observing the minute voltages which accompany muscle contractions and the passage of nerve impulses. *Action voltages* of about 1/20 volt can be picked up in their immediate vicinity, but it is also possible to sense the much smaller voltages which are transmitted to the body surface by using electrodes applied to the skin to determine the activity of underlying nerves and muscles. Specially constructed amplifiers are used to display the observed waveform by deflection of the spot on a cathode-ray tube or of the pen in a paper recorder.

A widely used electrophysiological instrument is the *electrocardiograph* (ECG) which gives information about activity of the heart from voltages picked up on the chest wall or even from the extremities. A comparison of the waveforms recorded from various electrode positions is useful in determining the location and extent of damage which may have occurred in, for example, the muscular wall of the heart. It is also possible to observe whether the muscle mass of the heart contracts in regular sequence, so that defects in the nervous pathways which co-ordinate the atrial and ventricular contractions may be detected.

Another application of electrocardiography is to the detection of rhythm disturbances (*arrythmias*). Occasional irregularities occur in normal health—'when I saw it happen, my heart missed a beat'—but potentially life-threatening ones may develop during a heart attack. Electrocardiographs are therefore widely used in coronary care units for patient-monitoring. Treatment of arrythmias in the early stages often prevents them from progressing to *asystole* (total stoppage of heart action) or a condition known as *ventricular fibrillation* in which the co-ordination of different parts of the ventricular muscle is totally lost and effective pumping stops.

A *defibrillator* can be used to restore co-ordinated contractions in the latter case. As Galvani showed when he applied a battery to a frog's leg—or anyone who has experienced an electric shock will remember—powerful muscular contractions are produced by currents which pass through the body. A defibrillator applies an electric shock of controlled magnitude, from a capacitor which has been charged to a high voltage, to the patient's heart via large electrodes placed on the chest. If the current is sufficient to cause the whole of the cardiac musculature to contract strongly at the same instant, synchronous contractions will often continue, so that co-ordinated heart action is restored.

The instrument which is used to record electrical activity from the brain is called an *electroencephalograph* (ecg). This differs from the electrocardiograph in that a number of recording channels are used simultaneously to display the electrical activity picked up by electrodes applied to various regions of the scalp, and that more sensitive amplifiers are required to amplify the weaker signals which reflect neuronal activity in a broad region underneath the electrodes. The waveform shape and frequency content of the recordings gives information on the nature of brain activity in alert, sleeping or unconscious subjects and allows regions of abnormal activity to be identified.

Typewriters

Science Museum

Adler Collection

Adler Collection

Top left: The Oliver No. 3 typewriter of 1898.

Above: The Blickensderfer Oriental, a manual single element machine, could print languages reading from right to left if required.

Left: The 1891 Hall Braille typewriter.

The manual typewriter relies on such simple mechanical principles that it is surprising that the first really practical machine was not developed until 1873. Although attempts at producing writing machines had been made by numerous inventors since the early eighteenth century, no real progress was made until 1867. In that year, Christopher Sholes and Carlos Glidden in the US produced the first working model of their typewriter which, after much modification, was taken up by the Remington company in 1873. The first Remington machines were built in 1874, and were exhibited at the American Centennial Exposition in 1876.

Two of the most important mechanisms of the typewriter, namely a keyboard and lever system and an escapement mechanism, had been perfected over a century earlier, being fundamental features of pianos and clocks respectively. Like the piano, the typewriter has a keyboard and lever system by means of which a small hammer is made to strike a target when a key is pressed.

In the typewriter, the target is a sheet of paper in front of which is an inked ribbon. Each of the hammers, which are more correctly called *typebars*, is fitted with a *typeslug* which carries a raised, reversed image of a character, so that when it strikes the ribbon an ink image of that character is transferred to the paper.

The paper is passed around a rubber roller called the *platen*. The paper must move one space to the left after each character is typed to make room for the next, and this is accomplished by mounting both paper and platen on a movable *carriage*. This carriage is pulled along a pair of rails by a spring which is wound up when the carriage moves to the right at the beginning of a line.

An escapement mechanism, actuated by an extension of the type-bar lever system, allows the carriage to move a half space when each key is pressed, stops the carriage just before the impact of the type on the paper, and lets it move another half space as the key is released.

Some early typewriters had separate keys and typebars for capital letters, but the typebars of all modern machines have the capital on the same bar as the lower case letter but slightly higher up, so that it normally does not make contact with the ribbon and paper. On most machines, when a capital is to be typed, a shift key is pressed which lowers the *typebasket*, that carries the typebars, so that the capital and not the lower case strikes the ribbon.

To allow the typist to see what has already been typed the ribbon is not normally in position over the paper, but is fed through a small guide which is raised into place when a key is pressed and is released after the typebar impact. At the same time the ribbon is wound a short distance from one spool to another.

Electric typewriters

Manufacturers tried for many years to harness electric power to the manual typewriter, but it was not until the 1950s that electric machines enjoyed substantial commercial success outside the US. Early designers found it simple enough to drive

Picturepoint

Above: Three early and unusual typewriters: a 1900 Lambert, left; an 1886 Columbia, rear; and an 1893 Blick (Blickensderfer) typewheel portable, on the right.

BERKELEY SQUARE.
W.

20th July, 1901.

My dear Mr. Ponsonby,

We should be so glad if you would come over to dinner next Wednesday, the 24th. Reggie is going away on the 30th and so this is to be by way of a send-off party. Do try to come.

With kind regards,
Believe me,
Yours sincerely,
Gladys Norrys-Lenton.

Facsimile of the "Handwriting" Type.

Radio Times Hulton Picture Library

Left: A facsimile of the print produced by the Remington 'Handwriting' typewriter.

Below: A simplified diagram of the basic manual typewriter print mechanism. When a keybutton is pressed downwards, the system of links and pivots draws the bottom end of the typebar downwards and forwards. This throws the other end, which carries the typeslug up and back towards the platen.

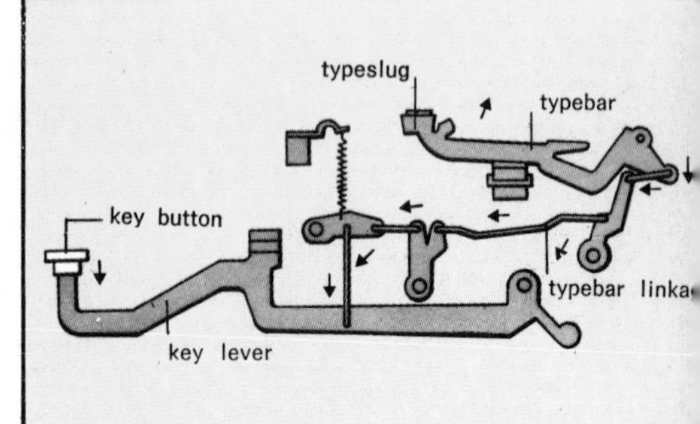

Radio Times Hulton Picture Library

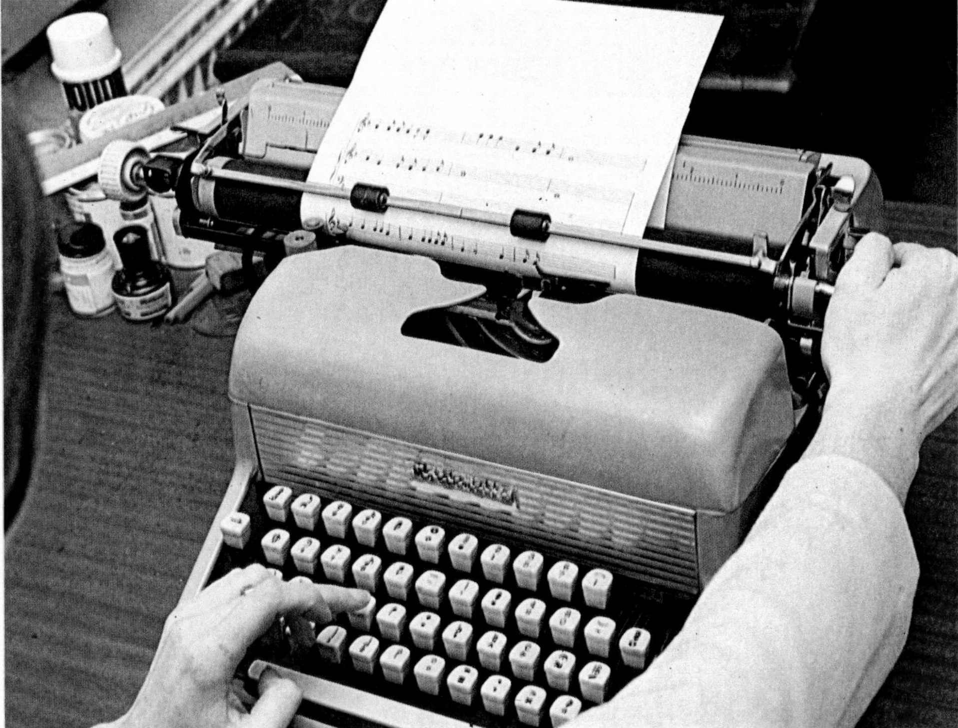

Spectrum

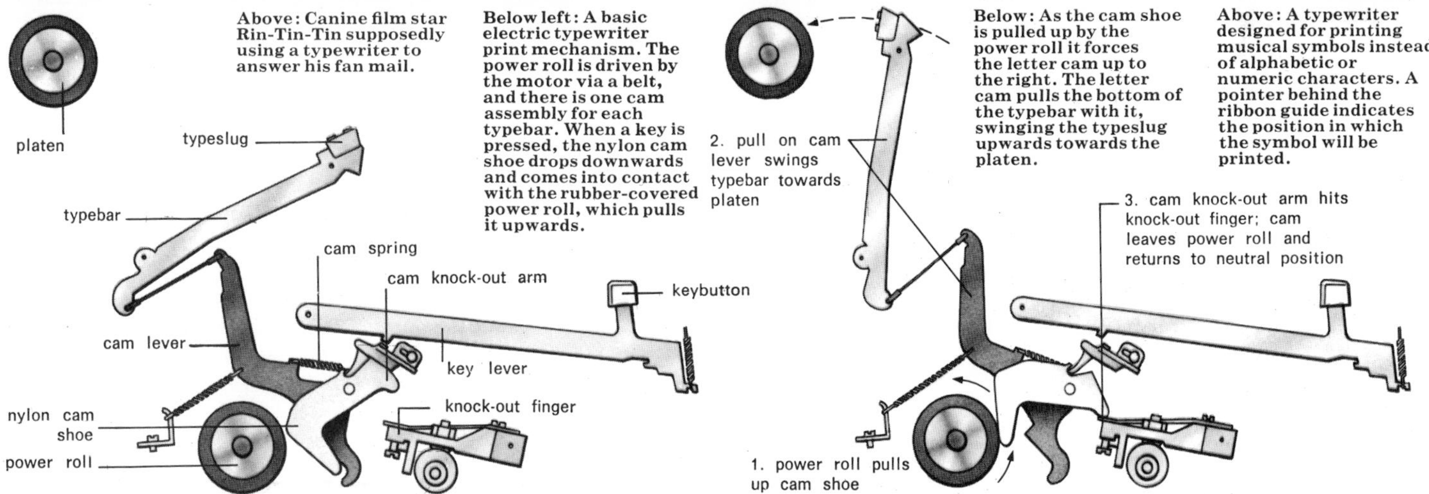

Above: Canine film star Rin-Tin-Tin supposedly using a typewriter to answer his fan mail.

Below left: A basic electric typewriter print mechanism. The power roll is driven by the motor via a belt, and there is one cam assembly for each typebar. When a key is pressed, the nylon cam shoe drops downwards and comes into contact with the rubber-covered power roll, which pulls it upwards.

Below: As the cam shoe is pulled up by the power roll it forces the letter cam up to the right. The letter cam pulls the bottom of the typebar with it, swinging the typeslug upwards towards the platen.

Above: A typewriter designed for printing musical symbols instead of alphabetic or numeric characters. A pointer behind the ribbon guide indicates the position in which the symbol will be printed.

Below: The typebasket area of a manual typewriter, an Olivetti Linea 98. A typebar is about to strike the ribbon, which has been lifted into place by the ribbon lift guide, and transfer its image to the paper. The paper is held in place against the front of the platen by the paper bail rollers.

British Olivetti Ltd.

the typebars by electric motor, but the chief difficulty was to isolate the bars from the vibration of the motor. Until this was achieved electric typewriters inevitably produced an inferior text because typebar vibration led to a slight blurring of the image on the paper.

Most modern electric machines are powered by an ac motor which continuously rotates a drive roller by means of a flexible belt. The belt isolates the roller from much of the motor vibration and the roller itself acts as a flywheel to maintain smooth rotation. In some machines the roller is fluted and depressing one of the keys causes a metal tooth to engage with the roller, whose momentum jerks it forward to activate the typebar lever system and hammer the type on to the paper. Others have a rubber roller which snatches at a metal or nylon cam when a key is pressed, the cam transmitting this motion to the typebar mechanism.

In either case the drive roller transmits only a brief impulse to the typebar and is already disconnected from it by the time the typebar hits the paper. Hence at the moment of impact the type is moving freely under its own momentum and makes a crisp image.

An even neater appearance can be achieved if the typewriter carriage motion is modified to allow for the different widths of letters. A normal typewriter allows the same space for a wide letter 'W' as for a narrow 'i' or a comma. This leads to an uneven appearance as compared with a printed text where each letter is allotted a different width. Such *proportional spacing* can be obtained on a typewriter by breaking up the carriage motion into smaller units and arranging for it to move, for example, 5 units for the 'W' and 2 units for the 'i'.

Single element typewriters

In the early 1960s IBM introduced the first *single element* electric typewriter, the Selectric, whose radically new design greatly extended its scope of application. Two main features distinguish the single element machine from its conventional rivals—there are no typebars and there is no moving carriage. All the type characters on the Selectric are arranged around the surface of a single typing element (also called a *typehead* or 'golf ball'), which is roughly spherical in shape. Pressing a key causes the element to rotate until the desired character is in front of the ribbon. It is then locked in this position and driven towards the

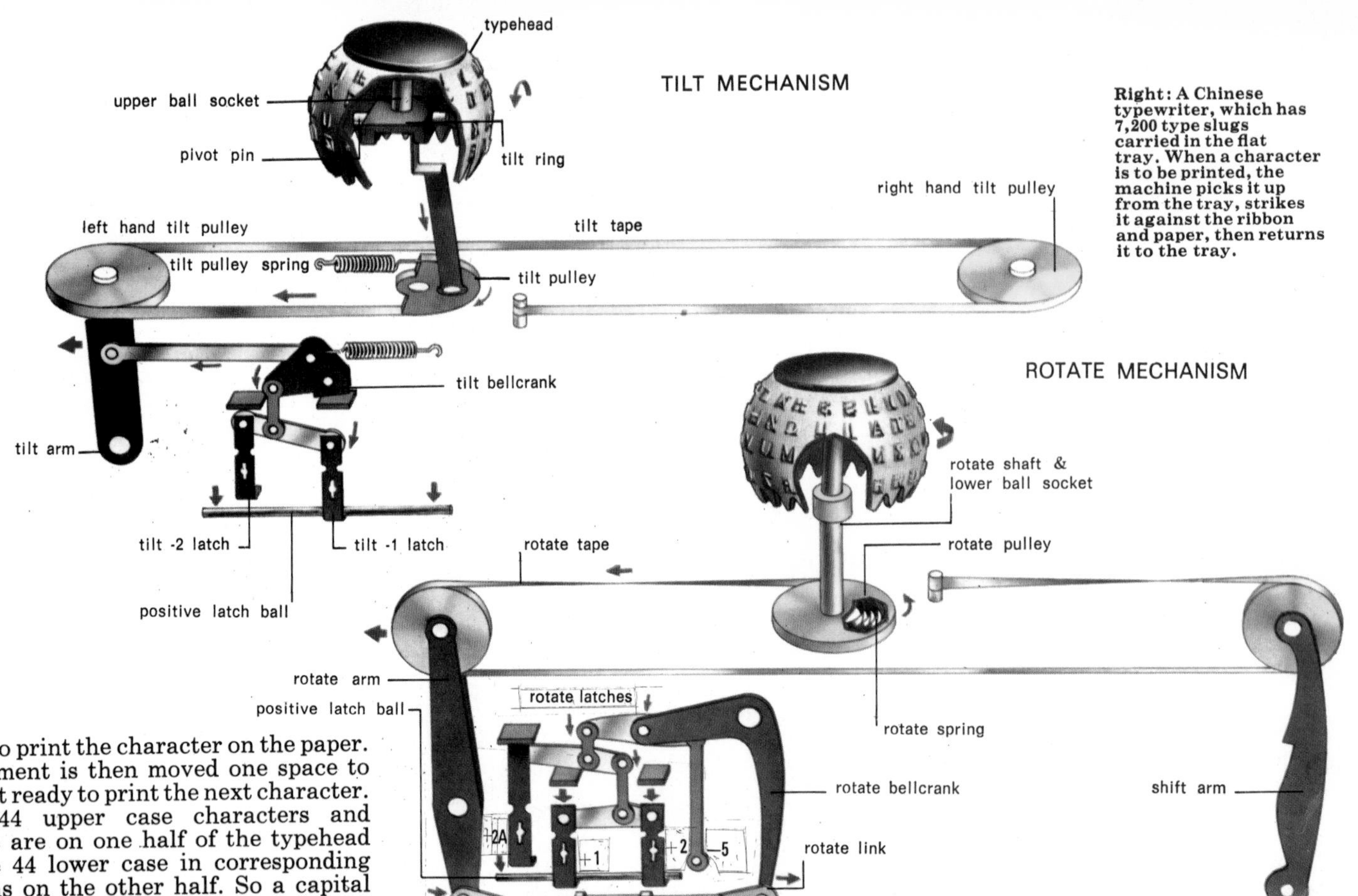

Right: A Chinese typewriter, which has 7,200 type slugs carried in the flat tray. When a character is to be printed, the machine picks it up from the tray, strikes it against the ribbon and paper, then returns it to the tray.

ribbon to print the character on the paper. The element is then moved one space to the right ready to print the next character.

The 44 upper case characters and symbols are on one half of the typehead and the 44 lower case in corresponding positions on the other half. So a capital letter can be typed, as on conventional machines, by pressing the shift key and the character key. The shift key, however, does not raise a carriage but rotates the element through 180° so that its back half faces the ribbon.

The characters on each half of the typehead are arranged in four horizontal rows with eleven characters in each row. The rest position for the typehead is such that, if no tilt or rotate motion is *selected*, it will print the character which is in the top horizontal row (tilt-0) and the centre column (rotate-0) of the columns of characters on that half of the element. In order to print any of the other characters on that half of the element, the machine has a system of pulleys and steel tapes which tilt and rotate the element to bring the required character into the print position.

Methods of selection

Selection is accomplished by means of a system of *latches* connected to the pulleys that operate the tilt and rotate tapes. During a print operation or *cycle*, these latches are driven downwards by a *latch bail*, which is itself driven by a set of cams. There are two tilt latches, which are used singly or as a pair to give the three tilt motions. When the tilt-1 latch only is used, the element is moved to the tilt-1 position; when the tilt-2 latch only is used, the element is moved to the tilt-2 position; and when both are used the element is moved to the tilt-3 position.

The rotate linkage operates in a similar, but more complex, fashion. There are four rotate latches, R-1, R-2, R-2A and the negative-5 latch. There are two directions in which the element must rotate from its home (rotate-0) position. It can move up to five positions in an anti-clockwise or 'positive' direction, or up to five positions in a clockwise or 'negative' direction.

When positive rotate positions are required, the negative-5 latch is not activated. The latch combinations used for the positive rotate positions are R-1

Above: The tilt and rotate systems of an IBM single element typewriter. The tilt and rotate latches are, in fact, mounted side by side in the machine, and all except the -5 latch are operated by the positive latch bail. The tilt system is shown with the T-2 latch pulled clear of the bail; the T-1 latch is left under it and is pulled down to give a tilt-1 selection. The rotate system is set up for a positive-3 selection. The -5 latch itself is not shown; for a positive rotate selection the -5 latch stays in its place, preventing the -5 link from moving upwards to give negative motion to the typehead.

Right: The IBM Memory Typewriter, used in word processing, has a 4,000 character electronic memory, plus a 50-track magnetic tape memory which can hold 4,000 characters per track.

IBM

British Olivetti Ltd.

British Olivetti Ltd.

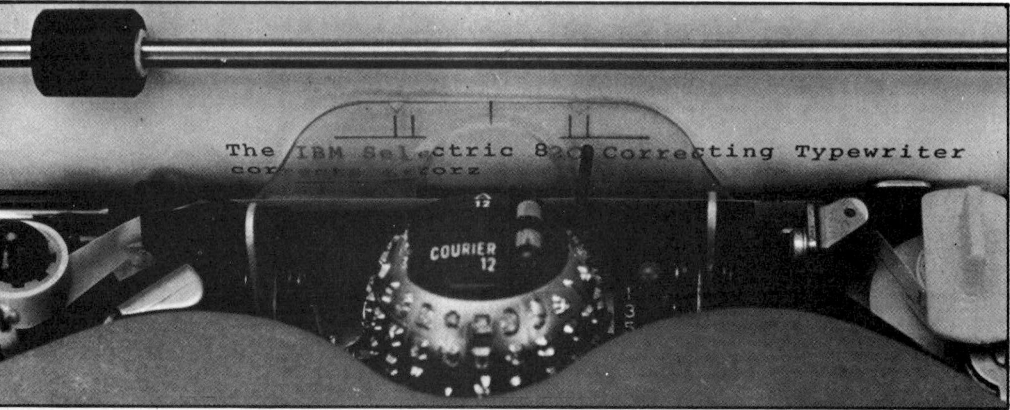

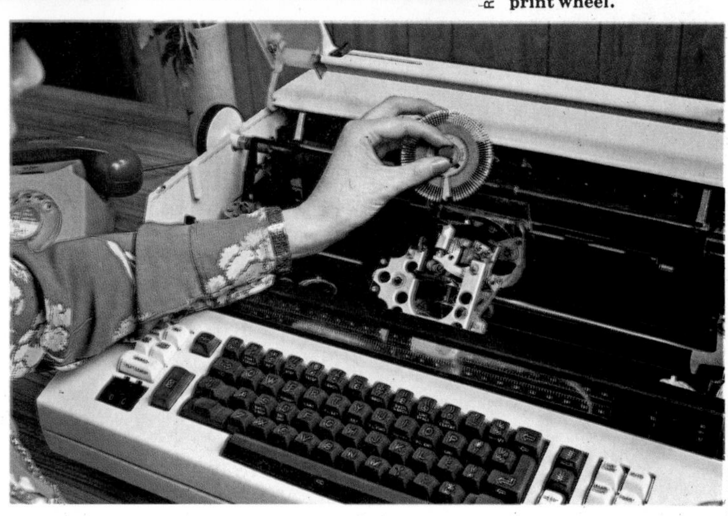

Above: The IBM 82C Correcting Typewriter is fitted with an error-correction tape (behind the ribbon) which can lift the image of an incorrect character from the paper. To correct a mistyped character, the operator presses the correction key, which backspaces the typehead and engages the correction tape. The incorrect character is then typed again, and the correction tape lifts the error from the paper. The correct character can then be typed in.

Left: The Xerox 800 electronic typing system can record characters either on magnetic cards or, as shown here, on cassettes of magnetic tape.

Below: The Xerox 800 is a single element machine, and the characters are carried on an interchangeable print wheel.

Far left: The Olivetti Lexicon 83 DL single element typewriter.

Left: The carrier and type element of an Olivetti Lexicon 90C. The barrel-shaped element is rotated horizontally and vertically, by a system of shafts, gears and levers, to bring the required character into position for printing. As is the case with the other makes of single element machine, the elements are produced in many different typestyles and are interchangeable. Most single element typewriters print either 10 or 12 characters per inch ('10' pitch or '12' pitch), and proportional spacing is available on some.

ZEFA

IBM

Rank Xerox

Rank Xerox

for position 1, R-2 for position 2, R-1 and R-2 for position 3, R-2 and R-2A for position 4, and R-1, R-2, and R-2A for position 5.

When the negative latch is activated the typehead is rotated five positions in a clockwise direction. In order to obtain the other four negative positions, the negative-5 latch is used in combination with one or more of the positive latches. For example, the negative-3 rotate position is obtained by using the negative-5 latch in conjunction with the R-2 latch, two units of positive motion combining with five of negative motion to give a net result of three units of negative motion. A selector mechanism beneath the keyboard activates the latches required when a key is depressed.

The typehead is carried along the typing line by a *carrier*, which travels along a grooved *print shaft*. The print shaft passes through a hollow *print sleeve* in the carrier which carries a set of cams that drive the typehead against the ribbon and paper during a print cycle, and drive the ribbon feed and lift mechanisms. A small metal peg, the *print key*, fixed in the print sleeve engages with the groove in the print shaft. During a print cycle the print shaft rotates 360°, turning the print key, and thus the print sleeve and its cams, with it. The ribbon feed and take-up spools, which may be enclosed within a plastic cartridge, are mounted on the carrier and travel along with it.

Other forms of single element typewriter are now available in addition to the IBM machines. These include Adler, Remington and Olivetti machines, which use typing elements not unlike the IBM ones, and the Xerox machine which has the characters mounted around a *print wheel*.

Word Processing

The general move towards using electric typewriters, particularly single element machines, introduced some new concepts to office typing. At first, 'automatic' typewriters were introduced for the easier handling of repetitive work. These machines used a variety of recording media, such as punched paper rolls, not unlike the old 'Pianola' rolls, or punched paper tape, an offshoot from computer technology.

It became obvious, however, that although these machines could speed up the production of standard work, they could not overcome the basic problems of errors and re-types of one-off letters and reports. Large sums of money were invested in finding solutions to these problems, and gradually the concept of *word processing* (as opposed to data processing) was formed.

Basically, the typist produces copy at draft speed (upwards of 60 words per minute) without regard to errors or layout. The rough draft is recorded, at the time of typing, on to magnetic tape, magnetic cards, or even in an electronic memory.

The typed draft is then read by the author and corrected or altered as necessary. Any revisions that are necessary are made by the typist to the recorded version of the draft; only the areas which need revision must be retyped, not, as might be the case with conventional machines, the entire text. The final copy can then be played out at speeds of up to 120 words per minute or more.

Calculators

One of the most widely-used calculating machines, the *abacus*, is also the most ancient. In one form or another it has been around for thousands of years, and millions are still in use all over Asia and the Soviet Union. The abacus consists of rows of beads, which represent the numbers, strung on rods or wires set in a rectangular frame, and although its operations are limited to basic arithmetic a skilled operator can use it as fast as most people can use a modern electronic calculator.

The first real advances in calculating, after the abacus, came in the seventeenth century. In 1614, John Napier invented the system of calculating by means of *logarithms*. Ordinary logarithms are calculated as *powers* of the number 10, for example $100 = 10^2$, or 10 to the *power* of 2, and so its logarithm (to base 10) is 2.0000. The number 3, on the other hand, is $10^{0.4771}$, and so its logarithm is 0.4771.

Sets of tables, known as *log tables*, have been drawn up for use in calculations, and by using these it is possible to perform complicated multiplication and division by simply adding or subtracting logarithms. As a simple example, to multiply 3 by 4 the logarithms of 3 and 4, which are 0.4771 and 0.6021, are added together. This gives 1.0792, which, by reference to the tables, we find is the logarithm of 12, and so the result is 3 x 4 = 12. Division is carried out by the subtraction of logarithms; 12 divided by 3 would be 1.0792 — 0.4771, which is 0.6021, the logarithm of 4. The adding or subtracting of logarithms to perform multiplication or division is based on the *exponent law*, $10^a.10^b = 10^{a+b}$.

The invention of logarithms led to the development of the *slide rule* by Edmund Gunter and William Oughtred during the first part of the seventeenth century. In its simplest form the slide rule has two scales, one fixed and one moving, which are marked off in distances which are proportional to the logarithms of the numbers they represent. Adding or subtracting these distances, by sliding the moving scale along the fixed one, effectively adds or subtracts the logarithms of the numbers indicated on the scales, and so multiplies or divides them. The modern version of the slide rule is based on a design by Amédée Mannheim in 1859.

Mechanical calculators

The first mechanical calculating machine was invented by Blaise Pascal in France in 1642. This machine used the rotation of gear wheels to represent the numbers, and its design was subsequently refined by Gottfried Leibniz in 1671. Leibniz was the inventor of the *stepped wheel*, a device which was still used in certain types of mechanical calculator built as recently as the 1960s.

The ideas of Pascal and Leibniz were later bettered by the work of Baldwin, Odhner and Burkhardt in the late nineteenth century, who developed more compact and efficient designs. The design of mechanical calculators was steadily refined during the first half of the twentieth century, and electro-mechanical machines, which used an electric motor

Picturepoint

Above: The abacus is a form of calculating machine that has been in use for thousands of years. The original version, which was used in ancient Babylon, was probably a tray or board covered in sand, in which marks were made to perform the calculations. This picture shows a modern Japanese abacus.

Below: The first practical mechanical calculator was built by the French mathematician Blaise Pascal (1623-1662) in 1642. It consisted of a system of gears and numbered wheels. Although it could perform addition and subtraction it could not do multiplication or division.

Right: The linear slide rule consists of two sets of fixed scales, with a sliding set of scales in between them. The scales are calibrated logarithmically, so that multiplication and division are performed, in effect, by the addition or subtraction of lengths along the scales.

Erich Lessing/John Hillelson Agency

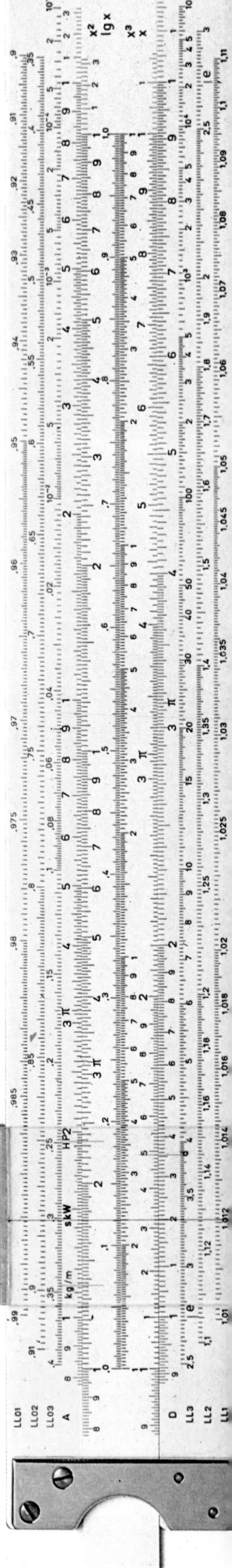

Dave Kelly

Left: A late 19th century adding machine.

Burroughs

Below: The upper two drawings show how a slide rule is used for multiplication. The top drawing shows how a slide rule multiplies 3 by 2; the *unity* ('1') mark on scale C is set at 2 on scale D. The cursor is placed over the 3 on the C scale, and the answer, 6, is where the cursor crosses the D scale. The middle drawing shows 5 x 3, and the way in which the position of the decimal point must be assessed by common sense—the answer is 15, not 1.5 as shown on the scale. The bottom drawing shows how D gives the square root of A, and C_1 gives the reciprocals of scale D.

to turn the gears that performed the calculations, were introduced.

Electronic calculators

The electronic calculator developed as a result of advances in electronic computer technology. The first computers were developed during the 1940s, and were enormous devices containing thousands of electronic valves. However, following the invention of the transistor in 1948, the size and power consumption of computer circuits decreased dramatically while their reliability and complexity increased.

The first electronic calculator as such, based on computer circuit technology, was the Bell Punch Anita machine produced in Britain in 1963. It used thousands of discrete transistors in its circuitry, and by today's standards it was a cumbersome machine, but it marked the end of the era of the mechanical calculator based on the gear wheels of Leibniz and Pascal, as well as that of the slide rule based on Napier's logarithms.

With the introduction of integrated circuits by Fairchild and Texas Instruments in the early 1960s, the success of the electronic calculator was assured. An integrated circuit contains the equivalent of many thousands of transistors and their associated components, and is built up from a single chip of silicon which is about 0.3 cm square. The first compact calculator, based on an integrated circuit and using a light-emitting diode (led) readout display, was introduced (by the Bowmar Corporation) as recently as 1971, and since then calculator production has expanded enormously, with a corresponding drop in prices.

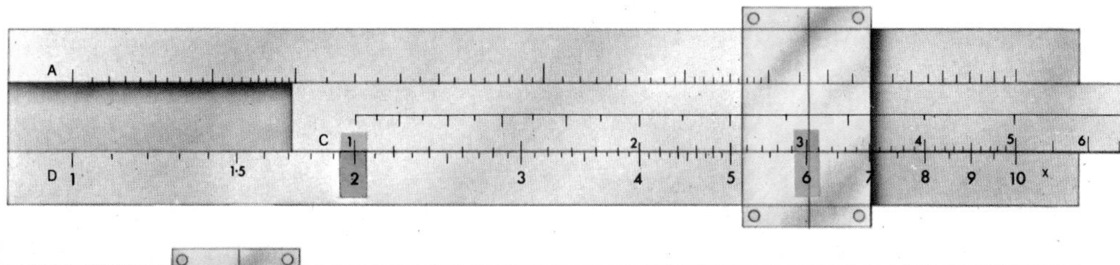

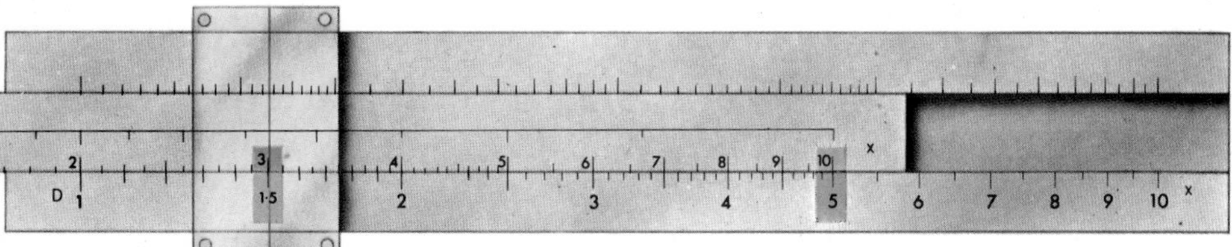

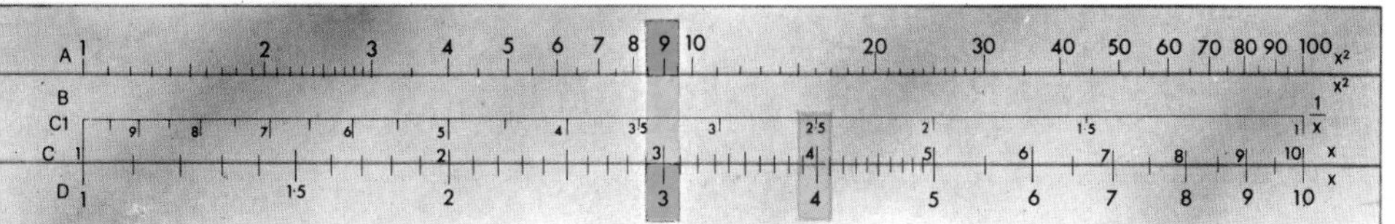

Basic principles

The actual way in which an electronic calculator works is quite complex, but the basic principles can be explained by reference to the way in which simple calculations are performed.

The operation of a calculator is regulated by a *clock* circuit which, as its name implies, generates timing pulses that are used to synchronize the operations of the other sections of the machine. In a simple calculator the clock may operate at a rate of about 250,000 pulses per second, which would enable it to perform 250,000 operations in one second.

Calculators use a form of binary arithmetic to perform their calculations since, being based on the number 2, all binary numbers can be represented by

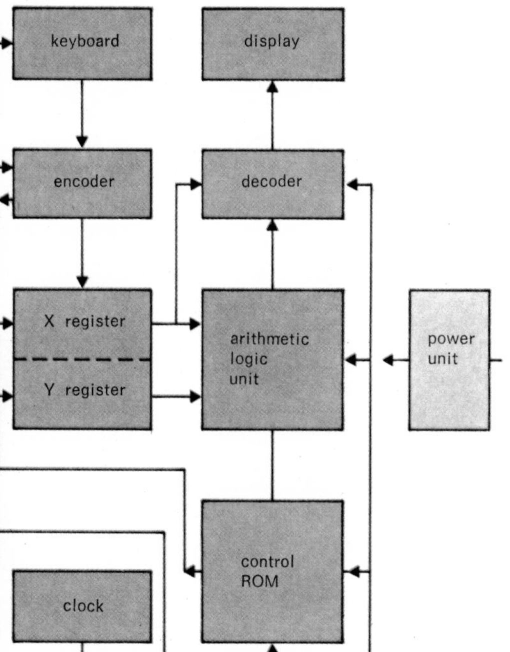

Left: A block diagram showing the relationships between the main sections of an electronic calculator. In the latest calculator designs, all the components apart from the keyboard, display and batteries are incorporated into a single integrated circuit chip about 0.3 cm square.

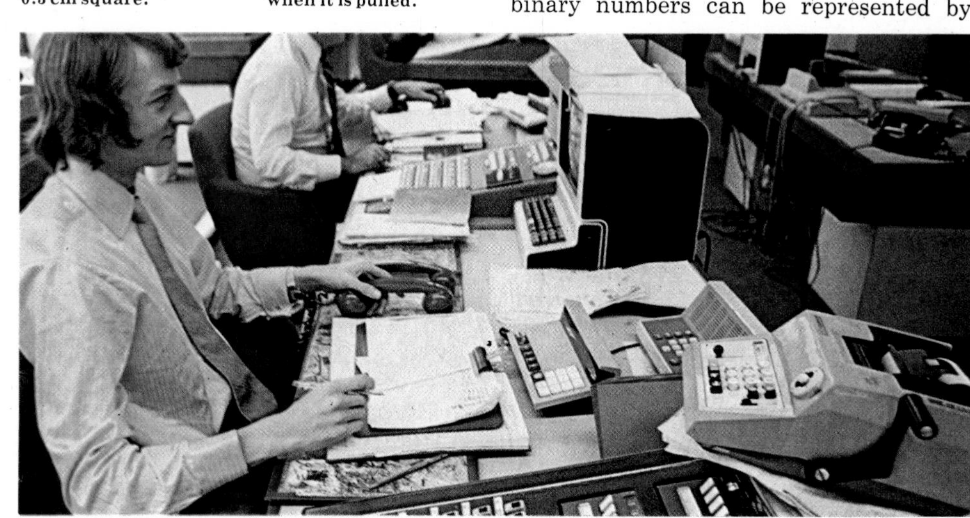

Below: A manually-operated mechanical printing calculator (bottom right) in the foreign exchange dealing room of an international bank. This type of machine has a lever on the right hand side which drives the internal gearing and the printing mechanism when it is pulled.

Syndication International

combinations of '1s' and '0s'. In a calculator, a '1' is present when a circuit is 'on', and a '0' when it is 'off'.

The form of binary arithmetic used by calculators is known as *binary coded decimal* (BCD), and the calculator contains an *encoder* which translates the decimal information from the keyboard into BCD, and a *decoder* which translates the BCD into decimal form to drive the output display.

In ordinary binary coding, the number '1010' represents the decimal number '10'; when read from right to left it represents no '1s', one '2', no '4s' and one '8'—a total of ten. In BCD, however, each *digit* of a decimal number is represented by a four-*bit* (binary digit) binary code, for example '87' would be 0001 1110 in BCD, which is read from left to right.

Simple calculations

Suppose we wish to do the calculation '5 + 9 = '. On each clock pulse the keyboard is *scanned*, and if there is a valid input present due to a key having been pressed it is sensed by the encoder, which then produces the BCD equivalent of the number.

The first number to be entered, 5, is encoded and then transferred to, and stored in, the *X register*, and it is also shown on the display. The next item to be entered from the keyboard is the *operator*, the '+' in this case, which is sensed by the encoder and sent to the *control ROM* (Read-Only Memory) where it is stored. The control ROM is the 'brain' of the whole calculator, and it controls the operations of the *arithmetic logic unit* which performs the actual calculations.

CBM

Left: A calculator assembly line. The girl in the foreground is fitting the integrated circuits to the keyboard assemblies.

Hewlett & Packard

Below: The Hewlett-Packard HP-65 is a fully programmable pocket calculator. It can be programmed either via the keyboard or by means of programs pre-recorded on magnetic cards, one of which is shown here, which can store up to 100 program steps each. In addition, 51 scientific and mathematic functions are pre-programmed into its internal storage. The HP-65 has nine storage registers into which data can be entered, and has another four separate working registers.

Below left and centre: The Sinclair Cambridge is a compact, pocket-sized electronic calculator with an 8-digit light-emitting diode display. The centre picture shows the machine with its back cover and batteries removed. The integrated circuit is housed within the rectangular black plastic moulding, and the smaller unit just above it is the rear of the display.

Below right: The CBM/Commodore SR 4148 R scientific calculator, with its top cover removed to show its internal circuits. This machine has two independent storage memories, and is powered by rechargeable batteries.

Dave Hosking

Dave Hosking

CBM

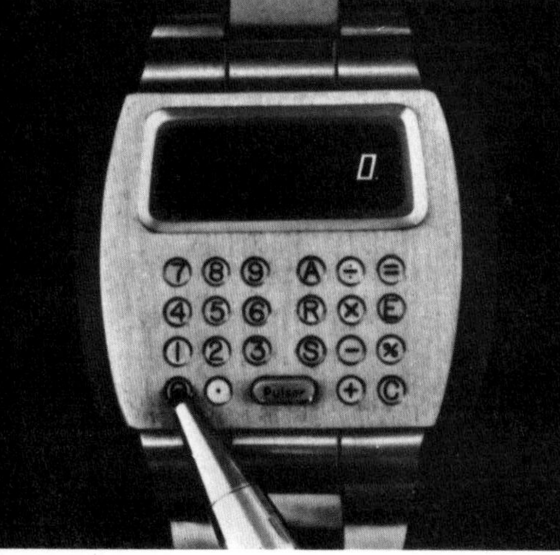

Left: This series of four pictures shows four functions of a miniature electronic calculator/digital wristwatch. From top to bottom, the pictures show: the time in hours and minutes; seconds; the date; and the calculator function.

Below: The Casio Biolator, which contains the additional feature of a program for calculating the state of a person's *biorhythms*, cycles of intellectual, physical and emotional conditions. To find which day of each cycle a person is at involves simply entering the current date and the person's birth date. It can also calculate the number of days since a given date.

John Hillelson Agency

Burroughs

Above: The Burroughs C 7200 programmable printing calculator has sixteen storage memories, and its programs are recorded on magnetic cards which each hold up to 408 program steps. Its program storage area can store 816 program steps, and the program cards can also be used for data storage.

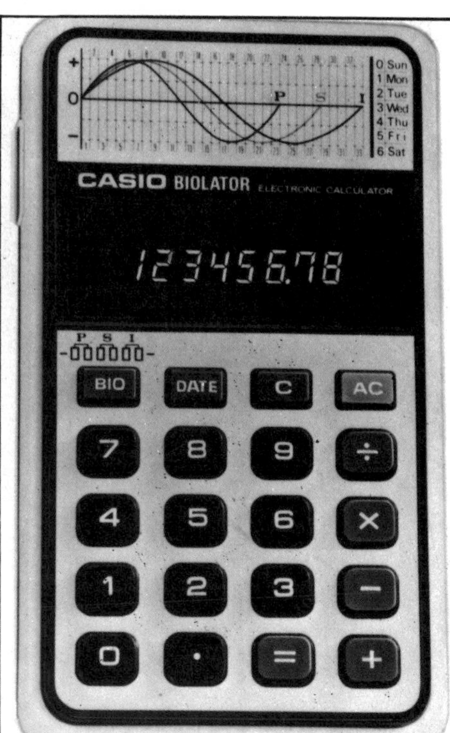

Automatic Business Machines Ltd

The next number, 9, is then entered, and after encoding it is put into the X register, displacing the previous number, 5, into the *Y register*. The number 9 is shown by the display. When the 'equals' key is pressed to complete the calculation, the contents of the X and Y registers are read into the arithmetic logic unit where they are processed according to the operator stored in the control ROM. The answer, 14, is decoded and shown in the display.

Other forms of calculation, such as multiplication, subtraction and division, are carried out in a similar manner, under the control of the pre-programmed instructions of the ROM.

Complex calculations

When we consider more complex functions of a calculator, such as the calculation of square roots or trigonometrical ratios, the computing power of the calculator becomes apparent. Once again, these are done by addition-type processes, but the numbers may pass through the arithmetic logic unit many times, with intermediate results being stored and recalled as required. These operations are controlled by built-in instruction programs called *algorithms*, the exact details of which are kept as trade secrets by the manufacturers. The better the algorithms used, the more accurate the calculator.

Simple calculators often have a *memory*, which is just another storage register similar to the X and Y registers, that can be controlled from the keyboard. A *constant* feature is often provided, which acts as a sort of limited memory in that the number is retained automatically in the Y register, and can thus be used for subsequent calculations without having to be re-entered through the keyboard each time it is needed.

On the newer and more advanced 'scientific' calculators, many extra features such as means, standard deviations, linear regression, combinations and factorials are available, in addition to logarithms, trigonometrical ratios and powers. These do not represent the peak of calculator design, however, because programmable machines, into which the user can program his or her own set of instructions to control the arithmetic logic unit, are now available.

In the less sophisticated programmables, the manufacturers have provided extra memory spaces so that a sequence of keystrokes for the solution of a particular equation can be 'remembered' and will operate on any number entered. This procedure obviously saves time if the calculation has to be performed repetitively.

Unfortunately, the program is lost once the machine is turned off, and so they must be programmed each time they are used. This drawback may, however, be overcome by the development of new forms of memory circuits which retain their information even when the power supply has been switched off.

The more advanced programmable calculators have the programs retained on a small magnetic card which is put into the machine when required, the information on it being read and stored by the machine. With this type of machine, computer-like techniques can be used since calculation methods such as looping and conditional statements are possible. These pocket-sized machines are so powerful that their computing capacity far exceeds that of the first-generation computers, which occupied whole rooms and consumed tremendous amounts of electrical power.

Computers

Throughout history, man has attempted to produce mechanical aids to assist in the organization and processing of information. The requirement has been for the storage of information, the processing of it in the form of sorting and arithmetic, and rapid retrieval of selected information.

Where the information to be processed is numeric, it can be represented either by a physical quantity, such as a length or voltage, or by a combination of digits. In the first of these two methods, the physical feature used is said to be an *analogue* of the number. Possibly the best known example of this is the slide rule, in which a number is represented by a length proportional to its logarithm. This choice of representation enables the multiplication of two numbers to be performed by the addition of two lengths.

The modern analogue computer generally uses variable voltages to represent quantities, and it is particularly suited to performing computations on quantities which vary with time, and require the solution of differential equations.

In a *digital* device, numbers are represented by positions on wheels, the fingers of the hands, or by a row of lights which represent the number in binary arithmetic. In the latter case, a light switched on would represent a binary '1' and a light switched off would represent a binary '0'.

Most examples of information processing do not require the particular aptitudes of analogue machines. They do, on the other hand, require an extensive storage capability and an ability to handle literal information, and for these requirements digital representation is appropriate. For this reason, the word 'computer' generally refers to the digital computer.

For any process to take place, with or without a computer, there must be some form of *input* to the process, the processing itself, and some result or *output*. The computer will always follow this essential pattern, and we may examine the features of input, processing and output in turn.

Input

The two commonest forms of input, punched paper tape and punched card, use patterns of holes to represent individual characters of data. Punched cards were first used, by a French mechanic called Falcon in 1728, as a means of controlling a weaving loom, and the successor of this type of loom, the Jacquard loom, still uses punched cards.

Cards were also used in a machine designed by Dr Herman Hollerith to analyze the results of the US Census of 1890. The Hollerith machines were the forerunners of the modern punched card machines used by computer systems.

The first card and tape readers for computers sensed ('read') the patterns of holes by having a small wire brush at each possible hole position. Where a hole had been punched, the brush at that position poked through the hole and completed an electrical circuit by contracting a metal roller beneath the card or tape, and so the pattern of holes was

Bavaria

Left: The operator's console of an IBM System/370 computer.

Right: A schematic diagram of a computer system: the arrows indicate the directions in which data flows around the system. Input/output devices, not shown here, perform both input and output functions.

backing stores
working store
input
control unit
arithmetic logic unit

IBM

Above: A general view of a computer system. The cpu is behind the operator's station in the centre background, with the magnetic tape units along the left hand side and the magnetic disk units on the far right. To the left of centre are two card machines and a display unit, and opposite these are two line printers. This system is an IBM 370/168.

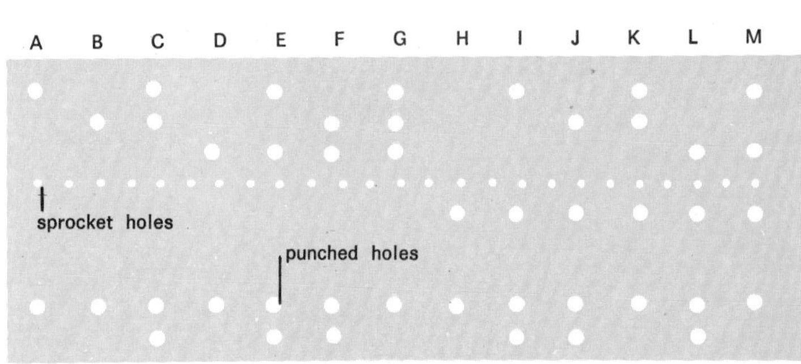

Right: Some of the patterns of holes used to represent letters in 8-hole punched paper tape. 5, 6 and 7-hole tapes are also used.

Below: 96-column punched cards have three rows of holes containing 32 columns each.

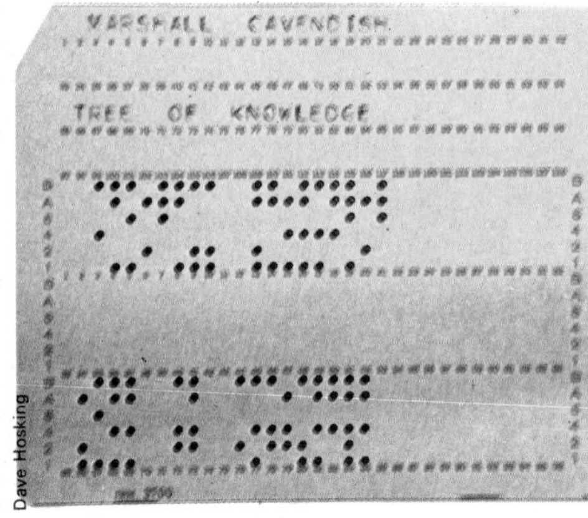

Dave Hosking

Right: The ferrite cores and wiring assembly of a magnetic core store.

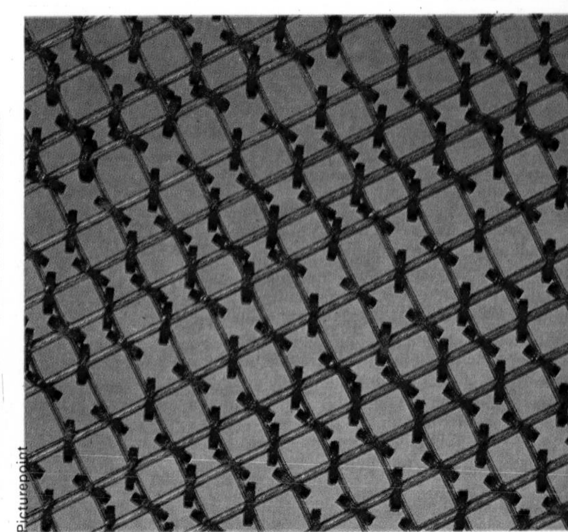
Picturepoint

Right: A row of magnetic tape units. The tape itself is similar to that used by domestic tape recorders, but it is 13 mm (0.5 in) wide and normally wound in 732 m (2,400 ft) lengths on to 25.4 cm (10 in) diameter spools. Tape speeds as high as 508 cm/sec (200 in/sec) are used.

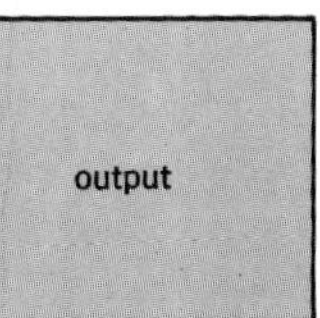

Picturepoint

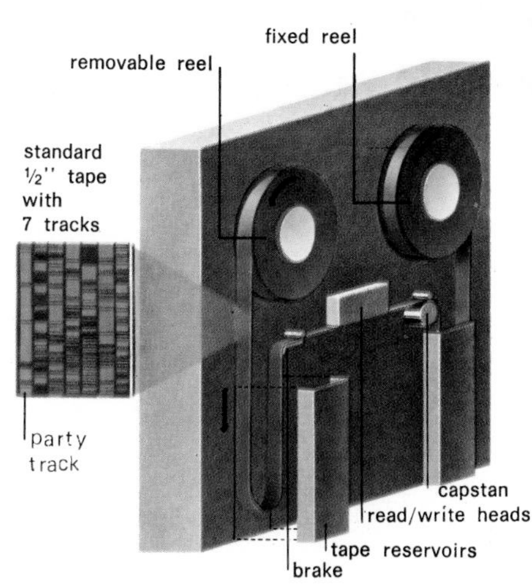

Above: A simplified diagram of a magnetic tape drive. The bits of data are written in rows across the tape, with one bit per track; one of the edge tracks is used for recording the *parity bits* which are part of an in-built error checking system. The capstan and brake shown are those used for forward tape motion.

Right: Digital information can be stored in the form of patterns in a laser-activated holographic plate. Holographic memories are just one of the many forms of storage under investigation by computer manufacturers; others include thin films of magnetizable alloy deposited on to non-magnetic base materials, and patterns of magnetic 'bubbles' in specially developed alloys. Most of the latest equipment, however, uses integrated circuit memory devices for the main storage. Integrated circuit memories operate at about ten times the speed of core storage.

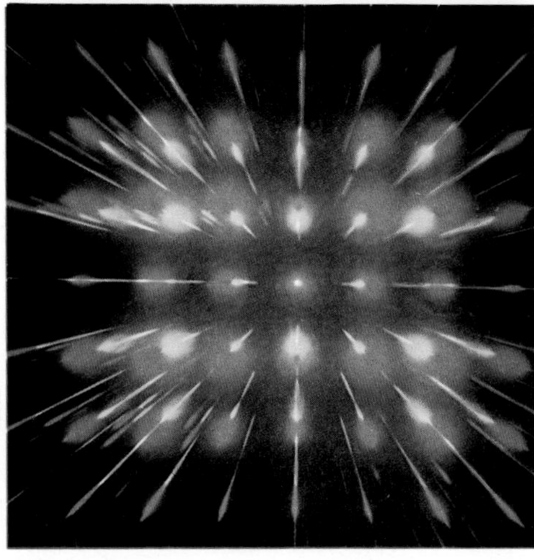

Photri

Below: Magnetic disks are usually used in packs, mounted on a central hub with spaces between them to allow the read/write heads to scan the disk surfaces. The method used to move the heads across the disks varies from one manufacturer to another. Typical operating speed is 2,400 rpm.

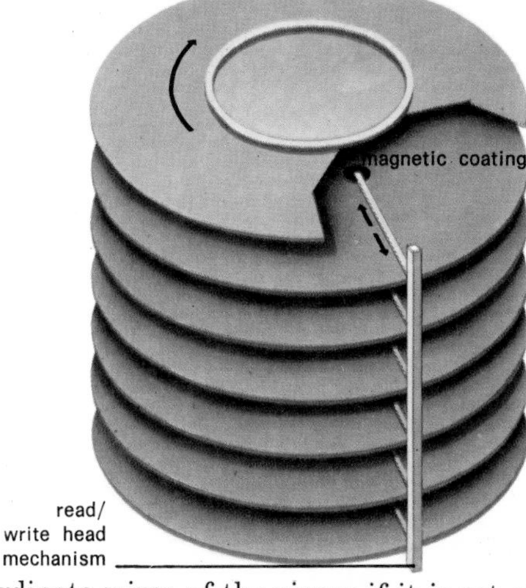

inputs			out put
A	B	C	
0	0	0	0
0	0	1	0
0	1	0	0
0	1	1	0
1	0	0	0
1	0	1	0
1	1	0	0
1	1	1	1

output			inputs	
A	B	C	or	ex or
0	0	0	0	0
0	0	1	1	1
0	1	0	1	1
0	1	1	1	0
1	0	0	1	1
1	0	1	1	0
1	1	0	1	0
1	1	1	1	0

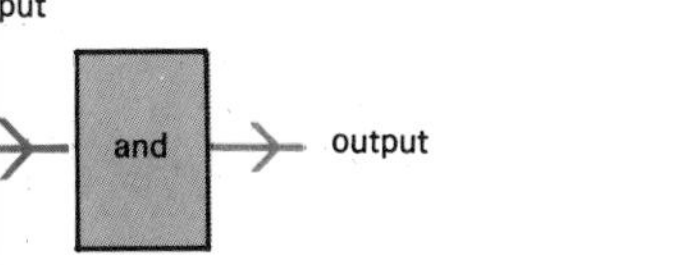

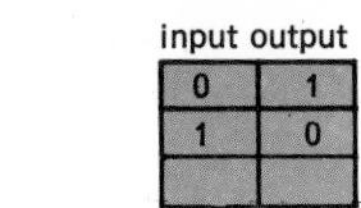

input	output
0	1
1	0

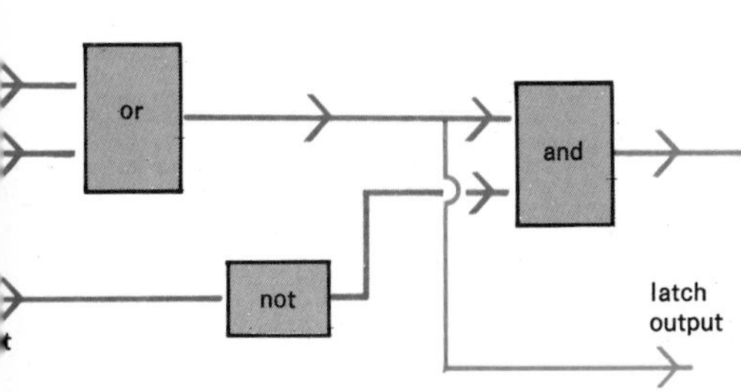

Above: Schematic representations of four types of *logic circuit* used in computers. These circuits are some of the basic elements of a computer, and are built up into complex combinations which enable the computer to perform its calculations. The *truth tables* next to the AND, OR and NOT circuits show what their outputs would be for any possible combination of inputs; for example the AND circuit only gives an output of '1' if A *and* B *and* C are '1'. The latch circuit is the basic element of an integrated circuit memory. Once it has been *set* 'on', it remains on until it is *reset*.

translated into a pattern of completed circuits. The modern machines use a photo-electric system to detect the presence of holes by shining a light through them.

Paper tape readers are capable of reading up to 1,000 characters per second, and card readers up to 2,000 cards per minute. There are two types of card in general use, one with 80 columns of possible character positions and one with 96 columns.

Processing

The input signals, which may represent data or instructions, pass as a pattern of pulses to the heart of the computer, the *central processing unit* (cpu). Here, the patterns are stored in an *immediate access* or *working* store. As with the input devices, the store employs a two-state system—a pattern of 'ons' and 'offs'—to represent the data and instructions.

Two methods of storage are currently employed, namely *magnetic core* (or *core storage*) and the solid-state store based on electronic circuits known as *bistable multivibrators*, *latches*, or *flip-flops*. In a core store the binary digits of the information are represented by the direction of magnetization of tiny rings or *cores* of ferrite, each of which has two *co-ordinate wires* passing through it at 90° to each other.

A ring is magnetized by currents passed in one direction to magnetize the ring as a '1', and in the other direction to magnetize it to represent a '0'. The ring is 'read' by means of a *sense* wire which is threaded through all the rings in turn. A '0' current is passed through the co-ordinate wires of the rings; if it is set at '0' nothing will happen, but if it is set at '1' the current will make it change its direction of magnetism and as it changes it will induce a tiny current in the sense wire. Other circuitry is provided to return the ring to its former state after reading, otherwise the data will have been lost during the read operation.

Each core represents one *bit* (*binary digit*) of information, and a pattern of bits represents a *word* of data. Typical word lengths used by computers are 16, 24 and 32 bits long, and in many cases the 8-bit *byte* is used.

Core store is *non-volatile*, that is, the stored patterns remain even if the power is switched off. Flip-flop storage is *volatile*, and takes the form of circuits, representing one bit each, which can be switched by pulses to either of two states, '1' or '0'. The early forms used valve circuits, with two valves per bit, and were bulky, power-consuming and relatively unreliable. The modern versions use integrated circuits, and are cheaper and faster in operation than core storage.

In addition to the working store, the cpu has two other main components: the *control unit* and the *arithmetic logic unit* (alu). The control unit takes procedural

Nixdorf Computers

IBM 3800 PRINTING SUBSYSTEM

fuser roller
preheat platen
form stacker
charge
cleaner
transfer station
toner supply
photoconductive surface
form supply
rotating mirror
forms overlay
modulator
laser

Right: Programs are the computer's operating instructions. This simplified flow chart shows some of the steps of a payroll calculation program.

Right: The IBM 3800 printer uses a laser to 'write' characters on a photoconductive drum, which picks up toner 'ink' and transfers it to the paper.

Above: Following the development of large computer systems, a wide variety of smaller systems were developed for use either as small-scale individual computers or as satellite units linked to a larger system. The machine shown here is a Nixdorf 8870, which includes a printer and a display.

Below: 'Viewdata' is a public computer system being developed by the British Post Office. Subscribers are linked to a central computer system by telephone line, and the data they request can be displayed via an ordinary tv set, or on a purpose-built terminal such as this one shown here.

Right: The IBM System 360 Model 30 computer, introduced in 1964, weighed about 2,545 kg (5,600 lb). This machine, the IBM 5100 portable computer, was introduced twelve years later; its processing functions are roughly the same as those of the 360/30, but it weighs only about 23 kg (50 lb).

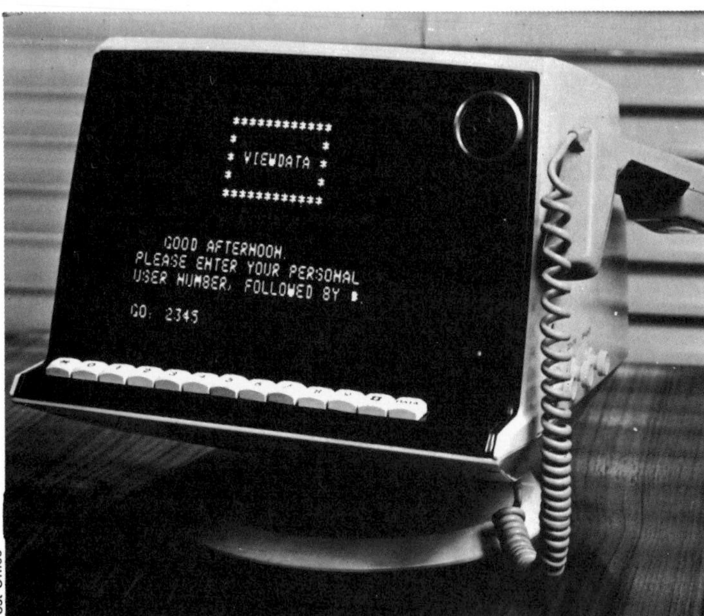
VIEWDATA
GOOD AFTERNOON.
PLEASE ENTER YOUR PERSONAL
USER NUMBER, FOLLOWED BY
GO: 2345

Post Office

IBM

Right: Two forms of voice synthesizer. The upper one is the phonetic keyboard of a Votrax system, which is used to enable computer systems to talk to their users. The lower one is a Marconi Marvox unit which can encode speech into digital information, and decode it again to reproduce the original speech.

Federal Screwworks

MARVOX

Right: The computer of the Skylab 3 orbital laboratory. Computers have been essential to the development of spaceflight, not only by making it possible to perform all the necessary navigational calculations, but also by their ability to supervise functions such as spacecraft life-support systems.

instructions from the store, and sets up circuits to enable each instruction to be carried out, for example the transfer of data from an input device to the store, or from the store to the alu. A complete set of instructions is called a *program*, and the control unit will action each instruction of a program until an instruction indicates that it is the final one.

The arithmetic logic unit is the part of the cpu where the actual computation takes place. Words from store are passed to the alu so that, for example, they may be added or subtracted, multiplied or divided, compared or modified, according to the program instructions from the control unit. Comparison is one of the most important features of the alu; one simple example is to determine which of two names is alphabetically earlier so that sorting can take place.

Output

The output from the cpu can be obtained in various forms, such as the printed output from a *line printer*, as the display on the tv-like screen of a *visual display unit*, as punched cards or paper tapes produced by *card* or *tape punches*, or recorded onto a magnetic storage medium such as *magnetic tape* or *magnetic disk*.

The input and output devices which support the processor are known collectively as *peripheral units*. Among the commonest peripherals found in the computer installation are those, such as magnetic tape or disk units, which extend the system's storage capability. In the tape units, the data is 'written' in blocks of bits along the tape, and so the tape

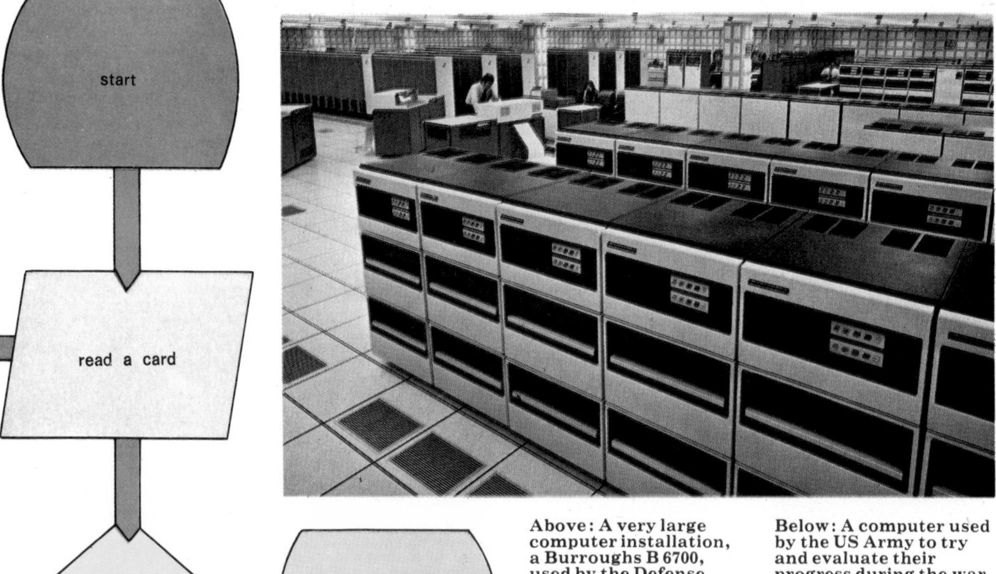

Burroughs

Above: A very large computer installation, a Burroughs B 6700, used by the Defense Logistics Services Center in Battle Creek, Michigan, USA. The system incorporates a disk storage *data base* or file of data which contains 13 billion bytes of information. This picture shows some of the disk units.

Below: A computer used by the US Army to try and evaluate their progress during the war in Vietnam. This is an example of the use of a computer 'model' of a situation such as war; the machine analyzes changes in various aspects of the situation, and predicts their probable consequences.

John Hillelson Agency

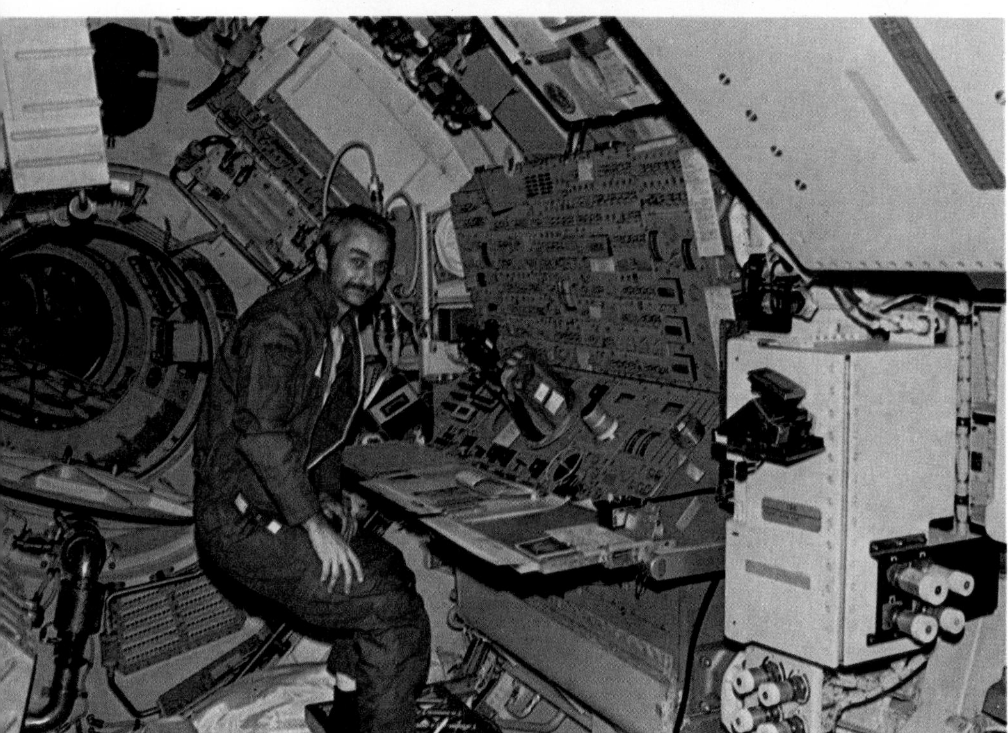

Aspect

must be wound through the machine in order to reach a given piece of data. This increases the time taken to retrieve information from the tape, and so this form of *backing storage* is used for data which is generally accessed *serially*, that is, in sequence, such as payroll records.

In the magnetic disk unit, on the other hand, the data is written in concentric tracks on each surface of the disk, and a set of read/write heads, or a single head capable of moving across the disk, can access an item of data in about a hundredth of a second. Since any required part of the data can be accessed without having to run through the data recorded before it, disk storage is said to give *random access*.

Programs

The program instructions are stored and handled within the machine in the same way as the other data, in the form of words of bit patterns. In the early days of computers, the program writers had to know the bit patterns for every instruction, and also the storage location for every item of data.

It was soon realized that programming could be made easier by getting the machine itself to do some of the work. The programs themselves are now written in *symbolic* programming languages, in which the instructions are written in abreviated forms such as 'ADD' or 'MLT' (multiply) known as *mnemonics*. A program held within the computer then translates these mnemonics into the bit patterns or *machine codes*. In addition, the data storage locations can be written in denary form, and the translation program will convert these into the necessary binary address.

Such translator programs are said to 'assemble' other programs and so are known as *assemblers*. Assemblers, however, are only the first level of sophistication in translator programs. Computer languages have been designed which require programs to translate one instruction into several machine instructions, and for which addresses may be designated by letters or words.

These translators, which also detect some programming errors, may be *compilers*, which translate a whole program before it is executed, or *interpreters* which translate and execute each instruction in turn. Languages which are far removed from the fundamental machine codes are said to be *high level*, in contrast to the *low level* machine code and assembly languages.

There are now a large number of high level languages, each designed for certain types of application. Thus FORTRAN (FORmula TRANslation language) is used for scientific and mathematical programs, and COBOL (COmmon Business Oriented Language) is used for business programs in which files of data, such as invoicing details, are to be processed.

Reduced costs and improved technology are bringing computer access within the reach of many more people. Just as the pocket calculator is commonplace today, so within a few years the pocket computer or the computer terminal, combined with high level easily-understood program languages, will bring sophisticated computing power to the individual, and provide immediate access to vast amounts of information held on large, centralized public computer systems.

Pollution Control

Action to reduce pollution to acceptable limits is now known to be essential if man is to survive. Such action can be taken only by governments, who are notoriously reluctant to take appropriate measures unless forced to by a major catastrophe, and even then only if little economic sacrifice is involved. Pollution may conveniently be discussed in terms of its effect on the rivers and seas, the atmosphere and the land.

Water pollution

When man was a nomadic creature and his numbers were small, water pollution problems were negligible as the rivers into which his waste passed were largely self-cleansing. As communities grew and became more or less static, they tended to settle near large sources of clean water which could accept the polluting load without serious detrimental effect. The River Thames at London, for example, was reasonably clean up to the early nineteenth century as it received only surface water drainage, domestic soil going into cesspits. With the introduction of the water closet, which coincided with a significant increase in population, cesspits overflowed and it was found necessary to connect them to the street drains discharging to the river. Not surprisingly, a rapid deterioration of the river ensued with, as a consequence, several massive cholera epidemics.

The public alarm which followed eventually resulted in a metropolitan sewage system with somewhat rudimentary sewage works at the end of the line. This improved matters for a time, but the growth of population and industry in the London area produced so much pollution in the tidal part of the Thames that as recently as 1950 the river frequently

Picturepoint Ltd

CEGB

Above: The ecological balance of many lakes and river systems, such as the Norfolk Broads in eastern England, is being disturbed by increasing nitrate levels in the water. These nitrates enter the water from nearby farmland where nitrate fertilizers are widely used, and lead to *eutrophication*—an overabundance of aquatic plants such as algae.

Right: Examining fish caught in the River Thames.

Below: Some of the fish now found in the tidal section of the River Thames. Over 90 species have now been found there; in 1957, because of pollution, there were virtually none.

Thames Water

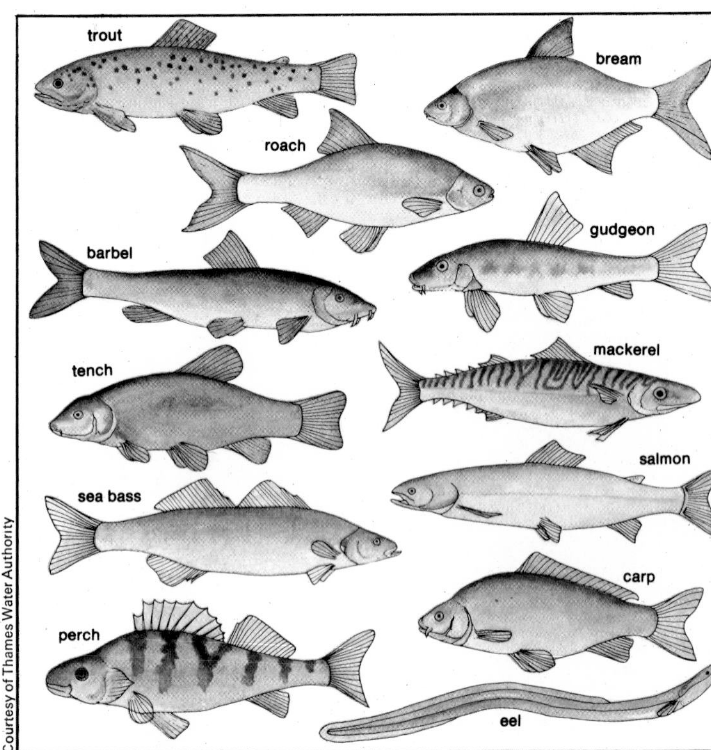

Courtesy of Thames Water Authority

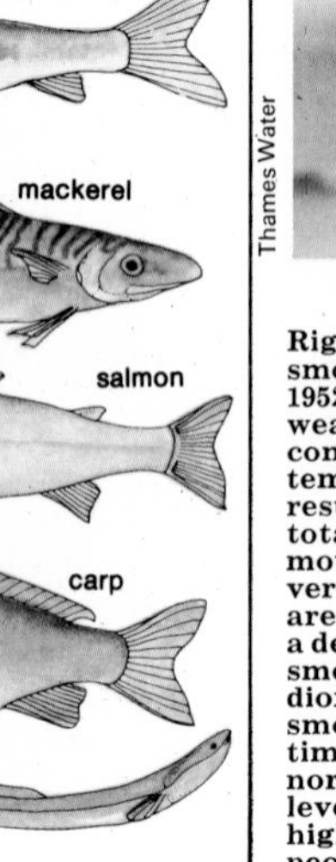

Right: In the notorious smog of December 5-8 1952, anticyclonic weather conditions, combined with temperature inversions, resulted in an almost total lack of air movement, horizontal or vertical, in the London area. This resulted in a dense accumulation of smoke and sulphur dioxide in the air; smoke levels were 16 times higher than normal, sulphur dioxide levels were 12 times higher, and over 4,000 people died.

Radio Times Hulton Picture Library

POLLUTANT SPECIES	MAJOR SOURCES
sulphur dioxide	electricity generation, oil refineries, iron and steel works
smoke, dust, grit	iron and steel works, power stations, foundries, gas works, cement works
carbon monoxide	combustion of fossil fuels
carbon dioxide	combustion of fossil fuels
oxides of nitrogen	nitric acid works, electricity generation, iron and steel works, fertilizer plant
ammonia	ammonia works
sulphur trioxide	sulphuric acid works, brick works
sulphides and sulphur	generating stations, metal smelting, rubber vulcanizing, coke ovens
chlorine and hydrogen chloride	chlorine works, secondary aluminium works, chromium works
chlorinated hydrocarbons	dry cleaning works, aerosol sprays
mercaptans	oil refineries, coke ovens
zinc oxide	copper works

Above: Coal- or oil-fired power stations have tall, multi-flue chimneys and separation equipment that removes most of the smoke and sulphur dioxide from the flue gases. Any pollutants that are not removed are carried high into the air by the chimneys so that they are dispersed well above the ground (the white plumes issuing from the cooling towers are steam, not smoke). Tall chimneys are used by many industrial plants to disperse the smoke away from ground level, but if the flue gases are not cleaned the pollutants can be carried a long way before returning to the ground; it has been suggested that the 'acid rain' falling in southern Scandinavia is a result of sulphur compounds 'exported' there from British factory chimneys.

Above right: The main sources of common air pollutants.

Right: The Taj Mahal, built by Shah Jahan in the seventeenth century, is beginning to turn brown because of air pollution from factories in the area. Steps are being taken to reduce this pollution and thus protect both the Taj and the health of the local population.

Below: Some major air pollution episodes of the past century.

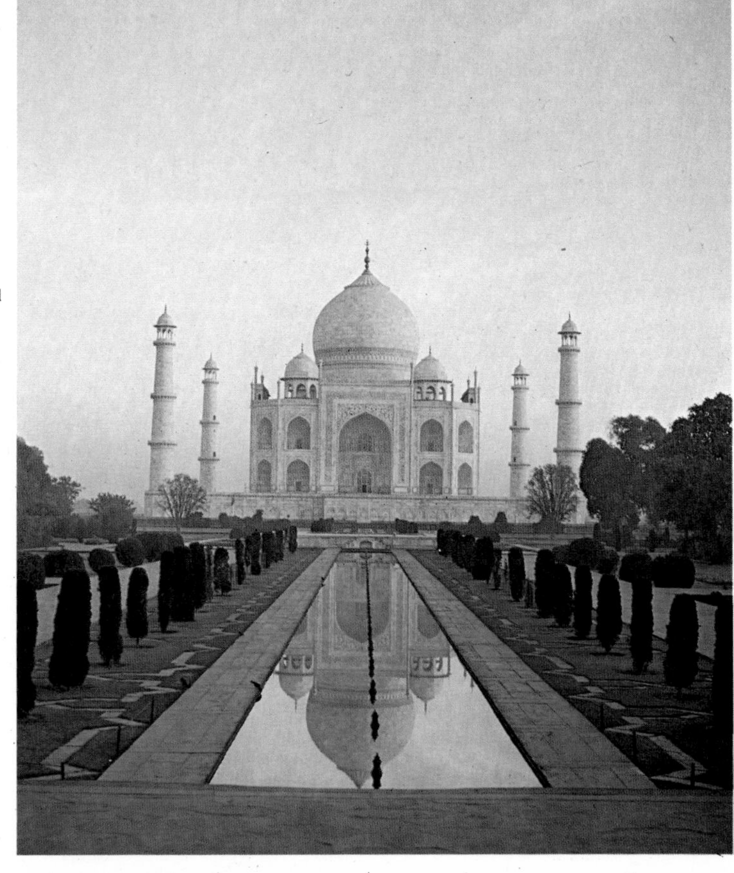

Spectrum

DATE		PLACE	EXCESS DEATHS
Feb.	1880	London, England	1,000
Dec.	1930	Meuse Valley, Belgium	63
Oct.	1948	Donora, Penn., U.S.	20
Nov.	1950	Poca Rica, Mexico	22
Dec.	1952	London, England	4,000
Nov.	1953	New York, U.S.	250
Jan.	1956	London, England	1,000
Dec.	1957	London, England	700–800
Dec.	1962	London, England	700
Jan./Feb.	1963	New York, U.S.	200–400
Nov.	1966	New York, U.S.	168

stank during the summer months, and fish had long since disappeared. The commissioning of new, larger and much more efficient sewage works has markedly improved the condition of the river, in which over 90 different species of fish have now been identified.

This improvement arose after the passing of various laws, for example the Control of Pollution Act, 1974, which set out to control pollution of water and the atmosphere, noise pollution, and the disposal of solid waste on land. Control of rivers and other sources of water was placed in the care of the newly-formed water authorities, who extended and improved control of the industrial use of water and of industrial discharges. Trade effluent control sections organize the issue to industry of licences which include rigid limits for pollutants in the discharges, and sample and analyze the discharges to ensure conformity with the licence conditions.

These are set at levels which safeguard the receiving sewers and the workers who maintain them, the sewage treatment processes and the quality of the final effluent and the sewage sludge. Industry has for the most part learned to consult trade effluent officers at the planning stage, to ensure the requirements of the water authorities are met, and to contact them immediately for advice when accidental spillages occur.

Several water authorities have installed automatic unmanned control stations which sample rivers at specified intervals, monitoring the samples for such parameters as pH (which indicates the acidity or alkalinity of the water), and the amounts of ammonia, nitrate, and dissolved oxygen present. The results are then transmitted to a central control station.

The World Health Organization and, more recently, the EEC, have drawn up official standards for drinking water to which water supply authorities conform to ensure the purity of their supplies. These standards cover *organoleptic* factors (detectable by the senses) such as colour, turbidity (cloudiness), odour and palatability; *physiochemical* factors which include pH, electrical conductivity, total and individual mineral contents, presence of acid radicals, and the total and ammoniacal nitrogen contents; *biological* factors, such as dissolved oxygen and oxidability; *microbiological* factors including the count of coliform bacteria and other pathogenic organisms; and other undesirable or toxic factors, which include metals, mineral oils, pesticides and similar organochlorine compounds, and selected carcinogens such as polycyclic aromatic hydrocarbons.

Air pollution

The principal pollutants of the atmosphere are smoke and sulphur dioxide (SO_2) from fires and furnaces. As usual it took a massive disaster, the London *smog* (a combination of smoke and fog) of 1952 in which over 4,000 bronchial sufferers died, to produce protective legislation in the form of the Clean Air Acts, of 1956 and 1968. These controlled the amount of smoke which could be emitted from industrial chimneys, and authorized the creation of 'smokeless zones' where only approved smokeless fuels could be burnt in domestic premises.

The importance of data acquisition in

the production of control procedures has been emphasized, and large numbers of air pollution monitors have been installed throughout the UK and in many other countries. These monitors measure suspended particulates and sulphur dioxide, (the major pollutants), and also carbon monoxide and oxides of nitrogen and lead, which are emitted from road vehicles. In the presence of strong sunlight, vehicles' exhaust gases can combine by a photochemical reaction to produce unpleasant *lachrymatory* substances (which make the eyes water), characterized by the presence of ozone (O_3) and nitrogen dioxide (NO_2).

This *photochemical smog* first appeared in American cities which have large concentrations of motor vehicles and which also experience the phenomenon of *temperature inversion*, a meteorological condition under which the air temperature increases with height instead of decreasing, and contaminants are concentrated. Similar occurrences in Tokyo in 1970 and, more recently, in Holland, aroused concern in other large cities such as London.

Although the presence of prevailing winds suggest that photochemical smog in London is unlikely, the Greater London Council has commenced systematic monitoring for nitrogen dioxide and ozone. There are no official standards for atmospheric pollutants, but the following guidelines for large urban areas have been suggested. Sulphur dioxide: 60 microgrammes per cubic metre ($\mu g/m^3$); suspended particulates: 40 $\mu g/m^3$; ozone: 160 $\mu g/m^3$; and carbon monoxide: 10 milligrammes per cubic metre (mg/m^3).

Some concern has been expressed over the concentration of lead in the atmosphere. This has been cited as an active contributor to a level of human ingestion which, while below the threshold of potential clinical poisoning, could by its persistence produce subtle but generally adverse effects. Lead has been cited as one factor in the causes of still-birth, diseases such as gout, and of brain disorders (especially in children where high blood levels of lead are associated with behavioural disturbances leading to delinquency).

Its presence in the atmosphere comes from the use of tetraethyl lead as an anti-knock ingredient in petrol, which as a result may contain up to 600 mg of lead per litre. A guideline maximum concentration of 3 $\mu g/m^3$ of lead in air has been suggested, a figure not uncommon in city streets carrying heavy traffic. Reductions in lead anti-knock ingredients have been recommended by the EEC and other bodies but, not surprisingly, implementation is more dependent on economic considerations than on health requirements.

Noise pollution

Although noise in the urban environment is not a new problem, it is strange that the systematic investigation of noise pollution is of quite recent origin—the first major noise survey in the world was made in London in 1960. In addition to the technical problems associated with such investigations, which involve extremely sophisticated equipment, the presentation of noise data in an understandable form is complicated. Sound pressure levels can be measured and expressed in decibels (dB). However, a modifying factor must be introduced to take account of the fact

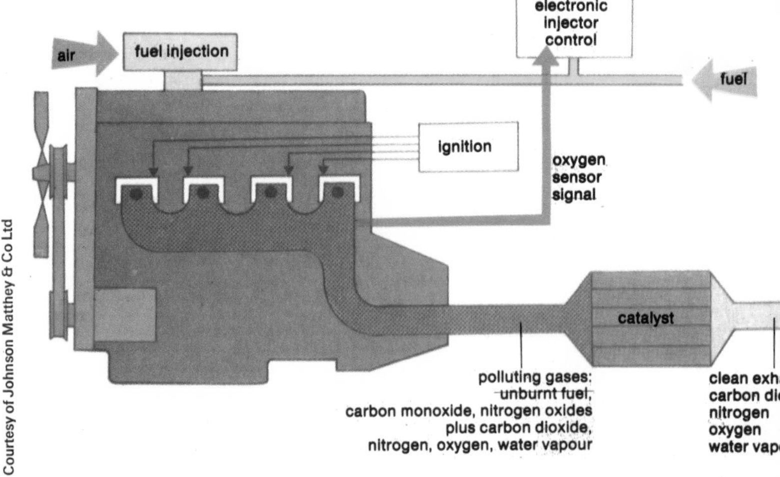

Right: The more dangerous gases contained in the exhaust from vehicle engines can be converted into relatively harmless compounds by means of a suitable catalyst, such as platinum or rhodium, fitted into the exhaust system. In the system represented here, the hydrocarbons (unburnt fuel), carbon monoxide and oxides of nitrogen in the exhaust are converted into carbon dioxide, water vapour and nitrogen gas.

Below: A car exhaust system incorporating a catalytic emission control system. Within the catalytic unit, the catalyst itself (which is usually platinum) is carried on a ceramic or metal alloy support.

Courtesy of Johnson Matthey & Co Ltd

Johnson Matthey & Co Ltd

	Hydro-carbons	Carbon monoxide	Nitroge oxide
1957–67 autos, averaged	8.7	87	not know
1970/71 standards	4.1	34	non
1972/73/74 standards	3.0	28	3.
1975 interim standard			
United States	1.5	15	3.
California	0.9	9	2.
statutory standard	0.41	3.4	0

Above: In the US the Air Quality Act of 1967 was revised in 1970 by the Clean Air Amendments, which introduced standards governing the level of exhaust emissions permissible from new vehicles. This chart shows how the legislation aims to reduce the emissions (in grams per mile).

Below: A team from the UK Atomic Energy Authority's Hazardous Materials Service examining a drum of chemicals washed ashore on a Cornish beach. Rapid identification of unknown substances washed ashore in this manner is essential, as they may be extremely poisonous or even explosive.

UKAEA

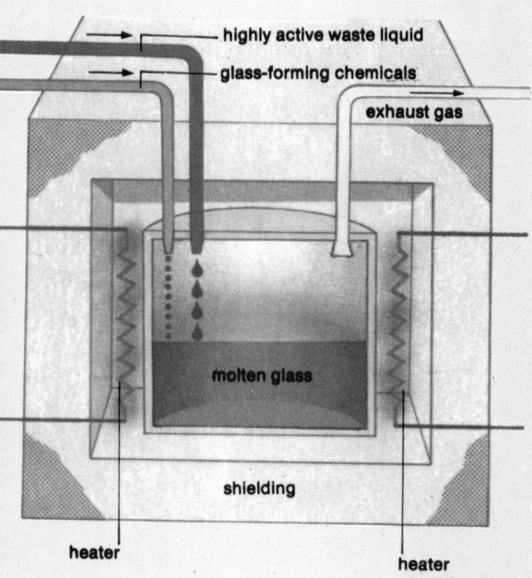

Above: A diagram of a proposed process for turning the highly active, long-lived liquid waste from reprocessed fast breeder reactor fuel into a type of glass so that it can be stored more safely. The vitrified waste would be sealed in stainless steel containers and stored under water.

Above: A section of a cylinder containing simulated vitrified nuclear waste.

Below: Containers of vitrified waste might be stored in special storage 'ponds', or else buried in stable geological formations such as salt domes, or beneath the bed of the ocean.

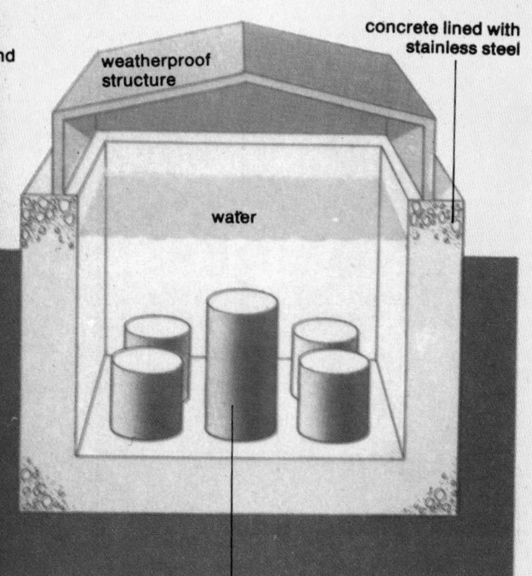

acceptable noise limits for working areas (in dB(A))	
workshops and machinery buildings where communication is necessary	70
workshop offices, plant offices and control rooms, and other areas where easy communication is necessary	60
general offices	50
private offices and small conference rooms	45
offices and conference rooms where a high standard is required	35

estimated community response to noise

amount in dB(A) by which the corrected measured noise level exceeds the corrected criterion	estimated community response
0	no observed reaction
5	sporadic complaints
10	widespread complaints
15	threats of community action
20	vigorous community action

Left: The generally acceptable noise limits for various types of working areas, and the estimated responses of a community to noise levels exceeding those which normally prevail in its neighbourhood.

Below left: Measuring aircraft noise levels in a street near London's Heathrow Airport.

Below: The noise levels produced by a Concorde airliner on take-off from Heathrow Airport. The Concorde, powered by turbojets, is noisier than the latest sub-sonic jets because they use turbofan engines.

GLC

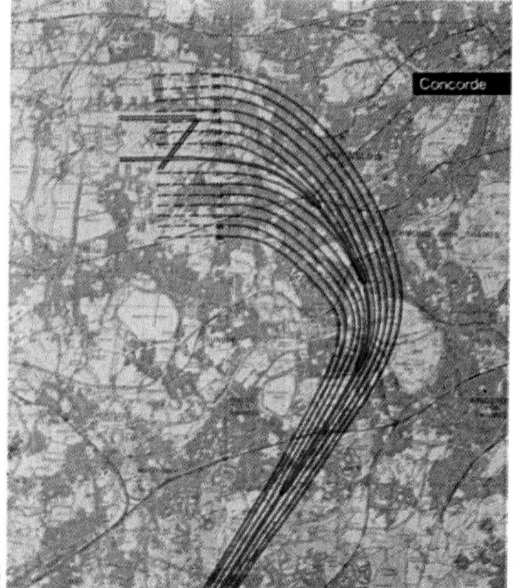

GLC

that the response of the human ear to a noise varies according to the frequency of the noise, high frequency noises appearing louder than lower frequencies at the same pressure levels.

To overcome this, it is necessary to 'weight' readings to give emphasis to certain frequencies so as to reproduce the response of an 'average' human ear. Instruments used for measuring sound pressure levels incorporate electronic circuits which automatically compensate for this subjective response. The scale usually used is the 'A' weighted scale, expressed as the dB(A) reading. A further complication is that this scale cannot be treated arithmetically in the same way as can, for instance, measurements of speed.

If the speed of a car increases from 50 kph to 100 kph, its speed has doubled. However, a noise level of 60 dB(A) is doubled by a change to 70 dB(A), an increase of 10 dB(A), not 60 dB(A). The effect of noise sources is not what might intuitively be expected. A single car horn may produce a noise level of 70 dB(A), while the addition of a second, identical horn at the same distance would increase the sound level to only 73 dB(A), a perceptible change but not a doubling of the noise level.

Aircraft noise is a major environmental problem which is being tackled in two ways; reducing the noise at source, and ensuring that no new noise-sensitive developments are permitted at or near a busy airport. The effect of aircraft noise may be reduced by the use of quieter engines, and by the gradual introduction of internationally-agreed improved noise standards for new aircraft. Alternatively, 'minimum noise routes' for flight paths may be selected, in theory planned to affect the minimum number of people. A third method is the use of noise abatement procedures which plan the rate of climb of an aircraft after take-off so as to cause the minimum of noise to the smallest number of people. Safety considerations for aircraft are very important, and have on many occasions prevented such plans from operating.

Land pollution

Pollution of land is the most difficult form of pollution to measure and control. The land's resources for self-cleansing are fewer and more easily destroyed than are those of the air or water. Land is used for the deposition of domestic and trade wastes and for the construction of special tips to receive poisonous waste. Sludge from sewage works is generally deposited on land either as a suspension in water or in the dry or semi-dried condition.

The sludge contains useful amounts of soil nutrients, such as nitrogen and phosphorus, but it can also contain undesirable amounts of toxic metals, which necessitates not only monitoring of the sludge but also constant control of trade discharges which are the main sources of the sludge metals. Domestic and most ordinary trade wastes can, however, be broken down by contact with soil and their deposition on waste land may make a significant contribution towards its reclamation.

Many countries now carry out general monitoring of levels of hazardous substances on polluted land, and measurement of these substances in plant tissue, in terrestrial animal life, in foodstuffs and in people.

Index

Entries and numerals in italics refer to illustrations.

D

E

F

G

H

I

J

K

L

M

N